W9-CPW-341

Ita-Kuv

12

THE NEW ILLUSTRATED COLUMBIA ENCYCLOPEDIA

THE NEW

ILLUSTRATED

COLUMBIA

ENCYCLOPEDIA

This edition is published by Rockville House Publishers by arrangement with
COLUMBIA UNIVERSITY PRESS
NEW YORK

Peaks of the Mont Blanc massif in northern Italy.

Ruins of the Roman Forum of Trajan, with the Column of Trajan (foreground) and the monument to King Victor Emmanuel II (background), in Rome, Italy.

White-tailed jackrabbit of North America.

Indian miniature depicting Krishna and Radha.

ROCKVILLE HOUSE PUBLISHERS
GARDEN CITY, N.Y. 11530

LIBRARY OF CONGRESS CATALOG CARD NO.: 78-56359

MANUFACTURED IN THE UNITED STATES OF AMERICA

PICTURE CREDITS

Illustrations courtesy of:
Key to picture position: t-top; c-center; b-bottom; r-right; l-left.
Combinations: tr-top right; tl-top left; etc.

Alabiso / A2 - 3569
Albright - Knox Art Gallery, Gift of Seymour H. Knox, Buffalo, N.Y. - 3551
AP - 3650
Archivio P2 - 3598
Art Institute of Chicago, Chicago, Ill. - 3653
W. W. Bacon III / Researchers - 3632
C. Bevilacqua - 3627
Bibliothèque de l'Opéra, Paris (France) - 3629
Bibliothèque Nationale, Paris (France) - 3537
J. B. Blossom / Natural History Photographic Agency - 3701
R. Borea - 3748
P. Breining / Mc Carthy Coll. - 3506
Brunoni - 3441 b
Bureau of Engraving and Printing, Washington, D.C. - 3508
Camera Press - 3596, 3635, 3644
Dr. Catalucci - 3513
CBS - 3462
Centro Documentazione Ebraica Contemporanea, Milan (Italy) - 3530 t
Certosa di Pavia, Pavia (Italy) - 3453 t
Cesati - 3684
Civica Raccolta di Stampe Bertarelli, Milan (Italy) - 3446
Columbia Pictures / Sam Spiegel - 3638
C.L.I. / I.C.P. - 3501
DAIEI - 3753
DPA - 3541, 3585
Dulevant - 3633
«Ebony», October 1966 - 3687
Egyptian National Museum, Cairo (Egypt) - 3528 t
Florida Department of Commerce - 3669
Fox - 3535, 3564
Fratelli Fabbri Editori, Milan (Italy) - 3443, 3444 b, 3445, 3453, 3468, 3469, 3476, 3491, 3492 t, 3493, 3494, 3496, 3504, 3520, 3528, 3530 b, 3539, 3548, 3551, 3562, 3584, 3591, 3593, 3601, 3606, 3609, 3629, 3636, 3653, 3706, 3717, 3741
Galleria degli Uffizi, Florence (Italy) - 3586, 3636
G. Gerster - 3455 r, 3485 b
Giorcelli - 3745
Gotoh Art Museum, Tokyo (Japan) - 3495
B. Hays / Researchers - 3579
I.C.P. - 3501
Istituto Luce - 3447
Jodrell Bank, Cheshire (U.K.) - 3539
Johnson - 3556
Kansas Department of Economic Development - 3616
Kentucky Department of Public Information - 3656, 3657
Keystone - 3731
Kitty Peak National Observatory, Tucson, Ariz. - 3702
P. Klee - Stiftung Kunstmuseum, Berne (Switzerland) - 3705
Koch Institut, Berlin (West Germany) - 3717
P. Koch / Researchers - 3708
Kunsthaus, Zurich (Switzerland) - 3720
Kunstmuseum, Berne (Switzerland) - 3705
H. Levart / Researchers - 3465
Magnum - 3487 b
Mairani - 3441 t
A. Margiocco - 3459, 3516
A. Margiocco / Köster - 3485 t
Marka - 3690
A. M. Mascheroni - 3661
Masuda Collection, Odawara (Japan) - 3496
Metro Goldwyn Mayer - 3648
The Metropolitan Museum of Art, New York, N.Y. - 3528 bl
W. Miller / Magnum - 3588
Mossotti / Transafrica - 3484 b, 3735
Musée des Antiquités Nationales, Paris (France) - 3453 b
Musée des Beaux Arts d'Ixelles, Brussels (Belgium) - 3568
Musée du Louvre, Paris (France) - 3572
Musée Guimet, Paris (France) - 3469
Museum of Natural History, London (U.K.) - 3591
N. Myers / Marka - 3681
NASA - 3734
National Portrait Gallery, London (U.K.) - 3476, 3700
News and Information Bureau, Canberra (Australia) - 3612, 3716
New York Public Library - Picture Collection, New York, N.Y. - 3748
L. Nicholson / Researchers - 3510, 3618
Palazzo Ducale, Urbino (Italy) - 3593
Palazzo Municipale, Genova (Italy) - 3548
R. Parent - 3504 b
L. Pellegrini - 3484 b
Picturepoint / I.C.P. - 3521
PIME - 3729
Prince of Wales Museum of Western India, Bombay (India) - 3741
Private Collection, Frankfurt (West Germany) - 3693
Publifoto - 3497
Researchers - 3707
SEF - 3455 l, 3617, 3672
L. Sillner / ZEFA - 3533
Sirman / Dimt - 3502
The Solomon R. Guggenheim Museum, New York, N.Y. - 3609
C. Stewart - 3504
Sudance / Jacana - 3600
Tennessee Department of Economic Development - 3715
Titus - 3457, 3597, 3679
Tomsich - 3460
UPI - 3461, 3552 b, 3555, 3643, 3651, 3675, 3698
USIS - 3463, 3687
C. Vergara / Researchers - 3519
Victoria and Albert Museum, London (U.K.) - 3528 br
Villani - 3524
Whitney Museum of American Art, Gift of Howard and Jean Lipman Foundation, Inc., New Yok, N.Y. - 3584

KEY TO PRONUNCIATION

ə	sofa (sō′fə), item (ī′təm), easily (ē′zəlē), cannon (kăn′ən), circus (sûr′kəs)
ă	act (ăkt), bat (băt)
ā	ape (āp), fail (fāl), day (dā)
â	air (âr), care (kâr)
ä	art (ärt), father (fä′~~th~~ər)
b	back (băk), labor (lā′bər), cab (kăb)
ch	chin (chĭn), hatchet (hăch′ət), rich (rĭch)
d	dock (dŏk), lady (lā′dē), sad (săd)
ĕ	end (ĕnd), steady (stĕd′ē), met (mĕt)
ē	eve (ēv), clear (klēr), see (sē)
f	fat (făt), phase (fāz), cough (kôf)
g	get (gĕt), bigger (bĭg′ər), tag (tăg)
h	hand (hănd), ahead (əhĕd′)
hw	wheel (hwēl), which (hwĭch)
ĭ	it (ĭt), pill (pĭl), mirror (mĭr′ər)
ī	iron (ī′ərn), eye (ī), buyer (bī′ər)
j	jam (jăm), ginger (jĭn′jər), edge (ĕj)
k	kit (kĭt), tackle (tak′əl), cook (ko͝ok)
l	little (lĭt′əl), holly (hŏl′ē), pull (po͝ol)
m	man (măn), hammer (hăm′ər), climb (klīm)
n	new (no͞o), known (nōn), winner (wĭn′ər)
ng	singing (sĭng′ĭng), finger (fĭng′gər), sang (săng), sank (săngk)
ŏ	hot (hŏt), body (bŏd′e)
ō	over (ō′vər), hope (hōp), grow (grō)
ô	orbit (ôr′bit), fall (fôl), saw (sô)
o͝o	foot (fo͝ot), wolf (wo͝olf), put (po͝ot), pure (pyo͝or)
o͞o	boot (bo͞ot), lose (lo͞oz), drew (dro͞o), true (tro͞o)
oi	oil (oil), royal (roi′əl), boy (boi)
ou	out (out), crowd (kroud), how (hou)
p	pipe (pīp), happy (hăp′ē)
r	road (rōd), appeared (əpērd′), carpenter (kär′pəntər)
s	so (sō), cite (sīt), baste (bāst)
sh	shall (shăl), sure (sho͝or), nation (nā′shən)
t	tight (tīt), better (bĕt′ər), talked (tôkt)
th	thin (thĭn), bath (băth)
~~th~~	then (~~th~~ĕn), father (fä′~~th~~ər), bathe (bā~~th~~)
ŭ	but (bŭt), flood (flŭd), some (sŭm)
û	curl (kûrl), girl (gûrl), fern (fûrn), worm (wûrm)
v	vest (vĕst), trivial (trĭv′ēəl), eve (ēv)
w	wax (wăks), twins (twĭnz), coward (kou′ərd)
y	you (yo͞o), onion (ŭn′yən)
z	zipper (zĭp′ər), ease (ēz), treads (trĕdz)
zh	pleasure (plĕzh′ər), rouge (ro͞ozh)

Foreign Sounds

ö	as in French peu (pö), German Goethe (gö′tə)
ü	as in French Cluny (klünē′)
kh	as in German ach (äkh), ich (ĭkh); Scottish loch (lŏkh)
N	this symbol indicates that the preceding vowel is nasal as in French cinq (săNk), un (öN), sans (säN), tombe (tôNb), en (äN)

Accents and Hyphens

′	primary accent, written after accented vowel or syllable: Nebraska (nəbrăs′kə), James Buchanan (byo͞okă′nən)
″	secondary accent: Mississippi (mĭs″əs-sĭp′ē)
–	dash, replacing obvious portion of pronunciation: hegemony (hĭjĕm′ənē, hē–, hĕj′əmō″nē, hĕg′ə–)
-	hyphen, to prevent ambiguity in syllabification: Erlanger (ûr′lăng-ər), dishearten (dĭs-här′tən)

Cross-references are indicated by SMALL CAPITALS

Italy, Ital. *Italia,* republic (1973 est. pop. 55,300,000), 116,303 sq mi (301,225 sq km), S Europe, bordering on France in the northwest, the Ligurian Sea and the Tyrrhenian Sea in the west, the Ionian Sea in the south, the Adriatic Sea in the east, Yugoslavia in the northeast, and Austria and Switzerland in the north. The country includes the large Mediterranean islands of SICILY and SARDINIA and several small islands, notably ELBA, CAPRI, ISCHIA, and the LIPARI ISLANDS. Vatican City (see under VATICAN) and SAN MARINO are two independent enclaves on the Italian mainland. ROME is Italy's capital and largest city; other important cities include MILAN, NAPLES, TURIN, GENOA, PALERMO, BOLOGNA, FLORENCE, CATANIA, VENICE, BARI, TRIESTE, MESSINA, VERONA, PADUA, CAGLIARI, TARANTO, BRESCIA, and LEGHORN. The country is divided into 20 regions, which are subdivided into a total of 94 provinces. The great majority of the population speaks Italian (including several dialects); there are small German-, French-, and Slavic-speaking minorities. Almost all Italians are Roman Catholic. About 75% of Italy is mountainous or hilly, and roughly 20% of the country is forested. There are narrow strips of low-lying land along the Adriatic coast and parts of the Tyrrhenian coast. Northern Italy, made up largely of a vast plain that is contained by the Alps in the north and drained by the Po River and its tributaries, comprises the regions of LIGURIA, PIEDMONT, Valle d'Aosta (see AOSTA, VALLE D'), LOMBARDY, TRENTINO-ALTO ADIGE, VENETIA, FRIULI-VENEZIA GIULIA, and part of EMILIA-ROMAGNA (which extends into central Italy). It is the richest part of the country, with the best farmland, the chief port (Genoa), and the largest industrial centers. Northern Italy also has a flourishing tourist trade on the Italian Riviera, in the Alps (including the Dolomites), on the shores of its beautiful lakes (Lago Maggiore, Lake Como, and Lake Garda), and in Venice. Gran Paradiso (13,323 ft/4,061 m), the highest peak wholly situated within Italy, rises in Valle d'Aosta. The Italian peninsula, bootlike in shape and traversed in its entire length by the Apennines (which continue on into Sicily), comprises central Italy (MARCHE, TUSCANY, UMBRIA, and LATIUM regions) and southern Italy (CAMPANIA, BASILICATA, ABRUZZI, MOLISE, CALABRIA, and APULIA regions). Central Italy contains great historic and cultural centers such as Rome, Florence, PISA, SIENA, PERUGIA, ASSISI, URBINO, Bologna, RAVENNA, RIMINI, FERRARA, and PARMA. The major cities of S Italy, generally the poorest and least developed part of the country, include Naples, Bari, BRINDISI, FOGGIA, and Taranto. Except for the Po and Adige, Italy has only short rivers, among which the Arno and the Tiber are the best known. Most of Italy enjoys a Mediterranean climate; however, that of Sicily is subtropical, and in the Alps there are long and severe winters. The country has great scenic beauty—the majestic Alps in the north, the soft and undulating hills of Umbria and Tuscany, and the romantically rugged landscape of the S Apennines. The Bay of Naples, dominated by Mt. Vesuvius, is one of the world's most famous sights. Italy began to industrialize late in comparison to other European nations, and until World War II was largely an agricultural country. However, after 1950 industry was developed rapidly so that by the early 1970s it contributed about 40% of the annual national product and agriculture only about 11%. The principal farm products are wheat, sugar beets, maize, potatoes, tomatoes, citrus fruit, olives, and livestock (especially cattle, pigs, sheep, and goats). In addition, much wine is

Peak of Aiguille du Géant in the Mont Blanc massif, Italy.
Coast of the Italian island of Sardinia.

Bern
SWITZERLAND
LIECHTENSTEIN
Innsbruck
AUSTRIA
HUNGARY
FRANCE
A L P S
ALPS
Aosta
VALLE D'AOSTA
Lake Maggiore
Lake Lugano
Lake Como
Como
Milan
LOMBARDY
PIEDMONT
Turin
Po R.
Cremona
Brescia
Lake Garda
Bolzano
TRENTINO ALTO-ADIGE
Trent
Belluno
FRIULI-VENEZIA GIULIA
Udine
VENETO
Verona
Padua
Venice
Trieste
Mantua
Ferrara
Parma
Modena
Bologna
EMILIA-ROMAGNA
Ravenna
Genoa
LIGURIA
La Spezia
YUGOSLAVIA
Rimini
SAN MARINO
LIGURIAN SEA
Pisa
Arno R.
Florence
Leghorn (Livorno)
Arezzo
Siena
TUSCANY
Ancona
MARCHE
Perugia
UMBRIA
ADRIATIC SEA
ELBA
CORSICA
Ajaccio
Tiber R.
L'Aquila
ABRUZZI
LATIUM
VATICAN CITY
Rome
MOLISE
Campobasso
ITALY
APULIA
Bari
PONTINE ISLANDS
CAMPANIA
Naples
Sassari
ISCHIA
CAPRI
Salerno
Potenza
TYRRHENIAN SEA
SARDINIA
BASILICATA
Taranto
Gulf of Taranto
Cagliari
CALABRIA
Catanzaro
LIPARI ISLANDS
Palermo
Messina
Reggio di Calabria
EGADI ISLANDS
Strait of Messina
IONIAN SEA
SICILY
Catania
Agrigento
Syracuse
MEDITERRANEAN SEA
Tunis
PANTELLERIA
Malta Channel
TUNISIA
ALGERIA
MALTA
Valletta

produced from grapes grown throughout the country. Industry is centered in the north, particularly in the "golden triangle" of Milan-Turin-Genoa. The chief manufactures of the country include iron and steel, refined petroleum, chemicals, textiles, motor vehicles, and machinery. There is a small fishing industry. Italy has only limited mineral resources; the chief minerals produced are petroleum (especially in Sicily), lignite, iron ore, iron pyrites, bauxite, sulfur, and mercury. There are also large deposits of natural gas (methane). Much hydroelectricity is generated, and there are several nuclear power stations in the country. In order to further the economic development of the south, the *Cassa per il mezzogiorno* (Southern Italy Development Fund) was founded in 1950; it has since allocated considerable funds, especially for improving the economic infrastructure of the region. Italy has a large foreign trade, facilitated by its sizable commercial shipping fleet. The leading exports are machinery, motor vehicles, food products, and textiles; the main imports are food and food products, minerals (especially petroleum), machinery, and chemicals. Tourism is a major source of foreign exchange. The chief trade partners are West Germany, France, and the United States. Italy is a member of the European Economic Community (Common Market). There are numerous universities in Italy, including ones at Bari, Bologna, Genoa, Milan, Naples, Padua, Palermo, and Rome. The following generalized outline of the highly complex history of Italy can be supplemented by the articles on individual cities and regions and by such general articles as ETRUSCAN CIVILIZATION; PAPACY; ITALIAN ART; ITALIAN LITERATURE; and RENAISSANCE.

Ancient Italy and the Barbarian Invasions. Little is known of Italian history before the 5th cent. B.C., except for the regions (S Italy and Sicily) where the Greeks had established colonies (see MAGNA GRAECIA). The earliest known inhabitants seem to have been of Ligurian stock. The Etruscans, coming probably from Asia Minor, established themselves in central Italy before 800 B.C. They reduced the indigenous population to servile status and established a prosperous empire with a complex culture. In the 4th cent. B.C., the Celts (called Gauls by Roman historians) invaded Italy and drove the Etruscans from the Po valley. In the south, the Etruscan advance was checked about the same time by the Samnites (see SAMNIUM), who had adapted the civilization of their Greek neighbors and who in the 4th cent. B.C. drove the Etruscans out of Campania. The Latins, living along the coast of Latium, had not been fully subjected to the Etruscans; they and their neighbors, the SABINES, were the ancestors of the Romans. The history of Italy from the 5th cent. B.C. to the 5th cent. A.D. is largely that of the growth of Rome and of the Roman Empire, of which Italy was the core. Augustus divided Italy into 11 administrative regions (Latium and Campania, Apulia and Calabria, Lucania and Bruttium, Samnium, Picenum, Umbria, Etruria, Cispadane Gaul, Liguria, Venetia and Istria, Transpadane Gaul). By that time, at the beginning of the Christian era, all of Italy had been thoroughly latinized, Roman citizenship was extended to all free Italians, an excellent system of roads had been built, and Italy, made tax exempt, shared fully in the wealth of Rome. Never since has Italy known an equal degree of prosperity or as long a period of peace. Christianity spread rapidly. Like the rest of the Roman Empire, Italy in the early 5th cent. A.D.

Ruins of the Roman Forum of Trajan, with the Column of Trajan (foreground) and the monument to King Victor Emmanuel II (background), in Rome, the capital of Italy.

Fiat automobile factory in Turin, northwestern Italy (above). Vineyards in the Piedmont region of northwestern Italy.

began to be invaded by successive waves of barbarian tribes—the Germanic VISIGOTHS, the HUNS, and the Germanic Heruli and OSTROGOTHS. The deposition (476) of Romulus Augustulus, the last Roman emperor of the West, and the assumption by ODOACER of the rule over Italy is commonly regarded as the end of the Roman Empire. The Eastern emperors, residing at Constantinople (see BYZANTINE EMPIRE), never renounced their claim to Italy and to succession to the West. On the urging of Zeno, the Eastern emperor, the Ostrogoth THEODORIC THE GREAT invaded Italy, took (493) Ravenna (which had replaced Rome as capital), killed Odoacer, and began a long and beneficent rule over Italy. Roman institutions were maintained with the help of scholars and administrators such as Boethius and Cassiodorus. After Theodoric's death (526), the murder (535) of the Gothic queen, AMALASUNTHA, was followed by the reconquest of Italy by Emperor JUSTINIAN I of the East and his generals, BELISARIUS and NARSES. Except, however, in the exarchate of Ravenna, the PENTAPOLIS and the coast of S Italy, Byzantine rule was soon displaced by that of the LOMBARDS, who under ALBOIN established (569) a new kingdom. The papacy emerged as the chief bulwark of Latin civilization. GREGORY I (reigned 590–604), without assistance from Byzantium, succeeded in saving Rome and the Patrimony of St. Peter from the Lombard conquest, thus laying the basis for the creation of the PAPAL STATES. At the same time, he effectively freed Rome from allegiance to the Byzantine conquerors. The Lombards warded off Byzantine efforts at reconquest and in 751 took Ravenna; their advance on Rome resulted in the appeal of Pope Stephen II to PEPIN THE SHORT, ruler of the Franks, who expelled the Lombards from the exarchate of Ravenna and from the Pentapolis, which he donated (754) to the pope. Pepin's intervention was followed by that of his son CHARLEMAGNE, who defeated the Lombard king, Desiderius, was crowned king of the Lombards, confirmed his father's donation to the papacy, and in 800 was crowned emperor of the West at Rome. These events shaped much of the later history of Italy and of the papacy. Among the direct results were the claim of later emperors to Italy and the temporal power of the popes.

Medieval Italy. In the divisions (9th cent.) of the Carolingian empire (see VERDUN, TREATY OF; MERSEN, TREATY OF), Italy passed to the successive emperors LOTHAIR I, LOUIS II, and CHARLES II; however, their control was largely nominal. Under CARLOMAN (d. 880) and Emperor CHARLES III (reigned 881–87), local power became increasingly strong in Italy. Emperor ARNULF (reigned 896–99) failed to reassert authority. From 888 to 962 Italy was nominally ruled by a series of weak kings and emperors including Guy of Spoleto, Berengar I of Friuli, Louis III of Burgundy, and BERENGAR II of Ivrea. The petty nobles were constantly feuding, and by the end of the period the papacy had sunk to its lowest point of degradation. The Magyars plundered N Italy, and in the south the Arabs seized (917) Sicily and raided the mainland. In 961, heeding an appeal by the pope for protection against Berengar II, the German king OTTO I invaded Italy. In 962 he was crowned emperor by the pope. This union of Italy and Germany marked the beginning of the HOLY ROMAN EMPIRE. Although the Alps had never prevented invaders from entering Italy, they did prevent the emperors from exercising effective control there. Again and again the emperors and German kings crossed the Alps to assert their authority; each time their authority virtually vanished when they left Italy. At best, their power was limited to the territories north of the Papal States. The popes, by exerting their influence and by arranging alliances with other powers, were important in frustrating imperial control. Apulia and Calabria, after being briefly held again by the Byzantines, were conquered (11th cent.) by the Normans under ROBERT GUISCARD and his successors, who also wrested Sicily from the Arabs and established the Norman kingdom of Sicily. In central and N Italy, the prevailing chaos was increased by the conflict between the emperors and the popes over INVESTITURE and by the contested succession to Tuscany after the death (1115) of Countess MATILDA. Because the many petty lords were independent of imperial authority and because the cities gradually gained control over these lords, FEUDALISM did not gain a firm foothold in central and N Italy. However, in the south the Norman kings and their successors, the HOHENSTAUFEN and ANGEVIN dynasties, firmly entrenched the feudal system, the worst features of which were later perpetuated by the Spanish rulers of Naples and Sicily. Thus, the great difference in social and economic structure between N and S Italy, which continued well into the 20th cent., can be traced back to the 11th cent. The characteristic development in central and N Italy was the rise of the city (see COMMUNE and CITY-STATE), beginning in the 10th cent. The rise was partly political in origin—the burghers were drawing together to protect themselves from the nobles—and partly economic—contact with the Muslim world was making the Italian merchants the middlemen and the Italian cities the entrepôts of Western Europe. The survival of Roman institutions and the example of the commune of Rome facilitated the process. To protect their commerce and their industries (particularly the wool industry) cities grouped together in leagues, which often were at war with each other. The leagues were particularly strong in Lombardy. The attempt by Emperor FREDERICK I to impose imperial authority on some cities led to the formation of the LOMBARD LEAGUE, which defeated the emperor in 1176. Rivalry among the cities, however, prevented the formation of any union strong enough to consolidate even a part of Italy. In the 13th cent. the struggle between Emperor FREDERICK II and the papacy divided the cities and nobles into two strong parties, the GUELPHS AND GHIBELLINES. Their fratricidal warfare continued long after the death (1250) of Frederick, which marked the virtual demise of imperial rule in Italy and the ascendancy of the papacy. In 1268, Frederick's grandson, Conradin, was executed at Naples, thus ending Hohenstaufen aspirations. The factional strife led to the rise of despots in some cities. These despots, who were of noble or bourgeois origin, were generally factional leaders, who, having obtained the magistracy, made it hereditary. Some of them managed to restore order in the cities. In many cities, however, the republican institutions were upheld with little interruption. In other cities, dynasties were established and invested (14th and 15th cent.) with titles by the emperors, who still claimed suzerainty over N Italy. The most powerful princes (e.g., the VISCONTI and SFORZA of Milan, the GONZAGA of Mantua, the ESTE of Ferrara, and the dukes of SAVOY) and the most powerful republics (e.g., Florence, Venice, and Genoa) tended to increase their territories at the expense of weaker neighbors. The cities in the Papal States passed under local tyrants during the Babylonian captivity of the popes at Avignon (1309–78) and during the

Detail of the Antonine column in Rome, depicting scenes of Marcus Aurelius's victory over the Marcomanni.

Giuseppe Garibaldi (left) meeting with King Victor Emmanuel II in 1860, during the unification of Italy.

Great Schism (1378–1417). By the end of the 15th cent. Italy had fallen into the following chief component parts: in the south, the kingdoms of Sicily and Naples, torn by the rival claims of the French Angevin dynasty and the Spanish house of Aragón; in central Italy, the Papal States, the republics of Siena, Florence, and Lucca, and the cities of Bologna, Forlì, Rimini, and Faenza (only nominally subject to the pope); in the north, the duchies of Ferrara and Modena, Mantua, Milan, and Savoy. The two great merchant republics, Venice and Genoa, with their far-flung possessions, colonies, and outposts, were distinct in character and outlook from the rest of Italy. Constant warfare among these many states resulted in political turmoil, but did little to diminish their wealth or to hinder their cultural output. The wars were generally fought in a desultory manner by hired bands led by professional commanders (see CONDOTTIERE). Compared to the Black Death, the plague that ravaged Italy in 1348, the local wars did little harm. Material prosperity had been furthered considerably by the Crusades; by the expanding trade with the Middle East; and by the rise of great banking firms, notably in Genoa, in Lucca, and in Florence (where the MEDICI rose from bankers to dukes). The prosperity facilitated the great cultural flowering of the Italian Renaissance, which permanently changed the civilization of Western Europe.

Political Disintegration and Rebirth. The Renaissance reached its peak in the late 15th cent. Meanwhile, Italy's political independence was threatened by the growing nations of France, Spain, and Austria. Quarrels among Italian states invited foreign intervention. The invasion (1494) of Italy by CHARLES VIII of France marked the beginning of the ITALIAN WARS, which ended in 1559 with most of Italy subjected to Spanish rule or influence. Early in the wars, in which France and Spain were the main contenders for supremacy in Italy, several Italian statesmen, notably MACHIAVELLI, came to the belief that only unity could save Italy from foreign domination. Pope JULIUS II consolidated the Papal States, but his HOLY LEAGUE, devised (1510) to drive out the French, failed to create a wider Italian unity. After 1519 the Italian Wars became part of the European struggle between FRANCIS I of France and Emperor CHARLES V. By the Treaty of CATEAU-CAMBRÉSIS (1559), Spain gained the kingdoms of Sicily and Naples and the duchy of Milan. Foreign domination continued with the War of the SPANISH SUCCESSION (1701–14; see also UTRECHT, PEACE OF) and the War of the POLISH SUCCESSION (1733–35). By 1748, Naples, Sicily, and the duchies of Parma and Piacenza had passed to branches of the Spanish Bourbons, and the duchies of Milan, Mantua, Tuscany, and Modena to Austria. Remaining independent were the Papal States, the declining republics of Venice, Genoa, and Lucca, and the kingdom of Sardinia (see SARDINIA, KINGDOM OF), created in 1720 by the union of Piedmont, Savoy, and Sardinia under the house of Savoy. These centuries of political weakness were also a period of economic decline. The center of European trade shifted away from the Mediterranean, and commerce and industry suffered from the mercantilist policies of the European states. Taxes rose under Spanish rule, the amount of land under cultivation declined, the population decreased, and brigandage increased. Nevertheless, Italy continued to have considerable influence on European culture, especially in architecture and music. Yet to subsequent generations in Italy (especially in the 19th cent.), preoccupied with the concepts of national independence and political power, the political condition of 18th-century Italy represented national degradation. The French Revolution rekindled Italian national aspirations, and the FRENCH REVOLUTIONARY WARS swept away the political institutions of 18th-century Italy. General Bonaparte (later NAPOLEON I), who defeated Sardinian and Austrian armies in his Italian campaign of 1796–97, was at first acclaimed by most Italians. Napoleon redrew the Italian map several times. Extensive land reforms were carried out, especially in N Italy. The Cispadane and Transpadane republics, established in 1796, were united (1797) as the CISALPINE REPUBLIC, recognized in the Treaty of CAMPO FORMIO (1797). In 1802 the Cisalpine Republic, comprising Lombardy and Emilia-Romagna, was renamed the Italian Republic; in 1805 it became the kingdom of Italy (enlarged by the addition of Venetia), with Napoleon as king and Eugène de BEAUHARNAIS as viceroy. From 1795 to 1812, Savoy, Piedmont, Liguria, Tuscany, Parma, and the Papal States were annexed by France. In 1806, Joseph BONAPARTE was made king of Naples; he was replaced in 1808 by Joachim MURAT, Napoleon's brother-in-law. Sardinia remained under the house of Savoy and Sicily under the Bourbons. Napoleon's failure to unite Italy and to give it self-government disappointed Italian patriots, some of whom formed secret revolutionary societies such as the CARBONARI, which later played a vital role in Italian unification. The Congress of Vienna (1814–15) generally restored the pre-Napoleonic status quo and the old ruling families. However, Venetia was united with Lombardy as the Lombardo-Venetian kingdom under the Austrian crown, and Liguria passed to Sardinia. Naples and Sicily were united (1816) as the kingdom of the TWO SICILIES. Austrian influence became paramount in Italy. Nevertheless, the efforts of Metternich and of the Holy Alliance (e.g., in quelling insurrections in Naples and in Palermo) could not suppress the nationalist movement. The RISORGIMENTO, as the movement for unification was called, included three groups: the radicals, led by MAZZINI, who sought to create a republic; the moderate liberals, who regarded the house of Savoy as the agency for unification; and the Roman Catholic conservatives, who desired a confederation under the presidency of the pope. In 1848–49, there were several short-lived revolutionary outbreaks, notably in Naples, Venice, Tuscany, Rome, and the kingdom of Sardinia (whose new liberal constitution survived). Unification was ultimately achieved under the house of Savoy, largely through the efforts of CAVOUR, GARIBALDI, and VICTOR EMMANUEL II, who became king of Italy in 1861. At that time, the kingdom of Italy did not include Venetia, Rome, and part of the Papal States. By siding against Austria in the AUSTRO-PRUSSIAN WAR of 1866, Italy obtained Venetia. To NAPOLEON III of France, who had helped Sardinia defeat Austria in 1859, Sardinia had ceded Nice and Savoy. The protectorate of Napoleon III over the Papal States delayed the Italian annexation of the city of Rome until 1870. Relations between the Italian government and the papacy, which refused to concede the loss of its temporal power, remained a major problem until 1929, when the LATERAN TREATY made the pope sovereign within Vatican City. After 1870, Austria still retained areas with largely Italian populations (e.g., S Tyrol and Trieste); Italian agitation for their annexation (see IRREDENTISM) went unfulfilled until World War I.

1861 to World War II. From 1861 until the Fascist dictatorship (1922–43) of Benito Mussolini, Italy was governed under the liberal constitution adopted by Sardinia in 1848. The reigns of Victor Emmanuel II (1861–78) and HUMBERT I (1878–1900), and the first half of the reign of VICTOR EMMANUEL III (1900–46) were marked by moderate social and political reforms and by some industrial expansion in N Italy (mainly in the 20th cent.). Periodic social unrest was caused by the dislocations attending industrialization and by occasional economic depression. In the underdeveloped south, rapid population growth led to mass emigration, both to the industrial centers of N Italy and to the Americas. The outstanding statesmen of the pre-Fascist period were Agostino DEPRETIS, Francesco CRISPI, and Giovanni GIOLITTI. Colonial expansion was emphasized under Crispi, but was otherwise sporadic. A severe setback to Italian colonial aspirations was the establishment (1881) of a French protectorate over TUNISIA; it was an important motive for the conclusion (1882) of Italy's alliance with Germany and Austria (see TRIPLE ALLIANCE AND TRIPLE ENTENTE). Later, Italy acquired part of Somaliland in 1889 and Eritrea (now part of Ethiopia) in 1890, but further advances in NE Africa were checked by the Ethiopian victory (1896) at Aduwa. Libya and the Dodecanese were conquered in the Italo-Turkish War (1911–12). In World War I, Italy at first remained neutral. After the Allies offered substantial territorial rewards, Italy denounced the Triple Alliance and entered (1915) the war on the Allied side. Although the Italians initially suffered serious reverses, they won (1918) a great victory at VITTORIO VENETO, which was followed by the surrender of Austria-Hungary. At the Paris Peace Conference, Italy obtained S Tyrol, Trieste, Istria, part of Carniola, and several of the Dalmatian islands. Italian possession of the Dodecanese was confirmed. However, these terms granted far less than the Allies had secretly promised in 1915. Italian discontent was evident in the seizure (1919) of Fiume (see RIJEKA) by a nationalist band led by Gabriel D'ANNUNZIO. Within Italy, political and social unrest increased, furthering the growth of Fascism. The Fascist leader (Ital. *Il Duce*) MUSSOLINI, promising the restoration of social order and of political greatness, directed (Oct. 27, 1922) a successful march on Rome and was made premier by the king. Granted dictatorial powers, Mussolini quashed opposition to the state (especially that of socialists and Communists), regimented the press and the schools, imposed controls on industry and labor, and created a CORPORATIVE STATE controlled by the Fascist party and the militia. The Fascist economic program as a whole was a failure, but some programs of lasting value (e.g., the draining of the Pontine marshes and the construction of a network of superhighways) were undertaken. The problems caused by an increasing population were aggravated by drastic immigration restrictions in the United States and by the economic depression of the 1930s. Mussolini followed an aggressive foreign policy, and after 1935

Alcide De Gasperi (second from left) and Luigi Einaudi (third from right), two important Italian politicians of the period following World War II.

he turned increasingly to militarist and imperialist solutions to Italy's problems. Italy conquered ETHIOPIA in 1935–36, easily overcoming the ineffective sanctions imposed by the League of Nations (from which Italy withdrew in 1937). At the same time, Italy drew closer to Nazi Germany and to Japan; in 1936, Italy formed an entente with Germany (see AXIS). Italy intervened on the Insurgent side in the Spanish civil war (1936–39), and in 1939 it seized ALBANIA. At the outbreak of World War II, Italy assumed a neutral stance friendly to Germany, but in June, 1940, it declared war on collapsing France and on Great Britain. In 1940, Italian forces were active in North Africa (see NORTH AFRICA, CAMPAIGNS IN) and attacked Greece; however, they were unsuccessful until German troops came to their aid in early 1941. Later in 1941, Italy declared war on the Soviet Union and on the United States. Soon Italy suffered major reverses, and by July, 1943, it had lost its African possessions, its army was shattered, Sicily was falling to U.S. troops, and Italian cities (especially ports) were being bombed by the Allies. In July, 1943, discontent among Italians culminated in the rebellion of the Fascist grand council against Mussolini, Mussolini's dismissal by Victor Emmanuel III, the appointment of BADOGLIO as premier, and the dissolution of the Fascist party. In September, 1943, Italy surrendered unconditionally to the Allies, while German forces quickly occupied N and central Italy. Aided by the Germans, Mussolini escaped from prison and established a puppet republic in N Italy. Meanwhile, the Badoglio government declared war on Germany, and Italy was recognized by the Allies as a cobelligerent. The Allied Italian campaign was a slow, grueling, and costly struggle (see CASSINO; ANZIO). The fall of Rome (July, 1944) was followed by a stalemate. In April, 1945, partisans captured and summarily executed Mussolini. In May, 1945, the Germans surrendered. After the war, Italy's borders were established by the peace treaty of 1947, which assigned several small Alpine districts (see BRIGUE AND TENDE) to France; the Dodecanese to Greece; and Trieste, Istria, most of Venezia Giulia, and several Adriatic islands to Yugoslavia and to the Free Territory of Trieste. In 1954, Trieste and its environs were returned to Italy. As a result of the war, Italy also lost effective control over its holdings of Libya, Eritrea, and Italian Somaliland.

Postwar Italy. In 1944 the unpopular Badoglio cabinet had resigned, and thereafter various coalition cabinets followed each other until Dec., 1945, when Alcide DE GASPERI, a Christian Democrat, became premier. De Gasperi remained an important influence on Italian politics until his death in 1954. In May, 1946, Victor Emmanuel abdicated, having previously transferred his powers to his son, HUMBERT II. After a month's rule, Humbert was exiled when the Italians in a plebiscite voted by a small majority to make the country a republic. A new republican constitution went into effect on Jan. 1, 1948. Enrico de Nicola was provisional president of Italy from 1946 to 1948; he was followed as president by Luigi Einaudi, Giovanni Gronchi (1955), Antonio Segni (1962), Giuseppe Saragat (1964), and Giovanni Leone (1971). The Christian Democrats, Communists, and Socialists emerged from the war as the chief parties. The split of the Socialists into the majority Socialists (the left wing) and the minority Social Democrats (the right wing) enabled the Christian Democrats to maintain power at the head of successive coalition governments with the Social Democrats (until 1959) and other center parties and to exclude the Communists from the government. However, the Communists dominated the local politics of Tuscany, Umbria, and Emilia-Romagna. In 1962, Premier Amintore FANFANI, a Christian Democrat, formed a center-left coalition with a cabinet that again included the Social Democrats, as well as the parliamentary support of the Socialist party, led by Pietro Nenni. However, Fanfani's government fell after general elections in 1963, and, in a manner characteristic of the 1960s and early 1970s, there was considerable uncertainty before Aldo Moro, also a Christian Democrat, was able to form a center-left coalition in late 1963. The Moro government fell in 1964 and in 1966, but on each occasion was reformed after a brief hiatus. However, following the general elections of May, 1968, the Moro government fell again and a government crisis began that was only ended in Dec., 1968, when Mariano Rumor, a Christian Democrat, formed a coalition government with Socialist support. In 1969–70, Rumor's government fell twice, but each time it was reconstructed after a period of uncertainty. However, after Rumor's coalition fell for a third time in July, 1970, he was replaced (Aug., 1970) as premier by Emilio Colombo, a Christian Democrat. Colombo resigned in Jan., 1972. After a long period of crisis, Giulio Andreotti, also a Christian Democrat, formed a new coalition government in June, 1972; for the first time in 10 years, the government had a center-right, rather than a center-left, character. But this combination also did not last long and was replaced (July, 1973) by a slightly left of center coalition headed by Rumor. After several attempts at reconstruction, Rumor's government fell in Nov., 1974, and he was succeeded by Aldo Moro. His government served until July, 1976, when Giulio Andreotti formed an all-Christian Democratic cabinet. In regional elections in 1975, and in the general election in 1976, the Communist party made its greatest advances of the postwar period, receiving some 33% of the vote to the Christian Democrats 38%. Nonetheless, Communists continued to be excluded from ministerial responsibility at the national level, although a Communist was elected president of the chamber of deputies. The Christian Democrats, lacking the support of non-Communist parties of the left, rely on the tacit support of the Communists. Despite pervasive instability, Italy's economy, particularly in the industrial sector, has expanded dramatically in the postwar period. The major problems of the 1970s were inflation, trade deficits, and labor unrest. Italy was a charter member of the North Atlantic Treaty Organization (1949) and its foreign policy has been firmly aligned to the West. Despite skepticism among Western nations, the Communist party has reaffirmed its commitment to Italian participation in NATO and the Common Market.

Government. Under the 1948 constitution, legislative power is vested in a bicameral parliament consisting of the 630-member chamber of deputies, which is popularly elected, and the senate, made up of 315 members elected by region, plus 5 life members nominated by the president of Italy and all living former presidents. The chamber is the more important body. The council of ministers, led by the premier, is the country's executive; it must have the confidence of parliament. The head of state is the president, chosen in a joint session by parliament. The country's 20 regions also have parliaments and governments with limited powers.

Bibliography. Among general histories of Italy are Vernon Bartlett, *Introduction to Italy* (1967); Muriel Grindrod, *Italy* (1968); Great Britain, Naval Intelligence Division, *Italy* (4 vol., 1944–45, repr. 1969–); Peter Gunn, *A Concise History of Italy* (1972). A bibliography of the early period and the barbarian invasions is listed under ROME. For the medieval period, see D. P. Waley, *The Italian City-Republics* (1969); J. K. Hyde, *Society and Politics in Medieval Italy* (1973). For the Renaissance, see bibliography under RENAISSANCE. For the modern period, see Benedetto Croce, *History of Italy, 1871–1915* (tr. 1929, repr. 1963); Norman Kogan, *A Political History of Postwar Italy* (1966); Giuseppe Mammarella, *Italy after Fascism: A Political History, 1943–1965* (rev. and enl. ed. 1966); Bolton King, *A History of Italian Unity* (2 vol., 1924, repr. 1967); S. B. Clough and Salvatore Saladino, *A History of Modern Italy* (1968); Denis Mack Smith, *Italy, A Modern History* (rev. and enl. ed. 1969); F. R. Willis, *Italy Chooses Europe* (1971); J. C. Adams, *The Government of Republican Italy* (3d ed. 1972); S. J. Woolf, ed., *The Rebirth of Italy, 1943–50* (1972).

Itami (ētä'mē), city (1970 pop. 155,763), Hyogo prefecture, S Honshu, Japan, on the Muko River and Osaka Bay. It is a residential suburb of Osaka and the site of Osaka International Airport.

Itasca, Lake (ītăs'kə), shallow lake, 2 sq mi (5.2 sq km), in a pine-wooded swampy region, NW Minn. Henry R. Schoolcraft identified it (1832) as the source of the Mississippi. Later geographers consider the source to be above the lake. In 1891 the region was included in a state park, which has a historical and natural history museum.

Iténez: see GUAPORÉ.

Ithaca, Greece: see ITHÁKI.

Ithaca (ĭth'əkə), city (1970 pop. 26,226), seat of Tompkins co., S central N.Y., at the southern end of Cayuga Lake, in the Finger Lakes region; settled 1789, inc. as a city 1888. It is important chiefly as an educational center, the seat of Cornell Univ. and of Ithaca College. It is also a major producer of salt in the state, and, with access to the New York State Barge Canal, it is an inland shipping point. A state hospital is in Ithaca. The city is situated on hills above the lake and is traversed by creeks that cut deep, scenic gorges.

Ithai (ĭ''thā'ī, ĭthā'ī), variant of ITTAI **2.**

Itháki (ēthä'kē) or **Ithaca** (ĭth'əkə), island (1971 pop. 4,156), c.37 sq mi (96 sq km), W Greece, one of the IONIAN ISLANDS. It is mountainous, rising to c.2,650 ft (810 m) at Mt. Anoyi, and has little arable land. The chief products are olive oil, currants, and wine. The main town is Itháki (1971 pop. 2,293), located on the island's east coast. The island is traditionally celebrated as the home of ODYSSEUS. Cyclopean walls and remains of a Corinthian colony (c.8th cent. B.C.) have been found. In 1953, Itháki was devastated by tidal waves.

Ithamar (ĭth'əmär), son of Aaron. Ex. 6.23; 28.1; 38.21; Lev. 10.6; 1 Chron. 24.3; Ezra 8.2.

Ithiel (ĭth'ĭēl, ĭthī'-). **1** Benjamite. Neh. 11.7. **2** See UCAL.

Ithmah (ĭth'mə), Moabite member of David's guard. 1 Chron. 11.46.

Ithnan (ĭth'năn), unidentified town, S Palestine, perhaps to be read Hazor-ithnan and identified with HAZOR **1.** Joshua 15.23.

Ithra (ĭth'rə), variant of JETHER **2.**

Ithran (ĭth'răn). **1** Descendant of Asher. 1 Chron. 7.37. He is probably the same as Jether in verse 38. **2** Chief of the Horites. Gen. 36.26.

Ithream (ĭth'rēəm), son of David. 2 Sam. 3.5; 1 Chron. 3.3.

Ithrite (ĭth'rīt), family name of two of David's guard. 2 Sam. 23.38; 1 Chron. 11.40.

Ito, Hirobumi (hērō'bo͞omē ē'tō), 1841–1909, Japanese statesman, the outstanding figure in the modernization of Japan. As a young Choshu samurai, he was a xenophobe. In 1863 he visited Europe, studied science in England, and became convinced of the necessity of adopting Western ways. After the MEIJI RESTORATION, Ito served in the ministries of foreign affairs, finance, and industry. He was a member of the mission sent abroad (1871) under Prince Iwakura to revise the unequal treaties with the Western powers and study Western technology. In 1873, Ito became a member of the ruling council and worked to modernize Japan and solidify the power of the oligarchs. By 1881 he forced Shigenobu OKUMA to resign and thus became the foremost political power in Japan. In 1882 he headed the mission sent abroad to study foreign governments. Returning, he established a cabinet and civil service (1885) and a privy council (1888), which he headed. He supervised (1883–89) the drafting of the constitution of 1889 and was intimate adviser to the emperor. In 1885 he negotiated the Li-Ito Convention, which postponed war with China over Korea. As prime minister (1892–96) he supported the Sino-Japanese War and negotiated the Treaty of Shimonoseki. After the war he became a supporter of party government, opposing Prince YAMAGATA. He was the first president of the Seiyukai party. Again prime minister (1898, 1900–1901), he tried to negotiate a peaceful settlement with Russia, but, failing, was forced to increase military appropriations. From 1901 to 1913 the premiership alternated between his protégé, Kammoche Saionji, and Taro Katsura, a follower of Yamagata. In 1905, Ito forced an agreement making Korea a virtual protectorate of Japan and became (1906) resident general there. His assassination (1909) by a Korean fanatic served as a pretext for annexation.

Ito, city (1970 pop. 63,003), Shizuoka prefecture, central Honshu, Japan, on the Izu Peninsula and the Sagami Sea. It is a port and hot spring resort.

Itsuku-shima (ētso͞oko͞o'-shĭm'ä), sacred island, 12 sq mi (31 sq km), in the Inland Sea, Japan, SW of Hiroshima. It is the site of an ancient Shinto shrine, famous for its magical beauty. It is also known for a 9th-century Buddhist temple, a pagoda (built 1407), a 16th-century hall built by Hideyoshi, and a huge torii (1875). Miya-jima, or Shrine Isle, is another name for the island.

Ittah-kazin (ĭt'ə-kā'zĭn), unidentified place, N Palestine. Joshua 19.13.

Ittai (ĭt'āī, ĭtā'ī). **1** Gittite follower of David. He stood by David in Absalom's revolt. 2 Sam. 15.19–22; 18.2,5,12. **2** Benjamite, one of David's mighty men. 2 Sam. 23.29. Ithai: 1 Chron. 11.31.

Ituraea (ĭtyo͞orē'ə), ancient country on the northern border of Palestine. Jetur, the son of Ishmael, was its founder. Ancient geographers are not agreed as to the exact limits of the country. The inhabitants were Arabians with their capital at Chalchis and their religious center at Heliopolis (Baalbek). Ituraea was conquered in 105 B.C. by Aristobulus, king of Judaea, who annexed it to Judaea and converted many of the inhabitants to Judaism. Later, after a brief period of independence, the country was subdued by Pompey. It remained thereafter chiefly in Roman hands, being united (A.D. c.50) to the Roman province of Syria. Many Ituraeans served in the armies of Rome and were renowned for their skill as horsemen and archers.

Iturbi, José (hōsā' ētōōr'bē), 1895–, Spanish-American pianist, b. Valencia, Spain. Iturbi studied at the Valencia and Paris conservatories on scholarship. His worldwide concert tours were brilliantly successful. He excelled as an interpreter of Spanish music. In New York City in 1929 he made his American debut; he made his first appearance as a conductor in Mexico City in 1933. He was conductor of the Rochester (N.Y.) Philharmonic Orchestra from 1936 to 1944. Iturbi appeared as an actor-performer in several filmed musicals of the 1940s.

Iturbide, Agustín de (ägōōstēn' dā ētōōrbē'thä), 1783–1824, Mexican revolutionist, emperor of Mexico (1822–23). An officer in the royalist army, he was sympathetic to independence but took no part in the separatist movement led by Miguel Hidalgo y Costilla, and in fact helped to suppress the peasant revolt. His forces were instrumental in checking MORELOS Y PAVÓN. In 1820 he was commissioned by Viceroy APODACA to lead royalist troops against Vicente GUERRERO. Iturbide undertook the command with the intention of overthrowing the viceroyalty and establishing Mexican independence. After Guerrero had inflicted minor defeats on his troops, Iturbide opened negotiations with the insurgent leader, and the result was the Plan of IGUALA (1821). Iturbide's army swept the country. The new viceroy, O'DONOJÚ, capitulated to their demands in the Treaty of CÓRDOBA (1821). The independence of Mexico was assured, but without the social reforms advocated by Hidalgo; instead of a new liberal state, Iturbide had ushered in a new conservative one. He headed a provisional government which in time became dictatorial. When no Bourbon prince could be found to accept the crown of Mexico and Spain repudiated the Treaty of Córdoba, his soldiers proclaimed him emperor as Agustín I. Congress, hostile but intimidated, ratified the proclamation (1822). It was not long before a revolution was in the field, with SANTA ANNA and GUADALUPE VICTORIA as its principal leaders. In 1823, Iturbide was forced to abdicate and go into exile in Europe. Congress decreed him a traitor and an outlaw, forbidding his reentry into Mexico. Iturbide, ignorant of the decree, sailed back to Mexico in 1824. He was captured, tried by the Congress of Tamaulipas, and shot. Iturbide has been regarded by conservatives as the champion of Mexican independence, rather than Hidalgo or Morelos y Pavón. In 1838 a conservative government placed his body in the Cathedral of Mexico. See biography by W. S. Robertson (1968).

Iturrigaray, José de (hōsā' thā ētōō'rēgärä'ē), 1742–1815, Spanish colonial administrator, viceroy of New Spain (1803–8). During his rule, all of Spanish America was disturbed by the Napoleonic invasion of Spain and the abdication of Ferdinand VII. A quasi-separatist movement arose among the creoles of Mexico, and Iturrigaray lent his ear to their schemes. The Spanish-born officials of the viceroyalty resisted the liberal creoles and, suspecting Iturrigaray, deposed him (Sept. 15, 1808), confiscated his fortune, and shipped him to Spain. The separatist spirit of the creoles burst forth two years later in the uprising of Miguel Hidalgo y Costilla.

Ituzaingó, battle of (ē''tōōsīn-gō'), fought in S Uruguay, Feb. 20, 1827. A combined Argentine-Uruguayan force under Carlos María de Alvear decisively defeated Brazil. The United Provinces of La Plata (Argentina) and Brazil had both claimed Uruguay. In the peace treaty that followed (1828), an independent Uruguay was created as a buffer state.

Itys (ī'tĭs) or **Itylus** (ĭt'ələs): see PHILOMELA; AËDON.

Itzá (ētsä'), Maya Indians of Yucatán (Mexico) and PETÉN (Guatemala). Probable founders of CHICHÉN ITZÁ, which they occupied at various times from c.514 to 1194, they moved (1450?) S from Campeche to Lake Petén. Here, in spite of sporadic attempts by the Spanish to convert or subdue them after the visit of Cortés in 1525, the Itzá (the last strong, independent Mayan tribe) remained until driven from their capital, Tayasal, in 1697.

Itzamna (ētsäm' nä), chief deity of the Maya. Son of Hunab Ku, the creator, he was believed to be lord of the heavens, day, and night. Thought by the Maya to have been the inventor of writing and books, Itzamna was, by extension, creator of the calendar and chronology. He was a benevolent deity.

Itzehoe (ĭt'səhō), city (1970 pop. 36,176), Schleswig-Holstein, N West Germany, on the Stör River. It is a commercial center; manufactures include cement and machinery. Itzehoe was founded c.810 by Charlemagne and is one of the oldest cities in Schleswig-Holstein. It passed to Prussia in 1866.

Iulis, ancient Greece: see KÉA.

Ivah (ī'və), unidentified city of Mesopotamia, perhaps the same as AVA. 2 Kings 18.34; 19.13; Isa. 37.13.

Ivan II or **Ivan Asen** (ē'vän ä'sən), d. 1241, czar of Bulgaria (1218–41). On the death (1207) of his father, Kaloyan, founder of the second Bulgarian empire, the throne was usurped by Ivan's cousin Boril. Ivan fled to the duchy of Galich and secured its aid. Returning in 1218, he captured Trnovo, had Boril blinded, and was crowned czar. Under Ivan II the Bulgarian empire reached its zenith, becoming the strongest power in the Balkans; he added Macedonia, Epirus, and much of Albania and Serbia to his lands. He campaigned (1235) with JOHN III of Nicaea against the Latin Empire of Constantinople, but later helped the Latins oppose John. Ivan's generally mild conduct and sincere faith endeared him even to his foes. He restored the autonomy of the Bulgarian church, established a central administration, and encouraged the settlement of Ragusan merchants. For his repudiation (1232) of the union with Rome and his support of the heretic Bogomils, he was excommunicated (1236) by Pope Gregory IX. Ivan II was succeeded by his sons Kaliman I, who reigned 1241–46, and Michael, who reigned 1246–57. With Michael's death the direct Asen line became extinct.

Ivan III or **Ivan the Great,** 1440–1505, grand duke of Moscow (1462–1505), creator of the consolidated Muscovite (Russian) state. He subjugated (1478) Great NOVGOROD, asserted his sway over Vyatka, Tver, Yaroslavl, Rostov, and other territories, and checked the eastward expansion of Lithuania, from which he gained some former Russian lands. In 1480 he freed Muscovy from allegiance to the Tatars of the GOLDEN HORDE. To prevent insurrection in annexed territories, Ivan transplanted their ruling classes to Old Muscovy and replaced them with loyal Muscovites. Prudence and wisdom were said to be his dominant traits. He established autocratic government and took as his second wife Sophia, niece of the last Byzantine emperor. The two-headed eagle of Byzantium was added to the arms of Muscovy, Sophia introduced customs of the Byzantine court, and the idea of Moscow as a "third Rome" (successor to the might of Rome and the Byzantine Empire) became popular in official circles. Laws were codified, foreign artisans were introduced, and Italian architects erected churches, palaces, and fortifications. Ivan was succeeded by his son, Vasily III.

Ivan IV or **Ivan the Terrible,** 1530–84, grand duke of Moscow (1533–84), first to assume formally the title of czar. He succeeded his father VASILY III, who died in 1533, under the regency of his mother. When she died (1538), the regency alternated among several feuding boyar families. Boyar rule ended only in 1546, when Ivan announced his intention of becoming czar. He was crowned in 1547. As czar, Ivan attempted to establish czarist autocracy at the expense of boyar power. In the early years of his reign, he reduced the arbitrary powers of the boyar provincial governors, transferring their functions to locally elected officials. The former boyars' council was replaced by a "chosen council" consisting of members who owed their status to the czar. In 1566, Ivan summoned what was probably the first general council of the realm *(Zemsky Sobor),* composed of representatives of different social ranks, including merchants and lower nobility. After reorganizing the army, Ivan conquered Kazan (1552) and Astrakhan (1556), thereby inaugurating Russia's eastward expansion. The conquest of Siberia by the Cossack YERMAK took place late in his reign (1581–83). Ivan also began trade with England via the White Sea in the mid-1550s. To improve his access to the Baltic Sea, he undertook (1558) a campaign against Livonia. In the resulting war with Poland and Sweden, he was at first successful but was later defeated by Stephen BATHORY, king of Poland and Lithuania. The peace treaties (1582, 1583) forced the czar to renounce his territorial gains and cede additional territory to Sweden. In his later years, Ivan's character, always stern, grew tyrannical. Apart from the reverses of the war, the change has been attributed to humiliations at the hands of the boyars during his childhood; a serious illness (1553) and resistance at that time to his efforts to secure the succession of his infant son; the death of his wife, Anastasia Romanov (1560), whom historians credit with exercising a moderating influence; and the defection to Poland of his favorite, Prince Andrew Kurbsky (1564). Suspecting conspiracies everywhere, he acted ruthlessly to consolidate his power. In 1565 he set aside an extensive personal domain, the *oprichnina,* under his direct control. He established a special corps *(oprichniki),* responsible to him alone, to whom he granted part of this domain at will. With the help of this corps, he diminished the political influence of the boyars and forcibly confiscated their lands in a reign of terror. Many boyars were executed or exiled. He formally abolished the *oprichnina* in 1572, although in effect it continued until 1575. Fits of rage alternated with periods of repentance and prayer; in one of his rages he killed (1581) his son and heir, Ivan. Although the exact number of his wives is uncertain, Ivan probably married seven times, ridding himself of unwanted wives by forcing them to take the veil or arranging for their murder. Despite his cruelty, he was a man of intelligence and learning. Printing was introduced into Russia during his reign, and his correspondence with the mutinous Prince Kurbsky reveals literary talent. Two sons, FEODOR I and DMITRI, survived the czar, but after his death his favorite, Boris GODUNOV, gained power. See biographies by Stephen Graham (1933, repr. 1968), Hans von Eckhardt (tr. 1949), and Ian Grey (1964); J. L. I. Fennell, ed., *The Correspondence between Prince A. M. Kurbsky and Tsar Ivan IV of Russia, 1564–1579* (1955).

Ivan V, 1666–96, czar of Russia (1682–96), son of Czar Alexis by his first wife. Ivan was retarded, and on the death of his elder brother, Feodor III, his succession was widely opposed by the supporters of his half brother, PETER I (Peter the Great). However, Ivan and Peter jointly succeeded under the regency of Ivan's sister SOPHIA ALEKSEYEVNA. After the overthrow (1689) of Sophia's regency, Ivan was excluded from state affairs and Peter assumed control. Ivan's elder daughter, Catherine, was the grandmother of Ivan VI; his younger daughter, Anna, became czarina of Russia in 1730. See C. B. O'Brien, *Russia under Two Tsars* (1952).

Ivan VI, 1740–64, czar of Russia (1740–41), great-grandson of Ivan V. He was the son of Prince Anthony Ulric of Brunswick-Wolfenbüttel and of ANNA LEOPOLDOVNA. An infant, he succeeded his great-aunt, Czarina Anna, on the Russian throne under the unpopular regency of his mother. In 1741, ELIZABETH, daughter of Peter I (Peter the Great), overthrew Anna Leopoldovna's regime and became czarina. Ivan grew up in solitary confinement. An attempt by a young officer to liberate him and make him czar resulted in his murder in the fortress of Schlüsselburg, according to standing instructions given by Czarina Catherine II.

Ivan Asen: see IVAN II, czar of Bulgaria.

Ivano-Frankovsk (ĭvä'nô-fräng'kôfsk), formerly **Stanislav** (stənyĭsläf'), city (1970 pop. 105,000), capital of Ivano-Frankovsk oblast, extreme SW European USSR, in Ukraine, on the Bystritsa River. It is a rail junction and industrial center situated in a fertile agricultural zone of the Carpathian foothills. The city has oil refineries, railroad repair shops, engineering and food processing plants, and factories that produce farm machinery, metal goods, leather footwear, furniture, cement, clothing, and other items. Oil fields are nearby. An old Ukrainian settlement, Stanislav was chartered in 1662 and, despite Tatar and Turkish raids, flourished as a trade center in the 17th and 18th cent. It became the bishopric of the Ukrainian Catholic Uniate Church in 1850. It passed to Austria in 1772 and to Poland in 1919 and was incorporated into the Ukraine in 1939. The city and oblast were renamed in 1962 in honor of the Ukrainian poet and writer Ivan Franko. Landmarks include a wooden church (1601), a Catholic Uniate cathedral, and an 18th-century palace.

Ivanov, Lev (lyĕf ēvä'nôf), 1834–1901, Russian dancer, teacher, choreographer, and ballet-master. Ivanov was assistant to chief ballet-master Marius PETIPA at the Imperial St. Petersburg Theatres and was instrumental in the development of the classic romantic ballet in Russia. When Petipa fell ill, Ivanov created the choreography for *The Nutcracker* (1892) to the music of Tchaikovsky. After Tchaikovsky's death, the previously unsuccessful *Swan Lake* (1877) was revised with choreography by Petipa and Ivanov, each doing alternate acts in varying styles. His other major works include revivals or stagings of *La Fille Mal Gardée, The Enchanted Forest, The Magic Flute,* and *Cinderella*. Ivanov sought a closer relationship of dance and music, thereby influencing the work of later choreographers, including Michel FOKINE.

Ivanov, Vsevolod Vyacheslavovich (fəsyĕ'vələt vyĕ"chĭslä'vəvĭch), 1895–1963, Russian short-story writer, novelist, and dramatist, b. Siberia. Ivanov had an adventurous early life as a sailor, circus performer, fakir, and partisan fighter. His talent for vivid description and ironic point of view was discovered and encouraged by Gorky. The novel *Armoured Train 14–69* (1922, tr. 1933), based on an episode of Soviet expansion in Siberia, is considered the most important of his many works. A long, semiautobiographical novel, *The Adventures of a Fakir,* was translated in abridged form in 1935. His later work includes *Saga of the Sergeant* (tr. 1952).

Ivanovo (ēvä'nəvə), city (1970 pop. 419,000), capital of Ivanovo oblast, central European USSR, in the Moscow industrial region. A great Soviet textile center, the city was the historic center of Russia's cotton-milling industry. From the 1880s it was a center of labor unrest. During the revolution of 1905, 60,000 workers went on strike and formed one of the first soviets of workers' representatives. After six weeks the strike was crushed. The city was called Ivano-Voznesensk until 1932.

Ivan the Great: see IVAN III.

Ivan the Terrible: see IVAN IV.

Ives, Charles, 1874–1954, American composer and organist, b. Danbury, Conn., grad. Yale, 1898; pupil of Dudley Buck and Horatio Parker. He was organist (1893–1904) in churches in Connecticut, New Jersey, and New York. In the insurance business from 1898 to 1930, Ives was at the same time composing music that was advanced in style, anticipating some of the innovations of Schoenberg and Stravinsky, but not influencing the trend of music because most of his works were not published. They were little known until 1939, when performance of his second piano sonata, *Concord* (1909–15), won him wide recognition. In 1947 his Third Symphony was awarded the Pulitzer Prize. His works include symphonies, orchestral suites, sonatas, organ pieces, choral works, a great deal of chamber music, and about 150 songs. He often used American folk music in compositions evoking the spirit of various aspects of American life such as revival meetings and brass-band parades. See his *Essays before a Sonata* (new ed. 1962) and his *Memos,* ed. by J. E. Kirkpatrick (1972); biography by Henry and Sidney Cowell (rev. ed. 1969); Vivian Perlis, *Charles Ives Remembered* (1974); R. S. Perry, *Charles Ives and the American Mind* (1974).

Ives, Frederic Eugene, 1856–1937, American inventor, b. Litchfield, Conn. A pioneer in the development of orthochromatic and trichromatic photography and of photoengraving, he followed an earlier suggestion by James Clerk Maxwell and produced in 1881 the first set of trichromatic plates. In 1878 he devised the first practical halftone process of photoengraving, developing it in 1886 to the process which came into general use. Among his other inventions are the short-tube, single-objective binocular microscope; the parallax stereogram; and a process for moving pictures in natural colors. His son **Herbert Eugene Ives,** 1882–1953, inventor and physicist, b. Philadelphia, was active in the development of television. He demonstrated the transmission via telephone wires of black-and-white pictures in 1924 and of color pictures in 1929. He made a number of important contributions to color science and invented the first practical artificial-daylight lamp.

Ives, James Merritt: see CURRIER & IVES.

Ivigtut (ē'vĭgtŏŏt), town (1969 pop. 75), SW Greenland, on the Arsuk Fjord. The world's largest known cryolite deposit was discovered there in 1806. Mined since 1864, the deposit has been recently exhausted; stockpiled cryolite has been exported since 1969.

Iviza: see IBIZA.

Ivo of Chartres, Saint (ī'vō, shär'trə), c.1040–c.1116, French churchman, bishop of Chartres (after 1090). He was fearlessly outspoken and was briefly imprisoned for opposing the irregular second marriage of King PHILIP I of France. He worked to obtain a compromise in the imperial struggle over investitures. His principal fame was for his knowledge of CANON LAW. His *Decretum* and *Panormia,* collections of canons, were perhaps the most extensive until supplanted by the work of GRATIAN. Feast: May 24.

ivory, type of dentin present only in the tusks of the ELEPHANT. In commerce, ivory is classified as live (from recently killed animals) and dead (tusks long stored or on the ground for extended periods and lacking the resilience of live ivory). Ivory may be of a soft or hard variety; the former type is more moist, cracks less easily than the brittle hard ivory, and is easier to work. Green, or guinea, ivory denotes certain types of ivory obtained from a wide belt in north central Africa, from the east to the west coasts. Ivory is obtained mainly from Africa, where elephant tusks are larger than they are in Asia, the second major source, and much dead ivory has been taken from remains of extinct mammoths found in Canada, Alaska, and Siberia. African tusks of about 55 lb (25 kg) each are common, although tusks of more than 200 lb (91 kg) have been recorded. At various periods in Africa native peoples, Arabs, and European colonial powers have dominated the trade in ivory. Zanzibar, Antwerp, and London have been major centers of ivory commerce. Europe, the United States, and India are major importers. In the West, soft ivory, obtainable primarily from the eastern half of Africa, is in greater demand than the hard variety from W Africa. Commercial uses of ivory include the manufacture of piano and organ keys, billiard balls, handles, and minor objects of decorative value. In modern industry, ivory is used in the manufacture of electrical appliances, including specialized electrical equipment for airplanes and radar. Large surfaces suitable for veneer are obtained by cutting spiral sheets around the tusk. Ivory is prized for its close-grained texture, adhesive hardness, mellow color, and pleasing smoothness. It may be painted or bleached, and is an excellent material for carving. Its use in art dates back to prehistoric times, when representations of animals were incised on tusks. Objects in ivory were created in ancient Egypt, Assyria, Crete, Mycenae, Greece, and Italy, and there are many Biblical references to its use at least from the time of Solomon. Large Greek statues, such as the Athena of PHIDIAS, were made in gold and ivory (chryselephantine), and the Romans made lavish use of ivory in furniture, implements of war, and decorative items. A considerable number of diptychs and panels in ivory, given as gifts primarily by Roman consuls, still exist. Ivory plaques, diptychs, boxes, liturgical objects, book covers, and small statues were made in great numbers from early Christian times until c.1400, but the production of

Italian early Renaissance triptych made of wood, ivory, and hippopotamus teeth (right).

Sculpted ivory horse of the Paleolithic period, found in a cave near Lourdes, southwestern France (below).

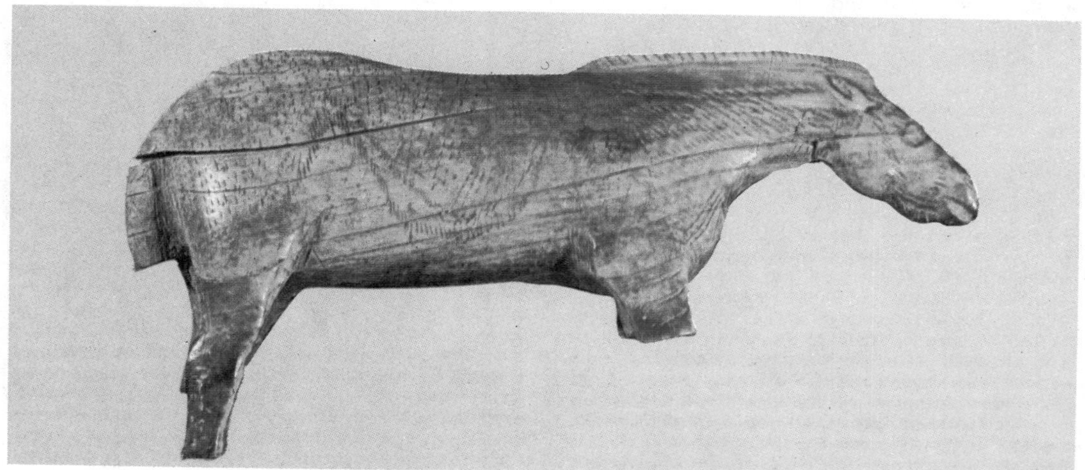

these objects declined thereafter. Ivory carving was practiced both in W Europe and in the Byzantine Empire. In India, ivory carving and turning has been done from ancient times. In China and Japan ivory has been used for inlay and small objects, especially for statues and carvings of small size and great precision and beauty of detail. In the last few centuries in Europe and North America, ivory has been employed to decorate furniture, for small statues, and occasionally as a surface for miniature painting. The diminishing number of elephants, to a large extent the result of wholesale slaughter for tusks, and the resulting increased cost of ivory have encouraged the making of imitations. Natural substitutes (e.g., TAGUA, or vegetable ivory) or near equivalents have long been used. In the past, the tooth structure of many other animals, such as the hippopotamus, walrus, narwhal, sperm whale, and wild boar, was also called ivory. See O. Beigbeder, *Ivory* (1965); M. Carra, *Ivories of the West* (1970).

ivory-billed woodpecker, common name for the largest of the North American woodpeckers, *Campephilus principalis*. Believed since 1952 to be nearing extinction, the last known members of this species were reported from the deepest forests of NW Florida and central Louisiana. A shiny blue-black in color with extensive white markings on its wings and neck, this bird is distinguished by its pure white bill and by a prominent top crest, red in the male and black in the female. A true WOODPECKER, it has a strong and straight chisellike bill and a long, mobile, hard-tipped, sticky tongue. It measures from 18 to 20 in. (46–51 cm) in length, with short legs and feet ending in large, curved claws. The ivory-bill deposits from three to five glossy white eggs per clutch in an unlined hole, preferably drilled in a cyprus tree. Of its reproductive habits little more than this is known. The disappearance of the ivory-bills may be blamed on the cutting and eventual disappearance of the trees in which they lived. It is thought that a few ivory-bills are surviving today in the forests of the Gulf Coast of North America and in Cuba. Ivory-billed woodpeckers are classified in the phylum CHORDATA, subphylum Vertebrata, class Aves, order Piciformes, family Picidae.

Ivory Coast, Fr. *Côte d'Ivoire*, independent republic (1973 est. pop. 4,585,000), 124,503 sq mi (322,463 sq km), W Africa, on the Gulf of Guinea of the Atlantic Ocean. The capital and chief port is ABIDJAN. The Ivory Coast is bordered by Liberia and Guinea on the west, by Mali and Upper Volta on the north, and by Ghana on the east. The country consists of a coastal lowland in the south, a densely forested plateau in the interior, and a region of high savannas in the north. Rainfall is heavy, especially along the coast. Among the major ethnic groups in the Ivory Coast are the Agni, Baoulé, and Senufo tribes. The population is about 65% animist, 23% Muslim, and 12% Christian. French is the official language, and French personnel play an important role in the economy. The wealthiest member of what was formerly French West Africa, the Ivory Coast has enjoyed a high economic growth rate since independence. Despite steady industrialization during the 1960s, the country is still predominantly agricultural. The Ivory Coast is one of the world's largest coffee producers. Cotton, cocoa, bananas, pineapples, and palm kernels are raised for export. Mahogany and other hardwood forests provide timber, which is also a valuable export. Livestock is raised in the savannas. Fishing and the canning of tuna are also important occupations. Among the country's industries are the production of flour, palm oil, petroleum, textiles, cigarettes, and the assembly of motor vehicles and bicycles. France is the chief trading partner of the Ivory Coast, which belongs to the French franc zone and is an associate member of the European Common Market. In precolonial times the Ivory Coast was dominated by native kingdoms. The Portuguese established trading settlements along the coast in the 16th cent., and other Europeans later joined the burgeoning trade in slaves and ivory. In 1842 a French military mission imposed a protectorate over the coastal zone. After 1870, France undertook a systematic conquest; although a protectorate over the entire country was proclaimed in 1893, strong resistance by native tribes delayed French occupation of the interior. The Ivory Coast was incorporated into the Federation of French West Africa, and several thousand troops from the Ivory Coast fought with the French during World War I; but effective French control over the area was not established until after the war. Vichy forces held the Ivory Coast during World War II, but many Ivorians left to join the Free French forces in the Gold Coast. As the desire for independence mounted, Félix HOUPHOUËT-BOIGNY, a planter and founder of the federation-wide Rassemblement Démocratique Africain (RDA), formed (1946) the nationalist Parti Démocratique de la Côte d'Ivoire (PDCI). In the French constitutional referendum of 1958, the Ivory Coast chose autonomy within the French Community. The following year Houphouët-Boigny played an instrumental role in the formation of the Council of the Entente, a customs union with Dahomey, Nigeria, and Upper Volta (Togo joined later). In 1960 the Ivory Coast withdrew from the French Community and declared itself independent. The new republic joined the Organization of African Unity in 1963. The Ivory Coast is a one-party state. Houphouët-Boigny has headed the government as well as the PDCI since independence. As president of the republic, he is elected for a five-year term by universal adult suffrage. The national assembly is elected concurrently on a single slate. Despite student and

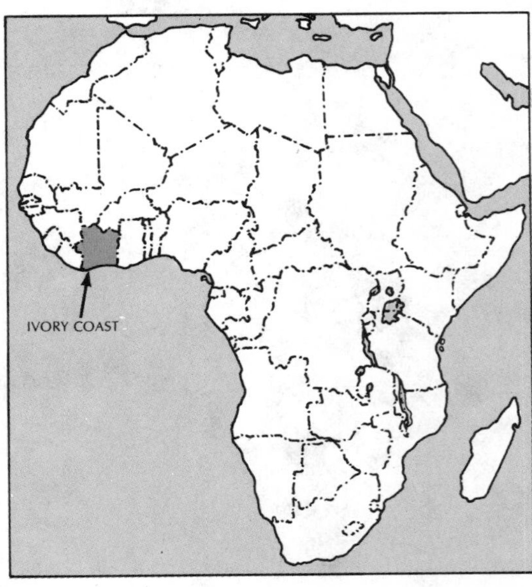

Woman of the Ivory Coast sorting coffee beans, the country's major product (above).

Timber, a valuable Ivory Coast export, being loaded on trucks to be transported to various ports (right).

worker unrest, Houphouët-Boigny's leadership has not been seriously challenged. In 1966 a treaty signed at Abidjan provided for a new West African customs union (superseding the Council of the Entente), including Mauritania and Senegal as well as the old council members. The Ivory Coast was one of the few African states to recognize Biafra during the Nigerian civil war (1967–70); this action, as well as Houphouët-Boigny's advocacy of dialogue with white-ruled South Africa, estranged the country somewhat from many other African states. See Immanuel Wallerstein, *Road to Independence: Ghana and the Ivory Coast* (1964); Aristide R. Zolberg, *One-Party Government in the Ivory Coast* (rev. ed. 1969); Christian P. Potholm, *Four African Political Systems* (1970); Philip Foster and Aristide R. Zolberg, ed., *Ghana and the Ivory Coast: Perspectives in Modernization* (1971).

ivory nut: see TAGUA.

Ivrea (ēvrĕ'ä), city (1971 pop. 29,358), Piedmont, NW Italy, on the Dora Baltea River. It is a commercial and industrial center. Manufactures include typewriters and calculating machines, textiles, and silverware. A Roman town (*Eporedia*), it was later the capital of a Lombard duchy and then the seat of a marquisate. BERENGAR II, one of its rulers, was briefly king of Italy (mid-10th cent.). Ivrea passed to the house of Savoy in the 14th cent. The city is dominated by a picturesque castle (14th cent.), which has four red brick towers.

Ivry-sur-Seine (ēvrē'-sür-sĕn), industrial and commercial suburb SE of Paris (1968 pop. 60,616), Val-de-Marne dept., N central France. Its port, on the Seine River, deals in wholesale trade in fuel, timber, barrels, and foodstuffs. Its manufactures include chemicals, metals, pharmaceuticals, and oils. There are churches dating from the 13th, 16th, and 17th cent. A thermal-power station is in the town.

ivy, name applied loosely to any trailing or CLIMBING PLANT, particularly cultivated forms, but more properly a designation for *Hedera helix,* the so-called English ivy, and some related species of the family Araliaceae (GINSENG family). Native to Europe and temperate Asia, English ivy is a woody evergreen vine, usually sterile, whose berries contain the poisonous principle hederin. Grown in numerous varieties, it is the most popular house and wall vine. The Boston, or Japanese, ivy (*Parthenocissus tricuspidata,* of Japan and China) and the American ivy, or VIRGINIA CREEPER (*P. quinquefolia,* of North America), are similar species of the family Vitaceae (GRAPE family). Both are sometimes called AMPELOPSIS, a name usually reserved for another related genus. Kenilworth ivy, *Cymbalaria muralis,* of the family Scrophulariaceae (FIGWORT family) is common to old ruins in Europe; it is often cultivated as a ground cover. Ivy was sacred to Bacchus and was associated with various pagan religions. It was formerly hung as a tavern sign in England. Ivy is classified in the division MAGNOLIOPHYTA, class Magnoliopsida. The ginseng family ivies are in the order Umbellales, the grape family ivies in the order Rhamnales, and the figwort family ivies in the order Scrophulariales.

Iwaki (ēwä'kē), city (1970 pop. 327,164), Fukushima prefecture, NE Honshu, Japan, on the Iwaki River. It is a major coal-mining center, railway hub, and industrial city where machinery, chemicals, and chemical fertilizers are produced.

Iwakuni (ēwä'ko͞onē), city (1970 pop. 106,116), Yamaguchi prefecture, SW Honshu, Japan, on the Aki Sea. It is an important industrial center with petroleum refineries and rayon, chemical fiber, paper pulp, and metal machine-tool industries. Iwakuni castle (1603) is an important historical site.

Iwakura, Tomomi, Prince (tōmō'mē ēwä'ko͞orä), 1825–83, Japanese statesman. A court noble, he supported the Meiji restoration and became a minister of state (1871–83). In 1871 he headed a mission to Europe and the United States that failed to secure abolition of the unequal treaties but brought back much useful information on foreign institutions and technology. He returned to Japan in 1873 to forestall the threat of war with Korea. From 1873 until his death Iwakura, a conservative, was a leader of the peace party.

Iwasa Matabei: see MATABEI, IWASA.

Iwata (ēwä'tä), city (1970 pop. 63,002), Shizuoka prefecture, central Honshu, Japan, on the estuary of the Tenryu River. It is an agricultural and industrial center.

Iwatsuki (ēwä'tso͞okē), city (1970 pop. 56,449), Saitama prefecture, central Honshu, Japan, on the Edo River. It is an industrial center where textiles and dolls are manufactured.

Iwo (ē'wō), city (1969 est. pop. 189,000), SW Nigeria. It is the trade center for a farm region specializing in cacao. A coffee plantation is located nearby. Iwo was the capital of a YORUBA kingdom (founded in the 17th cent.) that grew rapidly in the 19th cent. by taking in refugees during the Yoruba civil wars.

Iwo Jima (ē'wō jē'mə, ē'wô), Jap. *Io-jima,* volcanic island, c.8 sq mi (21 sq km), W Pacific, largest and most important of the VOLCANO ISLANDS. Mt. Suribachi, 546 ft (166 m) high, on the south side of the island, is an extinct volcano. The main industries are sulfur mining and sugar refining. During World War II the island, site of a Japanese air base, was taken (Feb.–March, 1945), at great cost by U.S. forces. Iwo Jima was formerly called Sulphur Island.

IWW: see INDUSTRIAL WORKERS OF THE WORLD.

Ixelles (ēksĕl'), Flemish *Elsene,* city (1970 pop. 86,450), Brabant prov., central Belgium, an industrial suburb of Brussels.

Ixion (ĭk'sēən), in Greek mythology, king of the Lapithes. Ixion murdered his father-in-law to avoid paying a price for his bride. When no one on earth would purify him, Zeus took Ixion to Olympus and purified him. While there Ixion attempted to seduce Hera, but Zeus created a phantom of her and by it Ixion became the father of the centaur monsters. As punishment for his impious act, Ixion was chained eternally to a revolving, fiery wheel in Tartarus.

Ixtacalco (ēstäkäl'kō), city (1970 pop. 474,700), Federal District, S central Mexico. It is an industrial center adjacent to Mexico City. Several historic landmarks have been preserved.

Ixtacihuatl, Ixtaccihuatl, or **Iztaccihuatl** (all: ēs"-täsē'wätəl) [Aztec,=white woman], dormant volcano, 17,342 ft (5,286 m) high, central Mexico, on the border between Puebla and Mexico state. Irregular in outline, and snow-capped, it is also popularly known as the Sleeping Woman.

Ixtapalapa (ēstäpälä'pä), city (1970 pop. 533,569), Federal District, S central Mexico. It is a commercial and industrial center. Ixtapalapa was founded on the site of an important pre-Colombian Indian city.

Iyeyasu: see IEYASU.

Izabal (ēsäbäl'), lake, c.30 mi (48 km) long and 15 mi (24 km) wide, E Guatemala, largest lake in the country. Known also as the Golfo Dulce, it drains to the Caribbean Sea through the Golfete Dulce, a small adjacent lake, and the Rio Dulce, a broad tropical river. In Spanish colonial times Lake Izabal was the scene of lively trading between the seacoast and the highlands, and the small town of Izabal on its south shore was a thriving port, constantly subjected to raids in the 17th cent. by English and Dutch buccaneers. Today shipping is negligible, although Lívingston, at the mouth of the Rio Dulce, is of some importance. Nearby are many pre-Columbian ruins, the most outstanding being at Quiriguá.

Izalco (ēsäl'kō), volcano, 7,828 ft (2,386 m) high, W El Salvador. Constantly active and still increasing in height, it is sometimes called the Lighthouse of the Pacific. There have been severe eruptions. The crater was first studied in 1956 by a French expedition.

Izard, Ralph (ĭz'ərd), 1742–1804, American diplomat and legislator, b. near Charleston, S.C. After an education in England, he returned (1764) to South Carolina but in 1771 again went to London. Because of his sympathy with the colonial cause, Izard moved (1776) to Paris. Appointed (1777) commissioner to Tuscany by the Continental Congress, he was not received by that government, but he felt that, as an American diplomat, he should take part in American negotiations with France and thus won the enmity of Benjamin Franklin. Izard's connection with the De Lanceys, New York Loyalists, led to accusations that he was a Tory; however, his sincere devotion to the patriot cause was demonstrated, and after his return (1779) to America he served (1782–84) in the Continental Congress. A Federalist, he strongly supported the Constitution and was (1789–95) Senator from South Carolina. See his *Correspondence, 1774–1804* (1844).

Izehar (ĭz'ēhär) or **Izhar** (ĭz'här), grandson of Levi. 1 Chron. 6.2,18,38; 23.12,18; Ex. 6.18,21; Num. 3.19. Amminadab: 1 Chron. 6.22.

Izhevsk (ēzhĭfsk'), city (1970 pop. 422,000), capital of Udmurt Autonomous SSR, E European USSR. A major steel-milling and metallurgical center, Izhevsk has ironworks dating back to 1760.

Izmail (ēzməēl'), city (1967 est. pop. 63,000), SW European USSR, in the Ukraine, on an arm of the Danube delta and near the Rumanian border. It is a rail junction, river port, commercial center, and the naval base of the Soviet Danube flotilla. Orchards and vineyards surround the city. Izmail's industries include food and fish processing, winemaking, auto and ship repair, and the manufacture of bricks and tiles. First known in the 16th cent., the city was a Turkish fortress and capital of a Turkish sanjak. Russian forces took the city twice (1770, 1790) during the Russo-Turkish Wars of Catherine II. Recaptured by the Russians in 1809, it was ceded to them by the Treaty of Bucharest (1812). At the Congress of Paris in 1856, Izmail was returned to Turkey; but Russia seized the city again in 1878 and held it until 1918, when Rumania took it. Transferred to the USSR in 1940, it was reconquered by the Rumanians the following year but restored to the USSR in 1947. Remains of the old Turkish fortress have been preserved.

İzmir (ĭzmĭr'), formerly **Smyrna** (smûr'nə), city (1970 pop. 520,686), capital of İzmir prov., W Turkey, on the Gulf of İzmir, an arm of the Aegean Sea. The largest Turkish seaport after İstanbul, its exports include agricultural products, cotton, and carpets. It is also an important commercial and industrial center, whose manufactures include paper, metal goods, dyes, textiles, and processed food and tobacco. It is a road and rail transportation center, and an annual trade fair is held there. İzmir prov. is rich in mineral resources. The city was settled during the Bronze Age (c.3000 B.C.). It was colonized (c.1000 B.C.) by Ionians and was destroyed (627 B.C.) by the Lydians.

It was rebuilt on a different site in the early 4th cent. B.C. by Antigonus I, was enlarged and beautified by Lysimachus, and became one of the largest and most prosperous cities of Asia Minor. Its wealth and splendor increased under Roman rule. The city had a sizeable Jewish colony, was an early center of Christianity, and was one of the Seven Churches in Asia (Rev. 2–8). It was pillaged by the Arabs in the 7th cent., fell to the Seljuk Turks in the 11th cent., was recaptured for Byzantium by Emperor Alexius I during the First Crusade, and formed part of the empire of Nicaea from 1204 to 1261, when the Byzantine Empire was restored. Also in 1261 the Genoese obtained trading privileges there, which they retained until the city fell (c.1329) to the Seljuk Turks. The Knights Hospitalers captured the city in 1344, restored Genoese privileges, and held the city until 1402, when it was captured and sacked by Tamerlane. The Mongols were succeeded in 1424 by the Ottoman Turks. A Greek Orthodox archiepiscopal see, the city retained a large Greek population and remained a center of Greek culture and the chief Mediterranean port of Asia Minor. After the collapse of the Ottoman Empire in World War I, the city was occupied (1919) by Greek forces. The Treaty of Sevres (1920) assigned İzmir and its hinterland to temporary Greek administration, but fighting soon erupted between Greek and Turkish forces. İzmir fell to the Turks in Sept., 1922, and a few days later was destroyed by fire. Thousands of Greek civilian refugees fled from the city. The Treaty of Lausanne (1923) restored İzmir to Turkey. A separate convention between Greece and Turkey provided for the exchange of their minorities, which was carried out under League of Nations supervision. Thus the population of İzmir became predominately Turkish. The city suffered greatly from severe earthquakes in 1928 and 1939. By the 1970s, however, it was a thriving, modern city. It is the site of Ege Univ. and several museums and was probably the birthplace of the poet Homer.

City of Izmir, an important commercial center in Turkey.

İzmit (ĭzmēt′) or **Kocaeli** (kō″jäĕl′ē), city (1970 pop. 123,016), capital of Kocaeli prov., NW Turkey, a port on the Bay of İzmit, at the eastern end of the Sea of Marmara. It is the center of a rich tobacco- and olive-growing region. Manufactures of the city include beer and paper and paper products. Founded c.712 B.C., the city became famous after Nicomedus I of Bithynia rebuilt it in 264 B.C. as his capital, NICOMEDIA.

Iznik: see NICAEA.

Izrahiah (ĭz″rəhī′ə), chief man of Issachar. 1 Chron. 7.3.

Izrahite (ĭz′rəhīt), patronymic: see ZERAH **1.**

Izri (ĭz′rī), temple musician. 1 Chron. 25.11. In verse 3 he is called Zeri.

Izumi (ēzo͞o′mē), city (1970 pop. 95,987), Osaka prefecture, S Honshu, Japan. It is a residential and commercial suburb of Osaka, with numerous textile mills.

Izumiotsu (ēzo͞omē′ōtso͞o), city (1970 pop. 59,437), Osaka prefecture, S Honshu, Japan, on Osaka Bay. It is a commercial port with chemical and textile industries.

Izumisano (ēzo͞omē′sänō), city (1970 pop. 77,000), Osaka prefecture, S Honshu, Japan, on Osaka Bay. It is a fishing and commercial port.

Izumo (ēzo͞o′mō), city (1970 pop. 69,708), Shimane prefecture, SW Honshu, Japan, on the Hii River. It is an important commercial, agricultural, and stock-raising center.

Izu-shichito (ē′zo͞o-shēchē′tō), island group, extending c.300 mi (480 km) S of Tokyo Bay, Japan. O-shima is the largest of these volcanic islands, which are now tourist attractions. The islands were formerly used for penal settlements. They are also called the Seven Isles of Izu.

Izvolsky, Aleksandr Petrovich (əlyĭksän′dər pētrô′-vĭch ēzvôl′skē), 1856–1919, Russian diplomat instrumental in fostering the Triple Entente with France and Great Britain. He rose in the diplomatic service and in 1906 was appointed foreign minister by Czar Nicholas II. In 1907 he reached an agreement with Great Britain ending the rivalry between the two powers in the Middle East: Persia was divided into three zones, one Russian, one British, with a neutral zone between; Afghanistan was recognized as being under British protection; and Tibet was declared neutral. This agreement, in conjunction with the Franco-Russian alliance formed in the 1890s and the Anglo-French accord in 1904, marked the emergence of the Triple Entente. In 1908, Izvolsky attempted to open the Dardanelles to Russian warships through an agreement with the Austro-Hungarian foreign minister AEHRENTHAL. In return for Russian acceptance of Austrian annexation of Bosnia and Hercegovina, Austria agreed to support the opening of the straits. Austria failed to keep its part of the pact, and Izvolsky suffered a humiliating diplomatic defeat. Appointed (1910) ambassador to France, he endeavored to strengthen Franco-Russian ties. After the Russian Revolution he remained in France. See his memoirs (tr. 1920).

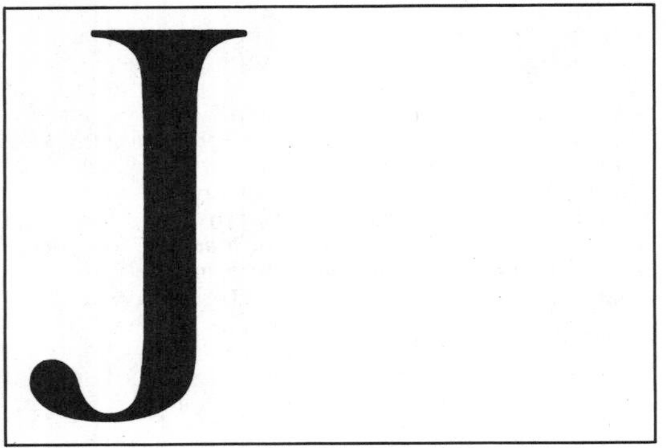

J, 10th letter of the ALPHABET, a Western European medieval development of *I*, with which it was formerly quite interchangeable in writing. It is pronounced as a consonant in English and often as a *y* in other languages, as in the Hebrew *hallelujah*.

Jaakobah (jā"əkō'bə), prince of the family of Simeon. 1 Chron. 4.36.

Jaala or **Jaalah** (both: jā'ālə), post-Exilic family. Ezra 2.56; Neh. 7.58.

Jaalam (jā-ā'ləm, jā'əlăm), son of Esau. Gen. 36.5,14, 18; 1 Chron. 1.35.

Jaanai (jā'ānī, jā-ā'-), chief Gadite. 1 Chron. 5.12.

Jaare-oregim (jāăr'ē-ŏr'ēgĭm), father of David's man Elhanan. 2 Sam. 21.19. Jair: 1 Chron. 20.5.

Jaasau (jā'əsô), Jew who married a foreign wife. Ezra 10.37.

Jaasiel (jā-ā'sēĕl), ruler of Benjamin. 1 Chron. 27.21. See JASIEL.

Jaazaniah (jā"āzənī'ə). **1** Head of a number of idolatrous priests whom Ezekiel saw in a vision. Ezek. 8.11. **2** Captain active in the politics of Palestine at the time of the fall of Jerusalem. 2 Kings 25.23. Jezaniah: Jer. 40.8. Azariah: Jer. 43.2. **3** Rechabite. Jer. 35.3. **4** Prince. Ezek. 11.1.

Jaazer (jā-ā'zər), variant of JAZER.

Jaaziah (jā"əzī'ə), descendant of Merari. 1 Chron. 24.26,27.

Jaaziel (jā-ā'zēĕl), Levite. 1 Chron. 15.18. Aziel: 1 Chron. 15.20.

Jabal (jā'bəl), son of Lamech. Gen. 4.19,20.

Jabal ad Duruz (jăbäl' äd do͝oro͞oz'), mountain, c.5,900 ft (1,800 m), S Syria, highest point of the Druses mts.

Jabalpur (jŭb"əlpôr'), city (1971 pop. 533,751), Madhya Pradesh state, central India, on the Narmada River. It is a district administrative center and an important rail junction and military post. Manufactures include weapons, ammunition, and cigarettes. Jabalpur Univ. is in the city.

Jabal Shammar (jă'băl shă'mər), former emirate, N Saudi Arabia. Its capital was at Hail. In 1921, Ibn Saud conquered the forces of the emir, Ibn Rashid, and annexed the territory to his kingdom of Nejd.

Jabbar, Kareem Abdul (kərēm' ăb'do͞ol jəbär'), 1947–, American basketball player, b. New York City. The towering Jabbar (7 ft 1⅜ in./217 cm) joined the Milwaukee Bucks of the National Basketball Association after brilliant accomplishments as a high school and college basketball star. He led the Univ. of California at Los Angeles to three consecutive National Collegiate Athletic Association basketball championships (1967–69). Originally named Ferdinand Lewis (Lew) Alcindor, he adopted his Muslim name in 1970. Jabbar led the Bucks to the championship in the 1970–71 season. In his first five years in professional basketball (1969–74), he was voted most valuable player three times and scored well over 10,000 points.

Jabbok, river, Jordan: see ZARQA.

Jabesh-gilead (jā'bĕsh-gĭl'ēăd), city of Gilead. After the affair at Gibeah, wives were provided for the Benjamites by sacking Jabesh. Later, Saul saved Jabesh, and at his death the grateful city buried him. Judges 21; 1 Sam. 11; 31.11; 2 Sam. 2.4.

Jabez (jā'bĭz). **1** Judahite. 1 Chron. 4.9,10. **2** Unidentified place, S Palestine. 1 Chron. 2.55.

Jabin (jā'bĭn), name of two kings of Hazor. Joshua 11.1; Judges 4.2.

Jabir (jā'bĭr) or **Geber** (jē'bər), fl. 8th cent., Arab alchemist and physician, originally named Jabir ibn Hayyan. He is believed to have lived at Kufa and at Baghdad. A great number of works on alchemy, many of them unpublished, have been attributed to him, but scholars disagree as to their authenticity. Recent studies indicate that many of the extant works in Arabic were written in the 9th and 10th cent. by later Arab alchemists and issued under Jabir's name. The works influenced the development of medieval alchemy and indicate the use of laboratory experiments. They perpetuated the theory that metals are composed of mercury and sulfur and can be transmuted into gold. In the early 14th cent. a Spanish alchemist wrote under the Latinized form of the name, Geber; his works are considered the clearest expression of alchemical thought to appear before the 16th cent. Several of the Arabic works were translated by E. J. Holmyard and published in 1928.

jabiru: see STORK.

Jablonec nad Nisou (yä'blônĕts nät nĭ'sôo͞o), Ger. *Gablonz,* city (1970 pop. 34,218), N Czechoslovakia, in Bohemia, on the Lausitzer Neisse. The glassware center of Czechoslovakia, it also has industries that manufacture automobile equipment, textiles, plastics, and buttons and costume jewelry. The city has a 14th-century Gothic church.

Jabneel (jăb'nēĕl) [Heb.,=God causes to build]. **1** Place, NE Palestine. Joshua 19.33. **2** See JAMNIA.

Jabneh (jăb'nē), variant of JAMNIA.

Jabotinsky, Vladimir (yăb"ətĭn'skē), 1880–1940, Jewish Zionist leader, b. Russia. A fiery orator and an accomplished writer in several languages, he was a militant Zionist and a persistent advocate of Jewish self-defense against pogroms in Russia. He formed the first Jewish self-defense unit in Palestine during the clashes with the Arabs in 1920; this brought him into open conflict with the British. He strongly condemned the official policy of the Zionist organization, charging it with weakness and appeasement of the British in Palestine. In 1925 he founded the Zionist Revisionist organization, which advocated large-scale Jewish immigration into Palestine and the creation of a Jewish state on both sides of the Jordan River. At the beginning of World War II he worked for the creation of a Jewish army. He was the author of several books, including *The Story of the Jewish Legion* (tr. 1945). See biography by Joseph B. Schechtman (2 vol., 1956–61).

Jaca (hä'kä), town (1970 pop. 11,134), Huesca prov., NE Spain, in Aragón, in the Pyrenees (alt. c.2,700 ft/820 m), near the French border on the Aragón River. A communications center and an episcopal see, it is a processing center for lumber and for the farm products of the fertile Aragón valley. After its recapture from the Moors it was (11th cent.) the cradle of the Aragonese kingdom. Huesca, taken in 1097, replaced it as the capital. Jaca has ancient walls and towers and a Romanesque cathedral (11th–15th cent.).

jaçana (jəkăn'ə, jəkän'ə), common name for members of the Jacanidae, a family of tropical and subtropical wading birds. Jaçanas, also called lily-trotters and lotus-birds, have long toes and toenails that enable them to walk delicately on floating vegetation as they search for insects and mollusks. Like certain of the related plovers, jaçanas have defensive spurs on the angles of their wings. The American jaçana (10 in./25 cm long), *Jacana spinosa,* is cinnamon red with striking yellow-green wing patches. The female jaçana is slightly larger than the male, but has similar coloration. It lays about 4 eggs per clutch, which is incubated by the male for three to four weeks. Jaçanas are excellent swimmers and divers and build their nests to float on water. They are classified in the phylum CHORDATA, subphylum Vertebrata, class Aves, order Charadriiformes, family Jacanidae.

jacaranda (jăk"ərăn'də): see BIGNONIA.

Jachan (jā'kăn), chief of the house of Gad. 1 Chron. 5.13.

Jachin (jā'kĭn). **1** Son of Simeon. Gen. 46.10; Ex. 6.15; Num. 26.12. Jarib: 1 Chron. 4.24. **2** Chief priest. 1 Chron. 9.10; 24.17; Neh. 11.10.

Jachin and Boaz (bō'ăz), two pillars in front of Solomon's Temple, probably symbolic of God's presence. 1 Kings 7.21; 2 Chron. 3.17.

Jáchymov (yä'khĭmôf), Ger. *Joachimsthal,* town, W Czechoslovakia, in Bohemia, in the Erzgebirge [ore mountains]. A major pitchblende-mining center of Europe, the city also produces iron, uranium, radium, lead, zinc, nickel, and cobalt. It is also a noted health resort, with thermal radioactive springs. Jáchymov was the main center of silver mining in Europe after the 16th cent., but its present output is negligible. The word *Thaler,* from which *dollar* is derived, is an abbreviation of *Joachimsthaler,* the name of a coin first struck there in the 16th cent.

jacinth (jā'sĭnth): see HYACINTH, in mineralogy.

jack: see POMPANO; TUNA.

jack, mechanical device used to multiply a relatively small applied force so that it can lift and support heavy loads, or sometimes, move massive objects into a desired position. The lever jack, often used in lifting automobiles, has a lever combined with a ratchet; the lever is used to lift the load a small distance and the ratchet prevents the load from falling back while the lever is reset so that the process can be repeated. In the screw jack the load is moved or lifted by the turning of a screw; the pitch of the screw threads is arranged so that friction is sufficient to hold the load in place when the torque applied to the screw is released. In yet another form of jack a hydraulic device is used. See HYDRAULIC MACHINE.

jackal, name for several Old World carnivorous mammals of the genus *Canis,* which also includes the DOG and the WOLF. Some authorities classify jackals in a separate genus (*Thos*). Jackals are found in Africa and S Asia, where they inhabit deserts, grasslands, and brush country. They are similar in size and behavior to the North American prairie wolf, or COYOTE, and like the coyote, they howl in the early evening. Although renowned as scaven-

Black-backed jackal, a carnivorous nocturnal mammal.

White-tailed jackrabbit of North America.

gers, jackals also hunt small animals. Secretive animals, they forage by night and spend the day in holes or hidden in grass or brush. The black-backed jackal, *Canis mesomelas,* the simenian jackal, *C. simensis,* and the side-striped jackal, *C. adustus,* are all found in Africa, and are generally solitary animals. The golden, or Asiatic, jackal, *C. aureus,* is found in S Asia and N Africa; golden jackals are more social than the African jackals and usually hunt in small packs. Jackals are classified in the phylum CHORDATA, subphylum Vertebrata, class Mammalia, order Carnivora, family Canidae.

jackass: see ASS.

jack-in-the-pulpit: see ARUM.

Jackman, Wilbur Samuel, 1855–1907, American educator, b. Mechanicstown, Ohio, grad. Harvard, 1884. Jackman was a leader of the nature study movement in elementary schools. He taught (after 1889) at the Cook County Normal School in Chicago and, beginning with *Nature Study for the Common Schools* (1891), wrote texts and manuals. He was appointed dean of the new college of education in the Univ. of Chicago in 1901, but resigned in 1904 to become principal of the University Elementary School and to edit the *Elementary School Teacher.*

jack-o'-lantern, common name for the MUSHROOM species *Clitocybe illudens.*

jackrabbit, popular name for several HARES of W North America, characterized by very long legs and ears. Jackrabbits are powerful jumpers and fast runners. In normal progress leaps are alternated with running steps; when pursued the hare runs fast and close to the ground. Jackrabbits are found W of the Great Lakes and the Mississippi River, from S Canada to Central America. They are brownish gray above and white below. The white-tailed jackrabbit (*Lepus townsendi*) is the most northerly species and ranges from plains to high mountains. It has an entirely white tail, and its coat turns white or light gray in winter. It averages 20 in. (51 cm) in length, with ears 5 to 6 in. (12.7–15.3 cm) long. It is closely related to the varying hare and the arctic hare. The black-tailed jackrabbit (*L. californicus*) found on the plains and in arid regions from the NW United States to Mexico, is slightly smaller, with longer ears; its tail is black above. The antelope jackrabbit (*L. alleni*) of Mexico and the extreme SW United States is a large, heavy hare with white sides and ears up to 8 in. (20.3 cm) long. It has been known to leap as high as 5 ft (1.5 m) and as far as 22 ft (6.7 m). Jackrabbits are classified in the phylum CHORDATA, subphylum Vertebrata, class Mammalia, order Lagomorpha, family Leporidae.

jackscrew: see SCREW.

Jackson, Abraham Valentine Williams, 1862–1937, American Orientalist, b. New York City. From 1895 to 1935 he taught at Columbia. His particular interest was Persia, and he became a great authority on ancient Persian religion, language, and literature as well as the modern Parsis.

Jackson, Andrew, 1767–1845, 7th President of the United States (1829–37), b. Waxhaw settlement on the border of South Carolina and North Carolina (both states claim him). A child of the backwoods, he was left an orphan at 14. His long military career began in 1781, when he fought against the British in a skirmish at Hanging Rock. He and his brother were captured and imprisoned at Camden, S.C. After studying law at Salisbury, N.C., he was admitted to the bar in 1787 and practiced in the vicinity until he was appointed solicitor for the western district of North Carolina (now Tennessee). In 1788 he moved west to Nashville. He was prosperous in his law practice and in land speculation until the Panic of 1795 struck, leaving him with little more than his estate, the HERMITAGE, on which he lived as a cotton planter during the intervals of his political career and where he is buried. Jackson married Rachel Donelson before she had secured a legal divorce from her first husband, and though the ceremony was later repeated, his enemies made capital of the circumstance. He rose in politics, was a member of the convention that drafted the Tennessee Constitution, and was elected (1796) as the sole member from the new state in the U. S. House of Representatives. The next year when his political chief, William Blount, was expelled from the Senate, Jackson resigned and, to vindicate his party, ran for the vacant seat. He won, but in 1798 he resigned. From 1798 to 1804 he served notably as judge of the Tennessee superior court. In the War of 1812 he defeated the Creek warriors at Horseshoe Bend (March, 1814) after a strenuous campaign and won the rank of major general in the U.S. army. He was given command of an expedition to defend New Orleans against the British. The decisive victory gained there over seasoned British troops under Gen. Edward Pakenham, though it came after peace had already been signed in Europe, made Jackson the one great military hero of the War of 1812. In 1818 he was sent to take reprisals against the Seminole, who were raiding settlements near the Florida border, but, misinterpreting orders, he crossed the boundary line, captured Pensacola, and executed two British subjects as punishment for their stirring up the Indians. He thus involved the United States in serious trouble with both Spain and Great Britain. John Q. Adams, then Secretary of State, was the only cabinet member to defend him, but the conduct of Old Hickory, as Jackson was called by his admirers, pleased the people of the West. He moved on to the national scene as the standard-bearer of one wing of the old Republican party. The greatest popular hero of his time, a man of action, and an expansionist, he became associated with the movement toward increased popular participation in government. He was regarded by many as the symbol of the democratic feelings of the time, and later generations were to speak of Jacksonian democracy. Although in broadest terms this movement often attacked citadels of privilege or monopoly and sought to broaden opportunities in many areas of life, there has been much dispute among historians over its essential social nature. At one time it was characterized as being rooted in the democratic nature of the frontier. Later historians pointed to the workingmen of the Eastern cities as the defining element in the Jacksonian political coalition. More recently the older interpretations have been challenged by those seeing the age as one that primarily offered new opportunities to the middle class—an era of liberal capitalism. Jackson had appeal for the farmer, for the artisan, for the small businessman; he was viewed with suspicion and fear by men of established position, who considered him a dangerous upstart. He rode on a wave of popularity that almost took him ino the presidency in the election of 1824. The vote was split with Henry CLAY and John Quincy ADAMS, and when the election was decided in the House of Representatives, Clay threw his influence to Adams, and Adams became President. By the time of the election of 1828, Jackson's cause was more assured. John C. CALHOUN, who was the candidate for Vice President with Jackson, brought most of William H. Crawford's former following to Jackson, while Martin VAN BUREN and the Albany Regency swung liberal-controlled New York state to him. The result was a sweeping victory; Jackson polled four times the popular vote that he had received in 1824. His inauguration brought the "rabble" into the White House, to the distaste of the established families. There was a strong element of personalism in the rule of the hotheaded Jackson, and the KITCHEN CABINET—a small group of favorite advisers—was powerful. Vigorous publicity and violent journalistic attacks on anti-Jacksonians were ably handled by such men as the elder Francis P. BLAIR, Duff GREEN, and Amos KENDALL. Party loyalty was intense, and party members were rewarded with government posts in what came to be known as the SPOILS SYSTEM. Personal relationships were of utmost importance, and the social slights suffered by the wife of Secretary of War John H. Eaton (see O'NEILL, MARGARET) helped to break up the cabinet. Calhoun's antagonism was more fundamental, however. Calhoun and the South generally felt threatened by the protective tariff that favored the industrial East, and Calhoun evolved the doctrine of NULLIFICATION and resigned from the vice presidency. Jackson stood firmly for the Union and had the force bill of 1833 (see FORCE BILL) passed to coerce South Carolina into accepting the Federal tariff, but a compromise tariff was rushed through and the affair ended. Jackson, on the other hand, took the part of Georgia in its insistence on states' rights and the privilege of ousting the Cherokee; he refused to aid in enforcing the Supreme Court's decision against Georgia, and the Indians were removed. More important than the estrangement of Calhoun was Jackson's long fight against the BANK OF THE UNITED STATES. Although its charter did not expire until 1836, Henry Clay succeeded in having a bill to recharter it passed in 1832, thus bringing the issue into the 1832 presidential election. Jackson vetoed the measure, and the powerful interests of the bank were joined with the other opponents of Jackson in a bitter struggle with the antibank Jacksonians. Jackson in the election of 1832 triumphed over Clay. His second administration—more bitterly resented by his enemies than the first—was dominated by the bank issue. Jackson promptly removed the funds from the bank and put them in chosen state banks (the "pet banks"). Secretary of Treasury Louis MCLANE refused to make the transfer as did his successor W. J. DUANE, but Roger B. TANEY agreed with Jackson's views and made the transfer (see also INDEPENDENT TREASURY SYSTEM). Jackson was a firm believer in a specie basis for currency, and the Specie Circular in 1836, which stipulated that all public lands must be paid for in specie, broke the speculation boom in Western lands, cast suspicion on many of the bank notes in circulation, and hastened the Panic of 1837. The panic, which had some of its roots in earlier crop failures and in overextended speculation, was a factor in the administration of Martin Van Buren, who was Jackson's choice and successful candidate for the presidency in 1836. Jackson retired to the Hermitage and lived out his life there, still despised as a high-handed and capricious dictator by his enemies and revered as a forceful democratic leader by his followers. Although he was known as a frontiersman, Jackson was personally dignified, courteous, and gentlemanly—with a devotion to the "gentleman's code" that led him to fight several duels. See biographies by Marquis James (2 vol., 1933–37, repr. 1968), Harold Syrett (1953, repr. 1971), J. W. Ward (1955, repr. 1962), and R. V. Remini (1966, repr. 1969); A. M.

Andrew Jackson, 7th President of the United States.

Schlesinger, Jr., *The Age of Jackson* (1945); G. G. Van Deusen, *The Jacksonian Era* (1959, repr. 1963); R. V. Remini, *Andrew Jackson and the Bank War* (1967); R. V. Remini, ed., *The Age of Jackson* (1972).

Jackson, Claiborne Fox, 1806–62, governor of Missouri, b. Fleming co., Ky. In 1822 he moved to Missouri, where he practiced law. Speaker of the state legislature (1844–46), he later was a leader of the proslavery Democrats who eventually defeated Sen. Thomas H. BENTON. Elected governor in 1860, Jackson recommended the calling of the state convention that voted against both secession and coercion of the South (1861). He attempted to arm the state militia from the Federal arsenal in St. Louis but was frustrated by Francis P. BLAIR and Nathaniel LYON. Lincoln's request for troops was refused by Jackson, who characterized the Union cause as an "unholy crusade." Upon Lyon's seizure of Camp Jackson, the governor called for volunteers but was forced to withdraw with them to SW Missouri. When the convention, assuming constituent powers, deposed the state government, Jackson, at Neosho, convened an ineffective rump legislature (1862).

Jackson, Frederick George, 1860–1938, British arctic explorer. He explored (1893–94) the tundra in arctic Russia and in Lapland, and he commanded (1894–97) the Jackson-Harmsworth expedition that explored Franz Josef Land. Jackson proved that Franz Josef Land was an archipelago, not a continent as had been suspected. His chance encounter (1896) with Fridtjof Nansen and F. H. Johansen, who were returning by sledge from their attempted journey to the North Pole, probably saved the lives of these two explorers. In later years Jackson became a well-known African traveler. His writings include *The Great Frozen Land* (1895) and *A Thousand Days in the Arctic* (1899).

Jackson, Frederick John Foakes-: see FOAKES-JACKSON, FREDERICK JOHN.

Jackson, Glenda, 1938–, English actress. Jackson's first starring role was as Charlotte Corday in *Marat/Sade* (1966) for the ROYAL SHAKESPEARE COMPANY. Her strong performance in the film *Women in Love* (1969) won her an Academy Award. Jackson's other major films include *Sunday Bloody Sunday* (1972), *A Touch of Class* (1973), and *The Maids* (1974). In 1971 she played Elizabeth I in a critically acclaimed television series.

Jackson, Helen (Fiske) Hunt, 1830–85, American writer whose pseudonym was H. H., b. Amherst, Mass. She was a lifelong friend of Emily Dickinson. In 1863, encouraged by T. W. Higginson, Jackson began writing for periodicals. She is the author of poetry, novels, children's stories, and travel sketches. In 1881 she published *A Century of Dishonor*, a historical account of the government's injustice to American Indians. This book led to her appointment (1882) as government investigator of the Mission Indians of California. She subsequently wrote *Ramona* (1884), her famous romance, which presented even more emphatically the plight of the Indians.

Jackson, Mahalia (məhăl'yə), 1911–72, American gospel singer and civil rights worker, b. New Orleans, La. She sang in church choirs during her childhood. Moving to Chicago in 1927, she worked at various menial jobs and sang in churches and revival meetings, attracting attention for her vigorous and joyful gospel style. As her reputation grew she made numerous recordings, and she was afforded national recognition with her Carnegie Hall debut in 1950. Jackson toured abroad and appeared on radio and at jazz festivals, refusing to sing the blues in favor of her more hopeful devotional songs. At Newport in 1958 she sang in Duke Ellington's *Black, Brown and Beige*. Deeply committed to the civil rights movement, she was closely associated with the work of Dr. Martin Luther King, Jr. See her autobiography (1966); biography by Jesse Jackson (1974).

Jackson, Robert Houghwout (hou'ət), 1892–1954, Associate Justice of the U.S. Supreme Court (1941–54), b. Spring Creek, Pa. Despite the fact that he did not have a law degree, he was admitted to the bar (1913) after a brief period of study at Albany law school. In 1934 he was appointed general counsel of the Bureau of Internal Revenue. From 1936 to 1938 he served as Assistant Attorney General in charge of the antitrust division. A strong advocate of New Deal policies, Jackson became (1938) U.S. Solicitor General and argued many Supreme Court cases involving constitutional law. In 1940 he became U.S. Attorney General, and in 1941 President Franklin D. Roosevelt appointed him to the Supreme Court. There his opinions continued to reflect his opposition to monopolies. He went on leave (1945–46) from the bench to be U.S. chief counsel at the Nuremberg war crimes trial. His feud with Justice Hugo L. Black probably eliminated him from consideration for Chief Justice when Harlan Stone died. An advocate of judicial restraint, he remained a firm defender of civil liberties. Known for his eloquent literary style, he defended freedom of religion with particular distinction. He wrote *The Struggle for Ju-*

Mahalia Jackson (center).

Robert H. Jackson.

dicial Supremacy (1940), *The Case Against the Nazi War Criminals* (1945), and *The Supreme Court in the American System of Government* (1955). See biography (1958) and study (1961) by E. C. Gerhart.

Jackson, Samuel Macauley, 1851–1912, American Presbyterian clergyman and encyclopedist, b. New York City. He was associate editor in the preparation of the original *Schaff-Herzog Encyclopedia* (1884) and editor in chief of the greatly enlarged *New Schaff-Herzog Encyclopedia of Religious Knowledge* (13 vol., 1908–14). He also edited the *Concise Dictionary of Religious Knowledge* (rev. ed. 1891) and the "American Church History" series (13 vol., 1893–97). Jackson was religious editor of several encyclopedias and dictionaries. He wrote a standard biography of Huldreich Zwingli (1901), part of the "Heroes of the Reformation" series, which he sponsored. He was long the moving spirit of the American Society of Church History and edited its papers.

Jackson, Sheldon, 1834–1909, American missionary and educator, b. Montgomery co., N.Y., grad. Union College, 1855, and Princeton Theological Seminary, 1858. After an active career as a Presbyterian home missionary in Minnesota and Wisconsin and (after 1870) as missionary superintendent in the Rocky Mt. area, he went to Alaska in 1884 as superintendent of missions, having already established missions and schools in that territory. In 1885 he became the first Federal superintendent of public instruction for Alaska, with the task of organizing a free school system for Indian, Eskimo, and white children. He succeeded in the next 20 years through work and travel in bringing school facilities to all corners of Alaska. He urged the introduction and raising of reindeer in the territory to supplement the dwindling food resources and in 1892, with government aid, brought the first reindeer into Alaska from Siberia. He aided in organizing the territorial government and in establishing mail routes. He was active in Alaskan politics as the moving spirit in the "missionary" party. He wrote numerous governmental and religious reports and *Difficulties at Sitka in 1885* (1886). See biography by J. A. Lazell (1960).

Jackson, Shirley, 1919–65, American writer, b. San Francisco. She is best known for her stories and novels of horror and the occult, rendered more terrifying because they are set against realistic, everyday backgrounds. Her works include *The Lottery* (1949), *We Have Always Lived in the Castle* (1953), and *The Haunting of Hill House* (1959). She was married to the critic Stanley Edgar Hyman. *The Magic of Shirley Jackson* (1966) and *Come Along With Me* (1968) are posthumous collections of her works.

Jackson, Stonewall (Thomas Jonathan Jackson), 1824–63, Confederate general, b. Clarksburg, Va. (now W. Va.), grad. West Point, 1846. He served with distinction under Winfield Scott in the Mexican War and from 1851 to 1861 taught at the Virginia Military Institute. He resigned from the army in Feb., 1852. At the beginning of the Civil War, Jackson, practically unknown, was made a colonel of Virginia troops and sent to command at Harpers Ferry. After J. E. JOHNSTON superseded him there in May, 1861, Jackson was given a brigade in Johnston's army and made a Confederate brigadier general. At the first battle of BULL RUN, he and his brigade earned their sobriquet by standing (in the words of Gen. Barnard Bee) "like a stone wall." He was promoted to major general, and in November, Johnston assigned him to command in the Shenandoah valley. Jackson's attack on James Shields's division at Kernstown on March 23, 1862, was repulsed but forced the retention of Union troops in the valley. In April, Robert E. LEE suggested that Jackson fall upon Nathaniel P. Banks's force in the lower valley, hoping that Irvin McDowell's army would thereby be diverted from joining George McClellan before Richmond (see PENINSULAR CAMPAIGN). Jackson's renowned Valley campaign resulted. He first defeated part of John C. Frémont's force at McDowell (c.25 mi/40 km W of Staunton) on May 8, 1862, and then, returning to the Shenandoah, routed Banks at Front Royal and Winchester (May 23–25) and drove him across the Potomac. The Federal administration, fearing that Jackson would now advance on Washington, sent Shields from McDowell's army to join Frémont, advancing from the west, in cutting off Jackson. Stonewall, however, retreated rapidly to the head of the valley and on June 8–9 defeated his pursuers at Cross Keys and PORT REPUBLIC. With the diversion a complete success, Jackson joined Lee in the SEVEN DAYS BATTLES. After the brilliance of the Shenandoah campaign, his service in that week of fighting was disappointing. But he soon redeemed himself. The speedy turning movement executed by his "foot cavalry" against Pope late in Aug., 1862, at the battle of Cedar Mt. set the stage for the crushing victory at the second battle of Bull Run, and in the ANTIETAM CAMPAIGN he marched promptly to Lee's aid after he had captured the Harpers Ferry garrison. When Lee reorganized the Army of Northern Virginia after Antietam, he made Jackson commander of the 2d Corps, and Stonewall was promoted to lieutenant general. He ably commanded the Confederate right in the battle of FREDERICKSBURG in December. In the battle of CHANCELLORSVILLE, Lee and Jackson repeated the tactics of second Bull Run. Jackson's turning movement completely crumbled Hooker's right (May 2, 1863). Pressing on in the darkness, Stonewall Jackson was mortally wounded by the fire of his own men. His death was a severe blow to the Southern cause. Jackson was a tactician of first rank and, though a strict disciplinarian, had the affection of his men. His devout Calvinism, fighting ability, and arresting personal quirks make him one of the most interesting figures of the war. He was Lee's ablest and most trusted lieutenant. See biographies by G. F. R. Henderson (1898, new ed. 1961), Burke Davis (1954, repr. 1961), Lenoir Chambers (1959), R. B. Cook (4th ed. 1963), and J. M. Selby (1968); H. K. Douglas, *I Rode with Stonewall* (1940).

Jackson, William Henry, 1843–1942, American artist and pioneer photographer of the West, b. Keeseville, N.Y. After serving with the Union army in the Civil War he traveled overland to California (1866–67), part of the way on a Mormon wagon train, and then settled in Omaha, Neb. (1868). Engaged in photography after 1858, Jackson devoted himself to recording the scenic grandeur and historic sites of the West. He photographed the building of the Union Pacific RR, the mining booms at Cripple Creek and Leadville, and the cliff dwellings at Mesa Verde. His photographic series on the Yellowstone region was instrumental in having the area set aside in 1872 as the first national park. In 1924, Jackson moved to Washington, D.C., began painting, and at the age of 93 executed a series of murals on the Old West for the new Dept. of the Interior Building. See his autobiography (1940) and his diaries, ed. by L. R. and A. W. Hafen (1959); C. S. Jackson, *Picture Maker of the Old West* (1947).

Jackson. **1** City (1970 pop. 45,484), seat of Jackson co., S Mich., on the Grand River; inc. 1857. It is an industrial and commercial center in a farm region. Several automobile models were pioneered in Jackson in the early 20th cent., and today the city's chief manufactures are a great variety of automobile and aircraft parts and accessories. Food products, tires, electronic equipment, sheet-metal items, and metal toys are also made. The Republican party was founded in Jackson on July 6, 1854; a tablet marks the site. A junior college is in the city. Nearby are Spring Arbor College and a state prison. **2** City (1970 pop. 153,968), state capital and seat of Hinds co., W central Miss., on the Pearl River; inc. 1833. It is the state's largest city and geographic center, with major rail, warehouse, and distributing operations. Industries include the production of oil and natural gas, food processing, and the manufacture of lumber, metal, glass, and wood products. The site of the city, a trading post known as Le Fleur's Bluff near the Natchez Trace, was chosen and laid out as the state capital in 1821 and named for Andrew Jackson. The first U.S. law giving property rights to married women was passed there in 1839. During the Civil War, Jackson was a military center for the VICKSBURG CAMPAIGN and was largely destroyed by Sherman's forces in 1863. The old capitol (1839) is preserved as a museum; the new capitol was completed in 1903. Among the many points of interest are the governor's mansion (erected 1839); city hall, which was used as a hospital during the Civil War; a 220-acre (89-hectare) scale model of the Mississippi River flood control system; Mynelle's gardens; a state wildlife museum; an art gallery; a notable Confederate monument; and many antebellum homes. Belhaven College, Jackson State College, the Univ. of Mississippi Medical Center, and several state institutions for the physically and mentally handicapped are there. Nearby are Tougaloo College and Mississippi College. During the 1960s Jackson was the scene of considerable racial unrest. In May, 1970, demonstrations at the predominantly black Jackson State College resulted in the death of two students. **3** City (1970 pop. 39,996), seat of Madison co., W Tenn., on the South Fork of the Forked Deer River; inc. 1823. It is a processing and rail shipping point for an extensive farm area. The city has railroad shops and industries producing a great variety of manufactures. The town was founded by a nephew of Andrew Jackson. It is the seat of Lane College, Lambuth College, Union Univ., and a junior college. Nearby are the West Tennessee Agricultural Experiment Station of the Univ. of Tennessee and a state park with Indian mounds. Casey Jones is buried in Jackson; his home and the Casey Jones railroad museum are of interest.

Jackson, Port, or **Sydney Harbour,** inlet of the Pacific Ocean, 22 sq mi (57 sq km), 12 mi (19 km) long and 1.5 mi (2.4 km) wide at its mouth, New South Wales, Australia, forming Australia's finest harbor. The Parramatta River forms its western arm. Sydney on the south shore is connected with its northern suburbs by Sydney Harbour Bridge (1932), the second longest steel-arch bridge in the world, with an arch span of 1,650 ft (503 m). In the inlet is Cockatoo Island, which has large shipyards.

Jackson College: see TUFTS UNIV.

Jackson Hole, fertile Rocky Mt. valley, c.50 mi (80 km) long and 6 to 8 mi (9.6–12.8 km) wide, NW Wyo., in Grand Teton National Park. Jackson Lake, 39 sq mi (101 sq km), a natural lake through which the Snake River flows, was dammed in 1916 to control the river's flow. The valley has been popular with hunters and trappers from the time U.S. trapper David Jackson, for whom it was named, wintered there in 1828–29. In the late 1880s, Jackson Hole was settled; two homesteads have been restored as historic sites. Jackson Hole Wildlife Park, 1,500 acres (607 hectares), est. 1948, is the winter home of the largest elk herd in North America. Many animals and birds inhabit the area, including the bald eagle and the rare trumpeter swan.

Jacksonville. **1** City (1970 pop. 19,832), Pulaski co., central Ark., inc. 1941. The nearby Little Rock Air Force Base, a tactical air command installation, is important to the city's economy. **2** City (1970 pop. 528,865), coextensive (since 1968) with Duval co., NE Fla., on the St. Johns River near its mouth on the Atlantic Ocean; inc. 1832. The largest city in the state and the second largest U.S. city in area (c.830 sq mi/2,150 sq km), it is a great rail, air, and highway focal point and a busy port of entry, with ship repair yards and extensive freight-handling facilities. Lumber, phosphate, paper, and wood pulp are the principal exports; automobiles and coffee are the major imports. The city is a leading manufacturing center, with lumber, paper, chemicals, food products, and cigars the principal products. Jacksonville is one of the most important Southern centers of commerce, finance, and insurance on the Atlantic coast. It is also a major East Coast center of U.S. navy operations; three important naval installations are in the area, including a naval air training station and the large base at the mouth of the St. Johns River. Jacksonville is also a tourist resort, with ocean beaches, fishing and yachting facilities, and inland hunting areas. It was settled in 1816 by Lewis Hogan. Named

for Andrew Jackson, first territorial governor of Florida, the city was laid out in 1822. The Seminole War and the Civil War (in which much of the city was destroyed) interrupted its growth, but with the development of a good deepwater harbor and railroads in the late 19th cent., industry and commerce increased. A fire in 1901 destroyed a large part of the city; it was quickly rebuilt. Educational facilities include Jacksonville Univ., Edward Walters College, Jones College, and a junior college. The city has a symphony orchestra, a municipal zoo, and several museums and art galleries. It is the home of the enormous Gator Bowl. Points of interest include the Confederate monument in Hemming Park and nearby Fort Caroline National Memorial (see NATIONAL PARKS AND MONUMENTS, table). Jacksonville has an international airport. **3** City (1970 pop. 20,553), seat of Morgan co., W central Ill.; laid out 1825, inc. 1867. Its industries include bookbinding and the manufacture of clothing, plastics, phonograph records, and metal products. It is the seat of Illinois College, MacMurray College, a state mental hospital, and schools for the deaf and blind. Stephen A. Douglas and William Jennings Bryan lived there. Jacksonville was a station on the Underground Railroad. **4** City (1970 pop. 16,289), seat of Onslow co., E N.C., on the New River; settled c.1757. It is a trade center in a farm area, with sawmills and plants making clothing, mobile homes, food products, and farm equipment. It is also a summer resort. Camp Lejeune, a U.S. marine corps training base, is adjacent to the city, and Petersburg Point, a marine air station, is to the south. A junior college is in the city, and a state park is nearby.

City hall in Jackson, Miss., built in 1854 and used as a hospital during the Civil War.

Jackson Whites, name applied to a racially mixed (black, white, and Indian) group of people living in the Ramapo Mts. along the New Jersey–New York state line. The origins of these people have for years been surrounded by myth and legend, e.g., that they are descended from a mixture of the Tuscarora Indians, Hessian deserters, women kidnapped in England by a man named Jackson, and runaway slaves. Recent research suggests that the origin of these people is to be found among remnants of the Algonquin Indians, early white settlers (mainly British and Dutch), and free, landholding Negroes who pioneered the Hackensack River valley before migrating to the Ramapo Mts. in the early 19th cent. The term Jackson Whites probably developed as a result of the continued joint reference to the mountain people as Jacks (an 18th-century term for freed slaves or blacks in general) and Whites, i.e., it became Jackson Whites by elision.

Jacob (jā'kəb). **1** Ancestor of the Hebrews, the younger of the twin sons of Isaac and Rebecca. The older was Esau. Jacob got his brother's birthright by a bargain (a mess of pottage) and, with his mother's help, received the blessing that the dying Isaac had intended for Esau. His brother was so enraged at this that Jacob was forced to flee to his uncle, Laban, in Padanaram. On his way, at Bethel, he had a vision of angels ascending and descending the ladder to heaven. After serving the crafty Laban for 20 years Jacob started back to the land of his fathers with his two wives, Leah and Rachel, his many sons, and rich possessions. On the banks of the Jabbok he wrestled with an angel and received the name of ISRAEL. Later, in the days of famine, he migrated with his family to Egypt and was reunited with his son Joseph. There in the land of Goshen he died, but they buried him in the family burying ground of Machpelah. His sons were the ancestors of the 12 tribes of Israel. Gen. 25–50; Hosea 12.2–4,12; Mal. 1.2; Acts 7.12–16; Heb. 11.20,21. Some biblical scholars have questioned the historicity of Jacob. **2** Father of Joseph. Mat. 1.15,16.

Jacob, François, 1920–, French biologist, educated at the Sorbonne. His medical studies were interrupted by World War II. He joined the Free French Forces and fought in Africa and during the liberation of Paris. In 1950 he joined the Pasteur Institute, and in 1964 he became professor at the Collège de France. He shared the 1965 Nobel Prize in Physiology and Medicine with André Lwoff and Jacques Monod for discoveries concerning genes, the tiny structures in cells that determine hereditary characteristics and control production of enzymes and other proteins. Jacob and Monod coined the term *messenger RNA.* Jacob's writings include *The Logic of Life: A History of Heredity* (1974).

Jacob, Max (mäks zhäkôb'), 1876–1944, French writer and painter, b. Brittany, of a Jewish family. His dream-inspired verse, plays, and novels bridged and gave impetus to the symbolist and surrealist schools. His conversion (1914) to Roman Catholicism had great impact on his work. Among Jacob's novels are *Saint Matorel* (1911) and *Filibuth; ou La Montre en or* (1922); his verse, usually light and ironic, includes *Fond de l'eau* (1927) and *Rivages* (1932). Prose and poetry are combined in his *Défense de Tartufe* (1919) and the play *Le Siège de Jérusalem: drame céleste* (1912–14). His critical study, *Art poétique* (1922), had wide influence. One-man shows of Jacob's paintings were held in New York in 1930 and 1938. He died in a Nazi concentration camp. See study of his paintings by Gerald Kamber (1971).

Jacobean style (jăkəbē'ən), an early phase of English Renaissance architecture and decoration. It formed a transition between the Elizabethan and the pure Renaissance style later introduced by Inigo JONES. The reign of James I (1603–25), who was a disciple of the new scholarship, saw the first decisive adoption of Renaissance motifs, in a free form communicated to England through German and Flemish carvers rather than directly from Italy. Although the general lines of Elizabethan design remained, there was a more consistent and unified application of formal design, both in plan and elevation. Gothic influence did not cease completely; it lingered both in the building of the court and in the houses of the lesser gentry. Much use was made of columns and pilasters, round-arch arcades, and flat roofs with openwork parapets. These and other classical elements appeared in a free and fanciful vernacular rather than with any true classical purity. With them were mixed the prismatic rustications and the ornamental detail composed of scrolls, straps, and lozenges also characteristic of Elizabethan design. The style influenced furniture design and other decorative arts. Increase of wealth and the abundant construction of colleges, hospitals, almshouses, and manors encouraged innovations. Jacobean buildings of note are Hatfield House, Hertford; Knole House, Kent; and HOLLAND HOUSE by John Thorpe. See M. Whiffen, *An Introduction to Elizabethan and Jacobean Architecture* (1952).

Jacobi, Abraham (jəkō'bē), 1830–1919, American pediatrician, founder of pediatrics in the United States, b. Westphalia, Germany, M.D. Bonn, 1851. He was imprisoned for participating in the Revolution of 1848, but he escaped and in 1853 came to the United States. He was renowned as a lecturer on pediatrics and as professor of children's diseases at New York Medical College (where in 1860 he opened the first children's clinic in the country) and at Columbia (1870–1902). He was a founder and editor of the *American Journal of Obstetrics* and author of numerous works. Mary Putnam Jacobi, a physician and the first woman student at L'École de Médicine, Paris, was his wife.

Jacobi, Carl Gustav Jacob (kärl gōōs'täf yä'kôp yäkô'bē), 1804–51, German mathematician. He was an outstanding teacher and was professor of mathematics at Königsberg (1827–42) and lectured at Berlin from 1844. One of the greatest algorists of all time, he is noted for his work on elliptic functions, described in his *Fundamenta Nova Theoriae Functionum Ellipticarum* (1829), and on determinants, the theory of numbers, differential equations, and dynamics. His brother, **Moritz Hermann Jacobi** (1801–74), was a physicist and engineer who was the more famous of the two during their lifetimes. He was known for his supposed discovery (1837) of galvanoplastics, but his reputation faded when his ideas were later shown to be mistaken.

Jacobi, Friedrich Heinrich, 1743–1819, German philosopher. Although educated for commerce, he early gave up business and became in 1770 a member of the council for the duchies of Berg and Jülich. A brilliant personality, he attracted to his home near Düsseldorf a notable literary and philosophic circle. His later years were spent in Holstein and in Munich, where he was appointed (1807) president of the newly founded Academy of Sciences. His collected works were published in 1812–25. Among them are *Briefe über die Lehre des Spinoza* (1785) and *David Hume über den Glauben; oder, Idealismus und Realismus* (1787). Jacobi criticized both Kant and Spinoza, arguing that philosophy cannot maintain distinct realms of existence and that it must be consistent and consider everything in the same cause and effect sequence. If this is done, however, then the originality and individuality of our experiences are lost. Jacobi's solution involved a unity and consistency based entirely on faith. He felt that even immediate sense perception is miraculous. Reason, then, must be restricted to its immediate material, and the ultimate reality is to be intuitively sensed. See A. W. Crawford, *The Philosophy of F. H. Jacobi* (1905).

Jacobins (jăk'əbĭnz), political club of the FRENCH REVOLUTION. Formed in 1789 by the Breton deputies to the States-General, it was reconstituted as the Society of Friends of the Constitution after the revolutionary National Assembly moved (Oct., 1789) to Paris. The club derived its popular name from the monastery of the Jacobins (Parisian name of Dominicans), where the members met. Their chief purpose was to concert their activity and to secure support for the group from elements outside the Assembly. Patriotic societies were formed in most French cities in affiliation with the Parisian club. The members were, for the most part, bourgeois and at first included such moderates as Honoré de Mirabeau. The Jacobins exercised through their journals considerable pressure on the Legislative Assembly, in which they and the FEUILLANTS were (1791–92) the chief parties. They sought to limit the powers of the king, and many of them had republican tendencies.

The group split on the issue of war against Europe, which the majority, the GIRONDISTS, sought. The minority, connected with the democratic, lower-class organizations in Paris, opposed foreign war and insisted on reform. This group of the Jacobins grew more radical, adopted republican ideas, and advocated universal manhood suffrage, popular education, and separation of church and state, although it adhered to orthodox economic principles. In the National Convention, which proclaimed the French republic, the Jacobins and other extremist opponents of the Girondists, notably the CORDELIERS, sat in the raised seats and were called the MOUNTAIN. Their leaders—Maximilien ROBESPIERRE and Louis de SAINT-JUST, among others—relied mainly on the strength of the Paris commune and the Parisian working class; the Girondists drew their strength from the provinces. After the fall of the Girondists (June, 1793), for which the Jacobins were largely responsible, the Jacobins instituted the REIGN OF TERROR. Under Robespierre, who came to dominate the government, the Terror was used not only against counterrevolutionaries, but also against former allies of the Jacobins, such as the Cordeliers and the Dantonists (followers of Georges DANTON). The fall of Robespierre on 9 Thermidor (July 27, 1794) meant the fall of the Jacobins, but their spirit lived on in revolutionary doctrine. The party reappeared in the DIRECTORY and in altered form much later in the Revolution of 1848. See Crane Brinton, *The Jacobins* (1930, repr. 1961); Isser Woloch, *Jacobin Legacy: The Democratic Movement under the Directory* (1970); M. L. Kennedy, *The Jacobin Club of Marseilles* (1973).

Jacobite Church (jăk'əbīt), Christian church of Syria, Iraq, and India, recognizing the Syrian Orthodox patriarch of Antioch as its spiritual head, regarded by Roman Catholics and Eastern Orthodox as heretical. It was founded (6th cent.) as a Monophysite church in Syria by Jacob Baradaeus, greatly helped by Empress Theodora. It is thus analogous in position to the Coptic Church, the Monophysite church of Egypt. For many centuries the Jacobites were under Muslim dominion. Most Jacobites live in Iraq, while their patriarch resides at Damascus. They resemble other Eastern Christians in custom; their rite is the Antiochene or West Syrian; the liturgical language is Syriac. Since the 17th cent. there has been constant contact with Rome; as a result there is a community in communion with the pope having practices and rite in common with the Jacobites. These "Syrian Catholics" number about as many as the Jacobites; their head, another patriarch of Antioch, lives at Beirut. They have a separate church organization from the Melchites, Maronites, and Chaldean Catholics, which are other communities of Syria and Iraq in communion with Rome. In Malabar, India, there is a Christian sect of "Malabar Jacobites"; this group came into existence in the 17th cent., when the bulk of the Malabar Christians left the Roman communion and established relations with the Jacobite patriarch. They now use the Antiochene rite, with some differences. They are divided into two disputing jurisdictional parties, and there is a quasi-Protestant group of "Reformed Jacobites." In the 20th cent. a large number of Malabar Jacobites entered into communion with the pope, retaining their liturgy and practices. These "Malankarese Catholics" are ecclesiastically separate from both the Syrian Catholics, whose rite they share, and from the "Syro-Malabar Catholics" (Chaldean rite), who represent the Malabar Christians who did not leave the Roman communion when the Malabar Jacobites did. See Donald Attwater, *The Christian Churches of the East* (1947–48).

Jacobites (jăk'əbīts), adherents of the exiled branch of the house of STUART who sought to restore JAMES II and his descendants to the English and Scottish thrones after the GLORIOUS REVOLUTION of 1688. They take their name from the Latin form (*Jacobus*) of the name James. When WILLIAM III and MARY II ascended the throne after the flight of James II to France, strong Stuart partisans remained to offer rebellion. However, the death (1689) of John Graham, Viscount DUNDEE, at Killiecrankie ended armed resistance in Scotland, and William III quashed Jacobite hopes in Ireland by his victory over James's forces at the battle of the BOYNE (1690). Thereafter the exiled English court in France became a center of intrigue for men like Henry ST. JOHN, Viscount Bolingbroke, and others like him who were out of favor in London. At home many Roman Catholics, high churchmen, and extreme Tories adhered to the Stuart cause. At the death (1701) of James II his son James Francis Edward STUART, the Old Pretender, was recognized as James III by the courts of France and Spain and proclaimed by the Jacobites. An invasion of Scotland in 1708 by the new claimant proved totally abortive. Each subsequent attempt also failed, and in each the Jacobites were the dupes of French or Spanish policy. After the death (1714) of Queen Anne and the accession of the Hanoverian George I, there was the rising known by its date as "the '15." Led by the incompetent John Erskine, 6th earl of MAR, it ended in the disastrous battles of Preston and Sheriffmuir. The Old Pretender, discredited by failure, retired first to Avignon and finally to Rome. Spain supported another Jacobite invasion of Scotland in 1719. After its failure hope lay dormant until the Old Pretender's son Charles Edward STUART (the Young Pretender or Bonnie Prince Charlie) reached manhood. Acting on the assumption that renewed French hostility toward England would bring support for a Jacobite invasion, the prince rashly sailed for Scotland, raised the clans in what was called "the '45," and won an initial victory at Prestonpans in Sept., 1745. An advance into England stalled at Derby for lack of support from English Jacobites and French allies. Despite Charles's objections, his council of war voted to retreat, an action skillfully managed by Lord George MURRAY. Disaster followed for the Jacobites at the battle of Culloden Moor (1746). Charles escaped to France, and Stuart hopes were extinguished, although a claimant to the throne lived on until 1807, in the person of Henry STUART, Cardinal York. Theoretical justification for the Stuart claim was found in the writings of the NONJURORS, who maintained the principles of hereditary succession and the divine right of kings. But the Stuarts' continued adherence to Roman Catholicism, the rash and incompetent leadership of their military ventures, and the duplicity of foreign courts had cost the Jacobite cause much support. Jacobite sympathies lingered, particularly in Scotland and Ireland, where Jacobitism had been practically synonymous with national discontent, but the movement ceased to be a serious political force. Jacobite activities gave rise to much ballad literature and were the theme of such later literary works as Sir Walter Scott's *Rob Roy, Waverley,* and *Redgauntlet,* William Thackeray's *Henry Esmond,* and R. L. Stevenson's *Kidnapped.* See studies by G. P. Insh (1952),

Rødovre Town Hall (1954–56), near Copenhagen, Denmark, designed by Arne Jacobsen.

G. H. Jones (1954), Sir Charles Petrie (rev. ed. 1959), and J. C. M. Baynes (1970); J. Prebble, *Culloden* (1961).

Jacobs, Helen Hull, 1908–, American tennis player, b. Globe, Ariz. She won wide recognition on the courts by taking the U.S. women's singles title for four consecutive years (1932–35) and by beating Alice Marble for the British women's singles crown in 1936. She was (1943–45) an officer in the Waves in World War II. She wrote *Modern Tennis* (1933) and *Beyond the Game* (1936).

Jacobs, Joseph, 1854–1916, Jewish writer, historian and folklorist, b. Australia. He lived in England until 1900, when he went to the United States to edit a revision of *The Jewish Encyclopedia.* He was later a teacher at the Jewish Theological Seminary in New York City and editor of the *American Hebrew.* His major contributions to Jewish history include *Jews of Angevin England* (1893), *An Inquiry into the Sources of the History of the Jews in Spain* (1894), and *Jewish Contributions to Civilization* (1919), an incomplete fragment. His *Story of Geographical Discovery* (1899) went through a number of editions. From 1889 to 1900 he edited *Folk-Lore,* the journal of the Folk-Lore Society. He compiled several collections of fairy tales and edited scholarly editions of Aesop's fables (1889) and the *Thousand and One Nights* (6 vol., 1896).

Jacobs, William Wymark, 1863–1943, English author. His humorous sea stories were first collected in *Many Cargoes* (1896). Of his several horror stories, the most famous is "The Monkey's Paw."

Jacobsen, Arne (är′nə yä′kŏpsən), 1902–71, Danish architect and designer. Attentive to detail, Jacobsen suited his buildings to the surrounding landscape. He chiefly designed private housing, particularly in Søholm. The Bellevue seaside resort (1930–35) and Copenhagen's Jespersen (1955) and Scandinavian Airlines (1959–60) buildings are among his best-known works. Professor of architecture at the Royal Danish Academy after 1955, Jacobsen also designed cutlery, furniture, and textile and wallpaper patterns.

Jacobsen, Jens Peter (yĕns pā′tər yä′kôpsən), 1847–85, Danish writer. His great historical romance *Marie Grubbe* (1876, tr. 1925) deals with spiritual degeneration in 17th-century Denmark. Jacobsen's other works include *Nils Lyhne* (1880, tr. 1919), a semiautobiographical work about a dreamer unable to cope with the realities of his life, and a volume of poems. Jacobsen created a curt prose that had great influence on naturalistic style, both in Denmark and abroad. He translated Darwin's *Origin of Species* and *Descent of Man* into Danish. See Alrik Gustafson, *Six Scandinavian Novelists* (1940).

Jacob's ladder: see PHLOX.

Jacobus da Varagine (jəkō′bəs dä väräj′ĭnē), c.1230–1298, Italian hagiographer, b. Varazze (then Voraggio), near Savona; also known as Jacobus de Voragine. He became a Dominican in 1244, was provincial of Lombardy, and after 1292 was archbishop of Genoa. Noted for his piety and great charity, he was beatified in 1816 and is revered as a saint in Genoa and Savona. He is remembered chiefly as the compiler of *The Golden Legend* (see GOLDEN LEGEND, THE).

Jacopone da Todi (yäkōpô′nā dä tô′dē), 1230?–1306, Italian religious poet, whose name was originally Jacopo Benedetti. After the sudden death of his wife, he renounced (c.1268) his career as an advocate, gave his goods to the poor, and after 10 years of penance became a Franciscan tertiary. Jacopone was excommunicated and imprisoned (1298) for signing a manifesto against Pope Boniface VIII. After his release, he retired to a hermitage. He wrote many ardent, mystical poems and is probably the author of the hymn *Stabat Mater Dolorosa.* The spiritual value of poverty is frequently the theme of his poetry. See Evelyn Underhill, *Jacopone da Todi, Poet and Mystic* (with selections, 1919); Helen White, *A Watch in the Night* (1933).

Jacquard, Joseph Marie (zhôzĕf′ märē′ zhäkär′), 1752–1834, French inventor, whose loom is of the greatest importance in modern mechanical figure weaving. After several years of experimentation, he received a bronze medal for his model exhibited at the Industrial Exposition at Paris (1801). In 1806 his perfected loom was bought by the state and declared public property, and he was granted an annuity of 3,000 francs and a royalty on all looms sold. The Jacquard LOOM, the first machine to weave in patterns, has had countless adaptations in modern textile industry.

Jacqueline (1401–36), countess of Hainaut, Holland, and Zeeland (1417–28). The daughter and heiress of William IV, duke of Bavaria and count of Hainaut, Holland, and Zeeland, and of Margaret of Burgundy, Jacqueline was passed over for the succession to the counties on her father's death in 1417 in favor of her uncle, John of Bavaria. Jacqueline married a cousin,

John IV, duke of Brabant, nephew of Philip the Good of Burgundy, but found him useless in helping her recover her inheritance and soon left him. She sought refuge in England, where, although her previous marriage had been dubiously annulled, she married (c.1422) Humphrey, duke of Gloucester, the brother of King Henry V. A subsequent invasion of Hainaut (1424–25) proved unsuccessful, and Jacqueline was abandoned by Humphrey and obliged to make peace with Duke Philip the Good of Burgundy, who sought to avenge her repudiation of John IV. Imprisoned at Ghent, she escaped but submitted after a struggle. The treaty of Delft (1428) recognized her as nominal countess and Philip as her administrator and heir. Four years later she attempted in vain to incite a rebellion in Holland against Philip, after which she abdicated her countships in Philip's favor in 1433.

Jacquerie (zhäk"ərē') [Fr.,=collection of *Jacques,* which is, like *Jacques Bonhomme,* a nickname for the French peasant], 1358, revolt of the French peasantry. The uprising was provoked by the depressed economic condition of the Hundred Years War, by the pillaging of the *écorcheurs,* and by the extortionate demands of the nobles. Beginning around Beauvais, north of Paris, the revolt spread over a wide area; castles were demolished, provisions stolen, and other violent acts committed. The leader, Guillaume Karle (or Cale), was captured and beheaded by Charles II of Navarre, and the mob was easily dispersed. The nobles took revenge by massacring thousands of the insurgents.

Jada (jā'də), Jerahmeelite. 1 Chron. 2.28,32.

Jadau (jā'dô), Jew who married a foreign wife. Ezra 10.43.

Jaddua (jădyo͞o'ə). **1** High priest after the Exile. Neh. 12.11,22. **2** Signer of the Covenant. Neh. 10.21.

jade, common name for either of two minerals used as gems. The rarer variety of jade is jadeite, a sodium aluminum silicate, $NaAl(SiO_3)_2$, usually white or green in color; the green variety is the more valuable. The commoner and less costly variety of jade is nephrite, a calcium magnesium iron silicate of varying composition, white to dark green in color. Jade has been prized by the Chinese and Japanese as the most precious of all gems. The Chinese in particular are known for the objets d'art they carve from it, and they traditionally associated it with the five cardinal virtues: charity, modesty, courage, justice, and wisdom; they also attributed healing powers to it. It was much used for implements by primitive people, especially in Mexico, Switzerland, France, Greece, Egypt, Asia Minor, and New Zealand. Jadeite is found in Upper Burma, in Japan, and in Guatemala; nephrite in New Zealand, Turkistan, Siberia, China, Silesia, Wyoming, California, and British Columbia. See J. L. Kraft, *Adventure in Jade* (1947); S. C. Nott, *Chinese Jade throughout the Ages* (2d ed. 1962); Richard Gump, *Jade* (1962); J. M. Hartman, *Chinese Jade of Five Centuries* (1969); Geoffrey Wills, *Jade of the East* (1972).

jadeite: see JADE.

Jadida, El: see AL-JADIDA, Morocco.

Jadon (jā'dŏn), worker on the wall at Jerusalem. Neh. 3.7.

Jadotville, Zaïre: see LIKASI.

Jadwiga (yädvē'gä), 1374–99, Polish queen (1384–99), daughter of LOUIS I of Hungary and Poland. To satisfy Polish demands for autonomy at Louis's death, she reigned in Poland and her sister reigned in Hungary. Jadwiga married (1386) Jagiello, grand duke of Lithuania (see LADISLAUS II), in order to unite Poland and Lithuania and to convert the Lithuanians to Christianity. They ruled jointly, and after she died without children he ruled alone. Jadwiga restored (1387) to Poland the regions of Lvov and Galich that her father had given to Hungarian governors. She founded (1397) a theological college in Kraków and effected the restoration of the Univ. of Kraków. She is nationally venerated as a saint. See Charlotte Kellogg, *Jadwiga, Queen of Poland* (1936).

jaeger (yā'gər), common name for several members of the family Stercorariidae, member of a family of hawklike sea birds closely related to the gull and the tern. The skua is also a member of this family. Jaegers and skuas are stocky, powerfully muscled birds with long, pointed wings, long tails, strong, hooked bills, and sharp, curved talons. They are tireless, wide-ranging flyers of the open seas. Their piratical habits give them the names robber gull and sea hawk. Jaegers and skuas rob the food of their smaller relatives, teasing and harassing them until they drop their prey. They also feed on the eggs of colonial sea birds, especially those of penguins. The skua (*Catharacta skua*) is the largest and darkest of the family, a denizen of the N Atlantic, though it breeds south to the antarctic. Of the three jaegers (*Stercorarius* species), all of northern oceans, the largest is the pomarine jaeger (also called jiddy hawk), the most common the parasitic jaeger, and the most graceful the long-tailed jaeger. All these birds are mostly blackish-brown above and white below, with a gilding of the head and neck in the older birds. Jaegers are classified in the phylum CHORDATA, subphylum Vertebrata, class Aves, order Charadriiformes, family Stercorariidae.

Jael (jāl), heroine of the time of Deborah. She murdered Sisera, her guest. Judges 4; 5.

Jaén (häān'), city (1970 pop. 78,156), capital of Jaén prov., S Spain, in Andalusia. It is a marketing and distribution center for a fertile area producing olive oil and wine. Nearby lead mines are believed to be among the richest in Europe; iron and copper are also exploited. Once the seat of a small Moorish kingdom, Jaén was conquered by Ferdinand III of Castile in 1246. There are remains of a Moorish castle and walls; an imposing cathedral (16th–18th cent.); and several palaces.

Chinese jade plaque of the Sung dynasty (960–1279).

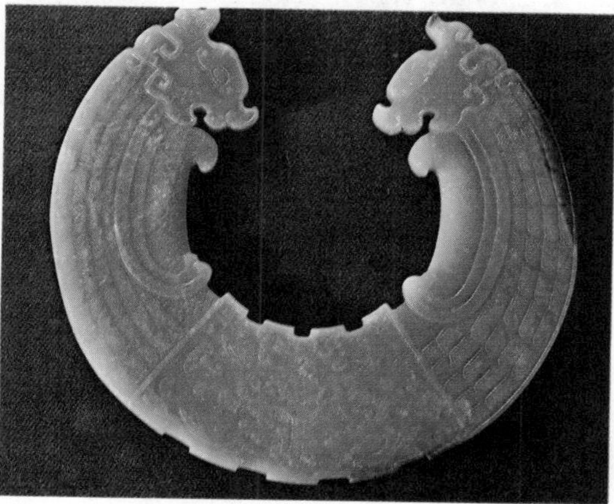

Jaffa (jăf'ə, yä'fä), Heb. *Yafo,* part of TEL AVIV-JAFFA, W central Israel, on the Mediterranean Sea. Originally a Phoenician city, Jaffa has been historically important largely because of its port (which was closed in 1965, when the port of Ashdod was completed). It was captured by Egypt in 1472 B.C. and made a provincial capital. In 701 B.C. the city was besieged by Sennacherib, king of Assyria. It was often held by Philistia, and not until after the Captivity in Babylon (6th cent. B.C.) did it become Hebrew territory. The Bible relates that Jonah set forth from there for Tarshish and that St. Peter restored Dorcas to life in Jaffa. Alexander the Great took Jaffa in the late 4th cent. B.C. The city changed hands frequently in the fighting between the Maccabees and the Syrians (2d and 1st cent. B.C.) and was destroyed by Vespasian in A.D. 68. The rebuilt city of Jaffa was conquered by the Arabs in 636. The Crusaders took it in 1126, Saladin recaptured it in 1187, and Richard I retook the city in 1191. In 1196 the Arabs again captured Jaffa, and in the 16th cent. the city, then in decline, was annexed by the Ottoman Empire. In the late 17th cent. Jaffa began to develop again as a seaport. It was captured by Napoleon in 1799. In World War I British troops took Jaffa, which became part of the British-administered PALESTINE mandate (1922–48). In 1947 and 1948 there was sharp fighting between Jaffa, which was largely inhabited by Arabs, and the adjoining all-Jewish city of Tel Aviv. The Arabs in Jaffa surrendered on the day (May 14, 1948) that the state of Israel was proclaimed. Most of the Arab population soon left. In 1950 the city was incorporated into Tel Aviv. Jaffa is mentioned in the Bible (2 Chron. 2.16) as marking the boundary of the tribe of Dan and is the Japho of Joshua 19.46. In the Apocrypha it is often spelled Joppe, but the usual Bible spelling is Joppa.

Jaffna (jăf'nə), peninsula, northernmost part of Sri Lanka (Ceylon), separated from India by Palk Strait. The peninsula is densely inhabited, largely by Tamil-speaking people. There are remains of ancient Tamil culture and of Portuguese and Dutch occupations of the 17th–18th cent. Tobacco, rice, coconuts, palmyra palm, and vegetables are grown, and fishing is an important occupation. The main industries are salt, cement, chemical, and tobacco production; cottage industries include textile weaving and gold filigree work. There is trade in elephants, peppers, and other commodities.

Jaffna moss: see AGAR.

Jagan, Cheddi (chĕd'ē jä'gän), 1918–, prime minister of British Guiana (1961–64), which later became Guyana. Of East Indian descent, he was trained as a dentist. In 1950 he founded, with Forbes BURNHAM, the country's first formal political party, and he was chief minister from April to Oct., 1953, when, in the wake of strikes and riots, the British authorities suspended the constitution and established an interim government. Jagan launched a civil disobedience campaign and was jailed (April–Sept., 1954) for violating an order restricting him to Georgetown. His extreme leftist views caused a rift with Burnham, who formed his own party in 1955. In 1957 elections, Jagan's party received a plurality, and he was named minister of trade and industry; his U.S.-born wife became minister of labor, health, and housing. In 1961, Jagan became prime minister. He attempted to impose a rigid austerity program, vigorously pushed social and economic reform, and worked for independence. Jagan's party led in the 1964 elections, but Burnham became prime minister after forming a coalition with a small third party. Jagan subsequently led the opposition to Burnham.

Jagannath, India: see PURI.

Jagatai (jăgətī'), d. 1242, Mongol conqueror; son of Jenghiz Khan. He led large armies on his father's campaigns of conquest. When the empire was divided in 1227 among Jenghiz Khan's three living sons and a grandson, Jagatai was rewarded with vast territories that correspond to present-day Turkistan and Afghanistan. He held this domain, a key area in the Mongol empire, as a satrapy under the rule of his brother Ogadai, who, although younger than Jagatai, had become grand khan. After Ogadai's death in 1241, dissension erupted between the Ogadai and Jagatai lines, and a third branch, which had descended from Jenghiz Khan's youngest son, Tule, dominated the Mongol empire. In the early 14th cent. Jagatai's descendants, the **Jagataids**, divided his khanate into two sections, the western region with its capital at Samarkand, and the eastern region, centering around Kashgar. Often at war with one another, the two domains were reunited by TAMERLANE (Timur), who may have been related to the family ruling the western region. The name Jagatai is sometimes spelled Chagatai or Djagatai.

Jagello: see JAGIELLO.

Jägerndorf: see KRNOV, Czechoslovakia.

Jaggard, William, c.1568–1623, London printer and publisher. Although it seems that he had previously pirated some of Shakespeare's works, he was chosen by the editors John Heming and Henry Condell as publisher of the First Folio edition of Shakespeare's plays. He died before the work was completed. To this book, undertaken after Jaggard became blind, are due the preservation of 18 of the plays and the correction of many textual errors in the plays printed in earlier editions, in quarto. See E. E. Willoughby, *A Printer of Shakespeare* (1934, repr. 1969).

Jagiello (yägyĕ'lō) or **Jagello** (yägĕ'lō), dynasty that ruled POLAND and LITHUANIA from 1386 to 1572, Hungary from 1440 to 1444 and again from 1490 to 1526, and Bohemia from 1471 to 1526. It took its name from Ladislaus Jagiello, grand duke of Lithuania, who became (1386) king of Poland as LADISLAUS II when he married Queen JADWIGA. His successors were LADISLAUS III (1434–44; as Uladislaus I also king of Hungary); CASIMIR IV (1447–92); John I (1492–1501); Alexander I (1501–5); SIGISMUND I (1506–48); and SIGISMUND II (1548–72), last ruler of the line. A son of Casimir IV became king of Bohemia (1471) as Ladislaus II and king of Hungary (1490) as ULADISLAUS II; his son was LOUIS II of Bohemia and Hungary (1516–26). The female line of Jagiello merged with the Swedish house of Vasa through the marriage of Catherine, sister of Sigismund II, with John III of Sweden; their son was king of Sweden and of Poland (see SIGISMUND III). Under Jagiello rule Poland reached its golden age.

jaguar (jăg'wär), large New World carnivore of the CAT family, *Panthera onca.* Jaguars range from the SW United States to S central Argentina. They have deep yellow or tawny coats marked with black rings, or rosettes, and spots. In all individuals at least some of the rings surround spots. This feature distinguishes the jaguar from the Old World LEOPARD, which has similar markings, but never has rosettes with internal spots. The jaguar is also shorter-limbed and stockier than the leopard. An adult male jaguar is up to 7 ft (2.2 m) long, including the 2½-ft (76-cm) tail, stands about 2½ ft (76 cm) high at the shoulder

Jaguar, large New World carnivore of the cat family.

and weighs about 200 lb (90 kg). Jaguars are very adaptable animals. They are primarily forest dwellers but may be found on the South American pampas, or even in rocky semidesert areas of Mexico and the United States. They are the best tree climbers of all the big cats and in some regions live an almost entirely arboreal existence for months at a time when the forest floor is flooded. They are also good swimmers and sometimes catch fish for food. Jaguars hunt deer, agouti, capybara, and especially peccaries. They are retiring animals, not particularly inclined to attack people, but a jaguar may launch an attack or even stalk a human being if threatened. In Mexico the jaguar is known as *el tigre,* "the tiger," although true tigers are found only in Asia. Jaguars are classified in the phylum CHORDATA, subphylum Vertebrata, class Mammalia, order Carnivora, family Felidae.

Jagur (jā'gər), unidentified town, S Palestine. Joshua 15.21.

Jah (yä), abbreviation of one of the reconstructions (Jahveh, Jahweh) of the ancient Hebrew ineffable name of GOD.

Jahangir or **Jehangir** (both: jəhän"gēr'), 1569–1627, Mogul emperor of India (1605–27), son of Akbar. An indolent and pleasure-loving man, he nonetheless continued his father's policy of expansion. The Rajput principality of Mewar (Udaipur) capitulated in 1614. In the Deccan, Ahmadnagar was taken in 1616 and half of its kingdom annexed. In the northwest, however, the Persian ruler, Shah Abbas, retook (1622) Kandahar. In 1611, Jahangir married a Persian widow, Nur Jahan, and she and her relatives soon dominated politics, while Jahangir devoted himself to cultivation of the arts, especially miniature painting, and to drinking. He welcomed foreign visitors to his court, granting trading privileges first to the Portuguese and then to the British East India Company. Civil strife and court intrigues marked the last years of Jahangir's reign. Shah Jahan, his son, succeeded him. See Beni Prasad, *History of Jahangir* (1922).

Jahath (jā'hăth). **1** Descendant of Gershom. 1 Chron. 6.20,43. **2** Chief of a Gershonite family. 1 Chron. 23.10. **3** Descendant of Judah. 1 Chron. 4.2. **4** Levite. 1 Chron. 24.22. **5** Temple overseer. 2 Chron. 34.12.

Jahaz (jā'həz), **Jahaza** (jāhā'zə), **Jahazah** (jāhā'zə), or **Jahzah** (jä'zə), unidentified town, E of the Dead Sea. Israel's defeat there of the Amorites is recorded on the Moabite stone. Num. 21.23; Deut. 2.32; Joshua 13.18; 21.36; Judges 11.20; 1 Chron. 6.78; Isa. 15.4; Jer. 48.21,34.

Jahaziah (jā"həzī'ə), one associated with Ezra in the expulsion of the foreign wives. Ezra 10.15.

Jahaziel (jəhā'zēĕl, jā"hāzī'əl, jāhăz'ēĕl). **1** Man who joined David at Ziklag. 1 Chron. 12.4. **2** One who inspired Jehoshaphat to oppose the invading Ammonites. 2 Chron. 20.14. **3** Priest before the Ark. 1 Chron. 16.6. **4** Kohathite Levite. 1 Chron. 23.19; 24.23. **5** Head of a family that returned from the Exile. Ezra 8.5.

Jahdai (jä'dāī), Calebite. 1 Chron. 2.47.

Jahdiel (jä'dīĕl), head of a Manassite family. 1 Chron. 5.24.

Jahdo (jä'dō), one of the tribe of Gad. 1 Chron. 5.14.

Jahleel (jä'lēĕl), founder of a Zebulonite family. Gen. 46.14; Num. 26.26.

Jahmai (jä'māī, jämā'ī), head of the house of Tola. 1 Chron. 7.2.

Jahn, Friedrich Ludwig (frē'drĭkh lo͞ot'vĭkh yän), 1778–1852, German patriot. A high school teacher in Berlin, he was active in efforts to free Germany from Napoleonic rule. He organized the TURNVEREIN, a gymnastic association, to build strength and fellowship among young people of all classes. The gymnastic groups Jahn fostered became centers for nationalism and for the movement to unify Germany. After serving (1813–15) in the war against Napoleon, Jahn continued his work until his political agitation caused his imprisonment (1819–25). Jahn, who also was influential in the organization of the BURSCHENSCHAFT movement, was a delegate to the FRANKFURT PARLIAMENT in 1848.

Jahnn, Hans Henny (häns hĕn'ē yän), 1894–1959, German novelist, dramatist, music publisher, and organ builder. Jahnn's early dramas, including *Pastor Ephraim Magnus* (1919) and *Medea* (1926), were laden with sexual-pathological images. Among his later novels, of greater substance, are *Thomas Chatterhorn* (1955) and a trilogy, *Fluss ohne Ufer* [shoreless river] (1949–50; tr. Vol. I, *The Ship*, 1961), which explores the dangers of delving into the secrets of creation. Jahnn also published 17th-century organ music and gained an international reputation as a builder and renovator of organs.

Jahve, Jahveh, or **Jahweh** (yä'vā,-wā), modern reconstructions of the ancient Hebrew ineffable name of GOD.

Jahzah (jä'zə), variant of JAHAZ.

Jahzeel (jä'zēĕl), Naphtalite. Num. 26.48. Jahziel: 1 Chron. 7.13.

Jahzerah (jä'zērə), the same as AHASAI.

Jahziel (jä'zēĕl), variant of JAHZEEL.

jai alai (hī'lī''), handball-like game of Spanish Basque origin, now also popular in Latin America and Florida. It is also called pelota. Jai alai is played on a three-walled court, called a *cancha*, with a hard rubber ball that must be hurled against the front wall with the *cesta*, a wicker basket attached to the player's arm. The *cancha* is usually about 175 ft (53 m) long, 55 ft (17 m) wide, and 40 ft (12 m) high. Spectators sit behind a wire fence on the fourth side of the court. To their right is the front wall, or *frontis*. The object is to hurl the ball against the front wall in such a way that it cannot be returned. The ball may hit the side or rear wall before striking the *frontis;* it may not hit the spectators' fence. Jai alai is one of the fastest of all games. It is played as either singles or doubles with scoring similar to that of handball. The first player or team to reach the required number of points (usually 6 or 7 in singles and as high as 25 in doubles) wins. Betting on games is popular and gambling is legal at the Florida jai alai courts.

jail: see PRISON.

Jailolo: see HALMAHERA, Indonesia.

Jaime. For Spanish rulers thus named, see JAMES.

Jainism (jī'nĭzəm) [i.e., the religion of Jina], religious system of India practiced by about 2,000,000 persons. Jainism, AJIVIKA, and BUDDHISM arose in the 6th cent. B.C. as protests against the overdeveloped ritualism of HINDUISM, particularly its sacrificial cults, and the authority of the Veda. Jaina tradition teaches that a succession of 24 tirthankaras (saints) originated the religion. The last, Vardhamana, called Mahavira [the great hero] and Jina [the victor], seems to be historical. He preached a rigid asceticism and solicitude for all life as a means of escaping the cycle of rebirth, or the TRANSMIGRATION OF SOULS. Thus released from the rule of KARMA, the total consequences of past acts, the soul attains NIRVANA, and hence salvation. Mahavira organized a brotherhood of monks, who took vows of celibacy, nudity, self-mortification, and fasting. Since the 1st cent. A.D., when a schism developed over the issue of nudity, there have been two great divisions of Jains, the Digambaras [space-clothed, i.e., naked] and the Svetambaras [white-clothed]. Jainists, then as now, accumulate merit through charity, through good works, and in occasional monastic retreat. Early Jainism, arising in NE India, quickly spread west, and according to tradition CHANDRAGUPTA, the founder of the Maurya empire, was converted to the sect, as were several kings of Gujarat. The Jaina canon, however, is preserved in an ancient dialect of NE India (see PRAKRIT LITERATURE). As Jainism grew and prospered, reverence for Mahavira and for other teachers, historical and legendary, passed into adoration; many beautiful temples were built and cult images set up. However, as time passed, the line between Hindu and Jain became more and more unclear. Soon Hindu gods such as Rama and Krishna were drawn into the Jaina pantheon, and Hindu Brahmans began to preside at Jaina death and marriage ceremonies and temple worship. The caste system, which primitive Jainism had rejected, also became part of later Jaina doctrine. Modern Jainists, eschewing any occupation that even remotely endangers animal life, are engaged largely in commerce and finance. Among them are many of India's most prominent industrialists and bankers as well as several important political leaders. A distinctive form of charity among Jains is the establishment of asylums for diseased and decrepit animals. See M. S. Stevenson, *The Heart of Jainism* (1915, repr. 1970); M. L. Mehta, *Jaina Philosophy* (1970); Subramania Gopalan, *Outlines of Jainism* (1973).

Jaipur (jī'po͝or), former native state, W India. It is now part of Rajasthan state. The region of Jaipur is mostly level, and, despite light rainfall, fair crops of maize, millet, and cotton are raised. Salt is mined and cotton and woolen cloth and metal products are manufactured. Jaipur was founded in the 12th cent. by the Kachwaha clan of the RAJPUTS. It became (c.1550) a feudatory of the MOGUL empire. In 1818, Great Britain exacted a treaty providing for an annual tribute. **Jaipur,** city (1971 pop. 613,144), capital of Rajasthan, was founded in 1728. Known as the pink city from the color of its houses, it is a transportation junction and a commercial center. It is enclosed by a crenellated wall 20 ft (6 m) high. An unusual feature for an Indian city of this size is the system of wide, regular streets. The grounds of the former maharaja's palace occupy one seventh of the municipal area. Among Jaipur's famed art products are jewelry, enamels, and muslins. Rajasthan Univ. is there. Jaipur has a large banking business. The deserted city of Amber, which was the capital of Jaipur state until 1728, is 5 mi (8 km) from Jaipur. The palace there is a fine example of Rajput architecture.

Jair (jā'ər). **1** Manassite. Num. 32.41; Deut. 3.14. **2** Judge of Israel. Judges 10.3. **3** Mordecai's father. Esther 2.5. **4** See JAARE-OREGIM. See also HAVOTH-JAIR.

Jairus (jāī'rəs) [Gr. form of JAIR], prominent Jew whose daughter was raised from the dead by Jesus. Mat. 9.18–26; Mark 5.22–43; Luke 8.41–56.

Jaisalmer (jəsäl'mər), former principality, Rajasthan state, NW India. Its terrain is largely a sandy waste. Jaisalmer was brought under the Mogul empire by Akbar in 1570. It became a British protectorate in 1818. In 1949 the region was incorporated in Rajasthan state.

Jaja (jä'jə), fl. 1869–1887, Nigerian merchant prince. A former slave, he became an important trader in Bonny in the 1860s as a middleman between the coastal markets and the Nigerian interior. In 1869 he founded his own state at Opobo on the Gulf of Guinea. From there he controlled supplies of palm oil and opposed the efforts of British firms to penetrate the interior. The traders persuaded the British vice consul, Henry Hamilton (Sir Harry) Johnston, to act against Jaja, who was seized in 1887 and then deported to the West Indies.

Jakan (jā'kən), the same as AKAN.

Jakarta: see DJAKARTA, Indonesia.

Jakeh (jā'kĕ), father of Agur. Prov. 30.1.

Jakim (jā'kĭm). **1** Chief priest in David's reign. 1 Chron. 24.12. **2** Chief Benjamite. 1 Chron. 8.19.

Jakobshavn (yäkôps-houn'), town (1969 pop. 2,544), Jakobshavn dist. (1969 pop. 2,992), W Greenland, on Disko Bay. Founded in 1741, it is a sealing and fishing port.

Jalalabad (jəlä"läbäd', jəlăl'əbăd), city (1969 pop. 48,919), capital of Nangarhar prov., E Afghanistan, near the KHYBER PASS. The city dominates the entrances to the Laghman and Kunar valleys and is a leading center for trade with India and Pakistan. Oranges, rice, and sugarcane grow in the fertile surrounding area, and the city has cane-processing and sugar-refining as well as papermaking industries. Jalalabad has long been both a military center and a winter resort. The site of the city belonged to the ancient Greco-Buddhist center of GANDHARA. Babur, founder of the Mogul empire of India, chose the site for the modern city, which was built c.1570 by his grandson, Akbar. During the First Afghan War, British troops held (1842) Jalalabad against a determined Afghan siege. Pathan tribesmen constitute most of the population. The city has a university and medical school.

Jalapa de Enriquez (hälä'pä thā ānrē'kās), city (1970 pop. 127,081), capital of Veracruz state, E central Mexico, on the slopes of the Sierra Madre Oriental. It is located in a rich agricultural region of fertile valleys. Its cool climate and the proximity of colorful Indian villages and of scenic Mt. Orizaba also make Jalapa a popular resort. The site of a pre-Columbian city, Jalapa was captured by Cortés in 1519. It was an important commercial center during the Spanish colonial era, but declined in the late 18th cent., after which it served as an important military base. The local museum has an excellent archaeological collection, notably a group of colossal Olmec heads, which are displayed in the open air.

Jalgaon (jäl'goun), town (1971 pop. 106,739), Maharashtra state, W central India. It is the center of a cotton-growing district.

Jalisco (hälē'skō), state (1970 pop. 3,322,750), 31,152 sq mi (80,684 sq km), W Mexico, bounded on the west by the Pacific. GUADALAJARA is the capital. Jalisco is dominated by the southern end of the Sierra Madre Occidental and the western extremity of the chain of volcanic mountains extending across central Mexico. The hot, tropical plains of the coast are broken by spurs of the Sierra, and most of the eastern part of the state lies within the central plateau. In the central part of Jalisco is an intermontane basin containing Lake Chapala; it is drained by the Lerma-Santiago system. Because of the variety of climate, landform, and elevation, nearly every kind of fruit and vegetable grows somewhere in Jalisco. Maize and wheat from the central plateau make it known as the "granary of Mexico"; rice and wheat are grown in the south; and the mountains yield timber and minerals (silver, iron, tin, cinnabar, and some gold.) The raising of livestock and the production of textiles and food products are also important. Although Jalisco was explored as early as 1522, serious conquest of the area, later included in NUEVA GALICIA, was not undertaken until 1529 by Nuno de GUZMÁN. Shortly before the War of the Reform (1858–61), Jalisco became a leading state in the great liberal revolution heralded by the Plan of AYUTLA. It was occupied by the French in the wars of intervention but was recaptured in 1866. In 1884 the territory of NAYARIT was separated from Jalisco. The state has two universities and a technological institute.

Jalon (jā'lŏn), descendant of Judah. 1 Chron. 4.17.

Jalpaiguri (jəlpī'go͝orē), town (1971 pop. 55,345), West Bengal state, NE India, on the Tista River. It is the administrative center for a district that produces tea, rice, jute, tobacco, timber, and medicinal herbs.

Jaluit (jä'lo͞oĭt), atoll (1970 pop. 492), c.40 mi (60 km) long and c.20 mi (30 km) wide, central Pacific, one of the Ralik Chain in the U.S. MARSHALL ISLANDS. It comprises some 85 islets, of which Jaluit Island (4 sq mi/10.4 sq km) is the largest. In World War II it was the headquarters of the Japanese admiralty for the Marshall Islands. U.S. forces captured the atoll in 1944. Jaluit is a seaport and trade center for the Marshalls.

jam: see JELLY AND JAM.

Jamaica (jəmā'kə), republic (1973 est. pop. 2,000,000), 4,232 sq mi (10,962 sq km), coextensive with the island of Jamaica, West Indies, S of Cuba and W of Haiti. Jamaica is the largest island in the Caribbean after Cuba and Hispaniola. The capital is KINGSTON; other important cities are SPANISH TOWN and MONTEGO BAY. Although largely a limestone plateau more than 3,000 ft (914 m) above sea level, Jamaica has a mountainous backbone that extends across the island from the west and rises to the Blue Mts. in the east; Blue Mt. (7,402 ft/2,256 m) is the highest point. Rainfall is heavy in this region (where there are extensive timber reserves) but diminishes westward across the plateau, which is a rugged area deeply dissected by streams and underlain by subterranean rivers. The heart of the plateau, known as the Cockpits, is used mostly for livestock grazing. A narrow plain along the northern coast and several larger plains near the south shore are Jamaica's major agricultural zones. The north coast also has fine beaches and is the focus of the tourist industry. The Rio Grande and the Black River are the country's chief waterways, but neither is navigable for long distances. The coastal bands widened by broad river valleys, as well as the mountain slopes, support the bulk of Jamaica's export crops: the famed Blue Mt. coffee, sugarcane, from which rum and molasses are also made, bananas, ginger, citrus fruits, cocoa, pimento, and tobacco. Most of these crops are grown on large plantations. Small peasant farms produce

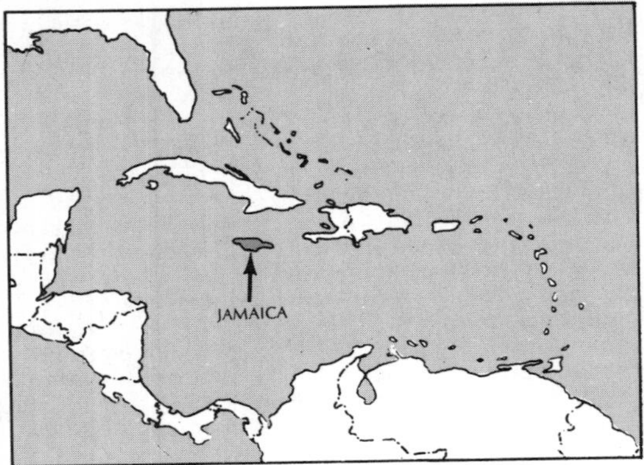

some ginger, bananas, and sugarcane for export but mainly raise such subsistence crops as yams, breadfruit, and cassava. Mining is a major source of wealth; since large, easily accessible deposits of bauxite were discovered in 1942, Jamaica has become one of the world's leading suppliers of this ore. Along with the alumina made from it, bauxite accounts for about half of Jamaica's foreign exchange. Tourism is the second biggest earner of exchange. Clothing constitutes the chief export item of the manufacturing sector. Jamaica's other industries (mainly concentrated in the Kingston area) include oil refining, tobacco processing, flour milling, and the production of cement, textiles, and processed foods. Since the late 1960s industry has generated a greater share of the national income than agriculture, which, however, still employs the largest percentage of the work force. The United States, Great Britain, and Canada, Jamaica's top trading partners, also provide much-needed capital for economic development. About 75% of the population is rural, but migration to the cities continues; the greatest urban concentration is around Kingston. People of African descent predominate in Jamaica. The small upper class is mainly white. Afro-Europeans and such Middle Eastern and Asian groups as Lebanese, Syrians, Chinese, and Indians, make up the rest of the population. Although English is the official language, most Jamaicans speak a patois, creole English. The chief religion is Protestantism. Discovered by Christopher Columbus in 1494, Jamaica was conquered and settled in 1509 by Spaniards under a license from Columbus's son. Spanish exploitation decimated the native Arawaks. The island remained Spanish until 1655, when Admiral William Penn and Robert Venables captured it; it was formally ceded to England in 1670, but the local white population obtained a degree of autonomy. Jamaica prospered from the wealth brought by buccaneers, notably Sir Henry MORGAN, to Port Royal, the capital; in 1692, however, the city sank into the sea during an earthquake, and Spanish Town became the new capital. A huge, mostly Negro, slave population grew up around the sugarcane plantations in the 18th cent., when Jamaica was a leading world sugar producer. Freed slaves and runaways, sometimes aided by the MAROONS (slaves who had escaped to remote areas after Spain lost control of Jamaica), collaborated in fomenting frequent rebellions against the white colonials. The sugar industry declined in the 19th cent., partly because of the abolition of slavery in 1833 (effective 1838) and partly because of the elimination in 1846 of the imperial preference tariff for colonial products entering the British market. Economic hardship was the prime motive behind the Morant Bay rebellion by freedmen in 1865. The British ruthlessly quelled the uprising and also forced the frightened white legislature to surrender its powers; Jamaica became a crown colony. Poverty and economic decline led many Negroes to seek temporary work in neighboring Caribbean areas and in the United States; many left the island permanently. Indians were imported to meet the labor shortage on the plantations after the Negro slaves were freed, and agriculture was diversified to lessen dependence on sugar exports. A new constitution in 1884 marked the initial revival of local autonomy for Jamaica. Despite labor and other reforms, Negro riots recurred, notably those of 1938, which were caused mainly by unemployment and resentment against British racial policies. Jamaican blacks had been considerably influenced by the theories of black nationalism promulgated by the American expatriate Marcus Garvey. A royal commission investigating the 1938 riots recommended an increase of economic development funds and a faster restoration of representative government for Jamaica. In 1944 universal adult suffrage was introduced, and a new constitution provided for a popularly elected house of representatives. By 1958, Jamaica became a key member of the British-sponsored West Indies Federation (see under WEST INDIES). The fact that Jamaica received only one third of the representation in the federation, despite its having more than half the land area and population of the grouping, bred resentment; a campaign by the nationalist labor leader Sir Alexander Bustamante led to a 1961 decision, by popular referendum, to withdraw from the federation. The following year Jamaica won complete independence from Great Britain and became a member of the Commonwealth of Nations and the United Nations. It joined the Caribbean Free Trade Association in 1968. In March, 1974, Jamaica became one of the seven charter members of the International Association of Producers of Bauxite and later announced large increases in bauxite taxes and royalties. The country has a two-party system: the Jamaica Labor Party (JLP) favors private enterprise, while the People's National Party (PNP) advocates moderate socialism. Bustamante, leader of the JLP, became the first prime minister of independent Jamaica. The party continued in power under Donald B. Sangster after the 1967 elections; he died in office and was succeeded by Hugh Shearer. In 1972 the PNP won an impressive victory, and Michael Manley became prime minister. The prime minister and his cabinet are responsible to the bicameral Parliament. See M. M. Carley, *Jamaica* (1963); R. W. Palmer, *The Jamaican Economy* (1968); Edward Brathwaite, *The Development of Creole Society in Jamaica, 1770–1820* (1971); Frank Cundall, *Historic Jamaica* (1915, repr. 1971), S. J. Hurwitz and E. F. Hurwitz, *Jamaica: A Historical Portrait* (1971); R. M. Nettleford, *Identity, Race and Protest in Jamaica* (1972).

Jamaica Bay, c.20 sq mi (50 sq km), SW Long Island, SE N.Y., separated from the Atlantic Ocean by Rockaway Peninsula; the Rockaway Inlet links it to the sea. The shallow bay has many islands, and its shores are generally marshy. There is a minimum of water movement, and pollution is a problem. Nearly all of the bay is in New York City; since 1950 much of the adjacent area has been reclaimed for housing.

Kingston, capital of the Caribbean island of Jamaica.

John F. Kennedy International Airport extends into the bay. Part of Gateway National Recreation Area, the bay is used for boating and fishing and is a wildlife refuge.

Jambi: see DJAMBI, Indonesia.

Jamblichus: see IAMBLICHUS.

Jambol: see YAMBOL, Bulgaria.

Jambres: see JANNES AND JAMBRES.

James, Saint, d. A.D. c.43, one of the Twelve Disciples, called St. James the Greater. He was the son of Zebedee and the brother of St. John; these brothers were the Boanerges, or Sons of Thunder. St. James was killed by Herod Agrippa I. Mark 3.17; 5.37; 9.2; 10.35–45; 14.33; Mat. 20.20–29; Acts 12.1–2. Veneration of St. James has been widespread, especially in Spain (where he is called Santiago); the shrine of the apostle at Compostela, Spain, is one of the most celebrated of Europe. Feast: July 25.

James, Saint, one of the Twelve Disciples, called St. James the Less or St. James the Little. He was the son of Alphaeus; his mother, Mary, was one of those at the cross and tomb (Mat. 10.3; 27.56; Mark 15.40; 16.1; Acts 1.13). The Western Church identifies him with Saint James, "the Lord's brother" (see separate article). Feast (with St. Philip): May 1.

James, Saint, the "brother" of Jesus Christ. The Gospels make several references to the brothers of Jesus (Mat. 12.46; 13.55; Mark 6.3; John 2.12), and St. Paul speaks of "James the Lord's brother" (Gal. 1.19). However, since belief in the perpetual virginity of Mary precludes a blood relationship between Jesus and James, it has been posited that they were stepbrothers (assuming a previous marriage for Joseph) or cousins. The latter hypothesis, which is favored by the Roman Catholic Church, identifies James with St. James the Less. The James whom Paul calls "the Lord's brother" witnessed the Resurrection and became a leader of the church in Jerusalem, by tradition the first bishop there. He apparently opposed the imposition of Jewish Law on gentile Christians but believed that Jewish Christians should continue to observe it. (Acts 12.17; 15.13–21; 21.18; Gal. 2.9,12.) He is probably the James of the epistle of that name. Some scholars believe that he wrote it himself, others that it was written at a later date under his name. The Jewish historian Josephus records that James was stoned to death at the instigation of the priests A.D. c.62.

James I (James the Conqueror), 1208–76, king of Aragón and count of Barcelona (1213–76), son and successor of Peter II. After a minority disturbed by private wars among the nobles, James soon consolidated royal power and tried to create a new nobility dependent on him. He seized the Balearic Islands (1229–35) and Valencia (1238) from the Moors and helped Castile to recover control of Murcia after a Moorish rebellion (1266). A crusade to Palestine (1269) was unsuccessful. By the Treaty of Corbeil (1258) with Louis IX of France, James gave up several claims in S France, while the French king renounced his rights in Catalonia, derived from Charlemagne. James's own chronicle of his reign has been translated into English. He was succeeded in Aragón by his son Peter III. Another son became king of Majorca as James I. See biographies by C. R. Beazley (1890) and F. D. Swift (1894).

James II, c.1260–1327, king of Aragón and count of Barcelona (1291–1327), king of Sicily (1285–95). He succeeded his father, Peter III, in Sicily and his brother, Alfonso III, in Aragón. James defended Sicily against the claims of CHARLES II of Naples until 1295, when he relinquished the island in exchange for the title to Sardinia and Corsica. (Sardinia was annexed in 1323–24, but he did not take Corsica.) James later supported Charles against the former's own brother, who had been proclaimed king of Sicily as FREDERICK II. James was succeeded in Aragón by his son Alfonso IV.

James I, 1566–1625, king of England (1603–25) and, as James VI, of Scotland (1567–1625). The son of Lord Darnley and MARY QUEEN OF SCOTS, he succeeded to the Scottish throne on the forced abdication of his mother. He was placed in the care of John Erskine, 1st earl of MAR, and later of Mar's brother, Sir Alexander Erskine. The young king progressed in his studies under various teachers, notably George BUCHANAN, and acquired a taste for learning and theological debate. During James's minority, Scotland was ruled by a series of regents—the earls of MURRAY, LENNOX, Mar, and MORTON. The king was the creature of successive combinations of the nobility and clergy in a complicated struggle between the remnants of his mother's Catholic party, which favored an alliance with France, and the Protestant faction, which wished an alliance with England. In 1582, James was seized by William Ruthven, earl of Gowrie (see RUTHVEN, family), and other Protestant adherents. He escaped in 1583 and began his personal rule, though influenced by his favorite, James STUART, earl of Arran. James considered an alliance with his mother's French relatives, the GUISE, but in 1586, to improve his prospects of succeeding to the English throne, he allied himself with Elizabeth I. This caused a break with his mother's party, and he accepted her execution in 1587 calmly. James, by clever politics and armed force, succeeded in subduing the feudal Scottish baronage, in establishing royal authority, and in asserting the superiority of the state over the Presbyterian Church. In 1589, against the wishes of Elizabeth, James married ANNE OF DENMARK. He succeeded in 1603 to the English crown by virtue of his descent from MARGARET TUDOR, daughter of Henry VII.

Portrait of James I, king of England and, as James VI, king of Scotland.

King of England. Although at first welcomed in England, James brought to his new kingdom little understanding of its Parliament or its changing political, social, and religious conditions. On his arrival in England, the king was presented with the Millenary Petition, a plea for the accommodation of Puritans within the Established Church. However, at the Hampton Court Conference (1604), called to consider the petition, James displayed an uncompromising anti-Puritan attitude, which aroused great distrust. (This conference commissioned the translation of the BIBLE that resulted in the Authorized, or King James, Version.) James's inconsistent policy toward English Roman Catholics angered both Catholic and Protestant alike. The GUNPOWDER PLOT (1605), which sprang from Catholic anger at the reimposition of fines and penalties that James had earlier relaxed, led to greater harshness toward Catholics and prevented any cordial relations thereafter. Yet the suspicion arose that the king favored the Catholics, because he sought to conciliate Spain and attempted to arrange a marriage between the Spanish infanta and Prince Charles (later CHARLES I). James's reliance on favorites whose qualifications consisted more of personal charm than talent for government, the extravagance and looseness of the court, and the scandalous career of James's favorite, Robert Carr, earl of SOMERSET, all furthered discontent.

Conflict with Parliament. James's relations with the English Parliament were strained from the beginning because of his insistence upon the concept of divine right of monarchy and his inability to recognize Parliament as representative of a large and important body of opinion. As it was, Parliament—and particularly the House of Commons, where Puritanism was strong—soon became the rallying point of the forces opposing the crown. The Commons blocked (1607) James's cherished project of a union with Scotland. They also complained bitterly about James's methods of raising revenue by imposing new customs duties and selling monopolies. The Great Contract of 1610, a compromise whereby James would relinquish some of his feudal rights in return for a yearly income, did not come to fruition. In 1611, James dissolved Parliament and except for the Addled Parliament of 1614, which produced no legislation, ruled without one until 1621. After the death (1612) of his capable minister, Robert Cecil, earl of SALISBURY, the king exercised the royal prerogative with even less restraint and entered into battle with the courts of common law, whose position was strongly defended by Sir Edward COKE. After the fall of Somerset, George Villiers, later 1st duke of BUCKINGHAM, rose to favor and by 1619 was in complete possession of the king's confidence. At the Parliament of 1621, called in order to raise money for the cause of the German Protestants and James's son-in-law, FREDERICK THE WINTER KING, in the Thirty Years War, James was forced to abolish certain monopolies that had been abused by their holders. This Parliament also impeached the lord chancellor, Francis BACON. It was dissolved by James for asserting its right to debate foreign policy. The unpopular Spanish policy was pursued until the 1623 expedition of Prince Charles and Buckingham to Spain to facilitate the marriage arrangements ended in failure. A marriage treaty with France was concluded in 1624, and James was unable to prevent Parliament from voting a subsidy for war against Spain. James left to his son, Charles I, a foreign war and events leading up to the ENGLISH CIVIL WAR. During James's reign occurred the beginnings of English colonization in North America (Jamestown was founded in 1607) and the plantation of Scottish settlers in Ulster. The king was active as an author. He produced several youthful essays on literary theory, poetry, and numerous political works. Two other important writings are his *True Law of Free Monarchy* (1598), an assertion of the concept of divine right of kings, and BASILIKON DORON (1599), a treatise on the art of government. His political works have been edited by C. H. McIlwain (1918, repr. 1965). See biographies by D. H. Willson (1956, repr. 1967) and David Mathew (1967); Godfrey Davies, *The Early Stuarts* (2d ed. 1959); J. P. Kenyon, *The Stuarts* (1958); G. P. V. Akrigg, *Jacobean Pageant* (1962, repr. 1967).

James II, 1633–1701, king of England, Scotland, and Ireland (1685–88); second son of Charles I, brother and successor of CHARLES II. As the young duke of York he was surrendered (1646) to the parliamentary forces at the end of the first civil war, but he escaped (1648) to the Continent and served in the French (1652–55) and Spanish (1658) armies. At the Restoration (1660) he returned to England, married Anne Hyde, daughter of the 1st earl of Clarendon, and was made lord high admiral, in which capacity he served (1665, 1672) in the DUTCH WARS. Charles II granted him sweeping proprietary rights in America, and the captured Dutch settlement New Amsterdam was renamed (1664) New York in his honor. James was converted to Roman Catholicism probably in 1668—a step that was to have grave consequences. After his resignation (1673) as admiral because of the TEST ACT and his marriage (1673) to the staunchly Catholic MARY OF MODENA (his first wife having died in 1671), he became increasingly unpopular in England. James consented to the marriage (1677) of his daughter Mary (later MARY II) to the Protestant prince of Orange (later WILLIAM III), and the couple became the heirs presumptive, after James, to the English throne. In the anti-Catholic hysteria that accompanied the false accusations of Titus OATES about the Popish Plot (1678), efforts were made by the so-called WHIGS to exclude James from the succession. Charles stood by his brother, preventing passage of the Exclusion Bill, but sent him out of the country. After a period as commissioner (1680–82) in Scotland, James returned to England, and particularly after the RYE HOUSE PLOT (1683) his fortunes rose a little. When Charles died in 1685, James succeeded peacefully to the throne. An uprising led by the duke of MONMOUTH was crushed (1685), but the severe reprisals of the Bloody Assizes under Baron JEFFREYS OF WEM added to the animosity toward James. The king favored autocratic methods, proroguing the hostile Parliament (1685), reviving the old ecclesiastical court of high commission, and interfering with the courts and with local town and county government. His principal object was to fill positions of authority and influence with Roman Catholics, and to this end he issued two declarations of indulgence (1687, 1688), suspending the laws against Catholics and dissenters. Defiance and dislike of him grew, fed by the trial (1688) of seven bishops who had refused to read his second declaration. The birth of a son, who would have succeeded instead of the Protestant William and Mary, helped to bring the opposition to a head. William of Orange was invited to England by Whig and TORY leaders. The unpopular, autocratic, and Catholic king had few loyal followers and was unable to defend himself. He fled, was captured, and was allowed to escape to France, and William and Mary took the throne. The so-called GLORIOUS REVOLUTION had succeeded. James made an effort to restore himself by crossing over to Ireland in 1689 and raising his standard there, but the effort failed dismally in the battle of the BOYNE (1690). Other projects for restoration failed, and James's supporter, Louis XIV, recognized William III in the Treaty of Ryswick (1697). The cause of James's son and grandson was upheld later by the JACOBITES long after James had died in inglorious exile. See his early memoirs (tr. 1962); biographies by Hilaire Belloc (1928, repr. 1971), F. G. Turner (1948), and Vincent Buranelli (1962); David Ogg, *England in the Reigns of James II and William III* (1955, repr. 1969); J. P. Kenyon, *The Stuarts* (1958, repr. 1966).

James I, 1243–1311, king of Majorca (1276–1311), count of Roussillon and Cerdagne, lord of Montpellier, son of James I of Aragón. In 1278 he was forced to become a vassal of his brother, Peter III of Aragón. Having supported the French crusade against Peter, he was expelled (1285) from his territories by Peter's son, Alfonso III, but was restored 10 years later as the vassal of James II of Aragón. He was succeeded by his son Sancho IV (reigned 1311–24).

James II, 1315–49, king of Majorca (1324–49), count of Roussillon and Cerdagne, lord of Montpellier; grandson of James I, nephew and successor of Sancho IV. In 1329 he declared himself a vassal of the Aragonese crown. Accusing James of illegal acts, Peter IV of Aragón invaded and conquered Majorca (1343) and Roussillon (1344) and annexed them to Aragón. James tried to recover his kingdom, but was defeated and killed in battle on Majorca. His son, James III, tried unsuccessfully to recover the kingdom in 1375.

James I, 1394–1437, king of Scotland (1406–37), son and successor of Robert III. King Robert feared for the safety of James because the king's brother, Robert STUART, 1st duke of Albany, who was virtual ruler of the realm, stood next in line of succession after the young prince. Albany had already been suspected of complicity in the death of James's older brother, David Stuart, duke of Rothesay. Accordingly, in 1406 the king sent James to France for safety, but the prince was captured on the way by the English and held prisoner until 1424. So, although James technically succeeded his father in 1406, the regent Albany ruled until his own death and was succeeded by his son, and the king's ransom was arranged only at the insistence of Archibald DOUGLAS, 4th earl of Douglas, and other nobles. The king had been well educated by his captors, Henry IV and Henry V of England, who had treated him as a royal guest. Shortly before his return to Scotland in 1424, James married Joan Beaufort, daughter of the earl of Somerset. *The Kingis Quair* [the king's book] (rev. ed. by W. W. Skeat, 1911), the story of his captivity and his romance with Joan, is usually considered to have been written by him. It and other poems attributed to him would establish him as one of the leading poets in the Chaucerian tradition. James was crowned at Scone and set about governing energetically. He asserted his authority over the nobility, ruthlessly exterminating members of the Albany family and a number of other barons and reducing the Highland clans to order. He also achieved important financial and judicial reforms and sought to remodel the Scottish Parliament, which he convened annually, along English lines. His plans for including burghers in the Parliament and improving commerce and the army were opposed by his militantly feudal nobles, and his vindictiveness, cupidity, and quick temper understandably diminished his popularity. He was assassinated by a group of nobles, one of whom, the earl of Atholl, probably hoped to claim the throne. However, James was succeeded by his son, James II. See biographies by E. W. M. Balfour-Melville (1936) and John Norton-Smith (1971).

James II, 1430–60, king of Scotland (1437–60), son and successor of James I. During his minority successive earls of Douglas vied for power with factions led by Sir William Crichton and Sir Alexander Livingstone. The power of the Douglases was temporarily broken (1440) by the judicial murder of William DOUGLAS, the 6th earl, but the king later allied himself with William DOUGLAS, the 8th earl, to overthrow Crichton and Livingstone. By 1450, James ruled in his own right. When in 1452 the king discovered Douglas in a conspiracy, James called him to Stirling, charged him with betrayal, and stabbed him. After the resulting rebellion, the king attainted James DOUGLAS, the 9th earl, and seized the Douglas lands. During his reign James improved the courts of justice and regulated the coinage. A Lancastrian partisan in the Wars of the ROSES, he invaded England and was accidentally killed at the siege of Roxburgh. His son James III succeeded him.

James III, 1452–88, king of Scotland (1460–88), son and successor of James II. During his minority he was under the care of his mother, Mary of Guelders, and her adviser, James Kennedy, bishop of St. Andrews. After their deaths, James was seized (1466) by the Boyd family, who ruled Scotland until 1469. In that year James married Margaret, daughter of the Danish king, and began to rule personally. He was a cultivated prince but lacked the force needed in so turbulent a period. James quarreled with and imprisoned (1479) his brother, Alexander STUART, duke of Albany, but Alexander escaped to France. In 1482, Albany, aided by the English, invaded Scotland. James moved to resist, but Archibald DOUGLAS, 5th earl of Angus, nominally one of his supporters, headed a group that hanged certain of James's favorites and briefly held the king prisoner. A period of peace followed, but in 1488 the nobles rebelled again, this time with the support of James's son, the future James IV. They defeated and murdered the king at Sauchieburn.

James IV, 1473–1513, king of Scotland (1488–1513), son and successor of James III. He was an able and popular king, and his reign was one of stability and progress for Scotland. After suppressing an insurrection of discontented nobles early in his reign, he set about restoring order, improving administrative and judicial procedure in the kingdom, and encouraging manufacturing and shipbuilding. A conflict with Henry VII of England over James's support of Perkin WARBECK, pretender to the English throne, ended with the conclusion of a seven-year truce in 1497. In 1503, James married Henry's daughter, MARGARET TUDOR. This marriage was to bring the Stuart line to the English throne in 1603. When Henry VIII ascended (1509) the English throne, relations between Scotland and England deteriorated. In 1512, Louis XII of France, already at war with England, urged and secured a renewal of his alliance with the Scottish king. In 1513, James, against the counsel of his advisers, invaded England, where at the battle of FLODDEN he was killed and the Scottish aristocracy was almost annihilated. See biography by R. L. Mackie (1958, repr. 1964).

James V, 1512–42, king of Scotland (1513–42), son and successor of James IV. His mother, MARGARET TUDOR, held the regency until her marriage in 1514 to Archibald DOUGLAS, 6th earl of Angus, when she lost it to John STUART, duke of Albany. The factions of Albany, Angus, and the queen mother struggled for control until Angus seized (1526) the young king. In 1528, James escaped, and Angus fled to England. James began to ally himself with France against his uncle, HENRY VIII of England. In 1537 he married Madeleine, daughter of Francis I of France, and after her death in the same year he married (1538) MARY OF GUISE. James rejected Henry's attempts to win his support for the English religious policy, and in 1542 war broke out between the two countries. James's nobles gave him little support, and his army was routed at Solway Moss in 1542. He died shortly thereafter and was succeeded by his infant daughter, MARY QUEEN OF SCOTS.

James VI, king of Scotland: see JAMES I, king of England.

James, kinsman of St. Jude. Luke 6.16. The original does not specify the relationship.

James, Henry, 1811–82, American student of religion and social problems, b. Albany, N.Y.; father of the philosopher William James and of the novelist Henry James. He rebelled against the strict Calvinist theology of his family and of Princeton Theological Seminary, to which he was sent, and sought a personal solution. Swedenborgian teachings opened for him a way and provided the framework for his own thought as expressed in *Substance and Shadow; or, Morality and Religion in Their Relation to Life* (1863), *Society the Redeemed Form of Man, and the Earnest of God's Omnipotence in Human Nature* (1879), and other books. He later developed a social philosophy based upon the principles of Charles Fourier. He was a close friend of many literary figures, including Ralph Waldo Emerson and Thomas Carlyle. See Austin Warren, *The Elder Henry James* (1934, repr. 1970); F. O. Matthiessen, *The James Family* (1947, repr. 1961).

James, Henry, 1843–1916, American novelist and critic, b. New York City. A master of the psychological novel, James was an innovator in technique and one of the most distinctive prose stylists in English. He was the son of Henry James, Sr., a Swedenborgian theologian, and the brother of William James, the philosopher. Educated privately by tutors in Europe and the United States, he entered Harvard law school in 1862. Encouraged by William Dean Howells and other members of the Cambridge literary circle in the 1860s, James wrote critical articles and reviews for the *Atlantic Monthly,* a periodical in which several of his novels later appeared in serial form. He made several trips to Europe, and while there he became associated with such notable literary figures as Turgenev and Flaubert. In 1876 he settled permanently in London and became a British subject in 1915. Having never married, he devoted himself to literature and travel, gradually assuming the role of detached spectator and analyst of life. In his early novels, including *Roderick Hudson* (1876), *The American* (1877), *Daisy Miller* (1879), and *The Portrait of a Lady* (1881), as well as some of his later work, James contrasts the sophisticated, though somewhat staid, Europeans with the innocent, eager, though often brash, Americans. In the novels of his middle period, *The Bostonians* (1886), *The Princess Casamassima* (1886), and *The Tragic Muse* (1890), he turned his attention from the international theme to reformers, revolutionaries, and political aspirants. During and after an unsuccessful six-year attempt (1889–95) to win recognition as a playwright, James wrote a series of short, powerful novels, including *The Aspern Papers* (1888), *What Maisie Knew* (1897), *The Spoils of Poynton* (1897), *The Turn of the Screw* (1898), and *The Sacred Fount* (1901). In his last and perhaps his greatest novels, *The Wings of the Dove* (1902), *The Ambassadors* (1903), and *The Golden Bowl* (1904), all marked by a return to the international theme, James reached his highest development in the portrayal of the intricate subtleties of character and in the use of a complex, convoluted style to express delicate nuances of thought. Perhaps more than any previous writer, James refined the technique of narrating a novel from the point of view of a character, thereby laying the foundations of modern STREAM OF CONSCIOUSNESS fiction. The series of critical prefaces he wrote for the reissue of his novels (beginning in 1907) won him a reputation as a superb technician. He is also famous for his finely wrought short stories, including "The Beast in the Jungle" and "The Real Thing," which are masterpieces of the genre. In addition to fiction and literary criticism, James wrote several books on travel and three autobiographical works. See his notebooks, ed. by F. O. Matthiessen and K. B. Murdock (1947); his plays, ed. by Leon Edel (1949); biographies by Leon Edel (5 vol., 1953–71) and F. W. Dupee (1951, repr. 1973); studies by F. O. Matthiessen (1944), J. W. Beach (rev. ed. 1954), Sallie Sears (1968), Peter Buitenhuis (1970), and Oscar Cargill (1961, repr. 1971).

James, Jesse, 1847–82, American outlaw, b. Clay co., Mo. At the age of 15 he joined the Confederate guerrilla band led by William QUANTRILL and participated in the civil warfare in Kansas and Missouri. In 1866, Jesse and his brother Frank became the leaders of a band of outlaws whose trail of robberies and murders led through most of the central states. At first they robbed only banks, but in 1873 they began to rob trains. The beginning of their downfall came in 1876 when, after killing two people and failing to secure any money in an attempted bank robbery at Northfield, Minn., they lost several members of the gang, including the Younger brothers, three of their most trusted followers, who were captured and imprisoned (see YOUNGER, COLE). The James brothers escaped and were quiet until 1879, when they robbed another train. The reward offered by Gov. Thomas T. Crittenden of Missouri for the capture of the James brothers, dead or alive, tempted one of the gang, Robert Ford, who caught Jesse (then living under the name of Thomas Howard) off guard and killed him. Frank James surrendered but was twice acquitted and lived out his life peacefully on his farm near Excelsior Springs, Mo. The melodramatic style of the exploits of the James gang attracted wide public admiration, giving rise to a number of legends, the famous song "The Ballad of Jesse James," and much popular literature. See biography by Robertus Love (1926); Homer Croy, *Jesse James Was My Neighbor* (1949, repr. 1962); C. W. Breihan, *The Complete and Authentic Life of Jesse James* (1953, repr. 1970); J. L. James, *Jesse James and the Lost Cause* (1961); W. A. Settle, *Jesse James was his Name* (1966).

James, Thomas, 1593?–1635?, English navigator and explorer (1631) of James Bay. Financed by Bristol merchants, he sailed in command of the *Henrietta Maria* in the spring of 1631 to find the NORTHWEST PASSAGE to the East. Having explored James Bay (the south extension of Hudson Bay), which was named for him, he wintered on Charlton Island, and in the summer of 1632 continued his attempt to find the passage, a quest that Luke Fox was also undertaking independently (1631). Upon his return to England, James wrote his *Strange and Dangerous Voyage* (1633), which was later to have a strong influence on the poet Samuel Taylor Coleridge. See R. B. Bodilly, *The Voyage of Captain Thomas James* (1928); C. M. MacInnes, *Captain Thomas James and the North West Passage* (1967).

James, Thomas, 1782–1847, American fur trader and pioneer, b. Maryland. He accompanied the 1809 expedition of the Missouri Fur Company up the Mis-

Crowd gathering in front of the house in St. Joseph, Mo., where the outlaw Jesse James was killed by Robert Ford.

souri River. He left the expedition at the Mandan Indian villages (in the vicinity of Bismarck, N. Dak.) and returned to St. Louis, where he became a merchant. With Robert McKnight he led an early expedition (1821–23) over the Santa Fe Trail. Later he settled in S Illinois. He is chiefly remembered for his valuable account of his early expedition, *Three Years among the Indians and Mexicans* (1846, ed. by W. B. Douglas, 1916).

James, William, 1842–1910, American philosopher, b. New York City, M.D. Harvard, 1869; son of the Swedenborgian theologian Henry James and brother of the novelist Henry James. In 1872 he joined the Harvard faculty as lecturer on anatomy and physiology, continuing to teach until 1907, after 1880 in the department of psychology and philosophy. In 1890 he published his brilliant and epochmaking *Principles of Psychology,* in which the seeds of his philosophy are already discernible. James's fascinating style and his broad culture and cosmopolitan outlook made him the most influential American thinker of his day. His philosophy has three principal aspects—his voluntarism, his pragmatism, and his "radical empiricism." He construes consciousness as essentially active, selective, interested, teleological. We "carve out" our world from "the jointless continuity of space." Will and interest are thus primary; knowledge is instrumental. The true is "only the expedient in our way of thinking." Ideas do not reproduce objects, but prepare for, or lead the way to, them. The function of an idea is to indicate "what conceivable effects of a practical kind the object may involve—what sensations we are to expect from it and what reactions we must prepare." This theory of knowledge James called PRAGMATISM, a term already used by Charles S. PEIRCE. James's "radical empiricism" is a philosophy of "pure experience," which rejects all transcendent principles and finds experience organized by means of "conjunctive relations" that are as much a matter of direct experience as things themselves. Moreover, James regards consciousness as only one type of conjunctive relation within experience, not as an entity above, or distinct from, its experience. James's other philosophical writings include *The Will to Believe* (1897), *The Varieties of Religious Experience* (1902), *Pragmatism* (1907), *A Pluralistic Universe* (1909), *The Meaning of Truth* (1909), *Some Problems in Philosophy* (1911), and *Essays in Radical Empiricism* (1912). See his letters (ed. by his son Henry James, 1920); biographies by E. C. Moore (1965) and G. W. Allen (1967); studies by B. P. Brennan (1968), John Wild (1969), and P. K. Dooley (1974); R. B. Perry, *The Thought and Character of William James* (2 vol. 1935, abr. ed. 1948) and *In the Spirit of William James* (1938, repr. 1958).

James. 1 Unnavigable river, 710 mi (1,143 km) long, rising in central N.Dak. and flowing across S.Dak. to the Missouri River at Yankton, S.Dak. Jamestown Dam on the river is an irrigation and flood control unit of the MISSOURI RIVER BASIN PROJECT of the U.S. Bureau of Reclamation. **2** River, 340 mi (547 km) long, formed in W central Va. by the union of the Jackson and Cowpasture rivers and winding E across Va. to enter Chesapeake Bay through Hampton Roads. One of Virginia's chief rivers, it is navigable for large ships to Richmond, c.100 mi (160 km) upstream; Norfolk, Newport News, and Portsmouth are large ports at its mouth. The James's upper course flows through scenic gorges in the Blue Ridge Mts. and the Piedmont; waterfalls and rapids provide power. English colonists founded Jamestown on the lower river in 1607. During the Civil War, Union forces used the river in vain attempts to capture Richmond (see PENINSULAR CAMPAIGN; SEVEN DAYS BATTLES).

James, epistle of the New Testament, the 20th book in the usual order, traditionally classified among the Catholic, or General, Epistles. The James of its ascription (1.1) is traditionally St. James the Less. The content is not very orderly, for the work, practical in stress, gives many diverse admonitions, some recurrent. It opens with a section on temptation (1.2–18; cf. 5.7–11), then goes on to two general ethical principles, "be doers of the word, not hearers only" (1.19–27) and "faith without works is dead" (2.14–26; cf. Heb. 11.17–40). The rest consists of specific points—human respect (2.1–13), bridling the tongue (1.26; 3.1–18; 5.12), living in harmony (4.1–17), the wickedness of the rich (2.2–7; 5.1–6), the efficacy of prayer (5.13–18), saving sinners (5.19–20). The scriptural authority cited for the anointing of the sick is here (5.14–15). Scholars differ widely on the origin and date of this epistle. It was one of the later books to be accepted as canonical. Martin Luther rejected it because it seems to deny his interpretation of justification by faith.

James, Protevangelium of: see PSEUDEPIGRAPHA.

James Bay, shallow southern arm of Hudson Bay, c.300 mi (480 km) long and 140 mi (230 km) wide, E central Canada, in the Northwest Territories between Ont. and Que. Numerous rivers flow into the bay. Of its many islands, the largest is Akimiski (898 sq mi/2,326 sq km). The bay was discovered (1610) by Henry Hudson but was named for Capt. Thomas James, an Englishman who explored much of it in 1631. An early fur-trading post established by Groseilliers and Radisson became (1670) Rupert House, the first post established there by the Hudson's Bay Company. Other important posts on James Bay are Fort Albany, Fort George, and Eastmain. The shores of the bay and some of its islands are wildlife reserves.

James Francis Edward Stuart: see STUART, JAMES FRANCIS EDWARD.

James Island: see CHARLESTON, S.C.

Jameson, Anna Brownell (Murphy), 1794–1860, English essayist, b. Dublin. The diary of her travels on the Continent as governess to a wealthy family was later published as *The Diary of an Ennuyée* (1826). Jameson's works—especially *Shakespeare's Heroines* (1932)—were popular in her day, but only *Sacred and Legendary Art* (1848–60; ed. by E. M. Hurll, 1896) had lasting currency.

Jameson, John Franklin, 1859–1937, American historian, b. Somerville, Mass. After teaching at Johns Hopkins, Brown, and the Univ. of Chicago he was director (1905–28) of the department of historical research of the Carnegie Institution, Washington, D.C., and from 1928 to his death he was chief of the division of manuscripts in the Library of Congress. As chairman of the committee of management of the *Dictionary of American Biography* he was largely responsible for the inauguration and completion of that monumental work. In these and other undertakings, Jameson exercised much influence in American historical scholarship. He wrote *Willem Usselinx, Founder of the Dutch and Swedish West India Companies* (1887), *The History of Historical Writing in America* (1891), *Dictionary of United States History* (1894, rev. ed. 1931), and *The Ameri-*

can Revolution Considered as a Social Movement (1926) and edited *Correspondence of John C. Calhoun* (1900, repr. 1969) and *Original Narratives of Early American History* (19 vol., 1906–17).

Jameson, Sir Leander Starr, 1853–1917, British colonial administrator and statesman in South Africa. He went to Kimberley (1878) as a physician, became associated with Cecil Rhodes in his colonizing ventures, and was appointed (1891) administrator of Mashonaland. On December 29, 1895, he led a band of volunteers on the famous Jameson Raid into the Boer colony of Transvaal in an effort to support a brewing rebellion by foreign settlers (mainly British), and to further Rhodes's ambition for a united South Africa. The raid was premature. Jameson was captured within a few days and turned over by President Kruger to the British to be punished for his unauthorized venture. He was returned to London for trial and sentenced to imprisonment for 15 months. On his release he returned to South Africa, served in the Cape Colony Parliament (1900–1902), and was premier (1904–8). He played an important role in the South African National Convention (1908–9), which achieved the union of the South African colonies. See Jean Van der Poel, *The Jameson Raid* (1952); E. H. Pakenham, *Jameson's Raid* (1960).

Jameson, Storm (Margaret Storm Jameson), 1891–, English novelist and critic, b. Whitby, Yorkshire, grad. Leeds Univ., 1912. Descended from a shipbuilding family, she drew on her knowledge of that business for her first three novels, a family chronicle trilogy reprinted as *The Triumph of Time* (1932). Most of her novels treat ethical and moral problems. Among them are *Cousin Honoré* (1940), *The White Crow* (1968), and *There Will Be a Short Interval* (1973). See her autobiography (1969).

Jameson Raid: see JAMESON, SIR LEANDER STARR.

Jamestown. 1 City (1970 pop. 39,795), Chautauqua co., W N.Y., on Chautauqua Lake; founded c.1806, inc. as a city 1886. It is the business and financial center of a dairy, livestock, and vineyard area, and its chief industries are food processing and furniture making. Two insurance companies have their headquarters there. The city has a junior college. Nearby are Allegany State Park and the Chautauqua Institution, a cultural and recreational center on the lake. **2** City (1970 pop. 15,385), seat of Stutsman co., SE N.Dak., on the James River, in a farm area; settled 1872 when Fort Seward was established to protect railroad workers, inc. 1896. It is the trade center for an agricultural area. Jamestown College, a state home for crippled children, and a state mental hospital are in the city. Fort Seward State Monument and a restored frontier village are on the outskirts. **3** Former village, SE Va., first permanent English settlement in America; est. May 14, 1607, by the LONDON COMPANY on a marshy peninsula (now an island) in the James River and named for the reigning English monarch, James I. Disease, starvation, and Indian attacks wiped out most of the colony, but the London Company continually sent more men and supplies, and John Smith briefly provided efficient leadership (he returned to England in 1609 for treatment of an injury). After the severe winter of 1609–10 (the "starving time"), the survivors prepared to return to England but were stopped by the timely arrival of Lord De la Warr with supplies. John Rolfe cultivated the first tobacco there in 1612, introducing a successful source of livelihood, and in 1614 he assured peace with the Indians by marrying Pocahontas, daughter of the Indian chief Powhatan. In 1619 the first representative government in the New World met at Jamestown, and Jamestown remained the capital of Virginia throughout the 17th cent. The village was almost entirely destroyed during BACON'S REBELLION; it was partially rebuilt but fell into decay with the removal of the capital to Williamsburg (1698–1700). Of the 17th-cent. settlement, only the old church tower (built c.1639) and a few gravestones were visible when National Park Service excavations began in 1934. Except for the land owned by the Association for the Preservation of Virginia Antiquities, Jamestown Island is today the property of the U.S. government. It is included in Colonial National Historical Park (see NATIONAL PARKS AND MONUMENTS, table). A tercentenary celebration was held in 1907, and in 1957 the Jamestown Festival Park was built to commemorate the 350th anniversary. The park contains exhibit pavilions and replicas of the first fort, the three ships that brought the first settlers, and an Indian lodge. See J. L. Kibler, *Cradle of the Nation* (1931); report by the Celebration Commission, *The 350th Anniversary of Jamestown, 1607–1957* (1958).

Jamestown weed: see JIMSON WEED.

Jami (jä'mē), 1414–92, Persian poet, b. Jam, near Herat. His full name was Nur ad-Din Abd ar-Rahman Jami. His poetic influence was widespread. Nearly 100 works are attributed to him, of which some 40 are considered authentic. He was also known as a saint for his devotion to dervish teaching and to Sufi philosophy. Among his works is the collection of poems *Haft Aurang* [the seven thrones], including the allegory "Salaman and Absal" (tr. by Edward FitzGerald in the 19th cent.), and a version of the tale of Joseph and Potiphar's wife. His *Baharistan* [abode of spring] is a collection of short stories.

Jamin (jā'mĭn). **1** Simeonite, Gen. 46.10; 1 Chron. 4.24. **2** Hezronite. 1 Chron. 2.27. **3** Reader of the Law. Neh. 8.7.

Jamitzer, Wenzel: see JAMNITZER, WENZEL.

Jamlech (jăm'lĕk), chief of the tribe of Simeon. 1 Chron. 4.34.

Jammes, Francis (fräNsēs' zhäm), 1868–1938, French poet. He lived most of his life in the Pyrenees. Jammes is usually grouped with the symbolists, but he is distinguished from them by the simplicity and artlessness of his pastoral poetry. *De l'angélus de l'aube à l'angélus du soir* (1898) brought him wide acclaim. Later works, including *Clairières dans le ciel* (1906) and *Géorgiques Chrétiennes* (1911–12), are suffused with Catholic spirit. He also wrote charming stories about rustic people. See Amy Lowell, *Six French Poets* (1915).

Jammu (jŭ'mo͞o), town (1971 pop. 155,249), Jammu and Kashmir state, N India, on the Tawi River and in the Himalayan foothills. The former winter capital of Jammu and Kashmir state, it is strategically important as the southern terminus of a highway linking the Vale of Kashmir with the North Indian plain. Once the seat of a Rajput dynasty, Jammu became the nucleus of the dominions of Gulab Singh, founder of the last ruling house of Kashmir. On one bank of the river is Jammu's old Fort of Bahu; on the other bank is the maharaja's palace, which dominates the city.

Jammu and Kashmir: see KASHMIR.

Jamnagar (jäm'nəgər), city (1971 pop. 214,853), Gujarat state, W central India. A port on the Gulf of Kutch, which is an arm of the Arabian Sea, Jamnagar has naval and aeronautical schools. A radium institute is also in the city. Jamnagar is a district administrative center and is known for its silk, embroidery, and marble. There are cotton-textile mills.

Jamnia (jăm'nēə), biblical *Jabneel* (jăb'nēĕl, jăb'-nēl) and *Jabneh* (jăb'nə,-nē) [Heb.,=God causes to build], ancient city, central Israel. The modern name is Yibna. It was a central city of Philistia, and in the Bible there is a reference to its walls being destroyed by Uzziah. It was pillaged by Judas Maccabaeus and later rebuilt. In the last years before the sack of Jerusalem (A.D. 70) Jamnia became a great Jewish cultural center, and at the prayer of JOHANAN BEN ZAKKAI, Vespasian spared Jamnia and permitted Johanan to settle there as leader of the Jewish community after the fall of Jerusalem. The Great Sanhedrin was moved to Jamnia, and under Johanan's guidance the city became the capital of the Jews. With great care the ceremonial and practices of the cult were preserved in the academy at Jamnia, and Jewish scholarship continued as before. Except for a short period Jamnia remained the seat of the rulers of Judaism until the rising of BAR KOKBA. In the Middle Ages the Crusaders fortified the city. See Joshua 15.11; 2 Chron. 26.6.

Jamnitzer, Jamitzer, or **Gemniczer, Wenzel** (vĕn'tsəl yäm'nĭtsər, yä'mĭtsər, gĕm'nĭtsər), 1508–85, leading member of a German family of goldsmiths and engravers. Born in Vienna, he settled in Nuremberg where, as a leading craftsman of his day, he executed work for emperors and officials of the court and the church. Examples of his refined workmanship, showing the German adaptation of Italian mannerist forms, are to be seen in the Louvre and in the Victoria and Albert Museum. His gilt bronze nude *Spring* is in Vienna.

Jamshedpur (jŭm"shĕdpo͝or'), city (1971 pop. 355,783), Bihar state, E central India, at the confluence of the Subarnarekha and Kharkai rivers. A great steel-producing center, it is sometimes called the "Pittsburgh of India." It was built in the early 20th cent. and was named for Jamshedji Tata, founder of the Tata Iron and Steel Works. Nearby are extensive coal and iron deposits. The National Metallurgical Laboratory is in the city.

Jamuna, river, Bangladesh: see BRAHMAPUTRA.

Janáček, Leoš (lĕ'ôsh yä'nächĕk), 1854–1928, Czech composer, theorist, and collector of Slavic folk music. He studied in Prague and Leipzig and founded a music conservatory at Brno in 1881. His works include the operas *Jenufa* (1904), his best-known work; *Katia Kabanova* (1921), after Ostrovski's *Storm; The Makropulos Affair* (1926); and *From the House of the Dead* (1930), after a novel by Dostoyevsky. Also of note are Jaňaček's song cycle, *The Diary of One Who Vanished* (1916–19), and his *Glagolitic Festival Mass* (1926), with a text in Old Slavonic. See biographies by Hans Hollander (1963) and Jarosla Vogel (1963).

Janesville, city (1970 pop. 46,426), seat of Rock co., S central Wis., on the Rock River; inc. 1853. It is an industrial and commercial center in a grain, dairy farm, and tobacco area. Manufactures include fountain pens, automobile bodies, and electronic and electrical equipment. A state school for the blind is in Janesville. Points of interest include the 26-room Tallman House, where Lincoln spent a weekend in 1859; the Stone House (1842), of Greek Revival style; and the Milton House (1844), which is connected with a log cabin by a slave tunnel.

Janet: see CLOUET, FRANÇOIS, and CLOUET, JEAN.

Janet, Pierre (pyĕr zhänā'), 1859–1947, French physician and psychologist. As director (1890–98) of the laboratory of pathological psychology at Salpêtrière and as professor of experimental and comparative psychology at the Collège de France from 1902, he made important contributions to the knowledge of mental pathology and the origins of hysteria through the use of hypnosis. In 1904 he founded the *Journal de psychologie normal et pathologique,* to which he contributed numerous articles. Among his important works were *L'Automatisme psychologique* (1889), in which he founded automatic psychology, and *Les Obsessions et la psychasthénie* (1903), which contains the first description of psychasthenia. *Major Symptoms of Hysteria* (1907) contains lectures delivered at Harvard. He wrote also *Principles of Psychotherapy* (1924), *Psychological Healing* (1925), and *Cours sur l'amour et la haine* (1933).

Janiculum: see *Rome before Augustus* under ROME.

Janina, Greece: see IOÁNNINA.

Janissaries (jăn'ĭsâr"ēz) [from Turkish,=recruits], elite corps in the service of the Ottoman Empire (Turkey). It was composed of war captives and Christian youths pressed into service; all the recruits were converted to Islam and trained under the strictest discipline. It was originally organized by Sultan Murad I. The Janissaries gained great power in the Ottoman Empire and made and unmade sultans. By 1600, Muslims had begun to enter the corps, largely through bribery, and in the 17th cent. membership in the corps became largely hereditary, while the drafting of Christians gradually ceased. In 1826, Sultan MAHMUD II rid himself of the unruly (and by now inefficient) Janissaries by having them massacred in their barracks by his loyal SPAHIS.

Jan Mayen (yän mī'ən), island, c.145 sq mi (380 sq km), in the Arctic Ocean, c.300 mi (480 km) E of Scoresby Sound, E Greenland. It was annexed by Norway in 1929. The island is barren tundra land rising abruptly to Håkon VII Toppen (c.7,450 ft/2,270 m) on Mt. Beerenberg, an extinct volcano. Fog and stormy weather characterize the island. Except for a meteorological and wireless station, the island is uninhabited, but it is visited by sealers. It was discovered (1607) by Henry Hudson and named for Jan Jacobsz May, a Dutch whaler who landed there in 1614.

Janna (jăn'ə), name in the Gospel genealogy. Luke 3.24.

Jannequin, Clément (klāmäN' zhänəkăN'), French composer, fl. 16th cent. Jannequin is famous for his descriptive four-part chansons about birds, battles, hunts, and other subjects. He is thought to have been a disciple of Josquin des Prés. See Alfred Einstein, *The Italian Madrigal* (1949).

Jannes and Jambres (jăn'ēz, jăm'brēz), opponents of Moses. 2 Tim. 3.8. Tradition gave these names to Pharaoh's magicians. Ex. 7.11. One of the PSEUDEPIGRAPHA bears their name.

Janoah (jənō'ə), unidentified town, N Palestine, captured by Tiglath-pileser III. 2 Kings 15.29.

Janohah (jənō'hə), town, Palestine, SE of Shechem. Joshua 16.6,7.

Jansen, Cornelis (kôrnā'lĭs yän'sən), 1585–1638, Dutch Roman Catholic theologian. He studied at the Univ. of Louvain and became imbued with the idea of reforming Christian life along the lines of a return to St. Augustine. He established a close friendship with DUVERGIER DE HAURANNE, a fellow student, with whom he shared and developed many of his theological ideas. In 1630, Jansen became professor at Louvain, and in 1636 bishop of Ypres. Out of his life work, the posthumous *Augustinus* (1642, in Latin), arose the great movement called **Jansenism.** This was strictly a Roman Catholic movement, and it had no repercussions in the Protestant world. Its fundamental purpose was a return of people to greater personal holiness, hence the characteristically mystical turn of Jansenist writings. St. Augustine's teaching on grace was especially appealing to Jansen, who stressed the doctrine that the soul must be converted to God by the action of divine grace, without which conversion could not begin. Predestination was accepted in an extreme form and was so essential to Jansenism that its adherents were even referred to as Calvinists by their opponents. But Jansenism had no appeal to Protestants, for it held the necessity of the Roman Catholic Church for salvation and opposed justification by faith alone. Jansenism, however, came into conflict with the church for its predestinarianism, for its discouragement of frequent communion for the faithful, and for its attack on the Jesuits and the new casuistry, which the Jansenists thought was demoralizing the confessional. Jansenism took root in France, especially among the clergy. There it early became involved with GALLICANISM, and high officials of church and state often sided with Jansenists to thwart the Holy See. The second great Jansenist work was *De la fréquente communion* (1643) of Antoine ARNAULD, which stirred the opposition of Jesuits and Dominicans. In 1653, Pope Innocent X condemned five of Jansen's doctrines, and in 1656 Arnauld was expelled from the Sorbonne. Meanwhile, Blaise PASCAL, the greatest Jansenist, aroused a storm by his anti-Jesuit *Provincial Letters,* and there was persecution of the Jansenists for a while. Pasquier QUESNEL published late in the 17th cent. a vernacular New Testament with Jansenist notes, which was condemned by Pope Clement XI. The aged Louis XIV undertook to suppress Jansenism, and the bulls *Vineam Domini* (1705) and *Unigenitus* (1713) virtually put the Jansenists out of the church. (Gallicanism, however, prevented the legal registration of *Unigenitus* in France until 1730.) The convent of PORT-ROYAL, the greatest center of Jansenism, was closed, and most Jansenists fled France. Jansenism survived as a tendency within the church, especially in France, taking the form usually of extreme scruples with regard to communion. In the Netherlands an organization not in submission to the pope was set up. There are Jansenist bishops of Utrecht, Haarlem, and Deventer. The independent Jansenists recognize the Council of Trent and are, except for their special differences, like Roman Catholics. The first Old Catholic bishop was consecrated by Jansenists (see OLD CATHOLICS). See Nigel Abercrombie, *The Origins of Jansenism* (1936); Marc Escholier, *Port-Royal: The Drama of the Jansenists* (tr. 1968).

Janson, Nicolas: see JENSON, NICOLAS.

Janssen, Cornelis van Ceulen: see JANSSENS, CORNELIS VAN CEULEN.

Janssen, Pierre Jules César (pyĕr zhül săzär' zhäN-sĕn'), 1824–1907, French astronomer. In 1857–58, in Peru, he worked on the determination of the magnetic equator; in Italy (1861–62, 1864) he observed the telluric lines in the solar spectrum; in the Azores (1867) he examined magnetic and topographical conditions; and in Japan (1874) and in Algeria (1882) he observed the transit of Venus. Janssen accompanied various solar eclipse expeditions, notably that to Guntur, India, in 1868, where he devised a new method of studying the solar prominences spectroscopically and discovered, almost simultaneously with J. N. Lockyer, the chemical constitution of the prominences. He was active in the establishment of the astrophysical observatory of Meudon (in Paris) and in 1876 became its director. There he gathered an important series of solar photographs included in his *Atlas de photographies solaires* (1904). He later became director of the observatory on Mont Blanc.

Janssens, Janssen, or **Jonson, Cornelis van Ceulen** (kôrnā'lĭs vän kö'lən yän'səns, -sən, -sôn), 1593–c.1662, Dutch portrait painter who worked in England. He was the fashionable portrait painter of the English court from 1618 until the advent of Van Dyck. In 1643 Janssens moved to Holland. His portraits, one of which is in the Metropolitan Museum, are in many famous English collections.

January: see MONTH.

Janum (jăn'ĭm), unidentified town, apparently near Hebron. Joshua 15.53.

Janus, in astronomy, one of the 10 known moons, or natural satellites, of SATURN.

Janus (jā'nəs), in Roman religion, god of beginnings. He was one of the principal Roman gods, the custodian of the universe. The first hour of the day, the first day of the month, the first month of the year (which bears his name) were sacred to him. His chief function was as guardian deity of gates and doors. The gates of his temple in the Roman Forum were closed in time of peace and opened in time of war. Janus was usually represented with two bearded heads placed back to back so that he might look in two directions at the same time. His principal festival was celebrated on the first day of the year.

Japan, Jap. *Nihon* or *Nippon,* country (1970 pop., including Okinawa, 104,665,171), 142,811 sq mi (369,881 sq km), occupying an archipelago off the coast of E Asia. The capital is TOKYO, the world's most populous city. Japan proper has four main islands which are, from north to south, HOKKAIDO, HONSHU (the largest island, where the capital and most major cities are located), SHIKOKU, and KYUSHU. There are also many smaller islands stretched in an arc between the Sea of Japan and the East China Sea and the Pacific proper. Honshu, Shikoku, and Kyushu enclose the Inland Sea. The general features of the four main islands are shapely mountains, sometimes snowcapped, the highest and most famous being the sacred FUJIYAMA; rushing short rivers; forested slopes; irregular and lovely lakes; and small, rich plains. Mountains, many of them volcanoes, cover two thirds of Japan's surface, hampering transportation and limiting agriculture. Less than 20% of the land is arable, and on the arable sections the population density is among the highest in the world. The climate ranges from chilly humid continental to humid subtropical. Rainfall is abundant, and typhoons and earthquakes are frequent. (For a more detailed description of geography, see separate articles on the individual islands.) Mineral resources are meager, except for coal, which is an important source of industrial energy. The rapid streams supply plentiful hydroelectric power. Imported oil, however, is the major source of energy. Some nuclear energy is also produced. The rivers are

Tokyo, the capital of Japan.

Buddhist monks in the garden of a temple near Tokyo.

generally unsuited for navigation (only two, the Ishikari and the Shinano, are over 200 mi/322 km long), and railroads and ships along the coast are the chief means of transportation. High-speed train service, the fastest in the world, was inaugurated in 1964 between Tokyo and Osaka. Japan's farming population has been declining steadily and was less than 30% of the total population in the early 1970s. Arable land in Japan is intensively cultivated; farmers use irrigation, terracing, and multiple cropping to coax rich crops from the overworked soil. Rice and other cereals are the main crops; some vegetables and industrial crops, such as mulberry trees (for feeding silkworms), are also grown, and livestock is raised. Fishing is highly developed, and the annual catch is one of the biggest in the world; Japan's fishing fleet ranges all over the world. In the late 19th cent. Japan was rapidly and thoroughly industrialized. Textiles were a leading item, vast quantities of light manufactures were also produced, and, in the 1920s and 1930s, heavy industries were greatly expanded, principally to support the military ambitions of the imperialists. Japan's economy collapsed after the defeat in World War II, and its merchant marine, one of the world's largest in the 1930s, was almost totally destroyed. In the late 1950s, however, the nation reemerged as a major industrial power. It is now the most industrialized country in Asia and the third greatest economic power in the world. Japanese industry is concentrated mainly in S Honshu and N Kyushu, with centers at Tokyo, YOKOHAMA, OSAKA, KOBE, and NAGOYA. In the 1950s and 1960s textiles became less important in Japanese industry while the production of heavy machinery expanded. Japan is the world's leading producer of ships and also ranks high in the production of cars and trucks, steel, and textiles. The manufacture of electronic equipment is also important. Japanese industry depends heavily on imported raw materials, which make up a large share of the country's imports. Japan receives all it needs of bauxite, phosphate, steel scrap, cotton, wool, and crude rubber, 99% of its crude oil, and 98% of its iron ore from imports. Exports are mainly manufactured goods, notably iron and steel, ships, and motor vehicles.

Japanese Society. The Japanese people are primarily the descendants of various peoples who migrated from Asia in prehistoric times; the dominant strain is N Asian or Mongoloid, with some Malay and Indonesian admixture. One of the earliest groups, the AINU, who still persist to some extent in Hokkaido, are physically somewhat similar to Caucasians. Non-Japanese, mostly Koreans, make up less than 1% of the population. Japan's principal religions are SHINTO and BUDDHISM. While the development of Shinto was radically altered by the influence of Buddhism, which was brought from China in the 6th cent., special varieties of Japanese Buddhism have developed in sects such as Jodo, Shingon, Nicheren, and Zen. Numerous cults formed after World War II and called the "new religions" have attracted many members. One of these, the Sokagakkai, a Buddhist sect, built up a large following in the 1950s and 1960s and became a strong social and political force. Less than 1% of the population are Christians. CONFUCIANISM has deeply affected Japanese thought and was part of the generally significant influence that Chinese culture wielded on the formation of Japanese civilization (see JAPANESE ARCHITECTURE; JAPANESE ART; JAPANESE LITERATURE). The family has long been the basic social unit in Japan. Family elders command much respect, and even in the 20th cent.

Rice paddies in Japan (right).

"Bullet train" connecting the Japanese cities of Tokyo and Osaka (below).

many parents continued to select marriage partners for their children. The status of women improved after the end of World War II when they received the right to vote, but social customs still tend to restrict their freedom. The Japanese educational system, established during the Allied occupation after World War II, is modeled on the U.S. system. Nine years of schooling is compulsory. The two leading national universities are at Tokyo and Kyoto. The standard of living improved dramatically between the 1950s and the early 1970s, and the Japanese have the highest per capita income of all Asians. Programs for social welfare and health insurance exist but are financially limited. Trade unions, organized by enterprise rather than by occupation, represent about one third of all employed workers. The two largest unions are the General Council of Trade Unions and the General Council of Japan Labor Organization. Japanese traditional sports include judo; kendo, a kind of fencing; and suma, a stylized form of wrestling. Baseball, though not native to Japan, is also very popular.

Early History and the Shoguns. Japan's early history is lost in legend. The divine design of the empire—supposedly founded in 660 B.C. by the emperor Jimmu, a lineal descendant of the sun goddess and alleged ancestor of the present emperor—was held as official dogma until 1945. Actually, reliable records date back only to about A.D. 400. In the first centuries of the Christian era the country was inhabited by numerous clans or tribal kingdoms ruled by priest-chiefs. Contacts with Korea were close, and bronze and iron implements were probably introduced by invaders from Korea around the 1st cent. By the 5th cent. the Yamato clan, whose original

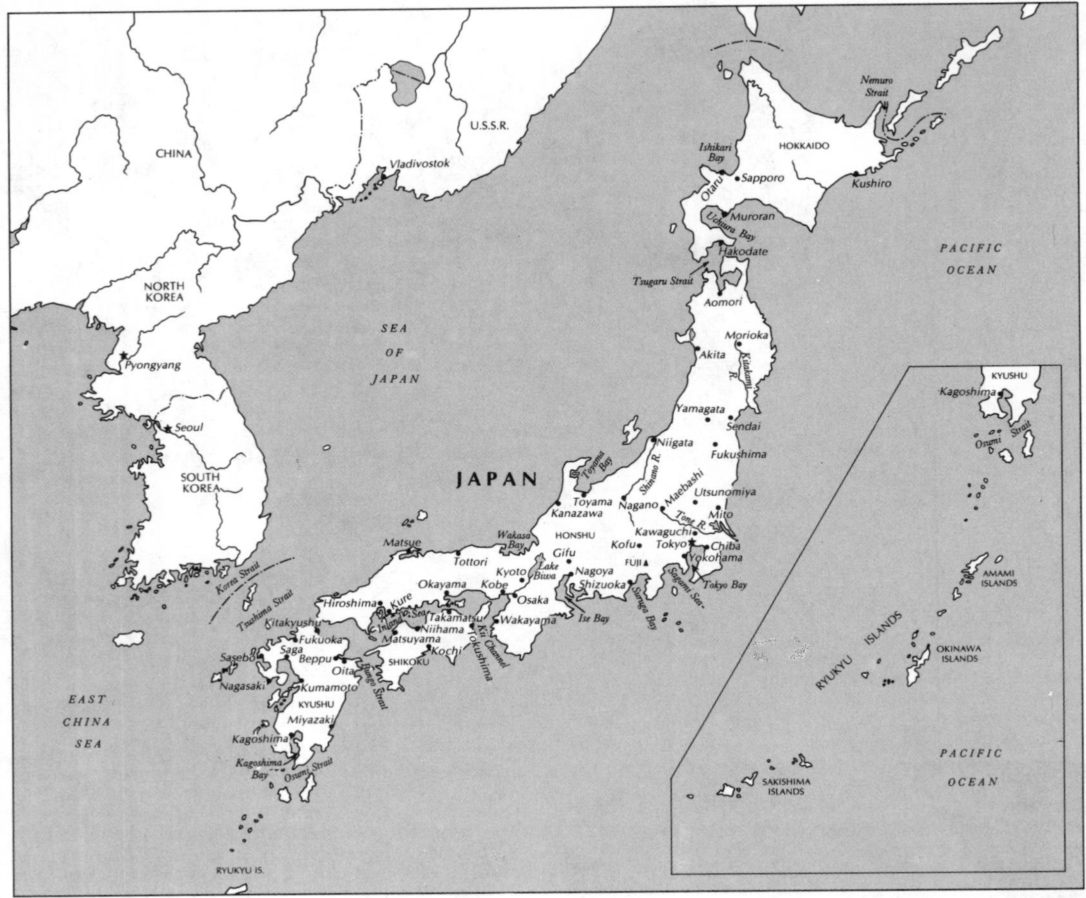

home was apparently in Kyushu, had settled in the vicinity of modern Kyoto and had established a loose control over the other clans of central and W Japan, laying the foundation of the Japanese state. From the 6th to the 8th cent. the rapidly developing society gained much in the arts of civilization under the strong cultural influence of China, then flourishing in the splendor of the T'ang dynasty. Buddhism was introduced, and the Japanese upper classes assiduously studied Chinese language, literature, philosophy, art, science, and government, creating their own forms adapted from Chinese models. A partially successful attempt was made to set up a centralized, bureaucratic government like that of imperial China. The Yamato priest-chief assumed the dignity of an emperor, and an imposing capital city, modeled on the T'ang capital, was erected at Nara, to be succeeded by an equally imposing capital at Kyoto. By the 9th cent., however, the powerful Fujiwara family had established a firm control over the imperial court. The Fujiwara influence and the power of the Buddhist priesthood undermined the authority of the imperial government. Provincial gentry—particularly the great clans who opposed the Fujiwara—evaded imperial taxes and grew strong. A feudal system developed. Civil warfare was almost continuous in the 12th cent. The Minamoto family defeated their rivals, the Taira, and became masters of Japan. Their great leader, YORITOMO, took the title of SHOGUN, established his capital at Kamakura, and set up a military dictatorship. For the next 700 years Japan was ruled by warriors. The old civil administration was not abolished, but gradually decayed, and the imperial court at Kyoto fell into obscurity. The Minamoto soon gave way to the Hojo, who managed the Kamakura administration as regents for puppet shoguns, much as the Fujiwara had controlled the imperial court. In 1274 and again in 1281 the Mongols under Kublai Khan tried unsuccessfully to invade the country (see KAMIKAZE). In 1331 the emperor Daigo II attempted to restore imperial rule. He failed, but the revolt brought about the downfall of the Kamakura regime. The Ashikaga family took over the shogunate in 1338 and settled at Kyoto, but were unable to consolidate their power. The next 250 years were marked by civil wars, during which the feudal barons (the daimyo) and the Buddhist monasteries built up local domains and private armies. Nevertheless, in the midst of incessant wars there was a brisk development of manufacturing and trade, typified by the rise of Sakai (later Osaka) as a free city not subject to feudal control. This period saw the birth of a middle class. Extensive maritime commerce was carried on with

Emperor Meiji, under whose reign was consolidated the Meiji restoration, which transformed Japan into a modern industrial state and an important military power.

Japanese aerial attack on Pearl Harbor on Dec. 7, 1941, which brought the United States into World War II.

the continent and with SE Asia; Japanese traders and pirates dominated Far Eastern waters until the arrival of the Europeans in the 16th cent.

Military Might and the Foreigners. The first European contact with Japan was made by Portuguese sailors in 1542. A small trade with the West developed. Christianity was introduced by St. FRANCIS XAVIER, who reached Japan in 1549. In the late 16th cent. three warriors, NOBUNAGA, HIDEYOSHI, and IEYASU, established military control over the whole country and succeeded one another in the dictatorship. Hideyoshi unsuccessfully invaded Korea in 1592 and 1596 in an effort to conquer China. After Hideyoshi's death, Ieyasu took the title of shogun, and his family ruled Japan for over 250 years. They set up at Yedo (later Tokyo) a centralized, efficient, but repressive system of feudal government (see TOKUGAWA). Stability and internal peace were secured, but social progress was stifled. Christianity was suppressed, and all intercourse with foreign countries was prohibited except for a Dutch trading post at Nagasaki. Tokugawa society was rigidly divided into the daimyo, SAMURAI, peasants, artisans, and merchants, in that order. The system was imbued with Confucian ideas of loyalty to superiors, and military virtues were cultivated by the ruling aristocracy (see BUSHIDO). Oppression of the peasants led to many sporadic uprisings. Yet despite feudal restrictions, production and trade expanded, the use of money and credit increased, flourishing cities grew up, and the rising merchant class acquired great wealth and economic power. Japan was in fact moving toward a capitalist system. By the middle of the 19th cent. the country was ripe for change. Most daimyo were in debt to the merchants, and discontent was rife among impoverished but ambitious samurai. The great clans of W Japan, notably Choshu and Satsuma, had long been impatient of Tokugawa control. In 1854 an American naval officer, Matthew C. PERRY, forced the opening of trade with the West. Japan was compelled to admit foreign merchants and to sign unequal treaties. Attacks on foreigners were answered by the bombardment of Kagoshima and Shimonoseki. Threatened from within and without, the shogunate collapsed. In 1867 a conspiracy engineered by the western clans and imperial court nobles forced the shogun's resignation. After brief fighting, in 1868 the boy emperor MEIJI was "restored" to power, and the imperial capital was transferred from Kyoto to Tokyo. This was the MEIJI RESTORATION.

Industries and Military Expansion. Although the Meiji restoration was originally inspired by anti-foreign sentiment, Japan's new rulers quickly realized the impossibility of expelling the foreigners. Instead they strove to strengthen Japan by adopting the techniques of Western civilization. Under the leadership of an exceptionally able group of statesmen (who were chiefly samurai of the western clans) Japan was rapidly transformed into a modern industrial state and a great military power. Feudalism was abolished in 1871. The defeat of the Satsuma rebellion in 1877 marked the end of opposition to the new regime. Emissaries were sent abroad to study Western military science, industrial technology, and political institutions. The administration was reorganized on Western lines. An efficient modern army and navy were created, and military conscription was introduced. Industrial development was actively fostered by the state, working in close cooperation with the great merchant houses. A new currency and banking system were established. New law codes were enacted. Primary education was made compulsory. In 1889 the emperor granted a constitution, modeled in part on that of Prussia. Supreme authority was vested in the emperor, who in practice was largely a figurehead controlled by the clan oligarchy. Subordinate organs of government included a privy council, a cabinet, and a diet consisting of a partially elected house of peers and a fully elected house of representatives. Universal manhood suffrage was not granted until 1925. After the Meiji restoration nationalistic feeling ran high. The old myths of imperial and racial divinity, rediscovered by scholars in the Tokugawa period, were revived, and the sentiment of loyalty to the emperor was actively propagated by the new government. Feudal glorification of the warrior and belief in the unique virtues of Japan's "Imperial Way" combined with the expansive drives of modern industrialism to produce a vigorous imperialism. At first concerned with defending Japanese independence against the Western powers, Japan soon joined them in the competition for an empire in the Orient. By 1899, Japan cast off the shackles of EXTRATERRITORIALITY, but not until 1911 was full tariff autonomy gained. The First SINO-JAPANESE WAR (1894–95) marked the real emergence of imperial Japan, with acquisition of Formosa and the Pescadores and also of the Liao-tung peninsula in Manchuria, which the great powers forced it to relinquish. An alliance with Great Britain in 1902 increased Japanese prestige, which reached a peak as a result of the RUSSO-JAPANESE WAR in 1904–5. Unexpectedly the Japanese smashed the might of Russia with speed and efficiency. The treaty of Portsmouth (see PORTSMOUTH, TREATY OF), ending the war, recognized Japan as a world power. A territorial foothold had been gained in Manchuria. In 1910, Japan was able to annex Korea. During World War I the Japanese secured the German interests in Shantung (later restored to China) and received the German-owned islands in the Pacific as mandates. In 1915, Japan presented the TWENTY-ONE DEMANDS designed to reduce China to a protectorate. The other world powers opposed the demands giving Japan policy control in Chinese affairs and prevented their execution, but China accepted the rest of the demands. In 1918, Japan took the lead in Allied military intervention in Siberia, and Japanese troops remained there until 1922. These moves, together with an intensive program of naval armament, led to some friction with the United States, which was temporarily adjusted by the Washington Conference of 1921–22 (see NAVAL CONFERENCES). During the next decade the expansionist drive abated in Japan, and liberal and democratic forces gained ground. The power of the diet increased, party cabinets were formed (see SEIYUKAI), and despite police repression, labor and peasant unions attained some strength. Liberal and radical ideas became popular among students and intelligentsia. Politics was dominated by big business (see ZAIBATSU), and businessmen were more interested in economic than in military expansion. Trade and industry, stimulated by World War I, continued to expand, though interrupted by the earthquake of 1923, which destroyed much of Tokyo and Yokohama. Agriculture, in contrast, remained depressed. Japan pursued a moderate policy toward China, relying chiefly on economic penetration and diplomacy to advance Japanese interests. This and other foreign policies pursued by the government displeased more extreme militarist and nationalist elements developing in Japan, some of whom disliked capitalism and advocated state socialism. Chief among these groups were the Kwantung army in Manchuria, young army and navy officers, and various organizations such as the Amur River Society, which included many prominent men. Militarist propaganda was aided by the depression of 1929, which ruined Japan's silk trade. In 1931 the Kwantung army precipitated an incident at Mukden (Shen-yang) and promptly overran all of Manchuria, which was detached from China and set up as the puppet state of Manchukuo. When the League of Nations criticized Japan's action, Japan withdrew from the organization. During the 1930s the military party gradually extended its control over the government, brought about an increase in armaments, and reached a working agreement with the zaibatsu. Military extremists instigated the assassination of Prime Minister Inukai in 1932 and an attempted coup d'etat in 1936. At the same time Japan was experiencing a great export boom, due largely to currency depreciation. From 1932 to 1937, Japan engaged in gradual economic and political penetration of N China. In July, 1937, after an incident at Peking, Japanese troops invaded the northern provinces. Chinese resistance led to full-scale though undeclared war (see SINO-JAPANESE WAR, SECOND). A puppet Chinese government was installed at Nanking in 1940. Meanwhile relations with the Soviet Union were tense and worsened after Japan and Germany joined together against the Soviet Union in the Anti-Comintern Pact of 1936 (see COMINTERN). In 1938 and 1939 armed clashes took place on the Manchurian border. Japan then stepped up an armament program, extended state control over industry through the National Mobilization Act (1938), and intensified police repression of dissident elements. In 1940 all political parties were dissolved and were replaced by the state-sponsored Imperial Rule Assistance Association. After World War II erupted (1939) in Europe, Japan signed a military alliance with Germany and Italy, sent troops to Indochina (1940), and announced the intention of creating a "Greater East Asia Co-Prosperity Sphere" under Japan's leadership. In April, 1941, a neutrality treaty with Russia was triumphantly concluded. In Oct., 1941, the militarists achieved complete control in Japan, when Gen. Hideki TOJO succeeded a civilian, Prince Fumimaro KONOYE, as prime minister. Unable to neutralize U.S. opposition to its actions in SE Asia, Japan opened hostilities against the United States and Great Britain on Dec. 7, 1941, by striking at Pearl Harbor, Singapore, and other Pacific possessions. The fortunes of war at first ran in favor of Japan, and by the end of 1942 the spread of Japanese military might over the Pacific to the doors of India and of Alaska was prodigious (see WORLD WAR II). Then the tide turned; territory was lost to the Allies island by island; warfare reached Japan itself with intensive bombing; and finally in 1945, following the explosion of atomic bombs by the United States over Hiroshima and Nagasaki, Japan surrendered on Aug. 14, the formal surrender being on the U.S. battleship *Missouri* in Tokyo Harbor on Sept. 2, 1945.

Surrender and Occupation. The surrender was unconditional, but the terms for Allied treatment of the conquered power had been laid down at the POTSDAM CONFERENCE. The empire was dissolved, and Japan was deprived of all territories it had seized by force. The Japanese Empire at its height had included the southern half of SAKHALIN, the KURILE ISLANDS, the RYUKYU ISLANDS, Formosa (see TAIWAN), the PESCADORES, KOREA, the BONIN ISLANDS, the Kwantung leased territory in Manchuria, and the island groups held as mandates from the League of Nations (the CAROLINE ISLANDS, MARSHALL ISLANDS, and MARIANAS ISLANDS). In the early years of the war, Japan had conquered vast new territories, including a large part of China, SE Asia, the Philippines, and the Dutch East Indies. With defeat, Japan was reduced to its size before the imperialist adventure began. The country was demilitarized, and steps were taken to bring forth "a peacefully inclined and responsible government." Industry was to be adequate for peacetime needs, but war-potential industries were forbidden. Until these conditions were fulfilled Japan was to be under Allied military occupation. The occupation began immediately under the command of Douglas MacArthur. A Far Eastern Commission, representing 11 Allied nations and an Allied council in Tokyo, was to supervise general policy. The commission, however, suffered from the general rising tension between the USSR and the Western nations and did not function effectively, leaving the U.S occupation forces in virtual control. The occupation force controlled Japan through the existing machinery of Japanese government. A new constitution was adopted in 1946 and went into effect in 1947; the emperor publicly disclaimed his divinity. The general conservative trend in politics was tempered by the elections of 1947, which made the Social Democratic party headed by Tetsu Katayama the dominant force in a two-party coalition government. In 1948 the Social Democrats slipped to a secondary position in the coalition, and in 1949 they lost power completely when the conservatives took full charge under Shigeru Yoshida. An attempt was made to break up the zaibatsu. Many of the militarist leaders and generals were tried as war criminals and in 1948 many were convicted. Economic revival proceeded slowly with much unemployment and a low level of production, which improved only gradually. In 1949, however, MacArthur loosened the bonds of military government, and many responsibilities were restored to local authorities. At San Francisco in Sept., 1951, a peace treaty was signed between Japan and most of its opponents in World War II. India and Burma refused to attend the conference, and the USSR, Czechoslovakia, and Poland refused to sign the treaty. It nevertheless went into effect on April 28, 1952, and Japan again assumed full sovereignty. The elections in 1952 kept the conservative Liberal party and Premier Shigeru Yoshida in power. In Nov., 1954, the Japan Democratic party was founded. This new group attacked governmental corruption and advocated stable relations with the USSR and Communist China. In Dec., 1954, Yoshida resigned, and Ichiro Hatoyama, leader of the opposition, succeeded him. The Liberal and Japan Democratic parties merged in Nov., 1955, to become the Liberal Democratic party (LDP). Hatoyama resigned because of illness in Dec., 1956, and was succeeded by Tanzan Ishibashi of the LDP. Ishibashi was also forced to resign because of illness and was followed by his fellow party member Nobusuke Kishi in Feb., 1957. In the 1950s Japan signed peace treaties with Taiwan, India, Burma, the Philippines, and Indonesia. Reparations agreements were concluded with Burma, the Philippines, Indonesia, and South Vietnam, with reparations to be paid in the form of goods and services to stimulate Asian economic development. In 1951, Japan signed a security treaty with the United States, providing for U.S. defense of Japan against external attack and allowing the United States to station troops in the country. New security treaties with the United States were negotiated in 1960 and 1970. Many Japanese felt that military ties with the United States would draw them into another war. Student groups and labor unions, often led by Communists, demonstrated during the 1950s and 1960s against military alliances and nuclear testing. One such demonstration (June, 1960) forced U.S. President Eisenhower to cancel a scheduled trip to Japan. Prime Minister Kishi was forced to resign in 1960 following the diet's acceptance, under pressure, of the U.S.-Japanese security treaty. He was succeeded by Hayato Ikeda, also of the Liberal Democratic party. Ikeda led his party to two resounding victories in 1960 and 1963. He resigned in 1964 and was replaced by Eisaku Sato, under whose administration an agreement was reached whereby the United States returned (1972) the Ryukyu Islands. Sato was succeeded (1972) by Kakuei Tanaka, also a Liberal Democrat. Tanaka resigned in 1974 because of alleged irregularities in his personal finances and was replaced by Takeo Miki. It was during Miki's term that Japan's greatest postwar political scandal erupted when it was revealed that various high-ranking Japanese officials had received more than $12 million in bribes from the Lockheed Aircraft Corp., an American concern. Former Premier Tanaka was arrested, jailed, and indicted (1976) for having accepted a $1.6 million payment. In the midst of the scandal, an election was held for the house of representatives; the LDP, although retaining a bare majority, suffered a major setback; Miki resigned and was succeeded by Takeo Fukuda.

Government and Politics. Government in Japan is based on the constitution drafted by the Allied occupation authorities and approved by the Japanese diet. It declares that the emperor is the symbolic head of state but that sovereignty rests with the people. The national diet has sole legislative power. Article nine disavows war as an instrument of national policy and forbids the maintenance of armed forces for offensive purposes. The constitution may be amended by a two-thirds vote in the diet followed by a majority vote in a national referendum. The diet is composed of the house of representatives, a body of 511 members elected for terms of four years, and the house of councillors, having 252 members elected for terms of six years. Executive power is vested in an 18-member cabinet appointed and headed by the prime minister, who is elected by the diet and is usually the leader of the majority party in that body. The diet may force the resignation of the prime minister through a vote of no confidence, and the cabinet may dissolve the house of representatives and call for new elections. The latter is often done, and house members rarely serve their full terms. A supreme court heads an independent judiciary. Japan is divided into 47 prefectures, each governed by a popularly elected governor and single-house legislature. Cities, towns, and villages elect their own mayors and assemblies. The Liberal Democratic party has had control of the diet since 1955, when the party was formed. Relatively conservative, the LDP has supported the alliance with the United States and the mutual security pacts between the two countries. Most political parties in Japan are small and do not have broad, mass memberships. Their members are mainly professional politicians. The Socialist party, which opposes the defense relationship with the United States, was the second largest party in the diet in 1977. The Democratic Socialist party, originally a splinter group from the Socialists, favors a gradual phasing out of military dependence on the United States and is the fourth largest group in the diet. The Komeito, or Clean Government party, was formed in 1967, and became the third largest group in the diet following the 1976 election. The Communists suffered major losses in 1976 and reverted to fifth place in the lower house. The New Liberal Club, formed in 1976, is a splinter group from the LDP, and the sixth largest party in the diet.

International Relations. Japan's postwar foreign policy was aimed at the maintenance and expansion of foreign markets, and in the late 1960s the country had a sizable trade surplus. The United States is its chief ally and trade partner. In the early 1970s, however, U.S.-Japanese relations became strained after the United States pressured Japan to revalue the yen and again when it opened communications with Communist China without prior consultation with Japan. Partly in response, the Tanaka government established (1972) diplomatic relations with Communist China and announced plans for negotiation of a peace treaty. Relations also became strained with South Korea and Taiwan. Japan did not sign a peace treaty with the USSR because of a dispute over territory in the Kuril Islands formerly held by Japan but occupied by the USSR after the war. The two countries did, however, sign (1956) a peace declaration and established fishing and trading agreements. Beginning in late 1973, when the Arab nations began a cutback in oil exports, Japan faced a grave economic situation that threatened to reduce power and industrial production. In addition, a high annual inflation rate (19% in 1973), a price freeze, and the instability of the yen on the international money markets slowed Japan's economy as it entered the mid-1970s. Although article nine of the constitution forbids the maintenance of armed forces, Japan has a sizable military capability for defensive warfare.

See J. A. Murdoch, *A History of Japan* (3 vol., 1926; repr. 1964); G. J. Groot, *The Prehistory of Japan* (1951, repr. 1972); R. A. Scalapino, *Democracy and the Party Movement in Prewar Japan* (1953); D. M. Brown, *Nationalism in Japan* (1955); W. K. Bunce, ed., *Religions in Japan: Buddhism, Shinto, Christianity* (1955, repr. 1962); Herschel Webb, *An Introduction to Japan* (2d ed. 1957, repr. 1960); Nobutaka Ike, *Japanese Politics: An Introductory Survey* (1957); K. S. Latourette, *The History of Japan* (rev. ed. 1957); G. C. Allen, *Japan's Economic Recovery* (1958); G. B. Sansom, *A History of Japan* (3 vol., 1958–63); I. B. Taeuber, *The Population of Japan* (1958); Donald Keene, *Living Japan* (1959); Richard Storry, *A History of Modern Japan* (1960); J. M. Maki, *Government and Politics in Japan* (1962); A. E. Tiedemann, *Modern Japan* (rev. ed. 1962); G. C. Allen, *Japan's Economic Expansion* (1965); Shigeru Yoshida, *Japan's Decisive Century, 1867–1967* (1967); Richard Halloran, *Japan: Image and Realities* (1969); Hugh Borton, *Japan's Modern Century* (2d ed. 1970); E. O. Reischauer, *Japan: The Story of a Nation* (4th ed. 1970); F. C. Langdon, *Japan's Foreign Policy* (1973); R. H. P. Mason and J. G. Caiger, *A History of Japan* (1974).

Japan, Sea of, enclosed arm of the Pacific Ocean, c.405,000 sq mi (1,048,950 sq km), located between Japan and the Asian mainland, connecting with the East China Sea, the Pacific Ocean, and the Sea of Okhotsk through several straits. The shallower northern and southern portions of the sea are important fishing areas. The sea has depths of more than 10,000 ft (3,050 m). A branch of the warm Japan Current flows northeast through the sea, modifying the climate of the region; Vladivostok, the only ice-free port of the eastern USSR, is there.

Japan Current or **Kuroshio** (ko͝orōshē'ō)[Jap.,= black stream], warm ocean current of the Pacific Ocean, off E Asia. A northward flowing branch of the North Equatorial Current, it runs E of Taiwan and Japan; the Tsushima Current separates from the main current and flows into the Sea of Japan. At about lat. 35°N it divides to form an eastern branch flowing nearly to the Hawaiian Islands and a northern branch that skirts the coast of Asia and merges with the waters of the cold Oyashio Current to form the North Pacific Current. Dense fogs develop along the boundary between the Japan and Oyashio currents. Air moving over the warm Japan Current becomes more temperate and acts to moderate the climate of Taiwan and Japan.

Japanese, language of uncertain origin that is spoken by more than 100 million people, most of whom live in Japan. There are also many speakers of Japanese in the Ryukyu Islands, Korea, Taiwan, parts of the United States, and Brazil. Japanese appears to be unrelated to any other language; however, some scholars see a kinship with the Korean tongue because the grammars of the two are very similar. Some linguists also link both Japanese and Korean to the ALTAIC languages. Japanese exhibits a degree of agglutination. In an agglutinative language, different linguistic elements, each of which exists separately and has a fixed meaning, are often joined to form one word. Japanese lacks tones, but has a musical accent and usually stresses all syllables equally. There is no declension for nouns and pronouns, whose grammatical relationships are shown by particles that follow them. Verbs are inflected and generally are placed at the end of a sentence. Extensive use of honorific forms is especially characteristic of Japanese; varying constructions are used to indicate differences in the social status of the individual speaking, the individual addressed, and individual spoken about. In the 3d and 4th cent. A.D., the Japanese borrowed the Chinese writing system of ideographic characters. Since Chinese is not inflected and since Chinese writing is ideographic rather than phonetic, the Chinese characters do not completely fill the needs of the inflected Japanese language in the sphere of writing. In the 8th cent. A.D., two phonetic syllabaries, or *kana*, were therefore devised for the recording of the Japanese language. They are used along with the ideographic characters (or *kanji* characters) to indicate the syllables that form suffixes and particles. The direction of writing is usually from top to bottom in vertical columns and from right to left. In scientific texts horizontal writing from left to right is sometimes employed. The Roman alphabet has also been used increasingly to transcribe Japanese. Since several thousand characters and two sets of *kana* are necessary for reading Japanese literature and periodicals, a need for simplification was felt when universal literacy became a national goal. Thus, after World War II, many *kanji* characters were simplified, and the number generally used was limited to about 2,000. Through another reform, phonetic *kana* characters are now used to correspond more closely to modern pronunciation than previously was the case. The large number of its speakers and the high level of cultural, economic, and political development of the Japanese people make Japanese one of the leading languages of the world. See Patrick G. O'Neill and S. Yanada, *An Introduction to Written Japanese* (1963); Roy A. Miller, *The Japanese Language* (1967); Susumu Ono, *The Origins of the Japanese Language* (1970).

Japanese architecture. Evidence of prehistoric architecture in Japan has survived in the form of models of terra-cotta houses buried in tombs and by remains of pit houses of the Jomon, the neolithic people of Japan. The more highly developed religious architecture of China came to Japan with the introduction of Buddhism in the 6th cent. Late in the 7th cent. the great monastery of Horyu-ji, near Nara, was near completion. The gateway, temple, and pagoda remained practically untouched until the 20th cent., when they were faithfully restored. These buildings illustrate the first epoch of Japanese architecture (6th–8th cent.), which was characterized by gravity, frankness of construction, and simple, vital compositions, sparsely ornamented. Wood has always been the favorite material, and wood construction was brought to a structural and artistic culmination as complete as any of the great styles of masonry architecture. Interior wood columns receive the loads, while the thin exterior walls are of woodwork and plaster. As in Greek and Chinese architecture, little use is made of diagonal members, and the framing is almost exclusively a system of uprights and horizontals. Vitality and grace are contributed by the refined curvatures in the column outlines, in the shapes of rafters and brackets, and especially in the great overhanging roofs. Throughout the 8th cent., the Japanese continued to emulate the architects of China. The gigantic monastery of Todai-ji was begun in 745. A great hall was built to house the DAIBUTSU, in front of which stood twin pagodas, each seven stories high. A distinctly Japanese style of architecture was developed in the late Heian period (898–1185). The famous Phoenix Hall at Uji, near Kyoto, originally a nobleman's villa, was converted (c.1050) into a temple. It represents the apogee of Japanese design. Beautifully situated near a lotus lake, it has a new sense of airiness, with its open porch and lofty central roof. The emergence of Zen Buddhism coincided with a renewed interest in Chinese architecture during the 13th cent. The plan of the Japanese temple adhered to the symmetrical simplicity of Chinese design. The hall of worship contained a spacious chancel with a flat ceiling, usually painted with the Zen theme of dragons in clouds. By the mid-14th cent. Buddhist architecture tended toward eclecticism and an emphasis on rich sculptural adornment. Through the centuries Buddhist temples have varied little in general arrangement. In front of the main building, or *honden*, stands an imposing gateway. Accessory structures include the five-storied square PAGODA (often omitted), the drum tower, and the holy font protected by a shed. The Shinto temple, whose pre-Buddhist type is perpetuated, is a small and extremely simple structure, roofed with bark thatch and devoid of color adornment. Greatest importance was attached to the landscape setting, a forested and picturesque hillside being the favored location. This regard for a natural environment is also consistently reflected in secular building. In the Heian period complex building schemes, known as *shinden-zukuri*, were devised for the court nobles. A number of elegant rectangular houses were joined

Japanese architecture: Phoenix Hall at Uji near Kyoto, represents the apogee of Japanese design.

Two examples of Japanese architecture:
Daigoji temple, built in 951, a pagoda of the Shingon sect (above); interior of the National Indoor Stadium at Yoyogi, designed by Kenzo Tange for the 1964 Olympics (below).

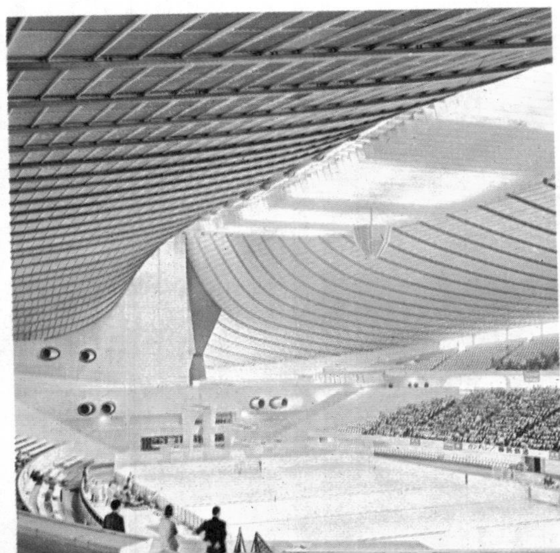

by long corridors that surrounded a landscaped garden and pond. During the Kamakura period (late 12th–14th cent.), the *shinden-zukuri* was modified for the samurai class, and clusters of separate buildings were united under one roof. During this period the standard for domestic architecture was set and has been maintained to the present day. The principal style of Japanese dwelling of the upper class is unexcelled for its refinement and simplicity. Interior posts form a supporting skeleton for the roof. The exterior walls usually consist of movable panels that slide in grooves. Wood panels (used at night or in rainy weather) alternate with screens of mounted rice paper (used in warm weather). The interior of the house is flexibly subdivided by screens (*shoji*) into a series of airy spaces. Important rooms are provided with a tokonoma, an alcove for the display of a flower arrangement and a few carefully chosen objects of art. Often a separate space is set aside for the tea ceremony, either incorporated within the house or constructed as a pavilion in the garden. An important development of the late 16th cent. arose as a result of feudal warfare. Fortified castles, of which one still exists at Himeji, were based on the European donjon and were erected on high bases formed of enormous stone blocks. In the Edo period (1615–1867) two particularly beautiful palaces were erected in and near Kyoto, both constructed on an asymmetrical and flexible plan. The Nijo palace is noted for its sumptuousness in terms of carved wood, black lacquer, gold decorations, and screen paintings. The Katsura palace is remarkable for its simplicity and elegance and its merging of outdoor and indoor spaces. Here Japanese taste is perhaps epitomized in the subtlety and delicacy of the landscaping, with an ingenious arrangement of rocks, pebbles, sand, plants, and water. The opening of Japan to the West in 1868 led to the adaptation of the European architectural tradition. After World War I the Japanese began to make their own original contributions to the development of the International style in modern architecture. Japanese architects incorporated Western technical innovations into buildings combining traditional and modern styles during the period following World War II. At first strongly influenced by Le Corbusier, Miës van der Rohe, and, to a lesser degree, Frank Lloyd Wright, major Japanese architects by the mid-1960s developed highly individual and imaginative visions that had worldwide following. Among the principal Japanese architects to gain international acclaim since 1950 are Kenzo TANGE, Sutemi Horiguchi, Kunio Maekawa, Togo Murano, Yoshiro Taniguchi, and Noriaki KUROKAWA. See A. L. Sadler, *A Short History of Japanese Architecture* (1941, repr. 1962); William Alex, *Japanese Architecture* (1963); Egon Tempel, *New Japanese Architecture* (1970); Ito Teiji, *Traditional Domestic Architecture of Japan* (1972); R. T. Paine and Alexander Soper, *The Art and Architecture of Japan* (1955, repr. 1973).

Japanese art. The earliest art of Japan, probably dating from the 3d and 2d millennia B.C., consisted of monochrome pottery in a cord pattern (*jomon*). This ware was gradually replaced by the art of the Yayoi culture, which produced bronze bells with simple designs, clay tomb figures (*haniwa*), and some painted burial chambers. The stylistic tradition of Japanese art was firmly established with the intro-

Japanese art: detail of a painted door of Phoenix Hall at Uji, of the Fujiwara period (898–1185) (opposite).

duction of Buddhism in the 6th cent. The teaching of the arts progressed under Korean monks and craftsmen, who created Buddhist sculpture and pictures representing divinities, saints, and legendary figures. After the 6th cent. and throughout its history Japanese art has relied heavily on forms and techniques borrowed from China. Rare examples of wall paintings in the golden hall at Horyu-ji, near Nara (end of the 7th cent. to early 8th cent.) were based on Chinese models, reflecting the T'ang style of painting. During the Nara period (710–784) the traditional technical methods of Japanese painting were established. The work is executed upon thin or gauzelike silk or soft paper with Chinese ink and watercolors. It is then mounted on silk brocade or its paper imitation and rolled upon a rod when not on view. The hanging scroll is called *kakemono*. The long, narrow horizontal scroll (*emakimono*), unrolled in the hands, usually portrays a procession or progressive scenes. In the sculpture of the Nara period, clay figures and statues made in the dry-lacquer process (lacquer applied to a solid core of wood or lacquered cloths placed over some kind of armature) attained great popularity. Representations of Buddhist deities and saints in wood and bronze evolved in style from a general flatness in the works of Kuratsukuri-no-Tori (active c.600–630) to the more massive figures of the 8th and 9th cent., which reflect the style of the later T'ang dynasty in China. The Jogan period (794–897) witnessed the beginning of an indigenous style of art. KANAOKA (late 9th cent.) was the first major native painter. The Fujiwara period (898–1185) is marked by the crystallization of the *Yamato-e* tradition of painting (based on national rather than on Chinese taste). The famous illustrated scroll of the *Tale of the Genji*—with its rich color and dreamy, almost expressionless treatment of men and women—reflects the extreme sensitivity and overrefinement of the court during that period. The same delicacy of taste can be seen in the sculpture of Jocho (11th cent.). The school of Jocho was continued by Kokei, Unkei, and Kaikei of the Kamakura period (late 12th–14th cent.). Vigor and realism were restored to the medium, although after this time sculpture ceased to develop in style. In painting most of the fine *emakimono* that survive today are from the Kamakura period. These scrolls are often executed in continuous narrative form, with the same figures appearing many times against a unified background. This method of representation was used with utmost skill and imagination in superb scrolls such as the *Tales of the Heiji Insurrection* (13th cent., Mus. of Fine Arts, Boston). In this art form man occupied the most important role, whereas in Chinese painting he is the least significant part of nature. In the Kamakura period the country was governed by the military, who preferred strength to refinement, movement to dreamy atmosphere, and realism to formality. The new class created a demand for paintings and sculptures portraying officials, warriors, priests, and poets. Takanobu and his son Nobuzane were the most highly esteemed portrait painters of the age. Unkei was the principal Kamakura sculptor. The Muromachi period (1392–1568) ushered in a renaissance of Chinese-style ink painting. The Zen sect of Buddhism, which enjoyed a growing popularity in the early Kamakura period, received the continued support of the new rulers. Ink painting was accepted as a means of teaching Zen doctrine. Such priest-painters as Cho Densu, Josetsu, Shubun, and Sesshu are

Bronze Shaka Triad (623) by the Japanese sculptor Kuratsukuri-no-Tori (active c. 600–630).

the most revered of Japanese landscapists. Their works are characterized by economy of execution, forceful brush strokes, and asymmetrical composition, with emphasis on unfilled space. Sculpture of the period began to lose its Buddhist inspiration. Architectural sculpture was on a par with the unprecedented grandeur and ostentation achieved in painted screens of the Momoyama period (1568–1615). At this time constant warfare created a need for many great fortresses. Their interiors were lavishly decorated with screens painted in strong, thick colors against a gold background. The KANO family of artists succeeded in fusing the technique of Chinese ink painting with the decorative quality of Japanese art. The school of painting started in the Edo period (1615–1867) by Koetsu and Sotatsu and continued by Korin and Kenzan represented a return to the native tradition of Japanese painting. *The Deer Scroll* (early 17th cent.; Seattle Art Mus.) by Koetsu and Sotatsu exemplifies the happy union of literature, calligraphy, and painting. A great demand for miniature sculptures in the form of ornamental buttons (*netsuke*) arose at this time and great masterpieces of carving were produced. Dutch engraving found its way to Japan in this period and influenced such painters as Okyo Maruyama, the leader of the naturalist school of painters, who worked from nature and created pictures with Western perspective. There arose a new type of art in the form of wood-block prints known as ukiyo-e (pictures of the fleeting or floating world), which appealed first to the taste of the lowest groups of feudal society. The color-print designers eventually won worldwide recognition and influenced Whistler and numerous other Western artists. Among the major ukiyo-e painters are Harunobu, Kiyonaga, Utamaro, Hokusai, and Hiroshige. Mid-19th-century contact with European culture had an enervating effect upon Japanese art. A few print designers attained distinction, but no masters appeared to equal their predecessors. In the 20th cent. the majority of painters and sculptors have been overwhelmingly influenced by Western styles. In lacquerware, ceramics, and textiles traditional forms have been retained and modern Japanese pottery is widely esteemed. See articles on individual artists, e.g., SESSHU. See R. T. Paine and Alexander Soper, *The Art and Architecture of Japan* (1955); James Michener, *Japanese Prints* (1959); J. E. Kidder, *Early Japanese Art* (1964) and *Japanese Temples* (1964); Kenji Toda, *Japanese Painting: A Brief History* (1965); Louis-Frédéric (pseud.), *Japan, Art and Civilization* (1971); Saburo Ienaga, *Painting in the Yamato Style* (1973).

Japanese beetle, common name for a destructive beetle, *Popillia japonica,* of the SCARAB BEETLE family. Accidentally imported to the United States from Japan, it was first discovered in New Jersey in 1916 and is now widespread in the northeastern states, where it is a serious pest of lawns, orchards, and gardens. The adult is about ½ in. (13 mm) long with a metallic-green head and thorax and reddish-brown wing covers. Metamorphosis is complete (see INSECT). The eggs are laid in the ground; the small white larvae, called grubs, feed on the roots of grasses, sometimes killing them, and hibernate during the winter. Pupation occurs in the spring, and the adult emerges in midsummer, feeding on and destroying leaves, flowers, and fruits. Many methods of control have been tried, especially those involving the insect's natural enemies—e.g., parasitic wasps and flies, some of them imported from Japan; bacteria that cause the "milky disease" of grubs; and certain parasitic nematodes. None, however, has been entirely successful in controlling the spread of the beetle. Japanese beetles are classified in the phylum ARTHROPODA, class Insecta, order Coleoptera, family Scarabaeidae. See bulletins of the U.S. Dept. of Agriculture.

Japanese flowering cherry, any of a variety of flowering CHERRY species native to the Far East.

Japanese literature. Although Japanese and Chinese are totally different languages, the Japanese borrowed and adapted Chinese ideographs early in the 8th cent. so that their spoken language could be written. Since, however, Japanese is better suited to phonetic transcription, the result is a language of extremely complicated linguistic construction. In 712 the new system of writing was used in the compilation of orally preserved poems and stories into the *Kojiki* [records of ancient matters], an account of the divine creation of Japan, its imperial family, and the rest of the world. Another historical work, the *Nihon-shoki* [chronicles of Japan] (721), was written in pure Chinese. The oldest anthology of Japanese verse, *Manyoshu* [collection of myriad leaves] (760), also written in Chinese, contains about 4,500 poems, many from much earlier times. A number of the poems in this collection are more varied in form and more passionate in statement than those written in later eras. The addition of two phonetic syllabaries (*kata-kana* and *hiragana*) during the Heian era (794–1185) opened the classic age, in which Japanese literature reached its first peak of development. Although classical Chinese still predominated in intellectual literary circles, literature in the native language gained increasing prestige. The poet Ki-no-Tsurayuki, in the preface to his travel journal *Tosa-Nikki* [Tosa diary] (936), apologized for writing in Japanese, but the book was widely read and respected. Much of Heian literature was written by women, foremost among whom was MURASAKI SHIKIBU. Her *Genji-Monogatari* [tale of Genji] (early 11th cent.) is ranked with the world's greatest novels. Sei Shonagon, another court lady of the time, wrote *Makura-no-soshi* [the pillow book], providing an excellent portrait of Heian aristocratic life, with its emphasis on elegance, always an important element of the Japanese aesthetic. The classic age closed in the 12th cent., followed by a period often called the dark age of Japanese letters, but

Japanese art: detail of the illustrated scroll of the Tale of the Genji, of the Fujiwara period (898–1185).

during which Japanese drama—with its unique and rich heritage—developed its four forms; No (serious drama), Kyogen (short, simple comedies), Kabuki (popular drama), and *Ningyo-shibai* (marionette drama). The greatest writers of No plays were Kanami Kiyotsugu (1333–84) and his son Zeami Motokiyo (1363–1443), who raised the No from its primitive origins to the highly purified art form that influenced such Western poets as W. B. Yeats and Ezra Pound. The *Heike-Monogatari* was one of several long narratives of the civil wars of the period. Establishment of the Tokugawa shogunate in 1603 brought an age of total cultural and physical isolation from other countries and a period of peace that lasted for more than 250 years. During this time the quality of Kabuki and *Ningyo-shibai* theater was much improved, largely due to the dramatist Monzaemon CHIKAMATSU. While Heian literature dealt mostly with the aristocracy, and Kamakura (1185–1333) and Muromachi (1333–1600) literatures dealt with the warrior class, the Tokugawa era was concerned with the bourgeoisie. Chikamatsu's plays are important in world literature as the first mature tragedies written about the common man. His contemporary Matsuo Basho (1648–94) was the greatest of haiku poets. The HAIKU, a 17-syllable poem, largely replaced the traditional tanka of 31 syllables. Buson Yosa (1716–81) and Issa Kabayashi (1763–1828) were also important haiku poets. The picaresque novel developed in Japan simultaneously with, but not influenced by, the rise of the genre in Europe. Saikaku Ihara (1642–93) was the foremost exponent of this form; his novel *Koshoku-ichida-onna* [the life of an amorous woman] presents a world of pleasure and eroticism that readers found appealing. The caliber of novel writing declined by the early 19th cent., not to be revivified until the dramatic opening of Japan to the West in 1858. The flood of translations from Western literature that followed induced the Japanese to give the novel a serious purpose. Shoyo Tsubouchi (1859–1935) had a great effect on the modern Japanese novel with his critical study *Shosetsu-shinzui* [the essence of the novel] (1885), in which he urged the use of colloquial speech rather than the special literary language that had been used by previous writers. *Ukigumo* [the drifting cloud] (1887–89), by Shimei Futabatei (1864–1909) was the first novel to be written in colloquial language. The "I novel," a type of extremely personal diary, was dominant for a time, followed by realistic and proletarian novels. Toson Shimazaki's *Hakai* [the broken commandment] (1906) deals with social problems, another example of European influence. Soseki Natsume (1867–1916), a major figure, was popular for *Wagahai-wa-neko-de-aru* [I am a cat] (1905) and *Botchan* (1906). Ryunosuke Akutagawa (1892–1907) is known for his unusual stories, notably "Rashomon." During World War II the military government suppressed literary expression. Kafu Nagai (1870–1959), with his talent for verbal portraiture, remained a popular figure during this time nevertheless. The immense public demand for fiction in postwar Japan has been fed by the prolific output of its writers, most of whom have faced the problem of reconciling Japanese tradition with Western influence. Possibly the most successful in combining these elements was Yasunari KAWABATA, who won the Nobel Prize for Literature in 1968. In the mid-20th cent. Japanese writers have attracted international attention and admiration. Junichiro TANIZAKI, Yukio MISHIMA, Kobo Abe, Shohei Ooka, the prewar writers Osamu Dazai and Ogai Mori, together with writers of earlier times, are among those whose works are available in English translation. Although modern Japanese poetry and drama have not kept pace with the development of novels and short stories, Japanese literature is now recognized as a major branch of world literature. See also ORIENTAL DRAMA. See Donald Keene, *Japanese Literature* (1955), and (ed.) *Anthology of Japanese Literature from the Earliest Era to the Mid-Nineteenth Century* (1955) and *Modern Japanese Literature: An Anthology* (1956); R. H. Brower and Earl Miner, *Japanese Court*

Illustration for Mubasaki Shikibu's Genji-Monogatari *(early 11th cent.), a masterpiece of Japanese literature.*

Yasunari Kawabata, Japanese novelist, winner of the 1968 Nobel Prize for Literature.

Poetry (1961); Geoffrey Bownas and Anthony Thwaite, ed., *The Penguin Book of Japanese Verse* (1964); W. G. Aston, *A History of Japanese Literature* (1899, repr. 1966); A. M. Janeira, *Japanese and Western Literature* (1970); E. O. Reischauer and J. K. Yamagiwa, *Translations from Early Japanese Literature* (2d ed. 1972); Yukio Mishima and Geoffrey Bownas, ed. *New Writing in Japan* (1973); Harry Guest et al., ed., *Post-War Japanese Poetry* (1973).

Japanese music, musical culture of a highly eclectic nature. It has borrowed musical instruments, scales, and styles from many neighboring areas. The indigenous music present before A.D. 453 consisted of chanted poems (*reyei* and *imayo*), traditional war and social songs (*kume-uta* and *saibara*), and the *kagura*, solemn Shinto temple music. All were recitations on a few notes. The importation of foreign music, particularly from China, began in the 5th cent. and continued into the 12th cent. The ancient ceremonial music imported from China, which the Japanese called *gagaku*, no longer exists in China but has been preserved almost intact since the 5th cent. by a continuing tradition of performance in the imperial court of Japan. It is orchestral music using the *sho* (a mouth organ, the Chinese SHENG), the *shakuhachi* (a long flute), and the *hichiriki* (a small oboe). The cantillations of the Buddhist religion came to Japan by way of Korea in the 6th cent. and were followed in the 7th cent. by the *bugaku* of Indian origin, a ceremonial dance with music. In the 9th and 10th cent. many instruments, including the *biwa* (a four-stringed bass lute used for accompaniment) and the KOTO (a long zither with 13 silk strings, used both as a solo instrument and in ensemble), were introduced from China. Midway between sacred and secular is the music of the No drama, dating from the 14th cent. It is restrained vocal recitative, *utai*, using very small intervals, Oriental ornamentation (e.g., sliding, tremolo, vibrato), and accompaniment by flute and drums. Popular secular music in Japan began in the 16th cent. with the introduction from China of the samisen, a three-stringed plucked instrument resembling a guitar, used for accompanying songs. Later secular music also included operalike creations and many varieties of *kumi* (chamber music for ensemble, voice, and koto) and koto solo (often sets of melodic variations on a short theme, or *damono*). *Hogaku* is the name for folk and popular music heard at open-air festivals. The Japanese use two basic types of scale, both pentatonic. The first, used in sacred music and common to the whole Far East, has two modes—*ryo*, the male mode, and *ritsu*, the female mode. The more frequently used scale, found also in Indonesia and S India, emphasizes semitones and exists in three modes, all used freely within the same composition—*hirajoshi*, the most important, roughly represented on the piano by the series ABCEFA; *kumoijoshi*, second in importance, approximated by EFABCE; and *iwato*, approximated by BCEFAB. Japanese music is of uneven phrase length, and the fourth is a particularly important interval. Ornamentation depends on the type and purpose of the piece. The rhythm is almost invariably in duple meter, with ternary or irregular passages occurring rarely. However, the independent drum rhythms, when these are present, tend to obscure the basic beat to Western ears. The music is primarily monophonic, although heterophony occurs in orchestral music and in pieces for voice and koto. The Meiji restoration saw the importation of Western music to Japan, beginning with the brass band. In the 1880s, Western music was introduced into the schools, and in 1887 the Academy of Music was established in Tokyo. Later, symphony orchestras were formed, and Western music became an integral part of the cultural life of Japan. Notable contemporary Japanese composers include Yasushi Akutagawa, Kan Ishii, and Akira Miyoshi. Seiji OZAWA, a conductor of international reputation, was born in Japan. See W. P. Malm, *Japanese Music and Musical Instruments* (1959); Hisao Tanabe, *Japanese Music* (rev. ed. 1959); Shigeo Kishibe, *The Traditional Music of Japan* (1966); Eta Harich-Schneider, *A History of Japanese Music* (1973).

Japanese quince: see QUINCE.

Japanese spaniel, breed of dainty, alert TOY DOG probably originating in ancient China and developed in Japan over many centuries. It stands about 9 in. (22.9 cm) high at the shoulder and weighs about 7 lb (3.2 kg). Its long, profuse coat is straight and silky and is usually black and white or any of various shades of red and white. Traditionally given as the gift of emperors, the Japanese spaniel was introduced into the West by Commodore Matthew Perry in the mid-19th cent. Today it is a popular house pet. See DOG.

japanning, method of varnishing a surface, such as wood, metal, or glass, to obtain a durable, lustrous finish. The term is derived from a process popular in England, France, the Netherlands, and Spain in the 17th cent. that imitated the Oriental lacquer work known as Japan ware. Japanning varnishes usually have a resin base and are colored by mineral and other pigments. Several coats of varnish are applied to the desired surface, the successive layers being heat-dried. Luster and hardness are attained by polishing each coat. Japanning has been applied to furniture, screens, and such small objects as trays and snuff-boxes.

Japheth (jā'fĕth), son of Noah and ancestor of those who were to occupy the isles of the Gentiles. This has been supposed to mean the Mediterranean lands of Europe and Asia Minor. Gen. 5.32; 6.10; 9.27; 10.1–5.

Japhia (jəfī'ə). **1** King of Lachish slain by Joshua. Joshua 10.3. **2** Son of David. 2 Sam. 5.15; 1 Chron. 3.7. **3** Town, N central Palestine, the present-day Yafa (Israel). Remains of an ancient synagogue were found there. Joshua 19.12.

Japhlet (jăf'lĕt), descendant of Asher. 1 Chron. 7.32,33.

Japhleti (jăflē'tī), clan, in a region between Ataroth-adar and lower BETH-HORON, probably in the vicinity of the present-day Ramallah (Jordan). It was either of Canaanite origin or of the tribe of Asher. Joshua 16.3.

Japho: see JAFFA, Israel.

japonica (jəpŏn'əkə): see QUINCE; CAMELLIA.

Japurá (zhəpōōrä'), river, c.1,300 mi (2,090 km) long, rising as the Caquetá in the Andes, SW Colombia. It flows SE into Brazil, where it is called the Japurá, and enters the Amazon through a network of channels. It is navigable in Brazil.

Jaques-Dalcroze, Émile (āmēl' zhäk-dälkrōz'), 1865–1950, Swiss educator and composer, b. Vienna, studied at the Geneva Conservatory, at the Paris Conservatory with Léo Delibes, and in Vienna with Anton Bruckner. From 1892 to 1909 he taught at the Geneva Conservatory, where he developed his system of EURYTHMICS as an aid to his own teaching. After successful demonstrations of his method he established (1910–14) the Jaques-Dalcroze School at Hellerau, near Dresden. In 1915 the Institut Jaques-Dalcroze was opened at Geneva. Jaques-Dalcroze also composed music and wrote several books, including an autobiography (1942).

Jarah (jā'rə), descendant of Saul. 1 Chron. 9.42. Jehoadah: 1 Chron. 8.36.

Jarbah: see JERBA, Tunisia.

Jareb (jâr'ĭb), Assyrian king, perhaps a symbolic name. Hosea 5.13; 10.6.

Jared (jâr'ĭd), father of Enoch. Gen. 5.15–20; Luke 3.37. Jered: 1 Chron. 1.2.

Jaresiah (jărēsī'ə), chief man of Benjamin. 1 Chron. 8.27.

jargon, pejorative term applied to speech or writing that is considered meaningless, unintelligible, or ugly. In one sense the term is applied to the special language of a profession, which may be unnecessarily complicated, e.g., "medical jargon." Jargon can also mean clumsy language that is hard to understand, synonymous with gibberish or gobbledygook, or a mixture of languages that serves different people (see LINGUA FRANCA).

Jarha (jär'hə), Egyptian slave to whom Sheshan gave his daughter. 1 Chron. 2.34,35.

Jarib (jâr'ĭb). **1** The same as JACHIN **1.** **2** Companion of Ezra. Ezra 8.16. **3** One who had a foreign wife. Ezra 10.18.

Jarmo: see MESOPOTAMIA.

Jarmuth (jär'məth). **1** City, SW Palestine. It allied itself against Gibeon and was defeated by Joshua. Joshua 10; 12; 15.35; Neh. 11.29. **2** See REMETH.

Jarnac (zhärnäk'), town (1968 pop. 4,831), Charente dept., in the Cognac region, on the Charente River. At Jarnac in 1569 French Catholics under the duke of Anjou (later Henry III) defeated the Huguenots, whose leader, Louis I, Prince of Condé, was killed.

Jaroah (jərō'ə), chief Gadite. 1 Chron. 5.14.

Jarosław (yärô'släf), town (1970 pop. 29,100), SE Poland, on the San River. Primarily an agricultural and trading center, it has food processing plants and flour mills. The town was founded by Yaroslav the Wise, duke of Kiev, in the 11th cent. It passed to Poland in 1382. Despite continuous Tatar raids, it developed as an important trade center in the 15th and 16th cent. It passed to Austria in 1772 and was restored to Poland in 1919.

Jaroszewicz, Piotr (pyô'tər yärôsh'ĕvĭch), 1909–, Polish political leader. A schoolmaster, he lived during World War II in the Soviet Union, where he joined the Polish army in 1943. In the postwar years he held several important positions in Poland and from 1952 to 1970 was vice premier. He became premier in 1970 following Józef Cyrankiewicz's resignation in the wake of serious rioting over inflation. He also became a full member of the politburo.

Jarrell, Randall, 1914–65, American poet and critic, b. Nashville, Tenn., grad. Vanderbilt Univ. (B.A., 1935; M.A., 1938). His poetry, reflecting an unusually sensitive and tragic view of life, includes *Blood for a Stranger* (1942), *Little Friend, Little Friend* (1945), *Losses* (1948), *The Seven-League Crutches* (1951), and *The Woman at the Washington Zoo* (1960). In 1953 his critical essays were collected and published as *Poetry and the Age.* Jarrell's other works include several delightful children's books; *Pictures from an Institution* (1954), a satirical novel set in a progressive women's college; and *A Sad Heart at the Supermarket* (1962), a collection of essays and fables. See Robert Lowell, Peter Taylor, and Robert Penn Warren, ed., *Randall Jarrell 1914–1965* (1967).

Jarring, Gunnar (gŭn'är yär'ĭng), 1907–, Swedish diplomat. He entered diplomatic service during World War II and was minister to India (1948–51), Ceylon (1950–51), and Iran, Iraq, and Pakistan (1951–52). In 1956, he became Sweden's ambassador and permanent delegate to the United Nations. He later served as ambassador to the United States (1958–64) and ambassador to the Soviet Union (1964–). Appointed (1967) special envoy to the UN Secretary General on the Middle East crisis, he held extensive but largely unsuccessful talks with Arab and Israeli leaders.

Jarrow, municipal borough (1971 pop. 28,779), Durham, NE England, on the Tyne estuary. Industries include the manufacture of iron and steel products and shipbuilding and repairing. The port exports coal. St. Paul's Church and an adjacent Benedictine monastery (now in ruins) were both founded in the 7th cent. The Venerable Bede lived, worked, and died in the monastery. In 1974, Jarrow became part of the new metropolitan county of Tyne and Wear.

Jarry, Alfred (älfrĕd' zhärē'), 1873–1907, French author. He was well known in Paris for his eccentric and dissolute behavior and for his insistence on the superiority of hallucinations over rational intelligence. His most famous work is the satirical farce *Ubu Roi* [Ubu the king] (1896, tr. 1961), with a repulsive and cowardly hero based on one of his old schoolteachers. He also wrote surrealistic verse stories, which, although witty, are also blasphemous and scatological. They include *Les Minutes de sable mémorial* [the moments of a monument in sand] (1894), *César-Antéchrist* [Caesar-Antichrist] (1895, tr. 1972), *L'Amour en visites* [love on visits] (1898), *L'Amour absolu* [absolute love] (1899), and *Le Surmale* (1902), as well as another play, *Ubu enchaîné* [Ubu in chains] (1902). See his *Ubu Plays* (tr. 1969).

Jarves, James Jackson (jär'vĭs), 1818–88, American art critic and art collector, b. Boston. He spent some years in Honolulu, where he founded and edited a weekly newspaper, the *Polynesia*; it became the official organ of the Hawaiian government. Jarves settled in Florence in 1852 and served (1880–82) as U.S. vice consul. His writings include *History of the Hawaiian or Sandwich Islands* (1843), several European travel books, and a number of works on art. Through his writings and exhibitions of his early Italian paintings, he did much to influence the artistic taste of the American public. His collection of paintings is at the Yale School of Fine Arts and at the Cleveland Museum of Art; the Metropolitan Museum has his collection of Venetian glass. See catalogs of his collections by Russell Sturgis, Jr. (1868), Osvald Sirén (1916), and Stella Rubinstein (1917); biography by Francis Steegmuller (1951).

Jarvis Island, island, 1.7 sq mi (4.4 sq km), central Pacific, one of the LINE ISLANDS, just south of the equator and c.1,300 mi (2,090 km) S of Honolulu. Known to British and American mariners, it was claimed in 1856 by the United States along with HOWLAND ISLAND and BAKER ISLAND but was annexed by Great Britain in 1889. American colonists were brought to Jarvis in 1935; the following year the island was placed under the U.S. Dept. of the Interior. Jarvis, on the air route from Hawaii to New Zealand, is now uninhabited.

Jashar or **Jasher, Book of** (both: jăsh'ər), lost Hebrew work, apparently a collection of songs celebrating national events. Fragments appear in Joshua 10.13; 2 Sam. 1.18.

Jashen (jā'shən), father of some of David's men. 2 Sam. 23.32. Hashem the Gizonite: 1 Chron. 11.34. The term *Gizonite* is obscure.

Jashobeam (jāshō'bēəm), one of David's mighty men. 1 Chron. 11.11; 12.6; 27.2.

Jashub (jā'shəb). **1** Son of Issachar. Num. 26.24; 1 Chron. 7.1. Job: Gen. 46.13. **2** Jew who had a foreign wife. Ezra 10.29.

Jashubi-lehem (jăsh'yo͞obī-lē'hĕm), obscure name in a genealogy. 1 Chron. 4.22.

Jasiel (jăs'ēĕl), one of David's mighty men. 1 Chron. 11.47. He is perhaps the same as JAASIEL.

jasmine (jăs'mĭn, jăz–) or **jessamine** (jĕs'əmĭn), any plant of the genus *Jasminum* of the family Oleaceae (OLIVE family). The genus includes shrubs and clambering plants, chiefly of Old World tropical and subtropical regions but cultivated elsewhere, outdoors in mild climates and in greenhouses farther north. The blossoms, mostly white or yellow, are usually very fragrant, some being used for scenting tea; the oil is utilized in perfumery. The common jasmine (*J. officinale*) has white flowers and glossy deciduous leaves. Both names are often given to other plants, such as Cape jasmine (see MADDER) and Carolina jasmine (see LOGANIA). Jasmine is classified in the division MAGNOLIOPHYTA, class Magnoliopsida, order Scrophulariales, family Oleaceae.

Jason. 1 St. Paul's host at Thessalonica. Acts 17.5–9. **2** Companion of Paul at Corinth, perhaps the same as **1.** Rom. 16.21.

Jason, in Greek mythology, son of Aeson. When Pelias usurped the throne of Iolcus and killed (or imprisoned) Aeson and most of his descendants, Jason was smuggled off to the centaur Chiron, who reared him secretly on Mt. Pelion. Later Pelias promised Jason his rightful kingdom if he would bring the GOLDEN FLEECE to Boeotia. Jason assembled Greece's bravest heroes and together they sailed in the *Argo* in quest of the fleece. On their journey the Argonauts were seduced by beautiful women, attacked by unfriendly warriors, buffeted by storms, and challenged by monstrous creatures. Finally the blind prophet Phineus told them how to make their way safely to Colchis, where the Golden Fleece was kept. When they arrived there, King Aeëtes demanded that before Jason take the fleece he yoke together two fire-breathing bulls, plough the field of Ares, and sow it with dragon's teeth obtained from CADMUS. Aeëtes' daughter MEDEA fell in love with Jason and gave him magical protection that allowed him to complete the tasks. In return Jason swore an oath of fidelity and promised to take her with him to Greece. When Aeëtes still refused to relinquish the fleece, Medea revealed its hiding place and drugged the guardian dragon. The Argonauts then fled Colchis with the fleece, pursued by Aeëtes. But Medea killed and cut to pieces his son Absyrtus, scattering the parts of his body in the sea. Aeëtes stopped to retrieve them. In another version, Absyrtus led the pursuit and, when Medea tricked him into an ambush, was killed by Jason. Jason and Medea stopped to be purified of the murder by Circe at Aeaea, and there they were married. When they returned to Iolcus they found that Pelias had continued his tyrannical rule. Medea persuaded Pelias that he could be rejuvenated by having pieces of his body boiled in a magical brew. She then convinced his daughters that they should perform the task of cutting up their father. Pelias was thus murdered by his innocent daughters. Jason seized the city, but he and Medea were expelled by Acastus, the son of Pelias. They sailed on to Orchomenses in Boeotia, where they hung the fleece in a temple. Then they went to Corinth. There Medea had rights to the throne, and Jason reigned for many years. But he forgot his oath and tried to divorce Medea so that he could marry Creusa, daughter of King Creon. In revenge, Medea, by magic and trickery, burned to death both the father and daughter. Because Jason had broken his oath of fidelity, the gods caused him to wander homeless for many years. As an old man he returned to Corinth, where, resting in the shadow of the *Argo*, he was killed when the prow toppled over on him. The story of Jason and Medea appears frequently in literature, most notably in Euripides.

Jason of Cyrene (sīrē'nē), 2d cent. B.C., Jewish historian. He wrote a history of the Maccabean uprising, used as the basis of 2 Maccabees.

Jasper, William, c.1750–79, American Revolutionary soldier, b. South Carolina (possibly near Georgetown). He joined William Moultrie's regiment early in the Revolution (1775), was made sergeant, and was ordered to Fort Sullivan (now Fort Moultrie) in Charleston harbor. There he bravely rehoisted the flag over the fort in the face of British gunfire (1776). He later distinguished himself as a scout before he was killed in the attack on Savannah.

Jasper, city (1970 pop. 10,798), seat of Walker co., NW central Ala., in a coal-mining area; inc. 1889. The city's industries produce coal, lumber, and textiles.

jasper, opaque, impure cryptocrystalline QUARTZ, usually red, but also yellow, green, and grayish blue. It is used as a gem. Ribbon jasper has the colors in stripes.

Jasper National Park, 4,200 sq mi (10,878 sq km), W Alta., Canada, in the Canadian Rocky Mts.; est. 1907. It is the second largest of the Canadian scenic national parks and contains many high peaks, glaciers, lakes, hot springs, and streams. It is a game reserve and a popular recreation area, with mountain climbing and excellent fishing. The park was named for Jasper Hawes, agent of the North West Company fur-trading post established (1813) on the Athabasca River. Jasper, a resort town, is the park headquarters and is a station on the Canadian National Railways system.

Jaspers, Karl (kärl yäs'pərs), 1883–1969, German philosopher and psychopathologist, b. Oldenburg. After receiving his medical degree (1909) he became (1914) lecturer in psychology and in 1922 professor of philosophy at the Univ. of Heidelberg. One of the leading figures in contemporary philosophy, he is generally placed within the orbit of existentialism. Jaspers, however, rejected this classification, as it tends to place him within a school. Nevertheless his basic philosophic concern was with the concrete individual, and he believed that genuine philosophy must spring from a man's individual existence and address itself to other individuals to help them gain a true understanding of their existence. The basic concept of his philosophy is the "encompassing," an essentially religious concept, intended to suggest the all-embracing transcendent reality within which human existence is enclosed. Although this idea is not in the realm of scientific thought, it is not an irrational concept, since Jaspers believed that the study of science is a necessary preparatory stage to grasping the "encompassing." Thus, while maintaining the value of science, Jaspers was profoundly aware of its limitations and believed that abstract sociological and psychological theories cause the individual to lose sight of his freedom and concrete situation. His works include *Psychologie der Weltanschauungen* (1919), *Die geistige Situation der Zeit* (1931; tr. *Man in the Modern Age,* 1933), *Reason and Existenz* (1935, tr. 1956), *Existenzphilosophie* (1938), *The Question of German Guilt* (tr. 1947), and *Philosophie und Welt* (1958). See C. F. Wallraff, *Karl Jaspers: An Introduction to His Philosophy* (1970); Sebastian Samay, *Reason Revisited: The Philosophy of Karl Jaspers* (1971); O. O. Schrag, *Existence, Existenz, and Transcendence: An Introduction to the Philosophy of Karl Jaspers* (1971).

jasper ware, kind of WEDGWOOD pottery in green, blue, lilac, and other colors, with characteristic Greek reliefs and designs.

Jassy, Rumania: see IAŞI.

Jastrow, Marcus, 1829–1903, American rabbi and Talmudic scholar, b. Poland. He was a rabbi (1866–92) in Philadelphia, editor of the Talmud material of *The Jewish Encyclopedia,* and author of *Dictionary of the Targumim, the Talmud Babli and Yerushalmi, and the Midrashic Literature* (1903).

Jászberény (yäs'bĕrānyə), town (1970 pop. 29,785), central Hungary, on the Zagyva River, a tributary of the Tisza. Attila the Hun was reputedly buried at Jászberény.

Jataka: see PALI LITERATURE.

Jathniel (jăth'nēĕl), doorkeeper of the tabernacle. 1 Chron. 26.2.

Játiva (hä'tēvä), town (1970 pop. 21,578), Valencia prov., E Spain, in Valencia. The town is a processing and distribution center for farm products. Its famous linen industry dates back to Roman times; knitted goods, bicycles, and toys are among other manufactures. Játiva was liberated from the Moors by James I of Aragón in the 13th cent. There are many fine public and private buildings, notably the well-preserved Spanish-Moorish castle, a former Mozarabic church, and the Gothic collegiate church (15th cent.). Játiva was long the residence of the Borgia, or Borja, family. Popes Calixtus III and Alexander VI were born there, as was the painter Jusepe Ribera.

Jattir (jăt'ər), town, S Palestine, the modern Horbat Yattir (Israel), S of Hebron. Joshua 15.48; 21.14; 1 Sam. 30.27; 1 Chron. 6.57.

jaundice (jôn'dĭs, jän'–), abnormal condition in which the body fluids and tissues, particularly the skin and eyes, take on a yellowish color as a result of an excess of bilirubin. During the normal breakdown of old erythrocytes (red blood cells), their hemoglobin is converted into bilirubin. Normally the bilirubin is removed from the bloodstream by the LIVER and eliminated from the body in the BILE, which passes from the liver into the intestines. There are several conditions that may interrupt the elimination of bilirubin from the blood and cause jaundice. Hemolytic jaundice is caused by excessive disintegration of erythrocytes; it occurs in hemolytic and other types of anemia and in some infectious diseases like malaria. Another type of jaundice results from obstruction in or about the liver; usually a stone or stricture of the bile duct blocks the passage of bile from the liver into the intestines. A third type of jaundice occurs when the liver cells are damaged by diseases such as hepatitis or cirrhosis of the liver; the damaged liver is unable to remove bilirubin from the blood. Treatment of jaundice is directed to the underlying cause. Many instances of obstructive jaundice may require surgery.

Jaunpur (jounpo͝or'), town (1971 pop. 76,040), Uttar Pradesh state, NE India, on the Gomati River. Now a district administrative center and market town where perfume is made, Jaunpur was in the 15th cent. a brilliant center of Muslim learning and architecture. Of the many buildings from this period the great Atala Devi Masjid mosque (completed 1408) is the most notable.

Jauregg, Julius Wagner: see WAGNER-JAUREGG.

Jaurès, Jean (zhäN zhōrĕs'), 1859–1914, French Socialist leader and historian. A brilliant student and teacher, he entered the chamber of deputies in 1885 and subsequently became a Socialist. In his Socialist journals, notably *Humanité,* he denounced nationalism and upheld socialism and world peace. Jaurès saw socialism as the economic equivalent of political democracy; he believed that economic equality would come as the result of peaceful revolution. He sought to reconcile Marxian materialism and his own idealistic beliefs and emphasized the importance of individual rights and initiative. As leader of the Socialists, he opposed Boulanger, defended Dreyfus, and worked for the separation of church and state. He was active in the formation (1905) of the unified French Socialist party, and he attempted to preserve party harmony. In 1914, Jaurès advocated arbitration instead of war and declared that capitalist nations, including France, were responsible for the war crisis. He was assassinated by a fanatical patriot in July, 1914. His *Histoire socialiste de la Révolution française* (new ed. by Albert Mathiez, 8 vol., 1922–24), an economic interpretation of the French Revolution, strikes a balance between the materialistic approach of Marx and the dramatic history of Michelet. See biographies by J. H. Jackson (1943) and Harvey Goldberg (1962).

Java (jä'və), island (1970 est. pop. 78,201,000), c.51,000 sq mi (132,090 sq km), Indonesia, S of Bor-

Jasper National Park in the Canadian Rocky Mts.(opposite).

Ruins of Buddhist monument of Borobudur, which dates from about the 9th cent., on the island of Java, Indonesia.

neo, from which it is separated by the Java Sea, and SE of Sumatra across Sunda Strait. Although Java is the fifth largest island of Indonesia, constituting only one seventh of the country's total area, it contains two thirds of the country's population; it is one of the most densely populated regions in the world. For centuries it has been the cultural, political, and economic center of the area. In Java are the republic's capital and largest city, DJAKARTA (formerly called Batavia), and the second and third largest cities, SURABAJA and BANDUNG. Tanjungpriok is the chief port, and JOGJAKARTA and SURAKARTA are cultural centers. A chain of volcanic mountains, most of them densely forested with teak, palms, and other woods, traverses the length of the island from east to west; Mt. Semeru rises to 12,060 ft (3,676 m). There are almost 2 million acres of planted teak forests, and although Java contains only about 3% of the country's forest land, it accounts for much of its timber production. The climate is warm and humid, and the volcanic soil is exceptionally fertile. There are elaborate irrigation systems, supplied by the island's numerous short, turbulent rivers. Most of Indonesia's sugarcane and kapok are grown in Java. Rubber, tea, coffee, tobacco, cacao, and cinchona are produced in highland plantations. While rice is the chief small-farm crop, other food crops are also grown. Cattle are raised in the east. In the northeast are important oil fields, and tin, gold, silver, coal, manganese, phosphate, and sulfur are also mined. Most of the country's manufacturing establishments are in Java; industry is centered chiefly in Djakarta and Surabaja, but Bandung is a noted textile center. Found mostly in the interior are such animals as tigers and leopards; birds of brilliant plumage are numerous. Java was a home of early man (see MAN, PREHISTORIC); there in 1891 were found the fossilized remains of the so-called Java man, or *Pithecanthropus erectus.* The typically Malayan inhabitants of the island comprise the Javanese (the most numerous), the Sudanese, and the Madurese. Numerous Chinese and Arabs live in the cities. Like Bali, Java is known for its highly developed arts. There is a rich literature, and the *wayang,* or shadow play, employing puppets and musical accompaniment, is an important dramatic form. Java has many state and private institutions of higher learning; most are in Djakarta, but Bandung, Bogor, Jogjakarta, and Surabaja all have several universities. Early in the Christian era Indians began colonizing Java, and by the 7th cent. "Indianized" kingdoms were dominant in both Java and Sumatra. The Sailendra dynasty (760–860 in Java) unified the Sumatran and Javan kingdoms and built in Java the magnificent Buddhist temple BOROBUDUR. From the 10th to the 15th cent., E Java was the center of Hindu-Javanese culture. The high point of Javanese history was the rise of the powerful Hindu-Javanese state of Majapahit (founded 1293), which extended its rule over much of Indonesia and the Malay Peninsula. Islam, which had been introduced in the 13th cent., peacefully spread its influence, and the new Muslim state of Mataram emerged in the 16th cent. Following the Portuguese, the Dutch arrived in 1596, and in 1619 the Dutch East India Company established its chief post in Batavia, thence gradually absorbing the native states into which the once powerful Javanese empire had disintegrated. Between 1811 and 1815, Java was briefly under British rule headed by Sir Thomas S. Raffles, who instituted certain reforms. The Dutch ignored these when they returned to power, resorting to a system of enforced labor, which, along with harsh methods of exploitation, led to a native uprising (1825–30) under Prince Diponegoro; the Dutch subsequently adopted a more humane approach. In the early phase of World War II, Java was left open to Japanese invasion by the disastrous Allied defeat in the battle of the Java Sea in Feb., 1942; Java was occupied by the Japanese until the end of the war. After the war the island was the scene of much fighting between Dutch and Indonesian forces; in 1946 the Dutch occupied many of the key cities, and the republic's capital was moved to Jogjakarta. Java now constitutes three provinces of Indonesia—West, Central, and East Java—as well as the autonomous districts of Jogjakarta and Djakarta. See Clifford Geertz, *The Religion of Java* (1960); Clive Day, *The Dutch in Java* (1904, repr. 1966); B. R. Anderson, *Java in a Time of Revolution* (1972).

Java man: see HOMO ERECTUS.

Javan (jā'văn). **1** Japheth's son, eponymous ancestor of the Greeks. Gen. 10.2,4; 1 Chron. 1.5,7; Isa. 66.19; Ezek. 27.13. **2** Unidentified place engaged in trade with Tyre, perhaps a Greek colony. Ezek. 27.19.

Javanese music, one of the richest and most distinctive of Oriental musical cultures. It was and is of enormous importance in religious, political, and entertainment functions. It possesses two separate tonal systems—*pélog* and *sléndro* or *salendro. Pélog* contains seven tones, only five of which are used in a given composition. The intervals of *pélog* are unequal, and the smaller ones approximate the semitone of Western music. *Sléndro* is a division of the octave into five roughly equal intervals. It was believed by the Javanese to be the older system, but contemporary musicologists find evidence that *sléndro* was derived from *pélog. Sléndro* is associated with that which is masculine, and *pélog* with that which is feminine. The Javanese *gamelan*, an orchestra of tuned percussion instruments, primarily of bronze, flourishes today in Bali, where it was introduced in the 15th cent. by Hindus escaping from the Muslim invasion of Java. The term *gamelan* includes percussion orchestras of varying function, style, size, and composition. The set of instruments known collectively as *gamelan* increase in value with age and with the concomitant stabilization of its individual sound. A complete double set, or *sapangkon*, half tuned to *pélog* and half to *sléndro*, may number as many as 80 separate instruments. They are played two ways: according to a subtle, flowing, quiet manner associated with singing and gentle dancing, and according to a powerful, louder manner associated with heroic dance. A fixed melody is the basis for complex vocal and instrumental improvisation. The archaic *gamelan*, no longer heard widely in Java, is best studied in BALINESE MUSIC. See Jaap Kunst, *Music in Java* (2 vol., 1949); D. A. Lentz, *The Gamelan Music of Java and Bali* (1965).

Javari (zhəvərē'), Span. *Yavarí*, river, c.500 mi (805 km) long, rising in the Cerro de Canchyuaya, E Peru. It flows northeast, forming part of the boundary between Brazil and Peru, before entering the Amazon near Tabatinga. It is navigable for most of its length.

javelina: see PECCARY.

Javelle water or **Javel water** (both: zhəvĕl') [Fr. *eau de Javelle*], aqueous solution of sodium or potassium hypochlorite. It was originally made near the French town of Javelle (now part of Paris) and was the first chemical bleach, a use first demonstrated by C. L. Berthollet in 1785. It was produced by passing chlorine gas through a water solution of potash (POTASSIUM CARBONATE). After the invention of BLEACHING POWDER Javelle water was sometimes produced by reacting the bleaching powder with potash or soda ash (SODIUM CARBONATE). Now usually sodium hypochlorite solution, it is used in BLEACHING and as a disinfectant.

Jawara, Sir Dauda Kairaba (dou'də kīrä'bə jäwär'ə), 1924–, president of Gambia (1970–). Trained as a veterinarian, he became active in politics in 1960, when he was chosen leader of the People's Progressive party. He entered the government as minister of education (1960–61) and served as first minister (1962–70). In 1970, Gambia became a republic with Jawara as president. He was knighted in 1966.

Jawlensky, Aleksey von (əlyĭksyā' vôn youlĕn'skē), 1864–1941, Russian painter. He went to Munich in 1896 and met Kandinsky, with whom he was associated in avant-garde groups. A hint of folk art and a sense of religious meditation distinguish his landscapes and later portraits. After 1916, Jawlensky concentrated on abstract representations of the human head. His *Fir Tree* and many other works are in the Pasadena Art Museum, California.

Jaxartes: see SYR DARYA, river, USSR.

Jay, John, 1745–1829, American statesman, first Chief Justice of the United States, b. New York City, grad. King's College (now Columbia Univ.), 1764. He was admitted (1768) to the bar and for a time was a partner of Robert R. Livingston. His marriage to Sarah, daughter of William Livingston, allied him with that influential family. In pre-Revolutionary activities he reflected the views of the conservative colonial merchant, opposing British actions but not favoring independence. Once the Declaration of Independence was proclaimed, however, he energetically supported the patriot cause. As a delegate to the First and Second Continental Congresses he urged a moderate policy, served on various committees, drafted correspondence, and wrote a famous address to the people of Great Britain. Returning to the provincial congress of New York, he guided the drafting (1777) of the first New York state constitution. Jay was appointed (1777) chief justice of New York but left that post to become (Dec., 1778) president of the Continental Congress. In 1779 he was sent as minister plenipotentiary to Spain, where he secured some financial aid, but failed to win recognition for the colonial cause. He was appointed (1781) one of the commissioners to negotiate peace with Great Britain and joined Benjamin FRANKLIN in Paris. Jay declined further diplomatic appointments in Europe and returned to America to find that Congress had appointed him Secretary of Foreign Affairs, a post he held (1784–89) for the duration of the government under the Articles of Confederation. Although he was able to secure minor treaties, he found it impossible under the Articles of Confederation to make progress in the settlement of major disputes with Great Britain and Spain, a situation that caused him to become one of the strongest advocates of a more powerful central government. He contributed five papers to *The Federalist,* dealing chiefly with the Constitution in relation to foreign affairs. Under the new government Jay became (1789–95) the first Chief Justice of the United States. He concurred in Justice James Wilson's opinion in *Chisholm* vs. *Georgia,* which led to the passing of the Eleventh Amendment. When the still-unsettled controversies with Great Britain threatened to involve the United States in war, Jay was drafted for a mission to England in 1794, where he concluded what is known as JAY'S TREATY. After having unsuccessfully opposed George CLINTON for governor of New York in 1792, Jay was elected and served (1795–1801) two terms. He declined reelection and also renomination to the U.S. Supreme Court and retired to his farm at Bedford in Westchester co. for the remaining 28 years of his life. Publication of the definitive edition of Jay's papers, under the editorship of Richard B. Morris, will be achieved in the 1970s. See H. P. Johnston, ed., *Correspondence and Public Papers of John Jay* (4 vol., 1890–93, repr. 1970); biographies by George Pellew (1890, repr. 1972), Frank Monaghan (1935, repr. 1972), and D. L. Smith (1968); Richard B. Morris, *John Jay, the Nation and the Court* (1967).

Jay, William, 1789–1858, American jurist and reformer, b. New York City; son of John Jay (1745–1829). For most of the period from 1818 to 1843 he served as judge of the county court of Westchester co., N.Y. An active abolitionist, Jay helped establish (1833) the New York City Anti-Slavery Society, was a strong opponent of the African colonization plan as a solution to slavery, and wrote vigorous pamphlets and articles, which were collected in his *Miscellaneous Writings on Slavery* (1853). He was a founder (1816) of the American Bible Society and president (1848–58) of the American Peace Society. His writings include a two-volume life of his father (1833). See study by Bayard Tuckerman (1893, repr. 1969).

jay, common name for a number of birds of the family Corvidae (crows and jays), found in Europe, Asia, and the Americas. The best-known representatives in America are the BLUE JAY, *Cyanocitta cristata,* and the Canada jay. The Canada jay is gray, about 12 in. (30 cm) long, with a white throat and forehead and black nape; it has no crest. Found in northern coniferous forests and swamps, it is known for its habit of stealing bright objects, and is called locally camp robber, whisky jack, and moose bird. The common jay is of wide distribution and is hunted for game in England and Europe. The female lays from five to seven eggs per clutch, and the male helps incubate them. The Florida, or scrub, jay has blue markings and no crest. The European jay is fawn-colored, with a black and white crest and wings of black, white, and blue. Jays are classified in the phylum CHORDATA, subphylum Vertebrata, class Aves, order Passeriformes, family Corvidae.

Jayhawkers, term applied to free-state guerrilla fighters opposed to the proslavery "border ruffians" during the struggle over Kansas in the years prior to the Civil War. Later, during the war, it was the nickname of the Seventh Kansas Cavalry, commanded by Colonel Charles R. Jennison. The origin of the word is uncertain, but it is believed to signify a bird that worries its prey. Today Kansans are sometimes called Jayhawkers. See S. Z. Starr, *Jennison's Jayhawkers* (1974).

Jay's Treaty, concluded in 1794 between the United States and Great Britain to settle difficulties arising mainly out of violations of the Treaty of Paris of 1783 and to regulate commerce and navigation. War threatened when the British admiralty ordered the seizure of American vessels trading with the French West Indies. To avert further difficulties, George Washington in April, 1794, named Chief Justice John Jay as envoy extraordinary for the negotiation of a treaty. The principal American objects were to secure surrender of the posts in the Old Northwest, to obtain compensation for losses and damages resulting from seizure of American vessels and provisions as contraband of war and for the impressment of American seamen, and to remove the restrictions on American commerce, especially on the British West Indies trade. Jay, arriving in England in June, was received favorably, and the treaty was signed on Nov. 19, 1794, by Jay and Lord GRENVILLE. It provided for British evacuation of the Northwestern posts by June 1, 1796, allowing settlers the option of becoming Americans or remaining British citizens, with full protection of property guaranteed. It referred settlement of the northwest and northeast boundaries and the questions of debts and compensations to mixed commissions; provided for unrestricted navigation of the Mississippi and free trade between the North American territories of the two countries; granted equal privileges to American and British vessels in Great Britain and the East Indies, but placed severe and humiliating restrictions upon American trade with the British West Indies; and permitted admission of British vessels to American ports on terms of the most-favored nation. No discrimination in duties was to be made, and articles provided for EXTRADITION of criminals and defined contraband material. Indemnity for those Americans whose Negro slaves were carried off by Britain's evacuating armies was not allowed; protection to American seamen against impressment was not guaranteed; and no recognition of the principles of international maritime law was secured. The treaty, which owed much to the influence of Alexander Hamilton, caused a storm of indignation in America. Jay was denounced and burned in effigy, Hamilton was stoned while speaking in its defense, and the treaty was called a complete surrender of American rights. It was submitted to the U.S. Senate, in special session, on June 8, 1795, and on June 24, after stormy debate, it was ratified with a special reservation on the clause relative to trade with the West Indies. It was signed by Washington. When the treaty was proclaimed as law, after the exchange of ratifica-

The Original Dixieland Jazz Band, one of two white bands that introduced jazz to the northern United States.

Duke Ellington, musician, composer, and big band leader, one of the most famous and innovative figures in jazz.

tions at London in 1796, the U.S. House of Representatives called upon the President for papers relating to the negotiation. In a special message Washington refused to comply with the request of the House. After lengthy debate the House passed a resolution, by three votes, declaring it expedient to pass laws making the treaty effective, and an act was finally passed (April 30, 1796) making appropriations for carrying the treaty into effect. See studies by S. F. Bemis (1923, rev. ed. 1962) and J. A. Combs (1970).

Jazer (jā′zər) or **Jaazer** (jā-ā′-), ancient city E of the Jordan River, probably about 10 mi (16.1 km) N of Hisban (Jordan). It was assigned to Gad. Num. 21.32; 32.1,3; Joshua 13.25; 21.39; 2 Sam. 24.5; 1 Chron. 26.31; Isa. 16.8; Jer. 48.32; 1 Mac. 5.8.

Jaziz (jā′zīz), shepherd of David. 1 Chron. 27.31.

jazz, the most significant form of musical expression of American black culture and America's outstanding contribution to the art of music. Jazz developed in the latter part of the 19th cent. from black work songs, field shouts, sorrow songs, hymns, and AMERICAN NEGRO SPIRITUALS whose harmonic, rhythmic, and melodic elements were predominantly African. Because of its spontaneous, emotional, and improvisational character, and because it is basically of black origin and association, jazz has yet to be accorded the degree of recognition it deserves. European audiences are far more receptive to jazz, and thus many American jazz musicians have become expatriates. At the outset, jazz was slow to win acceptance in the general public not only because of its racial origin but also because it suggested loose morals and general low life; however, it gained a wide audience when white orchestras adapted or imitated it, and became legitimate entertainment in the late 1930s when Benny GOODMAN led racially mixed groups in concerts at Carnegie Hall. Jazz, like athletics, has weakened racism to some degree and has forced acceptance of black Americans on the basis of their outstanding artistic abilities, although an enormous compromise was required of black musicians in terms of the music that white audiences would tolerate and understand. Show tunes became common vehicles for performance, and, while the results were exquisite, rhythmic and harmonic developments were impeded until the mid-1940s. Jazz is generally thought to have begun in New Orleans, spreading to Chicago, Kansas City, New York City, and the West Coast. The blues, vocal and instrumental, was and is a vital component of jazz, which includes, roughly in order of appearance: ragtime; New Orleans or Dixieland jazz; swing; bop, or bebop; progressive, or cool jazz; neo-bop, or hard-bop; third stream; mainstream modern; Latin-jazz; jazz-rock; and avant-garde jazz. All these styles are current except bebop, whose characteristics have become the material of modern jazz.

Blues. The blues, the heart of jazz, is a musical form now standardized as 12 bars, based on the tonic, dominant, and subdominant chords. The "blue notes" are the flatted third and seventh. A statement is made in the first four bars, repeated (sometimes with slight variation) in the next four, and answered or commented upon in the last four. In vocal blues the lyrics are earthy and direct and are mostly concerned with basic human problems—love and sex, poverty, and death. The tempo may vary, and the mood ranges from total despair to cynicism and satire. W. C. HANDY, basing his songs on traditional blues, greatly increased the popularity of the idiom. Important vocal blues stylists include Blind Lemon Jefferson, Huddie LEDBETTER (Leadbelly), Lightnin' Sam Hopkins, Robert Johnson, Gertrude (Ma) Rainey, Bertha (Chippie) Hill, Bessie SMITH, Billie HOLIDAY, and Dinah Washington.

Ragtime. The earliest form of jazz to exert a wide appeal, ragtime was basically a piano style emphasizing syncopation and polyrhythm. Scott JOPLIN was a major composer and performer of ragtime. From about 1893 to the beginning of World War I this music was popularized through sheet music and player-piano rolls. In the early 1970s, ragtime, particularly Joplin's works, had a popular revival.

New Orleans Jazz. New Orleans, or Dixieland, jazz is played by small bands usually made up of cornet or trumpet, clarinet, trombone, and a rhythm section that includes bass, drums, guitar, and sometimes piano. When the band marched, as it often did in the early days, the piano and bass were omitted and a tuba was used. The three lead instruments provide a contrapuntal melody above the steady beat of the rhythm, and individualities of intonation and phrasing, with frequent use of vibrato and glissando, give the music its warm and highly personal quality. The music ranged from funeral dirges to the exuberant songs of the Mardi Gras. The pioneer black New Orleans jazz band of Buddy Bolden was formed in the 1890s. The Original Dixieland Jazz Band and the New Orleans Rhythm Kings, both of them white bands, successfully introduced jazz to the northern United States. The closing in 1917 of the notorious Storyville district of New Orleans produced an exodus of jazz musicians. Many went to Chicago, where the New Orleans style survived in the bands of KING OLIVER, and later in the music of Louis ARMSTRONG, Jelly Roll MORTON, and Johnny Dodds. Fate Marable, who had played on Mississippi riverboats since 1910, now began to organize riverboat jam sessions with outstanding musicians. Meanwhile, distinctive styles developed in many cities, evolved by younger musicians who stressed a single melodic line rather than the New Orleans counterpoint. Bix BEIDERBECKE, a cornetist and trumpeter and a major

Miles Davis, a dominant figure in the development of progressive jazz.

Chicago-style musician, was influential in developing more complex melodic lines. Jazz spread to Kansas City, Los Angeles, and New York City.

Swing. Originating in Kansas City and Harlem in the late 1920s and becoming a national craze, swing was marked by the substitution of orchestration for improvisation. The average big band had about 15 members (five reeds, five brass, piano, bass, and drums) and could generate overwhelming volume or evince the most subtle articulations. The bands of Duke ELLINGTON and Count BASIE were, and remain, the finest practitioners of this idiom, while those of Fletcher HENDERSON, Jimmy Lunceford, Benny Goodman, Artie Shaw, Glenn Miller, Tommy Dorsey, and Harry James were also outstanding. The music was often written to showcase soloists who were be supported by the ensemble.

Bop. The vigor of the music notwithstanding, a revolt against the confining nature of the harmony, melody, and rhythm of swing arose in Kansas City and Harlem in the late 1930s and reached fruition in the mid-40s. The new music, called "bebop" or "rebop" (later shortened to "bop"), was rejected at first by many critics. Bop was characterized by the flatted fifth, a more elaborate rhythmic structure, and a harmonic rather than melodic focus. Charlie PARKER, Dizzy GILLESPIE, Thelonius MONK, Kenny Clarke, and Charlie Christian were major influences in the new music, which became the basis for modern jazz. The influence of two swing musicians, the tenor saxophonist Lester YOUNG and the drummer Jo Jones, was of paramount importance in influencing the harmonic and rhythmic direction of bop.

Progressive Jazz. After beginning in New York City, progressive, or cool, jazz developed primarily on the West Coast in the late 1940s and early 50s. Intense yet ironically relaxed tonal sonorities are the major characteristic of this jazz form, while the melodic line is less convoluted than in bop. Lester Young's style was fundamental to the music of the cool saxophonists Lee Konitz, Warne Marsh, and Stan Getz. Miles DAVIS played an important part in the early stages, and the influence of virtuoso pianist Lennie Tristano was all-pervasive. The music was accepted more gracefully by the public and critics than bop, and the pianist Dave BRUBECK became its most widely known performer.

Gerry Mulligan (left) and Sonny Rollins, two important contemporary jazz saxophonists.

Later Trends. By the mid-1950s a form of neo-bop, or hard-bop, had arisen on the East Coast. John COLTRANE, Sonny Rollins, Horace Silver, Art Blakey, and Max Roach led various small groups that represent an idiom marked by crackling, explosive, uncompromising intensity. About the same period, a number of outstanding musician-composers, including Charles Mingus, John Lewis, and Gunther Schuller, produced "third stream" jazz, essentially a blend of classical music and jazz. Jazz has also been successfully combined with Afro-Latin music, as in the music of Candido, Machito, Eddie Palmieri, and Mongo Santamaria. In the last half of the 1950s there were three major trends in contemporary jazz. First, a general modern jazz form had developed in the period since World War II, which can be called "mainstream," best exemplified by the music of Gerry Mulligan's various bands. Second, a number of instruments that either had never been used seriously in jazz, such as the flute, oboe, and flügelhorn, or had been unpopular, such as the soprano saxophone, were used to bring new instrumental voices into the music. Third, avant-garde leaders such as John Coltrane, Ornette Coleman, Eric Dolphy, Pharaoh Sanders, Archie Shepp, Cecil Taylor, and Rahsaan Roland Kirk continued to explore new harmonic, melodic, and rhythmic relationships. The new jazz is often atonal, and traditional melodic instruments often assume rhythmic-percussive roles and vice versa. In the late 1960s many jazz musicians, such as Miles Davis, Wayne Shorter, Larry Coryell, and Gary Burton, investigated the connections between rock and jazz. One of the most striking conceptions in the idiom is that of Mahavishnu John McLaughlin. Jazz artists in America have suffered much and received little. In many cases the misery of their lives and public indifference have driven them to find relief in drugs and alcohol. Despite hardships they have produced a richly varied art form in which improvisation and experimentation are imperative; jazz promises continued growth in directions as yet unforseeable. See L. G. Feather, *The Book of Jazz* (rev. ed. 1965); Gunther Schuller, *Early Jazz* (1968); Albert McCarthy et al., *Jazz on Record: The First Fifty Years* (1969); Martin Williams, *Where's the Melody* (rev. ed. 1969) and *The Jazz Tradition* (1970); Frank Kofsky, *Black Nationalism and the Revolution in Music* (1970); Donald Kennington, *The Literature of Jazz* (1971); L. G. Feather, ed., *The New Edition of the Encyclopedia of Jazz* (1972); Hughes Panassié, *The Real Jazz* (1960, repr. 1973). For blues see Charles Keil, *Urban Blues* (1966); Paul Oliver, *Aspects of the Blues Tradition* (1970). For ragtime see W. J. Schafer and Johannes Riedel, *The Art of Ragtime* (1974).

Jean, 1921–, grand duke of Luxembourg (1964–); son of Charlotte, grand duchess of Luxembourg, and Felix, prince of Bourbon-Parma. He fought with Great Britain's Irish Guards in World War II. In 1953, Jean married Princess Josephine Charlotte, daughter of Leopold III, former king of Belgium. Jean was made deputy to his mother in 1961, virtually assuming the powers of head of state. In 1964 he became grand duke.

Jean de Meun (zhäN də möN), d. 1305, French poet, also known as Jean Chopinel (or Clopinel) of

Meung-sur-Loire. He wrote the second part of the ROMAN DE LA ROSE and made translations from Latin, including the letters of Abelard to Heloise. Called by some the Voltaire of the Middle Ages, Jean de Meun was a man of encyclopedic knowledge, a fearless thinker, and a satirical writer.

Jeanne d'Albret (zhän dälbrā'), 1528–72, queen of Navarre (1555–72), daughter of Henri d'Albret and Margaret of Navarre, and mother of King Henry IV of France (Henry III of Navarre). She became queen of Navarre on her father's death. Unlike her consort, Antoine de BOURBON, whom she married in 1548, she remained one of the staunchest leaders of the French Protestants and one of the bitterest foes of the house of GUISE. See biography by N. L. Roelker (1968).

Jeanne d'Arc: see JOAN OF ARC.

Jeanneret, Charles Édouard: see LE CORBUSIER.

Jeannette (jənĕt'), city (1970 pop. 15,209), Westmoreland co., SW Pa., part of the greater Pittsburgh industrial area; laid out 1888, inc. as a city 1937. Its glassworks date from 1889.

Jean Paul: see RICHTER, JOHANN PAUL FRIEDRICH.

Jeans, Sir James Hopwood, 1887–1946, English mathematician, physicist, and astronomer. He was professor of applied mathematics at Princeton Univ. (1905–9), later lectured at Cambridge (1910–12) and Oxford (1922), and was research associate at Mt. Wilson Observatory (1923–44). He was knighted in 1928. He devoted himself to mathematical physics and contributed to the dynamical theory of gases and the mathematical theory of electricity and magnetism. Going on to astrophysics and cosmogony, he solved the problem of the behavior of rotating masses of compressible fluids. He was then able to explain the behavior of certain nebulae, discuss the origins of binary stars, and describe the evolution of gaseous stars. These ideas are presented in *Problems of Cosmogony and Stellar Dynamics* (1919). With Harold A. Jeffreys he developed the tidal hypothesis of the origin of the earth. In 1929, Jeans abandoned research and became one of the most outstanding popularizers of science and the philosophy of science. His later works include *The Universe around Us* (1929), *The Mysterious Universe* (1930), and *The Growth of Physical Science* (1947). See biography by E. A. Milne (1952).

Jearim, Mount (jē'ərĭm), the same as CHESALON.

Jeaterai (jēăt'ərā", jē"ātərā'ī), Gershonite Levite. 1 Chron. 6.21. See ETHNI.

Jebail: see BYBLOS.

Jebba (jĕb'ä), town, W Nigeria, the head of navigation on the Niger River. It is a port as well as a rail and road center. Paper is manufactured in the city. Jebba was conquered by the British in 1897 and served as the temporary capital of the Protectorate of Northern Nigeria from 1900 to 1902. The railroad reached Jebba in 1909, and in 1916 one of the few bridges across the Niger was built there.

Jebel Aulia (jĕb'əl' ou'lēə), Arab. *Jabal al Awliya*, village, N central Sudan. Nearby is a large dam (completed in 1937) that is used to control the flow of the Nile and that helps the Aswan Dam to store water for summer cultivation in parts of Egypt.

Jebel Shammar: see JABAL SHAMMAR, Saudi Arabia.

Jeberechiah (jē"bērĕkī'ə), father of ZECHARIAH **7.**

Jebus (jē'bəs), **Jebusi** (jĕb'yo͞osī), and **Jebusite** (jĕb'yo͞osīt), name of a tribe mentioned in the Bible as the inhabitants of Jerusalem before the Jews. They were apparently absorbed by their conquerors. Gen. 10.16; 15.21; Ex. 3.8; 34.11; Num. 13.29; Joshua 9.1; 11.3; 15.8; 18.16,28; Judges 1.21; 19.10,11; 2 Sam. 5.6; 1 Kings 9.20; 1 Chron. 11.4,5; 2 Chron. 8.7; Ezra 9.1.

Jecamiah (jĕkəmī'ə), descendant of David. 1 Chron. 3.18.

Jecholiah (jĕkōlī'ə), wife of King Amaziah. 2 Kings 15.2. Jecoliah: 2 Chron. 26.3.

Jechonias (jēkōnī'əs): see JEHOIACHIN.

Jecoliah (jĕkōlī'ə), variant of JECHOLIAH.

Jeconiah (jēkōnī'ə): see JEHOIACHIN.

Jedaiah (jēdā'yə, jĕd" āī'ə). **1** Simeonite chief. 1 Chron. 4.37. **2** Worker on the wall. Neh. 3.10. **3** Chief priest. 1 Chron. 24.7. **4** Priestly exile. Zech. 6.10,14.

Jedburgh (jĕd'bərə), burgh (1971 pop. 3,874), county town of Roxburghshire, SE Scotland, on the Jed River. The manufacture of rayon is the main industry. Jedburgh also has a tannery and woolen mills. The red sandstone ruins of an abbey founded in 1118 are notable. In 1975, Jedburgh became part of the Borders region.

Jedda: see JIDDA, Saudi Arabia.

Jediael (jēdī'āĕl). **1** Benjamite. 1 Chron. 7.6,11. **2** Doorkeeper. 1 Chron. 26.1,2. **3** One of David's guard. 1 Chron. 11.45; 12.20.

Jedidah (jēdī'də), wife of Amon of Judah. 2 Kings 22.1.

Jedidiah (jĕdĭdī'ə) [Heb.,=beloved of God], auspicious name that Nathan bestowed on the baby Solomon. 2 Sam. 12.24,25.

Jeduthun (jēdyo͞o'thən), Levite associated with the temple worship. 1 Chron. 9.16; 16.38; 25.3; 2 Chron. 29.14. It is not known why the name appears in the titles of Pss. 39; 62; 77.

jeep, small, durable automotive vehicle intended for heavy-duty applications and sometimes provided with the capability of delivering driving power to all four wheels. The last feature allows superior performance on slippery surfaces such as those formed by ice or mud. The earliest jeeps were used by U.S. military services during World War II.

Jeezer (jē-ē'zər), the same as ABIEZER.

Jefferies, Richard, 1848–87, English author. A naturalist, he wrote several books about the English countryside. He first achieved recognition with the sketches *The Gamekeeper at Home* (1878). His novels include *Wood Magic* (1881) and *Bevis* (1882). See his autobiography, *Story of My Heart* (1883).

Jeffers, Robinson, 1887–1962, American poet and dramatist, b. Pittsburgh, grad. Occidental College, 1905. From 1914 until his death Jeffers lived on an isolated section of the rocky California coast, finding his inspiration in its stern beauty. For Jeffers the world, viewed pantheistically, was marred only by man, a doomed and inverted animal. He frequently used Greek myth to illustrate man's tortured mind, his diseased introspection, and his alienation from nature. Jeffer's poetry is virile, intense, and rich in elemental power. Among his volumes of poetry are *Tamar and Other Poems* (1924), *Roan Stallion* (1925), *The Woman at Point Sur* (1927), *Cawdor* (1928), *Dear Judas* (1929), *Give Your Heart to the Hawks* (1933), *Such Counsels You Gave to Me* (1937), *The Double Axe & Other Poems* (1948), and *Hungerfield and Other Poems* (1954). His adaptations of Greek tragedy—*Medea* (1947), *The Tower Beyond Tragedy* (pub. 1924; produced 1950), and

The Cretan Woman (1954)—brought him wide recognition. See his letters, ed. by A. N. Ridgway (1968); biography by M. B. Bennett (1966); studies by M. C. Monjian (1958, repr. 1970), A. B. Coffin (1971), and R. J. Brophy (1973).

Jefferson, Joseph, 1829–1905, American actor. He was the foremost of an old and distinguished family of English and American actors. Jefferson spent the first 20 years of his life as a strolling player. His fame came with his creation of the role of Rip Van Winkle in a dramatization of Washington Irving's story, first in 1859 and later in 1865 as revised by Dion Boucicault. He performed the second version almost exclusively until 1880. He infused the character with human tenderness and dignity and heightened the "fairy-tale" elements of the play. Almost as famous was his interpretation of Bob Acres in *The Rivals,* a part he played hundreds of times. He was one of the first star actors in America to establish his own road company, the earlier practice being to depend for support on local stock companies. Jefferson was a painter of merit and was a member of the American Academy of Arts and Letters. In 1893 he succeeded Edwin Booth as president of the Players' Club, thus becoming the recognized dean of his profession. He retired in 1904. See his autobiography, ed. by A. S. Downer (1964); biography by Gladys Malvern (1945); William Winter, *The Jeffersons* (1881, repr. 1969).

Jefferson, Thomas, 1743–1826, 3d President of the United States (1801–9), author of the Declaration of Independence, and apostle of agrarian democracy. He was born on April 13, 1743, at "Shadwell," in Goochland (now in Albemarle) co., Va. The vicinity, which at that time was considered a Western outpost, was to remain his lifelong home, and from boyhood he absorbed the democratic views of his Western countrymen. After graduating from the College of William and Mary (1762), he studied law under George WYTHE. In the colonial house of burgesses he was (1769–75) a leader of the patriot faction. He helped to form, and became a member of, the Virginia Committee of Correspondence, and in his paper *A Summary View of the Rights of British America* (1774), prepared for the First Virginia Convention, he brilliantly expounded the view that Parliament had no authority in the colonies and that the only bond with England was that of voluntary allegiance to the king. Although never effective as a public speaker, he won a reputation as a draftsman of resolutions and addresses. A delegate to the Second Continental Congress (1775–76), he served as a member of the committee to draft the DECLARATION OF INDEPENDENCE. That historic document, except for minor alterations by John Adams and Benjamin Franklin and others made on the floor of Congress, was wholly the work of Jefferson. In spirit it reflects his debt to English political theorists, particularly John Locke, and to French and other continental philosophers. Jefferson returned to the Virginia legislature in the hope of being able to translate his ideals into reality in the establishment of a new state government. He urged the abolition of entail and primogeniture to prevent the continuance of an aristocracy of wealth and birth; both practices were abolished, although primogeniture existed until 1785. His bill for establishing religious freedom, grounded in the belief that the opinions of man cannot be coerced, was not successful until 1786, when James MADISON was able to carry part of the Jeffersonian program through to completion. In

Thomas Jefferson, 3d President of the United States.

1779, Jefferson succeeded Patrick Henry as governor of Virginia. He served through the trying last years of the American Revolution when Virginia was invaded by the British, and, hampered by lack of financial and military resources, he experienced great difficulty. His conduct as governor was investigated in 1781, but he was completely vindicated. In 1783–84 he was again in the Continental Congress, where he drafted a plan for a decimal system of coinage based on the dollar and drew up a proposed ordinance for the government of the Northwest Territory, which, although not then adopted, was the basis for the very important ORDINANCE OF 1787. In 1785 he succeeded Franklin as minister to France, remaining to witness the beginning in 1789 of the French Revolution, to which he gave his sympathetic interest. On the other hand, his unsuccessful attempt, with John Adams, to negotiate a trade treaty with England left him convinced of that country's essential selfishness. On his return he became (1790) Secretary of State. Though absent when the Constitution was drafted and adopted, Jefferson gave his support to a stronger central government and to the Constitution, particularly with the addition of the Bill of Rights. He failed to realize the power that conservative spokesmen had attained in his absence, and he did not seem to be aware at first of the threat to agrarian interests posed by the measures advocated by Alexander HAMILTON. He would call himself neither a Federalist nor an Anti-Federalist and was anxious to secure unity and cooperation in the new government. Jefferson did not begin to differ with Hamilton until they clashed as to the best method to persuade England to release the Northwest forts, which the British still held in violation of the Treaty of Paris of 1783. Jefferson favored the application of economic pressure by forbidding imports from England, but Hamilton objected, fearing that the resulting loss of revenue would endanger his plans for the nation's financial structure. Jefferson next opposed Hamilton by declaring against his Bank of the United States scheme on the ground that the Constitution did not specifically authorize it, rejecting the doctrine of "implied powers," invoked by Hamilton's supporters. In both these encounters Hamilton, to Jefferson's chagrin, emerged the victor. Fearing a return to monarchist ideals, if not to actual monarchy, Jefferson became virtual leader of the Anti-Federalist forces. He drew closer to himself a group of like-minded men who began to call themselves Republicans—a group to which the present DEMOCRATIC PARTY traces its origin. An organization was developed, and the *National Gazette,* edited by Philip Freneau, was established (1791) to disseminate Republican sentiments. Jefferson and Hamilton, from being suspicious of each other, became openly antagonistic, and President George Washington was unable to reconcile them. In 1793, Jefferson left the cabinet. Later he bitterly criticized JAY'S TREATY, which compromised the issues with Great Britain in ways outlined by Hamilton. Jefferson's party was able to elect him Vice President in 1796, when that office was still filled by the person who ran second in the presidential race. He took little part in the administration but presided over the Senate and wrote *A Manual of Parliamentary Practice* (1801). His followers kept up their agitation and under Jefferson's skillful direction extended the party's following both territorially and numerically, while the Federalists drifted into dissension. The passage of the ALIEN AND SEDITION ACTS immensely stimulated newspaper discussion, and Jefferson drafted, in protest against these laws, the Kentucky Resolutions (see KENTUCKY AND VIRGINIA RESOLUTIONS), the first statement of the STATES' RIGHTS interpretation of the Constitution. The Republicans triumphed easily at the polls in what is sometimes called "the Revolution of 1800." Aaron Burr, however, who had been slated for the office of Vice President, was found to have tied Jefferson for President, and the choice was automatically left to the House of Representatives. Jefferson was elected after a long deadlock, largely because Hamilton advised the Federalists to support Jefferson as less dangerous than Burr. Jefferson was the first President inaugurated in Washington, a city he had helped to plan (and where the THOMAS JEFFERSON MEMORIAL was dedicated in 1943). He instituted a republican simplicity in the new capital, cut expenditures in all branches of government, replaced Federalist appointees with Republicans, and sought to curb the powers of the judiciary, where he felt that the Federalists were attempting to entrench their philosophy. He believed that the Federal government should be concerned mostly with foreign affairs, leaving the states and local governments free to administer local matters. Despite his contention that the Constitution must be interpreted strictly, he pushed through the LOUISIANA PURCHASE, even though such an action was nowhere expressly authorized. His eager interest in the West and in exploration had already led him to plan and organize the LEWIS AND CLARK EXPEDITION. He held that West Florida was included in the Louisiana Purchase, but his attempts to secure Spanish recognition of this caused rifts in the party and made him the butt of sarcastic attacks by John Randolph in Congress. During his second administration, however, the chief difficulties resulted from attacks on the neutral shipping of the United States by the warring powers of Britain and Napoleonic France. Jefferson placed his faith in diplomacy backed by economic pressure as represented first by the Nonimportation Act (1806) and then by the EMBARGO ACT OF 1807. To enforce them, unfortunately, meant the impoverisnment of classes that had supported him and the infringement of that individual liberty he cherished. Shortly before he left office a rebellious people forced him to yield in his aims, although he maintained that the embargo had not been in effect long enough to achieve its objective. After 1809, Jefferson lived in retirement at his beloved MONTICELLO, although he often advised his successors, James Madison and James MONROE. One of his cherished ambitions was attained when he was able to bring about the founding of the Univ. of Virginia (see VIRGINIA, UNIVERSITY OF). President of the American Philosophical Society (1797–1815), the learned Jefferson was a scientist, an architect, and a philosopher-statesman, vitally interested in literature, the arts, and every phase of human activity. He had complete faith that a people enlightened by education, which must be kept free, could under democratic-republican institutions govern themselves better than under any other system. A 52-volume definitive edition of Jefferson's complete works is being published by Princeton Univ. Press under the editorial supervision of Julian P. Boyd. The projected multivolume *Jefferson and His Time* (Vols. I–IV, 1948–70) by Dumas Malone will doubtless be the definitive biography. See Jefferson's *Autobiography* (new ed., 1959), and a selection of his writings in *Jefferson Himself,* ed. by Bernard Mayo (1942); biographies by Gilbert Chinard (1929, repr. 1957), Nathan Schachner (1951), A. J. Nock (1956, repr. 1960), and F. M. Brodie (1974). See also Claude G. Bowers, *Jefferson and Hamilton* (1925, repr. 1966), *Jefferson in Power* (1936, repr. 1967), and *The Young Jefferson 1743–1789* (1945); Karl Lehmann, *Thomas Jefferson, American Humanist* (1947); Marie Kimball, *Jefferson* (3 vol., 1943–50); L. W. Levy, *Jefferson and Civil Liberties* (1963, repr. 1974); L. S. Kaplan, *Jefferson and France* (1967); Merrill Peterson, *The Jeffersonian Image in the American Mind* (1960), *Thomas Jefferson: A Profile* (1967), and *Thomas Jefferson and the New Nation* (1970).

Jefferson, Territory of, in U.S. history, region that roughly encompassed the present-day state of Colorado, although extending 2° farther south and 1° farther north, organized by its inhabitants (1859–61), but never given congressional sanction. After a great increase in emigration in the 1850s, settlers in Arapahoe co., Kansas Territory, felt the need to be closer to the seat of government. They met in convention in Denver on Aug. 1, 1859, to discuss alternatives to the region's status. The 166 delegates present debated the benefits of reorganization as a state or as a territory and submitted the question on Sept. 5 to the public, which voted overwhelmingly for territorial status. Subsequently, Beverly D. Williams was sent as a representative to Congress, which, however, refused his petition. Nevertheless, the constitution of the Territory of Jefferson was adopted on Oct. 24, and the first session of its legislature met on Nov. 7. Robert W. Steele was elected provisional governor. Although illegal, the new government coexisted peacefully with the official county institutions. Laws were passed regarding taxation, and the franchise was denied Indians and blacks. On Feb. 28, 1861, Congress passed the Organic Act, which created the Territory of Colorado. The provisional government quickly dismantled, and William Gilpin replaced Steele as governor.

Jefferson, city (1970 pop. 25,432), Fairfax co., N Va. It is a suburb of Washington. D.C.

State capitol building in Jefferson City, Mo.

Jefferson, Mount, N.H.: see PRESIDENTIAL RANGE.

Jefferson City, city (1970 pop. 32,407), state capital and seat of Cole co., central Mo., on the south bank of the Missouri River, near the mouth of the Osage; inc. 1825. The state government is the major employer, but the city, with rail and river facilities, is also the commercial and processing center of an agricultural area. The city has printing and publishing houses; other industries produce shoes, clothing, electrical appliances, and steel products. It was a small river village when it was chosen (1821) for the state capital; the legislature moved there from St. Charles in 1826. Because of divided loyalties and the difficulties of holding the state in the Union, Jefferson City was occupied by Federal troops during the Civil War. The Italian-Renaissance capitol of Carthage marble (completed 1917) contains murals by Thomas Hart Benton and N. C. Wyeth, and is the site of the Missouri state museum. In the city are Lincoln Univ., a junior college, the state penitentiary, and a national cemetery.

Jefferson Heights, uninc. town (1970 pop. 16,489), Jefferson parish, SW La., a suburb of New Orleans.

Jefferson Memorial: see THOMAS JEFFERSON MEMORIAL.

Jefferson National Expansion Memorial National Historic Site: see SAINT LOUIS, Mo.

Jeffersonville, city (1970 pop. 20,008), seat of Clark co., S Ind., at the falls of the Ohio River opposite Louisville, Ky. (with which it is connected by a bridge); inc. 1817. Its shipbuilding industry dates from the 19th cent.; kitchen cabinets are also made there. Jeffersonville was founded (1802) on the site of Fort Steuben (originally Fort Finney) by veterans of George Rogers Clark's northwest expedition, who were given the land in gratitude for their services. The town was built according to plans made by Thomas Jefferson, after whom it is named. It served (1813–16) as temporary capital of Indiana Territory. Mineral springs once attracted many visitors to Jeffersonville; today the city is the seat of Indiana Univ. Southeast and contains a steamboat museum.

Jeffords, Thomas, 1832–1914, American pioneer, b. Chautauqua co., N.Y. He went to Arizona in 1862 as a U.S. army scout and messenger and later became a stage driver. In 1866–67, he controlled mail service between Fort Bowie and Tucson. A number of his men were killed by Apaches, and he decided to meet with their chief, COCHISE. He won the Indians' respect by riding into their camp alone. A strong friendship developed between Jeffords and the chief, and it halted for a short period the Chiricahua Apaches' warfare against the whites. As Jeffords was the only white man whom Cochise trusted, Gen. O. O. Howard, the Indian Commissioner, used him as an agent in a treaty (1872). Cochise agreed to live on a reservation only if Jeffords were the Indian agent. Jeffords consented, and during the four years that he was the Indian agent, trouble with the warlike Chiricahua Apache virtually subsided.

Jeffrey, Francis, Lord Jeffrey, 1773–1850, Scottish critic and judge. He was a founder and editor of the *Edinburgh Review,* which printed his critical essays. See his *Contributions to the Edinburgh Review* (4 vol., 1844).

Jeffreys of Wem, George Jeffreys, 1st **Baron,** 1645?–1689, English judge under Charles II and JAMES II. A notoriously cruel judge, he presided over many of the trials connected with the Popish Plot (see OATES, TITUS) and was responsible for the judicial murder of Algernon SIDNEY and for the brutal trials of Richard BAXTER and many others. He was created baron in 1685 and was soon sent to W England to punish those concerned in the rebellion of the duke of MONMOUTH. In the resulting Bloody Assizes he caused nearly 200 persons to be hanged, some 800 transported, and many more imprisoned or whipped. James II made him lord chancellor later that year. When James fled the country in 1688, Jeffreys was imprisoned and died in the Tower of London. See biography by P. J. Helm (1967); study by G. W. Keeton (1966).

Jeffries, James J., 1875–1953, American boxer, b. Carroll, Fairfield co., Ohio. He began boxing in 1896, and in 1899 he won the heavyweight championship from Robert Fitzsimmons at Coney Island in New York City. He retired undefeated in 1905, but returned to the ring in 1910, when he was defeated by Jack Johnson at Reno, Nev.

Jegar-sahadutha: see GALEED.

Jehaleleel (jēhăl'ēlēl), descendant of Judah. 1 Chron. 4.16.

Jehalelel (jēhăl'ēlĕl), Levite. 2 Chron. 29.12

Jehangir: see JAHANGIR.

Jehannet: see CLOUET, FRANÇOIS, and CLOUET, JEAN.

Jehdeiah (jēdē'yə). **1** Descendant of Moses. 1 Chron. 24.20. **2** One in charge of David's asses. 1 Chron. 27.30.

Jehezekel (jēhĕz'əkĕl), chief priest. 1 Chron. 24.16.

Jehiah (jēhī'ə), doorkeeper. 1 Chron. 15.24.

Jehiel (jēhī'əl). **1** Ancestor of Saul. 1 Chron. 9.35. **2** One of David's mighty men. 1 Chron. 11.44. **3** Musician of David. 1 Chron. 15.18; 16.5. **4** Son of Jehoshaphat. 2 Chron. 21.2. **5** Levite under David. 1 Chron. 23.8; 29.8. Jehieli: 1 Chron. 26.21. **6** Tutor of David's sons. 1 Chron. 27.32. **7** Levite under Hezekiah. 2 Chron. 31.13. **8** Leader under Josiah. 2 Chron. 35.8. **9** Father of a postexilic family. Ezra 8.9. **10** Father of one who had a foreign wife. Ezra 10.2. **11, 12** Men who had foreign wives. Ezra 10.21,26.

Jehieli (jēhī'ēlī), variant of JEHIEL **5.**

Jehizkiah (jēhĭzkī'ə), one of the leaders under Pekah, in the northern kingdom, who insisted on restoring the captives from Judah. 2 Chron. 28.12.

Jehlam, river, Kashmir: see JHELUM.

Jehoadah (jēhō'ədä), the same as JARAH.

Jehoaddan (jēhōăd'ăn), mother of King Amaziah of Judah. 2 Kings 14.2; 2 Chron. 25.1.

Jehoahaz (jēhō'əhăz) or **Joahaz** (jō'əhăz). **1** King of Israel, son and successor of Jehu. Under Jehoahaz, the kingdom of Israel was at its lowest. 2 Kings 13.1–9; 14.1. **2** King of Judah. After the death in battle of his father, Josiah, he was made king at Jerusalem; but the Pharaoh Necho removed Jehoahaz to Egypt and substituted Jehoiakim, his brother, in his place. 2 Kings 23.30–35; 2 Chron. 36. Shallum: 1 Chron. 3.15; Jer. 22.11. **3** In 2 Chron. 21.17 and 25.23 AHAZIAH **2** is meant. **4** Father of a recorder. 2 Chron. 34.8.

Jehoash (jēhō'ăsh) or **Joash** (jō'ăsh). **1** King of Israel, son and successor of Jehoahaz. He was generally successful in a war with Damascus, and he conquered Amaziah of Judah. He was succeeded by his son Jeroboam II. 2 Kings 13; 14. **2** King of Judah, son of AHAZIAH **2.** When his father was murdered and his grandmother Athaliah seized the power and massacred the royal family, Jehoash, a baby, was saved by his aunt and uncle, Jehosheba and Jehoiada (see JEHOIADA **1**). He was dominated by his guardians when he became king six years later. He was responsible for religious reforms against Baal worship. After a long reign he was assassinated. 2 Kings 11; 12. **3** Gideon's father. Judges 6.11. **4** One of Ahab's sons. 1 Kings 22.26. **5** Judahite. 1 Chron. 4.22. **6** Benjamite. 1 Chron. 7.8. **7** One who joined David at Ziklag. 1 Chron. 12.3. **8** One of David's officers. 1 Chron. 27.28.

Jehohanan (jēhōhā'năn). **1** Officer of Jehoshaphat. 2 Chron. 17.15. **2** Father of an officer of Jehoiada. 2 Chron. 23.1. **3** Korahite porter. 1 Chron. 26.3. **4** Husband of a foreign wife. Ezra 10.28. **5, 6** Postexilic priests. Neh. 12.13,42.

Jehoiachin (jēhoi'əkĭn), King of Judah. He was king for a few months after the death of his father, JEHOIAKIM. He was carried away by Nebuchadnezzar to Babylon and imprisoned. On the death of Nebuchadnezzar he was freed and given honorable treatment. 2 Kings 24.6–16; 25.27–30. Jeconiah: 1 Chron. 3.16,17; Esther 2.6; Jer. 24.1; 27.20; 28.4; 29.2. Jechonias: Mat. 1.11,12. Coniah: Jer. 22.24,28; 37.1.

Jehoiada (jēhoi'ədə). **1** High priest. He married Jehosheba, a princess of Judah, and together they saved the infant Jehoash. They led the conspiracy against Athaliah that put Jehoash on the throne (see JEHOASH **2**). Jehoiada was buried with the kings of Judah. His son was Zechariah the martyr. 2 Kings 11; 12; 2 Chron. 22–24. **2** Priest and ally of David, father of Solomon's general Benaiah. 2 Sam. 8.18; 1 Chron. 12.27; 27.5. At one point he is apparently called Benaiah's son. 1 Chron. 27.34. **3** Priest. Jer. 29.26. **4** Worker on the wall of Jerusalem. Neh. 3.6. **5** Priest who held office in Nehemiah's regime. Neh. 12.10.

Jehoiakim (jēhoi'əkĭm), King of Judah, son of Josiah. On Josiah's death his son Jehoahaz became king. The Pharaoh Necho dethroned him and set up another of Josiah's sons, Eliakim, who took the name Jehoiakim. Jeremiah tried to arouse the king from his ways, but Jehoiakim had the book of Jeremiah's prophecies burned. Nebuchadnezzar took the hegemony of the West at Carchemish, but three years later the king of Judah revolted. Jehoiakim died just before Nebuchadnezzar took the city. He left a son, Jehoiachin. 2 Kings 23.34; 24.6–16; 25.27–30; Jer. 36.

Jehoiarib (jēhoi'ərĭb), the same as JOIARIB **2.**

Jehol (jəhôl', -hōl'), Mandarin *Je-ho,* former province (c.44,000 sq mi/114,000 sq km), NE China. Ch'eng-te was the capital. In 1955, Jehol was divided between the Inner Mongolian Autonomous Region and the provinces of Hopeh and Liaoning. The Tsungling is one of the ranges of this largely hilly and mountainous region, which is crossed by swift, unnavigable rivers. Jehol was the traditional gateway to Mongolia and from time to time was overrun by Tatars, Huns, and Khitan Mongols. It was the seat (10th–12th cent.) of the Liao (Khitan) empire. Conquered by the Manchus in the 17th cent., Jehol became an imperial pastureland. It was taken by the Japanese early in 1933 and included in Manchukuo; it was not restored to China until the end of World War II. From 1945 to 1955 it retained its provincial status but was administered as part of Manchuria.

Jehol: see CH'ENG-TE, China.

Jehonadab (jēhŏn'ədăb), the same as JONADAB.

Jehonathan (jēhŏn'əthən). **1** Levite. 2 Chron. 17.8. **2** Officer under David. 1 Chron. 27.25. **3** High priest. Neh. 12.18. **4** Teaching Levite. 2 Chron. 17.8.

Jehoram (jēhō'rəm) or **Joram** (jō'rəm). **1** King of Israel, brother and successor of AHAZIAH **1.** He compelled Jehoshaphat of Judah to help him put down a revolt in Moab. Jehoram was wounded in an attack on Ramoth-gilead and retired to Jezreel. JEHU, whom Elisha had earlier anointed king of Israel, put Jehoram to death and took the throne. This was the end of the house of Ahab in Israel. 2 Kings 1.17; 3.6. **2** King of Judah, son and successor of Jehoshaphat. His wife was the notorious ATHALIAH **1.** The Bible says that he followed her family in the worship of Baal. He was succeeded by his son AHAZIAH **2.** 2 Kings 8.16–24; 2 Chron. 21–22.1. **3** Priest. 2 Chron. 17.8.

Jehoshabeath (jēhōshăb'ēăth): see JEHOSHEBA.

Jehoshaphat (jēhŏsh'əfăt), **Josaphat** (jŏs'-), or **Joshaphat** (jŏsh'-). **1** King of Judah, son and successor of ASA **1.** He continued his father's reforms. He was an ally of Ahab, who was king of Israel, and his successors, and he was the first king of Judah to make a treaty with the kingdom of Israel. He was succeeded by his son, JEHORAM **2.** 1 Kings 22; 2 Kings 3; 2 Chron. 17–21. **2** Recorder under David and Solomon. 2 Sam. 8.16; 1 Kings 4.3. **3** One of Solomon's officers. 1 Kings 4.17. **4** Priest. 1 Chron. 15.24. **5** Father of King Jehu. 2 Kings 9.2, 14. The **Valley of Jehoshaphat,** mentioned in Joel 3 as a place of judgment, has been identified by tradition with the northern extension of the vale of Kidron to the E of Jerusalem.

Jehosheba (jēhŏsh'ēbə), daughter of King Jehoram of Judah and aunt of King JEHOASH. She married the high priest Jehoiada. 2 Kings 11.2. Jehoshabeath: 2 Chron. 22.11.

Jehoshua and **Jehoshuah** (jəhŏsh'o͞oə), variants of JOSHUA.

Jehovah (jəhō'və, jē–), modern reconstruction of the ancient Hebrew ineffable name of GOD.

Jehovah-jireh (jəhō'və-jī'rē), Abraham's name for the spot where the angel prevented the sacrifice of Isaac. Gen. 22.14.

Jehovah-nissi (jəhō'və-nĭs'ī), name Moses gave to the altar commemorating the victory over the Amalekites. Ex. 17.15.

Jehovah-shalom (jəhō'və-shā'lŏm), name Gideon gave to his altar in Ophrah after an angel appeared to him. Judges 6.24.

Jehovah's Witnesses, sect originating in the United States at the end of the 19th cent., organized by Charles Taze RUSSELL, whose doctrine centers on the second coming of Christ. The Witnesses believe that the event has already commenced; they also believe the battle of Armageddon is imminent and that it will be followed by a millennial period when repentant sinners will have a second chance for salvation. The Witnesses base their teaching on the Bible. They have no churches but meet in buildings that are always named Kingdom Hall. There are no official ministers because all Jehovah's Witnesses are considered ministers of the gospel. The views of the sect are circulated in *The Watchtower, Awake!,* and other publications and by the zealous house-to-house canvassing carried on by its members. Since their beginning, the Witnesses have been the subject of harassment virtually everywhere that they have been active. Regarding governments as the work of Satan, the Witnesses refuse to bear arms in war or participate in the affairs of government. Their refusal to salute the flag brought about a controversy that resulted in a decision in their favor by the U.S. Supreme Court in 1943. The Witnesses insist upon a rigid moral code and refuse blood transfusions. Before 1931, Jehovah's Witnesses were called Russellites; abroad the movement is usually known as the International Bible Students Association. It is active in almost every country in the world. See studies by H. H. Stroup (1945, repr. 1967), Royston Pike (1954), Marley Cole (1957), W. J. Whalen (1962), and W. C. Stevenson (1967).

Jehozabad (jēhŏz'əbăd). **1** One of the murderers of Joash. 2 Kings 12.21; 2 Chron. 24.26. **2** Captain in Jehoshaphat's army. 2 Chron. 17.18. **3** Porter. 1 Chron. 26.4.

Jehozadak (jēhŏz'ədăk), the same as JOZADAK.

Jehu (jē'hyo͞o). **1** King of Israel. He was anointed king by ELISHA, who led the revolt against the house of Ahab. Jehu murdered King JEHORAM of Israel and King AHAZIAH of Judah and the rest of the house of Ahab. Jehu's rapid chariot driving has become proverbial. To receive protection from Assyria, Jehu paid tribute to Shalmaneser III, an event depicted on the black obelisk in the British Museum. His son Jehoahaz succeeded him. 2 Kings 9. **2** Prophet under Kings Baasha and Jehoshaphat. 1 Kings 16; 2 Chron. 19. **3** Descendant of Judah. 1 Chron. 2.38. **4** Simeonite. 1 Chron. 4.35. **5** One of those who joined David at Ziklag. 1 Chron. 12.3.

Jehubbah (jēhŭb'ə), Asherite. 1 Chron. 7.34.

Jehucal (jē'hyo͞okăl", jēhyo͞o'kəl), Zedekiah's messenger to Jeremiah. Jer. 37.3. Jucal: Jer. 38.1.

Jehud (jē'həd), town, SW Palestine, the present-day Yehud (Israel), E of Jaffa. Joshua 19.45.

Jehudi (jēhyo͞o'dī), officer of Jehoiakim's court. Jer. 36.14,21,23.

Jehudijah (jēhyo͞odī'jə), wife of a Judahite. 1 Chron. 4.18.

Jehush (jē'hŭsh"), descendant of Saul. 1 Chron. 8.39.

Jeiel (jēī'ĕl). **1** Levite under David. 1 Chron. 15.18. **2** Musician of David. 1 Chron. 15.21; 16.5. **3** Ancestor of JAHAZIEL **2.** **4** Scribe of Uzziah. 2 Chron. 26.11. **5** Levite of Hezekiah. 2 Chron. 29.13. **6** Levite of Josiah. 2 Chron. 35.9. **7** Companion of Ezra. Ezra 8.13. **8** Husband of a foreign wife. Ezra 10.43. **9** Reubenite. 1 Chron. 5.7.

jejunum: see INTESTINE.

Jekabzeel (jēkăb'zēĕl), variant of KABZEEL.

Jekameam (jĕkəmē'əm), Kohathite Levite. 1 Chron. 23.19; 24.23.

Jekamiah (jĕkəmī'ə), descendant of Judah. 1 Chron. 2.41.

Jekuthiel (jēkyo͞o'thēĕl), Judahite. 1 Chron. 4.18.

Jelenia Góra (yĕlĕ'nyä go͞o'rä), Ger. *Hirschberg,* city (1970 pop. 55,720), SW Poland. It is an industrial and commercial center known especially for its woolen textiles. Chartered in 1312, the city passed to Bohemia in 1368 and to Prussia in 1741.

Jelgava: see YELGAVA, USSR.

Jellachich de Buzim, Joseph, Count (yĕ'lăchĭch, bo͞o'zĭm, -zhĭm), 1801–59, Austrian general, a Croatian nobleman. He was governor of Croatia when the REVOLUTION OF 1848 broke out in Hungary, and he commanded an army against the revolutionists. His purpose was to separate CROATIA from Hungary, and he was backed by the Austrian government. After the fall (1849) of the Hungarian revolutionary government of KOSSUTH, Jellachich was again governor of Croatia, which remained a part of Hungary.

Jellicoe, John Rushworth Jellicoe, 1st **Earl,** 1859–1935, British admiral. Crowning a naval career begun in 1872, he served (1914–16) as commander in chief of the Grand Fleet in World War I. His tactics at the inconclusive battle of JUTLAND won him some praise and much censure. As first sea lord (1916–17) he opposed the introduction of convoys to combat the German submarine campaign and was dismissed by Lloyd George. He was (1920–24) governor general of New Zealand, and became an earl in 1925. He wrote *The Grand Fleet, 1914–16* (1919) and *The Crisis of the Naval War* (1921).

jelly and jam, gelatinous, sweet food prepared by preserving fresh fruits. Since most fresh fruits contain about 80% water and from 10% to 15% sugar, they are subject to fermentation. They may be preserved by adding sugar and reducing the water content. Almost any fresh fruit can be made into jam by mashing or slicing it fine, adding an approximately equal amount of sugar, and simmering until it reaches the proper concentration or gel at 218° to 222°F (103°–105°C). Preserves differ from jam in that the fruit retains its form. For jelly, only those fruits may successfully be used that contain a sufficient amount of PECTIN (the chief gelling substance) and acid. Among these are plums, apples, grapes, and quinces and such berries as currants, gooseberries, raspberries, blackberries, and cranberries. Pectin or GELATIN may be added to other fruits, such as peaches and strawberries, but the results do not equal the natural jellies. Jelly is made by extracting the juice of fresh, sound, barely ripe fruit, combining with sugar, and cooking. Excess heating dissipates the flavor and may hydrolyze the pectin. Too little sugar yields a tough jelly; too much, a sticky one. Too much acid may cause separation of liquid. The manufacture of jams and jellies is now largely commercial.

jellyfish, common name for the free-swimming stage (see POLYP AND MEDUSA), of certain invertebrate animals of the phylum CNIDARIA (the coelenterates). The body of a jellyfish is shaped like a bell or umbrella, with a clear, jellylike material filling most of the space between the upper and lower surfaces. A mouth is located in the center of the undersurface and tentacles dangle from the bell margin. Many jellyfish are colored, with pink or orange internal structures visible through the colorless or delicately tinted bell, and all are exquisitely designed; they are among the most beautiful of animal types. Typically, jellyfish catch their prey with the aid of stinging cells located in the tentacles; many jellyfish can cause irritating or even dangerous stings to humans. Food is carried by the tentacles to the mouth, then is moved into the stomach and is distributed to the body through radial canals. Jellyfish move up and down by contracting and relaxing the bell, using muscles that circle the bell margin; they are carried horizontally by waves and currents. Jellyfish of the class Hydrozoa are small, ranging from ⅛ in. (0.32 cm) to several inches in diameter, and usually have four tentacles. They have several (often four) unbranched radial canals and simple sense organs. In this group the polyp, or attached stage, is often larger and more conspicuous than the medusa. Jellyfish of the class Scyphozoa, sometimes called true jellyfish, are larger and often have numerous tentacles; they have branched radial canals and complex sense organs. In this group the medusa is the prominent form and the polyp is reduced to a small larval stage. Scyphozoan jellyfish are commonly ¾ in. to 16 in. (2–40 cm) in diameter; *Aurelia,* the flattened

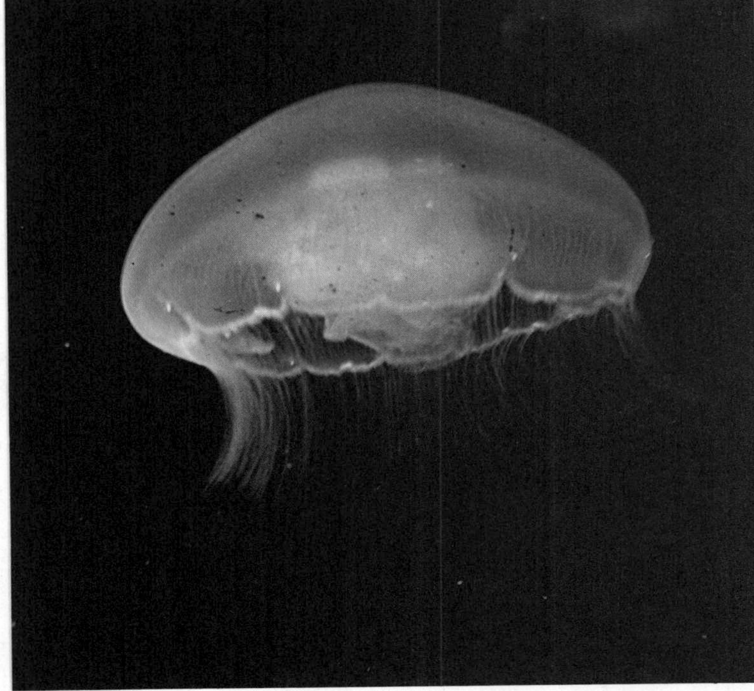

Flattened jellyfish, an invertebrate animal, common to the coasts of North America.

jellyfish common along North American coasts, may be as much as 1 ft (30 cm) across. One species of *Cyanea* found in cold northern seas may reach 6 ft (1.8 m) across and have tentacles over 100 ft (30 m) long. Tiny *Craspedacusta,* a hydrozoan jellyfish less than 1 in. (2.5 cm) long, occurs in freshwater lakes and ponds, but all other jellyfish are marine, living in ocean depths as well as along the coasts. The hydrozoan *Physalia,* or Portuguese man-of-war, is actually a large colony of modified individuals, some medusalike and some polyplike; a large gas-filled sac acts as a float for the colony. The tentacles of such a colony may extend 60 ft (18 m) into the water and can cause severe injuries to swimmers. *Physalia* is usually bright blue, sometimes with tints of pink and orange. The purple sail, *Velella,* a floating colony 1 to 3 in. (2.5–7.5 cm) across, may be blue or purple. Jellyfish are classified in the phylum Cnidaria, classes Hydrozoa and Scyphozoa.

Jemappes (zhəmäp'), town (1970 pop. 12,455), Hainaut prov., S Belgium. It is a coal-mining center of the Borinage region. Manufactures include iron and steel. At Jemappes in 1792 the French under Dumouriez defeated the Austrians under Duke Albert of Saxe-Teschen in one of the first important battles of the French Revolutionary Wars. The victory opened the way to Brussels for the French.

Jemez (hā'mās), pueblo (1970 pop. 1,197), Sandoval co., central N.Mex., on the East Fork of the Jemez River. In the 16th cent. there were several Jemez pueblos, but by 1622 there were only two. One of the remaining pueblos was abandoned prior to the Pueblo revolt of 1680. The other took a prominent part in the revolt; the Jemez Indians attacked the Spanish repeatedly and even made war on those neighbors who remained loyal to the Spanish. In 1694 the pueblo was stormed and captured by the Spanish. Although the Jemez promised to remain at peace, they revolted (1696) and killed the missionaries. Expecting a Spanish attack, they fled into Navaho country, where they remained for several years. Finally some of the Indians returned and built (c.1700) the present village. The inhabitants are PUEBLO INDIANS of the Tonoan linguistic stock. Their principal feast is on Nov. 12, for San Diego (St. Didacus). See E. W. Parsons, *The Pueblo of Jemez* (1925).

Jemima (jĕmī'mə), first daughter born to Job after his affliction. Job 42.14.

Jemison, Mary, 1743–1833, American frontierswoman. She was born at sea while her parents were en route from Ireland to America. In W Pennsylvania she was captured (1758) by a FRENCH AND INDIAN WAR party, taken to Fort Duquesne, and given to two Seneca women, who adopted her. She was married twice (to a Delaware and to a Seneca) and bore eight children. Known as the White Woman of the Genesee, Mary Jemison refused to leave the Senecas, and in 1817 New York confirmed her possession of a tract of land (given her in 1797) on the Genesee River. Her story is told in a classic tale of "Indian-capture," J. E. Seaver's *Narrative of the Life of Mrs. Mary Jemison* (1824; latest ed., 1967).

Jemuel (jĕmyo͞o'əl), first son of Simeon. Gen. 46.10; Ex. 6.15. Nemuel: Num. 26.12; 1 Chron. 4.24.

Jena (yä'nä), city (1970 pop. 88,346), Gera district, S East Germany, on the Saale River. Manufactures of this industrial center include pharmaceuticals, glass, and optical and precision instruments (the Zeiss works, partly removed after 1945 by the Soviet occupation forces). Jena was known in the 9th cent. and was chartered in the 13th cent. The city passed to the house of Wettin in the 14th cent. and in 1485 passed to its Ernestine line. In 1806, Napoleon I decisively defeated the Prussians at Jena. The Univ. of Jena was founded in 1557–58 and reached its height in the late 18th and early 19th cent. At that time the dramatist Friedrich von Schiller, the philosophers Hegel, Fichte, and Schelling, and the poet August Wilhelm von Schlegel taught there. Schiller wrote the Wallenstein trilogy and Goethe wrote *Hermann und Dorothea* at Jena. Noteworthy structures in the city include the Church of St. Michael (13th cent.), a 15th-century city hall, and parts of the city's medieval fortifications.

Jena, University of, at Jena, East Germany; founded 1548 as an academy, became a university 10 years later. The school gained an international reputation in the 18th cent. when Friedrich Hegel, Johann Fichte, and Friedrich Schiller taught there. In 1934 the university's official name became the Friedrich Schiller University of Jena. It includes sections of Marxism-Leninism, physics of instrument construction, instrument technology, mathematics, chemistry, biology, philosophy and history, literature and art, languages, education, physical education, and medicine (including dentistry); faculties of theology (Protestant) and law; and institutes of classical studies and archaeology and history of medicine and natural science.

Jenghiz Khan or **Genghis Khan** (both: jĕng'gĭz, -'gĭs kän), Mandarin *Ch'eng-chi-ssu-han,* 1167?–1227, Mongol conqueror, originally named Temujin. He succeeded his father, Yekusai, as chieftain of a Mongol tribe and then fought to become ruler of a Mongol confederacy. After subjugating many tribes of Mongolia and establishing his capital at Karakorum, Temu-jin held (1206) a great meeting, the khuriltai, at which he accepted leadership of the Mongols and assumed his title. He promulgated a code of conduct and reorganized his armies. He attacked (1213) the Jurchen-ruled Chin empire of N China and by 1215 had occupied most of its territory, including the capital, Yenching (now Peking). From 1218 to 1224 he conquered Turkistan, Transoxania, and Afghanistan and raided Persia and E Europe to the Dnepr River. Jenghiz Khan ruled one of the greatest land empires the world has ever known. He died while campaigning against the Jurchen, and his vast domains were divided among his sons and

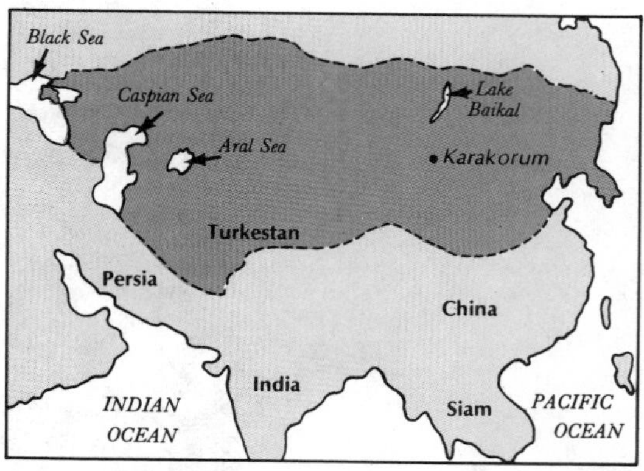

Empire of Jenghiz Khan (1227).

grandsons. His wars were marked by ruthless carnage, but Jenghiz Khan was a brilliant ruler and military leader. Tamerlane was said to be descended from him. See biographies by Harold Lamb (1927, repr. 1960), B. J. Vladimirtsov (1930, repr. 1969), Ralph Fox (1936, repr. 1962), René Grousset (tr. 1967), and R. P. Lister (1969); H. D. Martin, *The Rise of Chingis Khan and His Conquest of North China* (1950, repr. 1971).

Jenkins, John, 1728–85, American pioneer, b. probably Connecticut. In 1753, Jenkins explored the WYOMING VALLEY for the proposed Susquehanna Company. A settlement (1762) under his leadership was destroyed by the Indians, and in 1769, leading another group to the region, he founded Kingston. Jenkins lived there until the Wyoming Valley massacre (1778), then fled to Orange co., N.Y. After his retirement his son **John Jenkins** (1751–1827), b. New London, Conn., took his place as leader of the Connecticut settlers. During the American Revolution he took part in Gen. John Sullivan's punitive expedition against the Indians who had committed the Wyoming massacre. After the war Jenkins defended the Connecticut settlers in the Pennamite Wars and against Indian attacks. In 1786 he laid out the town of Athens, Pa.

Jenkins, Roy (Harris), 1920–, British politician. He entered the House of Commons in 1948 as a Labour member and soon became one of the most formidable debaters in Parliament. When the Labour party returned to power in 1964, he became minister of aviation. As home secretary from 1965 to 1967 he worked for broader laws against racial discrimination and played a large part in liberalizing the laws on abortion and homosexual activity. As chancellor of the exchequer from 1967 to 1970 he instituted a program of austerity in an effort to solve Britain's financial crisis. In 1971, in defiance of the Labour party majority, he supported Britain's entry into the Common Market. He served again as home secretary (1974–76) under Harold Wilson and made an unsuccessful bid to succeed Wilson when the latter resigned (1976). In 1977, Jenkins became president of the European Commission.

Jenkinson, Robert Banks: see LIVERPOOL, ROBERT BANKS JENKINSON, 2D EARL OF.

Jenkins's Ear, War of, 1739–41, struggle between England and Spain. It grew out of the commercial rivalry of the two powers and led into the larger War of the AUSTRIAN SUCCESSION. The incident that gave the name to the war occurred in 1731 when Robert Jenkins, master of the ship *Rebecca,* claimed he had had his ear cut off by Spanish coast guards. English smuggling and resentment at exclusion from the Spanish colonial trade caused the war, but Jenkins's story in the House of Commons, reinforced by the showing of his ear, had tremendous propaganda effect and forced the reluctant Sir Robert WALPOLE to declare war. The hostilities with Spain up to 1741 were marked only by the naval engagements of Admiral Edward Vernon in the West Indies.

Jenks, Jeremiah Whipple, 1856–1929, American economist, b. St. Clair, Mich., grad. Univ. of Michigan, 1878 , Ph.D. Univ. of Halle, 1885. He was professor of political economy (1891–1912) at Cornell and from 1912 was professor of government at New York Univ. Interested especially in the political aspects of economic problems, he served frequently on government boards and commissions and made many reports on trust, currency, labor, and immigration problems. Out of these experiences came his authoritative books *The Trust Problem* (1900; 5th ed. 1929) and *The Immigration Problem* (with W. J. Lauck, 1911; 6th ed. 1925). As a financial expert he advised the governments of Mexico, Nicaragua, China, and Germany. He also wrote *Principles of Politics* (1909) and *Governmental Action for Social Welfare* (1910).

Jenné: see DJENNÉ, Mali.

Jenner, Edward, 1749–1823, English physician; pupil of John Hunter. His invaluable experiments beginning in 1796 with the vaccination of eight-year-old James Phipps proved that cowpox provided immunity against smallpox. His discovery was instrumental in ridding many areas of the world of a dread disease and laid the foundations of modern immunology as a science. See W. R. Le Fanu, *A Bio-bibliography of Edward Jenner, 1749–1823* (1951).

Jenney, William Le Baron, 1832–1907, American engineer and architect, b. Fairhaven, Mass. He studied at Harvard Scientific School and the École des Beaux-Arts. Later he learned engineering, constructed a railroad in Panama before the Civil War, and was chief engineer on General Sherman's staff in Georgia. The Home Insurance Building, 10 stories high, which he designed and built in Chicago (1883; since demolished), was the first in which both the floors and the exterior masonry walls were borne by a skeleton framework of metal. Although this structural system did not receive clear architectural expression, technically Jenney's building has come to be known as the first skyscraper.

Sears, Roebuck and Company building (1889–90) in Chicago, Ill., designed by William Le Baron Jenney.

Jennings, Herbert Spencer, 1868–1947, American zoologist, b. Tonica, Ill., B.S. Univ. of Michigan, 1893, Ph.D. Harvard, 1896. He was professor of zoology at Johns Hopkins (1906–10) and did research on genetics (especially heredity and variation in microorganisms) and on animal behavior there from 1910 to 1938 and from 1939 at the Univ. of California. His demonstration that physical and chemical stimuli produce responses in lower animals disproved the current belief that their behavior was controlled by will and intelligence. His works include *Behavior of the Lower Organisms* (1906), *The Biological Basis of Human Nature* (1930); and *Genetics* (1935).

Jennings, Sarah, duchess of Marlborough: see MARLBOROUGH, SARAH CHURCHILL, DUCHESS OF.

Jennings. 1 City (1970 pop. 11,783), seat of Jefferson Davis parish, SW La., on the Mermentau River; inc. 1888. **2** City (1970 pop. 19,379), St. Louis co., E Mo., a residential suburb adjacent to St. Louis; settled 1870, inc. 1946.

jenny: see ASS.

Jennys, family of American painters, fl. 1770–1810. Little is known of the Jennys family. William Jennys and his son Richard painted portraits in Massachusetts and Connecticut. These are classed as primitives in style, yet they exhibit sophisticated psychological understanding of the sitters. William Jennys's portraits of the Bacon family (1795) are in the Rockefeller Folk Art Collection, Williamsburg, Va.

Jensen, Johannes Vilhelm (yōhän'əs vĭl'hĕlm yĕn'-sən), 1873–1950, Danish writer. As a young man he studied medicine; his interest in biology and anthropology is obvious throughout his works. Jensen created a distinctive literary form in his "myths," brief prose tales with an element of the essay. Selections have been translated as *The Waving Rye* (1959). His works, numbering more than 60 volumes, include essays, travel books, and lyrical poems. His epic novel cycle *The Long Journey* (6 vol., 1908–22; tr., 3 vol., 1923–24), a fantasy based on Darwinian theory, traces the story of man from primitive times to the age of Columbus. Jensen was awarded the 1944 Nobel Prize in Literature.

Jenson or **Janson, Nicolas** (both: nēkôlä' zhäN-sôN'), d. c.1480, Venetian printer, b. France. Jenson studied printing with Gutenberg at Mainz for three years. He was one of the first to design roman type, which was far superior in beauty and alignment of characters to that of JOHN OF SPEYER. He started publishing under his own name and with his own type in 1470 in Venice, producing numerous celebrated and beautiful editions. His roman type of 1470 furnished inspiration for Garamond, Caslon, William Morris, Bruce Rogers, and other masters. After his death, his type was used by the Aldine Press.

jeopardy, in law, condition of a person charged with a crime and thus in danger of punishment. At COMMON LAW a defendant could be exposed to jeopardy for the same offense only once; exposing a person twice is known as double jeopardy. Double jeopardy is prohibited in Federal and state courts by the Fifth and Fourteenth Amendments to the U.S. Constitution. The concept refers to an offense, not to an act giving rise to an offense; therefore, it is possible to try a person for multiple violations arising from a single act (e.g., assault, attempted murder, and carrying a deadly weapon). Jeopardy does not exist until the JURY is sworn in, or, if there is no jury, until evidence is introduced. The prohibition of double jeopardy does not preclude a second trial if the first court lacked jurisdiction (authority), if there was error in the proceedings, or if the jury could not reach a verdict. A similar principle, known as res judicata, operates in civil suits. It holds that once a civil case has been finally decided on the merits the same parties can not litigate it again.

Jephthae (jĕf'thē), Greek form of Jephthah.

Jephthah (jĕf'thə), son of Gilead and a judge of Israel. He vowed if victorious over his enemies to sacrifice the first of his household to greet him upon his return. His daughter and only child was the price of this vow. Judges 11;12. Jephthae: Heb. 11.32.

Jephunneh (jēfŭn'ē). **1** Father of Caleb. Num. 13.6. **2** Asherite. 1 Chron. 7.38.

Jequié (zhəkyĕ'), city (1970 pop. 100,411), Bahia state, E Brazil, on the Contas River. Cacao production and cattle breeding are the principal economic activities.

Jerah (jē'rə), descendant of Shem. Gen. 10.26; 1 Chron. 1.20.

Jerboa, small, jumping rodent that walks upright or hops like a kangaroo.

Jerahmeel (jĕrä'mēĕl). **1** Descendant of Judah. 1 Chron. 2.9,25; 1 Sam. 27.10. **2** Levite. 1 Chron. 24.29. **3** Prince commanded by Jehoiakim to imprison Jeremiah. Jer. 36.26.

Jerash (jĕr'ăsh), ancient city: see GERASA.

Jerba (jĕr'bə) or **Jarbah** (jär'-), island (1966 pop. 62,445), 197 sq mi (510 sq km), SE Tunisia, in the Mediterranean Sea. Fruits are grown on the island, once identified as the land of the lotus eaters. It has extensive Roman remains.

jerboa (jərbō'ə), name for the small, jumping RODENTS of the family Dipodidae, found in arid parts of Asia, N Africa, and SE Europe. Jerboas have extremely long hind feet and short forelegs; they always walk upright or hop like kangaroos. A jerboa can hop faster than a person can run, and a single leap may carry it more than 6 ft (1.8 m). Jerboas have long silky fur, buff colored above and pale below; members of most species have a black face mask and tail tuft. They have large eyes and long ears. The combined head and body length is between 2 and 8 in. (5-20 cm), depending on the species; the tail is usually somewhat longer than the body. When the animal sits, the tail is used as a prop. Solitary, nocturnal animals, with a low tolerance for heat, jerboas spend the day in individual burrows with plugged entrances. In the northern parts of their range they hibernate; some jerboas of the true deserts aestivate. They feed on plant matter, especially seeds, and insects. They do not drink, but survive on water obtained from food or produced by their own metabolism. The similar appearing KANGAROO RAT and JUMPING MOUSE of North America are not of the same family as the jerboa. There are about 25 jerboa species, 22 of them in Asia. They are classified in 10 genera of the phylum CHORDATA, subphylum Vertebrata, class Mammalia, order Rodentia, family Dipodidae.

Jered (jē'rĕd). **1** Variant of JARED. **2** Judahite. 1 Chron. 4.18.

Jeremai (jĕrĕmā'ī), husband of a foreigner. Ezra 10.33.

Jeremiah (jĕrĭmī'ə). **1** Prophet of the book of JEREMIAH. **2** Father-in-law of Josiah. 2 Kings 23.31; Jer. 52.1. **3** Rechabite contemporary with Jeremiah the prophet. Jer. 35.3. **4, 5, 6** Three who joined David at Ziklag. 1 Chron. 12.4,10,13. **7** Manassite. 1 Chron. 5.24. **8, 9** Priests. Neh. 10.2; 12.1,12,34.

Jeremiah or **Jeremias** (jĕrĭmī'əs), book of the Old Testament, 24th in the order of the Authorized Version (AV), 2d of the books of the Major Prophets. It tells of the career of Jeremiah, a prophet who preached (c.628-586 B.C.) in Jerusalem under King Josiah and his successors. His message was a summons to moral reform, personal and social, backed by threats of doom. Jeremiah realistically opposed resistance to Babylon, and his insistence on unpalatable truths brought him to prison and the stocks. When Jerusalem fell to Babylon (586 B.C.), Jeremiah was allowed to stay with the Jews who remained; they took him to Egypt, where he continued prophesying. The prophecies of the book were arranged by the prophet's secretary, BARUCH. They are not in strict chronological order, and there are important differences in texts; thus there is good reason for believing that chapters 46-51 (AV) belong with chapter 25. One analysis of the book would be as follows: introduction (1-3.5); prophecies under Josiah (3.6-25; 4-24); prophecies against Gentile nations (25; 46-51); prophecies under Josiah's successors (26-38); the capture of the city (39); later prophecies and events (40-45; 52). Among the well-known Messianic passages are 14.8-9; 23.5-6; 30.9-24; 32.37-44. There are other references to Jeremiah in the Bible: 2 Chron. 35.25; Ecclus. 49.8-9; Dan. 9.2; 2 Mac. 2.1-10; Mat. 2.17; Heb. 8.8. Jeremiah was greatly influenced by the prophecies of Amos and Hosea. See LAMENTATIONS. See E. W. Nicholson, *Preaching to the Exiles* (1971); see also bibliography under OLD TESTAMENT.

Jeremoth (jĕr'ĭmōth). **1** Benjamite. 1 Chron. 8.14. **2** Levite of David. 1 Chron. 23.23. Jerimoth: 1 Chron. 24.30. **3, 4** Men who had foreign wives. Ezra 10.26,27. **5** See JERIMOTH **5.**

Jeremy (jĕr'ĭmē), English form of JEREMIAH. The **Epistle of Jeremy** is a title given to the sixth chapter of Baruch.

Jerez de la Frontera (hārāth dā lä frōntā'rä), city (1970 pop. 149,867), Cádiz prov., SW Spain, in Andalusia. Jerez is an important commercial center noted for its sherry and cognac. Its horses of mixed Spanish, Arab, and English blood are world famous. Captured by the Moors in 711, the city was recovered by Alfonso X of Castile in 1264. Of interest are its Gothic churches and an 11th-century Arabian alcazar.

Jeriah (jērī'ə), Kohathite Levite. 1 Chron. 23.19; 24.23. Jerijah: 1 Chron. 26.31.

Jeribai (jĕr'ĭbā), soldier of David. 1 Chron. 11.46.

Jericho (jĕr'ĭkō) [Heb.,=fragrant, or city of the moon god], ancient city, Palestine, in the Jordan valley N of the Dead Sea. The modern Ariha, Jordan, lies near the ancient site. Jericho was captured from the Canaanites by Joshua, according to the biblical account in Joshua 6, and was destroyed, an event several times repeated in its history. One of its conquerors was Herod the Great, who sacked and rebuilt it. Later it fell to the Muslims. Deut. 34.3; Joshua 18.21; 2 Sam. 10.5; 1 Kings 16.34; 2 Kings 2.4; 25.5; Jer. 39.5; 52.8; 1 Mac. 9.50; Mat. 20.29; Luke 10.30. Excavations of the mound of Tell es Sultan, the original site, were begun early in the 20th cent. and have revealed the oldest known settlement in the world, dating perhaps from c.8000 B.C. Because the town of Joshua was destroyed by erosion, scholars have been unable to fix the date of the conquest of Palestine but generally place it between 1400 B.C. and 1250 B.C. At the nearby site of Herodian Jericho, 2 mi (3.2 km) S of Tell es Sultan, a Hellenistic fortress and the palace of Herod have been excavated. See John Garstang and J. B. E. Garstang, *The Story of Jericho* (1948); K. M. Kenyon, *Digging Up Jericho* (1958) and *Excavations at Jericho,* Vol. 1 (1960).

Jericho, uninc. residential town (1970 pop. 14,010), Nassau co., SE N.Y., on Long Island.

Jeriel (jērī'ĕl, jĕr'ēĕl), chief Issacharite. 1 Chron. 7.2.

Jerijah (jērī'jə), variant of JERIAH.

Jerimoth (jĕr'ĭmōth). **1** Benjamite. 1 Chron. 7.7,8. **2** One who joined David at Ziklag. 1 Chron. 12.5. **3** Officer of David. 1 Chron. 27.19. **4** Son of David. 2 Chron. 11.18. **5** Levite of David. 1 Chron. 25.4. Jeremoth: 1 Chron. 25.22. **6** Levite of Hezekiah. 2 Chron. 31.13. **7** See JEREMOTH **2.**

Jerioth (jērīŏth), woman named in a genealogy. 1 Chron. 2.18.

Jeritza, Maria (yərĭt'sə), 1887–, Austrian-American soprano. b. Brünn (now Brno). After Jeritza's debut as Elsa in *Lohengrin* at Olmütz in 1910, she was a member (1912-35) of the Vienna State Opera. She created the title role in the opera *Ariadne* by Richard Strauss. Jeritza sang (1921–32) at the Metropolitan Opera, New York City, where her Tosca was renowned. See her autobiography (1924).

Jeroboam I (jĕrəbō'əm), first king of the northern kingdom of Israel. He was an Ephraimite and led a revolt against Solomon, inspired probably by the restlessness of N Palestine under southern rule. Jeroboam fled to Egypt when the plot failed but returned on the accession of Solomon's son, REHOBOAM. When the new king would not satisfy the northerners, Jeroboam led a secession, leaving the house of David only Judah and some of the area of Benjamin. Jeroboam became notorious for fostering idolatry in his kingdom of Israel. His capital was first in Shechem and later at Tirzah. Jeroboam was succeeded by his son Nadab. 1 Kings 11.26–14.20; 2 Chron. 10; 13.

Jeroboam II, king of Israel, son of Jehoash, whom he succeeded. His reign was marked by increasing prosperity and expansion northward, but also by corruption. Amos and Hosea appeared under Jeroboam. 2 Kings 14.16,23–29.

Jeroham (jērō'hăm). **1** Samuel's grandfather. 1 Sam. 1.1; 1 Chron. 6.27. **2** Priest. 1 Chron. 9.12; Neh. 11.12. **3** Father of a chief Danite. 1 Chron. 27.22. **4, 5** Benjamites. 1 Chron. 8.27; 9.8. **6** One of David's men. 1 Chron. 12.7. **7** Father of a captain of Jehoiada. 2 Chron. 23.1.

Jerome, Saint (jərōm', jĕr'əm), c.347–420?, Christian scholar, Father of the Church, Doctor of the Church. He was born in Stridon on the border of Dalmatia and Pannonia of Christian parents (although he was not baptized until 366); his Roman name was Sophronius Eusebius Hieronymus. He studied in Rome (c.359–363) under Aelius Donatus. After further study at Trier and Aquileia, he journeyed to the East. At Antioch, in 375, he experienced a vision in which Christ reproved him for his pagan studies. Renouncing his classical scholarship, he fled to the desert to live as an ascetic and to devote himself to scriptural studies, for which he learned Hebrew. In 378 he returned to Antioch, was ordained there the following year, and then went to Constantinople to study under St. Gregory Nazianzen. In 382, Jerome returned to Rome with Gregory, when Pope DAMASUS I asked them to help settle some Eastern problems; Jerome remained as papal secretary. He was acclaimed for his exposition of Scripture, and Damasus requested him to begin on a new version of the Bible. Jerome was spiritual adviser to a number of noble ladies leading conventual lives, among whom the most eminent was St. Paula. Jerome's outspoken criticism of the secular clergy, however, caused antagonism, and when Damasus died he returned East. From 386 to his death, Jerome worked in the monastery that Paula established for him in Bethlehem. There he did the bulk of revision of his Latin translations of the Bible. He also wrote commentaries on Ecclesiastes and the epistles of St. Paul, translated Origen's homilies, revised part of the Latin version of the Septuagint, and translated from the Hebrew Isaiah and other prophets, Psalms, Kings, and Job. Jerome's texts were the basis of the VULGATE. In 393 he wrote *De viris illustribus* [concerning illustrious men], biographies of 130 Christian writers. Other works include *Adversus Jovinianum* [against Jovinian], which praises virginity; a dialogue against the Pelagians; panegyrics on deceased friends (e.g., St. Paula); and brilliantly written letters, of which over 100 remain, which furnish a rare account of his time. His correspondence with St. Augustine, with whom he sometimes quarreled, is of particular interest. St. Jerome was involved in many theological and scholarly controversies, even with a long-established friend such as Rufinus. Collections of patristic literature have translations of many of his works. St. Jerome is buried in the Church of St. Mary Major in Rome. Feast: Sept. 30. See his letters (ed. by James Duff, 1942); Paul Monceaux, *St. Jerome: the Early Years* (tr. 1933); D. S. Wiesen, *St. Jerome as a Satirist* (1964).

Jerome, Jerome Klapka, 1859–1927, English humorist and playwright. His *Idle Thoughts of an Idle Fellow* (1886) and *Three Men in a Boat* (1889) gave him his reputation for genial humor. Of his dramatic works, *The Passing of the Third Floor Back* (1907), a contemporary morality play, was the most famous. See study by R. M. Favrot (1973).

Jerome, William Travers, 1859–1934, American lawyer, b. New York City. Prominent in the cause of reform, he served (1894–95) on the Lexow commission to investigate political corruption and managed (1894) the successful campaign of William L. Strong for reform mayor of New York City. He helped frame the legislation that created the court of special sessions (1894) and became (1895) justice of that court. As district attorney (1901–9) of New York co., Jerome led a continuous and independent campaign against crime and political corruption. Frequently he led surprise raids in person, notably the one against the gambling house of Richard CANFIELD. Jerome was the prosecutor in the trial of Harry K. Thaw for the murder of Stanford WHITE. See biography by Richard O'Connor (1963).

Jerome of Prague, c.1370–1416, Bohemian religious reformer. During his studies at Prague and at Oxford, Jerome was influenced by the doctrinal views of John WYCLIF. He continued to study and travel widely abroad, in constant conflict with the authorities. In 1407 he returned to Prague, where he joined forces with John HUSS in advocating Bohemian control of the Univ. of Prague and in opposing the papal bulls against Lancelot of Naples. When Huss was summoned before the Council of Constance (see CONSTANCE, COUNCIL OF), Jerome went there to defend him in 1415. Arrested while attempting to escape from the hostile churchmen, Jerome was brought back to Constance and imprisoned. After the burning of Huss, Jerome recanted his defenses of Huss and Wyclif, but his sincerity was doubted and he was not released. In 1416 he withdrew his recantation and was burned as a heretic.

Jerrold, Douglas William (jĕr'əld), 1803–57, English humorist and playwright. His plays *Blackeyed Susan* (1829) and *Time Works Wonders* (1845) were highly successful. Jerrold is best known, however, for his contributions to *Punch,* collected as *Punch's Letters to His Son* (1843) and *Mrs. Caudle's Curtain Lectures* (1846). From 1852 until his death he edited *Lloyd's Weekly Newspaper.* See study by R. M. Kelly (1972). His son, **William Blanchard Jerrold,** 1826–84, succeeded his father as editor of *Lloyd's* and was the author of plays, novels, and biographies of his father (1859) and George Cruikshank (1882).

Jersey, island (1971 pop. 72,532), 45 sq mi (117 sq km), in the English Channel, largest of the CHANNEL ISLANDS, which are dependencies of the British Crown. It is 15 mi (24 km) from the Normandy coast of France and SE of Guernsey. SAINT HELIER, the capi-

Factories in Jersey City, N.J., on the Hackensack River.

tal, is on St. Aubin's Bay. The mild climate (plants requiring subtropical conditions grow without protection), the moderate rainfall (30–35 in./76–89 cm), and the scenery have contributed to make Jersey, like other Channel Islands, a vacation resort. The soil is generally good, and large quantities of vegetables (especially potatoes, tomatoes, and broccoli) and fruits are raised; cattle raising and dairying (Jersey cattle) are important. The inhabitants are mostly of Norman descent; English, French (the official language), and a Norman dialect are spoken.

Jersey cattle, breed of dairy cattle native to the island of Jersey in the English Channel. Jerseys, smallest of the dairy breeds, are usually a shade of fawn or cream, although darker shades are common. The lighter colors are attributed to Norman ancestors, while the darker cattle are thought to have decended from breeds native to Brittany. Jerseys are adaptable to many environments and are now found throughout the world. They were first brought to the United States c.1850; among the dairy breeds they now rank second in number to HOLSTEIN-FRIESIAN CATTLE. Their milk has the highest butterfat content of any dairy breed, and when they are crossed with native stock or other breeds they usually transmit good milking qualities.

Jersey City, city (1970 pop. 260,545), seat of Hudson co., NE N.J., a port on a peninsula formed by the Hudson and Hackensack rivers and Upper New York Bay, opposite lower Manhattan; settled before 1650, inc. as Jersey City 1836. The second largest city in the state and its second most important commercial and industrial center (surpassed only by Newark), it is a port of entry and a great shipping and manufacturing center. With 11 mi (17.7 km) of waterfront and one of the world's densest concentration of railheads, it is a major transportation terminal point and distribution center. It has railroad shops, oil refineries, warehouses, and more than 600 plants manufacturing a great variety of products. The area was acquired by Michiel Pauw c.1629 as the patroonship of Pavonia. The Dutch soon set up the trading posts of Paulus Hook, Communipaw, and Horsimus. In 1674 the site came permanently under British rule. The fort at Paulus Hook was captured by Light-Horse Harry Lee under Washington's plan, Aug. 19, 1779. Bergen, nearby, was a stockaded Dutch village dating from before 1620 and had New Jersey's first municipal government, church (Dutch Reformed), and school (1662). Its site is marked today by Bergen Square. Jersey City was consolidated with Bergen and Hudson City in 1869 after various changes of title and boundaries. The town of Greenville was added in 1873. The city's industrial growth began in the 1840s with the arrival of the railroad and the improvement of its water transport system. In 1916, Jersey City docks were the scene of the Black Tom explosion that caused widespread property damage and was attributed to German saboteurs. The city was the birthplace and center of many of the political operations of Frank Hague. It has a modern medical center and is the seat of Jersey City State College and St. Peter's College. Of interest is J. E. Fraser's statue of Lincoln (1929) in Lincoln Park.

Jerubbaal (jĕr′əbāl): see GIDEON.

Jerubbesheth (jērŭb′ĕshĕth): see GIDEON.

Jeruel (jēr″yōō′ĕl), unidentified wilderness, W of the Dead Sea. 2 Chron. 20.16.

Jerusalem, Heb. *Yerushalayim,* Arab. *Al Quds,* city (1972 pop. 304,500), capital of Israel. It is situated on a ridge 2,500 ft (760 m) high that lies W of the Dead Sea and the Jordan River. Jerusalem is an administrative, religious, and cultural center. Construction and tourism are the city's major industries. Manufactures include cut and polished diamonds, plastics, and shoes. The city is served by road, rail, and air transport. Jerusalem is the holy city for Jews, Christians, and Muslims. Often under the name of Zion, it figures familiarly in Jewish and Christian literature as a symbol of the capital of the Messiah. The eastern part of Jerusalem is the Old City, a quadrangular area built on two hills and surrounded by a wall completed in 1542 by Sulayman I. Within the wall are four quarters. The Muslim quarter, in the east, contains a sacred enclosure, the Haram esh-Sherif, within which, built on the old Mt. Moriah, are the Dome of the Rock (completed 691), or Mosque of Omar, and the Mosque of al-Aksa. In 1969 portions of al-Aksa were badly damaged by fire. The wall of the Haram incorporates the only extant piece of the Temple of Solomon; this, the western wall, or Wailing Wall, is a holy place for Jews. Nearby and SW of the Haram is the Jewish quarter, with several famous old synagogues. Largely destroyed in previous Arab-Israeli fighting, it was recaptured in 1967 by the Israelis, who began to rebuild and renovate it. To the W of the Jewish quarter is the Armenian quarter, site of the Gulbenkian Library. The Christian quarter occupies the northern and northwestern parts of the Old City. Its greatest monument is the Church of the Holy Sepulcher. Through the area runs the Via Dolorosa, where Jesus is said to have carried his cross. The New City, extending W and SW of the Old City, has largely developed since the 19th cent. It is the site of several educational institutions, as well as the Knesset (the Israeli parliament) and other government buildings. To the east of the Old City is the Valley of the Kidron, across which lie the Garden of Gethsemane and the Mount of Olives. To the north is Mt. Scopus, a Jewish intellectual center, which is the site of the Hadassah Medical Center and other branches of the Hebrew Univ. and the Jewish National Library. From 1948 to 1967, Mt. Scopus was an Israeli enclave in Arab territory. To the W and S of the Old City runs the Valley of Hinnom; this meets the Kidron near the pool of Siloam, which is next to the site of the original city of Jerusalem, now partly excavated and called the City of David (see OPHEL). Jerusalem's churches and shrines are innumerable. The traditional identifications vary in reliability from certainty (such as Gethsemane) to pious supposition (such as the Tomb of the Virgin). The most famous and most difficult identification is that of Calvary. Excavations have been made in Jerusalem since 1835, and after 1967 the Israelis increased this activity, uncovering remains of the Herodian period and ruins of a Muslim structure of the 7th or 8th cent. Despite the incomplete archaeological work, it is evident that Jerusalem was occupied as far back as the 4th millenium B.C. In the late Bronze Age (2000–1550 B.C.) it was a Jebusite (Canaanite) stronghold.

Old City of Jerusalem (background) as seen from the Mount of Olives, with the Mosque of Omar (center) and an ancient Hebrew burial ground (foreground).

DAVID captured it (c.1000 B.C.) from the Jebusites and walled the city. After SOLOMON built the Temple on Mt. Moriah in the 10th cent. B.C., Jerusalem became the spiritual and political capital of the Hebrews. In 586 B.C. it fell to the Babylonians, and the Temple was destroyed. The city was restored to Hebrew rule later in the 6th cent. B.C. by CYRUS THE GREAT, king of Persia. The Temple was rebuilt (538–515 B.C.; known as the Second Temple) by ZERUBBABEL, a governor of Jerusalem under the Persians. In the mid-5th cent. B.C., EZRA reinvigorated the Jewish community in Jerusalem. The city was the capital of the MACCABEES in the 2d and 1st cent. B.C. After Jerusalem had been taken for the Romans by POMPEY, it became the capital of the HEROD dynasty, which ruled under the aegis of Rome. The Roman emperor TITUS ruined the city and destroyed the Temple (A.D. 70) in order to punish and discourage the Jews. After the revolt of BAR KOKBA (132–35), HADRIAN rebuilt the city as a pagan shrine called Aelia Capitolina but forbade the Jews to live on the site. With the imperial toleration of Christianity (from 313), Jerusalem underwent a revival, greatly aided by St. Helena, who sponsored much building in the early 4th cent. Since that time Jerusalem has been a world pilgrimage spot. The Muslims, who believe that the city was visited by MUHAMMAD, treated Jerusalem well after they captured it in 637, making it their chief shrine after Mecca. From 688 to 691 the Dome of the Rock mosque was constructed. In the 11th cent. the FATIMIDS began to hinder Christian pilgrims; their destruction of the Church of the Holy Sepulcher helped bring on the CRUSADES. Jerusalem was conquered by the Crusaders in 1099 and for most of the 12th cent. was the capital of the Latin Kingdom of Jerusalem. In 1187, Muslims under SALADIN recaptured the city. Thereafter, under Mameluke and then Ottoman rule, Jerusalem was rebuilt and restored (especially by SULAYMAN I); but by the late 16th cent. it was declining as a commercial and religious center. In the early 19th cent. Jerusalem began to revive. The flow of Christian pilgrims increased, and churches, hospices, and other institutions were built. Jewish immigration accelerated (especially from the time of the Egyptian occupation of Jerusalem by MUHAMMAD ALI in 1832–41), and by 1900, Jews made up the largest community in the city. In 1917, during World War I, Jerusalem was captured by British forces under Gen. Edmund ALLENBY. After the war it was made the capital of the British-held League of Nations PALESTINE mandate (1922–48). As the end of the mandate approached, Arabs and Jews both sought to hold sole possession of the city. Christian opinion for the most part was strongly in favor of creating a free city safe for all religions. This view prevailed in the United Nations, which, in partitioning Palestine into Arab and Jewish states, declared that Jerusalem and its environs (including Bethlehem) would be an internationally-administered enclave in the projected Arab state. Even before the partition went into effect (May 14, 1948), fighting between Jews and Arabs broke out in the city. On May 28, the Jews in the Old City surrendered. The New City remained in Jewish hands. The Old City and all areas held by the Arab Legion were annexed by Jordan in Apr., 1949. Israel responded by announcing in Nov., 1949, that it would retain the area it held. On Dec. 14, 1949, the New City of Jerusalem was made the capital of Israel. In the Arab-Israeli War of 1967, Israeli forces took the Old City. Late in June of that year the Israeli government formally annexed the Old City and placed all of Jerusalem under a unified administration. Israel transferred many Arabs out of the Old City but promised access to the holy places there to people of all religions. Jerusalem is the seat of Hebrew Univ., the British School of Archaeology, the Dominican Fathers' Convent of St. Étienne, with the attached Bible School and French Archaeological School, the American College, the Greek Catholic Seminary of St. Anne, the Pontifical Biblical Institute, the Swedish Theological Institute, the Near East School of Archaeology, the Rubin Academy of Music, the Israel Academy of Sciences and Humanities, and the Israel Museum. See L. H. Cust, *Jerusalem* (1924); James Baikie, *Ancient Jerusalem* (1930); J. J. Simons, *Jerusalem in the Old Testament* (1952); A. N. Williams, *The Holy City* (1954); Michael Avi-Yonah, ed., *Jerusalem: The Saga of the Holy City* (1954); Teddy Kollek and Moshe Perlman, *Jerusalem: Sacred History of Mankind* (1968).

Orthodox Jews praying at the western wall in Jerusalem.

Jerusalem, Latin Kingdom of, feudal state created by leaders of the First Crusade (see CRUSADES) in the areas they had wrested from the Muslims in Syria and Palestine. In 1099, after their capture of Jerusalem, the Crusaders chose GODFREY OF BOUILLON king; he declined the title, preferring that of defender of the Holy Sepulcher, but with his election the kingdom may be said to have begun. His brother and successor, BALDWIN I, took the royal title. He and his successors were nominal overlords of the principality of Antioch and the counties of Edessa and Tripoli, which, with the royal domain of Jerusalem, constituted the great fiefs of the kingdom. Jerusalem itself contained the counties of Jaffa and Ashqelon, the lordships of Krak, Montreal, and Sidon, and the principality of Galilee. Coming into existence during the height of FEUDALISM, the kingdom was based on the purest forms of feudal theory. The kingship was elective, and the Assizes of Jerusalem, the law of the country, reflected the ideal feudal law. In practice, however, irregularities soon appeared, and the kings actually were chosen on dynastic considerations. The great feudal lords rarely felt bound to their overlord in the chronic struggles of the Latins among themselves and with the Mamelukes of Egypt, the Seljuk Turks, and the Byzantine emperors. The rise of the great military orders, the KNIGHTS TEMPLARS, the KNIGHTS HOSPITALERS, and the TEUTONIC KNIGHTS, as well as the intrusion of new Crusaders further undermined the royal authority. Edessa, captured by the Seljuks in 1144, was the first Latin state to fall to the infidel. The subsequent Crusades did not halt the Muslim advance, and in 1187 Jerusalem itself fell to Sultan SALADIN after his victory at Hattin. What remained of the Latin state was virtually destroyed by the complete rout of the Christians in the battle of Gaza (1244). The Crusades of Louis IX of France and Edward I of England were failures, and in 1291 Akko, the last Christian stronghold, fell. The kings of Jerusalem of the house of Bouillon were Baldwin I (reigned 1100–1118) and Baldwin II (reigned 1118–31). The crown then passed to the ANGEVIN dynasty, beginning (1131) with Fulk and ending (1186) with Baldwin V. Although it became an empty title, the kingship of Jerusalem continued nominally until the 20th cent. On Baldwin V's death the title passed to Guy of Lusignan and then to the successive husbands of Isabella, daughter of Amalric I: Conrad, marquis of Montferrat; Henry, count of Champagne; and Amalric II, king of Cyprus. In 1210, John of Brienne received the title, which passed (1225) to his son-in-law, Holy Roman Emperor Frederick II. After Frederick's death (1250) the title was held by various families who had a claim, notably the kings of Cyprus, the Angevins, and the houses of Lorraine and Savoy. The struggles of the Latin nobles of Jerusalem against the SARACENS have furnished the material for many chivalrous romances in subsequent ages, particularly for the poets of Renaissance Italy. See studies by D. C. Munro (1966), W. B. Stevenson (1968), Aharon Ben-Ami (1969), Meron Benvinistre (1970), and J. S. C. Riley-Smith (1973).

Jerusalem artichoke, tuberous-rooted perennial (*Helianthus tuberosus*) of the family Compositae (COMPOSITE family), native to North America, where it was early cultivated by the Indians. In this particular case the name Jerusalem is a corruption of *girasole* [turning toward the sun], the Italian name for SUNFLOWER, of which this plant is one species. The edible tubers are somewhat potatolike, but the carbohydrate present is inulin rather than starch, and the flavor resembles that of artichokes. Jerusalem artichoke is more favored as a food plant in Europe (where it was introduced in 1616) and China than in North America, where it is most frequently grown as stock feed. The inulin is valuable also as a source of fructose for diabetics. Jerusalem artichokes are classified in the division MAGNOLIOPHYTA, class Magnoliopsida, order Asterales, family Compositae.

Jerusalem cherry: see NIGHTSHADE.

Jerusalem thorn, name for various plants, particularly the CHRIST'S-THORN.

Jerusha or **Jerushah** (both: jērōō'shə), mother of King Jotham of Judah. 2 Kings 15.33; 2 Chron. 27.1.

Jervis, John, earl of St. Vincent (jär'vĭs, jûr'–), 1735–1823, British admiral. His most famous action as commander of the Mediterranean fleet was his defeat in 1797 of 27 Spanish ships off Cape St. Vincent with only 15 vessels. The victory was partly due to an unauthorized attack by Horatio NELSON and might have been more complete had Jervis realized the weakness of the enemy. However, it helped to reduce British concern at a time when a French invasion of Britain was threatened. Jervis received a peerage and pension. As first lord of the admiralty (1801–6), Jervis was especially concerned with the restoration of discipline and with problems of health and hygiene. He returned (1806–7) to a sea command until his health failed. See biographies by W. V. Anson (1913), O. A. Sherrard (1933), and W. M. James (1950).

Jervis Bay (jär'vĭs), sheltered inlet of the Pacific Ocean, 10 mi (16.1 km) long and 6 mi (9.7 km) wide, SE Australia. In 1915 the harbor and part of the coast were transferred to the federal government by New South Wales. Jervis Bay, connected by rail with Canberra, 85 mi (137 km) inland, then became the port of the landlocked Australian Capital Territory. The area around the bay is a popular summer resort.

Jesaiah (jēsā'yə). **1** Descendant of Zerubbabel. 1 Chron. 3.21. **2** Benjamite ancestor of Sallu. Neh. 11.7.

Jeshaiah (jēshā'yə). **1** Chief singer. 1 Chron. 25.3,15. **2** Tribal chief accompanying Ezra. Ezra 8.7. **3** Descendant of Moses. 1 Chron. 26.25. Isshiah: 1 Chron. 24.21. **4** Merarite who returned with Ezra. Ezra 8.19.

Jeshanah (jĕsh'ənə, jēshā'nə), unidentified town, probably N of Jerusalem. 2 Chron. 13.19.

Jesharelah (jĕshərē'lə), the same as ASARELAH.

Jeshebeab (jēshĕb'ēăb), chief priest of David. 1 Chron. 24.13.

Jesher (jē'shər), Caleb's son. 1 Chron. 2.18.

Jeshimon (jĕsh'ĭmŏn), desert, the Wilderness of Judah, between the hill country and the Dead Sea. Num. 21.20; 23.28; 1 Sam. 23.19,24; 26.1,3.

Jeshishai (jēshĭsh'ā), ancestor of Gadites of Gilead. 1 Chron. 5.14.

Jeshohaiah (jĕshōhā'yə), chief of a Simeonite family. 1 Chron. 4.36.

Jeshua or **Jeshuah** (both: jĕsh'yōōə) [Heb.,=God helps]. **1** See JOSHUA. **2** See JOSHUA **2.** **3** Head of a postexilic family. Ezra 2.6; Neh. 7.11. **4** Priestly family. 1 Chron. 24.11; Ezra 2.36; Neh. 7.39. **5** Head of a Levitical family. Ezra 2.40; 3.9; Neh. 10.9; 12.8. **6** Levite. 2 Chron. 31.15. **7** Unidentified town, S Palestine. Neh. 11.26.

Jeshurun (jĕshyōō'rən), affectionate name for Israel. Deut. 32.15; 33.5,26. Jesurun: Isa. 44.2.

Jesiah (jēsī'ə). **1** Ally of David at Ziklag. 1 Chron. 12.6. **2** See ISSHIAH.

Jesimiel (jĭsĭm'ēəl), Simeonite chief. 1 Chron. 4.36.

Jespersen, Otto (ŏ'tō yĕs'pərsən), 1860–1943, Danish philologist. Professor of English language and literature at the Univ. of Copenhagen and later rector there, Jespersen first earned a reputation for brilliant work in phonetics and later wrote widely used books on the English language and linguistics in general, notably *The Growth and Structure of the English Language* (1905), *A Modern English Grammar on Historical Principles* (in parts, 1909–31), *Language* (1922), *Philosophy of Grammar* (1924), and *Analytic Syntax* (1937).

jessamine: see JASMINE.

Jesse (jĕs'ē), in the Bible, the descendant of Rahab, the grandson of Boaz and Ruth and the father of

David. He is therefore in the Gospel genealogy. Ruth 4.17–22; 1 Sam. 16.1–22; 17.12,58; 1 Chron. 2.12,13; Isa. 11.1,10; Mat. 1.5,6; Luke 3.32. Because Jesse was ancestor of the House of David, a custom of medieval artists was to represent the genealogy of Jesus as beginning from him: hence the Jesse window (as at Chartres, France, and at Wells, England), a favorite device in stained glass; hence also the epithet of the Virgin: Jesse's Root.

Jesselton: see KOTA KINABALU, Malaysia.

Jessore (jĕsōr'), city (1961 est. pop. 46,400), SW Bangladesh, on the Bhairab River. Modern Jessore, a market town for rice and sugar, also has rice and oilseed mills and celluloid and plastics industries. Michael Madhusudan College, an affiliate of Rajshahi Univ., is in the city.

Jessup, Philip Caryl, 1897–, American authority on international law, b. New York City, grad. Hamilton College, 1919, LL.B. Yale, 1924, Ph.D. Columbia, 1927. He was admitted (1925) to the bar, and from 1925 to 1961 he taught international law and diplomacy at Columbia. He served (1943) in the foreign relief and rehabilitation office in the Dept. of State and later was (1943–44) assistant secretary general of the United Nations Relief and Rehabilitation Administration and a delegate (1944) at the Bretton Woods monetary conference. Then he served (1948) in the UN General Assembly. He became (1948) U.S. delegate on the UN Security Council and took a leading part in the UN debate on the Berlin blockade. He was appointed a delegate to the UN General Assembly in 1951 and an alternate delegate in 1952. He resigned (Jan., 1953) and returned to his teaching duties at Columbia. He was later (1961–70) a judge of the International Court of Justice at The Hague. His works include a biography of Elihu Root (2 vol., 1938), *A Modern Law of Nations* (1948), *Controls for Outer Space* (1959), *The Price of International Justice* (1971), and *The Birth of Nations* (1974).

Jesui (jĕs'yo͞oī), the same as ISUI.

Jesuit: see JESUS, SOCIETY OF .

Jesuit Estates Act, law adopted in 1888 by the Quebec legislature, partly to indemnify the Society of Jesus for Jesuit property confiscated by the British during the period after the suppression (1773) of the society by Pope Clement XIV. The act caused a violent controversy in Canada, and Protestants generally demanded that it be disallowed; the federal government finally decided not to interfere with provincial legislation, and the act was allowed to stand.

Jesuit Relations, annual reports and narratives written by French Jesuit missionaries at their stations in New France (America) between 1632 and 1673. They are invaluable as historical sources for French exploration and Indian relations and also as a record of the various Indian tribes of the region before the influence of settlers and missionaries had changed them. Published originally in Paris in annual volumes, they were translated and edited by R. G. Thwaites (73 vol., 1896–1901). See bibliography by J. C. McCoy, *Jesuit Relations of Canada, 1632–1673* (1937, repr. 1973).

Jesurun (jĕsyo͞o'rən), variant of JESHURUN.

Jesus or **Jesus Christ,** in the beliefs of CHRISTIANITY, the Son of God, the second person of the TRINITY. According to traditional Christian interpretation, Jesus was God made man, wholly divine, wholly human; he was born to MARY, a virgin, and died to make ATONEMENT to God for man's sin; his resurrection from the dead provides man's hope for salvation. Christians believe that Jesus fulfilled Hebrew prophecies of the MESSIAH. The name *Jesus* is Greek for the Hebrew *Joshua,* a name meaning *Savior; Christ* is a Greek translation of the Hebrew *Messiah,* meaning *Anointed.* The primary sources for the life of Jesus are the four Gospels of Matthew, Mark, Luke, and John and the epistles of the NEW TESTAMENT (see the articles on the separate books, e.g., MATTHEW, GOSPEL ACCORDING TO SAINT; JOHN, epistles). The first three Gospels are chronological biographies, the last a biography in essay form; hence the first three harmonize, with variation of detail, while the fourth uses an order suitable to its purpose. There are many contradictions between one Gospel and another, the most important bearing on chronological issues such as the date of the Last Supper, which the first three place on the first day of Passover, while John places it before the feast. The epistles, mostly written contemporaneously with the Gospels, add very few other details. There are brief references to Jesus in non-Christian writers of the period, especially in Tacitus, Suetonius, Pliny the Younger, and Josephus (perhaps interpolated). The interest of these writers, however, was not in Jesus but in the Christians. Second-century Christian writers furnish material, some undoubtedly reliable. The apocryphal Gospels and the traditional sayings of Jesus are quite unreliable, although some, such as the Gospel of Thomas, shed light on the development of the Gospel tradition (see PSEUDEPIGRAPHA and AGRAPHA OF JESUS). The study of the historicity of Jesus was until the end of the 19th cent. impeded by two facts: his followers assumed his historicity and regarded study of it as superfluous; others assumed the Gospels to be a tissue of myth and refused to apply to the study of his life such scientific historical methods as were applied to the study of Muhammad. According to the Gospels, Jesus was born of Mary, wife of Joseph, a carpenter of Nazareth, Galilee, who had brought his wife to Bethlehem, his ancestral home, for the Roman tax-census. The Christian era is computed according to a 6th-century reckoning to begin with Jesus' birth, A.D. 1. The date is placed several years too late, for Jesus was probably born between 8 B.C. and 4 B.C. The month and day are unknown; CHRISTMAS (Dec. 25) was set as the feast several centuries later. According to the Gospels, wonderful events surrounded the birth of Jesus, particularly its annunciation to Mary by an angel (Mat. 1.18–25; Luke 1.26–56). In accordance with Jewish law Jesus was circumcised, his mother purified, and he was confirmed at the end of his boyhood (Luke 2.21–52). Jesus lived at a critical period in Jewish history. The Jews were restive under Roman rule as administered by the corrupt house of HEROD; the Temple and the religion were under the control of a party allied with the Herodians; and the provincials of Galilee and Judaea, always eager for the Messiah, looked for an immediate deliverance from Roman control. Some time before A.D. 30 an ascetic preacher drew attention in the Jordan valley by his call to repentance to prepare for the Messiah. This was JOHN THE BAPTIST. Among those he baptized was his cousin Jesus. Jesus went from his baptism into solitude, thence to emerge on a three-year mission. He was about 30 at this time. (Mat. 3; 4; Mark 1; Luke 3; 4; John 1.) Jesus went about as a wandering rabbi, accompanied by a small band of disciples (see APOSTLE) depending for their few needs largely on the charity of the people. The first and principal

part of Jesus' mission was spent in Galilee. He apparently made a sensation in the country; the Gospels describe him as performing miracles of healing. His uncompromising demands on his hearers, repeated attacks on Pharisees and scribes, and his obvious preference for the company of social outcasts and the oppressed increased the popular enthusiasm. At the end of three years he set out with his disciples for Jerusalem for the Passover. Jesus' arrival there before the Passover was apparently marked by an outburst of messianic enthusiasm, and a day or so later, Jesus created a scene in the Temple by ousting the money-changers. The clique in power, whom he consistently upbraided, now felt they had to deal not only with a revolutionary preacher, but a violent reformer as well. So they induced one of his companions, JUDAS ISCARIOT, to betray him. Jesus ate a farewell supper (the Last Supper) with his disciples and went out of the city to pray in the garden of Gethsemane. There he was arrested. He was rushed to trial before the ecclesiastical court of the Sanhedrin. Jesus' claims to be the Messiah and the Son of God were taken as grounds to convict him of blasphemy, a crime in Jewish law worthy of death. The Roman governor, PONTIUS PILATE, who alone could order a man's death, tried to evade action, but he then yielded to the demand of Jewish authorities and delivered Jesus to be crucified. A sign was placed on the cross reading, "The King of the Jews." On the third day after his death, according to the Gospels, some women going to his tomb found it opened and the body of Jesus gone. An angel at the tomb told them that he had risen from the dead. Soon they saw him and talked with him, and his disciples (and others) met him as well. (Mat. 28; Mark 16; Luke 24; John 20; 21; 1 Cor. 15.3–8.) The

Jesus, depicted as the Good Shepherd in a Byzantine mosaic of the mausoleum of Galla Placida, Ravenna, Italy.

Gospels end at this point, but the book of Acts tells how, 40 days after the Resurrection, he ascended into heaven in the sight of his disciples. The Christian calendar revolves around the life of Jesus; his principal feasts are (in the Western Church) the Annunciation (March 25), Christmas (Dec. 25) with its preparation in ADVENT, the Circumcision (Jan. 1), the EPIPHANY (Jan. 6), CANDLEMAS (Feb. 2), and the Transfiguration (Aug. 6). The EASTER cycle of movable feasts and fasts begins with LENT, which ends in HOLY WEEK; after Easter comes the Ascension. Sunday is the Christian weekly memorial of the Resurrection, and among Roman Catholics and Orthodox Eastern, Friday commemorates the Crucifixion. The original source for the life of Jesus is the New Testament; biblical archaeology and studies of early Palestine have uncovered nothing unequivocally related to Jesus himself. Biographies repeat the Bible stories from particular points of view; Ernest Renan's *Life of Jesus* (1864) is rationalistic and skeptical, Giovanni Papini's biography (1921) is sentimentally pious; Albert Schweitzer's *Quest of the Historical Jesus* (1906, tr. 1910) is brilliantly selective and makes use of the knowledge of early Palestine.

Jesus in Art. No documented portraits of Jesus have survived. In EARLY CHRISTIAN ART AND ARCHITECTURE he was symbolized by a monogram, a fish, or a lamb, or was represented as the Good Shepherd. In the 4th cent. Jesus was depicted as an idealized, beardless youth, but this figuration was gradually altered to that of a bearded ascetic, particularly in BYZANTINE ART (see also ICON). In medieval art he was represented as Judge or Ruler, or as the Infant Jesus, usually with the Madonna.

Jesus. **1** Son of Sirach, author of ECCLESIASTICUS. **2** or **Jesus Justus,** converted Jew in Rome. Col. 4.11. **3** Hero of the book of JOSHUA.

Jesus, Society of, religious order of the Roman Catholic Church. Its members are called Jesuits. St. IGNATIUS OF LOYOLA, its founder, named it *Compañía de Jesús* [Span.,=(military) company of Jesus]; in Latin it is *Societas Jesu* (abbr. S.J.). The largest single religious order, it is characterized by a highly disciplined organization, especially devoted to the pope and ruled by its general, who lives in Rome. Jesuits have no choral office; like the secular clergy they are under obligation to individually recite the divine office each day. They have no distinctive habit. In principle they may accept no ecclesiastical office or honor. Jesuit training is famous and may last for more than 15 years. The novice spends two years in spiritual training, after which he takes the simple vows of the regulars—chastity, poverty, and obedience. Then as a scholastic he spends 13 years and sometimes longer in study and teaching, completed by an additional year of spiritual training. Toward the end of this period he is ordained and becomes a coadjutor. He may then take a fourth vow of special obedience to the pope and become professed. The society had its beginnings in the little band of six who together with St. Ignatius took vows of poverty and chastity while students at Paris. Their first plan was to work for the conversion of Muslims. Unable to go to the Holy Land because of the Turkish wars, they went to Rome and received ordination. Their constitution was approved by Pope Paul III (1540), and St. Ignatius was made (1541) general. The order then immediately began to expand. The society has distinguished itself in three principal fields: foreign missions, schools, and studies in the sciences and humanities. One of the most brilliant of all foreign missionaries was St. FRANCIS XAVIER (see also MISSIONS); his work in the East was continued by a host of Jesuits. The mission in Japan was wiped out by persecution in the early 17th cent., but when Japan was reopened to the West in the 19th cent. a number of Christians were found there, descendants of these martyrs. The most distinguished early figures of the Chinese mission were Fathers Matteo Ricci, Adam Schall, and Ferdinand Verbiest in the 17th cent.; a characteristic of their mission was their popularity at court, where they were revered as men of wisdom and science. There were persecutions and martyrdoms, but the original Jesuit foundation became the nucleus of the Roman Catholic Church in that country. The Indian mission began under the aegis of the Portuguese in Goa, whence it spread over the country; one of the most remarkable Jesuits in this mission was Robert de' Nobili, who, after arduous asceticism and study, won recognition as an equal of the Brahmans. The Jesuits worked all over Latin America; among their number was St. PETER CLAVER. The most remarkable missions were in Paraguay. In French North America the Jesuits came frequently into rivalry with the government and the other clergy; their missions among the Huron were especially successful, and they made headway among the Iroquois. The "Black-Robes," as the Indians called them, traveled as far afield as Oregon. Some of these Jesuits died as martyrs for their faith (c.1640); six of them have been canonized together, with two of their lay helpers, as the Jesuit Martyrs of North America (feast: Sept. 26). The JESUIT RELATIONS is a firsthand account of Jesuit work in New France. The suppression of the order in Canada in 1791 and its later readmission as a teaching order led to the JESUIT ESTATES ACT. In Europe the Jesuits were a major force in the Catholic Reformation. They sought to reclaim Protestant Europe for the church and to raise the spiritual tone of the Catholic countries. They enjoyed considerable success in W and S Germany, France, Hungary, and Poland. In nearly every important city the Jesuits established schools and colleges, and for 150 years they were leaders in European education. One of their boldest efforts was the English mission of 1580, distinguished by Saint Edmund CAMPION. Another celebrated English Jesuit was Robert Southwell. The Jesuits eventually became the object of criticism from vested ecclesiastical interests in every Catholic state. The Gallican party in France, being antipapal, was naturally anti-Jesuit. The polemics of Blaise Pascal and the Jansenists against Jesuit casuistry and alleged laxity in confessional practice were damaging. Through their loyalty to papal policies, the Jesuits were drawn into the struggle between the papacy and the Bourbon monarchies. Before the middle of the 18th cent. a combination of publicists (including Voltaire) and the absolute monarchs of Catholic Europe undertook to destroy them. In 1759 the Jesuits were expelled from Portugal and its colonies, France suppressed them in 1764, and in 1767 the Spanish dominions were closed to them. Pope Clement XIII denounced these acts, but, in 1773, CLEMENT XIV, under the coercion of the Bourbon monarchs and of some of his own cardinals, dissolved the order, and the Society of Jesus ceased to exist in the Catholic world. Frederick the Great and Catherine the Great refused to publish the brief suppressing them, and the Jesuits continued to exist in Prussia and Russia, especially as educators. As the 18th cent. drew to a close Catholic Europe, especially Italy, began to ask for restoration of the Jesuits, and, in 1814, Pius VII reestablished them as a world order. Today the society numbers over 31,000 members; in the United States, where there were approximately 5,000 Jesuits in 1973, there are many Jesuit schools and colleges (e.g., Georgetown, Fordham, and St. Louis universities). The order has a tradition of learning and science; e.g., the BOLLANDISTS are Jesuits, and Jesuits have made a specialty of the study of earthquakes. Pierre TEILHARD DE CHARDIN is the most famous Jesuit scientist of this century. Among the great organizers and theologians of the order are St. FRANCIS BORGIA, Claudio AQUAVIVA, Saint Robert BELLARMINE, Luis MOLINA, and Francisco SUÁREZ. See T. A. Hughes, *History of the Society of Jesus in North America* (3 vol., 1907–17, repr. 1970); T. J. Campbell, *The Jesuits, 1534–1921* (1921, repr. 1971); James Brodrick, *Origin of the Jesuits* (1940, repr. 1971) and *Progress of the Jesuits* (1947); Theodore Maynard, *Saint Ignatius and the Jesuits* (1956); T. J. M. Burke, ed., *Beyond All Horizons* (1957); Christopher Hollis, *History of the Jesuits* (1968); W. V. Baugert, *A History of the Society of Jesus* (1972).

Jesus Island or **Île-Jésus,** Que., Canada: see LAVAL.

Jesus Justus: see JESUS 2.

jet, black variety of lignite. Compact and homogeneous, it takes a good polish and is easily made into beads and other ornaments. The chief source of the world's supply is Yorkshire, England, although commercially valuable deposits exist in several countries, notably the United States, Spain, France, and Germany. Imitations of jet include anthracite, black glass, and black quartz.

Jether (jē'thər). **1** Eldest of Gideon's sons. He was killed by his brother Abimelech. Judges 8.20; 9. **2** Husband of David's sister Abigail. 1 Kings 2.5,32; 1 Chron. 2.17. Ithra: 2 Sam. 17.25. **3, 4** Judahites. 1 Chron. 2.32; 4.17. **5** Descendant of Asher. 1 Chron. 7.38. See ITHRAN **1.**

Jetheth (jē'thĕth), duke of Edom and descendant of Esau. Gen. 36.40; 1 Chron. 1.51.

Jethlah (jĕth'lə), unidentified town of Dan, NW of Jerusalem. Joshua 19.42.

Jethou: see CHANNEL ISLANDS.

Jethro (jĕth'rō), Midianite priest of the peninsula of Sinai who was the companion and father-in-law of Moses. Ex. 2.21; 3.1; 4.18; 18. Reuel: Ex. 2.18. Raguel: Num. 10.29. Hobab: Judges 4.11. Hobab is given once as the name of a brother-in-law of Moses. Num. 10.29.

jet propulsion, propulsion of a body by a force developed in reaction to the ejection of a high-speed jet of gas. In the combustion chamber of a jet propulsion engine the combustion of a fuel mixture generates expanding gases, which escape through an orifice to form the jet. Newton's third law of motion requires that the force which causes the high-speed motion of the jet of gas have a reaction force that is equal in magnitude and oppositely directed to push on the jet propulsion engine. Hence the term "reaction motor" is often applied to jet-propulsion engines. The first reaction engine, the aeolipile, was constructed by the inventor Heron of Alexandria. Developments through the centuries have resulted in two general types of reaction machines, the true ROCKET and the airstream engine, commonly known as the jet engine. Unlike a jet engine, a rocket engine carries with it chemicals that enable it to burn its fuel without drawing air from an outside source. Thus a rocket can operate in outer space, where there is no atmosphere. Fritz von Opel, a German automobile manufacturer, made the first flight entirely by rocket power in 1939. The American R. H. GODDARD did much of the important pioneer work in modern rocket development. The second category of jet-propulsion motor, the jet engine, is a development of the late 18th-century gas turbine engines, which directed the combustion gases against the blades of a turbine wheel. Not until 1908 was it suggested that an aircraft could be driven by jet propulsion. René Lorin, a French engineer, proposed using the reciprocating engine to compress air, mix it with fuel, and thus propel the aircraft by the pulses of hot gas produced by combustion of the mixture. In 1939 the English engineer Frank WHITTLE developed a jet engine that powered a full-sized aircraft, and a year later Secundo Campini in Italy flew for 10 min with a thermal jet engine. Both of their machines had the four basic parts of a jet engine—compressor, turbine, combustion chamber, and propelling nozzles. Air is compressed and led through chambers where its volume is increased by the heat of fuel combustion. On emergence it spins the compression rotors, which act on the inflow of air. Intermittent duct jet propulsion does not operate with a continuous blast, as does the thermal jet, but proceeds by a series of pulses, or intermittent explosions. The ram-jet, or continuous duct, engine relies on its own forward motion to compress the air that enters it. It can be used only as an auxiliary power supply because its action commences only after sufficient speed has been attained. Jet-propelled aircraft have almost completely replaced propeller-driven types in all cases where

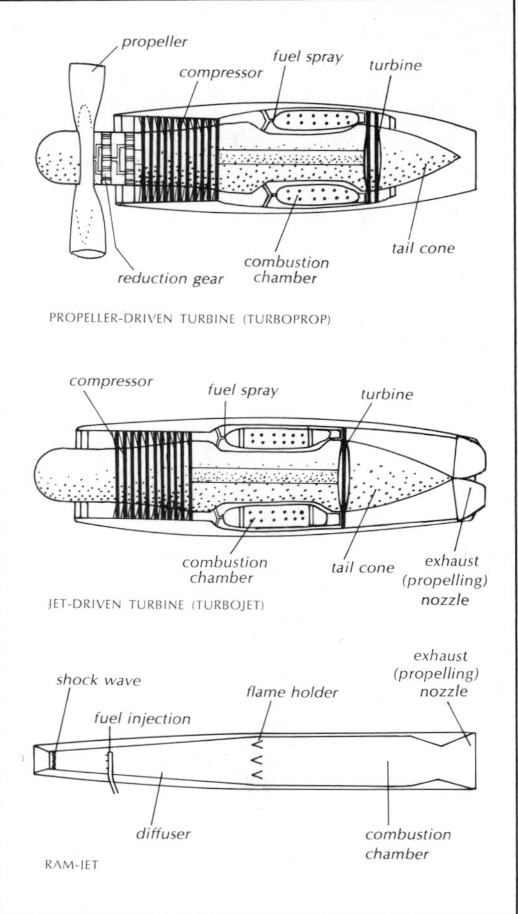

Types of jet engines: In the propeller-driven turbine a stream of high-velocity gases provides the power to drive the turbine and turn the propeller. In the jet-driven turbine the stream of gases is ejected through exhaust nozzles to provide propulsion. In the ram-jet the forward motion of the engine at high speeds compresses the entering air so that a separate compressor is not necessary.

high speed is desirable, as in long-range commercial airliners. Thrust-augmentation methods used to increase, at given moments, the effective driving force of jet engines are the afterburner, the water-injection, and air bleed-off methods. The afterburner method uses the exhaust gases from the engine for additional combustion with resulting higher compression; however, it consumes large amounts of fuel. The introduction of water into the air-compressor inlet also increases the thrust but can be used only at take-off because of the high water consumption. The air bleed-off, sometimes called the fan augmentation method, also makes more efficient use of air otherwise wasted. Some jet-propelled aircraft are capable of flight speeds well above the speed of sound. See TURBINE.

jetsam: see FLOTSAM.

jet stream, narrow, swift current of air found at heights ranging from 7 to 8 mi (11.3–12.9 km) above the surface of the earth. There are two major jet streams. Although discontinuous at some points, they circle the globe at mid-latitudes, one in each hemisphere, and move in an easterly direction. The mean winter position of the stream in the Northern Hemisphere is lat. 30°N, shifting northward to a mean summer position of lat. 40°N. Wind speeds average 35 mi (56.3 km) per hr in summer and 75 mi (120.7 km) per hr in winter, although speeds as high as 200 mi (321.9 km) per hr have been recorded. Instead of moving along a straight line, the jet stream flows in a wavelike fashion; the waves propagate eastward at speeds considerably slower than the wind speed itself. Since the progress of an airplane is aided or impeded depending on whether tail winds (in the direction of flight) or head winds (opposite to the direction of flight) are encountered, the jet stream is sought by eastbound aircraft, in order to gain speed and save fuel, and avoided by westbound aircraft. For this reason eastbound flights are usually faster.

jettison (jĕt'əsən, -zən) [O.Fr.,=throwing], in maritime law, casting all or part of a ship's cargo overboard to lighten the vessel or to meet some danger, such as fire. Such cargo, when found later, is known as jetsam (see FLOTSAM, JETSAM, AND LIGAN). The master of the ship has the absolute right to jettison cargo when he reasonably believes it to be necessary, and the owners of the ship incur no liability. If the vessel carries goods of more than one shipper, the rule of general average provides for apportioning the loss among all the shippers because all have benefited by the master's action. On the other hand, if some cargo is lost by accident, the shippers who suffered no loss do not contribute to indemnification.

jetty: see COAST PROTECTION.

Jetur (jē'tər), son of Ishmael, eponymous founder of Ituraea. 1 Chron. 1.31.

Jeuel (jo͞o'ĕl), chief of Judah. 1 Chron. 9.6.

Jeush (jē'əsh). **1** Son of Esau. Gen. 36.5,14,18; 1 Chron. 1.35. **2** Head of a Benjamite family. 1 Chron. 7.10. **3** Gershonite Levite. 1 Chron. 23.10,11. **4** Son of Rehoboam and Abihail. 2 Chron. 11.18,19.

Jeux Floraux, Académie des (äkädämē' dā jö flôrō') [Fr.,=academy of floral games], one of the oldest known literary societies. It was founded (c.1323) at Toulouse, France, by seven troubadours to uphold the traditions of courtly lyricism. It promulgated (c.1355) a code of poetry known as the laws of love. With the decay of troubadour tradition, its literary contest (established 1324 and held in modern times in Toulouse on May 3) began to change. In place of LANGUE D'OC, French became, after 1539, the sole language of contributions. The society received its present title from Louis XIV in 1694. The group supported romanticism; 19th-century winners of its traditional golden flower included Chateaubriand and Hugo. In 1895, on the urging of Frédéric Mistral, *langue d'oc* was readmitted on a par with French in its contests.

Jeuz (jē'əz), chief Benjamite. 1 Chron. 8.10.

Jevons, William Stanley (jĕv'ənz), 1835–82, English economist and logician. After working in Australia as assayer to the mint, he taught at Owens College, Manchester, and University College, London. His major contribution to economics was his theory of utility; Jevons held that value was determined by utility, and he demonstrated the relationship in mathematical terms. *The Theory of Political Economy* (1871) was his chief theoretical work. His practical application of economics in *The Coal Question* (1865) influenced government action. His several texts include *Pure Logic* (1863) and *The Principles of Science* (1874). See his *Letters and Journal* (ed. by his wife, 1886); study by E. W. Eckard (1940).

Jewel Cave National Monument: see NATIONAL PARKS AND MONUMENTS (table).

jewelry, personal adornments worn for ornament or utility, to show rank or wealth, or to follow superstitious custom or fashion. The most universal forms are the necklace, bracelet, RING, PIN, and EARRING. Its use antedates clothing, and it has been made of a variety of materials including berries, nuts, seeds, perforated stones, feathers, hair, teeth, bone, shells, ivory, and metals. Although bronze and silver have been used by primitive peoples and in modern handwrought jewelry, gold has been the preferred metal. Jewelry has been decorated by engraving, embossing, etching, and filigree, and by application of enamel, mosaic, GEMS, semiprecious stones, and glass. The art reached an elaborate development in the Orient with its wealth of precious stones and pearls. Egyptian relics show a rare craftsmanship. The jewelry is largely emblematic, very colorful, and displays lotus flower and scarab motifs. Beads were used extensively, as in broad collars, and were often used for bartering. Armlets and anklets were also worn. The Greeks were highly expert goldsmiths and preferred exquisitely wrought ornaments of metal unadorned with color. After 400 B.C. precious stones were set in gold; later the cameo was used. Roman jewelry, although based on Greek and Etruscan forms, was massive and valued rather for precious stones and cameos than for artistic settings. Ropes of pearls were especially prized. Byzantine jewelry, influenced by the East and lavish in color and design, was of composite Greek and Roman styles. Jewelry of the Middle Ages was massive; large brooches and girdles predominated. Amber was worn as a protection against evil spirits. After 1300 glass beads were used. The Renaissance brought a transformation in the art of the jeweler; noted artists and architects often designed or even rendered pieces of jewelry. Jewelry was splendid with enamel and precious stones; heavy gold link chains, jeweled collars, and the necklace with pendant were worn by both men and women. Jewelry, worn to excess, became overcrowded with stones, to the neglect of the design and setting. By the late 17th cent. the goldsmith and enameler gave way before the lapidary and mounter. A process of making imitation pearls was first discovered in 1680; thereafter, ropes of pearls became highly popular for women. In the late 18th cent. the fashion for decorative buttons, watches, and snuff boxes almost superseded the wearing of jewelry. After 1800 the bracelet, which had dwindled (c.1500) in importance with the ruffed and cuffed long sleeve, was again in favor. The 19th cent. also saw the revival of the cameo and the introduction of the watch and chain and sets of jewelry. With the introduction of factory-made ornaments, artistry of workmanship declined. In the 20th cent. platinum became popular for settings; costume jewelry, which followed the rapidly changing fashions in dress, was introduced (by Gabrielle Chanel), as was the wristwatch. There was a renewal of enthusiasm for handwrought pieces during the

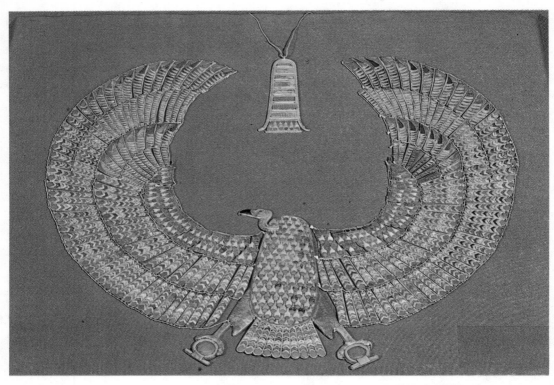

Examples of jewelry: ancient Egyptian ornamental collar representing a vulture made of gold, coralline, and glass, found in the tomb of King Tutankhamen (above).

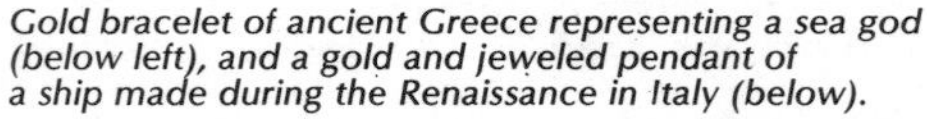

Gold bracelet of ancient Greece representing a sea god (below left), and a gold and jeweled pendant of a ship made during the Renaissance in Italy (below).

craft revival of the 1960s in the United States. See Frances Rogers and Alice Beard, *5,000 Years of Gems and Jewelry* (1940); Graham Hughes, *Modern Jewelry: 1890–1963* (1963); Joan Evans, *A History of Jewelry: 1100–1870* (2d ed. 1970); Anita Mason, *An Illustrated Dictionary of Jewellery* (1974).

jewelweed, common name for the Balsaminaceae, a family of widely distributed annual and perennial herbs. The principal genus is *Impatiens,* so named because of the sudden bursting of the seed capsules when touched. It is found in tropical and north temperate regions and is especially abundant in the mountains of India and Sri Lanka (Ceylon). A few species are commonly cultivated as ornamentals, e.g., the garden balsam (*I. balsamina*). *I. noli-me-tangere,* ranging from Europe to Japan, is the species most often called touch-me-not. The native American species (two in the East and three in the far West) are known as jewelweeds, snapweeds, and touch-me-nots, the names being used interchangeably and sometimes applied to the whole genus. They grow in damp, shady places. The orange or yellow flowers dangle from the branches and have spurs filled with nectar that attracts bumblebees and hummingbirds. The orange sap is a traditional remedy for poison ivy and has also been used as a dye. Water on the leaves produces a silvery sheen that gives these plants the local name silverleaf. The jewelweed family is classified in the division MAGNOLIOPHYTA, class Magnoliopsida, order Geraniales.

Jewett, Charles Coffin (jo͞o'ĭt), 1816–68, American librarian, b. Lebanon, Maine. Jewett prepared his first catalog of books as librarian of Andover Theological Seminary. He was appointed librarian of Brown Univ. in 1841, where he rearranged and cataloged that library by subjects. In 1848 he became librarian of the Smithsonian Institution. There he published a survey of U.S. libraries and started mechanical duplication of individual catalog entries. As superintendent of the Boston Public Library from 1858 to 1865, Jewett worked out catalog rules which were adopted internationally.

Jewett, Sarah Orne, 1849–1909, American novelist and short-story writer, b. South Berwick, Maine. As a child she accompanied her father, a physician, on his country visits and became well acquainted with the countryside and its people. Her studies of small-town New England life are perceptive, sympathetic, and gently humorous. After contributing to periodicals, she published her first collection of stories and sketches, *Deephaven,* in 1877. It was followed by such collections as *The King of Folly Island* (1888) and her masterpiece, *The Country of the Pointed Firs* (1896). Her novels include *The Marsh Island* (1885) and *The Tory Lover* (1901); her best-known novel, *A Country Doctor* (1884), relates the conflicts of a woman physician. See her letters (ed. by Richard Cary, rev. ed. 1967); biography by F. O. Matthiessen (1929, repr. 1965); studies by Richard Cary (1962) and Richard Cary, ed. (1973).

jewfish: see GROUPER.

Jewish Autonomous Oblast or **Birobidzhan** (bērōbējän'), autonomous region (1970 pop. 173,000), c.13,800 sq mi (35,700 sq km), Khabarovsk Kray, Far Eastern USSR, in the basins of the Biro and Bidzhan rivers, tributaries of the Amur. The capital is Birobidzhan. The region is bounded on the south by Mongolia and on the north by the Bureya and Khingan mts., which yield gold, tin, iron ore, and graphite. Mining, agriculture (chiefly carried on in the Amur plain), lumbering, and light manufacturing are the major economic activities. Formed in 1928 to give Soviet Jews a home territory and to increase settlement along the vulnerable borders of the Soviet Far East, the region was raised to the status of an autonomous oblast in 1934. Russians and Ukrainians outnumber the Jewish inhabitants, however, and the harsh climate has discouraged settlement. Despite some remaining Yiddish influences, Jewish cultural activity in the oblast has declined since an anti-Semitic campaign launched in the late years of Stalin's rule.

Jewish literature: see HEBREW LITERATURE; Yiddish language.

Jewish liturgical music. The Bible and the Talmud record that spontaneous music making was common among the ancient Jews on all important occasions, religious and secular. Hebrew music was both instrumental and vocal. Singing was marked by responsorial and antiphonal forms, and singing and dancing were accompanied by instruments. The first instruments mentioned in the Bible are the kinnor, evidently a lyre similar to the KITHARA and the *ugab,* possibly a vertical flute. Other instruments, more of ceremonial than of musical value, included the *hasosra,* a trumpet, and the *shofar,* a ram's or goat's horn, the least musical of all and the only one still in use. When the kingdom of Israel was established, music was developed systematically. The part played by music in the Temple was essential and highly developed. New instruments were the nevel, a harp; the *halil,* possibly a double oboe; the asor, a 10-stringed instrument probably like a psaltery; and the *magrepha,* an instrument of powerful sound, used to signal the beginning of the service. Various types of cymbals originally used in the Temple were prohibited after its restoration. Ritual music was at first only cantillation, i.e., recitative chanting, of the prose books of the Bible; later the prayers and biblical poetry were chanted, presumably in a modal system similar to the ragas of Hindu music or the *maqamat* of Arab music, i.e., melodies with improvisations. After the destruction of Jerusalem under Roman rule in A.D. 70, much of the chant was preserved among congregations of Oriental Jews and remains intact today, but the instrumental music was lost when the dispersed peoples, as an act of mourning, ceased playing instruments. A system of mnemonic hand signs for traditional chant had been developed in the Temple, and this after the Dispersion became the base for the development of a system of notation. In the 9th cent., Aaron ben Asher of Tiberias perfected the *te'amim,* or *neginoth,* a system of accent signs. His notation superseded all other systems and influenced the development of the earliest Christian neumes, which became a precise system while the *te'amim* retained their vague character (see MUSICAL NOTATION). With the growth in importance of the synagogue came the rise of the chazan, or CANTOR. Among the Sephardic Jews in Arab-dominated Spain, Arab music had great influence and was introduced into the synagogue. Later the Ashkenazim (Jewish communities that had their original European base in Germany) accepted some of the melodic forms of German folk song and Italian court song; this adaptation was more or less successfully opposed by traditionalists who reintroduced elements from the song of the Oriental Jews. The post-Renaissance cantors developed a distinct type of coloratura, which was popular in 17th-century Europe. In the early 19th cent., instruments were introduced into

Polish Jews arrested by German soldiers in World War II.

some German synagogues, and other changes resulted from adaptations of Christian music. In the reform movement of the 19th cent., the cantor was eliminated, the organ was employed, and Jewish hymns were written in the vernacular and often set to tunes of Protestant hymns. Reaction against this movement brought a more moderate reform in which the Viennese cantor Salomon Sulzer (1804–90) was an outstanding figure. Sulzer aimed to restore the traditional cantillation, but without improvisation, and to make use of new music composed for the synagogue. He used the organ and included hymns in the vernacular. Sulzer's compositions, together with those of Louis Lewandowski (1821–94), another great reformer and the leading cantor of his day in Berlin, formed the basis of much modern synagogue music. In Eastern Europe, Hasidic influence was felt from the late 18th cent. Two major Eastern European composers of traditional music were the Russian cantors Eliezer Gerowitch (1844–1914) and David Nowakowsky (1849–1921). In the United States, the reform synagogues make extensive use of hymns, mixed choirs and soloists, and organ compositions. There is a cantor in modern orthodox and conservative services but the organ is used only in some conservative services. Several 20th-century musicians, notably Ernest BLOCH and Gershon Ephros, have composed new works for the reformed and traditional services, respectively. See Eric Werner, *The Sacred Bridge* (1959); A. Z. Idelsohn, *Jewish Music in its Historical Development* (1967); A. M. Rothmüller, *The Music of the Jews* (tr. 1954, rev. ed. 1967); Alfred Sendrey, *Music in Ancient Israel* (1969).

Jews [from Judah], originally descendants of Judah, the fourth son of Jacob, whose tribe, along with that of his half brother Benjamin, made up the kingdom of Judah; the term later came to designate followers of the religion JUDAISM. Before World War II the Jewish population, scattered over the world, amounted to about 16 million; it is estimated that some 6 million Jews perished in massacres during the war. There were about 14 million Jews in the world in the early 1970s, with 7 million in the Americas, 4 million in Europe and 3 million in Africa and Asia. The nations with the largest Jewish populations were the United States (about 5.8 million), the Soviet Union (about 3 million), and Israel (about 2.8 million). HEBREW, the national language of Israel, is rapidly becoming the common language of usage between the Jews of many nations replacing YIDDISH and Ladino (see SEPHARDIM). In the Bible, Jewish history begins with the patriarchs Abraham, Isaac, and Jacob, who considered Canaan (an area comprising present-day Israel and parts of Egypt and Jordan) their home. Their history continues in Goshen, NE Egypt, where they settled as agriculturists many centuries before the Christian era. Under Ramses II the Jews were severely persecuted, and finally Moses led them out of Egypt; at Mt. Sinai he delivered to them the Ten Commandments. Many years of wandering in desert wildernesses followed before the Jews conquered Canaan. Their enemies at this time were the Philistines, and the Jews, who had been divided under tribal leaders called judges, came to see the need for union; Saul became the first king. Initially successful against the Philistines, he was finally defeated at Gilboa. David, of the tribe of Judah, ruled, conquered the enemies of the Jews, expanded his territory across the Jordan River, and brought prosperity and peace to his people. The reign of his son Solomon, who built the first TEMPLE, was the last before a period of disruption, caused partly by Solomon's system of heavy taxation. The tribes of the north united under Jeroboam, previously one of Solomon's officers, and formed the kingdom of Israel; those of the south, led by Solomon's son Rehoboam, formed the smaller but more strongly united

Menorah, an important Jewish ritual object, standing in the garden of Israel's Knesset in Jerusalem.

kingdom of Judah. The two kingdoms were constantly threatened during much of the following two centuries (935 B.C.–725 B.C.) as powerful states emerged to the east and west. In 722 B.C., Sargon II captured Samaria, capital of Israel, and most of the Israelites (the LOST TRIBES) were exiled. Judah passed under Assyrian domination, then under Egyptian, and in 586 B.C., under Babylonian, when the Temple was destroyed and the people were exiled until their return was permitted by CYRUS THE GREAT (538 B.C.). The rebuilding of the Temple was completed in 516 B.C. The Jews remained a strong religious group during the period of Hellenism, but regained political independence only under the MACCABEES. Strife between the PHARISEES and the SADDUCEES ended in Roman intervention and complete dominance, and Jerusalem was eventually destroyed in A.D. 70. A rebellion, led by BAR KOKBA against the Romans in the 2d cent. A.D., ended in defeat. As political aspirations subsided, Jewish life was increasingly led by scholars and rabbis. Its center remained in the Middle East until, following the organization of new kingdoms upon the ruins of the Roman Empire, Jews migrated to Western Europe and began to play an important part in its intellectual and economic life. From the 9th to the 12th cent. they enjoyed a golden age of literary efflorescence, particularly in Spain. From the time of the Crusades date the persecutions that persisted until the 18th cent. During this period the ownership of land and most occupations other than petty trading and moneylending were forbidden to them; the GHETTO came into existence. The Jews, who had earlier been an agricultural people became an urban population. In 1290 the Jews were expelled from England; in 1392 from France; in 1492 from Spain, under TORQUEMADA; in 1497 from Portugal. Many of the exiles perished; others found asylum in the Netherlands and in the Turkish possessions. The German Jews fled to Poland, but there too they were subjected to persecution. When a country suffered economically or in war, its Jews were likely to be the scapegoat. Their helplessness and their staunch religious faith gave rise to several messianic movements; one of the most important was led by SABBATAI ZEVI. The rise of capitalism provided the conditions for Jews to improve their economic lot throughout Europe, and the revolutionary sentiments at the end of the 18th cent. also contributed toward a more liberal attitude by many governments. Modern political emancipation of the Jews began with the American and French revolutions. In Germany and Austria emancipation of the Jews was proclaimed after the Revolution of 1848. In Russia, birthplace of the POGROM, equal rights were granted them shortly before the Bolsheviks took power in 1917; Soviet Russia established an autonomous Jewish state in remote Birobidzhan (see JEWISH AUTONOMOUS OBLAST, USSR), although Judaism, along with all other religions, was proscribed until 1936. In the late 1940s anti-Semitism again surfaced in the Soviet Union. In Rumania, Jews gained equal rights only at the end of World War I. The gradual emancipation of the Jews brought forth two opposed movements: cultural assimilation, first propounded by Moses MENDELSSOHN, and ZIONISM, founded by Theodor HERZL in 1896. A wave of persecution that had started in Russia after the assassination (1881) of Alexander II and moved westward to France temporarily abated. Then, beginning in 1933, with the rise to power in Germany of the Nazis, persecution of Jews became increasingly widespread and violent; their property was confiscated and thousands were driven into exile (see ANTI-SEMITISM; HOLOCAUST). After the Nazi concentration camps, massacres, and population displacements in World War II, great numbers of Jews sought refuge in Palestine. With the establishment of a Jewish state (see ISRAEL) in 1948, the Jews finally had a homeland that welcomed the immigration of Jews from other countries. Since then, Arab-Jewish relations have been marked by hostility, erupting in the Arab-Israeli Wars of 1956, 1967, and 1973. Jews have been in what is now the United States since 1654 and were prominent in its early history. However, it was not until the period c.1880 to 1922 that the great influx of European Jews, some 2.5 million, took place. A second, continuing, influx has taken place since the 1930s due to persecutions in various nations of Europe and Asia. See Heinrich Graetz, *History of the Jews* (6 vol., 1926; repr. 1956); Poul Borchsenius, *The History of the Jews* (1965); Ruth Gay, *Jews in America* (1965); A. L. Sachar, *A History of the Jews* (5th ed. 1965); E. H. Flannery, *Anguish of the Jews* (1966); Charles Raddock, *Portrait of a People* (2d ed. 1967); Abba Eban, *My People* (1968); Cecil Roth, *The Jewish Contribution to Civilization* (3d ed. 1956) and *A Short History of the Jewish People* (rev. ed. 1969); S. W. Baron, *A Social and Religious History of the Jews* (14 vol., 1952–1969); Louis Finkelstein, ed., *The Jews* (3 vol., 4th ed. 1970–71).

Jewsbury, Geraldine Endsor, 1812–80, English novelist. She is remembered as much for her friendship with the Carlyles and other literary people as for her novels, which include *Zoe* (1845) and *The Sorrows of Gentility* (1856). See biography by Susanne Howe (1935).

jew's-harp or **jews'-harp,** musical instrument of ancient lineage composed of a small metal frame containing a flexible metal tongue. The frame is held between the teeth and the metal tongue is plucked with the fingers. Each jew's-harp can produce only one tone, the quality of which may be varied by modifying the shape of the mouth to emphasize different harmonics of the tone. The musical possibilities may be increased by the use of additional tongues, giving additional tones, and in the

Person playing a jew's-harp.

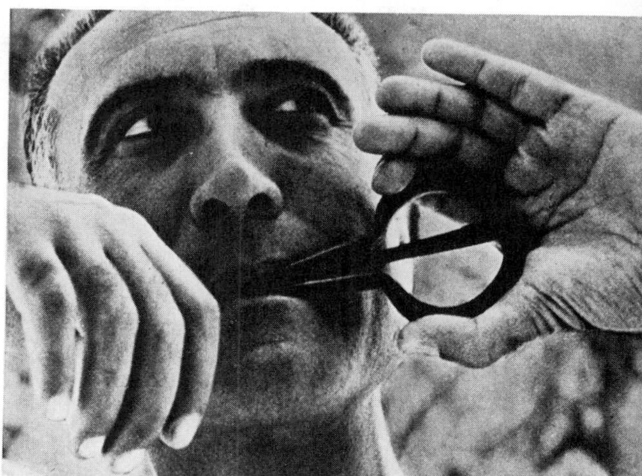

early 19th cent., particularly in Germany, jew's-harps were made with as many as 16 tongues. The instrument bears no traceable relationship to the Jewish people. It has also been called jaw's-harp, jew's-trump or jews'-trump.

Jex-Blake, Sophia, 1840–1912, English physician, active in opening the medical profession to women in England. A graduate of Queen's College, London, she began (1866) her medical studies in the United States and continued them in Edinburgh, but she met much opposition there and was unable to obtain a degree. She carried the battle to Parliament, which finally passed a law enabling the medical schools to give degrees to women. Jex-Blake was influential in founding medical schools for women in London and Edinburgh. See her *Medical Women* (1886, repr. 1970); biography by Margaret Todd (1918).

Jezaniah (jē"zənī'ə), the same as JAAZANIAH **3.**

Jezebel (jĕz'əbĕl), Phoenician princess who was the wife of King Ahab and the mother of Ahaziah, Jehoram, and Athaliah. She encouraged idolatrous worship of Baal and persecuted the prophets. Jezebel was the bitter foe of ELIJAH. Elijah's prophecy of Jezebel's doom was fulfilled when Jehu triumphed over the house of Ahab, and Jezebel, defiant to the last, was thrown from her window and killed; her body was eaten by dogs. 1 Kings 16.31; 21; 2 Kings 9.1–10, 30–37. In the Apocalypse the name is applied to a false prophetess of Thyatira. It is probably used symbolically for a wicked woman. Rev. 2.20.

Jezer (jē'zər), son of Naphtali. Gen. 46.24; Num. 26.49; 1 Chron. 7.13.

Jeziah (jēzī'ə), Jew who had a foreign wife. Ezra 10.25.

Jeziel (jē'zēəl), ally of David at Ziklag. 1 Chron. 12.3.

Jezliah (jĕzlī'ə), Benjamite. 1 Chron. 8.18.

Jezoar (jēzō'ər), Judahite. 1 Chron. 4.7.

Jezrahiah (jĕzrəhī'ə), singer at the dedication of the wall. Neh. 12.42.

Jezreel (jĕz'rēĕl) [Heb.,=God sows]. **1** Ancient city, Palestine, in the plain of ESDRAELON, halfway from Megiddo to the Jordan. It was a residence of King Ahab, whose family is therefore called the house of Jezreel. 1 Sam. 29; 2 Sam. 2.9; 1 Kings 21.1. The name is used for Israel in a pun in Hosea 2.22. It was later used for the whole valley. **2** Town of Judah. Joshua 15.56; 1 Sam. 27.3; 30.5. **3** Symbolic name for a son of Hosea. Hosea 1.4. **4** Judahite. 1 Chron. 4.3.

Jhang-Maghiana (jəng-məgyä'nə), twin cities (1972 metropolitan area est. pop. 127,000) c.2 mi (3.2 km) apart, central Pakistan, on the Chenab River. Metaled roads link the two cities, and a government college is halfway between them. Jhang has a government center that supplies blankets to the army and to hospitals. Maghiana, where many refugee weavers from India settled after the subcontinent's partition in 1947, is an important wool collection center. In the center of Jhang is the temple of Lal Nath, who founded the city in the late 17th cent.

Jhansi (jän'sē), city (1971 pop. 173,255), Uttar Pradesh state, N central India. An agricultural market and small industrial center, it has iron and steel mills and manufactures brassware. The city grew around a fort built in 1613 by the RAJPUTS and strengthened in 1742 by the MAHRATTAS. It reverted to Great Britain in 1853, when the ruling prince died without heirs. British residents in Jhansi were massacred during the INDIAN MUTINY (1857).

Jhelum (jā'lo͝om), town (1961 pop. 52,585), NE Pakistan, on the Jhelum River. It is an important market for timber, and has sawmills and plywood, textile, cigarette, and glass industries. An army supply corps training center and two colleges are also in the town. The area's history dates back at least to the 3d cent. B.C. Old Jhelum stood on the left bank of the river; boatmen crossed the river (c.1532) and founded the new town on the right bank. It became an important trade center owing its prosperity to the waterborne salt trade.

Jhelum or **Jehlam** (both: jā'ləm), westernmost of the five rivers of the PUNJAB, 480 mi (772 km) long. Rising in W Kashmir, it flows W through the Vale of Kashmir, S across the Punjab, where it forms part of the India-Pakistan border, then SW across NE Pakistan to the Chenab River. The Lower Jhelum Canal (opened 1901) and the Upper Jhelum Canal (1915) irrigate extensive areas of Pakistani Punjab. The Jhelum was crossed in 326 B.C. by Alexander the Great, who defeated the Indian king Porus. The river's ancient name was Hydaspes.

Jibsam (jĭb'săm), Issacharite. 1 Chron. 7.2.

Jibuti: see DJIBOUTI, French Territory of the Afars and the Issas.

Jidda (jĭ'də) or **Jedda** (jĕ–), city (1965 est. pop. 194,000), Hejaz, W Saudi Arabia, on the Red Sea. Jidda is the port of MECCA (c.45 mi/72 km to the east) and annually receives a hugh influx of pilgrims, mainly from Africa, Indonesia, and Pakistan. Unlike Mecca, Jidda has always accepted visitors of all religions. The diverse local population includes a large admixture of Negroes, Persians, and Indians. There are few exports, but many goods are imported to support the pilgrims. Several government ministries are in the city. Jidda was ruled by the Turks until 1916, when it became part of the independent HEJAZ. In 1925 it was conquered by Ibn Saud. The city, modernized in recent decades, is surrounded by a wall. There are many houses built of coral and embellished with ornate woodwork. Outside the wall was the reputed tomb of Eve, which was demolished in 1927. Present Jidda is not more than three centuries old, but Old Jidda, c.12 mi (19 km) south of the modern city, was founded c.646 by the caliph Uthman.

Jidlaph (jĭd'lăf), son of Abraham's brother, Nahor. Gen. 22.22.

jig, dance of English origin that is performed also in Ireland and Scotland. It is usually a lively dance, performed by one or more persons, with quick and irregular steps. When the jig was introduced to the United States, it was often danced in minstrel shows. In instrumental music the *gigue,* the successor to the jig, was used by Bach and Handel in their suites.

jigger: see CHIGOE.

jihad: see ISLAM.

Jih-k'a-tse (jŭr-kä-dzŭ) or **Shigatse** (shēgät'sē), town, S central Tibet Autonomous Region, China. It is in the center of a small, heavily populated alluvial plain near the Tsangpo (Brahmaputra) River. The second (after Lhasa) most important trade center in Tibet, it is on the ancient caravan route (now a modern highway) from Lhasa to Nepal, W Tibet, Kashmir, and Sinkiang (China). Jih-k'a-tse was the traditional seat of the Panchen Lama (see TIBETAN BUDDHISM), who ruled about 4,000 monks in the lamasery of Tashi Lumpo (founded 1446), west of the

Old Jidda, in western Saudi Arabia.

town. Jih-k'a-tse also has a large 17th-century fort. Other spellings of the name are Zhigatse and Zhikatse.

Jihlava (yēkh'lävä), Ger. *Iglau,* city (1970 pop. 40,920), W central Czechoslovakia, in Moravia, on the Jihlava River. Jihlava is a railway junction and has industries manufacturing linen and woolen cloth, machinery, footwear, and tobacco. Chartered in 1227, it was the site of the signing (1436) of the Compactata—the Magna Carta of the HUSSITES. The city has two medieval churches and a 16th-century town hall.

Jima or **Jimma** (both: jĭm'ä), city (1968 est. pop. 30,580), capital of Kefa (Kaffa) prov., SW Ethiopia. It is the commercial center for a coffee-producing region. An agricultural school is located there.

Jim Crow laws, in U.S. history, statutes enacted by Southern states and muncipalities, beginning in the 1880s, that legalized segregation between blacks and whites. The name is believed to be derived from a character in a popular minstrel song. The Supreme Court ruling in 1896 in Plessy v. Ferguson that separate facilities for whites and blacks were constitutional encouraged the passage of discriminatory laws that wiped out the gains made by Negroes during Reconstruction. Railways and streetcars, public waiting rooms, restaurants, boarding houses, theaters, and public parks were segregated; separate schools, hospitals, and other public institutions, generally of inferior quality, were designated for Negroes. By World War I, even places of employment were segregated, and it was not until after World War II that an assault on Jim Crow in the South began to make headway. In 1950 the Supreme Court ruled that the Univ. of Texas must admit a Negro, Herman Sweatt, to the law school, on the grounds that the state did not provide equal education for him. This was followed (1954) by the Supreme Court decision in Brown v. Board of Education of Topeka, Kansas, declaring separate facilities by race to be unconstitutional. Negroes in the South used legal suits, mass sit-ins, and boycotts to hasten desegregation. A march on Washington by over 200,000 in 1963 dramatized the movement to end Jim Crow. Southern whites often responded with violence, and federal troops were needed to preserve order and protect Negroes, notably at Little Rock, Ark. (1957), Oxford, Miss. (1962), and Selma, Ala. (1965). The Civil Rights Act of 1964, the Voting Rights Act of 1965, and the Fair Housing Act of 1968 finally ended the legal sanctions to Jim Crow. See CIVIL RIGHTS; INTEGRATION; NEGRO. See C. Vann Woodward, *The Strange Career of Jim Crow* (1966).

Jiménez, Juan Ramón (hwän rämōn' hēmä'nāth), 1881–1958, Spanish lyric poet, b. Andalusia, studied at the Univ. of Seville. In his youth Jiménez was influenced by the French symbolists; he wrote the romantic *Almas de violeta* in 1900. He later turned to greater simplicity of style in *Diario de un poeta recién casado* [diary of a recently married poet]. Later collections include *Unidad* (1925), *Sucesión* (1932), and *Presente* (1935). During the civil war he left Spain and lived for many years in the United States, Cuba, and, finally, Puerto Rico. Jiménez wrote some 32 volumes of poetry. The Nobel Prize in Literature was awarded to him in 1956. For English translations see *Juan Ramón Jiménez: Fifty Spanish Poems* (1951), *Platero and I* (1956), and *Selected Writings* (1957). See studies by P. R. Olson (1967) and H. T. Young (1967).

Jiménez de Cisneros, Francisco (fränthēs'kō hēmā'nāth dā thēsnā'rōs), 1436–1517, Spanish prelate and statesman, cardinal of the Roman Catholic Church. An austere Franciscan, he was appointed (1492) confessor to Queen Isabella I and later became (1495) archbishop of Toledo. He undertook the forcible conversion of the Moors in Granada, thus provoking a Moorish uprising (1500–1502). After acting (1506–7) as regent of Castile until the return of Ferdinand II from Italy, he was made inquisitor general and cardinal. He financed and personally led the expedition (1509) that captured Oran, in Africa. On Ferdinand's death (1516) he again assumed the regency pending the arrival of Charles I (later Holy Roman Emperor Charles V) from Flanders. When Charles arrived, he dismissed Jiménez peremptorily on the advice of his Flemish counselors, but the cardinal died before learning of his fall. Jiménez founded (1508) the Univ. of Alcalá de Henares and had the Polyglot Bible compiled at his expense. He enacted clerical reforms, eliminating many abuses and introducing better education of the churchmen. His name also appears as Ximénez and Ximenes.

Jiménez de Quesada, Gonzalo (gōnthä'lō hēmā'nĕth dā kāsä'thä), c.1499–1579, Spanish conquistador in Colombia. Chief magistrate of Santa Marta, he arrived there in 1535 or 1536 and was commissioned to explore the MAGDALENA in search of EL DORADO. He set out in 1536, and after incredible hardships he defeated the CHIBCHA and founded (1538) BOGOTÁ as capital of the New Kingdom of Granada (see NEW GRANADA). A hard taskmaster but an able leader, Quesada wavered between humane and brutal treatment of the Indians. He obtained fabulous amounts of emeralds and gold. Meeting FEDERMANN and BENALCÁZAR, who claimed the same territory, Quesada persuaded them to return with him to Spain, where settlement could be made. There he was ignored until 1550, when he was appointed marshal of New Granada and councilor of Bogotá for life. In 1569, still seeking El Dorado, he led a lavishly equipped expedition to the confluence of the Guaviare and Orinoco; he and what remained of his company returned wasted and penniless after three years. Still later, suffering from a skin disease and carried on a litter, Quesada put down an Indian revolt. Some think that he was the model for Cervantes's Don Quixote. His own account of his conquests has been lost, but excerpts copied by others from the original survive. See studies by A. F. Bandelier (1893, repr. 1962), C. R. Markham (1912, repr. 1971), Germán Arciniegas (tr. 1942, repr. 1968), and R. B. C. Graham (1922, repr. 1973).

Jimna or **Jimnah** (both: jĭm'nə), son of Asher. Num. 26.44; Gen. 46.17. Imnah: 1 Chron. 7.30.

Jimson weed or **Jamestown weed,** large, coarse annual plant (*Datura stramonium*) of the family Solanaceae (NIGHTSHADE family), considered a native of the American tropics but long widely distributed and often weedy. This and other species of the genus contain a narcotic poison, stramonium, similar to that of the related belladonna, that has been used by many peoples for various purposes, e.g., as a medicine (now chiefly inhaled for the relief of asthma or applied externally as a painkiller) and in the past as a poison and an instrument for obtaining prophetic dreams or messages in various cults (suggested as possibly the medium of priests at the Delphian oracle). The amusing antics of soldiers in colonial Virginia who ate Jimson weed have been recorded for history. Stramonium, comprised of several alkaloids (e.g., SCOPOLAMINE, ATROPINE, and hyoscyamine), may also be obtained from some other species of *Datura*. Jimson weed is classified in the division MAGNOLIOPHYTA, class Magnoliopsida, order Polemoniales, family Solanaceae.

jingle shell: see MUSSEL.

jingoism (jĭng'gōĭzəm), advocacy of a policy of aggressive nationalism. The term was first used in connection with certain British politicians who sought to bring England into the Russo-Turkish War (1877–78) on the side of the Turks. It apparently derived from a popular song of the period: "We don't want to fight, but, by jingo, if we do. . . ."

Jinja (jĭn'jə), city (1969 pop. 47,300), SE Uganda, on the Victoria Nile River, near Victoria Nyanza. It is an industrial city and the commercial and processing center for a region where cotton, sugarcane, maize, and groundnuts are grown. Manufactures include refined copper, metal goods, forest products, textiles, soap, and processed food. It is connected by rail with Mombasa on the Indian Ocean. Jinja was founded in 1901 as a trading post; with the development of the nearby Owen Falls hydroelectric project, it became (1950s) a major industrial center.

Jinnah, Muhammad Ali (məhäm'əd älē' jĭn'ə), 1876–1948, founder of Pakistan, b. Karachi. After his admission to the bar in England, he returned to India to practice law. Early in his career he was a fervent supporter of the INDIAN NATIONAL CONGRESS and an advocate of Hindu-Muslim unity. He was a member of the legislative council of the viceroy from 1910 to 1919. He joined the MUSLIM LEAGUE in 1913 and was elected its president in 1916 and 1920. He played a major role in negotiating the so-called Lucknow Pact (1916) between the League and the Congress, in which the latter conceded that Muslims should have a separate communal electorate to insure them adequate legislative representation. Hindu-Muslim cooperation soon broke down, however, and the Congress reversed its position on separate electorates. Finally totally disillusioned with the Congress, Jinnah resigned from that organization in 1930. From 1934 until his death he headed the Muslim League and guided its struggle for an independent Pakistan, a state that would include the pre dominantly Muslim areas of India. He supported the British during World War II while the Congress was under ban. The claim of Jinnah that the Muslim League represented the Muslims of India was substantiated in 1946, when in the elections for the Indian constituent assembly, the League won all the seats assigned to the Muslim electorate. Jinnah's firm stand and the widespread Hindu-Muslim riots forced the Congress to accept establishment of the separate state of Pakistan, and in Aug., 1947, India was partitioned. Jinnah was appointed the first governor general of the dominion of Pakistan and

Muhammad Ali Jinnah (right), the founder of Pakistan, with Sir Stafford Cripps.

elected president of its constituent assembly. He was called Quaid-i-Azam [great leader] by his followers. See Hector Bolitho, *Jinnah* (1954).

jinni (jĭnē′), feminine **jinniyah** (jĭnēyä′), plural **jinn** (jĭn), in Arabic and Islamic folklore, spirit or demon endowed with supernatural power. In ancient belief the jinn were associated with the destructive forces of nature. In Islamic tradition they were corporeal spirits similar to men in appearance but having certain supernatural powers, especially those of changing in size and shape. Capable of both good and evil, the jinn were popular in literatures of the Near East, notably in the stories of the *Thousand and One Nights.* The term *genie* is the English form and is sometimes confused with the Roman genius.

Jiphtah (jĭf′tə), unidentified town, SW Palestine. Joshua 15.43.

Jiphthah-el (jĭf′thə-ĕl), unidentified town, Palestine. Joshua 19.14,27.

Jipijapa (hēpēhä′pä), city (1962 est. pop. 13,400), W Ecuador, on the equatorial lowlands. A few miles inland from the Pacific, Jipijapa is famous for the manufacture of high-grade Panama hats, made from the jipijapa plant. It is also the trade center for an agricultural region.

Jirja (jĭr′jă) or **Girga** (gĭr′-), town (1966 pop. 44,300), central Egypt, on the Nile. It is noted for its pottery. The town is the seat of a Coptic bishop and derives its name from the old Mara Girgis Coptic monastery, which was dedicated to St. George. A Roman Catholic monastery, said to be the oldest in Egypt, is in Jirja. Nearby is the ancient city of Abydos.

jiujitsu or **jiujutsu** (jo͞ojĭt′so͞o): see JUDO.

Jívaro (hē′värō), linguistic stock of South American Indians, Ecuador. The peoples, N of the Marañón River and E of the Andes, engage in farming, hunting, fishing, and weaving. They have a patrilineal society, with some 15 to 20 people, the family group, living in each huge, isolated communal house. Though not unique to the Jívaro, head shrinking, accompanied by elaborate ceremony, made them famous, but the practice has virtually disappeared. The Jívaro long resisted government and missionary efforts to subdue them. See V. W. Von Hagen, *Off With Their Heads* (1937); Jirí Hanzelka and Miroslav Zikmund, *Amazon Headhunters* (tr. 1964); M. J. Harner, *The Jívaro* (1972).

Jizah, Al (äl jē′zö) or **Giza** (gē′zə), city (1966 pop. 345,261), capital of Al Jizah governorate, N Egypt, surburb of Cairo. It is a manufacturing and agricultural trade center. Products include cotton textiles, cigarettes, and footwear. It is also a resort, as well as the seat of Egypt's motion-picture industry. The Univ. of Cairo and a research center for schistosomiasis are located there. Nearby are the Great SPHINX, the pyramid of KHUFU (Cheops), and the tombs of Khufu's mother and daughter. The city is also known as Gizeh.

Joab (jō′ăb). **1** Son of David's sister Zeruiah and commander of his uncle's armies. A trusted and skillful administrator, he was often vindictive and cruel, as in his killing of Abner, Absalom, and Amasa. David's dying curse on Joab is remarkable. 1 Kings 2.5,6. For his support of Adonijah, Solomon had him put to death. 2 Sam. 2.12–32; 3.22–31; 8.16; 10.7–14; 11; 12.26; 14; 18; 19.1,5–7,13; 20.7–23; 24.1–9; 1 Kings 1.7; 2.28–34. **2** Chief craftsman of the valley of Charashim. 1 Chron. 4.14. **3** Family returned from exile. Ezra 2.6; 8.9; Neh. 7.11.

Joachim, Saint (jō′əkĭm), in tradition, the father of the Virgin and husband of St. ANNE; there is no mention of him in the Bible. His cult is ancient in the East, but modern in the Western Church. Feast: Aug. 16.

Joachim, Joseph (yō′sĕf yō′äkhĭm), 1831–1907, Hungarian violinist; friend of Mendelssohn, Brahms, and Schumann. In his long career his performances of violin masterpieces came to be accepted as models. Joachim was concertmaster under Liszt at Weimar, 1849–53; later he became (1868) musical director of the Berlin Hochschule. The Joachim quartet, which he founded in 1869, presented the conservative quartet repertory of the 19th cent. in definitive interpretations. He composed cadenzas for the violin concertos of Beethoven and Brahms.

Joachim of Floris (jō'əkĭm), c.1132–1202, Italian Cistercian monk. He was abbot of Corazzo, Italy, but withdrew into solitude. He left scriptural commentaries prophesying a new age. In his "Age of the Spirit" the hierarchy of the church would be unnecessary and infidels would unite with Christians. Joachim's works had a vogue in the 13th and the 14th cent.; many, especially religious zealots like the Franciscan spirituals, acclaimed him as a prophet. Dante places him in Paradise. One of Joachim's works was condemned as heretical. See study by Marjorie Reeves (1972).

Joachimsthal: see JÁCHYMOV, Czechoslovakia.

Joad, Cyril Edwin Mitchinson, 1891–1953, English philosopher. He became head of the department of philosophy at Birbeck College, Univ. of London, in 1930. As a rationalist, he was a successful lecturer and writer, his works including *Common Sense Ethics* (1920), *Matter, Life, and Value* (1929), and *Return to Philosophy* (1936). After his conversion to religion he wrote *Good and Evil* (1943) and *The Recovery of Belief* (1953).

Joah (jō'ä). **1, 2** Keepers of records. 2 Kings 18; Isa. 36; 2 Chron. 34.8. **3, 4** Gershonites. 1 Chron. 6.21; 2 Chron. 29.12. **5** Korahite doorkeeper. 1 Chron. 26.4.

Joahaz (jō'əhăz): see JEHOAHAZ.

Joanes, Vicente: see MACIP, VICENTE JUAN.

Joanna I, 1326–82, queen of Naples (1343–81), countess of Provence. She was the granddaughter of King Robert of Naples, whom she succeeded with her husband, Andrew of Hungary. The murder (1345) of Andrew at the queen's behest brought the wrath of Andrew's brother, LOUIS I of Hungary. Louis twice invaded Naples; each time Joanna fled, and in 1352 she made peace with Hungary. Joanna married twice more but remained childless and adopted young Charles of Durazzo (later CHARLES III of Naples) as her heir. When Pope Urban VI, angered by Joanna's support of the antipope Clement VII, urged Charles to dethrone her, she disinherited Charles in favor of Louis of Anjou (see LOUIS I, king of Naples). Charles conquered (1381) Naples, imprisoned the queen, and was granted the kingdom by the pope. Joanna died by Charles's orders. Her successive adoptions caused chronic warfare between the two claimants (continued by their heirs); thus began the decline of French hegemony in Italy.

Joanna II, 1371–1435, queen of Naples (1414–35), sister and successor of LANCELOT. The intrigues of her favorites kept her court in turmoil. Her second husband, James of Bourbon, tried to seize power but was imprisoned in 1416. Threatened (1420) by the ANGEVIN claimant to Naples, LOUIS III, Joanna asked the aid of ALFONSO V of Aragón in expelling Louis; she adopted (1421) Alfonso as her heir. After Alfonso attempted to take over Naples she transferred (1423) the adoption to Louis. Louis died (1434) after regaining most of Naples, and Joanna adopted his brother RENÉ. Joanna II was the last Angevin to reign in Naples; at her death Alfonso seized power, and René's claim was never secured.

Joanna (Joanna the Mad), 1479–1555, Spanish queen of Castile and León (1504–55), daughter of Ferdinand II and Isabella I. She succeeded to Castile and León at the death of her mother. Ferdinand II briefly assumed the regency until he was replaced by Joanna's ambitious husband, PHILIP I. After Philip's death (1506), Ferdinand again assumed the rule, for Joanna had by this time become quite insane. At Ferdinand's death (1516) Joanna's elder son, Charles (later Holy Roman Emperor CHARLES V), was proclaimed joint ruler of Castile with his mother. Joanna spent the rest of her life in the castle of Tordesillas. The pretence that she was not actually insane was sometimes used by the discontented, including Juan de PADILLA, to justify revolts against the "foreign" ruler, Charles. See Townsend Miller, *The Castles and the Crown* (1963).

Joanna, in the Bible. **1** Wife of Herod's steward Chuza. She was a follower of Jesus and was one who found the tomb empty. Luke 8.3; 24.10. **2** Ancestor of St. Joseph. Luke 3.27.

Joan of Arc, Fr. *Jeanne D'Arc* (zhän därk), 1412?–31, French saint and national heroine, called the Maid of Orléans; daughter of a farmer of Domrémy on the border of Champagne and Lorraine. At a young age she began to hear "voices"—those of St. Michael, St. Catherine, and St. Margaret. When she was about 16, the voices exhorted her to bear aid to the dauphin, later King CHARLES VII, then kept from the throne by the English in the HUNDRED YEARS WAR. Joan won the aid of Robert de Baudricourt, captain of the dauphin's forces in Vaucouleurs, in obtaining an interview with the dauphin. She made the journey in male attire, with six companions. Meeting the dauphin at Chinon castle, she conquered his skepticism as to her divine mission. She was examined by theologians at Poitiers, and afterwards she was furnished with troops by Charles. Her leadership provided spirit and morale more than military prowess. In May, 1429, she succeeded in raising the siege of Orléans, and in June she took other English posts on the Loire and defeated the English at Patay. After considerable persuasion the dauphin agreed to be crowned at Rheims; Joan stood near him at his coronation. This was the pinnacle of her fortunes. In Sept., 1429, Joan unsuccessfully besieged Paris. The following spring she went to relieve Compiègne, but she was captured by the Burgundians and sold to the English, who were eager to destroy her influence by putting her to death. Charles VII made no attempt to secure her freedom. In order to escape responsibility, the English turned her over to the ecclesiastical court at Rouen. She was tried for heresy and witchcraft before Pierre CAUCHON and other French clerics who supported the English. Probably her most serious crime was the claim of direct inspiration from God; in the eyes of the court this refusal to accept the church hierarchy constituted heresy. Throughout the lengthy trial and imprisonment she bravely fought her inquisitors. Only at the end of the trial, when Joan was sentenced to be turned over to a secular court, did she recant. She was condemned to life imprisonment. Shortly afterward, however, she retracted her abjuration, was turned over to the secular court as a relapsed heretic, and was burned at the stake (May 30, 1431) in Rouen. Charles VII made tardy recognition of her services by a rehabilitation trial that annulled the proceedings of the original trial in 1456. Joan was beatified in 1909 and canonized in 1920. Feast: May 30. Her career lent itself to numerous legends, and she has been represented in many paintings and statues. In literature and music she appears notably, though not always accurately, in works by many eminent

Joan of Arc (center), French saint and national heroine, captured by the Burgundians, from a 15th-cent. miniature.

writers and composers. Among her biographies, the best known is that of Jules Michelet (tr. 1957). See also biographies by Andrew Lang (1908) and Vita Sackville-West (1936); translations of the trial records by W. P. Barrett (1932 ed.) and W. S. Scott (1950) ; Régine Pernoud, *The Retrial of Joan of Arc* (tr. 1955) and *Joan of Arc by Herself and Her Witnesses* (tr. 1966); C. W. Lightbody, *The Judgements of Joan* (1961); Henri Guillemin, *Joan, Maid of Orleans* (1973).

Joan of Kent, 1328–85, English noblewoman; daughter of Edmund of Woodstock, earl of Kent, youngest son of Edward I. She early gained wide note for her beauty and charm, though the appellation Fair Maid of Kent, by which she became known, was probably not contemporary. Her marriage to the earl of Salisbury was annulled on the grounds of a precontract with Sir Thomas Holland, whom she then married. Upon the death of her brother in 1352 she became countess of Kent in her own right. In 1361, after Holland's death, she married Edward the Black Prince, by whom she had two sons, Edward (1365–70) and Richard (later Richard II). In 1378 she was instrumental in halting proceedings against John WYCLIF, though there is insufficient evidence to determine if she accepted his doctrines. As long as she lived, she was probably the principal influence on her son Richard II.

João Pessoa (zhwouN pəsô'ə), city (1970 pop. 197,398), capital of Paraíba state, NE Brazil, at the confluence of the Sanhauá and Paraíba do Norte rivers. Cotton, sugar, and minerals are exported through its port, Cabedelo. Industries in the city produce tobacco, shoes, and cement. The city was established in the late 16th cent. and named (1585) Filipea, in honor of Philip II of Spain and Portugal. During the brief Dutch occupation (17th cent.) it was called Frederickstadt, and, after its reconquest by the Portuguese, Paraíba. Its present name was acquired in 1930, in honor of the state governor who was assassinated in Recife during the VARGAS revolution. João Pessoa is the site of a state university. The city's Franciscan convent and church are excellent examples of colonial architecture. Nearby are several resort areas.

Joash (jō'ăsh): see JEHOASH.

Joatham (jō'əthəm): see JOTHAM.

Job (jōb), book of the Old Testament, in the 18th place in the Authorized Version. It is based on a folktale and is of unknown authorship and date, although many scholars assign it to a time between 600 B.C. and 400 B.C. The book is in a dialogue or dramatic form, all in verse except for the opening and close. The subject is the problem of good and evil in the world: "Why do the just suffer and the wicked flourish?" In the prologue (1–2) Satan obtains God's permission to test Job, whom God regards as "a perfect and an upright man"; accordingly, all that Job has is destroyed, and he is physically afflicted. The main part of the book (3–31) consists of speeches by Job and three friends who come to "comfort" him: Job speaks, then each of the three speaks in turn, with Job replying each time; there are three such cycles of discussion, although the third is incomplete. The friends insist alike that Job cannot really be just, as he claims to be, and Job reiterates his innocence of wrong. The sequence changes with the appearance of a fourth speaker, Elihu (32-37), who accuses Job of arrogant pride. He in turn is followed by God himself, who speaks out of a storm (38-41) to convince Job of his ignorance and rebuke him for his questioning. The epilogue (42) tells how God rebukes the friends for their accusations and how happiness is restored to Job. The ethical problem is not explicitly resolved. The author did not intend to solve the paradox of the righteous man's suffering, but rather to criticize a philosophy that associated sin with the sufferer. The texts are imperfect, and there may be serious losses, misplacements, or even additions to the original. The book contains many eloquent passages; among them are Job's declaration of faith in the "redeemer" (19) and his speech on wisdom (28) and God's discourse on animals (39-41). Job is mentioned elsewhere in the Bible: Ezek. 14.12-23; James 5.11. The Job of Gen. 46.13 is the same as JASHUB **1.** See studies by Robert Gordis (1965) and J. D. Levenson (1972); see also bibliography under OLD TESTAMENT.

Jobab (jō'băb). **1** Descendant of Shem. Gen. 10.29; 1 Chron. 1.23. **2** King of Edom. Gen. 36.33,34. **3** Chief defeated by Joshua. Joshua 11.1. **4, 5** Benjamites. 1 Chron. 8.9,18.

Job Corps, U.S. Government program to provide basic education for the most disadvantaged youths between the ages of 16 and 21. Established by the Economic Opportunity Act of 1964, its goal is to prepare these youths "for the responsibility of citizenship and to increase their employability." The Job Corps is administered by the Dept. of Labor, which works in conjunction with other Federal agencies in providing training. For example, the Forest Service maintains 20 Job Corps Conservation Centers on national forest land where youths receive vocational training. Job Corps recruiting is done primarily through state employment services. Enrollees spend from six months to two year in the program.

Jobert, Michel (mēshĕl' zhôbĕr'), 1921–, French diplomat, b. Morocco (then a French colony). He served for many years as a government official before joining (1963) Georges Pompidou's staff during Pompidou's premiership. After Pompidou's election as president (1969), Jobert was his adviser on foreign affairs. A skillful negotiator, he helped bring about Great Britain's entry into the European Economic Community in 1973. He was French foreign minister from April, 1973, to May, 1974.

Job's-tears, tall tropical plant of the family Gramineae (GRASS family), *Coix lacrymajobi,* native to E Asia and Malaya but elsewhere cultivated in gardens as an annual and naturalized in the S United States. The mature grains are enveloped by very hard, pearly white, oval structures which are used as beads for making rosaries, necklaces, and other objects. Some varieties are harvested for cereal food and are used medicinally in parts of the Orient. Job's-tears is classified in the division MAGNOLIOPHYTA, class Liliatae, order Cyperales, family Gramineae.

Jocasta (jōkăs'tə): see OEDIPUS.

Jocelin de Brakelond (jŏs'lĭn də brāk'lŏnd), fl. 1200, English chronicler, a monk of Bury St. Edmunds. His chronicle of St. Edmund's Abbey, covering the years 1173–1202, is written in a simple, vigorous style and is remarkable for its vivid pictures of monastic life and characters, particularly of the abbot Samson. Carlyle used it as the basis for the second part of his *Past and Present.* See edition by G. J. McFadden (1952).

Jochebed (jŏk'ēbĕd), mother of Moses. Ex. 6.20; Num. 26.59.

Jochumsson, Matthías (mät'tēäs yŏk'küms-sŏn), 1835–1920, Icelandic playwright, poet, and translator. Although Jochumsson was the founder of the modern drama in Iceland, with poetic plays such as *Útilegumennirnir* [the outlaws] (1864), he is best known as a lyric poet. After graduating from theological school he traveled abroad, returning to Iceland to work as a translator of Shakespeare, Byron, and Ibsen. His autobiography, *Sögukaflar af sjálfum mér* [stories from my life], was published in 1922. Jochumsson also composed hymns, including the Icelandic national hymn.

Jodelle, Estienne (ātyĕn' zhôdĕl'), 1532–73, French poet of the Pléiade (see under PLEIAD). He was the author of *Cléopatre captive* (1553), the first French tragedy that departed from medieval drama. His other plays were a comedy, *Eugène* (1552), and *Didon se sacrifiant* (1558), another tragedy.

Jodhpur (jŏd'po͝or) or **Marwar** (mär'wär), city and former principality, Rajasthan state, NW India. Except for the eastern section, it is largely an arid wasteland suitable only for the raising of camels. Gypsum and salt are mined, and cotton is raised. The state was founded in the 13th cent. by the Rahtor clan of RAJPUTS and was later a vassal of the MOGUL empire. The British brought it under their control in 1818, and in 1949 it was merged with the state of Rajasthan. **Jodhpur,** city (1971 pop. 318,894), capital of the former state and now a district administrative center, was founded in 1459. It is surrounded by a wall nearly 6 mi (9.7 km) long. Jodhpur is an important marketplace for wool. Its manufactures include textiles and electrical and leather goods. Towering above the city on a rock 400 ft (122 m) high is an old fortress housing several palaces and the treasury of the maharaja, which contains a famous gem collection. The Indian air force maintains a training center at Jodhpur.

Jodrell Bank Experimental Station (jŏd'rəl), observatory for RADIO ASTRONOMY located at Jodrell Bank, Macclesfield, Cheshire, England; its official name is the Nuffield Radio Astronomy Observatory. It was founded in 1945 and is administered by the Univ. of Manchester. The principal antennas are a fully steerable, altazimuth-mounted parabolic dish 250 ft (76 m) in diameter and a second altazimuth paraboloid measuring 125 ft (38 m) by 84 ft (26 m). In addition, the facility has a 50-ft (15 m) altazimuth paraboloid and a 50-ft polar-axis paraboloid. Research programs include studies of galactic structure, angular sizes and structure of radio sources, polarization of radio sources, quasars, pulsars, molecules in interstellar space, and lunar radar.

Joed (jō'ĕd), descendant of Benjamin. Neh. 11.7.

Joel (jō'əl). **1** Prophet of the book of JOEL. **2** Simeonite. 1 Chron. 4.35. **3** Reubenite. 1 Chron. 5.4,8. **4** Gadite. 1 Chron. 5.12. **5** Issacharite. 1 Chron. 7.3. **6** Manassite. 1 Chron. 27.20. **7, 8, 9** Levites. 1 Chron. 15.7, 11,17; 23.8; 26.22; 2 Chron. 29.12. **10** See IGAL. **11, 12** Men who returned from the Exile. Ezra 10.43; Neh. 11.9. **13** Ancestor of Samuel. 1 Chron. 6.36. Shaul: 1 Chron. 6.24. **14** Son of Samuel. 1 Sam. 8.2; 1 Chron. 6.33. Vashni: 1 Chron. 6.28.

Joel, book of the Old Testament, 29th in the order of the Authorized Version, 2d of the books of the Minor Prophets. It is the preaching of an otherwise

Control room at Jodrell Bank Experimental Station.

unknown prophet, dated variously from the 9th to the 3d cent. B.C. It gives an account of a plague of locusts, divinely sent (1-2.17); the people, on repentance, will be rewarded with present (2.18–27) as well as future blessings, this being a Messianic prophecy (2.28-3.21). Peter used Joel as a text in his Pentecost sermon. Acts 2. See Mariano DiGangi, *The Book of Joel* (1970); G. W. Ahlström, *Joel and the Temple of Jerusalem* (1971).

Joelah (jōē'lə), warrior with David at Ziklag. 1 Chron. 12.7.

Joensuu (yô'ĕnsōō), city (1970 pop. 36,281), capital of Pohjois-Karjala prov., SE Finland. It is the trade center of the forest region of NE Karelia, has plywood mills, and is an important lake port. It was chartered in 1848. The modern city hall was designed by Eliel Saarinen.

joe-pye weed (jō-pī'), name for a tall North American plant (*Eupatorium purpureum*) of the family Compositae (COMPOSITE family), having small, usually pinkish-purple blossoms in large terminal clusters. The name comes from that of an Indian who reputedly effected many cures with the herb. An infusion of the leaves and roots was formerly, and is sometimes yet, employed as a diuretic and an astringent among other things. It is also called gravelroot, trumpetweed, and purple BONESET or thoroughwort. Two related species, *E. maculatum* and *verticillatum,* are also called joe-pye weed. Joe-pye weed is classified in the division MAGNOLIOPHYTA, class Magnoliopsida, order Asterales, family Compositae.

Joezer (jōē'zər), one of David's captains. 1 Chron. 12.6.

Joffe, Abram (əbräm' yô'fyə), 1880–1960, Soviet scientist, b. Ukraine, grad. St. Petersburg (now Leningrad) Technological Institute, 1902. From 1902 to 1906 he worked in Munich as an assistant to W. C. Roentgen. In 1932, Joffe became director of the Leningrad Physico-Agronomy Institute. As a member of the Soviet Academy of Science, he helped found (1951) the Physico-Technical Institute of the academy. He is best known for his work on semiconductors, for his research on thermoelectric generators, and for his inventions in radio and aerodynamics, including a dynamo of a new type and a powerful accumulator for storing energy.

Joffre, Joseph Jacques Césaire (zhôzĕf′ zhäk säzĕr′ zhô′frə), 1852–1931, marshal of France. He began his career as a military engineer in the French colonies and was appointed French commander in chief in 1911. Like other members of the French general staff, he underestimated German strength at the outbreak of World War I, but his operations helped achieve an orderly French retreat. He deserves partial credit for the victory of the Marne (1914) in which he took advantage of an opportunity to counterattack. After the Germans nearly captured Verdun (1916) Joffre was made chief military adviser to the government, a powerless post from which he soon resigned. He was replaced by Gen. Robert Georges Nivelle as commander in chief. Joffre later served as chairman of the Allied War Council. See his memoirs (tr. 1932).

Joffrey Ballet: see ROBERT JOFFREY BALLET.

Jogbehah (jŏg′bēhä), town, E of the Jordan River, NW of Amman (Jordan). Num. 32.35; Judges 8.11.

Jogjakarta (jōg″yəkär′tə, jōk″-) or **Djokjakarta** (jōk″-), city (1961 pop. 312,698), S Java, Indonesia, at the foot of volcanic Mt. Merapi, capital of the autonomous district of Jogjakarta, a former sultanate. It is the cultural center of Java, known for its artistic life, particularly its drama and dance festivals and handicraft industries. It is also the trade hub of a major rice-producing region, and there is some manufacturing. Tourism is important; the magnificent BOROBUDUR temple is in the area. The vast walled palace (18th cent.) of the sultan of Jogjakarta was the provisional capital (1949–50) of the republic of Indonesia; part of it now houses Gadjah Mada Univ. Also in the city are the Islamic Univ. of Indonesia and several colleges. The town was founded (1749) by a sultan in an area which had been the center of previous cultures. It was the focus of the revolt against the Dutch (1825–30) and was the stronghold of the Indonesian independence movement from 1946 to 1950.

Jogli (jŏg′lī), chief Danite. Num. 34.22.

Jogues, Isaac (Saint Isaac Jogues) (ēzäk′ zhôg), 1607–46, French Jesuit missionary and martyr in the New World; one of the Jesuit Martyrs of North America. He arrived in Quebec in 1636, and immediately was sent to Christianize the Huron Indians on Georgian Bay. In 1641 he journeyed N to Sault Ste Marie, which he named. On his return from a journey to Quebec in 1642, the party was captured by the Iroquois; several were killed, and the rest were subjected to cruel tortures. Jogues was held captive until July, 1643, when he was ransomed by the Dutch and brought to New Amsterdam; from there he embarked for France. Later he returned to Canada. In April, 1646, he was sent among the Mohawks as an ambassador of peace. He discovered Lake George, which he named Lac du St. Sacrement. In May, 1646, he returned to Quebec to make plans for establishing a mission among the Mohawks. On his return, accompanied by Father Jean Lalande, he was met by a hostile band of Mohawks near the present Auriesville, N.Y., where both priests were murdered. Feast: Sept. 26 or (among the Jesuits) March 16. See G. D. Kittler, *Saint in the Wilderness* (1964).

Joha (jō′hə). **1** Son of BERIAH **3.** 1 Chron. 8.16. **2** One of David's guard. 1 Chron. 11.45.

Johanan (jōhā′năn) [short form of JEHOHANAN]. **1** Captain who led in the rescue of the captives of Ishmael. Jer. 40.8–43; 2 Kings 25.23. **2** Descendant of David. 1 Chron. 3.24. **3, 4** Two of David's men. 1 Chron. 12.4,12. **5** Chief priest. Neh. 12.22,23; Ezra 10.6. Jonathan: Neh. 12.11. **6** Son of King Josiah. 1 Chron. 3.15. **7** Father of AZARIAH **6.** **8** Father of AZARIAH **19.** **9** Head of a family in the return from the Exile. Ezra 8.12. **10** Son of TOBIAH **1.** Neh. 6.18.

Johanan ben Zakkai (jōhăn′ən bĕn zăk′āī), leader of the Pharisees of Jerusalem before the destruction of the Temple in A.D. 70, afterward founder of the academy of Jabneh (see JAMNIA). He emphasized the study of the Torah as the primary religious duty for which man was created. After A.D. 70 he taught that deeds of loving kindness might replace sacrifice in achieving atonement. His success at Jabneh assured the continuation of Judaism.

Johannesburg (jōhăn′ĭsbörg″, yōhä′nəsbörkh″), city (1970 metropolitan pop. 1,407,963), Transvaal, NE South Africa, on the southern slopes of the WITWATERSRAND at an altitude of 5,750 ft (1,753 m). Johannesburg is the largest city in South Africa, the center of its important gold-mining industry, its manufacturing and commercial center, and the hub of its transportation network. Gold mining is the sprawling city's chief industry. Manufactures include cut diamonds, industrial chemicals, plastics, cement, electrical and mining equipment, paper and paper products, glass, food products, and beer. South Africa's main stock exchange (founded 1887) is in the city. Jan Smuts International Airport is nearby. Johannesburg was founded as a mining settlement in 1886, when gold was found on the Witwatersrand; by 1900 the city had a population of c.100,000. Johannesburg's large black African population provides labor for the mines. Today most black Africans live in a group of townships (known collectively as Soweto) southwest of the city. Rand Afrikaans Univ. (1966), the Univ. of the Witwatersrand (1922), and Witwatersrand College for Advanced Technical Education (1925) are in Johannesburg, which also houses several museums, an art gallery, a planetarium, a zoo, a bird sanctuary, and numerous parks. Jan Smuts House is in the city. Nearby is Kyalami Circuit, where international motor races are held.

Johannes von Saaz (Johannes von Tepl) (yōhän′əs fən zäts, tĕp′əl), c.1350–c.1414, Bohemian humanist and writer. Johannes is best known for his powerful work *Der Ackermann aus Böhmen* (tr. *Death and the Plowman*) (c.1400), a dialogue between Death and a recently widowed farmer. Among the first prose works in Modern High German, it is characterized by medieval style and form but it embodies Renaissance spirit in its defense of mankind.

Johannes von Tepl: see JOHANNES VON SAAZ.

Johannisberg (yōhä′nĭsbĕrkh), village, Hesse, central West Germany, near the Rhine River. A health resort, it is also noted for its magnificent wine.

John, Saint, one of the Twelve Disciples, traditional author of the fourth Gospel, three epistles, and the Revelation (see JOHN, GOSPEL ACCORDING TO SAINT; JOHN, epistles; REVELATION). He and his brother, St. James (the Greater), were sons of Zebedee. Jesus called them Boanerges or Sons of Thunder (Mark 3.17). The two brothers, together with Peter, were the three apostles closest to Jesus; they witnessed the Transfiguration and accompanied Jesus to Gethsemane (Mat. 17.1–13; 26.36–46; Mark 9.2–13; 14.33–

45). John is thought to have been the disciple "whom Jesus loved"; to his care Jesus, in his dying moments, committed the Virgin Mary (John 13.23; 19.26; 21.20–23). He is mentioned occasionally in Acts (3,4; 8.14–25), and St. Paul refers to him (Gal. 2.9); inferences may also be drawn from the books bearing his name. According to 2d-century authorities John died at an advanced age at Ephesus (A.D. c.100), where he had chiefly lived except for a visit to Rome and a period of exile on Patmos (Rev. 1.9). However, many scholars believe that St. John the apostle and St. John of Ephesus were two different persons. He is variously called St. John the Evangelist, because of the Gospel; St. John the Divine (i.e., theologian), because of the theological interest of the books; and the Beloved Disciple. His symbol as evangelist is an eagle. Feast: Dec. 27; the Feast of St. John before the Latin Gate, commemorating the dedication of a Roman basilica to him on the traditional site of his miraculous escape from martyrdom: May 6.

John VIII, d. 882, pope (872–82), a Roman; successor of Adrian II. John strenuously opposed the activities of St. IGNATIUS OF CONSTANTINOPLE in Bulgaria. When Ignatius died, John recognized PHOTIUS as patriarch and called the council (879–80) that momentarily reconciled the differences between East and West. John was deeply involved in imperial politics. He crowned CHARLES II (Charles the Bald) emperor and excommunicated the future Pope Formosus for opposition to his policy. When Charles II lost his power, John favored Charles the Fat, who became emperor as Charles III. The pope had to bribe the Saracens to keep them from entering Rome. He did much to root out corruption in the church in Rome, and, except for Nicholas I, he was the strongest pope of the 9th cent. He was assassinated by his own relatives. Marinus I succeeded him.

John XII, c.937–964, pope (955–64), a Roman (count of Tusculum) named Octavian; successor of Agapetus II and predecessor of either Leo VIII or Benedict V. His father, Alberic, secured John's election before the latter was 20 years old. John's life was notoriously immoral and his pontificate a disgrace. He called on OTTO I to help him against Berengar II of Italy. John crowned (962) Otto the first German emperor, and the two, in the famous *Privilegium Ottonis,* pledged loyalty to each other. Disliking the emperor's new influence in papal affairs, John sided with Berengar's party against Otto. In retaliation, Otto invaded Rome and called a synod that deposed John and elected Leo VIII as pope. John was restored by Roman insurrectionists shortly before he was mysteriously murdered. Scholars differ on the

Johannesburg, the largest city in South Africa.

legitimacy of Leo VIII's reign, as they do on the brief pontificate of Benedict V, elected upon John's death and deposed by Otto shortly thereafter again in favor of Leo. Leo died in 965.

John XXI, d. 1277, pope (1276–77), a Portuguese named Pedro Giuliano; successor of Adrian V. Known generally as Peter of Spain (Petrus Hispanus), he is the only Portuguese pope. Peter's reputation as a scholastic philosopher was widespread, and he was the reputed author of an extensively used book on logic. Nine months after his election the ceiling of his library at Viterbo fell and killed him. John was actually the 20th canonical pope named John, but through chronological errors he called himself John XXI; this numbering is usually maintained. He was succeeded by Nicholas III.

John XXII, 1244–1334, pope (1316–34), a Frenchman (b. Cahors) named Jacques Duèse; successor of Clement V. Formerly, he was often called John XXI. He reigned at Avignon. John was celebrated as a canon jurist under Boniface VIII, whom he supported. After the death of Clement there was a period of more than two years before the conclave could agree. Before John's election a contest had begun in the empire between LOUIS IV and his rival, Frederick of Austria. John was neutral at first; then in 1323, when Louis had won and became Holy Roman emperor, pope and emperor began a serious quarrel. This was partly provoked by John's extreme claims of authority over the empire and partly by Louis's support of the radical Franciscans, whom John XXII condemned for their insistence on evangelical poverty. Louis was assisted by Marsilius of Padua, who published his theories in 1324, and later by William of Ockham. The emperor invaded Italy and set up (1328) as an antipope Pietro Rainalducci (as Nicholas V). The project was a fiasco, but Louis silenced the papal claims. In John's last years he advanced a theory concerning the vision of God in heaven; the novelty he proposed (that this vision will begin only after the Last Judgment) was everywhere denied and scorned by theologians, and John abandoned it. He was an excellent administrator and did much efficient reorganizing. He was succeeded by Benedict XII.

John XXIII, antipope: see COSSA, BALDASSARRE.

John XXIII, 1881–1963, pope (1958–63), an Italian (b. Sotto il Monte, near Bergamo) named Angelo Giuseppe Roncalli; successor of Pius XII. He was of peasant stock. Educated at Bergamo and the Seminario Romano (called the Apollinare), Rome, he was ordained in 1904. While secretary to the bishop of Bergamo (1904–14) he wrote scholarly works, among them a life of St. Charles Borromeo (completed in 5 vol., 1936–52). Called up for service in World War I, he was first in the medical corps and was later a chaplain. After the war he held posts in Rome and reorganized the Society for the Propagation of the Faith. In 1925 he was made archbishop and sent as Vatican diplomatic representative to Bulgaria. Later he was representative in Turkey and Greece, and in 1944 he was named papal nuncio to France. There he acted as mediator between the conservative churchmen and the more socially "radical" clergy; he gained popularity. In 1953 he was made cardinal and the patriarch of Venice. He was elected pope Oct. 28, 1958. As pope, he put reforms into practice: He laid stress on his own pastoral duties as well as those of other bishops and the lesser clergy; he was active in promoting social reforms for workers, the

Pope John XXIII (seated on throne), at the opening of the Second Vatican Council in Oct., 1962.

poor, orphans, and the outcast; he advanced cooperation with other religions (among his innumerable visitors were many Protestant leaders, the head of the Greek Orthodox Church, the archbishop of Canterbury, and a Shinto high priest). In April, 1959, he forbade Roman Catholics to vote for parties supporting Communism, but his encyclical *Mater et Magistra*—a vigorous social document issued July 14, 1961, just 30 years after Pius XI's *Quadragesimo Anno*—advocated social reform, assistance to underdeveloped countries, a living wage for all workers, and support for all socialist measures that promised real benefit to society. Pope John XXIII almost doubled the number of cardinals, making the college the largest in history. On Jan. 25, 1959, he quietly announced the intention of calling an ecumenical council to consider measures for renewal of the church in the modern world, promotion of diversity within the encasing unity of the church, and the reforms that had been earnestly promoted by the ecumenical movement and the liturgical movement (see LITURGY). The convening of the council on Oct. 11, 1962, was the high point of his reign (see VATICAN COUNCIL, SECOND). His heartiness, his overflowing love for humanity individually and collectively, and his freshness of approach to ecclesiastical affairs made John one of the best-loved popes of modern times. He was succeeded by Paul VI. In 1965 the process of beatification of John XXIII was begun. See his memoirs, *Journal of a Soul* (tr. 1964) and *Letters to his Family* (1970); biographies by Meriol Trevor (1967) and Lawrence Elliott (1973).

John I (John Tzimisces)(tsĭmĭs'ēz), c.925–976, Byzantine emperor (969–76). Of a noble Armenian family, he was the leading general of Emperor NICEPHORUS II, but fell from favor in 969. With the aid of the emperor's wife, Theophano, he had Nicephorus murdered and himself proclaimed emperor. John gained the favor of the patriarch of Constantinople by revoking his predecessor's anticlerical legislation. He regained E Bulgaria from the Russians and extended Byzantine power in the east at the expense of the Arabs. He was succeeded by Basil II.

John II (John Comnenus)(kŏmnē'nəs), 1088–1143, Byzantine emperor (1118–43), son and successor of Alexius I. He was crowned despite the intrigues of his sister, ANNA COMNENA, and of his mother, Irene. His attempts to cancel the commercial privileges granted the Venetians by Alexius were unsuccessful, but his campaigns against the Magyars, Serbs, and Pechenegs were victorious. He successfully defied Roger II of Sicily, made an alliance with Emperor Conrad III to check growing Norman power, and conquered Cilicia from the Armenians. He died while preparing to fight the Latin prince of Antioch. John II was respected for his lofty character and for leniency toward his adversaries. He was succeeded by his son Manuel I.

John III (John Ducas Vatatzes) (dŏŏ'kəs vətăt'zēz), d. 1254, Byzantine emperor of Nicaea (1222–54), successor and son-in-law of Theodore I. He extended his territory in Asia Minor and the Aegean islands but failed (1235) to take Constantinople from the Latins, although he was aided by IVAN II of Bulgaria. Subsequently Ivan, the Cumans, and the Latins of Constantinople allied themselves against John, who held his own. John joined the Turks against the Mongol invaders. He annexed Salonica (Thessaloníki) in 1246 and reduced the despotat of Epirus to vassalage, thus nearly recovering the territories of the Byzantine Empire. He maintained close relations with the German emperor, Frederick II, whose daughter he married. During his reign the empire flourished. He was succeeded by his son Theodore II.

John IV (John Lascaris)(lăs'kərĭs), b. c.1250, d. after 1273, Byzantine emperor of Nicaea (1258–61), son and successor (under a regency) of Theodore II and last of the Lascarids. Michael Palaeologus (later MICHAEL VIII) overthrew the regency and in 1259 was crowned coemperor. He postponed John's coronation and in 1261 had the boy blinded and imprisoned. It is possible that John escaped from his fortress and went (c.1273) to the court of Charles of Anjou.

John V (John Palaeologus) (pālēŏl'əgəs), 1332–91, Byzantine emperor (1341–91), son and successor of Andronicus III. Forced to fight John VI (John Cantacuzene), who usurped the throne during his minority, he came into power in 1354. In his reign the Ottoman Turks took Adrianople and Philippolis, conquered Serbia, and exacted tribute from the emperor. John vainly tried to heal the schism between East and West in order to secure Western aid against the Turks. He professed (1369) the Roman Catholic faith at Rome; while returning to Constantinople he was briefly imprisoned for debt in Venice. In 1371 he recognized the suzerainty of the Ottoman sultan Murad I. Deposed (1376) by his son Andronicus IV, he was restored in 1379. In 1390 his grandnephew, John VII, briefly usurped the throne. John V was succeeded by his son Manuel II.

John VI (John Cantacuzene) (kăn"təkyŏŏzēn'), c.1292–1383, Byzantine emperor (1347–54). He was chief minister under Andronicus III, after whose death he proclaimed himself emperor and made war on the rightful heir, John V. He was aided by the Ottoman Turks. The war allowed STEPHEN DUSHAN to build his Serbian empire. John's reign briefly quieted civil and religious strife within the empire. In 1354 he abdicated in favor of John V and retired to a monastery, where he wrote a history of the period 1320–56. A defender of the mystical theory known as Hesychasm, he was instrumental in its acceptance by the Orthodox Eastern Church.

John VII (John Palaeologus) (pā"lēŏl'əgəs), c.1370–1408, Byzantine emperor, grandson of John V. Backed by the sultan Bayazid I, he usurped (1390) the throne from John V but was dethroned by his uncle, Manuel II, six months later. He again ruled (1394–1403) as coemperor when Manuel II went to the West to seek aid against the Turks.

John VIII (John Palaeologus), 1390–1448, Byzantine emperor (1425–48), son and successor of Manuel II. When he acceded, the Byzantine Empire had been reduced by the Turks to the city of Constantinople. John sought in vain to secure Western aid by agreeing at the Council of Florence (1439) to the union of the Eastern and Western churches. His brother, Constantine XI, succeeded him in 1449 and was the last Byzantine emperor.

John I, 1350–95, king of Aragón and count of Barcelona (1387–95), son and successor of Peter IV. During his reign Aragón lost (1388) the duchy of Athens. An enthusiastic patron of learning and an imitator of French customs, he held one of the most brilliant courts of the time. He was succeeded by his brother, Martin I.

John II, 1397–1479, king of Aragón and Sicily (1458–79), king of Navarre (1425–79), count of Barcelona. He succeeded his brother, Alfonso V, in Aragón,

Catalonia, and Sicily and became king of Navarre through his marriage with Blanche, heiress of that kingdom. After Blanche's death (1442) Navarre was ruled by their son, CHARLES OF VIANA, but conflict between father and son plunged Navarre into civil war, and Charles fled to Italy. In 1461 a Catalan uprising forced John to recognize Charles as heir, but Charles died in the same year. John was expelled from Catalonia, and René of Anjou was chosen count of Barcelona. Only in 1472 did John succeed in pacifying Catalonia. At John's death Navarre passed to the house of FOIX through the marriage of John's daughter Leonor; Aragón, Catalonia, and Sicily passed to his son, Ferdinand II, who as Ferdinand V also became king of Castile.

John, 1167–1216, king of England (1199–1216), son of HENRY II and ELEANOR OF AQUITAINE. The king's youngest son, John was left out of Henry's original division of territory among his sons and was nicknamed John Lackland. He was, however, his father's favorite, and despite the opposition of his brothers (whose rebellion of 1173–74 was provoked by Henry's plans for John), he later received scattered possessions in England and France and the lordship of Ireland. His brief expedition to Ireland in 1185 was badly mismanaged. John deserted his dying father in 1189 and joined the rebellion of his brother Richard, who succeeded to the throne as RICHARD I in the same year. The new king generously conferred lands and titles on John. After Richard's departure on the Third Crusade, John led a rebellion against the chancellor, William of LONGCHAMP, had himself acknowledged (1191) temporary ruler and heir to the throne, and conspired with PHILIP II of France to supplant Richard on the throne. This plot was successfully thwarted by those loyal to Richard, including the queen mother, Eleanor of Aquitaine. Richard pardoned John's treachery. On Richard's death, John ascended the English throne to the exclusion of his nephew, ARTHUR I of Brittany. The supporters of Arthur, aided by King Philip, began a formidable revolt in France. At this time John alienated public opinion in England by divorcing his first wife, Isabel of Gloucester, and made enemies in France by marrying Isabel of Angoulême, who had been betrothed to Hugh de Lusignan. In 1202, Arthur was defeated and captured, and it is thought that John murdered him in 1203. Philip continued the war and gradually gained ground until by 1206 he was in control of Normandy, Anjou, Brittany, Maine, and Touraine. John had lost all his French dominions except Aquitaine and a part of Poitou. The death (1205) of John's chancellor, Hubert WALTER, archbishop of Canterbury, not only removed a moderating influence on the king but precipitated a crisis with the English church. John refused (1206) to accept the election of Stephen LANGTON as Walter's successor at Canterbury, and as a result Pope INNOCENT III placed (1208) England under interdict and excommunicated (1209) the king. The quarrel continued until 1213 when John, threatened by the danger of a French invasion and by increasing disaffection among the English barons, surrendered his kingdom to the pope and received it back as a papal fief. Submission improved John's situation greatly. Now backed by the pope, he formed an expedition to wage war on Philip in Poitou. However, while John was at La Rochelle, his allies, Holy Roman Emperor OTTO IV (his nephew) and the count of Flanders, were decisively beaten by Philip at Bouvines in 1214. John had resorted to all means to secure men and money for his Poitou campaign, and after returning home he attempted to collect SCUTAGE from the barons who had refused to aid him on the expedition. Abuses of feudal customs and extortion of money from the barons and the towns, not only by John but by Henry II and Richard I, had aroused intense opposition, which increased in John's unfortunate reign. The barons now rose in overwhelming force against the king, and John in capitulation set his seal on the MAGNA CARTA at Runnymede in June, 1215. Thus, the most famous document of English constitutional history was the fruit not of popular but of baronial force. John, supported by the pope, gathered forces and renewed the struggle with the barons, who sought the aid of Prince Louis of France (later LOUIS VIII). In the midst of this campaign John died, and his son, Henry III, was left to carry on the royal cause. John, though often cruel and treacherous, was an excellent administrator, much concerned with rendering justice among his subjects. The basic cause of his conflicts with the barons was not that he was an innovator in trying to wield an absolute royal power, but that in so doing he ignored and contravened the traditional feudal relationship between the crown and the nobility. The modern bitter and hostile picture of John is primarily the work of subsequent chroniclers, mainly ROGER OF WENDOVER and MATTHEW OF PARIS. John is the central character of one of Shakespeare's plays. See biographies by Kate Margate (1902, repr. 1970), John T. Appleby (1958), W. L. Warren (1961), J. C. Holt (1963), and Alan Lloyd (1972); A. L. Poole, *From Domesday Book to Magna Carta, 1087–1216* (2d ed. 1955).

John I or **John the Posthumous,** 1316, king of France, posthumous son of King Louis X. He lived only five days and was succeeded by his uncle, Philip V. According to legend, a dying child was substituted for John, who was then brought up by a merchant in Siena.

John II (John the Good), 1319–64, king of France (1350–64), son and successor of King Philip VI. An inept ruler, he began his reign by executing the constable of France (whose office he gave to his favorite, Charles de La Cerda) and by appointing dishonest and unpopular advisers. Because of a general economic crisis, he subsequently debased the coinage for the expenses of the Hundred Years War between France and England. His quarrels with his ambitious son-in-law, CHARLES II of Navarre, lasted throughout his reign. John was captured (1356) by the English at the battle of Poitiers. During his captivity, the dauphin (later King CHARLES V) acted as regent and dealt with several rebellions, such as the JACQUERIE. In 1360, by the Treaty of BRÉTIGNY, John was released in exchange for a ransom and hostages. In 1364 one of the hostages escaped, and John saved his honor by returning to England, where he died.

John I (John Zapolya) (zä'pôlyŏ), 1487–1540, king of Hungary (1526–40), voivode [governor] of Transylvania (1511–26). He was born John Zapolya, the son of Stephen ZÁPOLYA. The leader of the antiforeign party of the Hungarian nobles, he secured a decree at the diet of 1505 by which no foreign ruler would be chosen king of Hungary after the death of the ruling king, ULADISLAUS II. To strengthen his own candidacy for the crown he sought to marry the king's daughter, Anna, but his suit was rejected and he was removed from the court through his appointment as voivode of Transylvania. He ruthlessly crushed a peasant uprising in 1514. His anger at the marriage of Anna to Ferdinand of Austria (later Holy Roman Emperor FERDINAND I) probably motivated his failure to assist Uladislaus' son, King Louis II of Hungary, at the battle of MOHACS (1526). Louis II was killed in the battle. John was crowned king by the Hungarian nobles, but Ferdinand claimed the crown on the basis of his marriage with Anna as well as previous agreements. In 1527, Ferdinand defeated John and was crowned by John's opponents. John retired to his stronghold in the Carpathians. In 1529 the Turks began to overrun Hungary. John now descended upon and defeated Ferdinand's army and, after surrendering the crown to Sultan Sulayman I, was confirmed king by the sultan, who exercised real control. The struggle between John and Ferdinand ended in 1538, when John, who was then childless, agreed that the crown should pass to Ferdinand after his death. John set aside the agreement when, a few months before his death, a son, John Sigismund (John II), was born.

John II (John Sigismund Zapolya), 1540–71, king of Hungary and prince of Transylvania, son of John I. Through his mother, Isabel (daughter of Sigismund I of Poland), he was related to the Jagiello dynasty. As an infant, he was crowned king of Hungary on his father's death (1540). Sultan SULAYMAN I, on the pretext of protecting John's interests, invaded (1541) Hungary and took the capital, Buda, which remained in Turkish hands for 150 years. John and Isabel received the principality of Transylvania under Turkish suzerainty, but actual power was held by John's guardian, the monk George Martinuzzi, who sought to restore a unified Hungary. In 1551, Martinuzzi procured the deposition of John and Isabel and reunited Transylvania with Hungary, recognizing Ferdinand of Austria and Bohemia (later Holy Roman Emperor FERDINAND I) as king.. Martinuzzi, made prince-primate and a cardinal, soon fell out with Ferdinand, who had him assassinated. On the pressure of Sulayman I the diet of Transylvania recalled (1556) John and Isabel, and when Ferdinand made peace (1562) with Sulayman, he also recognized John as ruler of Transylvania. Thus Hungary remained split into three states—an Austrian part, a Turkish part, and Transylvania. It was under John II that the Transylvanian diet adopted (1564) Calvinism as the state religion. John was succeeded as prince of Transylvania by Stephen Bathory.

John II (John Casimir), 1609–72, king of Poland (1648–68), son of Sigismund III. He was elected to succeed his brother, Ladislaus IV. The turbulent period of his reign is known in Polish history as the Deluge. The uprising of the Cossacks under CHMIELNICKI, supported by the khan of Crimea, had begun under his predecessor. John II defeated (1651) the allied Cossack, Tatar, and Turkish forces, but in 1654 the Cossacks accepted Russian suzerainty over the UKRAINE, and Czar Alexis promptly invaded Poland. In 1655, CHARLES X of Sweden nearly overran Poland and was checked only by the successful Polish defense of CZESTOCHOWA, which inspired the Poles to renewed resistance. George II Rákóczy, prince of Transylvania, attacked Poland from the south but was defeated. FREDERICK WILLIAM of Brandenburg (the Great Elector), originally a Swedish ally, joined (1657) the Polish side in the struggle; in return John recognized his full sovereignty over East Prussia. The fighting in the west was concluded in 1660 (see OLIVA, PEACE OF). War with Russia ended only in 1667, with the cession of the eastern part of Ukraine to the czar. During John's reign the *liberum veto* (by which any deputy could dissolve the diet and annul its decisions) was greatly abused. The king and his French consort, Louise Marie de Gonzague (widow of Ladislaus IV), were childless; their efforts to nominate a successor evoked several rebellions of the nobles. A year after the death (1667) of his queen, who had exerted much influence over him, John abdicated and retired to an abbey at Nevers, France. Michael Wisniowiecki was elected his successor; disorder continued during his reign (1668–73), which was followed by that of John III.

John III (John Sobieski), (sôbyĕ'skē), 1624–96, king of Poland (1674–96), champion of Christian Europe against the Turks. Born to an ancient noble family, he was appointed (1668) commander of the Polish army. He defeated (1673) the Turks at Khotin shortly after the death of King Michael, and in 1674 he was elected to succeed Michael. John's plans to recover East Prussia led him to conclude alliances with France (1675) and Sweden (1677) against Frederick William of Brandenburg (the Great Elector). However, the emphasis of his foreign policy changed when Sultan Muhammad IV and the Hungarians under Thököly advanced against Austria. Realizing the danger to all Europe, John allied (1683) with Holy Roman Emperor Leopold I and, leading combined imperial and Polish forces, raised the siege of VIENNA and defeated the much larger Turkish army under Kara Mustapha. Despite Leopold's ungrateful reception, John continued his campaign and pursued the Turks into Hungary. In 1684 he formed a Holy League with the pope, the emperor, and Venice. In 1686 he made a treaty with Russia that confirmed Russian suzerainty in E Ukraine. However, John's attempts (1684–91) to secure access to the Black Sea by wresting Moldavia and Walachia from the Ottoman Empire were unsuccessful. His loss of military prestige encouraged the nobles to oppose him at home. John's death, followed by the choice of the elector of Saxony as King Augustus II of Poland, marked the virtual end of Polish independence.

John I (John the Great), 1357?–1433, king of Portugal (1385–1433), illegitimate son of Peter I. He was made (1364) grand master of the Knights of Aviz and exercised his influence in opposition to Leonor Teles, the queen of his half brother, FERDINAND I. After Ferdinand's death (1383), his widow and her lover, the conde de Ourém, set up a regency in the name of Ferdinand's daughter Beatrice, wife of John I of Castile. This provoked a popular national revolt, led by John of Aviz, who murdered Ourém, and Nun' Álvares PEREIRA. The Castilians invaded (1384) Portugal, but their forces were decimated by the plague while they laid siege to Lisbon. John was elected king in 1385, and in the same year a great victory over the Castilians at Aljubarrota assured Portuguese independence (though peace was not finally concluded until 1411). John's position was strengthened by an alliance with England, sealed by a treaty (1386) and by John's marriage (1387) to Philippa, daughter of JOHN OF GAUNT. The reign of John the Great was one of the most glorious in medieval Portuguese history. His popularity was heightened by his administrative reforms. His sons, Duarte, Peter, Henry the Navigator, John, and Ferdinand, were important in inaugurating the era of Portuguese colonial and maritime expansion. Ceuta in N Africa was conquered from the Moors in 1415. John was succeeded by his son Duarte.

John II (John the Perfect), 1455–95, king of Portugal (1481–95), son and successor of Alfonso V. He was an astute politician and statesman and a patron of Renaissance art and learning. He reduced the power of the feudal nobility and had his chief opponent, the duke of BRAGANZA, executed for treason. John maintained peace with Spain and signed (1494) the Treaty of TORDESILLAS, setting bounds for Spanish and Portuguese colonial expansion. Supporting Portuguese exploration, he sent land expeditions to India and Ethiopia in search of Prester John and sent a vessel N past North Cape. John refused to help Columbus, whom he thought a dreamer, but he encouraged the search for an eastern sea route to India. Diogo Cão discovered (1484) the Congo, and Bartholomew Diaz rounded (1488) the Cape of Good Hope during his reign. John's son Alfonso predeceased him, so he was succeeded by his cousin and brother-in-law, Manuel I.

John III (John the Fortunate), 1502–57, king of Portugal (1521–57), son of MANUEL I. His reign saw the Portuguese empire at its apogee. The great Asiatic possessions were extended by further conquest, and systematic colonization of Brazil was begun. However, in Portugal itself decadence had set in with the decline of both agriculture and the population. Portugal's African exploits were abandoned, but many Negro slaves were brought into the country. The Inquisition was introduced (1536) by John, who was devoted to the clerical party. The court was corrupt, though the king was not. Literature flourished early in his reign, but Portugal was falling into the stagnation that characterized the disastrous reign of Sebastian, who succeeded him.

John IV, 1604–56, king of Portugal (1640–56). He succeeded as duke of BRAGANZA in 1630. Descended from Manuel I and in illegitimate line from John I, he had the strongest claim to the Portuguese throne when a revolution was planned to cast off the rule of Philip IV of Spain. In 1640 the revolution was successfully carried out, and John became king of independent Portugal. John's policy was to secure foreign alliances, especially with France, in order to consolidate his position against Spain (which did not recognize Portuguese independence until 1668). During his reign the Dutch were expelled (1654) from Brazil, where they had seized territory during the period of Spanish rule. John was unwarlike himself and was devoted to hunting, music, and the arts. The first king of the Braganza line, he was succeeded by his son Alfonso VI. His daughter Catherine married Charles II of England.

John V (John the Magnanimous), 1689–1750, king of Portugal (1706–50), son and successor of Peter II. Before his accession the Methuen Treaty (1703) with England had brought Portugal into the War of the SPANISH SUCCESSION, but after a major defeat at Almansa (1707), the Portuguese played little part in the fighting. After the war, John sought to maintain Portugal's alliance with England and to keep peace, except in giving assistance (1716–17) to the Venetians against the Turks. Enriched by gold from Brazil, John was a patron of arts and letters, had a sumptuous court, and erected beautiful buildings in Lisbon. However, his wealth also made him independent of the Cortes, so he ruled with increasing absolutism. He has been criticized for subservience to the church, from which he drew most of his ministers, especially in later years. John was succeeded by his son Joseph.

John VI, 1769–1826, king of Portugal (1816–26), son of Maria I and Peter III. When his mother became insane, John assumed the reins of government (1792), although he did not formally become regent until 1799. He joined the coalition against revolutionary France, adopted a repressive policy in Portugal, and sought the friendship of England. The English alliance made Napoleon I an inveterate enemy of Portugal. French and Spanish forces in 1801 quickly defeated Portugal and forced on John the humiliating Treaty of Badajoz (1801). John was completely submissive to Napoleon, but nonetheless in 1807 the French again marched against Portugal. John and the royal family fled (1807) Lisbon and arrived (1808) in Brazil, where John set up his court. After the British defeated the French in Portugal, they set up a regency to rule the country. John, however, remained in Brazil even after succeeding as king on his mother's death (1816). It was only after the overthrow of the regency in Portugal by revolution (1820) and the proclamation of a liberal constitution that John was persuaded by the British to return (1821) to Portugal. He left his son Pedro (PEDRO I) as regent of Brazil. After accepting the constitution, he took advantage of every opportunity to modify it. He put down temporarily an absolutist revolt headed by his wife, Queen Carlota Joaquina, and his son Dom MIGUEL and in 1825 recognized Brazilian independence (proclaimed in 1822). On his death John left the regency of Portugal to his daughter Isabel, who recognized Pedro as Peter IV of Portugal.

John I, 1358–90, Spanish king of Castile and León (1379–90), son and successor of Henry II. He tried unsuccessfully to unite the Portuguese and Castilian crowns but was twice defeated by the Portuguese, notably in the battle of Aljubarrota (1385). He defended his crown against JOHN OF GAUNT and married his son Henry to John of Gaunt's daughter. Henry succeeded him as Henry III.

John II, 1405–54, Spanish king of Castile and León (1406–54), son and successor of Henry III. He was little interested in government, which he entrusted to his favorite Alvaro de LUNA. Literature, particularly poetry, flourished at his court, which was also celebrated for tournaments and brilliant festivals. John was succeeded by his son Henry IV.

John, in the Bible. **1** See JOHN, SAINT. **2** See JOHN THE BAPTIST. **3** See MARK, SAINT. **4** One of the high priest's family. Acts 4.6. There are also several persons named John in the books of the Maccabees. See MACCABEES and 1 Mac. 9.36–38; 13.53; 16.2; 2 Mac. 4.11; 11.17.

John, Augustus Edwin, 1879–1961, British painter and etcher, b. Wales. John studied at the Slade School, London. A leading portrait painter, he had many important sitters, among them Elizabeth II, Lloyd George, G. B. Shaw, T. E. Lawrence, Sean O'Casey, and Dylan Thomas. His portraits show vigorous characterization without flattery. His celebrated *Smiling Woman* is a portrait of his wife (1910; Tate Gall., London). John's etchings include several self-portraits as well as portraits of W. B. Yeats, Jacob Epstein, and James Joyce. See his autobiographical *Chiaroscuro* (1952); studies by T. W. Earp (1934) and John Rothenstein (1945). John's sister **Gwen John** (1876–1939) was a student of Whistler and a painter in the Pre-Raphaelite manner.

John, three epistles of the New Testament, the 23d, 24th, and 25th books in the usual order. By universal tradition they are ascribed to St. John, the disciple. This authorship is necessarily denied by the many critics who do not admit St. John to be the writer of the Gospel, for First John was certainly written by the man who wrote the Gospel, and Second and Third John are widely agreed to be by the same author also. The date of First John is about that of the Gospel; nothing can be said of the dates of the other two. These epistles are traditionally classed with the Catholic, or General, Epistles, but they were apparently addressed to definite churches or persons. First John is a homily on the blending of mystical and practical religion, intended for persons long Christian. A division of the book gives: prologue (1.1–4); God is light (1.5–2.28); God is righteous (2.29–4.6); God is love (4.7–5.12); epilogue (5.13–21). The necessity of good works to reveal the Christian heart is reiterated, e.g., 2.3–5; 3.24; 4.7–11,20. There is an allusion to the gnostic error of denying Jesus' historicity (4.2–3). Second John, in 13 verses, is the shortest book of the Bible. The author refers to himself as elder (presbyter or priest) and is addressing some "elect lady," probably an allegorical title, perhaps for a particular church. The letter warns against false teachers who deny the historicity of Jesus. Third John, in 14 verses, has the same author; it is addressed to a Gaius, of an unidentified church. It protests against the failure of the leader of the church to receive teaching missionaries.

John, Gospel according to Saint, fourth book of the New Testament. This life of Jesus is clearly set off from the other three Gospels (see SYNOPTIC GOSPELS), although it is probable that John knew and used both Mark and Luke as sources. The aim of the evangelist seems to be twofold—to show that Jesus is the vital force in the world now and forever and that he lived on earth in order to reveal himself to men in the flesh. These two ideas are, for the evangelist, complementary, and one of the artistic beauties of the Gospel is the way Jesus' acts as a human being introduce discourses upon his mystical nature. The Gospel opens with a philosophical prologue (1.1–18), in which Jesus is identified with the Word (or LOGOS). The author adopted this term from contemporary metaphysicians who used it to designate the link between God and man. Hence "the Word was made flesh" (1.14) is the explicit classical statement of the Incarnation. The book falls into two main sections, the ministry of Jesus (1.19–12.50) and the Passion and Resurrection (13–21). The first portion is a series of selected incidents from the ministry of Christ. The last part consists of a long account of the Last Supper (13–17), the Passion proper (18–19), and the Resurrection (20–21). The traditional date of composition is A.D. c.100; according to 20th-century scholarship it was composed probably between A.D. 95 and 115. The ascription to St. JOHN is very ancient, but it has been questioned by modern critics. Most scholars agree that 7.53–8.11 was not part of the Gospel as first composed; otherwise the book is usually considered to have been written almost exactly as it stands. The influence of the Gospel of St. John in Christianity has been tremendous. The unique position of Jesus Christ in Christian theology as God and man, which involves the dogmas of the Trinity, the Incarnation, and the Atonement, is first enunciated in this Gospel. See E. F. Scott, *The Fourth Gospel* (2d ed. 1930); C. H. Dodd, *The Interpretation of the Fourth Gospel* (1953, repr. 1960); J. L. Martyn, *History and Theology in the Fourth Gospel* (1968).

John Baptist de la Salle, Saint, 1651–1719, French educator, founder of the Christian Brothers, b. Rheims. He became a priest and canon of the cathedral. He spent his life teaching children of the poor. In 1684 (having resigned his canonry) he formed of his assistants a new order, the Christian Brothers. In 1685 to train his teachers, St. John Baptist founded at Rheims what is called the first normal school. He was a careful pedagogical thinker and ranks as one of the distinguished educators of modern times. His name in French is Jean Baptiste de la Salle. Feast: May 15. See W. J. Battersby, *De la Salle* (3 vol., 1945–52).

John Birch Society, ultraconservative, anti-Communist organization in the United States. It was founded in Dec., 1958, by manufacturer Robert Welch and named after John Birch, an American intelligence officer killed by Communists in China (Aug., 1945). The most prominent of the extreme right-wing groups active in the United States, the society was founded to fight subversive Communism within the United States. Its other objectives include the abolition of the graduated income tax, the repeal of social security legislation, the impeachment of various high government officials, and the end to bussing for the purpose of integrating the public schools. These objectives, together with charges made by Welch in his book, *The Politician*, to the effect that Dwight D. Eisenhower and John Foster Dulles had actively aided the so-called Communist conspiracy, tend to discredit the organization. See Richard Vahan, *The Truth about the John Birch Society* (1962); J. A. Broyles, *The John Birch Society* (1964); B. R. Epstein and Arnold Foster, *Radical Right* (1967).

John Bosco, Saint, 1815–88, Italian priest, b. Piedmont. As a priest at Turin he was very successful in work with boys. He founded (1841) the Salesian order (i.e., order of St. Francis of Sales) for this work and for foreign missions. Later he founded an order of women, Daughters of Mary Auxiliatrix, for similar work among girls. These orders have become very large. He was canonized in 1934. Feast: Jan. 31. See Henri Ghéon, *The Secret of Saint John Bosco* (1936).

John Bull: see ARBUTHNOT, JOHN.

John Carter Brown Library: see BROWN, JOHN CARTER.

John Chrysostom, Saint (krĭs'əstəm, krĭsŏs'-) [Gr.,=golden-mouth], c.347–407, Doctor of the Church, greatest of the Greek Fathers. He was born in Antioch and studied Greek classics there. As a young man he became an anchorite monk (374), a deacon (c.381) and a priest (386). Under Flavian of Antioch he preached brilliantly in the cathedral for 12 years, winning wide recognition. In 398 he was suddenly made patriarch of Constantinople, where he soon gained the admiration of the people by his eloquence, his ascetic life, and his charity. His attempts to reform the clergy, however, alienated many monks and priests, and the court of the Roman emperor of the East came to resent his denunciation of their ways. He lost favor when he demanded mercy for the dishonored EUTROPIUS and when he refused to condemn without a hearing certain monks accused of heresy. Empress Eudoxia and Theophilus, bishop of Alexandria, succeeded in having St. John condemned (403) by an illegal synod on false charges. The indignation of the people was reinforced by an opportune earthquake, and the superstitious Eudoxia had St. John recalled. He continued to attack the immorality of the court, and Emperor Arcadius exiled him to Cucusus in Armenia.

There he continued to exert influence through his letters, and Arcadius moved him to a more isolated spot on the Black Sea. St. John, already ill, died from the rigors of the journey. Although not a formal polemicist, John Chrysostom influenced Christian thought notably. He wrote brilliant homilies, interpreting the Bible literally and historically rather than allegorically. His treatise on the priesthood (381) has always been popular. His sermons and writings, remarkable for their purity of Greek style, afford an invaluable picture of 4th-century life. His influence was already great in his own day, and the pope withdrew (406–16) from communion with Constantinople because of his banishment. In 438, St. John's body was returned to Constantinople, and Emperor Theodosius II did penance for his parents' offenses. John Chrysostom was not the author of the liturgy that bears his name. In 1909, Pope Pius X declared him patron of preachers. Feasts: in the Eastern Church, Sept. 14, Nov. 13, and Jan. 27; in the Western Church, Jan. 27. See studies by W. R. W. Stephens (3d ed. 1883; Anglican) and Donald Attwater (1939; Roman Catholic).

John Climax, Saint [Gr.,=ladder], d. c.649, Syrian hermit of Mt. Sinai. Little is known of his life, but his guide to the spiritual life in 30 steps, *The Ladder of Paradise,* was widely read in the Middle Ages. He is also known as John Climacus or John Scholasticus. Feast: March 30.

John Crerar Library: see CRERAR, JOHN.

John Damascene, Saint: see JOHN OF DAMASCUS, SAINT.

John Day, river, 281 mi (452 km) long, rising in several branches in the Strawberry Mts., NE Oregon, and flowing W, then N to the Columbia River. Unnavigable, the river is used to irrigate vegetable farms.

John Day Dam, 219 ft (67 m) high and 5,640 ft (1,719 m) long, on the Columbia River between Oregon and Wash.; one of the world's largest hydroelectric generating plants. Built between 1959 and 1968 by the U.S. Army Corps of Engineers, the dam will have an ultimate generating capacity of 2,700,000 kw. The dam's reservoir regulates navigation upstream; locks provide ship passage from The Dalles Dam reservoir to McNary Dam (see COLUMBIA BASIN PROJECT).

John Dory: see ROCKFISH.

John D. Rockefeller, Jr., Memorial Parkway, Wyo.: see NATIONAL PARKS AND MONUMENTS (table).

John Fisher, Saint: see FISHER, JOHN.

John Fitzgerald Kennedy National Historic Site: see NATIONAL PARKS AND MONUMENTS (table).

John Frederick I, 1503–54, elector (1532–47) and duke (1547–54) of Saxony; last elector of the Ernestine branch of the house of WETTIN. Like his father, John the Steadfast, whom he succeeded, John Frederick was a devout Lutheran. A leader of the SCHMALKALDIC LEAGUE, he vacillated in loyalty to Holy Roman Emperor CHARLES V, but he was thrown into opposition when Charles undertook the Schmalkaldic War to crush the independence of the imperial states in Germany and to restore Christian unity. Captured (1547) in the battle of Mühlberg, John Frederick was forced to renounce the electorate in favor of his cousin and enemy, MAURICE, duke of Saxony. He retained only a remnant of his lands and the title of duke. He refused to abandon his religious beliefs during subsequent imprisonment (1547–52).

John George, 1585–1656, elector of Saxony (1611–56). A drunkard, he nonetheless ruled the leading

Spanish admiral and general John of Austria (center), commander of the Christian fleet of the Holy League against the Turkish fleet at the battle of Lepanto.

German Protestant state during the THIRTY YEARS WAR. He vacillated in his policy between support of the Holy Roman Empire against the Lutheran princes and aid to his fellow Lutherans. He backed (1620) Holy Roman Emperor FERDINAND II against Protestant rebels in Bohemia under FREDERICK THE WINTER KING, and in return was promised Lusatia. After Frederick's defeat, however, he opposed the transfer (1623) of the Palatinate to Duke MAXIMILIAN I of Bavaria. The Edict of Restitution (1629), abrogating Protestant rights, increased his opposition to imperial policy. John George joined the Swedes against the emperor, and the Saxon army invaded Bohemia. The Saxons were driven back by the imperial general WALLENSTEIN, who turned on Saxony (1632) and devastated it. In 1635, John George deserted the Swedish alliance and concluded the Peace of Prague with Ferdinand II, which confirmed his possession of Lusatia. War continued and Saxony was repeatedly destroyed by opposing armies. In 1645, John George signed an armistice with the Swedes. After the war, the Holy Roman emperor made him titular leader of the Protestant estates.

John Henry, legendary American Negro famous for his strength, celebrated in ballads and tales. In the most popular version of the story, John Henry tries to outwork a steam drill with only his hammer and steel bit. Although he succeeds in beating the machine, he dies of the strain. His legend originated c.1870 among the miners drilling the Big Bend Tunnel of the Chesapeake & Ohio Railway in West Virginia and may have some historical basis.

John Hyrcanus: see MACCABEES, Jewish family.

John Jay College of Criminal Justice of the City University of New York; est. 1964 as the College of Police Science, opened 1965. Its present name was adopted in 1966. The school offers a basic college curriculum, but its emphasis is on both undergraduate and graduate training in the field of criminal justice. The majority of its students are police and law enforcement officers; however, the college is open to civilian students. See NEW YORK, CITY UNIVERSITY OF.

John Mark: see MARK, ST.

John Maurice of Nassau, 1604–79, Dutch general and colonial administrator, a prince of the house of Nassau-Siegen; grandnephew of William the Silent. The Dutch West India Company appointed him (1636) governor-general of its newly acquired possessions in Brazil. He conquered NE Brazil from the Portuguese and, in order to insure the supply of slave labor, seized several Portuguese strongholds on the Guinea coast of Africa. An able administrator, John Maurice made broad plans for the development of Brazil. He built up the state of Pernambuco and rebuilt the city of Recife. However, the directors of the company criticized his expenses, while John Maurice was opposed to undertaking the new hostilities that they ordered. On his request he was recalled in 1643. He subsequently held commands in Europe in the Thirty Years War, governed, after 1647, Cleves, Mark, and Ravensberg for the elector of Brandenburg, and in 1652 was made a prince of the Holy Roman Empire; he also was made grand master of the Knights Hospitalers. Despite his advanced age, he won new distinction in the Dutch Wars. After his retirement in 1675 he lived at Cleves. His residence at The Hague is the celebrated Mauritshuis.

John Muir National Historic Site: see NATIONAL PARKS AND MONUMENTS (table).

Johnny Appleseed: see CHAPMAN, JOHN.

Johnny-jump-up: see VIOLET.

John of Austria, 1545–78, Spanish admiral and general; illegitimate son of Holy Roman Emperor Charles V. He was acknowledged in his father's will and was recognized by his half brother, Philip II of Spain. In 1569 he fought against the Morisco rebels in Granada. As admiral of the Holy League, formed against the Turks by Pope Pius V, Spain, and Venice, he won the famous naval victory of LEPANTO (1571). He later took Tunis and served as governor-general in Italy. In 1576 he was sent by Philip as governor-general to the Netherlands, then in rebellion against Spain under the leadership of WILLIAM THE SILENT. John was forced to make concessions but then resumed hostilities. His victorious general, Alessandro FARNESE, succeeded him as governor-general on his death. See Sir William Stirling-Maxwell, *Don John of Austria* (1883).

John of Austria, 1629–79, Spanish general and statesman; illegitimate son of Philip IV. He helped put down Masaniello's revolt (1647) in Naples, was viceroy of Sicily (1648–51), and fought (1651–52) against the rebels in Catalonia. In 1656, while France was at war with Spain (see FRONDE), he was appointed governor of the Spanish Netherlands. He was defeated by Turenne at the battle of the DUNES (1658) and recalled. His campaign (1661–64) for the reconquest of Portugal also failed. During the minority of CHARLES II, he overthrew the regency of the queen-mother Mariana and seized power (1677). His government lost Franche-Comté to France by the peace of Nijmegen (1678).

John of Brienne (brēĕn'), c.1170–1237, French crusader. He was a count and in 1210 married Mary, titular queen of Jerusalem. Mary died in 1212, and their daughter, Yolande (1212–28), succeeded to the title under John's regency. John played a conspicuous part in the Fifth Crusade (see CRUSADES), capturing Damietta in 1219, and in 1222 he went to Europe in search of support. He arranged the marriage (1225) between Yolande and Holy Roman Emperor FREDERICK II, who promptly claimed the crown of Jerusalem. John, claiming the title for himself, joined with a papal army in invading (1229) Frederick's kingdom in S Italy, while Frederick was absent on crusade. In 1228, John was chosen regent during the minority of BALDWIN II, Latin emperor of Constantinople (see CONSTANTINOPLE, LATIN EMPIRE OF), and he became coemperor in 1231. He successfully defended (1236) Constantinople against the joint forces of Emperor John III of Nicaea and Czar Ivan II of Bulgaria.

John of Damascus, Saint, or **Saint John Damascene** (dăm'əsēn), c.675–c.749, Syrian theologian, Father of the Church and Doctor of the Church. He was brought up at the court of the caliph in Damascus, where his father was an official, and he was educated by a Sicilian monk. John inherited his father's office but resigned it (c.726) and entered a monastery in Palestine. His life was spent largely in fighting with his pen for orthodoxy against ICONOCLASM. His fame rests on his theological masterpiece, *The Fountain of Wisdom,* a Greek work in three parts—a theological study of Aristotle's categories; a history of heresies, based on Epiphanius and Theodoret, with supplementary material on iconoclasm and Islam; and a formal exposition of the Christian faith (*De fide orthodoxa,* tr. by F. N. Chase, 1958). This last work was extensively used by the scholastics and is still a prime source for the dogmatic opinions of the principal Eastern Fathers. John also wrote hymns and regulated the choral parts of the Byzantine liturgy. He stimulated the production of Byzantine painting. The elegance of his Greek brought him the epithet Chrysorrhoas [gold-pouring]. His name appears also as John Damascenus. Feast: in Western calendars, March 27. See F. P. Cassidy, *Molders of the Medieval Mind* (1944).

John of Ephesus (ĕf'əsəs), c.505–c.585, Syrian Monophysite historian, bishop of Ephesus. He became a leader of the Monophysites (see MONOPHYSITISM), and Byzantine Emperor Justinian, whose favor he enjoyed, set him over the Monophysite community in Constantinople. John suffered greatly in the persecution of his sect after 571. His *Ecclesiastical History* makes an unusual effort to avoid prejudice. It is especially valuable for the events of the 6th cent. He is also called John of Asia.

John of Gaunt [Mid. Eng. *Gaunt*=Ghent, his birthplace], 1340–99, duke of Lancaster; fourth son of EDWARD III of England. He married (1359) Blanche, heiress of Lancaster, and through her became earl (1361) and duke (1362) of Lancaster. The Lancaster holdings made him the wealthiest and one of the most influential nobles in England. He served under his brother, EDWARD THE BLACK PRINCE, in the Hundred Years War and went (1367) on his campaign to aid PETER THE CRUEL of Castile. After the death of Blanche he married (1371) Peter's daughter, Constance, and thus gained a claim to the Castilian throne. When the Black Prince became ill during the French campaign of 1370–71, John took chief command. In 1373 he led his army from Calais to Bordeaux, but the expedition accomplished little. After a truce was reached (1375) he returned to England, where he allied himself with the corrupt court party led by Alice Perrers, mistress of the aging Edward III. For a short time John of Gaunt in effect ruled England. His party was temporarily dislodged from power by the Good Parliament of 1376, but John was soon able to restore his friends and assembled a hand-picked Parliament in 1377. Hostility to the strong clerical party, led by WILLIAM OF WYKEHAM, caused him to support the movement of John WYCLIF. After the accession (1377) of his nephew, RICHARD II, John remained the most powerful figure in the government, but he devoted himself primarily to military matters. In 1386, allied with John I of Portugal, who married one of his daughters, he led an expedition to make good his Castilian claims against John I of Castile. John of Gaunt finally agreed to peace in 1388, transferred his claims to his daughter by Constance of Castile, and married her to the future Henry III of Castile. He returned to England in 1389, was made duke of Aquitaine, and helped to restore peace between Richard II and the hostile barons led by Thomas of Woodstock, duke of GLOUCESTER. In 1396, John of Gaunt married Catherine Swynford, many years his mistress, and had his children by her, under the name of Beaufort, declared legitimate. He died soon after the king had exiled his eldest son, the duke of Hereford (later HENRY IV, first of the royal line of Lancaster). Another royal line, the Tudor, was descended from him and Catherine Swynford. John is also remembered as the patron of the poet Geoffrey Chaucer. See biography by Sydney Armitage-Smith (1904, repr. 1964); James R. Hulbert, *Chaucer's Official Life* (1912, repr. 1970).

John of Hollywood: see SACROBOSCO, JOHANNES DE.

John of Lancaster, duke of Bedford: see BEDFORD, JOHN OF LANCASTER, DUKE OF.

John of Leiden, c.1509–1536, Dutch ANABAPTIST leader. His original name was Beuckelszoon, Beuckelzoon, Bockelszoon, Bockelson, Beukels, or Buckholdt. John of Leiden was attracted to the extreme left of the early Reformation movement through the influence of Thomas MÜNZER. In 1533 he joined the Anabaptists and, as a follower of Johann Matthyszoon (Matthiesen) moved to Münster. There in 1534 the Anabaptists took up arms and deposed the civil and religious authorities of the town. After Matthyszoon's death in the siege, John of Leiden assumed leadership and set up a theocracy in the new Zion. Soon John declared himself "king," with Bernard Knipperdollinck second in command; during his brief and arbitrary rule general lawlessness prevailed, polygamy was legalized, and property communized. When the siege to recover the town, led by the expelled prince bishop, was successful in 1535, the leaders of the new "kingdom of Zion" were barbarously tortured and in the following year executed. See E. Belfort Bax, *Rise and Fall of the Anabaptists* (1903, repr. 1966).

John of Luxemburg, 1296–1346, king of Bohemia (1310–46). The son of Holy Roman Emperor HENRY VII, he married Elizabeth, sister of Wenceslaus III of Bohemia, and in 1310 he was chosen king of Bohemia, which had been in virtual anarchy since Wenceslaus's death (1306). As a condition of his accession John was forced to issue a charter guaranteeing the rights of the nobility and clergy. Perhaps disappointed that he was not elected to succeed his father, John spent much of his time in foreign wars. During his reign he extended Bohemian control to upper Lusatia and Silesia. He supported the Teutonic Knights in their wars against Lithuania. As a result of his campaigns he ruled parts of Lombardy and Tyrol briefly. He died fighting on the side of the French at CRÉCY though he had become blind. He was succeeded by his son, who later became Holy Roman emperor as Charles IV.

John of Nepomuk, Saint (nā'pōmo͝ok), d. 1393, patron saint of Bohemia, a martyr. He is also called John Nepomucen. He was vicar general of Bohemia under King Wenceslaus IV (later Holy Roman Emperor Wenceslaus). When the king wished uncanonically to convert an abbey into a cathedral, St. John opposed him, in spite of torture. The king had him drowned in the Moldau. An earlier story, since disproved, attributes his drowning to his refusal to disclose the confessional secrets of the queen. Feast: May 16.

John of Procida (prō'chēdä), c.1225–c.1302, Italian conspirator, lord of the island of Procida. He was an ardent supporter of the Hohenstaufen cause in Sicily and attempted to secure the island for MANFRED and CONRADIN against the claims of Charles of Anjou, who was given Sicily by the pope. After Manfred's defeat and Conradin's execution (1268) by Charles, John went into exile at the court of Manfred's son-in-law, PETER III of Aragón. Peter sent him to seek the aid of the Byzantine emperor, Michael VIII, for a projected invasion of Sicily. John probably also secretly visited Sicily, preparing the great uprising of the SICILIAN VESPERS (1282) against Charles, which ultimately brought Peter to the Sicilian throne. In 1283, John was made chancellor of Sicily.

John of Salisbury (sôlz'bərē), c.1110–1180, English scholastic philosopher, b. Salisbury. He studied in France at Paris and Chartres under Abelard and other famous teachers. He was secretary to Theobald, archbishop of Canterbury, and friend and secretary to St. Thomas à Becket, of whom he wrote a biography. From 1176 to 1180, John was bishop of Chartres. His two main works are the *Polycraticus,* a treatise on the principles of government, and the *Metalogicus,* which presents a picture of the intellectual life and the scholastic controversies of the age. He was well acquainted with the Latin classics, and the influence of Platonism on his writing is considerable. He was one of the originators of moderate REALISM as a solution to the controversy with nominalism. See two selections from the *Polycraticus—The Statesman's Book of John of Salisbury* (tr. by John Dickinson, 1927, repr. 1963) and *Frivolities of Courtiers* (tr. by J. P. Pike, 1938, repr. 1972); *The Pontificalis Historia of John of Salisbury* (ed. by Marjorie Chibnall, 1956); C. C. J. Webb, *John of Salisbury* (1931, repr. 1971).

John of Speyer (spī'ər), d. 1470, first printer in Venice, b. Bavaria. He designed and patented the first type purely roman in character. It appears in Cicero's *Epistulae ad familiares* and Pliny's *Historia naturalis,* both printed in 1469. On his death his patent on the roman design expired; Nicolas JENSON was enabled to print with roman type in 1470.

John of the Cross, Saint, Span. *Juan de la Cruz,* 1542–91, Spanish mystic and poet, Doctor of the Church. His name was originally Juan de Yepes. He was a founder of the Discalced Carmelites and a close friend of St. Teresa of Ávila, who guided him in his spiritual life. Because of his ardor in pursuing St. Teresa's reforms he antagonized the hierarchy. In 1577 he was imprisoned in Toledo and was subjected to physical and mental tortures. It was in his prison cell that St. John wrote his famous *Spiritual Canticle* and began his *Songs of the Soul.* These poems—a blend of exquisite lyricism and profound mystical thought—are among the finest creations of the Golden Age of Spanish literature. St. John is regarded by many as Spain's finest lyric poet. After an escape (1578) considered by many to be miraculous, he went to Andalusia, where his last years were spent in a constant struggle against his opponents and in the creation of masterly prose treatises on mystical theology, notably *The Dark Night of the Soul* and *The Ascent of Mount Carmel.* Feast: Nov. 24. See translation of his complete works by E. A. Peers (3 vol., 1953) and of his poems by J. F. Nims (1959); E. A. Peers, *The Spirit of Flame* (1943); Robert Sencourt, *Carmelite and Poet* (1944); Léon Cristiani, *St. John of the Cross* (tr. 1962); Gerald Brenan, *St. John of the Cross* (1973).

Johns, Jasper, 1930–, American artist, b. Augusta, Ga. Influenced by Marcel DUCHAMP in the mid-1950s, Johns attempted to transform common objects into art by placing them in an art context. His flags and target images executed from 1954 to 1959 heralded the POP ART movement. Johns based his painting technique on the informal brushwork and texture of ABSTRACT EXPRESSIONISM, attaching literal elements such as rulers and brooms to the canvas. His bronze castings, such as *Beer Cans* (1960), are also derived from common objects.

John Scotus: see DUNS SCOTUS, JOHN; ERIGENA, JOHN SCOTUS.

Johns Hopkins University, mainly at Baltimore, Md. Johns HOPKINS in 1867 had a group of his associates incorporated as the trustees of a university and a hospital, endowing each with $3.5 million. Daniel C. GILMAN became the first president in 1875, modeled the new school after European universities rather than American colleges, and emphasized graduate research rather than collegiate instruction. When it opened in 1876, Johns Hopkins was considered an experiment, but it was an immediate success. It was extremely influential, and the organizers of such schools as Clark Univ. and the Univ. of Chicago took many of their ideas from the plan of Johns Hopkins. The first American university press was opened at Johns Hopkins in 1878. In 1889, Johns Hopkins Hospital was completed, and in 1893 the famous medical school opened. Today the university includes undergraduate and graduate schools of arts and sciences, schools of engineering, medicine, hygiene and public health, McCoy College (adult education), and the school of advanced international studies (at Washington, D.C.), which has foreign study centers at Bologna, Italy; Rangoon, Burma; and Jogjakarta, Indonesia. The extensive facilities at Baltimore include a nuclear physics laboratory with an electrostatic accelerator. The university operates an applied physics laboratory at Silver Spring, Md.; and the Chesapeake Bay Institute for oceanographic research at Annapolis, Md. Johns Hopkins has a noted library system that houses a

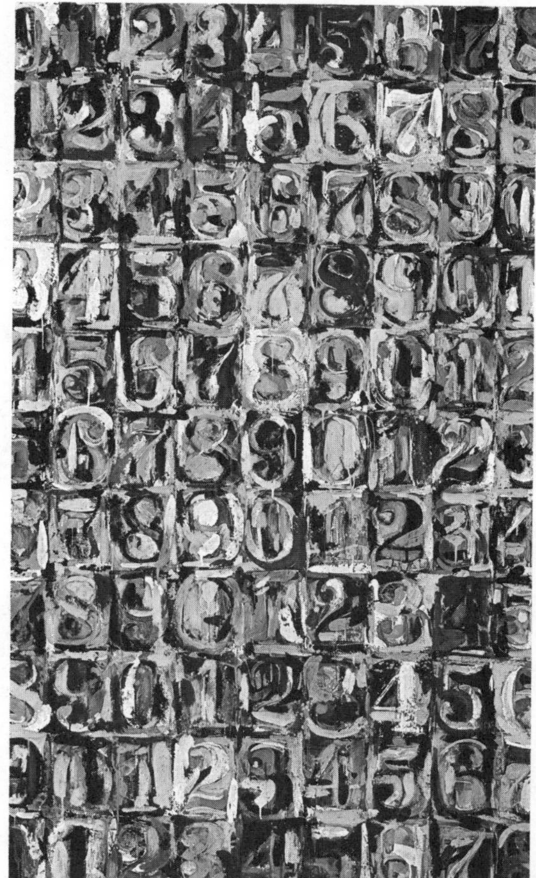

Numbers in Color, *detail of a painting by Jasper Johns, whose work often prefigured the pop art movement.*

number of important manuscript collections and documents. See history by J. C. French (1946).

Johnson, Alexander Bryan, 1786–1867, American philosopher and semanticist, b. Gosport, England. He emigrated (1801) to the United States and eventually became a wealthy banker in Utica, N.Y. Johnson anticipated many of the concerns of logical positivism and modern linguistic philosophy, but his views were ignored in his lifetime and were lost sight of for nearly a century. He held that a statement meant, for a speaker, whatever evidence he adduced or could adduce in its support: Language does not explain the world, rather the world explains language. He showed that many philosophical problems were the result of projecting distinctions of language onto nature, resulting in confusion. In addition to his philosophical works he wrote on politics, economics, and banking. His books included *The Philosophy of Human Knowledge; or A Treatise on Language* (1828), *Religion in its Relation to Present Life* (1841), *The Philosophical Emperor* (1841), and *The Meaning of Words* (1854). See *Centennial Conference on the Life and Works of Alexander Bryan Johnson*, ed. by C. L. Todd and R. T. Blackwood (1969).

Johnson, Allen, 1870–1931, American historian, b. Lowell, Mass. He was professor of history at Iowa (now Grinnell) College (1898–1905), Bowdoin College (1905–10), and Yale (1910–26). He achieved a notable success in editing the "Chronicles of America" (50 vol., 1918–21), a series both scholarly in material and popular in style, to which he contributed *Jefferson and His Colleagues* (Vol. XV, 1921). This success was partly responsible for his being selected as editor in chief of the *Dictionary of American Biography,* published under the auspices of the American Council of Learned Societies. Six volumes appeared before his death, setting the style and standard for the remainder of the enterprise. Among his other works are *Union and Democracy* (1915) and *The Historian and Historical Evidence* (1926, repr. 1965).

Johnson, Andrew, 1808–75, 17th President of the United States (1865–69), b. Raleigh, N.C. His father died when Johnson was 3, and at 14 he was apprenticed to a tailor. In 1826 the family moved to E Tennessee, and Andrew soon had his own tailor shop at Greeneville. A man of no formal schooling but of great perseverance and strength of character, he was greatly aided by his wife, Eliza McCardle, whom he married in 1827; she taught him to write and improved his reading and spelling. He prospered at his trade, and the tailor shop became the favored meeting place of other craftsmen, laborers, and small farmers interested in discussing public affairs. The best debater in the community, Johnson became the leader of his group in opposition to the slaveholding aristocracy. From 1830 onward he was almost continuously in public office, being alderman (1828–30) and mayor (1830–33) of Greeneville, state representative (1835–37, 1839–41), state senator (1841–43), Congressman (1843–53), governor of Tennessee (1853–57), and U.S. Senator (1857–62). As U.S. Representative and Senator, Johnson was principally interested in securing legislation to make land in the West available to homesteaders. He voted with other Southern legislators on questions concerning slavery, but after Tennessee seceded (June 8, 1861), he remained in the Senate, the only Southerner there. He vigorously supported Abraham Lincoln's administration, and in March, 1862, the President appointed him military governor of Tennessee with the rank of brigadier general of volunteers. His ability in filling this difficult position and the fact that he was a Southerner and a war Democrat made him an ideal choice as running mate to Lincoln on the successful Union ticket in 1864. On April 15, 1865, the day after Lincoln's assassination, he took the oath of office as President. Johnson's RECONSTRUCTION program (and he insisted that Reconstruction was an executive, not a legislative, function) was based on the theory that the Southern states had never been out of the Union. He therefore restored civil government in the ex-Confederate states as soon as it was feasible. Because he was not prepared to grant equal civil rights to Negroes and because he did not press for the wholesale disqualification for office of Confederate leaders, he was roundly denounced by the radical Republicans who, led by Thaddeus STEVENS, set out to undo Johnson's work on the convening of the 39th Congress in Dec., 1865. In April, 1866, Congress passed the Civil Rights Act over Johnson's veto, and his political power began to decline sharply. The remainder of his administration saw one humiliation after another. His "swing around the circle" in the congressional elections of 1866 was unsuccessful. Baited by mobs organized by the radicals and slandered by the press, he struck out at his enemies in such harsh terms that he did his own cause much harm. On March 2, 1867, the radicals passed over his veto the First Reconstruction Act and the TENURE OF OFFICE ACT. When Johnson insisted upon his intention to force out of office his Secretary of War, Edwin M. STANTON, whom he rightly suspected of conspiring with the congressional leaders, the radical Republicans sought to remove the President. Their first attempt failed (Dec., 1867), but on Feb. 24, 1868, the House passed a resolution of impeachment against him even before it adopted (March 2–3) 11 articles detailing the reasons for it. Most important of the charges, which were purely political, was that he

Andrew Johnson, 17th President of the United States.

had violated the Tenure of Office Act in the Stanton affair. On March 5 the Senate, with Chief Justice Salmon P. Chase presiding, was organized as a court to hear the charges. The President himself did not appear. In spite of the terrific pressure brought to bear on several Senators, the court narrowly failed to convict; the vote, on the 11th article (May 16) and on the second and third articles (May 26), was 35 to 19, one short of the constitutional two thirds required for removal. Although the problems of Reconstruction dominated Johnson's administration, there were important achievements in foreign relations, notably the purchase (1867) of Alaska, negotiated by Secretary of State William H. SEWARD. Johnson's name figured in the balloting at the Democratic convention of 1868, but he did not actively seek the nomination. In 1875, on his third attempt to resume public office, he was returned to the Senate from Tennessee, but died a few months after taking his seat. Publication of his papers, ed. by L. P. Graf and R. W. Haskins, was begun in 1967. See biography by R. W. Winston (1928, repr. 1969); D. M. Dewitt, *The Impeachment and Trial of Andrew Johnson* (1903, repr. 1967); H. K. Beale, *The Critical Year* (1930, new introd. 1958); G. F. Milton, *The Age of Hate* (1930, repr. 1965); Milton Lomask, *Andrew Johnson: President on Trial* (1960, repr. 1973); E. L. McKitrick, *Andrew Johnson and Reconstruction* (1960) and *Andrew Johnson, A Profile* (1969, repr. 1972); M. L. Benedict, *The Impeachment and Trial of Andrew Johnson* (1973).

Johnson, Cave, 1793–1866, American political leader, b. Robertson co., Tenn. He practiced law in his native state and served (1829–37, 1839–45) in the U.S. House of Representatives. Johnson gave active support to James K. Polk in the presidential campaign of 1844 and served (1845–49) as Postmaster General in Polk's cabinet, introducing postage stamps in the U.S. postal system. He later became (1853) a circuit judge in Tennessee. During the Civil War he opposed secession but afterwards supported the Confederacy.

Johnson, Eastman, 1824–1906, American portrait and genre painter, b. Lovell, Maine. He studied with a lithographer in Boston and later in Düsseldorf, then for almost four years at The Hague, where he was greatly influenced by the 17th-century Dutch masters. In 1855 Johnson returned to the United States and in 1860 settled in New York City. His fame rests primarily upon his skillfully executed genre pictures, such as *Old Kentucky Home* (N.Y. Public Lib.) and *Corn Husking at Nantucket* (Metropolitan Mus.). After 1885, however, he devoted himself to portraiture. Among his sitters were Presidents Hayes, Cleveland, and Harrison, as well as Cornelius Vanderbilt, Emerson, and Longfellow. See study by Patricia Hills (1972).

Johnson, Edward, 1881–1959, Canadian tenor and operatic manager, b. Guelph, Ont. After singing light opera and oratorio in New York from 1907, he went to Italy, where he sang operatic roles, using the name Eduardo di Giovanni, in many theaters, including Milan's La Scala (1913–18). In 1920 he joined the Chicago Opera Company and in 1922, the Metropolitan, where he created the leading tenor roles in Deems Taylor's *King's Henchman* (1927) and *Peter Ibbetson* (1931). In 1935 he became general manager of the Metropolitan Opera, retiring in 1950. He was succeeded by Rudolf Bing.

Johnson, Emily Pauline, 1862–1913, Canadian poet, b. near Brantford, Ont.; daughter of an Indian chief and his English wife. Although she had little formal training, Johnson's early poems praising Indian life were highly popular in recitals, and in 1892 she began a series of successful tours through the United States and England. Her poems, noted for their passion and dramatic intensity, appeared in *White Wampum* (1895), *Canadian Born* (1903), and *Flint and Feather* (1913), her collected poems. She also published a volume of tales of the Indians of the Pacific Northwest entitled *Legends of Vancouver* (1911).

Johnson, Emory Richard, 1864–1950, American economist, b. Waupun, Wis., Ph.D. Univ. of Pennsylvannia, 1893. He joined the faculty of the Univ. of Pennsylvania in 1893 and was dean of its Wharton School of Finance and Commerce from 1919 to 1933. He served on several government commissions as a transportation expert and wrote many books on the subject, including *Elements of Transportation* (1909), *Government Regulation of Transportation* (1938), and *Transport Facilities, Services, and Policies* (1947).

Johnson, Eyvind (ü'vĭnt), 1900–1976, Swedish novelist and short-story writer. After working as a laborer in the north of Sweden, Johnson moved to Stockholm in 1919 and began to write. He is best known outside Sweden for his cycle of four autobiographical novels entitled *Romanen om Olov* [the novel about Olov] (1934–37), which is noted for its extraordinary psychological penetration. Of his relatively few works translated into English the most celebrated is the novel *Return to Ithaca* (tr. 1952), concerning ancient and modern Greek culture. Johnson wrote more than 40 works, including the novels *Grupp Krilon* (1941), *Krilon själv* (1943), and *Livsdagen lang* (1964) and the collection of short stories *Sju liv* (1944). Considered one of the foremost Swedish writers of the 20th cent., Johnson shared the 1974 Nobel Prize in Literature with his countryman Harry Martinson.

Johnson, Guy, c.1740–1788, Loyalist leader in colonial New York, b. Ireland. He emigrated to America as a boy and married (1763) a daughter of Sir William Johnson, whom he succeeded as superintendent of Indian affairs in 1774. He had served in the French and Indian War and had acted as a deputy of Sir William after 1762. In the American Revolution he helped to keep most of the Iroquois loyal to the British. He made his headquarters (1779–81) at Niagara and with his deputy, John BUTLER, directed Loyalist raids against the patriot frontier settlements. He was succeeded as superintendent of Indian affairs by Sir John JOHNSON in 1782.

Johnson, Herschel Vespasian, 1812–80, U.S. political leader, b. Burke co., Ga. Admitted to the bar in 1834, he filled (1848–49) an unexpired Senate term before serving as circuit court judge (1849–53) and Democratic governor of Georgia (1853–57). A proponent of both states' rights and unionism, Johnson in 1860 ran unsuccessfully for the vice presidency with Stephen A. Douglas against Abraham Lincoln. Although he opposed secession, Johnson later served (1862–65) in the Confederate senate, where he refused to support conscription and the suspension of the writ of habeas corpus. Johnson was president of the 1865 Georgia constitutional convention and was elected (1866) to the U.S. Senate, but he was not allowed to take his seat. He was again a circuit court judge from 1873 until his death. See biography by P. S. Flippin (1931).

Johnson, Hiram Warren, 1866–1945, American political leader, U.S. Senator from California (1917–45), b. Sacramento, Calif. His role as attorney in the successful prosecution of Abe RUEF, political boss of San Francisco, led to his election (1910) as governor of California. Johnson broke the political domination of the Southern Pacific RR in California and secured the enactment of much reform legislation. A founder of the Progressive party, he was Theodore Roosevelt's running mate on the unsuccessful Progressive ticket of 1912. He was reelected governor in 1914. In 1916, Johnson refused to support Charles E. Hughes, the Republican presidential candidate, and Hughes lost California and the election to Woodrow Wilson. Johnson himself was elected U.S. Senator on the Progressive ticket and, reelected four times, served in the Senate until his death. In 1920 he was a leading contestant for the Republican presidential nomination, but after Warren G. Harding was nominated, Johnson declined offers of the vice-presidential nomination. Although he at first supported the Hoover administration, he later became its bitter opponent, and in 1932 he gave Franklin D. Roosevelt strong support. Johnson had been a stubborn opponent of the League of Nations, and he remained one of the most consistent of the isolationists in Congress. See study by S. C. Olin, Jr. (1968).

Johnson, Hugh Samuel, 1882–1942, American army officer, government administrator, b. Fort Scott, Kansas. After graduation (1903) from West Point, he entered the U.S. army as a second lieutenant. In World War I he formulated (1917) plans for selective service in the U.S. army, administered the draft, and served on the War Industries Board. Johnson resigned (1919) from the army as brigadier general and became a business executive. He was summoned (1933) to Washington, D.C., to help formulate the National Industrial Recovery Act, and after its passage he served (1933–34) as head of the NATIONAL RECOVERY ADMINISTRATION.

Johnson, Jack (John Arthur Johnson), 1878–1946, American boxer, b. Galveston, Texas. He defeated (1908) Tommy Burns at Sydney, Australia, and claimed the world's heavyweight championship. Responding to popular urging, James J. JEFFRIES came out of retirement to fight Johnson. Johnson won (1910) at Reno, Nev., and became the first Negro heavyweight boxing champion. He lost his title (1915) to Jess Willard in Havana, Cuba.

Johnson, James Weldon, 1871–1938, American author, b. Jacksonville, Fla., educated at Atlanta Univ. (B.A, 1894) and at Columbia. Johnson was the first Negro to be admitted to the Florida bar and later was American consul (1906–12), first in Venezuela and then in Nicaragua. In 1930 he became a professor at Fisk Univ., and in 1934 a visiting professor at New York Univ. He helped found and was secretary (1916–30) of the National Association for the Advancement of Colored People. His novel *Autobiography of an Ex-Coloured Man* (1912), published anonymously, caused a great stir and was republished under his name in 1927. Among his other works are *God's Trombones* (1927), Negro sermons in verse, and *Black Manhattan* (1930). He wrote songs with his brother, John Rosamond JOHNSON. See his autobiography, *Along This Way* (1933, repr. 1973); study by Eugene Levy (1973).

Johnson, Sir John, 1742–1830, Loyalist leader in the American Revolution, b. Mohawk valley, N.Y.; son of Sir William Johnson. He fought against the Indians in Pontiac's Conspiracy and was one of his father's chief lieutenants. For his services he was knighted in 1765. In the Revolution, like his brother-in-law, Guy Johnson, he set out to organize the settlers and Indians of the Mohawk region against the Revolutionaries. The plan failed, and he fled to Montreal. In the Saratoga campaign (1777) he served with Barry St. Leger and led a detachment at Oriskany. Later he led several raids on the Mohawk and Schoharie valleys. After the Revolution, he moved to Canada and in 1782 succeeded Guy Johnson as superintendent of Indian affairs.

Johnson, John Albert, 1861–1909, American political leader, governor of Minnesota, b. St. Peter, Minn. The son of poor parents, he left school early and worked at various trades until 1887, when he became editor and half owner of the St. Peter *Herald*, a Democratic journal. His editorials brought him into public notice, and in 1898 he was elected state senator. In 1904 he was elected governor on the Democratic ticket in a Republican state that gave Theodore Roosevelt a two-to-one majority that year. Johnson's victory won him national fame, increased by his reelections in 1906 and 1908. His progressive administration, gracious personality, and talent for speaking made him one of Minnesota's most popular governors. See biography by W. G. Helmes (1949).

Johnson, John Rosamond, 1873–1954, American composer and singer, b. Jacksonville, Fla., studied at Atlanta Univ. and the New England Conservatory of Music, Boston. After a career in music halls and light opera in England and on the Continent, Johnson toured Europe and the United States giving programs of Negro spirituals. He composed several hundred songs, including *Lift Every Voice and Sing*, for which his brother, James Weldon Johnson, wrote the words; it has been called the Negro national anthem. He edited several collections of American Negro songs and spirituals.

Johnson, Lady Bird, 1912–, b. Karnack, Texas, originally named Claudia Alta Taylor. She married (1934) Lyndon B. Johnson and played an active role in his political career. As first lady (1963–69) she sponsored environmental causes and national beautification projects. A successful businesswoman, she bought (1943) a debt-ridden radio station in Austin, Texas, and built it into a multimillion dollar broadcasting company. She also owns and manages extensive ranching lands in Texas. She is the author of *A White House Diary* (1970). See biographies by M. D. Smith (1964) and G. L. Hall (1967).

Johnson, Lionel Pigot, 1867–1902, English poet and critic, b. Broadstairs, Kent, educated at Oxford. He lived an ascetic, scholarly life in London, converting to Roman Catholicism in 1891. His keen interest in the IRISH LITERARY RENAISSANCE is reflected in many of his poems. As a whole Johnson's poetry is spare and austere, often spiritual in content and rather medieval in outlook. His works include *Poems* (1895) and *Ireland and Other Poems* (1897), and a critical work, *The Art of Thomas Hardy* (1894). An alcoholic, Johnson died at 35 of a fractured skull, the result of a fall. An autopsy revealed that his body had never developed beyond the age of 15. See his complete poems, ed. by Iain Fletcher (1953); his essays and critical papers, ed. by Thomas Whittemore (1912, repr. 1968).

Johnson, Lyndon Baines, 1908–73, 36th President of the United States (1963–69), b. near Stonewall, Texas. Born into a farming family, he graduated

Lyndon B. Johnson, 36th President of the United States.

(1930) from Southwest Texas State Teachers College (now Southwest Texas State Univ.), in San Marcos. He taught in a Houston high school before becoming (1932) secretary to a Texas Congressman in Washington. In 1934 he married Claudia Alta Taylor (nicknamed Lady Bird) and they had two daughters, Lynda Bird and Luci Baines. A staunch New Dealer, Johnson gained the friendship of the influential Sam Rayburn, at whose behest President Franklin Delano Roosevelt made him (1935) director in Texas of the National Youth Administration. In 1937, Johnson won election to a vacant congressional seat, and he was consistently reelected to the House through 1946. Despite Roosevelt's support, however, he was defeated in a special election to the Senate in 1941. He served (1941–42) in the navy, returning to Washington when President Roosevelt recalled all Congressmen from active service. In 1948, Johnson was elected U.S. Senator from Texas after winning the Democratic primary by a mere 87 votes. A strong advocate of military preparedness, he persuaded the Armed Services Committee to set up (1950) the Preparedness Investigating Subcommittee, of which he became chairman. Rising rapidly in the Senate hierarchy, Johnson became (1951) Democratic whip and then (1953) floor leader. As majority leader after the 1954 elections he wielded great power, exhibiting unusual skill in marshaling support for President Eisenhower's programs. He suffered a serious heart attack in 1955 but recovered to continue his senatorial command. Johnson lost the 1960 Democratic presidential nomination to John F. Kennedy, but accepted Kennedy's offer of the vice-presidential nomination. Elected with Kennedy, he energetically supported the President's programs, serving as an American emissary to nations throughout the world and as chairman of the National Aeronautics and Space Council and of the President's Committee on Equal Employment Opportunities. After Kennedy's assassination on Nov. 22, 1963, Johnson was immediately sworn in as President, and he announced that he would strive to carry through the late President's programs. Congress responded to Johnson's skillful prodding by enacting an $11 billion tax cut (Jan., 1964) and a sweeping Civil Rights Act (July, 1964). In May, 1964, Johnson called for a nationwide war against poverty and outlined a vast program of economic and social welfare legislation designed to create what he termed the Great Society. Elected (Nov., 1964) for a full term in a landslide victory over Senator Barry Goldwater, he pushed hard for his domestic program. The 89th Congress (1965–66) witnessed more major legislative action than any since the New Deal. A medicare bill, providing free medical care to the aged under Social Security, was enacted; Federal aid to education at all levels was greatly expanded; the Voting Rights Act of 1965 provided new safeguards for Negro voters; more money went to the antipoverty programs; and a Dept. of Transportation and Dept. of Housing and Urban Development were added to the Cabinet. Johnson's domestic achievements were soon obscured by foreign affairs, however. When North Vietnam attacked (Aug., 1964) American destroyers, Congress passed the Gulf of Tonkin resolution, giving the President authority to take any action necessary to protect American troops. Convinced that South Vietnam was about to fall to Communist forces, Johnson began (Feb., 1965) the bombing of North Vietnam. Within three years he increased American forces in South Vietnam from 20,000 to over 500,000. Johnson's actions eventually aroused widespread opposition in Congress and among the public, and a vigorous antiwar movement developed. As the cost of the war shot up, Congress scuttled many of Johnson's domestic programs. Large-scale riots in the Negro ghettos of major American cities further darkened his presidency, and by the beginning of 1968 he was under sharp attack from all sides. After Senators Eugene McCarthy and Robert Kennedy began campaigns for the Democratic nomination, Johnson announced (March, 1968) that he would not run for reelection. At the same time he called a partial halt to the bombing of North Vietnam; two months later peace talks began in Paris. When Johnson retired from office (Jan., 1969), he left the nation bitterly divided by the war. He retired to Texas, where he died on Jan. 22, 1973. See his memoirs, *The Vantage Point* (1971); biographies by Harry Provence (1964), E. F. Goldman (1969), Louis Heren (1970), G. E. Reedy (1970), and Richard Harwood and Haynes Johnson (1973).

Johnson, Martin Elmer, 1884–1937, American explorer and author, b. Rockford, Ill. He left home at 14 to work his way to Europe on a cattle boat, returning as a stowaway. He then joined the crew of Jack London's round-the-world cruise on the *Snark,* and was the only member of the party to complete the trip. His interest in photographing wildlife and native tribes seen on this voyage led him to make several trips for this purpose to the South Sea Islands and Borneo before undertaking (1921) the African expeditions for which he is best known. His films include *Simba, Congorilla,* and *Baboona,* as well as the film of vanishing wildlife in Africa that was made (1924–29) for the American Museum of Natural History. He was killed in an airplane crash in the United States. His wife, **Osa Helen (Leighty) Johnson,** 1894–1953, accompanied him on all his expeditions and was coauthor of *Cannibal Land* (1917), *Camera Trails in Africa* (1924), *Safari* (1928, repr. 1972), and *Lion* (1929). She also wrote *I Mar-*

Glass-walled house (1949) in New Canaan, Conn., designed by Philip Johnson.

ried Adventure (1940) and *Bride in the Solomons* (1944).

Johnson, Pamela Hansford: see under SNOW, C. P.

Johnson, Philip Cortelyou, 1906–, American architect, museum curator, and historian, b. Cleveland. After studying the new European architecture, Johnson wrote (with H.R. Hitchcock) *The International Style: Architecture since 1922* (1932). As chairman of the department of architecture at the Museum of Modern Art (1932–34; 1945–54), he became an important advocate of the new architecture in America. He founded his own firm in 1953. Johnson's sumptuous, glass-walled house in New Canann, Conn. (1949), reveals the influence of MIËS VAN DER ROHE, with whom he collaborated on the Seagram Building in New York City (1958). His later works include the Munson-Williams-Proctor Institute, Utica, N. Y. (1960), the New York State Theater (1964) at LINCOLN CENTER FOR THE PERFORMING ARTS, the Investors Diversified Services Project in Minneapolis (1973), and the addition to the Boston Public Library (1973). He is the author of *Miës van der Rohe* (1947). See studies by J. M. Jacobus, Jr. (1962), and Charles Noble (1972).

Johnson, Reverdy, 1796–1876, American lawyer and statesman, b. Annapolis, Md. Admitted to the bar in 1816, he served in the Maryland legislature (1821–28) and the U.S. Senate (1845–49) and was attorney general under President Taylor. Johnson won a reputation as one of the ablest constitutional lawyers of the period. His constitutional argument as counsel for the defense in the DRED SCOTT CASE is known to have greatly influenced the Supreme Court, particularly Chief Justice Roger Taney. A Whig and then a conservative Democrat, Johnson was sympathetic with the South but was absolutely opposed to secession and used his influence to keep Maryland in the Union. He played an important role in the unsuccessful defense of Mary E. SURRATT, alleged accomplice of John Wilkes Booth. In his second term in the U.S. Senate (1863–68), he supported President Andrew Johnson's Reconstruction program, and his opposition to the impeachment of Johnson influenced other senators in voting for the President's acquittal. In 1868 he was appointed minister to Great Britain, where he negotiated the Johnson-Clarendon Treaty to settle the ALABAMA CLAIMS; the treaty was rejected by the U.S. Senate largely for party reasons, and Johnson was recalled in 1869. See biography by B.C. Steiner (1914, repr. 1970).

Johnson, Richard Mentor, 1780–1850, Vice President of the United States (1837–41), b. Kentucky, on the site of present Louisville. Admitted (1802) to the bar, he became prominent in state politics as a Jeffersonian Republican and sat (1804–7) in the Kentucky legislature. He served (1807–1819) in the U.S. House of Representatives and commanded a regiment of Kentucky riflemen in the War of 1812, in which he served under William Henry Harrison in the Canadian campaign. At the battle of the Thames (1813), Johnson was severely wounded in action, and he is said to have killed Tecumseh. He resigned (1819) from the House to fill an unexpired term in the U.S. Senate, where he served until 1829. Again (1829–37) in the House, Johnson supported President Jackson's administration and pushed the bill

(1832) abolishing imprisonment for debt. Backed by Jackson, Johnson was nominated (1836) for Vice President on the Democratic ticket with Martin Van Buren. None of the vice presidential candidates received a majority of the electoral vote, so the election was decided by the U.S. Senate, which gave the office to Johnson. He was defeated (1840) in his bid for reelection by the Whig candidate, John Tyler. See biography by L. H. Meyer (1932).

Johnson, Richard W., 1827–97, Union general in the Civil War, b. Livingston co., Ky., grad. West Point, 1849. Before the Civil War he served principally on the frontier. Johnson, made a brigadier general of volunteers in Oct., 1861, served as a division commander in the Armies of the Ohio and the Cumberland. He fought at Shiloh and Murfreesboro and in the Chattanooga and Atlanta campaigns. After his service at the battle of Nashville in Dec., 1864, he was brevetted major general. Following his retirement from the army in 1867 Johnson taught military science at the Univ. of Missouri and the Univ. of Minnesota.

Johnson, Rossiter, 1840–1931, American editor, b. Rochester, N.Y. He was associate editor (1873–77) of the *American Cyclopaedia,* editor (1883–1902) of the *Annual Cyclopedia,* and managing editor (1886–89) of the *Cyclopedia of American Biography.* He originated and edited the "Little Classics" (18 vol., 1875–80) and was editor in chief of "The World's Great Books" (40 vol., 1898–1901). He also lectured widely and wrote a variety of books.

Johnson, Samuel, 1696–1772, American clergyman, educator, and philosopher, b. Guilford, Conn., grad. Collegiate School (now Yale), 1714; father of William Samuel Johnson. He became a Congregationalist minister, but in 1722 joined the Church of England. In 1724 he opened the first Anglican church in Connecticut at Stratford, remaining its minister until 1754, when he became the first president of an Anglican institution, King's College (now Columbia), in New York City. He resigned in 1763 to return to Stratford. A friend and correspondent of the English philosopher George Berkeley, Johnson became the principal exponent in America of Berkeleian idealism. His chief work was *Ethica* (1746), republished in an enlarged edition by Benjamin Franklin as *Elementa Philosophica* (1752). See Herbert Schneider and Carol Schneider, ed., *Samuel Johnson . . . His Career and His Writings* (4 vol., 1929, repr. 1972); study by J. J. Ellis (1973).

Johnson, Samuel, 1709–84, English author, b. Lichfield. The leading literary scholar and critic of his time, Johnson helped to shape and define the Augustan Age. But he was equally celebrated for his brilliant and witty conversation. His rather gross appearance and manners were viewed tolerantly, if not with a certain admiration. The son of a bookseller, Johnson excelled at school in spite of illness (he suffered the effects of scrofula throughout his life) and poverty. He entered Oxford in 1728 but was forced to leave after a year for lack of funds. He sustained himself as a bookseller and schoolmaster for the next six years, during which he continued his wide reading and published some translations. In 1735 he married Elizabeth Porter, a widow 20 years his senior, and remained devoted to her until her death in 1752. He settled in London in 1737 and began his literary career in earnest. He wrote at first primarily for Edward Cave's *Gentleman's Magazine*—poetry and prose on subjects literary and political. His poem "London," published anonymously in 1738, was praised by Pope and won Johnson recognition in literary circles. His *Life of Savage* (1744) is a bitter portrait of corruption in London and the miseries endured by writers. Also of note are *The Vanity of Human Wishes* (1749) and his essays in the periodical *The Rambler* (1750–52). Johnson's first work of lasting importance, and the one that permanently established his reputation in his own time, was his *Dictionary of the English Language* (1755), the first comprehensive lexicographical work on English ever undertaken. *Rasselas,* a moral romance, appeared in 1759, and *The Idler,* a collection of his essays, in 1761. Although Johnson enjoyed great literary acclaim, he remained close to poverty until a government pension was granted him in 1762. The following year was marked by his meeting with James BOSWELL, whose famous biography presents Johnson in exhaustive and fascinating detail, recreating his conversations verbatim. In 1764, Johnson and Joshua Reynolds founded "The Club" (known later as The Literary Club): Its membership included Oliver Goldsmith, Edmund Burke, David Garrick, and Boswell. The brilliance of this intellectual elite was, reportedly, dazzling, and Dr. Johnson (he had received a degree in 1764) was its leading light. His witty remarks are remembered to this day. He was a master not only of the aphorism—e.g., his definition of angling as "a stick and a string, with a worm on one end and a fool on the other"—but also of the quick, unexpected retort, as when, while listening with displeasure to a violinist, he was told that the feat being performed was very difficult: "Difficult," replied Johnson, "I wish it had been impossible!" In 1765, Johnson met Henry and Hester THRALE, whose friendship and hospitality he enjoyed until Thrale's death and Mrs. Thrale's remarriage. In that same year Johnson's long-heralded edition of Shakespeare appeared. Its editorial principles served as a model for future editions, and its preface and critical notes are still highly valued. In the 1770s, Johnson wrote a series of Tory pamphlets. His political conservatism was based upon a profound skepticism as to the perfectibility of human nature. Although personally generous and compassionate, he held that a strict social order is necessary to save man from himself. In 1773 he toured the Hebrides with Boswell and published his account of the tour in 1775. Johnson's *Lives of the Poets* (1779–1781), his last major work, comprises ten small volumes of acute criticism, characterized, as is all of Johnson's work, by both classical values and sensitive perception. Dr. Johnson, as he is universally known, was England's first full-dress man of letters, and his mind and personality helped to create the traditions that have guided English taste and criticism. Besides the classic biography by Boswell, see biographies by J. W. Krutch (1944), J. L. Clifford (1955), Sir John Hawkins (1787; ed. by Bertram Davis, 1961), and Donald Greene (1970); critical studies by W. J. Bate (1955), R. B. Schwartz (1971), and Peter Quennell (1973); J. L. Clifford, Johnsonian Studies, 1887–1950 (1951; supplement, 1962); J. L. Clifford and D. J. Greene, *A Survey and Bibliography of Critical Studies* (1970).

Johnson, Thomas, 1732–1819, American political leader, b. Calvert co., Md. A lawyer, he served (1762–73) in the Maryland colonial assembly, where he became prominent in the fight against the Stamp Act (1765). He was a member (1774–77) of the Continental Congress, and he nominated (1775) George Washington as commander in chief of the Continental army. Johnson served as governor of Maryland (1777–79) and helped bring about Maryland's adoption of the Constitution. He served briefly (1791–93) as Associate Justice of the U.S. Supreme Court. See biography by E. S. Delaplane (1927).

Johnson, Tom Loftin, 1854–1911, American municipal reformer, mayor of Cleveland (1901–10), b. Georgetown, Ky. He acquired a substantial fortune from streetcar and steel interests, and, deeply influenced in the 1880s by the writings of Henry GEORGE, he devoted himself to reform. After two terms (1891–95) as a Democratic member of the U.S. House of Representatives, he became (1901) mayor of Cleveland, serving four terms. He fought strenuous battles for municipal reform against political bosses (especially Mark Hanna) and business interests. Although his plans for municipal ownership of public utilities were not realized, he helped create civic consciousness in Cleveland, initiated sanitary measures, and improved facilities to help the city's poor. Cleveland, in the time of Johnson's mayoralty, was called "the best governed city in the United States." See his autobiography (1911); biography by Carl Lorenz (1911).

Johnson, Uwe (ü'vā yôn'zôn), 1934–, German novelist. Johnson's works explore the complex effects on the average man of divided modern Germany, both halves of which he sees as zones of moral poverty. His best-known novels include *Mutmassungen über Jakob* (1959; tr. *Speculations about Jacob,* 1963) and *Das dritte Buch übei Achim* (1961; tr. *The Third Book about Achim,* 1966). In the latter, as in *Zwei Ansichten* (1965; tr. *Two Views,* 1966), and *Absence* (tr. 1970), Johnson leaves to the reader any analysis of the problems he describes. See biography by Mark Boulby (1974).

Johnson, Walter Perry, 1887–1946, American baseball player, b. Humboldt, Kansas. He began playing with the Washington Senators of the American League in 1907. A right-handed pitcher, he won 416 games while losing 278 before he retired from active play in 1927. The numerous records he established include the greatest number of shutouts (113), the greatest number of strike-outs (3,510), and the most consecutive scoreless innings pitched (56). The "Big Train," as he was often called, later managed the Newark team (1928) of the International League and the Senators (1929–32) and the Cleveland Indians (1933–35) of the American League. He was elected to the National Baseball Hall of Fame in 1936. See biography by R. L. Treat (1948).

Johnson, Sir William, 1715–74, British colonial leader in America, b. Co. Meath, Ireland. He settled (1738) in the Mohawk valley, became a merchant, and gained great power among the Mohawk Indians and the other Iroquois. He had large landed properties, founded (1762) Johnstown, N.Y., and lived in baronial splendor at Johnson Hall. Because of his influence over the Indians, he was a key figure in the French and Indian Wars, first becoming prominent in King George's War. At the Albany Congress (1754) he helped formulate British Indian policy, and he was made (1755) superintendent of Iroquois affairs. In the French and Indian War, although his expedition against Crown Point did not capture that fort, he soundly defeated (1755) the French under Baron Dieskau at Lake George and built Fort William Henry. Johnson was rewarded with a baronetcy. In 1759 he captured Niagara, and in 1760 he served with Gen. Jeffrey Amherst in the capture of Montreal. He had been appointed general superintendent of Indian affairs N of the Ohio in 1756, and after the Peace of Paris (1763) his office was of great significance in the vast new areas gained from France. His chief lieutenants were George CROGHAN; Johnson's son-in-law, Guy JOHNSON; his son, Sir John JOHNSON; and Daniel Claus. Although Pontiac's Rebellion and British economy measures prevented him from establishing the centralized control over Indians and fur traders that he desired, he did much to further British rule in the formerly French territories. He presided at the council of FORT STANWIX (1768). His papers have been edited by the New York State Division of Archives (13 vol., 1921–62). See biographies by Arthur Pound and Richard Day (1930, repr. 1971) and J. T. Flexner (1959).

Johnson, William Samuel, 1727–1819, American political leader and president of Columbia College (1787–1800), b. Stratford, Conn. A lawyer in Connecticut, he soon became a leading figure in the colony, serving as a member of the lower house and in the governor's council. Although conservative in his views, he was sent (1765) as a delegate to the Stamp Act Congress. From 1767 to 1771 he was an agent of Connecticut in England and after his return was a judge of the superior court (1772–73). Because of his opposition to political independence of the colonies, he declined to serve when elected as a delegate to the Continental Congress (1774) and soon retired from politics. He was called from retirement to represent (1785–87) Connecticut in the Confederation Congress and at the Federal Constitutional Convention (1787), in which he took a prominent part in the debate on represention. He served (1787–1800) as president of the newly reorganized Columbia College, formerly King's College, of which his father, Samuel Johnson (1696–1772), had been president. He was elected U. S. Senator from Connecticut in 1789, but retired in 1791. See biographies by E. E. Beardsley (1876) and G. C. Groce, Jr. (1937).

Johnson City. 1 Village (1970 pop. 18,025), Broome co., S N.Y., in a tri-city area including Endicott and Binghamton; inc. 1892. It is noted for its Endicott-Johnson shoes. Originally called Lestershire, the area remained rural until a shoe company built a factory there in 1890. The name was changed in 1916. **2** City (1970 pop. 33,770), Washington co., NE Tenn., in a mountainous region; settled before 1800, inc. 1869. It is an important burley tobacco and dairy market and a railroad center. East Tennessee State Univ. and a large veterans hospital are there. The oldest church in the state (built 1782) is in Johnson City, and nearby is Rocky Mount historic shrine, a log cabin (built 1770) that served (1790–92) as the first capitol of the territory south of the Ohio River. Four Tennessee Valley Authority lakes in the area offer recreation. **3** City (1970 pop. 767), seat of Blanco co., central Texas. It is the site of the "LBJ Ranch," known as the Texas White House when Lyndon B. Johnson was President. The Lyndon B. Johnson National Historic Site includes the former President's boyhood home in the town and his birthplace 13 mi (21 km) to the west.

Johnson grass: see SORGHUM.

Johnston, Albert Sidney, 1803–62, Confederate general, b. Washington, Ky. After serving in the Black Hawk War, he resigned (1834) from the U.S. army and went to Texas where he enlisted (1835) in the revolutionary army. Johnston became its commander in 1837 and served as Texas secretary of war,

1838–40. In the Mexican War, he commanded a regiment of volunteers and saw action at Monterrey. Reentering the U.S. army in 1849, Johnston served on the Texas frontier, was commander of the Dept. of Texas (1856–58), led the expedition against the Mormons (1857), and commanded the Dept. of Utah (1858–60). When Texas seceded from the Union in April, 1861, Johnston, commanding the Dept. of the Pacific, again resigned his commission in the U.S. army and was soon made general in charge of Confederate operations in the West. Union victories, especially at Fort Donelson (Feb., 1862), forced him to withdraw from the line of defense he had established in 1861. He concentrated an army at Corinth, Miss., and on April 6, 1862, attacked Ulysses S. Grant at Shiloh (see SHILOH, BATTLE OF). Johnston was killed at the height of battle, and the Confederacy lost one of its ablest generals. See biography by his son W. P. Johnston (1878, repr. 1964).

Johnston, Alexander Keith, 1804–71, Scottish cartographer and geographer royal of Scotland. He issued many notable atlases, maps, and gazetteers, including *The National Atlas of Historical, Commercial, and Political Geography* (1843), *The Physical Atlas of Natural Phenomena* (1848), *The Dictionary of Geography* (1850; known as *Johnston's Gazetteer*), and *The Royal Atlas of Modern Geography* (1861). A son, **Alexander Keith Johnston,** 1844–79, carried on the work of the map-publishing house founded by his father. He assisted (1873–75) in a survey of Paraguay and died in Africa while leading an expedition of the Royal Geographical Society to Lake Nyasa.

Johnston, Gabriel, 1699–1752, colonial governor of North Carolina (1734–52). An efficient and popular Scot, he nevertheless had constant difficulties with the assembly over quitrents and other financial matters and several times dissolved that body. During his administration numerous land grants to immigrants were issued, free schools were established, and Wilmington was developed.

Johnston, Sir Harry Hamilton, 1858–1927, British explorer and colonial official. His early interest in the natural sciences was combined with his concern for the political problems of colonial Africa. He began his first trip to sub-Saharan Africa in 1882 and in 1883 encountered Henry Morton Stanley in the Congo Basin. In 1884 he made an expedition to Mt. Kilimanjaro that uncovered valuable scientific data and strengthened Britain's political hold in East Africa. Johnston entered the foreign service in 1885; he served in colonial administrative positions in many parts of Africa and established a British protectorate over Nyasaland (present-day Malawi). After his retirement (1902) he continued his naturalist studies. He was knighted in 1896.

Johnston, Joseph Eggleston, 1807–91, Confederate general, b. Prince Edward co., Va., grad. West Point, 1829. He served against the Seminole Indians in Florida and with distinction under Winfield Scott in the Mexican War. Johnston was quartermaster general with the rank of brigadier general when he resigned (April, 1861) to fight for the Confederacy. In May he was made a brigadier general and assigned to command at Harpers Ferry. He evaded the Union army under Gen. Robert Patterson and marched to the aid of General Beauregard at BULL RUN, where his part in the Confederate victory won him a generalcy and the command of the Army of Northern Virginia (July). Johnston opposed General McClellan in the PENINSULAR CAMPAIGN until he was wounded at Fair Oaks in May, 1862. Upon resuming service in November, he was assigned to command the Dept. of the West. Although it seems certain that President Davis intended him to give orders to John Clifford PEMBERTON at Vicksburg and Braxton BRAGG in Tennessee, Johnston chose to interpret his position as merely nominal. When he finally did take command in the VICKSBURG CAMPAIGN, it was too late to save Pemberton. Johnston, placed in command of the Army of the Tennessee (Dec., 1863), adopted the policy of strategic retreat against William Tecumseh SHERMAN in the ATLANTA CAMPAIGN—a policy that did not suit Davis, who appointed John Bell HOOD to succeed him. He was restored to command in Feb., 1865, by Lee, now commander in chief. He obstructed General Sherman's advance through North Carolina, but upon hearing of Lee's surrender to General Grant, he capitulated to Sherman on April 26. After the war Johnston served (1879–81) in the House of Representatives from Richmond, Va., and by appointment of President Cleveland, was (1885–91) Federal commissioner of railroads. Cautious as he was, Johnston was not a brilliant offensive commander but was probably the peer of Lee in defensive generalship. Davis's hostility to Johnston was widely known and seriously disrupted Confederate military organization. See Johnston's *Narrative of Military Operations* (1874; new ed. 1959, repr. 1969); biographies by R. M. Hughes (1893) and G. E. Govan and J. W. Livingood (1956).

Johnston, Mary, 1870–1936, American novelist, b. Buchanan, Va. Her books combine romance with history. She is chiefly remembered for *To Have and to Hold* (1900), a story of colonial Virginia, and its successor, *Audrey* (1902). Her other novels include two Civil War stories, *The Long Roll* (1911) and *Cease Firing* (1912); *The Great Valley* (1926); and *Miss Delicia Allen* (1932).

Johnston, Richard Malcolm, 1822–98, American author, b. Hancock co., Ga., grad. Mercer Univ., 1841. He is known for his stories and sketches of rural Georgia, of which the collection *Dukesborough Tales* (1871) is best known. See his autobiography (1900).

Johnston, Samuel, 1733–1816, political leader in the American Revolution, b. Dundee, Scotland. He emigrated as a child to North Carolina, where his uncle, Gabriel JOHNSTON, was royal governor. After being admitted to the bar, he was a member of the colonial assembly (1759–75) and of its standing Committee of Correspondence after 1773. He was elected to the four provincial congresses (1774–76), presiding at the third and at the fourth, which passed the Halifax Resolves declaring for independence of the colonies; served in the new state senate; and represented North Carolina in the Continental Congress (1780–82). Johnston was governor of North Carolina (1787–89) and presided over the convention that rejected the Federal Constitution (1788) and over the one (1789) at which North Carolina finally ratified it. He was one of the state's first U.S. Senators (1789–93), a judge of the superior court (1800–1803), and one of the first trustees of the Univ. of North Carolina.

Johnston, town (1970 pop. 22,037), Providence co., N central R.I., a suburb of Providence; inc. 1759. Among its manufactures are jewelry, textiles, and fabricated metals. Johnston is the home of several insurance companies. Its many historic landmarks include the Clemence-Irons House (c.1680).

Johnstone (jŏn'stən), burgh (1971 pop. 22,629), Renfrewshire, W Scotland. There are flax and cotton mills and engineering works. Chemicals, machine tools, and shoelaces are manufactured. In 1975, Johnstone became part of the Strathclyde region.

Johnston Island, central Pacific, c.3,000 ft (910 m) long and c.600 ft (180 m) wide, c.700 mi (1,130 km) SW of Honolulu. It was discovered by the British in 1807 and claimed by the United States in 1858. A bird reservation for years, the island became a U.S. naval base in 1941. In 1962 the United States conducted a series of nuclear tests in the area.

Johnstown. 1 City (1970 pop. 10,045), seat of Fulton co., E central N.Y.; founded 1772, inc. 1895. Its leather glove industry began in 1800. Knitted goods, boats, gelatin, and chemicals are also made. Johnson Hall, built by the city's founder, Sir William Johnson, houses many of his relics. Other notable old buildings include the county courthouse (1774) and Fort Johnstown (1771), now the county jail. The last Revolutionary battle in New York was fought in Johnstown on Oct. 25, 1781. Elizabeth Cady Stanton was born in the city. A junior college is there. **2** Industrial city (1970 pop. 42,476), Cambria co., SW Pa., on the Conemaugh River at the mouth of Stony Creek; settled 1770, inc. as a city 1936. Situated in a beautiful mountain region, it is a center of heavy industry. Manufactures include iron, steel, coal products, refractories, chemicals, wearing apparel, and mining, telegraph, railroad, and industrial equipment. Branches of U.S. Steel and Bethlehem Steel are there. In 1834 the Pennsylvania Canal and the Portage RR were joined in Johnstown. The first Kelly pneumatic converter for the transformation of crude iron into steel was built there in 1862. The city expanded with the rapid growth of iron and steel industries after the Civil War. On May 31, 1889, the dam across the river c.12 mi (19 km) above the city broke as a result of heavy rains, and the city was flooded, with the loss of about 2,200 lives. Flooding occurred again in 1936, but the river has since been channeled (completed 1943) for flood prevention. The Univ. of Pittsburgh at Johnstown and a state rehabilitation center are in the city. Johnstown Flood National Memorial and Allegheny Portage Railroad National Historic Site are nearby (see NATIONAL PARKS AND MONUMENTS, table). See D. G. McCullough, *The Johnstown Flood* (1968).

Johnstown Flood National Memorial: see JOHNSTOWN **2**; NATIONAL PARKS AND MONUMENTS (table).

John the Baptist, Saint, d. A.D. c.28–30, Jewish prophet, the forerunner of Jesus. He was the son of Zacharias and Elizabeth, who was a kinswoman of the Virgin Mary, and his birth was miraculously foretold. After spending some time in the desert, he received a divine call to preach repentance to the people of the Jordan valley in preparation for the Messiah. He baptized his followers, and he baptized Jesus, whom he recognized as the Son of God. John's vigorous preaching and great popularity enraged the aristocracy, and he offended Herodias, wife of HEROD, by rebuking her publicly. At her instigation and at the direct request of her daughter SALOME he was beheaded. (Mat. 11.1–19; 17.11–13; Mark 6.14–29; Luke 1.5–80; 3.1–20; John 1.15–36.) John is also mentioned by the Jewish historian Josephus. Christians have always venerated St. John the Baptist as high among the saints; he is the only saint besides the Virgin Mary whose birthday is celebrated: June 24. The feast of his beheading is Aug. 29. See Carl Kraeling, *Saint John the Baptist* (1951).

John the Fearless, 1371–1419, duke of Burgundy (1404–19); son of PHILIP THE BOLD. He fought against the Turks at NIKOPOL in 1396 and was a prisoner for a year until he was ransomed. He continued his father's feud with Louis, duc d'ORLÉANS, brother of King Charles VI, and became popular by advocating governmental reforms. In 1407 he had Louis assassinated; he was forced to leave Paris but later returned and obtained control of the French government. Rivalry between his party and the supporters of Orléans led to open civil war in 1411 (see ARMAGNACS AND BURGUNDIANS). In 1413, John was again forced to flee Paris as a result of a reaction against the violence of his supporters, the CABOCHIENS. He did not aid the government, now under Armagnac control, against the English invaders under King Henry V, and in 1418 he took advantage of French defeats to seize Paris and the king. John negotiated both with Henry V and with the dauphin (later King Charles VII), who now led the Armagnacs. At a meeting in Montereau with the dauphin, John was assassinated (1419). He was succeeded by his son, Philip the Good.

John the Posthumous: see JOHN I, king of France.

Johor or **Johore** (jōhôr', jə–), state (1971 pop. 1,273,-900), 7,360 sq mi (19,062 sq km), at the southern extremity of the Malay Peninsula, Malaysia, opposite Singapore. It is largely covered with rain forests and swamps. The principal rivers and communication routes are the Muar and the Johor; the capital is JOHOR BAHARU, across the strait from Singapore. The Chinese and the Malays are the two largest groups in the population, and there is a significant Indian minority. Johor has extensive rubber plantations; other agricultural products are rice, copra, pineapples, gambier, and palm products. Tin and bauxite are mined. After the fall of Malacca (Melaka) to the Portuguese (1511), the former sultan of Malacca continued to rule over Johor and the Riau Archipelago. In the 18th cent. the Bugis, a Malay people from Celebes, became dominant in Johor. In 1819 a British-installed sultan granted the site of Singapore to the British East India Company and became for practical purposes an independent ruler. Thereafter relations with Great Britain were friendly; Johor remained one of the most peaceful of the Malay states. In 1885, Johor and Great Britain established formal treaty relations, and in 1914 Johor became a British protectorate. Until 1948, when it entered the Federation of Malaya, Johor was classified as one of the Unfederated Malay States. See MALAYSIA, FEDERATION OF.

Johor Baharu (bəhär'o͞o), **Johore Bharu,** or **Johore Bahru** (both: bär'o͞o), city (1971 pop. 135,936), capital of Johor, Malaysia, S Malay Peninsula, opposite Singapore. The city is connected with Singapore by a stone causeway across the narrow Johore Strait. It is a trade center for rubber and tropical produce. The seat of the sultan of Johor is in Johor Baharu; his residence, Bakit Serene, contains priceless art treasures. The population of the city is mainly Chinese.

Johore Strait, arm of the Singapore Strait, c.40 mi (60 km) long and from 1 to 3 mi (1.6–4.8 km) wide, between Singapore Island and the Malay Peninsula. The eastern part of the strait has a deep channel leading to a port on N Singapore. A causeway (3,443 ft/1,049 m long; opened 1924) connects Johor Baharu, Malaysia, and Woodland, Singapore.

Joiada (joi'ədə), high priest. Neh. 12.10,11,22.

Joiakim (joi'əkĭm) [short for JEHOIAKIM], high priest. Neh. 12.10.

Joiarib (joi'ərĭb). **1** Exile returned from Babylon. Ezra 8.16. **2** Chief priest. Neh. 11.10; 12.6,19. Jehoiarib: 1 Chron. 9.10; 24.7. **3** Judahite. Neh. 11.5.

joinery, craft of assembling exposed woodwork in the interiors of buildings. Where CARPENTRY refers to the rougher, simpler, and primarily structural elements of wood assembling, joinery has to do with difficult surfaces and curvatures, such as those of spiral stairs, with complex intersections of members or moldings, and with the handling of the finer qualities and varieties of woods. The joiner's skill and art thus approach those of the cabinetmaker. One must have an extensive knowledge of geometrical relations and projections, in addition to being manually proficient. In modern woodworking, however, the hand processes of the joiner have, to a large degree, been superseded by mechanical means.

joint, in anatomy, juncture between two bones. Some joints are immovable, e.g., those that connect the bones of the skull, which are separated merely by short, tough fibers of cartilage. The movable joints are found for the most part in the limbs. Hinge joints provide a forward and backward motion as at the elbow and knee. Pivot joints permit rotary movement, like the turning of the head from side to side. Ball-and-socket joints, like those at the hip and shoulder, allow the greatest range of movement, as the rounded end of one bone fits into the hollow or socket of another bone, separated by elastic cartilage. Further ease of movement is assured by a lubricating liquid, the synovial fluid, supplied by the synovial membrane that lines movable joints. In addition, some joints contain a cushioning, fluid-filled sac, called a BURSA. Holding the joints in place are strong LIGAMENTS fastened to the bones above and below the joint. Joints are subject to SPRAINS and dislocations as well as to infections and disorders caused by diseases such as ARTHRITIS.

joint, in geology, fracture in rocks along which no appreciable movement has occurred (see FAULT). Most rocks are jointed, but the origin of these joints is not always clear. Nearly vertical joints that result from shrinkage during cooling are commonly found in igneous rocks. The prismatic joints of the Palisades of New Jersey and Devil's Tower, Wyoming, are examples of joints caused by contraction during the cooling of fine-grained igneous rock masses. Deep-seated igneous rocks often have joints approximately parallel to the surface, suggesting that they formed by expansion of the rock mass as overlying rocks were eroded away. Some joints in sedimentary rocks may have formed as the result of contraction during compaction and drying of the sediment. In some cases, jointing of the rock may result from the action of the same forces that cause FOLDS and faults. In relatively undisturbed sedimentary rocks, such joints are often in two vertical sets perpendicular to one another. Commonly, streams develop along zones of weakness caused by joints in rocks, and thus the regional pattern of joint orientation often exerts a strong control on the development of drainage patterns.

Joint Chiefs of Staff, U.S. statutory agency, created in 1949 within the Dept. of Defense, whose members are the principal military advisers to the President, the National Security Council, and the Secretary of Defense. Its four permanent members are the chairman; the chief of staff, U.S. army; the chief of naval operations; and the chief of staff, U.S. air force. The commandant of the U.S. Marine Corps attends meetings regularly and sits as a coequal with the other members when they are considering matters that directly concern the corps.

joint stock company: see CHARTERED COMPANIES.

Joinville, Jean, sire de (zhäN sĕr də zhwăNvēl'), 1224?–1317?, French chronicler, biographer of LOUIS IX of France (St. Louis). As seneschal (governor) of Champagne, Joinville was a close adviser to Louis, whom he accompanied (1248–54) on the Seventh Crusade. He opposed and refused to take part in the Eighth Crusade. His memoir of St. Louis, dictated between 1304 and 1309 for the instruction of Louis X, is an invaluable record of the king, of feudal France, and of the Seventh Crusade. It is written in a simple, delightful style, with moving reverence for the saintly and chivalrous king, with a sharp eye for graphic and psychological detail, and with occasional sly humor. Filled with digressions and personal recollections, it is less the work of a historian than that of a wise, experienced gentleman. There are several English translations of Joinville's memoirs, notably those by Sir Frank Marzials (1908), Joan Evans (1938), and René Hague (1955).

Jókai, Mór (mōr yō'koi), 1825–1904, Hungarian romantic novelist and journalist. Jókai was a fervent nationalist who, after the Hungarian defeat in 1848, became a fugitive from the Austrians. He was later a member (1861–97) of the Hungarian parliament. Often compared to both Dickens and Scott, Jókai was an enormously prolific and popular writer. His novels, national in character, often earthy and humorous in style, have been translated into 25 languages. Among them are *An Hungarian Nabob* (1853–54, tr. 1898) and *Black Diamonds* (1870, tr. 1896).

Jokdeam (jŏk'dēăm, jŏkdē'ăm), unidentified town, S Palestine. Joshua 15.56. Jorkeam: 1 Chron. 2.44.

Jokim (jō'kĭm), son of Shelah the Judahite. 1 Chron. 4.22.

Jokmeam (jŏk'mēăm). **1** Unidentified Levitical town of Ephraim, in central Palestine. 1 Chron. 6.68. Kibzaim: Joshua 21.22. **2** Town, in Solomon's 5th district. 1 Kings 4.12. Some scholars correct the text to read Jokneam, but this interpretation is doubtful.

Jokneam (jŏk'nēăm), Canaanite royal city, later a Levitical city of Zebulun, SW of Mt. Carmel (in present-day Israel). Joshua 12.22; 19.11; 21.34.

Jokshan (jŏk'shăn), son of Abraham. Gen. 25.2,3; 1 Chron. 1.32.

Joktan (jŏk'tăn), descendant of Shem. Gen. 10.25–30.

Joktheel (jŏk'thēĕl, –thēl). **1** Unidentified city, SW Palestine. Joshua 15.38. **2** City of Edom. 2 Kings 14.7. See also SELA.

Jökulsá (yö'külsou), name of several Icelandic rivers formed by glaciers. The best known is the Jökulsá á Fjöllum, which rises on the north slope of the Vatnajökull in SE Iceland and flows c.130 mi (210 km) N into the Axarfjörður, forming the Dettifoss c.30 mi (50 km) from its mouth.

Jokyakarta: see JOGJAKARTA, Indonesia.

Joliet, Louis: see JOLLIET, LOUIS.

Joliet (jō'lēĕt"), city (1970 pop. 78,887), seat of Will co., NE Ill., on the Des Plaines River; inc. 1857. It is an important river port and an industrial and railroad center, with limestone quarries and coal mines in the area. Earth-moving equipment; wire, radio and television parts; wallpaper; chemicals; and paper and metal products are made in the city. The state penitentiary is there. Joliet is the seat of the College of St. Francis and a junior college.

Joliette (zhôlyĕt'), city (1971 pop. 20,127), S Que., Canada, on L'Assomption River, NE of Montreal. Its industries include steel, paper, and textile manufacturing, tobacco processing, and limestone quarrying. The Séminaire de Joliette, affiliated with the Univ. of Montreal, is there.

Joliot-Curie (zhôlyō'-kürē'), French scientists who were husband and wife. **Frédéric Joliot-Curie**(frādārēk'), 1900–1958, formerly Frédéric Joliot, and **Irène Joliot-Curie** (ērĕn'), 1897–1956, daughter of Pierre and Marie Curie, were married in 1926. Both were assistants at the Radium Institute in Paris, of which Irène, succeeding her mother, was director in 1932. Together the Joliot-Curies continued the work of the Curies on radioactivity. For their artificial production of radioactive substances, by bombarding certain elements with alpha particles, they shared the 1935 Nobel Prize in Chemistry. In 1940 they collaborated on research on the chain reaction in nuclear fission. In 1946 they helped to organize the French atomic energy commission, and in the same year Frédéric was appointed chairman of the commission. He was forced to resign in 1950, however, because of his Communist activities, and in 1951 Irène was also dropped from the commission because of her Communist affiliations. In 1947, Irène became a professor and the director of the radium laboratory at the Sorbonne. In 1956, Frédéric was a member of the French Communist party's Central Committee, and in the same year he was appointed to the chair of nuclear physics at the Univ. of Paris.

Jolliet or **Joliet, Louis** (both: jō'lēĕt", jō"lēĕt', Fr. lwē zhôlyā'), 1645–1700, French explorer, joint discoverer with Jacques MARQUETTE of the upper Mississippi River, b. Quebec prov., Canada. After a year's study of hydrography in France and some years as a trader and trapper on the Great Lakes, Jolliet was appointed (1672) as leader of an expedition in search of the Mississippi. He and Father Marquette, with five voyageurs, set out from St. Ignace in May, 1673, went to Green Bay, ascended the Fox River, portaged (at the site of Portage, Wis.) to the Wisconsin River, and descended to the Mississippi. The group followed the west bank south until they passed the mouth of the Arkansas River; then, having convinced themselves that the river emptied into the Gulf of Mexico, they ascended its eastern bank. They came to the Illinois River, ascended it, and, on the site of modern Chicago, portaged to the Chicago River, and again reached Lake Michigan. Marquette remained in the West while Jolliet went east to make his report, but in the Lachine Rapids, near Montreal, Jolliet's canoe overturned and his records were lost. His brief narrative, written from memory, is in essential agreement with Marquette's, the chief source account of the journey. Jolliet was rewarded with the gift of Anticosti Island in the Gulf of St. Lawrence, which was, however, seized by the British while Jolliet was absent on explorations in Labrador and around Hudson Bay. In 1697 he was made royal professor of hydrography and given a small seigniory near Quebec. See biographies by Jean Delanglez (1948) and V. L. S. Eifert (1961); M. S. Scanlon, *Trails of the French Explorers* (1956).

Al Jolson with May McAvoy in a scene from The Jazz Singer, *the first major film with sound.*

Jolo (hō'lō, hōlō'), island (345 sq mi/894 sq km), SULU ARCHIPELAGO, the Philippines. The seaport city, Jolo (1969 est. pop. 46,800), on the northwest coast of the island, is the capital of Sulu prov., the trading and shipping hub of the archipelago, and a Muslim center. An ancient walled city, it was once a pirate base and served as the residence of a sultan until the sultanate was abolished in 1940. The city was almost completely destroyed in 1974 when fighting erupted between government forces and Muslim insurgents who were seeking to establish a secessionist state. After the battle, the rebels withdrew into the island's interior to fight a war of attrition.

Jolson, Al, 1888–1950, American entertainer, whose original name was Asa Yoelson, b. Russia. He emigrated to the United States c.1895. The son of a rabbi, Jolson first planned to become a cantor but soon turned to the stage. After his New York City debut in 1899, he worked in circuses, in minstrel shows, and in vaudeville; in 1909 in San Francisco he first sang "Mammy" in black face, and his style brought him fame and many imitators. The first of his many Broadway appearances was in *La Belle Paree* (1911); his film work began with *The Jazz Singer* (1927), the first major film with sound and a landmark in the history of motion pictures. After 1932 he had his own radio show. Among the songs he made famous were "April Showers," "Swanee," "Sonny-Boy," and "Mammy." See Harry Jolson, *Mistah Jolson* (1951); Michael Freedland, *Jolson* (1972).

Jomini, Antoine Henri (äNtwän' äNrē' zhômēnē'), 1779–1869, Swiss general and military writer. He organized (1799) the militia of the Helvetic Republic and after 1804 served as staff officer in the French army. In Aug., 1813, after a clash with Marshal Berthier, he defected to the enemy, joining the Russian army, in which a commission had previously been arranged. He rose to high rank in Russia, becoming a celebrated authority on strategy. His works include a study of the campaigns of Frederick the Great, *Traité des grandes opérations militaires* (5 vol., 1804–10; tr. *Treatise on Grand Military Operations*); *Histoire critique et militaire des guerres de la Révolution* (1819–24), on the French Revolutionary Wars; and the influential *Précis de l'art de la guerre* (1836; tr. *The Art of War*, 1862), which he wrote while military tutor to the future Czar Alexander II. Jomini emphasized the capture of major points and the importance of superior numbers, and he advocated the employment of speed and maneuver rather than battle whenever possible.

Jommelli, Niccolò (nēk-kōlô' yōm-mĕl'lē), 1714–74, Italian opera composer of the Neapolitan school.

His earliest works, such as *L'errore amoroso* (1737) and *Ezio* (1741), were very successful. He produced operas in Vienna (1749–50). While he was choir director (1751–54) at St. Peter's in Rome, he composed church music. Jommelli was musical director (1754–69) to the duke of Württemberg at Stuttgart. After his return to Naples his last operas, such as *Armida abbandonata* (1770) and *Ifigenia in Tauride* (1771), were rejected by the public as too learned and too German. Despite an attack of apoplexy in 1773, he was still able, in his last year, to compose a Miserere that is considered his masterpiece. In his operas he introduced *recitativo accompagnato* and anticipated many of the reforms of Gluck.

Jona, variant of JONAH. See also BAR-JONA.

Jonadab (jō'nədăb). **1** Nephew of David. 2 Sam. 13.3,32–36. **2** Founder of the Rechabites and a companion of Jehu. Jer. 35. Jehonadab: 2 Kings 10.15–23.

Jonah (jō'nə), **Jonas** (jō'nəs), or **Jona,** book of the Old Testament, 32d in the order of the Authorized Version, 5th of the books of the Minor Prophets. It tells of the career of a Hebrew prophet sent to reform Nineveh; he is specifically dated (2 Kings 14.25) as living under Jeroboam II (reigned c.793–c.753 B.C.) of Israel. His story is famous: to avoid the divine mission he sails for Tarshish but is thrown overboard by the crew because his disobedience has brought down a storm on the ship. Swallowed by a "great fish," he is vomited up on shore after three days. Now willing, he preaches his mission so successfully that God is moved by the people's repentance and revokes the doom Jonah had foretold. The prophet, irritated by the divine change of heart, sulks, but he is shown by an example how God's mercy prevails. Allusions to the story are frequent in the Bible: Mat. 12.39–41; 16.4; Luke 11.29–30; Tobit 14.4. Jonah's coming forth from the fish or whale after being swallowed is famous as a prefiguration of the Resurrection of Christ. See study by R. H. Bowers (1971); see also bibliography under OLD TESTAMENT.

Jonan (jō'nən), ancestor of Joseph. Luke 3.30.

Jonas (jō'nəs), Greek form of Hebrew JONAH. For the father of St. Peter, see BAR-JONA.

Jonas, Franz (fränts yō'näs), 1899–1974, Austrian Socialist politician. Jonas was mayor of Vienna (1951–65) and a member of parliament (1962–65). In 1965 he was elected president, and in 1971 he was reelected, defeating Kurt Waldheim.

Jonas, Justus (yo͝os'to͝os yō'näs), 1493–1555, German Protestant reformer. In 1521, Jonas, then a professor at the Univ. of Erfurt, accompanied Martin Luther to the Diet of Worms. During an intimate friendship Jonas assisted Luther with the translation of the Bible. He also translated the Latin works of Luther and Melanchthon into German. He was present at Luther's death and preached his funeral sermon.

Jonathan (jŏn'əthən) [short for JEHONATHAN]. **1** Saul's son and David's friend, killed at the battle of Mt. Gilboa. 1 Sam. 13; 14.18–20; 20.16–18; 31.1,2. **2** David's nephew. 2 Sam. 21.21. This is probably the Jonathan called David's uncle in the translations of 1 Chron. 27.32. **3** Courtier under David. 2 Sam. 15; 17.17,20; 1 Kings 1.42. **4** One of David's men. 2 Sam. 23.32; 1 Chron. 11.34. **5** Official under David. 1 Chron. 27.25. **6** Levite. 2 Chron. 17.8. **7** Jerahmeelite. 1 Chron. 2.32,33. **8** Israelite in the return to Jerusalem. Ezra 8.6. **9** Priest involved with the foreign marriages. Ezra 10.15. **10** The same as JOHANAN **5.** **11** Priest. Neh. 12.14. **12** Levite. Neh. 12.35. **13** Scribe in whose house Jeremiah was imprisoned. Jer. 37.15; 38.26. **14** Captain under Gedaliah. Jer. 40.8. **15** One of the MACCABEES. 1 Mac. 9–13; 2 Mac. 8.22.

Jonathan, Joseph Leabua (lēä'bwä), 1914–, prime minister of Lesotho (1965–). He worked in South African mines (1933–37), returned to Basutoland, and later became active in politics (1952). A founder of the Basutoland National party (1959), he led it from its inception and worked for independence from South Africa. He became prime minister (1965) under a constitution that preceded Basutoland's independence as Lesotho in 1966. In 1970, when it appeared that he had lost the national election, he seized additional powers and suspended the constitution.

Jonath-elem-rechokim: see AIJELETH SHAHAR.

Jones, Anson, 1798–1858, last president of the Texas republic (1844–46), b. near Great Barrington, Mass. He studied medicine and after an itinerant business and medical career went (1833) to Texas and became a doctor. He joined the revolutionary forces in the war against Mexico and was present at the battle of San Jacinto (1836). Entering politics, Jones was a member of the Texas congress, was appointed (1838) by President Sam Houston as minister to the United States, was dismissed (1839) by President Mirabeau B. Lamar, and served as a senator. His appointment as secretary of state in the second Houston administration (1841–44) prepared the way for his election as president in 1844. Following the annexation of Texas, Jones resigned (1846) his authority to the new governor of the state. He committed suicide in 1858. See biography by Herbert Gambrell (1948).

Jones, Casey, 1864–1900, American locomotive engineer celebrated in ballad and song, probably b. Jordan, Fulton co., Ky. His real name was John Luther Jones, but at the age of 17 he went to Cayce, Ky., and there he was employed as a telegraph operator; from the name of the town he was given the nickname "Casey." In 1888 he entered the service of the Illinois Central RR as a locomotive fireman and soon (1890) was promoted to engineer. He was famous among railroad men for his boast that he always brought his train in on schedule and for his peculiar skill with a locomotive whistle. Given the "crack" assignment of driving the *Cannon Ball* express from Memphis, Tenn., to Canton, Miss.—a particularly dangerous run on which several accidents had occurred—Casey Jones was determined to bring the overdue train in on time but met with disaster. On the morning of April 30, 1900, confronted with a stationary freight train a few feet ahead of his speeding locomotive at Vaughan, Miss., he ordered his fireman to jump. He applied the brakes, and although the *Cannon Ball* crashed and Jones was killed, the passengers were saved. A fellow railroad worker, Wallace Saunders, soon composed a popular ballad about him; one version of it, *Casey Jones,* was published by T. Lawrence Siebert and Eddie Newton. Monuments commemorating Jones stand at Cayce, Ky., and Jackson, Tenn. He was buried at Jackson, Tenn. See biography by F. J. Lee (1939).

Jones, Davy: see DAVY JONES.

Jones, Sir Edward Burne-: see BURNE-JONES.

Jones, Ernest, 1879–1958, British psychoanalyst, b. Wales, M.D. Univ. of London, 1903. He taught (1910–13) at the Univ. of Toronto and was director (1908–13) of the Ontario Clinic for Nervous Diseases. In 1913 he returned to England, where he founded (1925) the London clinic for Psycho-Analysis and served as its director until 1935. Jones was instrumental in introducing the study of psychoanalysis into England and the United States. He is considered an authoritative biographer of Freud, whom he visited several times in Vienna; he also accompanied Freud on trips to Austria and the United States. His writings include *The Life and Work of Sigmund Freud* (3 vol., 1953–57) and *Free Associations: Memories of a Psychoanalyst* (1959).

Jones, Ernest Charles, 1819–69, English agitator, lawyer, journalist, and poet. He was a prominent leader of the more militant wing of the Chartists (see CHARTISM). After imprisonment for sedition (1848–50), he edited a radical journal and later practiced as a lawyer. *The Battle Day and Other Poems* (1855) and his other labor verse have more literary merit than his sensational novels. See his writings and speeches (ed. by John Saville, 1952).

Jones, Henry: see CAVENDISH.

Jones, Henry Arthur, 1851–1929, English playwright. His reputation was first established with the melodrama *The Silver King* (with Henry Herman; 1882). Strongly influenced by the great Norwegian playwright Henrik Ibsen, Jones turned to writing dramas of social and moral criticism. He was the author of over 60 plays, of which *The Middleman* (1889), *Michael and His Lost Angel* (1896), *The Liars* (1897), and *Mrs. Dane's Defense* (1900) are among the most important. His critical works include *The Renascence of the English Drama* (1895) and *The Theatre of Ideas* (1915).

Jones, Howard Mumford, 1892–, American man of letters, b. Saginaw, Mich., grad. Univ. of Wisconsin, 1914. A noted scholar and critic, he wrote on various phases of American literature and culture. He was professor of English and later of humanities at Harvard from 1930 to 1962. Among his works are *Ideas in America* (1944), *The Bright Medusa* (1952), *American Humanism* (1957), and *O Strange New World* (1964; Pulitzer Prize), a study of American culture from the 15th to the 19th cent. His *Education and World Tragedy* (1946) concerns the problems of higher education. His other writings include plays; translations of Heine; and a biography of Thomas Moore, *The Harp That Once—* (1937).

Jones, Inigo, 1573–1652, one of England's first great architects. Son of a London clothmaker, he was enabled to travel in Europe before 1603 to study paintings, perhaps at the expense of the earl of Rutland. On a second trip to Italy (1613–14) he thoroughly studied the remains of Roman architecture and the Renaissance buildings by Palladio. At the English courts of both James I and Charles I he designed settings for elaborate MASQUES, some of which he wrote. Besides performing various architectural services for the crown, he was also sponsored by the earl of Arundel. After renewed visits to Italy, Jones became (1615) king's surveyor of the works. In 1616 he began work on the Queen's House, Greenwich, the first English design to embody Palladian principles. He then built (1619–22) the royal banqueting hall in Whitehall, London, again adapting the classical proportions and use of architectural elements he had learned in Italy. He also made designs for St. Paul's church, Covent Garden, with its square (1631–38). He built other houses in London and in the country; especially outstanding is his advisory work (1649–53) on Wilton House, Wiltshire. Making a clean break from the prevailing Jacobean style, he achieved a magnificent coherence of design. The work of Inigo Jones marked a starting point for the classical architecture of the late Renaissance and Georgian periods in England. See study by Stephen Orgel and Roy Strong (2 vol., 1973).

Jones, James, 1921–77, American novelist, b. Robinson, Ill. Written in the tradition of NATURALISM, his novels often celebrate the endurance of man. *From Here to Eternity* (1951), his best-known work, is a powerful story of army life in Hawaii before the attack on Pearl Harbor. His other novels include *Some Came Running* (1957), *The Thin Red Line* (1962), and *A Touch of Danger* (1973). *Viet Journal* (1974) is an account of his trip to Vietnam.

Queen's House (begun in 1616) in Greenwich, England, designed by Inigo Jones.

Jones, James Earl, 1931–, American actor, b. Tate co., Miss. Jones achieved Broadway stardom with his powerful portrayal of the fighter Jack Johnson in *The Great White Hope* (1968). He made his stage debut at the Univ. of Michigan, and appeared thereafter for seven years with the New York Shakespeare Festival in *Macbeth* (1962), *Othello* (1963), and *King Lear* (1973), among many others. In 1973 he played Hickey in *The Iceman Cometh* and in 1974 Lenny in *Of Mice and Men,* both in New York.

Jones, Jesse Holman, 1874–1956, U.S. Secretary of Commerce (1940–45), b. Robertson co., Tenn. A lumber magnate, banker, and millionaire of Houston, Texas, Jones was appointed (1932) by President Hoover as a member of the RECONSTRUCTION FINANCE CORPORATION (RFC). He became (1933) its chairman under Franklin Delano Roosevelt, and, with the merging of the RFC with other Federal agencies, he was appointed (1939) Federal loan administrator. Jones's performance in the RFC won such high praise that, after his appointment (1940) as Secretary of Commerce, Congress transferred the RFC from the Federal Loan Administration to the Department of Commerce. His close ties with the business community made him indispensable to the Roosevelt administration, and during World War II he was one of the most powerful men in Washington, D.C. He retired from government service in 1945. See his *Fifty Billion Dollars* (1951); biography by B. N. Timmons (1956).

Jones, John Paul, 1747–92, American naval hero, b. near Kirkcudbright, Scotland. His name was originally simply John Paul. He went to sea when he was 12, and his youth was adventure-filled. He was chief mate on a slave ship in 1766 but, disgusted with the work, soon quit. In 1769 he obtained command of the *John,* a merchantman that he captained until 1770. In 1773, while Jones was in command of the *Betsy* off Tobago, members of his crew mutinied and he killed one of the sailors in self-defense. To avoid trial he fled, and in 1775 he was in Philadelphia, with the Jones added to his name. Joseph Hewes of Edenton, N.C., obtained for him a commission in the Continental navy. In 1777, Jones was given command of the *Ranger,* fresh from the Portsmouth shipyard. He sailed to France, then daringly took the war to the very shores of the British Isles on raids and in 1778 captured the *Drake,* a British warship. It was, however, only after long delay that he was given another ship, an old French merchantman, which he rebuilt and named the *Bon Homme Richard* ("Poor Richard"), to honor Benjamin Franklin. He set out with a small fleet but was disappointed in the hope of meeting a British fleet returning from the Baltic until the projected cruise was nearly finished. On Sept. 23, 1779, he did encounter the British merchantmen, convoyed by the frigate *Serapis* and a smaller warship. Despite the superiority of the *Serapis,* Jones did not hesitate. He sailed close in, to cut the advantage of the *Serapis,* and finally in the battle lashed the *Bon Homme Richard* to the British ship. The battle, which began at sunset and ended more than three and a half hours later by moonlight, was one of the most memorable in naval history. Both ships were heavily damaged. The *Serapis* was afire in at least 12 different places. The hull of the *Bon Homme Richard* was pierced, her decks were ripped, her hold was filling with water, and fires were destroying her, unchecked; yet when the British captain asked if Jones was ready to surrender, the answer came proudly, "Sir, I have not yet begun to fight." When the *Serapis* surrendered, Jones and his men boarded her while his own vessel sank. He was much honored in France for the victory but received little recognition in the United States. After the Revolution he was sent to Europe to collect the prize money due the United States. In 1788 he was asked by Catherine the Great to join the Russian navy; he accepted on the condition that he become a rear admiral. His command against the Turks in the Black Sea was successful, but political intrigue prevented his getting due credit. In 1789 he was discharged from the Russian navy and returned to Paris. There in the midst of the French Revolution he died, without receiving the commission that Jefferson had procured for him to negotiate with the dey of Algiers concerning American prisoners. Although he is today generally considered the greatest of American naval heroes and the founder of the American naval tradition, his grave was forgotten until the ambassador to France, Horace E. Porter, discovered it in 1905 after the expenditure of much of his own time and money. The remains were removed to Annapolis and since 1913 have been enshrined in a crypt at the U.S. Naval Academy. See his memoirs (1830, repr. 1972); Anna De Koven, *Life and Letters of John Paul Jones* (1913); F. A. Golder, *John Paul Jones in Russia* (1927); Lincoln Lorenz, *John Paul Jones* (1943, repr. 1969); Gerald W. Johnson, *The First Captain* (1947); Samuel Eliot Morison, *John Paul Jones* (1959, repr. 1964).

Jones, LeRoi, also known as **Imamu Baraka,** (ēmä'mo͞o bərä'kə), 1934–, American author and political activist, b. Newark, N.J. His writings express the violent hatred of a black man for all aspects of white society. Among his plays are *Dutchman, The Toilet,* and *The Slave* (all 1964). His other works include poems, essays, stories, and a novel, *The System of Dante's Hell* (1965). Jones has been active in black politics in Newark, and in 1972 he was one of the leaders of the National Black Political Caucus.

Jones, Mary Harris, 1830–1930, American labor agitator, called Mother Jones, b. Ireland. For many years interested in the labor movement, she became active in it after the death of her husband and children in 1867. She won fame as an effective speaker, always appearing at the scene of any major strike. In 1936 the Progressive Miners of America erected a memorial on her grave in Mt. Olive, Ill. Her autobiography (ed. by M. F. Parton, 1925, repr. 1969) contains some factual inaccuracies. See biography by Dale Fetherling (1974).

Jones, Robert Edmond, 1887–1954, American scene designer, b. Milton, N.H. With his design in 1915 for *The Man Who Married a Dumb Wife,* a new era of scene design began in the United States. His use of color and dramatic lighting enhanced his imaginative sets. Some of Jones's most notable designs were for *Macbeth, Richard III, Hamlet* (for John Barrymore), and *The Green Pastures.* After work with the Washington Square Players, he joined Kenneth Macgowan at the Greenwich Village Theatre; working in conjunction with the Provincetown Players, he created sets for the plays of Eugene O'Neill. Jones did the designing for the early three-color-process film *La Cucaracha* (1933). He wrote *Drawings for the Theatre* (1925), *The Dramatic Imagination* (1941), and, with Kenneth Macgowan, *Continental Stagecraft* (1922). See *The Theatre of Robert Edmond Jones* (ed. by Ralph Pendleton, 1958).

Jones, Robert Tyre, Jr. (Bobby Jones), 1902–71, American golfer, b. Atlanta, Ga. A lawyer, he became a golf devotee. Jones won the National Open

(1923, 1926, 1929), the National Amateur (1924–25, 1927–28), and the British Open (1926–27). The first golfer to win the National and the British Open tournaments in the same year (1926), Jones became the only player ever to make the grand slam in golf—winning the National Open, the National Amateur, the British Open, and the British Amateur championships in 1930. He then retired from tournament play. See his *Down the Fairway* (1927; with O. B. Keeler); *Golf Is My Game* (1960); *Bobby Jones on Golf* (1966); *Bobby Jones on the Basic Golf Swing* (1969); O.B. Keeler, *The Bobby Jones Story* (1953).

Jones, Rufus Matthew, 1863–1948, American minister of the Society of Friends, educator, and author, b. South China, Maine. He taught philosophy and ethics at Haverford College, Pa., from 1893 to 1934. One of the founders of the noted American Friends Service Committee (1917), he was its chairman until 1928 and thereafter honorary chairman. His many books, mainly on the Quakers and on mysticism, include *Quakerism, a Religion of Life* (1908), *The Quakers in the American Colonies* (1911), *The New Quest* (1928), *George Fox, Seeker and Friend* (1930), *Radiant Life* (1944), and *The Luminous Trail* (1947). See anthology of his writings ed. by H. E. Fosdick (1951); biographies by David Hinshaw (1951, repr. 1970) and E. J. G. Vining (1958).

Jones, Samuel Milton, 1846–1904, American political reformer, known as "Golden Rule" Jones, b. Wales. He was brought to America as a child and worked in the oil fields of Pennsylvania and Ohio. He invented improvements in oil-drilling machinery, and after the oil trust refused to handle these inventions, Jones manufactured them himself—very successfully—in Toledo, Ohio. He was noted for his advanced program of employee-management relations. Elected (1897) mayor of Toledo on the Republican ticket, he put into operation a comprehensive program of municipal reform. When refused renomination in 1899, he ran as an independent and overwhelmingly defeated both political machines. He was reelected in 1901 and 1903 and died in office. During his administration he established civil service and instituted the eight-hour day and minimum wages for city employees. See his autobiography, *The New Right* (1899).

Jones, Thomas ap Catesby, 1789–1858, American naval officer, b. Westmoreland co., Va. He joined the navy in 1805 and helped suppress piracy and the slave trade in the Gulf of Mexico (1808–12). In the War of 1812 he made a desperate and unsuccessful effort to halt the fleet carrying the British army to New Orleans from crossing Lake Borgne (1814). In 1826 he made a visit to Hawaii that increased U.S. prestige in those islands. In 1842, acting upon a rumor that the United States and Mexico were at war, he captured Monterey, Calif. For this action he was removed from command but not otherwise censured.

Jones, Sir William, 1746–94, English philologist and jurist. Jones was celebrated for his understanding of jurisprudence and of Oriental languages. He published an *Essay on the Law of Bailments* (1781), widely used in America as well as in England. For 11 years he was a supreme court judge in Calcutta. Jones founded the Asiatic Society of Bengal at Calcutta. Through the Society, as well as through his publications, he had a great influence on literature, Oriental study, and philology in Western Europe. Jones was the first to suggest that Sanskrit originated from the same source as Latin and Greek, thus laying the foundation for modern comparative philology. See his letters, ed. by Garland Cannon (2 vol., 1970).

Jones Beach, state park, 2,413 acres (977 hectares), on an offshore bar, SW Long Island, SE N.Y., in Nassau co.; est. 1929. It is noted for its wide, white sand beaches, outdoor marine theater, and varied recreational facilities.

Jonesboro, city (1970 pop. 27,050), a seat of Craighead co., NE Ark., on Crowley's Ridge; founded 1859, inc. 1883. It is the trade, distributing, and industrial center for a large farm area. Arkansas State Univ. is there, and a state park is nearby. Parts of the city were devastated by tornadoes in May, 1973.

Jong, Petrus Josef Sietse de: see DE JONG, PETRUS JOSEF SIETSE.

Jongkind, Johann Barthold (yōhän' bär'tôlt yông'kĭnt), 1819–91, Dutch landscape painter and etcher. He studied in Paris with Isabey. Jongkind's work was a transition between the Barbizon school and the impressionists, and he notably influenced the latter group. He painted chiefly in France, though many of his scenes are Dutch. He was a fine watercolorist and one of the foremost etchers of the 19th cent. In these media he achieved a fresh rendering of atmospheric effects, especially in his marine scenes. Jongkind is represented in the Rijks Museum and in the Louvre.

jongleurs (zhông-glör'), itinerant entertainers of the Middle Ages in France and Norman England. Their repertoire included dancing, conjuring, acrobatics, the feats of the modern juggler, singing, and storytelling. Many were skilled in playing musical instruments. The jongleurs were often collaborators or assistants of TROUBADOURS or TROUVÈRES.

Jönköping (yön'chö"pĭng), city (1970 pop. 96,944), capital of Jönköping co., S Sweden, at the southern end of Lake Vättern. It is a commercial and industrial center. The safety match was developed there, and the city has large match factories (founded 1844). Other manufactures include machinery, paper, textiles, and airplanes. Jönköping was chartered in 1284 by Magnus I. Gustavus Adolphus gave (1620) it special privileges after its citizens had burned the city to prevent the Danes from sacking it. Jönköping's modern prosperity began in the 19th cent. with the opening of the Göta Canal and the coming of the railroad.

Jonquière (zhôNkyĕr'), city (1971 pop. 28,430), S Que., Canada, on the Saguenay River, adjacent to its twin city, Kénogami, W of Chicoutimi. Its chief industries produce paper and pulp. Jonquière has a college and a school of technology.

jonquil: see AMARYLLIS.

Jonson, Ben, 1572–1637, English dramatist and poet, b. Westminster, London. The high-spirited buoyancy of Jonson's plays and the brilliance of his language have earned him a reputation as one of the great playwrights in English literature. After a brief term at bricklaying, his stepfather's trade, and after military service in Flanders, he began working for Philip Henslowe as an actor and playwright. In 1598 he was tried for killing another actor in a duel but escaped execution by claiming right of clergy (that he could read and write). His first important play, *Every Man in His Humour*, was produced in 1598, with Shakespeare in the cast. In 1599 its companion piece, *Every Man out of His Humour*, was produced. In *The Poetaster* (1601) Jonson satirized several of his fellow playwrights, particularly Dekker and Marston, who were writing at that time for a rival company of child actors. He collaborated with Chapman and Marston on the comedy *Eastward Ho!* (1604). A passage in the play derogatory to the Scots offended James I, and the three playwrights spent a brief time in prison. Jonson's great period, both artistically and financially, began in 1606 with the production of *Volpone.* This was followed by his three other comic masterpieces, *Epicoene* (1609), *The Alchemist* (1610), and *Bartholomew Fair* (1614). Jonson became a favorite of James I and wrote many excellent masques for the court. He was the author of two Roman tragedies, *Sejanus* (1603) and *Catiline* (1611). With the unsuccessful production of *The Devil Is an Ass* in 1616 Jonson's good fortune declined rapidly. His final plays were failures, and with the accession of Charles I in 1625 his value at court was less appreciated. His plays, written along classical lines, are marked by a pungent and uncompromising satire, by a liveliness of action, and by numerous HUMOR characters, whose single passion or oddity overshadows all their other traits. He was a moralist who sought to improve the ways of men by portraying human foibles and passions in exaggeration and distortion. Jonson's nondramatic poetry includes *Epigrams* (1616); *The Forrest* (1616), notable for the two beautiful songs: "Drink to me only with thine eyes" and "Come, my Celia, let us prove"; and *Underwoods* (1640). His principal prose work *Timber or Discoveries* (1640) is a collection of notes and reflections on miscellaneous subjects. Jonson exerted a strong influence over his contemporaries. Although arrogant and contentious, he was a boon companion, and his followers, sometimes called the "sons of Ben," loved to gather with him in the London taverns. Examples of his conversation were recorded in *Conversations with Ben Jonson* by Drummond of Hawthornden. See Jonson's works (11 vol., 1925–52); biography by Marchette Chute (1953); studies by E. B. Partridge (1958), J. A. Barish (1960), Wesley Trimpi (1962), G. B. Jackson (1969), J. G. Nichols (1970), J. B. Bamborough (1970), J. A. Bryant (1973), and W. D. Wolf (1973).

Jonson, Cornelis van Ceulen: see JANSSENS, CORNELIS VAN CEULEN.

Jónsson, Einar (ā'när yōn'sôn), 1874–1954, Icelandic sculptor and painter. His subjects were drawn from Nordic mythology, Icelandic folklore, and the Bible. His statue of the explorer Thorfinn Karlsefni is in Fairmount Park, Philadelphia. In Reykjavik, Iceland, there is a museum of his work.

Joos of Ghent: see JUSTUS OF GHENT.

Jooss, Kurt (ko͞ort yōs), 1901–, German dancer, producer, and choreographer. Jooss was a student of Rudolf von Laban and was influenced by Émile Jaques-Dalcroze. *The Green Table* (1932), his most famous ballet, was an expressionistic view of the origins of war. Leaving Germany after the rise of Hitler, he worked in England with his Ballets Jooss and toured in many European and American cities, returning to Germany after the war. His group was disbanded in 1962; Jooss continued to perform with other Western European companies. His ballets, including *Chronica, The Big City, A Spring Tale,* and *Pandora,* have influenced the development of psychological themes in ballet. See A. V. Coton, *The New Ballet: Kurt Jooss and his Work* (1946).

Joplin, Scott, 1868–1917, American ragtime pianist and composer, b. Texarkana, Texas. Self-taught, Joplin left home in his early teens to seek his fortune in music. From 1885 to 1893 he lived in St. Louis, playing in saloons and bordellos. In 1894 he moved to Sedalia, Mo., and played second cornet in a local band. For the next two years Joplin toured with a vocal ensemble he had formed and made his first efforts at composing ragtime. When the group disbanded (1896), he returned to Sedalia, where he stayed about four years. During this time he studied music at George Smith College, an educational institution for blacks sponsored by the Methodist Church. In 1899 he published the "Maple Leaf Rag," and its success was instantaneous. However, his next two major efforts, a folk ballet titled *Rag Time Dance* (1902) and a ragtime opera called *A Guest of Honor* (never published) were failures. Joplin continued to write ragtime music and moved (1909) to New York City, where he had considerable success until 1915, when at his own expense he produced a second ragtime opera, *Treemonisha* (1911), that failed to gain recognition. This failure and the declining interest in ragtime is thought to have affected his personality, which became moody and temperamental. In 1916 he was confined to the Manhattan State Hospital, where he died the following year. Joplin's rags were highly innovative, characterized by a lyricism and suppleness that elevated ragtime from honky-tonk piano music to a serious art form. Some of his compositions are "The Entertainer" (1902), "Rose Leaf Rag" (1907), "Gladiolus Rag" (1908), "Fig Leaf Rag" (1908), and "Magnetic Rag" (1914). A revival of interest in ragtime occurred in the 1970s. Several of Joplin's rags were used as background music for the Hollywood film *The Sting* (1973), and a Joplin Festival was held at Sedalia in 1974. See Rudi Blesh and Harriet Janis, *They All Played Ragtime* (rev. ed. 1966).

Joplin (jŏp'lĭn), city (1970 pop. 39,256), Jasper and Newton counties, SW Mo., at the edge of the Ozarks; settled c.1839, inc. 1873. It is a railroad center, the shipping and processing point of a grain and livestock region with dairy and fruit farms, and the industrial center of a lead and zinc area. The city has a mineral museum and is the seat of Missouri Southern State College.

Joppa: see JAFFA, Israel.

Jorah (jō'rə), the same as HARIPH.

Jorai (jō'rāī, jōrā'ī), Gileadite. 1 Chron. 5.13.

Joram (jō'rəm). **1, 2** Kings of Israel and Judah: see JEHORAM **1, 2.** **3** Son of Toi, king of Hamath, sent to congratulate David on the defeat of Hadadezer. 2 Sam. 8.9–10. Hadoram: 1 Chron. 18.10. **4** Levite. 1 Chron. 26.25.

Jordaens, Jacob (yä'kôp yôr'däns), 1593–1678, Flemish baroque painter, b. Antwerp. After the deaths of Rubens and Van Dyck, by whom he was influenced, he became the leading Flemish painter of his day and worked in Antwerp nearly all his life. Like Rubens, Jordaens produced portraits and religious and allegorical paintings, often expressing a joy of life. In early works (c.1612–25), such as *The Artist's Family* (Hermitage, Leningrad) and *Allegory of Fertility* (Brussels), he reveals the influence of Caravaggio in his firm modeling and realistically treated surface. Works executed c.1625–35 show increased grandeur and richness (*Triumph of Bacchus*; Kassel), and in the next years Rubens and Van Dyck influences are especially clear. In the last 25 years of his life, Jordaens stressed increasingly the classicist elements in baroque art, moving from the energetic *Triumph of Prince Frederik Hendrik of Orange* (The Hague) to the more rigidly composed *Christ and the Doctors*

Allegory of Fertility, *detail of a painting by the Flemish baroque artist Jacob Jordaens.*

(Mainz). Examples of his work may be seen in many of the major museums of Europe and the United States. See study by Max Rooses (tr. 1908).

Jordan, Camille (kämē'yə zhôrdäN'), 1771–1821, French writer and political figure. A moderate supporter of the French Revolution, he fled France during the REIGN OF TERROR and again after the coup d'etat of Sept. 4, 1797. He befriended Johann von Goethe, J. C. F. von Schiller, and Johann von Herder. Returning to France after Napoleon Bonaparte (later Emperor Napoleon I) came to power, he wrote (1802) the widely read pamphlet, *Vrai sens du vote national* [the true meaning of the national vote], directed against Napoleon. After the Bourbon restoration Jordan was elected (1816) to the chamber of deputies.

Jordan, David Starr, 1851–1931, American scientist and educator, b. Gainesville, N.Y., M.S. Cornell, 1872, M.D. Indiana Medical College, 1875, and studied under Louis Agassiz at Penikese Island. He taught (1875–79) at Butler Univ. and in 1879 became professor of zoology and head of the department of natural science at Indiana Univ.; there he was president from 1885 to 1891. He served as the first president (1891–1913) of Stanford Univ. and as chancellor (1913–16). A prolific writer and a popular speaker, he was active as director (1910–14) of the World Peace Foundation and president (1915) of the World Peace Congress. Peace and international arbitration were the subjects of his books *The Human Harvest* (1907) and *War and Waste* (1913). As a leading ichthyologist Jordan served on international commissions for fisheries and as assistant (1877–91, 1894–1909) to the U.S. Fish Commission. His earliest important work, *A Manual of the Vertebrate Animals of Northern United States* (1876), went through many editions. He also wrote *The Fishes of North and Middle America* (4 vol., 1896–1900), *A Guide to the Study of Fishes* (2 vol., 1905), *Your Family Tree* (with S. L. Kimball, 1929), and *Trend of the American University* (1929). See his autobiographical *Days of a Man* (2 vol., 1922); biography by H. A. Moran (1969).

Jordan, officially Hashemite Kingdom of Jordan, formerly Transjordan, kingdom (1970 est. pop. 2,348,000), 37,737 sq mi (97,740 sq km), SW Asia, bordering on Israel in the west, on Syria in the north, on Iraq in the northeast, and on Saudi Arabia in the east and south. AMMAN is the country's capital and largest city; other cities include Zarqa, HEBRON, Irbid, the Old City of JERUSALEM, and NABLUS. In the Arab-Israeli War of 1967, Israel captured and occupied all of Jordan located W of the Jordan River and the Dead Sea (the area known collectively as the West Bank), which comprises about 2,165 sq mi (5,607 sq km) and includes Hebron, JERICHO, the Old City of Jerusalem, and Nablus. Jordan falls into three main geographical regions. East Jordan, which encompasses about 92% of the country's land area, is made up of a section (average elevation: 2,500 ft/760 m) of the Arabian Plateau that in the northeast includes part of the Syrian Desert. In the western

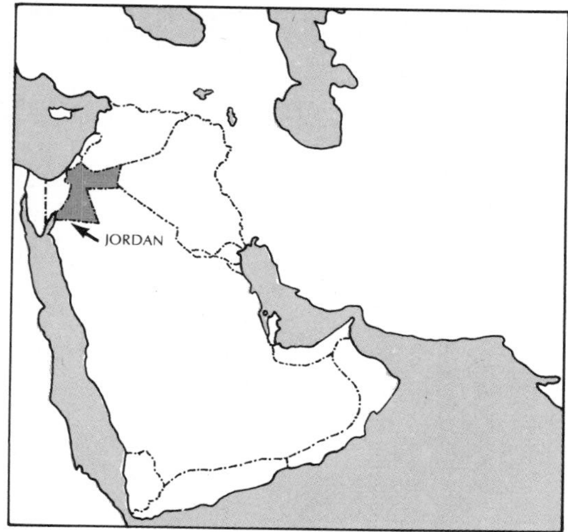

part of the plateau are the Jordanian Highlands, which include Jabal Ramm (5,755 ft/1,754 m), Jordan's loftiest point. Central Jordan is made up of a segment of the Great Rift Valley (which continues southward into Africa) and includes the Jordan River, the Dead Sea, and the Arabah (a dry riverbed). West Jordan, which is part of historic Palestine, is composed of the hilly regions of SAMARIA (in the north) and JUDAEA (in the south). Samaria has abundant fertile soil, and Judaea is largely stony and barren. The inhabitants of Jordan are mostly of Arab descent; however, the Palestinians are also descended from the people who lived in Palestine before the Arab conquest (7th cent.), whereas the inhabitants of E Jordan (many of whom belong to BEDOUIN tribes) are of purer Arab ancestry. There are small minorities of Armenians and Circassians. Arabic, the official language, is spoken by virtually everyone. About 90% of the people are Sunni Muslims. There are approximately 100,000 Christians, about half of whom are Greek Orthodox. Jordan's economy is largely agricultural. Only about 10% of the country's land is arable, and farm output is further limited by the small size of most farms, inefficient methods of tilling the soil, inadequate irrigation, and the dislocations caused by the Arab-Israeli Wars. The principal crops are wheat, barley, lentils, tomatoes, eggplants, citrus fruits, and grapes. Many Jordanians support themselves by raising sheep and goats. Manufactures are largely limited to basic items such as foodstuffs, beverages, clothing, construction materials (especially cement), soap, dairy products, and cigarettes. Numerous artisans make items of leather, wood, and metal. Phosphate rock and potash are the only minerals produced in significant quantities. Jordan's transportation system is limited to a small network of all-weather roads and a narrow-gauge railroad (formerly part of the Hejaz RR) that enters Jordan from Syria and runs through Amman and into S Jordan. Aqaba is the country's only seaport. The annual cost of Jordan's imports usually far exceeds its earnings from exports. The principal imports are foodstuffs, textiles, machinery, iron and steel, and chemicals; the main exports are phosphates and tomatoes. Jordan's leading trade partners are the United States, Saudi Arabia, Lebanon, and Syria. The history section of this article is primarily concerned with the region E of the Jordan River; for the history of the area to the west see PALESTINE. The region of present-day Jordan roughly corresponds to the biblical lands of AMMON, BASHAN, EDOM, and MOAB. The area was conquered by the Seleucids in the 4th cent. B.C. and was part of the Nabatean empire, whose capital was Petra, from the 1st cent. B.C. to the mid-1st cent. A.D., when it was captured by the Romans under Pompey. In the period between the 6th and 7th cent. it was the scene of considerable fighting between the Byzantine Empire and Persia. In the early 7th cent. the region was invaded by the Muslim Arabs, and after the Crusaders captured Jerusalem in 1099, it became part of the Latin Kingdom of Jerusalem. In 1516 the Ottoman Turks gained control of what is now Jordan, and it remained part of the Ottoman Empire until the 20th cent. After the fall of the Ottoman Empire in World War I the region came under (1919) the government of Faisal I centered at Damascus. When Faisal was defeated by the French, Transjordan (as Jordan was then known) was made (1920) part of the British League of Nations mandate of Palestine. In 1921, ABDULLAH ibn Husain, a member of the Hashemite dynasty and the brother of Faisal, was made head of Transjordan, which was administered separately from Palestine and was specifically exempted from being part of a Jewish national home. A Jordanian army, called the Arab Legion, was created by the British largely through the work of Sir John Bagot GLUBB. In a treaty signed with Great Britain in 1928, Transjordan became a constitutional state ruled by a king (to be hereditary in the family of Abdullah). The country supported the Allies in World War II, and, by a treaty with Great Britain signed in 1946, it became (May 25) independent as the Hashemite Kingdom of Transjordan. By an agreement signed in 1948, Britain guaranteed Transjordan an annual military subsidy. Abdullah opposed Zionist aims, and when Palestine was partitioned and the state of ISRAEL was established in 1948, Transjordan, like other members of the ARAB LEAGUE, sent forces to fight Israel (see ARAB-ISRAELI WARS). The troops of the Arab Legion were unsuccessful against the Israeli forces, but they did gain control of most of that part of W central Palestine that the United Nations had designated as Arab territory. In April, 1949, the country's name was changed to Jordan, thus reflecting its ac-

Tombs of the ancient city of Petra, in present-day Jordan.

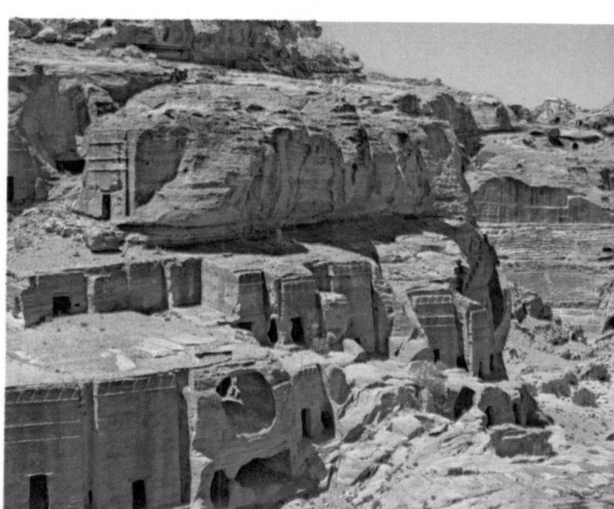

quisition of land W of the Jordan River. In Dec., 1949, Jordan concluded an armistice with Israel, and early in 1950, it formally annexed the West Bank, a move that was deeply resented by other Arab states, which favored the establishment of an independent state of Palestine. The annexation of the West Bank increased Jordan's population by about 450,000 persons, many of them homeless refugees from Israel. In 1951, Abdullah was assassinated in Jerusalem by a Palestinian and was succeeded by his son Talal. Talal, however, was mentally ill, and in 1952 parliament replaced him with his son HUSSEIN I. In 1953 and 1954 border clashes with Israel threatened a renewal of major hostilities, and Jordan received promises of aid from other Arab countries. After a series of anti-Western riots in Jordan, Hussein early in 1956 dismissed Glubb as commander of the Arab Legion, and following the Suez crisis later in the year, he ended Jordan's treaty relationship with Great Britain. In Feb., 1958, Jordan and Iraq formed the Arab Federation as a countermove to the newly formed United Arab Republic (UAR); however, the federation was short-lived; Hussein dissolved it in August, following the July revolution in Iraq that toppled the monarchy there. At the time of the Iraqi revolution, the UAR called for the overthrow of the governments in Jordan and Lebanon. To stabilize politics in these countries, the British sent troops to Jordan, and the United States dispatched forces to Lebanon (in both cases at the request of the governments involved). Tensions were soon reduced, and by early November the troops had been withdrawn. However, for the next few years Jordan remained on poor terms with Iraq and the UAR. The terrorist killing in 1960 of Jordan's prime minister, Hazza Majali, was alleged to have been directed from Syria. In 1961, Hussein was among the first to recognize Syria after it withdrew from the UAR. Following the establishment in 1963 of a revolutionary Jordanian government-in-exile in Damascus, a state of emergency was declared in Jordan. The crisis ended only after the United States and Great Britain announced their support of Hussein and the U.S. 6th Fleet was placed on alert. In the mid-1960s, Jordanian politics were calm, Jordan's economy expanded as its international trade increased, and Jordan was on good terms with Egypt. In 1966 relations with Syria deteriorated, and there were serious border clashes with Israel. Following Egypt's declaration in 1967 of a blockade of Israeli shipping in the Gulf of Aqaba, Hussein signed a mutual defense pact with President Gamal Abdal Nasser of Egypt. In the brief Arab-Israeli War in June, Jordanian forces were routed by Israel, and Jordan lost the West Bank. In 1968–69 there were clashes along the frontier with Israel, but of greater significance was the growing hostility between the Jordanian government and the Palestinian guerrilla organizations (notably Al Fatah, the Palestine Liberation Organization, and the Popular Front for the Liberation of Palestine) operating in Jordan. The guerrillas sought to establish an independent Palestinian state, a goal that conflicted with Hussein's intention of reestablishing Jordan's control over the West Bank. There was major fighting between the guerrillas and the Jordanian army in Nov., 1968, and in Sept., 1970, the country was engulfed in a bloody 10-day civil war, which ended when other Arab countries (especially Egypt) arranged a cease fire. In July, 1971, the army carried out a successful offensive that destroyed the guerrillas' bases. Jordan played a minor role in the Arab-Israeli War of Oct., 1973, sending a small number of troops to fight on the Syrian front but not actually attacking Israel across their common border. Bowing to intense pressure from other Arab states, Hussein formally renounced all Jordanian claims to the West Bank in 1974. He also agreed to recognize the Palestine Liberation Organization as the sole negotiating representative of the Palestinian people. Although the policy of "Jordanization" (the removal of Palestinian influence in Jordanian affairs) remained in effect, Hussein moved (1976) to reassert some influence over the West Bank. In 1975–76, Jordan and Syria agreed to coordinate their military forces in order to achieve a common "eastern front" policy against Israel.

Government. Under the 1952 constitution as amended, the most powerful political and military figure in the country is the king. He appoints a cabinet (headed by a prime minister), which is responsible to the bicameral parliament that consists of a 30-member senate (appointed by the king) and a 60-member house of representatives (popularly elected to 4-year terms). See Sir John Bagot Glubb, *The Story of the Arab Legion* (1952) and *Syria, Lebanon, and Jordan* (1967); F. G. Peake, *A History of Jordan and its Tribes* (1958); Raphael Patai, *The Kingdom of Jordan* (1958); P. J. Vatikiotis, *Politics and the Military in Jordan: A Study of the Arab Legion, 1921–57* (1967); H. C. Reese et al., *Area Handbook for the Hashemite Kingdom of Jordan* (1969); N. H. Aruri, *Jordan: A Study in Political Development, 1921–1965* (1972); Sir Charles Johnston, *The Brink of Jordan* (1972).

Jordan, river, c.200 mi (320 km) long, formed in the Hula basin, N Israel, by the confluence of three headwater streams and meandering S through the Sea of Galilee to the Dead Sea; longest and most important river of Palestine. It flows through the northern section of the Jordan trough, a part of the Great Rift Valley; between the Sea of Galilee and the Dead Sea, the Jordan valley is called the Ghor. The Jordan is fed by many small streams; the Yarmuk River is its largest tributary. Deep and turbulent during the rainy season, the Jordan is reduced to a sluggish, shallow stream during the summer. As it nears the Dead Sea, its salinity increases. Although the river is not navigable, its waters are potentially very valuable for irrigation. Plans for the integrated development of the water of the entire Jordan basin collapsed in 1953 because of Arab-Israeli enmity. Individual mutually harmful schemes have been initiated, e.g., Israel's National Water Carrier Project, which uses the Sea of Galilee as a reservoir, and Jordan's East Ghor project, which diverts water from the Yarmuk River. Irrigation projects in Syria and Lebanon divert water from the Jordan's headstreams. The Jordan, scene of Christ's baptism, is frequently mentioned in the Bible. The southern half of the river formerly flowed through Jordan, but after the 1967 Arab-Israeli War this part of the river became a section of the defacto Israel-Jordan border.

Jordan, river, 60 mi (97 km) long, draining Utah Lake N into Great Salt Lake, N central Utah; it passes through Salt Lake City. Fed by numerous streams flowing off the Wasatch Range, the Jordan is used for irrigation and forms the heart of the Utah Oasis. Mormons settled along its banks in the mid-1800s.

Jordanes (jôrdā'nēz), fl. 6th cent., historian of the Ostrogoths. Born in the lower Danube region, he entered the priesthood and lived much of his life at

Ravenna. His *History of the Goths*, an abridgment of the lost work of CASSIODORUS, is the only source for Ostrogothic history. It is one of the few works written in Vulgar Latin.

Jorga, Nicolas: see IORGA, NICOLAE

Jørgensen, Jens Johannes (yĕns yōhä'nəs yör'gənsən), 1866–1956, Danish poet and religious writer. He reacted against the naturalism of Georg Brandes and, in such works as *Poems* (1898), turned to symbolism and emotion. Jørgensen's conversion (1896) to Roman Catholicism is described in his autobiography (7 vol., 1916–28; tr., 2 vol., 1928–29). Among his works are *Saint Francis of Assisi* (1907, tr. 1912) and *Saint Catherine of Siena* (1915, tr. 1938). *Flowers and Fruit* (1907) and *The Brig Marie of Svendborg* (1926) are collections of his poems.

Jorim (jôr'ĭm), ancestor of Joseph. Luke 3.29.

Jorkoam (jôrkō'əm), descendant of Caleb. 1 Chron. 2.44.

Jos (jôs), city (1969 est. pop. 105,000), central Nigeria, on the Jos Plateau. It is a mining center for tin ore, which is processed in the city, and a collection point for hides and skins and for market-garden produce to be sent to Lagos. It is also a resort. Jos was developed in the early 20th cent. by the British as an administrative center and mining town. The railroad reached here in 1927. The Jos Museum includes a collection of neolithic Nok TERRA-COTTA figurines (see AFRICAN ART). The UNESCO School for Museum Technicians is attached to the museum.

Josabad (jō'zəbăd), officer of David. 1 Chron. 12.4.

Josaphat (jŏs'əfăt), in the Bible: see JEHOSHAPHAT.

Josaphat, in literature: see BARLAAM AND JOSAPHAT.

Jose (jō'zē), in the Gospel genealogy. Luke 3.29.

Josedech (jŏs'ədĕk), variant of JOZADAK.

Joselito (hōsālē'tō), 1895–1920, Spanish matador, b. Seville as José Gómez. A prodigy, he appeared first as a torero in 1908 and later toured Spain as one of a child-bullfighting group known as the Niños Sevillanos. His rivalry with Juan BELMONTE between 1914 and 1920 is known as the Golden Age of Bullfighting. It ended with Joselito's fatal goring at Talavera de la Reina on May 16, 1920, in a corrida in which both matadors appeared. Joselito and Belmonte are considered the two greatest matadors of all time.

Joseph, Saint, husband of the Virgin, a carpenter, a descendant of the house of David. He was apparently dead at the time of the Passion, for his last appearance in the Gospels is at the finding of the 12-year-old Jesus in the temple (Luke 2.42–50). As the foster father of Jesus and the chaste spouse of Mary, St. Joseph is highly honored by Orthodox and Roman Catholics. The latter regard him as patron of the Church. Feast: March 19; another feast, the Solemnity of St. Joseph: third Wednesday after Easter.

Joseph I, 1678–1711, Holy Roman emperor (1705–11), king of Hungary (1687–1711) and of Bohemia (1705–11), son and successor of Leopold I. Joseph became Holy Roman emperor in the midst of the War of the SPANISH SUCCESSION and died before it ended. He vigorously supported the claim of his brother (who succeeded him as CHARLES VI) to the Spanish throne. During his reign Hungary was in revolt under Francis II RÁKÓCZY, but by 1711 the rebellion had been quelled. Joseph made some attempts at internal reform. A musician and an admirer of art, he encouraged cultural life in Vienna.

Joseph II, 1741–90, Holy Roman emperor (1765–90), king of Bohemia and Hungary (1780–90), son of MARIA THERESA and Holy Roman Emperor FRANCIS I, whom he succeeded. He was the first emperor of the house of Hapsburg-Lorraine. From the death of his father (1765) to the death of his mother (1780) he ruled the Hapsburg lands jointly with his mother but had little authority. After his mother's death Joseph instituted far-reaching reforms that were more the result of Joseph's personal philosophy and principles than of the philosophy of ENLIGHTENMENT. As a young man he was profoundly impressed by the subhuman conditions of the peasantry that he saw while touring the provinces. He was impatient with the slowness of Maria Theresa's reforms. On her death, he was ready with a full revolutionary program. He contemplated nothing less than the abolition of hereditary and ecclesiastic privileges and the creation of a centralized and unified state administered by a civil service based on merit and loyalty rather than birth. He planned a series of fiscal, penal, civil, and social laws that would have established some measure of social equality and security for the masses. A strong exponent of absolutism, he used despotic means to push through his reforms over all opposition in order to consolidate them during his lifetime. Although Joseph was a faithful Roman Catholic he instituted a series of religious reforms aimed at making German Catholicism independent of Rome. Joseph's main piece of legislation was the abolition (1781) of serfdom and feudal dues; he also enabled tenants to acquire their own lands from the nobles for moderate fees and allowed peasants to marry whom they wished and to change their domicile. He forbade religious orders to obey foreign superiors, suppressed all contemplative orders, and even sought to interfere with the training of priests. A personal visit (1782) of Pope PIUS VI to Vienna did not halt these measures. The Patent of Tolerance (1781) provided for extensive, although not absolute, freedom of worship. In judicial affairs Joseph liberalized the civil and criminal law codes, abolishing torture altogether and removing the death penalty. In fiscal matters Joseph was influenced by the PHYSIOCRATS. He ordered a general reassessment of land preparatory to the imposition of a single land tax. This reform met widespread opposition. Still more unpopular, however, was his attempt to abrogate local governments, customs, and privileges in his far-flung and multilingual dominions, which he divided into 13 circles centrally administered from Vienna. He even sought to impose German as the sole official language; a multilingual administration seemed irrational to him. Revolts broke out in Hungary and in the Austrian Netherlands (see NETHERLANDS, AUSTRIAN AND SPANISH); these were subsequently halted during the reign of LEOPOLD II, Joseph's brother and successor, who rescinded Joseph's reforms in these lands. Joseph founded numerous hospitals, insane asylums, poorhouses, and orphanages; he opened parks and gardens to the public; and he legislated to provide free food and medicine for the indigent. Most of Joseph's reforms did not outlive him. His failure to make them permanent was largely caused by his lack of diplomacy, by his untimely death, by the reaction produced by the French Revolution, and by his unsuccessful foreign policy. Moreover, his scattered and varied lands offered poor conditions for reform. His plan to annex Bavaria to Austria and thus to consolidate his state was frustrated in the War of the BAVARIAN SUCCESSION (1778–79); his project to exchange the Austrian Netherlands for Bavaria was thwarted (1785) by King Frederick II of Prussia,

Josephine, empress of the French as consort to Napoleon I, in a portrait by Pierre Paul Prud'hon (detail).

who formed the *Fürstenbund* [princes' league] for that purpose. Joseph allied himself with Czarina CATHERINE II of Russia (whom he accompanied incognito on her Crimean journey), hoping to share in the spoils of the Ottoman Empire (Turkey). Austria joined Russia in the war of 1787–92 against Turkey but was unsuccessful. Obsessed with his social responsibility, Joseph found only occasional time to interest himself in any but the utilitarian arts. With the exception of the pliable KAUNITZ, Joseph's ministers found it difficult to collaborate with him. Joseph was hated and ridiculed by the clergy and nobles, but he was the idol of the common people. Judgments on Joseph II vary widely, but it is certain that he left a socially freer state on his death than he had found on his accession. See Saul K. Padover, *The Revolutionary Emperor, Joseph II* (rev. ed. 1967); P. P. Bernard, *Joseph II* (1968).

Joseph, 1714–77, king of Portugal (1750–77), son and successor of John V. His reign was dominated by his minister, the marquês de POMBAL. Joseph was succeeded at his death by his daughter, Maria I, and Peter III.

Joseph. **1** One of the early heroes of the Bible, the favored son of Jacob and Rachel, sold as a boy into slavery by his brothers who were jealous of Joseph's dreams and of his coat of many colors given him by Jacob. In Egypt, Joseph, after gaining a position of authority in the household of his master, Potiphar, was imprisoned on the false accusations of Potiphar's wife. He was released after interpreting Pharaoh's dream of the lean and fat kine. Pharaoh renamed him Zaphnath-paaneah and took him into favor. Joseph's recognition of his brothers in the famine years when he was governor over Egypt is a famous scene of literature. His wife was Asenath, an Egyptian, and their sons Manasseh and Ephraim were ancestors of 2 of the 12 tribes of Israel. Gen. 30; 37; 39–50. The story has been retold and reworked, as in Joseph and Asenath, among the PSEUDEPIGRAPHA, and in the works of Thomas MANN. **2** Issacharite. Num. 13.7. **3** Asaphite. 1 Chron. 25.2,9. **4** One who had a foreign wife. Ezra 10.42. **5** Priest. Neh. 12.14. **6, 7, 8** Ancestors of St. Joseph. Luke 3.24,26,30. See JOSES; BARNABAS.

Joseph (Chief Joseph), c.1840–1904, chief of a group of NEZ PERCÉ INDIANS. On his father's death in 1871, Joseph became leader of one of the groups that refused to leave the land ceded to the United States by the fraudulently obtained treaty of 1863. Faced with forcible removal (1877), Joseph and the other nontreaty chiefs prepared to leave peacefully for the reservation. Misinformed about the intentions of the Nez Percés, Gen. Oliver Otis HOWARD ordered an attack, which the Indians repulsed. Pursued by the U.S. army, the warriors, with many women and children, began a masterly retreat to Canada of more than 1,000 mi (1,609 km). The Indians won several engagements, notably one at Big Hole, Montana, but 30 mi (48 km) short of the Canadian border they were overtaken by troops under Gen. Nelson A. MILES and forced to surrender. The whites had assumed that Joseph, spokesman for the Indians in peacetime, was responsible for their outstanding strategy and tactics, which actually had been agreed upon in council by all the chiefs. He became, however, a symbol of the heroic, fighting retreat of the Nez Percés. He was taken to Fort Leavenworth, then spent the remainder of his life on the Colville Indian Reservation in the state of Washington and strove to improve the conditions of his people. In 1903 he made a ceremonial visit to Washington, D.C. See biographies by O. O. Howard (1881, repr. 1972), H. A. Howard (1941, repr. 1965), and M. D. Beal (1963, repr. 1973).

Joseph, Father (François Leclerc du Tremblay), 1577–1638, French Capuchin monk, a confidant and agent of Cardinal Richelieu, generally known as the Éminence Grise [gray eminence]. Combining the elements of a mystic and of a Machiavellian politician, he devoted his life with equal energy to missionary work and to the shady and delicate diplomatic negotiations with which Richelieu entrusted him. He dreamed of a crusade against the Turks and of the restoration of Roman Catholicism throughout Europe, yet he lent his services to a policy that strengthened Protestantism and the Ottoman Empire at the expense of the Catholic house of Hapsburg. Rumors ascribed to him an evil influence over the cardinal. It is more likely, however, that Father Joseph was a pliable instrument in the cardinal's hands and that his influence on the events that led to the entry of France into the Thirty Years War has been vastly exaggerated. Unlike his master, Father Joseph sought no material rewards. He is the subject of a study by Aldous Huxley, *Grey Eminence* (1941, repr. 1969).

Joseph Barsabas, Saint (bär'səbəs), surnamed Justus, Matthias' competitor for the place among the disciples left vacant by Judas Iscariot. Lots were drawn, and Matthias won. Acts 1.23. Feast: July 20.

Josephine, 1763–1814, empress of the French (1804–9) as the consort of NAPOLEON I. Born Marie Josèphe Rose Tascher de La Pagerie, in Martinique, she was married in 1779 to Alexandre de Beauharnais. Two children were born, Eugène (later viceroy of Italy) and Hortense (later queen of Holland). Josephine's husband was guillotined during the French Revolution, in 1794, but she escaped with brief imprisonment. In 1796 she was married, by a civil ceremony, to Napoleon Bonaparte, whom she had met through Paul BARRAS. Before Napoleon became emperor, they were remarried in a religious ceremony. Josephine took a prominent part in the social life of the time. Napoleon had the marriage annulled in 1809 because of her alleged sterility, so that he might marry Marie Louise, daughter of the Austrian emperor Francis I (formerly Holy Roman Emperor Francis II). Thereafter Josephine lived in retirement at Malmaison. See biographies by R. M. Wilson (1930) and André Castelot (tr. 1967); studies by Frédéric MASSON.

Joseph of Arimathea, Saint (âr"ĭməthē'ə), wealthy man, probably a member of the Sanhedrin, who gave the body of Jesus a decent burial. (Mat. 27.57–61; Mark 15.42–47; Luke 23.50–56; John 19.38–42.) The Christian Church has always honored him. The stories connecting him with the Holy GRAIL and with the founding of GLASTONBURY are probably literary fictions of the Middle Ages and have never received the approval of the church. Feast: March 17.

Joseph of Exeter, fl. c.1190, English poet who wrote in Latin. He is best known for *De Bello Trojano* (c.1184), an epic poem in six books, written in the style of Vergil. His adventures in the Third Crusade were recounted in *Antiocheis*, most of which is lost. He lived much of his life in France.

Josephus, Flavius (flā'vēəs jōsē'fəs), A.D. 37–A.D. 95?, Jewish historian and soldier, b. Jerusalem. Having studied the tenets of the three main sects of Judaism—Essenes, Sadducees, and Pharisees—he became a Pharisee. At the beginning of the war between the Romans and Jews, he was made governor of Galilee. He displayed valor and shrewdness in the war, but when the stronghold he defended was taken, he won the favor of the Roman general Vespasian (Titus Flavius Vespasianus) and took his name, Flavius. The conduct of Josephus toward the Roman conquerors has been both criticized and defended; however, our knowledge of his conduct is based on his own writings. It is as a historian of the Jews that Josephus is renowned. He wrote *The Jewish War;* the famous *Antiquities of the Jews*, a history of the race from creation to the war with Rome; *Against Apion*, an exalted defense of the Jews; and his autobiography, or apologia. His complete works have appeared in English editions. See H. St. John Thackeray, *Josephus: The Man and the Historian* (1929, rev. ed. 1968); F. J. Foakes Jackson, *Josephus and the Jews* (1930); R. J. H. Shutt, *Studies in Josephus* (1961); G. A. Williamson, *The World of Josephus* (1965).

Joses (jō'sēz) [Gr. form of Heb. JOSEPH]. **1** Kinsman of Jesus. Mark 6.3; Mat. 13.55. **2** Brother of St. JAMES (the Less); same as **1,** if the traditional interpretation is accepted. Mat. 27.56; Mark 15.40,47. **3** See BARNABAS, SAINT.

Josetsu (jō"sä'tso͞o), fl. 1425, Japanese landscape painter, teacher, and priest. His work shows the formal characteristics of Chinese *suiboku-ga* (black-and-white) painting. He worked in Kyoto, where SHUBUN was his pupil.

Joshah (jō'shə), Simeonite chief. 1 Chron 4.34.

Joshaphat (jŏsh'əfăt): see JEHOSHAPHAT.

Joshaviah (jŏshəvī'ə), one of David's guard. 1 Chron. 11.46.

Joshbekashah (jôshbĕk'əshä), Hemanite temple musician. 1 Chron. 25.4, 24.

Joshua (jŏsh'o͞oə, -əwə). **1** Central figure of the book of JOSHUA. **2** High priest associated with Zerubbabel in rebuilding the Temple. Hag. 1; 2; Zech. 3; 6.11. Jeshua: Ezra 3.2; 4.3; 10.18; Neh. 12.26. Jesus: Ecclus. 49.12. **3** Owner of the field where the Ark of the Covenant stood. 1 Sam. 6.14. **4** Governor of Jerusalem. 2 Kings 23.8.

Joshua (jŏsh'o͞oə) or **Josue** (jŏs'yo͞oē), book of the Old Testament, the sixth in the order of the Authorized Version (AV). It is a historical sequel to Deuteronomy, telling of the occupation of Palestine by the Hebrews. The chief figure of the book is Joshua, Moses' successor as leader of Israel. He appears in Moses' lifetime in increasingly important positions, as a warrior (Ex. 17.9, 14), as the assistant to Moses (Ex. 24.13; 33.11), as one of the spies (Num. 13; 14), and finally as Moses' designated successor (Deut. 31.1-8, 14-23; 32.44). The Book of Joshua may be divided into three sections: first, the conquest of the Promised Land (1-12), including the divine appointment of Joshua (1.1-9), the dry crossing of the Jordan River (3), the fall of Jericho (6), and the battle where the sun and moon stood still (10); second, the allotment of the land to the people by tribes (13-22), mainly lists of names, but including an account of how the tribes east of the Jordan acquitted themselves of the charge of setting up a sanctuary of their own (22); and, third, the farewell sermon of Joshua and his death (23-24). Joshua's name appears variously in AV: Jehoshua (Num. 13.16); Jehoshuah (1 Chron. 7.27); Jeshua (Neh. 8.17); Jesus (Acts 7.45;

Heb. 4.8). He is also called Hoshea (Deut. 32.44) and Oshea (Num. 13.8, 16), both variants of Hosea. He is one of the great heroes of biblical history. Ecclus. 46.1–6; 1 Mac 2.55. For critical views of the composition of Joshua see study by J. A. Soggin (tr. 1972); see also bibliography under OLD TESTAMENT.

Joshua tree: see YUCCA.

Joshua Tree National Monument: see NATIONAL PARKS AND MONUMENTS (table).

Josiah (jōsī'ə) or **Josias** (jōsī'əs). **1** King of Judah, son and successor of Amon. The great event of his reign came in its 18th year, when the book of the law, apparently DEUTERONOMY, was found in the Temple. Josiah had it read publicly, and a reform movement began, led by the young king. The basis of the reforms, which extended to the northern kingdom of Israel, was the removal of all outlying religious centers so as to concentrate everything in worship at Jerusalem. When the pharaoh Necho set out to help the Assyrians in Haran, Josiah opposed him and fell, at Megiddo. He was succeeded by his son Jehoahaz. 2 Kings 22–23; 2 Chron. 34–35. **2** Man at whose house the prophet Zechariah was to crown the high priest. Zech. 6.10–11.

Josibiah (jŏsĭbī'ə), father of Jehu the Simeonite. 1 Chron. 4.35.

Jósika, Miklós, Baron (bä'rōn mĭk'lōsh yō'shĭkō), 1794–1865, Hungarian novelist and patriot. The originator of the Hungarian historical novel, he was often superficial and inaccurate, but was nevertheless responsible for a renewed interest in Hungary's history. His many novels include *Abafi* (1836) and *Az utólsó Bátory* (1840). Forced to flee abroad after his part in the unsuccessful revolution of 1848–49, he directed the central office of Polish émigrés in Brussels.

Josiphiah (jŏsĭfī'ə), father of one who returned with Ezra. Ezra 8.10.

Jos Plateau (jôs), region, c.3,000 sq mi (7,770 sq km), alt. c.4,200 ft (1,280 m), central Nigeria, W Africa. The plateau, composed mainly of granite, slopes gently to the north and is covered by grasslands; the Gongola River rises there. The region has one of the higher population densities in Nigeria and is freer from disease than the surrounding lowlands. Tin is mined and processed on the plateau, and farming and grazing are important. The town of Jos is the region's chief center. In the 19th cent. the plateau was a refuge for non-Islamic tribes fleeing from the Islamic Fulani people.

Josquin Desprez or **Des Prés** (both: zhōs'kăN dāprā'), c.1440–1521, Flemish composer, b. Hainaut, regarded by his contemporaries as the greatest of his age. Luther spoke highly of Desprez who may have instructed Erasmus in music. He was in Milan from 1459 to 1479, and he sang in the papal choir intermittently from 1486 to 1494. After brief service under the duke of Ferrara, he ended his days as provost of the Collegiate Church of Condé. His earlier works exhibit a preoccupation with contrapuntal skills, while his later works are more chordal. He wrote Masses and miscellaneous Italian pieces, but he was particularly noted for his chansons and motets.

Jostedalsbreen (yô'stədälsbrā''ən), largest glacier of the European mainland, 315 sq mi (816 sq km), Sogn og Fjordane co., SW Norway. Located W of the Jotunheimen mts., between Nordfjord and Sognafjord, the glacier is 60 mi (97 km) long and 15 mi (24 km) wide, with its head c.6,700 ft (2,040 m) above sea level. It has many tributary glaciers.

Josue (jŏs'yo͞oē), variant of JOSHUA.

Jotbah (jŏt'bə), unidentified place, probably in S Palestine. 2 Kings 21.19.

Jotbath (jŏt'bəth) or **Jotbathah** (-bəthə), unidentified desert place. Num. 33.33; Deut. 10.7.

Jotham (jō'thəm). **1** The only one of Gideon's sons not killed by Abimelech; noted for his parable of the trees electing the bramble to be their king. Judges 9.5–21. **2** King of Judah, son of Uzziah. He was a contemporary of Isaiah, Hosea, and Micah. 2 Kings 15.5,32–38. Joatham: Mat. 1.9. **3** Descendant of Caleb. 1 Chron. 2.47.

Jotunheimen (yō'to͝onhāmən), mountain group, S central Norway; highest of Scandinavia. It culminates in Galdhøpiggen (8,098 ft/2,468 m high) and Glittertinden (8,104 ft/2,470 m). The Jostedalsbreen, a huge glacier, is to the west. Sparsely inhabited, the region is used for summer pasture. In Norse mythology, it was the home of the giants, the Jotun.

Joubert, Joseph (zhôzĕf' zho͞obĕr'), 1754–1824, French moralist. His *Pensées* (of which there are many English translations) rank with those of La Rochefoucauld in their finished style but have a greater range, including ethics, politics, theology, and literature.

Joubert, Petrus Jacobus (pā'tro͞os yäkō'bo͞os yo͞obĕr'), 1831–1900, Boer general and politician. With Paul Kruger and Martinus Wessel Pretorius he governed the Transvaal from 1880 to 1883. In 1881 he defeated the British twice before routing them at Majuba Hill. Joubert ran for president against Kruger in 1883, 1893, and 1898. At the outbreak of the South African War he directed the siege of Ladysmith until ill health forced him to retire.

Jouett, Matthew Harris, 1787–1827, American painter, b. Mercer co., Ky., studied in Boston with Gilbert Stuart. He was the first prominent painter in the West. Among his more than 300 portraits are one of Lafayette in the state capitol at Frankfort, Ky., and one of John Grimes in the Metropolitan Museum. James Edward Jouett was his son.

Jouffroy, Théodore Simon (tāôdôr' sēmôN' zho͞ofrwä'), 1796–1842, French philosopher. He was professor at the Collège de France and librarian at the Univ. of Paris. His translations of Thomas Reid and Dugald Stewart spread the influence of the Scottish school of philosophy. His writings stressed the distinction between psychology and physiology. He was influenced by Victor Cousin. His works include *Cours de droit naturel* (1835), *Mélanges philosophiques* (1833), and *Cours d'esthétique* (1843).

Jouhaux, Léon (lāôN' zho͞o-ō'), 1879–1954, French Socialist labor leader. He headed the Confédération générale du Travail from 1909 to 1947, when he resigned in protest against its alliance with Communist interests. In 1949 he helped found the anti-Communist International Confederation of Free Trade Unions. Long prominent in the International Labor Organization and active in the service of peace, Jouhaux received the 1951 Nobel Peace Prize. His works include studies on labor and on disarmament.

Joule, James Prescott (jo͞ol, joul), 1818–89, English physicist. His scientific researches began in his youth when he invented an electromagnetic engine. Joule made valuable contributions to the fields of heat, electricity, and thermodynamics. His work established the mechanical theory of HEAT, and he was the first to determine the relationship between heat energy and mechanical energy (the mechanical equivalent of heat). Joule discovered the first law of THERMODYNAMICS, which is a form of the law of conservation of energy (see CONSERVATION LAWS). He was one of the great experimental scientists of the 19th cent. The electrical unit of work is named for him.

joule (jo͞ol, joul), abbr. J, unit of WORK or ENERGY in the MKS SYSTEM of units, which is based on the METRIC SYSTEM; it is the work done or energy expended by a force of 1 newton acting through a distance of 1 meter. The joule is named for James P. Joule.

Joule's law: see THERMOELECTRICITY.

Jourdan, Jean Baptiste (zhäN bätēst′ zho͞ordäN′), 1762–1833, marshal of France. He fought in the American Revolution, and in the French Revolutionary Wars he commanded the Army of the North to Wattignies (1793), won a decisive victory at Fleurus (1794), and led the army of Sambre-et-Meuse into Cologne (1794). He sponsored the law of general conscription (1796) that bore his name. Although initially opposed to the coup d'etat of 18 Brumaire (1799), he served Napoleon as ambassador to the Cisalpine Republic (1801) and was made councilor of state (1802) and marshal of France (1804). After Napoleon's fall, he rallied to the Bourbons, who later made him a peer.

journalism, the collection and periodical publication of news. It includes writing for, editing, and managing such media as the NEWSPAPER and the PERIODICAL. Journalism dates at least from the *Acta Diurna* of Rome (a series of public announcements that can be considered the prototype of the modern newspaper), but it was not until the 15th cent. that the invention of printing made possible its rapid growth. Modern journalism, however, began in the latter years of the 18th cent. Up to that time journalistic enterprise had been hampered by government control, which the American and French Revolutions and the political freedom they fostered helped to break. Until the institution of freedom of speech and of the press, journalism had generally served as the handmaiden of politics or business. Even in the 19th cent. journalists, despite their increased liberties in England and America, were largely controlled by political parties. The advance of universal education, growing popular support of newspapers and periodicals, and new inventions such as the typewriter and linotype helped to extend the prestige and independence of journalism. Enterprising editors in the American newspaper field in the mid-19th cent. influenced other journalistic media (e.g., the muckraking magazine and the independent periodical). In the 20th cent. journalism has undergone profound changes. The personal power of the journalist declined in the face of tremendous technological advances, the growth of the NEWS AGENCY, vast strides in reporting techniques, heavier dependence on advertisement, and the development of other mass media such as radio, television, and motion pictures. However, interest in major political events, the two world wars, and a marked spirit of internationalism led to a great expansion of facilities. Journalism has tended to become more standardized, impersonalized, and sensationalized in England and in the United States and has expanded considerably beyond its original methods of publishing the news in printed form. Joseph Pulitzer, W. R. Hearst, Henry Luce, and Joseph Patterson have been influential names in the style development of contemporary American journalism. Radio and television have become an important and controversial aspect of journalism because they can render events as they actually occur; the psychological effect of the American landing on the coast of Normandy on June 6, 1944, was undoubtedly augmented by the fact that the event was broadcast on radio. Television has had an even stronger impact. Indeed, it has been noted that television not only reports events, it also, by its very presence, influences the course and outcome of these events. There has been controversy about television coverage of numerous events, including the Army-McCarthy hearings, the assassination of President Kennedy, occurrences in the Vietnam War, the Democratic and Republican conventions of 1968 and 1972, and the hearings of the Senate Select Committee on 1972 Campaign Activities. The importance of journalism has been testified to by the establishment of schools of journalism at most of the world's leading universities. The earliest in the United States was established at the Univ. of Wisconsin (1905). Other early schools were the Univ. of Missouri (1908) and Columbia Univ. school of journalism, which was endowed in 1903 but which did not open until 1912. See F. L. Mott, *News in America* (1952) and *American Journalism* (3d ed. 1962); John Hohenberg, *The New Front Page* (1966); A. K. MacDougall, ed., *The Press* (1972); R. A. Rutland, *The Newsmongers* (1973).

joust: see TOURNAMENT.

Jouvenel, Henry de (äNrē′ də zho͞ovənĕl′), 1876–1935, French statesman and journalist. Although from an early age influential in politics, he refused to join a party, claiming that existing groups only pandered to the masses. He advocated a modified form of syndicalism. Long editor of the *Matin*, Jouvenel was elected (1921) to the senate, where he generally aligned himself with the left. He was minister of public instruction in 1924 and a delegate to the League of Nations in 1922 and in 1924. As French high commissioner (1925–26) in Syria he employed stern methods to quell a rebellion. Ambassador to Italy in early 1933, he labored to bring Benito Mussolini into the French camp. In 1912, Jouvenel married the French novelist Colette; they were later divorced. See Rudolph Binion, *Defeated Leaders* (1960).

Jouvenet, Jean Baptiste (zhäN bätēst′ zho͞ovənā′), 1644–1717, French painter, one of a family of painters. He worked in Paris in the studio of Charles Le Brun, whose manner he acquired and whose favor at court he shared. He is best known for his religious paintings; the most important are the series of four canvases for St. Martin des Champs, including the *Miraculous Draught of Fishes* (1706; Louvre). These later works are characterized by a baroque force, with naturalistic details.

Jouvet, Louis (lwē zho͞ovā′), 1887–1951, French actor, producer, and director. A member of Copeau's Théâtre du Vieux Colombier after 1913, he left in 1922 to organize his own theater. He was director of the Comédie des Champs Élysées (1924–34) and from 1934 of the Athénée in Paris. He was the first to produce and act in many of the plays of Giraudoux. Jouvet also created highly original décors and stage lighting.

Jove: see JUPITER.

Jovellanos, Gaspar Melchor de (gäspär′ mĕlchôr′ dā hōvĕlyä′nōs), 1744–1811, Spanish statesman and writer. Jovellanos's poetry is philosophical and reflective; his best-known poem is *Epístola de Fabio a*

Anfriso [epistle from Fabio to Anfriso]. His personal integrity put him at odds with church and state, and he was imprisoned for seven years (1801–8). In his prose writing he appealed for prison reform. Jovellanos's report on agrarian law and his memoir in defense of the Central Junta at the time of the French invasion in 1808 had a wide influence. A firsthand view of Jovellanos's life and times is afforded by his diary, covering the years from 1790 to 1801.

Jovian (Flavius Claudius Jovianus) (jō'vēən), c.331–364, Roman emperor (363–64). The commander of the imperial guard under JULIAN THE APOSTATE in his Persian campaign, Jovian was proclaimed emperor by the soldiers when Julian was killed. He made a humiliating peace with SHAPUR II of Persia. He returned Christianity to the privileged position it had enjoyed before Julian, and he restored his friend St. Athanasius to the episcopal see of Constantinople. After a reign of only eight months Jovian died and was succeeded by the joint emperors Valentinian I and Valens.

Jovian planets, the planets JUPITER, SATURN, URANUS, and NEPTUNE. They are all larger and more massive than the earth. Uranus has a radius about 4 times that of the earth and is about 15 times as massive, while Jupiter has a radius about 11 times that of the earth and is about 318 times as massive. However, they are all much less dense than the earth. Since they rotate faster, they are more flattened at the poles than are the TERRESTRIAL PLANETS.

Jowett, Benjamin (jou'ĕt), 1817–93, English educator and Greek scholar, b. London. Jowett was a Church of England clergyman, master of Balliol College, Oxford (1870–93), and vice chancellor of Oxford. His influence on his pupils was profound. Jowett's translation of the dialogues of Plato (1871) is an outstanding work both of English literature and of classical scholarship. See biography by G. C. Faber (1957).

Joyce, James, 1882–1941, Irish novelist. Probably the most significant British writer of the 20th century, Joyce was a master of language, exploiting its total resources. His novel *Ulysses,* which is among the great works of world literature, utilizes many radical literary techniques and forms. The effect of Joyce on other 20th-century writers is incalculable. Born one of ten children in a Dublin suburb, Joyce was educated at Jesuit schools—Clongowes Wood College in Clane (1888–91), Belvedere College in Dublin (1893–99)—and was graduated from University College in Dublin (1899–1902). Although a brilliant student, he paid little attention to his official studies; instead, repelled by the narrow orthodoxy of Catholicism, he abandoned his religion and led a dissolute life. In 1902 he lived briefly in Paris, returning to the Continent in 1904 with Nora Barnacle, the girl who would eventually become his wife. For the next 25 years Joyce, Nora, and their children (George, b. 1905, and Lucia Anna, b. 1907) lived at various times in Paris, Trieste, and Zürich. Joyce returned to Ireland twice: in 1909 in a futile attempt to start a chain of motion picture theaters in Dublin, and in 1912 to arrange for the publication of *Dubliners.* The book was published there but subsequently burned by the printers because the names of actual persons, places, and institutions were mentioned. It was finally published in England in 1914. Joyce and his family spent the years of World War I in Zürich, where he worked on his novel *A Portrait of the Artist as a Young Man.* It first appeared in *The Egoist,* a periodical edited by Harriet Shaw Weaver, and was published in book form in 1916. In 1917, Joyce contracted glaucoma and for the rest of his life endured pain, periods of near blindness, and innumerable operations. During these years he lived mainly on money donated by patrons, notably Harriet Shaw Weaver. His great novel *Ulysses,* written between 1914 and 1921, was published in parts in *The Little Review* and *The Egoist,* but Joyce encountered much opposition to publishing the novel in book form because charges of obscenity were leveled against it. It was finally published in Paris by Shakespeare & Company, a bookstore owned by an American, Sylvia Beach. Its publication was banned in the United States until 1933. From 1922 until 1939 Joyce worked on *Finnegans Wake* (1939). In 1931 he married Nora. Although she was unintellectual and rather uninterested in his work, their union was a happy one, marred only by the progressive insanity of their daughter. Joyce died in Zürich in 1941 after an operation for a malignant duodenal ulcer. With each of Joyce's four major works there is an increase in the profundity of his vision and the complexity of his literary technique, particularly his experiments with language. His first book, *Dubliners,* is a linked collection of 15 short stories treating the squalid lives of various Dublin residents. The stories often center on moments of spiritual insight, which Joyce called epiphanies. *A Portrait of the Artist as a Young Man* is a fairly realistic, highly autobiographical account of the adolescence and youth of Stephen Dedalus, who comes to realize that before he can be a true artist he must rid himself of the stultifying effects of the religion, politics, and essential bigotry of Ireland. *Ulysses* recreates the events of one day in Dublin, June 16, 1904, centering on the activities of a Jewish advertising-space salesman, Leopold Bloom, his wife Molly, and the aforementioned Stephen Dedalus, now a teacher. The fundamental design of *Ulysses* is based on Homer's *Odyssey.* Each of the novel's major characters has a counterpart in the *Odyssey,* and the novel's theme is Bloom's search for a son and Stephen's for a father. Each incident in the novel parallels one in the epic and is also associated with an hour of the day, color, art, and part of the body. Attempting to recreate the total life of his characters—the surface life and the inner life—Joyce mingles realistic descriptions with verbal representations of his characters' most intimate and random thoughts, for which he utilized

Irish novelist James Joyce with Sylvia Beach, who first published the writer's great novel, Ulysses.

the stream of consciousness technique. Interspersed throughout the work are historical, literary, religious, and geographical allusions, evocative patterns of words, word games, and many-sided puns, all of which imbue the ordinary events of the novel with the significance of those in an epic. *Ulysses* is a complex book, intricate in structure and proceeding on several levels of meaning. Yet it is also an extraordinarily satisfying book, a celebration of life unparalleled in its humor, characterization, and tragic irony. Joyce's last work, *Finnegans Wake,* is the book of night to supplement the day of *Ulysses.* Although appearing at times to present the dreams of a Dublin publican, the novel also seems to represent a universal consciousness. In order to present this new reality Joyce manipulated and disoriented language, pushing it to the furthest limits of comprehensibility and then beyond. Because of its complexity, *Finnegans Wake* is seldom read and is probably, despite much scholarly treatment, not thoroughly understood. The canon of Joyce's works includes volumes of poems, *Chamber Music* (1907), *Pomes Penyeach* (1927), and *Collected Poems* (1937); *Exiles* (1918), a play in the manner of Ibsen; and part of an early version of *A Portrait of the Artist as a Young Man* called *Stephen Hero* (1944). In June, 1962, a Joyce museum, containing pictures, papers, and first editions of Joyce's books, was dedicated in Dublin. Selections from his work appear in *The Portable James Joyce* (ed. by Harry Levin, 1947). See his letters (Vol. I ed. by Stuart Gilbert, 1957; Vol. II and III ed. by Richard Ellman, 1966); biographies by Richard Ellman (1959) and C. G. Anderson (1968); studies by Anthony Burgess (1965); R. M. Adams (1962 and 1966), John Gross (1970), A. Walton Litz (1961, 1966 and 1972) and Richard Ellman (1974); Don Gifford and R. J. Seidman, *Notes For Joyce: An Annotation of James Joyce's Ulysses* (1974); bibliography by J. J. Slocum and Herbert Cohoon (1953, repr. 1972).

Joyce, William, 1906–46, British Nazi propagandist, b. Brooklyn, N.Y., called Lord Haw-Haw. Taken to England as a child, Joyce became involved there in the fascist movement. He went to Germany just before the outbreak of World War II and throughout the war broadcast German propaganda in English from Berlin. He was captured by British soldiers in Germany in 1945. Despite his American birth, he was adjudged subject to British jurisdiction because he held a British passport. He was convicted of treason and hanged. See biography by J. A. Cole (1964); Rebecca West, *The New Meaning of Treason* (rev. ed. 1967).

Jozabad (jō'zəbăd). **1, 2** Two of David's captains. 1 Chron. 12.20. **3, 4** Important Levites. 2 Chron. 31.13; 35.9. **5** Man who had married a foreigner. Ezra 10.22. **6, 7, 8, 9** Levites in the return from the Exile. Ezra 8.33; 10.23; Neh. 8.7; 11.16. These four may be identical.

Jozachar (jŏz'əkär), murderer of Joash. 2 Kings 12.20,21. Zabad: 2 Chron. 24.26.

Jozadak (jō'zədăk), one in the high priests' line who probably never held office, because he was carried away to Babylon. Ezra 3.2; 10.18; Neh. 12.26. Jehozadak: 1 Chron. 6.14,15. Josedech: Hag. 1.1; Zech. 6.11.

József, Attila (ä'tĭlä yō'zhĕf), 1905–37, Hungarian poet. Born in Budapest of a poor family, József had to support himself from the age of seven with menial jobs; he was never able to earn a living from his writing. He was dismissed from the Univ. of Szeged for publishing a poem that was considered blasphemous. After two years abroad he returned to Budapest, where he joined the illegal Communist Party. After suffering periodic struggles with schizophrenia, he committed suicide. His poetry, known abroad only after his death, deals with proletarian life, based largely on his personal experiences.

Juana, Spanish queen of Castile: see JOANNA.

Juana Inés de la Cruz (hwä'nä ēnās' dā lä kro͞os), 1651–95, Spanish American poet, b. Mexico. She is considered the greatest lyric poet of the colonial period. A beautiful and intellectually precocious girl, Sor Juana was a favorite at the viceregal court before entering a convent at the age of 16. Forced to study outside the university, she devoted herself to amassing a fine library. Her classical erudition and her scientific curiosity led to reprimands from her convent superiors. The bishop of Puebla published one of her studies but criticized her for neglecting religious duties. Sor Juana answered the bishop's objections to the education of women in a spirited autobiographical letter (1691) that became a classic. Her spontaneous and original lyric poetry won enduring fame. *Primer sueño,* one of her major poetic works, nearly 1,000 lines long, is the metaphoric interpretation of a dream and of awakening. Sor Juana sold her books and devoted her last years to the spiritual life. She died trying to help the convent victims of an epidemic.

Juana la Beltraneja (hwä'nä lä bĕltränā'hä), 1462–1530, Castilian princess; daughter of Juana of Portugal, queen of HENRY IV of Castile. Her paternity was generally attributed to the court favorite Beltrán de la Cueva, whence her name. Juana was recognized as legitimate heiress to the throne by the Cortes of Castile, but later Henry IV designated as successor first his half brother Alfonso (d.1468) and then his half sister Isabella (later ISABELLA I). In 1470, Henry recognized Juana again, but when he died (1474) Isabella seized the throne. Juana's partisans called upon Alfonso V of Portugal for help and arranged his marriage to the young princess. After five years of struggle Alfonso was decisively defeated at Toro (1476), and Isabella was recognized (1479) as queen of Castile. Juana retired to a convent in Portugal.

Juan Carlos (hwän kär'lōs), 1938–, king of Spain (1975–), b. Rome, the son of Don Juan de Borbón y Battenberg, count of Barcelona, and Doña María de las Mercedes de Borbón y Orleans and the grandson of Alfonso XIII. As part of his grooming as Franco's successor, he graduated from Spain's three military academies and received commissions in the army, navy, and air force. In 1962 he married Princess Sophia of Greece, by whom he had three children. In 1969 he was designated heir to the Spanish throne and Franco's successor and was empowered (1971) to serve as acting chief of state in the event of Franco's incapacitation. He briefly served as provisional chief of state when Franco was ill in 1974 and assumed this position again on Oct. 30, 1975. Upon Franco's death (Nov. 20, 1975), he ascended the throne as Juan Carlos I. He attempted to move Spain gradually toward parliamentary democracy; political parties, including those of the left, were legalized and most political prisoners released. His foreign policy was aimed at the eventual integration of Spain into the North Atlantic Treaty Organization and the Common Market.

Juan de Fuca Strait (wän də fyo͞o'kə), inlet of the Pacific Ocean, 100 mi (161 km) long and 11 to 17 mi (18–27 km) wide, between Vancouver Island, British Columbia, and Washington state, linking the Strait of Georgia and Puget Sound with the Pacific; forms part of the U.S.-Canada border. Victoria, British Columbia, the strait's largest city, is located at its eastern end; ferries connect it with the U.S. mainland. Discovered by the English captain Charles W. Barkley in 1787, the strait was named for a sailor, Juan de Fuca, who reputedly had discovered it for Spain in 1592.

Juanes, Juan de: see MACIP, VICENTE JUAN.

Juan Fernández (hwän fărnän'dās), group of small islands, S Pacific, c.400 mi (640 km) W of Valparaiso, Chile. They belong to Chile and are administered as a part of Valparaiso prov. The two principal islands are Más a Tierra and Más Afuera. Volcanic in origin, they have a pleasant climate and are rugged and heavily wooded. The chief occupation is lobster fishing. Discovered by an obscure Spanish navigator in 1563, the islands achieved fame with the publication of Daniel Defoe's *Robinson Crusoe* (1719), generally acknowledged to have been inspired by the confinement on Más a Tierra (1704–9) of Alexander SELKIRK, a Scottish sailor. Occupied by the Spanish in 1750, the islands passed to Chile when it won independence. In the 19th cent. Más a Tierra was used as a penal colony.

Juan Manuel, Infante de Castile (hwän mänwĕl', ēnfän'tā thā kästē'lā), 1282–1349?, Spanish nobleman, soldier, and writer; nephew of Alfonso X (called the Wise). Juan Manuel was a wealthy and powerful prince. His masterpiece is the *Libro del Conde Lucanor* (1323–35, tr. 1868), a collection of 50 didactic tales that were source material for several major writers, including Boccaccio, Chaucer, and Calderón. See study by H. T. Sturcken (1974).

Juárez, Benito (bānē'tō hwä'rās), 1806–72, Mexican liberal statesman and national hero, an Indian. Revered by Mexicans as one of their greatest political figures, Juárez, with great moral courage and honesty, upheld the civil law and opposed the privileges of the clericals and the army. A lawyer, he was governor of Oaxaca from 1847 to 1852. In 1853 he was imprisoned for his opposition to SANTA ANNA. After a period of exile in the United States, Juárez was a chief figure in drawing up the Plan of AYUTLA and in the subsequent revolution that overthrew Santa Anna. Juárez became minister of justice in the new government and issued the Ley Juárez, which, with the Ley Lerdo (see LERDO DE TEJADA, MIGUEL), attacked the privileges of the church and the army. The conservatives rose against the liberal constitution of 1857. When COMONFORT resigned, Juárez became acting president. He showed his mettle as a high-minded leader of the liberal revolution, which transferred political power from the creoles to the mestizos and forged Mexico's national consciousness. Forced to flee to Guanajuato, then to Guadalajara, and finally to Veracruz with his government, he resisted the conservatives, and ultimately the liberals were successful in the War of the Reform (1858–61). After establishing the government in the capital, Juárez was immediately faced with new difficulties. The intervention of France, Spain, and Great Britain because of unpaid debts to their nationals was followed by the French attempt to establish a Mexican empire (1864–67) under MAXIMILIAN. Juárez, with the adherence of such notable Mexicans as Ignacio Manuel ALTAMIRANO, continued gallant resistance to the French soldiers and moved his capital to El Paso del Norte (later renamed Juárez city). The Mexican people rallied to Juárez, and the empire fell. Reelected in 1867, he instituted the program of reform in full force, but political divisions among the liberals hampered real accomplishments, and by his political maneuvers Juárez somewhat tarnished the glory gained by his defense of Mexico. He was again elected in 1871. An insurrection against him by Porfirio DÍAZ was being suppressed when Juárez died. See biography by U. R. Burke (1894); Ralph Roeder, *Juárez and His Mexico* (1947, repr. 1968); studies by W. V. Scholes (1969) and I. E. Cadenhead, Jr. (1973).

Juárez, city (1970 pop. 436,054) Chihuahua state, N Mexico, on the Rio Grande opposite El Paso, Texas. Connected with the United States by three international bridges, it is a shipping point and highway and rail terminus. It is also the commercial and processing center for the surrounding cotton-growing area. Except for the river valley, under intense cultivation southeast of the city, Juárez is hemmed in by desert. It is a straggling town with the nondescript air of most Mexican-American border settlements. Developing (1659) as the focal point for Spanish colonial expansion to the north, it was originally called El Paso del Norte and included settlements on both sides of the river, until they were split by the Treaty of Guadalupe Hidalgo (1848), which ended the Mexican War. In 1888 the name of the Mexican town was changed to honor Benito Juárez, who made it his capital when exiled from central Mexico. The city was captured by Pascual Orozco and Francisco Villa in the early days of the revolution in 1910.

Juárez Celman, Miguel (mēgĕl' hwä'rās sĕl'män), 1844–1909, president of Argentina (1886–90). After political service in the province of Córdoba, he became president for a six-year term. Speculation, flagrant under his predecessor Julio A. ROCA, now reached its height, and the administration was notorious for corruption. Political opposition to his government increased after he left his party. A revolt in July, 1890, was suppressed, but Juárez Celman was forced to resign (Aug., 1890). He was succeeded by Carlos Pellegrini.

Juba I, c.85 B.C.–46 B.C., king of Numidia. He joined Pompey's party and in 49 B.C. routed Caesar's legate, Curio. He fought on the side of Metellus SCIPIO and took his life after Caesar's victory at Thapsus. Despite his defeat, his son, **Juba II,** d. c.20 A.D., was educated in Rome and reinstated as king, probably first in Numidia, then in Mauretania (c.25 B.C.). Augustus gave to him in marriage Cleopatra Selene, the daughter of Antony and Cleopatra. Highly learned, Juba II wrote lengthy historical and geographical works.

Juba (jo͞o'bä), city, S Sudan, a port on the White Nile. It is the southern terminus of river traffic in the Sudan, and it is also a highway hub, with roads radiating into Uganda, Kenya, and Zaïre. At a conference in Juba in 1947, representatives of the northern and southern parts of Sudan agreed to unify the country, thus dashing Britain's hopes of adding the south to Uganda. As the administrative capital of S Sudan, Juba became the spearhead of southern resistance to alleged northern dominance of the country. Beginning with a mutiny of southern troops at Juba in 1955, southern unrest led to a Sudanese civil war that was not settled until 1969.

Juba, Ital. *Giuba,* river, c.1,000 mi (1,610 km) long, formed at the Ethiopia-Somali Republic border, E Africa, by the confluence of the Daua and Ganale Doria rivers, both of which rise in the highlands of S Ethiopia. The Juba River meanders S through SW Somali Republic to the Indian Ocean near Kismayu. It

Street in downtown Juarez, Mexico.

is navigable for shallow craft to Bardero. The only perennial river of the Somali Republic, the Juba has flood seasons in both spring and autumn. The valley is part of the nation's chief agricultural region, and the river is extensively used for irrigation.

Jubal (jo͞o'băl), son of Lamech and originator of musical instruments. Gen. 4.21.

jubilee (jo͞o'bĭlē) [Hebrew], in the Bible, a year when slaves were manumitted, debts were forgiven, and a general sabbatical year was observed. It occurred once in 50 years, as prescribed by Lev. 25.8–55. In the Roman Catholic Church the name is applied to a holy year when special privileges are given by the church for pilgrimage to Rome and an unusual jubilee indulgence is announced. The first holy year was celebrated in 1300. In 1343 the pope proclaimed that holy years would recur at 50-year intervals, and in 1470 the interval was reduced to 25 years. The most recent holy year proclaimed was 1975. On occasion an extraordinary jubilee is declared, such as that to celebrate the 50th anniversary of Pope Pius XI's ordination (1929) and that celebrating the conclusion of the Second Vatican Council (1966).

Jubilees, Book of: see PSEUDEPIGRAPHA.

Jucal (jo͞o'kəl), variant of JEHUCAL.

Juchitán (ho͞ochētän'), town (1970 pop. 27,907), Oaxaca state, S Mexico. Located on a vast expanse of flat, fertile plain only slightly above sea level, the old town, largely Indian in population, rivals Tehuantepec (20 mi/ 32 km to the east) as the cultural center of the ZAPOTEC. It is linked to Veracruz and the Guatemala border by railroad and is on the Inter-American Highway.

Juda (jo͞o'də) [variant of JUDAH]. **1** See JUDAH **1.** **2** See JUDE, SAINT. **3, 4** Ancestors of St. Joseph. Luke 3.26,30.

Judaea or **Judea** (both: jo͞odē'ə) [Lat. from JUDAH], Greco-Roman name for S Palestine. It varied in size in different periods. In the time of Christ it was both part of the province of Syria and a kingdom ruled by the Herods. It was the southernmost of the Roman divisions of Palestine, the others being Galilee, Samaria, and Peraea. Idumaea was S of Judaea. A strip of Samaria lay between Judaea and the Mediterranean.

Judah I, 135?–220?, leader of the Palestinian Jews, called *ha-Nasi* [prince] and Rabbi. He was redactor of the MISHNA and president of the Sanhedrin.

Judah (jo͞o'də). **1** Fourth son of Jacob and Leah and the eponymous ancestor of one of the 12 tribes of Israel. Judah is a distinctive figure, a leader in the family counsels. With Reuben he interceded for Joseph's life, and he was the spokesman for his brothers before Joseph in Egypt. In the exodus his tribe was in the lead, and it settled in the rich land of S Palestine, extending c.45 mi (72 m) north and south, from the Dead Sea to the Mediterranean. Within its borders was Jerusalem. It gave its name to the Kingdom of Judah. The royal and Messianic family of David was of the tribe of Judah. Gen. 29.35; 35.23; 37.26; 38; 43.3; 44.14; 46.12,28; 49.8; Num. 2.3; 10.14; 13.6; 26.22; Joshua 15.1; 1 Chron. 2–5. Juda: Luke 3.33; Heb. 7.14; Rev. 5.5; 7.5. Judas: Mat. 1.2. **2** Levitical family. Neh. 12.8. **3** Levite. Ezra 10.23. **4** Overseer. Neh. 11.9. **5** Priest's son. Neh. 12.36. **6** The same as HODAVIAH **3.**

Judah, Theodore Dehone, 1826–63, American railroad builder, b. Bridgeport, Conn. He built the Niagara Gorge RR and did canal work before going (1854) to lay out a railroad near Sacramento, Calif. There he promoted the idea of a railroad across the mountains eastward from the Central Valley and interested a number of men in the scheme. The Central Pacific RR was formed, with Judah as chief engineer. He became dissatisfied with his associates and was on his way to the East to obtain capital and support when he died. See biography by Helen Hinckley (1969).

Judah, the southern of the two kingdoms remaining after the division of the kingdom of the JEWS that occurred under REHOBOAM. The northern kingdom, Israel, was continually at war with Judah. In the Bible the southern kingdom is regarded as usually more loyal to God than the northern kingdom was. Judah's capital was Jerusalem and its dynasty was the house of David. It lasted from 931 B.C. to 586 B.C.

Judah ha-Levi or **Judah Halevy** (both: hä″lē′vī), c.1075–1141, Jewish rabbi, poet, and philosopher, b. Tudela, Spain. His poems—secular, religious, and nationalist—are filled with a serene and lofty spirit. In his great philosophic work, *Sefer ha-Kuzari,* he emphasized the superiority of religious truths, arrived at through intuition, over philosophical and speculative truths, arrived at through logic and reason. In this work he developed a philosophy of history wherein he explains the force of the "divine influence" at work in the world, known first by the patriarchs (Abraham, Isaac, and Jacob), through them by the Jewish people, and ultimately, through the martyrdom of the Jews, by all mankind. See *The Kuzari* (tr. by Hartwig Hirschfeld, 1964).

Judaism, broadly defined, the religious beliefs and practices and the way of life of the JEWS. The term itself is of predominantly modern usage; it is not used in the Bible or in Rabbinic literature and only rarely in the literature of the medieval period. The term closest to *Judaism* (Heb. *Yahadut*) in the Rabbinic literature is *Yehudit,* which refers to a specific law, custom, or practice; the word TORAH is employed when referring to what is now subsumed under the name Judaism. Today, the two terms are used interchangeably, although *Torah* usually connotes the divinely revealed teachings, while *Judaism* includes also the totality of human interpretation and practice. Thus, one may speak of "secular Judaism," referring to an adherence to values expressed by Judaism but removed from their religious context. The history of Judaism predates the period to which the term itself actually refers, in that Judaism formally applies to the post-Second Temple period, while its antecedents are to be found in the biblical "religion of Israel." The Bible is no longer considered a homogeneous work; the many traditions represented in it demonstrate variance and growth. While the historicity of the patriarchs' existence and of MOSES as the giver of all laws is under question, certain dominant themes can be seen developing in this early period that have importance for later Judaism. Central to these is the notion of monotheism, which most scholars believe to have been the outgrowth of a process that began with polytheism, progressed to henotheism (the worship of one god without denying the existence of others), and ended in the belief in a single Lord of the universe, uniquely different from all His creatures (Deut. 6.4). He is compassionate toward His creation, and in turn man is to love and fear (i.e., stand in awe of) Him. Because God is holy He demands that His people be holy, righteous, and just, a kingdom of priests (Ex. 19.6) to assist in the fulfillment of His designs for mankind and the world (Isa. 43.10). Israel's chosenness consists of this special designation and the task that accompanies it. God promises the land of Canaan to Israel as their homeland, the place in which the Temple will be built and sacrificial worship of God carried out (Deut. 12.11). The holy days consisted of the Sabbath, Passover, Shavuot, and Sukkoth; and circumcision, dietary laws, and laws pertaining to dress, agriculture, and social justice characterized the structure of the biblical religion. Three types of leaders existed during this period: the priest (*kohen*), who officiated in the Temple and executed the laws; the prophet (*navi*), to whom was revealed God's messages to His people; and the sage (*hacham*), who taught practical wisdom and proper behavior. There was developing already in this early period a belief in the ultimate coming of God's kingdom on earth, a time of peace and justice (Isa. 2.1–4). To this was added, after the destruction (586 B.C.) of the First Temple and the Babylonian captivity (which many saw as the consequence of idolatry and which may have been responsible for the final stage of the development from polytheism to monotheism), the expectation of national restoration under the leadership of a descendant of the Davidic house, the MESSIAH. It was during this post-exilic period (not later than the 5th cent. B.C.) that a compilation of earlier texts and oral traditions was made, forming the core of the Pentateuch, the Five Books of Moses (to which 19 others were later added to form the Hebrew Bible or OLD TESTAMENT, canonized perhaps as late as the 2d cent. A.D.). Attributed to Moses (although some scholars believe its legal portions were formulated by EZRA), these books were studied publicly, and were accompanied by expositions and explanations in which the Oral Law, as distinct from the Written Law (the Torah text), is rooted. While it is widely held that the PHARISEES further developed the Oral Law, in opposition to the literalness of the SADDUCEES, it is inconceivable that the latter group could have administered the biblical laws without reinterpreting them in accordance with a changing world, or in the face of a lack of specificity in the text. The Babylonian exile had exposed the Israelites to new ideas, and it is to that period that the notions of identifiable angels (such as Michael and Raphael), of the personification of evil (Satan), and of the resurrection of the dead (Dan. 12.2) can probably be traced. The conquests of Alexander the Great once again brought the Jews into contact with new ideas, most significantly that of the immortality of the soul. Conflict arose within the community of Israel concerning the level of Hellenization acceptable, out of which came the revolt of the MACCABEES against the Seleucid rulers of Syria and their Judean sympathizers. The resulting martyrdom of many gave added impetus to the belief in collective resurrection of the dead and the immortality of the soul after the body's death. Basically contradictory, these concepts were wed in such a way that while the body awaited its resurrection, the soul was seen as living on in another realm. This new development in no way supplanted the earlier notion of earthly reward; life on earth, however, was viewed by many as preparatory for the next. As the conditions of life deteriorated, apocalyptic beliefs grew—national catastrophe and the Messianic kingdom were seen as imminent events. Some groups (see ESSENES; QUMRAN) fled into the desert to lead righteous lives in anticipation, others followed claimants to the mantle of Messiah (most notably Jesus), while still others became adherents of one of the numerous mystery religions of the period. Out of these numerous ingredients came both Christianity and classical, or rabbinic, Judaism. Developing over a period of five centuries (until A.D. c.500), rabbinic Judaism was characterized by the replacement of the Temple by the SYNAGOGUE (the Second Temple was destroyed in A.D. 70), of the now defunct priesthood by the RABBI, and of the sacrificial ceremony by the prayer service and study. Basic to these changes was the development of the Oral Law (see MISHNA; TALMUD) and the MIDRASH, which, as outgrowths of the biblical religion, centered on the relationships between God, His Torah, and His people, Israel. Emphasis was placed upon study of the Torah (in its broadest sense) as the most important religious act, leading to an understanding of the proper way of life; upon the growing need for national restoration in the face of continued Exile from the Promised Land; and upon the function of this world as preparatory for the World to Come (*Olam ha-Bah*), while not devaluing the importance of life in this world. Significantly, a place in the World to Come could be achieved by persons of all nations. During the medieval period, these trends continued and were basic to the several important codifications of the legal material and to the many biblical and talmudic commentaries that were composed at this time (most notably by RASHI and MAIMONIDES). Two new developments arose in the medieval period. Built upon earlier mystical commentaries of biblical passages, the CABALA flowered during the Middle Ages under the impetus of ideas external to Judaism, predominant among them Neoplatonism, and due to the needs of a persecuted people for redemption. A Jewish philosophy developed in answer to the questions raised by the exposure to Greek thought as distilled through the Islamic philosophers' natural philosophy and metaphysics. Central to these issues was the conflict between reason and revelation: whether revelation was necessary if all could be ascertained through reason, or whether reason was imperfect and revelation was God's assisting man to know the truth. Biblical anthropomorphism had to be dealt with by the rationalists. Maimonides posited the untraditional notion of negative attributes, which tended to depersonalize God. He argued that one can say nothing positive about the personal nature of God, which is beyond human comprehension; one can only indicate what He is not (thus, the statement that God is wise says only that God is not ignorant, not how wise He actually is). The cabalists, taking a more comprehensive view, retained the idea that the totality of God's nature is ultimately beyond human grasp ("Ein Sof" [Heb., literally,= without end] as the "Nothing"), yet, in keeping with tradition, held to a vision of a personal God who exists as the active, creative, and sustaining force within the cosmos ("Ein Sof" as the "Everything"). While the Jewish Middle Ages is usually defined by scholars as extending at least into the 18th cent. (and by some into the 19th cent. to the 1807 convening by Napoleon I of the "French Sanhedrin" to map out the role of the Jews after their emancipation within his empire), there was a Jewish counterpart to the general European Renaissance of the 15th–16th cent. While being influenced by the period (as demonstrated by Judah ABRAVANEL), the Jews of N Italy, S France, and the Levant also came under Sephardic, and particularly under Marrano, influence, which forced them to reevaluate their traditions (see SEPHARDIM). Marrano skepticism, the result of living in two worlds, tended to be a liberalizing influence. Yet, as the victims of years of persecution, the Marranos harbored hopes that added fuel to the fires of Messianism. Both tendencies were present in the community of Amsterdam (and to a degree in Hamburg) that was established by the Marranos at the end of the 16th cent. and flourished as a creative entity (helping to establish the Jewish communities in New Amsterdam and London) until the collapse of the Messianic hope that had been centered on SABBATAI ZEVI. While the reaction to this episode led to a stiffening of rabbinic traditions wherever Sabbatianism had caught on, the spirit of skepticism and the renewed Messianism could not be extinguished. Both elements would add much to the future of the Reform movement (one of whose major centers was Hamburg) and Zionism (two of whose lights, Yehudah Alkalai and Theodor Herzl, claimed Sephardic Marrano descent). The 18th cent. produced both the great traditionalist rabbinic figure ELIJAH BEN SOLOMON and the untraditional figures of BAAL-SHEM-TOV, the founder of HASIDISM (which Elijah himself fought against), and Moses MENDELSSOHN, the spiritual progenitor of later reformers whom Elijah's spiritual descendants repeatedly condemned. The events of the early decades of the 19th cent., subsumed under the name of the Emancipation, brought most Western Jews and their Judaism into contact with modernity, resulting in more than one serious conflict. Particularly acute for many was the problem of maintaining claims of distinctiveness, of being "chosen," while at the same time wishing to participate in the general society. In addition, how were they to maintain Jewish traditions when the non-Jewish world demanded their abandonment, threatening otherwise to label Jews as antisocial or unassimilable. As the century progressed these problems, first dealt with by the Reform leaders of Germany (most notably Abraham GEIGER), were met head-on in Eastern Europe, giving rise to the Haskalah movement whose members (e.g., Nachman KROCHMAL) sought to revitalize Jewish life by recreating it along the lines of the best in European culture. Finally, in reaction both to the needs of a persecuted people and to the nationalistic desires growing in the late 19th cent., ZIONISM promised a return to the Holy Land. This again created problems for the traditionalists whose religious ideas and religiously oriented life-style were rooted in the Diaspora. For many Jews still unanswered is the question of whether a full Jewish life is possible in Exile, or whether residing in Zion is essential. Theologically, Zionism posed the problem of whether man can work for the Messianic return or whether this would be counter to another traditional belief that saw man awaiting the divine intervention. Today, traditionalists of both camps can be found in residence in the state of Israel, due in part to the necessities of emigration occasioned by the Holocaust of the Nazi era. Ultimately, it was the halakah (the law) over which the religion of the Jews divided beginning in the 19th cent. and continuing to the present. The Orthodox hold both the written law (the Scriptures) and the Oral Laws (the commentaries on the legal portions of the Scriptures) as authoritative, derived from God, while the Reform see them as neither derived from God nor authoritative in any absolute sense, but binding only in their ethical content. While Orthodox Jews maintain the traditional rituals of Ashkenazic Jewry [German Jews and their descendants], the Reform Jews continue to perform only those rituals that they believe can promote and enhance a Jewish, God-oriented life. The "historical school," or Conservative movement, attempts to formulate a middle position, maintaining most of the traditional rituals, but recognizing the need to make changes in accordance with overriding contemporary considerations. Conservative Jews believe that the history of Judaism proves their basic assumptions: that tradition and change have always gone hand in hand and that what is central to Judaism and has remained constant throughout the centuries is the people of Israel (and their needs), not the rigidified fundamentalism of Orthodoxy nor the abandonment of the traditions and uniqueness of the Jewish people by Reform. All three positions have softened to an extent in recent years, the more moderate elements in each group having expressed more tolerance toward the others, but the lines between them remain distinct. Also part of contemporary Judaism are the several Sephardic traditions maintained in Israel, France, Canada, and the United States by immigrants from the Near East and North Africa and by European Sephardim in Europe and the Americas; the several Hasidic groups in Israel and the United States predominantly; the religious and secular Zionists in Israel and the Diaspora; the unorganized secular Jews who maintain an atheist's or agnostic's adherence to Jewish values and culture; and those unorganized Jews who seek a religious life outside the synagogue, where they can no longer find fulfillment. These many positions represent the most recent attempts at defining the "essence of Judaism," a process that has been continuous throughout the ages, variously emphasizing one of the three major components of Judaism (God, Torah, Israel) over the remaining two. Among the most important holy days in Judaism are the SABBATH, ROSH HA-SHANAH, Yom Kippur (see ATONEMENT, DAY OF), Sukkoth (see TABERNACLES, FEAST OF), PASSOVER, SHAVUOT, HANUKKAH, and PURIM. See Kaufmann Kohler, *Jewish Theology Systematically and Historically Considered* (1918, repr. 1968); W. R. Smith, *Lectures on the Religion of the Semites* (1927, repr. 1956); G. F. Moore, *Judaism in the First Centuries of the Christian Era* (3 vol., 1927–30, repr. 1958); Hayyim Schauss, *Guide to Jewish Holy Days* (1938, repr. 1966); Leo Baeck, *The Essence of Judaism* (1948, repr. 1961); Louis Finkelstein, *The Beliefs and Practices of Judaism* (2d ed. 1952); S. W. Baron, *A Social and Religious History of the Jews* (15 vol., 1952–73); Gershom Scholem, *Major Trends in Jewish Mysticism* (3d ed. 1954, repr. 1961); M. M. Kaplan, *Judaism as a Civilization* (2d ed. 1957, repr. 1967); J. B. Agus, *The Evolution of Jewish Thought* (1959, repr. 1973); John Bright, *A History of Israel* (1959); Isidore Epstein, *Judaism, A Historical Presentation* (1959); Yehezkel Kaufmann, *The Religion of Israel* (tr. 1960); Jacob Katz, *Tradition and Crisis* (tr. 1961); J. L. Blau, *The Story of Jewish Philosophy* (1962), *Modern Varieties of Judaism* (1966), and, ed., *Reform Judaism: A Historical Perspective* (1973); Martin Buber, *On Judaism* (1967); M. A. Meyer, *The Origins of the Modern Jew* (1967); Jacob Neusner, *There We Sat Down* (1972); Nathan Glazer, *American Judaism* (2d ed. 1973).

Judas, in the Bible. **1** See JUDE, SAINT. **2** Judas Maccabeus: see MACCABEES. **3** See JUDAS ISCARIOT. **4** See JUDAH (of which Judas is the Greek form) **1.** **5** Owner of a house in Damascus where St. Paul went after his conversion. Acts 9.11. **6** See JUDAS BARSABAS. **7** "Brother" of Jesus. Matt. 13.55; Mark 6.3.

Judas Barsabas (bär'səbəs), missionary apostle. Acts 15.22–33.

Judas Iscariot (ĭskâr'ēət), Jesus' betrayer, one of the Twelve Disciples, said to have been their treasurer. Judas went to the chief priests and offered to betray Jesus, for which he was paid the sum of 30 pieces of silver. After the Last Supper he led an armed band to Gethsemane and there identified Jesus to the soldiers by kissing him. Later he repented and killed himself. The blood money went to buy a potter's field, ACELDAMA. Mat. 26.14–16, 20–25, 47–49; 27.3–10; Mark 14.10,11,43–45; Luke 22.3–6; John 6.71; 12.4–6; 13.26–30; 18.1–5; Acts 1.16–20. The name Iscariot may be a corruption of *sicarius* (Lat.,=murderer), indicating that Judas, or his father (who was also called Iscariot), belonged to a radical anti-Roman Jewish sect, the Sicarii. This possibility would support the theory that Judas betrayed Jesus out of disappointment and anger that Jesus was not the political Messiah he looked for.

Judas Maccabeus: see MACCABEES, Jewish family.

Judas of Galilee, fl. A.D. 6, a leader of the Zealots, a radical revolutionary Jewish sect. He raised an insurrection against the taxation census of Cyrenius (A.D. 6) on the grounds that no one but God was Israel's master, and he was killed. Acts 5.37.

Judas tree: see REDBUD.

Judd, Donald, 1928–, American artist, b. Excelsior Springs, Mo. Judd's sculpture, allied with the minimalist school of the late 1960s (see MODERN ART), has the appearance of industrial fabrication. He uses a variety of rectangular forms fashioned from painted wood, polychrome, or steel. Examples of his work are in the Whitney Museum, New York City.

Judd, Gerrit Parmele, 1803–73, missionary and statesman, b. Paris, N.Y. He arrived in Hawaii as a medical missionary. He ended his mission service in 1842 and became a Hawaiian government official under King Kamehameha III, playing a leading role in establishing the constitution of the Hawaiian monarchy and gaining recognition of Hawaii as a sovereign nation.

Judd, Orange, 1822–92, American agricultural editor and publisher, b. near Niagara Falls, N.Y., grad. Wesleyan Univ., 1847. At Wesleyan he built (1871) the Orange Judd Hall of Natural Science and secured through his gifts the establishment of the first agricultural experiment station in the country. He became in 1853 joint editor and owner of the *American Agriculturist,* which he made into one of the leading farm papers of the country.

Jude, Saint, or **Saint Judas** [Jude is an English form to distinguish him from Judas Iscariot], one of the Twelve Disciples, also called Lebbaeus and Thaddaeus. He is thought to have been the brother of St. James the Less. It does not seem likely that he was the Judas called the brother of Jesus (Mat. 13.55; Mark 6.3) or the author of the epistle of St. Jude. (Mat. 10.3; Mark 3.18; Luke 6.16; John 14.22; Acts 1.13.) According to Western tradition he suffered martyrdom in Persia with St. SIMON, with whom he shares a feast: Oct. 28.

Jude, epistle of the New Testament, the next to last book of the Bible. The Jude who wrote it has been identified since ancient times with St. Jude the apostle; but most modern scholars deny the identity and date the letter as late as A.D. 100. It is called a Catholic (or General) Epistle, but it is clearly intended for a particular audience (3), which it warns against some heresy that led to immorality (4,8,10). The dangers are shown from Old Testament examples (5–11). The book contains references to Jewish apocryphal books, Enoch (14–15) and the Assumption of Moses (9). It ends with a doxology (24–25). Jude has a close literary relationship with Second PETER.

Judea (jo͞odē'ə): see JUDAEA.

Judenburg (yo͞o'dənbo͝orkh), city (1971 pop. 11,300), Styria prov., S central Austria, on the Mur River. It is an industrial city and winter sports center. Originally a settlement along a Roman road, Judenburg was settled by Jewish merchants in the 11th cent. and became an important regional commercial center. It has a Romanesque church and a 15th-century bell tower.

Judge, William Quan, 1851–96, American theosophist, b. Ireland. He emigrated as a boy to the United States. Becoming interested in theosophy, he associated himself with Madame BLAVATSKY and others in 1875 in founding the Theosophical Society, and he edited and published (1886–96) its organ, the *Path*. After a schism in the society, he became president (1894) of the American section of the Theosophical Society. He wrote *The Ocean of Theosophy* (14th ed. 1937).

Judges, book of the Old Testament, seventh in the order of the Authorized Version. It is the sequel of Joshua in the biblical history, telling of the Hebrews in the Promised Land from Joshua's death until, but not including, the time of Samuel. The religious interpretation is stated in an introduction (2.6–3.4): the book is an account of Israel's successive apostasies from God and their consequences, first, punishment at the hands of a foreign nation, then, delivery from it by God, who raises up a leader. The leaders are called judges; they are primarily military leaders, the heads of tribes. The chronology of the book is impossible to untangle, partly because of occasional failure to give the length of time between the judges. The book consists mainly of lengthy accounts of a few judges: Deborah with Barak (4–5), Gideon (6–8), Gideon's usurping son Abimelech (9–10), Jephthah (11–12), and Samson (13–16). The other judges receive less attention, some a bare mention: Othniel, Ehud, and Shamgar (3) before Deborah; Tola and Jair (10) before Jephthah; and Ibzan, Elon and Abdon (12) before Samson. The opening chapter of the book is out of order, for it belongs to the period of Joshua; the closing chapters contain two appended stories of violence, one laid in Dan (17–18), the other in Benjamin (19–21). For critical views of the composition and for bibliography, see OLD TESTAMENT.

judgment, decision of a court of law respecting the issues before it. The term ordinarily is not applied to the DECREE (order) of courts of EQUITY. The outstanding characteristic of a legal judgment in contrast to an equitable decree is its finality and fixity; thus, except for error justifying an APPEAL, the judgment may not be reconsidered (see JEOPARDY). The judgment, which in most cases of consequence follows the VERDICT of a JURY, is the determination of the judge that the defendant is guilty or innocent of the alleged offense. If the judgment is one of criminal guilt, the court proceeds to impose SENTENCE. In civil cases, when judgment is for the plaintiff, the court usually awards a sum as DAMAGES. The damages thereupon constitute a debt that takes priority over all other obligations of the defendant except taxes and previous judgments. If the debtor fails to pay, the sheriff, to execute the judgment, will seize and sell first his personal property and then his realty. The sheriff may also garnish monies owed to the defendant, e.g., his wages (see GARNISHMENT). Certain property of the debtor is exempt from seizure, including clothing, equipment needed to carry on his trade or profession, and the family homestead. In some jurisdictions a defendant who willfully refuses to pay a judgment may be punished for a CONTEMPT of court. A judgment rendered by the courts of one state is entitled to recognition by the courts of all other states.

Judgment Day or **Doomsday,** central point of Christian eschatology. The origin of Christian belief in the Last Judgment lies in the New Testament, from which comes the doctrine that this world will come to an end, the dead will be raised up in the general RESURRECTION, and Christ will come in glory to judge the living and the dead; then the sinners shall be cast into HELL, and the righteous shall live in HEAVEN forever. (Mat. 24.3–25.46; Luke 21.5–36; 1 Cor. 15; 1 Thess. 4.13–5.3.) There is no generally accepted teaching among Christians as to when the Second Coming shall take place, but many individuals have ventured to prophesy its date. Those who lay stress on the end of the world are called chiliasts, millenarians, or, specifically, ADVENTISTS. According to many, the book of REVELATION (the Apocalypse) gives notions of the end of the world. See ANTICHRIST; ARMAGEDDON; MILLENNIUM; APOCALYPSE.

Judith [Heb.,=Jewess], biblical book included in the Old Testament of the Western canon and Septuagint, but not included in the Hebrew Bible and placed in the Apocrypha in the Authorized Version. It tells of an attack on the Jews by an army led by Nebuchadnezzar's general Holofernes. Bethulia, a besieged Jewish city, is about to surrender when Judith, a Jewish widow of great beauty and devotion, enters the enemy camp, gains the favor of Holofernes, and murders him. Judith returns to the city with his head, and the Jews rout the armies. The story is informed with a spirit of God's interest in His people, and Judith is pictured as a woman of great self-sacrifice and nobility. The texts of Judith are in great confusion. The book was written probably by a Palestinian before 100 B.C., but some scholars date it in a later period. By identifying Nebuchadnezzar as the king of Assyria (he was king of Babylon), the author appears to be giving notice that the book is not historical. However, there are historical parallels for the invasion. Another Judith, a wife of Esau, is named in Gen. 26.34. For bibliography, see OLD TESTAMENT.

judo, sport of Japanese origin that makes use of the principles of jujitsu, a weaponless system of self-defense. Jujitsu was developed over a period of 2,000 years by Buddhist monks in China, Japan, and Tibet as a system of defense that could be used against armed marauders and yet would not be in conflict with their religion. Judo was created (1882) by Jigoro Kano, a Japanese jujitsu expert, who modified or dropped many holds that were too dangerous to be used in sport. It depends for success upon the skill of using an opponent's weight and strength against him, thus enabling a weak or light individual to overcome a physically superior opponent. A method of applying pressure to sensitive parts of an opponent's body, usually by means of blows with the side of the hand, is also used. This art, known in judo as *atemi,* has been separately developed and is known as karate. A judo match begins with a ceremonial bow, after which each player grasps the other by the collar and sleeve of his jacket, or *gi.* A point is scored when a player forcefully throws the other onto his back, when one is held down for 30 seconds, when one is caught in a judo "choke," or when a player is forced to submit because of a twisted elbow joint. Proficiency in judo is indicated by the color of a player's belt; white indicates a beginner, black an expert. There is a wide range of color in between. Jujitsu, the unmodified form of judo, has been taught to military and police forces. In 1953 judo was recognized in the United States as a sport by the Amateur Athletic Union; and annual championships are now held. Numerous schools throughout the world now teach judo. See Eric Dominy, *Judo, Techniques and Tactics* (1969); G. R. Gleeson, *Better Judo* (1972).

Judson, Adoniram (ădənī'rəm), 1788–1850, American Baptist missionary, b. Malden, Mass. At Andover Theological Seminary, he became the leader of a missionary movement out of which grew the American Board of Commissioners for Foreign Missions. As a Congregational minister, Judson sailed (1812) for India. After conversion to the Baptist faith, he went (1813) to Burma, where he remained for 30 years. In 1845 he visited the United States, and on his return to Moulmein (1846) he completed and published (1849) his *Dictionary, English and Burmese.* He had also translated the Bible into Burmese. The Judson Memorial Church in New York City is named for him. See biographies by his son Edward Judson (1883), S. R. Warburton (1937), and Courtney Anderson (1956); V. E. Robinson, *The Judsons of Burma* (1966).

Judson, Edward Zane Carroll: see BUNTLINE, NED.

Jugendstil: see ART NOUVEAU.

Juggernaut, India: see PURI.

Jugoslavia: see YUGOSLAVIA.

Jugurtha (jo͞ogûr'thə), c.156–104 B.C., king of Numidia, a grandson of MASINISSA. On the death of Micipsa (118 B.C.), the royal power devolved upon his two sons and upon his adopted son Jugurtha. The latter ousted the other two heirs and united Numidia under his rule. In the process, however, some Italians were murdered, leading Rome to invade Numidia; peace was reestablished in 111 B.C. Jugurtha, on a visit to Rome to explain his acts, ordered a rival murdered. War was resumed, and the Romans under Quintus Caecilius Metellus Numidicus gained some notable successes. Under a new commander, Caius MARIUS, the Romans continued to apply pressure on Jugurtha, who was being supported by his father-in-law, Bocchus, king of Mauretania. Jugurtha was captured (106 B.C.) when Bocchus betrayed him, and he was put to death in prison in Rome.

Juilliard School, The (jo͞ol'yärd), in New York City; school of music, drama, and dance; coeducational; est. 1905 as the Institute of Musical Art, chartered 1926 as the Juilliard School of Music with two separate units—the Juilliard Graduate School (1924) and Institute of Musical Art. These were amalgamated into a single school in 1946. In 1968 the dance department became a separate division, and a division of drama was created. In 1969 the school moved to the Lincoln Center for the Performing Arts and adopted its present name.

Juiz de Fora (zhwēzh dĭ fô'rə), city (1970 pop. 238,052), Minas Gerais state, SE Brazil. It is an indus-

Untitled, *a stainless steel and plexiglas sculpture by the American artist Donald Judd.*

trial and commercial city with more than half of the labor force engaged in textile production. Foodstuffs are also produced. The city, founded at the end of the 18th cent., grew rapidly because of its strategic location on the road to Rio de Janeiro. In the 19th cent., coffee cultivation was the main economic activity. The first railroad in Brazil was constructed (1861) between Juiz de Fora and Petrópolis.

jujitsu: see JUDO.

jujube (jo͞o'jo͞ob): see BUCKTHORN.

jujutsu: see JUDO.

Jujuy (ho͞ohwē'), city (1960 pop. 44,188), capital of Jujuy prov., NW Argentina, on the Bermejo River. In the scenic foothill region of the E Andes, it is the center of an agricultural, mining, and cattle-raising area. It was in Jujuy that Manuel Belgrano, the patriot general, created the first Argentine national flag. Juan Lavalle, after a futile attempt to depose the caudillo Juan Manuel de Rosas, was killed in Jujuy in 1841. There are interesting Indian ruins nearby. Jujuy is also known as San Salvador de Jujuy.

Jukes: see DUGDALE, RICHARD LOUIS.

julep (jo͞o'lĭp) or **mint julep,** alcoholic beverage of the S United States. Its basis is properly bourbon whiskey, which is combined with water, sugar, crushed ice, and mint leaves.

Julia, feminine name in the Julian gens. **1** Died 54 B.C., daughter of Julius CAESAR and wife of POMPEY. By her grace and tact she maintained the bond between her father and her husband. After her death the two statesmen became open enemies. **2** 39 B.C.–A.D. 14, daughter of Augustus and wife, in turn, of Marcus Claudius Marcellus (d. 23 B.C.), Marcus Vipsanius Agrippa, and Tiberius. Her infidelities caused her banishment by Augustus to Pandataria Island in the Tyrrhenian Sea. Soon after Tiberius became emperor, she died of starvation. **3** 18 B.C.–A.D. 28, daughter of Julia and Agrippa (see above); wife of Lucius Aemilius Paullus. Because of her licentious conduct, she was banished by Augustus to the island of Tremerus off the coast of Apulia, where she died.

Julia, Christian at Rome. Rom. 16.15.

Julian, George Washington, 1817–99, American abolitionist, U.S. Representative from Indiana (1849–51, 1861–71), b. Wayne co., Ind. Elected to the Indiana legislature as a Whig in 1845, he later became prominent in the Free-Soil party and in 1849 was sent to Congress by a coalition of Free-Soilers and Democrats. There he continued his radical antislavery activities. In 1852 the Free-Soil party nominated him for Vice President on the ticket with John P. Hale. He joined the Republican party at the time of its formation and in 1861 returned to Congress, where he became chairman of the committee on public lands and a member of the committees on the conduct of the war, on Reconstruction, and on the impeachment of President Andrew Johnson. In 1872 he joined the Liberal Republican party and after its demise was associated with the Democratic party. From 1885 to 1889 he was surveyor general of New Mexico by appointment of President Cleveland. Among his writings are *Speeches on Political Questions* (1872); *Political Recollections, 1840 to 1872* (1884); *Later Speeches on Political Questions, with Select Controversial Papers,* by his daughter, Grace J. Clarke (1889); and a biography of his father-in-law, Joshua R. Giddings (1892). See biography by P. W. Riddleberger (1966).

Juliana, 1909–, queen of the Netherlands (1948–).

Judo match between two black belt opponents.

She succeeded on the abdication of her mother, Queen WILHELMINA. She was married (1937) to Prince Bernhard of Lippe-Biesterfeld, to whom she bore four daughters. The eldest, Princess Beatrix (b. 1938), is the heiress apparent.

Julian Alps, mountain range, NE Italy and NW Yugoslavia, between the Carnic Alps and the Dinaric Alps, rising to 9,396 ft (2,864 m) in Triglav, the highest peak in Yugoslavia. The forested, glacier-scoured region is a popular resort area.

Juliana of Norwich (nôr'ĭch), d. c.1443, English religious writer, an anchoress, or hermit, of Norwich called Mother (or Dame) Juliana or Julian. Her work, completed c.1393, *Revelations of Divine Love,* is an expression of mystical fervor in the form of 16 visions of Jesus. Dominant ideas are the great love of God for men and the detestable character of human sin. She is considered one of the greatest English mystics. See edition of her book by George Tyrell, S.J. (1920); study by P. F. Chambers (1955)

Julian Day calendar, system of astronomical dating that allows the difference between two dates to be calculated more easily than conventional civil calendars. The Julian Period begins on Jan 1, 4713 B.C., and dates have been numbered in consecutive order since then, regardless of the various changes made in civil calendars based on changing definitions of the year. The Julian Day number for Jan. 1, 1976, is 2,442,779, for Jan. 1, 1977, is 2,443,145, for Jan. 1, 1980, is 2,444,240, and so on. The Julian Day is from noon, Greenwich mean time, on the given date to noon of the following date.

Julianehåb (yo͞olyä'nəhôp''), town (1969 pop. 2,703), in Julianehåb dist. (1969 pop. 3,213), SW Greenland. It is a fishing port with canneries. Sheep are raised in the surrounding region.

Julian the Apostate (Flavius Claudius Julianus), 331?–363, Roman emperor (361–63), nephew of Constantine I; successor of Constantius II. He was given an education that combined Christian and Neoplatonic ideas. He and his half brother Gallus were sent (c.341) to Cappadocia. When Gallus was appointed Caesar (351), Julian was brought back to Constantinople. After Gallus had been put to death, Julian was called from the quiet of a scholar's life and made (355) Caesar. Sent to Gaul, he was unexpectedly successful in combating the Franks and the Alemanni and was popular with his soldiers. When Constantius, fearing Julian, ordered him (360) to send soldiers to assist in a campaign against the Persians, Julian obeyed, but his soldiers mutinied and proclaimed him augustus. He accepted the title, but Constantius refused to yield the western provinces to him. Before the two could meet in battle to decide the claim, Constantius died, naming Julian as his successor. Sometime in the course of his studies, Julian abandoned Christianity. Although as emperor he issued an edict of religious toleration, he did try unsuccessfully to restore paganism; the result was much confusion since Christianity was rent by the quarrel over Arianism. His short reign was just, and he was responsible for far-reaching legislation. During a campaign against the Persians, he was killed in a skirmish. He was succeeded by JOVIAN. Julian was a writer of some merit, and his works have been translated into English by W. C. Wright (3 vols., 1913–24). See study by Giuseppe Ricciotti (tr. 1960).

Jülich (yü'lĭkh), former duchy, West Germany, between Cologne and Aachen. The town of Jülich was the capital. At first a county, Jülich was raised to a duchy in 1356, and in 1423 it was united with the county of BERG. After the extinction of the Jülich line, both Jülich and Berg passed (1521) to Duke John III of Cleves (see CLEVES, DUCHY OF). The struggle that broke out in 1609 for the succession to the territories of the dukes of Cleves ended in 1666. Jülich and Berg passed to the Palatinate-Neuburg branch of the Bavarian house of Wittelsbach and the rest to the electors of Brandenburg. Occupied by the French from 1794 to 1814, the territory was assigned (1815) to Prussia at the Congress of Vienna.

Jülich, town (1970 pop. 19,439), North Rhine–Westphalia, W West Germany. It has some light industry and is the seat of a nuclear research center. Originally a Roman settlement known as Juliacum, Jülich was chartered in the mid-13th cent. and served as the capital of the former duchy of Jülich. The town was almost totally destroyed in World War II.

Julier (yo͞ol'yər), pass, 7,504 ft (2,287 m) high, Grisons canton, SE Switzerland, connecting the Upper Engadine Valley to the Oberhalbstein Valley. Used since ancient times, it is crossed by the Julier Road (built 1820–40).

Julius I, Saint, pope (337–52), a Roman; successor of St. Marcus. In the controversy over ARIANISM, when both sides appealed to him for support, he convened a synod at Rome (340), at which were present St. ATHANASIUS, Marcellus of Ancyra, and many other Catholic exiles from the East. The Arians of the East seem to have evaded his invitation. The principal result of the entire incident was a letter from the pope to the Arians, questioning their sincerity in the matter of the council, acquitting Athanasius of every charge, and chiding the Arians for not appealing to the pope at the beginning, since, he said, he had the principal see and the appellate jurisdiction over the whole church. As an early example of the papal claims the letter is remarkable. He was succeeded by Liberius. Feast: April 12.

Julius II, 1443–1513, pope (1503–13), an Italian named Giuliano della Rovere, b. Savona; successor of Pius III. His uncle Sixtus IV gave him many offices

Pope Julius II, in a portrait by Raphael.

and created him cardinal. Innocent VIII, successor to Sixtus IV, was entirely under Cardinal della Rovere's influence, and it was in reaction to the cardinal's power that the rest of the cardinals elected (1492) his bitter enemy, Rodrigo Borgia, as Pope ALEXANDER VI. Giuliano went into voluntary exile and had little to do with ecclesiastical affairs until Alexander's death (1503). Pius III succeeded for less than a month, and Giuliano succeeded him. Pope Julius showed himself first of all a warrior, and he ably completed the work, begun by his enemy Cesare Borgia, of restoring the Papal States to the church. Having joined the League of Cambrai, he was at war with Venice until 1509 and won back Ravenna, Rimini, and Faenza. He then formed (1510) the anti-French HOLY LEAGUE. The resultant struggle was a draw (see ITALIAN WARS). In 1512 he assembled the Fifth LATERAN COUNCIL, which condemned the Gallicanism of the church in France and abolished simony in the college of cardinals. Julius was a great patron of art, and Raphael (who painted his portrait), Michelangelo, and Bramante enjoyed his favor. He laid the cornerstone of St. Peter's. Worldly as Julius was, he was one of the first to suppress nepotism and to try, albeit feebly, to break the hold of Renaissance corruption on Rome. He was succeeded by Leo X.

Julius, centurion in whose charge Paul was sent to Rome. Acts 27.1.

Julius Caesar: see CAESAR, JULIUS.

Jullian, Camille (kämē'yə zhülyäN'), 1859–1933, French historian. His monumental *Histoire de la Gaule* (8 vol., 1908–26) combines scholarly erudition with colorful style and remains the most authoritative work on Gaul from 600 B.C. to the end of Roman rule. A disciple of FUSTEL DE COULANGES, Jullian also prepared the revision of Fustel's study of medieval institutions.

Jullundur (jŭl'əndər), city (1971 pop. 296,103), Punjab state, NW India. It has flour and silk mills. Jullundur was the capital of Punjab from the time of India's independence (1947) until Chandigarh was built in 1953.

July: see MONTH.

July Revolution, revolt in France in July, 1830, against the government of King CHARLES X. The attempt of the ultraroyalists under Charles to return to the ancien régime provoked the opposition of the middle classes, who wanted more voice in the government. The banker, Jacques LAFFITTE, was typical of the bourgeois who supported liberal journalists, such as Adolphe THIERS, in opposing the government. Liberal opposition reached its peak when Charles called on the reactionary and unpopular Jules Armand de POLIGNAC to form a new ministry (Aug., 1829). When the chamber of deputies registered its disapproval, Charles dissolved the chamber. New elections (July, 1830) returned an even stronger opposition majority. Charles and Polignac responded with the July Ordinances, which established rigid press control, dissolved the new chamber, and reduced the electorate. Insurrection developed, and street barricades and fighting cleared Paris of royal troops. Charles X was forced to flee and abdicated in favor of his grandson, Henri, conte de CHAMBORD. Henri was set aside and, although there was a movement for a republic, the duc d'Orléans was proclaimed (July 31) king of the French as LOUIS PHILIPPE. His reign was known as the July Monarchy. See study by D. H. Pinkney (1972).

Jumel Mansion (jo͞omĕl', zho͞o-), historic house, New York City. The sturdy Georgian mansion was completed in 1766 by Roger Morris, one of the city's wealthy merchants. In the American Revolution it served as headquarters of George Washington and Sir Henry Clinton, American and British commanders in chief. After the war it was used as a tavern. It was purchased (1810) by a rich wine merchant, Stephen Jumel (d. 1832), for his wife, Eliza Brown Jumel (1775–1865). After Jumel's death she married (1833) Aaron Burr, wrangled with him over family finances, and procured (1834) a divorce. When she died, the mansion passed to members of her family. In 1903 it was purchased by the city. By 1945 it was completely restored and opened to the public under the auspices of the Daughters of the American Revolution. See W. H. Shelton, *The Jumel Mansion* (1916).

Jumet (zhümā'), city (1970 pop. 28,029), Hainaut prov., S Belgium. Manufactures include metal products, glass, and beer.

Jumna (jŭm'nə) or **Yamuna** (yä'mənə), river, c.850 mi (1,370 km) long, rising in the Himalayas, N India, and flowing generally SE, through the Siwalik Range, past Delhi, to the Ganges River at Allahabad, Uttar Pradesh state; the Chambal and Betwa rivers are its main tributaries. The Jumna's confluence with the Ganges is sacred to Hindus; Allahabad is a major pilgrimage center. Along the Jumna's banks are many historic monuments including the TAJ MAHAL at Agra. Formerly an important trade artery, the Jumna is now the source of irrigation for Uttar Pradesh and Punjab states. The East Jumna, West Jumna, and Agra are the major canals on the river.

jumping bean: see SPURGE.

jumping mouse, RODENT slightly larger than the common mouse, found in North America and N Asia, also called the kangaroo mouse. Its long hind legs and tail enable it to leap distances up to 12 ft (3.7 m). Jumping mice have gray to brown fur and are white underneath. They can scurry as well as leap and are good swimmers. Solitary, nocturnal animals, they are found in marshes and on stream banks in coniferous and deciduous forests of both coasts of North America, and also in fields and pastures. Two genera, *Zapus* and *Napaeozapus,* are North American, ranging from the Arctic Circle S to New Mexico and Tennessee; a related genus, with one species, *Eozapus setchuanus,* the Szechuan jumping mouse, is native to China. Jumping mice feed on a diet of grass seeds, fruit, and insect larvae. They gain weight in autumn and hibernate in fur-lined burrows during winter. Litters, containing from three to six young, are born in late spring. Jumping mice are classified in the phylum CHORDATA, subphylum Vertebrata, class Mammalia, order Rodentia, family Zapodidae.

Junagadh (jo͞o'nəgäd") or **Junagarh** (-gär"), former principality, Kathiawar peninsula, W India, on the Arabian Sea. The region of Junagadh became a district of Gujarat state in 1960. Grains, cotton, and tobacco are grown there, and the fishing industry is important. Junagadh was wrested from the MOGUL empire in the mid-18th cent. by Sher Kahn Babi, a Muslim freebooter who established a dynasty that was later supported by the British. In 1947 the Muslim ruler ceded his state to Pakistan, although the population was overwhelmingly Hindu. He was forced to flee when Indian forces invaded the state. The town of **Junagadh** (1971 pop. 95,945) was formerly the state capital and is now a district administrative center. It is also a market for gold and silver embroidery, perfume, and copper and brass vessels. The town has ancient Buddhist caves and RAJPUT forts, as well as a modern college. Nearby is the Girnar forest, the only place in Asia where lions are found.

junco or **snowbird,** common name for a bird of the family Fringillidae (FINCH family). Juncos are small seed-eaters with white underparts and gray (sometimes also brown) backs. They travel in flocks, seeking weed seeds in fields. The slate-colored junco is common in the East; there are a number of Western juncos. Juncos belong to the genus *Junco* and are classified in the phylum CHORDATA, subphylum Vertebrata, class Aves, order Passeriformes, family Fringillidae.

Junction City, city (1970 pop. 19,018), seat of Geary co., NE Kansas, at the confluence of the Republican and Smoky Hill rivers; inc. 1859. The rail and trade center of an agricultural and dairy area, it grew as the supply point for nearby FORT RILEY. Limestone quarries are near the city.

Jundiaí (zho͞ondyī'), city (1970 pop. 169,096), São Paulo state, S Brazil, on the Jundiaí River. It is an agricultural and industrial center. Among its products are textiles, ceramics, furniture, soap, wines, foodstuffs, brushes, shoes, paper, matches, chemicals, and agricultural tools. The city was established in the 17th cent.

June, Jennie: see CROLY, JANE CUNNINGHAM.

June: see MONTH.

Juneau, Solomon Laurent (jo͞onō', jo͞o'nō), 1793–1856, French Canadian fur trader and founder of

Milwaukee, Wis., b. near Montreal. In 1818, as an agent of the American Fur Company, he moved to their new post at Milwaukee. He amassed a fortune in independent trade, acquired large tracts of land there, and was revered by the Indians. He became an American citizen in 1831. He surveyed the town site, built the first store and first tavern, became Milwaukee's first postmaster (1835) and first president of the village (1837). His fortune was reduced by the Panic of 1837, but he remained a leading citizen of Milwaukee, becoming its first mayor in 1846.

Juneau (jo͞o'nō), city (1970 pop. 13,556), state capital, SE Alaska, in the Alaska Panhandle; settled by gold miners 1880, inc. 1900. A port on Gastineau Channel, Juneau is a trade center for the Panhandle area, with an ice-free harbor, a seaplane base, and an airport. The state and Federal government is the major employer. Salmon and halibut fishing, lumbering, and tourism are also important economic activities. Joseph Juneau and a partner discovered gold nearby in 1880, and the city developed as a gold rush town. It was officially designated as capital of the Territory of Alaska in 1900 but did not function as such until the government offices were moved from Sitka in 1906. In 1959 it became state capital with the admission of Alaska to the Union. Juneau lies at the foot of two spectacular peaks, Mt. Juneau and Mt. Roberts. Douglas Island lies across the channel. The huge boxlike Federal Building dominates the skyline. The Alaska Historical Library and Museum are in the city. A junior college (a unit of the Univ. of Alaska) serves the area. In 1970 the municipal boundaries were extended, making Juneau the largest city in area in the United States, at 3,108 sq mi (8,050 sq km). Glacier Bay National Monument is to the northwest. In 1974, Alaskans voted to move the state capital away from Juneau.

June beetle or **May beetle,** a blackish or mahogany-colored beetle of the SCARAB BEETLE family, widely distributed in North America and especially abundant in the NE United States and the adjacent parts of Canada. It is also known as June bug, although true bugs belong to a different insect order. The adults, which may swarm in great numbers in early summer and are attracted to lights, feed by night on the foliage of deciduous trees and hide during the day. The eggs are laid in the soil, where the larvae, called white grubs, remain for two or three years, eating the roots and other underground parts of grasses, grains, and trees. The grubs cause great destruction to lawns and fir trees. Many birds and small mammals, such as skunks and pigs, root out the grubs and eat them. The insects pupate underground in the fall and emerge as adults the following spring. June beetles are sometimes called cockchafers, a name used primarily for some of their close relatives in the Old World. They are closely allied to the leaf chafers, including the rose chafer. June beetles are classified in the phylum ARTHROPODA, class Insecta, order Coleoptera, family Scarabaeidae.

Juneberry: see SHADBUSH.

June bug, name for JUNE BEETLE and MAYFLY.

June Days, in French history, name usually given to the insurrection of workingmen in June, 1848. The working classes had played an important role in the FEBRUARY REVOLUTION of 1848, but with the triumph of the bourgeois, their hopes for economic and social reform were ignored. Their increasing unrest was due to continued economic crisis and rising unemployment and to the inadequacy of the national workshops, which, although proposed by Louis BLANC, were never organized as he planned them. Instead of providing work, the workshops became a system of registering the unemployed for a meager dole. When a decree of June 21 abolished the work-

Juneau, Alaska, on the Gastineau Channel.

shops, dispersing the workers to the army and to the provinces, the workingmen rose in revolt. There were four days (June 23–26) of violent fighting in the barricaded streets of Paris. General CAVAIGNAC was given dictatorial powers and used harsh measures to suppress the insurrection. The June Days further alienated the lower classes from the revolution.

Jung, Carl Gustav (kärl go͞os'täf yo͝ong), 1875–1961, Swiss psychiatrist, the founder of analytical psychology, studied at Basel (1895–1900) and Zürich (M.D., 1902). After work at the University Psychiatric Clinic in Zürich, he studied (1902) under Eugen Bleuler at the Burghölzli Clinic. He wrote valuable papers, but more important was a book on the psychology of dementia praecox (1906). In 1907 he met Sigmund Freud, whose work had impressed him. Jung edited the *Jahrbuch für psychologische und psychopathologische Forschungen* and was made (1911) president of the international psychoanalytic society. However, a formal break with Freud came when Jung's revolutionary work appeared as *Wandlungen und Symbole der Libido* (1912; tr. *Psychology of the Unconscious,* 1916; rev. ed. 1952; tr. *Symbols of Transformation,* 1956). Jungian psychology is based on psychic totality and psychic energism; he postulated two dimensions in the unconscious—the personal (repressed events of a person's life) and the archetypes of a collective unconscious. His *Psychologische Typen* (1921, tr. 1923) elucidated EXTROVERSION AND INTROVERSION. Other major concepts are those of anima/animus and of synchronicity, the coincidence of causally unrelated events having identical or similar meaning. To Jung, the most important and lifelong task imposed upon any person is fulfillment through the process of individuation, achievement of harmony of conscious and unconscious, which makes a person one and whole. Among Jung's many works are *Two Essays on Analytical Psychology* (tr. 1953); *Psychology and Alchemy* (tr. 1953); *Modern Man in Search of a Soul* (1933); *The Structure and Dynamics of the Psyche* (tr. 1960); *Psychology and Religion: West and East* (tr. 1958). Publication of the definitive edition of Jung's works in English translation was begun in 1953. See the autobiographical *Memories, Dreams, Reflections* (recorded and ed. by Aniela Jaffe, 1963); his letters, ed. by Gerhard Adler (Vol. I, 1973); his correspondence with Sigmund Freud, ed. by William McGuire (1974); studies by Jolande Jacobi (6th rev. ed. 1961), A. M. Dry (1962), Antonio Moreno (1970), and E. A. Bennet (1966, repr. 1972); C. S. Hall and V. J. Nordby, *A Primer of Jungian Psychology* (1973).

Jungaria: see DZUNGARIA, China.

Jungbunzlau: see MLADÁ BOLESLAV, Czechoslovakia.

Jünger, Ernst (ĕrnst yüng'ər), 1895–, German writer. Jünger's early war novels were based on arduous army experience. They glorified war and its sacrifice as the greatest physical and mental stimulants. Among these works are *Storm of Steel* (1920, tr. 1929), *Feuer und Blut* (1924), and *Copse 125* (1925, tr. 1930). Later he opposed Hitler and rejected his own militarism in a mystical plea for peace, expressed in his diaries of the war years, *On the Marble Cliffs* (1939, tr. 1947), *Gärten und Strassen* (1942), and *Heliopolis* (1949). Jünger's later works include *The Glass Bees* (1957, tr. 1961). See study by J. P. Stern (1953).

Jungfrau (yo͝ong'frou), peak, 13,642 ft (4,158 m) high, S central Switzerland, in the Bernese Alps. It was first ascended in 1811. Aletsch Glacier is on the south side. The **Jungfraujoch** (-yôkh") is a mountain saddle 11,333 ft (3,454 m) high, the highest point in Europe reached by rail. It has a scientific institute and is popular with tourists. A meteorological station is on the nearby Sphinx summit, 11,723 ft (3,573 m) high. The region is noted for its scenery and winter sports.

Jungius, Joachim (yō'äkhĭm yo͝ong'ēo͞os), 1587–1657, German mathematician, logician, and systematizer of natural history. In 1608 he made his inaugural dissertation at the University of Giessen, proclaiming in it the doctrine, endorsed by progressive 17th-century scientists, that science must be based on mathematics. A practicing physician as well as a professor of mathematics, he subsequently elaborated an empirical philosophy of science, a morphological system of botany, and a corpuscular chemistry that assumed the conservation of mass. Difficulties with religious authorities forced Jungius to refrain from publishing many of his later works.

jungle [Hindustani *jangal*=desert, forest; from Skt. *jangala*=wasteland, uncultivated land], densest form of tropical FOREST (usually second growth or later) found throughout tropical lowland regions. Jungle is characterized by high humidity and resultant abundance (both in numbers and variety) of flora and concomitantly of fauna. *Jungle* is not a strict ecological term and is often applied to any impenetrable thicket or tangled mass of vegetation.

jungle cat: see LYNX.

jungle fowl, common name for small, terrestrial wild fowl comprising four species in the genus *Gallus.* Most important of these is the red jungle fowl, which Charles Darwin determined to be the ancestor of all domesticated fowl. It is the only wild fowl that can crossbreed fertilely with domesticated species. It is yellow-headed with a red comb and wattles, and its multicolored plumage resembles a jester's costume. The female is slightly smaller and less brightly colored than its mate. Jungle fowl are found in large numbers from India through S China and the Malayan archipelago, where they inhabit thickly wooded areas. They feed on a diet of seeds, buds, fruit, and insects. The polygamous males are highly aggressive (the modern game cock is thought to be the domestic form closest to the ancestral species) and they take no part in nest building, incubation, or the care of the young. From archaeological evidence, it would seem that the jungle fowl was first domesticated in India as much as 5,200 years ago, and that by the 6th cent. B.C. it had entered Europe. The jungle fowl is classified in the phylum CHORDATA, subphylum Vertebrata, class Aves, order Galliformes, family Phasianidae.

Junia (jo͞o'nēə), man or woman early converted to Christianity. Rom. 16.7.

Junín (ho͞onēn'), city (1970 pop. 69,731), Buenos Aires prov., E Argentina, on the Salado River. It is a busy commercial center for an agricultural and livestock area. There are important railroad repair shops. Junín began as a frontier fort (est. 1827) during the struggle against the Indians of Pampa.

Junín, village (1961 est. pop. 5,000), W central Peru, in the Andes. In the vicinity on Aug. 6, 1824, Simón BOLÍVAR, aided by Antonio José de SUCRE, defeated the Spanish general, José Canterac, in the first important battle leading to Peruvian independence.

junior college: see COMMUNITY COLLEGE.

junior high school: see SCHOOL.

juniper, any tree or shrub of the genus *Juniperus,* aromatic evergreens of the family Cupressaceae (CYPRESS family), widely distributed over the north temperate zone. Many are valuable as a source of lumber and oil. The small fleshy cones are berrylike in appearance. The so-called common juniper (*J. communis*) is found throughout the genus range and is also much cultivated in different varieties, e.g., dwarf and pyramidal. Its fruits are the juniper berries used for flavoring gin and other beverages and sometimes in cooking. The juniper most common in North America is usually called red cedar (*J. virginiana*) and is found over most of the E United States. Its fragrant, insect-repellent wood, closegrained but brittle, is much used for chests, closets, posts, woodenware, and pencils, for which uses the large forests of these trees have been depleted. Oil of red cedar is used in medicine, perfumery, and microscopy. Other trees are sometimes called red cedar. Western juniper, *J. occidentalis,* of the W United States (not to be confused with the western ARBORVITAE, although both are also called western red cedar) has edible fruits. Indians also used the fruits of other Western species as food and the bark for fiber. Junipers have been used for incense in the Orient and by the Plains Indians in religious ceremonies. Juniper is classified in the division Pinophyta, class Pinopsida, order Coniferales, family Cupressaceae.

Junius, English political author, known only by the signature Junius, which he signed to various letters written to the London *Public Advertiser* from Jan., 1769, to Jan., 1772, attacking George III and his ministers. The letters, centering on John WILKES and the controversy over the Middlesex election, were written by a passionate opponent of the government familiar with secret government matters. Junius used scandal and invective rather than argument as his major tools of attack. The letters were reprinted by the publisher of the *Advertiser* in 1772, and a new edition, with additional letters, appeared in 1812. Although the identity of Junius has never been definitely established, the political beliefs, handwriting, and life of Sir Philip FRANCIS have led many to ascribe the authorship to him. Arguments have also been offered in favor of the authorship of Lord SHELBURNE and of Laughlin Macleane, British army surgeon and secretary to Shelburne.

Junius, Franciscus, 1589–1677, French philologist; son of Franciscus Junius (1545–1602), French Huguenot theologian. The younger Franciscus Junius was born in Heidelberg and lived chiefly in Holland and England. He was a pioneer in the study of Gothic and Anglo-Saxon. A unique manuscript of Anglo-Saxon poems formerly attributed to CÆDMON was owned and edited by him and is known as the Junius Manuscript (Bodleian Lib., Oxford). For a modern edition, see G. P. Krapp, *The Junius Manuscript* (1931).

Junkceylon: see PHUKET, Thailand.

Juno (jo͞o′nō), in astronomy, 3d ASTEROID to be discovered. It was found in 1804 by C. Harding. It has a diameter of c.120 mi (190 km). Its average distance from the sun is 2.67 ASTRONOMICAL UNITS, and its orbital period is 1,594 days.

Juno, in Roman religion, wife and sister of Jupiter. In early Roman times she, like the Greek Hera (with whom she was later identified), was goddess and protector of women, concerned especially with their sexual life. In later religion she became, however, the great goddess of the state and was worshiped, in conjunction with Jupiter and Minerva, at the temple on the Capitol.

Junot, Andoche (äNdôsh′ zhünō′), 1771–1813, French general. Having served under Napoleon Bonaparte in Italy and Egypt, he became ambassador to Portugal (1804–5) and commanded the French invasion of that country in 1807, thus opening the PENINSULAR WAR. Appointed governor general of Portugal, he was forced to evacuate after his defeat by Arthur Wellesley (later the duke of Wellington) in 1808. He also served in Spain, Germany, and Russia. Napoleon created him duke of Abrantès, under which name his wife, Laure Junot, duchesse d'Abrantès, is generally known. Near the end of his life he became insane, and he may have committed suicide.

Jupiter, in astronomy, 5th planet from the sun and largest planet of the solar system. Jupiter's orbit lies beyond the ASTEROID belt at a mean distance of c.483 million mi (773 million km) from the sun; its period of revolution is c.11.9 years. In order from the sun it is the first of the Jovian planets (Jupiter, Saturn, Uranus, and Neptune), very large, massive planets of relatively low density, having rapid rotation and a thick, opaque atmosphere. Jupiter has a diameter of c.88,700 mi (142,000 km), nearly 11 times that of the earth, and its volume is more than 1,300 times greater than the earth's. Its mass is 318 times that of the earth and about 2½ times the mass of all other planets combined. The heavy atmosphere of Jupiter, which blocks any possible observation of its surface, is composed mainly of hydrogen, helium, methane, and ammonia. It appears to be divided into a number of light and dark bands parallel to its equator and shows a range of complex features, most notably the Great Red Spot, located in its southern hemisphere and measuring c.30,000 mi long by 10,000 mi wide (48,000 by 16,000 km). The Spot is taken by some as evidence of solid surface features beneath the atmosphere. Others think that because of its low density a definite surface might not exist. One theory pictures a gradual transition from the outer ammonia clouds to a thick layer of frozen gases and finally to a liquid or solid hydrogen mantle. The Spot and other markings of the atmosphere also provide evidence for Jupiter's rapid rotation, which has a period of about 9 hr 55 min. This rotation causes a polar flattening of over 6%. The temperature of the visible surface of its atmosphere is about −190°F (−124°C), yet Jupiter radiates about four times as much heat energy as it receives from the sun, suggesting higher temperatures deeper within the atmosphere. This energy is thought to be due in part to a slow contraction of the planet. Jupiter is also characterized by intense nonthermal electromagnetic radiation. In the 15-m range it is the strongest radio emitter in the sky. Thirteen natural satellites are known to orbit Jupiter. The four largest—Io, Europa, Ganymede, and Callisto (also designated I, II, III, and IV)—were discovered by Galileo in 1610, shortly after he invented the telescope, and are known as the Galilean satellites. Ganymede is the largest satellite in the solar system; with a diameter exceeding 3,000 mi (4,800 km), it is larger than the planet Mercury. Satellite V, discovered by E. E. Barnard in 1892, is closest to Jupiter and has a diameter of c.100 mi (160 km). The eight remaining satellites orbit at greater distances from the planet, and none is larger than c.50 mi (80 km) in diameter. The outer four satellites—VIII, IX, XI, and

XII—located from 14 million to 16 million mi from Jupiter (22 million–26 million km), have RETROGRADE MOTION, i.e., motion opposite to that of the planet's rotation, and may be captured asteroids.

Jupiter, in Roman religion, the supreme god, also called Jove. Originally a sky deity associated with rain and agriculture, he developed into the great father god, prime protector of the state, concerned, like the Greek Zeus (with whom he is identified), with all aspects of life. At his temple on the Capitol, triumphant generals honored him with their spoils and magistrates paid homage to him with sacrifices. Jupiter was the son of Saturn and Ops and the brother and husband of Juno.

Jura (zhürä'), department (1968 pop. 233,547), E France, in FRANCHE-COMTÉ. It borders on Switzerland. LONS-LE-SAUNIER is the capital.

Jura (jo͝or'ə, Fr. zhürä', Ger. yo͞o'rä), mountain range, part of the Alpine system, E France and NW Switzerland, occupying parts of the French region of Franche-Comté and the Swiss cantons of Vaud, Neuchâtel, Bern, Solothurn, and Basel. It extends in narrow, parallel ridges c 160 mi (260 km) from the Rhine River at Basel to the Rhône River SW of Geneva; Crêt de la Neige (5,652 ft/1,723 m), in France, is the highest peak. The Jura's rounded crests and summits are covered with dense pine forests and good pasture lands. The region is drained by the Doubs, the Ain, the Loué, and smaller streams. Major cities include La Chaux-de-Fonds, Neuchâtel, and Biel, Switzerland, and Besançon, France. Hydroelectric plants in the Jura supply power to pulp and paper, textile, and woodworking industries. Important watch industries, particularly in the Swiss towns of Le Locle, La Chaux-de-Fonds, and Grenchen, are also there. Export products from the French Jura include brierwood (for pipes), plastics, and cheese. The Jura mts. are a popular year-round resort region. Composed of sandstone and limestone and rich in fossils, the Jura gives its name to the JURASSIC PERIOD. The mountains N of the Lake of Constance in SW West Germany are called the Swabian Jura.

Fossils of the Jurassic period: fossilized remains of a marine reptile (above), cycad plant fossil (below).

Jura, island, Great Britain: see HEBRIDES, THE.

Jurassic period (jərăs'ĭk) [from the Jura mts.], second period of the MESOZOIC ERA of geologic time. In the Jurassic period, E North America was mostly elevated and subject to erosion, which reduced the Appalachian region to a peneplain. Before the end of the period, the Appalachian borderland began to founder as the Atlantic Ocean continued to widen. The Pacific border of North America, from California to Alaska, was submerged for most of the period. In the Early Jurassic, large areas of Arizona, Colorado, and Utah were apparently desert, and the sand was later consolidated into the white and pinkish Glen Canyon and Navaho sandstones, which now enhance the scenic beauty of the district. During the Upper Jurassic the Logan Sea entered this area from the north. In its various advances and retreats, this body of water covered large areas of Montana, Idaho, Wyoming, Colorado, and Utah, depositing sandstone, shale, limestone, and some gypsum. The retreat of the Logan Sea toward the end of the period was followed, probably in the Upper Jurassic but possibly in the Lower Cretaceous Period, by the deposition of the Morrison continental series of clays and sandstones, noted for its richness in fossil dinosaurs. The close of the Jurassic in North America was marked by widespread folding along the western border of the continent, accompanied by the intrusion of lava as the eastern edge of the plate that carries the Pacific Ocean was thrust beneath the westward drifting plate that carries the North American continent. In this disturbance the Sierra Nevada, Klamaths, Cascades, Coast Ranges, and coastal mountains of Canada and Alaska were formed. The history of the European Jurassic is very well known, the system being one of the most complete on the Continent. Studies of oxygen isotopes, the extent of land flora, and marine fossils indicate that climates during Jurassic times were mild—perhaps 15°F (8°C) warmer than those of today. No glaciers existed during this period. The plant life of the Jurassic was dominated by the cycads, but conifers, ginkgoes, horsetails, and ferns were also abundant. Of the marine invertebrates, the most important were the ammonites. The dominant animals on land, in the sea, and in the air were the reptiles. Dinosaurs, more numerous and more extraordinary than those of the Triassic period, were the chief land animals; crocodiles, ichthyosaurs, and plesiosaurs ruled the sea; while the air was inhabited by the pterodactyls and relatives. Mammals, making their first appearance, were few and small but undoubtedly became well established during the Jurassic period. The Jurassic saw the appearance of the first bird, Archaeopteryx. See GEOLOGIC ERAS (table).

Jurieu, Pierre (pyĕr zhüryö'), 1637–1713, French Calvinist theologian. He was (1674–81) professor at Sedan. In 1681 in an attempt to preserve Huguenot liberties he published anonymously *La Politique du clergé de France;* his authorship soon became known, and he left France. From 1681 he was pastor of the Walloon Church in Rotterdam, writing in behalf of the French Reformed Church and giving aid to exiles from France after the revocation of the Edict of Nantes. His controversial works, often bitter and aggressive, were directed against such contemporaries as Antoine Arnauld, Bishop Bossuet, Archbishop Fénelon, and Pierre Bayle. Important writings are the *Pastoral Letters Addressed to the Faithful in France* (1686, tr. 1689) and *Critical History of Dogmas and Cults* (1704, tr. 1705). See G. H. Dodge, *The Political Theory of the Huguenots of the Dispersion* (1947).

jurisprudence (jo͝or"ĭspro͞od'əns), study of the nature and the origin and development of LAW. It is variously regarded as a branch of ethics or of sociology. Many of the major systematic philosophers (e.g., Aristotle, St. Thomas Aquinas, and Kant) have expounded jurisprudential theories. Before the 19th cent. most jurisprudents adhered to NATURAL LAW, which maintained that sound legal doctrine was derivable only from a supposed law of nature established by divine ordinance. The natural-law school did not deny that the details of legal regulation depended upon the will of the sovereign. However, the positivist, or analytical, school, which first became important in the late 18th cent., insisted that law was entirely a matter of sovereign decree, distinct from morality and theology. Among important 19th-century trends was the view, represented by SAVIGNY, that a people's legal system expressed the national spirit. In the mid-19th cent. many jurisprudents attempted to avoid what they felt were theoretical preconceptions and to demonstrate a uniform evolution from primitive times to modern industrialized society. Other thinkers were skeptical of evolutionary explanations and sought the basic principles underlying all systems of law in various fields, including economics and psychology. Among the more important legal thinkers in the United States have been Learned HAND, Oliver Wendell HOLMES, and Roscoe POUND. See Jerome Hall, ed., *Readings in Jurisprudence* (1938); W. S. Carpenter, *Foundations of Modern Jurisprudence* (1958); Denis Lloyd, *Introduction to Jurisprudence* (3d ed. 1972).

Jurjan: see GORGAN, town, Iran.

Jurong Industrial Estate: see SINGAPORE.

Juruá (zho͞orwä'), river, c.1,500 mi (2,410 km) long, rising in the Cerros de Canchyuaya, E Peru. It flows in a winding course generally NE through Acre and Amazonas states, W Brazil, to the Amazon River E of Fonte Boa. One of the Amazon's longer tributaries, it is navigable along one third of its course and was important for transport during the wild-rubber boom.

jury, body convened to make decisions of fact in legal proceedings. Historians do not agree on the origin of the English jury. Although some authorities trace it to Anglo-Saxon or even more remote Germanic times, most believe that it was brought to England by the Normans. The first jurors were not triers of fact in legal disputes but were persons acquainted with the situation in question who spoke out of personal knowledge. Thus, in compiling the DOMESDAY BOOK inquests of neighbors were convened to furnish information on property holdings. In the enforcement of criminal justice the earliest function of the jury (mid-12th cent.) appears to have been the presentation of accusations, and it was only later that jurors were convened to answer on oath the question of guilt. These early jury trials, while supplanting the ORDEAL and other irrational procedures, were not themselves satisfactory, because they depended entirely on the unsupported oath of the jurors. A verdict could not be overturned except by attaint, that is, by summoning a second jury to give its sworn verdict on the question as to whether the first jury had committed perjury. By the 16th cent. the jury was used in civil as well as criminal cases, and the practice of calling witnesses was well developed. However, not until the mid-18th cent. were methods other than the attaint available to set aside an improper verdict. To Englishmen and other peoples who have adopted the English common-law system trial by jury became a cherished protection against the possibility of judicial and administrative tyranny. Among the abuses recited in the American Declaration of Independence is "depriving us in many cases, of the benefits of Trial by Jury." The Sixth and Seventh Amendments to the U.S. Constitution, reflecting this concern, require a jury in Federal trials in criminal prosecutions and in civil suits at common law where the damages sought exceed $20; the traditional exemption of cases in EQUITY was left unchanged. The merger of law and equity has led to the development of various tests to determine if a case can be tried before a jury. In 1967 the U.S. Supreme Court held that the

Fourteenth Amendment guaranteed the right to a jury in state criminal trials. Most U.S. states preserve jury trials for a variety of civil cases. Great Britain has limited the use of civil juries to cases in which community attitudes are especially important (e.g., defamation and fraud). In most criminal cases the charge is first considered by a GRAND JURY with 12 to 23 members. It hears witnesses against the accused, and if 12 jurors believe that there is sufficient evidence to prosecute, an INDICTMENT or the like is presented. The jury sitting at the trial proper is called a petit (or petty) jury from its smaller size (usually 12 members). The selection of a jury is essentially alike in civil and in criminal cases. The venire, a panel of prospective jurors living in the district where the trial is to be held, is summoned for examination. Counsel for the parties may first challenge the array, that is, object that the venire as a whole was improperly chosen or is for some reason unfit. The challenges to the poll (the veniremen taken individually) that follow are designed to secure as jurors unbiased persons without special knowledge of the matters in issue. Included are challenges for principal cause, i.e., some grounds such as relationship to a party that requires dismissal of the venireman; challenges to the favor, i.e., suspicion of unfitness on which the judge rules; and a limited number of peremptory challenges. Once selected, the jury (usually with several alternates) takes an oath to act fairly and without preconceptions. At the close of the evidence and after the summations of counsel the judge instructs the jury concerning the VERDICT. The value of juries in civil trials is disputed. Opponents of juries argue that they are ineffective, irrational, and cause delay; proponents argue that juries bring community standards to bear, can modify the effects of harsh laws, and are a protection against incompetent judges. Outside of the English-speaking countries there is generally less recourse to the jury and less care in the selection of jurors. See A. T. Vanderbilt, *Judges and Jurors: Their Functions, Qualifications, and Selection* (1956); P. A. Devlin, *Trial by Jury* (1956).

Jushab-hesed (jo͞oshăb'-hēsĕd"), son of Zerubbabel. 1 Chron. 3.20.

Jusserand, Jean Jules (zhäN zhül zhüsəräN'), 1855–1932, French diplomat and author, b. Lyon. After service in London, Constantinople, and Copenhagen, he was ambassador to the United States (1902–25). A close friend of every U.S. President during the period, he did much to promote friendly Franco-American relations and to win the United States to the Allied side in World War I. Jusserand was also a noted scholar; his works include *English Wayfaring Life in the Middle Ages* (tr. 1889), *Shakespeare in France* (1898), a life of Ronsard (1913), and *With Americans of Past and Present Days* (1916), the first work on U.S. history to be awarded a Pulitzer Prize. See his reminiscences, *What Me Befell* (1933).

Jussieu (zhüsyö'), name of a French family of distinguished botanists. **Antoine de Jussieu,** 1686–1758, was director of the Jardin des Plantes, Paris. He edited Jacques Barrelier's posthumously published *Plantae per Galliam, Hispaniam et Italiam observatae* (1714) and the third edition (1719) of J. P. de Tournefort's *Institutiones rei herbariae.* **Bernard de Jussieu,** 1699–1777?, brother of Antoine, was director of the gardens at the Trianon, Versailles; there he arranged the plants according to his new system of classification, which he never published. He revised (1725) Tournefort's *Histoire des plantes qui naissent aux environs de Paris.* Another brother, **Joseph de Jussieu,** 1704–79, accompanied La Condamine to South America, where he remained until c.1771. He introduced into Europe many plants, including the heliotrope. A nephew, **Antoine Laurent de Jussieu,** 1748–1836, assisted Bernard de Jussieu, whose system of classification by natural affinities he elaborated in *Genera plantarum* (1789), which influenced later systems of classification. He was professor at the Museum of Natural History, Paris, and organized its botanical collection. His son, **Adrien de Jussieu,** 1797–1853, also professor of botany at the museum, wrote a standard text, *Cours élémentaire de botanique* (1842–44).

Justice, United States Department of, Federal executive department established in 1870 and charged with providing the means for enforcing Federal laws, furnishing legal counsel in Federal cases, and construing the laws under which other Federal executive departments act. The department is headed by the U.S. Attorney General, the chief U.S. law officer and an original cabinet member. Before the formation of the Dept. of Justice the Attorney General

Communion of the Apostles, *detail of a painting by the Flemish artist Justus of Ghent.*

had represented the government in legal matters and given legal advice to the executive branch under the authority of the Judiciary Act of 1789, but he had had no executive department to assist him. Because of the mounting responsibilities of the Attorney General and because of the growing need for uniformity in the administration of law, a department was created. The act of 1870 also set up the office of Solicitor General to represent the government in Supreme Court cases. The Dept. of Justice comprises eight specialized divisions (the Antitrust Division, the Civil Division, the Criminal Division, the Land and Natural Resources Division, the Tax Division, the Civil Rights Division, the Administrative Division, and the division responsible for enforcing Federal narcotics laws). The Justice Dept. also comprises the FEDERAL BUREAU OF INVESTIGATION, the Immigration and Naturalization Service, the Bureau of Prisons, the Drug Enforcement Administration, the Law Enforcement Assistance Administration, the Board of Immigration Appeals, and the Board of Parole.

justice of the peace, official presiding over a type of POLICE COURT. In some states of the United States the justices, who are usually elected, have jurisdiction over petty civil and criminal cases as well as having such duties as the issuing of search warrants and the performance of marriage services. The justice of the peace was formerly of greater importance than he is at present. The establishment of the office throughout England in 1360 represented a further extension of royal authority to local government, especially to rural areas. The justices, selected from the gentry, enjoyed extensive administrative and police authority, and they had judicial power over most crimes. The office was established also in the American colonies, but by the latter part of the 19th cent. it had been relegated to a much less central role, especially in administrative areas, in both England and the United States.

Justin I, c.450–527, Byzantine emperor (518–27); successor of Anastasius I. He was chief of the imperial guard and became emperor when Anastasius died. Justin persecuted the Monophysites and maintained close relations with the Western church. An uneducated man, he entrusted the government largely to his nephew, who eventually succeeded him as JUSTINIAN I. See Alexander Vasiliev, *Justin the First* (1950).

Justin II, d. 578, Byzantine emperor (565–78), nephew and successor of Justinian I. He allied himself with the Turks and resumed the wars with Persia. During his reign Slavs and Avars attacked the empire, and Italy was invaded by the Lombards under ALBOIN. He severely persecuted the Monophysites. Subject to fits of insanity, he adopted (574) the general Tiberius as his son. Tiberius was made Caesar and exercised power until he succeeded Justin (578) on the latter's death. Tiberius was in turn succeeded (582) by Maurice.

Justin (Marcus Junianus Justinus), fl. 3d cent., Roman historian. He made a collection of excerpts from TROGUS, which gives many facts not recounted elsewhere.

Justinian I, 483–565, Byzantine emperor (527–65), nephew and successor of JUSTIN I. He was responsible for much imperial policy during his uncle's reign. Soon after becoming emperor, Justinian instituted major administrative changes and tried to increase state revenues at the expense of his subjects. Justinian's fiscal policies, the discontent of the Monophysites at his orthodoxy, and the loyalty of the populace to the family of Anastasius I produced the Nika riot (532), which would have cost Justinian his throne but for the firmness of his wife, Empress THEODORA, and the aid of his great generals, BELISARIUS and NARSES (see BLUES AND GREENS). Justinian, through Belisarius and Narses, recovered Africa from the Vandals (533–48) and Italy from the Ostrogoths (535–54). He was less successful in fighting the Persians and was unable to prevent the raids of the Slavs and the Bulgars. Justinian's policy of caesaropapism (i.e., the supremacy of the emperor over the church) included not only matters of organization, but also matters of dogma. In 553, seeking to reconcile the Monophysites to the church, he called a council (see CONSTANTINOPLE, SECOND COUNCIL OF) but accomplished nothing and finally tended to drift into heresy himself. Justinian's greatest accomplishment was the codification of Roman law, commonly called the CORPUS JURIS CIVILIS, executed under his direction by TRIBONIAN. It gave unity to the centralized state and greatly influenced all subsequent legal history. Justinian erected many public works, of which the church of HAGIA SOPHIA is the most notable. He was succeeded by his nephew, Justin II. The writings of PROCOPIUS are the main source of information on Justinian's reign. See Charles Diehl, *Justinien et la civilisation byzantine au VIe siècle* (1901, repr. 1969); W. G. Holmes, *The Age of Justinian and Theodora* (1912); J. W. Barker, *Justinian and the Later Roman Empire* (1966); Robert Browning, *Justinian and Theodora* (1971).

Justinian II (Justinian Rhinotmetus), 669–711, Byzantine emperor (685–95, 705–11), son and successor of Constantine IV. He unsuccessfully warred against the Persians. His extravagance and despotism and his ministers' extortions caused a revolution (695). Justinian had his nose cut off; hence he was given the epithet Rhinotmetus [Gr.,=with the cut-off nose]. He was then exiled. Restored (705) with the help of the Bulgars, he was deposed and beheaded. A series of usurpers occupied the throne from 711. In 717 Leo III established a new dynasty. See study by Constance Head (1972).

Justin Martyr, Saint, A.D. c.100–c.165, Christian apologist, called also Justin the Philosopher. Born in Samaria of pagan parents, he studied philosophy, and after his conversion in Ephesus to Christianity at about the age of 38, he went from place to place trying to convert men of learning by philosophical argument. He opened a school of Christian philosophy at Rome, where he and some disciples were finally martyred under Marcus Aurelius. Of his writings (in Greek), only two undisputed works remain, the *Apology* (with an appendix called the *Second Apology*) and the *Dialogue*. The *Apology* is a learned defense of Christians against charges of atheism and sedition in the Roman state; it contains an exposition of Christian ethics and invaluable records of the customs and practices of 2d-century Christianity. The *Dialogue* sets forth in the form of an argument with Trypho (or Tryphon) the Jew a philosophic defense of Christian beliefs, particularly with reference to Jewish writings; it has references to the Gospels that have been of much interest to students of the Bible. Feast: April 14.

Justin Morgan, 1792–1821, American horse, the foundation sire of the Justin Morgan breed of horses. Originally called "Figure," the stallion was renamed for his first owner, Justin Morgan (1747–

97), after both owner and horse were dead. The horse—small, weighing about 800 lb (363 kg), of tremendous endurance, and with a delicate head, heavy shoulders, and a short neck—was bought and sold many times. The Morgan breed preceded the Hambletonian strain as the favored type of trotting horses in America.

Justo, Agustín Pedro (ägōōstēn' pä'thrō hōōs'tō), 1876–1943, president of Argentina (1932–38). An army general, he rose to prominence (1922) as minister of war under Marcelo Torcuato de Alvear and later participated in the conservative revolution that overthrew Hipólito Irigoyen (1930). As president he became a leading exponent of Pan-Americanism and the League of Nations; together with his foreign minister, Carlos SAAVEDRA LAMAS, he was instrumental in ending the Chaco War. In World War II, Justo supported the Allied cause and was, in the face of much pro-Axis sentiment in Argentine political circles, the chief advocate of the United Nations in Argentina. When Brazil declared war on the Axis he requested and received the rank of honorary general in the Brazilian army.

Justus. **1** Surname of JOSEPH BARSABAS. **2** or **Titus Justus,** Corinthian host of St. Paul. Acts 18.7. **3** Jesus Justus: see JESUS **2.**

Justus of Ghent, fl. c.1460–c.1480, Flemish religious and portrait painter, now generally identified with Joos van Wassenhove; also known as Jodocus or Joos of Ghent. His simple, quiet style provides a clear link between Flemish and Italian art. In 1460 he was admitted to the painters' guild in Antwerp, and in 1464 he was at Ghent, where he remained until his departure (c.1469) for Italy and the court of Federigo da Montefeltro, duke of Urbino. His Flemish works are the *Adoration of the Magi* (Metropolitan Mus.) and the *Calvary* (St. Bavo, Ghent); the *Communion of the Apostles* (Urbino) is his only certain Italian work, although he surely worked on a series of panels of poets and philosophers (Urbino and Louvre). His Flemish technical achievements interested the Italians, who must also have recognized affinities to their own art in Justus's graceful yet monumental figures and rhythmically arranged forms.

Justus of Tiberia, fl. 1st cent. A.D., Jewish historian. Friendly to Rome, he opposed the Jewish war against the Romans and fled to Beirut where he became the private secretary of Agrippa II. He is mainly known for his lost *History of the Jewish War,* written from a different point of view than the work of the same title by his rival Josephus. Justus' book is known to us through its mention by Josephus and the early Fathers of the Church.

jute (jōōt), name for any plant of the genus *Corchorus,* tropical annuals of the family Tiliaceae (LINDEN family), and for its fiber. Many species yield fiber, but the chief sources of commercial jute are two Indian species (*C. capsularis* and *C. olitorius*), grown primarily in the Ganges and Brahmaputra valleys. Although jute adapts well to loamy soil in any hot and humid region, cultivation and harvesting require abundant cheap labor, and India remains the unrivaled world producer as well as the chief fiber processor. Calcutta is the main center. Europe and the United States import large quantities of jute fiber and cloth; Dundee, Scotland, is also a major jute-textile manufacturer. The fiber strands in the bark are 6 to 10 ft long (2–3 m) and are separated from the woody stalk centers by retting. The fiber deteriorates quickly and, because of its uneven diameter and comparatively low cellulose content, is relatively weak. However, because of its low cost and the ease of dyeing and spinning, jute is the principal coarse fiber in commercial production and use. About 90% is spun into yarn for fabrics; the better qualities supply burlap and the poorer grades are used for baling and sacking (e.g., gunny sacks). It is also used for twine, rope, carpet and linoleum backing, and insulation. The discarded lower ends, called jute butts, are used for paper manufacture. The plant, cultivated in India from remote times, has been known to Western commerce only since about 1830. Jute is classified in the division MAGNOLIOPHYTA, class Magnoliopsida, order Malvales, family Tiliaceae.

Jutes: see ANGLO-SAXONS.

Jutland (jŭt'lənd), Dan. *Jylland,* Ger. *Jütland,* peninsula, c.250 mi (400 km) long and up to 110 mi (177 km) wide, N Europe, comprising continental Denmark and N Schleswig-Holstein state, West Germany. It is bounded by the Skagerrak in the north, the North Sea in the west, the Kattegat and Lille Baelt in the east, and the Eider River in the south. The term usually is applied only to the Danish territory. Danish Jutland, including adjacent islands, has an area of 11,441 sq mi (29,632 sq km) and contains about half the population of Denmark. The Limfjørd strait cuts across N Jutland. A glacial ridge extending through central Jutland divides the peninsula into two sections. Western Jutland is windswept and sandy and has poor soil. Its coast is marshy, with many lagoons, and Esbjerg is the only good port. The east coast of Jutland is fertile and densely populated. Dairying and livestock raising are the main occupations of E Jutland; Århus and Ålborg are the chief ports. The peninsula has many lakes and is traversed by the Gudenå, Denmark's principal river. Yding Skovhøj, the highest point (568 ft/173 m) in Denmark, is in E Jutland. Sønderjylland (South Jutland) is the name applied in Denmark to the northern part of the former duchy of Schleswig, including the towns of Åbenrå, Haderslev, and Sønderborg. Jutland was known to the ancients as the Cimbric Peninsula (Lat. *Chersonesus Cimbrica*). In 1916, off the coast of W Jutland, British and German fleets engaged in the largest naval battle of World War I.

Jutland, battle of, only major engagement between the British and German fleets in World War I. On May 31, 1916, a German squadron under Admiral Hipper met a British squadron under Admiral Beatty, c.60 mi (100 km) west of the coast of Jutland. The German high seas fleet, under Admiral Scheer, approached later in the day, and Beatty turned north to join the main body of the British grand fleet under Admiral Jellicoe. Although outnumbered in the ensuing engagement, the Germans displayed brilliant naval tactics, and the encounter ended only when fog and darkness permitted their escape to their home base. The tactics employed by Jellicoe and the heavy losses of the British navy in the battle caused one of the great controversies of the war. The battle is known in Germany as the battle of the Skagerrak. See studies by H. H. Frost (1934, repr. 1970), Donald Macintyre (1958), and J. J. C. Irving (1966).

Juttah (jŭt'ə), city, S Palestine, the present-day Yattah (Jordan), S of Hebron. Joshua 15.55; 21.16.

Juvarra, Filippo (fēlēp'pō yōōvär'rä), 1678–1736, Italian architect of the late baroque and early rococo periods. Trained in the studio of Carlo Fontana in Rome, he entered (1714) the service of Victor Amadeus II of Savoy and was soon appointed first architect to the king. Juvarra acquired an unparalleled reputation throughout Europe. In 1719 he was in Portugal planning the palace at Mafra for King John V, after which he traveled to London and Paris. He died in Madrid, where he had gone (1735) to design a royal palace for Philip V. The main body of his work, however, is in Piedmont, where he planned many royal residences and churches. Among them are the Palazzo Madama, Turin; the castle at Stupinigi; and the churches of the Superga near Turin and of the Carmine, Turin. Drawing mainly from Italian and German Renaissance and baroque works, Juvarra integrated a variety of elements, achieving unity and grandeur of design. See R. Pommer, *Eighteenth Century Architecture in Piedmont* (1967).

Juvenal (Decimus Junius Juvenalis) (jo͞o'vənəl), fl. 1st to 2d cent. A.D., Roman satirical poet. His verse established a model for the satire of indignation, in contrast to the less harsh satire of ridicule of Horace. Little is known about his life except that during much of it he was desperately poor. A tradition tells that as a youth he was banished from court for satirizing an imperial favorite; later his work reveals a deep hatred for the Emperor Domitian. He is known chiefly for his 16 satires, which contain a vivid representation of life in Rome under the empire. They were probably written in the years between A.D. 100 and A.D. 128. The biting tone of his diatribes has seldom been equaled. From the stern point of view of the older Roman standards he powerfully denounces the lax and luxurious society, the brutal tyranny, the affectations and immorality of women, and the criminal excesses of Romans as he saw them, especially in his earlier years. The rhetorical form of his verse is finished, exact, and epigrammatic, furnishing many sayings that have become familiar through quotation. See translations by Rolfe Humphries (1958), G. G. Ramsay (rev ed. 1961), and Jerome Mazzaro (1965); studies by I. G. Scott (1927), Gilbert Highet (1955, repr. 1961), and W. S. Anderson (1964).

juvenile delinquency, legal term for behavior of children and adolescents that in adults would be judged criminal under law. In the United States definitions and age limits of juveniles vary, the maximum age being set at 14 years in some states and as high as 21 years in others. The 16- to 20-year age group, considered adult in many places, has one of the highest incidences of serious crime. A high proportion of adult criminals have a background of early delinquency. Theft is the most common offense by children; more serious property crimes and rape are most frequently committed in later youth. The causes of such behavior, like those of crime in general, are found in a complex of psychological, social, and economic factors. Clinical studies have uncovered emotional maladjustments, usually arising from disorganized family situations, in many delinquents. Other studies have indicated that there are persisting patterns of delinquency in poverty neighborhoods regardless of changing occupants; here the GANG, a source of much delinquency, is strong. Not until the development, after 1899, of the juvenile court was judgment of youthful offenders effectively separated from that of adults. The system emphasizes informal procedure and correction rather than punishment. In some states psychiatric clinics are attached, and there has been a tendency to handle cases in public welfare agencies outside the court. Juvenile correctional institutions have been separated from regular prisons since the early 19th cent. and although most are inadequate, some have developed intensive rehabilitation programs, providing vocational training and psychiatric treatment. The English BORSTAL SYSTEM for youth is notable. The parole system, foster homes, child guidance clinics, and public juvenile protective agencies have contributed to the correction of delinquent and maladjusted children. Especially important for prevention is action by community groups to provide essential facilities for the well-being of children. On an international level, delinquency rates are highest in the more economically and technologically advanced countries. See W. C. Kvaraceus, *Juvenile Delinquency* (1964); T. C. N. Gibbens, ed., *Cultural Factors in Delinquency* (1966); Travis Hirschi, *Causes of Delinquency* (1969); Sheldon and Eleanor Glueck, *Toward a Typology of Juvenile Offenders* (1970); Sol Rubin, *Crime and Juvenile Delinquency* (3d ed., 1970); LaMar Empey, *Explaining Delinquency* (1971); W. C. Reckless, *The Prevention of Delinquency* (1972).

juvenile literature: see CHILDREN'S LITERATURE.

Jylland: see JUTLAND, peninsula, Denmark.

Jyväskylä (yü'väskü"lä), city (1970 pop. 57,370), capital of Keski-Suomi prov., S central Finland. Situated on Lake Päijänne, it is an important port. Paper and wood products are made. There is an arts festival held in July. The city was chartered in 1837 and was the site (1858) of the first Finnish-language secondary school.

British ships during the battle of Jutland.

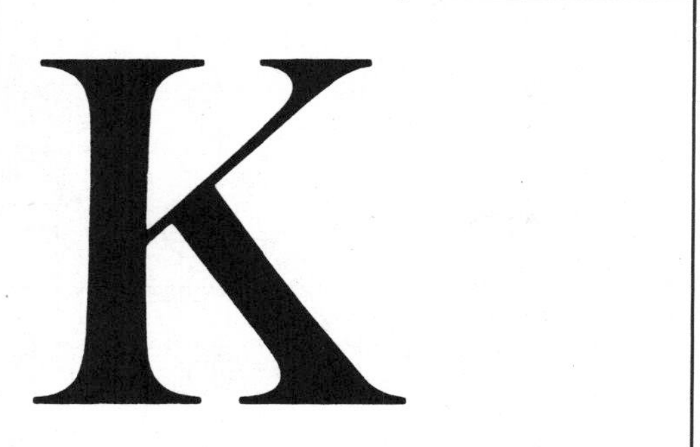

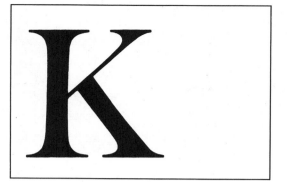

K, 11th letter of the ALPHABET. It is a usual symbol for a voiceless velar stop, as in the English *cook.* It corresponds to Greek kappa. In chemistry K is the symbol for the element POTASSIUM.

K2, peak, Kashmir: see GODWIN-AUSTEN, MOUNT.

Kaaba or **Caaba** (both: kä'bə, kä'əbə), in ISLAM, the most sacred sanctuary, the center of the Muslim world and the chief goal of pilgrimage. It is a small building in the Great Mosque of MECCA nearly cubic in shape, built to enclose the Black Stone, which is the most venerated Muslim object. The Kaaba was a pagan holy place before Muhammad, and many legends surround its origin. Around the Kaaba is a road along which pilgrims perform the *tawaf,* or sevenfold circuit of the sanctuary, an old pagan ritual. The Kaaba stone, worn hollow by centuries of ritual kissing, is held together by a wide silver band. Its custody is keenly sought after in the Islamic world; in the 5th cent. it passed to the KURAISH, in the 10th cent. the KARMATHIANS carried it away, and in 1932 an Afghan attempted to steal it. Nonbelievers are forbidden to approach it. The Kaaba is the place toward which Muslims face when praying.

Kabalevsky, Dmitri (dəmē'trē kä"bəlĕf'skē), 1904–, Soviet composer. Kabalevsky studied at the Scriabin Music School and the Moscow Conservatory, where he became a professor of composition. His music is melodic and harmonically conservative. His large output includes the opera *Colas Breugnon* (1938); *The Commedians* suite (1940); a Requiem (1963); concertos for piano, for violin, and for cello; orchestral and choral symphonies; and piano and chamber works. His music often reflects the influence of folk tradition.

Kabardino-Balkar Autonomous Soviet Socialist Republic (kăb"ərdē'nō-bălkâr'), autonomous republic (1970 pop. 589,000), c.4,800 sq mi (12,400 sq km), SE European USSR, in the northern part of the Caucasus mts. NALCHIK is the capital. The area is a largely unsettled, roadless mountain wilderness. The population—Kabardins, Balkars, Russians, and Ukrainians—is concentrated in the narrow gorges of the streams flowing into the Terek River. The Kabardins speak a Caucasian language and are Muslims (Sunnites); the Balkars speak a Turkic language. Livestock and poultry are raised, and wheat, corn, hemp, and fruit are grown. Much of the republic's industry is related to agricultural processing. Lumbering, metallurgy, and mining are also important. The Kabardins were known in the 9th cent. They occupied the land in the foothills of the central Caucasus between the 13th and 15th cent. It is not known when the Balkars settled. They were formed from the Black Bulgars, the Alans, and the Cumans. The Kabardin area became a Muscovite protectorate in 1557. Its annexation by Russia began with the treaty of Kuchuk Kainarji (1774) and was completed in 1827. The area was organized as an oblast in 1922 and became an autonomous republic in 1936. In 1943 the Balkars, accused of collaborating with the Germans, were deported, and their area, the upper Baksan valley, was ceded to the Georgian SSR. The area was then renamed Kabardinian Autonomous SSR. In 1956 the Balkars were returned, and in 1957 the area assumed its old name.

kabbalah: see CABALA.

Kabeiroi (käbē'rē, kəbī'rī), in ancient religion of the Middle East, nature deities of obscure origin, possibly Phoenician. They were connected with several fertility cults, particularly at Lemnos and at Samothrace, where important mysteries were celebrated. According to one legend they were also patrons of navigation. In Greek religion they were associated with Hephaestus, Hermes, and Demeter and were similar to the Corybantes, Curetes, and Dactyls, who were attendants to the Gods.

Kabir (kəbēr'), 1440–1518, Indian mystic and poet. A Muslim by birth, he was a weaver in Benares (Varanasi) and early in life became the disciple of the famous Hindu saint Ramananda. Kabir opposed caste practices, ritual, image-worship, and all forms of religious sectarianism; he taught the brotherhood of Hindu and Muslim under one God. Because of his anti-institutional ideas he was subject to persecution and banished from Benares c.1495. Thereafter he traveled from one N Indian city to another and died at Maghar near Gorakhpur. His songs in Hindi show the fusion of Muslim and Hindu devotional traditions. See *Poems of Kabir,* tr. by Rabindranath Tagore, 1972; I. A. Ezekiel, *Kabir, the Great Mystic* (1966).

Black-shrouded Kaaba in the Great Mosque of Mecca.

kabuki (käbo͞o'kē): see ORIENTAL DRAMA.

Kabul (kä'bo͝ol, kəbo͞ol'), city (1971 pop. 318,094), capital of Afghanistan and its largest city and economic and cultural center, E Afghanistan, on the Kabul River. It is strategically located in a high narrow valley, wedged between two mountain ranges that command the main approaches to the KHYBER PASS. A paved road links Kabul with the USSR border. The city's chief products are woolen and cotton cloth, beet sugar, ordnance, textiles, plastics, leather goods, furniture, glass, matches, soap, and machinery. Kabul's history dates back more than 3,000 years, although the city has been destroyed and rebuilt on several different sites. Conquered by Arabs in the 7th cent., it was overshadowed by Ghazni and Herat until Babur made it the capital (1504–26) of the Mogul empire. It remained under Mogul rule until its capture (1738) by Nadir Shah of Persia. It succeeded KANDAHAR as Afghanistan's capital in 1773. During the Afghan Wars a British army took (1839) Kabul. In 1842 the withdrawing British troops were ambushed and almost annihilated after the Afghans had promised them safe conduct; in retaliation another British force partly burned Kabul. The British again occupied the city in 1879, after their resident and his staff were massacred there. Kabul's old section, with its narrow, crooked streets, contains extensive bazaars; the modern section has administrative and commercial buildings. An educational center, Kabul has a university (est. 1931), numerous colleges, and a fine museum. Also in the city are Babur's tomb and gardens; the mausoleum of Nadir Shah; the Minar-i-Istiklal (column of independence), built in 1919 after the Third Afghan War; the tomb of Timur Shah (reigned 1773–93); and several important mosques. The fort of Bala Hissar, destroyed by the British in 1879 to avenge the death of their envoy in Kabul, is now a military college. The royal palace and an ancient citadel stand outside the present city.

Kabwe (käb'wā), formerly **Broken Hill,** city (1972 est. pop., with suburbs, 83,000), central Zambia. It is a lead and zinc mining center.

Kabyles (kəbīlz'), tribal people, predominantly agricultural, of North Africa, whose center is the rugged Kabylia region of Algeria. Of uncertain origin, they form one of the larger divisions of the BERBERS. Known for their fierce resistance to the successive conquerors of the region, they were slow to adopt the Muslim religion and Arabic speech and in Great Kabylia (the central and southern region of Algeria) they still retain their vernacular.

Kabzeel (kăb'zēĕl), unidentified city, extreme S Palestine. Joshua 15.21; 2 Sam. 23.20; 1 Chron. 11.22. Jekabzeel: Neh. 11.25.

kachina, spirit of the invisible life forces of the Pueblo Indians of North America. The kachinas, or kachinam, are impersonated by elaborately costumed masked male members of the tribes who visit Pueblo villages the first half of the year. In a variety of ceremonies, they dance, sing, bring gifts to the children, and sometimes administer public scoldings. Although not worshiped, kachinas are greatly revered, and one of their main purposes is to bring rain for the spring crops. The term *kachina* also applies to cottonwood dolls made by the Hopi and Zuni that are exquisitely carved and dressed like the dancers. Originally intended to instruct the children about the hundreds of kachina spirits, the finer carvings have become collector's items. The name is also spelled katchina.

Kachin State (kəchĭn'), state (1969 est. pop. 687,000), 33,903 sq mi (87,809 sq km), extreme N Burma. It is a mountainous region bounded on the NW by India and on the N and E by China and traversed by tributaries of the Irrawaddy River. MYITKYINA, the capital, and BHAMO are the chief towns. Rice and sugarcane are grown, jade and amber mined, and

Kabul, the capital and largest city of Afghanistan.

timber and bamboo cut. The state is sparsely populated; Jinghpaw-speaking Kachins constitute the largest group. They maintain the tribal forms of organization under chiefs, practice shifting cultivation, and are mostly animists. The territory was never subject to the Burman kings, and after the establishment of British rule it was governed by the British directly, not as part of Burma. Antigovernment insurgents have been active in Kachin State since Burma achieved independence in 1948.

Kádár, János (yä'nôsh kä'där), 1912–, Hungarian Communist leader. In 1932 he joined the then illegal Communist party and held high government and party posts from 1942, becoming home secretary in 1948, when the Communist party took control in Hungary. In 1951, Kádár was accused of pro-Titoism and imprisoned until 1954. After his release he quickly regained power, becoming a member of the party's central committee in July, 1956, and first secretary of the party (the Socialist Workers' party from Sept., 1956) in October. In the Hungarian revolution of 1956, Kádár at first aligned himself with the rebels and joined the cabinet of Imre NAGY. However, in November he formed a countergovernment with Soviet support, and Soviet troops crushed the revolt. In 1958 he tried and executed Nagy and other leaders of the revolt. Kádár resigned as premier in 1958 but resumed that post from 1961 to 1965. In 1962 he carried out a drastic purge of former Stalinists. In the early 1960s, Kádár permitted limited domestic liberalization but adopted a strong pro-Moscow policy during the 1968 Soviet invasion of Czechoslovakia. See his selected speeches and articles, *Socialist Construction in Hungary* (tr. 1962) and *On the Road to Socialism* (tr. 1965); William Shawcross, *Crime and Compromise* (1974).

Kadesh (kā'dĕsh), ancient city of Syria, on the Orontes River. There Ramses II fought (c.1300 B.C.) the Hittites in a great battle that ended in a truce.

Kadesh (kā'dĕsh) or **Kadesh-barnea** (-bärnē'ə), oasis in the desert S of Palestine, mentioned frequently in the Bible, notably as a limit of Edom. Another biblical name is En-mishpat. Gen. 14.7; 16.14; Num. 20; 32.8; Deut. 1.46; 2.14.

Kadmiel (kăd'mēĕl), family that returned with Zerubbabel. Ezra 2.40; 3.9; Neh. 7.43; 9.4,5; 10.9; 12.8,24.

Kadmonites (kăd'mənīts), unidentified tribe, whose land was promised to Abraham's descendants. Gen. 15.19.

Kadoma (kädō'mä), city (1970 pop. 141,041), Osaka prefecture, Honshu, Japan, on the Furu River. It is an industrial and residential suburb of Osaka, with mechanical and textile industries.

Kaduna (kä"do͞onä'), town (1969 est. pop. 174,000), N Nigeria. A leading commercial and industrial center of N Nigeria, Kaduna has cotton textile, beverage, and furniture factories. It is also a rail and road junction and the trade center for the surrounding agricultural area. Cotton, peanuts, sorghum, and ginger are shipped. The city was founded by the British in 1913 and became the capital of Nigeria's Northern Region in 1917. Training colleges for teachers, police, and the military and a technical institute are in Kaduna.

Kael, Pauline (kāl), 1919–, American motion picture critic, b. Petaluma, Calif. Possessed of an extensive knowledge of the technical aspects of movie-making, Kael is noted for her perceptive and tough-minded film criticism. She became movie critic for the *New Yorker* magazine in 1968. Her books, mostly collections of reviews, include *I Lost It at the Movies* (1965), *Kiss Kiss Bang Bang* (1968), *The Citizen Kane Book* (1971), and *Deeper into Movies* (1973).

Kaesong or **Kaisong** (both: kă'sŭng'), Jap. *Kaijo,* city (1966 est. pop. 265,000), S North Korea. A longtime commercial center, it is important chiefly for its exports of ginseng, a valuable medicinal root. There is also active trade in rice, barley, and wheat. Fine porcelain is made in the city, and there is some heavy industry. In the 10th cent. Wang, founder of the Koryo dynasty, made Kaesong his capital; the city, then called Songdo, remained Korea's capital until 1392, when the Yi dynasty moved the capital to Seoul. Intersected by the 38th parallel, Kaesong served as the main contact point between North and South Korea from 1945 to 1951 and passed from United Nations to North Korean forces several times during the Korean War. The armistice talks, first held at Kaesong, were later transferred to PANMUNJOM. Historic landmarks include the tombs of several Korean kings, the old city walls, and the remains of a royal palace from the Koryo period.

Kaffa: see FEODOSIYA, USSR.

kaffir or **kaffir corn:** see SORGHUM.

Kaffraria (kəfrăr'ēə), former name for a region in the Transkei, E South Africa. Founded in 1848 as the dependency of British Kaffraria, it was added to Cape Colony in 1865.

Kafiristan, Afghanistan: see NURISTAN.

Kafirs or **Kaffirs** (both: kăf'ərz) [Arabic,=infidel], name applied by European settlers to the Xhosa branch of the Bantu-speaking people of S Africa. Originally used only for the inhabitants of the Transkeian Territories (then called Kaffraria), the name came to be commonly employed as a derogatory term for all Negro Africans. The South African government encourages use of the term *Bantu* rather than Kafir or native.

Kafka, Franz (fränts käf'kä), 1883–1924, German novelist and short-story writer, b. Prague, Czechoslovakia. Of a middle-class Jewish family, he studied law and then obtained a position in the workmen's-compensation division of the Austrian government. His slow and conscientious methods made it impractical for him to gain a living by writing, and most of his works were published posthumously, including his symbolic novels *Der Prozess* (1925, tr. *The Trial,* 1937), *Das Schloss* (1926, tr. *The Castle,* 1930), and *Amerika* (1927, tr. 1938). In prose that is remarkable for its clarity and precision, Kafka presents a world which is at once real and dreamlike and in which modern man, burdened with guilt, isolation, and anxiety, makes a futile search for personal salvation. Important stories appearing during his lifetime were "Das Urteil" (1913, tr. "The Judgment," 1945), *Die Verwandlung* (1915, tr. *The Metamorphosis,* 1937), "Ein Landarzt" (1919, tr. "A Country Doctor," 1945), *In der Strafkolonie* (1920, tr. "In the Penal Colony," 1941), and "Ein Hungerkünstler" (1922, tr. "A Hunger Artist," 1938). See his diaries ed. by M. Brod (tr. 1948–49); his letters to Felice Bauer, ed. by Erich Heller and Jürgen Born (tr. 1973); biographies by Max Brod (new ed. 1964) and Gustav Janouch (rev. ed. 1971); studies by W. H. Sokel (1966), R. M. Albérès (1968),Wilhelm Emrich (1968), Martin Greenburg (1968), Anthony Thorlby (1972), and R. D. Gray (1973).

Kafue (käfo͞o'ā), river, c.600 mi (970 km) long, rising along the Zambia-Zaïre border, S central Africa, near Lubumbashi, and meandering through central

Zambia to the Zambezi River. It provides water to Zambia's copperbelt. The lower Kafue valley is fertile. The river has a good hydroelectricity-generating potential, especially at Kafue Gorge.

Kafue National Park, c.8,650 sq mi (22,400 sq km), S central Zambia, S Africa; est. 1950. It is a haven for the animal and bird life of a diverse region that includes desert, grasslands, forests, and marshes.

Kaga (kä'gä), city (1970 pop. 56,514), Ishikawa prefecture, W Honshu, Japan. It is an agricultural market, hot spring resort, and industrial center with mechanical and textile industries.

Kagawa (kägä'wä), prefecture (1970 pop. 907,897), N Shikoku, Japan. TAKAMATSU is the capital. It is an agricultural region (rice, barley) with a mountainous and forested interior. The coast has fishing ports and salt-producing centers.

Kagera (kägā'rə), river, c.250 mi (400 km) long, formed on the Rwanda-Tanzania border, E central Africa, by the confluence of the Nyaburongo and Ruvubu rivers. The Kagera's headwaters, which rise in the highlands of Rwanda and Burundi, are the remotest sources of the Nile. The Kagera flows north and east, forming part of Tanzania's borders with Rwanda and Uganda, before emptying into Victoria Nyanza. There is a small hydroelectric plant at Kikagati, Uganda.

Kagoshima (kä"gō'shĭmä), city (1970 pop. 403,309), capital of Kagoshima prefecture, extreme S Kyushu, Japan, on Satsuma Peninsula and Kagoshima Bay. An important port, it has a navy yard. The city's industries produce Satsuma porcelain ware, silk and cotton clothing, tinware, and wood products. Kagoshima is the site (since 1961) of a major Japanese rocket base. It is the seat of two universities and is historically important as the castle town of the Shimazu family and as the birthplace of Takamori Saigo, Toshimichi Okubo, and Heihachiro Togo. The center of the Satsuma Rebellion, the city was destroyed in 1877. In 1914 it suffered damage from the eruption of a volcano on Sakurajima, an island in the bay, and it was bombed (1945) in World War II. It was at Kagoshima that St. Francis Xavier landed in 1549. Kagoshima prefecture (1970 pop. 1,729,010), 3,515 sq mi (9,104 sq km), is largely mountainous, with gold, silver, iron, and copper mines. There is some subtropical vegetation.

kagu (kä'gōō), common name for a long-legged, heronlike bird, *Rhynochetos jubatus.* It has a loose, gray plumage with darker bandings; broad, rounded wings marked with white, black, and red; and a striking orange-red bill and feet. About the size of domestic fowl, the kagu has a large head endowed with a long erectile topcrest. Once abundant on the islands of the Coral Sea, the shy, nocturnal kagu is now close to extinction, and may only be found in the remotest mountains of New Caledonia in the South Pacific. Like the dodo, the kagu suffered greatly from the ravages of domestic animals, especially pigs and dogs. A forest-floor dweller, it lives on a diet of insects and snails. It is practically flightless, but is a rapid runner with a curious manner of progress; it moves in short spurts, then stands motionless before moving on again. Its courtship behavior consists of a wild, skipping dance. The female lays a single, pale brown, rust-streaked egg, depositing it in a ground nest of leaves and twigs. Both sexes share in the incubation. Kagus are classified in the phylum CHORDATA, subphylum Vertebrata, class Aves, order Gruiformes, family Rhynochetidae.

Kahn, Albert (kän), 1869–1942, American architect, designer of factories, b. Germany. He organized a large office in Detroit that applied the techniques of mass production to architecture, and he designed a great number of factories, war plants, and naval bases. Kahn was a pioneer in the use of reinforced concrete and steel. From 1928 to 1932 he was in

Kagu, a heronlike bird of New Caledonia.

Richards Medical Research Laboratories at the Univ. of Pennsylvania in Philadelphia, designed by the American architect Louis Kahn.

charge of the industrial building program in the USSR. See George Nelson, *Industrial Architecture of Albert Kahn, Inc.* (1939).

Kahn, Julius, 1861–1924, American legislator, b. Germany. He arrived (1866) in California as a child. He studied law in San Francisco, was elected (1892) to the state legislature, and was admitted (1894) to the bar. Kahn served (1899–1903, 1905–24) in the U.S. House of Representatives and became noted chiefly as an advocate of military preparedness. He helped draft and secure the passage of the National Defense Act of 1915, the Selective Draft Act of 1917, and the National Defense Act of 1920. His wife, **Florence Prag Kahn,** 1868–1948, succeeded him in Congress and served until 1937.

Kahn, Louis Isadore, 1901–74, American architect, b. Estonia. From the 1920s through World War II, Kahn worked on numerous housing projects including Carver Court (1944), in Coatesville, Pa. He also planned the Yale Univ. Art Gallery and the American Federation of Labor Medical Building, Philadelphia. Kahn was widely acclaimed for his design of the Richards Medical Research Laboratories at the Univ. of Pennsylvania (1958–60). In this work he arrived at a new and dynamic integration of formal and functional elements, ingeniously relating mechanical services to the total architecture. His notable later designs include the Olivetti-Underwood Corp. factory (1969) at Harrisburg, Pa., and the Kimbell Art Museum, Fort Worth, Texas. He exerted a wide influence as professor at the Univ. of Pennsylvania and at Yale. See his notebooks and drawings, ed. by R. S. Wurman and Eugene Feldman (1962); study by Vincent Scully, Jr. (1962).

Kahn, Otto Hermann, 1867–1934, American banker and patron of the arts, born and educated in Germany. He emigrated to the United States in 1893 and in 1897 joined the banking firm of Kuhn, Loeb & Company in New York City. He was closely associated with E. H. Harriman in the reorganization of the Union Pacific and other railroads and had a part in numerous international finance organizations. Among the many theatrical and musical groups he helped underwrite were the Russian ballet and the Paris Conservatory orchestra in their American appearances. From 1903 he was active on the board of the Metropolitan Opera Company; in 1908 he brought, from Milan, Giulio Gatti-Casazza as director and Arturo Toscanini as principal conductor, launching the company on one of its most successful periods. A collection of his writings and speeches was published as *Of Many Things* (1926). See biography by M. J. Matz (1963).

Kahoolawe (kähō'ōlä'vä, –wä, kähō'lä'–), uninhabited island, 45 sq mi (117 sq km), central Hawaii; separated from Maui island to the NE by Alalakeiki Channel. The island, low and unfertile, has served as a prison and as a military target range.

Kaieteur Falls (kīətōōr'), waterfall, 741 ft (226 m) high, in the Potaro River, W Guyana. It plunges over an escarpment of the Guiana Highlands. One of the most impressive falls in South America, it is included in a national park.

K'ai-feng or **Kaifeng** (both: kī-fŭng), city (1970 est. pop. 330,000), NE Honan prov., China, on the Lunghai RR. It is a commercial, agricultural, and industrial center. Manufactures include agricultural machinery, motor vehicles, electrical and electronic equipment, fertilizer, chemicals, and processed foods. The Huang Ho (Yellow River), just to the north, has frequently flooded the city. K'ai-feng has often been a major center of Chinese political and cultural life. Founded in the 3d cent. B.C., it was, as Pienliang, capital of the Five Dynasties (906–59) and then capital of the northern Sung dynasty (960–1127). Zoroastrians worshipped there, and in the 12th cent. a Jewish colony was established. The city fell to the Mongols in the 13th cent. K'ai-feng was the provincial capital until superseded (1954) by Cheng-chou.

Kaigetsudo (kīgĕt'sōōdō), school of Japanese artists painting in the ukiyo-e style (see JAPANESE ART). Kaigetsudo was founded by Kaigetsudo Ando in the early 18th cent. Characterized by broad lines, majestic poses, restrained color, and boldly designed costumes, Kaigetsudo paintings depicted the life of courtesans. These works reflect the rise of the mercantile classes and their enthusiasms. Principally painters, the Kaigetsudo artists are better known in the West for their prints, which had a wider distribution.

Kai Islands or **Kei Islands** (both: kī), island group (c.550 sq mi/ 1,420 sq km), E Indonesia, SE of Ceram, in the Banda Sea, in the Moluccas. It is densely forested with valuable timber; the people are skilled boat builders. The chief island is Great Kai. The group is sometimes called the Key Islands.

kail: see KALE.

Kailas (kīläs'), peak, c.22,280 ft (6,790 m) high, SW Tibet (China), highest point of the Kailas Range, in the Himalayas. It is near the sources of the Sutlej, Indus, and Brahmaputra rivers. The dwelling place of the Hindu god Shiva, Kailas is the goal of pilgrimages. The pilgrim road that girdles the mountain reaches 18,000 ft (5,486 m).

Kailasa, India: see ELLORA.

Kailua (käēlo͞o'ə), uninc. city (1970 pop. 33,783), Honolulu co., Hawaii, on the southeastern coast of Oahu, on Kailua Bay. An agricultural experiment station is in Kailua, and a U.S. marine corps air station is nearby.

Kain (kān): see KENITES.

Kainan (kīnäN'), city (1970 pop. 53,370), Wakayama prefecture, S Honshu, Japan, on the Kii Sound. It is a port, railway junction, and industrial center with spinning, textile, and print-dyeing industries.

Kairouan: see AL QAYRAWAN, Tunisia.

Kaisaria, Turkey: see KAYSERI.

Kaiser, Georg (gā'ôrkh kī'zər), 1878–1945, German expressionist playwright. His early plays dealt with the erotic and the psychological. In maturity Kaiser turned to social themes, glorifying the ideal of sacrifice for the mass interest and attacking the brutality of the machine age. Among his many dramas are *The Citizens of Calais* (1914, tr. 1946), *From Morn to Midnight* (1916, tr. 1920), and the trilogy *The Corals* (1917, tr. 1929), *Gas* (1918, tr. 1924), and *Gas II* (1920). See studies by B. J. Kenworthy (1957) and Ernst Schürer (1972).

Kaiser, Henry John, 1882–1967, American industrialist, b. Sprout Brook, N.Y. He organized his first construction company in 1913, soon entered the road-paving business, and by 1930 was a leader in the field. In 1931 he was named chairman of the executive committee of the company formed to build Hoover Dam. He also participated in the construction of Bonneville, Grand Coulee, and Shasta dams and the San Francisco–Oakland Bridge. During World War II he and his corporations made exceptional contributions to the war effort, producing ships, planes, and military vehicles in vast numbers. From 1945 until his death he served as chairman of Kaiser Industries, an enterprise involving steel, aluminum, and home building. His effort to become an automobile manufacturer after World War II was not successful.

Kaiserslautern (kī"zərslou'tərn), city (1970 pop. 99,617), Rhineland-Palatinate, W West Germany, on the Lauter River. It is a commercial, industrial, and cultural center. There are ironworks, textile mills, and sewing-machine, furniture, and automobile factories. Charlemagne built a castle in Kaiserslautern that was later enlarged (1153–58) by Emperor Frederick I (Barbarossa); some ruins of the castle remain today. The city was repeatedly devastated by warring armies, notably by the Spanish (1635) in the Thirty Years War. During the French Revolutionary Wars the Prussians defeated (1793) the French there. Kaiserslautern has a noted early Gothic collegiate church (13th–14th cent.) and an art gallery. It is the seat of part of the Univ. of Trier and Kaiserslautern (founded 1970).

Kaiser Wilhelm Canal: see KIEL CANAL.

Kaiser-Wilhelmsland: see PAPUA NEW GUINEA.

Kaizuka (kīzo͞o'kä), city (1970 pop. 73,265), Osaka prefecture, S Honshu, Japan, on Osaka Bay. It is a commercial port and industrial center where textiles and flour are produced.

Kajaani (kä'yänē), Swed. *Kajana,* city (1970 pop. 19,677), Oulu prov., central Finland, on the Kajaaninjoki River. Forest products (including paper goods and cellulose) and sports equipment are manufactured. The city is also a road, rail, and water transportation center. Kajaani was chartered in 1651. The Kajaneborg fortress, around which the city grew, was taken by the Russians in 1716. Restored in 1937, the fortress is today a tourist attraction.

Kakamigahara (käkä"mēgähä'rä), city (1970 pop. 78,107), Gifu prefecture, central Honshu, Japan. It is an agricultural and commercial center.

Kakhetia (kəkhĕt'yēə), historic region, SE European USSR, in Georgia. TELAVI is the chief town. Kakhetia was an independent kingdom from the 8th cent. until 1010, when it became part of Georgia. Again independent between 1468 and 1762, it then became part of the East Georgian kingdom that was joined with Russia in 1801.

Kakinada (kəkĭnä'də) or **Cocanada** (kōkənä'də), town (1971 pop. 164,172), Andhra Pradesh state, SE India, on the Godavari River delta. Formerly an important port on the Bay of Bengal, it is now a district administrative center and a market for sugarcane, oilseed, cotton, rice, jute, and iron ore.

Kakogawa (käkō'gäwä), city (1970 pop. 127,112), Hyogo prefecture, S Honshu, Japan, on the Kako River. It is an industrial center where woolen and rubber goods and chemical fertilizers are produced.

Kalahari (kä"lähä'rē), arid plateau region, c.100,000 sq mi (259,000 sq km), in Botswana, South West Africa, and the Republic of South Africa. The Kalahari, covered largely by reddish sand, lies between the Orange and Zambezi rivers and is studded with dry lake beds. Yearly rainfall varies from 5 in. (12.7 cm) in the southwest, where there are active sand dunes, to 20 in. (50.8 cm) in the northeast. Grass grows throughout the Kalahari in the rainy season, and some parts also support low thorn scrub and forest. Grazing and a little agriculture are possible in certain areas. Many game animals live in the Kalahari. Its human inhabitants are mainly SAN, who are nomadic hunters, and KHOIKHOI, who are hunters and farmers.

Kalahari Gemsbok National Park, c.8,030 sq mi (20,800 sq km), SW Botswana and N Cape Prov., Republic of South Africa, S Africa; est. 1931. One of Africa's largest game reserves, it is a sanctuary for the animals and birds of the Kalahari desert.

Kalakh: see CALAH.

Kalámai (kälä'mā) or **Kalamata** (käləmä'tə, kăl–), city (1971 pop. 39,133), capital of Messinia prefecture, S Greece, in the Peloponnesus; a port on the Gulf of Messinia. It is an agricultural trade center and ships olive oil and fruits. Silk and flour are manufactured. The city developed after c.1205, when it became a fief of the Villehardouin family. It later came under the rule of Venice and (1459–1821) the Ottoman Turks. It was destroyed (1825) by Ibrahim Pasha during the Greek War of Independence.

Kalamata, Greece: see KALÁMAI.

Kalamazoo (kăl″əməzo͞o′), city (1970 pop. 85,555), seat of Kalamazoo co., SW Mich., on the Kalamazoo River at its confluence with Portage Creek; inc. 1838. It is an industrial and commercial center in a fertile farm area that produces celery, peppermint, and fruit. Kalamazoo has a large paper industry, as well as many other industries. The city is the seat of Western Michigan Univ., Kalamazoo College, a junior college, and a state mental hospital. It has a natural history museum, an art institute, and a symphony orchestra.

kalang: see FRUIT BAT.

Kalanianole, Honah Kuhio, 1871–1922, delegate to U.S. Congress from the Territory of Hawaii. He was educated in Hawaii, the United States, and England and held minor posts in the Hawaiian monarchy before it was overthrown in 1893; he served as a delegate to the U.S. Congress from 1902 until his death. His great achievement was gaining the adoption of the Hawaiian Homes Commission Act, which preserved land for the native Hawaiians.

Kalávrita (kəlä′vrĭtə), ancient *Cynaetha,* town (1971 pop. 1,948), central Greece, in the Peloponnesus. It is chiefly a summer resort. At the nearby monastery of Hagia Laura (founded 961) the Greeks first rallied (1821) in the War of Independence. The monastery of Megaspelaion, said to date from the 4th cent., is in a vaulted cave just northeast of the town.

Kalb, Johann (Ger. yō′hän kälp), 1721–80, American general in the Revolution, known generally as Baron de Kalb, b. Hüttendorf, Germany. He assumed his title for military reasons and as Jean de Kalb served France in the War of the Austrian Succession and the Seven Years War. He again served France in 1768 as a secret agent in the English colonies in America. Silas DEANE offered (1776) commissions to Kalb, Lafayette, and other European soldiers of fortune, which the Continental Congress at first refused to honor. Finally Kalb was made general and was with Washington at Valley Forge. In 1780 he was made second in command to Horatio Gates in the CAROLINA CAMPAIGN, and he died (Aug. 19, 1780) from wounds received in the battle of Camden.

Kalckreuth, Leopold Karl Walter, Graf von (lā′ōpôlt kärl väl′tər gräf fən kälk′roit), 1855–1928, German painter and graphic artist. He taught at the Weimar and Karlsruhe academies and directed the Stuttgart Academy (1900–1905). Although noted for his somber early paintings of peasant women, he later abandoned naturalism for symbolist art.

kale, borecole (bôr′kōl), and **collards,** common names for nonheading, hardy types of CABBAGE (var. *acephala* and sometimes others), with thick stems and curly leaves, belonging to the family Cruciferae (MUSTARD family). They are grown for greens and, in Europe, for fodder. In the Channel Islands a tall fodder variety, known as Jersey kale, Jersey cabbage, or cow cabbage, grows to more than 7 ft (2.1 m). Kale (or kail) is a cool-weather crop—frost improves the flavor. In the United States the principal commercial growing regions are in Virginia and on Long Island. Kale is closest in form to the wild cabbage. In Scotland the word *kale* is used for cabbages of any kind. Sea kale is a European herb of the genus *Crambe* (also of the mustard family), found along the northern coasts and often used as a potherb. Kale, borecale, and collards are all classified in the division MAGNOLIOPHYTA, class Magnoliopsida, order Capparales, family Cruciferae.

kaleidoscope (kəlī′dəskōp), device consisting of a tube through which changing symmetrical patterns can be viewed. At one end of the tube is an eyepiece; at the other end colored chips of glass are loosely sandwiched between two glass disks. Between the ends of the tube are two rectangular plane mirrors. The long edge of one of the two mirrors lies against the long edge of the other at an angle, their intersection lying close to the axis of the tube. The glass chips form patterns where they lie, and these patterns change as the chips fall into new positions when the tube rotates. Each pattern undergoes multiple reflections in the mirrors in such a way as to produce a resulting symmetrical pattern that can be seen through the eyepiece. Invention of the device is credited to the Scottish physicist Sir David Brewster.

Kalemi (kälā′mē), formerly **Albertville** (älbĕrvēl′), city (1967 est. pop. 87,000), Shaba region, SE Zaïre, on Lake Tanganyika at the mouth of the Lukuga River. It is a commercial center and a rail-steamer transfer point, handling goods moving between Zaïre and Tanzania. Manufactures include textiles and cement. The city was founded in 1892 by Belgians as a military post in their campaign against Arab traders.

Kalends: see CALENDAR.

Kalevala (kä′lĕvä″lä), Finnish national epic. It is a compilation of folk verses, dealing mainly with the extraordinary deeds of three semidivine brothers whose abode was in mythical Kaleva, land of the heroes. The epic was once thought to date from the first millennium B.C. and to reveal primitive Finnish life, but it is now thought that parts were created in the Middle Ages and perhaps later. Although known to scholars as early as 1733, the verses were largely ignored until the 19th cent., when, under the impetus of the romantic movement, they were collected by two Finnish physicians, Zakarias Topelius, who published the first fragments in 1822, and Elias LÖNNROT, who gave the cycle its present form. From the miscellaneous episodes chanted to him by the rune singers Lönnrot created a poetic whole, editing the material and sometimes writing transitional verses himself. A collection of 25 runes (about 12,000 lines) was published in 1835; a second edition containing 50 runes (nearly 23,000 lines) was published in 1849. The epic is rich in mythology, magic, enigma, and folklore; its expeditions are reminiscent of the *Odyssey,* with underlying themes of love, egoism, and the struggles of spirit against matter and man against nature. Its effect on Finnish art in all its branches has been great. The eight-syllable trochaic line of the *Kalevala* was imitated by Longfellow in *Hiawatha.* See tr. by W. F. Kirby (1907, new ed. 1956) and F. P. Magoun (1963).

Kalgan: see CHANG-CHIA-KOU, China.

Kalgoorlie (kălgo͞or′lē), town (1971 pop. 9,170), Western Australia, SW Australia. It is the chief mining town of the state and the center of the East Coolgardie Goldfield. Gold was found at nearby Coolgardie in 1892; nickel is also mined. The Western Australia School of Mines (1902) was transferred (1903) from Coolgardie to Kalgoorlie.

Kali (kä′lē) [Hindi, = the Black One], important goddess in popular Hinduism and TANTRA. Known also as Durga [the Inaccessible] and as Chandi [the Fierce], Kali is associated with disease, death, and destruction. As Parvati she is the consort of SHIVA.

Arid plateau region of the Kalahari in South Africa.

Although often represented as a terrifying figure, garlanded with skulls and bearing a bloody sword in one of her many arms, she is worshiped lovingly by many as the Divine Mother. Her cult, popular among many lower castes in India, especially in Bengal, frequently includes animal sacrifice. Kali was patroness of the THUGS.

Kalidasa (kä″lĭdä′sə), fl. 5th cent.?, Indian dramatist and poet. He is regarded as the greatest figure in classical Sanskrit literature. Except that he was retained by the Gupta court, no facts concerning his life are known. His three surviving plays are *Sakuntala* (or *Shakuntala*), *Vikramorvasi,* and *Malavikagnimitra*. These court dramas in verse (*nataka*) relate fanciful or mythological tales of profound romantic love intensified and matured by adversity. *Sakuntala,* which is generally considered his masterpiece, tells of a maiden, Sakuntala, whom King Dushyanta marries. The king is bewitched so that he forgets his bride until a ring he gave her is discovered in the body of a fish. In Kalidasa's two epics, *Raghuvansa* and *Kumarasambhava,* delicate descriptions of nature are mingled with battle scenes. The other poems of Kalidasa are shorter and almost purely lyrical. *Meghaduta* [cloud messenger] is a description of the regions of India crossed by a cloud traveling between a tree spirit and his wife. *Ritusamhara* describes the course of pastoral love through the six seasons into which Indians divided the year. See A. W. Ryder, *Shakuntala and Other Writings by Kalidasa* (1959); studies by M. B. Harris (1936) and K. Krishnamoorthy (1972).

Kalimantan: see BORNEO.

Kálimnos (kä′lēmnôs), mountainous island (1971 pop. 13,281), 41 sq mi (106 sq km), SE Greece, one of the DODECANESE, 11 mi (18 km) off the coast of Asia Minor. A sponge-fishing center, it also produces figs, olives, citrus fruits, and almonds. The main town is Kálimnos, on the southeastern shore of the island.

Kalinin, Mikhail Ivanovich (mēkhəyēl′ ēvä′nəvĭch kəlyē′nyĭn), 1875–1946, Russian revolutionary. Of the working class, he was active in revolutionary affairs from his youth. He became the first chairman of the central executive committee of the USSR (now chairman of the presidium), or titular head of state (1919–46), and was a member (1925–46) of the politburo.

Kalinin, formerly **Tver,** city (1970 pop. 345,000), capital of Kalinin oblast, central European USSR, at the confluence of the Volga and Tver rivers. A major port on the upper Volga as well as an industrial center, it has industries producing linen textiles, heavy machinery, and rolling stock. The city grew around a fort established in the late 12th cent. It was early an important trade center, and from the mid-13th cent. until the late 14th cent. it was the seat of a powerful principality that rivaled Moscow. It was subjugated (1475–85) by Ivan III, grand duke of Moscow. Tver was renamed (1931) for M. I. Kalinin. There are a cathedral and castle, both from the 17th cent., in Kalinin.

Kaliningrad (kəlyē″nyĭn-grät′), formerly **Königsberg,** city (1970 pop. 297,000), capital of Kaliningrad oblast, W European USSR, on the Pregolya River near its mouth on the Vislinski Zalev, which empties into the Gulf of Kaliningrad on the Baltic Sea. A major ice-free Baltic seaport and naval base, and an important industrial and commercial center, Kaliningrad has industries that produce ships, machinery, food products, metals, automobile parts, and textiles. The city has an institute of oceanography and botanical and zoological gardens. The city was founded (1255) as a fortress of the Teutonic Knights by King Ottocar II of Bohemia, for whom it is supposedly named. It joined (1340) the Hanseatic League and became (1457) the seat of the grand master of the Teutonic Order after the knights lost Marienburg to Poland. It was the residence of the dukes of Prussia from 1525 until the union (1618) of Prussia and Brandenburg and became (1701) the coronation city of the kings of Prussia. The Univ. of Königsberg (founded 1544) reached its greatest fame when Kant (who was born and lived his entire life at Königsberg) taught there. The university building, the old castle, the 14th-century cathedral, and most of the old city were severely damaged by Soviet troops in World War II. As part of the northern section of East Prussia, the city was transferred to the USSR in 1945. The new Soviet city (named Kaliningrad for Mikhail Kalinin in 1946) was laid out after 1945 in the former residential suburbs of Königsberg; its population is almost entirely Russian.

Kalisch, Isidor (ēzēdôr' kä'lĭsh, kä'-), 1816–86, Jewish rabbi and author, b. Prussia. Forced to leave Germany because of his liberal political views, he emigrated to the United States in 1849 and served as rabbi in various American cities. He is chiefly known for his place in the polemical controversy of the day over Reform Judaism, of which he was a leader. He wrote several books on Judaism.

Kalisch: see KALISZ, Poland.

Kalispel Indians: see PEND D'OREILLE INDIANS.

Kalispell (kăl'ĭspĕl'', -pĕl'), city (1970 pop. 10,526), seat of Flathead co., NW Mont., at the head of Flathead Lake near Glacier National Park; inc. 1892. It is the tourist and trade center of a rich agricultural, fruit, and timber region. The headquarters of the Flathead National Forest are in Kalispell. Hungry Horse Dam and a state park are nearby. A junior college is in the city.

Kalisz (kä'lēsh), Ger. *Kalisch,* city (1970 pop. 81,227), central Poland. An industrial center, it has industries producing textiles, machinery, metals, and chemicals. One of the oldest Polish towns, it has been identified as the Slavic settlement of Calissia mentioned in the 2d cent. A.D. by Ptolemy. It flourished as a trade center from the 13th cent. At Kalisz Casimir III signed (1343) the treaty with the Teutonic Knights by which he conceded his rule over East Pomerania. The city passed to Prussia in 1793, was transferred to Russia in 1815, and was restored to Poland in 1919. In a treaty signed (1813) at Kalisz, Prussia and Russia formed an alliance against Napoleon I.

kalium, Latin name for POTASSIUM.

Kalkbrenner, Friedrich Wilhelm Michael (frē'drĭkh vĭl'hĕlm mĭkh'äĕl kälk'brĕnər), 1785–1849, German-French pianist and composer, son of the composer Christian Kalkbrenner (1755–1806). Kalkbrenner studied with his father and in 1798 enrolled in the Paris Conservatory. He was highly influential as a piano teacher, particularly in octave, left-hand, and pedal technique. His many compositions for the piano include four concertos.

Kallai (kəlā'ī), priest of Joiakim. Neh. 12.20.

Kallio, Kyösti (kü'östē käl'lyô), 1873–1940, Finnish political leader. Of peasant background, he entered politics and was a vocal advocate of Finnish independence from Russia. Minister of agriculture in the newly independent government (1917–20, 1921–22), he was instrumental in inaugurating land redistribution. He served a number of times as prime minister (1922–24, 1925–26, 1929–30, and 1936–37) and was president of Finland from 1937 to Nov., 1940. Illness and strain brought on by the Finnish-Russian War of 1939–40 led to his resignation.

Kalmar (käl'mär), city (1970 pop. 34,680), capital of Kalmar co., SE Sweden, on the Kalmarsund (an arm of the Baltic Sea) opposite Öland Island. It is a commercial, industrial, and tourist center and is connected by ferry with Öland. Manufactures include matches, glass, processed food, and ships. It has been an important trade center since the 8th cent. The KALMAR UNION was negotiated there in 1397. Kalmar has a 12th-century castle, the Kalmarnahus, which withstood numerous sieges in the Danish-Swedish wars of the 16th-17th cent. The name is also spelled Calmar.

Kalmar Union, combination of the three crowns of Denmark, Sweden, and Norway, effected at Kalmar, Sweden, by Queen MARGARET I in 1397. Because the kingship was elective in all three countries, the union could not be maintained by inheritance. Nationalist forces used the election procedure to modify terms of the union. Margaret's successors controlled Sweden only for brief periods; the accession (1523) of GUSTAVUS I as king of Sweden dissolved the union. The union of Denmark and Norway lasted, however, until 1814.

Kalmyk Autonomous Soviet Socialist Republic (kăl'mĭk), autonomous republic (1970 pop. 268,000), c.29,400 sq mi (76,150 sq km), SE European USSR, on the Caspian Sea. Elista is the capital. Lying mostly in the vast depression of the N Caspian lowland, the republic is largely a steppe and desert area. There are salt lakes but no permanent waterways. Stock raising (horses, cattle, sheep, goats, and some pigs and camels) is by far the leading economic activity, and fishing is important. Irrigation has made limited agriculture possible; winter wheat, maize, and fodder crops are grown. Industry revolves primarily around the processing of agricultural products, fish, and minerals. The population is primarily Russian and Kalmyk. A seminomadic branch of the Oirat Mongols, the Kalmyks migrated from Chinese Turkistan to the steppe W of the Volga's mouth in the mid-17th cent. They became allies of the Russians and were charged by Peter I with guarding the eastern frontier of the Russian Empire. Under Catherine II, however, the Kalmyks became vassals. In 1771 about 300,000 Kalmyks E of the Volga set out to return to China but were decimated en route by Russian, Kazakh, and Kirghiz attacks. The Kalmyks W of the Volga remained in Russia, where they retained their Lamaist Buddhist religion and their seminomadic life. The word *Kalmyk* in Turkish means "remnant," referring to those who stayed behind. The Kalmyk Autonomous Oblast was established in 1920; it became an autonomous republic in 1936. During World War II, Kalmyk units fought the Russians in collaboration with the Germans. As a result, the Kalmyks were deported to Siberia in 1943, and their republic was dissolved. In 1956, Nikita Khrushchev denounced the deportation as a Stalinist crime, and the following year about 6,000 Kalmyks were returned. The Kalmyk Autonomous SSR was officially reestablished in 1958.

Kalocsa (kŏ'lôchŏ), town (1970 pop. 16,004), S Hungary, near the Danube River. It is an agricultural center and is famed for its embroidery. Created a bishopric by St. Stephen, it became the seat of an archbishop in 1260. The town has a Roman Catholic academy, a cathedral, and an archiepiscopal palace (built in 1786).

Kaluga (kəlo͞o'gə), city (1970 pop. 211,000), capital of Kaluga oblast, central European USSR, on the Oka River. It is a river port and an industrial center producing machinery, electrical equipment, and textiles. Known since 1389 as a Muscovite outpost, Kaluga was the scene of the murder (1610) of the second false DMITRI.

Kalundborg (kä'lo͞onbôr), city (1970 com. pop. 19,216), Vestsjaelland co., central Denmark, a port on the Kalundborg Fjord, an arm of the Store Baelt. It is a commercial, industrial, and communications center. Manufactures include chemicals and machinery. Founded c.1170, the city has a 12th-century church laid out in the form of a Greek cross. The novelist Sigrid Undset (1882–1949) was born in Kalundborg.

kalunite: see ALUM.

Kama (kä'mə), river, c.1,260 mi (2,030 km) long, E European USSR, the chief left tributary of the Volga. It rises in the foothills of the central Urals and flows N, then E, and then SW past Perm, Sarapul, and Chistopol to join the Volga below Kazan. The Vyatka is its principal tributary. The Kama is an important transportation artery. There is a large hydroelectric station at Perm.

Kamakura (kämä'ko͞orä), city (1970 pop. 139,253), Kanagawa prefecture, central Honshu, Japan, on Sagami Bay and at the base of the Miura Peninsula. It is a resort and residential area but is chiefly noted as a religious center, the site of more than 80 shrines and temples. Kamakura is especially famous for its *daibutsu* [Jap., = great Buddha], a 42-ft-high (12.8-m) bronze figure of Buddha, cast in 1252, and for a 30-ft-high (9.1-m) gilt and camphor statue of Kannon, the goddess of mercy. Kamakura was splendid as the seat of YORITOMO and his descendants (1192–1333); under the Ashikaga Shogunate (1333–1573) it was the government headquarters of eastern Japan. An earthquake in 1923 severely damaged the city.

Kamarhati (kämärhä'tē), city (1971 pop. 169,222), West Bengal state, NE India. It is a suburb of Calcutta.

Kamban, Guðmundur (gvüth'müntür käm'bän), 1888–1945, Icelandic dramatist and novelist. Many of Kamban's plays, among them *Hadda-Padda* (1914, tr. 1917), were produced in Denmark. His spirited and erudite historical novels, based upon the Icelandic sagas, include *Skalholt* (4 vol., 1930–32; tr. of Vol. I and II, *The Virgin of Skalholt*, 1935) and *I See a Wondrous Land* (1936, tr. 1938).

Kamchatka (kămchăt'kə), peninsula, 104,200 sq mi (269,878 sq km), Far Eastern USSR, separating the Sea of Okhotsk in the west from the Bering Sea and the Pacific Ocean in the east. Extending from lat. 51°N to lat. 61°N, it is 750 mi (1,207 km) long and terminates in the south in Cape Lopatka, beyond which lie the Kuril Islands. Petropavlovsk-Kamchatski is the chief city. There are many rivers and lakes, and the eastern shore is deeply indented by gulfs and bays. The peninsula's central valley, drained by the Kamchatka River, is enclosed by two parallel volcanic ranges that extend north-south; there are about 20 active volcanoes, the only active ones in the USSR. The highest point is Klyuchevskaya Sopka (15,600 ft/4,755 m), itself an active volcano. Kam-

Monumental bronze figure of Budda at Kamakura, Japan.

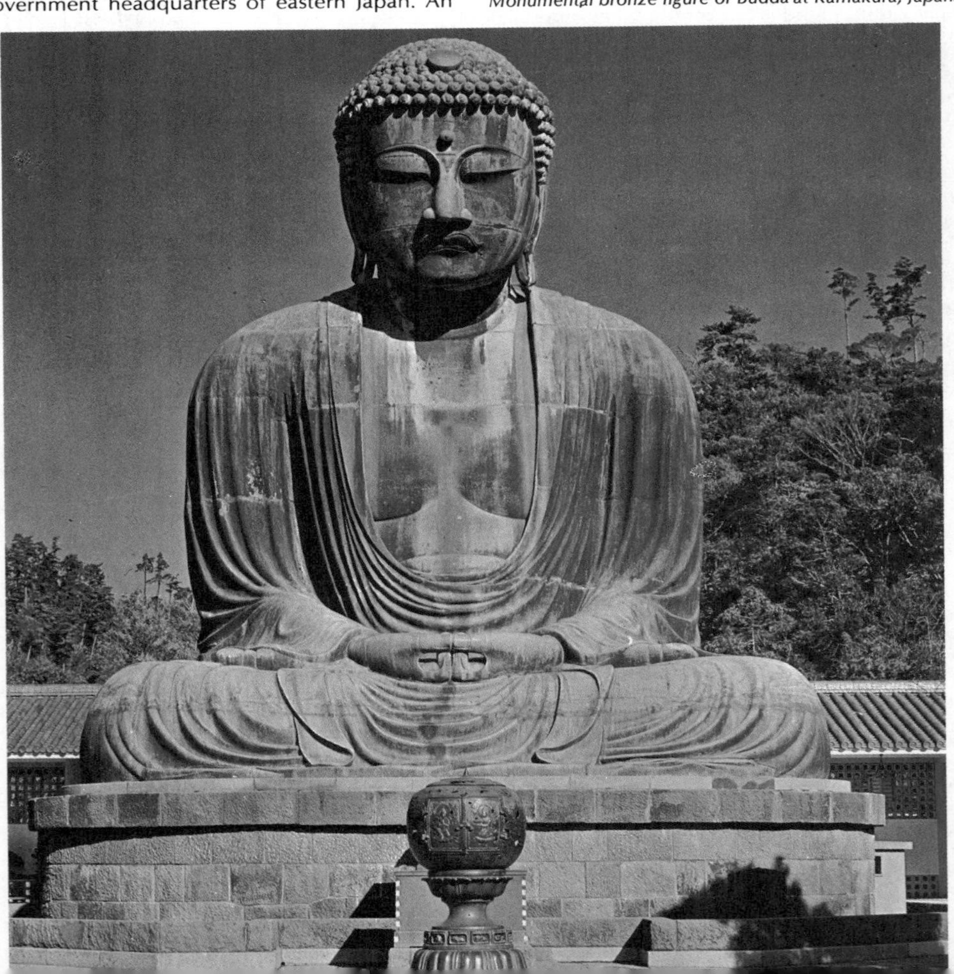

chatka is covered with mountain vegetation, except in the central valley and on the west coast, which has peat marshes and tundralike moss. The climate is cold and humid. There are numerous forests, mineral springs, and geysers. Kamchatka's mineral resources include oil, coal, gold, mica, pyrites, sulfur, and tufa. Fishing, sealing, hunting, and lumbering are the main occupations. As a Soviet fishing area (notably for crabs, which are exported worldwide), Kamchatka is surpassed only by the Caspian Sea region. Fur trapping on the peninsula yields most of the furs of the Soviet Far East. Cattle breeding is carried on in the south and farming (rye, oats, potatoes, vegetables) in the Kamchatka valley and around Petropavlovsk-Kamchatski. Reindeer are also raised on the peninsula. Industries include fish processing, shipbuilding, and woodworking. The majority of the population is Russian, with large minorities of Koryak peoples. The Russian explorer Atlasov discovered Kamchatka in 1697. Its exploration and development continued in the early 18th cent. under Czar Peter I. Russian conquest was complete by 1732. Heavy Russian colonization occurred in the early 19th cent. From 1926 to 1938, Kamchatka formed part of the Far Eastern Territory.

kame (kām), low, steep, rounded hill or ridge of layered sand and gravel drift, developed from glacial deposits. Kames were probably formed by streams of melting glacial ice that deposited mud and sand along the ice front. The subsequent retreat of the glacier left them as more or less isolated hills and ridges, ranging in height from a few feet to 100 ft (30 m) or more. Kames generally occur in clusters and are situated directly behind a mass of rock and soil called a terminal MORAINE. They are common in the glaciated valleys of the Scottish Lowlands, where the name originated.

Kamehameha (kämä'hämä'hä), dynasty of Hawaiian monarchs. **Kamehameha I** (Kamehameha the Great), c.1738–1819, was king of the island of Hawaii after 1790. Through conquest he became (1810) ruler of all the Hawaiian islands, which were previously governed by warring chiefs. Law and order were established for the first time, and the islands became prosperous. Although he was cordial to the traders who visited the islands and encouraged the introduction of their technology, he also insisted on the preservation of the ancient customs and religious beliefs of Hawaii. See biographies by H. H. Gowen (1919) and J. T. Pole (1959). His son, **Kamehameha II,** 1797–1824, succeeded to the throne in 1819. During his short reign, American missionaries were admitted to the islands for the first time. Upon his death in London during a ceremonial visit, his younger brother, **Kamehameha III,** 1814–54, became (1824) king. His mother, Kaahumanu, who served as regent during his minority, encouraged the spread of Christianity in the islands. American traders entered the islands in large numbers, and there was a growing danger of filibustering expeditions and even annexation from the United States. Under these pressures, Kamehameha III gave in to Western influences. Hawaii was converted from semifeudalism into a constitutional monarchy. A constitution adopted in 1840 provided for religious freedom, representative government, and an independent judiciary; a later constitution (1852) granted suffrage to all adult males. His son, **Kamehameha IV,** 1834–63, attempted to resist American influence during his reign (1854–63) but without much success. When his brother, **Kamehameha V,** 1831–72, became (1863) king, he tried to restore the old tribal ways. The constitution of 1852 was abrogated, and he proclaimed a new one that restored power to the monarch, weakened the legislature, and restricted suffrage. Under his reign, the influence of American missionaries waned rapidly. He died without an heir, however, and the legislature chose his successor, thus bringing to an end the Kamehameha dynasty.

Kamenets-Podolski (käm'mĭnyĭts-pədôl'skē), city (1969 est. pop. 69,000), SW European USSR, in the Ukraine. It is a rail terminus and has industries that produce foodstuffs, tobacco, machinery, machine tools, and automobile parts. Kamenets-Podolski was part of the duchy of Galich-Volhynia from the 12th to the 14th cent., when it passed to Poland. It came under Russian control in 1793. Historic landmarks include the fortress (15th–16th cent.), which is now a museum, and some cathedrals and monasteries dating from the 14th cent.

Kamenev, Lev Borisovich (lyĕf bərē'səvĭch kä'mĭnyĭf), 1883–1936, Soviet Communist leader. His original name was Rosenfeld. He joined (1901) the Social Democratic party and sided with the Bolshevik wing when the party split (1903). Banished (1915) to Siberia for his revolutionary activities, he returned after the February Revolution of 1917 and became a member of the first Politburo of the Communist party. On Lenin's death (1924), Kamenev, STALIN, and ZINOVIEV formed a triumvirate of successors and excluded TROTSKY, Kamenev's brother-in-law, from power. In 1925 the Stalinist majority in the party defeated Kamenev and Zinoviev, who joined (1926) Trotsky's opposition. Kamenev was expelled from the party in 1927, but he recanted, was readmitted, and held minor offices. He was arrested late in 1934 on charges of complicity in the murder of KIROV and was sentenced to imprisonment. In 1936 he, Zinoviev, and 14 others were tried for treason in the first big public purge trial. They confessed and were executed.

Kamensk-Shakhtinskiy (kä'myĭnsk-shäkh'tyĭnskē), city (1970 pop. 68,000), SE European USSR, on the Donets River. A mining center of the Donets coal basin, the city is also an important producer of artificial fibers. Kamensk-Shakhtinskiy was founded in 1817.

Kamerlingh Onnes, Heike (hī'kə kä'mərlĭng ôn'əs), 1853–1926, Dutch physicist. He was, from 1882, professor of physics at the Univ. of Leiden. He made important studies of the properties of helium and, in attempting to solidify it, produced a temperature within one degree of absolute zero. In the course of his low temperature experiments, he discovered the property of SUPERCONDUCTIVITY in certain metals. For these researches he received the 1913 Nobel Prize in Physics.

Kamerun: see CAMEROONS.

Kames, Henry Home, Lord (hyo͞om), 1696–1782, Scottish judge and philosopher. A man of broad interests and a wide-ranging intellect, his works included dissertations on Scottish law, agriculture, and problems of moral and aesthetic philosophy. Among his writings were *Introduction to the Art of Thinking* (1761) and *Elements of Criticism* (1762). See studies by W. C. Lehmann (1971) and I. S. Ross (1972).

kamikaze (kä″məkä'zē) [Jap.,=divine wind], the typhoon that destroyed Kublai Khan's fleet, foiling his invasion of Japan in 1281. In World War II the term was used for a Japanese suicide air force, composed of fliers who crashed their bomb-laden planes into their targets, usually ships. The kamikaze was first used extensively at Leyte Gulf and was especially active at Okinawa.

Kamina (kämē'nä), city (1967 est. pop. 115,000), Shaba region, S Zaïre. It is an administrative and transportation center. A major military airfield is located there. Kamina was used by the Belgians as a center for interventionist actions in the early months of Zaïre's independence (1960). It later served as a center for UN operations during the crisis caused by the secession (1960–63) of Katanga.

Kaministikwia (kəmĭn''ĭstĭk'wēə), river, c.60 mi (100 km) long, rising in Dog Lake, W Ont., Canada, and flowing S, then E into Lake Superior at Thunder Bay. In fur trade days it was the chief alternate to the Grand Portage–Pigeon River route into the northwest. After 1783, when the Pigeon River formed part of the U.S. boundary, it became the main route used by the North West Company to Fort William, their western headquarters at the mouth of the river. Kakabeka Falls (130 ft/40 m high), W of Fort William, is used to generate hydroelectricity.

Kamloops (kăm'lo͞ops), city (1971 pop. 26,168), S British Columbia, Canada, at the junction of the North Thompson and South Thompson rivers. A trading post was first established on the site in 1812. A village grew up at the time of the Cariboo gold rush (1860), and in 1885 the main line of the Canadian Pacific reached Kamloops. It is now a tourist and supply center for an extensive lumbering, mining, and farming district.

Kammersee, lake, Austria: see SALZKAMMERGUT.

Kampala (kämpä'lä), city (1969 pop. 331,889), capital of Uganda, on Victoria Nyanza. It is Uganda's largest city and its administrative, communications, economic, and transportation center. Manufactures include processed foods, beverages, shoes, enamelware, furniture, and machine parts. It is linked by railroad with Kasese, a mining center in SW Uganda, and with Mombasa, Kenya, on the Indian Ocean coast. Steamers on Victoria Nyanza link the city with ports in Kenya and Tanzania. An international airport is nearby, at ENTEBBE. Kampala grew up around a fort constructed (1890) by Capt. Frederick LUGARD for the British East Africa Company. In 1962, Kampala replaced Entebbe as the capital of Uganda. Despite its proximity (20 mi/32 km) to the equator, the city has a moderate climate, largely because of its altitude (c.4,000 ft/1,220 m). The city is built on and around six hills and has modern government and commercial quarters as well as wide avenues that fan out toward the surrounding suburbs. Kampala is the seat of the East African Development Bank and Makerere Univ.

Kampen (käm'pən), town (1971 pop. 29,087), Overijssel prov., central Netherlands, on the IJssel River, near the IJsselmeer. It is a trade and industrial center. Kampen was first mentioned in the 13th cent., and in the 15th cent. it was a member of the Hanseatic League. Notable structures in the town include the 14th-century town hall and several churches and buildings dating from the 14th and 15th cent. Two theological schools are there.

Kamperduin, Netherlands: see CAMPERDOWN.

Kampot (kämpôt') town, capital of Kampot prov., S Cambodia, on the Gulf of Siam. It is a seaport on the Phnom Penh–Kompong Som RR and the center of the Cambodian pepper culture. A cement plant is located nearby.

Kan (gän), river, c.550 mi (885 km) long, flowing north through the plain of central Kiangsi prov., SE China, past Nan-ch'ang to P'o-yang lake. Despite many rapids, it is navigable for junks below Kan-chou and for steamers up to Nan-ch'ang. The lower Kan valley is fertile; rice and tea are the main crops.

Kanagawa (känä'gäwä), prefecture (1970 pop. 5,472,247), E central Honshu, Japan. Yokohama is the capital. Other important cities include Kawasaki, Yokosuka, and Kamakura (a religious center). The urban belt of the eastern part of the prefecture merges with Tokyo to the north.

Kanah (kā'nə). **1** Unidentified town, N Palestine. Joshua 19.28. **2** River, central Palestine. Joshua 16.8; 17.9.

Kanalit, mts.: see CERAUNIAN MOUNTAINS, Albania.

Kananga (kənäng'gə), formerly **Luluabourg** (lo͞olwäbo͞or'), city (1971 est. pop. 483,400), capital of Kasai-Occidental prov., S central Zaïre, on the Lulua River. It is the commercial and transportation center of an agricultural region where cotton is grown. The city was founded in 1884 by the German explorer Hermann von Wissmann. In 1895, Batetela troops stationed there revolted after their chief was executed by authorities of the Belgian-run Independent State of the Congo. At first successful, the mutineers were finally defeated in 1901. Kananga grew rapidly in the early 20th cent. with the coming of the railroad. Many Luba tribesmen settled there and became economically dominant over the indigenous Lulua people. After Zaïre (then called the Democratic Republic of the Congo) achieved independence (1960), there were violent clashes between the Luba and Lulua, and many Luba fled to the short-lived (1960–61) Mining State of South KASAI. In 1961–62, the city was held by rebel troops from Equateur prov., who were loyal to Antoine Gizenga.

Kanaoka (känä'ōkä), fl. 2d half of 9th cent., Japanese landscape and figure painter, founder of the Kose school of painting. None of his works survives, but tradition says that he was the first Japanese painter to paint Japanese subject matter. He is also known as Kose no Kanaoka.

Kanarak: see KONARAK.

Kanarese (känərēz'), Dravidian language of India. See DRAVIDIAN LANGUAGES.

Kanaris, Constantine (känä'rĭs), 1790–1877, Greek patriot, admiral, and politician. He distinguished himself in the Greek War of Independence, notably at Tenedos, where he destroyed (1822) the flagship of the Turkish admiral. Kanaris served several terms as minister of the navy and as premier in 1848–49, and he became increasingly active in political life. In 1862 he was a leader in the revolution that ousted King Otto and put George I on the Greek throne. Under George I, he was premier in 1864–65 and in 1877. The name also appears as Canaris.

Kanatha: see DECAPOLIS.

Kanawha (kənô'wə), principal river of W.Va., 97 mi (156 km) long, formed by the confluence of the New and Gauley rivers, S central W.Va., and flowing NW to the Ohio River at Point Pleasant; Charleston, W.Va., is the largest city on the river. The Kanawha flows through a rich coal, natural-gas, and salt-brine

Twilight, *an abstract work by the Russian painter Wassily Kandinsky (opposite).*

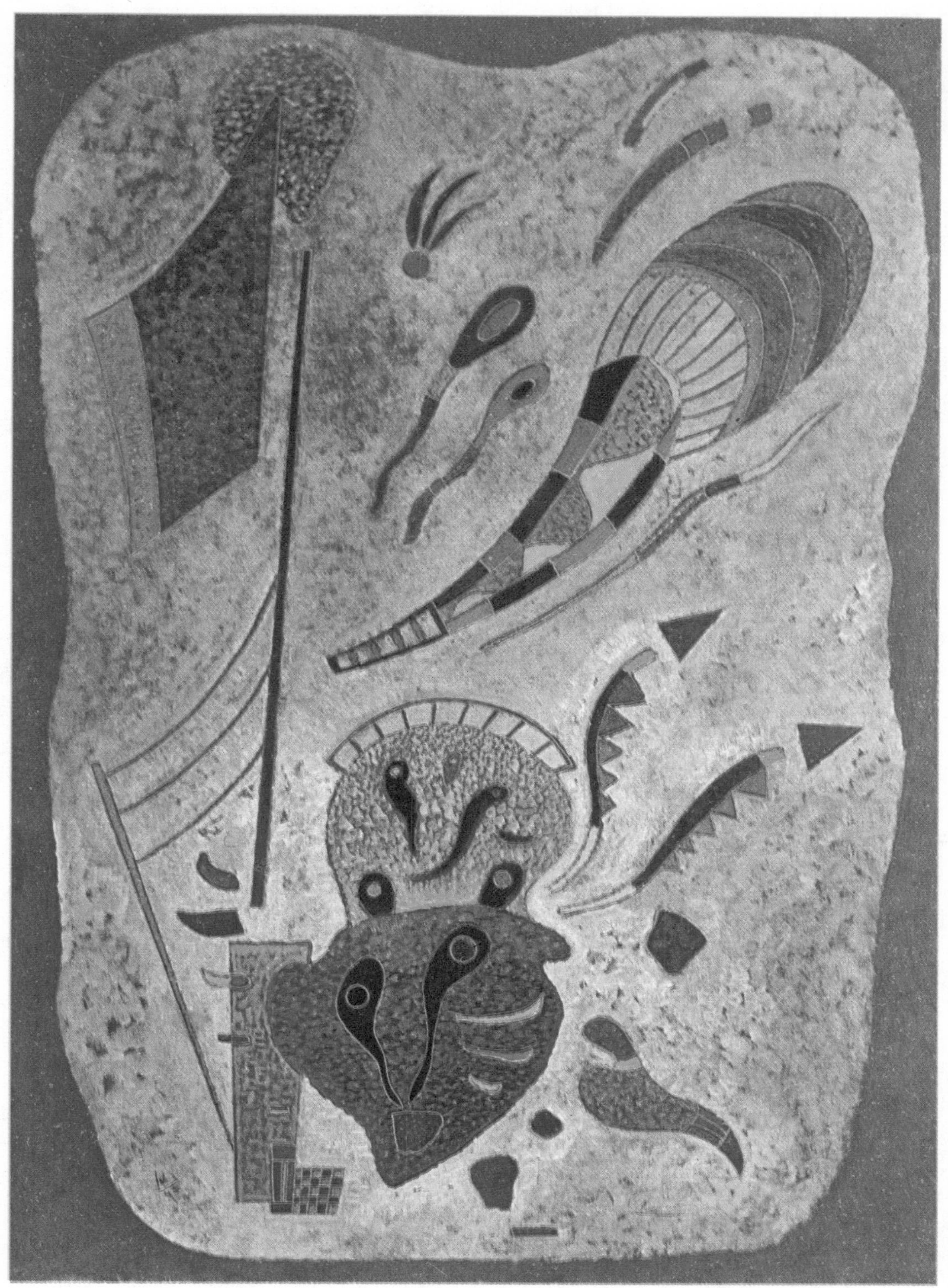

3609

region; its valley is one of the world's largest chemical-manufacturing centers. There are navigation locks and power dams on the river; its tributaries have flood-control works.

Kanazawa (kä"nä'zäwä), city (1970 pop. 361,373), capital of Ishikawa prefecture, central Honshu, Japan, on the Sea of Japan. It produces cotton and silk textiles, machinery, rolling stock, iron, and fine porcelain and lacquer ware. The city, built on the site of the old village of Yamazaki, was the seat of the Maeda clan (16th-19th cent.) and gradually became an industrial center. Kenrokuran Park (rebuilt 17th cent.), with its splendid landscape gardens and a famous No theatre and school, is in Kanazawa.

Kanchenjunga, Kanchanjanga (both: kän"chənjo͝ong'gə, kăn'chĕnjŭng'gə), or **Kinchinjunga** (kĭn"chənjo͝ong'gə), mountain, on the Sikkim-Nepal border, E Himalayas; geologically regarded as the main axis of the Himalayan range. The third-highest mountain in the world, it has five peaks, of which the tallest is 28,208 ft (8,598 m). In 1955 a British expedition under Charles Evans climbed the mountain, but in deference to the wishes of Sikkimese authorities the party stopped a few yards short of the summit.

Kanchi or **Kancheepuram,** India: see KANCHIPURAM.

Kanchipuram (kŭn'chēpo͝orəm), formerly Conjeeveram, city (1971 pop. 110,505), Tamil Nadu state, S India. Sacred to Hindus, it is known as the "golden city" and the "Benares of the south." Several temples in the Dravidian style survive from the period when it was the capital of the Pallava empire (3d–8th cent.) of S India and Sri Lanka and a center of Brahmanical and Buddhist culture. The city was captured (8th cent.) by the Chalukya dynasty and subsequently passed to the Chola (11th–13th cent.), to the Vijayanagar (early 15th cent.), and to the Orissa (late 15th cent.) kingdoms. After 1481 it fell to several different Muslim sultanates. A base of French power in India, it was captured by Robert Clive in 1758. Its ancient name was Kanchi. The patterns and texture of its saris are famous.

Kan-chou or **Kanchow** (both: gän-jō), city, SW Kiangsi prov., China, on the Kan River. It is a large transportation, distribution, and commercial center. Fertilizer is manufactured in the city, and tungsten mines are nearby. The city was formerly known as Kanhsien.

Kanchow: see KAN-CHOU, China.

Kandahar (kăn"dəhär'), city (1971 pop. 133,795), capital of Kandahar prov., S Afghanistan. The country's second largest city and chief trade center, Kandahar is a market for sheep, wool, cotton, food grains, fresh and dried fruit, and tobacco. It has an international airport and is linked by road with the USSR border. Woolen cloth, felt, and silk are manufactured. The surrounding irrigated region produces fine fruits, especially grapes, and the city has plants for canning, drying, and packing fruit. Kandahar may have been founded by Alexander the Great (4th cent. B.C.). India and Persia long fought over the city, which was strategically located on the trade routes of central Asia. It was conquered by Arabs in the 7th cent. and by the Turkic Ghaznivids in the 10th cent. Jenghiz Khan sacked it in the 12th cent., after which it became a major city of the Karts (Mongol clients) until their defeat by Tamerlane in 1383. Babur, founder of the Mogul empire of India, took Kandahar in the 16th cent. It was later contested by the Persians and by the rulers of emerging Afghanistan, who made it the capital (1748–73) of their newly independent kingdom. British forces occupied Kandahar during the First Afghan War (1839–42). The British again held the city from 1879 to 1881, when they finally recognized Abd ar-Rahman as emir of Afghanistan. The old city, sections of whose mud wall still survive, was laid out by Ahmad Shah (1724–73) and is dominated by his octangular, domed mausoleum. There are also numerous mosques (one said to contain the Prophet Muhammad's cloak) and bazaars. Modern Kandahar adjoins the old city. It has a technical college. Together with Peshawar, Pakistan, Kandahar is the principal city of the Pathan people.

Kandalaksha (kəndəläk'shə), Finnish *Kannanlahti,* city (1970 pop. 43,000), NW European USSR, on the Kandalaksha Bay of the White Sea. It is a seaport and has aluminum plants and hydroelectric stations. A settlement at the present site was known to the Vikings.

Kandinsky, Wassily (kăndĭn'skē, Rus. vəsē'lyē kəndyēn'skē), 1866–1944, Russian abstract painter and theorist. Usually regarded as the originator of abstract art, Kandinsky abandoned a legal career for painting at 30 when he moved to Munich. In subsequent trips to Paris he came into contact with the art of Gauguin, the neo-impressionists, and the fauves. He then developed his ideas concerning the power of pure color and nonrepresentational painting. His first work in this mode was completed in 1910, the year in which he wrote an important theoretical study, *Concerning the Spiritual in Art* (1912, tr. 1947). In this work he examines the psychological effects of color with analogies between music and art. He exhibited with the BRÜCKE group, and with Franz Marc and others he founded the BLAUE REITER group. In 1915, Kandinsky returned to Moscow, where he taught and directed artistic activities. During the early 1920s his style evolved from riotous bursts of color in his "Improvisations" to more precise, geometrically arranged compositions. In 1921 he returned to Germany and the next year joined the BAUHAUS faculty. In 1926 he wrote *Point and Line to Plane* (tr. 1947), which includes an analysis of geometric forms in art. At the outset of World War II, he went to France, where he spent the rest of his life. Kandinsky is well represented in the Solomon R. Guggenheim Museum, New York City, and the Pasadena Art Museum, California. See his *Reminiscences* (1913; tr. in *Modern Artists on Art,* ed. by R. L. Herbert, 1964); biographies by Will Grohmann (tr. 1958) and Jacques Lassaigne (1964); study by Paul Overy (1969).

Kandy (kăn'dē), city (1970 pop. 91,942), capital of Central prov., Sri Lanka (Ceylon), on the Kandy Plateau. It is a mountain resort and the market center for an area producing tea, rubber, rice, and cacao. The main part of the city overlooks a scenic artificial lake built by the last king of Kandy in 1806. Near the lake is the Temple of the Tooth, said to house one of Buddha's teeth. This sacred relic, brought to Ceylon in the 4th cent. (reputedly by a princess who hid it in her hair), may have been destroyed (1560) by the Portuguese. The relic, which has made Kandy a pilgrimage and tourist attraction, is honored in the annual *Esala Perahera* pageant. Kandy is noted for such local handicrafts as reed and lacquer work and silver and brassware. Although the city's history dates back to the 5th cent. B.C., it did not become the capital of the Sinhalese kings until 1592. It was temporarily occupied by the Portuguese (16th cent.)

and the Dutch (18th cent.); but, as a stronghold, it remained free until 1815, when the British captured it and exiled the last king to India. A palace, an art museum, and an Oriental library are remains of the royal period. In the suburb of Peradeniya is the Univ. of Sri Lanka (1942) and the famous botanical gardens, noted especially for their orchids.

Kane, Elisha Kent, 1820–57, American physician and arctic explorer, b. Philadelphia. Seeking adventure after medical school, Kane entered naval service and before he was 30 had seen many parts of the world and had served in the Mexican War. As senior medical officer he sailed (1850) on the first Grinnell expedition in search of the lost Franklin party. Kane's *U.S. Grinnell Expedition in Search of Sir John Franklin* (1853; repr. in part as *Adrift in the Arctic Ice Pack,* 1915) stirred such interest that he was able to organize and lead the second Grinnell expedition (1853–55). This expedition, of which I. I. HAYES was medical officer, passed northward through Smith Sound at the head of Baffin Bay, discovered and explored Kane Basin, and discovered Kennedy Channel beyond. Several sledging journeys were undertaken, on one of which a record of lat. 80°10′N was achieved. Humboldt Glacier was sighted, and scientific observations resulted in valuable new information on the arctic regions. Frozen in at Rensselaer Bay, the party abandoned ship, and Kane led a difficult retreat by land to Upernavik, Greenland. Kane's expedition had contributed more knowledge of Greenland than that of anyone before him. His health, never robust, was weakened by the rigors of his adventurous life, and he lived only long enough to complete his narrative of the second expedition, *Arctic Explorations* (1856), which had a tremendous sale. The spiritualist Margaret Fox claimed after his death that she had been his wife. Kane's *Love Life of Dr. Kane* (1866) contains many of his letters to Margaret Fox. See studies by Jeannette Mirsky (1954, repr. 1971), Oscar M. Villarejo (1965), and G. W. Corner (1972).

Kane, John, 1860–1934, American primitive painter, b. Scotland. He came to Pittsburgh at the age of 19, and worked for years as a day laborer, painting in his spare time. His paintings exhibit a delight in precise pattern and a sturdy disregard for academic conventions. Examples of his work are *Across the Strip* (Phillips Memorial Gall., Washington, D.C.) and his striking self-portrait (1929; Mus. of Modern Art, New York City). See his autobiography (1938).

Kane, Paul, 1810–71, Canadian painter, b. Ireland. Kane went to Toronto as a child. He studied art in the United States (1836–41) and in Europe (1841–45). After his return to Canada (1845) he made an extended journey into the Hudson's Bay Company territories of W Canada, traveling by snowshoe, horseback, and canoe to paint the Indians of the region. He returned to E Canada in 1848. Most of the paintings resulting from his journey are in the Royal Ontario Museum, Toronto, and in the Parliament buildings, Ottawa. His account of his journey appeared as *Wanderings of an Artist among the Indians of North America* (1859; new ed. with title *Paul Kane's Frontier,* incl. biography and catalog by J. R. Harper, 1971).

Kane Basin, 110 mi (177 km) long, part of the channel between NW Greenland and E Ellesmere Island. The Humboldt Glacier flows into the basin. It is named for the U.S. explorer Elisha K. Kane.

Kanellopoulos, Panayotis (pänäyô'tēs känälō'-po͞olōs), 1902–, Greek writer and political leader. A professor of sociology at the Univ. of Athens, he was active in World War II in the resistance and in the government-in-exile, in which he served as deputy premier and war minister. He held the premiership for a brief period in 1945. In the government of Constantine Karamanlis he was (1959–63) deputy premier, and he became leader of the National Radical Union after Karamanlis's electoral defeat and voluntary exile in 1963. In April, 1967, King Constantine II appointed him head of the caretaker cabinet charged with preparations for the May, 1967, elections; his rightist cabinet was soon toppled by George Papadopoulos in the coup of April 21, 1967. An outspoken opponent of authoritarianism, Kanellopoulos was subjected to arrest and house detention under the junta. After the junta was overthrown in 1974, he declined to serve in the new Karamanlis government or to take part in the elections. Kanellopoulos is the author of books, poems, and dramas in the fields of sociology and cultural philosophy.

Kanem (känēm'), former empire in Africa in the areas near Lake Chad that are now part of Chad and N Nigeria. The empire began in the 9th cent., when the Sefawa migrated to the area from the Sahara. The rulers eventually embraced Islam and extended their control to neighboring BORNU. After attacks by the Bulalas forced the rulers of Kanem to shift their capital to Bornu (c.1380), Bornu gradually emerged as the center of a revitalized empire of which Kanem became a protectorate.

Kaneohe (kä'nāōhā), uninc. city (1970 pop. 29,903), Honolulu co., Hawaii, on the east coast of Oahu, on Kaneohe Bay. Once the site of a pineapple plantation and cannery, it is now a lovely residential seaside community. A state mental hospital and a missile-tracking station are there. The U.S. Kaneohe Marine Corps Air Base is nearby; it was attacked by the Japanese on Dec. 7, 1941. Many ancient fishponds built by Hawaiian chiefs are in the area.

Kaneohe Bay, Hawaii, on the east coast of Oahu, protected by coral reefs and dotted with islands. The shores of the bay are rimmed with ancient fishponds built by the Hawaiian chiefs. A U.S. marine corps air base is there.

Kangar (käng''är'), town (1970 pop. 8,757), capital of Perlis state, Malaysia, central Malay Peninsula, on the Perlis River. It is a port and the center of a rice-growing region.

kangaroo, name for a variety of hopping MARSUPIALS, or pouched mammals, of the family Macropodidae, found in Australia, Tasmania, and New Guinea. The term is applied especially to the large kangaroos of the genus *Macropus.* Kangaroos have powerful hind legs designed for leaping, long feet, short forelimbs, and long muscular tails. The hind legs are also used to deliver blows at enemies when the animal is cornered; the feet are sharply clawed. The tail serves as a balance when the animal leaps and as a prop when it stands; the usual posture is bipedal. The handlike forepaws are used for grasping. As in most marsupials, females have a pouch surrounding the teats. Kangaroos feed on grass and other vegetation; they are the chief grazers of the Australian plains. Day-active animals, they move about in herds called mobs and sleep on the ground at night. Males are called boomers, females flyers; the young are called joeys. The single young is born in an immature state after a gestation period of about 40 days and is suckled in the mother's pouch for about six months. After it begins to graze it returns frequently to the

Female kangaroo with young in her pouch.

pouch for shelter and transport until it is too large to be carried. The largest kangaroo, and largest of all marsupials, is the great red kangaroo, *M. rufus,* which inhabits the inland plains of Australia. Males of this species may be over 7 ft (210 cm) tall and weigh over 200 lbs (90 kg). They are bright maroon in color, with white faces and underparts. Females, called blue flyers, are blue-gray; smaller and faster than the males, they may achieve speeds of 30 mi (48 km) per hr. The great gray kangaroo, *M. canguru,* is almost as large; it is found in open forest areas of E and W Australia and in Tasmania. A related kangaroo, *M. robustus,* is known as the wallaroo and inhabits rocky hills throughout most of the continent. Smaller, but quite similar in appearance and behavior, are members of the kangaroo family called wallabies and pademelons, of which there are many species, classified in several genera. Some of these are plains dwellers, others live among rocks or in scrub country; most are about the size of a rabbit. Of similar size are the tree and rat kangaroos. Tree kangaroos, species of the genus *Dendrolagus,* are the only arboreal members of the family. Found in the rain forests of New Guinea and N Australia, they climb well and can leap from branch to branch. Rat kangaroos are omnivorous animals of ratlike appearance. They feed largely on roots and fungi; members of many species live in burrows. They are classified in several genera and are distributed throughout the Australian region. Because many types of kangaroo have valuable hides, and because they compete with domestic livestock for grazing land, kangaroos have been extensively hunted and are now extremely reduced in numbers. They are classified in the phylum CHORDATA, subphylum Vertebrata, class Mammalia, order Marsupialia, family Macropodidae.

Kangaroo Island, small island, South Australia, S Australia, at the entrance to Gulf St. Vincent. It is 90 mi (145 km) long and 34 mi (55 km) wide. The chief products are barley, sheep, salt, gypsum, and eucalyptus oil. At its west end is Flinders Chase, a large reservation for native flora and fauna. There are many summer resorts. Kingscote (1971 pop. 2,665) is the principal settlement.

kangaroo mouse: see KANGAROO RAT.

kangaroo rat, small, jumping desert rodent, genus *Dipodomys,* related to the POCKET MOUSE. There are about 20 kangaroo rat species, found throughout the arid regions of Mexico and the S and W United States. Kangaroo rats have large, mouselike heads with big eyes, external fur-lined cheek pouches for food storage, and extremely long, tufted tails. In many species the tail is longer than the combined head and body length. The total length, including the tail, is 10 to 15 in. (25–37.5 cm), depending on the species. The front limbs are very short and the back limbs extremely long and stiltlike. The animal moves by long leaps, like a kangaroo, using its tail for balance and as a rudder for turning at high speeds. Kangaroo rats have long silky fur, pale brown above and white beneath, with black and white tail tufts and black face markings. Solitary, nocturnal creatures, they live in burrows by day and forage at night for seeds, grass, and tubers. Active hoarders, they sometimes dry their food in shallow pits just below the surface of the ground, then dig it up and store it in their burrows. Like a number of other desert animals, the kangaroo rat has physiological mechanisms for conserving the water that it obtains from food or produces metabollically, so that it does not need to drink. A related genus, *Microdipodops,* is called the kangaroo mouse, or dwarf kangaroo rat. It is about 6 in. (15 cm) in total length and is found in the Great Basin of the W United States. Kangaroo rats are classified in the phylum CHORDATA, subphylum Vertebrata, class Mammalia, order Rodentia, family Heteromyidae.

K'ang Hsi (käng shē), 1654–1722, 2d emperor of the Ch'ing dynasty of China (1661–1722). He extended Manchu control and promoted learning in the arts and sciences. K'ang Hsi conquered the feudatories of S China (1673–81), took Taiwan (1683), established China's first diplomatic relations with Russia (1689), and pushed the Ölöds from Outer Mongolia (1697). Repeated tax reductions, attention to water conservation, and imperial tours of inspection earned him a reputation for benevolence. Under his patronage, a Ming history, two monumental dictionaries, and a literary encyclopedia were completed. He employed Jesuit missionaries to map the empire and to teach mathematics and astronomy. See study by J. D. Spence (1974).

Kanghwa or **Kanghoa** (both: käng'hwä'), island, 163 sq mi (422 sq km), off SW South Korea, in the Yellow Sea. Farming and fishing are important occupations. Kanghwa was briefly the site of the Korean capital in the 13th cent. It was early fortified as an outer defense for Seoul and was stormed by the French in 1866 and by the Americans in 1871.

Kangnung (käng'nŏŏng'), city (1970 est. pop. 74,500), NE South Korea, a port on the Sea of Japan. It is also an agricultural center and is famed for its beautiful scenery.

Kang Teh: see PU YI, HENRY.

K'ang-ting or **Kangting** (both: käng-dĭng), city, W Szechwan prov., China, in the Kan-tzu Tibetan Autonomous Region. It is a transportation center on the main road from Ch'eng-tu to Lhasa, Tibet. Until 1950 it was the capital of Sikang prov.

Kangwon (käng'wŭn'), province (1970 pop. 1,873,-908), N South Korea. CHUNCHON is the capital. The 38th parallel that divided Korea after World War II ran through Kangwon, but after the Korean War truce of 1953 much of the province returned from North to South Korean rule. Mining, farming, and fishing are chief economic activities in the province.

K'ang Yu-wei (käng yo͞o-wē), 1858–1927, Chinese philosopher and reform movement leader. He was a leading philosopher of the new text school of Confucianism, which regarded Confucius as a utopian political reformer. K'ang first gained fame in 1895 when he sent a memorial to the emperor unsuccessfully urging continuation of the war with Japan, rejection of the Treaty of Shimonoseki, and adoption of extensive administrative reforms. That same year with LIANG CH'I-CH'AO he founded a reform newspaper and a reform organization, but both were quickly suppressed (1896). Enthusiasm for his ideas spread, however, and several provincial reform associations were founded (1896–97). Again confronted with foreign pressure for concessions, Emperor KUANG HSU (1898) summoned K'ang to Peking and asked him to draw up reform plans. In a series of decrees known as the "hundred days' reform," the emperor changed the civil service examination system to include essays on current affairs, established Peking Univ. as well as western-style provincial schools, abolished many sinecure posts, and revised administrative regulations. Backed by conservative officials, Dowager Empress TZ'U HSI imprisoned the emperor and rescinded most of the reforms. K'ang fled to Japan and spent the years before the 1911 revolution working for constitutional monarchy. He and Liang were bitterly opposed to the T'ung-meng-hui, an anti-Manchu revolutionary party founded in 1905 under the leadership of SUN YAT-SEN. After the revolution, K'ang remained in opposition to the republican government, participating (1917) in an unsuccessful attempt to restore the last Ch'ing emperor, PU YI. See M. E. Cameron, *The Reform Movement in China, 1898–1912* (1931, repr. 1963); biography ed. and tr. by Lo Jung-pang (1967).

Kanhsien: see KAN-CHOU, China.

Kaniapiskau (kănyəpĭs'kô"), river, c.575 mi (930 km) long, issuing from Kaniapiskau Lake, NE Que., Canada. It flows generally NW past Fort Mackenzie to the Koksoak River, which then flows NE to Ungava Bay at Fort Chimo. The river's lower course drains part of the iron belt of N Quebec. An alternate spelling is Caniapiscau.

Kanin (kä'nyĭn), peninsula, N European USSR, projecting into the Barents Sea between the White Sea (in the west) and Chesha (Cheshskaya) Bay (in the east). Its northernmost cape is called Kanin Nos. The native Nentsy (Samoyed) people engage in fishing, hunting, and reindeer raising.

Kanishka (kənĭsh'kə), fl. A.D. c.120, king of GANDHARA. He was the most powerful and renowned ruler of the Kushan dynasty, one of the five tribes of the Yüeh-chih who had divided (1st cent. B.C.) Bactria among them. Earlier Kushan kings had extended their dominion into N India, and Kanishka ruled over an empire that stretched from the Pamirs to Bengal. His capital was at Peshawar. A patron of Buddhism, he built many Buddhist monuments, helped found the Gandharan school of sculpture, and encouraged the spread of Buddhism to central Asia.

Kankakee (kăngkəkē'), city (1970 pop. 30,944), seat of Kankakee co., E Ill., on the Kankakee River; inc. 1855. It is an industrial and shipping center for a farm area. Kankakee's varied manufactures include ranges, water heaters, furniture, tractors, farm and garden equipment, biochemicals, and pharmaceuticals. Limestone quarries are nearby. A state mental hospital, a state park, Olivet Nazarene College, and a junior college are in the city.

Kankan (känkän', käNkäN'), city (1964 est. pop. 50,000), E Guinea, a port on the Milo River, a tributary of the Niger. It is the commercial center for a farm area where rice, sesame, maize, tomatoes, oranges, mangoes, and pineapples are grown. Diamonds are mined, and the national diamond exchange is there. Bricks and fruit juices are made in Kankan, which also has a tomato canning factory and a sawmill. The city is connected by rail with Conakry. Kankan was probably founded in the 18th cent. as a trade center that linked the Sudan region with the forest belt and the Atlantic coast. SAMORY began (c.1866) his career as a military leader and empire builder in the Kankan district, and in 1873 took Kankan itself. The French occupied the city in 1891. Kankan has a polytechnic institute and a center for research on rice cultivation.

Kanko: see HAMHUNG, North Korea.

Kannanlahti: see KANDALAKSHA, USSR.

Kannapolis (kənăp'əlĭs), uninc. city (1970 pop. 36,293), Cabarrus and Rowan counties, W central N.C.; founded c.1905. It is a planned company town owned by Cannon Mills, known for its production of household linens.

Kannauj (kənouj'), town (1971 pop. 28,189), Uttar Pradesh state, N central India, on the Ganges River. It is a market center for food grains, oilseed, fruit, perfume, and rose water. An ancient town, Kannauj was a brilliant cultural center and the capital of Harsha's empire in the 7th cent. In the 9th cent. it became the capital of the Pratihara empire. During that period, it was famous for its poets. Kannauj declined after being conquered by Turkish tribes under Mahmud of Ghazni in 1018.

Kano (kä'nō), family or school of Japanese painters. **Kano Masanobu,** c.1434–c.1530, the forerunner of the school, was attached to the shogun Yoshimasa's court. He painted landscapes, birds, and figure pieces, chiefly in ink with occasional touches of pale tints. His work is Japanese in spirit, reflecting the influence of Chinese art in technique and style. Only a few of his works survive. His son, **Kano Motonobu,** c.1476–1559, was the actual founder of the school and one of the foremost artists of Japan. Into Chinese-style ink painting he introduced heavily stressed outlines and bold decorative patterns. His screen paintings served well as architectural decorations and appealed to the tastes of the warrior class. Many of his screen paintings are still preserved in temples of Kyoto. **Kano Eitoku,** 1543–90, grandson of Motonobu, painted screens with landscapes and figures and decorated the interiors of the royal palaces. His art differs from that of the earlier Kano painters; it is less precise and is characterized by energy, ease, and inventiveness. His screen paintings were done in brilliant colors against a ground of gold leaf. He had many pupils and imitators, but most of his own work has perished. **Kano Tanyu,** 1602–74, first known as Morinobu, was the grandson of Eitoku and was called the reviver of the Kano school. He was appointed official painter of the Tokugawa government (1621) and established a school of his own. He became one of the most vigorous and versatile of Japanese painters. He worked in both Edo and Kyoto, decorating castles and royal palaces. Although much of his work has since disappeared, some screen paintings are still preserved at Nijo Castle in Kyoto and at Nagoya Castle. His *Confucius and Disciples* is at the Museum of Fine Arts, Boston. See S. E. Lee, *A History of Far Eastern Art* (1964).

Kano (kä'nō), city (1971 est. pop. 357,000), N Nigeria. It is the trade and shipping center for an agricultural region where cotton, cattle, and about half of Nigeria's groundnuts are raised. Kano is the major industrial center of N Nigeria; peanut flour and oil, cotton textiles, steel furniture, processed meat, concrete blocks, shoes, and soap are the chief manufactures. The city has long been known for its leatherwork; its tanned goatskins were sent (from about 15th cent.) to N Africa and were known in Europe as morocco leather. One of the seven HAUSA city-states, Kano's written history dates back to A.D. 999, when the city was already several hundred years old. It was a cultural, handicraft, and commercial center, with wide trade contacts in W and N Africa. In the early 16th cent. Kano accepted Islam, and c.1600 it was temporarily held by the Muslim state of BORNU. Kano reached the height of its power in the 17th and 18th cent. In 1809 it was conquered by the FULANI, but it soon regained its leading commercial position. In 1903 a British force under Frederick LUGARD captured the city. In Kano are Abdullahi Bayero College (1960; part of Ahmadu Bello Univ., Zari); Gidan Makama Museum, with examples of local art; and the palace of the emir, the former ruler of the Kano city-state.

Kanonji (känōn'jē), city (1970 pop. 43,162), Kagawa prefecture, E Shikoku, Japan, on the Hiuchi Sea. It is a religious center and agricultural market noted for its Kanonji (Buddhist) Temple.

Kanoya (känō'yä), city (1970 pop. 66,995), Kagoshima prefecture, S Kyushu, Japan, on the Osumi Peninsula. It is an agricultural market with a silk-rayon weaving industry.

Kanpur (kän'po͝or), city (1971 pop. 1,151,975), Uttar Pradesh state, N central India, on the Ganges River. A major industrial center, it produces chemicals, textiles, leather goods, and food products. It is also a transportation hub. An agricultural college is nearby. Kanpur was a village until its cession to the British in 1801 by the Nawab of Oudh. During the INDIAN MUTINY (1857), Nana Sahib, whose claim to a pension had been rejected, slaughtered the entire British garrison, including women and children.

Kansa Indians (kăn'sô), people whose language belongs to the Siouan branch of the Hokan-Siouan linguistic stock (see AMERICAN INDIAN LANGUAGES), also known as the Kansas or Kaw Indians. Closely related to the OSAGE INDIANS, from whom they separated probably not long before the settlers met them, they shared the typical Plains culture and began farming only after the buffalo had disappeared from the Plains. They were at the mouth of the Kansas River when traders reached them, but had moved westward to the mouth of the Saline River by 1815, when the United States made its first treaty with them. By treaties of 1825 and 1846, the Kansa Indians ceded most of their lands and accepted a reservation on the Neosho River at Council Grove, where they lived until 1873. They were then placed on a new reservation in Oklahoma, next to the Osage tribe. Their lands were allotted to them on an individual basis rather than to the whole tribe. See W. E. Unrau, *The Kansa Indians* (1971).

Kansas, state (1970 pop. 2,249,071), 82,264 sq mi (213,064 sq km), central United States, admitted to the Union in 1861 as the 34th state. TOPEKA is the capital; other major cities are WICHITA (the largest city in the state) and KANSAS CITY (adjoining Kansas City, Mo.). Almost rectangular in shape, Kansas is bounded on the N by Nebraska, on the E by Missouri (the Missouri River forms the boundary for a short distance), on the S by Oklahoma, and on the W by Colorado. The geographical center of the United States (exclusive of Alaska and Hawaii) is located in Kansas between Smith Center and Lebanon. Part of the GREAT PLAINS, Kansas is famous for its seemingly endless fields of ripe golden wheat. The land rises more than 3,000 ft (914 m) from the eastern alluvial prairies of Kansas to its western semiarid high plains, which stretch toward the foothills of the Rocky Mts. The rise is so gradual, however, that

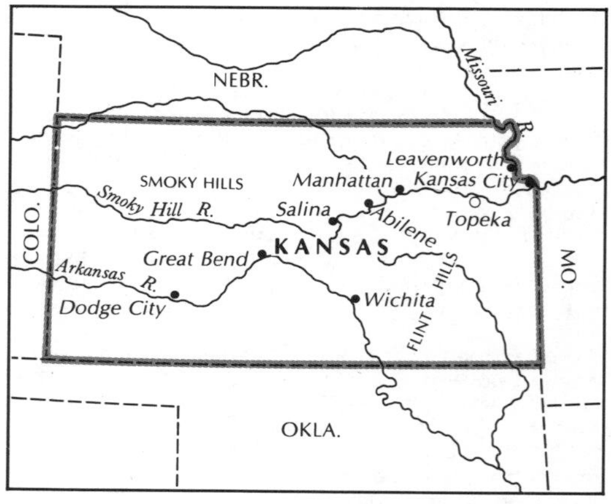

it is imperceptible, although the terrains of the east and the west are markedly different. The state is drained by the Kansas and Arkansas rivers, both of which generally run from west to east. The average annual rainfall of 27 in. (69 cm) is not evenly distributed: the eastern prairies receive up to 40 in. (102 cm) of rain, while the western plains average 17 in. (43 cm). Occasional dust storms plague farmers and ranchers in the west. The climate is continental, with wide extremes—cold winters with blizzards and hot summers with tornadoes. Floods also wreak havoc in the state; hence, flood-control projects, such as dams, reservoirs, and levees, are a major undertaking. Kansas was once primarily an agricultural state, but manufacturing has surpassed agriculture as a source of income. However, farming is still important to the state's economy, and Kansas is the nation's leading producer of wheat and second largest producer of sorghum for grain. Corn and hay are also major crops. Cattle and calves are raised on the state's abundant grazing lands and constitute the single most-valuable agricultural item. Meat-packing and dairy industries are major economic activities, and the Kansas City stockyards are among the nation's largest. Food processing ranked as the state's third largest industry in the early 1970s. The two leading industries are the manufacture of transportation equipment and of chemicals. Wichita is a leader in the aircraft industry, especially in the production of private planes. Other important manufactured items are petroleum and coal products and nonelectrical machinery. The state is a major producer of crude petroleum and has large reserves of natural gas and helium. Kansas was once a great shallow sea, and salt deposits in commercially profitable quantities still remain. When the Spanish explorer Francisco Vásquez de Coronado visited (1541) the Kansas area in his search for Quivira, a fabled kingdom of riches, the area was occupied by various Plains Indian tribes, notably the Kansa Indians, the Wichita Indians, and the Pawnee Indians. Another Spanish explorer, Juan de Oñate, penetrated the region in 1601. A result of Spanish entry into the region was the introduction of the horse, which revolutionized the life of the Plains Indians. While not actually exploring the Kansas area, Robert Cavelier, sieur de La Salle, claimed (c.1682) for France all territory drained by the Mississippi River, including Kansas. French traders were active among the Indians during most of the 18th cent. By the Treaty of Paris of 1763 (see PARIS, TREATY OF) ending the French and Indian Wars, France ceded the territory of W Louisiana (including Kansas) to Spain. In 1800, Spain secretly retroceded the territory to France, from whom the United States acquired it in the Louisiana Purchase in 1803. The region was little known, however, and subsequent explorations to include Kansas were the Lewis and Clark expedition (1803–6), the Arkansas River journey of Zebulon M. Pike in 1806, and the scientific expedition of Stephen H. Long in 1819. Most of the territory that eventually became Kansas was in an area known as the "Great American Desert," considered unsuitable for white settlement because of its apparent barrenness. In the 1830s the region was designated permanent Indian country, and northern and eastern tribes were relocated there (see INDIAN TERRITORY). Forts were constructed for frontier defense and for the protection of the growing trade along the Santa Fe Trail, which crossed Kansas. Fort Leavenworth was established in 1827, Fort Scott in 1842, and Fort Riley in 1853. Kansas, at this time mainly a region to be crossed on the way to California and Oregon, was organized as a territory in 1854. Its settlement, however, was spurred not so much by natural westward expansion as by the determination of both proslavery and antislavery factions to achieve a majority population in the territory. The struggle between the factions was further complicated by the conflict over the location of a transcontinental railroad, with proponents of a central route (rather than a southern route) eager to resolve the slavery issue in the area and promote settlement. The KANSAS-NEBRASKA ACT (1854), an attempted compromise on the extension of slavery, repealed the Missouri Compromise and reopened the issue of extending slavery north of lat. 36°30′ by providing for SQUATTER SOVEREIGNTY in Kansas and Nebraska, allowing settlers of territories to decide the matter themselves. Meanwhile, the EMIGRANT AID COMPANY was organized in Massachusetts to foster antislavery emigration to Kansas, and proslavery interests in Missouri and throughout the South took counteraction. Towns were established by each faction—Lawrence and Topeka by the free staters and Leavenworth and Atchison by the proslavery settlers. Soon all the problems attendant upon organizing a territory for statehood became subsidiary to the single issue of slavery. The first elections in 1854 and 1855 were won by the proslavery group; armed Missourians intimidated voters and election officials and stuffed the ballot boxes. Andrew H. Reeder was appointed the first territorial governor in 1854. The first territorial legislature ousted (1855) all free-state members, secured the removal of Gov. Reeder, moved the capital to Lecompton, and adopted proslavery statutes. In retaliation the abolitionists set up a rival government at Topeka in Oct., 1855. Violence soon came to the territory. The murder of a free-state man in Nov., 1855, led to the so-called Wakarusa War, a bloodless series of encounters along the Wakarusa River. The intervention of the new governor, Wilson Shannon, kept proslavery men from attacking Lawrence. However, civil war ultimately turned the territory into "bleeding Kansas." On May 21, 1856, proslavery groups and armed Missourians known as "Border Ruffians" raided Lawrence. A few days later a band led by the abolitionist crusader John Brown murdered five proslavery men in the Pottawatomie massacre. Guerrilla warfare between free-state men called Jayhawkers and proslavery bands—both sides abetted by desperadoes and opportunists—terrorized the land. After a new governor, John W. Geary, persuaded a large group of "Border Ruffians" to return to Missouri, the violence subsided. The Lecompton legislature met in 1857 to make preparations for convening a constitutional convention. Gov. Geary resigned after it became clear that free elections would not be held to approve a new constitution. Robert J. Walker was appointed governor, and a convention held at Lecompton drafted a constitution. Only that part of the resulting proslavery constitution dealing with slavery was submitted to the electorate, and the question was drafted to favor the proslavery group. Free-state men refused to participate in the election with the result that the constitution was overwhelmingly approved. Despite the dubious validity of the Lecompton constitution, President Buchanan recommended (1858) that Congress accept it and approve statehood for the territory. Instead, Congress returned it for another territorial vote. The proslavery group boycotted the election, and the constitution was rejected. Lawrence became de facto capital of the troubled territory until after the Wyandotte Constitution (framed in 1859 and totally forbidding slavery) was accepted by Congress. The Kansas conflict and the issue of statehood for the territory became a national issue and figured in the 1860 Republican party platform. Kansas became a state in 1861, with the capital at Topeka. Charles Robinson was the first governor and James H. Lane, an active free-stater during the 1850s, one of the U.S. Senators. In the Civil War, Kansas fought with the North and suffered the highest rate of fatal casualties of any state in the Union. Further hardships developed as Kansas was scourged by Indian raids in the west and border warfare in the east, climaxed by the burning of Lawrence in 1863 by the Confederate William C. Quantrill and his guerrilla band. With peace came the development of the prairie lands. The construction of railroads made cowtowns such as ABILENE and DODGE CITY, with their cowboys, saloons, and frontier marshals, the shipping point for large herds of cattle driven overland from Texas. The buffalo herds disappeared (today some buffalo roam in state parks and game preserves), and cattle took their place. Pioneer homesteaders, adjusting to life on the timberless prairie

Dwight D. Eisenhower's family homestead in Abilene, Kansas.

Reenactment of Kansas settlement; in background are large landmark rocks along the Butterfield Trail.

and living in sod houses, suffered privation. In 1874, Mennonite emigrants from Russia brought the Turkey Red variety of winter wheat to Kansas. This wheat was instrumental in making Kansas the Wheat State as winter wheat replaced spring wheat on an ever-increasing scale. Corn, too, soon became a major money crop. Agricultural production was periodically disrupted by national depressions and natural disasters. Repeated and prolonged droughts accompanied by dust storms, occasional grasshopper invasions, and floods caused severe economic dislocation. Mortgages often weighed heavily on farmers, and discontent was expressed in farmer support of radical farm organizations and third-party movements, such as the GRANGER MOVEMENT, GREENBACK PARTY, and POPULIST PARTY. Tax relief, better regulation of interest rates, and curbs on the power of railroads were sought by these organizations. Twice in the 1890s, Populist-Democrats were elected to the governorship. As conditions improved, Kansas returned largely to its allegiance to the Republican party and gained a reputation as a conservative stronghold with a bent for moral reform, indicated in the state's strong support of prohibition; laws against the sale of liquor remained on the books in Kansas from 1880 to 1949. Over the years improved agricultural methods and machines increased crop yield. Irrigation proved practicable in some areas, and winter wheat and alfalfa could be cultivated in dry regions. Wheat production greatly expanded during World War I, but the end of the war brought financial difficulties. During the 1920s and 30s, Kansas was faced with labor unrest and the economic hardships of the depression. As part of the Dust Bowl, Kansas sustained serious land erosion during the long drought of the 1930s. Erosion led to the implementation of conservation and reclamation projects, particularly in the northern and western parts of the state. In 1924 an effort of the Ku Klux Klan to gain political control was fought by William Allen White, editor of the Emporia *Gazette*, who supported many liberal causes. Alfred M. Landon, elected governor in 1932, was one of the few Republican candidates in the country to win election in the midst of the sweeping Democratic victory that year. He was nominated as the Republican presidential candidate in 1936. During World War II agriculture thrived and industry expanded rapidly. The food-processing industry grew substantially, the cement industry enjoyed a major revival, and the aircraft industry boomed. After the war agricultural prosperity once again declined when the state was hit by a severe drought and grasshopper invasion in 1948. Prosperity returned briefly during the Korean War, but afterwards farm surpluses and insufficient world markets combined to make the state's tremendous agricultural ability part of the national "farm problem." Kansas has become increasingly industrialized and urbanized, however, and industrial production has surpassed farm production in economic importance. Flood damage in the state, especially after a major flood in 1951, spurred the construction of dams (such as the Tuttle Creek, Milford, and Wilson dams) on major Kansas rivers, and their reservoirs have vastly increased water recreational facilities for Kansans. Points of historical interest in Kansas include the boyhood home of Dwight D. Eisenhower and the Eisenhower Library in Abilene. In Medicine Lodge is the home of Carry Nation, who, at the turn of the century, became convinced of her divine appointment to destroy the saloons; her home there is now a museum. Fort Leavenworth is the site of a large Federal penitentiary. Government in Kansas is based on the constitution of 1859, adopted just before Kansas attained statehood. An elected governor heads the executive and serves a term of two years. The legislature has a house of representatives and a senate, with the 125 members of the house elected for two-year terms and the 40 members of the senate elected for four-year terms. Kansas is represented in the U.S. Congress by five Representatives and two Senators and has seven electoral votes in presidential elections. Although Kansas has long been a Republican stronghold, a Democrat, Robert Docking, was elected governor in 1966 and was reelected in 1968, 1970, and 1972. In 1974, Robert F. Bennett, a Republican, was elected governor. Institutions of higher learning include the Univ. of Kansas, at Lawrence; Kansas State Univ., at Manhattan; Wichita State Univ., at Wichita; and Washburn Univ. of Topeka, at Topeka. See Paul Gates, *Fifty Million Acres: Conflicts over Kansas Land Policy, 1854–1890* (1954); W. F. Zornow, *Kansas: a History of the Jayhawk State* (1957); A. E. Castel, *A Frontier State at War: Kansas, 1861–1865* (1958); R. S. Brownlee, *Gray Ghosts of the Confederacy* (1960); R. W. Baughman, *Kansas in Maps* (1961); W. T. Nugent, *The Tolerant Populists: Kansas Populism and Nativism* (1963); J. R. Cook, *The Border and the Buffalo* (1967); Federal Writers' Project, *Kansas: a Guide to the Sunflower State* (1939, repr. 1973).

Kansas or **Kaw,** river, 170 mi (274 km) long, formed by the junction of the Smoky Hill and Republican rivers in NE Kansas and flowing E to the Missouri River at Kansas City; the system drains parts of Kansas, Nebraska, and Colorado. Heavy floods (especially in 1951) on the Kansas and its tributaries caused great damage in this primarily agricultural region. Since 1954 numerous dams, reservoirs, and levees have been built.

Kansas, University of, mainly at Lawrence; coeducational; state supported; chartered 1864, opened 1866 with aid from the philanthropist Amos A. Lawrence. Its school of medicine is partly at Kansas City. The university's library collections and the Dyche Museum of Natural History are noteworthy.

Kansas City, two adjacent cities of the same name, one (1970 pop. 168,213), seat of Wyandotte co., NE Kansas (inc. 1859), the other (1970 pop. 507,187), Clay, Jackson, and Platte counties, NW Mo. (inc. 1850). They are at the junction of the Missouri and Kansas (or Kaw) rivers and together form a large commercial, industrial, and cultural center. They are a port of entry, the focus of many transportation lines, and a huge market for wheat, hay, poultry, and seed. Both cities have large stockyards, grain elevators, food-processing establishments (especially for meat-packing and flour milling), oil refineries, steel mills, soap and farm-machinery factories, automobile-assembly plants, and railroad shops. The area was the starting place of many Western expeditions; the Santa Fe and Oregon trails passed through there. Several historic settlements of the early 19th cent. (including Westport) were predecessors to the present-day cities. Kansas City, Kansas, is the seat of two junior colleges, two theological seminaries, the Univ. of Kansas Medical Center, and a state school for the blind (est. 1868). It has an agricultural hall of fame, a Shawnee mission (1839), and several museums. A 19th-century Indian cemetery there is being incorporated into a unique center city mall. Kansas City Mo., with its fine parks and residential districts, is the site of the noted Nelson Art Gallery and the

Cattle stockyards near Dodge City, southwestern Kansas.

Nelson Art Gallery in Kansas City, Mo.

Atkins Museum of Fine Arts. Among its educational institutions are the Univ. of Missouri-Kansas City, Avila College, Park College, Rockhurst College, Kansas City Art Institute, a college of osteopathy and surgery, a conservatory of music, two junior colleges, and a number of theological schools. The city has a philharmonic orchestra and several theaters. The Kansas City *Star* is nationally known; it was founded (1880) by William Rockhill Nelson and headed by him until 1915. Extensive flood damage in 1951 led to several river-control projects in the region. Richards-Gebaur Air Force Base is to the south. See J. H. McDowell, *Building a City: A Detailed History of Kansas City, Kansas* (1969).

Kansas-Nebraska Act, bill that became law on May 30, 1854, by which the U.S. Congress established the territories of Kansas and Nebraska. By 1854 the organization of the vast Platte and Kansas river countries W of Iowa and Missouri was overdue. As an isolated issue territorial organization of this area was no problem. It was, however, irrevocably bound to the bitter sectional controversy over the extension of slavery into the territories and was further complicated by conflict over the location of the projected TRANS-CONTINENTAL RAILROAD. Under no circumstances did proslavery Congressmen want a free territory (Kansas) W of Missouri. Because the West was expanding rapidly, territorial organization, despite these difficulties, could no longer be postponed. Four attempts to organize a single territory for this area had already been defeated in Congress, largely because of Southern opposition to the MISSOURI COMPROMISE. Although the last of these attempts to organize the area had nearly been successful, Stephen A. DOUGLAS, chairman of the Senate Committee on Territories, decided to offer territorial legislation making concessions to the South. Douglas's motives have remained largely a matter of speculation. Various historians have emphasized Douglas's desire for the Presidency, his wish to cement the bonds of the Democratic party, his interest in expansion and railroad building, or his desire to activate the unimpressive Pierce administration. The bill he reported in Jan., 1854, contained the provision that the question of slavery should be left to the decision of the territorial settlers themselves. This was the famous principle that Douglas now called "popular sovereignty" (see SQUATTER SOVEREIGNTY), though actually it had been enunciated four years earlier in the COMPROMISE OF 1850. In its final form Douglas's bill provided for the creation of two new territories—Kansas and Nebraska—instead of one. The obvious inference—at least to Missourians—was that the first would be slave, the second free. The Kansas-Nebraska Act flatly contradicted the provisions of the Missouri Compromise (under which slavery would have been barred from both territories); indeed, an amendment was added specifically repealing that compromise. This aspect of the bill in particular enraged the antislavery forces, but after three months of bitter debate in Congress, Douglas, backed by President Pierce and the Southerners, saw it adopted. Its effects were anything but reassuring to those who had hoped for a peaceful solution. The squatter sovereignty provision caused both proslavery and antislavery forces to marshal strength and exert full pressure to determine the "popular" decision in Kansas in their own favor, using groups such as the EMIGRANT AID COMPANY. The result was the tragedy of "bleeding" Kansas. Northerners and Southerners were aroused to such passions that sectional division reached a point that precluded reconciliation. A new political organization, the REPUBLICAN PARTY, was founded by opponents of the bill, and the United States was propelled toward the Civil War. See P. O. Ray, *The Repeal of the Missouri Compromise* (1909, repr. 1965).

Kansas State University, at Manhattan; coeducational; land-grant and state supported; chartered and opened 1863.

Kansu or **Kan-su** (both: kăn'sōō, gän'sōō'), province (1968 est. pop. 13,000,000), NW China. The capital is LAN-CHOU. Kansu is bordered by the Mongolian People's Republic on the north. Its mountains include part of the Nan Shan range and an extension of the Kunlun. The loess soil is very fertile, but rainfall is inadequate and irrigation and land reclamation programs have had to be developed. Winter wheat, kaoliang, millet, corn, rice, cotton, and tobacco are grown, especially in the Huang Ho (Yellow River) and Wei River valleys. Large state farms have been established in the province. Livestock (cows, sheep, goats, horses, and camels) are raised in the mountainous areas. Kansu's mineral resources include coal, copper, gold, and large deposits of iron ore and oil; two important oil fields are in the province. Lan-chou is a flourishing industrial center, with one of the largest oil refineries in the country, and Yu-men is an oil center; other towns are developing rapidly. Roads and railways have been extensively improved. Lan-chou is an important transportation hub; the Lan-chou–Sinkiang RR crosses the province, and the Lan-chou–Peking RR has a connection through Mongolia to the USSR. Long isolated from the center of Chinese power, the Kansu area has traditionally been independent of all but the strongest central governments. After the 13th cent., Muslim strength grew, and fierce Muslim rebellions often plagued the central government. Today the province's strategic importance is enhanced by its control of communications into Sinkiang, Mongolia, and the USSR. Although Mandarin Chinese comprise most of the population, there are 11 major minorities, of which Muslims and Mongols are the largest. Kansu's boundaries have been changed several times in recent years. The former province of Ninghsia was joined to it in 1954, then detached in 1958 and reconstituted as an autonomous region. In the 1969–70 redistricting, Kansu received a portion of W Inner Mongolian Autonomous Region.

Kant, Immanuel (ĭmän'ōōĕl känt), 1724–1804, German metaphysician, one of the greatest figures in philosophy, b. Königsberg (now Kaliningrad, USSR), where he was educated. He tutored in several families and after 1755 lectured at the Univ. of Königsberg in philosophy and various sciences. He became professor of logic and metaphysics in 1770 and achieved wide renown through his writings and teachings. His early work, reflecting his studies of Christian Wolff and G. W. Leibniz, was followed by a period of great development culminating in the *Kritik der reinen Vernunft* (1781, tr. *Critique of Pure Reason*). This work inaugurated his so-called "critical period"—the period of his major writings. The more important among these writings were *Prolegomena zu einer jeden künftigen Metaphysik* (1783, tr. *Prolegomena to Any Future Metaphysics*), *Grundlegung zur Metaphysik der Sitten* (1785, tr. *Foundations of the Metaphysics of Morals*), *Kritik der praktischen Vernunft* (1788, tr. *Critique of Practical Reason*), and *Kritik der Urteilskraft* (1790, tr. *Critique of Judgment*). His *Religion innerhalb der Grenzen der blossen Vernunft* (1793, tr. *Religion within the Limits of Reason Alone*) provoked a government order to desist from further publications on religion. According to Kant, his reading of David Hume awakened him from his dogmatic slumber and set him on the road to becoming the "critical philosopher," whose position can be seen as a synthesis of the Leibniz-Wolffian rationalism and the Humean skepticism. Kant termed his basic insight into the nature of knowledge "the Copernican revolution in philosophy." Instead of assuming that our ideas, to be true, must conform to an external reality independent of our knowing, Kant proposed that objective reality is known only insofar as it conforms to the essential structure of the knowing mind. He maintained that objects of experience—phenomena—may be known, but that things lying beyond the realm of possible experience—noumena, or things-in-themselves—are unknowable, although their existence is a necessary presupposition. Phenomena that can be perceived in the pure forms of sensibility, space, and time must, if they are to be understood, possess the characteristics that constitute our categories of understanding. Those categories, which include causality and substance, are the source of the structure of phenomenal experience. The scientist, therefore, may be sure that the natural events he observes are knowable in terms of the categories. Man's field of knowledge, thus emancipated from Humean skepticism, is nevertheless limited to the world of phenomena. All theoretical attempts to know things-in-themselves are bound to fail. This inevitable failure is the theme of the portion of the *Critique of Pure Reason* entitled the "Transcendental Dialectic." Here Kant shows that the three great problems of metaphysics—God, freedom, and immortality—are insoluble by speculative thought. Their existence can be neither affirmed nor denied on theoretical grounds, nor can they be scientifically demonstrated, but Kant shows the necessity of their existence in his moral philosophy. Kant's ethics centers in his categorical imperative (or moral law)—"Act as if the maxim from which you act were to become through your will a universal law." This law has its source in the autonomy of a rational being, and it is the formula for an absolutely good will. However, since man is a member of two worlds, the sensible and the intelligible, he does not infallibly act in accordance with this law but on the contrary almost always acts according to inclination. Thus what is objectively necessary, i.e., to will in conformity to the law, is subjectively contingent; and for this reason the moral law confronts man as an "ought." In the *Critique of Practical Reason* Kant went on to state that morality requires the belief in the existence of God, freedom, and immortality, because without their existence there can be no morality. In the *Critique of Judgment* Kant applied his critical method to aesthetic and teleological judgments. The chief purpose of this work was to find a bridge between the sensible and the intelligible worlds, sharply distinguished in his theoretical and practical philosophy. This bridge is found in the concepts of beauty and purposiveness that suggest at least the possibility of an ultimate union of the two realms. The results of Kant's work are incalculable. In addition to being the impetus to the development of German idealism by J. G. Fichte, F. W. Schelling, and G. W. F. Hegel, Kant's philosophy has influenced almost every area of thought. Among the major outgrowths of Kant's influence was the Neo-Kantianism of the late 19th cent. This movement had many branches in Germany, France, and Italy; the two chief ones were the Marburg school, founded by Hermann Cohen and including Ernst Cassirer, and the Heidelberg school, led by Wilhelm Windelband and Heinrich Rickert. The Marburg school was primarily concerned with the application of Kantian insights to the understanding of the physical sciences, and the Heidelberg school with the application of Kant to the historical and cultural sciences. Closely connected with the latter group was the social philosopher Wilhelm Dilthey. Kant influenced English thought through the philosophy of Sir William Hamilton and T. H. Green, and some Kantian ideas are found in the pragmatism of William James and John Dewey. In theology, Kant's influence can be seen in the writings of Friedrich Schleiermacher and Albrecht Ritschl; his ideas in biology were developed by Hans Driesch, and in Gestalt psychology by Wolfgang Köhler. All of Kant's important works have been translated into English. See Lucien Goldmann, *Immanuel Kant* (1945, tr. 1972); H. W. Cassirer, *A Commentary on Kant's Critique of Judgment* (1938, repr. 1970) and *Kant's First Critique* (1954); John Kemp, *The Philosophy of Kant* (1968); L. W. Beck, *Studies in the Philosophy of Kant* (1965) and (ed.) *Kant Studies Today* (1969).

Kantara, El: see QANTARAH, AL, town, Egypt.

Kantrowitz, Adrian, 1918–, American surgeon. The son of a physician, Kantrowitz received his M.D. from Western Reserve Univ. (1943), returning after World War II to study cardiovascular physiology under Carl John Wiggers. He devised (with Alan Lerrick) a plastic heart valve (1954), a heart-lung machine (1958), an internal pacemaker (1961–62), and (with Tetsuzo Akutsu) an auxiliary left ventricle (1964). In 1966 he performed the first implantation of a partial mechanical heart in a human, and on Dec. 6, 1967, the second human cardiac transplant. He also published pioneer motion pictures taken inside the living heart.

Kanuma (känōō'mä), city (1970 pop. 77,746), Tochigi prefecture, central Honshu, Japan. It is an industrial center where brooms, hemp yarn and rope, and wood fittings are produced.

Kanye (kän'yə), town (1971 pop. 10,664), SE Botswana. It is a commercial and administrative center. Asbestos is mined nearby.

Kao-hsiung or **Kaohiung** (both: gou-shyōōng), city (1971 est. pop. 845,900), S Taiwan. It is the second largest city of Taiwan, the leading port in the southern part of the island, and a major industrial center. The leading industries produce sugar, petroleum products, cement, aluminum, wood and paper products, fertilizers, metals, and machinery; shipbuilding is also carried on. The city grew up from a small fishing village and was developed as a manufacturing center and port by the Japanese, who occupied Taiwan in 1895. Kao-hsiung has an important naval base.

Kaolack (kou'läk), city (1969 est. pop. 95,000), W Senegal, a port on the Saloum River. Lying in a farm area, Kaolack is a major peanut marketing and exporting center and has a large peanut oil factory. Brewing, leather tanning, cotton ginning, and fish processing are also important industries. Salt is produced from nearby salines. The city is on the railroad from Dakar to the Niger River in Mali. Kaolack is the center of the Sufi Muslim Tijaniyya brotherhood, whose mosque is on the city's outskirts.

kaoliang (kä"ōlēăng'): see SORGHUM.

kaolin (kā'əlĭn): see CHINA CLAY.

kaolinite (kā'əlĭnīt), clay mineral crystallizing in the monoclinic system and forming the chief constituent of CHINA CLAY and kaolin. It is a hydrous aluminum silicate commonly formed by the weathering and decomposition of rocks containing aluminum silicate compounds; feldspar is a chief source. Kaolinite has the same chemical composition as dickite and nacrite (both of which are also clay or kaolin minerals) but differs from them in origin, in optical properties, in reaction to heat, and in certain other physical properties. Kaolinite is the basic raw material for ceramics, and large quantities are also used in the manufacture of coated paper.

Kao Tsu: see LIU PANG.

Kapilavastu (kä"pĭləvä'stōō), ancient town, S Nepal. According to legend, the Buddha, whose father ruled the state of Kapilavastu, passed his early years there and was born nearby.

Kapitza, Peter (kä'pētsə), 1894–, Russian physicist, educated at the polytechnic institute of Petrograd (now Leningrad) and at Cambridge. He developed equipment (for a laboratory at Cambridge) capable of producing very powerful magnetic fields for his experiments in LOW TEMPERATURE PHYSICS. In 1934, Kapitza returned to the USSR, and the equipment he designed was bought by the Soviet government. Kapitza was made director of the Institute for Physical Problems of the Academy of Sciences of the USSR. In 1938 he discovered the SUPERFLUIDITY of liquid helium. He resigned as head of the Institute for Physical Problems in 1946, but returned as director in 1955 and also became editor of the *Journal of Theoretical and Experimental Physics.* He has been an outspoken advocate of open scientific thought in the USSR.

Kaplan, Mordecai Menahem, 1881–, American rabbi, educator, and philosopher, b. Lithuania, grad. College of the City of New York, 1900, M.A. Columbia, 1902. He went to the United States when he was eight years old. In 1909 he became principal and in 1931 dean of the Teachers Institute of the Jewish Theological Seminary of America. In 1922 he founded the Society for the Advancement of Judaism. He is best known, however, as the originator and leader of the Reconstructionist movement (see JUDAISM). Among his many books are *Judaism as a Civilization* (enl. ed. 1957), *The Meaning of God in Modern Jewish Religion* (1937), *The Future of the American Jew* (1948), *Judaism without Supernaturalism* (1958), *The Greater Judaism in the Making* (1960), *The Religion of Ethical Nationhood* (1970), *And If Not Now When? Toward a Reconstitution of the Jewish People* (1973). See Ira Eisenstein and Eugene Kohn, ed., *Mordecai M. Kaplan: An Evaluation* (1952).

kapok (kā'pŏk, kăp'ək), name for a tropical tree of the family Bombacaceae (BOMBAX family) and for the fiber (floss) obtained from the seeds in the ripened pods. The floss has been important in commerce since the 1890s; the chief source is *Ceiba pentandra,* the kapok (or silk-cotton) tree, cultivated in Java, Ceylon, the Philippines, and other parts of the Far East and in Africa, where it was introduced from its native America. The floss is removed by hand from the pods, dried, freed from seeds and dust, and baled for export. The lustrous, yellowish floss is light, fluffy, resilient, and resistant to water and decay. It is used as a stuffing, especially for life preservers, bedding, and upholstery, and for insulation against sound and heat. The seed kernels contain about 25% fatty oil used for soap or refined as edible oil. The residual cake is valuable as a fertilizer and as livestock fodder. Kapok is classified in the division MAGNOLIOPHYTA, class Magnoliopsida, order Malvales, family Bombacaceae.

Kaposvár (kŏ'pôshvär), city (1970 pop. 58,099), SW Hungary, on the Kapos River. It is a road and rail junction, a market for agricultural goods and livestock, and an industrial center. Landmarks include an 18th-century church, a 19th-century town hall, and the ruins of an old castle.

Kapp, Wolfgang (vôlf'gäng käp), 1858–1922, German right-wing politician. In 1920 he led the uprising known as the Kapp putsch, an armed revolt in Berlin aimed at restoring the German monarchy. He seized the Berlin government, but a general strike broke his power. Kapp fled to Sweden, returned (1922) to Germany, and died while awaiting trial for treason.

Kapteyn, Jacobus Cornelius (yäkō'bəs kôrnā'lēəs käptīn'), 1851–1922, Dutch astronomer. He was an authority on the Milky Way, of which he made notable statistical studies; he constructed a model of the galaxy known as the "Kapteyn universe." He computed the positions of the stars of the Southern Hemisphere photographed by Sir David Gill and in 1904 announced the discovery of two streams of stars moving in opposite directions in the plane of the Milky Way.

Kapuas (kä'po͞oäs), river, c.710 mi (1,140 km) long, rising in the mountains of central Borneo and flowing SW through W Kalimantan, Indonesia, to the South China Sea near Pontianak. Its valley is intensively cultivated; rice is the chief crop. The river is navigable for c.560 mi (900 km).

Kapuskasing (kăpəskā'sĭng), town (1971 pop. 12,834), central Ont., Canada, on the Kapuskasing River, N of Timmins. It has lumbering and pulp and paper mills. A federal experimental farm is nearby.

Kara (kä'rə), river, c.140 mi (230 km) long, NE European and NW Siberian USSR. It flows N from the N Urals into the Kara Sea, forming part of the traditional border between European and Asian Russia. It is navigable in its lower course.

Karabakh: see NAGORNO-KARABAKH, USSR.

Kara-Bogaz-Gol (kä'rə-bəgäz'-gôl), shallow bay, c.7,000 sq mi (18,100 sq km), Central Asian USSR, in Turkmenistan. An arm of the Caspian Sea, it acts as a natural evaporating basin, drawing off the water of the Caspian and depositing salts along its shores. The town of **Kara-Bogaz-Gol** is a Caspian seaport at the entrance of the bay and produces chemicals, sulfates, and mirabilite.

Karabük (kärä'bük), city (1970 pop. 64,770), N Turkey. It was built in the 1930s as the seat of the iron and steel industry of Turkey. Nearby are the Zonguldak coal fields.

Karachay-Cherkess Autonomous Oblast (kärächī'-chĕrkĕs'), administrative division (1970 pop. 345,000), c.5,500 sq mi (14,200 sq km), Stavropol Kray, SE European USSR, in the Greater Caucasus, along the upper Kuban River. CHERKESSK is the capital. The oblast consists of lowland steppe in the north and the Caucasian foothills in the south. Grains, fruits, and vegetables are grown and livestock is raised. The oblast has coal, lead, zinc, copper, and gold mines. Industrial products include building materials, foodstuffs, and machinery. Though there are Cherkess, the overwhelming majority of the population are Karachay, Turkic-speaking Muslims who arrived in the region in the 14th cent. In the 16th cent. they became vassals of Kabardinian princes, then passed (1733) to Turkish suzerainty, and in 1828 were conquered by the Russians. The region was included (1921) in the Mountain People's Republic, but in 1922 it became the Karachay-Cherkess Autonomous Oblast. In 1924 it was divided into the Karachay Autonomous Oblast and the Cherkess National Okrug; the latter became an autonomous oblast in 1928 (see CIRCASSIA). In 1943 the Karachay, accused of collaborating with the Germans in World War II, were deported to Siberia and their autonomous oblast was abolished. However, the Karachay-Cherkess Autonomous Oblast was reestablished in 1957, when the "rehabilitation" of deported peoples was decreed.

Karachi (kərä'chē), city (1972 est. pop. 3,469,000), largest city and former capital of Pakistan, SE Pakistan, on the Arabian Sea near the Indus River delta. The capital of Sind prov., it is Pakistan's chief seaport and industrial center, as well as a transportation, commercial, and financial hub and a military headquarters. It has a large automobile assembly plant, an oil refinery, a steel mill, shipbuilding and repair and railroad yards, jute and textile factories, printing and publishing plants, food processing plants, and chemical and engineering works. Filmmaking and fishing are also important. Karachi airport, one of the busiest in Asia, is a major link in international air routes. An old settlement, Karachi was developed as a port and trading center by Hindu merchants in the early 18th cent. In 1843 it passed to the British, who made it the seat of the Sind government and a military center. Steady improvements in harbor facilities made Karachi a leading Indian port by the late 19th cent., while agricultural development of the hinterland gave it a large export trade in wheat and cotton. Karachi served as Pakistan's capital from 1947, when the country gained independence, until 1959, when Rawalpindi became the interim capital pending completion of Islamabad. In Karachi are a university and several other educational institutions; the national museum, with a fine archaeological collection; and the tomb of Muhammad Ali JINNAH, founder of Pakistan. Karachi's port was bombed and shelled during the 1971 India-Pakistan War.

Karadjordje: see KARAGEORGE.

Karadjordjević or **Karageorgevich** (both: kărəjôr'jəvĭch), Serbian dynasty, descended from Karageorge (Karadjordje). Its ruling members were ALEXANDER, prince of Serbia, and kings PETER I, ALEXANDER, and PETER II, of Yugoslavia. It was long involved in a feud with the OBRENOVIĆ dynasty. The Karadjordjević dynasty lost the throne in 1945 when Yugoslavia became a federal republic.

Karadžić, Vuk Stefanović (vo͞ok stĕfä'nôvich kä'räjĭch), 1787–1864, Serbian philologist and folklorist, of Moldavian descent. During his lifetime Karadžić published 10 volumes of Serbian folk poetry. He inaugurated language reforms and adopted the Serbian vernacular. His introduction of phonetic spelling and invention of new letters to complete the Cyrillic alphabet were major contributions to Serbian linguistics. Among his most important lexicographical works are a grammar of vernacular Serbian (1814) and a Serbian dictionary (1818). In 1847 he translated the New Testament into Serbian for the British and Foreign Bible Society.

Karafuto: see SAKHALIN, USSR.

Karaganda (kä'rəgəndä'), city (1970 pop. 522,000), capital of Karaganda oblast, Central Asian USSR, in Kazakhstan, on the Trans-Kazakhstan RR. It consists of about 50 coal-mining settlements scattered around the central part of the city, and it is a leading industrial and cultural center of Kazakhstan. Its industries include iron and steel foundries, flour mills, food and beverage plants, ship repair yards, and factories that produce mining equipment, building materials, machinery, and footwear. Karaganda was founded in 1857 as a copper-mining settlement. The Karaganda coal basin, developed in the late 1920s, is one of the USSR's largest producers of bituminous coal. Near the city is the gigantic Novo-Karaganda power station.

Karageorge (kăr'əjôrj', kä"räjôr'jā), 1768?–1817, Serbian patriot. Born George Petrović, he was known as Karageorge, or Black George. He led the Serbs in their insurrection (1804) against the Turks, took (1806) Belgrade, where the Turkish population was massacred, and was proclaimed (1808) hereditary chief of the Serbs. He fought with Russia against Turkey (1809–12). Abandoned by the Russians when peace was signed, he fled to Austria. On his return to Serbia he was murdered, probably at the instigation of Miloš Obrenović (see MILOŠ). Although an illiterate peasant, Karageorge showed great military ability. The name also appears as Karadjordje, and the dynasty descended from him is known as Karadjordjević.

Karageorgevich: see KARADJORDJEVIĆ.

Kara Irtysh: see IRTYSH, river, USSR.

Karaites (kâr'əīts), Jewish schismatic sect, reputedly founded (8th cent.) in Persia by ANAN BEN DAVID and originally known as Ananites. Its adherents were called Karaites after the 9th cent. The Karaites attacked the Talmudic interpretation of the Bible, rejecting the oral law and interpreting the Bible literally, and they developed their own commentaries, which were in many respects more rigorous and ascetic than the Talmudic interpretations. In the 10th cent. they produced a splendid literature in both Arabic and Hebrew. The sect declined after the 12th cent., but remnants are still extant, notably in the Crimea and Israel. The name is also spelled Caraites. See *Karaite Anthology* (ed. and tr. by Leon Nemoy, 1952), Zvi Ankori, *Karaites in Byzantium: The Formative Years, 970–1100* (1957, repr. 1968); Philip Birnbaum, ed., *Karaite Studies* (1971).

Karaj (käräj'), city (1966 pop. 44,243), Tehran prov., N Iran, on the Karaj River. It is an agricultural market and a transportation center. Chemicals are manufactured there.

Karajan, Herbert von (käräyän'), 1908–, Austrian conductor. Karajan began his conducting career in 1927. After World War II his reputation spread through Europe to the United States. He toured with various orchestras (notably the Berlin Philharmonic) and participated in many of Europe's music festivals. He is musical director of the Berlin Philharmonic and was artistic director of the Vienna State Opera (1956–64). Karajan is especially noted for his numerous recordings.

Herbert von Karajan.

Kara-Kalpak Autonomous Soviet Socialist Republic (kä"rəkŭlpäk'), autonomous republic (1970 pop. 702,000), c.61,000 sq mi (158,000 sq km), Central Asian USSR, on the Amu Darya River. NUKUS is the capital. The republic comprises parts of the Ustyurt plateau, the Kyzyl-Kum desert, and the Amu Darya delta on the Aral Sea. The republic is the USSR's chief producer of alfalfa; other crops are cotton, rice, corn, and jute. Livestock raising (notably cattle and Karakul sheep) and silkworm breeding are widespread. There are many light industries. The population, concentrated in the delta, consists mostly of Kara-Kalpak (Turkic-speaking Muslims), Kazakhs, Uzbek, Turkomans, Russians, and Tatars. The Kara-Kalpak, known since the 16th cent., when they lived along the lower and middle courses of the Syr Darya River, were partly subjected by the Kazakhs. In the 18th cent. they migrated to their present homeland and in the 19th cent. came under the rule of the khanate of Khiva. The khanate passed under Russian control at the end of the 19th cent. and under Bolshevik control by 1920. The Kara-Kalpak Autonomous Oblast was formed in 1925 within the Kazakh Autonomous Republic. It became an autonomous republic itself in 1932 and was transferred to the Uzbek SSR in 1936.

Karakorum (kä"rəkō'rəm), ruined city, central Mongolian People's Republic, near the Orkhon River, SW of Ulan Bator. The area around Karakorum had been inhabited by nomadic Turkic tribes from the 1st cent. A.D., but the city itself was not laid out until c.1220, when Jenghiz Khan, founder of the Mongol empire, established his residence there. As capital of the MONGOLS, Karakorum was visited (c.1247) by a papal mission under Giovanni Carpini. The city was abandoned (and later destroyed) after Kublai Khan, grandson of Jenghiz, transferred (1267) the Mongol capital to Khanbaliq (modern Peking). The noted Lamaist monastery of Erdeni Dzu was built near Karakorum in 1586. The ruins of the ancient Mongol city were discovered in 1889 by N. M. Yadrinstev, a Russian explorer, who also uncovered the Orkhon Inscriptions (see under ORKHON). Karakorum is also the name of a nearby site, which in the 8th and 9th cent. was the capital of the UIGURS.

Karakorum, mountain system, extending c.300 mi (480 km), between the Indus and Yarkand rivers, N Kashmir, S central Asia; SE extension of the Hindu Kush. Karakorum's main range has some of the world's highest peaks, including Mt. Godwin-Austen (28,250 ft/8,611 m), the second-tallest peak in the world. Karakorum also has several of the world's largest glaciers. Its southern slopes are the watershed for many tributaries of the Indus River. The mountains, the greatest barrier between India and central Asia, are crossed above the perpetual snow line by two natural routes; **Karakorum Pass** (alt. 18,290 ft/5,575 m), the chief pass of the system, is on the main Kashmir-China route.

Kara-Kul (kä″rə-ko͞ol), mountain lake, c.140 sq mi (360 sq km), Gorno-Badakhshan Autonomous Oblast, Central Asian USSR, in the Pamir, near the Chinese border. It is c.12,840 ft (3,900 m) above sea level, and its greatest depth is 780 ft (240 m).

Karakul sheep (kăr′əkəl), breed native to central Asia. The newborn lambs usually have tightly curled black fur and are skinned before they are three days old to provide the commercial lambskin for which the sheep are raised. The finest pelts are often obtained from unborn lambs. A large percentage of this lambskin is classified as Persian lamb, though it may also be called karakul, broadtail, krimmer, or astrakhan, according to the quality and tightness of the curl. The lambs grow rapidly and produce good meat but are seldom raised for this purpose. The grown sheep are medium-sized and broad-tailed; their wool is a mixture of coarse and fine fibers, varying in color from black to shades of tan and gray, and is used in making carpeting and other heavy fabrics. Karakul sheep are raised in several countries of Asia, Europe, Africa, and the Americas. In the United States they are raised on a small scale, chiefly in Texas.

Kara-Kum (kär″ə-ko͞om′), two deserts, S USSR. The Caspian Kara-Kum, the larger desert (c.115,000 sq mi/297,900 sq km), is W of the Amu Darya River and includes most of the Turkmen Republic. The Murghab and Tedzhen rivers flow out of the Hindu Kush Mts. to the south and empty into the desert, providing water for irrigation. The oases of Mary (Merv) and Tedzhen are noted for cotton growing. The Kara-Kum Canal, one of the largest irrigation projects in the Soviet Union, carries water from the Amu Darya at Kelif westward across the desert to Mary and ultimately to Ashkhabad, a distance of c.500 mi (800 km). The canal water permits irrigated agriculture (mainly cotton) and industry to flourish along the southern margin of the desert. The Trans-Caspian RR, a leading transportation artery of Soviet Central Asia, crosses the desert from Krasnovodsk, on the Caspian Sea, to Ashkhabad, Mary, Bukhara, and Tashkent. Natural gas deposits have been discovered at Darvaza and Mary. The Aral Kara-Kum desert (c.15,440 sq mi/40,000 sq km) lies NE of the Aral Sea in the Kazakh Republic.

Karamai (kärämī′), Mandarin *K'o-la-ma-i,* city, N Sinkiang Uigur Autonomous Region, China, in the Dzungarian basin. Since the discovery (1955) there of one of the largest oil fields in China, it has grown into an oil-producing and refining center.

Karaman (kärämän′), town (1970 pop. 35,049), S central Turkey, at the northern foot of the Taurus mts. The ancient Laranda, Karaman was renamed after the chieftain of a Turkic tribe who conquered the city c.1250 and set up the independent Muslim state of Karamania, which at one time comprised most of Asia Minor. A successor state of the Seljuk empire, Karamania existed until its final subjugation by the Ottoman Turks in the late 15th cent. Karaman has retained ruins of the Karamanid castle and of two fine mosques.

Mountains in the Karakorum range in the western region of Pakistan near the Chinese border.

Karamanlis, Constantine (kôn'stäntēn kärämänlĭs'), 1907–, Greek political leader, b. Macedonia. Elected to parliament in 1936, he held various cabinet posts from 1946 to 1955. After the death of Marshal Papagos, Karamanlis was named (1955) premier. He held that post from Oct., 1955, to June, 1963, except for brief intervals from March to May, 1958, and from Sept. to Nov., 1961, while his right-wing National Radical Union, founded in 1956, continued to gain majorities in the general elections. A partisan of the North Atlantic Treaty Organization, Karamanlis reached (1959) agreement with Great Britain and Turkey over Cyprus. In 1959 he announced a five-year plan (1960–64) for the Greek economy, emphasizing improvement of agricultural and industrial production. After his cabinet fell in 1963, Karamanlis went into exile abroad. He was a vocal opponent of the military junta that seized power in Greece in 1967. In July, 1974, the junta fell, following a disastrous military venture in Cyprus. Karamanlis returned as premier. He scheduled parliamentary elections in Nov., 1974, and his party, the New Democratic party, won a substantial majority. His name also appears as Caramanlis.

Kara Mustafa: see MUSTAFA.

Karamzin, Nikolai Mikhailovich (nyĭkəlī' mēkhī'ləvĭch kərəmzēn'), 1766–1826, Russian historian and writer. *Letters of a Russian Traveler, 1789–90* (1792, abr. tr. 1957), dealing with a journey to Western Europe, brought a cosmopolitan awareness into Russian writing. Karamzin made the Russian literary language more polished, elegant, and rhythmic. These reforms were important for later writers, especially Pushkin. Karamzin's sentimental story of a betrayed peasant girl, "Poor Lisa" (1792), forecast the novel of social protest. His greatest work, an 11-volume *History of the Russian State* (1818–24), was a widely read dramatic account of the political actions of the Russian princes up to 1613. He believed in a strong monarchic state, but criticized 18th-century rulers in his vigorous *Memoir on Ancient and Modern Russia,* written in 1810–11 (1914, tr. 1959). See his *Selected Prose* (tr. 1969); studies by H. M. Nebel (1967) and A. G. Cross (1971).

Kara Sea, Rus. *Karskoye More,* shallow section of the Arctic Ocean, off N USSR, between Severnaya Zemlya and Novaya Zemlya. It is no deeper than 650 ft (198 m). It receives the Ob, the Yenisei, the Pyasina, and the Taimyra rivers, and is important as a fishing ground. Its main ports are Novyy Port and Dikson, but the ice-locked sea is navigable only during August and September. Ice floes menaced its early navigators and added to the difficulties of the Northeast Passage.

karate: see JUDO.

Karatsu (kärä'tso͞o), city (1970 pop. 74,223), Saga prefecture, NW Kyushu, Japan, on Karatsu Bay. It is a summer resort and fishing port important historically as Japan's ancient communications point with Korea.

Karbala (kär'bələ), city (1965 pop. 83,301), provincial capital, central Iraq, at the edge of the Syrian Desert. The city's trade is in religious objects, hides, wool, and dates. Karbala is the site of the tomb of the Shiite leader Husein, who was killed in the city in 680, and is second only to Mecca in being a holy place visited by Shiite pilgrims. The tomb, with a gilded dome and three minarets, is the most notable building; it was destroyed by the Wahabis in 1801 but was quickly restored by contributions from Persians and other Shiite Muslims. Iranian pilgrims to Mecca usually begin their journey at Karbala, and many pious Muslims bring the bones of their dead for burial there.

Karcag (kŏr'tsŏg), city (1970 pop. 24,631), E Hungary. A road and rail junction, Karcag is an important communications point.

Kardelj, Edvard (ĕd'värt kär'dĕlyə), 1910–, Yugoslavian politician. A Slovenian schoolteacher, he early joined the Yugoslav Communist party. In 1940 he became a politburo member. He was important in the underground in World War II and was vice premier of Josip Broz Tito's provisional government, a position that he continued to hold after the formal establishment of the Yugoslav Communist state in 1945. He later served as minister of foreign affairs (1948–53), vice chairman of the federal executive council (1953–63), and president of the federal parliament (1963–67). A leading ideologist, Kardelj helped in carrying out Yugoslavia's break with the USSR in 1948 and in adapting the official ideology to the new independent course.

Kareah (kārē'ə), father of JOHANAN **1.** Jer. 40.8. Careah: 2 Kings 25.23.

Karelia: see KARELIAN AUTONOMOUS SOVIET SOCIALIST REPUBLIC.

Karelian Autonomous Soviet Socialist Republic (kərē'lyən) or **Karelia** (kərĕ'lyēə), autonomous region (1970 pop. 714,000), c.66,540 sq mi (172,300 sq km), NW European USSR, extending from the Finnish border in the west to the White Sea in the east and from the Kola Peninsula in the north to Lakes Ladoga and Onega (Europe's largest freshwater bodies) in the south. PETROZAVODSK is the capital. A glaciated plateau, Karelia is covered by about 50,000 lakes and by coniferous forests; fishing and lumbering are major industries. Agriculture, generally hampered by cold climate and poor soil, is possible only in the south, where some grains, potatoes, fodder grasses, and vegetables are grown; dairy farming and livestock raising are also carried on. Karelia has valuable deposits of iron ore, magnetite, lead, zinc, copper, titanium, marble, and pyrite. Power for industry is supplied by the republic's many short, rapid rivers. Besides lumbering and related industries, Karelia has shipbuilding and repair yards, food-processing plants, ironworks, and factories that produce machinery, aluminum, building materials, and textiles. The republic is crossed by the Murmansk RR and by the Baltic–White Sea Canal, which is both commercially and strategically important. Russians constitute a majority of the population, the rest of which consists mainly of Karelians, Finns, and Lapps, who are very closely related and have an identical written language. The Karelians, a major division of the Finns, were first mentioned in the 9th cent. and formed a strong medieval state. Karelia, properly speaking the region N and E of Lake Onega, was conquered in the 12th–13th cent. by the Swedes, who took the west, and by Novgorod, which took the east. The eastern part was taken from Russia by Sweden in 1617 but restored in 1721 by the Treaty of Nystad. The western part shared the history of Finland until 1940. It was from oral traditions among the Karelians that the Finnish national epic, the *Kalevala,* was compiled in the 19th cent. by Elias Lönnrot. The Karelian area of the Russian Empire was economically backward and was often a place of exile for political prisoners. In 1920 an autonomous oblast, known as the Karelian Workers'

Commune, was set up in E Karelia; in 1923 it was made into the Karelian Autonomous SSR, which, after the Soviet-Finnish War of 1939–40, incorporated most of the territory ceded by Finland to the USSR. In March, 1940, the region's status was raised to that of a constituent republic, called the Karelo-Finnish SSR. During World War II, the Finns (allies of the Axis powers) occupied most of Karelia; but it was returned to the USSR in 1944. Karelia reverted to the status of an autonomous republic in 1956.

Karelian Isthmus, land bridge, NW European USSR, connecting Russia and Finland. Situated between the Gulf of Finland in the west and Lake Ladoga in the east, it is 25 to 70 mi (40–113 km) wide and 90 mi (145 km) long. LENINGRAD and VYBORG (Viipuri) are its chief cities. Originally part of the Grand Duchy of Sweden, the isthmus passed to Russia in 1721, and—except for its southernmost section—became part of Finland in 1917. The Mannerheim Line, which crossed the isthmus, was breached in 1940 by the Russians, who occupied the area. It was briefly held (1941–44) by Finnish and German units during World War II. The isthmus was formally ceded to the USSR in 1944, and more than 400,000 of its Finnish residents moved into Finland.

Karelo-Finnish Soviet Socialist Republic: see KARELIAN AUTONOMOUS SOVIET SOCIALIST REPUBLIC.

Karenni State: see KAYAH STATE, Burma.

Karens (kərĕnz′), members of a Thai-Chinese cultural group, one of the most important minorities in Burma, living in the KAYAH STATE, Tenasserim, and the Irrawaddy delta. They form 11% of the Burmese population. The Karen hill tribes have tended to remain animistic, but among those settled in the plains there are about 300,000 Christians and over a million Buddhists. The Karens speak the Karen languages, probably of the Sino-Tibetan family. They are mostly farmers, but Karen tribesmen were superior soldiers in the military units raised in Burma under British rule. A major unifying element among the Karens is a strong opposition to Burmese political domination. Their revolt (1948–49) against the union government aimed at separation from Burma. They scored important successes, and the government was forced to grant the Karenni State (later Kayah State) a large measure of autonomy.

Karfiol, Bernard (kär′fēŏl), 1886–1952, American painter, b. Budapest of American parents; educated in Brooklyn, N.Y. He studied at the National Academy of Design in New York City and at Julian's in Paris. From 1908 to 1913 he taught and painted in New York. From 1917, Karfiol's work was widely exhibited and received many awards. It is characterized by tenderness, simplicity, sensuous form, and harmonious color. Perhaps best known as a painter of nudes, Karfiol was also an admirable landscape and portrait painter. Many of his scenes were inspired by the landscape of Maine. *Fishing Village* and *Seated Nude* (both: Mus. of Modern Art, New York City) are characteristic works. Karfiol is represented in many leading American galleries. See study by J. P. Slusser (1931).

Kariba Dam (kärē′bä), hydroelectric project, in Kariba gorge of the ZAMBEZI River, on the Zambia-Rhodesia border, S central Africa; built 1955–59. One of the world's largest dams, it is 420 ft (128 m) high and 1,900 ft (579 m) long. Kariba Lake, the dam's vast man-made reservoir, extends c.175 mi (280 km) and has a maximum width of 20 mi (32 km). The creation of the lake forced resettlement of about 50,000

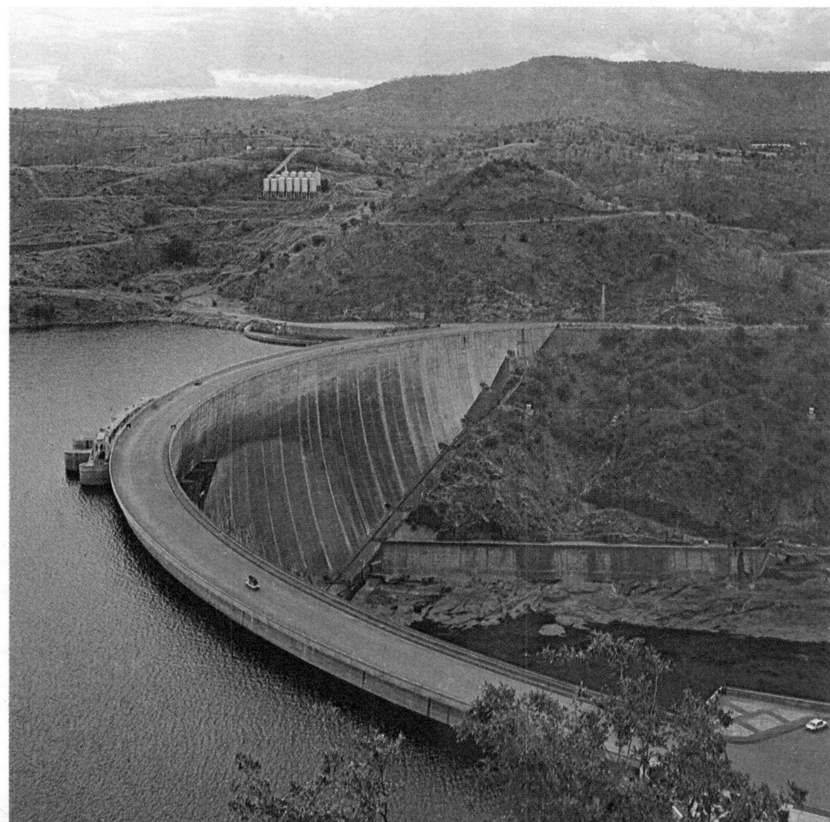

Kariba Dam, on the Zambia-Rhodesia border, one of the world's largest dams.

Africans living along the Zambezi. In 1960–61, Operation Noah captured and removed the animals threatened by the lake's rising waters. The Kariba project supplies electricity to the COPPERBELT in Zambia and to parts of Rhodesia.

Karikal, India: see FRENCH INDIA.

Karim Khan (kärēm' khän), d. 1779, ruler of Persia (1750–79), founder of the Zand dynasty. He emerged victorious from a contest for power and ruled under the title Vakil [representative]. His rule was one of tranquility, and he made Shiraz, his capital, beautiful with buildings including the Mosque of Vakil and the Bazaar of Vakil. A few northern tribes were left almost independent. One of them was the Kajars (or Qajars), and from them was to come AGA MUHAMMAD KHAN, who overthrew (1794) Lutf Ali Khan, the last ruler of the Zand dynasty.

Karisimbi, mountain, Africa: see VIRUNGA.

Kariya (kärē'yä), city (1970 pop. 87,671), Aichi prefecture, central Honshu, Japan. It is an industrial center with textile, mechanical, and food-processing industries.

Karkaa (kärkā'ə), unidentified place, S Palestine. Joshua 15.3.

Karkheh (kär'kĕ), ancient *Choaspes,* river, c.350 mi (560 km) long, rising in the Zagros mts., W Iran, and flowing S into the Khuzistan lowland, where it forms a swamp bordering the Tigris River. An ancient storage dam on the river at Shush made Khuzistan one of the most prosperous agricultural regions of Asia until the system fell into disrepair and the irrigated area reverted to desert. The area is now being reclaimed as part of the Khuzistan project.

Karkonosze: see KRKONOŠE, mountains.

Karkor, place, in Gilead. Judges 8.10.

Karl. For German and Swedish kings thus named, see CHARLES.

Karlfeldt, Erik Axel (ā'rĭk äk'səl kärl'fĕlt), 1864–1931, Swedish lyric poet. Little known outside Sweden, his work was greatly loved in his native land. Themes of nature, love, and peasant life predominate in *Songs of the Wilderness and of Love* (1895), *Fridolin's Ballads* (1898), and other collections. He was posthumously awarded the 1931 Nobel Prize in Literature, which he had refused in his lifetime. Selected poems were translated as *Arcadia Borealis* (1938).

Karli (kär'lē), village, Maharashtra state, W India. Nearby are Buddhist caves that may have been excavated as early as the 2d cent. B.C. The most famous of them measures 124 ft by 45 ft (38 m by 14 m) and is India's largest cave temple. Its ancient shrine, columns, and ornamentation survive in part.

Karl-Marx-Stadt (kärl-märks-shtät), formerly **Chemnitz** (kĕm'nĭts), city (1970 pop. 299,312), capital of Karl-Marx-Stadt district, S East Germany, on the Chemnitz River. It is a major industrial center and a road and rail junction. Manufactures include machine tools, machinery, chemicals, optical instruments, furniture, and textiles. Nearby is a large open-pit lignite mine. Of Wendish origin, the city was chartered in 1143, when it was also granted a linen-weaving monopoly. It grew as a trade center, was devastated in the Thirty Years War (1618–48), and recovered its prosperity after the introduction (late 17th cent.) of cotton milling. Noteworthy buildings of the city include the Renaissance-style city hall and a late-Gothic church, the Stadtkirche. The city was renamed Karl-Marx-Stadt in 1953.

Karl Marx University: see LEIPZIG, UNIV. OF.

Karloff, Boris, 1887–1969, Anglo-American actor, b. Dulwich, England; his original name was William Pratt. A distinguished character actor with a superb speaking voice, Karloff was famous for his monster roles in Hollywood horror films, notably *Frankenstein* (1931). His other movies include *The Ghoul* (1933), *The Bride of Frankenstein* (1935), *Isle of the Dead* (1945), and *Targets* (1968).

Karlovci, Sremski: see KARLOWITZ, TREATY OF.

Karlovy Vary (kär'lôvĭ vä'rĭ), Ger. *Karlsbad,* city (1970 pop. 43,708), NW Czechoslovakia, in Bohemia, at the confluence of the Teplá and Ohře rivers. A famous health resort, Karlovy Vary is one of the best-known spas of Europe; its hot mineral water is taken particularly for digestive diseases. The medicinal springs, known for centuries, attracted European aristocrats until World War I. Karlovy Vary is also noted for its china, glass, and porcelain industries, and bricks are produced in quantity. The city was chartered in the 14th cent. by Emperor Charles IV, who is said to have discovered its springs. In recent years, Karlovy Vary has hosted conferences of Soviet and East European Communist leaders.

Karlowitz, Treaty of (kär'lōvĭts), 1699, peace treaty signed at Sremski Karlovci (Ger. *Karlowitz*), N Serbia, Yugoslavia. It was concluded between the Ottoman Empire (Turkey) on the one side and Austria, Poland, and Venice on the other. The preceding war (1683–97) had resulted in the Turkish defeat in 1697, thereby forcing Turkey to consent to the treaty. All Hungary (including Transylvania but not the Banat of Temesvar), Croatia, and Slavonia were ceded to Austria by Turkey. Podolia passed to Poland, and the Peloponnesus and most of Dalmatia passed to Venice. Russia, also at war with Turkey, captured Azov in 1696 and concluded a separate peace treaty with Turkey in 1700. The Venetian gains were lost again at the Treaty of PASSAROWITZ (1718). The Treaty of Karlowitz, which crowned the successful campaign of Prince Eugene of Savoy, marked the beginning of the Ottoman Empire's disintegration.

Karlsbad: see KARLOVY VARY, Czechoslovakia.

Karlsefni, Thorfinn: see THORFINN KARLSEFNI.

Karlshamm (kärls-hä'mən, kärls'hä"-), city (1970 pop. 13,121), Blekinge co., SE Sweden, a busy port on the Baltic Sea; chartered 1664. It is the seat of a large fishing fleet and has a major concentrated food factory.

Karlskoga (kärl'sko͞o"gä), city (1970 pop. 36,963), Örebro co., S Sweden; chartered 1940. An industrial center, it is the seat of the Bofors iron and armaments works and has other industries that manufacture steel, machines, explosives, chemicals, and clothing.

Karlskrona (kärlskro͞o'nä), city (1970 pop. 34,145), capital of Blekinge co., SE Sweden, on the Baltic Sea. It is a seaport and fishing center with a large modern port. The city has been the headquarters of the Swedish navy since 1679 and has many service-connected industries. Manufactures include metal goods, canned food, and porcelain. A naval museum is in the city. A variant spelling is Carlscrona.

Karlsruhe (kärls'ro͞oə), city (1970 pop. 259,245), Baden-Württemberg, SW West Germany, on the northern fringes of the Black Forest, connected by canal with a port on the nearby Rhine River. It is a transportation, industrial, and cultural center and is the seat of the federal constitutional court and the federal court of justice. Manufactures include textiles, jewelry, pharmaceuticals, machinery, and refined oil. Karlsruhe was founded in 1715 by Karl Wilhelm, margrave of Baden-Durlach, to replace nearby Durlach (incorporated into Karlsruhe in 1938) as the margravial residence. After 1771 it was the capital of the duchy (later grand duchy and, after 1919, state) of Baden. The old part of Karlsruhe, badly damaged in World War II, was laid out as a vast semicircle with the streets converging radially upon the ducal palace (1752–85; restored after 1945). The city has a university (founded as a technical academy in 1825), a school of fine arts, a school of music, a center for atomic research, well-known theaters and art galleries, and a large conference center, the Schwarzwaldhalle (1953–54). It is sometimes spelled Carlsruhe.

Karlstad (kärl'städ), city (1970 pop. 64,458), capital of Värmland co., S Sweden, on Lake Vänern. It has ironworks and machine shops and other industries that manufacture forest products and heavy machinery. Known as Thingvalla (or Tingvalla) in the Middle Ages, it was chartered by Charles IX as Karlstad in 1584. A fire in 1865 destroyed much of the city. The treaty that severed the union of Norway and Sweden was negotiated and signed there in 1905.

Karlstadt, Reformation leader: see CARLSTADT.

karma or **karman** (kär'mə, kär'mən) [Skt.,=action, work, or ritual], basic concept common to HINDUISM, BUDDHISM, and JAINISM. The doctrine of karma states that one's state in this life is a result of actions (both physical and mental) in past incarnations, and action in this life can determine one's destiny in future incarnations. Karma is a natural, impersonal law of moral cause and effect and has no connection with the idea of a supreme power that decrees punishment or forgiveness of sins. Karmic law is universally applicable, and only those who have attained liberation from rebirth, called *mukti* (or *moksha*) or NIRVANA, can transcend it. *Karma yoga* (see YOGA), the spiritual discipline of detachment from the results of action, is a famous teaching of the BHAGAVAD-GITA.

Karman, Theodor von, 1881–1963, American aeronautical engineer, b. Hungary, grad. Royal Technical Univ., Budapest (1902) and Univ. of Göttingen (Ph.D., 1908). From 1909 to 1912 he served as director of the aeronautical institute at the Univ. of Aachen. He came to the United States in 1930, was naturalized in 1936, and was on the staff of the California Institute of Technology from 1930 to 1949. He made many contributions to the field of aerodynamics and is known especially for his mathematical formulas called the von Karman theory of vortex streets. These formulas are used in the calculation of the resistance by air to objects (e.g., aircraft, rockets) moving through it. His writings include *Aerodynamics* (1954) and his autobiography, *Wind and Beyond* (with Lee Edson, publ. posthumously, 1967).

Karmathians or **Carmathians** (kärmā'thēənz), a Muslim sect of the 9th and 10th cent., similar to the ASSASSIN sect. They were part of a movement for social reform which spread widely through Islam from the 9th to the 12th cent. They were organized according to initiation and illumination, like other similar sects of the period. Although heretical, their doctrine had a great influence on Islamic philosophy and remnants of it are today found in the religion of the Druses. The chief importance of the Karmathians came with their establishment of an independent communist community in lower Mesopotamia before 900. They were the source of rebellions in Khorasan and Syria, and after 900 they conquered all of Yemen. In spite of the efforts of the Abbasid caliph at Baghdad, the Karmathians continued their career until (c.930) they created a sensation that rocked Islam by carrying away the Black Stone from the Kaaba at Mecca. Ten years later the Karmathians returned the stone. They were in constant touch with the founders of Fatimid rule in Egypt, alternately at war or peace with them. They ceased to be a political power after 1000.

Karnak (kär'năk), village, central Egypt, on the Nile. It is 1 mi (1.6 km) E of LUXOR and occupies part of the site of THEBES. Remains of the pharaohs abound at Karnak. Most notable is the Great Temple of Amon. Although there was an older foundation, the

Ruins of the Great Temple of Amon at Karnak, Egypt.

temple was largely conceived and accomplished in the XVIII dynasty, and it is often considered the finest example of New Empire religious architecture. The temple grounds extend about 1,000 ft (300 m). The western half comprises a vast court and the great hypostyle hall (388 ft by 170 ft/118 m by 52 m), with 134 columns arranged in 16 rows. The eastern half is a complex of halls and shrines, many of the Middle Empire. There are smaller temples at Karnak dedicated to Mut and to Khensu, wife and son respectively of AMON.

Karnal (kərnäl′), town (1971 pop. 92,835), Haryana state, N central India. The town's name is derived from Karna, the rival of Arjuna in the Sanskrit MAHABHARATA epic. It is on the Delhi-Ambala railroad. Karnal is a market for rice, wheat, and maize, a cattle-breeding center, and the site of the National Dairy Research Institute. The British occupied the town in 1805.

Karnataka (kärnä′təkə), formerly **Mysore** (mīsôr′), state (1971 pop. 29,263,334), 74,122 sq mi (191,976 sq km), SW India, bordering on the Arabian Sea. The capital is BANGALORE. The Cauvery, the Tunga, and the Badhra rivers, are used for both power and irrigation. Coffee is the major crop, but cotton, millet, sugarcane, rice, and fodder are also grown. The state has the most valuable sandalwood forests in India. Karnataka produces nearly all of India's gold and chromite and has considerable deposits of iron ore and manganese. There is an excellent road and railway system, and the state has many industries. Steel and steel products, automobiles, and airplanes are among the manufactures. The population is Hindu and speaks Kannada (Kanarese). The linguistic uniformity of the state and its excellent education system contribute to one of India's highest literacy rates. The region was part of the empire of the Mauryas (c.325–185 B.C.). From the 3d to the 11th cent. it was ruled by the Gangas and Chalukyas. In 1313 it was conquered by the DELHI SULTANATE, but it was soon lost to the Vijayanagar kingdom. In the late 18th cent. the Muslim leaders HAIDER ALI and his son, TIPPOO SAHIB, conquered the Hindu rulers of Karnataka. They fought the British but were finally defeated in 1799. The British restored the Old Hindu dynasty and thereafter provided protection. The state acceded to the Indian Union in 1947 and in 1956 its area was doubled. Karnataka is governed by a chief minister and cabinet responsible to a bicameral legislature (with one elected house) and by a governor appointed by the president of India. The name was officially changed from Mysore to Karnataka in 1973.

Karo, Joseph ben Ephraim: see CARO, JOSEPH BEN EPHRAIM.

Karolostadt, Reformation leader: see CARLSTADT.

Károlyi, Count Julius (kä′rôlyĭ), 1871–1946?, Hungarian politician; cousin of Michael Károlyi. He became premier and finance minister in 1931. He resigned in 1932 after failing to satisfy either the nationalist right or the liberal left. Julius Gombos succeeded him.

Károlyi, Count Michael, 1875–1955, Hungarian politician, of an ancient noble family. A liberal, he organized (1918) a national council for Hungary after the dissolution of the Austro-Hungarian Monarchy and was made premier. His attempt to strike a balance between the extreme right and left undermined his position. A republic was set up and in Jan., 1919, Károlyi was elected provisional president, apparently in order to remove him from active control. Forced in the end to choose between the conservatives and the Communists, he surrendered the government to the Communists. The dictatorship of Bela KUN was set up in March, 1919. Károlyi left Hungary when Kun's regime collapsed. He returned from England to Hungary after World War II and was appointed (1947) Hungarian ambassador to France. In 1949 he resigned because of disagreement with the policy of his government. He remained in France until his death. His memoirs appeared in English in 1956.

Kárpathos (kär′päthôs), Ital. *Scarpanto,* Lat. *Carpathus,* island (1971 pop. 5,420), c.110 sq mi (280 sq km), SE Greece, in the Aegean Sea, one of the DODECANESE. It is mountainous, rising to c.4,000 ft (1,220 m).

Karpaty: see CARPATHIANS.

Karpinsky, Alexander Petrovich (əlyĭksän′dər pētrô′vĭch kärpēn′skē), 1846–1936, Soviet geologist. From 1869 to 1885 he was at the Mining Institute, St. Petersburg (now Leningrad), as student and teacher. He was imperial director (1885–1916) of mining research and in 1886 was elected to what is now known as the Soviet Academy of Sciences, of which he was president from 1916 until his death. Karpinsky was noted for his prolific research on various geological subjects, especially paleontology, mineralogy, and petrology. His work was chiefly in the Urals, and he completed the first geological map of European Russia; it appeared in *Outline of the Geological History of European Russia* (1883–94). At the time of the Soviet revolution he was influential in preserving much scientific equipment and many invaluable records and also in securing for the Academy of Sciences an important role in the new regime.

Karroo (kəro͞o′, kä–), the semiarid plateaus of W Cape Prov., Republic of South Africa. The Little Karroo is located N of the Cape Ranges and extends c.200 mi (320 km) from east to west at an altitude of from 1,000 to 2,000 ft (305–610 m). It is separated from the Great Karroo (c.300 mi/480 km long; alt. 2,000–3,000 ft/610–915 m) by the Zwartberg Mts. The Karroo, where irrigated, is very fertile. Livestock grazing is important there, and citrus fruits and grains are raised. The name is also applied to the low scrub vegetation found in semiarid regions and also to a system of rocks laid down over central and southern Africa during the late Paleozoic and early Mesozoic eras.

Kars (kärs), city (1970 pop. 53,473), capital of Kars prov., E Turkey, in Armenia, on the Kars River, near the Soviet border. Its manufactures include textiles, carpets, and food products. An old fortified city, well situated in the mountains, Kars was the capital of an Armenian state in the 9th and 10th cent. It was destroyed by Tamerlane in 1386 and was captured and rebuilt by the Ottoman Turks in the 16th cent. In 1828, 1855, and 1877 the city was occupied by Russia and together with the surrounding region was ceded to Russia by the Congress of Berlin in 1878. By a peace treaty (1921) between the nationalist Turkish government of Kemal Atatürk and the USSR, Kars and Ardahan were returned to Turkey. Kars has an 11th-century Armenian church.

Karsavina, Tamara (təmä′rə Kərsä′vyĭnə), 1885–, Russian prima ballerina. Karsavina was trained in the Imperial Theatre School and the Maryinsky Theatre in St. Petersburg, making her debut at the latter in 1902. At its inception in 1909 she joined the Dia-

Tamara Karsavina.

ghilev Ballets Russes in Paris and was considered the greatest ballerina to perform with the company. Partner to Nijinsky, she created principal roles in many works, including *Les Sylphides, Petrouchka, Firebird, Le Spectre de la rose, Daphnis and Chloë,* and *The Three-Cornered Hat.* She danced with the company until 1929 and was a leading exponent of Michael Fokine's dance theories. In the 1940s she coached the Sadler's Wells company. Her books include her reminiscences, *Theatre Street* (1931), *Classical Ballet: The Flow of Movement* (1962), and *Ballet Technique* (1968).

Karshi (kərshē'), city (1970 pop. 71,000), S Central Asian USSR, in Uzbekistan, on the Kashka-Darya River. It is the center of a fertile oasis that produces wheat, cotton, and silk. Karshi was founded in the 14th cent. and has a 16th-century mosque and mausoleum.

Karst (kärst), Ital. *Carso,* Serbo-Croatian *Kras,* limestone plateau, in the Dinaric Alps, NW Yugoslavia, N of Istria and extending c.50 mi (80 km) SE from the lower Isonzo valley. It is characterized by deep gullies, caves, sinkholes, and underground drainage—all the result of carbonation-solution. The best-known caves are at Postojna. The barren nature of the plateau deters human settlement. Rough pasture or forest covers much of the surface, and there is little arable land. The term *karst* is used to describe any area where similar geological formations are found.

Kartah (kär'tə), unidentified city, N central Palestine. Joshua 21.34.

Kartan (kär'tăn), the same as KIRJATHAIM **1.**

Karun (käro͞on'), river, c.450 mi (720 km) long, rising in the Zagros mts., W Iran, and flowing S to the Shatt al Arab on the Iraqi border. The Karun is navigable to Ahvaz for shallow draft vessels; rapids prevent further upstream passage except during high water in April and May. The river was opened to foreign trade in 1888; but since the construction of a rail line during World War II between the river port of Khorramshahr, Ahvaz, and the main Iranian system, this route has lost importance. At Shushtar there is a dam designed to irrigate an area of 500 sq mi (1,295 sq km); it is surmounted by a magnificent bridge (no longer in use), probably built in the 3rd cent. for Shapur I of Persia by captured Roman soldiers.

Karun, Lake, Egypt: see MOERIS.

Karur (kəro͞or'), city (1971 pop. 65,246), Tamil Nadu state, S central India. Milled rice, cotton fabrics, and brassware are the city's chief products. According to Hindu legend, Brahma began the work of creation in Karur, which is referred to as the "place of the sacred cow." Upon the dissolution of the Hindu VIJAYANAGAR empire in 1565, Karur fell to the Naik kings of Madurai. The British occupied the city in 1760.

Karviná (kär'vĭnä), Ger. *Karwin,* city (1970 pop. 76,215), N central Czechoslovakia, in Moravia, near the Polish border. It is an industrial center of the Ostrava-Karviná coal-mining region. Formerly in Austria, the city became (after 1918) an object of dispute between Poland and Czechoslovakia; after World War I a conference of Allied ambassadors awarded (1920) it to Czechoslovakia despite Polish claims. The city was seized by Poland in Oct., 1938, but was restored to Czechoslovakia in 1945.

Karyai, Greece: see ATHOS.

Kasai (käsī'), former province, c.124,000 sq mi (321,160 sq km), S central Zaïre. Luluabourg (present Kananga) was the capital. Between the Kasai and the Sankuru rivers the Kuba kingdom of the Shongo people existed from the early 17th cent. In the south of the province were the constantly warring Luba and Bena Lulua peoples. This ethnic conflict was partly responsible for the secession (Aug., 1960) of the Baluba-dominated Mining State of South Kasai, headed by Albert Kalonji, who proclaimed himself king of South Kasai. The central government reestablished control over the whole of Kasai in Dec., 1961. In 1967 the province was divided into two regions, Kasai-Oriental (capital, Mbuji-Mayi) and Kasai-Occidental (capital, Kananga).

Kasai or **Kassai,** river, c.1,100 mi (1,800 km) long, rising in central Angola, S central Africa, flowing E, N, and NW through W Zaïre to the Congo (Zaïre) River; it forms part of the Angola-Zaïre border. The Kasai, navigable for c.475 mi (760 km) above its mouth, is an important trade artery. Its tributaries include many navigable streams (some of which are rich in alluvial diamonds).

Kasan: see KAZAN, USSR.

Kasavubu, Joseph (kăs"əvo͞o'bo͞o, kä'sə–), 1917?–1969, African political leader, president of the Republic of the Congo (now Zaïre) from 1960 to 1965. He studied for the Roman Catholic priesthood but did not complete his training. Later, he became active in the nationalist movement while teaching school and working for the Belgian government in the Congo. In 1946 he asserted that the Congolese were the legitimate owners of the country and that the Belgians, as intruders, had to leave. In 1955 he became president of Abako, a cultural association of the Bakongo tribe. Under his leadership Abako became a powerful political organization. Briefly imprisoned in 1959 for inciting violence, he later attended (1960) the conference at Brussels that led to independence for the Congo. He became (1960) the Congo's first head of state. There ensued a struggle for power between him and Patrice LUMUMBA, the premier, in which each attempted to dismiss the other. Lumumba was ousted by Kasavubu with the aid of General MOBUTU SESE SEKO. In 1965, Mobutu deposed Kasavubu, who retired from politics.

Kasbek, Mount: see KAZBEK, MOUNT, USSR.

Kasbin, Iran: see QAZVIN.

Kaschau: see KOŠICE, Czechoslovakia.

Kashan (kăshän'), city (1966 pop. 58,468), Tehran prov., central Iran. The city has long been noted for its silk textiles, carpets, ceramics, copperware, and rose water. The Ardebil carpet and celebrated porcelain tiles were made there in the Safavid period. The present city is also a transportation center. Kashan is one of Iran's loveliest cities; the skyline is dominated by a 13th-century minaret that is 150 ft (45 m) high. Sialk, a prehistoric site, is nearby. The well-known rose fields of Qamsar, or Kamsar, are nearby.

Kashgar (kăsh'gär), Mandarin *K'a-shih,* city (1970 est. pop. 175,000), SW Sinkiang Uigur Autonomous Region, China, on the Kashgar River (a tributary of the Tarim). It is the hub of an important commercial district, the western terminus of the main road of the province, and a center for caravan trade with India, Afghanistan, and the USSR. Cotton and wool cloth, rugs, and gold and silver jewelry are manufactured. From Kashgar a mountain pass provides a route to Samarkand and thence to the Middle East. The city, predominantly Uigur in ethnic composition, first came under Chinese rule in the period of the Han dynasty (206 B.C.–A.D. 221). Romans traded there in the 6th cent. When Kashgar was the capital of the Uigur Turks (750–840), it was also a center of Manichaeism. Visited by Marco Polo in 1275, Kashgar was soon after conquered by Jenghiz Khan. From the 15th to the 17th cent. it was ruled by hereditary Khojar (Muslim) kings. The city passed definitively to China in 1760, but since then there have been uprisings and periods of contested control.

Kashing: see CHIA-HSING, China.

Kashiwazaki (kăshēwä'zäkē), city (1970 pop. 73,569), Niigata prefecture, central Honshu, Japan, on the Japan Sea. It is an agricultural center and a resort with hot springs.

Kashka-Darya (kəshkä'-dəryä'), river, c.200 mi (320 km) long, Central Asian USSR. It is the basis of a wide network of irrigation canals near the towns of Kitab and Kashi.

Kashmir, officially **Jammu and Kashmir** (kăshmēr', kăsh'mēr; jŭ'moo), former princely state, c.86,000 sq mi (222,800 sq km), NW India and NE Pakistan. The region is administered in two sections: the Indian state of Jammu and Kashmir (1971 pop. 4,615,176), c.54,000 sq mi (139,900 sq km), with its capital at SRINAGAR, the historic capital of the state; and the Pakistani-controlled Azad Kashmir, c.32,000 sq mi (82,900 sq km), with MUZAFFARABAD as its capital. Kashmir is bordered on the W by Pakistan, on the S by India, and on the N and E by China. One of the most beautiful regions of the East, Kashmir is covered with lofty, rugged mountains, including sections of the Himalayan and Karakorum ranges. Rivers, including the Indus, run through relatively narrow but heavily populated valleys. The valley of the Jhelum River, the celebrated Vale of Kashmir, is the most populous area and the economic heart of the region; it produces abundant crops of wheat and rice. The handicraft industry, particularly the making of woolen cloth and shawls (cashmeres), for which the state was renowned, has declined. In the late 14th cent., after years of Buddhist and Hindu rule, Kashmir was conquered by Muslims who converted most of the population to Islam. It became part of the Mogul empire in 1586, but by 1751 the local ruler was independent. After a century of disorder the British pacified Kashmir in 1846 and installed a Hindu prince as ruler of the predominantly Muslim region. When India was partitioned in 1947, a Muslim revolt, supported by tribesmen from Pakistan, flared up against the state government of Kashmir. The Hindu ruler fled to Delhi and there signed an agreement that placed Kashmir under the dominion of India. Indian troops were flown to Srinagar to engage the rebels. Pakistan, backing the rebels, later dispatched troops to oppose the Indian forces. The fighting was ended by a UN cease-fire in 1949, but the region was divided between India and Pakistan along the cease-fire line. A constituent assembly in Indian Kashmir voted in 1953 for incorporation into India, but this move was delayed by continued Pakistani-Indian disagreement and disapproval by the United Nations of annexation without a plebiscite. In 1955 an outbreak of fighting ended in an agreement between India and Pakistan to keep their respective forces in Kashmir 6 mi (10 km) apart. A new vote by the assembly in Indian Kashmir in 1956 led to the integration of Kashmir as an Indian state; Azad Kashmir remained, however, under the control of Pakistan. India refused to consider subsequent Pakistani protests and UN resolutions calling for a plebiscite. The situation was further complicated in 1959, when Chinese troops occupied the district of Ladakh and neighboring areas. China, rejecting Indian protests, held the territory. Indian-Pakistani relations became more inflamed in 1963 when a Sino-Pakistani agreement defined the Chinese border with Pakistani Kashmir. Serious fighting between India and Pakistan broke out again in Aug., 1965. A UN cease-fire took effect in September. In Jan., 1966, President Ayub Khan of Pakistan and Prime Minister Lal Bahadur Shastri of India met at Tashkent in the Soviet Union at the invitation of the Soviet government and an agreement was reached providing for the mutual withdrawal of troops to the positions held before the latest outbreak of fighting. In the Dec., 1971, war between India and Pakistan, however, there was further fighting in Kashmir in which India made some gains. In Dec., 1972, a new cease-fire line along the positions held at the end of the 1971 war was agreed to by India and Pakistan.

Kashmiri (kăshmē'rē), language belonging to the Dardic group of the Indo-Iranian subfamily of the Indo-European family of languages. See INDO-IRANIAN LANGUAGES.

Kasimir. For Polish rulers thus named, see CASIMIR.

Kaskaskia (kăskăs'kēə), village (1970 pop. 79), Randolph co., SE Ill., on Kaskaskia island in the Mississippi River where it is joined by the Kaskaskia River. It is now relatively unpopulated, mainly because it was inundated by the Mississippi toward the close of the 19th cent., but Kaskaskia's past is deeply rooted in the history of the region. The settlement was established by Jesuit missionaries in 1703 (four years after the founding of Cahokia) and named for the Kaskaskia Indians, a tribe of the Illinois, who inhabited the area. In time an agricultural community grew up on the fertile bottomlands surrounding the village, and traders made it a center of operations. The French built a fort there in 1721 and occupied it until 1755; it was destroyed when Kaskaskia was taken over by the British in 1763. In 1778, during the American Revolution, George Rogers Clark, with a company of Virginia militia, took possession of the village for the United States, and a period of turbulence followed the departure of Clark's troops in 1780. Kaskaskia declined for two decades, then thrived as the capital of Illinois Territory (1809–18) and state capital (1818–20). The first Illinois newspaper was started there in 1814. The community again declined after the capital of Illinois was shifted (1820) to Vandalia, and periodic floods discouraged further growth. Fort Kaskaskia State Park was set aside in 1927 across the Mississippi River near Chester, Ill.

Kasprowicz, Jan (yän käsprô'vēch), 1860–1926, Polish poet. His writings progressed from social revolt (e.g., *From a Peasant's Field*, 1891) to poems of spiritual struggle and philosophical intensity. Among his later works are *To a Dying World* (1902), *Ballad of the Sunflower* (1908), and *The Book of the Poor* (1916). Highly regarded by his contemporaries, Kasprowicz was also renowned for his translations of English, French, German, and Italian classics.

Kassa: see KOŠICE, Czechoslovakia.

Kassala (käsä'lä, kăs'əlä), city (1969 est. pop. 81,000), NE Sudan. It is a cotton market and rail transport center and has extensive fruit gardens. Founded in 1840 as a military camp for the troops of Muhammad Ali during his conquest of Sudan, Kassala was captured by the Mahdists in 1885 and by the Italians in 1894. Restored to Egyptian sovereignty in 1897, it became part of the Anglo-Egyptian Sudan.

Kassel (käs'əl), city (1970 pop. 214,156), Hesse, E West Germany, on the Fulda River. It is an industrial, rail, and cultural center. Manufactures include machinery, chemicals, textiles, optical and precision instruments, locomotives, and motor vehicles. Kassel was mentioned in 913 and was chartered in 1198. It became (1567) the capital of the landgraviate of Hesse-Kassel (raised to an electorate in 1803). Kassel also was the capital of the kingdom of Westphalia (1807–13) under Jérôme Bonaparte. After Electoral Hesse and Nassau passed (1866) to Prussia and were united as the province of Hesse-Nassau, Kassel was made the capital. As a center of German airplane and tank production in World War II, Kassel was severely damaged by Allied air raids. Many historic buildings were destroyed, but after 1945 much of the city's former beauty was restored. Kassel has several important museums. International exhibits ("Documenta") of modern art are periodically held in the city. A former spelling is Cassel.

Kassem, Abdul Karim (äbdo͝ol' kärēm' kässēm'), 1914–63, Iraqi general and politician. A graduate (1934) of the Iraqi military academy, he attended the army staff college. His outstanding bravery, shown in campaigns against the Kurds and in the Palestinian war of 1948, won him many military decorations. He organized the military coup d'etat that in July, 1958, overthrew the Iraqi monarchy and established Kassem as premier of the new republic. An Arab nationalist, he quelled a pro-Communist uprising in 1959. After this, Kassem's power and influence steadily deteriorated. He was overthrown and executed by military and civilian members of the BA'ATH PARTY in Feb., 1963.

Kasserine Pass, gap, 2 mi (3.2 km) wide, central Tunisia, in the Grand Dorsal chain (an extension of the Atlas Mts.). A key point in the Allied offensive in Tunisia in World War II, the pass was the scene of an Axis breakthrough (Feb. 20, 1943), but it was retaken with very heavy losses by U.S. forces on Feb. 25. See NORTH AFRICA, CAMPAIGNS IN.

Kassites or **Cassites,** ancient people, probably of Indo-European origin. They were first mentioned in historical texts as occupying the W Iranian plateau. In the 18th cent. B.C. they swept down on BABYLONIA, conquered the region, and ruled there until the 12th cent. B.C., when they returned to the Iranian plateau. They remained more or less independent until the beginning of the Christian era, when they disappeared from history.

Kastamonu (kä"stämōno͞o'), city (1970 pop. 29,303), capital of Kastamonu prov., N Turkey. It is a manufacturing center, noted for its textiles and copper utensils, and is the chief city of a region rich in minerals. Kastamonu was captured by the Ottoman Turks in 1393, was taken by Tamerlane in 1403, and was regained by the Ottomans in 1460.

Kastoría (kästôrē'ə), city (1971 pop. 15,407), capital of Kastoría prefecture, N Greece, in Macedonia, on a peninsula extending into Lake Kastoría. It is a market for farm produce, and it has fisheries. In the 17th and 18th cent. it was a major fur-trade center. In the city are many little Byzantine churches and palatial homes.

Kástron (kä'strôn), town (1971 pop. 3,982), E Greece, on Límnos island, in the Aegean Sea. It is a seaport trading in local produce. In ancient times it was known as Myrina. Today it is also called Kastro or Castro.

Kasugai (käso͞o'gī), city (1970 pop. 161,835), Aichi prefecture, central Honshu, Japan. It is a suburb of Nagoya and the site of silk and textile industries.

Katahdin (kətä'dĭn), mountain, 5,267 ft (1,605 m) high, between branches of the Penobscot River in N central Maine; highest point in Maine. The peak and the beautifully wooded, lake-dotted territory surrounding it constitute Baxter State Park, the gift of Gov. Percival P. Baxter in 1931. Katahdin mt. is the northern terminus of the Appalachian Trail.

Katanga: see SHABA, province, Zaïre.

Katar: see QATAR.

Katayama, Tetsu (tĕt'so͞o kätäyä'mä), 1887–, Japanese statesman. Active as a youth in the Japanese labor movement, he was a founder (1926) of the Social Democratic party. When the party was suppressed by the police, he helped organize (1931) its successor, the Social Mass party. He was forced to retire from prewar politics because of his opposition to the invasion of Manchuria (1931–32) and continuation of the second Sino-Japanese War (1937–45). After World War II he reentered politics as president of the Socialist party and was prime minister (1947–48) of a coalition cabinet.

Katayev, Valentin Petrovich (vəlyĭntyĕn' pētrô'vĭch kətī'əf), 1897–, Russian novelist, short-story writer, and playwright. Katayev's novels portray almost the entire range of Soviet life, from the period of the New Economic Policy (*The Embezzlers*, 1927, tr. 1929) through the first Five-Year Plan (*Time, Forward!*, 1932, tr. 1933) to World War II (*The Wife*, 1944, tr. 1946). In *Peace Is Where the Tempests Blow* (1936, tr. 1937) he described a pleasant childhood in

Katmai National Monument, Alaska.

Odessa against the background of the Revolution of 1905. Katayev's comedies became very popular, especially *Squaring the Circle* (1929, tr. 1934), a farce about Soviet marriage and housing conditions. His later works include *The Holy Well* (tr. 1967) and a volume of reminiscences, *Grass of Oblivion* (1967, tr. 1970). His younger brother, Yevgeny, used the surname Petrov in collaborating with Ilya ILF.

Kateríni (kätərē'nē), city (1971 pop. 28,808), capital of Piería prefecture, N Greece, in Macedonia. It is the commercial center for a productive tobacco-growing region.

Katharine or **Katherine.** For some persons so named, see CATHERINE.

Katharine of Aragón, 1485–1536, first queen consort of HENRY VIII of England; daughter of Ferdinand II of Aragón and Isabella of Castile. In 1501 she was married to Arthur, eldest son of Henry VII. He died in 1502, and the marriage of Katharine to his brother, Henry, was projected. A papal dispensation was obtained, but the marriage was delayed by diplomatic wrangling between Henry VII and Ferdinand and did not take place until the prince had ascended (1509) the throne as Henry VIII. As governor of the realm during Henry's expedition to the Continent in 1513, she organized the successful defense against Scottish invasion that ended in the English victory at Flodden. Only one of Katharine's six children survived infancy (see MARY I), and Henry was disappointed at her failure to produce a male heir. The English alliance with Katharine's nephew, Holy Roman Emperor CHARLES V, wavered and fell in 1525, and her political importance declined. Finally, Henry became strongly infatuated with Anne BOLEYN. In 1527, with the help of Cardinal Thomas WOLSEY, Henry began the attempt to have his marriage annulled. This move precipitated the chain of events that ended in the English Reformation. Katharine steadfastly refused to acknowledge the invalidity of the marriage or to retire to a convent. In 1529 at a trial conducted by cardinals CAMPEGGIO and Wolsey, she appealed vainly to Henry, denied the jurisdiction of the court because it was under pressure by the king, and withdrew. Pope CLEMENT VII recalled the hearing to Rome, in effect denying the divorce. Henry then proceeded on his own; after his secret marriage to Anne Boleyn in 1533, a court presided over by Thomas CRANMER pronounced the former marriage invalid. Katharine refused to accept the decision. The pope's formal declaration for her in 1534 came too late. She was separated from her daughter, Mary, never visited by Henry, and confined with few attendants at various inferior estates. Katharine nevertheless refused, despite all threats and mistreatment, to take the title of princess dowager or to acknowledge the Act of Succession and the Act of Supremacy. Her great popularity with the common people of England never waned throughout the long period of her misfortunes. She died after a prolonged illness. See Albert Du Boys, *Catherine of Aragon and the Sources of the English Reformation* (1881, repr. 1968); biographies by Garrett Mattingly (1941, repr. 1960) and Mary M. Luke (1967).

Kathiawar (kä'tēəwär"), peninsula, c.25,000 sq mi (64,750 sq km), W India, between the Gulf of Kutch and the Gulf of Cambay. Almost all of Kathiawar is included in Gujarat state; a small area is part of Goa, Damar, and Diu. The region, mostly level, produces much cotton and has stone quarries and cement and chemical industries. Bhavnagar is the chief port. Under British rule the region contained numerous princely states.

Katmai National Monument (kăt'mī), 2,792,137 acres (1,129,978 hectares), at the northern end of the Alaska Peninsula, S Alaska; has the second largest area in the U.S. National Park System; est. 1918. Mt. Katmai and Novarupta volcanoes and the Valley of the Ten Thousand Smokes are located in this dying volcanic region, which is the site of one of the greatest eruptions in history, that of Novarupta in 1912. All plant and animal life in the area was destroyed by the ash and lava, although no persons were reported killed. Kodiak Island, 100 mi (160 km) to the southeast, was covered with c.1 ft (.3 m) of ash. As lava beneath Mt. Katmai drained W to Novarupta, its top collapsed, forming a crater, 8 mi (12.8 km) in circumference and 3,700 ft (1,128 m) deep, in which a lake has formed. The Valley of the Ten Thousand Smokes (72 sq mi/186 sq km) has countless holes and cracks through which hot gases passed to the surface; all but a few are now extinct. The region is inaccessible except to specially equipped expeditions. The national monument also includes glacier-covered peaks and crater lakes. Moose and brown bear thrive in the area.

Katmandu (kätmändōō'), city (1971 pop. 332,982), capital of Nepal, central Nepal, c.4,500 ft (1,370 m) above sea level, in a fertile valley of the E Himalayas. It is the administrative, business, and commercial center of Nepal, and lies astride an ancient trade and pilgrim route from India to Tibet, China, and Mongolia. The Buddha was reputedly born near the city. Originally ruled by the Newars, Katmandu became independent in the 15th cent. and was captured in 1768 by the Gurkhas, who made it their capital. The Gurkhas timed their invasion to coincide with the annual Indra Jatra festival (in honor of the goddess Devi), knowing that the people of Katmandu would be engrossed in the celebration and unlikely to offer resistance. In the late 18th cent. the city became the seat of a British resident. Landmarks include the elaborate royal palace, several pagoda-shaped temples, and many Sanskrit libraries. Katmandu also has a number of colleges.

Kato, Komei (Takaaki) (kō'mā kä'tō, täkä-ä'kē), 1860–1926, Japanese statesman. He entered the foreign ministry after graduating from Tokyo Univ. He served (1909) as ambassador to Great Britain. He was foreign minister (1914–15), but his presentation of the Twenty-one Demands to China forced his resignation. Later he organized and headed the conservative Kenseikai party. During his term (1924–25) as prime minister his cabinet was called "the Mitsubishi government," because he and his foreign minister, SHIDEHARA, were both connected by marriage with the Mitsubishi interests. His administration reduced army strength and government expenditures, initiated universal military training, increased military instruction on all educational levels, sponsored the manhood-suffrage law, and favored the Peace Preservation Law, penalizing political heterodoxy.

Kato, Tomosaburo (tōmōs"ä"bōōrō', kä'tō), 1861–1923, Japanese admiral. He was naval chief of staff (1894–95) and chief assistant to Admiral Togo in the Russo-Japanese War. As navy minister from 1915 to 1923, he directed Japanese naval operations in World War I and the naval expansion thereafter. At the Washington Conference (1921–22) he accepted the principle of naval limitation. He was prime minister (1922–23).

Katona, József (yō'zhěf kŏ'tônŏ), 1791–1830, Hungarian dramatist. His classic tragedy *Bánk Bán* (1821) was among the first important works in Magyar. It was set to music by Francis Erkel (1810–93) and became Hungary's most popular opera. The work is remarkable for its portrayal of emotional conflict.

Katowice (kätôvē'tsě), Ger. *Kattowitz,* city (1970 pop. 303,264), S Poland. One of the chief mining and industrial centers of Poland, it has industries producing heavy machinery and chemicals; mines in the region yield coal, iron, zinc, and lead. The city was chartered in 1865 and passed from Germany to Poland in 1921. Katowice is also an important educational and cultural center.

Katrine, Loch (lŏkh kăt'rĭn), lake, 8 mi (12.9 km) long and 1 mi (1.6 km) wide, Perthshire, central Scotland. Its beauty is celebrated in Sir Walter Scott's *Lady of the Lake.* When Loch Katrine became Glasgow's main source of water, the lake was enlarged (1859), and the Silver Strand of Scott's poem disappeared. Glen Gyle, at the head of the lake, is Rob Roy's birthplace.

Katrineholm (kä"trēnəhôlm'), city (1970 pop. 22,045), Södermanland co., S Sweden; chartered 1917. It is a commercial, industrial, and transportation center. The city has one of Europe's largest dairies and other industries thát manufacture ball bearings, automobile bodies, furniture, and machinery.

Katsina (kätsē'nə, kät'sĭnə), city (1969 est. pop. 105,000), N Nigeria, near the Niger frontier. The city, surrounded by a wall 13 mi (21 km) long, is the trade center for an agricultural region where guinea corn and millet are grown for home consumption, and groundnuts, cotton, and hides are produced commercially. Leather handicrafts are made in Katsina. In the 17th and 18th cent. it was the largest of the seven HAUSA city-states and the cultural and commercial center of Hausaland. In 1807, Katsina was conquered by the FULANI and lost its preeminent position among Hausa cities to KANO. The city is the site of Katsina Training College and Gobaru Tower mosque.

Katsura, Taro (tärō' kät'sōōrä), 1847–1913, Japanese statesman. A Choshu clansman, and a protégé of

Pagoda-shaped temple in Katmandu, the capital of Nepal.

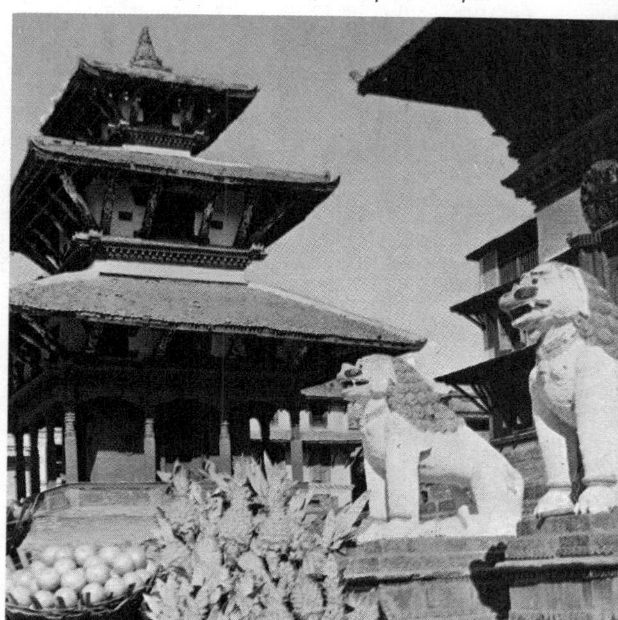

Aritomo YAMAGATA, he served as war minister, then (1901-6) as prime minister. During that administration, with the Anglo-Japanese Alliance in 1902 and the defeat (1904-5) of Russia, Japan emerged as the major power in the Far East and gained effective control over Korea. In the Taft-Katsura agreement of 1905, the United States recognized that control. In 1906, Katsura resigned because of public dissatisfaction with the Portsmouth Treaty. As prime minister again (1908-11), he annexed Korea and engaged in a struggle with the Diet over expansion of the military budget. His reappointment as prime minister in 1912 came after the overthrow of Kimmochi SAIONJI for failure to approve increased army spending, and was widely interpreted as an example of GENRO manipulation. The major parliamentary parties united in opposition, organized mass demonstrations, and passed a nonconfidence motion. Katsura lost support of the genro when he attempted to form a new party and sought imperial intervention to rescind the nonconfidence motion. He was forced to resign.

Katsuta (kätso͞o'tä), city (1970 pop. 66,754), Ibaraki prefecture, central Honshu, Japan, on the Naka River. It is a commercial center with mechanical, automotive, and electronics industries.

Kattath (kăt'tăth), unidentified city, N central Palestine. Joshua 19.15.

Kattegat (kăt'ĭgăt"), strait, c.140 mi (230 km) long and from 40 to 100 mi (60-160 km) wide, between Sweden and Denmark. It is connected with the North Sea through the Skagerrak, which begins at the northern tip of Jutland, and with the Baltic Sea by way of the Øresund, Store Baelt, and Lille Baelt. Göteborg (Sweden) and Århus (Denmark) are the chief ports.

Kattowitz: see KATOWICE, Poland.

Katun (kəto͞on'), river, c.415 mi (670 km) long, Altai Kray, S Siberian USSR. It rises in the Katun Alps and flows generally north to join the Biya, with which it forms the Ob River. The Katun is partly navigable.

katydid, common name of certain large, singing, winged INSECTS belonging to the long-horned GRASSHOPPER family (Tettigoniidae) in the order Orthoptera. Katydids are green or, occasionally, pink and range in size from 1¼ to 5 in. (3-12.5 cm) long. Katydids are nocturnal and arboreal; they sing in the evening. The males have song-producing, or stridulating, organs located on their front wings. The females chirp in response to the shrill song of the males, which supposedly sounds like "katy did, katy didn't," hence the name. The song serves a function in courtship, which occurs in late summer. The female lays eggs in the ground or in plant tissue; the eggs hatch in spring. Newly hatched katydids resemble the adults except for their smaller size and lack of wings. Katydids are common in the E United States and are also found in the tropics. They are classified in the phylum ARTHROPODA, class Insecta, order Orthoptera, suborder Ensifera, family Tettigoniidae.

Katyn (kətĭn'), village, W central European USSR. It was occupied by the Germans in Aug., 1941, during World War II. In 1943 the German government announced that the mass grave of some 4,250 Polish officers had been found in a forest near Katyn and accused the Soviets of having massacred them. The officers had been captured during the Soviet invasion of Poland in 1939. The Soviet government denied the German charges and asserted that the Poles, war prisoners, had been captured and executed by invading German units in 1941. The Soviets refused to permit an investigation by the International Red Cross. In 1944, a Soviet investigating commission alleged that the Germans killed the officers. In 1951-52, a U.S. Congressional investigation charged that the Soviets had executed the Poles. See J. K. Zawodny, *Death in the Forest* (1972).

Katzenbach, Nicholas deBelleville (kăt'sənbăk), 1922-, U.S. Attorney General (1965-66), b. Philadelphia. He served (1950-56) as adviser in the office of the general counsel to the Secretary of the Air Force and was on the law faculties of Yale (1952-56) and the Univ. of Chicago (1956-60). In 1961 he joined the Justice Department as Assistant Attorney General in charge of the Office of Legal Counsel. As Deputy Attorney General (1962-64) he played an important role in the enforcement of desegregation at the universities of Mississippi and Alabama, and he helped draft the Civil Rights Act of 1964. When Robert F. Kennedy resigned as Attorney General in Sept., 1964, President Lyndon B. Johnson named him acting Attorney General. In Feb., 1965, he was confirmed as Attorney General. He succeeded George Ball as Undersecretary of State in 1966. He resigned in 1968 to become vice president of IBM Corp.

Katzimo, New Mexico: see ENCHANTED MESA.

Kauai (kou"wī'), circular island (1970 pop. 29,524), 549 sq mi (1,422 sq km), 32 mi (52 km) in diameter, N Hawaii, separated from Oahu island to the southeast by Kauai Channel. Lihue (1970 pop. 3,124) is the largest town and Nawiliwili Harbor the chief port. Geologically, Kauai is the oldest of the Hawaiian Islands. It was formed by now extinct volcanoes; Kawaikini (5,170 ft/1,576 m high) and Waialeale (5,080 ft/1,548 m high) are the tallest peaks. High annual rainfall has eroded deep valleys in Kauai's central mountain mass. Waimea Canyon (2,000-3,000 ft/610-915 m deep; c.10 mi/16 km long) resembles a miniature Grand Canyon. The northeastern slopes of Waialeale, one of the wettest spots on earth, receive an annual average rainfall of 450 in. (1,143 cm). An independent kingdom when visited by English Capt. James Cook in 1778, Kauai became part of the Kingdom of Hawaii in 1810. The first major attempt at agricultural development in Hawaii took place there with the establishment of a sugar plantation in 1835. Most of the island's people live along the coast. Agriculture is the main industry, with sugarcane, rice, and pineapples the chief crops; ranching and tourism are also important.

Kauffmann, Angelica (äng-gā'lēkä kouf'män), 1741-1807, Swiss neoclassical painter and graphic artist. From her youth she was known for her artistic, musical, and linguistic abilities. She went to England, where she enjoyed success as a fashionable portrait painter and decorator. A protégée of Sir Joshua Reynolds, Kauffman was one of the original members of the Royal Academy. She often decorated houses designed by the ADAM brothers. After her marriage in 1781 to the Venetian painter Antonio Zucchi, she lived in Italy, where she flourished in artistic and literary circles. Reynolds, Winckelmann, Goethe, and Garrick commissioned her to paint their portraits. Representative works include *Religion* (National Gall., London); *Self-Portrait* (Staatliche Museen, Berlin); and the etchings of *L'Allegra* and *La Pensierosa*. The British Museum has a collection of her drawings and prints. See study by Lady Victoria Manners and G. C. Williamson (1924).

Kaufman, George S. (kôf'mən), 1889-1961, American dramatist and journalist, b. Pittsburgh. As a drama critic for various New York newspapers he was influential in raising the standards of criticism in the theater. He collaborated on more than 40 plays, many of them tremendously successful, which varied in mood from the rowdy farces of his early days to his later more sophisticated comedies. His collaboration with Marc Connelly produced such plays as *Merton of the Movies* (1922) and *Beggar on Horseback* (1924) and was followed by collaborations with Ring Lardner—*June Moon* (1929)—and Edna Ferber—*The Royal Family* (1927), *Dinner at Eight* (1932), and *Stage Door* (1936). In 1932, Kaufman won the Pulitzer Prize for the musical *Of Thee I Sing* (1931), written with Morrie Ryskind, to a score by George Gershwin. Some of his most famous plays were done in collaboration with Moss Hart, notably *Once in a Lifetime* (1930), *Merrily We Roll Along* (1934), *You Can't Take It with You* (1936; Pulitzer Prize), and *The Man Who Came to Dinner* (1939). Among his later works are *The Late George Apley* (with J. P. Marquand, 1944) and *The Solid Gold Cadillac* (with Howard Teichmann, 1954). Kaufman directed several successful plays including *The Front Page* (1928), *My Sister Eileen* (1940), and *Guys and Dolls* (1950). See biographies by Howard Teichmann (1972) and Scott Meredith (1974).

Kaufmann Peak: see LENIN PEAK, USSR.

Kaukauna (kôkô'nə), industrial city (1970 pop. 11,292), Outagamie co., E Wis., on the Fox River; settled 1793, inc. 1885. The city has a large paper plant; dairy items, foundry products, machine tools, and farm equipment are also manufactured. A fur-trading post was established on the site by Pierre Grignon in 1760. The Grignon mansion, built 1836–39 on the first land deeded in Wisconsin, has been restored. Outagamie County Teachers College is in Kaukauna.

Kaunas (kou'näs), Pol. *Kowno,* Rus. *Kovno,* city (1967 est. pop. 284,000), W European USSR, in Lithuania, on the Neman River. It is a river port and an industrial center with industries producing machinery, iron and steel, chemicals, plastics, and textiles. Probably founded as a fortress at the end of the 10th cent., Kaunas was a medieval trading center and a Lithuanian stronghold against the Teutonic Knights. It passed to a united Lithuanian-Polish state in 1569 and to Russia in the third partition of Poland (1795). Although strongly fortified by the Russians, it was captured (1915) by the Germans in World War I. From 1918 to 1940, Kaunas was the provisional capital of Lithuania—Vilnius (which Lithuania claimed as its rightful capital) being held by Poland until 1939 and by Russia in 1939–40. Kaunas was occupied by German forces from 1941 to 1944. During the German occupation the Jews of Kaunas (about 30% of the prewar population) were virtually exterminated. Before evacuating at the approach of Soviet troops the Germans destroyed much of the city. Nearby are a 16th-century town hall, the ruins of a castle (14th–15th cent.), the Vytautus church (15th cent.), and a noted 17th-century monastery. The city has a university (founded 1922), a polytechnical institute (founded 1950), a medical institute (founded 1951), and several museums.

Kaunda, Kenneth (koun'də), 1924–, African political leader, president of Zambia (1964–), b. Northern Rhodesia (now Zambia). Kaunda entered the nationalist movement after working as a teacher and welfare officer. He opposed (1953) the formation of the Federation of Rhodesia and Nyasaland. His party was banned in 1959, and Kaunda was imprisoned, but in 1960 he was released and became head of a new independence party, the United National Independence party (UNIP). In 1962 he rejected a constitution proposed by Great Britain for Northern Rhodesia, charging that it would perpetuate white supremacy. Nevertheless, he took part in elections that October, and after winning a parliamentary seat, formed a coalition government. He continued to press for dissolution of the federation, which eventually came about in Dec., 1963, and the following year, when Zambia gained its independence, Kaunda became its first president. He was reelected in 1968 and 1973. In 1969, he nationalized Zambia's copper mines. Faced with increasing tribal dissension, Kaunda, in 1972, pushed through a bill making the UNIP the only political party in Zambia. In foreign affairs, Kaunda became increasingly uncompromising toward the white-supremacist government of neighboring Rhodesia. Kaunda has written several books, including *Black Government,* (with C. M. Morris, 1960), *Zambia Shall be Free* (an autobiography, 1962), and *Humanism in Africa and a Guide to Its Implementation* (1967). See biography by R. S. Hall (1965).

Kenneth Kaunda.

Kaunitz, Wenzel Anton, Fürst von (vĕn'tsəl än'tôn fürst fən kou'nĭts), 1711–94, Austrian statesman. He distinguished himself as a negotiator of the Treaty of Aix-la-Chapelle (1748) and was (1750–53) ambassador to Paris. From 1753 until his retirement in 1792 he served the Hapsburg rulers, Maria Theresa, Joseph II, and Leopold II, as chancellor and foreign minister. Reversing 300 years of Hapsburg diplomacy, Kaunitz recognized Prussia rather than France as the chief enemy of Austria and was responsible for the coalition that led to the SEVEN YEARS WAR. Through Kaunitz, Austria shared in the first partition of Poland (1772). Kaunitz did not agree with all of the reforms of Joseph II, but he helped

One of the numerous self-portraits by the Swiss neoclassical painter Angelica Kauffmann.

Joseph centralize the administration. Kaunitz is regarded as one of the most astute statesmen of the 18th cent.

Kautsky, Karl Johann (kärl yō'hän kout'skē), 1854–1938, German-Austrian socialist, b. Prague. A leading figure in the effort to spread Marxist doctrine in Germany, he was the principal deviser of the Erfurt Program, which set the German Social Democratic party on an orthodox Marxist path and established him as a dominant figure in the Second INTERNATIONAL. He was a consistent opponent of Eduard BERNSTEIN and other socialists who advocated revision of Marxist doctrines. After initial hesitation he opposed the Social Democratic party's support of the German effort in World War I and helped form, with Hugo HAASE, the Independent Social Democratic party. Soon after the Bolshevik Revolution (1917) in Russia, he condemned it as undemocratic and non-Marxian. Kautsky wrote a great amount of socialist and other literature and edited the German documents on the origin of World War I (4 vol., 1919). Among his translated works are *The Economic Doctrines of Karl Marx* (tr. 1925), *Ethics and the Materialist Conception of History* (tr. 1907), and *Bolshevism at a Deadlock* (tr. 1931).

kava or **kavakava** (kä'vəkä''və): see PEPPER.

Kaválla or **Cavala** (both: kävä'lä), city (1971 pop. 46,234), capital of Kaválla prefecture, NE Greece, in Macedonia; a port on the Gulf of Kaválla, an inlet of the Aegean Sea. Surrounded by a rich tobacco-growing hinterland, it is a leading Greek city for processing and exporting tobacco. Fish and manganese are also shipped, and flour is manufactured. Known as Neapolis in ancient times, the city was the landing place of St. Paul on his way to Philippi, the ancient site of which is nearby. Kaválla was held by the Ottoman Turks from 1387 to 1913, when it passed to Greece.

Kaveri, river, India: see CAUVERY.

Kaverin, Veniamin Aleksandrovich (vĕnyəmēn' əlyĭksän'drəvĭch kəvyĕ'rĭn), 1902–, Russian novelist and short-story writer. He was a member of the literary group that called itself the Serapion Brothers, and he expounded that circle's creed of the artistic independence of politics in the story *The Unknown Artist* (1931, tr. 1947). Later Kaverin turned to a more conventional style. A long novel, *The Fulfillment of Desires* (1934–35, tr. *The Larger View,* 1938), deals with the adjustment of the intellectual to Soviet society. His later work includes *Open Book* (1953, tr. 1957). See study by Donald Piper (1970).

Kavir Buzurg, Iran: see DASHT-E KAVIR.

Kaw, river: see KANSAS, river.

Kawabata, Yasunari (yäso͞onä'rē käwä'bätä), 1899–1972, Japanese novelist. His first major work, *The Izu Dancer,* was published in 1925. He came to be a leader of the school of Japanese writers that propounded a lyrical and impressionistic style, in opposition to the proletarian literature of the 1920s. Kawabata's melancholy novels often treat, in a delicate, oblique fashion, sexual relationships between men and women. For example, *Snow Country* (tr. 1956), probably his best-known work in the West, depicts the affair of an aging geisha and an insensitive Tokyo businessman. All Kawabata's works are distinguished by a masterful, and frequently arresting, use of imagery. Among his works in English translation are the novels *Thousand Cranes* (tr. 1959), *The Sound of the Mountain* (tr. 1970), and *The Lake* (tr. 1974), and the volume of short stories, *The House of the Sleeping Beauties and Other Stories* (tr. 1969). In 1968, Kawabata became the first Japanese author to receive the Nobel Prize in literature. Four years later, in declining health and probably depressed by the suicide of his friend Yukio Mishima, he committed suicide. See his Nobel Prize speech, *Japan the Beautiful and Myself* (tr. 1969).

Kawagoe (käwä'gōā), city (1970 pop. 171,038), Saitama prefecture, central Honshu, Japan. Silk textiles are manufactured in the city. Kawagoe is the site of Kitain Temple (built 830), famed for its images of the 500 disciples of Buddha.

Kawaguchi (käwä'go͞ochē), city (1970 pop. 305,887), Saitama prefecture, central Honshu, Japan, on the Ajikawa and Kizagawa rivers. A Tokyo suburb, it has ironworks and textile mills.

Kawanishi (käwä'nēshē), city (1970 pop. 87,127), Hyogo prefecture, central Honshu, Japan, on the Ina River. It is an agricultural and commercial center and the site of a hat-manufacturing industry.

Kawartha Lakes (kəwôr'thə), group of 14 lakes, in a region c.50 mi (80 km) long and c.25 mi (40 km) wide, S Ont., Canada, near the towns of Lindsay and Peterborough. Balsam is the largest lake. They are popular as summer resorts. Many of the lakes form part of the Trent Canal system.

Kawasaki (käwä'säkē), city (1970 pop. 973,251), Kanagawa prefecture, central Honshu, Japan, on Tokyo Bay. Located in the Tokyo-Yokohama industrial area, it has steel mills, shipyards, oil refineries, engineering works, and factories that produce motors, electrical machinery and parts, petrochemicals, and cement. Heigenji Temple, dedicated to Kobo-Daishi, is in Kawasaki.

Kaw Indians: see KANSAS INDIANS.

Kay, John, 1704–64, English inventor. He patented in 1733 the fly shuttle, operated by pulling a cord that drove the shuttle to either side, freeing one hand of the weaver to press home the weft. Workers in the weaving industry who regarded Kay's invention as a threat to their jobs mobbed Kay and destroyed his model. Various factory owners duplicated his device but managed not to pay him a royalty. Kay went to France, resumed his work, and tried unsuccessfully to win recognition in England. Although he was the inventor of one of the most important principles of modern mechanical weaving, he died in poverty.

Kay, Ulysses, 1917–, American composer, b. Tucson, Ariz. He graduated from the Univ. of Arizona in 1938 and studied for several years at the Eastman School of Music and at Yale Univ. During World War II he served in the navy. He has won many awards and fellowships, including a Fulbright scholarship and a Rosenwald fellowship. Kay is one of the foremost black composers of serious neoclassical music. He has written several operas, choral works, and chamber and orchestra pieces. His works include *Of New Horizons* (1944), a piece for orchestra; *Jeremiah* (1945), a cantata; and *The Juggler of Our Lady* (1956), a one-act opera.

Kayah State (kəyä') or **Karenni State** (kərĕn'ē), state (1969 est. pop. 113,000), 4,506 sq mi (11,671 sq km), E Burma, on the Thai border. Loikaw is the capital. The terrain is mountainous and is traversed by the Salween, the principal river. The inhabitants of the state are Karens. In the south are the Mawchi mines, an important source of tungsten. Rice and vegetables are grown, and the forests yield teak. Under the 1947 Burmese constitution the Karenni State was constituted from the three states that had treaty relationships with the British crown. The name was changed to Kayah State in 1952.

kayak (kī'ăk), Eskimo canoe, originally made of sealskin stretched over a framework of whalebone or driftwood. It is completely covered except for the opening in which the paddler sits. Since the paddler wears a waterproof skin shirt which is laced to the boat, he can turn all the way over without sinking. The kayak is propelled by a double-bladed paddle and is primarily a hunting canoe. Because of its maneuverability in ice-infested waters, it is still in use over a great extent of the Arctic. The kayak is also popular today as a sporting boat. See also CANOE.

Kaye, Nora (Nora Koreff), 1920–, American ballerina, b. New York City. Kaye studied with Michel Fokine and Antony Tudor. She joined the Ballet Theatre in 1940 and scored a major triumph in 1942 in *Pillar of Fire*. Noted for her astounding versatility, she has performed in works ranging from *Giselle* and *Swan Lake* to the comic *Gala Performance* and *Age of Anxiety*.

Kayes (kāz), town (1970 est. pop. 30,000), W Mali, a port on the Senegal River. It is the administrative and commercial center for a region where peanuts and gum arabic are produced. The town has tanneries. Kayes is at the upper limit of navigation on the Senegal.

Kayibanda, Grégoire (grāgwär' kīēbän'dā), 1924–, political leader in Rwanda. A member of the Hutu tribe, he worked as a journalist and later founded the Ruanda (now Rwanda) Cooperative Movement (1952), the Hutu Social Movement (1957), and the Democratic Republican Movement (1959). In 1961 he became president of Rwanda. He was overthrown in a bloodless army coup just before the 1973 elections.

Kayser, Heinrich Gustav Johannes (hīn'rĭkh go͝os'täf yōhän'əs kī'zər), 1853–1940, German physicist. He was professor at Bonn from 1894 to 1920. He is known for his work in sound and, in association with C. D. T. Runge, in SPECTRUM analysis. He wrote a handbook of spectroscopy (1901–12) and a treatise on the electron theory (1905). In his later years he was widely respected as the dean of European spectroscopists.

Kayseri (kī'sĕrē''), city (1970 pop. 167,696), capital of Kayseri prov., central Turkey, at the foot of Mt. Erciyas. It is an important commercial center and has textile mills, sugar refineries, and cement factories. Carpets are made there. The ancient CAESAREA MAZACA, it was taken by the Seljuk Turks in the mid-11th cent., briefly held (1097) by the Crusaders, and captured (1243) by the Mongols. The city was occupied by the Mamelukes of Egypt in 1419. Sultan Selim I incorporated Kayseri into the Ottoman Empire in 1515. The city has numerous historical remains. Nearby is Kanesh, an archaeological site that dates back to the 3d millennium B.C.

Kazakh Soviet Socialist Republic (käzäk′, Rus. kə–) or **Kazakhstan** (kä″zäkstän′, Rus. kəzəkhstän′), constituent republic (1970 pop. 12,850,000), c.1,050,000 sq mi (2,719,500 sq km), S USSR. It borders on Siberia in the north, China in the east, the Kirghiz, Uzbek, and Turkmen republics in the south, and the Caspian Sea in the west. ALMA-ATA, the capital, Chimkent, Semipalatinsk, Aktyubinsk, Tselinograd, and Ust-Kamenogorsk are the major cities. It is the second largest constituent republic after the Russian Soviet Federated Socialist Republic (RSFSR) and the third largest in population after the RSFSR and the Ukraine. Kazakhstan is a vast flatland, bordered by a high mountain belt in the southeast. It extends nearly 2,000 mi (3,200 km) from the lower Volga and the Caspian Sea in the west to the Altai mts. in the east, comprising N Central Asian and SW Siberian USSR. It is largely lowland in the north and west (W Siberian, Caspian, and Turan lowlands), hilly in the center (Kazakh Hills), and mountainous in the south and east (Tien Shan and Altai ranges). Kazakhstan is a region of inland drainage; the Syr Darya, the Ili, the Chu, and other rivers drain into the Aral Sea and Lake Balkhash. Most of the region is desert or has limited and irregular rainfall; however, dry farming along the northern borders of Kazakhstan has been expanding at a considerable rate since cultivation began in 1954. As a result of the cultivation of these virgin lands, the Tselinny Kray (Virgin Lands Territory) was established in 1961. Kazakhstan produces much of the USSR's wool and cattle and a very great part of its wheat. The Kazakh Plateau covers the core of the region, and has important mineral resources. Coal is mined at Karaganda and Ekibatuz, and there are major oil fields at Emba, at the northern tip of the Caspian. Well over half the copper, lead, zinc, nickel, chromium, and silver mined in the USSR is from this area; in northern and central Kazakhstan there are huge iron ore deposits. The Irtysh hydroelectric stations are a major source of power. The republic's industries are located along the margins of the region: Agricultural and mining machinery is manufactured, and Temir-Tau is the iron and steel center. Superphosphate fertilizers, phosphorus acids, artificial fibers, synthetic rubber, textiles, and medicines are among the many products. The population of Kazakhstan consists of Kazakhs, Russians, Ukrainians, Uzbeks, Belorussians, and Uigurs. The Kazakhs, who make up about one third of the population, speak a Turkic language and are Muslims. The original Turkic tribes were conquered by the Mongols in the 13th cent. and ruled by various khanates until the Russian conquest (1730–1840). In 1916 the Kazakhs rebelled against Russian domination and were in the process of establishing a Western-style state at the time of the 1917 Bolshevik Revolution. Organized as the Kirghiz Autonomous SSR in 1920, it was renamed the Kazakh Autonomous SSR in 1925 and became a constituent republic in 1936. The culture of the Kazakh nomads featured the Central Asian epics, ritual songs, and legends. The 19th cent. saw the growth of the Kazakh intelligentsia. A written literature strongly influenced by Russian culture was then developed. The republic is the site of the Kazakh State Univ. (founded 1934) and the Kazakh Academy of Sciences (founded 1946).

Kazan, Elia (ĭlī′ə, ēl′yə kəzăn′, –zän′), 1909–, American stage and film director, producer, writer, actor, b. Turkey, as Elia Kazanjoglous. Emigrating to the United States in 1913, Kazan began his acting career with the New York Group Theatre in the 1930s. He became a founding member and director of the Actors' Studio. Kazan's outstanding stage productions include *The Skin of Our Teeth* (1942), *All My Sons* (1947), *A Streetcar Named Desire* (1947; film version, 1951), *Death of a Salesman* (1948), and *Tea and Sym-*

Scene from Elia Kazan's film On the Waterfront, *with Eva Marie Saint and Marlon Brando (center).*

pathy (1953). Among his major films are *A Tree Grows in Brooklyn* (1944), *Gentlemen's Agreement* (1947), *On the Waterfront* (1954), *East of Eden* (1955), *A Face in the Crowd* (1957), and *Wild River* (1960). He directed the films *America, America* (1963) and *The Arrangement* (1969) from his own novels.

Kazan (kəzän', -zăn', Rus. kəzä'nyə), city (1970 pop. 869,000), capital of the Tatar Autonomous Soviet Socialist Republic, E European USSR, on the Volga. It is a major historic, cultural, industrial, and commercial center. Manufactures include aircraft, machines and machine tools, chemicals, explosives, electrical equipment, building materials, food products, and furs. Kazan's port and shipyards on the Volga make it an important water transport center. Founded in 1401, Kazan became the capital of a powerful, independent Tatar khanate (1445), which emerged from the empire of the Golden Horde. The khanate was conquered and the city sacked in 1552 by Ivan IV. It became the capital of the Volga region in 1708 and was an outpost (18th cent.) of Russian colonization in the east. It was burned by Pugachev in 1774 and was rebuilt by Catherine II. Little remains of the Muslim period except the Suyumbeka tower in the impressive 16th-century kremlin. Lenin and Tolstoy studied at the Univ. of Kazan (founded 1804). The city also has a branch of the Soviet Academy of Sciences, an ancient cathedral, and several monasteries and mosques. The name is sometimes spelled Kasan.

Kazanlik (kä"zänlĭk'), town (1968 est. pop. 48,800), central Bulgaria, in the Kazanlik valley, a region famous for its rose fields. Kazanlik developed in the 17th cent. as a manufacturing center for attar of roses. Other manufactures include textiles and musical instruments.

Kazan-retto: see VOLCANO ISLANDS.

Kazantzakis, Nikos (nē'kôs kä"zändzä'kēs), 1883?–1957, Greek writer, b. Crete. After obtaining a law degree he studied philosophy under Henri Bergson in Paris and traveled widely in Europe and Asia. Although attracted to Communism early in life, he later grew disillusioned with revolutionary materialism and rationalism. From 1919 to 1927 he directed the Greek ministry of public welfare, and as minister of state (1945–46) he vainly tried to reconcile the factions of left and right. Of an intensely poetic and religious nature, Kazantzakis was torn between the active and the contemplative, between the sensual and the ascetic, and between nihilism and commitment. A tendency toward hero worship is revealed in his interpretative works on Bergson and Nietzsche. His most ambitious work, *The Odyssey, a Modern Sequel* (1938, tr. 1958), a verse tale, begins where Homer's *Odyssey* ends; the new adventures of Odysseus are used to explore the world views of Jesus, Buddha, Lenin, Nietzsche, and others. He presents the human struggle for spiritual freedom and philosophic maturity, showing particular enthusiasm for heroic pessimism and for nihilism. *Zorba the Greek* (1946, tr. 1952) reflects an enormous exuberance for life, and *Christ Recrucified* (1938, tr. *The Greek Passion,* 1953) is a darker tale of good and evil in which a modern man reenacts a Christlike destiny. Other works include *The Last Temptation of Christ* (1951, tr. 1960) and *The Poor Man of God* (1953, tr. *Saint Francis,* 1962). He also translated many classics into Greek. See biography by Helen Kazantzakis (1968); study by Pandelis Prevelakis (1958, tr. 1961).

Kazbek, Mount (kŏzbĕk', Rus. kəzbyĕk'), peak, 16,541 ft (5,042 m) high, SE European USSR, in Georgia, in the Greater Caucasus. An extinct volcano, it rises above the Daryal gorge and the Georgian Military Road. Its glaciers give rise to the Terek River. Mt. Kazbek was first scaled in 1868. An alternate spelling is Kasbek.

Kaz Dağı (käz däŭ'), anc. Ida Mts., range, NW Turkey, SE of the location of ancient Troy. Mt. Gargarus (5,797 ft/1,767 m) is the highest point. The mountain was dedicated in ancient times to the worship of Cybele who was therefore sometimes called Idae Mater.

Kazerun (kä"zĕro͞on'), city (1971 est. pop. 42,000), Fars prov., SW Iran. It is an agricultural trade center.

Kazimierz: For Polish rulers thus named, see CASIMIR.

Kazin, Alfred (kā'zĭn), 1915–, American critic, b. Brooklyn, N.Y., grad. College of the City of New York (B.S., 1935) and Columbia (M.A., 1938). His first book, *On Native Grounds* (1942), is a study of American prose literature starting with William Dean Howells. Kazin's later writings include *The Inmost Leaf* (1955) and *Contemporaries* (1962), and *Bright Book of Life* (1973), which carries his analysis of American literature up to 1972. *Walker in the City* (1951) is a lyrical reminiscence of his childhood in the Jewish immigrant section of Brooklyn; *Starting Out in the Thirties* (1965) recalls his young manhood.

Kazinczy, Ferencz (fĕ'rĕnts kŏ'zĭntsē), 1759–1831, Hungarian author and critic. The influence of Kazinczy's works made him a leading reformer of the Hungarian language. He was imprisoned (1794–1801) for revolutionary activity. His didactic verse (e.g., *Poetai Berke,* 1813) and works of biography brought him renown. Kazinczy's translations of Shakespeare and major European authors greatly benefited Hungarian literature. His voluminous correspondence is of great historical value.

Kazvin, Iran: see QAZVIN.

Kéa (kā'ä) or **Keos** (kā'ôs, kē'ŏs), Lat. *Ceos,* island (1971 pop. 1,666), c.61 sq mi (160 sq km), SE Greece, in the Aegean Sea; one of the Cyclades. Fruits, barley, and silk are produced. Kéa (1971 pop. 693), the main town, is situated on the site of ancient Iulis. The poets Bacchylides and Simonides were born on the island. Under Ottoman rule it was a pirates' haven.

kea: see PARROT.

Kealakekua Bay (kā'əläkākōo͞'ə), on the Kona (west) coast of the island of Hawaii. Capt. James Cook, who discovered the islands in 1776, stopped there on his second voyage to Hawaii and was killed during a beach fight with the natives on Feb. 14, 1779. A monument to him stands on the shore.

Kean, Edmund, 1787?–1833, English actor. Kean's acting expressed the ideal of the romantic temperament. With his energy and violent emotions, he brought about a radical change in the prevailing classical style of the period. His parentage is uncertain, although evidence favors Aaron Kean, a surveyor's clerk, and Ann Carey, one of a company of strolling players. He served an apprenticeship with groups of provincial and strolling players and in 1814 appeared at Drury Lane as Shylock, a triumph that is a landmark in the history of the theater. He further increased his reputation with portrayals of Richard III, Iago, Othello, Macbeth, Barabbas, and Sir Giles Overreach. In the United States in 1820–21

Kean had many triumphs, but a broken engagement in Boston ruined his popularity there. His personal life was as stormy as his career. In 1822 a suit against him for adultery resulted in Kean's separation from his wife and son and hastened the disintegration of his reputation. In 1825 he again visited the United States and in some measure retrieved his reputation. After his return to England in 1826 his health and dramatic powers declined. A small man with a wild spirit and a gruff voice, he was lauded for his facial mobility; according to Coleridge he had the power to reveal Shakespeare by "flashes of lightning." See biographies by H. N. Hillebrand (1933) and M. W. Disher (1950). His son, **Charles John Kean,** 1811?–1868, went on the stage against his father's wishes and proved best in melodrama. At his father's last appearance in 1833 he played Iago to his father's Othello at Covent Garden. He is best known for his spectacular and historically accurate productions of Shakespeare and contemporary works, especially Byron's *Sardanapalus,* at the Princess Theatre (1851–59). He often played opposite his wife **Ellen Tree Kean,** 1808–80, a noted comedienne, whom he married in 1842. See the letters of Charles and Ellen Kean, ed. by J. M. D. Hardwick (1954).

Kearney, Denis (kär'nē), 1847–1907, American political agitator, b. Co. Cork, Ireland. He was a sailor and then a San Francisco drayman. When California suffered a depression in 1877, Kearney began addressing the workingmen and the unemployed in vacant San Francisco sand lots. He denounced the Central Pacific RR monopoly, political and economic abuses, and particularly Chinese labor, ending many of his speeches with the words, "The Chinese must go." His inflammatory harangues attracted many followers, and after organizing the Workingmen's Party of California—often called the "Sand-Lotters"—he led in the 1870s in driving Orientals from their factories, in burning their laundries, and in threatening violence to those who employed Chinese workers. The party united with the Granger organization and sent a large number of delegates to the California constitutional convention of 1878, where their influence brought about many new laws. The state judicial system was reformed, a railroad commission was established, and home rule was set up in San Francisco. The Chinese were forbidden to hold property and to engage in specified occupations. The provisions denying the Chinese civil liberties were later voided by the courts. Kearney went East to popularize the Workingmen's party, but, gaining little success, he dropped back into obscurity after 1884.

Kearney, city (1970 pop. 19,181), seat of Buffalo co., S central Nebr., on the Platte River; inc. 1873. It is a commercial, industrial, and transportation center in an agricultural area. Farm and irrigation equipment are among its many products. Fort Kearny (named for Gen. Stephen W. Kearny), established nearby in 1848 to protect the Oregon Trail, was abandoned in 1871. The site is now a state park. A state college and a museum are in the city.

Kearns (kûrnz), uninc. town (1970 pop. 17,071), Salt Lake co., N Utah, a suburb of Salt Lake City. There are dairy farms in the area, and sugar beets are grown.

Kearny, Lawrence (kär'nē), 1789–1868, American naval officer, b. Perth Amboy, N.J.; cousin of Stephen Watts Kearny. He became a midshipman in 1807, served in the War of 1812, and later saw action in the Caribbean and Mediterranean against pirates. As commander (1840–43) of the East India squadron, he opened negotiations that resulted in the signing of a commercial treaty between China and the United States in 1844. On his way home he stopped at the Hawaiian Islands and protested the proposed cession of the islands to Great Britain. See biography by C. S. Alden (1937).

Kearny, Philip, 1814–62, Union general in the American Civil War, b. New York City; nephew of Stephen Watts Kearny. After studying law he joined (1837) the army. One of three officers sent to study the French cavalry service (1839), he served (1840) with the French in Algeria. In the Mexican War, Kearny lost an arm at Churubusco. He resigned from the army in 1851 to travel and in 1859 fought again with the French in the war for Italian liberation. Upon the outbreak of the Civil War he was appointed brigadier general of volunteers and given command of the 1st New Jersey Brigade. Kearny fought in the Peninsular campaign and at the second battle of Bull Run. While reconnoitering at Chantilly, he unknowingly entered the enemy's lines and was killed (Sept., 1862). Kearny was noted for his courage and dash and was idolized by his men. Kearny, N.J., was named for him. See biography by Irving Werstein (1962).

Kearny, Stephen Watts, 1794–1848, American general in the Mexican War, b. Newark, N.J. At the beginning of the Mexican War he was made commander of the Army of the West with the rank (June, 1846) of brigadier general. With about 1,600 men he marched over the Santa Fe Trail to New Mexico, entered the city of Santa Fe without opposition, and organized a civil government for the territory. On his way to join the forces of Commodore Robert F. STOCKTON in California he was besieged at San Pasqual, where he was wounded and suffered casualties of a third of his command before being rescued by relief forces from Stockton. After several skirmishes the combined forces reached Los Angeles and occupied the town. A dispute arose between Kearny and Stockton as to the chief command, and Col. John C. FRÉMONT, appointed civil governor of California by Stockton, refused to obey Kearny's orders. When orders from Washington sustained Kearny, he had Frémont court-martialed. Kearny was military governor of the territory until the end of May, 1847. Afterward he went to Mexico, where he was governor of Veracruz and then of Mexico City for brief periods in 1848. Fort Kearney, erected in 1848 on the Platte River in what is now Nebraska, was named for Kearny but misspelled.

Kearny (kär'nē), town (1970 pop. 37,585), Hudson co., NE N.J.; inc. 1899. The town is the site of shipyards (greatly enlarged in 1941) and dry docks. Its chief product is communications equipment. Kearny contains much of the tidal wastelands between the Passaic and the Hackensack rivers that is being reclaimed for industrial and recreational purposes.

Kearsarge (kēr'särj''), Union ship in the Civil War. See CONFEDERATE CRUISERS.

Keaton, Buster (Joseph Francis Keaton), 1895–1966, American movie actor, b. Piqua, Kans. Considered one of the greatest comic actors in film history, Keaton was featured in many silent comedies as a deadpan hero who survived against incredible odds. Among these movies are *The Navigator* (1924), *The General* (1926), and *Steamboat Bill Junior* (1927). He made a comeback as a supporting actor in such films as *Sunset Boulevard* (1959), *Limelight* (1952), and *A Funny Thing Happened on the Way to the Forum* (1966).

Keats, John, 1795–1821, English poet, b. London. He is considered one of the greatest of English poets. The son of a livery stable keeper, Keats attended school at Enfield, where he became the friend of Charles Cowden Clarke, the headmaster's son, who encouraged his early learning. Apprenticed to a surgeon (1811), Keats came to know Leigh Hunt and his literary circle, and in 1816 he gave up surgery to write poetry. His first volume of poems appeared in 1817. It included "I stood tip-toe upon a little hill," "Sleep and Poetry," and the famous sonnet "On First Looking into Chapman's Homer." *Endymion,* a long poem, was published in 1818. Although faulty in structure, it is nevertheless full of rich imagery and color. Keats returned from a walking tour in the Highlands to find himself attacked in *Blackwood's Magazine*—an article berated him for belonging to Leigh Hunt's "Cockney school" of poetry—and in the *Quarterly Review.* The critical assaults of 1818 mark a turning point in Keats's life; he was forced to examine his work more carefully, and as a result the influence of Hunt was diminished. However, these attacks did not contribute to Keats's decline in health and his early death, as Shelley maintained in his elegy "Adonais." Keats's passionate love for Fanny Brawne seems to have begun in 1818. Fanny's letters to Keats's sister show that her critics' contention that she was a cruel flirt was not true. Only Keats's failing health prevented their marriage. He had contracted tuberculosis, probably from nursing his brother Tom, who died in 1818. With his friend, the artist Joseph Severn, Keats sailed for Italy shortly after the publication of *Lamia, Isabella, The Eve of St. Agnes, and Other Poems* (1820), which contains most of his important work and is probably the greatest single volume of poetry published in England in the 19th cent. He died in Rome in Feb., 1821, at the age of 25. In spite of his tragically brief career, Keats is one of the most important English poets. He is also among the most personally appealing. Noble, generous, and sympathetic, he was capable not only of passionate love but also of warm, steadfast friendship. Keats is ranked, with Shelley and Byron, as one of the three great Romantic poets. Such poems as "Ode to a Nightingale," "Ode on a Grecian Urn," "To Autumn," and "Ode on Melancholy" are unequaled for dignity, melody, and richness of sensuous imagery. All of Keats's poetry is filled with a mysterious and elevating sense of beauty and joy. His posthumous pieces include "La Belle Dame sans Merci," in its way as great an evocation of romantic medievalism as "The Eve of St. Agnes." Among his sonnets, familiar ones are "When I have fears that I may cease to be" and "Bright star! would I were as steadfast as thou art." "Lines on the Mermaid Tavern," "Fancy," and "Bards of Passion and of Mirth" are delightful short poems. Some of Keats's finest work is in the unfinished epic "Hyperion." In recent years critical attention has focused on Keats's philosophy, which involves not abstract thought but rather absolute receptivity to experience. This attitude is indicated in his celebrated term "negative capability"—"to let the mind be a thoroughfare for all thought." Keats's letters (ed. by H. E. Rollins, 1958) vividly reveal his character, opinions, and feelings. See his poetical works, ed. by H. W. Garrod (2d ed. 1958); his autobiography, ed. by E. V. Weller (1933); biographies by Aileen Ward (1963), W. J. Bate (1963) and Robert Gittings (1968); studies by W. J. Bate (1945) and Morris Dickstein (1971).

Buster Keaton in the film The General.

Keble, John (kē'bəl), 1792–1866, English clergyman and poet. His career (1807–11) at Corpus Christi College, Oxford, was one of unusual distinction. Made fellow of Oriel College in 1811 and ordained in 1816, he became tutor and examiner, but resigned in 1823 to become his father's curate. He based the doctrine and devotion of his important poetical work *The Christian Year* (1827) on the Book of Common Prayer. It sold 150 editions in 50 years and led to a professorship of poetry at Oxford (1831–41). Alarmed at the suppression of 10 bishoprics in Ireland, Keble preached (1833) a sermon that he called "National Apostasy." J. H. Newman later called this the beginning of the OXFORD MOVEMENT. From 1836 he held the living of Hursley, Hampshire. His works include an edition of Richard Hooker's works (1836), a life of Bishop Wilson (1863), the Oxford Psalter (1839) and *Lyra Innocentium: Thoughts in Verse on Children* (1846). Among his poems are the well-known hymns *Red o'er the Forest, New Every Morning is Thy Love,* and *Sun of My Soul.* See biographies by J. T. Coleridge (1869) and Walter Lock (1892); study by G. Battiscombe (1964).

Kebnekaise (kĕb'nəkī''sə) [Lappish, = kettle top], mountain peak, 6,965 ft (2,123 m) high, Norrbotten prov., N Sweden; highest in Sweden. There are 16 small glaciers on the slopes.

Kechua: see QUECHUA; AMERICAN INDIAN LANGUAGES.

Kecskemét (kĕch'kĕmāt), city (1970 pop. 77,484), central Hungary, in a fruit-growing region. It is a county administrative center, a road and rail hub, and a manufacturing city whose industries produce food products, alcoholic beverages, textiles, and furniture. Known since the 4th cent., the city has several churches, a museum, and a law school with a large library. The Hungarian dramatist Joseph Katona was born in Kecskemét.

Kedah (kĕ'də, kā'dä), state (1971 pop. 955,374), 3,660 sq mi (9,479 sq km), central Malay Peninsula, Malaysia, on the Strait of Malacca. It is bordered on the N and NE by Thailand. The capital and chief city is ALOR SETAR; Sungai Patani is an important town. Along the coast are wide alluvial plains where rice is grown. South Kedah has rubber plantations, and tin is mined in the hills of the interior. Generally level, Kedah has on its east border a mountain range that rises to 6,600 ft (2,012 m). Several islands are also included in the state; Langkawi off the northwest coast is the largest. The majority of the inhabitants of Kedah are Malays; there are also many Chinese, Indians working on the rubber plantations, and small groups of aborigines. Kedah was the center of the early Hinduized kingdom of Langkasuka, according to Arab and Chinese reports of the 6th–8th cent. During the Sri Vijaya domination of the Malay Peninsula (8th–13th cent.), it was an important naval base and the terminus of transpeninsular trade routes. During the 15th cent. it fell under the domination of Malacca (see MELAKA) but maintained substantial independence and a profitable trade with India and Indonesia. At this time most of the inhabitants were converted to Islam. After the fall of Malacca (1511), Kedah was fought over by the Portuguese, Dutch, Bugis, Minangkabau, and Siamese. By ceding PINANG (1786) and Province Wellesley (1800) to the British, the sultan of Kedah embittered his relations with the Siamese court, which was not appeased by his subsequent conquest of PERAK for Siam. A bloody Siamese invasion (1821) drove him into exile until 1842; upon his return PERLIS was created as a separate state. In 1909, Siam transferred sovereignty over Kedah to Great Britain. Before the establishment of the Federation of Malaya (1948), Kedah was classed as one of the Unfederated Malay States. See MALAYSIA, FEDERATION OF.

Kedar (kē'dər), powerful nomadic tribe, descendants of the second son of Ishmael, living NW of the Sinai peninsula, E of Palestine. Gen. 25.13; Ps. 120.5; Cant. 1.5; Isa. 21.16; 42.11; 60.7; Jer. 2.10; 49.28; Ezek. 27.21.

Kedemah (kĕd'ēmə, kē'dēmə), son of Ishmael. Gen. 25.15; 1 Chron. 1.31.

Kedemoth (kĕd'əmŏth, kē'dē–), unidentified town E of the Dead Sea. Deut. 2.26; Joshua 13.18; 21.37; 1 Chron. 6.79.

Kedesh (kēdĕsh). **1** Town, S Judah. Joshua 15.23. **2** See KISHION. **3** or **Kedesh-naphtali,** city, extreme N Palestine, NW of Lake Huleh. Joshua 12.22; 19.37; 20.7; 21.32; Judges 4.6–11; 2 Kings 15.29; 1 Chron. 6.76.

Keeler, James Edward, 1857–1900, American astronomer, b. La Salle, Ill. At the age of 21 he went on the Naval Observatory expedition to Colorado to observe the solar eclipse of July, 1878. In 1886 he became an assistant and in 1888 full astronomer at Lick Observatory, Mt. Hamilton, Calif. He was director of the Allegheny Observatory from 1891 to 1898. In the course of his examination of the spectra of the heavenly bodies, he furnished confirmation for Clerk Maxwell's theory that the rings of Saturn are composed of meteoric particles. In 1898, Keeler returned to Lick Observatory as director, and there, working with the Crossley reflector, he observed and photographed vast numbers of nebulas whose existence had never before been suspected, arriving at the conclusion that the spiral nebula is the normal type. He contributed memoirs to the Royal Astronomical Society of England and many papers to the *Astrophysical Journal,* of which he was coeditor. He wrote *Spectroscopic Observations of Nebulae* (1894).

Keeling Islands: see COCOS ISLANDS.

Keelung: see CHI-LUNG, Taiwan.

Keene, Charles Samuel, 1823–91, English pen-and-ink artist and caricaturist. In 1851 he began his long association with *Punch,* where the bulk of his work appeared. His drawings ranged from interesting vignettes of the contemporary scene to tidy landscapes and interiors. See studies by Joseph Pennell (1897) and Derek Hudson (1947).

Keene, Laura, c.1826–1873, Anglo-American actress-manager, b. England. She played with Mme Vestris at the Lyceum, London. She emigrated to the United States in 1852 and became manager (1855) of Laura Keene's Varieties Theater, New York City. In 1856 she opened Laura Keene's Theater (later the Olympic) and successfully produced and acted in many foreign and American plays until 1863. Her most famous production was Tom Taylor's *Our American Cousin,* which she gave at Ford's Theater, Washington, when Lincoln was shot there in 1865.

Keene, city (1970 pop. 20,467), seat of Cheshire co., SW N.H., on the Ashuelot River; settled 1736, inc. as a city 1873. It is a trade and manufacturing center in a farming and resort area. The city is the seat of Keene State College. A state park is to the north, and Mt. Monadnock, a popular ski site, is to the east.

Keeshond (kās'hŏnd) (pl. Keeshonden), breed of medium-sized NONSPORTING DOG raised in Holland for several hundred years and introduced into England in the year 1900. It stands about 18 in. (46 cm) high at the shoulder and weighs from 32 to 40 lb (14.5–18.1 kg). Its weather-resistant double coat consists of a thick, downy underlayer and an abundant, straight, harsh topcoat that stands out from the body. The undercoat is gray or cream-colored, and the outer hairs are black-tipped. Undoubtedly of Arctic origin, the Keeshond is related to the Norwegian elkhound, the Samoyed, the chow chow, and, most closely, the Pomeranian. In Holland it was so common a sight in the barges on the Dutch canals that it was first registered in England under the name "Dutch barge dog." The Keeshond is raised as a pet and watchdog. See DOG.

Keetmanshoop (kēt'mäns-ho͝op"), town (1970 pop. 10,297), S South West Africa. It is the trade center for a region where karakul sheep are raised. Keetmanshoop was founded in 1866 as a German missionary station.

Keewatin (kēwä'tĭn, -wā'-), administrative district (228,160 sq mi/590,934 sq km), Northwest Territories, Canada, N of Manitoba and W of Hudson Bay. Its boundaries, set in 1920, include all of Hudson and James bays and all of the mainland of the Northwest Territories E of long. 102°W, except for the Boothia and Melville peninsulas.

Keewatin: see PRECAMBRIAN ERA.

Kefallinía (kĕfälēnē'ä) or **Cephalonia** (sĕfəlō'nyə), island (1971 pop. 31,787), c.300 sq mi (780 sq km), W Greece, the largest of the IONIAN ISLANDS. It has an irregular coastline and is largely mountainous, rising to c.5,340 ft (1,630 m) at Mt. Ainos, which in ancient times was crowned by a temple to Zeus. Argostolion, a port, is the island's main town and ships local products such as fruit and wine. Sheep raising and fishing are important occupations on the island. Kefallinía was an ally of Athens in the Peloponnesian War and later was a member of the Aetolian League. The island was taken by Rome in 189 B.C. After the division of the Roman Empire (A.D. 395), it was held by the Byzantine Empire until its occupation (1126) by Venice. It subsequently was ruled by several Italian families, was seized by the Ottoman Turks (1479), and was ceded (1499) to Venice, which held it until the Treaty of Campo Formio (1797). Its subsequent history is that of the Ionian Islands. In 1953 the island was devastated by earthquakes of such force that Mt. Ainos was split.

Kefauver, Carey Estes (kēfôvər), 1903–63, U.S. Senator from Tennessee (1949–63), b. Madisonville, Tenn., known as Estes Kefauver. He became a Chattanooga lawyer and in 1938 was elected to the U.S. House of Representatives, where he served until he entered the Senate in 1949. His victory in the senatorial race was conspicuous because it ended "Boss" Edward H. Crump's domination of Tennessee politics. As chairman of the Senate crime investigating committee in 1950 and 1951, Kefauver attracted nationwide publicity. *Crime in America* (1951) was Kefauver's own book on the results of this investigation. Reelected to the Senate in 1954, he won the Democratic party's nomination for Vice President in 1956, but, with Adlai Stevenson, was defeated in the Eisenhower landslide. A supporter of civil rights legislation, Kefauver won (1960) reelection after overcoming the active opposition of a staunch segregationist in Tennessee's Democratic primary. He was a principal sponsor of a law enacted in 1962 to protect the public from harmful and ineffective pharmaceuticals. See biography by J. B. Gorman (1971).

Keflavík (kĕp'lävēk''), town (1970 pop. 5,663), SW Iceland, on the Faxaflói, W of Reykjavík. It is a major fishing port, best known for its large international airport, which was built by the United States during World War II; in 1951 the United States was granted the right to use it as a military base.

Kehelathah (kē''hēlā'thə), unidentified desert encampment. Num. 33.22,23.

Keighley (kēth'lē), municipal borough (1971 pop. 55,263), West Riding of Yorkshire, N central England, at the junction of the Aire and Worth rivers. The Leeds and Liverpool Canal connects Keighley with Liverpool and Hull. Keighley's products include woolen, silk, and rayon goods; spinning machinery and looms; and sewing and washing machines. In 1938, Keighley absorbed nearby Haworth, home of the Brontë family and site of a Brontë museum. In 1974, Keighley became part of the new metropolitan county of West Yorkshire.

Keihin: see YOKOHAMA, Japan.

Kei Islands: see KAI ISLANDS, Indonesia.

Keijo: see SEOUL, South Korea.

Keilah (kēī'lə), town, SW Palestine. David rescued it from the Philistines and lived there until the treachery of its inhabitants caused him to leave. Joshua 15.44; 1 Sam. 23.1–13; Neh. 3.17.

Keita, Modibo (mōdē'bō kā'tä), 1915–77, African political leader in the Republic of Mali. He studied in France and taught in the French Sudan (later the Republic of Mali) before becoming active in nationalist politics in 1946. He represented the French Sudan in the French national assembly from 1956 to 1958. A strong supporter of African unity, Keita promoted the Mali Federation, formed in 1959, and after the federation was dissolved (1960) he was elected the first president of the Republic of Mali. He ruled until 1968, when he was ousted by an army coup.

Keitel, Wilhelm (vĭl'hĕlm kī'təl), 1882–1946, German general. A supporter of Hitler, he became (1938) chief of staff of the supreme command of the armed forces, a new post that marked the German army's subjection to Hitler. On May 8, 1945, Keitel ratified in Berlin the unconditional surrender of Germany. He was convicted at the Nuremberg war-crimes trial and hanged.

Keith, Sir Arthur, 1866–1955, British anatomist, b. Aberdeen, Scotland, educated at the Univ. of Aberdeen, University College, London, and the Univ. of Leipzig. He became conservator of the museum and professor at the Royal College of Surgeons (1908), then professor of physiology at the Royal Institution, London (1917–23). From 1933 he carried out research on tuberculosis as master of the Buckston Browne Research Farm at Downe, Kent. He also applied his knowledge of anatomy to an influential study of human origins, reconstructing prehistoric man based on fossil remains from Europe and N Africa. His writings include *Human Embryology and Morphology* (1902, 6th ed. 1949), *The Antiquity of Man* (1915, 2d ed. 1925), and *A New Theory of Evolution* (1948). See his autobiography (1950).

Keith, George, c.1638–1716, Scottish preacher. Joining the Quakers c.1663, he was closely associated with Robert Barclay, George Fox, and other influential Friends. Shortly after his arrival in America (1684) he became the leader of a separate faction known as Christian Quakers, for which he was denounced by William Penn in 1692. Keith returned to England where, in 1700, he was ordained a priest in the Anglican Church. He was again in America (1702–4), preaching and baptizing. His journeys in the colonies are recorded in his *Journal of Travels from New Hampshire to Caratuck* (1706). See biography by E. W. Kirby (1942).

Keith, George, 1693?–1778, Scottish Jacobite, 10th earl marischal [marshal] of Scotland. He took part in the Jacobite uprising of 1715 and after its failure escaped to the Continent. A leader of the Spanish expedition to Scotland (1719) in behalf of the Old Pretender, he again escaped. Later he joined his brother James Francis Edward Keith in Prussia and rose high in the favor of Frederick the Great, who appointed him ambassador to Paris (1751), governor of Neuchâtel (1752), and ambassador to Spain (1758). Although pardoned by George II of Britain, he spent most of the remainder of his life in Prussia. See biography by E. E. Cuthell (1915).

Estes Kefauver with Senate crime committee exhibit.

Keith, George Keith Elphinstone, Viscount 1746–1823, British admiral. After serving as a captain in the American Revolution and early French Revolutionary Wars, he was appointed (1795) vice admiral. He suppressed the mutinies at Nore and Spithead (1797) and commanded the Mediterranean fleet (1798–1801), the North Sea fleet (1803–7), and the Channel fleet (1812–15), receiving Napoleon's surrender after Waterloo. Not a military tactician, he won no notable battles but was a skilled administrator and commander.

Keith, James Francis Edward, 1696–1758, Scottish field marshal of Prussia; brother of George Keith, 10th earl marischal [marshal] of Scotland. He participated in the Jacobite uprising of 1715 and in the abortive invasion of 1719 with his brother. Escaping to the Continent, he first entered the Spanish service and then went to Russia, where he gained honor in both civil and military offices. Later he went to Prussia and became close friends with Frederick the Great, who made him a field marshal (1747). Keith entered the circle of Europe's leading intellectuals and rendered great service to Prussia in the early part of the Seven Years War. He was killed in the battle of Hochkirch. See Peter Wilding, *Adventurers in the Eighteenth Century* (1937).

Keith, Minor Cooper, 1848–1929, American magnate, a founder of the United Fruit Company, b. Brooklyn, N.Y. In the face of incredible hardships he built (1871–90) a railroad from the port of Limón, which he founded on the Caribbean, to San José, capital of Costa Rica. Banana plantations that he started experimentally near Limón in 1873 prospered, and he established the first steamship service to bring these bananas to the United States. He gained control of other plantations in Panama and Colombia and dominated the banana trade. In 1899 he combined his plantation interests with those of the Boston Fruit Company in the West Indies to form the United Fruit Company. He returned to railroad building, organized (1912) the International Railways of Central America, and completed an 800-mi (1,287-km) railway system, but died before realizing his dream of a line from Guatemala to the Panama Canal. His work profoundly altered the economic life of Central American countries. See Watt Stewart, *Keith and Costa Rica* (1964).

Keith, William, 1838–1911, American painter, b. Scotland. In 1851 he came to New York City, where he learned wood engraving and did illustrations for *Harper's Weekly*. He moved to San Francisco in 1860 and later turned to painting, studying in Düsseldorf in 1870 and in Munich in the 1880s. His Western landscapes evolved from early mountain epics to later intimate natural scenes. The Keith Memorial Gallery of the Oakland Art Museum is devoted entirely to his work. His *By the Creek, Sonoma* is in the Corcoran Gallery of Art, Washington, D.C. See Brother Cornelius, *Keith, Old Master of California* (2 vol., 1942, 1956).

Keizer (kī'zər), uninc. town (1970 pop. 11,405), Marion co., NW Oregon, a suburb of Salem.

Kejimkujik National Park, 140 sq mi (363 sq km), S central N.S., Canada, near Maitland Bridge; est. 1968. The park has a rolling landscape with numerous lakes and streams. Micmac Indian petroglyphs are found there.

Kekkonen, Urho Kaleva (o͞or'hô kä'lävä kĕ'kōnĕn), 1900–, president of Finland (1956–). The leading spokesman of the Center party (known as the Agrarian party until 1965), he held various cabinet posts from 1936 and was prime minister from 1950 to 1956. He succeeded Juho Paasikivi as president in 1956. His reelection in 1962 and 1968 affirmed his policy of maintaining friendly neutrality with the USSR. In 1973 the Finnish parliament voted to extend his term, which was to expire in March, 1974, for four years.

Kekulé von Stradonitz, Friedrich August (frē'-drĭkh ou'go͝ost kā'ko͞olā fən shträ'dōnĭts), 1829–96, German organic chemist. He was professor at Ghent (1858–65) and at Bonn from 1865. He made studies of various carbon compounds, especially BENZENE, for the molecular structure of which he developed the ring theory. This theory is of fundamental importance to modern chemistry.

Kelaiah (kēlā'yə) or **Kelita** (kēlī'tə), Levite active in the return to Palestine. Ezra 10.23; Neh. 8.7; 10.10. The texts could refer to different persons.

Kelantan (kəlăn'tən, kəlän''tän'), state (1971 pop. 680,626), 5,780 sq mi (14,970 sq km), central Malay Peninsula, Malaysia, on the South China Sea. It is bordered on the N by Thailand. The capital is KOTA BAHARU. It is drained by the Kelantan River (c.150 mi/240 km long), which flows into the South China Sea. Rice, the most important commercial crop, is grown on the wide coastal plains; other products are rubber and copra. Tin, gold, manganese, and iron are mined on a small scale in the hills of the interior. The people are mainly Malay, but there is a small Chinese minority. Kelantan was ruled by Sri Vijaya until the 13th cent.; it fell under the sway of Malacca (see MELAKA) in the 15th cent. After the fall of Malacca (1511), conflict among many powers resulted eventually in the establishment by Siam of sovereignty over the area (early 19th cent.). Kelantan became a protectorate of Great Britain in 1909. Before the establishment of the Federation of Malaya (1948), Kelantan was classed as one of the Unfederated Malay States. See MALAYSIA, FEDERATION OF.

Kelita (kēlī'tə): see KELAIAH.

Keller, Gottfried (gôt'frēt), 1819–90, Swiss novelist, poet, and short-story writer. His vital, realistic, and purposeful fiction gives him a high place among 19th-century authors. Chief among his works is the

Helen Keller.

"educational" novel *Der grüne Heinrich* (1854–55; tr. *Green Henry,* 1960), which he later revised. It is considered one of the outstanding works of the 19th cent. A number of short stories are included in *People of Seldwyla* (1856–74; tr. 1929); among them is the highly regarded tale which was the basis of Delius's opera *A Village Romeo and Juliet.* See J. M. Lindsay, *Gottfried Keller: Life and Works* (Am. ed. 1969).

Keller, Helen Adams, 1880–1968, American author and lecturer, blind and deaf from the age of two, b. Tuscumbia, Ala. In 1887 she was put under the charge of Anne Sullivan (see MACY, ANNE SULLIVAN), who was her teacher and companion. As a pupil Helen Keller made rapid progress and was graduated from Radcliffe in 1904 with honors. She lectured all over America and in Europe and Asia, raising funds for the training of the blind and promoting other social causes. Her books include *The Story of My Life* (1903), *The World I Live In* (1908), *Helen Keller's Journal, 1936–1937* (1938), *Let Us Have Faith* (1940), and *The Open Door* (1957). See biography by Margery Weiner (1970).

Kellermann, François Christophe (fräNswä' krĕstôf' kĕlĕrmän'), 1735–1820, marshal of France, b. Strasbourg. He served in the Seven Years War and won renown in the FRENCH REVOLUTIONARY WARS when he and General Dumouriez stopped the Prussians at VALMY (1792). In the Reign of Terror, he was accused of treason and imprisoned (1793–94), but was not convicted. Napoleon made him senator (1799) and duke of Valmy (1808). Rallying (1814) to Louis XVIII, Kellermann was raised to the peerage.

Kelley, Abby: see FOSTER, ABBY KELLEY.

Kelley, Edgar Stillman, 1857–1944, American composer and critic, b. Sparta, Wis., studied in Chicago and at the Stuttgart Conservatory. After his return to the United States he played the organ in Oakland, Calif., and in San Francisco and served as music critic of the San Francisco *Examiner.* He taught (1901–2) at Yale, replacing Horatio Parker, and afterward in Berlin until 1910, when he became dean of the composition department of the Cincinnati Conservatory. Among his works are an operetta, *Puritania* (1892); an orchestral suite, *Aladdin* (1915), based on Chinese music heard in San Francisco; two symphonies, *Gulliver* (1913–36) and *New England* (1914); incidental music to the play *Ben Hur* (1899); and an oratorio, *The Pilgrim's Progress* (1918). His writings include *Chopin the Composer* (1913).

Kelley, Florence, 1859–1932, American social worker and reformer, b. Philadelphia, grad. Cornell, 1882, and Northwestern Univ. law school, 1894. Married in 1884 to a Polish doctor, Lazare Wishnieweski, she divorced him six years later and became a Hull House resident. A confirmed socialist and active in many reforms, Kelley devoted most of her energies toward securing protective labor legislation, especially for women and children. From 1899 she served for many years as director of the National Consumer's League, which strove for industrial reform through consumer activity. Her writings include *Ethical Gains through Legislation* (1905) and *Modern Industry* (1914). See Josephine Goldmark, *Impatient Crusader* (1953); D. R. Blumberg, *Florence Kelley* (1966).

Kelley, Hall Jackson, 1790–1874, American propagandist for the settlement of Oregon, b. Northwood, N.H. A schoolmaster in Boston (1818–23) and later a railroad surveyor in Maine, he founded (1829) a society to promote American settlement in the disputed Columbia River country and wrote appeals to prospective colonists. He secured the aid of Nathaniel J. WYETH, but plans for a joint expedition to the West were delayed, and Wyeth went alone. In 1833, Kelley went to New Orleans, sailed to Veracruz, and crossed Mexico to California, where he met the trader Ewing Young. The two arrived in the Oregon country in 1834. A sick and discouraged man, Kelley was sheltered at Fort Vancouver by Dr. John MCLOUGHLIN until the spring of 1835, when he returned to Boston. He subsequently wrote a "memoir" on Oregon, which was presented to Congress by Caleb Cushing. See biography by Fred W. Powell (1917); Fred W. Powell, ed., *Hall J. Kelley on Oregon* (1932).

Kelley, Oliver Hudson, 1826–1913, American agriculturist, b. Boston. He was a founder of the National Grange of the Patrons of Husbandry, the central influence in the GRANGER MOVEMENT of the 1870s. Kelley took up land on the Minnesota frontier in 1849 and farmed until, in 1864, he became connected with the U.S. Bureau of Agriculture, traveling in the West and South to report on agricultural conditions. At this time he conceived the idea of the Grange as a social and fraternal organization of farmers, and in 1867 he and six others secured the charter and Kelley became secretary. After 1873 the leadership passed to others, and Kelley resigned as secretary in 1878. He wrote *Origin and Progress of the Order of the Patrons of Husbandry* (1875).

Kelley, William Darrah (dâr'ə), 1814–90, American legislator, b. Philadelphia. He was admitted (1841) to the bar and served (1847–56) as judge of the court of common pleas for Philadelphia. Originally a Democrat and a believer in free trade, he joined the Republican party when it was founded, because of its antislavery stand. The depression of 1857 and his fear that goods produced by low-paid foreign labor would flood the country converted him to protectionism. He was elected to Congress in 1860 and was continuously reelected for the rest of his life. As a staunch radical, he supported Negro suffrage and military reconstruction in the South. He served on the Committee on Ways and Means for 20 years. His sincerity and financial disinterestedness were never questioned, but his constant emphasis on protection as a cure-all and his frequent mention of Pennsylvania's iron industry led his colleagues to call him "Pig Iron" Kelley. He was an advocate of currency inflation for the sake of labor and the farmer. He published a number of books, including *Speeches, Addresses, and Letters on Industrial and Financial Questions* (1872), *Letters from Europe* (1879), and *The Old South and the New* (1888).

Kellogg, Clara Louise, 1842–1916, American operatic soprano, b. Sumterville, S.C. She made her debut in 1861 in New York City and in 1863 sang Marguerite in the first New York performance of Gounod's *Faust.* From 1873 to 1876 she toured the United States with her own company, producing opera in English.

Kellogg, Edward, 1790–1858, American economist, b. Norwalk, Conn. He advocated a financial scheme to abolish interest, which was often usurious at the time he wrote. Kellogg devised a system of financial control whereby the government would issue legal tender notes and then lend them on the security of real estate at a low rate of interest. At the same time the government would issue at the same rate of interest bonds that could be exchanged freely for the notes. By that system Kellogg hoped to keep the interest rate close to the estimated rate of accumulation of wealth in the United States. His pamphlet *Currency: The Evil and the Remedy* (1844) was circulated with Horace Greeley's aid; it was revised under the title *Labor and Other Capital* (1849) and went into many editions after Kellogg's death as *A New Monetary System;* the 1883 edition includes a biographical sketch by his daughter. Kellogg's views were favored by agrarian and labor organizations and led to the formation of a number of political parties (e.g., the Greenbacks, the Populists) whose aim was a national economy and currency not manipulable by banking and financial interests.

Kellogg, Frank Billings, 1856–1937, American lawyer, U.S. Senator (1917–23), and cabinet member, b. Potsdam, N.Y. As a child, he moved to Olmstead co., Minn. He later studied law and held several municipal posts. He entered private law practice in St. Paul, Minn., where he became an outstanding corporation lawyer and gained stature in the Republican party. Appointed (1904) special counsel to the U.S. Attorney General, Kellogg played an important role in antitrust prosecution, particularly in the dissolution of the General Paper and the Standard Oil companies. As special counsel to the Interstate Commerce Commission, he was active in the investigation of the railroads controlled by Edward H. Harriman. Elected U.S. Senator, he was one of the few Republicans who supported the League of Nations, although he believed minor changes were needed to permit U.S. entry. After serving (1924–25) as ambassador to Great Britain, he succeeded (1925) Charles E. Hughes as Secretary of State. He bettered relations with Mexico and helped to settle the TACNA-ARICA CONTROVERSY between Chile and Peru. Largely for his successful promotion of the KELLOGG-BRIAND PACT, he was awarded the 1929 Nobel Peace Prize. He resigned his cabinet post in 1929 and afterward served (1930–35) as a judge of the Permanent Court of International Justice. He established a foundation for the study of international relations at Carleton College in Minnesota. See biography by David Bryn-Jones (1937); L. E. Ellis, *Frank B. Kellogg and American Foreign Relations, 1925–1929* (1961).

Kellogg, Vernon Lyman, 1867–1937, American zoologist, b. Emporia, Kansas, B.A. Univ. of Kansas, 1889. He was professor (1894–1920) of entomology at Stanford Univ. He served (1915–16) as director in Brussels of the American Commission for Relief in Belgium and later held other positions with the American Relief Administration in Europe. From 1919 to 1931 he was permanent secretary of the National Research Council. He worked in insect taxonomy and in economic entomology and was also known for his interpretations of science for the layman.

Kellogg-Briand Pact (-brēäN′), agreement, signed Aug. 27, 1928, condemning "recourse to war for the solution of international controversies." It is more properly known as the Pact of Paris. In June, 1927, Aristide BRIAND, foreign minister of France, proposed to the U.S. government a treaty outlawing war between the two countries. Frank B. KELLOGG, the U.S. Secretary of State, returned a proposal for a general pact against war, and after prolonged negotiations the Pact of Paris was signed by 15 nations—Australia, Belgium, Canada, Czechoslovakia, France, Germany, Great Britain, India, the Irish Free State, Italy, Japan, New Zealand, Poland, South Africa, and the United States. The contracting parties agreed that settlement of all conflicts, no matter of what origin or nature, that might arise among them should be sought only by pacific means and that war was to be renounced as an instrument of national policy. Although 62 nations ultimately ratified the pact, its effectiveness was vitiated by its failure to provide measures of enforcement. The Kellogg-Briand Pact was given an unenthusiastic reception by many countries. The U.S. Senate, ratifying the treaty with only one dissenting vote, still insisted that there must be no curtailment of America's right of self-defense and that the United States was not compelled to take action against countries that broke the treaty. The pact never made a meaningful contribution to international order, although it was invoked in 1929 with some success, when China and the USSR reached a tense moment over possession of the Chinese Eastern RR in Manchuria. Ultimately, however, the pact proved to be meaningless, especially with the practice of waging undeclared wars in the 1930s (e.g., the Japanese invasion of Manchuria in 1931, the Italian invasion of Ethiopia in 1935, and the German occupation of Austria in 1938). See R. H. Ferrell, *Peace in Their Time* (1952, repr. 1968).

Kellogg Foundation, philanthropic institution established (1930) at Battle Creek, Mich., by food manufacturer W. K. Kellogg (1860–1951). Kellogg eventually gave the institution a total of $47 million, and by 1972 its endowment had increased to more than $490 million. After World War II the foundation broadened its interests, formerly restricted to Michigan, to include support of projects throughout the world, with an emphasis on activities in the Western Hemisphere. The foundation has concentrated on the application of knowledge rather than on basic research. Its major interests have been in the fields of agriculture, health, and education.

Kells, Republic of Ireland: see CEANANNUS MOR.

Kelly, Ellsworth, 1923–, American painter, b. Newburgh, New York. Kelly paints flat color areas usually having sharp contours and geometric shapes. *Atlantic* (1956) and *Green Blue Red* (1964) are in the Whitney Museum, New York City. The Walker Art Center, Minneapolis, Minnesota, owns *Blue Red Green* (1962).

Kelly, Gene, 1912–, American dancer, choreographer, and movie actor and director, b. Pittsburgh. Kelly first gained fame in the Broadway musical *Pal Joey* (1941). His best-known work has been in motion pictures, where he excelled in a novel combination of camera and dance techniques in such films as *On the Town* (1949), *An American in Paris* (1951), *Singin' in the Rain* (1952), and *Invitation to the Dance* (1956). A skillful and expressive performer, he has appeared in such film musicals as *Anchors Aweigh* (1945), *Take Me Out to the Ballgame* (1949), and *Brigadoon* (1954). He has also played dramatic film roles, as in *Inherit the Wind* (1960), and has directed several movies, including *The Happy Road* (1950) and *Hello Dolly* (1969).

Kelly, George, 1887–1974, American playwright, b. Philadelphia. He began his career as a vaudevillian, as both an actor and skit writer. His best-known plays, penetrating satires on American middle-class life, include *The Torch-Bearers* (1922), *The Show-off* (1924), *Craig's Wife* (1925; Pulitzer Prize), and *The Deep Mrs. Sykes* (1945).

Kelly, Hugh, 1739–77, English dramatist, b. Killarney. His first and best-known play, the sentimental comedy *False Delicacy,* was produced by Garrick in 1768 and was extremely popular in its time.

Kelly, John, 1822–86, American politician, boss of TAMMANY Hall, b. New York City. He entered politics at an early age. At first he opposed Tammany Hall, but later (1853) joined the organization and became city alderman. He served (1855–58) in Congress and was (1859–61, 1865–67) sheriff of New York County. After the exposure of William M. Tweed, Kelly, by then popularly known as "Honest John," reorganized the Tammany machine. By 1874 he held control of the organization and carried on continuous warfare with the faction of Samuel J. Tilden, who originally had cooperated with him in reorganizing Tammany. Kelly's refusal to back Tilden's candidate for governor, Lucius Robinson, and his decision to run for governor himself as an independent helped bring about the election (1879) of Alonzo Cornell. While he was head of Tammany, Kelly was able to determine the course of New York City elections, and he himself was city comptroller from 1876 to 1880. Upon retirement (1884) he yielded his political control to one of his lieutenants, Richard CROKER. See M. R. Werner, *Tammany Hall* (1932, repr. 1968).

Kelmscott Press, printing establishment in London. There William MORRIS led the 19th-century revival of the art and craft of making books (see ARTS AND CRAFTS). The first book made by the press was *The Story of the Glittering Plain* (1891), by William Morris. The masterpiece of the press was *The Works of Geoffrey Chaucer* (1896), a folio with illustrations by Sir Edward Burne-Jones and decorative designs and typeface by William Morris. After the death of Morris, in 1896, the press completed some work that he had planned, but no new work was undertaken. The final publication of the press was *A Note by William Morris on His Aims in Founding the Kelmscott Press* (1898). The three types designed by Morris and used by the press were the Golden type, named for *The Golden Legend* (1892); the Troy type, named for *The Recuyell of the Historyes of Troye* (1892); and the Chaucer type, named for the *Chaucer.* The Chaucer type is smaller than the Troy type; otherwise they are the same. The type designs were influenced directly by printers of the 15th cent. The enormous achievement of the press owes much to the art of Burne-Jones and to the inspiration and guidance of the master printer Emery Walker. It gave to the making of books new dignity and raised the level of printing craftsmanship, profoundly influencing book-design quality. See ASHENDENE PRESS; VALE PRESS; DOVES PRESS. See M. J. Perry, *A Chronological List of the Books Printed at the Kelmscott Press* (1928); Temple Scott, *A Bibliography of the Works of William Morris* (1877, repr. 1971).

Kelowna (kĭlō'nə), city (1971 pop. 19,412), S British Columbia, Canada, on Okanagan Lake. It is a tourist resort and serves as a trade center for a fruit-growing and lumbering area.

kelp: see SEAWEED.

kelpfish: see BLENNY.

Kelsey, Henry, c.1670–1729, English fur trader and explorer in Canada. He entered the service of the Hudson's Bay Company in 1684. He was sent (1689) inland to secure Indian trade and later (1691–92) made his much disputed journey into W Canada; some say he went southwest, but evidence points to his being west of Churchill in the region of Reindeer Lake. He was present when York Factory was surrendered to the sieur d'Iberville in 1694 and in 1697. He then served the company in a number of different posts. He returned to the Hudson's Bay region (1714) and served as second in command (1714–17), as governor of York (1717–18), and as governor of all the company's forts in the region (1718–22). He was replaced as governor in 1722 and returned to England. In 1719 he commanded an expedition to explore the northwest coast of Hudson Bay. See A. G. Doughty and Chester Martin, ed., *The Kelsey Papers* (1929).

Kelso, city (1970 pop. 10,296), seat of Cowlitz co., SW Wash., on the Cowlitz River near the Columbia, in a rich farm area; inc. 1889. Boatbuilding, meatpacking, and the manufacture of cement are the major industries. Settled in 1847, Kelso was an important stopping place for early steamboat travel along the Cowlitz River.

Kelt: see CELT.

Keltie, Sir John Scott, 1840–1927, Scottish geographer. He was inspector of geographical education for the Royal Geographic Society, librarian, and secretary of the society. In 1880 he became editor of *The Statesman's Yearbook,* and in 1925 joint editor of the *Geographical Journal.* His works include *A History of the Scottish Highlands and Clans* (1874), *Report on Geographic Education* (1886), *The Partition of Africa* (1894), *Applied Geography* (new ed. 1908), and *History of Geography* (with O. J. R. Howarth, 1914).

Kelvin, William Thomson, 1st **Baron,** 1824–1907, British mathematician and physicist, b. Belfast. He was professor of natural philosophy at the Univ. of Glasgow (1846–99). He is known especially for his work on heat and electricity. In THERMODYNAMICS his work of coordinating the theories of heat held by various leading scientists of his time established firmly the law of the conservation of energy as proposed by Joule. He introduced the Kelvin scale, or absolute scale, of TEMPERATURE. He also discovered the Thomson effect in THERMOELECTRICITY. The importance of the discoveries and improvements that he made in connection with the transmission of messages by submarine cables led to his establishment as a leading authority in this field. He invented the reflecting galvanometer and the siphon recorder, an instrument by which telegraphic messages are recorded in ink fed from a siphon. See biographies by S. P. Thompson (1910) and A. G. King (1925). His brother, **James Thomson,** 1822–92, an engineer, was professor at Queen's College, Belfast, from 1857 to 1873. He is known for his studies of the variation in melting point with pressure as well as for his research in hydraulics.

kelvin, abbr. K, official name in the INTERNATIONAL SYSTEM OF UNITS (SI) for the degree of temperature as measured on the KELVIN TEMPERATURE SCALE.

Kelvin temperature scale, a TEMPERATURE scale based on the properties of gases. It is found experimentally that all gases, when their temperature is reduced, contract at such a rate that their volume would be zero at a temperature of −273.15°C (degrees Celsius). The Kelvin scale is defined so that 0°K (degrees Kelvin) corresponds to this theoretical lowest temperature. The Kelvin degree is the same size as the Celsius degree (see CELSIUS TEMPERATURE SCALE); hence the two reference temperatures, the freezing point of water (0°C), and the boiling point of water (100°C), correspond to 273.15°K and 373.15°K, respectively. Because the Kelvin scale begins at the lowest possible temperature, it is known as an absolute scale; thus 0°K can be called absolute zero. The Kelvin scale is used only by scientists. An-

Gene Kelly (center) in a scene from the film Take Me Out to the Ballgame, *with Frank Sinatra (left).*

other absolute scale, the Rankine scale, is used by some engineers. It also begins at absolute zero but has degrees the same size as those of the FAHRENHEIT TEMPERATURE SCALE.

Kem (kĕm), river, c.240 mi (390 km) long, Karelian Autonomous Republic, NW European USSR. It rises SE of Kuusamo, Finland, and flows E into the White Sea. The first hydroelectric station along the Kem went into operation in 1967 at Putkinsk; others are planned.

Kemal Pasha, Mustafa: see ATATÜRK, KEMAL.

Kemano Dam: see NECHAKO, river, Canada.

Kemble, Roger, 1721–1802, English actor and manager. During his years as the leader of a traveling company, he married (1753) Sarah Wood, an actress, who bore him 12 children. They thus founded one of the most distinguished families of actors ever to grace the English stage. Five of the children became famous. See Percy Fitzgerald, *The Kembles* (1871); Stephen Kemble, *The Kemble Papers* (New-York Historical Society Collections, 1885). The best known of the children was Sarah Kemble (see SIDDONS, SARAH KEMBLE). The eldest son, **John Philip Kemble,** 1757–1823, was educated for the priesthood, but instead went on the stage and in 1783 made his London debut as Hamlet, in which role he was painted by Sir Thomas Lawrence. A stately, formal actor, suited only for tragedy, his best role was Coriolanus, which was also his farewell performance in 1817. At the Drury Lane from 1783 to 1803, he became manager in 1788 and often played opposite Mrs. Siddons. He managed Covent Garden (1803–8) and, when it was destroyed by fire, built a new one, opening it in 1809. Because of a heavy financial loss, he increased prices, setting off the Old Prices Riots which forced a compromise agreement. See biography by Herschel Baker (1942). His brother **George Stephen Kemble,** 1758–1822, lived always in his shadow. He gave up chemistry when his sister Sarah became famous and returned to the stage, achieving success in roles such as Falstaff. He managed at various times a provincial company, a theater in Edinburgh, where he introduced John Philip Kemble and Mrs. Siddons to the public, and a company in Ireland. His younger brother, **Charles Kemble,** 1775–1854, was most successful in comedy. He first appeared as Malcolm in *Macbeth* in 1794 with John Philip Kemble and Mrs. Siddons in the lead roles. He was poetic rather than emotional, and Romeo was considered his best role. He assumed (1822) the management of Covent Garden in 1822, but he had little financial success until the stage debut of his eldest daughter, Fanny, with whom he successfully toured the United States (1832–34). He retired in 1840. See biography by Jane Williamson (1970). His sister, **Elizabeth Kemble,** 1761–1836, married an actor, Charles Whitlock, in 1785 and, taking as her stage name Mrs. Whitlock, she attained considerable popularity during a visit to the United States in 1792. She retired in 1807 **Fanny Kemble** (Frances Anne Kemble), 1809–93, elder daughter of Charles Kemble, made her debut as Juliet in 1829 under her father's management at Covent Garden. Her success was great and immediate, and her stature as an actress grew in both comedy and tragedy. She was the original Julia in *The Hunchback,* written for her by Sheridan Knowles. She received extravagant praise on her American tour in 1832. In 1834 she married Pierce Butler of Philadelphia, went with him to an estate in Georgia, but later divorced him. During the Civil War she lived in England, writing against slavery for the London *Times.* Her *Journal of a Residence on a Georgia Plantation in 1838–1839* (1863, ed. by John A. Scott, 1961) and *Records of a Later Life* (1882) are much-used sources. See biographies by L. S. Driver (1933), Robert Rushmore (1970), and Constance Wright (1972). **Adelaide Kemble,** 1814–79, second daughter of Charles Kemble, was an opera singer. She studied in Italy and appeared with success in Germany and France (1837–38) and at Covent Garden (1841–42). In 1843 she married Edward Sartoris. She wrote *A Week in a French Country House* (1867).

Kemerovo (kĕm'ərō"vō), city (1970 pop. 385,000), capital of Kemerovo oblast, central Siberian USSR, on the Tom River and on a branch of the Trans-Siberian RR. It is a coal-mining center of the Kuznetsk Basin, with important chemical and synthetic fiber industries. Founded as Shcheglova in 1720, the city was renamed Kemerovo in 1863.

Kemi (kĕ'mē), city (1970 pop. 28,984), Lappi prov., W central Finland, on the Gulf of Bothnia at the mouth of the Kemijoki River. An old trading post, it was chartered in 1869. Kemi is a port and has large sawmills and pulp mills and a power station.

Kemijoki (kĕ'mēyôkē), longest river of Finland, c.345 mi (560 km) long, rising near Sokosti peak, NE Finland. It flows generally SW to Kemijärvi lake, then W into the Gulf of Bothnia at Kemi. With its many tributaries, the Kemijoki drains most of N Finland. It is an important logging route.

Kemnitz, Martin: see CHEMNITZ, MARTIN.

Kempe, Margery (kĕmp), d. 1438 or afterward, English religious writer, b. King's Lynn. She was the wife of a prominent citizen and the mother of 14 children. Her autobiography, *The Book of Margery Kempe* (complete ed. 1940; ed. with modern spelling 1944), was known only in small excerpts until 1934, when the whole was discovered. She was a religious enthusiast whose loud weeping in church and reproof of her neighbors kept her in public disfavor. She traveled abroad as a pilgrim, and her work has rich details of the everyday life of her time. The narrative is occasionally interrupted with visions, prayers, and meditations, many of them of great beauty. The book may be the earliest autobiography in English. See MYSTICISM. See biographies by Martin

Thornton (1961) and L. Collis (1964); study by R. K. Stone (1970).

Kempener, Pieter de (pē'tər də kĕm'pənər), c.1503–1580, Flemish painter, b. Brussels. He studied and painted for 10 years in Italy and about 1537 settled in Seville, Spain, where he was known as Pedro Campaña. For churches in Seville he painted religious pictures remarkable for the strong chiaroscuro and naturalistic detail that influenced the school of Seville. The development toward mannerism can be seen in the agitated movements and elongated figures of his masterpiece *The Descent from the Cross* in the Seville Cathedral. On his return to Brussels (1563) he became chief engineer to the duque de Alba and director of the tapestry works.

Kempenfelt, Richard: see ROYAL GEORGE.

Kempenland (kĕm'pənländ), Fr. *Campine,* region, Limburg and Antwerp provs., NE Belgium, and North Brabant prov., S Netherlands. It is a coal-mining and manufacturing area. Once covered by moors and marshes, it has been partially reclaimed. Hasselt and Turnhout are the main cities.

Kemper, Reuben, d. 1827, American adventurer, b. Virginia. With his brothers Nathan and Samuel he settled c.1800 in Feliciana, just above Baton Rouge, in West Florida, then Spanish territory. Expelled from their land by the Spanish authorities, they crossed the border into Mississippi Territory, where they organized a small force and declared West Florida independent of Spain. An attempt to take Baton Rouge in 1804 failed. The three were kidnapped in 1805 but were rescued by a U.S. force as they were being taken down the Mississippi River to Baton Rouge by the Spanish. Other forays were climaxed in 1810 by Reuben's attempt to occupy Mobile. He failed and was arrested and detained by U.S. authorities while the Spanish dispersed the rest of his band. See I. J. Cox, *The West Florida Controversy* (1918, repr. 1967).

Kempis, Thomas à: see THOMAS À KEMPIS.

Kempten (kĕmp'tən), city (1970 pop. 44,910), Bavaria, S West Germany, on the Iller River, in the Allgäu. It is the center of a dairying region. Among the city's manufactures are textiles, paper, and machinery. Of Celtic origin, Kempten became a flourishing Roman colony called Cambodunum. A free imperial city from the late 13th cent., it was sacked (1632) by the Swedes in the Thirty Years War. Kempten passed to Bavaria in 1803. The city is rich in historic architecture.

Kemuel (kēmyo͞o'ĕl). **1** Father of Aram. Gen. 22.21. **2** Ephraimite prince. Num. 34.24. **3** Levite prince. 1 Chron. 27.17.

Ken, Thomas, 1637–1711, English prelate and hymn writer, prominent among the nonjuring bishops. He became chaplain to Charles II in 1680 and was nominated by that monarch to the bishopric of Bath and Wells in 1684. Under James II, Ken refused to publish the Declaration of Indulgence in accordance with the king's order; for this he was sent to the Tower with six other bishops in 1688. On the accession of William of Orange (William III) Bishop Ken would not take the oath of allegiance to him after having given it to the Stuarts, and in 1691 his see was taken from him as a nonjuror. Most noted of his hymns is the doxology, "Praise God from whom all blessings flow." See biographies by E. H. Plumptre (1888), F. A. Clarke (1896), and H. A. L. Rice (1958).

Kenai Peninsula (kē'nī), S Alaska, jutting c.150 mi (240 km) into the Gulf of Alaska, between Prince William Sound and Cook Inlet. The Kenai Mts., c.7,000 ft (2,130 m) high, occupy most of the peninsula. The coastal climate is mild, with abundant rainfall and a growing season adequate for many crops. There are forest, mineral, and fishing resources in the east and, in the western section, good farmland. The Alaska RR crosses the peninsula from Seward (1970 pop. 1,587), the largest town.

Kenan (kē'nən), son of Enos. 1 Chron. 1.2. Cainan: Gen. 5.9–14; Luke 3.37.

Kenath (kē'năth), town, ancient Palestine, E of the Jordan. It was captured and renamed by Nobah after himself. It was later the Kanata of the Decapolis. Num. 32.42; 1 Chron. 2.23.

Kenaz (kē'năz). **1** Edomite. Gen. 36.15,42; 1 Chron. 1.36. **2** Kinsman of Caleb. 1 Chron. 4.13,15; Judges 1.13. One of these was the eponym of the Kenezites. Num. 32.12; Joshua 14.6–14; 15.17.

Kendal, Ehrengard Melusina von der Schulenburg, duchess of: see SCHULENBURG, EHRENGARD.

Kendal, Dame Madge (kĕn'dəl), 1849–1935, English actress, whose maiden name was Margaret Robertson. She was the 22d child of an actor-manager and the sister of T. W. Robertson, the dramatist. After early performances in juvenile roles, she made her debut (1865) as Ophelia at the Haymarket Theatre, London, and became prominent in both comedy and tragedy. She married William Kendal in 1869 and thereafter co-starred with him in productions of Shakespeare and contemporary comedies, touring the United States in 1889. Kendal was made Dame of the British Empire in 1927. See her *Dramatic Opinions* (1890) and *Dame Madge Kendal by Herself* (1933). Her husband, **William Kendal,** 1843–1917, whose original name was William Hunter Grimston, became a favorite in romantic roles after 1861, though his talent was never equal to that of his wife. In partnership with John Hare, the Kendals managed the St. James Theatre (1879–88). They both retired in 1908. See T. E. Pemberton, *The Kendals* (1900).

Kendall, Amos, 1789–1869, American journalist and statesman, b. Dunstable, Middlesex co., Mass. He edited (1816–29) at Frankfort, Ky., the *Argus of Western America,* one of the most influential Western papers of the day. At first a supporter of Henry Clay, he shifted allegiance to Andrew JACKSON and helped to build Jackson's political strength. In 1829 he went to Washington, D.C., and was appointed by President Jackson fourth auditor of the Treasury. His real importance was as one of the ablest and most influential members of the Kitchen Cabinet—a group of intimate advisers to President Jackson. He helped draft many of Jackson's more important state papers, was chief counselor to Jackson in the controversy over rechartering the Bank of the United States, and vigorously defended administration policies in the newspapers. He was appointed (1835) U.S. Postmaster General by Jackson, and he remained at the post under President Van Buren, thoroughly reorganizing a badly managed department. He became (1845) business manager for Samuel F. B. Morse and played an important role in the development of telegraph service. Kendall opposed secession and urged vigorous prosecution of the war against the South, although he was often critical of President Lincoln's policies. See his autobiography, ed. by his son-in-law, William Stickney (1872, repr. 1949).

Kendall, Edward Calvin, 1886–1972, American biochemist, b. South Norwalk, Conn., grad. Columbia (B.S., 1908; Ph.D., 1910). At St. Luke's Hospital, New

York City, he did research on the thyroid gland (1911–14). He became (1914) head of the biochemistry section at the Mayo Clinic and was (1921–51) professor of physiological chemistry at the Mayo Foundation (affiliated with the Univ. of Minnesota). After 1952 he was professor of chemistry at Princeton. He shared with Philip S. Hench and Tadeus Reichstein the 1950 Nobel Prize in Physiology and Medicine for his work on the hormones of the adrenal gland cortex. Kendall isolated and identified a series of compounds from the adrenal gland cortex, prepared cortisone by partial synthesis (with Merck & Co., Inc.), and with P. S. Hench, H. F. Polley, and C. H. Slocumb, investigated the effects of cortisone and of adrenocorticotropic hormone (ACTH) on rheumatoid arthritis. Other contributions include the isolation of thyroxine (1914) and the crystallization of glutathione and establishment of its chemical structure.

Kendall, George Wilkins, 1809–67, American journalist, b. near Amherst, N.H. After a succession of journalistic jobs, he was a partner in founding (1837) the New Orleans *Picayune.* In 1841 he joined the disastrous Texan expedition to Santa Fe, sponsored by the president of Texas, Mirabeau Lamar, in the hope of winning the allegiance of the New Mexico area to the republic of Texas. The surviving members, including Kendall, were marched to Mexico City and imprisoned. After his release Kendall wrote *Narrative of the Texan Santa Fe Expedition* (1844). He was an exponent of war with Mexico, and, when hostilities began, he served first under Gen. Zachary Taylor and then as aide to Gen. William Worth in Gen. Winfield Scott's campaigns. He sent back to his paper, by private express, narrative accounts that became famous and were widely copied, thus earning him a reputation as the first of the modern war correspondents. He also wrote *The War between the United States and Mexico* (1851).

Kendrick, John, c.1740–1794, American sea captain, b. Massachusetts. During part of the American Revolution he commanded privateers. As commander of an expedition composed of the *Columbia* and *Washington,* he explored (1788–89) the Pacific Northwest Coast in the neighborhood of Nootka Sound, managing to avoid conflict with the Spanish who were there at the time. Robert Gray, later discoverer of the Columbia River, sailed with him. Kendrick also visited Japan, becoming the first to fly the American flag in a port of that country.

Keneh: see QINA, Egypt.

Kenilworth (kĕn'əlwûrth''), urban district (1971 pop. 20,121), Warwickshire, central England. A market town, it is famous for the ruins of Kenilworth Castle, celebrated in Sir Walter Scott's novel *Kenilworth* and founded c.1120 by Geoffrey de Clinton. In the 13th cent. the castle became the property of Simon de Montfort. In the castle's Great Hall, Edward II was forced to relinquish his crown in 1327. The castle then passed by marriage to John of Gaunt, who made many alterations in the buildings. It became royal property through John's son, Henry IV, until Queen Elizabeth I presented it to Robert Dudley, earl of Leicester. The castle was donated to the government in 1937. Also in Kenilworth are ruins of an Augustinian priory founded c.1122.

Kenilworth ivy, an IVY of the FIGWORT family.

Kenites (kēn'īts), wilderness nomadic tribe friendly to the Jews. They came with the Jews into Palestine and made the south of the country their home up to the time of David. Moses' father-in-law was a Kenite, and so was the husband of Jael. Gen. 15.19; Num. 24.21; Judges 1.16; 4.11,17; 1 Sam. 15.6; 27.10; 30.29; 1 Chron. 2.55.

Kenitra (kənē'trə), city (1970 est. pop. 130,000), NW Morocco, on the Sebou River. It is a busy port exporting agricultural products. The city was built by the French and called by them Port Lyautey. American troops landed there in Nov., 1942, during World War II.

Kenmore, village (1970 pop. 20,980), Erie co., NW N.Y., a residential suburb adjacent to Buffalo; inc. 1899. Agnes B. McKirdy lived there.

Kennan, George, 1845–1924, American authority on Siberia, b. Norwalk, Ohio. In 1864 he made the first of his journeys to the Far East as an engineer. His articles on Siberia, for many years almost the sole authoritative source of information on that region, were published as *Tent Life in Siberia* (1870) and *Siberia and the Exile System* (2 vol., 1891).

Kennan, George Frost, 1904–, U.S. diplomat and historian, b. Milwaukee, Wis., grad. Princeton, 1925. After 1927 he served in various diplomatic posts in Europe, including Hamburg, Riga, Berlin, Prague, and Moscow. In 1947 he was on the policy-planning staff of the Dept. of State; later (1949–50) he was one of the chief advisers to Secretary of State Dean Acheson. He was appointed ambassador to the USSR in 1952, but was recalled at the demand of the Soviet government because of comments he made on the isolation of diplomats in Moscow and the campaign that Soviet propagandists were conducting against the United States. Retiring from the diplomatic service in 1953, he joined the Institute for Advanced Study at Princeton, N.J., and in 1956 became professor at its school of historical studies. He served (1961–63) as U.S. ambassador to Yugoslavia. Kennan, who had helped formulate the Truman administration's policy of "containment" of the USSR, eventually became an advocate of withdrawal of U.S. forces from Western Europe and of Soviet forces from the satellite countries. His works include *Soviet-American Relations, 1917–1920* (2 vol., 1956–58), *American Diplomacy, 1900–1950* (1951), *Realities of American Foreign Policy* (1954), *Russia and the West under Lenin and Stalin* (1961), and *Democracy and the Student Left* (1968). See his memoirs (2 vol., 1967–72).

George F. Kennan.

Members of the Kennedy family: Edward (left), Joseph (center), and Robert.

John Fitzgerald Kennedy, 35th President of the United States (below).

Kennebec (kĕn'əbĕk), river, 164 mi (264 km) long, rising in Moosehead Lake, NW Maine, and flowing S to the Atlantic; the Androscoggin River is its chief tributary. French explorer Samuel de Champlain explored it in 1604 and 1605; in 1607 English colonist George Popham established a short-lived colony, Fort St. George, at its mouth. Trading posts were established shortly after 1625. In 1775, American Gen. Benedict Arnold's expedition went up the Kennebec en route to Quebec. Lumber and, in the 19th cent., ice were shipped down the river to the coast, and shipbuilding flourished along its banks. Villages such as Augusta and Waterville, established near power sites, became industrial centers.

Kennebunk (kĕnəbŭngk'), town (1970 pop. 5,646), York co., S Maine; inc. 1820. The first settlement (c.1650) grew as a trading and, later, a shipbuilding and shipping center. The Wedding Cake House at Kennebunk is known for its scroll-saw architecture.

Kennebunkport (kĕn''ĭbŭngkpôrt', kĕn''ĭbŭngk'-pôrt), town (1970 pop. 2,160), York co., S Maine, on the Atlantic coast; settled 1629, inc. 1653. The early town, called Arundel, appears in Kenneth Roberts's books; the name was changed in 1821. The town is a summer resort, especially for authors, artists, and actors.

Kennedy, Charles Rann, 1871–1950, Anglo-American dramatist, b. Derby, England. He became a U.S. citizen in 1917. His plays, concerned with moral problems, include *The Servant in the House* (1908), *Winterfeast* (1908), and *The Terrible Meek* (1912).

Kennedy, Edward Moore, 1932–, U.S. Senator (1962–), brother of John Fitzgerald and Robert Francis Kennedy, b. Boston, Mass. Ted Kennedy served (1961–62) as an assistant district attorney in Massachusetts before being elected (1962) as a Democrat to the U.S. Senate. After the assassination of his brother, Robert, in June, 1968, he became the acknowledged leader of Senate liberals and served (1969–71) as assistant majority leader. His political future was marred somewhat by his involvement in the Chappaquiddick incident (July, 1969), in which Mary Jo Kopechne, a passenger in the car he was driving, drowned when the car crashed and fell into a creek. Kennedy's reputation survived, however, and he continued to advocate such liberal reforms as a national health insurance program and tax reform. He was considered a leading Democratic presidential candidate, but in Sept., 1974, announced that he would not run for President in 1976. Kennedy is the author of *Decisions for a Decade* (1968) and *In Critical Condition* (1972). See biographies by W. H. Honan (1972) and Burton Hersh (1972).

Kennedy, John Fitzgerald, 1917–63, 35th President of the United States (1961–63), b. Brookline, Mass.; son of Joseph P. Kennedy. While an undergraduate at Harvard (1936–40) he served briefly in London as secretary to his father, who was then ambassador there. His Harvard honors thesis on the British failure to judge adequately the threat of Nazi Germany was published as *Why England Slept* (1940). Enlisting in the navy in Sept., 1941, he became commander of a PT boat in the Pacific in World War II. In action off the Solomon Islands (Aug., 1943), his boat was sheared in two and sunk, and Kennedy was credited with saving the life of at least one of his crew. After the war he was briefly a journalist. As Congressman from Massachusetts (1947–53), he consistently supported the domestic programs of the Truman administration but criticized its China policy. In 1952, despite the Eisenhower landslide, he defeated Henry Cabot Lodge for a seat in the U.S. Senate, where he served on the Labor and Public Welfare Committee and on the Foreign Relations

Committee. In 1953, Kennedy married Jacqueline Lee Bouvier. While recuperating in 1955 from a serious operation to repair a spinal injury, he wrote *Profiles in Courage* (1956), brief portraits of American political leaders who have defied public opinion to vote according to their consciences; for this work he received the Pulitzer Prize. Although Kennedy narrowly lost the Democratic vice-presidential nomination in 1956, his overwhelming reelection as Senator in 1958 helped him toward the goal of presidential candidacy. In 1960 he entered and won seven presidential primaries and won the Democratic nomination on the first ballot. He selected Lyndon Baines JOHNSON as his vice-presidential candidate. In the campaign that followed, Kennedy engaged in a series of televised debates with his Republican opponent, Richard M. NIXON. Defeating Nixon by a narrow popular margin, Kennedy became at 43 the youngest man ever elected President and the first Roman Catholic President. Soon after his eloquent inaugural address (" . . . Ask not what your country can do for you—ask what you can do for your country"), Kennedy set out his domestic program, known as the New Frontier: tax reform, federal aid to education, medical care for the aged under social security, enlargement of civil rights through executive action, aid to depressed areas, and an accelerated space program. He was almost immediately, however, caught up in foreign affairs crises. The first (April, 1961) was the abortive BAY OF PIGS INVASION of Cuba by Cuban exiles trained and aided by the Central Intelligence Agency. Although the planning had been done under the Eisenhower administration, Kennedy had approved the invasion and was widely criticized for it. In June, 1961, the President met in Vienna with Soviet Premier Khrushchev. Hopes of a thaw in the cold war were dashed by Khrushchev's threat that the USSR would conclude a peace treaty with East Germany and thus cut off Western access to West Berlin. In the period of tension that followed, the United States increased its military strength while the East Germans erected the Berlin Wall. The danger of a confrontation between the United States and the USSR subsided for a time. But in Oct., 1962, U.S. reconnaissance planes discovered the existence of Soviet missile bases in Cuba. President Kennedy immediately ordered a blockade to prevent further weapons from reaching Cuba and demanded the removal of installations already there. After a brief interval of extreme tension when the world appeared to be on the brink of nuclear warfare, the USSR complied with U.S. demands. Kennedy won much praise for his stance in the Cuban crisis, but some have criticized him for what they felt was unnecessary "brinkmanship." The following year (Aug., 1963) tension with the USSR was eased by the conclusion of a nuclear test ban treaty that prohibited the atmospheric testing of nuclear weapons. In Southeast Asia, however, the Kennedy administration perceived a growing Communist threat to the South Vietnamese government. It steadily increased the number of U.S. military "advisers" in South Vietnam (from 685 to about 16,000) and for the first time placed U.S. troops in combat situations there. As disaffection in South Vietnam grew, moreover, the United States involved itself in local political maneuvering and finally connived at the overthrow (Oct., 1963) of the corrupt South Vietnamese dictator, Ngo Dinh Diem (see VIETNAM WAR). Within the Western Hemisphere, Kennedy established (1961) the ALLIANCE FOR PROGRESS, which provided economic assistance to the Latin American countries. He also initiated the PEACE CORPS program, which sent U.S. volunteers to work in the developing countries. Many of Kennedy's proposed domestic reforms were either killed or not acted upon by Congress. In the area of civil rights the administration pressed hard to achieve INTEGRATION in the South; it assigned Federal marshals to protect the Freedom Ride demonstrations and used Federal troops in Mississippi (1962) and a federalized National Guard in Alabama (1963) to quell disturbances resulting from enforced school desegregation. In June, 1963, the President proposed extensive civil rights legislation, but this, like his tax reform program, was not enacted until after his death. On Nov. 22, 1963, President Kennedy was shot while riding in an open car in Dallas, Texas. He died half an hour later and was succeeded as President by Lyndon Johnson. The WARREN COMMISSION, appointed by Johnson to investigate the murder, concluded that it was the work of a single assassin, Lee Harvey OSWALD. Kennedy's death shocked a nation grown accustomed to his eloquence and his idealistic concern for social justice and international accord. Many felt that had he not been killed at the age of 46 he would have gone on to achieve real greatness as a President. Kennedy was buried in Arlington National Cemetery. See biographies by J. M. Burns (1960) and Victor Lasky (1963); T. H. White, *The Making of the President, 1960* (1961); T. C. Sorenson, *Kennedy* (1965); A. M. Schlesinger, Jr., *A Thousand Days* (1965); Pierre Salinger, *With Kennedy* (1966); Tom Wicker, *JFK and LBJ* (1968); Earl Latham, ed., *J. F. Kennedy and Presidential Power* (1972).

Kennedy, Joseph Patrick, 1888–1969, U.S. ambassador to Great Britain (1937–40), b. Boston, grad. Harvard, 1912, father of John F. Kennedy, Robert F. Kennedy, and Edward M. Kennedy. He engaged in banking, shipbuilding, investment banking, and motion-picture distribution before he served (1934–35) as chairman of the Securities and Exchange Commission. He was (1936–37) head of the U.S. Maritime Commission until his appointment as ambassador. In London he supported the overtures of the Chamberlain government to Hitler and was generally noninterventionist. He resigned as ambassador in November, 1940. In his later years he continued to be successful in business (notably real estate) and devoted considerable time to philanthropic activities, especially the Joseph P. Kennedy, Jr., Memorial Foundation, dedicated to a son killed in World War II. He wrote *I'm for Roosevelt* (1936). See J. F. Dinneen, *The Kennedy Family* (1960) and biographies by R. J. Whalen (1964) and D. E. Koskoff (1974).

Kennedy, Robert Francis, 1925–68, American politician, U.S. Attorney General (1961–64), b. Brookline, Mass., younger brother of President John F. Kennedy. A graduate of Harvard (1948) and the Univ. of Virginia law school (1951), he managed John F. Kennedy's successful campaign for the U.S. Senate in 1952. From 1953 to 1956 he was counsel to the Senate subcommittee chaired by Sen. Joseph R. McCarthy. He then became (1957) chief counsel to the Senate subcommittee investigating labor rackets and there gained a reputation by exposing corruption in the Teamsters union. In 1960 he was manager of his older brother's presidential campaign. His inclusion in President Kennedy's cabinet gave rise to charges of nepotism, but he proved a vigorous Attorney General, especially in prosecuting cases relating to civil rights. He was also his brother's closest adviser. After John Kennedy's assassination, Robert Kennedy continued for a time to serve in President Lyndon Johnson's cabinet, but in 1964 he resigned to run for election as Senator from New York. Despite criticism that he was a carpetbagger from Massachusetts, he won the election. In the Senate he was a vigorous advocate of social reform and became identified particularly as a spokesman for the rights of the minorities. Although Kennedy had supported his brother's intensification of American aid to the South Vietnamese government, he became increasingly critical of Johnson's escalation of the Vietnam War and by 1968 was advocating that the Viet Cong be included in a South Vietnamese coalition government. Urged to run against President Johnson for the Democratic nomination in 1968, Kennedy appeared reluctant until Sen. Eugene McCarthy's showing in the New Hampshire Democratic primary convinced him that a challenge to Johnson could be successful. He announced his candidacy on March 16, 1968. Although Johnson withdrew (March 31) from the race, the administration's standard passed to Vice President Hubert Humphrey, while Senator McCarthy retained the support of many opponents of the Vietnam War, who accused Kennedy of opportunism. Kennedy conducted an energetic campaign and won a series of primary victories, culminating in the one in California on June 4. At the end of that day he gave a victory speech to his supporters in the Ambassador Hotel in Los Angeles, and then, while leaving by a rear exit, was shot. He died a day later (June 6, 1968). The gunman, Sirhan Bishara Sirhan, was captured at the scene of the crime and later convicted of first degree murder. Like his brother John F. Kennedy, Robert Kennedy was buried in Arlington National Cemetery. He wrote *The Enemy Within* (1960), *Thirteen Days: A Memoir of the Cuban Missile Crisis* (1969), and *To Seek a Newer World* (1969). See Penn Kimball, *Bobby Kennedy and the New Politics* (1968); David Halberstam, *The Unfinished Odyssey of Robert Kennedy* (1968); Douglas Ross, ed., *Robert Kennedy: Apostle of Change* (1968); Jack Newfield, *Robert Kennedy: A Memoir* (1969); Jules Witcover, *Eighty-Five Days* (1969); Victor Navasky, *Kennedy Justice* (1971).

Kennedy, Mount, 13,095 ft (3,991 m) high, SW Yukon Territory, Canada, in the St. Elias Mts. near the Alaskan border. It was named in honor of U.S. President John F. Kennedy in 1965. Although discovered in 1935, the mountain was climbed for the first time in 1965 by a team that included Robert F. Kennedy, the President's brother.

Kennelly, Arthur Edwin (kĕn'əlē), 1861–1939, American electrical engineer, b. Bombay, India, educated at University College School, London. He was Edison's chief electrical assistant (1887–94) and was later professor at Harvard (1902–30) and at the Massachusetts Institute of Technology (1913–24). Much of his research was on electromagnetism and alternating currents. In 1902 he advanced the theory, also proposed by Oliver Heaviside, that a layer of ionized air in the upper atmosphere might deflect downward electromagnetic waves. The theory was demonstrated as fact, and the deflecting layer is variously called the Heaviside layer or the Kennelly-Heaviside layer (see IONOSPHERE).

Kenner, city (1970 pop. 29,858), Jefferson parish, SE La., a suburb of New Orleans; inc. 1952. New Orleans International Airport is within the city limits, and a racetrack is nearby.

Kennesaw Mountain National Battlefield Park: see NATIONAL PARKS AND MONUMENTS (table).

Kenneth I ((Kenneth mac Alpin), d. 858, traditional founder of the kingdom of Scotland. He succeeded his father, Alpin, as king of Dalriada (the kingdom of the Gaelic Scots in W Scotland) and c.843 obtained the Pictish throne, thus establishing the nucleus of the kingdom of Scotland. Because of continual depredations by the Danes from the Irish coast, Kenneth moved his capital eastward to Scone.

Kenneth II, d. 995, Scottish king (971–995). The son of Malcolm I (reigned 943–54), he became king of the united Picts and Scots in 971 and immediately

Third Beach, Newport, *by the 19th-cent. American landscape painter John Frederick Kensett.*

led a savage raid on the British in Northumbria. He is later listed, however, as submitting to the Anglo-Saxon king Edgar c.973 and being granted by him the land between the Tweed and Forth rivers. This is the earliest mention of the Tweed as the border between England and Scotland. Kenneth's reign also saw consolidation of his kingdom in the central area north of the Tay River. He was murdered as a result of a conflict with the mormaor (high steward) of Argyll.

Kennewick, city (1970 pop. 15,212), Benton co., SE Wash., on the Columbia River near the influx of the Snake River, in an irrigated farm and vineyard region; inc. 1904. Food processing is the chief industry. The Atomic Energy Commission's nearby Hanford Works (established during World War II) is a major employer.

Kennicott, Benjamin, 1718–83, English clergyman and biblical scholar. His long career at Oxford was one of devotion to learning. He was rector of Culham, Oxfordshire, from 1753 to 1783. With the aim of preparing an improved Hebrew text of the Old Testament, he secured the assistance of other scholars in the study of Hebrew manuscripts. Besides the many printed editions, 615 Hebrew manuscripts and 16 manuscripts of the Samaritan Pentateuch were collated to produce his edition, the *Vetus testamentum Hebraicum cum variis lectionibus* (1776–80).

Kenny, Elizabeth, 1886–1952, Australian nurse, b. New South Wales, grad. St. Ursula's College, Australia, 1902. She became "Sister" Kenny as a first lieutenant nurse (1914–18) in the Australian army. While caring for poliomyelitis victims in her homeland, she developed a method using hot, moist applications in conjunction with passive exercise. She came to the United States in 1940 to demonstrate her techniques, which were used extensively with good results. She was coauthor with John F. Pohl of *The Kenny Concept of Infantile Paralysis and Its Treatment* (1942); with Martha Ostenso she wrote the autobiographical *And They Shall Walk* (1943). See biography by H. J. Levine (1954).

Kénogami (kānŏg'əmē), city (1971 pop. 10,970), SE Que., Canada, on the Saguenay River, adjacent to its twin city, Jonquière. It has pulp and paper mills and a hydroelectric station.

Kenora (kənô'rə), town (1971 pop. 10,952), W Ont., Canada, at the north end of the Lake of the Woods. There are fish-processing plants and lumber, flour, pulp, and paper mills in the town. Kenora contains an airport and serves as a base for fishing, hunting, and canoe trips.

Kenosha (kĭnō'shə), industrial city (1970 pop. 78,805), seat of Kenosha co., SE Wis., a port of entry on Lake Michigan; inc. 1850. Clothing, automobiles, electronic equipment, and metal products are among its many manufactures. The first public school in the state was begun there in 1849. A historical and art museum and the county courthouse (containing the county historical museum) are part of the civic center. Also in the city are Carthage College, a technical institute, and a library designed by Daniel Burnham.

Kenrick, Francis Patrick, 1797–1863, American Roman Catholic churchman, b. Dublin, Ireland, educated in Rome. In 1821 he was ordained priest and went to America to teach in the college at Bardstown, Ky. In 1829 he was made bishop coadjutor of Philadelphia. His charitable work in the cholera epidemic in 1832 and his courageous dignity in the anti-Catholic riots of 1844 won him considerable admiration. He was made archbishop of Baltimore and apostolic delegate in 1851. He wrote many works on the Bible. His brother, **Peter Richard Kenrick,** 1806–96, was also an American Roman Catholic churchman and was also born in Dublin. He was educated at Maynooth. Called by his brother in 1833 to be pastor of the Philadelphia cathedral and vicar general of the diocese, he was sent in 1841 at the request of the bishop of St. Louis to be coadjutor there. In 1843 he became bishop and in 1847 archbishop. At the First Vatican Council (1870) he at first opposed the enunciation of papal infallibility as a dogma. See J. J. O'Shea, *The Two Kenricks* (1904).

Kensett, John Frederick, 1818–72, American landscape painter, of the Hudson River school, b. Cheshire, Conn. He began painting while working as an engraver and in 1840 went to England to study. He spent some time in Paris and in Düsseldorf before going (1845) to Rome, where he became a popular member of the American art colony and perfected his technique. After a few years he returned to the United States and in 1848 became a member of the National Academy of Design. His delicately colored, poetic landscapes brought him fame and wealth. The Metropolitan Museum has several of his paintings. There are others in the Corcoran Gallery and the New York Public Library.

Kensico Reservoir (kĕn'zĭkō), c.4 sq mi (10 sq km), SE N.Y., N of White Plains, formed by Kensico Dam (completed 1915) on the Bronx River. A principal unit in the New York City water supply system, the reservoir receives water from sources in the Catskill Mts. and from the Delaware River.

Kensington, England: see KENSINGTON AND CHELSEA.

Kensington and Chelsea, borough (1971 pop. 184,392) of Greater London, SE England. It was created in 1965 by the merger of the metropolitan London boroughs of Kensington and Chelsea. Kensington is a largely residential district with fashionable shopping streets. Portobello Road is a well-known street market. The area has undergone extensive urban renewal and now contains blocks of large, tall flats. A large park, Kensington Gardens, adjoins Hyde Park. The gardens originally were the grounds of Kensington Palace (Nottingham House), partially built by Christopher Wren, which was the home of William and Mary, Queen Anne, and George I and George II. HOLLAND HOUSE was the residence of the Fox family and, for a time, of William Penn. South Kensington is a center of colleges and museums; it is the site of the natural history section of the BRITISH MUSEUM, the VICTORIA AND ALBERT MUSEUM, the Science Museum, the Royal College of Art, and the Royal College of Science, among others. Albert Hall, a concert hall, is also there. Chelsea is a literary and artistic quarter. Sir Thomas More, D. G. Rossetti, James Whistler, Charles Dickens, and many others were associated with it. Thomas Carlyle's house is there. Chelsea Old Church, part of which dates from the 13th cent., includes the Chapel of Sir Thomas More (1528). The church, as well as the Royal Hospital for Soldiers built (1682–92) by Christopher Wren, was badly damaged in World War II.

Kensington Rune Stone, much-disputed stone found (1898) on a farm near Kensington, Minn., SW of Alexandria. Inscribed on the stone in RUNES is an account of a party of Norse explorers, 14 days' journey from the sea, who camped nearby in 1362 and lost 10 of their men, presumably to Indians. Archaeological and philological disputes have been waged over the authenticity of the stone, with no definite conclusions having been reached. Most scholars argue that the stone is a hoax, i.e., that it is of more recent origin than the 14th cent., though some accept it with the corroborative archaeological evidence. See VINLAND. See Erik Wahlgren, *The Kensington Rune Stone: A Mystery Solved* (1958); H. R. Holand, *Norse Discoveries and Explorations in America, 982–1362* (1940, repr. 1969); T. C. Blegen, *The Kensington Rune Stone* (1968).

Kent, Edward Augustus, duke of, 1767–1820, fourth son of George III of Great Britain and father of Queen Victoria. Most of his mature life was spent in military service at Gibraltar, in Canada, and in the West Indies. He was married (1818) to Victoria Mary Louise of Saxe-Coburg.

Kent, George Edward Alexander Edmund, duke of, 1902–42, fourth son of George V of Great Britain. He traveled extensively as "salesman of the empire." A member of the Royal Air Force after 1940, he was killed on active service in a plane crash in Scotland. Three children were born of his marriage (1934) to Princess Marina (1906–68) of Greece: Prince Edward (b. 1935), who succeeded him as duke of Kent, Princess Alexandra (b. 1936), and Prince Michael (b. 1942).

Kent, James, 1763–1847, American jurist, b. near Brewster, N.Y. He was admitted to the bar in 1785 and began practice in Poughkeepsie, N. Y. Active in the Federalist party, he served several terms in the New York legislature. In 1793, Kent moved to New York City, where his reputation for learning established him as first professor of law at Columbia College. His lectures (1794–98) were not especially well received, and he welcomed the appointment in 1798 as a judge of the state supreme court. He was made chief judge in 1804, and from 1814 until his statutory retirement in 1823 he presided over the state court of chancery. Kent's written opinions as chancellor were instrumental in reviving EQUITY, which had largely lapsed in the United States after the American Revolution. He refashioned many of the doctrines in that area by combining concepts from English chancery jurisprudence with the principles of Roman law. After his retirement he again (1824–26) was professor of law at Columbia, but found the delivery of lectures tedious and soon resigned. He vastly expanded the material of his courses to prepare his *Commentaries on American Law* (4 vol., 1826–30), a systematic treatment of international law, American constitutional law, the sources of state law, and the law of personal rights and of property. It was enthusiastically received by the legal profession and in Kent's lifetime went through six editions. See *Memoirs and Letters of James Kent* by his great-grandson, William Kent (1898, repr. 1970); study by J. T. Horton (1939, repr. 1969).

Kent, Rockwell, 1882–1971, American painter, muralist, wood engraver, lithographer, and writer, b. Tarrytown, N.Y. Kent studied with Robert Henri. He lived in Labrador, Alaska, Greenland, and Tierra del Fuego and painted vigorous, exotic landscapes during his travels. His graphic art and his painting are notable for their stark, powerful style. Among his major works are *Winter* (Metropolitan Mus.), *Down to the Sea* (Brooklyn Mus.), and *Toilers of the Sea* (Art Inst., Chicago). He is the author of *Wilderness* (1921), *Voyaging Southward from the Strait of Magellan* (1924), *Salamina* (1935), *Greenland Journal* (1962), and the autobiographical *This Is My Own* (1940).

Kent, William, 1685–1748, English landscape gardener, architect, and painter. A very minor painter, Kent made ceiling decorations for Kensington Palace. He greatly influenced landscape gardening by changing the prevailing artificial style to one based more closely on nature, as in the gardens at Rousham. As an architect, he followed Neo-Palladian tenets and adhered to strictly symmetrical planning, especially in his masterpiece, Holkham Hall, Norfolk (begun 1734). In London he planned the treasury building (1734) and the Horse Guards building (erected posthumously, 1750–58). See study by Margaret Jourdain (1948).

Kent, county (1971 pop. 1,396,030), 1,525 sq mi (3,950 sq km), SE England. It lies between the Thames estuary and the Strait of Dover. The county town is MAIDSTONE. The Isle of SHEPPEY is separated from the north coast by the narrow Swale channel. The chalky North Downs cross the county from east to west, and to the south lie the fertile Weald and ROMNEY MARSH. The Medway, the Stour, and the Darent are the chief rivers. The region, largely agricultural, is a market-gardening center. Crops include fruit, grain, and hops. Sheep and cattle grazing, fishing, and dairying are also important. One of London's "Home Counties," Kent is becoming increasingly important industrially because of the encroachment of the London urban area into its western portion. Paper, pottery, tile and brick, cement, beer, malt, and chemicals are manufactured, and there is shipbuilding and oil refining. Kent has some coal deposits. Because of its strategic location on the path to the Continent through Dover, Kent has been important throughout English history. Julius Caesar landed at Kent in 55 B.C. Roman roads crossed the county. Kent was one of the seven Anglo-Saxon kingdoms. In the Middle Ages many religious houses were established in the old kingdom of Kent, and CANTERBURY became the goal of numerous pilgrims such as Chaucer described in the *Canterbury Tales.* The region was intimately associated with the rebellions of Wat Tyler, Jack Cade, and Sir Thomas Wyatt. The coast was heavily fortified during the two World Wars. In 1974, Kent was reorganized as a nonmetropolitan county.

Kent. **1** Industrial city (1970 pop. 28,183), Portage co., NE Ohio; settled in 1805 as Franklin Mills, combined with Carthage and renamed as Kent 1863, inc. as a city 1920. Electric motors, compressors, drilling rigs, fasteners, and locks are made there. The city is the seat of Kent State Univ. **2** City (1970 pop. 16,275), King co., W central Wash., near Puget Sound; inc. 1890. Formerly a farm area, Kent is now rapidly urbanizing. It has a large aerospace industry. Food is processed, and electrical supplies and chemical products are made.

Kent, kingdom of, one of the kingdoms of Anglo-Saxon England. It was settled in the mid-5th cent. by aggressive bands of people called Jutes (see ANGLO-SAXONS). Historians are in dispute over the authenticity of the traditional belief that HENGIST AND HORSA landed in 449 to defend the Britons against the Picts and whether Hengist and his son Aesc subsequently turned against their employer, VORTIGERN. The Jutes, at any rate, soon overcame the British inhabitants and established a kingdom that comprised essentially the same area as the modern county of Kent. ÆTHELBERT of Kent established his hegemony over

England S of the Humber River, received St. Augustine of Canterbury's first mission to England in 597, and became a Christian. During the following century, Kent was periodically subjugated and divided by Wessex and Mercia and finally became a Mercian province under OFFA. A Kentish revolt after Offa's death in 796 was put down. Conquered by Egbert of Wessex in 825, Kent was forced to acknowledge the overlordship of Wessex and became part of that kingdom. Although it suffered heavily from Danish raids, it remained one of the most advanced areas in pre-Norman England because of the archbishopric of Canterbury and because of its steady intercourse with the Continent. The metalwork and jewelry of Kent were distinctive and beautiful. See J. E. A. Jolliffe, *Pre-Feudal England: the Jutes* (1933, repr. 1963); F. M. Stenton, *Anglo-Saxon England* (3d ed., 1971).

Kent, Maid of: see BARTON, ELIZABETH.

Kenton, Simon, 1755–1836, American frontiersman, b. probably Fauquier co., Va. In 1771, believing he had killed a man, he fled westward, assuming the name Simon Butler. He settled in Boonesboro, Ky., in 1775 and defended the settlement against frequent Indian attacks; in one of these encounters he saved Daniel Boone's life. During the American Revolution he accompanied (1778) George Rogers Clark on his expedition to Kaskaskia and Vincennes and helped Boone in the raid on Chillicothe. He was later captured by the Indians, who brought him to the British in Detroit, but he escaped (1779) and again joined Clark as a scout. Learning that the man he thought he had killed was alive, he resumed his original name, and eventually settled (1799) in Ohio. Kenton was elected a brigadier general of militia in 1804 and served in the War of 1812 at the battle of the Thames. See biography by Edna Kenton (1930, repr. 1971); Patricia Jahns, *The Violent Years: Simon Kenton and the Ohio-Kentucky Frontier* (1962).

Kent's Cavern or **Kent's Hole,** limestone cave, Devonshire, SW England, near Torquay. The floor is

Fort Harrod, in Pioneer Memorial State Park, Ky. (above).

Abraham Lincoln Birthplace National Historic Site, Ky.

composed of several strata, with remains indicating the prehistoric coexistence there of man and now extinct animals. The Rev. J. McEnery explored (1825–29) the cave and put forth the coexistence theory. The cave was extensively explored from 1865 to 1880.

Kent State University, mainly at Kent, Ohio; coeducational; founded 1910 as a normal school, became Kent State College in 1929, gained university status in 1935. The university's schools include the Honors Experimental College (begun in 1961 as an honors program, became in 1970 a separate college). The university maintains two-year branches at Ashtabula, East Liverpool, Geauga County, Salem, Stark County, Trumbull County, and Tuscarawas County.

Kentucky (kəntŭk'ē, kĭn-), state (1970 pop. 3,219,311), 40,395 sq mi (104,623 sq km), S central United States, admitted as the 15th state of the Union in 1792. FRANKFORT is the capital, LOUISVILLE the largest city. The northern boundary is formed by the erratic course of the Ohio River, separating Kentucky from Ohio, Indiana, and Illinois. The river runs generally SW below Covington, in the north, until it joins the Mississippi River, which forms the western border with Missouri. At the southwest tip of the state about 5 sq mi (13 sq km) of Kentucky territory, created by a double hairpin turn in the Mississippi River, protrudes N from Tennessee into Missouri and is entirely separate from Kentucky. Tennessee borders Kentucky in a straight line on the south. In the east, the boundary with West Virginia is formed by the Big Sandy River and its tributary, the Tug Fork, while the Virginia border runs through the

Field of tobacco, Kentucky's chief crop.

Cumberland Mts., part of the Appalachian Mt. chain. Many rapid creeks in the mountains feed the Kentucky, the Cumberland, and the Licking rivers, which together with the Tennessee and the Ohio are the chief rivers of the state. The Kentucky Dam on the Tennessee River near Paducah, is a major part of the Tennessee Valley Authority system. From elevations of about 2,000 ft (610 m) on the Cumberland Plateau in the southeast, where Black Mt. (4,145 ft/1,263 m) marks the state's highest point, Kentucky slopes to elevations of less than 800 ft (244 m) along the western rim. The narrow valleys and sharp ridges of the mountain region are noted for forests of giant

hardwoods and scented pine and for springtime blooms of laurel, magnolia, rhododendron, and dogwood. To the west, the plateau breaks in a series of escarpments, bordering a narrow plains region interrupted by many single conical peaks called knobs. Surrounded by the knobs region on the south, west, and east and extending as far west as Louisville is the BLUEGRASS country, the heart and trademark of the state. To the south and west lie the rolling plains and rocky hillsides of the Pennyroyal, a section that takes its name from a species of mint that grows abundantly in the area. There underground streams have washed through limestone to form miles of subterranean passages, some of the notable ones being in Mammoth Cave National Park. Northwest Kentucky is generally rough, rolling terrain, with scattered but important coal deposits. The isolated far-western region, bounded by the Mississippi, Ohio, and Tennessee rivers, is referred to as the Purchase, or Jackson Purchase (for Andrew Jackson, who was a prominent member of the commission that bought it from the Chickasaw Indians in 1818). Consisting of flood plains and rolling uplands, it is the largest migratory bird route in the United States. Little remains of Kentucky's great forests that once spread over three quarters of the state and were renowned for their size and density. Kentucky's climate is generally mild, with few extremes of heat and cold. The state is noted for the distilling of Bourbon whiskey and for the breeding of thoroughbred racehorses. In 1973 the state was also the country's largest grower of tobacco after North Carolina. Tobacco has long been the state's chief crop, and it is also the chief farm product, followed by cattle, dairy products, and hogs. Hay, corn, and soybeans are other major crops raised in the state. Kentucky's economy, traditionally based on agriculture, now derives by far the greatest share of its income from industry. Even Lexington, long known as one of the world's largest loose-leaf tobacco markets, has become industrialized. The state's chief industries manufacture electrical equipment, food products, nonelectrical machinery, chemicals, and fabricated and primary metals. Kentucky is one of the country's major producers of coal, the state's most valuable mineral. Other mineral products include stone, petroleum, and natural gas. When the Eastern seaboard of North America was being colonized in the 1600s, Kentucky was part of the inaccessible country beyond the mountains. After Robert Cavelier, sieur de La Salle, claimed all regions drained by the Mississippi and its tributaries for France, British interest in the area quickened. The first major expedition to the Tennessee region was led by Dr. Thomas Walker, who explored the eastern mountain region in 1750 for the Loyal Land Company. Walker was soon followed by hunters and scouts including Christopher Gist. Further exploration was interrupted by the French and Indian War (1754–63) between the French and British for control of North America, and PONTIAC'S REBELLION, an Indian uprising (1763–66), but, with the British victorious in both, settlers soon began to enter Kentucky. They came in defiance of a royal proclamation of 1763, which forbade settlement W of the Appalachians. Daniel Boone, the famous American frontiersman, first came to Kentucky in 1767; he returned in 1769 and spent two years in the area. A surveying party under James Harrod established the first permanent settlement at Harrodsburg in 1774, and the next year Daniel Boone, as agent for Richard Henderson and the Transylvania Company, a colonizing group of which Henderson was a member, blazed the WILDERNESS ROAD from Tennessee into the Kentucky region and founded Boonesboro. Title to this land was challenged by Virginia, whose legislature voided (1778) the Transylvania Company's claims, although individual settlers were confirmed in their grants. Meanwhile, Kentucky was made (1776) a county of Virginia, and new settlers came through the Cumberland Gap and over the Wilderness Road or down the Ohio River. These early pioneers of Kentucky and Tennessee were constantly in conflict with Indians. The white population nevertheless increased, and many Kentuckians, feeling that Virginia had failed to give them adequate protection, worked for statehood in a series of conventions held at Danville (1784–91). Others, observing the weaknesses of the U.S. government, considered forming an independent nation. Since trade down the Mississippi and out of Spanish-held New Orleans was indispensable to Kentucky's economic development, an alliance with Spain was contemplated, and U.S. Gen. James Wilkinson, who lived in Kentucky at the time, worked toward that end. However, in 1792 a constitution was finally framed and accepted, and in the same year the Commonwealth of Kentucky (its official designation) was admitted to the Union, the first state W of the Appalachians. Isaac Shelby was elected the first governor, and Frankfort was chosen capital. Indian troubles in Kentucky were virtually ended with U.S. Gen. Anthony Wayne's victory over the Indians at the battle of Fallen Timbers in 1794. In 1795, Pinckney's Treaty between the United States and Spain granted Americans the right to navigate the Mississippi, a right soon completely assured by the Louisiana Purchase of 1803. Enactment by the Federal government of the ALIEN AND SEDITION ACTS (1798) promptly provoked a sharp protest in Kentucky (see KENTUCKY AND VIRGINIA RESOLUTIONS). The state grew fast as trade and shipping centers developed and river traffic down the Ohio and Mississippi increased. The War of 1812 spurred economic prosperity in Kentucky, but financial difficulties after the war threatened many with ruin. The state responded to the situation by chartering in 1818 a number of new banks that were allowed to issue their own currency. These banks soon collapsed, and the state legislature passed measures for the relief of the banks' creditors. However, the relief measures were subsequently declared unconstitutional by a state court. The legislature then repealed legislation that had established the offending court and set up a new one. The state became divided between prorelief and antirelief factions, and the issue also figured in the division of the state politically between followers of the Tennesseean Andrew Jackson, then rising to national political prominence, and supporters of the Whig Party of Henry Clay, who was a leader in Kentucky politics for almost half a century. In the first half of the 19th cent., Kentucky was primarily a state of small farms rather than large plantations and was not adaptable to extensive use of slave labor. Slavery thus declined after 1830, and for 17 years, beginning in 1833, the importation of slaves into the state was forbidden. In 1850, however, the legislature repealed this restriction, and Kentucky, where slave trading had begun to develop quietly in the 1840s, was converted into a huge slave market for the lower south. Antislavery agitation had begun in the state in the late 18th cent. within the churches, and abolitionists such as

James G. Birney and Cassius M. Clay labored vigorously in Kentucky for emancipation before the Civil War. Soon Kentucky, like other border states, was torn by conflict over the slavery issue. In addition to the radical antislavery element and the aggressive proslavery faction, there was also in the state a conciliatory group, in which John J. Crittenden, then U.S. Senator, was most conspicuous, that strove to preserve the Union at all costs. At the outbreak of the Civil War, Kentucky attempted to remain neutral. Gov. Beriah Magoffin refused to sanction President Lincoln's call for volunteers, but his warnings to both the Union and the Confederacy not to invade were ignored. A native son, Gen. Albert S. Johnston, and his Confederate forces invaded and occupied part of S Kentucky, including Columbus and Bowling Green. The state legislature voted (Sept., 1861) to oust the Confederates and Ulysses S. Grant crossed the Ohio and took Paducah. Johnston was forced to abandon his Kentucky positions completely, and the state was secured for the Union. After battles in Mill Springs, Richmond, and Perryville in 1862, there was no major fighting in the state, although the Confederate cavalryman John Hunt Morgan occasionally led raids into the state, and guerrilla warfare was constant. For Kentucky it was truly a civil war as neighbors, friends, and even families became bitterly divided in their loyalties. Over 30,000 Kentuckians fought for the Confederacy, while about 64,000 served in the Union ranks. After the war many in the state opposed federal Reconstruction policies, and Kentucky refused to ratify the Thirteenth and Fourteenth amendments to the U.S. Constitution. As in the South, an overwhelming majority of Kentuckians supported the Democratic party in the period of readjustment after the war, in many ways as bitter as the war itself. After the Civil War industrial and commercial recovery was aided by increased railroad construction, but farmers were plagued by the liabilities of the one-crop (tobacco) system. After the turn of the century, the depressed price of tobacco gave rise to a feud between buyers and growers, resulting in the Black Patch War. Night riders terrorized buyers and growers in an effort to stage an effective boycott against monopolistic practices of buyers. For more than a year general lawlessness prevailed until the state militia forced an agreement in 1908. Coal mining, which began on a large scale in the 1870s, was well established in mountainous E Kentucky by the early 20th cent. The mines boomed during World War I, but after the war, when demand for coal lessened and production fell off, intense labor troubles developed. The attempt of the United Mine Workers of America (U.M.W.) to organize the coal industry in Harlan co. in the 1930s resulted in outbreaks of violence, drawing national attention to "bloody" Harlan, and in 1937 a U.S. Senate subcommittee began an investigation into allegations that workers' civil rights were being violated. Further violence ensued, and it was not until 1939 that the U.M.W. was finally recognized as a bargaining agent for most of the state's miners. Labor disputes and strikes have persisted in the state; some are still accompanied by violence. After World War I improvements of the state's highways were made, and a much-needed reorganization of the state government was carried out in the 1920s and 30s. Since World War II, construction of turnpikes, extensive development of state parks, and a marked rise in tourism have all contributed to the development of the state. Tourist attractions include the famous Kentucky Derby at Churchill Downs in Louisville and the celebrated horse farms surrounding Lexington in the heart of the bluegrass region. The Abraham Lincoln Birthplace National Historic Site and Cumberland Gap National Historic Park are historic landmarks. At Fort Knox is the U.S. Depository. Kentucky is renowned for its former family feuds, such as the notorious Hatfield-McCoy affair in the early 19th cent. Kentucky's state constitution was adopted in 1891. The governor of the state is elected for a term of four years. The general assembly, or legislature, is bicameral with a senate of 38 members and a house of representatives of 100 members. State senators are elected to serve for terms of four years and representatives, for two years. Kentucky is represented in the U.S. Congress by seven Representatives and two Senators and has nine electoral votes in presidential elections. Wendell H. Ford, a Democrat, was elected governor in 1971. Upon his election (1974) to the U.S. Senate, he was succeeded by Lt. Gov. Julian Carroll. The Democratic party has long been dominant in Kentucky politics, but Republicans have been making significant inroads into Democratic strength in the state. A public school system was established in the state in the mid-19th cent. Except for a disturbance in Sturgis in 1956, compliance in Kentucky with the 1954 Supreme Court decision on the INTEGRATION of public schools has been general and without extreme resistance. Institutions of higher learning include the Univ. of Kentucky and Transylvania Univ., at Lexington; the Univ. of Louisville, at Louisville; Kentucky Wesleyan College, at Owensboro; Union College, at Barbourville, and Kentucky State Univ., at Frankfort. An excellent bibliography of Kentucky is J. Winston Coleman, Jr., *A Bibliography of Kentucky History* (1949). See F. G. Davenport, *Ante-bellum Kentucky: A Social History, 1800–1860* (1943); J. W. Coleman, *Historic Kentucky* (1967); T. D. Clark, *A History of Kentucky* (4th ed. 1961) and *Kentucky, Land of Contrast* (1968); Federal Writers' Project, *Kentucky: A Guide to the Bluegrass State* (1939, repr. 1973).

Kentucky, river, 259 mi (417 km) long, formed by the junction of the North Fork and the Middle Fork rivers, central Ky., and flowing NW to the Ohio River at Carrollton. Frankfort, Ky., is the river's largest city. The river is navigable for its entire length by means of locks. The Kentucky's upper course flows through a coal-mining district and the middle course through a deep gorge before entering the fertile bluegrass region.

Kentucky, University of, mainly at Lexington; coeducational; land-grant and state supported; opened 1865 as part of Kentucky Univ. (see TRANSYLVANIA UNIV.), became a state agricultural and mechanical college in 1878, and a university in 1908. It has several extension centers throughout the state.

Kentucky and Virginia Resolutions, in U.S. history, resolutions passed in opposition to the ALIEN AND SEDITION ACTS, which were enacted by the Federalists in 1798. The Jeffersonian Republicans first replied in the Kentucky Resolutions, adopted by the Kentucky legislature in Nov., 1798. Written by Thomas Jefferson himself, they were a severe attack on the Federalists' broad interpretation of the Constitution, which would have extended the powers of the national government over the states. The resolutions declared that the Constitution merely established a compact between the states and that the Federal government had no right to exercise powers not specifically delegated to it under the terms of the compact; should the Federal government assume such powers, its acts under them would be unauthoritative and therefore void. It was the right of the states and not the Federal government to decide as to the constitutionality of such acts. A further resolution, adopted in Feb., 1799, provided a means by which the states could enforce their decisions by formal nullification of the objectionable laws. A similar set of resolutions was adopted in Virginia in Dec., 1798, but these Virginia Resolutions, written by James Madison, were a somewhat milder expression of the strict construction of the Constitution and the compact theory of the Union. The resolutions were submitted to the other states for approval with no real result; their chief importance lies in the fact that they were later considered to be the first notable statements of the STATES' RIGHTS theory of government, a theory that opened the way for the NULLIFICATION controversy and ultimately for SECESSION. See E. D. Warfield, *The Kentucky Resolutions of 1798* (1887, repr. 1969); John C. Miller, *Crisis in Freedom* (1951, repr. 1964).

Kentucky saddler: see AMERICAN SADDLE HORSE.

Kentville, town (1971 pop. 5,198), W N.S., Canada, on the Cornwallis River, NW of Halifax. It is a tourist and trade center in the Annapolis valley, a fruit-growing region.

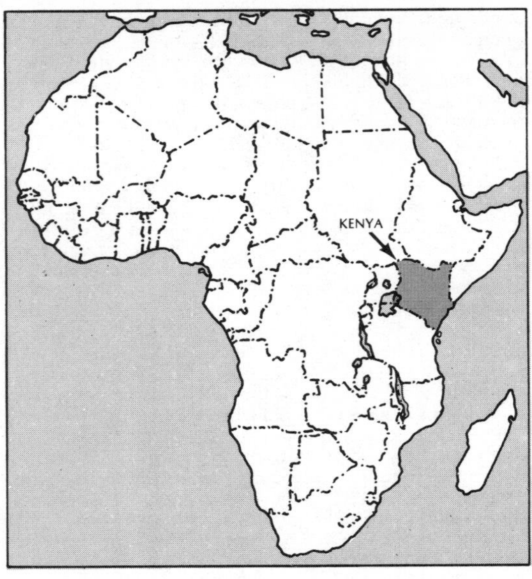

Kenya (kĕn'yə, kēn'-), republic (1969 pop. 10,942,708), 224,960 sq mi (582,646 sq km), E Africa. NAIROBI is the capital; other cities include MOMBASA (the chief port), NAKURU, KISUMU, Thika, and Eldoret. Kenya is bordered by the Somali Democratic Republic on the east, the Indian Ocean on the southeast, Tanzania on the south, Victoria Nyanza (Lake Victoria) on the southwest, Uganda on the west, the Sudan on the northwest, and Ethiopia on the north. The country, which lies astride the equator, is made up of several geographical regions. The first is a narrow, dry coastal strip that is low lying except for the Taita Hills in the south. The second, an inland region of bush-covered plains, constitutes most of the country's land area. In the northwest, straddling Lake Rudolf and the Kulal Mts., are high-lying scrublands. In the southwest are the fertile grasslands, and forests of the Kenya highlands. In the west is the Great Rift Valley, an irregular depression that cuts through W Kenya from north to south in two branches. It is also the location of some of the country's highest mountains, including Mt. Kenya (17,058 ft/5,199 m). Kenya's main rivers are the Tana and the Althi. Except for the temperate highlands, the country's climate is hot and dry. Black Africans make up about 97% of the population; they are divided into about 40 ethnic groups, of which the Bantu-speaking Kikuyu, Kamba, Gusii, and Luhya and the Nilotic-speaking Luo are predominant. Persons of Indian, Pakistani, Goanese, and European descent live in the interior, and there are some Arabs along the coast. The official language of Kenya is Swahili, which replaced English in 1974. Most of the population follows traditional religious beliefs, but about 30% are Christian and about 6% Muslim. The great majority of Kenyans are engaged in farming, largely of the subsistence type, but industry is growing. Coffee, tea, sisal, pyrethrum, maize, and wheat are grown in the highlands, mainly on small African-owned farms formed by dividing some of the large, formerly European-owned estates. Coconuts, cashew nuts, cotton, sugarcane, sisal, and maize are grown in the lower-lying areas. Much of the country remains grassland, where large numbers of cattle are pastured. Kenya's leading manufactures include refined petroleum, processed food, cement, textiles, leather goods, and metal products. The chief minerals produced are limestone, soda ash, gold, and salt. Kenya attracts many tourists, largely lured by its varied wildlife, which is protected in the expansive Tsavo National Park (8,034 sq mi/20,808 sq km) in the southeast. Kenya's chief exports are coffee, tea, pyrethrum, and sisal; the leading imports are petroleum and petroleum products, chemicals, and machinery; trade is mainly with Great Britain, West Germany, and the United States. In 1967, Kenya formed the East African Economic Community with Tanzania and Uganda.

History. During the 1950s and 60s, the anthropologist L. S. B. Leakey discovered in N Tanzania the remains of men who lived c.2 million years ago. These persons, perhaps the earliest men on earth, most likely also inhabited S Kenya. In the Kenya highlands, the existence of farming and domestic herds can be dated to c.1000 B.C. Trade between the Kenya coast and Arabia was brisk by A.D. 100. Arabs settled on the coast by the 8th cent., and they soon established several autonomous city-states (including Mombasa, Malindi, and Pate). Around the year 1000, ironworking reached the interior of Kenya, at about the same time that the first Bantu-speaking people arrived there. The Portuguese first visited the Kenya coast in 1498, and by the end of the 16th cent. they controlled much of it, including Mombasa. However, in 1729, the Portuguese were permanently expelled from Mombasa and were replaced as the leading power on the coast by two Arab dynasties: the Busaidi dynasty, based first at Masqat (in Oman) and from 1832 on Zanzibar, and the Mazrui dynasty, based at Mombasa. The Busaidi wrested Mombasa from the Mazrui in 1837. From the early 19th cent. there was long-distance caravan trading between Mombasa and Victoria Nyanza. Beginning in the mid-19th cent., European explorers (especially John Ludwig Krapf and Joseph THOMSON) mapped parts of the interior. The British and German governments agreed upon spheres of influence in E Africa in 1886,

focus. The sun is thus off-center in the ellipse and the planet's distance from the sun varies as the planet moves through one orbit. The second law specifies quantitatively how the speed of a planet increases as its distance from the sun decreases. If an imaginary line is drawn from the sun to the planet, the line will sweep out areas in space that are shaped like pie slices. The second law states that the area swept out in equal periods of time is the same at all points in the orbit. When the planet is far from the sun and moving slowly, the pie slice will be long and narrow; when the planet is near the sun and moving fast, the pie slice will be short and fat. The third law establishes a relation between the average distance of the planet from the sun (the semimajor axis of the ellipse) and the time to complete one revolution around the sun (the period): the ratio of the cube of the semimajor axis to the square of the period is the same for all the planets including the earth. Kepler's first and second laws were published in 1609 in *Commentaries on the Motions of Mars.* Mars was the planet whose motions were in greatest disagreement with existing theories. Kepler relied on the astronomical observations of Tycho Brahe, which were much more accurate than any earlier work. The third law appeared in 1619 in *Harmony of the Worlds.* Kepler's laws opened the way for the development of celestial mechanics, i.e., the application of the laws of physics to the motions of heavenly bodies. His work shows the hallmarks of great scientific theories: simplicity and universality. Earlier theories of planetary motion, such as the geocentric PTOLEMAIC SYSTEM and the heliocentric COPERNICAN SYSTEM, had allowed only perfect circles as orbits and were therefore compelled to combine many circular motions to reproduce the variations in the planets' motions. Kepler eliminated the epicycles and deferents that had made each planet a special case. His laws apply in generality to all the planets. Kepler believed that the sun did not sit passively at the center of the solar system but that through some mysterious power or "virtue" actually compelled the planets to hold to their orbits. Because the planets moved slower when they were farther from the sun, this power must diminish with increasing distance. The idea that the planets were controlled by the sun was developed by Isaac Newton in his laws of MOTION and law of GRAVITATION. Newton assumed that the sun continuously exerts a force on each planet pulling the planet toward the sun. He calculated that elliptical orbits would result if the force varied inversely as the square of the distance from the sun (i.e., when the distance doubles, the force becomes four times weaker). His law of universal gravitation predicts that the planets exert small forces on each other although subject to the dominant force of the sun. These small additional forces explain most of the small departures from Kepler's laws revealed by later, more accurate observations.

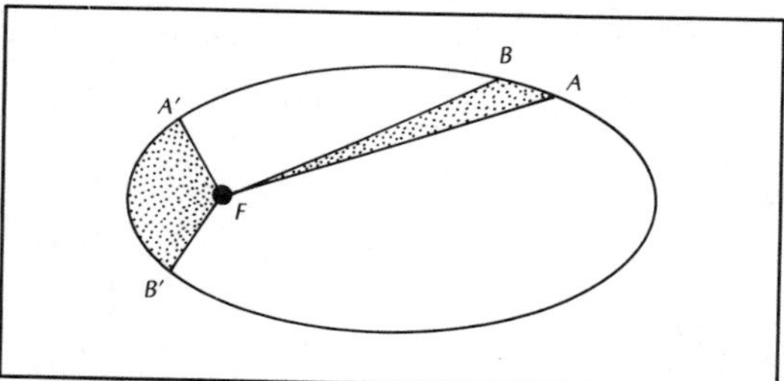

Schematic representation of Kepler's second law: The areas ABF and A′B′F are equal and are swept out in equal intervals of time by a planet orbiting around the sun (at F).

Keppel, Arnold Joost van: see ALBEMARLE, ARNOLD JOOST VAN KEPPEL, 1ST EARL OF.

Keppel Harbor: see SINGAPORE.

Keppler, Joseph, 1838–94, American cartoonist, b. Vienna. Emigrating to America in 1867, he established with Adolph Schwarzmann in St. Louis a humorous German periodical, *Puck* (1871). Upon its failure, Keppler joined the staff of *Frank Leslie's Illustrated Newspaper* in New York City and in 1876 started a second *Puck,* followed in 1877 by the English edition. Both magazines became famous for their political cartoons, which espoused the cause of the national Democratic party. Keppler's cartoons were skillfully drawn and notable for their penetrating satire. He was the first in the United States to apply color lithography to caricature.

Ker, Robert, earl of Somerset: see SOMERSET, ROBERT CARR, EARL OF.

Kerala (kä'rälä, kərä'lə), state (1971 pop. 21,280,397), 15,003 sq mi (38,858 sq km), SW India, on the Arabian Sea. TRIVANDRUM is the capital. The most densely populated Indian state, Kerala was created in 1956 from the Malayalam-speaking former princely states of Cochin and Travancore and Malayalam-speaking areas formerly in Madras state (now Tamil Nadu). About 60% of the population is Hindu; Christians and Muslims each make up about 20% of the remaining inhabitants. Although Kerala has the highest literacy rate in India, it suffers from economic underdevelopment and unemployment. In 1957, India's first Communist state administration was elected in Kerala, and a Communist coalition was again elected in 1967 and 1970. Maoist Naxalite groups are active in the state. Kerala takes its name from the ancient Tamil kingdom of Kerala (Chera), which traded with the Phoenicians, Greeks, and Romans. The state is governed by a chief minister responsible to an elected unicameral legislature and by a governor appointed by the president of India.

keratin (kĕr'ətĭn), any one of a class of fibrous PROTEIN molecules that serve as structural units for various living tissues. The keratins are the major protein components of hair, wool, nails, horn, hoofs, and the quills of feathers. These proteins generally contain large quantities of the sulfur-containing AMINO ACIDS, particulary cystine (see CYSTEINE); human hair is approximately 14% cystine in composition. The formation of a covalent chemical bond between two atoms of sulfur, called a disulfide bridge, on separate polypeptide chains of keratin allows for the cross-linkage of these molecules and results in a fairly rigid aggregation of the constituent proteins. This phenomenon is seen to be consistent with the physiological role of the keratins, which provide a tough, fibrous matrix for the tissues in which they are found. The keratins have been of particular interest to biochemists concerned with the three-dimensional geometry of proteins.

Kerbela: see KARBALA, Iraq.

Kerch (kyĕrch), city (1970 pop. 128,000), SE European USSR, in the Crimea. It lies on the Kerch Strait of the Black Sea and at the eastern end of the Kerch Peninsula, a land strip between the Sea of Azov and the

Black Sea. A seaport and major industrial center, it has iron and steel mills, machine, chemical, and coking plants, shipyards, fisheries, and canneries. Iron ore, vanadium, and natural gas are extracted nearby. The city was founded as Panticapaeum (6th cent. B.C.) by Greek colonists from Miletus and was the forerunner of all Milesian cities in the area. It was a large trade center and a terraced mountain city with self-government. It became (5th cent. B.C. to 4th cent. A.D.) the capital of the European part of the Kingdom of Bosporus (see CRIMEA). It was conquered (c.110 B.C.) by Mithridates VI of Pontus, then passed under Roman and Byzantine rule, and was taken by Novogorod in the 9th cent. and called Korchev. Later (13th cent.) it became a Genoese trade center called Cherkio and was conquered (1475) by the Crimean Tatars, who called it Cherzeti. It was captured (1771) by the Russians in the first Russo-Turkish War (1768–74), and the Treaty of Kuchuk Kainarji (1774) formally gave it to Russia. Under Russia, Kerch was a military port and then became (1820) a commercial port. There are ruins of the ancient acropolis on top of the steep hill of Mithridates. Archaeological remains, discovered in catacombs and burial mounds near the city, are in the archaeological museum (founded 1826), which is famous for its Greco-Scythian antiquities. The Church of St. John the Baptist dates from the 8th cent. The city has a marine fishery and oceanography research institute.

Kerch Strait, shallow channel, c.25 mi (40 km) long, S European USSR, connecting the Sea of Azov with the Black Sea and separating the Crimea in the west from the Taman peninsula in the east. Its northern end, opening into the Sea of Azov, is narrowed to a width of from 2 to 3 mi (3.2–4.8 km) by the narrow Chuska landspit; the southern end, opening into the Black Sea, is c.9 mi (14 km) wide. Its arm, the Taman Gulf, penetrates east into the Taman peninsula. The city of Kerch lies near the middle of the strait, on the Crimean side, in Ukraine. Kerch Strait was the Cimmerian Bosporus of the ancients; it is also known by its Tatar name, Yenikale.

Keren-Happuch (kĕr'ən-hăp'ək), Job's third daughter after his affliction. Job 42.14.

Kerensky, Aleksandr Feodorovich (kərĕn'skē, Rus. əlyĭksän'dər fyô'dərəvĭch kâ'rĭnskē), 1881–1970, Russian revolutionary. A lawyer, he was elected to the fourth Duma in 1912 as a representative of the moderate Labor party. He joined the Socialist Revolutionary party after the February Revolution of 1917 that overthrew the czarist government and became minister of justice, then war minister in the provisional government of Prince Lvov. He succeeded (July, 1917) Lvov as premier. Kerensky's insistence on remaining in World War I, his failure to deal with urgent economic problems (particularly land distribution), and his moderation enabled the Bolsheviks to overthrow his government later in 1917. Kerensky fled to Paris, where he continued as an active propagandist against the Soviet regime. In 1940 he fled to the United States; later he continued to travel and lecture. Among his writings are *The Prelude to Bolshevism* (1919) and *The Catastrophe* (1927).

Kerguelen (kûr'gəlĕn, Fr. kĕrgālĕn'), subantarctic island of volcanic origin, 1,318 sq mi (3,414 sq km), in the S Indian Ocean, c.3,300 mi (5,310 km) SE of the southern tip of Africa; largest of the 300 Kerguelen Islands (total area c.2,700 sq mi/7,000 sq km), part of the French Southern and Antarctic Territories. Kerguelen Island rises in the south to Mt. Rose (6,120 ft/1,865 m), and Cook Glacier covers its western third. Glacial lakes, peat marshes, lignite, and guano deposits are found on the island; it also has seals, rabbits, wild hogs, and wild dogs. The island, famous for the native Kerguelen cabbage, is used mainly as a research station and a seal-hunting and whaling base. Kerguelen was discovered in 1772 by the French navigator Yves Joseph de Kerguélen-Trémarec, who named it Desolation Island. It has belonged to France since 1893.

Kerintji (kərĭn'chē), peak, 12,467 ft (3,800 m) high, in the Pegunungan Barisan, W central Sumatra, Indonesia. It is Sumatra's highest point.

Kerioth (kĕr'ēŏth). **1** Unidentified town, E of the Jordan in Moab. Jer. 48.24,41. Kirioth: Amos 2.2. **2** Unidentified town, S Palestine. In AV what had been one name is given as two: "Kerioth and Hezron." Another name was Hazor. Joshua 15.25.

Kérkira (kĕr'kērä) or **Corfu** (kôr'fo͞o), Lat. *Corcyra* (kôrsī'rə), city (1971 pop. 28,630), capital of Kérkira prefecture, NW Greece, the only city on Kérkira island, a port on the channel that separates the island from the mainland. Olive oil, wine, and citrus fruits are shipped from Kérkira, and textiles are manufactured there. It is also a commercial and tourist center and has been the summer home of the Greek royal family. A Venetian fortress (c.1550) and the Church of St. Spyridon, containing the tomb of the patron saint of the island, are among Kérkira's historic buildings.

Kérkira or **Corfu** Lat. *Corcyra,* island (1971 pop. 89,578), 229 sq mi (593 sq km), NW Greece, in the Ionian Sea, the second largest of the IONIAN ISLANDS, separated by a narrow channel from the Albanian and Greek coasts. Though rising 2,980 ft (910 m) at Mt. Pantokrator in the northeast, Kérkira is largely a fertile lowland producing olive oil, figs, wine, and citrus fruit. Livestock raising (poultry, hogs, and sheep) and fishing are important sources of livelihood. Commerce and tourism are centered in Kérkira city, the capital. The island has been identified with Scheria, the island of the Phaeacians in Homer's *Odyssey.* It was settled c.730 B.C. by Corinthian colonists and shared with Corinth in the founding of Epidamnus on the mainland but became the competitor of Corinth in the Adriatic Sea. The two rivals fought the first recorded (by Thucydides) naval battle in 665 B.C. In 435 B.C., Kérkira (then Corcyra) made war on Corinth over the control of Epidamnus, and in 433 it concluded an alliance (often renewed) with Athens; this alliance helped to precipitate (431) the PELOPONNESIAN WAR. The island passed under Roman rule in 229 B.C. and in A.D. 336 became part of the Byzantine Empire. It was seized from the Byzantines by the Normans of Sicily in the 1080s and 1150s, by Venice (1206), and later by Epirus (1214–59) and the Angevins of Naples. In 1386 the Venetians obtained a hold that ended only with the fall of the Venetian republic in 1797. Under Venetian rule, the island had successfully resisted two celebrated Turkish sieges (1537, 1716). The island was under the protection of Great Britain from 1815 to 1864, when it was ceded to Greece. It was occupied (1916) by the French in World War I, and in 1917 the union of Serbia, Croatia, and Slovenia was concluded there. In 1923, after Italian officers trying to establish the Greek-Albanian border were slain in Greece, Kérkira was bombarded and temporarily occupied in retaliation by Italian forces.

Kerkrade (kĕrk'rä"də), city (1971 pop. 47,753), Limburg prov., SE Netherlands, on the West German border. It is one of Europe's oldest coal-mining centers; coal mining began there in the 12th cent.

Kermadec Islands (kərmăd'ĕk), uninhabited volcanic group (c.13 sq mi/34 sq km), South Pacific, a dependency of New Zealand. Sunday Island, the largest, is mountainous and fertile. The group was annexed to New Zealand in 1887.

Kerman (kĕrmän'), city (1971 est. pop. 88,000), capital of Kerman prov., E central Iran. It is noted for making and exporting carpets. Cotton textiles and goats-wool shawls are also manufactured. Kerman was under the Seljuk Turks in the 11th and 12th cent., but remained virtually independent, conquering Oman and Fars. Marco Polo visited (late 13th cent.) and described the city. Kerman changed hands many times in ensuing years, prospering under the Safavid dynasty (16th cent.) and suffering under the Afghans (17th cent.). In 1794 its greatest disaster occurred: Aga Muhammad Khan, shah of Persia, ravaged the city by selling 20,000 of its inhabitants into slavery and by blinding another 20,000. Kerman recovered very slowly. Historic reminders include medieval mosques, the beautiful faïence found among the extensive ruins outside the city walls, and 16th-century mosaics with Chinese motifs. Nearby is the shrine of Shah Vali Namatullah, a 15th-century Sufi holy man.

Kermanshah (kĕrmän"shä'), city (1971 est. pop. 190,000), capital of Kermanshah prov., W Iran. It is the trade center for a rich agricultural region that produces grain, fruits, and sugar beets. Manufactures include carpets, canvas shoes, textiles, and refined petroleum. The city has numerous caravansaries that are crowded semiannually with Shiite pilgrims to Karbala, Iraq. Kermanshah was founded by the Sassanids in the 4th cent. A.D. and became a secondary royal residence. It was captured by the Arabs in the 7th cent.; Harun ar-Rashid spent his summers there. It was later a frontier fortress against the Ottoman Turks, who occupied it a number of times including the period from 1915 to 1917. Nearby are the famed BEHISTUN INSCRIPTIONS and notable Sassanian rock reliefs.

kermes (kûr'mēz), brilliant red natural dye extracted from the bodies of the adult females of a scale insect parasitic upon oak trees; the females are large and similar in appearance to galls. A very ancient dye, kermes has largely been replaced by cochineal and artificial dyes.

Kern, Jerome (kûrn), 1885–1945, American composer of musicals, b. New York City. After studying in New Jersey and New York he studied composition in Germany and England. His first success was the operetta *The Red Petticoat* (1912). Among the numerous musicals that followed were *The Girl from Utah* (1914), *Leave It to Jane* (1917), *Sally* (1920), *Sunny* (1925), *The Cat and the Fiddle* (1931), and *Roberta* (1933). After 1931 he wrote scores for many films, including versions of several of his stage successes. His outstanding work is *Show Boat* (1927), for which Oscar Hammerstein II wrote an adaptation of Edna Ferber's novel. Kern's many famous songs include "Ol' Man River," from *Show Boat,* and "Smoke Gets in Your Eyes," from *Roberta.* He also wrote an orchestral work, *A Portrait of Mark Twain* (1942). See biography by David Ewen (1960).

Scene from Jerome Kern's musical Roberta, *with (from left) Bob Hope, Ray Middleton, Lyda Roberti, and Sydney Greenstreet.*

Kern, river, 155 mi (249 km) long, rising in the S Sierra Nevada Mts., E Calif., and flowing south, then southwest to a reservoir in the extreme southern part of the San Joaquin valley. The river, one of California's important power-generating streams, has Isabella Dam as its chief facility. Kern River is the southern terminus of the Friant-Kern Canal, constructed between 1945 and 1951 to bring the waters of the San Joaquin River to the region (see CENTRAL VALLEY PROJECT); irrigated agriculture (alfalfa, fruit, and cotton) and cattle grazing are practiced. U.S. explorer John Frémont named the river in honor of Edward M. Kern, the topographer of his third expedition. Gold was discovered along the river in 1853. The canyon of the upper Kern in Sequoia National Park is noted for its beauty.

Keros (kē'rŏs), family that returned from Babylon. Ezra 2.44; Neh. 7.47.

kerosine, colorless, thin mineral oil whose density is between 0.75 and 0.85 grams per cubic centimeter. A mixture of hydrocarbons, it is commonly obtained in the fractional distillation of petroleum as the portion boiling off between 150°C and 275°C (302°F–527°F). Kerosine has been recovered from other substances, notably coal (hence another name, coal oil), oil shale, and wood. At one time kerosine was the most important refinery product because of its use in lamps. Now it is most noted for its use as a carrier in insecticide sprays and as a fuel in jet engines.

Kerouac, Jack (John Kerouac) (kĕr'o͞oăk"), 1922–69, American novelist, b. Lowell, Mass., educated at Columbia. One of the leaders of the BEAT GENERATION, he was the author of *On the Road* (1957), the novel considered to be the testament of the beat movement. Kerouac's writings reflect a frenetic, restless pursuit of new sensation and experience. Among his works are the novels *The Subterraneans* (1958), *The Dharma Bums* (1958), *Big Sur* (1962), and *Desolation Angels* (1965); a volume of poetry, *Mexico City Blues* (1959); and a volume describing Kerouac's dreams, *Book of Dreams* (1961). See biography by Ann Charters (1973).

Kéroualle, Louise Renée de: see PORTSMOUTH, LOUISE RENÉE DE KÉROUALLE, DUCHESS OF.

Kerr, Archibald John Kerr Clark: see INVERCHAPEL OF LOCH ECK, ARCHIBALD JOHN KERR CLARK KERR, 1ST BARON.

Kerr, Clark, 1911–, American educational reformer, b. Reading, Pa., grad. Swarthmore (B.A., 1932), and the Univ. of California at Berkeley (Ph.D., 1939). He was a professor of industrial relations at Berkeley from 1945 until 1952 when he was named chancellor. In 1958 he was named president of the Univ. of California, a post he held until 1967, when he became director of the Carnegie Fund Study on the Future of Higher Education. His writings include *The Uses of the University* (1963).

Kerr, Philip Henry: see LOTHIAN, PHILIP HENRY KERR, 11TH MARQUESS OF.

Kerr, Walter Francis (kûr), 1913–, American drama critic and playwright, b. Evanston, Ill. He became drama critic for the New York *Herald Tribune* in 1951 and for the New York *Times* in 1966. Kerr believes that great theater must be popular theater, and his influential reviews have often aroused controversy. Among his plays are *Murder in Reverse* (1935) and the musical *Goldilocks* (1958), written with Jean Kerr. His other works include *How Not To Write A Play* (1956) and *Tragedy and Comedy* (1967). His wife is **Jean Collins Kerr,** 1923–, author and playwright, b. Scranton, Pa. Her plays, all comedies, include *Mary, Mary* (1961), *Poor Richard* (1964), and *Finishing Touches* (1973). She has also written amusing autobiographical works about her family, notably *Please Don't Eat the Daisies* (1957) and *The Snake Has All the Lines* (1960).

Kerrville (kûr'vĭl), city (1970 pop. 12,672), seat of Kerr co., S central Texas, on the Guadalupe River; settled 1846, inc. 1942. It is a vacation and health resort in the cool hill country on the edge of the Edwards Plateau. A military junior college and a number of art galleries are there. A state park is nearby.

Kerry, county (1971 pop. 112,941), 1,815 sq mi (4,701 sq km), SW Republic of Ireland. The county town is TRALEE. Kerry consists of a series of mountainous peninsulas that extend into the Atlantic. The shore line is deeply indented by Dingle Bay, Tralee Bay, and the Kenmare River. Carrantuohill (3,414 ft/1,041 m), in the mountains known as Macgillycuddy's Reeks, is the highest point in Ireland. The streams are short and precipitous, and there are many bogs. The Lakes of KILLARNEY are a popular tourist attraction. Farming (oats and potatoes), sheep and cattle raising, and dairying are the chief occupations. Peat is sold commercially. Footwear is made in Tralee and Killarney. There are many well-preserved dolmens, stone forts, round towers, castles, and abbeys. Irish Gaelic is still spoken by many of the inhabitants of Kerry.

Kerry blue terrier, breed of large, sturdy TERRIER perfected in Ireland more than 100 years ago. It stands from 17 to 19 in. (43.2–48.3 cm) high at the shoulder and weighs from 30 to 40 lb (13.6–18.2 kg). Its dense coat is soft and wavy, never harsh, and may be any shade of blue-gray or gray-blue. A truly all-purpose working terrier, the Kerry blue was used to hunt small game, destroy vermin, retrieve on land and water, and herd sheep and cattle. Today it is a popular house pet and show competitor. See DOG.

Kerulen (kĕr'o͞olĕn) or **Herelen** (hĕr'əlĕn), river, 785 mi (1,263 km) long, E Mongolian People's Republic, rising in the Kentei Mts., NE of Ulan Bator, and flowing S, then E to Hu-lun Lake, Heilungkiang prov., NE China. A road from Ulan Bator to Choybalsan, a railhead linked to the Trans-Siberian RR, follows the river.

Kesennuma (kāsān-no͞o'mä), city (1970 pop. 63,265), Miyagi prefecture, NE Honshu, Japan, on Kesennuma Bay. It is a fishing port.

Kesselring, Albert (äl'bĕrt kĕs'əlrĭng), 1885–1960, German field marshal. An artillery staff officer in World War I, he later joined the air force and rapidly rose in rank during the Hitler regime. In World War II, he commanded air operations in Poland, on the Western Front, in central Russia, and in the Mediterranean area. Late in 1943, Kesselring was made supreme commander in Italy, and in March, 1945, he replaced Rundstedt as commander in chief in the West. He was convicted of war crimes by a British tribunal in 1947, but his death sentence was commuted to life imprisonment. Freed by an act of clemency in 1952, he was elected (1953) president of the Stahlhelm, a veterans' organization in West Germany. See his memoirs (1953; tr. 1953, repr. 1970).

Kesten, Hermann (hĕr'män kĕst'ən), 1900–, German-American novelist, essayist, publisher, and dramatist. In Amsterdam, Kesten was director (1933–40) of the German-language publishing house Allert de Lange. He is well known for his attacks on Nazism, as in *Die Zwillinge von Nürnberg* (1946; tr. *The Twins of Nuremberg,* 1947). Kesten often uses a historical format for his works of social criticism, which include *Josef sucht die Freiheit* (1927; tr. *Joseph Breaks Free,* 1930); *Der Scharlatan* [the charlatan] (1932); and *Die Kinder von Gernica* (1939; tr. *The Children of Guernica,* 1939). His essay collection, *Ein Optimist* (tr. *The Optimist*) appeared in 1970.

Kesteven, Parts of: see LINCOLNSHIRE.

Ket (kĕ'tyə), river, c.845 mi (1,360 km) long, W central Siberian USSR. It rises in central Siberia, just N of Krasnoyarsk, and flows NW and W into the Ob. The Ket is navigable c.410 mi (660 km). It is connected with the Kas (a tributary of the Yenisei) by the Ob-Yenisei canal system.

ketch, fore-and-aft-rigged sailing vessel with a mainmast forward carrying a mainsail and jibs. It has a mizzenmast aft, stepped forward of the rudder post. In the United States, ketch-rigged vessels are widely used today as yachts. The term was formerly applied to a two-masted square-rigged vessel with the mainmast stepped amidship. Widely employed in offshore fishing by the Americans until about 1700, the ketch was also used until the mid-19th cent. as a warship in European navies.

Ketchikan (kĕ'chĭkăn''), city (1970 pop. 6,994), SE Alaska, a port of entry on Revillagigedo Island in the Alexander Archipelago. A supply point for miners in the gold rush of the 1890s, it has become a center of Alaska's fishing (especially salmon but also halibut) and pulp industries and a tourist hub. Its excellent ice-free harbor on Tongass Narrows makes it an important port on the Inside Passage and a distribution point for a large area.

Ketchwayo: see CETEWAYO.

ketone (kē'tōn), any of a class of organic compounds that contain the CARBONYL GROUP, C=O, and in which the carbonyl group is bonded only to carbon atoms. The general formula for a ketone is RCOR', where R and R' are alkyl or aryl groups. The simplest ketone, where R and R' are methyl groups, is ACETONE; this is one of the most important ketones used in industry. Low-molecular-weight ketones are used chiefly as solvents. Ketones may be prepared by several methods, including the oxidation of secondary alcohols and the destructive distillation of

$\mathrm{R{-}C({=}O){-}R'}$

general formula

$\mathrm{CH_3{-}C({=}O){-}CH_3}$

acetone (dimethyl ketone)

Ketones.

certain salts of organic acids. Ketones are related to the ALDEHYDES but are less active chemically.

Kett or **Ket, Robert,** d. 1549, English rebel. He led an agrarian revolt in 1549 as a protest against the enclosure of common land for sheep grazing. With 16,000 men he blockaded Norwich, but was defeated and executed.

Kettering, municipal borough (1971 pop. 42,628), Northamptonshire, central England. It is a center for the manufacture of shoes, other leather products, and textiles. There are also iron mining and smelting, engineering, and cardboard and brush-making industries.

Kettering, city (1970 pop. 71,864), Montgomery co., SW Ohio, a suburb of Dayton; settled c.1812, inc. 1952. Among Kettering's many manufactures are shock absorbers, electric motors, and tool and die products. The city is the seat of the Kettering College of Medical Arts and a defense electronics center, a supply facility for the U.S. armed forces.

kettle, oval depression found in glacial MORAINES, which are landforms made up of rock debris. When a glacier melts and draws away from an area, a block of ice may break off and be covered by earth and rock. As the block melts, the ground above it subsides, forming a kettle. Kettles may be deeper than 100 ft (30 m) in depth and more than 1 mi (1.6 km) in diameter. Pitted outwash plains contain many kettles.

kettledrum, in music, percussion instrument consisting of a hemispherical metal vessel over which a membrane is stretched, played with soft-headed wooden drumsticks. Of ancient origin, it appeared early in Europe, copied from the Saracens. These early kettledrums were small and appeared in pairs, often hung about the player's waist. The kettledrum was introduced into the opera orchestra by Lully in the 17th cent. and was commonly used to express joy or triumph in the music of the baroque period. Unique among Western percussion instruments, it can be tuned to definite pitches by adjusting the tension of the head. Usually there are two or more in the modern orchestra, the tuning of which varies. Berlioz used eight pairs in his *Requiem.* Several improved methods of tuning were developed in the 19th cent.; common today is a single pedal capable of giving the instrument a full chromatic range of over an octave. Kettledrums are also called timpani. See DRUM.

Kettle Rapids Dam: see NELSON, river, Canada.

Keturah (kētyo͞o'rə), mother of six sons of Abraham. Gen. 25.1; 1 Chron. 1.32.

Keuka Lake (kyo͞o'kə), 18 mi (29 km) long and .5 to 2 mi (.8–3 km) wide, W central N.Y., one of the FINGER LAKES; drains NE into Seneca Lake. Penn Yan at its northern end and Hammondsport at its southern end are trade centers for the surrounding resort, grape-growing, and wine-making region.

Kewanee (kĭwä'nē), industrial city (1970 pop. 15,762), Henry co., NW Ill., in a farm and livestock area; inc. 1855. Its manufactures include gloves, trailers and trucks, boilers, steel doors and windows, farm machinery, foundry equipment, valves, and pipe fittings. The city holds an annual "Hog Capital Festival." A junior college is there.

Keweenaw (kē'wĭnô), peninsula, 60 mi (97 km) long, projecting NE from the W Upper Peninsula, NW Mich., into Lake Superior. Portage Lake and a connecting ship canal cut across the middle of the peninsula, converting its upper portion into an island and creating an important waterway. The canal is crossed by a bridge with one of the heaviest lift spans in the world. The peninsula has the richest and longest-mined copper deposits in the United States. Tourism and lumbering are also important.

Kew Gardens (kyo͞o), Surrey, S England, on the Thames just W of London; Royal Botanic Gardens is the official name. The gardens were founded by the dowager princess of Wales in 1761 and consisted of about 9 acres (3.6 hectares). In 1841 they were presented to the nation as a royal gift. They now cover 288 acres (117 hectares) and contain thousands of species of plants, four museums, and laboratories and hothouses. The Chinese Pagoda, c.165 ft (50 m) high, was designed by William Chambers in 1761; it is still a famous landmark. Near the main entrance is Kew Palace, a red-brick mansion, once the home of George III and Queen Charlotte.

Key, David McKendree, 1824–1900, American politician and jurist, b. Greene co., Tenn. He practiced law in Chattanooga, Tenn., from 1853 to 1870, except during the Civil War, when he was an officer in the Confederate army. He served in the U.S. Senate (1875–77) to complete Andrew Johnson's term. In 1877, President Hayes chose Key to be his Postmaster General, an action that provoked sharp criticism from Republicans, who felt that the presence of an ex-Confederate in the cabinet violated party principles. From 1880 to 1894, Key served as U.S. judge for the eastern and middle districts of Tennessee.

Key, Ellen (kā), 1849–1926, Swedish author and feminist. Believing that women are primarily fitted for motherhood, she advocated political and educational equality to prepare them for this role but deplored feminist claims to equality in competitive occupations. Her ideas influenced social legislation in many countries. Among her best-known works published in English are *Love and Marriage* (1911, repr. with critical and biographical notes by Havelock Ellis, 1931), *The Century of the Child* (1909), *The Woman Movement* (1912), *The Younger Generation* (1914), and *War, Peace, and the Future* (1916). See biographies by John Landquist (1909) and L. S. Nyström (1913).

Key, Francis Scott (kē), 1779–1843, American poet, author of the STAR-SPANGLED BANNER, b. present Carroll co., Md. A lawyer, he was U.S. attorney for the District of Columbia (1833–41). His works include *The Power of Literature and Its Connection with Religion* (1834) and the posthumous collection *Poems* (1857), which contains several hymns.

key, in mechanics: see LOCK AND KEY.

key. **1** In music, term used to indicate the SCALE from which the tonal material of a given composition is derived. To say, for example, that a composition is in the key of C major means that it uses as its basic tonal material the tones of the C major scale and that its harmony employs the chords built on the tones of that scale. C is then the keynote, and the C major triad, or the notes CEG, the tonic chord of the composition. In addition to the seven tones of the C major scale, however, the remaining five tones of the chromatic scale may appear as auxiliary tones, and chords may be borrowed from other keys. MODULATION to another key may take place, but if there is a return to the original key the whole composition is said to be in the key of C. At the beginning of a composition, its key is usually indicated by a key signature (see MUSICAL NOTATION). A term usually used synonymously with key is TONALITY. Absence of a feeling of key is called ATONALITY. The concept of keynotes was developed during the 16th cent. and has been to some extent abandoned, temporarily at least, in the 20th cent. Polytonality, the employment of two or more keys simultaneously, has been used by some 20th-century composers. **2** Also in music, in reference to musical instruments the term *key* refers to a lever depressed by the player's finger or, in the case of the pedal keyboard of the organ, his foot. In woodwind instruments the keys control covers on the holes that shorten the vibrating column of air. In brass winds they control the valves that lower the pitch of the instrument by lengthening the tube.

Keyes, Roger John Brownlow Keyes, 1st **Baron** (kēz), 1872–1945, British admiral. In World War I he achieved his greatest fame as commander of the Dover patrol when he raided Zeebrugge and Ostend in Belgium (April 23, 1918) to cripple the last German submarine campaign in the English Channel. He became admiral of the fleet in 1930 and retired in 1935, but he was recalled to active duty in World War II. As director of combined operations (1940–41) he influenced the early developments in amphibious warfare. From 1934 to 1943 he served as a Conservative member of Parliament, and in 1943 he was raised to the peerage as Baron Keyes of Zeebrugge and Dover.

Key Islands: see KAI ISLANDS, Indonesia.

Key Largo, narrow island, c.30 mi (48 km) long, off S Fla., largest of the FLORIDA KEYS.

Keynes, John Maynard, Baron Keynes of Tilton (kānz), 1883–1946, English economist and monetary expert, studied at Cambridge. He served (1906–8) in the India Office of the civil service, where he was concerned with problems of Indian currency. In 1919 he became principal British treasury representative at the peace conference ending World War I, but he resigned in protest against what he considered the inequitable and unworkable economic provisions of the Versailles Treaty. His *Economic Consequences of the Peace* (1919) vividly presented his views and won him world fame. Keynes criticized the Versailles Treaty from the viewpoint of a classical economist, unfavorably contrasting the economic nationalism inherent in the treaty with the relatively free pre-1914 economy based on gold and low tariffs. He foresaw that German economic weakness stemming from the Versailles provisions would involve the whole of Europe in ruin. Keynes's departure from classical concepts of free economy dates from 1929, when he endorsed David Lloyd George's campaign pledge to promote employment by a program of government spending on public works. Keynes came to believe that such a program would increase national purchasing power as well as promote employment in complementary industries. Instead of simply relying on the free economy to solve most economic problems, Keynes advocated active government intervention in the market. For the sake of full employment Keynes also abridged his classical belief in international free trade. In the world depression of the 1930s, Keynes's theories influenced governments in several nations to adopt spending programs, such as those embodied in the New Deal, aimed at maintaining a high level of national income. Today Keynesian economics stands as the most influential economic formulation of the 20th cent.; Keynes's ideas appeal to both practical politicians and theoretical economists with equal force, perhaps because he attacked the real problems of national employment and income while still remaining faithful to the requirements of rigorous economic thought. His ideas, based on large-scale government economic planning, are best expressed in his chief work, *The General Theory of Employment, Interest, and Money* (1936). In the years following 1936, Keynes contributed little to economic theory, spending most of his time in public service. During World War II he was a consultant to the chancellor of the exchequer and a director of the Bank of England. He was raised to the peerage in 1942. At Bretton Woods (1944) he influenced proposals for the establishment of a world bank to stimulate the development of underdeveloped areas. Although he favored a planned economy and wide control of the economic life by democratic public-service corporations, he never wavered in his faith in the capitalist system. In Keynesian theory, government action is designed to influence the market, not to eliminate it. Other works by Keynes include the *Tract on Monetary Reform* (1923) and the *Treatise on Money* (1930). An edition of his complete works was begun in 1971. See biography by R. F. Harrod (1951, repr. 1969); S. E. Harris, *John Maynard Keynes* (1955) and *The New Economics* (1960); L. R. Klein, *The Keynesian Revolution* (2d ed. 1966).

Keyser, Thomas de, c.1596–1667, Dutch portrait and figure painter of Amsterdam. He was the outstanding practitioner in his field prior to Rembrandt. De Keyser's work is distinguished for its clear, warm color, masterly characterization, and strong light and shade. Among his best-known paintings are *Burgomasters of Amsterdam* (The Hague) and the portrait of Constantijn Huygens and *Merchant and His Clerk* (both: National Gall., London).

Keyserling, Eduard, Graf von (ā'do͞oärt gräf fən kī'sərlĭng), 1855–1918, German novelist. A member of an old and aristocratic family in the Baltic province of Courland, he depicts with delicate precision the life of his social class. Several of his novels have been translated—*Beate und Mareile* (1903, tr. *The Curse of the Tarniffs,* 1928), *Dumala* (1908, tr. *Man of God,* 1930), and *Wellen* (1911, tr. *Tides,* 1929).

Key West, city (1970 pop. 29,312), seat of Monroe co., S Fla., on an island at the southwestern extremity of the FLORIDA KEYS; inc. 1828. About 150 mi (240 km) from Miami (but only 90 mi/145 km from Cuba), it is the southernmost city of the continental United States. It is a port of entry; a winter and fishing resort, with a tropical climate; a shrimping and fishing center; and artists' colony; and a key military point. Its military installations include a major U.S. naval air station, a naval base, and a U.S. Coast

Key West, the southernmost city of the continental United States.

Guard base (at Fort Taylor, built 1844–46). Early Spanish sailors called the site Cayo Hueso (Bone Island), because of the human bones they found there. Key West became a center for ship salvaging, cigar manufacturing, sponge gathering, and fishing. A railroad (completed 1912) serving those industries linked the Keys with the mainland. It was abandoned after being damaged by a hurricane in 1935 and was replaced by a 123-mi (198-km) highway (completed in 1938). After a severe decline in industry, the Federal government took over (1934) the bankrupt city. Places of interest include a sponge pier, an aquarium, a lighthouse (1846; replacing one built in 1825), and two Civil War forts. There is a junior college in the city. John James Audubon and Winslow Homer painted in Key West, and the city, with its heterogeneous population, of Cuban, Spanish, Negro, and English descent, has been used as a setting in the works of Hemingway, who lived there at one time. Hemingway's home (built 1851) is now a museum. See Federal Writers' Project, *A Guide to Key West* (2d ed. 1950); W. C. Maloney, *A Sketch of the History of Key West, Florida* (1968).

Kezia (kēzī'ə), second daughter of Job after his affliction. Job 42.14.

Keziz (kē'zĭz), valley, in the vicinity of Jericho. Joshua 18.21.

KGB: see SECRET POLICE.

Khabarovsk (khəbä'rəfsk, khəbərôfsk'), city (1970 pop. 436,000), capital of Khabarovsk Kray, Far Eastern USSR, on the Amur River near its junction with the Ussuri. An industrial center and a major transportation point on the Trans-Siberian RR, the city has oil refineries, shipyards, and factories that produce farm machinery, trucks, aircraft, diesel engines, and machine tools. Khabarovsk, formerly a fortified trading post, prospered greatly after the coming of the railroad in 1905. The city was the capital of the Soviet Far East from 1926 to 1938.

Khabarovsk Kray or **Khabarovsk Territory**, administrative division (1970 pop. 1,346,000), 305,000 sq mi (789,950 sq km), Far Eastern USSR. Situated in the eastern and northeastern extremity of Siberia, the territory is bounded by the Sea of Okhotsk in the east, Primorsky Kray and Manchuria in the south, and the Kolyma range in the north. It includes the JEWISH AUTONOMOUS OBLAST. The mountainous territory is crossed by the Dzhugdzhur and Bureya ranges, where gold, oil, tin, and coal are extracted. Major cities are the capital, Khabarovsk, the industrial center Komsomolsk-on-Amur, and the ports Sovetskaya Gavan and Nikolayevsk-on-Amur; 75 percent of the total population (Russians, Ukrainians, Byelorussians, Jews, Tatars, and Yakuts) is concentrated in the cities. The territory was founded in 1938 and reorganized in 1953 and 1957. For history, see SOVIET FAR EAST.

Khabur (khäbo͞or'), river, c.200 mi (320 km) long, rising in SE Turkey, and flowing generally south through NE Syria to enter the Euphrates River, near Dayr az Zawr. The Khabur River project, begun in the 1960s, seeks, by the construction of a series of dams and a drainage scheme, to remove salt from the soil and to bring c.250,000 acres (101,200 hectares) of land under cultivation. In ancient times the Khabur was known as the Habor; along its banks in Gozan the Israelite captives from Samaria were settled in the 8th cent. B.C. (2 Kings 17.6; 18.11).

Khachaturian, Aram Ilich (ərăm' ĭlyĕch' khä"chəto͞oryän'), 1903–, Russian composer of Armenian parentage. Khachaturian graduated from the Moscow Conservatory in 1934. He first studied the cello and c.1926 began to compose. His music, colorful and energetic, uses Armenian and Oriental folk idioms. His piano concerto (1935), violin concerto (1940), the ballet *Gayané* (1942), containing the popular *Sabre Dance,* and the orchestral suite *Masquerade* (1944) are especially popular. Despite official Soviet criticism of his "modernistic" style, he continues to create works of harmonic complexity. His name also appears in English as Khatchatourian.

Khafre (khä'frä) or **Chephren** (kĕf'rĕn), fl. 2565 B.C., king of ancient Egypt, of the IV dynasty, and builder of the second pyramid at Gizeh. His face is perhaps that represented on the Sphinx. An obscure king, Dedefre, may have come between Khufu and Khafre in the dynasty.

Khair ad-Din: see BARBAROSSA.

Khairpur (khīr'po͝or), city (1961 pop. 34,144), SE Pakistan, in Sind prov. It trades in wheat, cotton, tobacco, and dates. Manufactures include textiles, armaments, and pharmaceuticals. The city was the capital of the former princely state of Khairpur, which was founded in 1783 and merged into Pakistan in 1955. It is a cultural center with fine historic buildings, notably the Faiz Palace, and with several educational facilities.

Khakass Autonomous Oblast (khəkäs'), administrative division (1970 pop. 446,000) 23,900 sq mi (61,900 sq km), S central Siberian USSR, in Krasnoyarsk Kray. ABAKAN (the capital) and Chernogorsk (a coal-mining center) are the major cities. The oblast, largely consisting of black-earth steppe, is bounded by the upper Yenisei River on the east and by the wooded Kuznetsk Ala-Tau and Sayan ranges on the west and south, respectively. The Abakan (a tributary of the Yenisei) and Chulym rivers drain the area. Railroads are the chief mode of transportation. The oblast's swift-flowing rivers provide hydroelectric power. Gold, coal, iron ore, barite, copper, lead, and molybdenum are mined, and gypsum, limestone, marble, and other building stones are quarried. The forests of the taiga zone yield lumber and wood products. Although the oblast's population is primarily Russian (with some Ukrainians), there is a large Khakass minority. The Khakass are an ancient Turkic-Mongol nationality that inhabited the S Yenisei valley for many centuries. They speak a Turkic language and are Orthodox Christians. The region, known for mining and trade from the 8th to the 11th cent., came under Russian control in the 17th cent. Numerous Russian settlers were attracted by copper mining in the 18th cent. The Khakass sided with counterrevolutionary forces during the Russian civil war. The autonomous oblast was formed in 1930.

khaki (kăk'ē, kä'kē) [Hindi,=dust-colored], closely twilled cloth of linen or cotton, dyed a dust color. It was first used (1848) for uniforms for the English regiment of Sir Harry Burnett Lumsden in India and later became the official color for British army uniforms, as well as for those of other countries. It became popular for hunting and outdoor wear, as in the uniforms of groups such as the Boy Scouts and for heavy working clothes.

Khalid (khä'lēd) (Khalid ibn al-Walid), d. 642, Arab warrior. He assisted the Meccans in attacking (625) Muhammad and the inhabitants of Medina after the battle of Badr. Khalid and the Meccans were victorious in the battle of Ohud but did not follow up their victory. In 629, Khalid accepted Islam. He became the chief Muslim general in the conquest of Syria, Egypt, Iraq, and Persia. Muhammad gave him the title "The Sword of God."

Khalid ibn Abd al-Aziz al Saud, 1913–, king of Saudi Arabia (1975–). Son of Ibn Saud, Khalid was named crown prince and deputy premier by his brother, King Faisal, in 1965. He succeeded to the throne in March, 1975, after Faisal's assassination. A quiet man with a heart condition who had long shunned public life, Khalid proved to be a surprisingly strong monarch. He decentralized the Saudi government and accelerated Faisal's program of economic and social modernization. In 1976 he called the Arab summit conference that briefly ended the civil war in Lebanon.

Khalkidhikí (khälkēthēkē') or **Chalcidice** (kălsĭd'-ĭsē), peninsula (1971 pop. 75,582), NE Greece, projecting into the Aegean Sea from SE Macedonia. Its southern extremity terminates in three peninsulas: Kassandra (anc. Gr. *Pallene*) in the west, Sithonia in the center, and ATHOS in the east. The region is largely mountainous, dry, and agricultural. Olive oil, wine, wheat, and tobacco are produced; magnesite is mined. In antiquity the peninsula was famous for its timber. OLYNTHUS and POTIDAEA were the chief towns in antiquity; Poliyiros is today the leading town and an administrative center. The peninsula was named for KHALKÍS, which established colonies there in the 8th and 7th cent. B.C. In the 4th cent. B.C. the peninsula was conquered by Philip II of Macedon, and in the 2d cent. B.C. by Rome. The subsequent history of Khalkidhikí is essentially that of THESSALONÍKI.

Khalkís (khälkēs') or **Chalcis** (kăl'sĭs), city (1971 pop. 36,300), capital of Évvoia (Euboea) prefecture, E Greece, on the island of ÉVVOIA. Connected to the mainland by a bridge, the city is a trade center for local products, including wine, cotton, and citrus fruits. Soap and cement are manufactured. The chief city of ancient Euboea, Khalkís was settled by the Ionians and early became a commercial and colonizing center. It established (8th–7th cent. B.C.) colonies on KHALKIDHIKÍ and in Sicily. The city was subdued by Athens (c.506 B.C.) and led the revolt of Euboea against Athens in 446 B.C. Again defeated, it came under Athenian rule until 411 B.C. In 338 B.C. it passed to Macedonia. Aristotle died there (322 B.C.). In succeeding centuries the city was used as a base for invading Greece. In the Middle Ages it was named Negropont by the Venetians, who occupied it in 1209. It passed to the Ottoman Turks in 1470 and in 1830 became part of Greece. A diamond-shaped Venetian citadel is there.

Khama (kä'mə), d. 1923?, chief of the Bamangwato people of Bechuanaland (now Botswana) from 1875 until his death; grandfather of Sir Seretse Khama. To counter threats from neighboring Africans and from the Boers of S Africa, he and other chiefs arranged (1885) for Great Britain to make Bechuanaland a protectorate. Despite the opposition of many British imperialists wishing to undermine the chief's authority, this status was confirmed when Khama made a journey to England in 1895. Khama's firm leadership eliminated much of the internal dissension that had divided his people.

Khama, Sir Seretse (sĕrĕt'sā kä'mä), 1921–, president of Botswana (1966–); grandson of Chief Khama. After studying in England he returned to Bechuanaland (now Botswana) but was banished (1950) in a dispute with the British government over his succession to the chieftaincy of the Bamangwato tribe. He renounced (1956) his claim, returned, and launched the Bechuanaland Democratic party. He served (1965–66) as prime minister; when Bechuanaland became independent as Botswana, he assumed the presidency. He was knighted in 1966.

Khanabad (khän'äbäd), city (1967 est. pop. 30,000), NE Afghanistan, near the USSR border. It is a market town for wool and silk.

Khanaqin (khän'äkēn), town (1965 pop. 23,527), E Iraq, on a tributary of the Diyala. It is located in an oil-producing region and has an oil refinery.

Khandwa (kŭnd'və), town (1971 pop. 85,513), Madhya Pradesh state, central India. Khandwa is a district administrative center and a market for cotton, timber, and grain. There are cotton gins and oilseed mills. The town is believed by some authorities to be the city of Kognabanda mentioned by the ancient Hellenistic geographer Ptolemy. During the 12th cent. it was a center of JAINISM. Two colleges in the town are affiliated with Sagar Univ.

Khangai (khän'gī'), massive mountain range, W central Mongolian People's Republic, extending from east to west for c.500 mi (800 km); rises to c.13,000 ft (3,960 m). Many rivers, notably the Orkhon and the Selenga, rise on the range's wooded slopes.

Khaniá (khänyä') or **Canea** (kənē'ə), ancient Gr. *Cydonia* (sīdō'nēə), city (1971 pop. 40,564), capital of Khaniá prefecture, NW Crete, Greece, a port on the Gulf of Khaniá, an arm of the Sea of Crete. Olives, citrus fruits, and wine are shipped. One of the oldest Cretan cities, it was conquered in 69 B.C. by the Romans and in A.D. 826 fell under Arab rule. Reconquered (961) by the Byzantine Empire, it became (13th cent.) a Venetian colony. The Ottoman Empire took the city in 1645. It was the capital of Crete from 1841 to the mid-20th cent. The city has a synagogue, a mosque, and several churches. Among its historic sites are medieval fortifications and an old Venetian arsenal.

Khanty-Mansi National Okrug (khŭntē'-mŭnsē'), administrative division (1970 pop. 272,000), 201,969 sq mi (523,100 sq km), W Siberian USSR. Khanty-Mansisk is the capital. The region, mostly forest and swamp with numerous lakes and peat bogs, is drained by the lower Irtysh and the Ob rivers, which are also important transportation arteries. The territory is very sparsely populated; the largest concentrations of people are in the Ob and Irtysh valleys. Lumbering, fishing, fur farming and trading, and reindeer breeding are the okrug's chief occupations. Farming and fish processing are carried on. Oil and natural gas production is increasingly important, notably at Berezovo, where large natural gas fields have been developed. Lumbering is hampered by the okrug's great distance from markets. Russians comprise the majority of the okrug's population, but there are large minorities of Khanty (Ostyaks) and Mansi (Yugra or Voguls), both of whom belong to the Finno-Ugric linguistic family. Some Komi and Nentsy people also inhabit the region. The Khanty, who were under the control of the Siberian Tatars, opposed Russian conquest and rule from the 16th through the 18th cent. The Mansi have been in the area since the 11th cent.; they, too, resisted Muscovite domination. The okrug, formed in 1930, was known until 1940 as the Ostyak-Vogul National Okrug.

Kharagpur (käräg'pər), city (1971 pop. 161,911), West Bengal state, E central India. It is an industrial city and has a scientific-research center.

Kharbin: see HARBIN, China.

Kharga: see KHARIJAH, AL, Egypt.

Kharijah, Al (äl khär'ēnjä) or **Kharga** (khär'gə), large oasis, S central Egypt, in the Libyan (Western) Desert. Populated chiefly by Bedouins and Berbers, the irrigated oasis produces cereals, vegetables, dates, citrus fruits, and alfalfa. Cattle and poultry are also raised. Al Kharijah, the chief settlement, is a rail terminus. The oasis was prosperous in ancient times, and there are ruins of temples built by the Achaemenids of ancient Persia and by the Romans.

Khark (khärk), island, c.4 mi (6 km) long and c.2 mi (3 km) wide, SW Iran, in the Persian Gulf. Site of one of the world's largest deep-water oil ports, it is linked to the mainland by a 25-mi (40-km) pipeline. The name is also spelled Kharg.

Kharkov (khär'kəf), city (1970 pop. 1,223,000), capital of Kharkov oblast, S European USSR, in the Ukraine, at the confluence of the Kharkov, Lopan, and Udy rivers in the upper Donets valley. The USSR's sixth largest city, Kharkov is also one of the country's main rail junctions and economic and cultural centers. Proximity to the iron mines of KRIVOY ROG and the coal of the DONETS BASIN has provided the basis for engineering industries that produce a wide variety of other heavy metal items. Kharkov's industries also include food and tobacco processing, printing, and the manufacture of chemicals. Founded in 1656 as a military strongpoint to defend Moscow's southern border, it became an important frontier headquarters of the Ukrainian Cossacks. They kept the city loyal to the czar during the Cossack uprisings of the late 17th cent., and, as a result, Kharkov received more autonomy than most other Ukrainian cities. Developing as an intellectual and commercial center, Kharkov became the site of large annual trade fairs, which were held from the second half of the 18th cent. until the Russian Revolution. Russia's annexation of the Crimea in 1783 and colonization of the steppes further stimulated Kharkov's economic growth. The coal and metallurgical industries developed after the 1860s, and railroads were built in the late 19th cent. Kharkov also became an important center of the 19th-century Ukrainian national and literary movements. The city became the capital of the Ukraine in 1919 but was superseded by Kiev in 1934. Kharkov's landmarks include the cathedral of the Protectoress (1686), the cathedral of the Assumption (1771), and a bell tower that was built to celebrate Napoleon's defeat in 1812. The university dates from 1805, and there are numerous scientific research institutes. Heavy fighting raged in Kharkov during World War II.

Khartoum (kärtōōm'), city (1969 est. pop. 231,000), capital of the Sudan, a port at the confluence of the Blue Nile and White Nile rivers. Khartoum is the Sudan's second largest city and its administrative center. Food, beverages, cotton, gum, and oil seeds are processed in the city. Manufactures include cotton textiles, knitwear, glass, and tiles. Khartoum is a railroad hub and is connected by road to the heart of the adjacent cotton-growing region. The city also has an international airport. Founded in 1821 as an Egyptian army camp, Khartoum developed as a trade center and slave market. In the war between Great Britain and the forces of the MAHDI, Gen. Charles GORDON was killed there (1885) after resisting a long siege, which was one of the most notable events in British imperial history and during which the city was severely damaged. Khartoum was retaken by H. H. KITCHENER in 1898 and rebuilt. An educational center, Khartoum is the site of the Univ. of Khartoum (founded 1903 as Gordon Memorial College), a branch of the Univ. of Cairo, and Khartoum Polytechnic. The city's Sudan Museum has important

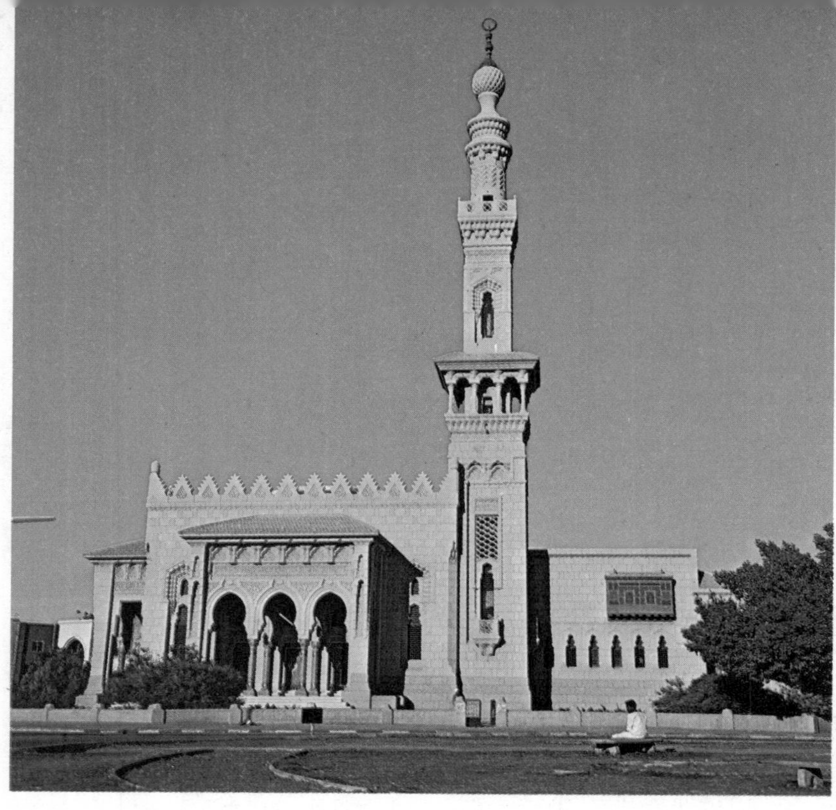

Mosque in the city of Khartoum, capital of the Sudan.

archaeological holdings. Bridges link Khartoum with Khartoum North and Omdurman.

Khaskovo, or **Haskovo,** city (1968 est. pop. 68,000), S Bulgaria, in an agricultural region noted for its tobacco. The city has one of Bulgaria's largest cigarette factories.

Khatanga (khətän'gə), river, Krasnoyarsk Kray, N central Siberian USSR, formed by the union of the Kotui and the Kheta rivers. From the Kotui it is c.715 mi (1,150 km) long and flows north through the central Siberian Plateau past Khatanga village and NE into the Khatanga Gulf of the Laptev Sea, forming the southeastern border of the Taymyr peninsula. The river is navigable.

Khatchatourian, Aram Ilich: see KHACHATURIAN.

Khatti: see HITTITES.

Khayr ad-Din: see BARBAROSSA.

Khayyam, Omar: see OMAR KHAYYAM.

Khazars (khä'zärz), ancient Turkic people who appeared in TRANSCAUCASIA in the 2d cent. A.D. and subsequently settled in the lower Volga region. They emerged as a force in the 7th cent. and rose to great power. The Khazar empire extended (8th-10th cent.) from the northern shores of the Black Sea and the Caspian Sea to the Urals and as far westward as Kiev. The Khazars conquered the Volga Bulgars and the Crimea, levied tribute from the eastern Slavs, and warred with the Arabs, Persians, and Armenians. In the 10th cent. they entered into friendly relations with the Byzantine Empire, which attempted to use them in the struggle against the Arabs. In the 8th cent. the Khazar nobility embraced Judaism. Cyril and Methodius subsequently made some Christian converts among them. Religious tolerance was complete in the Khazar empire, which reached a relatively high degree of civilization. Itil, its capital in the Volga delta, was a great commercial center. The Khazar empire fell when Sviatoslav, duke of Kiev, defeated its army in 965. The Khazars (or Chazars) are believed by some to have been the ancestors of many East European Jews.

Kherson (khĕrsôn'), city (1970 pop. 261,000), capital of Kherson oblast, S European USSR, in the Ukraine, on the Dnepr River near its mouth on the Black Sea. It is a rail junction and a sea and river port, exporting grain, timber, and manganese ore and importing oil from the Caucasus. Kherson has one of the Ukraine's largest cotton textile mills; the city's other industries include shipbuilding and food processing. Kherson was founded in 1778 by Potemkin as a naval station, fortress, and shipbuilding center. Its name derives from its location on the probable site of the Greek colony Chersonesus Heracleotica. The city became the administrative center for Russia's newly acquired holdings along the Black Sea. By the late 19th cent. it was an important export center. The dredging of a deepwater canal along an arm of the Dnepr to the sea in 1901 further stimulated Kherson's growth as a port. The city's importance was enhanced still more with the building of the DNEPROGES power station in 1932 and the development of navigation on the Dnepr. Kherson's landmarks include the fortress with earthen ramparts and stone gates and the 18th-century cathedral that contains Potemkin's tomb.

Khibinogorsk: see KIROVSK, USSR.

Khingan, Great (khĭn'gän', shĭng'än'), Mandarin *Ta-hsing-an,* mountain range, Heilungkiang, Kirin, and Liaoning prov., NE China, extending c.750 mi (1,210 km) from the Amur River S to the Liao River; the highest point is 5,657 ft (1,724 m). The range forms the eastern edge of the Mongolian Plateau. Heavily forested, it has some of China's richest timber resources. The **Lesser Khingan,** Mandarin *Hsiao-hsing-an,* Heilungkiang prov., is a continuation of the Bureya range in the Siberian USSR. It extends c.400 mi (640 km) NE from the Sungari River and is linked to the Great Khingan by the I-lo-hu-li range, N Heilungkiang prov.

Khíos (khē'ôs) or **Chios** (kī'ŏs), island (1971 pop. 52,487), c.350 sq mi (910 sq km), E Greece, in the Aegean Sea, just W of Asia Minor. It is mountainous and is famous for its scenic beauty and good climate. The highest point is Mt. Elias (c.4,160 ft/1,270 m). The island produces olives, figs, and mastic and has marble quarries, lignite deposits, and sulfur springs. Sheep and goats are raised. Khíos was colonized by Ionians and later held (494–479 B.C.) by the Persians. In 479 B.C. it recovered its independence and joined the DELIAN LEAGUE. It rebelled several times against Athenian ascendancy in the league. The island was on good terms with Rome, maintaining its independence until the reign of Vespasian (1st cent. A.D.). It became part of the Byzantine Empire and later passed (1204) to the Latin emperors of Constantinople and then (1261) to the Genoese. The Ottoman Turks conquered the island in 1566 and held it until the First Balkan War (1912), when it was taken by Greece. A rebellion against Turkish rule resulted (1822) in a ruthless massacre of the population. Khíos claims to be the birthplace of Homer. **Khíos**, a seaport (1971 pop. 24,084), is the island's chief town and the capital of Khíos prefecture.

Khiva (khē'və, khēvä'), city (1967 est. pop. 22,000), Central Asian USSR, in Uzbekistan, in the Khiva oasis and on the Amu Darya River. Industries include metalworking, cotton and silk spinning, wood carving, and carpetmaking. The city, in existence by the 6th cent., was the capital of the Khorezm kingdom in the 7th and 8th cent. From the late 16th until the early 20th cent., Khiva was the capital of the khanate of the same name. The city was a significant trade and handicraft center in the late 18th and early 19th cent. It passed to Russia in 1873. It served as the capital of the Khorezm Soviet People's Republic from 1920 to 1923 and of the Khorezm SSR in 1923 and 1924. The ancient quarter of the city has been set aside to preserve such landmarks as an 18th-century fort, the khan's palace (now a museum), and a 19th-century mausoleum and minaret.

Khiva, khanate of, former state of central Asia, based on the Khiva (Khorezm) oasis along the Amu Darya River. The khanate lay S of the Aral Sea and included large areas of the Kyzyl-Kum and Kara-Kum deserts. Founded c.1511 as part of the Khorezm state, Khiva rose in the late 16th cent. as a Muslim Uzbek state. It flourished in the early 19th cent. but was conquered by Russia in 1873; the khans subsequently continued to rule under Russian protection. Khiva's economy was based on agriculture, livestock breeding, brigandage, and handicrafts. The territory comprised the Khorezm Soviet People's Republic from 1920 to 1924, when the area was divided between the Uzbek SSR and the Turkmen SSR. For earlier history, see KHOREZM.

Khlesl, Melchior: see KLESL, MELCHIOR.

Khmelnitsky, Bohdan: see CHMIELNICKI, BOHDAN.

Khmelnitsky (khmĕlnēt'skē), city (1970 pop. 113,000), capital of Khmelnitsky oblast, SW European USSR, in the Ukraine, on the Southern Bug River. It is a rail terminus and highway hub and has metal forges, food-processing (notably sugar-refining) plants, and factories that produce machine tools, equipment for power stations, reinforced concrete items, clothing, and footwear. Known since the 15th cent., the city was a fortress by the late 16th cent. and became part of Russia in 1795. Formerly called Proskurov, it was renamed in 1954 on the 300th anniversary of a treaty between the Russians and the Cossacks led by Bohdan Chmielnicki (Khmelnitsky).

Khmer Empire, ancient kingdom of SE Asia. In the 6th cent. the Cambodians, or Khmers, established an empire roughly corresponding to modern CAMBODIA and LAOS. Divided during the 8th cent., it was reunited under the rule of Jayavarman II in the early 9th cent.; the capital was established in the area of ANGKOR by the king Yasovarman I (889–900). The Angkor period (889–1434), the golden age of Khmer civilization, saw the empire at its greatest extent; it held sway over the valleys of the lower Menam (in present-day Thailand) and the lower Mekong (present-day Cambodia and South Vietnam), as well as N into Laos. The Khmer civilization was largely formed by Indian influences. Buddhism flourished side by side with the worship of Shiva and of other Hindu gods, while both religions coalesced with the cult of the deified king. In the Angkor period many Indian scholars, artists, and religious teachers were attracted to the Khmer court, and Sanskrit literature flourished with royal patronage. The great achievement of the Khmers was in architecture and sculpture. The earliest known Khmer monuments, isolated towers of brick probably date from the 7th cent. Small temples set on stepped pyramids next appeared. The development of covered galleries led gradually to a great elaboration of plan. Brick was largely abandoned in favor of stone. Khmer architecture reached its height with the construction of Angkor Wat by Suryavarman II (1113–50) and Angkor Thom by Jayavarman VII (1181–c.1218). Sculpture, which also prospered at Angkor, showed a steady development from relative naturalism to a more conventionalized technique. Bas-reliefs, lacking in the earliest monuments, came to overshadow in importance statues in the round; in the later stages of Khmer art hardly a wall was left bare of bas-reliefs, which conveyed in the richness of their detail and vitality a vivid picture of Khmer life. The Khmers fought repeated wars against the Annamese and the Chams; in the early 12th cent. they invaded Champa, but, in 1177, Angkor was sacked by the Chams. After the founding of Ayuthia (c.1350), Cambodia was subjected to repeated invasions from Thailand, and the Khmer power declined. In 1434, after the Thai captured Angkor, the capital was transferred to Phnom Penh; this event marks the end of the brilliance of the Khmer civilization. See L. P. Briggs, *The Ancient Khmer Empire* (1951); John Audric, *Angkor and the Khmer Empire* (1972).

Khmer Republic: see CAMBODIA.

Khmer Rouge (ro͞ozh), or National United Front of Cambodia, Communist-dominated insurgent movement formed in Cambodia in 1970. With the aid of North Vietnam and the Viet Cong, the Khmer Rouge launched a massive guerrilla war against the regime of Lon Nol, who had overthrown Prince Sihanouk in Mar., 1970. Although numbering only 3,000 in 1970, the Khmer Rouge forces recruited supporters from guerrilla-held areas and by 1975 had grown to some 60,000. Following the Communist victory (April, 1975), the Khmer Rouge leader, Khieu Samphan, became the Cambodian chief of state.

Khodzhent: see LENINABAD, USSR.

Khoi, Iran: see KHVOY.

Khoikhoi (koi'koi"), people numbering about 39,000 mainly in South West Africa and in NW Cape Prov., Republic of South Africa. The Khoikhoi have been called Hottentots by whites in South Africa. In language and in physical type the Khoikhoi appear to be related to the SAN (Bushmen), i.e., they speak a variation of the Khoisan, or Click, language (see AFRICAN LANGUAGES); they are generally much lighter in complexion than the neighboring Bantu. A pastoral people, inhabiting the coast of the Cape of Good Hope in historic times, the Khoikhoi were the first native people to come into contact (mid-17th cent.) with the Dutch settlers. As the Dutch took over land for farms, the Khoikhoi were dispossessed, exterminated, or enslaved, and their numbers dwindled. They were formerly divided into 10 clans, each ruled by a headman and councillors elected by universal male suffrage. The Khoikhoi have largely disappeared as a group, except for the Namas (see NAMAQUALAND) of SW Africa, who still live as pastoral nomads. Most Khoikhoi have settled in villages, living as farmers and laborers. See Isaac Schapera, *The Khoisan Peoples of South Africa* (1930, repr. 1965); Peggy Heap, *The Story of Hottentots Holland* (1970).

Khokand: see KOKAND, USSR.

Kholmogory (khŭl"məgô'rē), village, NW European USSR, SE of Arkhangelsk and at the mouth of the Northern Dvina River. Known since 1355, Kholmogory was a major trade center for Novgorod merchants in the 15th and 16th cent. and became a shipping and cattle raising center in the 18th cent. Its significance declined with the rise of Arkhangelsk.

Khoper (khəpyôr'), river, c.625 mi (1,010 km) long, S European USSR. It rises SW of Penza and flows SW, then S into the Don. It is partly navigable.

Khorasan (khôräsän'), province (1966 pop. 2,497,-381), c.125,000 sq mi (323,750 sq km), NE Iran. Mashhad is the capital and chief city; other cities include Sabzevar, Bojnurd, and Neyshabur. It is mainly mountainous and arid. Products include agricultural goods, refined sugar, textiles, carpets, turquoises, opium, and wool. Khorasan was occupied by the Arabs in the mid-7th cent., and it was there that Abu Muslim began (8th cent.) his campaign against the Umayyads. The province contributed to the military power of the early Abbasid caliphs. Khorasan was devastated by the Oghuz Turks in 1153 and 1157 and by the Mongols from 1220 to 1222. In 1383 the province was invaded by Tamerlane. It is also known as Khurasan.

Khorezm (khərĕz'əm) or **Khwarazm** (khwärăz'əm), ancient and medieval state of central Asia, situated in and around the basin of the lower Amu Darya River; now an oblast, NW Uzbek Republic, USSR. Khorezm is one of the oldest centers of civilization in central Asia. It was a part of the Achaemenid empire of Cyrus the Great in the 6th cent. B.C. and became independent in the 4th cent. B.C. It was later inhabited by Persians who adhered to Zoroastrianism and used Aramaic script. Khorezm was conquered by the Arabs in the 7th cent. and was converted to Islam. In 995 the country was united under the emirs of N Khorezm, whose capital URGENCH became a major seat of Arabic learning. The capital was a center of agriculture and trade and the residence of the ruling shahs. In the late 12th cent., Khorezm gained independence from the Seljuk Turks, the successors to the Arabs. With independence it expanded its rule, and at the height of its power in the early 13th cent. ruled from the Caspian Sea to Bukhara and Samarkand. It was conquered in 1221 by Jenghiz Khan and was included in the Golden Horde. The development of caravan trade by the Mongols was profitable to Khorezm. In the late 14th cent., Khorezm, along with its vast irrigation system, was destroyed by Tamerlane. A century of struggle over Khorezm between the Timurids, the descendants of Tamerlane, and the Golden Horde was followed by the Uzbek conquest in the early 16th cent. Khorezm became an independent Uzbek state and was known as the khanate of Khiva after Khiva became the capital. There are ruins of ancient forts, one of which dates back to the 6th cent. B.C.

Khorog (khərôk'), city (1970 pop. 12,000), capital of Gorno-Badakhshan Autonomous Oblast, Central Asian USSR, in Tadzhikistan, in the Pamir. Khorog has shoe factories and metal-working plants, and building materials are produced.

Khorramabad (khōräm"äbäd'), city (1971 est. pop. 62,000), capital of Luristan governorate, Khuzistan prov., W Iran. It is the trade center of a mountainous region where fruit, grain, and wool are produced.

Khorramshahr (khōräm"shä'hər), city (1971 est. pop. 90,000), Khuzistan prov., SW Iran, at the confluence of the Karun River and the Shatt al Arab, near the Persian Gulf. It is a busy port. Its development dates to the late 19th cent., when steam navigation on the Karun was started. The city was known as Muhammerah until the mid-1920s, when Reza Shah took it out of the hands of a semi-independent local sheikh and placed it under the control of the central government.

Khorsabad (khôrsäbäd'), village, NE Iraq, near the Tigris River and 12 mi (20 km) NE of Mosul. It is built on the site of Dur Sharrukin, an Assyrian city (founded 8th cent. B.C. by Sargon), which covered 1 sq mi (2.6 sq km). Its mounds were excavated by P. E. Botta in 1842 and in 1851, and statues of Sargon and of huge, winged bulls that guarded the gates of the royal palace were taken to the Louvre. In 1932 there were discovered hundreds of cuneiform tablets in the Elamite language and a list of kings ruling from c.2200 B.C. to 730 B.C.

Khortitsa: see ZAPOROZHYE, USSR.

Khosru I (Khosru Nushirvan) (khŏsrōō'; nōōshĭrvän'), d. 579, king of Persia (531–79), greatest of the Sassanid or Sassanian monarchs. He is also known as Chosroes I. He succeeded his father, Kavadh I, but before becoming king, Khosru was responsible for a great massacre (c.528) of the communistic Mazdakites. He extended Persian rule E to the Indus River with the capture (560) of Bactria, W across Arabia by establishing (570) at least nominal rule over Yemen, and north and northwest by taking part of Armenia and Caucasia from the Byzantine Empire. He fought against Belisarius and the other generals of Justinian I and against Justin II. Khosru is revered by the Persians as a just though despotic ruler who encouraged learning, stimulated commerce, rebuilt cities, and set up a reformed system of taxation.

Khosru II (Khosru Parviz) (pärvēz'), d. 628, king of Persia of the Sassanid, or Sassanian, dynasty; grandson of Khosru I. He is also called Chosroes II. He succeeded his father Hormizd, or Hormoz, in 590, but he was opposed by the usurper Bahram Chukin, and forced to flee to the Byzantine Empire. Emperor Maurice aided him in overthrowing Bahram, but Khosru had to cede practically all of Armenia. When Maurice was murdered by the tyrant Phocas, Khosru declared a war of revenge against his murderer and conquered much Byzantine territory until he was finally defeated by Heraclius I. Khosru was murdered by his son and successor, Kauadh II Shiruya.

Khotan: see HO-T'IEN, China.

Khotin (khətyēn'), city, SW European USSR, in the Ukraine, on the Dnestr River. It lies in Bessarabia in an agricultural district and has agricultural and food-processing industries. Located on the site of an ancient fortified Slavic settlement, the city is named for Kotizon, a 3d-century Dacian chief. It was included in Kievan Russia in the 10th cent. and later became part of the Galich and Galich-Volhynian duchies. Khotin developed into an important trade and craft center and in the 13th cent. was the site of a Genoese trading colony. The city was included in the Hungarian and Moldavian states in the 14th and 15th cent. Its strategic location at an important Dnestr River crossing caused the city to change hands frequently from the 16th to 18th cent. Seized by Russia in 1739, Khotin was incorporated into the Russian Empire in 1812 as part of Bessarabia. The city was under Rumanian rule from 1918 to 1940 and under German occupation from 1941 to 1944. Khotin has remains of an imposing fortified castle that was built (13th cent.) by the Genoese, enlarged (14th–15th cent.) by the Moldavians, and restored (18th cent.) by the Turks.

Khrushchev, Nikita Sergeyevich (nyĭkē'tə syĭrgā'yəvĭch khro͝oschôf'), 1894–1971, Soviet Communist leader, premier of the USSR (1958–64), and first secretary of the Communist party of the Soviet Union (1953–64). Of a peasant family, he worked in the plants and mines of Ukraine, joined the Communist party in 1918, and in 1929 was sent to Moscow for further study. He became a member of the central committee of the Communist party of the Soviet Union (CPSU) in 1934 and first secretary of the powerful Moscow city and oblast party organization in 1935. Made first secretary of the Ukrainian Communist party in 1938, he carried out Stalin's ruthless purge of its ranks. As a full member of the politburo, the ruling body of the central committee of the CPSU after 1939, Khrushchev was one of Stalin's close associates. In World War II he served on the military councils of several fronts. He was recalled from Ukraine to his Moscow post in 1949. After the death of STALIN on March 5, 1953, a "collective leadership" replaced the single ruler of the USSR; from the ensuing struggle for power Khrushchev emerged victorious. He replaced MALENKOV as first secretary of the party in Sept., 1953, and, in 1955, Malenkov resigned as premier and was succeeded by BULGANIN, a change clearly leaving Khrushchev with the advantage. In 1954 he initiated the virgin lands program to increase grain production and headed a delegation to Communist China. At the 20th All-Union Party Congress (1956), Khrushchev delivered a "secret" report on "The Personality Cult and Its Consequences," bitterly denouncing the rule, policies, and personality of Stalin. The program of destalinization, which had already begun, was supported and continued by Khrushchev. Legality of procedure was restored, the secret police became less of a threat, concentration camps and many forced labor camps were closed, and some greater degree of meaningful public controversy was permitted. The new atmosphere of relative freedom constituted a great change from the days of Stalin. Destalinization had, however, repercussions in other Communist countries, creating unrest that exploded in the Polish defiance of the USSR in 1956 and in the quickly quelled Hungarian revolution of the same year. These events and the abandonment of the sixth FIVE-YEAR PLAN weakened Khrushchev's position, but he gained strength in 1957 with his program for decentralization of industry. In 1957 a faction headed by Malenkov, MOLOTOV, and Kaganovich tried in vain to remove Khrushchev from leadership; they were instead removed from important posts, as, soon after, was ZHUKOV, who had supported Khrushchev against them. Khrushchev replaced Bulganin as premier in March, 1958, becoming undisputed leader of both state and party. Jovial in manner, often deliberately uncouth, he showed himself capable of alternating belligerence with camaraderie. He soon was known throughout the world as a leader of great shrewdness, fully attuned to the realities of the international scene. In foreign affairs Khrushchev's announced policy, opposite to that of Stalin, was one of "peaceful coexistence" in the COLD WAR. He toured the United States in 1959 and met with President Eisenhower at Camp David, Md., thus helping to improve the tense international relations created by his threats (1958) to sign a separate peace with East Germany. In 1960, however, Khrushchev cancelled the Paris summit conference after a U.S. reconnaissance plane was shot down over the USSR. In the fall of 1960 he headed the Soviet delegation to the UN General Assembly, where he raged against UN interference in the Republic of the Congo (now Zaïre). Khrushchev's policies at home and abroad involved him in an increasingly bitter struggle with Communist China, which continued to adhere strongly to a bellicose Stalinist ideology. International tension was created by Khrushchev's adamant stand over BERLIN, but was lessened somewhat by his withdrawal of Soviet missiles from CUBA in 1962 and by small compromises in the Soviet proposals for disarmament. In Oct., 1964, Khrushchev was removed from power. Repeated failures in agricultural production as well as Khrushchev's retreat in the Cuban missile crisis and the rift with Commu-

Nikita Khrushchev.

nist China had intensified the opposition to him. He lived in obscurity outside Moscow until his death in 1971. See UNION OF SOVIET SOCIALIST REPUBLICS. See biographies by George Paloczi-Horvath (1960), Lazar Pistrak (1961), Edward Crankshaw (1966), and Mark Frankland (1969); Strobe Talbott, ed., *Khrushchev Remembers* (2 vol., tr. 1970 and 1974).

Khufu (kho͞o'fo͞o) or **Cheops** (kē'ŏps), fl. c.2680 B.C., king of ancient Egypt, founder of the IV dynasty. He was king for 23 years and was famous as the builder of the greatest PYRAMID at Gizeh.

Khulna (ko͝ol'nə), town (1961 est. pop. 128,000), SW Bangladesh, near the Ganges delta. It is a river port and the trade and processing center for the products of the Sundarbans, a swampy, forested region. Agricultural products, especially rice and jute, are processed, and there is some textile manufacturing and shipbuilding. Khulna is also an educational center.

Khurasan, Iran: see KHORASAN.

Khuzistan (kho͞ozēstän'), province (1966 pop. 1,578,079), c.24,000 sq mi (62,160 sq km), SW Iran, bordering on Iraq in the west and the Persian Gulf in the south. Its major cities include Ahvaz (the capital), Khorramshahr, Dezful, and Abadeh. Khuzistan has large petroleum deposits and major oil refineries. Mountainous in the east, it has a hot climate; agricultural products include dates, citrus fruit, rice, and vegetables. Dams on the Dez River in the northern part of the province provide water for irrigation and hydroelectricity. Khuzistan was the biblical Elam, called Susiana in classical times. The area was conquered (7th cent.) by the Arabs and invaded (13th cent.) by the Mongols; it passed to Tamerlane in the 14th cent. About half the population today is made up of Shiite Muslims. The province was formerly called Arabistan.

Khvoy (khvō'ē), city (1971 est. pop. 51,000), West Azerbaijan prov., NW Iran. It is the trade center for a fertile farm region. Because of its strategic location near Turkey and the Soviet Union, control of the city has frequently been in dispute. Khvoy was attacked by Russia in 1827, occupied by Turkey in 1911, and held by the Soviet Union during World War II. Nearby, in 1514, Selim I, an Ottoman sultan, defeated Shah Ismail of Persia at the battle of Chaldiran. The city is also known as Khoi.

Khwarazm: see KHOREZM.

Khyber Pass (kī'bər), narrow, steep-sided pass, 28 mi (45 km) long, winding through the Safed Koh Mts., on the Pakistan-Afghanistan border; highest point is 3,500 ft (1,067 m). It links the cities of Peshawar, Pakistan, and Kabul, Afghanistan. For centuries a trade and invasion route from central Asia, the Khyber Pass was one of the principal approaches of the armies of ALEXANDER THE GREAT, TAMERLANE, BABUR, MAHMUD OF GHAZNI, and NADIR SHAH in their invasions of India. The pass was also important in the Afghan Wars fought by the British in the 19th cent. The Khyber Pass is now traversed by a modern road, an old caravan route, and a railroad (built 1920–25), which passes through 34 tunnels and over 92 bridges and culverts. Pakistan controls the entire pass.

Kiakhta: see KYAKHTA, USSR.

Kialing, river, China: see CHIA-LING.

Kiamusze: see CHIA-MU-SSU, China.

Kian: see CHI'AN, China.

kiang: see ASS.

Kiangsi (kyăng'sē', jēäng'sē'), Mandarin *Chiang-hsi*, province (1968 est. pop. 22,000,000), c.66,000 sq mi (170,940 sq km), SE China. NAN-CH'ANG is the capital. The largely hilly and mountainous surface is drained by many rivers; the longest is the navigable Kan, which flows NE to P'o-yang lake. In Kiangsi's fertile soil and mild climate agriculture flourishes; the growing season is 9 to 11 months long, and more than 30% of the area is cultivated. Kiangsi is one of China's leading rice producers; other food crops include wheat, sweet potatoes, barley, and corn. Commerical crops are cotton, oil-bearing plants (rapeseed, sesame, soybeans, and peanuts), ramie, tea, sugarcane, tobacco, and oranges. Ten percent of the province is forested, and a lumbering industry has developed. Tung and mulberry trees are grown; a large, integrated silk complex is at Nan-ch'ang. Fish culture is important. Kiangsi is China's main source of tungsten; it also has high-grade coking coal (near P'ing-hsiang) and kaolin, which supplies the ancient porcelain industry of Ching-te-chen. Uranium is mined at Ch'üan-nan, and manganese, tin, and antimony are also found. Cities, such as Nan-ch'ang, Chiu-chiang, Kan-chou, and Fu-chou, are generally situated along the Kan River or on the province's two main railroads. The population in the north consists of largely Chinese who speak the Kan (Kiangsi) variety of Mandarin, while in the south, adjoining Kwangtung, there is a large Hakka minority. Kiangsi, linked with Kwangtung by the Meiling Pass, has been for centuries China's main north-south corridor for migration and communication. Traditionally known as Kan, Kiangsi was ruled by the Chou dynasty (722–481 B.C.); it received its present name only under the Southern Sung dynasty (A.D. 1127–1280). The province, whose present boundaries date from the Ming dynasty, passed under Manchu rule in 1650. The Chinese Communist movement began (1927) in Kiangsi; the province was a stronghold for the Communists until they were dislodged in 1934. The famous LONG MARCH began from Kiangsi. Following World War II, during which Kiangsi was largely free of Japanese forces, the province passed (1949) to the Communists.

Kiangsu (kyăng'so͞o, jēäng'so͞o'), Mandarin *Chiangsu*, province (1968 est. pop. 47,000,000), c.41,000 sq mi (106,190 sq km), E China, on the Yellow Sea. NANKING is the capital. Kiangsu consists largely of the alluvial plain of the Yangtze River and includes much of its delta; in elevation it rarely rises above sea level. The fairly warm climate, moderate rainfall, and fertile soil make Kiangsu one of the richest agricultural regions of China and one of the most densely populated. The province straddles two agricultural zones, with wheat, millet, koaliang, corn, soybeans, and peanuts cultivated in the north and rice, tea, sugarcane, and barley raised in the south. Cotton is grown along the coast (north and south) in the saline soil, which is not suited for other crops. Tea is planted in the western hills, and some experimenting with oak trees for silk culture has been initiated. Intensive land reclamation has been accomplished, with extensive dikes and the use of the raised-field system. Fish are abundant in the many lakes (of which T'ai is the most famous), in the streams and canals, and off the Yangtze delta; Kiangsu, which is known to the Chinese as "the land of rice and fish," is rich in marine products. It is also a major salt-producing area. Kiangsu is bisected by the Yangtze, which can be navigated by steamers up to 15,000 tons, and by a portion of the Grand Canal. Its first-class roads and extensive railroad system, including the busiest railway in China, the

Shanghai-Nanking line, make for excellent communications. Perhaps the most prosperous province in China, Kiangsu is deficient only in timber and minerals. A major part of China's foreign trade clears through the port of SHANGHAI into Kiangsu. Shanghai, one of the world's great seaports and the chief manufacturing center of China, is in Kiangsu prov. but is administered directly by the central government. Nanking has been developed into an industrial center, with a great variety of manufactures. SU-CHOU, WU-HSI, and CHEN-CHIANG are known for their silk. Textile, food-processing, cement, and fertilizer industries are found throughout the province. Kiangsu was originally part of the Wu kingdom, and the name Wu is still its traditional name. Kiangsu received its present name, derived from Kiangning (Nanking) and Su-chou (Soochow), in 1667, when it was formed from the old Kiangnan prov. The gateway to central China, Kiangsu became the main scene of European commercial activity after the Treaty of Nanking (1842). The capture of Kiangsu in 1937 was an important phase of Japan's effort to conquer all China (see SINO-JAPANESE WAR, SECOND). Liberated by the Chinese Nationalists in 1945, Kiangsu fell to the Communists in 1949. For a time Kiangsu was administered as two regional units, North and South Kiangsu, but in 1952 the province was reunited. Many archaeological sites have been excavated in Kiangsu since 1956.

Kiangtu: see YANG-CHOU, China.

Kiaochow (kyou'chou', jēou'jō'), Mandarin *Chia-chou,* former German territory, area c.200 sq mi (520 sq km), along the southern coast of Shantung prov., China. Its administrative center was the city of Ch'ing-tao. Germany leased Kiaochow in 1898 for 99 years, but in 1914 Japan seized it. Through agreements reached at the Washington Conference in 1922, Kiaochow was returned to China.

Kiating: see LO-SHAN, China.

kibbutz: see COLLECTIVE FARM.

Kibo, peak, Africa: see KILIMANJARO.

Kibroth-hattaavah (kĭb'rŏth-hătā'āvə), unidentified desert camp. There the Israelites were punished with a plague. Num. 11.34; 33.16; Deut. 9.22.

Kibzaim (kĭb'zāĭm, kĭbzā'-): see JOKMEAM.

Kickapoo Indians (kĭk'əpo͞o), North American Indians, whose language belongs to the Algonquian branch of the Algonquian-Wakashan linguistic stock (see AMERICAN INDIAN LANGUAGES) and who in the late 17th cent. occupied SW Wisconsin. They were closely related to the SAC AND FOX INDIANS. The culture of the Kickapoo Indians was essentially that of the Eastern Woodlands area, but they also hunted buffalo, one of the few traits that the Kickapoo adopted from their neighbors in the Plains area. After the allied Kickapoo, Ojibwa, Ottawa, Potawatomi, and Sac and Fox tribes massacred (c.1769) the ILLINOIS INDIANS, they partitioned the Illinois territory. The Kickapoo, numbering about 3,000, moved south to central Illinois. Later they split in two; the Vermilion group settled on the Vermilion River, a tributary of the Wabash, and the Prairie group on the Sangamon River. The Kickapoo, a power in the region, sided with the British in the American Revolution and in the War of 1812, when they aided the Shawnee chief Tecumseh. By the Treaty of Edwardsville (1819) the Kickapoo ceded all their lands in Illinois to the United States. They were prevented from entering Missouri, which had been set aside for them, because that region was occupied by the hostile Osage Indians. Kanakuk, a prophet, exhorted the Kickapoo to remain where they were, promising that if they avoided liquor and infractions of the white man's law, they would inherit a land of plenty. His pleas were futile, and the Kickapoo, after aiding the Sac and Fox in the Black Hawk War, were forced to leave Illinois. The Kickapoo moved first to Missouri and then to Kansas. A large group, dissatisfied with conditions on the reservation, went (c.1852) to Mexico, where they became known as the Mexican Kickapoo. After the U.S. Civil War, the Mexican Kickapoo proved so constant an annoyance to border settlements that the United States made efforts to induce them to return. The negotiations were successful, and a number returned to settle (1873–74) on a reservation in Oklahoma. The remaining Mexican Kickapoo are settled on a reservation in Chihuahua, Mexico. The Kickapoo living on reservations in Kansas and Oklahoma number some 1,000. See R. E. Ritzenthaler, *The Mexican Kickapoo Indians* (1956, repr. 1970); A. M. Gibson, *The Kickapoos* (1963).

Kicking Horse, river of SE British Columbia, Canada, rising in the Rocky Mts., and flowing SW and NW to Golden, where it enters the Columbia River. Its course is rapid, with several high falls. **Kicking Horse Pass,** 5,339 ft (1,627 m) high, NW of Lake Louise, in Banff National Park, connects the Bow River with the Kicking Horse and is one of the principal rail and highway passes over the Continental Divide.

Kid, Thomas: see KYD, THOMAS.

Kidd, Benjamin, 1858–1916, English social philosopher. His most noted work, *Social Evolution* (1894), sets forth his doctrine of the constant strife between individual and public interest. His works also include *Control of the Tropics* (1898) and *The Principles of Western Civilization* (1902).

Kidd, William, 1645?–1701, British privateer and pirate, known as Captain Kidd. He went to sea in his youth and later settled in New York, where he married and owned property. In 1691 he was rewarded for his services against French privateers. While in London in 1695 he was commissioned by the earl of Bellomont, recently appointed governor of New York, as a privateer to defend English ships from pirates in the Red Sea and the Indian Ocean. In 1696, Kidd set sail for New York and from there to Madagascar. Disease, mutiny, and failure to take prizes apparently caused him to turn pirate. Returning (1699) to the West Indies with his richest prize, the Armenian *Quedagh Merchant,* he learned of piracy charges against him. He sailed to New York to clear himself by claiming that the vessels he had attacked were lawful prizes. He was arrested and taken to London, where in 1701 he was tried on five charges of piracy and one of murder. The trial was complicated by the fact that four Whig peers who had backed him were politically embarrassed by his career. He was convicted and hanged. The barbaric cruelty and buried treasure of Captain Kidd are unsubstantiated bits of the legends about him. The Kidd legend has often been referred to in literature, for instance in Edgar Allen Poe's *Gold Bug* and Robert Louis Stevenson's *Treasure Island.* See D. C. Seitz, ed., *The Tryal of Captain William Kidd* (1935); biographies by W. H. Bonner (1947) and D. M. Hinrichs (1955).

Kidder, Alfred Vincent, 1885-1963, American archaeologist, b. Marquette, Mich., grad. Harvard (B.A. 1908; Ph.D. 1914). From 1915 to 1929 he conducted excavations at Pecos, N.Mex., for the Phillips Academy, Andover, Mass. This research is considered to have laid the foundation for modern archaeological field methods. In the late 1920s he started the Pecos conferences for archaeologists and ethnologists. As an associate in charge of archaeological investigations (1927–29) and as chairman of the division of historical research (1929–50) at the Carnegie Institution, he conducted a broad-scale research program in the Guatemalan highlands which established the framework of Mayan stratigraphy. In 1939 he became honorary curator of Southwestern American archaeology at the Peabody Museum, Harvard. His writings include *Introduction to the Study of Southwestern Archaeology* (1924), regarded as the first comprehensive archaeological study of a New World area; *The Pottery of Pecos* (2 vol., 1931–36); *The Artifacts of Pecos* (1932); and *Pecos, New Mexico: Archaeological Notes* (1958). See biography by R. B. Woodbury (1973).

Kidderminster, municipal borough (1971 pop. 47,255), Worcestershire, W central England. It is a market town. Kidderminster carpets have been produced since 1735; other industries include spinning, dyeing, metal forging, and the production of beet sugar. In 1974, Kidderminster became part of the new nonmetropolitan county of Hereford and Worcester.

Kiddush (kĭd'əsh) [Heb.,=sanctification], Jewish ceremonial blessing indicating the beginning of the Sabbath or any other Hebrew festival. Kiddush is also said at mealtime and consists of a prayer of benediction over the occasion and the wine or bread.

kidnapping, in law, the unlawful and willful taking away of a person by force, threat, or deceit with intent to cause him to be detained against his will. Kidnapping is usually done for RANSOM but may be for political or other purposes. A parent whose legal rights to custody of a child have been taken away can be guilty of the crime if he takes his own child. Consent of the kidnapped person is a defense, unless he was legally incompetent at the time (e.g., a minor or an insane person). The crime differs from abduction, in that the intent of sexual intercourse is not required, and from false imprisonment, in which there is no attempt to abduct. Under English common law it was only a MISDEMEANOR, but in most states of the United States it is punishable by death or life imprisonment if there are no extenuating circumstances. The kidnapping and murder of the son of Charles A. Lindbergh in 1932 stirred public sentiment and led to a Federal statute prescribing very severe penalties for persons transporting the victims of kidnapping across state or national boundaries. The practice of kidnapping, in the wider and not strictly legal sense, has been known since the beginnings of man's history. It was common as a method for procuring slaves, and it has been prominent as a more or less systematic means for groups of brigands and revolutionary bands to obtain money through ransom. In the 1970s, kidnapping became a common tactic of revolutionary groups. Public officials, businessmen, and diplomats were held for ransom or as hostages whose safe release was dependent on the freeing of political prisoners.

kidney, artificial, mechanical device capable of assuming the functions ordinarily performed by the kidneys. In treating cases of kidney failure a tube is inserted into an artery in the patient's arm, and the blood is channeled through a cellophane tube immersed in a bath containing all the normal blood chemicals except urea and other metabolic waste products. When the blood flows through the tube the poisonous wastes pass out through the cellophane and into the bath because of the difference in concentration of the solutions on either side of the cellophane membrane. The purified blood is returned to the body through a vein in the arm. This process of blood purification, called hemodialysis (see DIALYSIS), is usually repeated twice a week and requires several hours to complete.

kidneys: see URINARY SYSTEM.

Kidron (kĭd'rŏn) or **Cedron** (sē'-), brook or field, the present-day Qidron (Jordan), E of Jerusalem between the city and the Mount of Olives. 2 Sam. 15.23; 1 Kings 2.37; 2 Kings 23.4, 6,12; John 18.1. See also JEHOSHAPHAT.

Kieft, Willem (vĭl'əm kēft), 1597–1647, Dutch director general of NEW NETHERLAND. Arriving in New Amsterdam in 1638 to succeed Wouter VAN TWILLER, Kieft immediately assumed absolute control. His arbitrary rule and tactless handling of the Indians resulted in almost continuous Indian warfare during his administration. He was replaced by Peter STUYVESANT (1647) and was lost at sea on his way to Holland.

Kiel (kēl), city (1970 pop. 271,719), capital of Schleswig-Holstein, N West Germany, on Kiel Bay, an arm of the Baltic Sea. Situated at the head of the Kiel Canal, the city was Germany's chief naval base from 1871 to 1945, when the naval installations were dismantled. Kiel is now a shipping and industrial center, with large shipyards and factories that manufacture textiles, processed foods, and printed materials. Chartered in 1242, Kiel joined the Hanseatic League in 1284. It became the residence of the dukes of Holstein. Kiel passed to Denmark in 1773; with Holstein it was annexed by Prussia in 1866. The sailors' mutiny that began at Kiel at the end of World War I touched off a socialist revolution in Germany. In World War II the city suffered severe damage from Allied air attacks. The city is the seat of a university (founded 1665) and several museums. The sailing and yachting events of the 1972 Olympic summer games were held there.

Kiel Canal, artificial waterway, 61 mi (98 km) long, in Schleswig-Holstein, N West Germany, connecting the North Sea with the Baltic Sea. At sea level, the canal extends from Kiel on the Baltic to Brunsbüttelkoog at the mouth of the Elbe River. Locks at each end of the canal minimize tidal variation. Built (1887–95) to facilitate movement of the German fleet, the Kiel Canal was widened and deepened from 1905 to 1914. Large oceangoing ships can pass through the canal. Because of its great military and commercial importance the canal was internationalized by the Treaty of Versailles (1919). Hitler repudiated its international status in 1936. The canal is also known as the Kaiser Wilhelm Canal, for William II of Germany, and as the North Sea-Baltic Canal (Ger. *Nord-Ostsee-Kanal*).

Kielce (kyĕl'tsĕ), city (1970 pop. 126,000), S central Poland. It is a railway junction and manufacturing center where metals, agricultural machinery, and chemicals are produced. It also has marble quarries. Founded in 1173, Kielce obtained municipal rights in the 14th cent. It belonged to the bishops of Kraków until 1789. The city passed to Austria in 1795 and to Russia in 1815 and reverted to Poland in 1919.

Its most notable buildings are a 12th-century cathedral and a 17th-century palace.

Kielland, Alexander Lange (äləksän'dər läng'ə khĕl'län), 1849–1906, Norwegian novelist, short-story writer, and playwright. Two early volumes of short stories—*Tales of Two Countries* (1879, tr. 1891) and *Norse Tales and Sketches* (1897)—placed him among the important realists. His witty and ironic novels, written with the purpose of social reform, include *Skipper Worse* (1882, tr. 1885). His writing was greatly influenced by George BRANDES.

Kierkegaard, Søren (sö'rən kyĕr'kəgôr), 1813–55, Danish philosopher and religious thinker. Kierkegaard's outwardly uneventful life in Copenhagen contrasted with his intensive inner examination of self and society, which resulted in many diversified and profound writings; their dominant theme is that "truth is subjectivity." Kierkegaard argued that in religion the important thing is not truth as objective fact but rather the individual's relationship to it. Thus it is not enough to believe the Christian doctrine; one must also live it. He attacked what he felt to be the sterile metaphysics of G. W. Hegel and the worldliness of the Danish church. His writings fall into two categories—the aesthetic and the religious. The aesthetic works, which include *Either/Or* (1843), *Philosophical Fragments* (1844), *Stages on Life's Way* (1845), and *The Concluding Unscientific Postscript* (1846), were all published under pseudonyms and interpret human existence through the eyes of various poetically delineated characters. In those works Kierkegaard developed an "existential dialectic" in opposition to the Hegelian dialectic, and described the various stages of existence as the aesthetic, the ethical, and the religious. As the individual advances through these stages he becomes increasingly more aware of his relationship to God. This awareness leads to despair as the individual realizes the antithesis between temporal existence and eternal truth. The specifically religious writings include *Works of Love* (1847) and *Training in Christianity* (1850). Kierkegaard also kept an extensive journal that contains many of his deepest insights. Although practically unknown outside of Denmark during the 19th cent., he later exerted a tremendous influence upon both contemporary Protestant theology and the philosophic movement known as EXISTENTIALISM. His major works have been translated into English. See James Collins, *The Mind of Kierkegaard* (1953, repr. 1965); P. P. Rohde, *Søren Kierkegaard* (1963); Louis Mackey, *Kierkegaard* (1971).

kieselguhr (kē'zəlgo͝or''): see DIATOM.

Kiev (kē'ĕf, Rus. kē'yəf), Ukrainian *Kyyiv*, Rus. *Kiyev*, city (1970 pop. 1,632,000), capital of the Ukrainian Soviet Socialist Republic and of Kiev oblast, SW European USSR, a port on the Dnepr River. The largest city of the Ukraine and the third largest of the USSR, Kiev is a leading industrial, commercial, and cultural center. Food processing (notably the processing of beet sugar), metallurgy, and the manufacture of machinery, machine tools, rolling stock, chemicals, building materials, and textiles are the major industries. Known to Russians as the "mother of cities," Kiev is one of the oldest towns in Europe. It probably existed as a commercial center as early as the 5th cent. A Slavic settlement on the great trade route between Scandinavia and Constantinople, Kiev was tributary to the Khazars when the VARANGIANS under Oleg established themselves there in 882. Under Oleg's successors it became the capital of medieval Kievan Russia (the first Russian state) and was a leading European cultural and commercial center. It was also an early seat of Russian Christianity. The city reached its apogee in the 11th cent., but by the late 12th cent. it had begun to decline. From 1240, when it was devastated by the Mongols, until the 14th cent., the city paid tribute to the Golden Horde. Kiev then passed under the control of Lithuania, which in 1569 was united with Poland. With the establishment of the Kievan Academy in 1632, the city became a center of Ukrainian learning and scholarship. In 1648, when the Ukrainian Cossacks under Bohdan Chmielnicki rose against Poland, Kiev became for a brief period the center of a Ukrainian state. After the Ukraine's union with Russia in 1654, however, the city was acquired (1686) by Moscow. In Jan., 1918, Kiev became the capital of the newly proclaimed Ukrainian republic; but in the ensuing civil war (1918–20), it was occupied in succession by German, White Russian, Polish, and Soviet troops. In 1934 the capital of the Ukrainian SSR was transferred from Kharkov to Kiev. German forces held the city during World War II and massacred thousands of its inhabitants, including 50,000 Jews. Postwar reconstruction of the heavily damaged city was not completed until c.1960. Lying amid hills along the Dnepr and filled with gardens and parks, Kiev is one of Europe's most beautiful cities, as well as a treasury of medieval art and architecture. Its most outstanding buildings include the Tithes Church, the ruins of the Golden Gate (11th cent.), and the 11th-century Cathedral of St. Sophia (now a museum), which was modeled on Hagia Sophia in Constantinople and contains splendid mosaics, frescoes, and icons. The Uspensky Cathedral, virtually destroyed during World War II, has been fully restored. The celebrated Lavra cave monastery (11th cent.) is now a museum and a sacred place of pilgrimage. The St. Vladimir Cathedral (9th cent.) is famed for its murals. Among the city's educational

Cathedral of St. Sophia (11th cent.) in Kiev, USSR.

and cultural institutions are the Univ. of Kiev (1833) and the Ukrainian Academy of Sciences (1918).

Kievan Russia (kē'ĕfən), medieval state of the Eastern Slavs. It was the earliest predecessor of the present-day Union of Soviet Socialist Republics. Flourishing from the 10th to the 13th cent., it included nearly all of present-day UKRAINE and BELORUSSIA and part of NW European USSR, extending as far N as Novgorod and Vladimir. According to the Russian *Primary Chronicle*, a medieval history, the Varangian RURIK established himself at Novgorod c.862 and founded a dynasty. His successor, OLEG (d. c.912), shifted his attention to the south, seized Kiev (c.879), and established the new Kievan state. The Varangians were also known as *Rus* or *Rhos*; it is possible that this name was early extended to the Slavs of the Kievan state, which became known as Kievan Rus. Other theories trace the name *Rus* to a Slavic origin. Oleg united the Eastern Slavs and freed them from the suzerainty of the KHAZARS. His successors were IGOR (reigned 912–45) and Igor's widow, St. Olga, who was regent until about 962. Under Olga's son, SVIATOSLAV (d. 972), the Khazars were crushed, and Kievan power was extended to the lower Volga and N Caucasus. Christianity was introduced by VLADIMIR I (reigned 980–1015), who adopted (c.989) Greek Orthodoxy from the Byzantines. The reign (1019–54) of Vladimir's son, YAROSLAV the Wise, represented the political and cultural apex of Kievan Russia. After his death the state was divided into principalities ruled by his sons; this soon led to civil strife. A last effort for unity was made by VLADIMIR II (reigned 1113–25), but the perpetual princely strife and the devastating raids of the nomadic CUMANS soon ended the supremacy of Kiev. In the middle of the 12th cent. a number of local centers of power developed: Galich in the west, Novgorod in the north, Vladimir-Suzdal (see VLADIMIR) in the northwest, and Kiev in the south. In 1169, Kiev was sacked and pillaged by the armies of Andrei Bogolubsky of Suzdal, and the final blow to the Kievan state came with the Mongol invasion (1237–40). The economy of the Kievan state was based on agriculture and on extensive trade with Byzantium, the Orient, and Scandinavia. Culture, as well as religion, was drawn from Byzantium; CHURCH SLAVONIC was the literary and liturgical language of the state. According to Soviet and some Western scholars the history of the Kievan state is the common heritage of modern Russians, Ukrainians, and Belorussians, although their existence as separate peoples has been traced as far back as the 12th cent. See S. H. Cross, ed., *The Russian Primary Chronicle* (tr. 1953, repr. 1973); George Vernadsky, *Kievan Russia* (vol. II of *A History of Russia,* 2d ed. 1973).

Kievan Russia (c.1000).

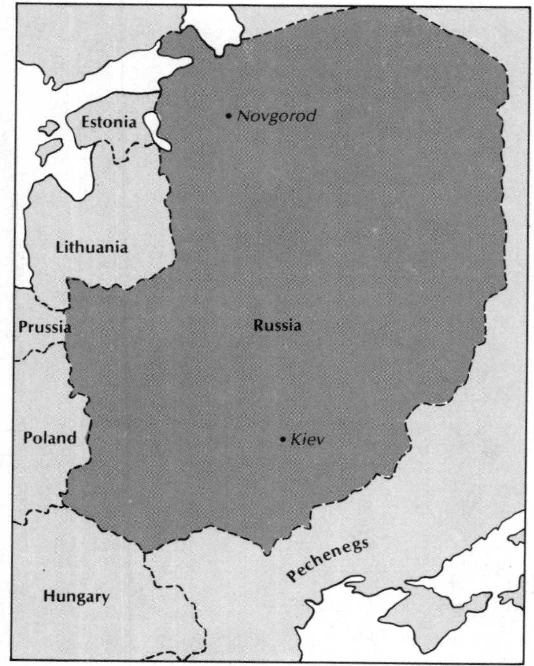

Kigali (kēgä'lē), town (1970 est. pop. 60,000), capital of Kigali prefecture and of Rwanda, central Rwanda. It is the country's main administrative and economic center. The town has an international airport. Iron ore (cassiterite) is mined nearby.

Kigoma-Ujiji (kēgō'mä'-o͞ojē'jē), municipality (1967 pop. 21,369), capital of Kigoma prov., W Tanzania, a port on Lake Tanganyika. It is the terminus of the railroad from Dar es Salaam (completed 1914) and is connected by ship with Zaïre and Burundi. There are fisheries. Ujiji and Kigoma were important settlements of Arab and Swahili ivory and slave traders between c.1850 and c.1890. The explorer Henry M. Stanley successfully ended his search for David Livingstone at Ujiji on Nov. 10, 1871. The region was occupied by the Germans in the 1890s. Kigoma and Ujiji were combined into a single municipality in the 1960s.

Kikuyu (kĭko͞o'yo͞o), Bantu-speaking people, numbering over 1.5 million, forming the largest tribal group in Kenya. The Kikuyu live in the highlands NE of Nairobi. Before the British conquest they were the most influential people in the country. During the 1950s, under the leadership of Jomo KENYATTA, the Kikuyu fought the British colonialists in what was known as the Mau Mau Emergency. Although the Kikuyu traditionally lived in separate family homesteads, most were moved into villages during the rebellion. After the removal of the colonists, a large number chose to remain in the villages. The Kikuyu economy centers mainly around agriculture, with little or no hunting or fishing. See H. E. Lambert, *Kikuyu Social and Political Institutions* (1956, repr. 1965); R. M. Gatheru, *Child of Two Worlds* (1964, repr. 1972).

Kilauea (kē'läwä'ə), crater, 3,646 ft (1,111 m) deep, central Hawaii island, Hawaii, on the southeastern slope of Mauna Loa in HAWAII VOLCANOES NATIONAL PARK. One of the largest active craters in the world, Kilauea has a circumference of c.8 mi (13 km) and is surrounded by a wall of volcanic rock 200 to 500 ft (61–152 m) high. In its floor is Halemaumau, a fiery pit. The usual level of the lake of molten lava is c.740 ft (230 m) below the pit's rim.

Kildare, James Fitzgerald, 20th **earl of** (kĭldâr'), 1722–73, Irish nobleman. He sat in the Irish House of Commons from 1741 until 1744, when he succeeded as earl of Kildare. He was created Viscount Leinster (in the English peerage) in 1747 and duke of Leinster in 1766. He emerged as a popular hero when he successfully opposed attempts to divert surplus Irish

Gnus at the foot of Kilimanjaro, Tanzania (opposite).

revenues to the British crown. He became lord deputy of Ireland in 1756.

Kildare, Thomas Fitzgerald, 10th **earl of,** 1513–37, Irish nobleman, called Silken Thomas. When his father, the 9th earl and lord deputy of Ireland, was summoned to London on charges of maladministration in 1534, Thomas became vice deputy. The same year, hearing the rumor that his father had been executed (he actually died later in the Tower of London), he renounced his allegiance to King Henry VIII and rose in rebellion. Thomas was excommunicated for the murder of his enemy, the archbishop of Dublin. The rebellion was crushed the following year, and Thomas eventually surrendered and was hanged in London with five of his uncles.

Kildare, county (1971 pop. 71,522), 654 sq mi (1,694 sq km), E central Republic of Ireland. The county town is Naas, the ancient seat of the kings of Leinster. The region is a flat plain, containing the greater portion of the Bog of Allen and the CURRAGH. The principal rivers are the Liffey, the Greese, and the Barrow. Agriculture is the chief occupation; the breeding of racehorses is significant. The county is named for the oak (*Cill Dara*) under which St. Bridget constructed her cell. There are many pre-Christian and early Christian remains.

Kilham, Alexander (kĭl'əm), 1762–98, English Methodist minister, founder of the Methodist New Connection. He took a leading part in Methodist affairs after the death of John Wesley, advocating separation from the Church of England (see METHODISM). He supported the right of preachers to administer the Lord's Supper and sought to have powers of church government distributed between clerical and lay members. For a series of pamphlets that he wrote, he was brought to trial at the conference of 1796 and expelled from the connection. In 1798 he and three other preachers formed the Methodist New Connection, the first group of Methodists to break away.

Kilimanjaro (kĭl"ĭmənjä'rō), highest mountain of Africa, NE Tanzania. An extinct volcano, it rises in two snow-capped peaks, Kibo (19,340 ft/5,895 m) and Mawenzi (17,564 ft/5,354 m), which are joined by a broad saddle (alt. c.15,000 ft/4,600 m). Coffee and plantains are the chief crops raised on Kilimanjaro's intensively cultivated lower southern slopes.

Kilindini: see MOMBASA, Kenya.

Kilkenny (kĭlkĕn'ē), county (1971 pop. 61,811), 796 sq mi (2,062 sq km), S Republic of Ireland. The county town is KILKENNY. It is mainly a rolling plain, part of the central plain of Ireland, with low hills to the south. The principal rivers are the Suir, the Nore, and the Barrow. Grains and vegetables are grown, and livestock is raised. There are food-processing and brewing industries. In the northeast is a large anthracite coal field. Castlecomer is the coal-mining center. Kilkenny is roughly coextensive with the ancient kingdom of OSSORY. It is rich in antiquities.

Kilkenny, urban district (1971 pop. 10,292), county town of Co. Kilkenny, S Republic of Ireland, on the Nore River. The districts of Irishtown and Englishtown, separated by a stream, were legally united in 1843. Strife between the inhabitants of the two districts, to the near destruction of both, may have given rise to the stories of the Kilkenny cats, who ate each other up. A third district is High Town. Kilkenny was the seat of the kings of OSSORY. The first earl of Pembroke founded a castle in the 12th cent. (restored c.1835) overlooking the Nore. Parliaments and assemblies were held in the 14th, 16th, and 17th cent. Among noted pupils at the Protestant school of Kilkenny were Swift, Bishop Berkeley, and Congreve. In Irishtown is the great Cathedral of St. Canice (13th cent.), the seat of the Protestant dioceses of the United Dioceses of Ossory, Ferns, and Leighlin. The Roman Catholic Cathedral of St. Mary (seat of the diocese of Ossory), a round tower, and remains of Dominican and Franciscan monasteries (mostly 13th cent.) are noteworthy. The Statute of Kilkenny (1366) forbade the English settlers from marrying the Irish inhabitants, speaking Irish, or wearing Irish dress.

Killarney, urban district (1971 pop. 7,179), Co. Kerry, SW Republic of Ireland. The town, which has footwear and other industries, is a tourist center for the three Lakes of Killarney. They occupy a wooded valley stretching south between the mountains. Lough Leane or Lower Lake is the largest; it has about 30 islands. The largest island is the "sweet Innisfallen" of Thomas Moore's poem. On the island are the ruins of an abbey founded c.600 by St. Finian. There the Annals of Innisfallen, an important historical document, were written (11th–14th cent.). The ruins of the 15th-century Muckross Abbey lie on the shore of Muckross Lake (Middle Lake or Lough Torc), which has picturesque waterfalls and limestone caves. Upper Lake is the third lake. In the town is the cathedral of the diocese of Kerry, designed by A. W. N. Pugin.

killdeer, common North American shorebird related to the PLOVER and the SANDPIPER. It is about 10 in. (25 cm) in length and its plumage is grayish brown with a double black band across a white breast. Its simple nest is a depression in the soil or gravel. The killdeer is classified in the phylum CHORDATA, subphylum Vertebrata, class Aves, order Charadriiformes, family Charadriidae.

Killeen (kĭlēn'), city (1970 pop. 35,507), Bell co., central Texas, in a ranching and cotton region; inc. 1893. The city has some varied light manufacturing, but adjacent Fort Hood is the major source of employment. Founded in 1882 and named for a Santa Fe RR official, Killeen remained a small farming and ranching village until the establishment (1942) of Camp Hood. The camp's redesignation (1950) as a fort with a permanent status spurred a great population growth in the city. A junior college is in Killeen, and nearby Belton and Stillhouse Hollow lakes provide recreational facilities.

killer whale, or **grampus,** a large, rapacious marine mammal, *Orcinus orca,* of the DOLPHIN family. Male killer whales may reach a length of 30 ft (9 m) and females half that length. The killer whale is black above, with a sharply contrasting white oval patch around each eye; its belly is white with white markings projecting up along the animal's sides. It has a high, triangular dorsal fin midway between head and tail, and broad, paddle-shaped flippers. The killer whale is worldwide in distribution. It is a swift and ferocious animal, armed with more than four dozen sharp teeth, and is the only cetacean (see WHALE) that feeds regularly on birds or mammals. Killer whales eat seals, sea birds, and fish, and in packs they will even attack larger whales. The female gives birth to a single calf, up to 7 ft (2.1 m) long, following a gestation period of approximately one year. Females mature in 6 to 7 years, males in 12. They are classified in the phylum CHORDATA, subphylum Vertebrata, class Mammalia, order Cetacea, family Delphinidae.

Killiecrankie, Pass of (kĭlĭkrăng'ke), wooded pass, Tayside region, central Scotland, through which the river Garry flows, near Pitlochry. There Jacobite Highlanders defeated (1689) a large government force under Hugh MacKay and the Jacobite leader, Viscount Dundee, was killed.

killifish, northern representative, especially the genus *Fundulus,* of the Cyprinodontidae or toothed minnows, a family that includes also the topminnows and many popular aquarium fishes (e.g., the guppy or rainbow fish, *Lebistes reticulatus)* among its brightly colored tropical species. Most North American toothed minnows are oviparous, i.e., bearing young hatched from eggs, and some are quite colorful; however, the tropical viviparous species (i.e., bearing live young) are preferred for aquariums, since they are easier to raise. Killifishes average from 2 to 4 in. (5–10 cm) in length and have compressed bodies, small mouths with projecting lower jaws, unforked tails, and large scales. They live in ponds, streams, ditches, and salt marshes throughout the United States and feed on insect larvae, crustaceans, and small water plants. The banded killifish is found in the Mississippi basin; the common killifish (5 in./12.5 cm) is an eastern species. Guppies can survive temperatures of up to 100°F (38°C) as can certain topminnows of the W United States. The greenish-gray female guppy (1½ in./3.75 cm) produces from 12 to 25 live offspring every few weeks; in captivity they must be separated from the cannibalistic adults. The rainbow colors of the male guppy (1 in./2.5 cm) are marked with black spots and bars. Like the guppy, the 2-in. (5-cm) *Gambusia,* a topminnow of the S Atlantic and the Gulf, bears live young and is important in controlling mosquitoes, on whose larvae both the guppy and the minnow feed. Killifishes are classified in the phylum CHORDATA, subphylum Vertebrata, class Osteichthyes, order Cyprinodontiformes, family Cyprinodontidae.

Killigrew, Thomas, 1612–83, English dramatist and theater manager, b. London. Before the closing of the theaters by the Puritans in 1642, he wrote several tragicomedies, including *The Prisoners* and *Claracilla.* His most popular play was the coarse comedy, *The Parson's Wedding* (1637). In 1647 he followed Prince Charles into exile and at the Restoration was rewarded by being made groom of the bedchamber to Charles II and chamberlain to the queen. Charles granted to Killigrew and to Sir William D'Avenant exclusive patents in 1660 to build two new theaters and to form companies of players. Killigrew was first to establish his company, the King's Servants, at Gibbon's tennis court, Vere St.; three years later he moved to his new building, the Theatre Royal, in Drury Lane. He produced garbled versions of Shakespeare, the plays of Dryden and Aphra Behn, and his own plays. See study by A. B. Harbage (1930, repr. 1967).

Killingly (kĭl'ĭng-lē), town (1970 pop. 13,573), Windham co., NE Conn., on the Quinebaug River and the R.I. border, in a farm area; settled 1693, inc. 1708. Once a great textile town, it still has some textile manufactures.

Killingworth, rural town (1970 pop. 2,435), S Conn., bordered on the W by the Hammonasset River and on the S by Clinton; organized c.1667. It has 18th-century houses, a noted church (1817), and Ely House, in which Longfellow supposedly wrote "The Birds of Killingworth."

Kill Van Kull (kĭl văn kŭl), channel, 4 mi (6.4 km) long and .5 mi (.8 km) wide, connecting Upper New York Bay with Newark Bay, between Bayonne, N.J., and Staten Island, N.Y. It is the main route for ships docking at Port Elizabeth and Port Newark, N.J. Bayonne Bridge (1931; 1,652 ft/504 m long), the world's longest steel-arch bridge, spans the channel.

Killy, Jean-Claude (zhäN-klōd kēlē'), 1943–, French skier. He grew up at his father's ski resort and began skiing at the age of 3. At 18 he was a senior member of the French national team. A daring athlete with superb reflexes, Killy has reached speeds of more than 80 mi (129 km) per hr. The dominant male in the sport from 1966 to 1968, Killy won the triple Olympic crown (downhill, slalom, and giant slalom) in the 1968 Winter Olympics, the second person ever to do so. A World Cup winner in 1966–67 and 1967–68, he also led the French team to world championships in those years. In 1968, Killy retired to race automobiles and pursue commercial ventures, but he returned in 1972, becoming a professional skier.

Kilmainham (kĭlmān'əm), suburb of Dublin, Co. Dublin, E Republic of Ireland. The commander of the British forces in Ireland had his headquarters there. Parnell was imprisoned there until he agreed (1882) to the "Kilmainham Treaty" with the English government (see PARNELL, Charles Stewart).

Kilmarnock (kĭlmär'nək), burgh (1971 pop. 48,785), Ayrshire, SW Scotland. An industrial town in a mining region, it has industries that manufacture carpets, hosiery, farm and hydraulic machinery, whiskey, and shoes. Its textile industry (bonnets) dates from 1603. Robert Burns's first poems were published there in 1786; the Burns Monument has a museum. In 1975, Kilmarnock became part of the Strathclyde region.

Kilmer, Joyce, 1886–1918, American poet, b. New Brunswick, N.J., educated at Rutgers College and Columbia (B.A., 1908). He is known chiefly for his poem "Trees," in *Trees and Other Poems* (1914).

kiln (kĭl, kĭln), furnace for firing pottery and enamels, for making brick, charcoal, lime, and cement, for roasting ores, and for drying various substances (e.g., lumber, chemicals). Kilns may be updraft or downdraft; round, conical, annular, or rectangular; arranged for intermittent or continuous firing; and of the muffle (double-wall) or direct-contact type, as required. Rotary kilns are much used in continuous processes, including cement manufacturing and the drying of granular materials. They consist of long tubes lying almost horizontally that are rotated slowly as heat is applied to the material being treated inside the tubes. The fuel used may be electricity, oil, gas, or coal. The temperature of firing and the length of time required depend on the design of the kiln and the type of material being fired.

kilogram, abbr. kg, fundamental unit of mass in the METRIC SYSTEM, defined as the mass of the International Prototype Kilogram, a platinum-iridium cylinder kept at Sèvres, France, near Paris. Copies of this standard are deposited at bureaus of standards throughout the world, and other units of mass are defined in terms of it. When the metric system was originally devised, the kilogram was defined so that 1,000 cubic centimeters (1 cubic decimeter) of pure water has a mass of exactly 1 kilogram.

kilowatt: see WATT.

Kilpatrick, William Heard, 1871–1965, American philosopher, b. White Plains, Ga., grad. Mercer College, 1891, Ph.D. Columbia, 1912, and studied at Johns Hopkins Univ. He taught at Teachers College,

Columbia, from 1909, becoming professor of the philosophy of education in 1918; he retired in 1938. Acclaimed as the great popularizer of the philosophy of John DEWEY, Kilpatrick rejected organized subjects; his child-centered emphasis, however, represented a sharp divergence from the position of Dewey. Among his writings are *Source Book in the Philosophy of Education* (1923), *Foundations of Method* (1925), and *Education and the Social Crisis* (1932).

Kilung: see CHI-LUNG, Taiwan.

Kimball, Fiske (Sidney Fiske Kimball), 1888–1955, American architect and writer, b. Newton, Mass. He was professor of architecture and fine arts at the Univ. of Michigan (1912–19) and of art and architecture at the Univ. of Virginia (1919–23) and was in charge of the fine arts department, New York Univ. (1923–25). From 1925 until his retirement in 1955 he was director of the Philadelphia Museum of Art and was responsible for the acquisition of many important collections. Much of his architectural work consisted of the restoration of old houses, e.g., of Monticello, the Jefferson home, near Charlottesville, and Stratford, the seat of the Lees, both in Virginia. With G. H. Edgell he wrote *A History of Architecture* (1918). He was also the author of *Domestic Architecture of the American Colonies* (1922), *American Architecture* (1928), and *The Creation of the Rococo* (1943).

Kimball, Sumner Increase, 1834–1923, organizer of the U.S. Life-Saving Service, b. Lebanon, Maine. A lawyer, he became (1871) head of the revenue marine service of the Treasury Dept., and his investigations into shipwrecks along the Atlantic coast led to a reorganization of LIFESAVING methods. Kimball commanded the Life-Saving Service from its inception in 1878 until it became part of the U.S. coast guard in 1915. He wrote *Organization and Methods of the U.S. Life Saving Service* (1889) and *Joshua James, Life Saver* (1909).

Kimball, William Wirt, 1848–1930, American naval officer, b. Paris, Maine, grad. Annapolis, 1869. One of the first to serve on torpedo boats, he did much in the 1880s to develop magazine and machine guns, and he designed armored cars. In the '90s he did important work in the development of the submarine, and in the Spanish-American War, having organized the navy's first torpedo-boat flotilla, he commanded the Atlantic torpedo-boat flotilla. Kimball was made rear admiral in 1908, and in 1909 he commanded the expeditionary forces sent to Nicaragua. He retired from active duty in 1910.

Kimberley (kĭm'bərlē), town (1971 pop. 7,641), SE British Columbia, Canada. At an elevation of more than 3,000 ft (914 m), it is the site of the Sullivan mine, where large quantities of silver, lead, and zinc are mined.

Kimberley (kĭm'bərlē), city (1970 pop. 113,681), Cape Prov., central South Africa. The city is primarily a diamond-mining center, although textiles, construction materials, and machinery are manufactured. The city is also an important railroad junction. Kimberley was founded in 1871 when diamonds were discovered on a nearby farm. The De Beers Consolidated Mines, organized by Cecil RHODES, assumed control of the diamond fields in 1888. In 1899–1900, during the SOUTH AFRICAN WAR, the city was besieged by BOER forces. Northern Cape Technical College, Alexander McGregor Memorial Museum, and the Duggan-Cronin Bantu Gallery are in Kimberley.

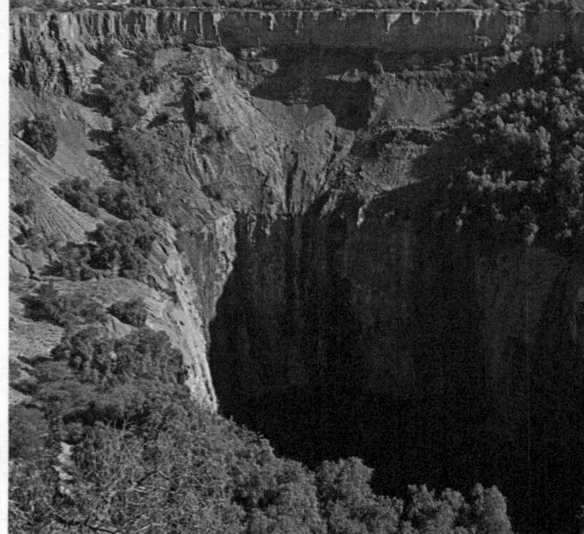

Kimberley Mine, now abandoned, in Kimberley, South Africa.

Kimberley, geographical area, c.139,000 sq mi (360,010 sq km), Western Australia, NW Australia. The Kimberley Goldfield was the site (1882) of the first major Western Australian gold strike. Little gold was mined after 1900.

kimberlite: see DIAMOND.

Kimhi (kĭm'hē) or **Kimchi** (kĭm'khē), family of Jewish scholars and grammarians in Spain and France. **Joseph ben Isaac Kimhi,** 1105?–1170?, besides writing a Bible commentary, making numerous translations, and writing poems of merit, introduced the long and short divisions of Hebrew vowels (increasing their number from 7 to 10) and elaborated the passive verb forms. He is the author of what may be the first European Jewish anti-Christian polemic, *Sefer Ha-Berit.* **Moses Kimhi,** d. 1190?, son of Joseph, wrote *The Paths of Knowledge*, a grammatical textbook, which is a mine of philological information and which was heavily used by the 16th cent. Christian Hebraists. **David Kimhi,** known as Redak, 1160?–1235?, another son, wrote *Mikhlol* [completeness], long the leading Hebrew grammar, *The Book of Roots,* a dictionary of the Bible, and *The Pen of the Scribe,* a manual of punctuation. His learned and lucid commentaries on the Old Testament were included in the standard editions of the Hebrew Bible. The Latin translations of his commentaries greatly influenced Christian translators of the Bible.

Kim Il Sung (kēm ēl so͝ong), 1912–, North Korean political leader, chief of state of the Democratic People's Republic of Korea (1948–); originally named Kim Sung Chu. While fighting Japanese occupation forces in the 1930s, he renamed himself Kim Il Sung after a famous Korean guerrilla leader of the early 20th cent. He was trained in Moscow before World War II, and in 1945 he became chairman of the Soviet-sponsored People's Committee of North Korea. In 1948, when the People's Republic was established, he became its first premier. Between 1950 and 1953 he led his nation in the KOREAN WAR. In 1972 he relinquished the premiership, but retained his position as North Korea's leader by assuming the presidency under a revised constitution. Under his rule, North Korea increased its military forces, embarked on a program of industrialization, and maintained close relations with both Communist China and the Soviet Union.

Kinabalu or **Kinibalu, Mount** (both: kĭn″əbəlo͞o′), peak, 13,455 ft (4,101 m) high, N Sabah, Malaysia, NE of Kota Kinabalu; highest peak on Borneo.

Kinah (kī′nə), unidentified town, extreme S Palestine. Joshua 15.22.

Kincardine (kĭnkär′dĭn, kĭng-), town (1971 pop. 3,239), S Ont., Canada, on Lake Huron, W of Walkerton. It is a resort, with knitting and woolen mills and a furniture factory. Just to the north is Douglas Point, the site of a nuclear power plant.

Kincardineshire (kĭngkär′dĭnshĭr), county (1971 pop. 26,050), 379 sq mi (982 sq km), E Scotland; sometimes called the Mearns. STONEHAVEN is the county town. The Grampian mountains, which extend into the county, rise to 2,555 ft (779 m) at Mt. Battock and slope to a fertile lowland between the Dee and the North Esk rivers behind the rocky coast. Pastoral agriculture (sheep and dairy and beef cattle) is more important than cultivation (oats, barley, and potatoes). Fishing is pursued from North Sea ports. Woolens, whiskey, and leather goods are made at Stonehaven; Johnshaven and Inverbervie have flax-spinning factories. Kincardineshire, long inhabited by Picts, was occupied briefly by the Romans. Remains of their forts and of Pictish castles are found in the county. Dunnottar Castle was a seat of the earls marischal of Scotland. In 1975, Kincardineshire became part of the Grampian region.

Kinchinjunga: see KANCHENJUNGA.

kindergarten (Ger., = garden of children), system of preschool education. Friedrich FROEBEL designed (1837) the kindergarten to provide an educational situation less formal than that of the elementary school but one in which children's creative play instincts would be organized constructively. Through the use of songs, stories, games, simple manual materials, and group activities for which the furnishings of a kindergarten are adapted, children develop habits of cooperation and application, and the transition from home to school is thought to be made less formidable. The theory implicit in the kindergarten system, that education develops through expression and social cooperation, has greatly influenced elementary education and PARENT EDUCATION, especially in the United States, where kindergartens are generally a part of public school systems. The first kindergarten in America was founded (1856) at Watertown, Wis., by Margaretta Schurz, wife of Carl Schurz. It was followed by a school opened (1861) by Elizabeth Peabody in Boston and by a public kindergarten established (1873) in St. Louis by Susan Blow. See also NURSERY SCHOOL. See J. C. Foster and N.E. Headley, *Education in the Kindergarten* (4th ed., 1965); Helen Peterson, *Kindergarten: the Key to Child Growth* (1958); H. F. Robison, *New Directions in the Kindergarten* (1965); Clancy Goode, *World of Kindergarten* (1970).

Kinderhook (kĭn′dərho͝ok″), village (1970 pop. 1,233), Columbia co., SE N.Y.; settled before the Revolution, inc. 1838. Richard Upjohn designed St. Paul's Church (1851) there. Martin Van Buren was born and is buried in Kinderhook; the Van Buren homestead, "Lindenwald," is south of the village. The House of History, maintained by the county historical society, occupies an early 19th-century mansion.

Kindi, al- (Abu Yusuf Yakub ibn Ishak al-Kindi) (ä′-bo͞o yo͞oso͞of′ yäko͞ob′ ĭb′ən ēshäk′ ăl-kĭn′dē), 9th cent. Arab philosopher, b. Basra, Iraq. He studied at Basra and at Baghdad and is noted as one of the earliest scholars in the Middle East to become thoroughly versed in the writings of Aristotle. In his own teachings al-Kindi undertook to demonstrate the essential harmony between the views of Plato and those of Aristotle. His philosophical ideas show some elements of NEOPLATONISM. He is regarded as one of the Peripatetics in Islam, and, as one of the earliest of the Muslim philosophers of Arabic descent, he has been called "the philosopher of the Arabs." He emphasized the righteousness as well as the unity of God and considered that the Creator revealing Himself in prophecy was a reasonable truth and the highest form of knowledge. In his doctrine of manifold intelligence, he defined four types of reason. Besides his translations and commentaries on Aristotle's works, he produced over 250 treatises on a great variety of subjects; although only a few on medicine and astrology are extant, in the 1940s 24 of his hitherto unknown philosophical works were found. Al-Kindi was well known to the Christian scholars of the Middle Ages. He wrote strongly in opposition to alchemy and some kinds of belief in miracles. Al-Kindi's library was confiscated later in his life by the caliph al-Mutawakkil, who looked upon philosophy with suspicion.

Kindia (kĭn′dyə), town (1964 est. pop. 25,000), W Guinea. It is the trade center for an area where bananas, manioc, rice, fruits, and vegetables are grown and bauxite is mined. The bottling of tonic water and the manufacture of soap are carried on in the town, and wood is processed for use in furniture factories outside Conakry. Kindia has a fruit research center.

kinematics: see DYNAMICS.

Kineshma (kē′nyĭshmə), city (1970 pop. 96,000), N central European USSR, on the Volga River. A river port and a rail terminus, it is an old textile center with sawmills and chemical plants.

kinetic art, term referring to sculptured works that include motion as a significant dimension. The form was pioneered by Marcel DUCHAMP, Naum GABO, and Alexander CALDER. Kinetic art is either nonmechanical, e.g., Calder's MOBILES, or mechanical, e.g., works by Gabo and Jean TINGUELY. The latter sort of kineticism developed in response to an increasingly technological culture.

kinetic-molecular theory of gases, physical theory that explains the behavior of gases on the basis of the following assumptions: (1) Any gas is composed of a very large number of very tiny particles called molecules; (2) The molecules are very far apart compared to their sizes, so that they can be considered as points; (3) The molecules exert no forces on one another except during rare collisions, and these collisions are perfectly elastic, i.e., they take place within a negligible span of time and in accordance with the laws of mechanics. A gas corresponding to these assumptions is called an *ideal gas*; as the temperature of a real gas is lowered, or its pressure is raised, its behavior no longer resembles that of an ideal gas because one or more of the assumptions of the theory is no longer valid. The analysis of the behavior of an ideal gas according to the laws of mechanics leads to the general gas law, or ideal gas law: The product of the pressure and volume of an ideal gas is directly proportional to its absolute temperature, or $PV = kT$ (see GAS LAWS). Boyle's law, Charles's law, and Gay-Lussac's law, which are special cases of the general gas law, may also be easily derived. The theory further shows that the absolute temperature is directly proportional to

Billie Jean King.

the average kinetic energy of the molecules, thus providing an interpretation of the nature of temperature in general in terms of the detailed structure of matter (see TEMPERATURE; KELVIN TEMPERATURE SCALE). Pressure is seen to be the result of large numbers of collisions between the molecules and the walls of the container in which the gas is held. See THERMODYNAMICS.

kinetics: see DYNAMICS.

kinetin, one of a group of chemically similar plant hormones, the cytokinins, that promote cell division. In some instances kinetin acts together with another hormone, indoleacetic acid, or AUXIN; in other cases it acts in opposition to auxin.

King, Billie Jean, 1943–, American tennis player, b. Long Beach, Calif. Her original name was Billie Jean Moffitt. She began playing tennis at age 11 and enjoyed success from age 15 when she won the S California championship in her age group. In 1961 (and again in 1962, 1965, 1967, 1968, 1971, and 1972) she won the women's doubles title at Wimbledon and the singles title in 1966, 1967, 1968, 1972, 1973, and 1975. She was the U.S. Lawn Tennis women's singles champion in 1967, 1971, 1972, and 1974. In 1973 she defeated Bobby RIGGS in a "battle of the sexes." An aggressive hard-hitting competitor, she turned professional in 1968. Active in the women's rights movement, particularly in the area of equality of wages, she began publishing (1974) with her husband Larry King, a magazine, *Womensport.* See her autobiography written with Kim Chapin (1974).

King, Charles Bird, 1785–1862, American portrait painter, b. Newport, R.I. He studied under Edward Savage and with Benjamin West in London. His work, executed in Washington, D.C., included Indian portraits for a 3-volume work on the tribes of North America, still lifes, and portraits of eminent Americans. His portraits of Henry Clay and John C. Calhoun are in the Corcoran Gallery, Washington, D.C.

King, Ernest Joseph, 1878–1956, American admiral, commander in chief of the U.S. fleet (1941–45), b. Lorain, Ohio. A graduate of Annapolis, he distinguished himself in many branches of naval service, including the submarine and air arms. In World War I he was assistant chief of staff to Admiral Henry T. Mayo, commander of the Atlantic Fleet. King himself commanded (Feb.–Dec., 1941) the Atlantic Fleet and then became commander of the U.S. naval forces. King also became (March, 1942) chief of naval operations and directed the naval strategy that took the U.S. fleet into Japanese waters. He was made (1944) admiral of the fleet ("five-star admiral") and retired from the navy a year later. See his autobiographical *Fleet Admiral King: A Naval Record* (with W. M. Whitehill, 1952).

King, Henry, 1592–1669, English poet. He became bishop of Chichester in 1642. Elegies constitute nearly half his work, his most notable being "The Exequy," written on the death of his young wife. However, he is chiefly remembered for his love poem "Tell me no more how fair she is." See his poems, ed. by Margaret Crum (1965); Ronald Berman, *Henry King & the Seventeenth Century* (1964).

King, Henry Churchill, 1858–1934, American theologian and educator, b. Hillsdale, Mich. At Oberlin from 1884, he taught in succession mathematics, philosophy, and theology. He was president of the college from 1902 to 1927. Prominent in the councils of the Congregational Church, he was moderator (1919–21) of its National Council and chairman (1921–27) of the Congregational Foundation for Education. Among his many books are *Rational Living* (1905), *The Ethics of Jesus* (1910), *Fundamental Questions* (1917), and *Seeing Life Whole* (1923). See study by Ronald Berman (1964).

King, James Gore: see KING, RUFUS.

King, John Alsop: see KING, RUFUS.

King, Martin Luther, Jr., 1929–68, American clergyman and civil rights leader, b. Atlanta, Ga., grad. Morehouse College (B.A., 1948), Crozer Theological Seminary (B.D., 1951), Boston Univ. (Ph.D., 1955). The son of the pastor of the Ebenezer Baptist Church in Atlanta, King was ordained in 1947 and became (1954) minister of a Baptist church in Montgomery, Ala. He led the boycott (1955–56) by Montgomery blacks against the segregated city bus lines, and he attained national prominence by advocating a policy of passive resistance to segregation. In 1956, he gained a major victory and prestige as a civil rights leader when the Montgomery buses began to operate on a desegregated basis. After the Montgomery success, King organized the Southern Christian Leadership Conference, which gave him a base to pursue further civil rights activities, first in the South and later nation-wide. His philosophy of nonviolent resistance led to his arrest on numerous occasions in the 1950s and 60s. He organized (1963) the massive March on Washington, which brought more than 200,000 people together. In 1964 he was awarded the Nobel Peace Prize. King's leadership in the civil rights movement was challenged in the mid-1960s as others grew more militant. However, King's interests widened from civil rights to criticism of the Vietnam War and to a deeper concern for poverty. His plans for a Poor People's March to Washington were interrupted (1968) for a trip to Memphis, Tenn., in support of striking sanitation workers. On April 4, 1968, he was shot and killed by an assassin's bullet on the balcony of the motel where he was staying. James Earl Ray was later convicted of his murder. See his *Stride Toward Freedom* (1958), *Why We Can't Wait* (1964), and *Where Do We Go From Here: Chaos or Community?* (1967). See biographies by W. R. Miller (1968), C. E. Lincoln, ed. (1970), D. L. Lewis (1971), J. A. Bishop (1971), L. G. Davis (1969, repr. 1973), K. L. Smith and I. G. Zepp, Jr. (1974); Coretta King, *My Life With Martin Luther King, Jr.* (1969).

King, Rufus, 1755–1827, American political leader, b. Scarboro, Maine (then a district of Massachusetts). He served briefly in the American Revolution and practiced law in Massachusetts before serving (1783–85) as a member of the Massachusetts General Court. He was (1784–87) a delegate to the Continental Congress, where he helped draft the Ordinance of 1787 and was chiefly responsible for the exclusion of slavery from the Northwest Territory. At the Federal Constitutional Convention (1787), he was an effective supporter of a strong central government and helped to secure Massachusetts's ratification of the Constitution. Moving to New York City, King was elected to the state assembly and was chosen (1789) as one of New York's first two U.S. Senators. He strongly supported Alexander Hamilton's financial measures and later defended Jay's Treaty. As minister to Great Britain (1796–1803) he reconciled many differences between the two countries and proved himself an able diplomat. He was the unsuccessful Federalist party candidate for Vice President in 1804 and 1808 and for President in 1816. From 1813 to 1825 he again served as U.S. Senator. Although at first an opponent of the War of 1812, he later came to support the administration's war measures. King opposed the Missouri Compromise and advocated solving the slavery problem by emancipating and colonizing the Negroes outside the country on the proceeds of the sale of public lands. In 1824 he declined reelection but was again minister to Great Britain (1825–26). Charles King (1789–1867) was his son. See Charles King, ed., *The Life and Correspondence of Rufus King* (6 vol., 1894–1900, repr. 1971); biography by E. H. Brush (1926); study by Robert Ernst (1968).

King, William, 1650–1729, Irish clergyman and author. He was made archbishop of Dublin in 1702. An ardent believer in the rights of the Church of Ireland, he published in 1691 his *State of the Protestants in Ireland under the late King James's Government.* His chief work is *De origine mali* (1702, tr. 1730).

King, William, 1663–1712, English poet. He supported the Tory and High Church party. He is noted for his humorous and satirical writings, which include *Dialogues of the Dead* (attacks against Richard Bentley, pub. 1699) and *Miscellanies in Prose and Verse* (1709).

King, William Lyon Mackenzie, 1874–1950, Canadian political leader, b. Kitchener, Ont.; grandson of William Lyon Mackenzie. An expert on labor questions, he served in Wilfrid Laurier's Liberal administration as deputy minister of labor (1900–1908) and minister of labor (1909–1911) and was editor (1900–1908) of the *Labour Gazette.* He first served in the House of Commons from 1909 to 1911, and during World War I he was engaged (1914–1917) in investigating industrial relations in the United States. Chosen in 1919 to succeed Laurier as leader of the Liberal party, Mackenzie King led the opposition in Parliament until 1921, when he became prime minister, a post he filled, except for a brief interval in

Civil rights leader Martin Luther King, Jr., addressing demonstrators during the 1963 March on Washington.

1926, until 1930. Leader of the opposition during Richard Bedford Bennett's government (1930–35), he afterward again served (1935–48) as prime minister. Called upon to guide Canadian affairs during World War II, King enunciated his position in *Canada at Britain's Side* (1941) and *Canada and the Fight for Freedom* (1944). In 1940 he concluded with President Franklin Delano Roosevelt the Ogdensburg Agreement and in 1941, the Hyde Park Declaration; by these Canada and the United States agreed to create a permanent joint board of defense and to cooperate in the production of defense materials. King served as chairman of the Canadian delegation at the conference (1945) in San Francisco to draft the Charter of the United Nations and at the Paris Conference of 1946. With President Harry Truman and Prime Minister Clement Attlee of Great Britain, he signed in 1945 the Washington declaration on atomic energy. See biography by R. M. Dawson (Vol. I, 1958) and H. B. Neatby (Vol. II, 1963); J. W. Pickersgill and D. F. Forster, *The Mackenzie King Record* (4 vol., 1960–70).

King, William Rufus Devane, 1786–1853, U.S. Senator from Alabama (1819–44, 1848–52), b. Sampson co., N.C. A Democratic Congressman from North Carolina (1811–16), he settled (1818) in Alabama and became one of its first Senators. King resigned in 1844 to become minister to France; he successfully urged France to refrain from joining England in a protest against U.S. annexation of Texas. Later he again entered (1848) the Senate. Elected (1852) Vice President under Franklin Pierce, he died in Alabama soon after taking the oath of office.

King Arthur: see ARTHURIAN LEGEND.

kingbird: see FLYCATCHER.

King Charles Land: see KONG KARLS LAND.

king crab: see HORSESHOE CRAB.

king crow: see DRONGO.

king devil: see HAWKWEED.

kingdom, in taxonomy: see CLASSIFICATION.

kingfish, common name for several fishes, among them the CROAKER and POMPANO.

kingfisher, common name for members of the family Alcedinidae, essentially tropical and subtropical land birds, with affinities to trogons and swifts and related to the hornbill. Kingfishers have chunky bodies, short necks and tails, large heads with erectile crests, and strong, long beaks. Most kingfishers are carnivorous. The family is divided into two subfamilies, the fishing and the forest kingfishers, the American species being in the former category. The common eastern American belted kingfisher, *Megaceryle alcyon,* perches above the banks of freshwater streams and dives for small fish, crustaceans, reptiles, amphibians, and aquatic insects, returning to its perch to eat. It is 12 to 14 in. (30–35 cm) long, blue-gray above and white beneath; the female has chestnut breast markings. The Texas kingfisher is green above, has no crest, and is smaller (8 in./20 cm). Of the forest kingfishers, the best known is the Australian kookaburra, *Dacelo gigas,* famous for its laughing cry and valued as a destroyer of harmful snakes and lizards. The related (family Todidae) colorful West Indian tody is insectivorous. The genus *Halcyon,* of the forest kingfishers, is the largest group, comprising some 33 species. Fishing kingfishers nest in deep burrows dug out along streams. The burrows may extend up to 10 ft (300 cm) vertically, and from five to eight eggs are laid in the chamber rounded out at the end of the tunnel. Both male and female share the incubation duties. Many forest kingfishers nest in the same fashion as the fishing kingfishers, but some, e.g., the kookaburra, never go near the water and nest in trees. Kingfishers are classified in the phylum CHORDATA, subphylum Vertebrata, class Aves, order Coraciiformes, family Alcedinidae.

King George's War: see FRENCH AND INDIAN WARS.

King Horn, probably the earliest English-language romance, written c.1250 and containing about 1,500 lines. It is anonymous and is based on an earlier work in French. Emphasizing action and adventure, the poem relates the story of a heroic Scottish prince's successful fight to regain his kingdom after his expulsion by invaders. See edition ed. by Joseph Hall (1901); W. H. French, *Essays on King Horn* (1940).

Kingisepp, town: see SAREMA, USSR.

Kingisepp (kēn"gĭsyĕp'), city, NW European USSR, SW of Leningrad, near the Estonian border, on the Luga River. A river port, it has leather and shoe industries. The site was settled in the 9th cent., and the fortress of Yam was founded there in 1384 as a frontier post of Novgorod. The fortress was taken by Sweden in 1585 and passed to Russia in 1703, when it was renamed Yamburg. In 1922 it was renamed for an Estonian Communist leader.

Kingis Quair, The: see JAMES I, king of Scotland.

kinglet, common name for members of a subfamily of five species of Old and New World warblers, similar to the thrushes and the Old World flycatchers. Kinglets are small birds (4 in./10 cm) with soft, fluffy, olive or grayish green plumage and bright crown patches. Their distribution is circumpolar in the conifer belt. The two American species, the ruby-crowned and golden-crowned kinglets, breed in Canada and winter in Mexico. Similar are the Old World goldcrest and the European firecrest. They are active, insectivorous birds, traveling in loose bands together with nuthatches, woodpeckers, creepers, and titmice. Their hanging nests are purse-shaped. In the same order as the kinglets are the gnatwrens of Central and South America and the gnatcatchers, both of the family Polioptilidae, found from the N United States to Argentina. These dainty, slender birds are colored in soft grays and have thin, pointed bills; they feed on small insects. The blue-gray gnatcatcher of the United States and Mexico is typical of the group. Kinglets are classified in the phylum CHORDATA, subphylum Vertebrata, class Aves, order Passeriformes, family Sylviidae.

Kingman Reef, uninhabited reef, less than 1 sq mi (2.6 sq km), central Pacific, one of the LINE ISLANDS, 1,075 mi (1,730 km) SW of Honolulu. It was discovered by Americans in 1798 and annexed by the United States in 1922. Formerly an airport on the route from Honolulu to Pago Pago, Kingman Reef is now under the jurisdiction of the U.S. navy.

King Philip's War, 1675–76, the most devastating Indian war in New England. The war is named for King Philip, the son of MASSASOIT and chief of the WAMPANOAG INDIANS. His Indian name was Metacom, Metacomet, or Pometacom. Upon the death (1662) of his brother, Alexander (Wamsutta), whom the Indians suspected the English of murdering, Philip became sachem and maintained peace with the colonists for a number of years. However, hostility developed over the steady succession of land sales forced on the Indians by their growing dependence on English goods. Suspicious of Philip, the English colonists in 1671 questioned and fined him and demanded that the Wampanoag surrender their arms, which they did. In 1675 a Christian Indian who had been acting as an informer to the English was murdered, probably at Philip's instigation. Three Wampanoags were tried for the murder and executed. Incensed by this act, the Indians in June, 1675, made a sudden raid on the border settlement of Swansea. Other raids followed; towns were burned and many whites—men, women, and children—were slain. Unable to draw the Indians into a major battle, the colonists resorted to similar methods of warfare in retaliation and antagonized other tribes. The Wampanoag were joined by the Nipmuck and by the NARRAGANSETT INDIANS (after the latter were attacked by the colonists), and soon all the New England colonies were involved in the war. Philip's cause began to decline after he made a long journey west in an unsuccessful attempt to secure aid from the Mohawk. In 1676 the Narragansett were completely defeated and their chief, Canonchet, was killed in April of that year; the Wampanoag and Nipmuck were gradually subdued. Philip's wife and son were captured, and he was killed (Aug., 1676) by an Indian in the service of Capt. Benjamin Church after his hiding place at Mt. Hope (Bristol, R.I.) was betrayed. His body was drawn and quartered and his head exposed on a pole in Plymouth. The war, which was extremely costly to the colonists in men and money, resulted in the virtual extermination of tribal Indian life in S New England and the disappearance of the fur trade. The New England Confederation then had the way completely clear for white settlement. See G. M. Bodge, *Soldiers in King Philip's War* (1891, 3d ed. 1906, repr. 1967); G. W. Ellis and J. E. Morris, *King Philip's War* (1906); J. T. Adams, *The Founding of New England* (1921, repr. 1963); D. E. Leach, *Flintlock and Tomahawk* (1958, repr. 1966).

King Ranch, 1,000,000 acres (404,700 hectares), S Texas, SW of Corpus Christi with headquarters at Kingsville, Texas; one of the largest ranches in the world. Larger than the state of Rhode Island, it has several divisions, of which the best known is Santa Gertrudis, the "home" ranch. The Santa Gertrudis, the only true cattle breed developed in North America, was developed there. Thoroughbred racehorses are also raised on the ranch. The ranch was founded in 1853 by Richard King, a steamboat captain. After King's death, the giant holdings were managed by his son-in-law, Robert Kleberg; later, Kleberg's son succeeded to the management. The property was divided in 1935, but the central ranches are still large enough to resemble a semifeudal domain. Profits from oil and natural-gas rights and farming have been added to income gained from the great beef herds, which total more than 50,000 head.

Kings, county, N.Y.: see BROOKLYN, borough.

Kings, river, 125 mi (201 km) long, rising in three forks in the Sierra Nevada, E Calif., and flowing SW to Tulare Lake in the San Joaquin valley. Its middle and southern forks flow through the great gorges of Kings Canyon National Park (see NATIONAL PARKS AND MONUMENTS, table). Part of the Central Valley project, the Kings River has been linked with the San Joaquin River; Pine Flat Dam (completed 1954) impounds a huge reservoir used for flood control, irrigation, and river regulation.

Kings, books of the Old Testament, originally a single work in the Hebrew canon, called First and Second Kings in the Authorized Version, where they occupy the 11th and 12th place, and called Third and Fourth Kings in the Greek versions and the Western canon (the books of Samuel are called First and Second Kings in this enumeration). They continue the historical narrative of First and Second Samuel from the death of David until the destruction of the southern Hebrew kingdom (Judah), i.e., roughly from 1000 B.C. to 560 B.C. The major divisions of the history are as follows: first, the reign of Solomon (1 Kings 1-11), including the end of David's reign (1 Kings 1-2) and a lengthy account of the Temple (1 Kings 5-8); second, a synchronizing parallel account of the two Hebrew kingdoms (1 Kings 12 to 2 Kings 17), beginning with the division between Rehoboam and Jeroboam (1 Kings 12-14) and including as its major single portion the rise and fall of the house of Ahab of Israel, with which is woven the careers of the prophets Elijah and Elisha (1 Kings 17 to 2 Kings 9); and, third, the end of the southern kingdom (2 Kings 18-25). Although the books of Kings continue Samuel, they differ in having more frequent condemnation and praise of actions. The events of Kings are told with a different point of view in Chronicles. A noteworthy feature is the constant allusion to books containing historical data left out of Kings. The books of Kings have a persistent note of catastrophe caused by the sins of the Jews. See John Gray, *I & II Kings: A Commentary* (1963).

Kings Bay, Spitsbergen: see KONGSFJORDEN.

Kings Canyon National Park: see NATIONAL PARKS AND MONUMENTS (table); SEQUOIA NATIONAL PARK.

King's College, former name of COLUMBIA UNIV.

King's College, University of: see DALHOUSIE UNIV.

King's County, Republic of Ireland: see OFFALY.

Kingsley, Charles, 1819-75, English author and clergyman. Ordained in 1842, he became vicar of Eversley in Hampshire in 1844. From 1848 to 1852 he published tracts advocating CHRISTIAN SOCIALISM. These views were embodied in his first two novels, *Alton Locke* (1850) and *Yeast* (1851), both of which deal with contemporary social problems. In his subsequent novels, including *Hypatia* (1853), *Westward Ho!* (1855), and *Hereward the Wake* (1866), he used historical settings to communicate his ideas. A statement denigrating the Roman Catholic clergy, made by Kingsley in an article, started a controversy with John Henry NEWMAN that resulted in Newman's famous *Apologia*. In 1859, Kingsley was made chaplain to Queen Victoria. From 1860 to 1869 he was professor of modern history at Cambridge and in 1873 was appointed canon of Westminster. Several collections of his sermons were published during his lifetime. Included among his other notable work is the well-known children's book *The Water Babies* (1863). See *Letters and Memories* (ed. by his wife, 2 vol., 1877 repr. 1973); biographies by M. F. Thorp (1937, repr. 1969) and Una Pope-Hennessy (1948, repr. 1973).

King's Lynn, municipal borough (1971 pop. 30,102), Norfolk, E England, on the Great Ouse River near its influx into The Wash. The town's large harbor serves foreign as well as coastal trade and is the base for a fishing fleet. A farm market, it is also a center of fertilizer production, canning, flour milling, beet-sugar refining, shipbuilding, and metalworking. King's Lynn dates from Saxon times. Red Mount Chapel was visited by pilgrims in the 15th and 16th cent. The two market places are interesting for their ancient buildings and for the fairs that are still held.

King snake, of North America, eating another snake.

There is a Norman church and other old buildings. King's Lynn was the birthplace of the novelist Fanny Burney and the mystic Margery Kempe.

Kings Mountain National Military Park: see NATIONAL PARKS AND MONUMENTS (table).

king snake, name for a number of species of the genus *Lampropeltis*, nonvenomous, egg-laying, constricting SNAKES of North America which show much variation in color and markings. The common king snake, or chain snake, (*Lampropeltis getulus*), of the E United States is usually about 3 to 5 ft (90–150 cm) long and black or brown with yellow and white rings or bands that form a chainlike pattern. It eats rodents, birds, and snakes. It is immune to the venom of the rattlesnake and the copperhead, which it kills by constriction. The scarlet king snake (*L. doliata*), has a pattern of black, red, and yellow bands similar to that of the unrelated coral snake. Other less brightly marked varieties of the same species are called milk snakes, because they are reputed by legend to milk cows. King snakes are valuable destroyers of rodents. They are classified in the phylum CHORDATA, subphylum Vertebrata, class Reptilia, order Squamata, family Colubridae.

Kings Peak, Utah: see UINTA MOUNTAINS.

Kingsport, city (1970 pop. 31,938), Hawkins and Sullivan counties, NE Tenn., on the Holston River near the Va. line; inc. 1917. Industries include bookbinding and the manufacture of film, textiles, and plastics. The city, which is encircled by mountains, stands on the site of forts Robinson (1761) and Patrick Henry (1775) on the old Wilderness Road.

Kingston, city (1971 pop. 59,047), S Ont., Canada, on Lake Ontario, near the head of the St. Lawrence River and at the end of Rideau Canal from Ottawa. Kingston has probably the best harbor on the lake. Industries include the manufacture of locomotives, textiles, aluminum products, synthetic yarn, and ceramics. On the site stood FORT FRONTENAC, of great importance in the French and Indian War. The present city was founded by United Empire Loyalists in 1783 and prospered during the War of 1812 as the Canadian naval base for operations against the Americans. From 1841 to 1844 it served as the capital of Canada. Fort Henry, built during the War of 1812 and rebuilt from 1832 to 1836, is now a museum. Kingston is the seat of Queen's Univ. (1842), of the Royal Military College, and of Anglican and Roman Catholic bishoprics and cathedrals. In 1953 the village of Portsmouth was joined to Kingston.

Kingston, city (1970 pop. 111,879), capital and largest city of Jamaica, SE Jamaica. The country's chief port, it has one of the finest harbors in the West Indies and exports sugar, rum, molasses, and bananas. The city's industries include tourism, food processing, and oil refining. Kingston was founded in 1693 on a deep, landlocked harbor. The former capital, Port Royal, at the tip of the long, narrow peninsula forming the harbor, was inundated after an earthquake in 1692; the capital was then moved to Spanish Town and, in 1872, to Kingston. After fire destroyed the new Port Royal in 1703, Kingston became Jamaica's leading commercial city. It has suffered from severe hurricanes and was leveled by an earthquake in 1907. Kingston is famed for its lively calypsos and its relics of buccaneering days. In the suburb of Mona are the University College of the West Indies and the Royal Botanical Gardens, noted especially for their orchids.

Kingston. 1 City (1970 pop. 25,544), seat of Ulster co., SE N.Y., on the Hudson River at the mouth of Rondout Creek; inc. as a village 1805, and as a city through the union (1872) of Kingston and Rondout. The eastern gateway to the Catskill-Shawangunk vacationland and the center of an expanding industrial region, it has plants making electronic computers, farm machinery, and apparel. Fur trading posts were built there between 1611 and 1615. The first permanent settlement (called Wiltwyck) was established in 1652. Kingston served as the first capital of New York state until it was burned by the British in Oct., 1777. Its growth in the early 19th cent. was stimulated by the Delaware and Hudson Canal. Among notable landmarks are many old Dutch stone houses; the senate house (1676), meeting place of the first New York state legislature and now a museum; the old Dutch church (1659) and cemetery (1661); the burial place of James Clinton; and nearby "Slabsides," former cottage of John Burroughs. To the west is Ashokan Reservoir. 2 Borough (1970 pop. 18,325), Luzerne co., NE Pa., on the Susquehanna River opposite Wilkes-Barre; settled 1769, inc. 1857. Although chiefly residential, it has railroad shops and varied manufactures. It was devastated by a flood in June, 1972.

Kingston upon Hull: see HULL, England.

Kingston upon Thames, borough (1971 pop. 140,210) of Greater London, SE England. The borough was created in 1965 by the merger of the municipal boroughs of Kingston upon Thames, Malden and Coombe, and Surbiton. Mainly residential, it has light-engineering works and manufactures electronic equipment. In the 10th cent. several Anglo-Saxon kings were crowned at Kingston upon Thames; the stone believed to have been used during the coronations is preserved in the market place. Kingston College of Further Education and Kingston Polytechnic are in the borough. Kingston Grammar School was founded in 1561.

Kingstown, borough, Republic of Ireland: see DÚN LAOGHAIRE.

Kingstown, town (1970 pop. 17,258), capital of St. Vincent, British West Indies. The chief port of entry, it is also a popular winter resort.

Kingsville, city (1970 pop. 28,915), seat of Kleberg co., S Texas; inc. 1911. It is headquarters of the gigantic KING RANCH, part of which is nearby. The city is a processing center for a farm, oil, and gas area. Large petrochemical and gas plants are in the vicinity. Kingsville is the seat of Texas Arts and Industries (A&I) Univ.

Kingswood, urban district (1971 pop. 30,269), Gloucestershire, SW England. A residential suburb of Bristol, Kingswood has a footwear industry. It is noted for its open-air chapel, which marks the site of Methodist open-air sermons on Hanham Mount by John Wesley and George Whitefield in the 18th cent. In 1974, Kingswood became part of the new nonmetropolitan county of Avon.

King William Island, part of the Arctic Archipelago, in the Arctic Ocean, central Northwest Territories, Canada, between Boothia Peninsula and Victoria Island. The island was discovered (1831) by Sir James C. Ross, who also explored the northern coast. In 1837, Thomas Simpson of the Hudson's Bay Company traced the southern coast. The ships of the expedition of Sir John Franklin were wrecked off the west coast, and the island was further explored by searchers for Franklin, notably John Rae and Sir Francis L. McClintock. Roald Amundsen wintered there in 1903–4 while on his way through the Northwest Passage. See P. F. Cooper, *Island of the Lost* (1961).

King William's War: see FRENCH AND INDIAN WARS.

Kinhwa: see CHIN-HUA, China.

Kinibalu, Mount: see KINABALU, MOUNT, Malaysia.

kinkajou (kĭng'kəjo͞o"), nocturnal, arboreal mammal, *Potos flavus,* found from Mexico to Brazil and related to the RACCOON. It has a long, slender body with soft, short, woolly hair of any of various shades of brown or yellow. Its tail is prehensile and is used to grasp branches when the animal climbs. The kinkajou spends most of its time in trees. It eats small animals, fruits, and honey and is sometimes called honey-bear, a name also applied to a true BEAR of SE Asia. Kinkajous are classified in the phylum CHORDATA, subphylum Vertebrata, class Mammalia, order Carnivora, family Procyonidae.

Kinnarodden: see NORDKYN, CAPE, Norway.

Kinneret, Lake: see GALILEE, SEA OF.

Kino, Eusebio Francisco (āo͞osā'byō fränsēs'kō kē'nō), c.1644–1711, missionary explorer in the American Southwest, b. Segno, in the Tyrol. He was in 1669 admitted to the Jesuit order. A distinguished mathematician, he observed the comet of 1680–81 at Cádiz, publishing his results in his *Exposición astronómica de el* [sic] *cometa* (1681). He arrived as a missionary in New Spain in 1681 and was appointed royal cosmographer to accompany the expedition to colonize Lower California. When the settlement in S California was abandoned, he went to Pimería Alta (now N Sonora and S Arizona), where he labored as a missionary, explorer, and colonizer until his death. He made more than 50 journeys from his base, the mission of Nuestra Señora de los Dolores in Sonora, frequently with only Indian guides as companions. He established agriculture at the missions he founded and brought in cattle, horses, and sheep; he distributed cattle and seed grain among the Indian tribes. In 1701–2 he made two expeditions down the Colorado, on the second reaching the head of the Gulf and proving anew that California was not an island. He was the first to map Pimería Alta on the basis of actual exploration, and his map, published in 1705, and many times reproduced, remained the basis for maps of the region until the 19th cent. His valuable historical and autobiographical chronicle, *Favores celestiales,* was edited by H. E. Bolton as *Kino's Historical Memoir of Pimería Alta* (1919, repr. 1948). See E. J. Burros, *Kino and the Cartography of Northwestern New Spain* (1965); F. J. Smith, J. L. Kessell, and F. J. Fox, *Father Kino in Arizona* (1966).

Kinorhyncha (kĭn"ərĭng'kə), class of organisms belonging to the phylum ASCHELMINTHES.

Kinross, burgh (1971 pop. 2,418), county town of Kinross-shire, E Scotland, on Loch Leven. It is a market town. Kinross House, in the style of an Italian Renaissance mansion, was built for James II of England (then duke of York) in 1685. In 1975, Kinross became part of the Tayside region.

Kinross-shire (kĭnrŏs'shĭr), county (1971 pop. 6,422), 81 sq mi (210 sq km), E Scotland. KINROSS is the county town. The central plain is sheltered by hills to the east and the northwest. Loch Leven lies in SE Kinross-shire. There are stock and dairy farms, and oats and barley are grown. Wool and linen weaving are other industries. Mary Queen of Scots was imprisoned in Loch Leven Castle for 11 months (1567–

68).In 1975, Kinross-shire became part of the Tayside region.

Kinsale (kĭnsāl'), urban district (1971 pop. 1,628), Co. Cork, S Republic of Ireland, on the Bandon River estuary. It is a fishing port and seaside resort. Kinsale was an Anglo-Norman settlement. In 1601, Kinsale was held for 10 weeks by a Spanish force. Charles Fort, built in 1677, was several times the object of siege and was burned by Irish nationalists in 1922. James II landed at Kinsale in 1689. The town surrendered to the English under the duke of Marlborough in 1690. St. Multose Church dates from the 12th cent.

Kinsey, Alfred Charles, 1894–1956, American biologist, b. Hoboken, N.J., grad. Bowdoin (B.S., 1916), Harvard (D.Sc., 1920). He was associated with the Univ. of Indiana from 1920, becoming professor of zoology in 1929. His early work dealt with the life cycle, evolution, geographic distribution, and speciation of the gall wasp. He is most widely known for his later extensive studies of human sexual behavior. His program of research on this subject received financial support from the National Research Council, the Rockefeller Foundation, and the Univ. of Indiana. Kinsey and his assistants interviewed many thousands of individuals in all parts of the country. Their findings met with considerable popular response when they were presented in *Sexual Behavior of the Human Male* (1948) and *Sexual Behavior of the Human Female* (1953). Kinsey's program of studies is continuing at the Institute for Sex Research, Inc., Bloomington, Ind.

Kinshasa (kēn'shäsə), formerly **Leopoldville,** city (1970 pop. 1,323,039), capital of Zaïre, W Zaïre, a port on Stanley (Malebo) Pool of the Congo River. It is Zaïre's largest city and its administrative, communications, and commercial center. Major industries are food and beverage processing, tanning, construction, ship repairing, and the manufacture of chemicals, mineral oils, textiles, and cement. A transportation hub, Kinshasa is the terminus of the railroad from MATADI and of navigation on the Congo River from Kisangani; the international airport is a major link for African air traffic with Europe and the Americas. There is motorboat service to BRAZZAVILLE, Congo Republic, on the opposite bank of Stanley Pool. Kinshasa was founded in 1881 by Henry M. Stanley, the Anglo-American explorer, who named it Leopoldville after his patron, Leopold II, king of the Belgians. In 1898 the rail link with Matadi was completed, and in 1926 the city succeeded Boma as the capital of the Belgian Congo (see ZAÏRE). Its main growth occurred after 1945. A major anti-Belgian rebellion that took place there in Jan., 1959, started the country on the road to independence (June, 1960). In 1966 the city's name was changed from Leopoldville to Kinshasa, the name of one of the African villages that occupied the site in 1881. Modern Kinshasa is an educational and cultural center and is the seat of Lovanium Univ. of Kinshasa (1954), which has an archaeological museum, the National School of Law and Administration, a telecommunications school, a research center for tropical medicine, and a museum of Africana. Historical buildings in the city include the chapel of the American Baptist Missionary Society (1891) and a Roman Catholic cathedral (1914). There is a large stadium (seating capacity about 70,000). An international trade fair is held annually in July.

kinship, relationship by blood or marriage between persons; also, in anthropology and sociology, a system of rules, based on such relationships, governing descent, inheritance, marriage, extramarital sexual relations, and sometimes residence. All societies recognize consanguineal and affinitive ties between individuals, but there is great divergence in the manner of reckoning descent and relationship. Kinship patterns are so specific and elaborate that they constitute an important and independent field of anthropological and sociological investigation. In many societies the concept of kinship extends beyond FAMILY ties, which vary in breadth and inclusiveness, to less precisely defined groupings such as the CLAN, where consanguinity is often hypothetical if not actually mythological. As a rule, however, these groups maintain INCEST rules as strict as those for close biological relatives. See Robin Fox, *Kinship and Marriage* (1967); Ira Buchler and H. A. Selby, *Kinship and Social Organization* (1968); Bernard Farber, *Comparative Kinship Systems* (1968); J. R. Goody, *Comparative Studies in Kinship* (1969).

Kinston, city (1970 pop. 23,020), seat of Lenoir co., E N.C., on the Neuse River; settled c.1740, inc. 1849. It is a market for bright leaf tobacco and an industrial city where lumber, textiles, and fertilizers are produced. A junior college is in Kinston.

Kintyre (kĭntīr'), peninsula, 42 mi (68 km) long and 10 mi (16 km) wide, Argyllshire, W Scotland, joined to the mainland at the isthmus of Tarbert between East Loch Tarbert and West Loch Tarbert. The Mull of Kintyre, at the southwestern tip, is 13 mi (21 km) from Ireland. The terrain is hilly and uncultivated. Campbeltown is the main town.

Kioga: see KYOGA, lake, Africa.

Kiowa Indians (kī'əwə), North American Indians, whose language is thought to form a branch of the Aztec-Tanoan linguistic stock (see AMERICAN INDIAN LANGUAGES). The Kiowa, a nomadic people of the Plains area, had several distinctive traits, including a pictographic calendar and the worship of a stone image, the *taimay*. In the 17th cent. they occupied W Montana, but by about 1700 they had moved to an area SE of the Yellowstone River. Here they came into contact with the Crow Indians, who gave the Kiowa permission to settle in the Black Hills. While living there, they acquired (c.1710) the horse, probably from the Crow. Their trade was mainly with the Arikara, the Mandan, and the Hidatsa. After the invading Cheyenne and the Sioux drove the Kiowa from the Black Hills, they were forced to move south to Comanche territory; in 1790, after a bloody war, the Kiowa reached a permanent peace with the Comanche. According to Lewis and Clark, the Kiowa were on the North Platte River in 1805, but not much later they occupied the Arkansas River region. Later the Kiowa, who allied themselves with the Comanche, raided as far south as Durango, Mexico, attacking Mexicans, Texans, and Indians, principally the Navaho and the Osage. In 1837 the Kiowa were forced to sign their first treaty, providing for the passage of Americans through Kiowa-Comanche land; the presence of settlers in increased numbers accelerated hostilities. After 1840, when the Kiowa made peace with the Cheyenne, four groups—the Kiowa, the Cheyenne, the Comanche, and the Apache—combined to fight the eastern Indians, who had migrated to Indian Territory. This caused more hostility between the Indians and the U.S. government, and U.S. forces finally defeated the confederacy and imposed the Treaty of Medicine Lodge (1867). This confederated the Kiowa, the Comanche, and the Apache and provided that they should settle in

Oklahoma. However, parts of the Kiowa remained hostile until the mid-1870s. Oncoming settlers, unaware of treaty rights, caused friction with the Kiowa, resulting in a series of minor outbreaks. In 1874 the Kiowa were involved in a serious conflict, which was suppressed by the U.S. army. American soldiers killed the horses of the Kiowa, and the government deported the Kiowa leaders to Florida. By 1879 most of them were settled on their present reservation in Oklahoma, where they number about 2,000. The **Kiowa Apache,** a small group of North American Indians traditionally associated with the Kiowa from the earliest times, now live with them on their reservation. The Kiowa Apache retain their own language. See R. H. Lowie, *Societies of the Kiowa* (1916); A. L. Marriott, *Kiowa Years* (1968); M. P. Mayhall, *The Kiowas* (rev. ed., 1972).

Kipawa: see TÉMISCAMING, Que., Canada.

Kipchaks: see CUMANS.

Kipling, Rudyard, 1865–1936, English author, b. Bombay, India. Educated in England, Kipling returned to India in 1882 and worked as an editor on a Lahore paper. His early poems were collected in *Departmental Ditties* (1886), *Barrack-Room Ballads* (1892), and other volumes. His first short stories of Anglo-Indian life appeared in *Plain Tales from the Hills* (1888) and *Soldiers Three* (1888). In 1889 he returned to London, where his novel *The Light That Failed* (1890) appeared. Kipling's masterful stories and poems interpreted India in all its heat, strife, and ennui. His romantic imperialism and his characterization of the true Englishman as brave, conscientious, and self-reliant did much to enhance his popularity. These views are reflected in such well-known poems as "The White Man's Burden," "Loot," "Mandalay," "Gunga Din," and *Recessional* (1897). In London in 1892, Kipling married Caroline Balestier, an American, and lived in Vermont for four years. There he wrote children's stories, *The Jungle Book* (1894) and *Second Jungle Book* (1895), *Kim* (1901), *Just So Stories* (1902), and *Captains Courageous* (1897). Returning to England in 1900, he lived in Sussex, the setting of *Puck of Pook's Hill* (1906). Other works include *Stalky and Co.* (1899) and his famous poem "If" (1910). England's first Nobel Prize winner in literature (1907), he was buried in Westminster Abbey. See his *Something of Myself* (1937); biographies by C. E. Carrington (1955) and J. I. M. Stewart (1966); studies by J. M. S. Tompkins (2d ed. 1965), Bonamy Dobrée (1967), and V. A. Shashane (1973).

Kipnis, Alexander, 1891–, Russian-American operatic bass. He studied conducting at the Warsaw Conservatory and voice in Berlin. He made his operatic debut (1915) in Hamburg. Imprisoned by the Germans in World War I as an enemy alien, he was freed and permitted to sing in Wiesbaden. From 1922 to 1925 he was the principal bass of the Berlin Opera Company. He appeared with the Chicago Opera Company (1924–32) and toured extensively. His debut at the Metropolitan Opera House (1940) was as Gurnemanz in *Parsifal.* He is noted for his performance of the role of Boris Godunov.

Kir (kûr). **1** Unidentified land to which Tiglath-pileser III banished the Syrians, credited by Amos as the original home of the Aramaeans. 2 Kings 16.9; Isa. 22.6; Amos 1.5; 9.7. **2** Place in Moab, identified with Kir-haraseth, Kir-hareseth, Kir-haresh, and Kir-heres. 2 Kings 3.25; Isa. 15.1; 16.7, 11; Jer. 48.31, 36.

Kirby, William, 1817–1906, Canadian author, b. England. He was a journalist and civil servant. Besides volumes of verse and tales, he wrote *The Golden Dog* (1877), also published as *Le Chien d'or* (1884), a popular romance of 17th-century Quebec.

Kirby-Smith, Edmund: see SMITH, EDMUND KIRBY.

Kircher, Athanasius (ätänä'zēo͞os kĭrkh'ər), 1601?–1680, German Jesuit archaeologist, mathematician, biologist, and physicist. He was interested in all branches of science, especially in subterranean phenomena (volcanic forces in particular), in the deciphering of hieroglyphics, and in linguistic relations. At first professor of ethics and mathematics at the Univ. of Würzburg, he later became (1635) professor of physics, mathematics, and Oriental languages at the College of Rome, resigning in 1643 to devote himself to archaeological research. His studies with the microscope led him to the belief, which he was possibly the first to hold, that disease and putrefaction were caused by the presence of invisible living bodies. He also perfected the aeolian harp. His remarkable collection of antiquities became the nucleus of the Museum Kircherianum of the College of Rome. His writings filled 44 folio volumes and included an autobiography.

Kirchhoff, Gustav Robert (go͞os'täf rō'bĕrt kĭrkh'-hôf), 1824–87, German physicist. He served as professor of physics at the universities of Breslau (1850–54), Heidelberg (1854–74), and Berlin (from 1875). He is known especially for his work with the SPECTROSCOPE in association with R. W. Bunsen, with whom he discovered the elements cesium and rubidium, and for his explanation of the Fraunhofer lines in the solar SPECTRUM. He also did important research in electricity (he formulated KIRCHHOFF'S LAWS) and thermodynamics.

Kirchhoff's laws [for Gustav R. Kirchhoff], pair of laws stating general restrictions on the current and voltage in an electric network or CIRCUIT. The first of these states that at any given instant the sum of the voltages around any closed path, or loop, in the net-

Sick Woman, *by the German expressionist Ernst Kirchner.*

work is zero. The second states that at any junction of paths, or node, in a network the sum of the currents arriving at any instant is equal to the sum of the currents flowing away.

Kirchner, Ernst Ludwig (ĕrnst lo͝otʹvĭkh kĭrkhʹnər), 1880–1938, German expressionist painter and graphic artist. He studied art in Munich and was greatly impressed by the neo-impressionists. Kirchner studied Oceanic and other primitive sculpture at the Dresden Museum of Ethnology in 1904. This art was of great importance for him and for the movement known as the BRÜCKE, which he cofounded the following year. Also inspired by late Gothic woodcuts and the art of Edvard Munch, Van Gogh, and the Fauves, Kirchner merged their expressive forces into powerful and original creations. With startling contrasts of pure color and aggressive forms, Kirchner explored the world of night cafés and the streets of metropolitan Berlin. His savagely executed woodcuts are among the outstanding works in this medium produced in the 20th cent. and are among the most powerful creations of the expressionist vision. He suffered an emotional breakdown in 1914 and moved to a sanatorium in Davos, Switzerland, after World War I. In the next few years, his art became less tortured and more abstract. In 1938, following the Nazi condemnation of "degenerate art," including some 600 of Kirchner's works, the artist, in failing health, committed suicide. Characteristic works are the portrait of Erich Heckel and his wife (Smith College Mus.); *The Street* (1913; Mus. of Modern Art, New York City); and the illustrations for *Peter Schlemihl* (1916). See biographical study by D. E. Gordon (1968).

Kirchner, Leon, 1919–, American composer, b. Brooklyn, N.Y. Kirchner studied at the Univ. of California at Berkeley with Ernest Bloch, Arnold Schoenberg, and Roger Sessions. He became professor of music at Harvard in 1961. Although he uses many of the most modern techniques of composition, including electronics, he is a self-proclaimed romantic. Among his works are two piano concertos (1953 and 1963); three string quartets (1949, 1958, and 1967), the third for strings and tape; and the opera *Lily,* in progress in 1974.

Kirghiz Soviet Socialist Republic (kĭrgēzʹ, kûrʹgēz, Rus. kĭrgēsʹ), **Kirghizia** (kĭrgēʹzhə), or **Kirghizstan** (kĭrgēstänʹ), constituent republic (1970 pop. 2,933,000), c.76,600 sq mi (198,400 sq km), Central Asian USSR. It borders on China in the southeast and on the Kazakh SSR, the Uzbek SSR, and the Tadzhik SSR in the north, west, and southwest. FRUNZE, the capital, and Osh are the chief cities. Kirghizia is a mountainous country in the Tien Shan and Pamir systems, rising to 24,409 ft (7,440 m) at Pobeda Peak on the Chinese border. It has rich pasturage for goats, sheep, cattle, and horses. Over 80% of the cultivated area is irrigated. Cotton, sugar beets, tobacco, fruit, and grapes are grown; sericulture is carried on; and grain crops are cultivated in the nonirrigated areas. There are coal, antimony, lead, tungsten, mercury, uranium, petroleum, and natural gas deposits. Industries include food processing, sugar refining, nonferrous metallurgy, and the manufacture of agricultural machinery, textiles, and building materials. The Kirghiz, a Muslim, Turkic-speaking pastoral people with definite Mongol strains, constitute about one half of the population; the rest are Russians, Uzbeks, and Ukrainians. Formerly known as Kara [black] Kirghiz to distinguish them from the Kazakhs (at one time called Kirghiz), the Kirghiz migrated to Kirghizia from the region of the upper Yenisei, where they had lived from the 7th to the 17th cent. The area came under the rule of the Kokand khanate in the 19th cent. and was gradually annexed by Russia between 1855 and 1876. The nomadic Kirghiz resisted conscription into the czarist army in 1916 and fought the establishment of Bolshevik control from 1917 to 1921. As a result of war devastation, there was a famine in 1921–22 in which over 500,000 Kirghiz died. The area was formed into the Kara-Kirghiz Autonomous Oblast within the Russian Soviet Federated Socialist Republic in 1924, an autonomous republic in 1926, and a constituent republic in 1936. The Kirghiz state university was established in 1951 and the Kirghiz Academy of Sciences in 1954. The republic's cultural life stresses epic poems, tales, and folk songs, and the Kirghiz have traditionally excelled in wood carving, rug weaving, and jewelry making.

Kir-haraseth, Kir-hareseth, Kir-haresh, and **Kir-heres:** see KIR **2.**

Kiriathaim (kĭrʹēəthāʹĭm), town of Moab. Jer. 48.1,23; Ezek. 25.9. Kirjathaim: Num. 32.37; Joshua 13.19.

Kirin (kēʹrĭnʹ), Mandarin *Chi-lin* [propitious forest], province (1968 est. pop. 17,000,000), NE China; one of the original Manchurian provinces. The capital is CH'ANG-CH'UN. It is bordered by the USSR on the northeast, by North Korea on the southeast, and by the Inner Mongolian Autonomous Region on the west. Kirin, crossed by the Sungari River and forming part of the fertile alluvial Manchurian plain, enjoys great agricultural prosperity; soybeans, wheat, upland rice, sweet potatoes, and beans are grown. Mountains in the east rise to more than 9,000 ft (2,740 m). Vast timberlands, among the best in China, are exploited, and iron, coal, gold, and lead are extracted. The province has a good network of railroads, including the line between Shen-yang, Ch'ang-ch'un, and Harbin. and its branches. The population, mainly Chinese, is concentrated in the industrial cities of CH'ANG-CH'UN, CHI-LIN, SSU-P'ING, and LIAO-YÜAN. Near the North Korean border is the Yenpien Korean autonomous region (est. 1952), which has a large Korean population. Kirin Univ. is in CH'ANG-CH'UN.

Kirin, city: see CHI-LIN, China.

Kirioth (kĭrʹēŏth), the same as KERIOTH **1.**

Kirjath (kûrʹjăth), the same as KIRJATH-JEARIM.

Kirjathaim (kərjəthāʹĭm). **1** Town, N Palestine. 1 Chron. 6.76. Kartan: Joshua 21.32. **2** See KIRIATHAIM.

Kirjath-arba: see HEBRON, Jordan.

Kirjath-arim (kûrʹjăth-āʹrĭm) and **Kirjath-baal** (-bāʹəl), alternative names of KIRJATH-JEARIM.

Kirjath-huzoth (kûrʹjăth-hyo͞oʹzŏth), unidentified place, E of the Dead Sea. Num. 22.39.

Kirjath-jearim (kûrʹjăth-jēʹərĭm), ancient fortress and holy place, Palestine, W of Jerusalem. Joshua 9.17; 1 Sam. 6.21; 1 Chron. 2.50, 52; 13.5, 6; 2 Chron. 1.4; Neh. 7.29. Kirjath: Joshua 18.28. Kirjath-arim: Ezra 2.25. Kirjath-baal: Joshua 15.60; Judges 18.12. Baalah: Joshua 15.9, 10. Baale of Judah: 2 Sam. 6.2.

Kirjath-sannah (kûrʹjăth-sănʹə) and **Kirjath-sepher** (-sēʹfər), alternative names of DEBIR **2.**

Kirk, Grayson Louis, 1903–, American educator, b. Jeffersonville, Ohio, grad. Miami Univ., 1924, Ph.D. Univ. of Wisconsin, 1930. He taught at Wisconsin from 1929 to 1940, when he became associate professor of government at Columbia. In 1942 he became full professor of government and in 1947 professor of international relations. After 1959 Kirk served as Bryce Professor of History of International Relations. In 1953 he succeeded Dwight D. Eisenhower as president of Columbia, a post he held until 1968. He is the author of *Philippine Independence* (1936), *Contemporary International Politics* (with W. R. Sharp, 1940), and *The Study of International Relations in American Colleges and Universities* (1947).

Kirk, Norman Eric, 1923–74, New Zealand political leader. A Labour party member, he rose in New Zealand politics, entering Parliament in 1957, and becoming vice president (1963) and then president (1964) of the Labor party. In the Nov., 1972, elections Kirk's party gained a parliamentary majority and he assumed the posts of prime minister and foreign minister. He was a supporter of increased social security, housing, and welfare benefits.

Kirkaldy of Grange, Sir William (kərkôl'dē), d. 1573, Scottish soldier and politician. Associated with his father in the murder of Cardinal BEATON in 1546, he was captured by the French in 1547 and held prisoner in France until 1550, when he escaped to become a secret agent of England in France. On the accession of Mary I to the English throne in 1553 he entered the service of the king of France. Pardoned for his part in the murder of Beaton, he returned to Scotland in 1557 and became a prominent Protestant leader. He opposed the marriage of MARY QUEEN OF SCOTS to Lord Darnley and was implicated in the assassination of Rizzio. After Mary's marriage to Lord Bothwell, Kirkaldy was the leader to whom the queen surrendered at Carberry Hill in 1567. While she was a prisoner in England, Kirkaldy shifted his allegiance to Mary's supporters and held Edinburgh castle for her, bringing upon himself the denunciation of his former friend, John Knox, and of other Presbyterian leaders. In 1573 he was forced to surrender the castle to an Anglo-Scottish force and was hanged.

Kirkcaldy (kərkô'dē, -kôl'-), burgh (1971 pop. 50,338), Fife, E Scotland, on the Firth of Forth. It is composed of seven villages, including Dysart, strung along the shore, giving rise to the name "Lang Toun." It is one of the largest producers of linoleum and oilcloth in Great Britain. Other industries include textile printing and the manufacture of farm machinery. The port is engaged in coastal trade. The city is the birthplace of Adam Smith.

Kirkcudbright (kûrko͞o'brē), burgh (1971 pop. 2,506), county town of Kirkcudbrightshire, SW Scotland, at the head of the Dee estuary. It has granaries and creameries and is a market town and artists' colony. There are traces of an ancient wall and moat and of a McClellan clan castle (1582). In 1975, Kirkcudbright became part of the Strathclyde region.

Kirkcudbrightshire (kûrko͞o'brēshĭr), county (1971 pop. 27,450), 897 sq mi (2,323 sq km), SW Scotland, in the GALLOWAY district. KIRKCUDBRIGHT is the county town. The land is mountainous, sloping to a rugged coastline along the Solway Firth. The Cree, the Dee (the western border), and the Urr are the main rivers. Stock raising and dairy farming are the main occupations; oats, barley, and turnips are also grown. There is a forestry industry. The county has a number of ruined abbeys and castles. In 1975, Kirkcudbrightshire became part of the Strathclyde region.

Kirke, Sir David (kûrk), 1597–1655?, English merchant adventurer, b. France. In 1627 he and his brothers Lewis and Thomas sailed in a fleet outfitted by their father, Gervase Kirke, and Sir William Alexander (later earl of Stirling) on a royal patent to expel the French settlements in Canada and establish a monopoly of trade in Nova Scotia. Near Newfoundland they seized a fleet of French vessels. They then attacked the French stations in Nova Scotia and went back to England with captives and spoils. In 1629, David returned and forced Samuel de CHAMPLAIN to surrender Quebec. Meanwhile Charles I had made peace with France and all French possessions taken after April 24, 1629, had to be restored. Knighted in 1633, Sir David went to Newfoundland in 1638 as governor and colonizer. Royalist in sympathy during the English civil war, he was deprived of his governorship after the execution of the king. A portion of his properties was restored to him shortly before his death. See Henry Kirke, *First English Conquest of Canada* (1871).

Kirkenes (kēr'kənēs), town, Finnmark co., NE Norway, a port on the Varangerfjord, near the Soviet border. It is the processing and shipping center of an iron ore mining region. It was severely damaged in World War II.

Kirkintilloch (kûrkĭntĭl'ŏkh), burgh (1971 pop. 25,185), Dumbartonshire, W Scotland, on the Forth and Clyde Canal. An engineering center, the burgh has factories that produce mining machinery and valves. The electrical power system of S Scotland is controlled from Kirkintilloch. Chartered in the 13th cent., the burgh is located on the line of the Roman Antonine wall. In 1975, Kirkintilloch became part of the Strathclyde region.

Kirkland, Samuel, 1741–1808, American missionary to the Oneida Indians, b. Norwich, Conn. He made a trip among the Oneida in 1764. In 1766 he went among them again and lived with them according to their customs, preached to them, and became their valued counselor. Kirkland kept the Oneida loyal to the colonists throughout the American Revolution; after the war he assisted in making treaties of peace with the Iroquois and in working out plans for their welfare. He again (1790–92) pacified the Six Nations, when there was some danger of their joining the Ohio tribes in revolt. He realized one of his life's ambitions when (1793) he received—through the aid of Alexander Hamilton—a charter from New York state to found Hamilton Oneida Academy for the education of both white and Indian youths. Few Indians attended, however, and as Hamilton College it changed over to a regular curriculum.

Kirkland, city (1970 pop. 15,249), King co., W Wash., a suburb of Seattle on Lake Washington; inc. 1905. Furniture is the principal manufacture.

Kirkland Lake, mining town, E Ont., Canada. It is one of Canada's largest gold-mining centers. Gold was discovered there in 1911.

Kırklareli (kərklär'ĕlĕ"), city (1970 pop. 28,290), capital of Kırklareli prov., NW Turkey. It is a transportation hub and a trade center for butter and cheese. During the First Balkan War the Bulgarians defeated (1912) the Turks there. The city has numerous mosques and Greek churches. It was formerly known as Kırk-Kilise.

Kirksville, city (1970 pop. 15,560), seat of Adair co., N Mo.; inc. 1857. Among its manufactures are shoes, gloves, machinery, and hospital equipment. Andrew Taylor Still founded a school of osteopathy there in 1892; it is now the Kirksville College of Medicine. A state college and a state park are also in the city.

Kirkuk (kĭrkōōk′), city (1965 pop. 167,413), NE Iraq. It is the center of Iraq's oil industry and is connected by pipelines to ports on the Mediterranean Sea. It is also a market for the region's produce, including cereals, olives, fruits, and cotton. There is a small textile industry. Kirkuk is built on a mound containing the remains of a settlement dating back to 3000 B.C. The majority of the inhabitants are Kurds.

Kirkwall (kûrk′wôl, -wəl), burgh (1971 pop. 4,618), county town of Orkney, N Scotland, on the east coast of Mainland Island. It is the trading center of the Orkney Islands, with exports of eggs, fish, whiskey, cattle, and sheep. It is also a boatbuilding center. Kirkwall was founded sometime prior to 1046 (when it was mentioned in a saga) and became important as a port on the northern trade route to Scandinavia and the Baltic states. St. Magnus Cathedral dates from 1137, the bishop's palace from c.1200, and the earl's palace from 1600. The latter two are ruins.

Kirkwood, Samuel Jordan, 1813–94, American politician, b. Harford co., Md. Moving to Ohio in 1835, he served (1845–49) as prosecuting attorney for Richland co. and was a member (1850–51) of the Ohio constitutional convention. After settling in Iowa in 1855, he was elected (1856) to the state legislature and then to the governorship (1860–64). A thoroughgoing radical Republican, he successfully quelled internal dissension and supplied the Union Army with over 50 regiments of infantry and cavalry, partly fitted out with his own money. In 1866–67, Kirkwood filled out a term in the U.S. Senate. He was again governor (1876–77), U.S. Senator (1877–81), and Secretary of the Interior (1881–82). See biography by D. E. Clark (1917).

Kirkwood, city (1970 pop. 31,769), St. Louis co., E Mo., a suburb of St. Louis; inc. 1865. Lime, cement, and lumber products are made. A junior college is in the city.

Kirkwood's gaps, regions in the ASTEROID belt within which no asteroids are found; first observed (1886) by the astronomer D. Kirkwood. None of the asteroids has an orbital period close to ½, ⅓, or ⅖ that of Jupiter. It was at first believed that the orbits of these "missing" asteroids had been altered by a resonant gravitational PERTURBATION caused by Jupiter; recent calculations indicate that the gaps are probably due to mutual interactions of the asteroids themselves.

Kirov, Sergei Mironovich (syĭrgā′ mērô′nəvĭch kē′rəf), 1888–1934, Russian Soviet leader. He fought in the civil war of 1918–20 and rose to power as one of Stalin's most trusted aides. A member of the Communist party Politburo from 1930, he was secretary of the party at Leningrad when he was assassinated, probably at Stalin's order. However, Stalin used Kirov's murder to institute the party purge and the treason trials of the late 1930s. Among those tried and executed were ZINOVIEV, KAMENEV, and RYKOV, who were charged with association with TROTSKY and counterrevolutionary conspiracy.

Kirov (kē′rəf), formerly **Vyatka** (vyät′kə), city (1970 pop. 332,000), capital of Kirov oblast, central European USSR, on the Vyatka River. It is a river port and an industrial center with sawmills and machine and metalworking plants. Founded in 1174 as Khlynov by Novgorod colonists, it was fortified against Votyak (Udmurt) and Cheremiss (Mari) attacks. It soon became the capital of an independent republic which was annexed to Moscow by Ivan III in 1489. Its location made for favorable trade conditions with Ustyug, the Volga region, and Archangelsk. In the 17th cent. it grew in importance because it was on the road from Moscow to Siberia. The city was renamed Vyatka in 1780. In the 19th cent. it was used as a place of political exile. The city was renamed in 1934 for S. M. Kirov. In Kirov are a 17th-century cathedral and a library (1837) founded by Alexander Herzen, who was an exile in the city.

Kirovabad (kē″rəvəbät′), city (1970 pop. 190,000), SE European USSR, in Azerbaijan, on the Gandzha River. The largest Azerbaijan industrial center after Baku, Kirovabad produces cotton and silk textiles, building materials, carpets, cottonseed oil, agricultural implements, copper sulfate, and wine. Formerly named Gandzha or Ganja, it was founded in the 6th cent., c.4 mi (6 km) east of the modern city, but was demolished by earthquake in 1139, after which the survivors settled on the present site. The medieval city was an important textile and wine center. It was destroyed by the Mongols in 1231 and recovered slowly. It was the seat of a khanate under Persian suzerainty from the 17th cent. until its conquest (1804) by the Russians, who named it Elisavetpol. It became Gandzha again after the Russian Revolution, but in 1935 it was renamed in honor of S. M. Kirov. Ancient Gandzha was the native city of the 12th-century poet, Nizami Gandzhevi, whose tomb still remains. There is also a 17th-century mosque.

Kirov Ballet, one of the two major ballet companies of the Soviet Union, the other being the BOLSHOI BALLET. It was originally the Imperial Russian Ballet, performing in St. Petersburg, now Leningrad. Under the direction of Marius PETIPA the company premiered the Tchaikovsky ballets *Sleeping Beauty* (1890) and *Swan Lake* (1895). The company went into decline after the Russian Revolution in 1917. The great teacher and ballet mistress Agrippina Vaganova (1879–1951) helped perpetuate its traditions by training the company's principal dancers. Her work became the foundation of modern Soviet ballet instruction. In 1935 the company was renamed the Kirov Ballet. The Kirov again declined in the 1970s; its repertoire included few new works, and such Kirov stars as Rudolf Nureyev, Natalia Makarova, and Mikhail Baryshnikov had defected.

Kirovograd (kē″rəvəgrät′), city (1972 est. pop. 201,000), capital of Kirovograd oblast, S central European USSR, in the Ukraine, on the Ingul River. It is an agricultural trade center, with one of the USSR's largest farm machinery plants. Other industries include metallurgy, food processing, and the manufacture of building materials. Founded as a fortress in 1754, it was named Elisavetgrad for Empress Elizabeth. Between 1881 and 1919 it was the scene of several pogroms. It was renamed Zinovievsk in 1924, Kirovo in 1936, and Kirovograd in 1939.

Kirovsk (kē′rəfsk), city (1970 pop. 38,000), N European USSR, on the Kola Peninsula. The city is the center of a mining complex that produces apatite and nephelite, raw materials for the superphosphate and aluminum industries. It was founded in 1929 as Khibinogorsk.

kirsch or **kirschwasser** (kĭrsh, -väs′ər) [Ger., = cherry water], a LIQUEUR made principally in France, Germany, and Switzerland from the pulp and crushed stones of the cherry, fermented, then distilled and sweetened. It is distilled in earthenware or paraffin-lined casks to prevent it from taking on the color imparted by wood.

Kırşehir (kŭr″shĕhĕr′), city (1970 pop. 32,580), capital of Kırşehir prov., central Turkey. It is noted for its carpets. Grains are grown nearby.

Kirshon, Vladimir Mikhailovich (vlədyē′mĭr mēkhī′ləvĭch kērshôn′), 1902–38, Russian dramatist. He began his career with *Red Dust* (1927, tr. 1930), a play showing the degeneration of a revolutionist under the reconstruction program known as the New Economic Policy. His play *Bread* (1930, tr. 1934) deals with the struggle against private hoarding on collective farms. The majority of his plays concerned the social problems of the new order. Kirshon was expelled from the Communist party in 1937 because of his leading role in the suspect Russian Association of Proletarian Writers.

Kirstein, Lincoln, 1907–, American dance and theater executive and writer, b. Rochester, N.Y. Kirstein was cofounder of the American Ballet in 1934. In 1948 he helped establish the New York City Ballet, becoming its general director. Together with the choreographer George BALANCHINE he encouraged the development of a truly American style of dance. He is the author of many books including *Dance* (1935), a compendious history; *Ballet Alphabet* (1939); *The Classic Ballet, Basic Technique and Terminology* (with Muriel Stuart, 1952); *Movement and Metaphor* (1970); a history of the New York City Ballet (1973); and the definitive biography of Elie Nadelman (1973). Kirstein was instrumental in recovering for their owners works of art plundered by Nazi officials during World War II. As a producer he has worked with the Shakespeare Memorial Theater at Stratford, Conn., and for many years presented the 12th-century musical drama *The Play of Daniel* annually at Christmas in New York. Kirstein has also promoted cultural exchange programs between Japan and the United States.

Kirun: see CHI-LUNG, Taiwan.

Kiruna (kē′rünä), city (1970 pop. 25,034), Norrbotten co., N Sweden. The northernmost city in Sweden, it is the center of the Lapland iron-mining region. The ore, more than 70% pure, is shipped on the Lapland railroad (completed 1902) either to Narvik, Norway, an ice-free Atlantic port, or to Luleå, Sweden, on the Gulf of Bothnia. Kiruna became the most extensive city (c.5,500 sq mi/14,250sq km) in the world in 1948, when several distant mining villages were incorporated into it. The city is also a winter sports center and has a geophysical institute.

Kiryu (kĭryo͞o′), city (1970 pop. 133,141), Gumma prefecture, central Honshu, Japan. A major center of silk production since the 8th cent., it now manufactures rayon as well.

Kisangani (kēsangä′nē), formerly **Stanleyville,** city (1970 pop. 230,000), capital of Haut-Zaïre region, N central Zaïre, a port on the Congo River. The city is the terminus of steamer navigation on the Congo from Kinshasa and is a transportation center for NE Zaïre. It is on a short rail line (to Ubundi) that skirts the Stanley Falls. Manufactures include metal goods and beer, and cotton and rice are shipped from the city. Founded in 1883 by the explorer Henry M. Stanley and originally located on a nearby island in the river, the city, as Stanleyville, became the stronghold of Patrice Lumumba in the late 1950s. After the assassination of Lumumba in 1961, Antoine Gizenga set up a government there that rivaled the central government in Leopoldville (now Kinshasa). Gizenga's regime was quashed in 1962, but in 1964, 1966, and 1967 the city was the site of temporarily successful revolts against the central government. Kisangani has a university and a museum.

Kisarazu (kēsärä′zo͞o), city (1970 pop. 73,319), Chiba prefecture, E central Honshu, Japan, on Tokyo Bay. It is a residential and industrial suburb of Tokyo noted for its Shojoji (Buddhist) temple.

Kiselevsk (kēsĭ′lyôfsk″), city (1970 pop. 127,000), S Siberian USSR. It is a major coal-mining center in the Kuznetsk Basin and also manufactures mining machinery.

Kisfaludy, Károly (kä′roi kĭsh′fŏlo͞odē), 1788–1830, Hungarian dramatist, founder of the Hungarian national drama. Kisfaludy traveled abroad extensively and studied painting before he returned to Hungary and began his literary career. His *Tatars in Hungary* (1819) was the first genuinely dramatic Hungarian play and the first of the many successes by which he established the national drama and the Hungarian romantic movement. With his brother Sándor he was cofounder (1822), editor, and a major contributor of the vigorous, influential literary journal *Aurora.* Among his works are the comedies *The Suitors* and *The Rebels* and the tragedy *Irene.* His brother, the poet **Sándor Kisfaludy,** 1772–1844, is considered the first major romantic poet of Hungary. He is especially celebrated for his two volumes of love lyrics, *The Loves of Himfy* (1801, 1807).

Kish (kĭsh). **1** Father of Saul. 1 Sam. 9.1; 10.21. Cis: Acts 13.21. **2** Uncle of Saul. 1 Chron. 8.30; 9.36. **3** Ancestor of Mordecai. Esther 2.5. **4** Merarite. 1 Chron. 23.21; 24.29; 2 Chron. 29.12.

Kish, ancient city of Mesopotamia, in the Euphrates valley, 8 mi (12.9 km) E of Babylon and 12 mi (19 km) east of the modern city of Hillah, Iraq. It was occupied from very ancient times, and its remains go back as far as the protoliterate period in Mesopotamia. In the early 3d millennium B.C., Kish was a Semitic city. Although it was one of the provincial outposts of Sumerian civilization, it had a cultural style of its own. There is an excavated palace of Sargon I of Agade, a native of Kish, and a great temple built by Nebuchadnezzar and Nabonidus in the later Babylonian period. The site also yielded a complete sequence of pottery from the Sumerian period to that of Nebuchadnezzar.

Kishi (kĭsh′ī), Levite: see KUSHAIAH.

Kishi, Nobusuke (nōbo͞os′kā kē′shē), 1896–, Japanese statesman. The son of a minor official, he attended the law college of Tokyo Univ. He entered government service in 1920 and rose to high office in the ministry of commerce and industry. After 1935 he played a key role in the industrial development of MANCHUKUO. During World War II he was minister of commerce and industry in Hideki Tojo's cabinet; he was imprisoned for three years after the war. As secretary general of the postwar Democratic party, he was instrumental in uniting all conservative factions into the powerful Liberal Democratic party (1955). He became party president and prime minister in 1957, but widespread public agitation over the new UNITED STATES-JAPAN SECURITY TREATY forced Kishi to resign from both posts in 1960. He was succeeded by Hayato Ikeda. See Dan Kurzman, *Kishi and Japan* (1960).

Kishinev (kĭshĭnyĕf′,–nĕf′), Rumanian *Chisinau,* city (1972 est. pop. 400,000), capital of the Moldavian Soviet Socialist Republic, SW European USSR, on the Byk River, a tributary of the Dnestr. Major industries include food and tobacco processing, metalworking, and the manufacture of building materials, machinery, plastics, rubber, and textiles. Founded in the early 15th cent. as a monastery town, Kishinev was taken in the 16th cent. by the Turks and in 1812 by the Russians, who made it the center of Bessarabia. Rumania held the city from 1918 to 1940, when it was seized by the USSR. The Jewish population, which formerly constituted about 40% of the total, was largely exterminated in World War II. Kishinev's educational and cultural facilities include a university (1945) and the Academy of Sciences of the Moldavian SSR.

Kishion (kĭsh'ēŏn), unidentified Levitical border town, W of the Sea of Galilee. Joshua 19.20. Kishon: Joshua 21.28. Kedesh: 1 Chron. 6.72.

Kishiwada (kēshēwä'dä), city (1970 pop. 162,022), Osaka prefecture, SW Honshu, Japan, on Osaka Bay. It is an industrial and residential suburb of Osaka.

Kishon (kī'shŏn) [Heb. *Qishon*=tortuous], intermittent river, c.45 mi (70 km) long, rising below Mt. Gilboa, N Israel, and flowing NW to the Mediterranean Sea near Haifa; only the lower 7-mi (11.3-km) section is a permanent stream. The defeat of Sisera and the slaying by Elijah of the prophets of Baal occurred on the river bank (Judges 4.7,13; 5.21; 1 Kings 18.40. Kison: Ps. 83.9). For Kishon, the town, see KISHION.

Kiska, island: see ALEUTIAN ISLANDS.

Kiskunfélegyháza (kĭsh'koŏnfā'lĕdyəhä"zŏ), city (1970 pop. 34,127), S central Hungary. It is a road and rail junction; trade and industry are based on the agricultural products of the surrounding region.

Kislovodsk (kēsləvôtsk') [Rus.,=sour water], city (1970 pop. 90,000), S European USSR, in the N Caucasus mts. It is a famous health resort with mineral springs, sanatoriums, and a physico-therapeutical institute. Kislovodsk was founded in 1803.

Kismayu (kĭsmī'ōō), town (1968 est. pop. 18,000), SW Somalia, on the Indian Ocean. It is the principal town and port of the Juba region. Kismayu was founded in 1872 by the sultan of Zanzibar, passed to Great Britain in 1887, and was held until 1924, when it was transferred to Italian control. The town has several mosques and a palace that was constructed by the sultan.

Kispest: see BUDAPEST, Hungary.

Kissidougou (kēsēdōō'gōō), town (1961 est. pop. 12,000), S Guinea. It is a market town for an agricultural area that produces coffee, rice, palm products, kola nuts, and other crops. There are sawmills in the town, and diamonds are mined nearby.

Kissimmee, Lake, 55 sq mi (142 sq km), central Fla.; one of the largest freshwater lakes in Florida. The Kissimmee River, 140 mi (225 km) long, rises in small lakes and flows S through Lake Kissimmee to Lake Okeechobee. The lake and river region is a major U.S. cattle-raising area; truck crops and citrus fruits are also grown.

kissing bug: see ASSASSIN BUG.

Kissinger, Henry Alfred (kĭs'ənjər), 1923–, American political scientist and U.S. Secretary of State (1973–77), b. Fürth, Germany. He emigrated to the United States in 1938 and later became (1943) a citizen. As a leading expert on international relations and nuclear defense policy, Kissinger taught (1957–69) at Harvard and served as a consultant to government agencies and private foundations. The national security adviser (1969–75) to Presidents Nixon and Ford, Kissinger played a major role in the formulation of U.S. foreign policy. Kissinger helped initiate (1969) the Strategic Arms Limitation Talks (SALT) with the Soviet Union and arranged President Nixon's 1972 visit to the People's Republic of China. He supported U.S. disengagement from Vietnam and won (1973) the Nobel Peace Prize for negotiating the cease-fire with North Vietnam. His negotiating skill also led to a cease-fire between Israel and Egypt, and the disengagement of their troops after the 1973 Arab-Israeli War. Kissinger continued in office after Gerald R. Ford succeeded (1974) to the presidency. He is the author of many articles and books, including *Nuclear Weapons and Foreign Policy* (1957), *The Necessity for Choice* (1961), and *The*

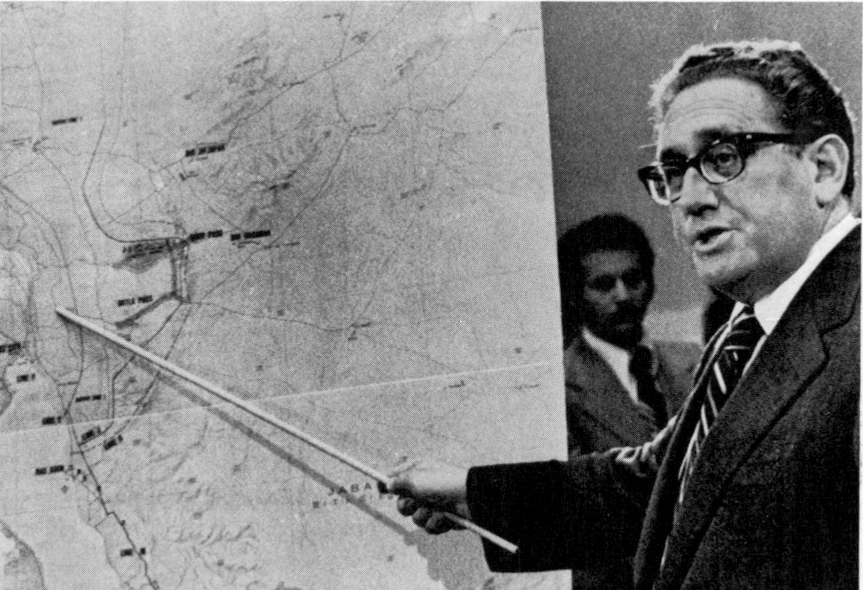

Henry Kissinger.

Troubled Partnership (1965). See biographies by David Landau (1972) and S. R. Graubard (1973); studies by C. R. Ashman (1972) and Bernard and Marvin Kalb (1974).

Kistna (kĭst'nə) or **Krishna** (krĭsh'nə), river, c.800 mi (1,290 km) long, rising in Maharashtra state, central India, in the Western Ghats, and flowing SE through Andhra Pradesh state to the Bay of Bengal. The river supplies water for irrigation. Its source is sacred to Hindus; the river is named for the god Krishna.

Kisumu (kēso͞o'mo͞o), city (1969 pop. 30,700), capital of Nyanza prov., SW Kenya, on Kavirondo Gulf (an arm of Victoria Nyanza). It is the principal lake port of Kenya and the commercial center of a prosperous farm region. Manufactures include refined sugar, frozen fish, textiles, and processed sisal. The railroad from Mombasa reached Kisumu in 1901. The city was formerly called Port Florence.

Kitab al-Aghani (kētäb' äl-ägänē') [Arabic,=book of songs], collection of poems in many volumes compiled by ABU AL-FARAJ ALI OF ESFAHAN. It contains poems from the oldest epoch of Arabic literature down to the 9th cent. The poems were put to music, but the musical signs are no longer readable. Because of the accompanying biographical annotations on the authors and composers, the work is an important historical source.

Kitai: see CH'I-T'AI, China.

Kitakyushu (kētä'kyo͞osho͞o), city (1970 pop. 1,042,-321), Fukuoka prefecture, N Kyushu, Japan, on the Shimonoseki Strait between the Inland Sea and the Korea Strait. It was formed in 1963 by the union of the cities of Kokura, Moji, Tobata, Wakamatsu, and Yawata (or Yahata), which are now wards of the city. Kitakyushu is one of Japan's most important manufacturing regions and one of its chief ports and railroad centers. It has a great variety of industries, the chief of which produce iron and steel (especially in Yawata ward), textiles, chemicals, machinery, ships, porcelain, and glass. Its ports (especially in Moji and Wakamatsu wards) receive raw materials and export manufactured goods. Kokura ward is the city's commercial and financial center. Tobata ward has a major coal-handling facility; a deep-sea fishing fleet is based there. There are several institutions of higher learning in Kitakyushu. The city is connected by tunnel and bridge with Shimonoseki on Honshu.

Kitami (kētä'mē), city (1970 pop. 82,727), Hokkaido prefecture, NE Hokkaido, Japan, on the Tokoro River. It is an agricultural market and a major center for the production of peppermint.

Kitasato, Shibasaburo (shĭbä'säbo͞orō kē'täsä'tō), 1852–1931, Japanese physician. He worked with Robert Koch in Germany (1885–91), and with Emil Behring he studied the tetanus bacillus and developed (1890) an antitoxin for diphtheria. After returning to Japan he founded an institute for the study of infectious diseases and became its director in 1891. His most noted contribution to bacteriology was the discovery (1894) of the infectious agent of bubonic plague, which he described simultaneously with Alexandre Yersin.

Kit-Cat Club, London political and literary club, active c.1700–1720. The membership of some four dozen included leading Whig politicians and London's best young writers. Among them were Charles Seymour, 6th duke of Somerset; Sir Robert Walpole; Thomas Pelham-Holles, duke of Newcastle; William Congreve; Joseph Addison; Sir Richard Steele; and Sir Godfrey KNELLER, who did portraits of the members. The club was the center of opposition during Queen Anne's Tory ministry (1710–14).

kitchen, separate room or other space set aside for the cooking or preparation of meals. When cooking first moved indoors, it was performed, with other domestic labors, in the common room, where the fire burned on the hearth, or—even earlier, before chimneys were known—on the floor in the center of the room. With the building of larger houses, the kitchen became a separate room. Little is known of the culinary arrangements of antiquity. Excavations at Pompeii show separate rooms fitted with the simple equipment still used in some Oriental cooking. A large brazier, or metal basket on legs, held burning charcoal over which a single basin could be simmered. In homes of wealthy Romans a bench of brick or masonry contained several holes, so that a number of dishes could be cooked at once. Water was kept in jars and heated in large caldrons. Although the peoples of N Europe used stoves from ancient times for heating, they cooked over open fires and baked in outdoor ovens. In the Middle Ages, many of the finest kitchens were in the monasteries; the kitchens were in separate buildings and were equipped for cooking, brewing, and baking on a large scale. In North American colonial and pioneer days the kitchen was large enough to accommodate the operations of spinning, weaving, sewing, knitting, and harness mending as well as cooking. Early American manor houses, especially in the South, usually had separate kitchens, often connected with the house by a covered way or porch. Many farmhouses, before the use of gas or electricity, had a separate summer kitchen, where canning or preserving and the preparation of meals for harvest workers could be carried on without heating the house. See Molly Harrison, *The Kitchen in History* (1973).

Kitchen Cabinet, in U.S. history, popular name for the group of intimate, unofficial advisers of President JACKSON. Early in his administration Jackson abandoned official cabinet meetings and used heads of departments solely to execute their departmental duties, while the policies of his administration were formed in meetings of the Kitchen Cabinet. The members of the informal cabinet included the elder Francis P. BLAIR, Duff GREEN, Isaac Hill, Amos KENDALL, and William B. Lewis. John H. EATON of the regular cabinet met with the group; Martin VAN BUREN also was taken into its confidence. Several members of the Kitchen Cabinet were able journalists, editors of influential regional newspapers. They continued to wield effective pens in defense of the administration measures after they came to Washington. Kendall—perhaps the ablest and most influential member—vigorously defended the policies of Andrew Jackson in the *Globe*, the administration journal edited by Francis P. Blair. Following the cabinet reorganization of 1831, the Kitchen Cabinet became less important.

Kitchener, Horatio Herbert Kitchener, 1st **Earl,** 1850–1916, British field marshal and statesman. Trained at the Royal Military Academy, Woolwich (1868–70), he had a brief period of service in the French army before being commissioned (1871) in the Royal Engineers. After duty in Palestine and Cyprus, he was attached (1883) to the Egyptian army, then being reorganized by the British. He took part (1884–85) in the unsuccessful attempt to relieve Charles George GORDON at Khartoum. He was then

Horatio Herbert Kitchener.

(1886–88) governor general of Eastern Sudan and helped (1889) turn back the last Mahdist invasion of Egypt. In 1892 he was made commander in chief of the Egyptian army and in 1896 began the reconquest of the Sudan, having prepared the way by a reorganization of the army and the construction of a railway along the Nile. A series of victories culminated (1898) in the battle of OMDURMAN and the reoccupation of Khartoum. He forestalled a French attempt to claim part of the Sudan (see FASHODA INCIDENT) in the same year and was made governor of the Sudan. In 1899, Kitchener was appointed chief of staff to Lord ROBERTS in the SOUTH AFRICAN WAR. He reorganized transport, led an unsuccessful attack on Paardeberg, and suppressed the Boer revolt near Prişka. When Roberts returned to England late in 1900, believing the Boer resistance crushed, Kitchener was left to face continued guerrilla warfare. By a slow extension of fortified blockhouses, the use of concentration camps for civilians, and the systematic denudation of the farm lands—methods for which he was much criticized—Kitchener finally secured Boer submission (1902). He was created viscount and sent to India as commander in chief of British forces there. He redistributed the troops and gained greater administrative control of the army in the face of serious opposition from the viceroy Lord CURZON. He left India in 1909, was made field marshal, and served (1911–14) as consul general in Egypt. He was made an earl in 1914. At the outbreak of World War I, Kitchener was recalled to England as secretary of state for war. Virtually alone in his belief that the war would last a number of years, he planned and carried out a vast expansion of the army from 20 divisions in 1914 to 70 in 1916. However, his relations with the cabinet were strained. In 1915 when he was attacked by the newspapers of Lord NORTHCLIFFE for the shortage of shells, responsibility for munitions was taken away from him, and later in the same year he was stripped of control over strategy. He offered to resign, but his colleagues feared the effect on the British public, which still idolized him. In 1916, Kitchener embarked on a mission to Russia to encourage that flagging ally to continued resistance. His ship, the H.M.S. *Hampshire*, hit a German mine and sank off the Orkney Islands, and he was drowned. See biography by Philip Magnus (1958, repr. 1968).

Kitchener, city (1971 pop. 111,804), S Ont., Canada, in the Grand River valley. Settled largely by Mennonites from Pennsylvania in 1806, it was known as Berlin until 1916, when it was renamed in memory of Lord Kitchener. Its products include packaged meats, metal goods, and rubber products. The city of Waterloo adjoins Kitchener. Woodside National Historic Park commemorates the birthplace of W. L. McKenzie King.

kitchen midden, refuse heap left by a prehistoric settlement; kitchen middens have been found throughout the world. First studied (1848) in Denmark, middens are an important source of ecological and cultural information. Kitchen middens, sometimes known as shell mounds, usually date from the late MESOLITHIC period. Their contents include artifacts that can be dated, suggesting the mode of life and technology of ancient peoples. Analysis of animal remains can indicate the climate, season, length of occupation, hunting patterns, and the possible presence of domestication. Estimates of population density are derived from the size and depth of the middens and from the distribution of sites.

kite, in aviation, aircraft restrained by a towline and deriving its lift from the aerodynamic action of the wind flowing across it. Commonly the kite consists of a light framework upon which paper, silk, or other thin material is stretched. Kites having one plane surface require flexible tails for lateral and directional stability. Kite making has been popular in China and other Far Eastern countries for centuries. It is thought that the first use of kites to secure meteorological information was made by Alexander Wilson of Scotland, who in 1749 used them to carry thermometers aloft. In 1752, Benjamin Franklin used kites to study the lightning. The box kite was invented c.1893 by Lawrence Hargrave, an Australian, and was used effectively in meteorological and aerodynamic studies. The tetrahedral kite was used by Alexander Graham Bell for making experiments on problems of airplane construction. See Clive Hart, *Kites: An Historical Survey* (1967); Otto Piene, *More Sky* (1973).

kite, in zoology, common name for a bird of the family Accipitridae, which also includes the HAWK. Kites are found near water and marshes in warm parts of the world. They prey chiefly on reptiles, frogs, and insects. The swallow-tailed, white-tailed, and Mississippi kites are found in the Gulf states and in Central and South America. The Everglade kite, *Rostrhamus sociabilis,* feeds exclusively on a large freshwater snail. The common kite of England, now rare, was once a scavenger in the streets of London. Kites are classified in the phylum CHORDATA, subphylum Vertebrata, class Aves, order Falconiformes, family Accipitridae.

kithara (kĭth'ərə) or **cithara** (sĭth'–), musical instrument of the ancient Greeks. It was a plucked instrument, a larger and stronger form of the LYRE, used by professional musicians both for solo playing and for the accompaniment of poetry and song. It consisted of a relatively square wooden box that extended at one end into heavy arms. Originally it had 5 strings, but later there were 7 and finally 11 strings. These were stretched from the sound box across a bridge and up to a crossbar fastened to the arms. Since the strings were of equal length, tuning was determined only by the thickness and tension of each string. Because of its size and weight, it rested against the body of the player and was held in position by a band. The player usually stood when performing.

Kíthira (kē'thērä) or **Cythera** (sĭthēr'ə), island (1971 pop. 3,961), c.109 sq mi (282 sq km), S Greece, in the Mediterranean Sea, southernmost of the IONIAN ISLANDS, off the S Peloponnesus. Mostly rocky with many streams, it produces wine, goat cheese, olives, corn, and flax. On the south shore is Kíthira (1971 pop. 349), the chief village, formerly called Kapsali. Ancient Kíthira was a center of the cult of Aphrodite. The island passed to Greece in 1864.

Kithlish (kĭth'lĭsh), unidentified town, SW Palestine. Joshua 15.40.

Kitimat (kĭt'ĭmăt), town (1971 pop. 11,803), W British Columbia, Canada, at the head of Douglas Channel. It is the site of a huge aluminum smelter (opened 1954). There are also pulp and paper mills. Kitimat has a deep-water anchorage.

Kitron (kĭt'rŏn), unidentified town, N central Palestine. Judges 1.30.

kitsch [Ger.,=trash], term most frequently applied since the early 20th cent. to works considered pretentious and tasteless. Exploitative commercial objects such as Mona Lisa scarves and abominable plaster reproductions of sculptural masterpieces are described as kitsch, as are works that claim artistic value but are weak, cheap, or sentimental. A museum of kitsch was opened in Stuttgart.

Kittatinny Mountain (kĭtətĭn'ē), ridge of the Appalachian system, extending across NW N.J. from Shawangunk Mt., SE N.Y., to Blue Mt., E Pa.; rises to High Point (1,803 ft/550 m), the highest peak in New Jersey. Kittatinny Mt. is a major resort and recreation area; the Appalachian Trail follows the ridge. The Delaware River cuts through the western part of the ridge forming Delaware Water Gap.

Kittery (kĭt'ərē), town (1970 pop. 11,028), York co., extreme SW Maine, at the mouth of the Piscataqua River opposite Portsmouth, N.H.; inc. 1647. Its economy centers around tourism and the Portsmouth Naval Shipyard, which is located on two islands (formerly part of Kittery and now Federal property) and connected with Kittery by two bridges. The old-

Swallow-tailed kite.

Aerial view of the Kitt Peak National Observatory complex, near Tucson, Ariz.

est town in Maine (settled c.1623), it grew as a trading, fishing, lumber-shipping, and shipbuilding center. John Paul Jones's ship *Ranger* (built in 1777), and the *Kearsarge* of Civil War fame were both built in Kittery. There are several 18th-century houses in the town, and in the village of Kittery Point, a resort, is the William Pepperrell house (1682). William Whipple, a signer of the Declaration of Independence, was born in Kittery.

Kittikachorn, Thanom: see THANOM KITTIKACHORN.

Kittim or **Chittim** (both: kĭt'ĭm), biblical term for Cyprus, but often extended to include lands in general W of Syria. The name was originally used for the Phoenician port of CITIUM in Cyprus. Gen. 10.4; Num. 24.24; 1 Chron. 1.7; Isa. 23.1,12; Jer. 2.10; Ezek. 27.6; Dan. 11.30; 1 Mac. 1.1.

kittiwake: see GULL.

Kitt Peak, 6,875 ft (2,095 m) high, on the Papago Indian reservation in the Quinlan Mts., S Ariz., SW of Tucson. It is the site of KITT PEAK NATIONAL OBSERVATORY.

Kitt Peak National Observatory, astronomical OBSERVATORY located on the Papago Indian reservation near Tucson, Arizona; it was founded in 1960 under contract with the National Science Foundation and is administered by the Association of Universities for Research in Astronomy. Its principal instrument is the Mayall 158-in. (401-cm) reflector, which was the second largest in the United States at the time of its completion (1973). The observatory's equipment also includes one 84-in. (213-cm), one 50-in. (127-cm), two 36-in. (91-cm), and two 16-in. (41-cm) reflecting telescopes as well as the 60-in. (152-cm) Robert McMath Solar Telescope, the largest instrument of its kind in the world. The 50-in. reflector is operated by remote control from the Tucson headquarters of the observatory and is a prototype of future space telescopes. Principal programs of study conducted by the observatory are in three general areas. The stellar division performs basic research on galaxies, stars, nebulas, and the solar system. The solar division, using the solar telescope in coordination with a vacuum spectrograph, analyzes the composition, magnetic field strength, motion, and physical nature of the sun. The planetary sciences division performs planetary research by means of ground-based observations and rocket-borne experiments.

Kittredge, George Lyman, 1860–1941, American scholar, b. Boston. A member of the Harvard faculty (1888–1936), Kittredge was a noted authority on the English language, Shakespeare and Chaucer. His one-volume edition of the complete works of Shakespeare appeared in 1936. He began a more detailed edition of the separate plays in 1939, which was not completed. His books on English include *The Mother Tongue* (with Sarah Arnold; 1900).

Kitty Hawk or **Kittyhawk,** sandy peninsula, NE N.C., E of Albemarle Sound. Nearby is Kill Devil Hill, where the Wright brothers experimented successfully (1900–1903) with gliders and airplanes. Wright Brothers National Memorial (see NATIONAL PARKS AND MONUMENTS, table), commemorating their first successful flight, is there.

Kitwe (kē'twā), city (1972 est. pop., with suburbs, 251,600), N central Zambia, near Zaïre; founded 1936. It is the main commercial and industrial center of the COPPERBELT. Copper is mined, and food products, clothing, and plastics are manufactured there. The Zambia Institute of Technology is in Kitwe.

Kitzbühel (kĭts'bü"həl), town (1971 pop. 8,000), in Tyrol prov., W Austria, in the Kitzbühel Alps. It is a famous winter sports and resort center.

Kiukiang: see CHIU-CHIANG, China.

Kiungshan: see CH'IUNG-SHAN, China.

Kiuprili: see KÖPRÜLÜ.

kiva (kē'və), large, underground ceremonial chamber, peculiar to the ancient and modern PUEBLO INDIANS. The modern kiva probably evolved from the slab houses (i.e., storage pits and dwellings that were partly underground and lined with stone slabs set on edge) of their cultural ancestors, the BASKET MAKERS. A modern kiva is either a rectangular or a circular structure, with a timbered roof. It is entered through a hatchway by means of a ladder. The floor is made of smooth sandstone slabs, and the walls of fine masonry. There is a dais at one end, a fire pit in the center, and an opening in the floor at the other end. This orifice represents the entrance to the lower world and the place of emergence through which life came to this world. The walls also have a symbolic significance and are decorated with mythological figures. Women are traditionally restricted from entering a kiva. Men use the kiva for secret ceremonies, as a lounging place, and as a workshop where weaving is done.

Kivu (kē'vo͞o, kēvo͞o'), region (1970 pop. 3,361,883), c.89,000 sq mi (230,510 sq km), E Zaïre. It borders on Uganda, Rwanda, Burundi, and Lake Tanganyika on the east. Bukavu is the capital. Coffee, cotton, rice, and palm oil are produced, and some tin and gold are mined. The Ruwenzori mts. and Albert National Park, a vast game preserve, are in the region. Most of Kivu was controlled (1961–62) by the breakaway regime of Antoine Gizenga, which was centered at Kisangani (then Stanleyville). The central government reestablished control over Kivu in 1962, but rebel activity continued there in the later 1960s.

Kivu, lake, 1,042 sq mi (2,699 sq km), 55 mi (89 km) long, on the Zaïre-Rwanda border, E central Africa; highest lake in Africa (4,788 ft/1,459 m). It is drained by the Ruzizi River, which flows S into Lake Tanganyika. Lake Kivu is a tourist center.

Kiwanis International (kĭwä'nĭs), community service organization of business and professional men, founded in 1915 at Detroit, Mich. Local Kiwanis clubs meet weekly; their activities are carried on through committees that include agriculture and conservation, public affairs, business standards, support of churches, children's aid, and vocational guidance. Kiwanis sponsors Key Club International, a service organization for outstanding male high school students. Each local Kiwanis club has a voice in Kiwanis International, which is organized throughout the United States and Canada.

kiwi (kē'wē) or **apteryx** (ăp'tərĭks), common name for the smallest member of an order of primitive flightless birds related to the ostrich, the emu, and the cassowary. The kiwi, named by the Maoris for its shrill, piping call, is most closely related to the extinct MOA. It is the size of a large chicken and has short, stout legs and coarse, dark plumage that hides the rudimentary wings. It lacks wing and tail plumes and walks with a rolling gait. It is the only bird whose nostrils open at the tip of the bill, which is 6 in. (15 cm) long, slender, and curved. Kiwis hide during the day and forage at night for grubs and worms. Their eyesight is poor; the long, hairy bristles at the base of the bill are believed to have a tactile function which is thought to supplement their keen sense of smell in hunting. Kiwis nest in underground burrows, the male performing the incubational duties. The one or two chalky white eggs are 5 in. (12.5 cm) long, weigh almost 1 lb. (0.5 kg), and take from 75 to 80 days to hatch. The three living species of kiwi, genus *Apteryx,* have dwindled with the advance of agriculture and the introduction of predators such as cats, weasels, and stoats, but they are now rigidly protected by law. The kiwi is the symbol of New Zealand and appears on the seal, coins, stamps, and on various products of its homeland; overseas New Zealand troops are popularly called kiwis. Kiwis are classified in the phylum CHORDATA, subphylum Vertebrata, class Aves, order Apterygiformes, family Apterygidae.

Kiyonaga (kēyōnä'ga), 1752–1815, Japanese painter and designer of woodcuts of the Torii school. After working as a bookseller in Tokyo, he took lessons from the Torii master Kiyomitsu but created a more individual linear style. He is best known for his cuts of beautiful women and of warriors. He published (1771–1811) over 100 illustrated books. His unmannered, vivid style had wide appeal and won him many followers. See study by Seiichiro Takahashi (1956).

Kiyonobu I (Torii Kiyonobu I) (kēyōnō'bo͞o), 1664–1729, Japanese printmaker. Specializing in portraits of Kabuki actors, Kiyonobu I worked in the ukiyo-e print style (see JAPANESE ART), concentrating on intricate elements of costume design. Flat and vividly colorful, Kiyonobu's work was notable for its sweeping contour lines and for the boldness of its composition. Kiyonobu was closely allied with the world of theater and frequently painted the actors in their best-known roles. His son, Kiyonobu II, 1702–52, collaborated with him and helped perpetuate his style.

Kizel (kēzyĕl'), city (1970 pop. 54,000), E European USSR, on the Kizel River and on the western slopes of the Urals. It is a coal-mining and industrial center with coal-concentrating factories and plants that produce mining equipment, clothing, and food products. It was founded in the late 18th cent. when the coal mines of the Kizel basin were being developed.

Kizil: see KYZYL, USSR.

Kizil Adalar (kəzŭl' ädälär') or **Princes Islands,** group of nine small islands (1970 pop. 15,244), c.4 sq mi (10.4 sq km), NW Turkey, in the Sea of Marmara, near İstanbul. The islands are a popular resort area. They were used as places of exile in Byzantine times. There are several old monasteries and churches. Büyük Island is the largest of the group.

Kizil Irmak (kəzŭl' ərmäk'), anc. *Halys,* longest river of Turkey, c.715 mi (1,150 km) long, rising in the Kızıl Dağ, N central Turkey, and flowing in a wide arc SW, then N, and then NE into the Black Sea. It has an irregular volume and is not used for navigation. The river is an important source of hydroelectric power.

Kizil Kum, desert, USSR: see KYZYL-KUM.

Klabund (kläbo͝ont'), pseud. of **Alfred Henschke** (äl'frĕt hĕnsh'kə), 1890–1928, German poet, novelist, and dramatist. A skillful translator and adapter of Oriental literature, he wrote original poems in a Chinese style. His play *Kreidekreis* (1924, tr. *Circle of Chalk,* 1929), based on Chinese legend, was very popular. His novels include *Bracke* (1918, tr. *Brackie the Fool,* 1927) and *Pjotr* (1923, tr. *Peter the Czar,* 1925).

Kladno (kläd'nô), city (1970 pop. 58,069), NW Czechoslovakia, in Bohemia. An industrial center of the Kladno coal-mining region, it has large iron and steel plants, and manufactures chemicals and machinery. Known in 973, Kladno grew rapidly with the opening of its first coal mine in 1846.

Klagenfurt (klä'gənfo͝ort), city (1971 pop. 74,300), capital of Carinthia prov., S Austria, on the Glan River. Situated in a mountain lake region, it is a noted winter sports center. Manufactures include machinery, textiles, and leather goods. An annual timber fair is held there. Klagenfurt was chartered about the mid-13th cent. and became an episcopal see in the late 18th cent. The city has a cathedral (16th cent.), a theological seminary, and several museums.

Klaipeda: see KLAYPEDA, USSR.

Klamath (klăm'əth), river, c.265 mi (430 km) long, rising in Upper Klamath Lake in the Klamath Mts., SW Oregon and flowing generally SW across NW Calif. to the Pacific Ocean. Most of its course passes through national forests and wildlife refuges. The river is used for irrigation and power production. Klamath Falls is the largest city on the river.

Klamath Falls, city (1970 pop. 15,775), seat of Klamath co., SW Oregon, at the southern tip of Upper Klamath Lake; inc. 1905. It is the processing and distributing center of a lumber, livestock, and farm area, and is a resort center. There is some manufacturing. Klamath Falls was settled in 1867 as Linkville. The Klamath irrigation project (1900) and the coming of the railroad (1909) stimulated its growth from a hamlet to a thriving city. A junior college is in the city, and Crater Lake National Park, Lava Beds National Monument, and Klamath Indian Reservation are nearby.

Klamath Indians, North American Indians, who in the 19th cent. lived in SW Oregon. They speak a language of the Sahaptin-Chinook branch of the Penutian linguistic stock (see AMERICAN INDIAN LANGUAGES). The material for the first description of the Klamath was collected by Peter Skene Ogden, who visited them in 1829 and opened trade relations. They subsisted by hunting, fishing, and collecting roots and wokas, or water-lily seeds. The Klamath were peaceful toward the settlers but not toward the N California Indians. They raided those Indians periodically and carried off the women and children, keeping their captives as slaves or selling them to other Indians. By the treaty of 1864 with the United States, the practice of slavery was abolished and their land NE of Upper Klamath Lake in Oregon was set aside as the Klamath Indian Reservation. Today they are mostly farmers and number some 700. See Leslie Spier, *Klamath Ethnography* (1930); Theodore Stern, *The Klamath Tribe* (1965).

Klaproth, Martin Heinrich (mär'tēn hīn'rĭkh kläp'rōt), 1743–1817, German chemist. He is often referred to as the father of analytic chemistry. He recognized (1789) the presence of zirconium in the ore zirconia and of uranium in a precipitate of pitchblende. He also worked on other elements, including titanium and tellurium.

Klaus, Josef (yō'zĕf klous), 1910–, Austrian politician. He was drafted into the army and fought in World War II on the Axis side. Chosen leader (1963) of the business- and church-oriented People's party, Klaus tended to oppose compromises with the party's coalition partner, the Socialists. He became chancellor in 1964 and was succeeded in 1970 by the Socialist Bruno KREISKY.

Klaypeda (klī'pĕdä), formerly **Memel** (mā'məl), city (1970 pop. 140,000), NW European USSR, in Lithuania, on the Baltic Sea, at the entrance to the Kursky Zaliv. An ice-free seaport and an industrial center, it has shipyards and industries producing textiles, fertilizers, and wood products. One of the oldest cities of Lithuania, Klaypeda was the site of a settlement as early as the 7th cent. It was conquered and burned in 1252 by the Teutonic Knights, who built a fortress and named it Memelburg. The city was ceded (1629) by Prussia to Sweden but reverted to Prussia in 1635. In the Napoleonic Wars the city was (1807) the refuge and residence of Frederick William III of Prussia, who signed there the edict emancipating the serfs in his kingdom. From 1919 it shared the history of the MEMEL TERRITORY. The name also appears as Klaipeda.

Kléber, Jean Baptiste (zhäN bätēst' klābĕr'), 1753–1800, French general, b. Strasbourg. A trained architect, he attended military school in Munich and served in the Austrian army from 1777 to 1783. In 1789 he entered the French National Guard. He fought with distinction in the French Revolutionary Wars and crushed the 1793 royalist uprising in the Vendée. He accompanied Napoleon Bonaparte to Egypt in 1798. Left in command when Napoleon returned (1799) to France, Kléber defeated (March, 1800) the Turks at Heliopolis, near Cairo, and recaptured Cairo. He was assassinated (June) at Cairo by a Turkish fanatic.

Klebs, Edwin (klāps), 1834–1913, German-American pathologist, b. Prussia. He was an assistant of Rudolf Virchow and professor of pathology at Zürich (1872–92) and from 1896 at Rush Medical College, Chicago. He is known for his many original observations on the pathology of infectious diseases. He worked on tuberculosis, malaria, anthrax, and syphilis and described the diphtheria bacillus and typhoid bacillus although he did not demonstrate them to be the causes of these diseases. The diphtheria bacillus is also known as the Klebs-Löffler bacillus.

Klee, Paul (poul klā), 1879–1940, Swiss painter, graphic artist, and art theorist, b. near Bern. Klee's enormous production (more than 9,000 works) is unique in that it represents the successful combination of his sophisticated theories of abstraction with a very personal inventiveness that has the appearance of great innocence. The son of a music teacher, he was himself a musician, and musical analogies permeate his writing. He traveled through Europe, open to many artistic influences. The most important of these were the works of Blake, Beardsley, Goya, Ensor, and, especially, Cézanne. In 1911 he became associated with the BLAUE REITER group and later exhibited as one of the Blue Four. Klee's awakening to color occurred on a trip to Tunis in 1914, a year after he had met DELAUNAY and been made aware of new theories of color use. Thereafter his whimsical and fantastic images were rendered with a luminous and subtle color sense. Characteristic of his witty, often grotesque, pieces are *The Twittering Machine* (1922, Mus. of Modern Art, New York City) and *Fish Magic* (1925, Phila. Mus. of Art). Other works reveal the strong, rhythmic patterns of a relentless terror, as in *Revolutions of the Viaducts* (1937, Hamburg). World-famous by 1929, Klee

Death and Fire *(1940), by the Swiss painter Paul Klee.* *© 1978, Copyright by COSMOPRESS, Geneva (Switzerland).*

taught at the BAUHAUS (1922–31) and at the Düsseldorf academy (1931–33) until the Nazis, who judged his work degenerate, forced him to resign. In his series of *Pedagogical Sketchbooks* (tr. 1944) and lecture notes entitled *The Thinking Eye* (tr. 1961), Klee sought to define his intuitive approach to artistic creation. His last ten years were spent in Switzerland, and nearly 2,600 of his works are in the Klee Foundation, Bern. See his notebooks, ed. by Jürg Spiller (Vol I, tr. 1961, Vol II, tr. 1974); his diaries, ed. by his son Felix Klee (tr. 1964); his life and work in documents, ed. by Felix Klee (tr. 1962); studies by Will Grohmann (1958 and 1967), Werner Haftmann (1968), and Christian Geelhaar (1973).

Klein, Christian Felix (krĭs'tēän fā'lĭks klīn), 1849–1925, German mathematician. He is noted for his work in geometry and on the theory of functions. His Erlangen program (1872) for unifying the diverse forms of geometry through the study of equivalence in transformation groups was influential, especially in the United States, for over 50 years. In his *Lectures on the Icosahedron and the Solution of Equations of the Fifth Degree* (1884, tr. 1888) he showed how the rotation groups of regular solids could be applied to the solution of difficult algebraic problems. Klein was professor of mathematics successively at the Univ. of Erlangen, the Technical Institute, Munich, and the universities of Leipzig and Göttingen, and was a prolific writer and lecturer on the theory, history, and teaching of mathematics. His works include *Famous Problems of Elementary Geometry* (1895; tr., 2d ed. 1930) and *Elementary Mathematics from an Advanced Standpoint* (2 vol., 1907–8; tr. 1932–40).

Kleist, Heinrich von (hīn'rĭkh fən klīst), 1777–1811, German dramatic poet. His writings rank high in German romantic literature. Kleist served (1792–99) in the army and led an unhappy life that ended in suicide. His comedies include *The Broken Pitcher* (1806, tr. 1961) and *Amphitryon* (1807), after Molière. Among his passionate tragedies is *Penthesilea* (1808). *Käthchen von Heilbronn* (1810) is a tale of chivalry; his masterpiece is *The Prince of Homburg* (1821, tr. 1956), a historical tragedy. Kleist's terse, dynamic style and his sense of conflict—between reason and feeling, divine law and human law—are also evident in his *Novellen.* Best known of these is *Michael Kohlhaas* (1808, tr. 1967). See studies by Walter Silz (1961) and J. Gearey (1968).

Klemperer, Otto (ô'tō klĕm'pərər), 1885–1973, German conductor, b. Breslau. Klemperer studied in Frankfurt and Berlin. Working first in Prague, he later conducted the Berlin State Opera (1927–33), introducing new works by Janáček, Schoenberg, Stravinsky, and Hindemith. With the rise of the Nazi regime, he went to the United States where he conducted the Los Angeles Philharmonic (1933–40). Klemperer was celebrated for his interpretations of

Beethoven, Mahler, and Richard Strauss. In 1938 he directed the reorganization of the Pittsburgh Orchestra. In 1946 he returned to Europe where he conducted in Budapest, Germany, and England. See his *Minor Recollections* (1964).

Klenze, Leo von (lā'ō fən klĕn'tsə), 1784–1864, German architect and landscape and portrait painter. He was court architect to Jérôme Bonaparte of Westphalia and to Louis I of Bavaria, for whom he built many structures in the Italian Renaissance and neo-Greek styles. His chief works in Munich were the Glyptothek (1816–30), the Pinakothek, and the Odeon (1828). In 1839 he began additions to the Hermitage in Leningrad.

kleptomania (klĕp"təmā'nēə) [Gr.,=craze for stealing], irresistible compulsion to steal, motivated by neurotic impulse rather than material need. No specific cause is known. The condition is considered generally as the result of some underlying emotional disturbance rather than as a form of neurosis in itself. Legally kleptomania is not classified as insanity, and the individual is held responsible except when complete lack of control over his actions can be definitely established.

Klerksdorp (klĕrks'dôrp), town (1970 pop. 70,710), Transvaal, NE Republic of South Africa, on the Schoonspruit River. The town, which has grain elevators, lumberyards, and food-processing and beverage-making industries, is the mining and processing center for major gold and uranium deposits and is also the distribution center for neighboring farms. There are rail and road connections with Cape Town and Johannesburg. Klerksdorp was founded in 1837 by BOER farmers and, with POTCHEFSTROM, was one of the first European towns founded in the

Walhalla of Ludwig I, near Regensburg, West Germany, designed by Leo von Klenze.

Transvaal. Gold mining began in 1886 but declined in the late 1890s. Heavy fighting occurred in the area during the SOUTH AFRICAN WAR (1899–1902). Gold mining revived in 1932, and the town underwent an economic revival, which accelerated after World War II. Klerksdorp has a training school for nurses.

Klesl or **Khlesl, Melchior** (both: mĕl'khyôr klā'səl), 1552–1630, Austrian politician, cardinal of the Roman Catholic Church. The son of a Protestant baker, he was converted to Catholicism by the Jesuits and became chancellor of the Univ. of Vienna. Made (1581) an official of the bishop of Passau and then (1598) bishop of Vienna, he led the campaign to drive Protestantism from Lower Austria. Later, however, as adviser to Archduke (after 1612, Holy Roman Emperor) MATTHIAS, he concluded that only a policy of compromise would preserve intact the Hapsburg domains. In 1615 he was created cardinal. Archduke Ferdinand (later Holy Roman Emperor FERDINAND II), attributing the emperor's delay in putting down the Prague insurrection (the prelude to the THIRTY YEARS WAR) to Klesl's influence, had him imprisoned (1618). Later released (1622) and transferred to Rome, he returned to Vienna as bishop in 1627.

Kleve, city and former duchy, West Germany: see CLEVES.

Klikitat Indians (klĭk'ĭtăt"), North American Indians whose language belongs to the Sahaptin-Chinook branch of the Penutian linguistic stock (see AMERICAN INDIAN LANGUAGES), inhabiting S central Washington in the early 19th cent. Lewis and Clark visited (1805) them and estimated their population to be some 700. They were energetic traders, acting as middlemen between the Indians of the coast and those of the interior. By the Yakima treaty (1855) they ceded their territory to the United States, and most of them went to live on the Yakima Reservation, where they have lost their identity as a tribe. See C. O. Bunnell, *Legends of the Klikitats* (1933).

Klimt, Gustav (go͞os'täf klĭmt), 1862–1918, Austrian painter. He cofounded the Vienna Secession group, an alliance against 19th-century eclecticism in art, and in 1897 became its first president. In the following decade Klimt became the foremost painter of ART NOUVEAU in Vienna. He created many murals for public buildings, e.g., the frieze for the Palais Stoclet, Brussels (1908). Klimt achieved his greatest fame as a portrait and landscape painter of exotic and erotic sensibility. Delineating symbolic themes with extravagant rhythms, Klimt was the quintessential exponent of art nouveau. The Museum of Modern Art, New York City, has examples of his work. See his catalogue raisonné by Fritz Novotny and Johannes Dobai (tr. 1969).

Kline, Franz, 1910–62, American painter, b. Wilkes-Barre, Pa. He studied (1937–38) in England, then settled in New York City. From the early 1950s, Kline exhibited large canvases of dynamically painted black-and-white grids. His works often recall Chinese calligraphy but he himself denied Oriental influence. His subsequent works, sometimes with notes of bright color, established his reputation as an important figure in the movement known as ABSTRACT EXPRESSIONISM. See memoir by Fielding Dawson (1967).

Klinger, Friedrich Maximilian von (frē'drĭkh mäk"sēmē'lyän fən klĭng'ər), 1752–1831, German dramatist. A friend of the young Goethe, he was a playwright for a theatrical troupe and later an army officer. His early work typified the STURM UND DRANG period, so named after his play *Wirrwarr; oder, Sturm und Drang* [confusion; or, storm and stress] (1776); his later plays, influenced by Schiller and Iffland, are more reserved in tone. Klinger's other works include the play *The Twins* (1776) and the novel *Faust's Life, Deeds, and Journey to Hell* (1791, tr. 1825).

Klinger, Max (mäks), 1857–1920, German painter, sculptor, and etcher. Before 1886 he produced cycles of original and somewhat morbidly imaginative etchings, such as *Deliverances of Sacrificial Victims Told in Ovid* and *Brahms-Phantasie.* From 1886 to 1894 Klinger devoted himself primarily to painting, usually on a grandiose scale. Among his paintings are *Judgment of Paris* and *Christ on Olympus* (both: Vienna). After 1894 he worked predominantly in sculpture, his most successful medium. Notable examples are *Salome, Cassandra,* and the dramatic polychromed statue of Beethoven (all: Leipzig) and the bust of Nietzsche (Weimar).

klipspringer: see ANTELOPE.

Kłodzko (klôts'kô), Ger. *Glatz,* town (1970 pop. 26,100), SW Poland. It is a commercial center with textile mills, metalworks, slate quarries, and sugar refineries. Founded in the 10th cent., it was capital of a county created in 1462. It was seized by Frederick II of Prussia in the War of the Austrian Succession and was formally ceded to Prussia in 1745.

Klondike (klŏn'dīk), region of YUKON TERRITORY, NW Canada, just E of the Alaska border. It lies around Klondike River, a small stream that enters the Yukon River from the east at Dawson. The discovery in 1896 of rich placer gold deposits in Bonanza (Rabbit) Creek, a tributary of the Klondike, caused the Klondike stampede of 1897–98. News of the discovery reached the United States in July, 1897, and

Boat from Klondike gold rush era, beached at Dawson.

within a month thousands of people were rushing north. Most landed at Skagway at the head of Lynn Canal and crossed by Chilkoot or White Pass to the upper Yukon, which they descended to Dawson. Others went in by the Copper River Trail or over the Teslin Trail by Stikine River and Teslin Lake, and some by the all-Canadian Ashcroft and Edmonton trails. The rush continued by these passes all the following winter. The other main access route was up the Yukon River, c.1,600 mi (2,575 km), by steamer. Many of those using this route late in 1897 were caught by winter ice below Fort Yukon and had to be rescued. With unexpected thousands in the region a food famine threatened, and supplies were commandeered and rationed. The number in the Klondike in 1898 was c.25,000. Thousands of others who did not find claims drifted down the Yukon and found placer gold in Alaskan streams, notably at Nome, to which there was a new rush. Others went back to the United States. Gold is still mined in the area. The hardships of the trails and the color of Klondike days are described in many personal narratives; among the best are W. B. Haskell's *Two Years in the Klondike* (1898) and James Wickersham's *Old Yukon* (1938). See Pierre Berton, *Klondike, the Last Great Gold Rush, 1896–99* (rev. ed. 1972).

Kloos, Willem (vĭl'əm klōs), 1859–1938, Dutch poet and critic. In 1885 he founded the progressive literary journal *De Nieuwe Gids* [the new guide]. His personal anger against prevailing modes of literary expression is vented in the sonnets in *Verzen* (1894), notable for the fresh imagery and metaphor they introduced to Dutch poetry. Unlike some of his literary associates, Kloos never developed social concerns and remained primarily a literary reformer.

Klopstock, Friedrich Gottlieb (frē'drĭkh gôt'lēp klôp'shtôk), 1724–1803, German poet, important for his influence upon Goethe, the GÖTTINGEN poets, and the STURM UND DRANG movement. His epic *Messias* (4 vol., 1748–73, tr. *The Messiah*) created a literary storm when it first appeared in the *Bremen Beitrage*. The poem has the merit of being the first major modern work by a distinctively German poet, but the poem as a whole is weak, for Klopstock's genius was lyrical rather than epic. His rhapsodic, musical *Odes* (1747–80) strongly influenced German song composition. Gluck, C. P. E. Bach, Beethoven, Schubert, Mahler, and many others set them to music. Klopstock also wrote a trilogy of dramas on the Germanic hero *Hermann* (1769, 1784, 1787).

Klosterneuburg (klôs″tərnoi'bo͞orkh), city (1971 pop. 21,900), Lower Austria prov., NE Austria, on the Danube River and the north slope of the Wienerwald, near Vienna. Klosterneuburg was formed in 1938 through the merger of seven towns. It is the site of a wealthy Augustinian monastery (consecrated 1136), the oldest in Austria. The monastery has an extensive library, enormous wine cellars, and the famous Verduner Altar (1181) by Nicholaus of Verdun.

Kloster-Zeven, Convention of (klôs'tər-tsā'fən), 1757. Early in the Seven Years War the English army,

Huge masses of ice breaking away from the Lowell Glacier in the St. Elias Mts., Kluane National Park.

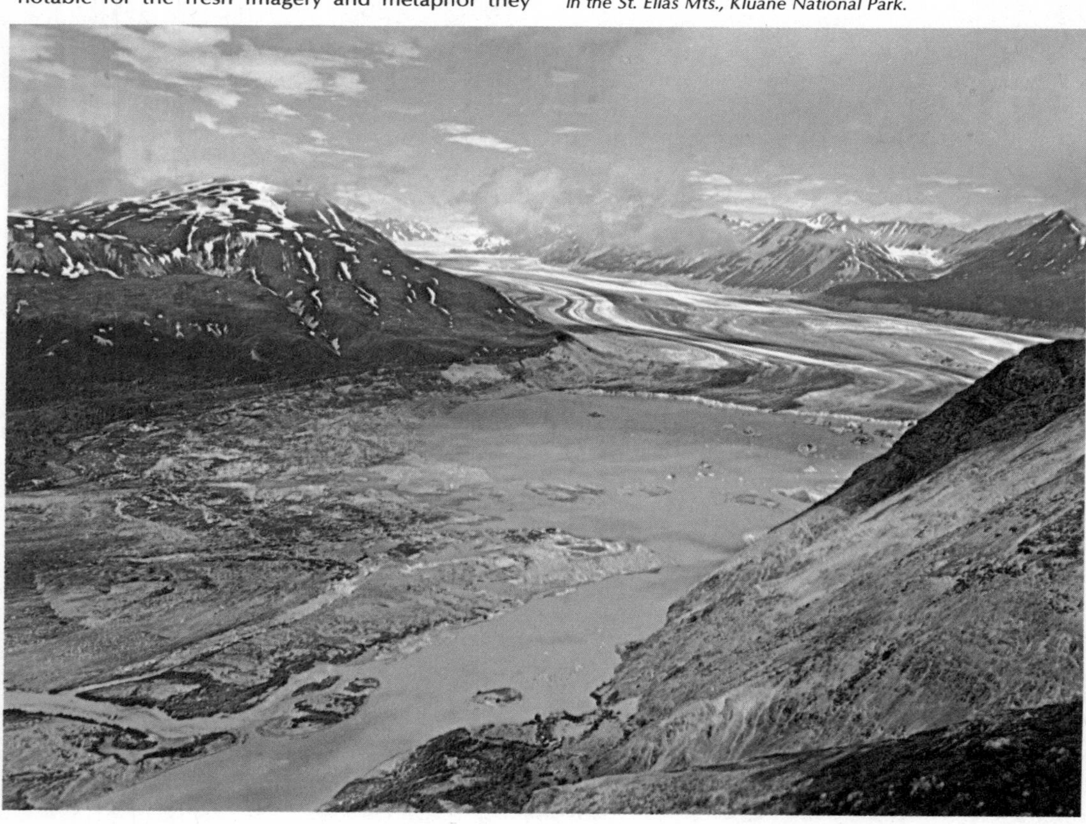

under the command of the duke of CUMBERLAND, was defeated by the French at Hastenbeck. Cumberland capitulated at the former Benedictine abbey near Zeven (a small town, formerly in Hanover, NE of Bremen) and allowed the French to occupy Hanover. The convention was disavowed by the English government, and Cumberland was dismissed.

Kluane National Park (klo͞oän'), c.8,500 sq mi (22,000 sq km), SW Yukon Territory, Canada, between Kluane Lake and the British Columbia and Alaska borders; est. 1972. Located in the St. Elias Mts., the park contains some of Canada's highest mountains (including Mt. Logan, the nation's highest peak) and one of the world's largest nonpolar systems of ice fields. There is a great variety of wildlife.

Kluckhohn, Clyde Kay Maben (klŭck'hōn), 1905–1960, American anthropologist, b. LeMars, Iowa, grad. Univ. of Wisconsin, 1928, M.A. Oxford, 1932, Ph.D. Harvard, 1936. He taught at the Univ. of New Mexico (1932–34) and at Harvard (1935–60). Kluckhohn is known primarily for his studies of the Navaho Indians and of personality and culture. His other works include an introduction to anthropology, *Mirror for Man* (1949) and *Culture: A Critical Review of Concepts and Definitions* (1952). See W. W. Taylor et al., ed., *Culture and Life* (1973).

klystron (klīs'trŏn, klīs'–), vacuum tube used in electronic circuits that operate at frequencies from about 200 megahertz to about 30,000 megahertz. A stream of electrons directed and focused by a series of electrodes is made to pass through one or more cavity resonators (spaces enclosed by electrically conducting surfaces). Signal voltages applied to the input cavity resonator modify the speed of the electrons, speeding some up and slowing others down. The output cavity resonator slows the electrons, causing them to emit radiation that constitutes the output signal. Klystrons may be adjusted to provide amplification or oscillation. Unlike the conventional electron tube, the output of the klystron is not measured by the electron flow in the cathode-anode circuit but by the high frequency currents produced in its resonant cavities. Klystrons are widely used in microwave radar and communications equipment and in linear accelerators for nuclear physics experiments.

Klyuchevsky, Vasily Osipovich (vəsē'lyē ô'sĭpəvĭch klyo͞ochĕv'skē), 1841–1911, Russian historian. Interpreting history from a sociological viewpoint, he emphasized geographic and economic conditions as the determining factors of social change. Klyuchevsky considered colonization a distinctive feature of Russian development and an important factor in the rise of a strong central state. Among his many writings, noted for scrupulous research and documentation, is his *Course of Russian History* (5 vol., 1902–21; tr. *A History of Russia,* 5 vol., 1960).

Knapp, Seaman Asahel, 1833–1911, agriculturist and teacher, b. Schroon Lake, N.Y., grad. Union College, Schenectady, 1856. He went to Iowa in 1866 and began publication in 1872 at Cedar Rapids of the *Western Stock Journal and Farmer.* In 1879 he became professor of agriculture and manager of the Iowa State College farm, and from 1884 to 1886 he was president of the college. He resigned to conduct in Louisiana farm demonstration work, an innovative method of instruction which he introduced, consisting of practical demonstrations on individual farms. Later, under James Wilson as Secretary of Agriculture, Knapp was employed by the department as a special agent to promote better farming methods in the South—particularly in the growing and handling of rice, for which he was sent to the Orient to study techniques there. His greatest work was the demonstration of methods of fighting the boll weevil. This led to the development in the Dept. of Agriculture of the Farmers Cooperative Demonstration Work division, which he headed. See biography by J. C. Bailey (1945). He was succeeded by his son, **Bradford Knapp,** 1870–1938, b. Vinton, Iowa, grad. Vanderbilt Univ., 1892, who after his father's death was director of the Farmers Cooperative Demonstration Work division until the department was reorganized in 1914; until 1920 he headed the extension work in the South. He served as president at Oklahoma Agricultural and Mechanical College (1923–28), at Alabama Polytechnic Institute (1928–32), and at Texas Technological College (from 1932). He wrote *Safe Farming* (1919).

kneecap (patella), saucer-shaped bone at the front of the knee joint; it protects the ends of the femur, or thighbone, and the tibia, the large bone of the foreleg. The kneecap is embedded in the tendon tissue of the quadriceps femoris, a large thigh muscle. As the leg bends and straightens, the kneecap glides up and down in a groove of the femur. Dislocation of the kneecap is a common athletic injury, occurring when stress on the powerful extensor muscles that straighten the leg pulls the kneecap to one side. See SKELETON.

Kneller, Sir Godfrey (nĕl'ər) or **Gottfried von Kniller** (gôt'frēt fən knĭl'ər), 1646–1723, English portrait painter, b. Germany. After study in Amsterdam, Rome, and Venice, he settled in England in 1675, achieving success in fashionable circles and at court, where he was named principal painter in 1688. Serving under the monarchs from Charles II to George I, Kneller and the factory of painters in his employ mass-produced such works as *Ten Beauties of the Court* (Hampton Court), *The Duchess of Portsmouth* (Goodwood, Sussex), and *Charles Beauclerk* (Metropolitan Mus.). From 1702 to 1717 he executed 42 portraits of the members of the KIT-CAT CLUB (National Portrait Gall., London), which are among his best works. His facile and standardized paintings are sometimes careless of execution. Kneller became the director, in 1711, of the first Academy of Painting in London and strongly influenced the subsequent generation of English portraitists.

Knickerbocker (nĭk'ərbŏk"ər), term used almost synonymously with the adjective "Dutch" in respect to Dutch families and customs and the Dutch region of early New York state. *A History of New York* (1809), written by Washington Irving under the pseudonym Diedrich Knickerbocker, popularized the term. There was an actual Knickerbocker family that came from Holland c.1674 and lived chiefly in Albany co.

knife: see CUTLERY.

Knight, Charles, 1874–1953, American artist, b. New York City. Knight painted and sculpted animal subjects. He is best known for his murals at the American Museum of Natural History, New York City. These depict scenes of prehistoric life based on information from fossil remains. His books include *Before the Dawn of History* (1935) and *Prehistoric Man* (1949).

Knight, George Wilson, 1897–, English writer and critic, grad. Oxford (B.A., 1923; M.A., 1925). He has written numerous books and essays on English literature, including *The Wheel of Fire* (1930), *The Imperial Theme* (1931), *The Crown of Life* (1946), *The Golden Labyrinth* (1962), and *Neglected Powers: Essays on 19th and 20th Century Literature* (1971), as well as studies of Byron, Milton, and Shakespeare. In addition he has written plays, poems, and an autobiography.

Knight, Sarah Kemble, 1666–1727, American teacher, b. Boston. She was known as Madam Knight in connection with her writing school and her work as a recorder of public documents. Her famous *Private Journal of a Journey from Boston to New York in the Year 1704* (1825) is a source of information on colonial customs and conditions, especially of inns. In later life she herself maintained an inn near New London, Conn.

knight. 1 In ancient history, as in Athens and Rome, a noble of the second class who in military service had to furnish his own mount and equipment. In Roman society, the knights (Latin *equites*) ranked below the senatorial class and above ordinary citizens. A knight forfeited his status if his fortune sank below the assessed value of 400,000 sesterces (about $16,000). **2** In medieval history, an armed and mounted warrior belonging to the nobility. The incessant private warfare that characterized early medieval times brought about a permanent military class, and by the 10th cent. the institution of knighthood was well established. The knight was essentially a military officer, although with the growth of FEUDALISM the term tended to assume a position not only in the ranks of nobility but also in the ranks of landholders. The knight generally held his lands by military tenure; thus knight service was a military service, usually 40 days a year, normally expected by an overlord in exchange for each fief held by a knight. All military service was measured in terms of knight service, and a vassal might owe any number of knight services. Although all true nobles of military age were necessarily knights, knighthood had to be earned. In the late Middle Ages the son of a noble would serve first as page, then as squire, before being made a knight. Knighthood was conferred by the overlord with the accolade (a blow, usually with the flat of the sword, on the neck or shoulder); the ceremony was preceded, especially in the later period of feudalism, by the religious ceremony of the vigil before an altar. A knight fighting under another's banner was called a knight bachelor; a knight fighting under his own banner was a knight banneret. Knights were ordinarily accompanied in battle by personal attendants (squires, pages) and by vassals (see YEOMAN) and servants. Military tenure was generally subject to the law of PRIMOGENITURE, which resulted in a class of landless knights; at the time of the Crusades those landless knights formed the great military orders of knighthood, which were religious as well as military bodies. Important among these were the KNIGHTS TEMPLARS, KNIGHTS HOSPITALERS, TEUTONIC KNIGHTS, LIVONIAN BROTHERS OF THE SWORD, Knights of CALATRAVA, and Knights of AVIZ. Secular orders, patterned loosely on the religious ones, but not limited to landless knights, also grew up, principally as honorary establishments by the kings or great nobles. Examples in England were the Order of the Garter and in Burgundy the Order of the Golden Fleece. The most important of these orders have survived and many more have been added (e.g., the orders of the Bath, of Victoria, and of the British Empire in Great Britain and the Legion of Honor in France; see DECORATIONS, CIVIL AND MILITARY). As the feudal system disintegrated, knight service was with growing frequency commuted into cash payments. In England the payment was known as SCUTAGE. Many landowners found the duties of knighthood too onerous for their meager resources and contented themselves with the rank of squire. This was particularly true in England, where gentlemen landowners are still termed squires. The military value of a cavalry consisting of heavily armored knights lessened with the rise of the infantry, artillery, and mercenary armies. In Germany, where the institution of knighthood persisted somewhat longer than in Britain and France, knighthood in its feudal meaning may be said to have come to an end in the early 16th cent. with the defeat of Franz von SICKINGEN. The title knight (Ger. *Ritter*, Fr. *chevalier*) was later used as a noble title in Germany and France. In the French hierarchy of nobles the title chevalier was borne by a younger son of a duke, marquis, or count. In modern Britain, knighthood is not a title of nobility, but is conferred by the royal sovereign (upon recommendation of the government) on commoners or nobles for civil or military achievements. A knight is addressed with the title Sir (e.g., Sir John); a woman, if knighted in her own right, is addressed as Dame.

knighthood: see CHIVALRY; COURTLY LOVE.

knight service: see KNIGHT **2.**

Knights Hospitalers, members of the military and religious Order of the Hospital of St. John of Jerusalem, sometimes called the Knights of St. John and the Knights of Jerusalem. Early in the 11th cent. the increasing number of pilgrimages to the holy city of Jerusalem led some Italian merchants to obtain from the city's Muslim rulers the right to maintain a Latin-rite church there. In connection with this church a hospital for ill or infirm pilgrims was established. When the Crusaders took Jerusalem, the master of the hospital was Gerard de Martignes, who created a separate order, the Friars of the Hospital of St. John of Jerusalem. In 1113, Pope Paschal II recognized the order.

The Knights in the Holy Land. The object of the order was to aid the pilgrims, and it soon became apparent that military protection was necessary. Gerard's successor, Raymond du Puy, reconstituted the order as a military one. The members were divided into three classes—the knights of justice, who had to be of noble birth and had to be knights already; the chaplains, who served the spiritual needs of the establishment; and the serving brothers, who merely carried out orders given them. Besides these, there were the honorary members called donats, who contributed estates and funds to the order. The Hospitalers obtained a great income through gifts, and the necessity of caring for their estates led to the formation of subsidiary establishments all over Europe, the preceptories. The knights took part in the major crusading campaigns, notably the capture (1154) of Ascalon. When Jerusalem fell (1187) to the Muslims, the Hospitalers established themselves at Margat and then (1189) at Acre. The subsequent period was marked by rivalry with the KNIGHTS TEMPLARS and by military failure. Meanwhile, the hospital work of the order went on. In 1291 the knights were driven from the Holy Land by the fall of Acre and established themselves in Cyprus. They continued to combat the Muslims but now by sea rather than by land; the Hospitalers became the principal agents of convoys for pilgrims. Cyprus, however, was not the ideal place for the establishment, and the grand master, William de Villaret, planned the conquest of Rhodes from the Saracens, a conquest achieved by his brother and successor, Fulk (or Foulques) de Villaret in a special crusade (1308–10). *On the Island of Rhodes.* The order grew stronger on Rhodes. They had received some benefit from the dissolution of the Knights Templars, and the wealth of their grand priories all over Europe had greatly increased. To some extent, at least, the change was accompanied by a decline in moral standards. The Knights of Rhodes, as they came to be known, maintained their reputation as fighting men. In 1344 the knights, with the Genoese, retook Smyrna and held it for a short time. In 1365, in conjunction with the king of Cyprus, they captured Alexandria, which, however, they were unable to retain. The island of Rhodes was an important strategic point, and the Turks on their advance after the capture of Constantinople determined to take it. A heroic episode in medieval military history was the successful defense of Rhodes by the grand master, Pierre (later Cardinal) d'Aubusson, against the forces sent by Sultan Muhammad II. But the knights could not summon the means to resist indefinitely, and in 1522 the grand master Philippe de L'Isle Adam was forced to capitulate. The knights wandered homeless until in 1530 Holy Roman Emperor Charles V conferred upon them the sovereignty of the island of Malta. *The Knights of Malta.* The island became the fixed home of the order and gave its name to the knights. Under Jean de La Valette they built the great fortifications and defended Malta against the Turks in 1565. Meanwhile, the Protestant Reformation had dealt a severe blow to the order. It refused to yield to Henry VIII in England, and the English branch was suppressed. In Malta the order continued to live in fear of the Turks. The city of Valetta was built, and, as in Rhodes, the rule of the order was beneficial. The battle of Lepanto (1571) checked the Turks in the Mediterranean and a time of relative quiet began. The hospital at Malta was the equal of any in Europe, and the knights continued their charitable work. There was some reorganization of the order, and admission became more and more a test of nobility of birth. The order received its death blow when Napoleon Bonaparte on his Egyptian campaign took Malta (1798). The knights were compelled to leave. They chose Czar Paul of Russia as grand master by an illegal election, which was later validated. Many of the knights went to St. Petersburg. Thus a Roman Catholic order, with the permission of the pope, passed under the rule of an Orthodox emperor. The order was practically at an end. Admiral Nelson took Malta, and although by earlier agreement the island was to be returned to the knights, it was by the Congress of Vienna permanently ceded to Great Britain. After Paul's death there was a period of some indecision and deliberation. The pope named Tommasi as grand master; in 1802 he became the last regular head of the order, which moved to Catania. After 1805 the knights had no regular head and the fraternity continued but had little more than nominal existence in Catania, then Ferrara, then Rome. In 1879 the pope restored the office of grand master, but the reconstructed order that resulted has little relation to the old Knights of Malta. It is a charitable organization especially devoted to the care of the sick and the wounded. It expanded considerably, and in 1926 an association was founded in the United States. The reestablishment of the grand priory in conjunction with the efforts of some French Hospitalers who had attempted to revive the order in France took place in 1827, but the reconstituted order had no organic connection with the old order. The symbol of the Order of St. John came to be a white cross worn on a black robe; thus the Hospitalers were the Knights of the White Cross, in contradistinction to the Templars, the Knights of the Red Cross. The Maltese cross (see CROSS) has been used by various secret organizations, which have been falsely alleged to have a connection with the Knights of St. John. See E. J. King, *The Knights Hospitallers in the Holy Land* (1931); E. E. Hume, *Medical Work of the Knights Hospitallers* (1940); Roger Peyrefitte, *Knights of Malta* (tr. 1959); Roderigo Cavaliero, *The Last of the Crusaders* (1960, repr. 1963); C. E. Engel, *Knights of Malta* (1963); Ernie Bradford, *The Shield and the Sword* (1973).

Knights of Columbus, American Roman Catholic society for men, founded (1882) at New Haven, Conn. (where its headquarters are still located). Its objects are to encourage fraternity and benevolence among its members, to promote tolerance, to encourage civic loyalty, and to protect the interests of the Roman Catholic Church.

Knights of Jerusalem: see KNIGHTS HOSPITALERS.

Knights of Labor, American labor organization, started by Philadelphia tailors in 1869, led by Uriah S. Stephens. It became a body of national scope and importance in 1878 and grew more rapidly after 1881, when its earlier secrecy was abandoned. Organized on an industrial basis, with women, Negro workers (after 1883), and employers welcomed, excluding only bankers, lawyers, gamblers, and stockholders, the Knights of Labor aided various groups in strikes and boycotts, winning important strikes on the Union Pacific in 1884 and on the Wabash RR in 1885. But failure in the Missouri Pacific strike in 1886 and the HAYMARKET SQUARE RIOT (for which it was, although not responsible, condemned by the press) caused a loss of prestige and strengthened factional disputes between the craft unionists and the advocates of all-inclusive unionism. With the motto "an injury to one is the concern of all," the Knights of Labor attempted through educational means to further its aims—an 8-hour day, abolition of child and convict labor, equal pay for equal work, elimination of private banks, cooperation—which, like its methods, were highly idealistic. The organization reached its apex in 1886, when under Terence V. Powderly its membership reached a total of 702,000. Among the causes of its downfall were factional disputes, too much centralization with a resulting autocracy from top to bottom, mismanagement, drainage of financial resources through unsuccessful strikes, and the emergence of the American Federation of Labor. By 1890 its membership had dropped to 100,000, and in 1900 it was practically extinct. See T. V. Powderly, *Thirty Years of Labor* (1889, repr. 1967); N. J. Ware, *The Labor Movement in the United States, 1860–1895* (1929, repr. 1964).

Knights of Malta and **Knights of Rhodes:** see KNIGHTS HOSPITALERS.

Knights of Saint Crispin, union of shoemakers, organized in 1867 by Newell Daniels of Milwaukee in protest against the increasing industrialization of the shoe industry, which was replacing the skilled workers with new unskilled factory labor. As a result of a series of successful strikes, it became for a time the largest trade union in the country, with a membership of from 40,000 to 50,000. Interference in politics, corruption among its officers, the combination of employers against it, and the financial crisis of 1873 caused its downfall. By 1878 it was defunct, many of its members having joined the KNIGHTS OF LABOR, in which they became the largest trade element. See D. D. Lescohier, *The Knights of St. Crispin, 1867–1874* (1910, repr. 1969).

Knights of Saint John of Jerusalem: see KNIGHTS HOSPITALERS.

Knights of the Golden Circle, secret order of Southern sympathizers in the North during the Civil War. Its members were known as COPPERHEADS. Dr. George W. L. Bickley, a Virginian who had moved to Ohio, organized the first "castle," or local branch, in Cincinnati in 1854 and soon took the order to the South, where it was enthusiastically received. Its principal object was to provide a force to colonize the northern part of Mexico and thus extend proslavery interests, and the Knights became especially active in Texas. Secession and the outbreak of the Civil War prompted a shift in its aims from filibustering in Mexico to support of the new Southern government. Appealing to the South's friends in the North, the order soon spread to Kentucky, Indiana, Ohio, Illinois, and Missouri. Its membership in these states, where it became strongest, was largely composed of Peace Democrats, who felt that the Civil War was a mistake and that the increasing power of the Federal government was leading toward tyranny. They did not, however, at this time engage in any treasonable activity. In late 1863 the Knights of the Golden Circle was reorganized as the Order of American Knights and again, early in 1864, as the Order of the Sons of Liberty, with Clement L. VALLANDIGHAM, most prominent of the Copperheads, as its supreme commander. Membership in the Sons of Liberty was perhaps between 200,000 and 300,000 in 1864, when it reached its maximum. Only a minority of this membership was radical enough—in some localities—to discourage enlistments, resist the draft, and shield deserters. Numerous peace meetings were held. A few extreme agitators, some of them encouraged by Southern money, talked of a revolt in the Old Northwest, which, if brought about, would end the war. Southern newspapers wishfully reported stories of widespread disaffection, and John Hunt Morgan's raid (1863) into Kentucky, Indiana, and Ohio was undertaken in the expectation that the disaffected element would rally to his standard. Gov. Oliver P. Morton of Indiana and Gen. Henry B. Carrington effectively curbed the Sons of Liberty in that state in the fall of 1864. With mounting Union victories late in 1864, the order's agitation for a negotiated peace lost appeal, and it soon dissolved. See Wood Gray, *The Hidden Civil War* (1942); G. F. Milton, *Abraham Lincoln and the Fifth Column* (1942, repr. 1962); F. L. Klement, *The Copperheads in the Middle West* (1960); R. O. Curry, *A House Divided* (1964).

Knights of the Sword: see LIVONIAN BROTHERS OF THE SWORD.

Knights of the White Camellia: see KU KLUX KLAN.

Knights Templars: see FREEMASONRY.

Knights Templars, in medieval history, members of the military and religious order of the Poor Knights of Christ, called the Knights of the Temple of Solomon from their house in Jerusalem. Like the Knights Hospitalers and the Teutonic Knights, the Templars were formed during the CRUSADES. They originally had a purely military function. Founded when Hugh de Payens and eight other knights joined together c.1118 to protect pilgrims, the order grew rapidly. St. Bernard of Clairvaux drew up its rules, and it was recognized at the Council of Troyes (1128) and confirmed by Pope Honorius III. The Templars received gifts of estates and money, and the organization soon became one of the most powerful in Europe. By combining monastic privilege with chivalrous adventure, they attracted many nobles. The order, organized under a grand master and general council, had its headquarters at Jerusalem. It was directly responsible only to the pope and thus was free from the control of the secular crusading leaders. As Crusaders the knights were important both in fighting the Muslims (notably at Gaza in 1244 and later at Damietta, during the Fifth Crusade) and in the internal struggles of the Latin Kingdom of Jerusalem (see JERUSALEM, LATIN KINGDOM OF). Although the Knights of the White Cross (the Hospitalers) were at first probably larger and richer, the Templars, who wore the red cross on a white ground, were greater warriors. In the later crusades the deadly rivalry of the three orders helped weaken the Crusaders' chances of success. When Jerusalem fell to the Muslims (1187), the Templars operated from Acre; after its fall (1291) the order retreated to Cyprus. By that time the Templars had ceased to be primarily a fighting organization and had become the leading money-handlers of Europe. From the beginning the knights aroused opposition because of their special privileges, their freedom from secular control, and their great military and financial strength. As their banking role increased—they served such kings as Henry II of England and Louis IX of France—and their landholdings grew, they aroused the hostility, fear, and jealousy of secular rulers and of the secular clergy as well. When the Crusades failed, the Hospitalers became a naval patrol in the East, but the Templars grew more worldly, more decadent, and more hated. In 1307, Philip IV of France, who needed money for his Flemish war and was unable to obtain it elsewhere, began a persecution of the Templars. With the aid of Pope Clement V, the king had members of the order arrested and their possessions confiscated. By 1308 the persecutions were in full process. The knights were put on trial and were tortured to extract confessions of sacrilegious practices. The pope at first opposed the trials but soon reversed his position, and at the Council of Vienne (1311–12) he dissolved the order by papal bull. The Templars were completely destroyed by 1314. Much of their property, theoretically designated for the Hospitalers, was acquired by secular rulers. The leaders of the order, including the last grand master, Jacques de Molay, were tried by ecclesiastic judges and sentenced to life imprisonment, but after denouncing their confessions they were burned at the stake (1314) as lapsed heretics by civil authorities. It is impossible to evaluate fairly the Templars and their fate; the injustices of their final treatment have led some to consider them blameless, yet the charges against them were not entirely unfounded. The literature on the Templars is vast. A defense of the order is C. G. Addison, *The History of the Knights Templars* (rev. ed. 1912). See also the studies by E. J. Martin (1928), G. A. Campbell (1937), Edith Simon (1959), and T. W. Parker (1963).

Kniller, Gottfried von: see KNELLER, SIR GODFREY.

knitting, construction of a fabric made of interlocking loops of yarn by means of needles. Knitting, allied in origin to weaving and to the netting and knotting of fishnets and snares, was apparently unknown in Europe before the 15th cent., when it began to be practiced in Italy and Spain. The Scots claimed its invention and also its introduction into France. Hand-knitting needles are of bone, wood, steel, ivory, or celluloid. Two needles with heads are required for flat or selvage work; three or more, pointed at both ends, for tubular work such as hose; and for larger tubular work, a circular needle. The first knitting machine, invented in England in 1589 by William Lee, was refused a patent by Queen Elizabeth on the grounds that it would curtail the work of hand knitters. Lee's machine, marketed in France, was the forerunner of the warp and circular frames used after 1790; these in turn developed into the two modern types of power machines, the warp and the weft. The springbeard needle of Lee's frame was supplemented in 1847 by Matthew Townsend's latch needle, commonly used for coarse work. In 1864, William Cotton patented a machine by which garments and the heels and toes of hosiery might be shaped. Automatic machines were first introduced in 1889. In weft knitting, which includes hand knitting, the fabric is constructed in horizontal courses with one continuous yarn. The basic stitches are the plain (or jersey), purl, and rib. Either flatbed or circular machines may be used. The warp, or chainloom, machine, generally flatbed, builds vertical chains, or wales, each having a separate yarn. The wales are tied together by zigzagging the yarns from needle to needle in the basic tricot or milanese stitches or variants of these. The warp-knit fabric is run-resistant but less elastic than the weft. See Barbara Abbey, *The Complete Book of Knitting* (1972).

Knob Lake: see SCHEFFERVILLE, Que., Canada.

Knolles or **Knollys, Sir Robert** (both: nōlz), d. 1407, English military commander in the Hundred Years War. He became a leader of a company of mercenaries, fought against Bertrand DU GUESCLIN, whom he captured in 1359, and assisted EDWARD THE BLACK PRINCE in his Spanish campaign, especially at Nájera (1367). Continuing to fight throughout France, either for the English or for his own plunder, he ravaged Normandy and the Loire valley. In 1381 he helped to disperse the Peasants' Revolt in England.

Knopf, Alfred A., 1892–, American publisher, b. New York City. After working (1912–14) for the Doubleday, Page Publishing Company, he founded (1915) his own firm (Alfred A. Knopf, Inc.), which remained independent until 1960, when the company was sold by Knopf to Random House, Inc.; the Knopf imprint remained in existence. Knopf emphasized translations of great contemporary European literature, at that time neglected by American publishers, and specialized in producing books that were outstanding for fine printing, binding, and design. His colophon, the borzoi, became synonymous with beauty and taste in book design and high standards in the selection of books for publication.

Knossos: see CNOSSUS.

knot, any fastening made with cord or rope, including such forms as the hitch, splice, tie, and bend. The art of tying knots, known to sailors as marlinespike seamanship, was used in building bridges and rigging ships by the early Egyptians, Phoenicians, Persians, and Greeks; it reached a high stage of development among the seafaring peoples of the West in the 19th cent. The kinds of knots used by sailors are innumerable, but almost any navigator of small pleasure craft will find four secure knots sufficient: the reef, or square, knot (for securing the ends of two lines); the bowline (for forming a loop); the half hitch (for forming a loop); and the eye splice (for any permanent loop, frequently formed around a metal lining called a thimble). In marine speed measurement, a knot is equal to one nautical mile per hour, a nautical mile being 6,076.1 ft (1,852.0 m). In architecture, an ornament of leaves, flowers, or the like on a projecting piece is called a knot. In heraldry, a knot is an ornamental design representing the interlacing of cordage.

Knowles, James Sheridan (nōlz), 1784–1862, Anglo-Irish dramatist; cousin of Richard Brinsley Sheridan. Although he was one of the leading playwrights of his time, his works are seldom produced today. His chief plays, which are noted for their professional, workmanlike construction, include the tragedies *Virginius* (1820) and *William Tell* (1825) and the comedies *The Hunchback* (1832) and *The Beggar of Bethnal Green* (1834). In 1845, Knowles became a Baptist minister.

Knowles, John, 1926–, American writer, b. Fairmont, W.Va., grad. Yale, 1949. He is best known for his first novel, *A Separate Peace* (1960), in which a boy in a New England prep school during World War II learns about love and hate, conflict and death, war and peace. Knowles's other novels include *Morning in Antibes* (1962), *The Paragon* (1971), and *Spreading Fires* (1974).

Know-Nothing movement, in U.S. history. The increasing rate of immigration in the 1840s encouraged nativism. In Eastern cities where Roman Catholic immigrants especially had concentrated and were welcomed by the Democrats, local nativistic societies were formed to combat "foreign" influences and to uphold the "American" view. The American Republican party, formed (1843) in New York, spread into neighboring states as the Native American party, which became a national party at its Philadelphia convention in 1845. The movement was temporarily eclipsed by the Mexican War and the debates over slavery. When the slavery issue was temporarily quieted by the Compromise of 1850 nativism again came to the fore. Many secret orders grew up, of which the Order of United Americans and the Order of the Star-spangled Banner came to be the most important. These organizations baffled political managers of the older parties, since efforts to learn something of the leaders or designs of the movement were futile; all their inquiries of supposed members were met with a statement to the effect that they knew nothing. Hence members were called Know-Nothings, although there was never a political organization bearing the name. Efforts were concentrated on electing only native Americans to office and on agitating for a 25-year residence qualification for citizenship. Growing rapidly, the Know-Nothings allied themselves with the group of Whigs who followed Millard Fillmore and almost captured New York state in the 1854 election, while they did sweep the polls in Massachusetts and Delaware and had local successes in other states. The disintegration of the Whig party aided them in their strides towards national influence. In 1854 they looked towards extension into the South, and in the following year they openly assumed the name American party and cast aside much of their characteristic secrecy. In June, 1855, a crisis developed; at a meeting of the national council in Philadelphia, Southerners seized control and adopted a resolution calling for the maintenance of slavery. The slavery issue, after the passage of the Kansas-Nebraska Act, again came to the front, and this time the slavery issue split apart the Know-Nothing movement as it had the Whigs. The antislavery men went into the newly organized Republican party. Millard Fillmore, the American party candidate for President in 1856, polled a small vote and won only the state of Maryland. The national strength of the Know-Nothing movement thus was broken. See R. A. Billington, *The Protestant Crusade, 1800–1860* (1938, repr. 1964); W. D. Overdyke, *The Know-Nothing Party in the South* (1950, repr. 1968); Carleton Beals, *Brass-Knuckle Crusade* (1960).

Knox, Frank (William Franklin Knox), 1874–1944, U.S. Secretary of the Navy (1940–44), b. Boston. He joined the Rough Riders in the Spanish-American War and also served in World War I. Knox was general manager (1928–31) of the Hearst papers and after 1931 owner of the Chicago *Daily News.* A strong opponent of the New Deal, he was the unsuccessful Republican candidate for Vice President in 1936. In 1940, President Franklin Delano Roosevelt, seeking to create national unity in defense preparations, made Knox Secretary of the Navy. He died in office and was succeeded by James V. Forrestal.

Knox, Henry, 1750–1806, American Revolutionary officer, b. Boston. He volunteered for service and went, in 1775, to Ticonderoga to retrieve the captured cannon and mortar there for use in the siege of Boston. The fortification of Dorchester Heights with this artillery compelled the evacuation of Boston by the British. From that time he was a trusted companion of George Washington. The artillery, under his charge, took a conspicuous part in the battles of Princeton, Brandywine, Germantown, Monmouth, and Yorktown. He commanded at West Point (1782–84) and was a founder (1783) of the Society of the Cincinnati. Knox was Secretary of War both under the Articles of Confederation and under the Constitution (1785–94). A conservative, he attempted to raise a force to oppose Shay's Rebellion, and he favored a strong Federal government. See biography by North Callahan (1958).

Knox, John, 1514?–1572, Scottish religious reformer, founder of Scottish PRESBYTERIANISM. Little is recorded of his life before 1545. He probably attended St. Andrews Univ., where he may have become acquainted with some of the new Protestant heresies. He entered the Roman Catholic priesthood, however, and from 1540 to 1544 was engaged as an ecclesiastical notary and as a private tutor. By late 1545 he had attached himself closely to the reformer George WISHART. When, after Wishart's execution (1546), a group of Protestant conspirators took revenge by murdering Cardinal David BEATON, Knox, now definitely a Protestant, took refuge with them in St. Andrews Castle and preached in the parish church. Attacked by both Scottish and French forces, the castle was eventually surrendered (1547), and Knox served 19 months in the French galleys before his release (1549) through the efforts of the English government of Edward VI. Knox spent the next few years in England, preaching in Berwick and Newcastle as a licensed minister of the crown and serving briefly as a royal chaplain. He helped to prepare the second Book of Common Prayer, but he declined a bishopric in the newly established Church of England. Shortly after the accession (1553) of the Catholic Mary I to the English throne, Knox went into exile on the Continent, living chiefly in Geneva and Frankfurt. In Geneva he consulted with John CALVIN on questions of church doctrine and civil authority. Meanwhile, through his frequent letters, he exerted considerable influence among Protestants in England and Scotland; in his "Faithful Admonition" pamphlet of 1554 he began to urge the duty of the righteous to overthrow "ungodly" monarchs. In 1555–56 he visited Scotland, preaching in private and counseling the Protestant congregations. After his return to Geneva, where he served (1556–58) as pastor to the English congregation, he wrote the *First Blast of the Trumpet against the Monstrous Regiment* [i.e., regimen] *of Women.* That fiery tract was directed against the Catholic MARY OF GUISE, regent of Scotland, and Queen Mary of England, but it also alienated the Protestant Elizabeth I, who succeeded to the English throne in 1558.

The Scottish Reformation. In 1557 the Scottish Protestant nobles signed their First Covenant, banding together to form the group known as the lords of the congregation (see SCOTLAND, CHURCH OF). When, in 1559, Mary of Guise moved against the Protestants, the lords of the congregation took up arms and invited Knox back from Geneva to lead them. Aided by England and by the regent's death in 1560, the reformers forced the withdrawal of the French troops that had come to Mary's aid and won their freedom as well as dominance for the new religion. Under Knox's direction, a confession of faith (basically Calvinist) was drawn up (1560) and passed by the Scottish Parliament, which also passed laws abolishing the authority of the pope and condemning all creeds and practices of the old religion. The Book of Discipline, however, which provided an organizational structure for the new church, failed to get adequate approval from the nobles in 1561. When MARY QUEEN OF SCOTS arrived from France to assume her crown in the same year, many Protestant lords deserted Knox and his cause, and some even joined the queen. From his pulpit and in personal debates with Mary on questions of theology and the loyalty owed by the subject to his monarch, Knox stubbornly defied Mary's authority and thundered against her religion. The queen's marriage to Lord Darnley, her suspected complicity in his murder, and her hasty marriage to James Hepburn, earl of Bothwell, stirred the Protestant lords to revolt. Mary was forced to abdicate (1567) in favor of her young son, James VI. All the acts of 1560 were then confirmed, thereby establishing Presbyterianism as the official religion. Despite the ill-health of his last years, Knox continued to be an outspoken preacher until his death. It has been said of Knox that "rarely has any country produced a stronger will." His single-minded zeal made him the outstanding leader of the Scottish Reformation and an important influence on the Protestant movements in England and on the Continent, but the same quality tended to close his mind to divergent views. His *History of the Reformation in Scotland,* finished in 1564 but published in 1584 after his death, is a striking record of that conflict, but includes a number of misstatements and omissions resulting from his strong bias. The standard edition of his works is that edited by David Laing (6 vol., 1846–64, repr. 1967). See biographies by P. Hume Brown (1895), E. S. C. Percy (1937, repr. 1965), Geddes MacGregor (1957), J. G. Ridley (1968), and W. S. Reid (1974); J. S. McEwen, *The Faith of John Knox* (1961); S. W. Reid, *Trumpeter of God* (1974).

Knox, Philander Chase, 1853–1921, U.S. cabinet member, b. Brownsville, Pa. He built up a fortune as a corporation lawyer in Pittsburgh. He was Attorney General (1901–4) in the cabinets of Presidents Wil-

Knoxville, a major trade and industrial center, in eastern Tenn.

liam McKinley and Theodore Roosevelt. He was prominently identified with trust prosecutions, but failed to dissolve any significant organizations, except that of the Northern Securities Company, a railroad holding corporation. He served as U. S. Senator by appointment (1904–5) and was elected for the succeeding full term, but resigned in 1909 to become Secretary of State under President Taft. Continuing the policies of his predecessors, John Hay and Elihu Root, Knox sought to protect financial interests abroad, particularly in Latin America and China—a policy that became known as "dollar diplomacy." Knox returned to the Senate in 1917 and allied himself with those who fought ratification of the Treaty of Versailles and participation in the League of Nations. See S. F. Bemis, ed., *The American Secretaries of State,* Vol. IX (1929, repr. 1963).

Knox, Ronald, 1888–1957, English theologian and author. He attended Eton and then Balliol College, Oxford, and in 1910 was ordained as an Anglican minister. Doctrinal preferences, however, led to his Roman Catholic ordination (1919) and appointment as Catholic chaplain at Oxford (1926). While chaplain, Knox wrote several detective novels until appointed to produce a new English Bible (complete ed. 1955). Other works include *Spiritual Aeneid* (1918), a defense of his adoption of Catholicism, and *Enthusiasm* (1950), a history of Christian sectarianism.

Knox, Fort: see FORT KNOX.

Knox College, at Galesburg, Ill.; coeducational; chartered 1837, opened 1841 with funds from George W. GALE; called Knox Manual Labor College until 1857. In 1930 it absorbed Lombard College (chartered 1851, opened 1852). The college was the scene of a Lincoln-Douglas debate in 1858.

Knoxville, city (1970 pop. 174,587), seat of Knox co., E Tenn., on the Tennessee River; inc. 1876. A port of entry, it is a major trade and shipping center for a farm, bituminous-coal, and marble area. Its industries include meat packing, tobacco marketing, and the manufacture of seat belts, plastics, textiles, and marble, wood, and metal products. Tourism is also important. The city is surrounded by mountains and lakes, and the Great Smoky Mts. National Park and several state parks are nearby. A house was built on this site c.1785, followed by a fort and then a town, named for Gen. Henry Knox. Knoxville was the capital of the Territory of the United States South of the River Ohio from 1792 to 1796 and twice (1796–1812, 1817–18) served as the state capital. During the Civil War the area was torn by divided loyalties. Federals under Gen. A. E. Burnside occupied the city in Sept., 1863, and successfully withstood a Confederate siege (Nov.–Dec., 1863) led by Gen. James Longstreet, after which the Confederates had no influence in the area. The Univ. of Tennessee at Knoxville and Knoxville College are there. Knoxville is headquarters of the TENNESSEE VALLEY AUTHORITY, and Norris Dam, from which the city procures its power, is nearby. Points of interest include the graves of John Sevier and William Blount, the Blount Mansion (1792), a replica of the old fort, Chisholm's Tavern (1792), and many other old buildings.

Knudsen, William Signius (nōōd'sən), 1879–1948, American industrialist and U.S. government official, b. Copenhagen, Denmark. He emigrated to the United States at age 20, worked in various factories, and became production manager in the Ford Motor Company during World War I. Employed (1922) by the General Motors Corp., Knudsen became (1937) president. From 1940 to 1945, during World War II, he served successively as director of industrial production for the National Defense Commission, the Office of Production Management, and, as lieutenant general in the U.S. army, for the War Dept. See biography by Norman Beasley (1947).

Knut: see CANUTE.

Knutson, Paul: see PAUL KNUTSON.

Knyphausen, Wilhelm, Baron von (vĭl'hĕlm bärôn' fən kənüp'houzən), 1716–1800, German general in British service in the American Revolution. He served in the army of Frederick the Great before coming to America with the Hessian troops in 1776. Knyphausen distinguished himself in the battles at White Plains, Brandywine, Germantown, and Monmouth. He commanded (1779–80) New York in the absence of Sir Henry Clinton.

Koa (kō'ə), obscure name associated with the Assyrians. Ezek. 23.23.

koala (kōä'lə), arboreal MARSUPIAL, or pouched mammal, *Phascolarctos cinereus,* native to Australia. Although it is sometimes called koala bear, or Australian bear, and is somewhat bearlike in appearance, it is not related to true bears. Once abundant, it is now found in much-reduced numbers in Queensland, Victoria, and New South Wales. It has thick grayish fur, a tailless body 2 to 2½ ft (60–75 cm) long, a protuberant, curved, black nose, and large furry ears. The five sharply clawed toes on each foot enable it to grasp and climb. A slow-moving, nocturnal animal, the koala has perhaps the most specialized diet of any living mammal; it feeds on leaves and shoots of a particular stage of maturation from particular species of eucalyptus. The single cub is about ¾ in (1.9 cm) long at birth and is nursed in the mother's pouch, from which it emerges for the first time when about six months old. Until it is about eight months old it continues to ride in the pouch, and until about a year of age it is carried on its mother's back or in her arms. The harmless and defenseless koala has been ruthlessly hunted, chiefly for fur but also for food; disease and the clearing of the eucalyptus forests have also taken a heavy toll. Protective measures have been adopted to prevent its extinction. The koala is classified in the phylum CHORDATA, subphylum Vertebrata, class Mammalia, order Marsupialia, family Phalangeridae.

koan (kō'än) [Jap.,=public case; Chin. *kung-ar*], a subject for meditation in ZEN BUDDHISM, usually one of the sayings of a great Zen master of the past. In the formative period of Zen in China, masters tested the enlightenment of their students and of one another through statements and dialogue that expressed spiritual intuition in nonrational, paradoxical language. In later generations records of such conversations began to be used in teaching, and the first collections of subjects, or koans, were made in the 11th cent. Koan practice was transmitted to Japan as a part of Zen in the 13th cent., and it remains one of the main practices of the Rinzai sect. The most famous koan collections are the *Wu-men-kuan* (Jap. *Mu-mon-kan*) or "Gateless Gate" and the *Pi-yen-lu* (Jap. *Heki-gan-roku*) or "Blue Cliff Records." An example of a well-known koan is: "What is the sound of one hand clapping?" See Isshu Mi-

Koala, an arboreal marsupial native to Australia.

ura and R. F. Sasaki, *Zen Dust* (1966); G. M. Kubose, *Zen Koans* (1973).

kob: see MARSH ANTELOPE.

Kobe (kō'bā), city (1970 pop. 1,288,754), capital of Hyogo prefecture, S Honshu, Japan, on Osaka Bay. One of the leading Japanese ports, it is also a major industrial center and railway hub. It has shipbuilding yards, vehicle factories, iron and steel mills, sugar refineries, and chemical, rubber, and food-processing plants. A cultural center, Kobe has seven colleges and universities and many temples and shrines. Since 1878 the city has included Hyogo (formerly Hiogo), an ancient port that was prominent during the Ashikaga period (14th–16th cent.) and regained importance after it was reopened to foreign trade in 1868. Kobe was heavily bombed during World War II but has since been rebuilt and enlarged.

København, Denmark: see COPENHAGEN.

Koberger, Anton (än'tōn kō'bĕr"gûr), c.1445–1513, German printer. He established in 1470 the first printery in Nuremberg. In 1483 he produced a German Bible and in 1484 the first book printed in the Hungarian language. Koberger was primarily a publisher. He had agencies in many cities, employed traveling salesmen, and issued one of the first advertising circulars.

Koblenz (kō'blĕnts), Eng. *Coblenz,* city (1970 pop. 119,423), Rhineland-Palatinate, W West Germany, at the confluence of the Rhine and the Moselle (Ger. *Mosel*) rivers. Its manufactures include machines, furniture, pianos, textiles, and printed materials. It is an important trade center for Rhine and Moselle wines. The city was founded (9 B.C.) as Castrum ad Confluentes by Drusus. It was prominent in Carolingian times as a residence of the Frankish kings and as a meeting place for churchmen. Koblenz was held by the archbishops of Trier from 1018 to the late 18th cent. In 1794 it was occupied by French troops and in 1798 was annexed by France and made the capital of the Rhine and Moselle department. The city passed to Prussia in 1815. After World War I it was occupied by Allied troops from 1919 to 1929. Noteworthy buildings in Koblenz include the Church of St. Castor (founded 836; rebuilt c.1200), the fortress of EHRENBREITSTEIN, and an 18th-century castle. Part of the West German state archives are located in the city.

Kobo-Daishi: see KUKAI.

Koch, Johannes: see COCCEIUS, JOHANNES.

Koch, Kenneth (kŏch), 1925–, American poet, novelist, and playwright, b. Cincinnati, Ohio. Since studying at Harvard and Columbia he has been associated with the Artist's Theatre and *Locus Solus* magazine. Koch's "antisymbolic" poetic style contains witty juxtapositions and dislocations of words. His works include *Poems* (1953); *Ko, or a Season on Earth* (1959), a novel in verse; *Bertha and Other Plays* (1966); *Wishes, Lies, and Dreams: Teaching Children to Write Poetry* (1970) and *Rose, Where Did You Get That Red?: Teaching Great Poetry to Children* (1973).

Koch, Lauge (lou'gə kôk), 1892–1964, Danish geologist and explorer, noted for his scientific work in Greenland. He accompanied Knud Rasmussen's second Thule expedition (1916–18) as geologist and cartographer and was chief of a notable expedition (1920–23) to N Greenland during which he completed the mapping of the Greenland coast and gave for the first time the geological picture of the northern portion of the island. Thereafter Koch was almost continuously in Greenland, as leader of Danish expeditions. In 1938 his air photographs over N Greenland proved the much-sought Peary Channel to be only a fjord.

Robert Koch.

Koch, Robert (rō'bĕrt kôkh), 1843–1910, German bacteriologist. He studied at Göttingen under Jacob Henle. As a country practitioner in Wollstein, Posen, he devoted much time to microscopic studies of bacteria, for which he devised not only a method of staining with aniline dyes but also techniques of bacteriological culture still in general use. He established the bacterial cause of many infectious diseases and discovered the microorganisms causing anthrax (1876), wound infections (1878), tuberculosis (1882), conjunctivitis (1883), Asiatic cholera (1884), and other diseases. He was professor at the Univ. of Berlin from 1885 to 1891 and head of the Institute for Infectious Diseases (founded for him) from 1891 to 1904. In the course of his bacteriological investigations for the British and German governments he traveled to South Africa, India, Egypt, and other countries and made valuable studies of sleeping sickness, malaria, bubonic plague, rinderpest, and other diseases. For his work in developing tuberculin as a test for tuberculosis he received the 1905 Nobel Prize in Physiology and Medicine.

Kochanowski, Jan (yän kôkhänôf'skē), 1530–84, esteemed as the greatest poet of the Polish Renaissance. Kochanowski assimilated the poetic traditions of Italy and France and created new rhythmic patterns, expressive phrases, and syntactic structures that were integrated into the Polish literary language. His philosophical, erotic, and patriotic lyrics lifted Polish literature out of its provincialism and brought it into the mainstream of the European Renaissance. His works include *Trifles* (1584), short poems on many subjects; *Laments,* elegies upon the death of his daughter; an epic, *The Standard*; and a tragedy, *The Dismissal of the Greek Envoys* (1578).

Of special note is his Polish version of the Psalms. Much of his work is available in English translation.

Kocher, Emil Theodor (ā'mĭl tā'ōdôr kôkh'ər), 1841–1917, Swiss surgeon, M.D. Univ. of Bern, 1865. He was professor of surgery at Bern (1872–1911). For his work on the physiology, pathology, and surgery of the thyroid gland—which he was the first (1876) to excise in cases of goiter—he received the 1909 Nobel Prize in Medicine. He was a skilled surgeon and a pioneer in the application of asepsis. His works include a textbook on operative surgery (1894).

Kochi (kō'chē), city (1970 pop. 240,321), capital of Kochi prefecture, S Shikoku, Japan. From its port, Urado, the city exports dried bonito, ornamental coral, cement, and paper. Kochi prefecture (1970 pop. 786,690), 2,743 sq mi (7,104 sq km), is a mountainous region with fertile coastal plains.

Ko-chiu or **Kokiu** (both: gô-jēo͞o), town, S Yünnan prov., China. Site of the country's largest tin reserves, it is the great tin-mining center of China, with smelters and concentrating plants. Iron is also found there, and chemicals are produced.

Kock, Hieronymus: see COCK, HIERONYMUS.

Kodaira (kōdī'rä), city (1970 pop. 137,373), Tokyo Metropolis, central Honshu, Japan. It is a suburb of Tokyo.

Kodály, Zoltán (zôl'tän kô'dī), 1882–1967, Hungarian composer and collector of folk music. In 1906 he began to teach at the Budapest Hochschule, of which he became assistant director in 1919. He lectured (1931–33) at the Univ. of Budapest. Kodály did much to raise the standards of music education in Hungary. With Bartók he collected thousands of Hungarian folk songs and dances, and the influence of this interest is strong in his compositions, which have a romantic style. Among his best-known works are the opera *Háry János* (1926, orchestral suite 1927), the *Psalmus Hungaricus* (1923) and *Missa Brevis* (1945) for chorus and orchestra, and orchestral dances.

Kodiak Island, 5,363 sq mi (13,890 sq km), c.100 mi (160 km) long and 10–60 mi (16–96 km) wide, off S Alaska, separated from the Alaska Peninsula by Shelikof Strait. Alaska's largest island, Kodiak is mountainous and heavily forested in the north and east; the native grasses in the south offer good pasturage for cattle and sheep. The island has many ice-free, deeply penetrating bays that provide sheltered anchorages and transportation routes. The Kodiak bear and the Kodiak king crab are native to the island. Most of the island is a national wildlife refuge. In 1912 the eruption of Mt. Katmai on the mainland blanketed the island with volcanic ash, causing widespread destruction and loss of life (see KATMAI NATIONAL MONUMENT). Discovered in 1763 by Russian fur trader Stepan Glotov, the island was the scene of the first permanent Russian settlement in Alaska, founded by Grigori Shelekhov, a fur trader, on Three Saints Bay in 1784. The settlement was moved to Kodiak village in 1792 and became the center of Russian fur trading. Kodiak is the island's chief town. Salmon fishing is now the main occupation, and the Karluk River is famous for its salmon run. Fish canning, fox breeding, and grazing are also important. A U.S. naval base is there.

Kodok (kō'dŏk), formerly **Fashoda** (fəshō'də), town, SE Sudan, on the White Nile. In 1898 it was the scene of the Fashoda Incident, which brought Britain and France to the brink of war and resulted, in 1899, in an Anglo-French agreement establishing the frontier between the Sudan and the French Congo along the watershed between the Congo and Nile basins. The formation of an Anglo-French entente in 1904 prompted the British to change the town's name in hopes of obliterating the memory of the incident.

Koechlin, Charles (shärl kāklăN'), 1867–1950, French composer. Koechlin studied composition with Massenet and Fauré. He composed in all forms and many styles, but his music is rarely performed. Koechlin was also active as a teacher and music theorist, and wrote books about Fauré and Debussy, for some of whose works he did orchestration.

Koelreuter, Joseph Gottlieb: see KÖLREUTER.

Koerber, Ernest von (fən kör'bər), 1850–1919, Austro-Hungarian prime minister. A career civil servant, he became prime minister (1900–1904) and made a vigorous but vain attempt to reconcile the national factions of the monarchy by liberal, parliamentary methods. His second tenure, after the assassination (1916) of Count STÜRGKH, was brief because of differences with the new emperor, Charles I.

Koestler, Arthur (kĕst'lər), 1905–, English writer, b. Budapest of Hungarian parents. He became a Communist in 1931 but left the party at the time of the Stalin purge trials of the 1930s. While a correspondent in the Spanish civil war, he was captured by Franco's forces and imprisoned; *Spanish Testament* (1937) relates his experiences. Released in 1937, he edited an anti-Nazi and anti-Soviet French weekly and served in the French foreign legion (1939–40). After the German invasion he was interned in a concentration camp. He escaped from France in 1940 and joined the British army. Koestler combines a brilliant journalistic style with an understanding of the great movements of his times and a participant's sense of commitment. His greatest influence has been as spokesman of the ex-Communist left. *Darkness at Noon* (1941), his most important novel, vividly describes the purge of an old Bolshevik for "deviationist" belief in the individual. Other novels include *Thieves in the Night* (1946), a powerful description of the Arab-Israeli struggle, *The Age of Longing* (1951), and *The Call Girls: A Tragicomedy* (1973). His later essays and studies are often philosophic, examining the nature of art, science, and man himself. They include "The Yogi and the Commissar" (1945), a famous essay in *The God That Failed* (ed. by R. H. Crossman, 1951), *The Lotus and the Robot* (1960), *The Ghost in the Machine* (1968), *The Case of the Midwife Toad* (1971), and *The Roots of Coincidence* (1972). See his autobiography in 2 vol., *Arrow in the Blue* (1952) and *The Invisible Writing* (1954); study by Wolfe Mays (1973).

Koffka, Kurt (kŏf'kə, Ger. ko͝ort kôf'kä), 1886–1941, American psychologist, b. Germany, Ph.D. Univ. of Berlin, 1908. Before settling permanently in the United States in 1928 as a professor at Smith, he taught at Cornell and at the Univ. of Wisconsin. With Max Wertheimer and Wolfgang Köhler he is credited with developing the theories that gave rise to the school of GESTALT psychology. His book *Growth of the Mind* (1924) was considered responsible for awakening much interest in Gestalt concepts. See his *Principles of Gestalt Psychology* (1935).

Koforidua (kōfōrēdo͞o'ä), town (1970 pop. 44,768), capital of the Eastern region, S Ghana. It is the commercial center for a region producing palm oil, cassava, and corn; it also serves as a road and rail center. Fruit juice is made in the town. Koforidua was founded (c.1875) by refugees from ASHANTI. It is also called New Juaben.

Kofu (kō'fo͞o), city (1970 pop. 182,604), capital of Yamanashi prefecture, central Honshu, Japan. It is an industrial center, with manufactures of silk textiles and crystal ware, as well as a collection point for silk cocoons and raw silk. In the 16th cent. Kofu was the castle town of the Takeda family. Yamanashi prefecture (1970 pop. 762,029), 1,724 sq mi (4,465 sq km), is a major production area for raw silk and grapes.

Koganei (kōgä'nā), city (1970 pop. 94,448), Tokyo Metropolis, central Honshu, Japan. It is a suburb of Tokyo.

Kohala (kōhä'lə), peninsula, Hawaii, on the northern tip of the island of Hawaii. The region is rich in relics of ancient Hawaii, such as burial caves and *heiau* (temples). Kamehameha I was born near the village of Kapaau-Halaula. The Kohala Mts. there rise to 5,489 ft (1,673 m).

Kohat (kō'hät), town (1961 pop. 49,854), N Pakistan, on the Kohat Toi River. The town, enclosed by a wall with 14 gates, is noted for its cotton fabrics and sarongs. Kohat contains a 19th-century British fort built on the site of an old Sikh fortress.

Kohath (kō'hăth), founder of a family of the Levites. It comprised four groups, the Amramites, Izeharites, Hebronites, and Uzzielites. Gen. 46.11; Num. 3.19,27,29,30; 4; 7.9; 10.21; Joshua 21; 1 Chron. 6; 9.32; 15.5; 26; 2 Chron. 20.19; 29.12; 34.12.

Koh-i-noor: see DIAMOND.

Kohler, Kaufmann (kouf'mən kō'lər), 1843–1926, American rabbi, scholar, and leader in Reform Judaism, b. Bavaria. He emigrated to the United States in 1869 and served with congregations in Detroit and Chicago before becoming (1879) rabbi of Temple Beth-El in New York City. From 1903 to 1921 he was president of the Hebrew Union College in Cincinnati. He called the conference (1885) at which the Pittsburgh Platform of Reformed Judaism was adopted. One of the editors of *The Jewish Encyclopedia,* he also wrote *Backwards or Forwards: Lectures on Reform Judaism* (1885), *Jewish Theology Systematically and Historically Considered* (1918), *Heaven and Hell in Comparative Religion* (1923), and the *Origins of the Synagogue and the Church* (1929). His *Studies, Addresses, and Personal Papers* (1931) contains a short autobiography. See R. J. Marx, *Kaufmann Kohler as Reformer* (1951).

Köhler, Wolfgang (kö'lər), 1887–1967, American psychologist, b. Estonia, Ph.D. Univ. of Berlin, 1909. From 1913 to 1920 he was director of a research station on Tenerife, Canary Islands. Later he served as both professor of psychology and director of the Psychology Institute, Berlin. He came to the United States in 1934, where he became professor of psychology at Swarthmore College. Köhler is best known for his experiments with problem-solving in apes at Tenerife and the influence of his writings in the founding of the school of GESTALT psychology. His writings include *Gestalt Psychology* (rev. ed. 1947) and *The Mentality of Apes* (rev. ed. 1948). See his selected papers, ed. by Mary Henle (1971).

Kohler, village (1970 pop. 1,738), Sheboygan co., E Wis., on the Sheboygan River; inc. 1912. The Kohler plumbing-fixtures plant there has been the scene of some of the longest and most bitter labor disputes in U.S. history. The last strike began in 1954 and ended in 1962.

kohlrabi (kōl'rä'bē) [Ger. partly from Ital.,=turnip cabbage], plant (*Brassica caulorapa,* sometimes classified as var. *caulorapa* of the CABBAGE species) of the family Cruciferae (MUSTARD family), with an edible turniplike, swollen stem. It is a cool-weather plant grown more in Europe, where some varieties are used for fodder, than in America. The flavor is more delicate than that of some of the other cabbage plants. Kohlrabi is classified in the division MAGNOLIOPHYTA, class Magnoliopsida, order Capparales, family Cruciferae.

Koiso, Kuniaki (ko͞onēä'kē koi'sō), 1880–1950, Japanese general. He was chief of staff of the Kwantung army, commander in chief in Korea, and governor-general of Korea before he replaced Tojo as prime minister in July, 1944. He resigned in April, 1945, after Iwo Jima, the Philippines, and Okinawa were lost. Sentenced (1948) to life imprisonment as a war criminal, he died in a U.S. army hospital.

Kokand or **Khokand** (kəkänt'), city (1972 est. pop. 139,000), Central Asian USSR, in Uzbekistan, in the Fergana Valley. It is a center for the manufacture of fertilizers, chemicals, machinery, and cotton and food products. Important since the 10th cent., Kokand became the capital of an Uzbek khanate which became independent of the emirate of Bukhara in the middle of the 18th cent. and flowered in the 1820s and '30s. Kokand was taken by the Russians in 1876 and became part of Russian Turkistan. It was the capital (1917–18) of the anti-Bolshevik autonomous government of Turkistan.

Koken, Johannes: see COCCEIUS, JOHANNES.

Kokiu: see KO-CHIU, China.

Kokkola (kōk'kōlä), Swed. *Gamlakarleby,* city (1970 pop. 20,932), Vaasa prov., W Finland, on the Gulf of Bothnia. It is a port with steel, engineering, and lumber industries. It was chartered in 1620.

Kokomo (kō'kəmō), city (1970 pop. 44,042), seat of Howard co., N central Ind., on Wildcat Creek; inc. 1865. Radios, automobile parts, and metal products are manufactured there. The first commercially built automobile was invented and tested in Kokomo in 1894 by Elwood Haynes. Points of interest include the Elwood Haynes Museum. Indiana Univ. has a campus at Kokomo, and Grissom Air Force Base is nearby.

Koko Nor or **Kuku Nor** (both: kōkō nōr), Chin. *Ch'ing Hai* or *Tsinghai* [blue sea], salt lake, c.1,625 sq mi (4,210 sq km), in the Tibetan highlands, NE Tsinghai prov., China; one of the largest lakes in China. At an altitude of 10,515 ft (3,205 m), it is shallow and brackish and of little economic value.

Kokoschka, Oskar (ôs'kär kōkôsh'kä), 1886–, Austrian expressionist painter and writer. After teaching at the art academy in Dresden (1920–24), Kokoschka traveled extensively in Europe and N Africa before moving to London in 1938. In 1937 his works in German galleries were removed by the Nazi regime. After World War II he lived in Switzerland and established an international summer school in Salzburg. Kokoschka was influenced by the elegant work of Klimt, but soon developed his own expressionist style. His early portraits emphasize psychological tension (e.g., the portrait of Hans Tietze and his wife, 1909; Mus. of Modern Art, New York City). The same restless, energetic draftsmanship is revealed in his expressionist landscapes and his striking posters and lithographs. His landscapes include *Jerusalem* (Detroit Inst. of Arts) and *View of Prague* (Phillips

Memorial Gall., Washington, D.C.). See his volume of watercolors, drawings, and writings (1962); reproductions of his work, comp. by Bernhard Bultmann (1961), Ludwig Goldscheider (1963), E. G. Rathenau (1970), and Jan Tomeš (1972); biography by Edith Hoffmann (1947).

Kokubunji (kōko͞o'bo͞onjē), city (1970 pop. 81,259), Tokyo Metropolis, central Honshu, Japan. It is a suburb of Tokyo and is noted for its Kokubunji (Buddhist) temple founded in 1588.

Kokura: see KITAKYUSHU, Japan.

kola: see COLA.

Kolaiah (kŏlā'yə). **1** Benjamite family in Jerusalem. Neh. 11.7. **2** Father of Ahab, a false prophet. Jer. 29.21.

Kola Peninsula (kō'lə, Rus. kô'lə), peninsula, c.50,000 sq mi (129,500 sq km), NW European USSR, in Murmansk oblast. Forming an eastern extension of the Scandinavian peninsula, it lies between the Barents Sea to the north and the White Sea to the south. In the northeastern part are tundras; the southwestern area is forested. The peninsula has rich mineral deposits in the Khibiny mts., which rise to c.4,000 ft (1,220 m). Hydroelectric plants have been built along the Tuloma, Voronya, and Niva rivers. The port of MURMANSK and the mining center of KIROVSK are the major cities of the peninsula. Along the coasts and in the mining centers, the population is primarily Russian; in the interior are Lapps, who subsist largely on reindeer raising. Near Murmansk is the ancient town of Kola founded in 1264 by Slavs from Novgorod.

Montana *(1947), detail of a painting by the Austrian expressionist artist Oskar Kokoschka.*

Kolar (kōlär'), city (1971 pop. 43,345), Karnataka state, SW India. Founded in the late 19th cent., it is the center of the Indian gold-mining industry. The first hydroelectric project in S India was built in 1902 to provide electricity for the gold fields.

Kolarovgrad: see SHUMEN, Bulgaria.

Kolas, Jakub (yä'ko͝ob kō'läs), 1882–1956, Belorussian poet and novelist, whose original name was Konstantin Mitskevich. With Janka Kupala, he was a leading figure in Belorussian national and literary life. Among his many works are novels concerned with moral themes, such as *Through Life* (1926), with collectivism, and with war themes, among them *The Fisherman's Hut* (1949). Kolas is best known for his stirring patriotic poems, including *New Earth* (1923).

Kolbe, Georg (gā'ôrkh kôl'bə), 1877–1947, German sculptor. Kolbe studied painting and after meeting Rodin turned to sculpture, working in Berlin from 1903 until his death. He is best known for his impressionist figure studies, many of which are in American museums. During the Nazi regime, Kolbe turned to works of a more aggressive nature, producing idealized figures of warriors and athletes.

Kolberg: see KOŁOBRZEG, Poland.

Kolchak, Aleksandr Vasilyevich (əlyĭksän'dər vəsē'lyəvĭch kəlchäk'), 1874–1920, Russian admiral, leader of the anti-Bolshevik forces in W Siberia during the civil war (1918–20). He distinguished himself in the Russo-Japanese War, and in World War I he commanded the Black Sea fleet. After the October Revolution of 1917, Kolchak became (Oct., 1918) minister of war in an anti-Bolshevik government set up in Omsk, Siberia. In November he carried out a coup d'etat against the Socialist Revolutionaries in the government and assumed dictatorship over Siberia. At first successful against the Bolshevik forces, he was recognized by the Allies as well as by General DENIKIN as representing the provisional Russian government. However, his great offensive of 1919 (in which he intended to join the British forces and the Russian counterrevolutionaries on the coast of the White Sea) collapsed rapidly and exposed Denikin's army in S Russia. Kolchak retreated to Irkutsk, lost most of his following (especially the Czechs, who controlled the Trans-Siberian RR) and was betrayed to the Bolsheviks, who shot him. Before his death, he recognized Denikin as head of all anti-Bolshevik forces in Russia. His defeat left all Siberia in Bolshevik control, except the Far Eastern portion, which was controlled by Japanese intervention troops.

Kölcsey, Ferenc (fĕ'rĕnts köl'chĕĭ), 1790–1838, Hungarian writer and orator. A student of the Enlightenment, he aided his friend Krasiński in a reform of the Hungarian language, investigated Hungarian literary history, and introduced the critical essay. As a member of parliament (1832–36), he spoke eloquently to urge freedom for the serfs. His prose and poetry are somber and elaborately classical in style; they reveal a strong moral sense. Kölcsey wrote the Hungarian national hymn (1823).

Kolding (kôl'dĭng), city (1970 com. pop. 52,510), Vejle co., S central Denmark, a port on Kolding Fjord, an arm of the Lille Baelt. It is a commercial, industrial, and fishing center. Of note in the city are Koldinghus, a royal castle built in 1248 that now houses a historical museum, and the oldest stone church (built in the 13th cent.) in Denmark.

Kolguyev (kəlgo͞o'yĭf), island, 1,350 sq mi (3,497 sq km), off NE European USSR, in the Barents Sea, E of the Kanin peninsula and 50 mi (80 km) from the mainland. It is a part of the NENETS NATIONAL OKRUG, Archangelsk oblast, and is inhabited mainly by Nentsy (Samoyedes). It is a tundra region, and the Nentsy engage in fishing, seal hunting, reindeer raising, and trapping. Burgino is the major settlement.

Kolhapur (kōləpo͝or'), former princely state, 3,219 sq mi (8,337 sq km), Maharashtra state, SW India. Largely agricultural, the region produces cotton and textiles. It also has large bauxite deposits. A center of the MAHRATTAS, Kolhapur was an important state of the Deccan. It was transferred to Maharashtra state in 1960. The city of **Kolhapur** (1971 pop. 259,068) was the capital of the former state. It occupies the site of an ancient Buddhist center. There are many Buddhist remains, notably a stupa, or shrine (3rd cent. B.C.), with inscriptions in characters of the Asoka period.

Kolín (kô'lēn), city (1970 pop. 26,769), N central Czechoslovakia, in Bohemia, on the Elbe (Labe) River. It is a river port and manufactures railroad cars, chemicals, light machinery, and metal products. The city also has a petroleum refinery and a hydroelectric station. Founded in the 13th cent., Kolín grew rapidly after the construction (19th cent.) of the Vienna-Prague railway. The 13th-century Church of St. Bartholomew is noted for its Gothic choir.

kolkhoz: see COLLECTIVE FARM.

Kollár, Jan (yän kō'lär), 1793–1852, Slovak poet who wrote in Czech. An Evangelist minister, he was an ardent proponent of Pan-Slavism. He promoted his ideas in a famous essay on Slavonic cultural unity (1836) and in his best-known poem, *The Daughter of Slava* (1821–24). Kollár is regarded as the greatest poet of the Czech revival.

Kölliker, Albert von (äl'bĕrt fən kö'lĭkər), 1817–1905, Swiss physiologist and histologist. He was professor of physiology and of microscopic and comparative anatomy at Würzburg from 1847. His researches and texts on histology and embryology and his recognition of Schwann's cell theory were pioneer contributions toward understanding the function of spermatozoa and of spontaneous variation in evolution. He also wrote numerous memoirs on his findings and an autobiography (1899).

Kollontai, Aleksandra Mikhailovna (əlyĭksän'drə mēkhī'ləvnə kələntī'), 1872–1952, Russian revolutionary, diplomat, and novelist, whose maiden name was Aleksandra M. Domontovich. The daughter of a general, she early rebelled against her society. Although she married an officer of the czarist army, she was active in revolutionary circles and in 1908 was forced to flee abroad. She visited the United States in 1916 and edited, with Bukharin, the Communist daily *Novy Mir* [new world] in New York City. In 1917 she returned to Russia to take part in the Bolshevik Revolution. In 1920 she became people's commissar for social welfare. She was a leader of the "Workers' Opposition" that opposed party and government control of trade unions; this position was defeated by Lenin in 1921. Kollontai joined the people's commissariat for foreign affairs and became (1923) minister to Norway—the first woman to hold that diplomatic rank. After several ministerial appointments she became (1930) minister to Sweden and remained there until 1945. She was raised to ambassadorial rank in 1943 and was instrumental in conducting the Soviet-Finnish armistice negotiations of 1944. Known as a proponent of free love, she wrote extensively on this and on other social questions. See her autobiography (tr. 1971); biography by Isabel de Palencia (1947).

Kollwitz, Käthe Schmidt (kā'tə shmĭt kôl'vĭts), 1867–1945, German graphic artist and sculptor. She first gained a reputation with her illustrations for Hauptmann's *Weavers* and Zola's *Germinal.* Kollwitz became known for her superb woodcuts and lithographs. An ardent socialist and pacifist, she produced stark and anguished portrayals of misery and hunger such as *Death and the Mother* (1934, Phila. Mus. of Art). These powerful images convey her compassion for the poor. In 1932 she was director of the department of graphic arts at the Berlin Academy, but the advent of the Nazi party ended her public career in Germany. See her diary and letters (1955); her prints and drawings, ed. by Carl Zigrosser (2d ed. 1969); study by Otto Nagel (tr. 1971).

Kolmar, France: see COLMAR.

Köln, West Germany: see COLOGNE.

Kol Nidre: see ATONEMENT, DAY OF.

Kołobrzeg (kôlôb'zhĕk) or **Kolberg,** town (1970 pop. 25,400), NW Poland, on the Baltic Sea at the mouth of the Prośnica River. It is a seaport, seaside resort, and rail junction. A salt-trading center in the Middle Ages, it was chartered in 1255. It was besieged three times by the Russians in the Seven Years War before it fell in 1761. Kołobrzeg was virtually obliterated during World War II.

Kolokotronis, Theodore (kôlôkôtrô'nyēs), 1770-1843, Greek patriot and general. A leader in the Greek War of Independence against Ottoman rule in the 1820s, he was instrumental in the capture of Trípolis, Návplion, Corinth, Pátrai, and Árgos. In 1823 he was appointed commander-in-chief of forces in the Peloponnesus. A supporter of Count CAPO D'ISTRIA, Kolokotronis was one of the leading pro-Russian advocates. He opposed the regency of Bavarian ministers during the minority of King Otto I and was charged with treason, but he was pardoned in 1835. Kolokotronis is the hero of numerous folk songs. See his *Memoirs from the Greek War of Independence, 1821–1833* (tr., new and enl. ed. 1969).

Kolomna (kəlôm'nə), city (1970 pop. 136,000), central European USSR, at the confluence of the Moskva and Oka rivers. Locomotives and machine tools are produced. Known in 1177, the city became a Muscovite outpost in 1301 and has been an industrial center since 1863. Remains of the towers of Kolomna's 16th-century kremlin are still standing.

Kolomyya (kələmĭ'yə), Ger. *Kolomea,* Pol. *Kołomyja,* city (1967 est. pop. 39,000), SW European USSR, in the Ukraine, on the Prut River and in the Carpathian foothills. It is a rail junction and agricultural trade center. Industries include food processing, woodworking, oil refining, and the manufacture of building materials, farm machinery, and textiles. First mentioned in 1240, Kolomyya was then a Ukrainian settlement in the Galich-Volhynian principality. It passed in the 14th cent. to the Poles, who fortified it. Kolomyya was taken by Austria during the Polish partition of 1772 and became part of the newly independent republic of Ukraine in 1918 but reverted to Poland in 1920. It was incorporated into the Ukrainian Soviet Socialist Republic in 1939.

Kolozsvár, Rumania: see CLUJ.

Kölreuter or **Koelreuter, Joseph Gottlieb** (both: yō'zĕf gôt'lēp kölʹroi"tər), 1733–1806, German botanist. In 1764 he became professor of natural history and director of the botanical gardens at Karlsruhe. He experimented with hybridization of plants, studied their fertilization and development, and pointed out the importance of insects and of wind in the pollination of flowers.

Koltsov, Aleksey Vasilyevich (əlyĭksyā' vəsē'lyəvĭch kəltsôf'), 1809–42, Russian poet. Although he had little formal education, he taught himself by studying great works of literature. He was encouraged by the critic Belinsky, and became well known for his fresh, unsophisticated lyrics on themes of peasant life published as *Stikhotvoreniya* [poetry-making] (1835).

Kolwezi (kōlwĕz'ē), city (1968 est. pop. 71,000), Shaba region, SE Zaïre. It is a center for copper and cobalt mining. There are copper-ore concentration plants, a zinc refinery, and a brewery.

Kolyma (kŏlĭmä', kōlē'mə, Rus. kəlĭ'mə), river, c.1,500 mi (2,410 km) long, rising in several headstreams in the Kolyma and Cherskogo ranges, Far Eastern USSR. It flows generally N to the Arctic Ocean at Nizhniye Kresty. It is navigable (June–October) for c.1,000 mi (1,610 km). Its upper course crosses the rich **Kolyma Gold Fields,** which supply much of the gold for Soviet foreign trade. Gold mining was begun in the 1930s, and both the fields and the surrounding area were developed with the use of forced labor. The **Kolyma Range** (or Gyda Range), E of the Kolyma River, extends NE from Magadan and rises to c.6,000 ft (1,830 m).

Komaki (kōmä'kē), city (1970 pop. 77,996), Aichi prefecture, Honshu, Japan, on the Nobi Plain. It is a suburb of Nagoya and an agricultural market.

Komandorski Islands (kŏməndôr'skē) or **Commander Islands,** Rus. *Komandorskiye Ostrova,* group of treeless islands, off E Kamchatka Peninsula, E Far Eastern USSR, in SW Bering Sea. They consist of Bering Island, Medny Island, and two islets. These hilly, foggy islands often have earthquakes. Their inhabitants, Russians and Aleuts, are engaged in fishing, hunting, and whaling. The largest village is Nikolskoye on Bering Island.

Komárno (kô'märnô) or **Komárom** (kô'märôm), Ger. *Komorn,* city of Czechoslovakia and Hungary, on both sides of the Danube, at its confluence with the Nitra and Váh rivers. Komárno (1970 pop. 27,031) is located on the left bank and belongs to Czechoslovakia. It is a shipbuilding center and has flour mills and machinery and textile plants. Hungarian Komárom (1968 est. pop. 26,800), on the right bank, has lumber yards, sawmills, and textile plants. Both parts of the city have port installations. The site of Komárno was fortified by the Romans. It became a free city in 1331. Later a part of the AUSTRO-HUNGARIAN MONARCHY, it was partitioned in 1920 between Hungary and Czechoslovakia.

Komatsu (kōmä'tso͞o), city (1970 pop. 95,684), Ishikawa prefecture, central Honshu, Japan. It is a flourishing market town noted for its production of silk, rayon, and pottery.

Komeito: see SOKA GAKKAI.

Komi (kō'mē, kô'-), Finnic people of the northeastern part of the European USSR. There are two traditional branches of the Komi—Zyrians and Permyaks. The Zyrians are now officially called Komi and make up over half of the population. The Permyaks are now called Komi-Permyaks. Both speak a Finno-Permian language. The Komi live in the Komi ASSR and the Komi-Permyaks live in the Komi-Permyak National Okrug, both administrative divisions of the Russian SFSR. There are about 370,000 Komi (both groups) in the USSR. Traditionally they have been Orthodox Christians since the 14th cent. The enlightener of the Komi and a saint of the Orthodox Eastern Church was Stephen of Perm (1340–96). He constructed an alphabet for the Komi and translated some parts of the Bible into their language.

Komi Autonomous Soviet Socialist Republic, autonomous region (1970 pop. 965,000), c.160,000 sq mi (414,400 sq km), NE European USSR. SYKTYVKAR is the capital. The region is a wooded lowland, stretching across the Pechora and the Vychegda river basins and the upper reaches of the Mezen River. The northern part is permanently frozen, wooded tundra. Mining is the most important economic activity. There are major coal fields in the Pechora basin, yielding heating and coking coal. Along the Ukhta River there are important oil fields. Leningrad receives most of its coal and oil from the region. Syktyvkar, the capital, is a major lumber center; Vorkuta is a coal-mining center; and there is extensive lumbering, stock raising, fishing, and hunting. Komi, Russians, and Ukrainians constitute the population. The Komi, formerly called Zyrians, speak a Finno-Ugric language and adhere to the Russian Orthodox religion. The area underwent a spectacular economic advance after the opening (1942) of the Kotlas-Vorkuta RR to transport the area's coal and oil.

The area belonged to the Novgorod Republic from the 13th cent. The Zyrian Autonomous Oblast was constituted in 1921; it became an autonomous republic in 1936.

Komi-Permyak National Okrug (kô'mē-pĭrmyăk'), administrative division (1970 pop. 212,000), 12,664 sq mi (32,800 sq km), E central European USSR, in the basin of the upper Kama River. The terrain is slightly hilly and heavily forested and is drained by the Kama and its tributaries. The navigable Kama is also the area's chief transportation artery. Lumbering is the major industry of the okrug. Among the crops grown are rye, oats, spring wheat, and flax. The territory is the oldest and most populous of the USSR's national okrugs. The Komi and the Permyaks, both Finno-Ugric peoples, make up around 75% of the population; the rest are mostly Russians. The okrug was established in 1925.

Komodo dragon: see LIZARD.

komondor (kŏm'əndôr") (pl. komondorok), breed of large, powerful WORKING DOG recognized as a distinct breed in Hungary since the 9th cent. It stands from 23½ to 31½ in. (60–80 cm) high at the shoulder and weighs from 75 to 90 lb (34.0–40.8 kg). Its long, smooth, dense coat is white and shaggy, tending to tangle. The ancestral home of the komondor is stated by many authorities to be Tibet, although others have traced its origin to the Russian Steppes, from whence it was thought to have been brought into Europe with the migration of Huns. Recently, however, evidence has come to light that strongly suggests that the komondor was the guard dog used by Sumerian shepherds in the Tigris-Euphrates valley 7,000 to 8,000 years ago. Whatever its origins, it is one of the oldest European breeds of dogs, the guardian of herds and homes for centuries. Today it is raised for show competition and as a watchdog and pet. See DOG.

Komorn: see KOMÁRNO.

Komotau: see CHOMUTOV, Czechoslovakia.

Komotiní (kômətĭnē'), city (1971 pop. 28,896), capital of Rodhópi prefecture, NE Greece, in Thrace. It is the commercial center for a region that produces grains, silk, and tobacco. The city has a sizable Muslim minority.

Kompong Cham (käm'pông' chäm), city (1967 est. pop. 31,000), capital of Kompong Cham prov., SE Cambodia, a port on the Mekong River. The third largest city in Cambodia, it has a large textile factory, built with aid from the People's Republic of China. In Sept., 1973, it was the scene of heavy fighting as government forces, reinforced and supplied via the Mekong River, withstood a massive attack by the Khmer Rouge. A technical university is located in the city.

Kompong Som (käm'pông' sôm), formerly **Sihanoukville,** city and seaport (1962 pop. 6,578), located in, but politically independent of Kampot prov., S Cambodia, on the Gulf of Siam. Although a new city (completed 1960), it is the principal deep-water port and commercial outlet of Cambodia. The city and port were built on mud flats, with French aid, and grew with the construction of a highway and railroad to Phnom Penh. The docks and warehouses have been greatly expanded with U.S. aid. The country's only oil refinery, located there, was destroyed (1971) by insurgent Khmer Rouge troops. Kompong Som has an international airport.

Komsomolsk (kəmsəmôlsk') or **Komsomolsk-on-Amur** (-ämo͝or'), Rus. *Komsomolsk-na-Amure,* city (1970 pop. 218,000), Khabarovsk Kray, S Far Eastern USSR, on the Amur River. It is a manufacturing center producing steel, refined oil, and wood products. Tin mines are nearby. The city was founded (1932) by the Komsomol (the Communist youth organization).

Kona (kō'nə), district, along the western coast of the island of Hawaii. It is Hawaii's coffee belt and the only coffee-producing area in the United States. The Kona coast, with fine deep-sea fishing offshore, is a favorite tourist spot. On Kealakelua Bay stands a monument to English explorer Capt. James Cook, killed there by natives in 1779. Kailua Bay to the north was the landing site in 1820 of the first U.S. missionaries to Hawaii.

Konakry: see CONAKRY, Guinea.

Konarak (kōnä'rək, kō'nərək), Hindu temple of the sun god, Orissa state, E India. Built during the reign of Narasimha I (1238–64), it is made of red sandstone and is called the Black Pagoda in contrast to the whitewashed temples of nearby Puri. Although Konarak is partially ruined, enormous wheels carved in high relief about the base have survived, suggesting the chariot of the sun god. Many of the carvings are erotic. Another form of the name is Kanarak.

Kondouriotis, Paul (kôndo͞oryô'tĭs), 1857–1935, Greek admiral and statesman. He became a national hero through his victories over the Turkish fleet in the Greco-Turkish War of 1897 and in the Balkan Wars of 1912–13. He was regent after the death (1920) of King Alexander and again after the departure (1923) of King George II from Greece. In 1924 he was elected provisional president of the newly formed Greek republic. Early in 1926 General PANGALOS compelled Kondouriotis to resign, but in August, General Kondylis overthrew Pangalos and recalled Kondouriotis. A new constitution was promulgated. Kondouriotis sought to resign several times during the premierships of ZAÏMIS (1926–28) and VENIZELOS, and in 1929 his resignation was final. Zaïmis succeeded him as president. The name also appears as Koundouriotis.

Kondylis, George (kônthē'lĭs), 1879–1936, Greek general and statesman. He fought in the Balkan Wars and at Salonica (now Thessaloníki) in World War I. Entering politics in the turbulent postwar years, he served (1924–25) as minister of war and of the interior in the republican government. He overthrew the dictatorship of General PANGALOS in 1926 and served briefly as premier. After 1933 he suddenly switched to the royalist camp. As minister of war (1932–35) under Panayoti TSALDARIS, he suppressed (1935) the Cretan uprising in favor of Eleutherios VENIZELOS; in Oct., 1935, he ousted Tsaldaris in a coup d'etat, became premier in his place, and induced the parliament to recall King GEORGE II, who, however, soon dismissed him. The name also appears as Condylis.

Konev, Ivan Stepanovich (ēvän' styĭpä'nəvĭch kô'-nyĭf), 1897–1973, Russian field marshal. In World War II he reconquered (1944–45) the Ukraine and S Poland from the Germans, took Silesia, and participated in the conquest of Czechoslovakia and the capture of Berlin. He became (1945) military governor of the Soviet occupation zone in Austria and (1946) commander in chief of Soviet ground forces. From 1955 to 1960 he commanded the unified military forces set up by the Warsaw Treaty. In 1961–62 he headed Soviet forces in East Germany.

Kong Karls Land (kông kärls län) or **King Charles Land,** island group, 128 sq mi (332 sq km), in the Barents Sea, part of the Norwegian possession of Svalbard, W of Spitsbergen. It includes Kongsøya, Svenskøya, and Abeløya islands.

Kongo, kingdom of the, former state of W central Africa, founded in the 14th cent. In the 15th cent. the kingdom stretched from the Congo (Zaïre) River in the north to the Loje River in the south and from the Atlantic Ocean in the west to beyond the Kwango River in the east. Several smaller autonomous states to the south and east paid tribute to it. The Kongo was ruled by the *manikongo,* or king, and was divided into six provinces, each administered by a governor appointed by the *manikongo.* In 1482, Diogo Cão, a Portuguese explorer, visited the kingdom, and the reigning *manikongo,* Nzinga Nkuwu, was favorably impressed with Portuguese culture. In 1491, Portuguese missionaries, soldiers, and artisans were welcomed at Mbanza, the capital of the kingdom. The missionaries soon gained converts, including Nzinga Nkuwu (who took the name João I), and the soldiers helped the *manikongo* defeat an internal rebellion. The next *manikongo,* Afonso I (reigned 1505–43), was raised as a Christian and attempted to convert the kingdom to Christianity and European ways. However, the Portuguese residents in the Kongo were primarily interested in increasing their private fortunes (especially through capturing black Africans and selling them into slavery), and, despite the attempts of King Manuel I of Portugal to channel the efforts of his subjects into constructive projects, the continued rapaciousness of the Portuguese played a major part in weakening the kingdom and reducing the hold of the capital (renamed São Salvador) over the provinces. After the death of Afonso, the Kongo declined rapidly and suffered major civil wars. The Portuguese shifted their interest southward to the Ndongo kingdom and helped the Ndongo defeat the Kongo in 1556. However, in 1569 the Portuguese aided the Kongo by helping to repel an invasion from the east by a LUNDA ethnic group. The slave trade, which undermined the social structure of the Kongo, continued to weaken the authority of the *manikongo.* In 1641, Manikongo Garcia II allied himself with the Dutch in an attempt to control Portuguese slave traders, but in 1665 a Portuguese force decisively defeated the army of the Kongo and from that time onward the *manikongo* was little more than a vassal of Portugal. The kingdom disintegrated into a number of small states, all controlled to varying degrees by the Portuguese. The area of the Kongo was incorporated mostly into Angola and partly into the Independent State of the Congo (now ZAÏRE) in the late 19th cent.

kongoni: see HARTEBEEST.

Kongsberg (kôngs'bĕr), city (1970 pop. 18,497), Buskerud co., SE Norway, on the Lågen River. It is a commercial, industrial, and winter sports center and has a hydroelectric power plant. Formerly a silver-mining center, Kongsberg has old mines and a great church (1761) that are tourist attractions.

Kongsfjorden (kôngs"fyôr'dən) [Kings Bay], inlet of the Arctic Ocean, 14 mi (23 km) long, NW Spitsbergen, Svalbard. Ny-Ålesund is on the inlet. The scenic fjord is often visited by tourist vessels.

Königgrätz: see HRADEC KRÁLOVÉ; SADOVÁ, Czechoslovakia.

Königinhof: see DVŮR KRÁLOVÉ NAD LABEM, Czechoslovakia.

König Rother (kön'ĭk rōt'ər), earliest heroic minstrel epic from the precourtly period of Middle High German literature. Written in Bavaria in popular verse style by an unknown Rhenish poet (c.1140–50), the epic has a fairy-tale quality. It recounts King Rother's adventurous quest to the Orient for his bride, portraying with sympathy the lord-vassal relationship. See *King Rother* (tr. 1962).

Königsberg: see KALININGRAD, USSR.

Königshütte: see CHORZÓW, Poland.

Königsmark, Countess Maria Aurora (märē'ä ouro͞o'rä kö'nĭksmärk), 1666–1728, Swedish noblewoman; sister of Count Philipp Christoph Königsmark. She went to Dresden in search of her missing brother and there became the mistress of Augustus II of Poland and Saxony. Their son, Maurice, was the famous Marshal de SAXE. In her last years she was abbess coadjutor at Quedlinburg.

Königsmark, Count Philipp Christoph (fē'lĭp krĭs'tôf), d. 1694?, Swedish nobleman, an officer in the service of Hanover. Accused of having an affair with SOPHIA DOROTHEA, wife of Elector George Louis (later George I of England), the count disappeared in 1694. It is believed that he was killed by order of the elector.

konimeter or **coniometer** (both: kōnĭm'ətər), instrument for determining the concentration of dust in air, e.g., in a mine or mill. A measured volume of air is passed over a plate to which dust particles adhere; the particles are later counted under a microscope. Other methods, now more widely used, involve the collection (by filtration or precipitation) of dust from a large volume of air and the subsequent weighing of the dust.

Koninck or **Coningh, Philips de** (fē'lĭps də kō'nĭngk, kō'nĭng), 1619–88, Dutch landscape and portrait painter. His panoramic landscapes, rich and warm in tone, suggest dramatic atmosphere and space. They are among the best in the Dutch landscape tradition. A number of his drawings have been preserved. Koninck's paintings include *Entrance to a Forest* and *Landscape* (both: Rijks Mus.), *Landscape with Hunting Party* (National Gall., London), and a landscape in the Metropolitan Museum.

Koninksloo, Gillis van: see CONINXLOO, GILLIS VAN.

Köniz (kö'nĭts), town (1970 pop. 32,505), Bern canton, W central Switzerland. It is a suburb of Bern. The Romanesque-Gothic church, founded in the 10th cent. by Rudolph II of Burgundy, has noteworthy 14th-century stained glass and frescoes.

Konotop (kŏnətŏp'), city (1969 est. pop. 62,000), central European USSR, in Ukraine, on the Ezuch River. It is a rail junction and agricultural center, with food-processing plants, railroad repair shops, an electromechanics industry, and factories that produce clothing and mining equipment. Konotop was founded in 1634 by the Poles, who made it a fortress. It was ruled briefly by the Ukrainian hetman Chmielnicki and his successor and later became a Polish district center.

Konoye, Fumimaro (fo͞o"mēmärō' kōnoyā'), 1891–1945, Japanese statesman. A scion of the ancient Fujiwara noble family and protégé of Kimmichi Saionji, he was president of the house of peers from 1933 to 1937. In June, 1937, he accepted the premiership. A former liberal, he now favored increased armament and centralized government control. Following the outbreak of war with China in July, 1937, he pressed Chiang Kai-shek to establish autonomous demilitarized regions in N China and to recognize the puppet state of MANCHUKUO. The National Mobilization Law was passed in March, 1938, and in November, Konoye proclaimed Japan's aim of a "new order in East Asia." He resigned in Jan., 1939, and became president of the privy council and minister without portfolio. Recalled to the premiership in July, 1940, he concluded an alliance with the Axis and founded (Oct., 1940) the Imperial Rule Assistance Association to replace the political parties. Having failed to reach an agreement with the United States, he resigned in Oct., 1941, to be followed by Hideki Tojo. In July, 1945, he was chosen as a peace envoy to Moscow and later became vice premier in the first postwar cabinet and head of the constitutional drafting committee. He was listed for trial as a war criminal but committed suicide in Dec., 1945.

Konstantinovka (kənstəntyē'nəfkə), Ukr. *Kostyantyniwka,* city (1970 pop. 105,000), S central European USSR, in the Donets Basin of the Ukraine. It is a zinc-refining and superphosphate-producing center.

Konstanz, West Germany: see CONSTANCE.

Kon Tiki: see HEYERDAHL, THOR.

Konya (kōn'yä), city (1970 pop. 200,760), capital of Konya prov., S central Turkey. It is the trade center of a rich agricultural and livestock-raising region. Manufactures include cement, carpets, and leather, cotton, and silk goods. As the ancient ICONIUM, the city was important in Roman times, but it reached its peak after the victory (1071) of Alp Arslan over the Byzantines at Manzikert, which resulted in the establishment (1099) of the sultanate of Iconium or Rum (so called after Rome), a powerful state of the Seljuk Turks. In the late 13th cent. the Seljuks of Iconium were defeated by the Mongols, and their territories subsequently passed to Karamania (see KARAMAN). In the 15th cent. the whole region was annexed to the Ottoman Empire by Sultan Muhammad II, the conqueror of Constantinople. Konya lost its political importance but remained a religious center as the chief seat of the whirling dervishes, whose order was founded there in the 13th cent. by the poet and mystic Celaleddin Rumi. The tomb of the founder, several medieval mosques, and the old city walls have been preserved. In 1832 an Egyptian army under Ibrahim Pasha completely routed the Turks at Konya. The Armenian population of the town, once very numerous, was largely deported during World War I. Konya prov., the largest in Turkey, has important mineral resources and produces much opium.

Koo, Vi Kuiyuin Wellington (vē jün wĕl'ĭngtən ko͞o), Mandarin *Ku Wei-chün,* 1887–, Chinese Nationalist diplomat, b. Shanghai. Koo was educated at Columbia (B.A., 1908; M.A., 1909; Ph.D., 1912), where he specialized in international law. In 1912, Wellington Koo was secretary to Yüan Shih-kai, president of China. He was ambassador to France (1936–41), Great Britain (1941–46), and the United States (1946–56). He served as delegate to the Paris Peace Conference (1919) and then was a representative on the Council of the League of Nations. At various times he was minister of foreign affairs and prime minister. He headed the Chinese delegation to the San Francisco conference which founded (1945) the United Nations. From 1957 to 1967 he served on the International Court of Justice at The Hague.

Kook, Abraham Isaac, 1864–1935, Jewish scholar and philosopher, b. Latvia. He settled (1904) in Palestine, where he became the chief rabbi of the Ashkenazi community in 1921. He was one of the first Orthodox rabbis to apply his Talmudic learning to current problems. He attempted to show that Palestine and Zionism were an integral part of Judaism: that those secularist Jews who worked to build up the Jewish homeland were unknowingly doing God's work, which one day would become evident to them; and that the present condition of nationalism was a necessary step on the way to universalism, as nations are the organizational units in which man will be educated for the fulfillment of this idea. He was the author of several books on Judaism. See biography by J. B. Agus (2d ed. 1972); S. H. Bergman, *Faith and Reason* (tr. 1963).

kookaburra (ko͝ok'əbûr''ə), common name for a squat, long-tailed Australian kingfisher, *Dacelo navaguinae.* It is one of the largest birds of the family Alcedinidae (kingfisher family). Because of its loud, maniacal-sounding call, it is also known as the laughing jackass, or jackass kingfisher. The kookaburra has dull plumage and is about the size of a raven. Like many forest kingfishers, it does not fish at all, but rather feeds mainly on a diet of snakes, which it picks up by the head and drops from great heights in order to kill before consuming them. It also feeds on lizards, young birds, and large insects. Today, the kookaburra is often found in the vicinity of human settlements, using its large, hooked bill to scavenge for scraps. It is chiefly a solitary, nonmigratory bird. The kookaburra lays its pure white eggs in a burrow carved out of a termite nest. Both sexes participate in the incubation and care of their virtually helpless young. Kookaburras are classified in the phylum CHORDATA, subphylum Vertebrata, class Aves, order Coraciiformes, family Alcedinidae. See study by V. A. Parry (1972).

Koolau Range (kō'əlou''), mountain chain, extending northwest-southeast, E Oahu island, Hawaii; rises to 3,105 ft (946 m) in Konahuanui. It is cut by two scenic passes, Nuuanu Pali and Waimanalo Pali, which shorten the route between E and W Oahu.

Kootenai (ko͞o'tĭnā), river, 407 mi (655 km) long, rising in the Rocky Mts., SE British Columbia, Canada. It flows S into NW Montana, NW through N Idaho, then N into Canada. There it flows through Kootenay Lake (64 mi/103 km long; 191 sq mi/495 sq km), an expansion of the river, before joining the Columbia River at Castlegar. The river is used to generate hydroelectricity. The Canadian name is spelled Kootenay.

Kootenai Indians (ko͞ot'ənā''), group of North American Indians, who in the 18th cent. occupied the so-called Kootenai country (i.e., N Montana, N Idaho, and SE British Columbia). Their language is thought by some scholars to form a branch of the Algonquian-Wakashan linguistic stock, although others argue that it has not been definitely related to any known linguistic family (see AMERICAN INDIAN LANGUAGES). The Upper Kootenai lived near the headwaters of the Columbia River, and the Lower Kootenai lived on the Lower Kootenai River. According to tradition the Kootenai once lived E of the Rocky Mts., but they were driven westward by their enemies the Blackfoot Indians. Kootenai culture was essentially that of the Plateau area, but after the advent of the horse the Kootenai adopted many Plains area traits including a seasonal buffalo hunt. Contact with whites began early in the 19th cent., when the North West Company established Rocky Mountain House on the upper Saskatchewan River.

In 1807 the same company opened the first trading post in Kootenai country. Today a group of the Kootenai live with the Salish Indians on the Flathead Reservation in NW Montana, where together they number some 2,800. The name is sometimes spelled Kootenay or Kutenai. See H. H. Turney-High, *Ethnography of the Kutenai* (1941, repr. 1974); O. W. Johnson, *Flathead and Kootenay* (1969).

Kootenay Lake, Canada: see KOOTENAI, river.

Kootenay National Park, 543 sq mi (1,406 sq km), SE British Columbia, Canada; est. 1920. In the Rocky Mts. near Kootenay Lake, it contains high peaks, glaciers, deep canyons, and hot springs. The Banff-Windermere Highway crosses the park.

Kooweskoowe: see ROSS, JOHN.

Köpenick (kö'pənĭk), district of East Berlin, E central East Germany, at the confluence of the Spree and Dahme rivers. It is an industrial center and a tourist spot, with forests and large lakes. Köpenick was the scene of the trial (1730) of Crown Prince Frederick (later FREDERICK II), who had attempted to escape from Prussia to England. In 1906, Wilhelm Voight, a shoemaker dressed as an army captain, imprisoned the mayor of Köpenick (then an independent town), an episode dramatized (1931) by Carl Zuckmayer in *Der Hauptmann von Köpenick.*

Koper (kô'pĕr), Ital. *Capodistria,* town (1971 pop. 35,407), NW Yugoslavia, in Slovenia, on the Istrian peninsula in the Gulf of Trieste. It is a fishing port and has small shipyards. From 1278 until 1797 the town was the capital of ISTRIA under Venetian rule. The Treaty of Campo Formio, which dissolved the republic of Venice, transferred Koper to Austria. The town passed to Italy after World War I and became part of the Free Territory of Trieste in 1947. In 1954, Koper was annexed to Yugoslavia. It preserves the aspect of a Venetian town, with a Romanesque cathedral and campanile, a Gothic loggia, and a pinnacled town hall.

Köping (chö'pĭng''), city (1970 pop. 21,740), Västmanland co., S central Sweden, at the western end of Lake Mälaren. It is an important lake port and a commercial and industrial center. Manufactures include machinery, textiles, and cement. It was the site of the strong Köpingshus fortress, destroyed in 1434.

Kopp, Hermann Franz Moritz (hĕr'män fräntz mō'rĭts kôp), 1817–92, German physical chemist and historian of chemistry. His research concerned the connection between the physical properties and the chemical structure of compounds. He continued Jöns Berzelius's annual reports on developments in chemistry, broadening their scope to include related sciences. Kopp is perhaps best known for his *Geschichte der Chemie* [history of chemistry] (4 vol., 1843–47).

Köprülü (köprülü'), family of humble Albanian origin, several members of which served as grand vizier (chief executive officer) in the Ottoman Empire (Turkey). The name is also spelled Kiuprili, Koprili, and Kuprili. **Mehmed Köprülü**, 1583–1661, became grand vizier of MUHAMMAD IV in 1656. He gained complete authority and control and displayed remarkable statesmanship and efficiency. He reorganized the Ottoman fleet, conquered (1658) Transylvania, restored internal order (by executing dissidents), reformed the finances, and built forts along the Don and Dnepr rivers. During his vizierate the Ottoman Empire regained some of its former prestige and vitality. He was succeeded as vizier by his son **Ahmed Köprülü,** 1635–76. An able statesman and soldier, he took (1669) the last Venetian stronghold in Crete, but he was severely defeated (1664) by MONTECUCCULI at Szentgotthárd in Hungary and suffered reverses in his campaigns against John III of Poland. Ahmed, who died from overindulgence, was succeeded as vizier by Kara Mustafa, his brother-in-law. Ahmed's brother, **Mustafa Köprülü,** 1637–91, became vizier in 1689, at a time when the Austrians and their allies were advancing victoriously into the Ottoman Empire. He continued his predecessors' administrative and fiscal reforms and improved the status of the Christian subjects. He drove the Austrians from Serbia but was killed in the battle of Slankamen. His cousin, **Hüseyin Köprülü,** d. 1702, became vizier after the Turkish defeat at Senta in 1697. Recognizing the exhaustion of Turkey, he negotiated a humiliating peace (see KARLOWITZ, TREATY OF). He too was a reformer and patronized the arts and letters. Mustafa Köprülü's son, **Numan Köprülü,** d.1719, was vizier in 1710–11. Another son, **Abdullah Köprülü,** d. 1735, was acting vizier from 1723 until his death.

Korah (kō'rə). **1** Levite leader, with Dathan and Abiram, of the unsuccessful revolt in the desert against Moses that ended by the rebels' being consumed by fire and earthquake. Num. 16; 26.9–11. Core: Jude 11. **2** Son of Esau. Gen. 36.5,14,18. **3** Another descendant of Esau. Gen. 36.16. **4** Descendant of Caleb. 1 Chron. 2.43. **5** Levitical family, perhaps descended from **1,** that had duties as doorkeepers and singers. Ex. 6.24; 1 Chron. 9.19,31; 2 Chron. 20.19; titles of Pss. 42; 44–49; 84; 85; 87; 88. Kore: 1 Chron. 26.19.

Koran or **Quran** (kōrăn', -rän') [Arab.,=reading, lection], the sacred book of Islam. According to Islamic belief, it was revealed by God to the Prophet MUHAMMAD in separate revelations over the major portion of the Prophet's life at Mecca and at Medina. The canonical text was established A.H. 30 (A.D. 651–52), under the caliph UTHMAN, by Arabic editors, who used for their basis a collection made by Zaid ibn Thabit, the Prophet's secretary. The caliph had all collections destroyed save Zaid's and thus made the new edition unique. The revelations are divided into 114 suras (chapters), but many of the suras include several revelations. The arrangement of the suras is mechanical: the first (Fatihah) is a short exultation in God, the rest are graded generally by length, from longest to shortest. It is thus impossible to tell from the book the chronological order of revelations; generally, however, the shorter suras, more electric and fervent than the rest, are the earlier, while many of the longer suras (and all of those revealed at Medina) are later. The Koran is in classical Arabic; that is to say, the Arabic of the Koran is the classic language. The Koran is undoubtedly the most influential book in the world after the Bible. Muslims memorize much or all of it, and Islam considers all science but a commentary on the Koran. It is probably true that the Koran accounts for the remarkable unity of Islam, one of the most widespread religions. Many Muslims believe it a sacrilege to translate the Koran, but despite their objections translations have been made. See A. J. Arberry, *The Koran Interpreted* (2 vol., 1955, repr. 1969); Izutsu Toshihiko, *God and Man in the Koran* (1964); Richard Bell, *Introduction to the Quran* (2d ed. 1970).

Korat: see NAKHON RATCHASIMA, Thailand.

Korçë (kôr'chə), city (1970 pop. 43,300), capital of Korçë prov., SE Albania, near the Greek border. Located in an agricultural region, it is a commercial and industrial center producing leather, tobacco and glass products, and knitwear. There are lignite, copper, and iron ore deposits nearby. Korçë is the seat of a Greek Orthodox metropolitan. Known in 1280, it was destroyed (1440) by the Turks but developed again after the 16th cent. Ever since Albania gained independence in the Balkan Wars, Korçë has been claimed by Greece. Greek troops occupied it in 1912–13 during the Balkan Wars and again early in World War I. From 1916 to 1920 it was occupied and administered by the French, and in World War II it was held (Nov., 1940–April, 1941) by the Greeks. Korçë has a large 15th-century mosque and several modern government buildings. It is also known as Korça and Koritsa.

Korčula (kôr'cho͞olä), Ital. *Curzola,* island (1971 pop. 20,176), 105 sq mi (272 sq km), in the Adriatic Sea, off Dalmatia, W Yugoslavia. It is covered with pine forests, pastures, and vineyards. Most of the inhabitants are sailors, farmers, or fishermen. The island was colonized by the Greeks in the 4th cent. B.C. The chief town Korčula, has retained its fine medieval cathedral and fortifications. According to some sources, Marco Polo was born there.

Kordofan (kôrdōfăn'), province (1969 est. pop. 2,400,000), central Sudan. AL UBAYYID is the capital. The terrain, generally level in the north, rises in the south to the Nuba Mts. Kordofan's economy is agricultrual, with millet as the staple crop. The government has sponsored many irrigation projects. Conquered for Egypt in 1821, Kordofan was under Turco-Egyptian rule until 1882, when the Mahdi fomented revolt. With the defeat of Mahdist forces in 1898, Kordofan became part of Anglo-Egyptian Sudan.

Kore (kō'rē). **1** Family of temple doorkeepers. 1 Chron. 9.19. **2** Levite under Hezekiah. 2 Chron. 31.14. **3** See KORAH **5.**

Kore, in Greek religion: see PERSEPHONE.

Korea (kôrē'ə, kə–), Korean *Choson,* Jap. *Chosen* or *Tyosen,* historic region (85,049 sq mi/220,277 sq km), E Asia. Seoul was the traditional capital. A peninsula, 600 mi (966 km) long, Korea separates the Yellow Sea (and Korea Bay, a northern arm of the Yellow Sea) on the west from the Sea of Japan on the east. On the south it is bounded by Korea Strait (connecting the Yellow Sea and the Sea of Japan) and on the north its land boundaries with China (c.500 mi/800 km) and with the USSR (only c.11 mi/18 km) are marked chiefly by the great Yalu and Tumen rivers. The Korean peninsula is largely mountainous; the principal series of ranges, extending along the east coast, rises (in the northeast) to 9,003 ft (2,744 m) at Mt. Paektu, the highest peak in Korea. Most rivers are relatively short and many are unnavigable, filled with rapids and waterfalls; important rivers, in addition to the Yalu and Tumen, are the Han, the Kum, the Taedong, the Naktong, and the Somjin. Off the heavily indented coast (c.5,400 mi/8,690 km long) lie some 3,420 islands, most of them rocky and uninhabited (of the inhabited islands, about half have a population of less than 100); the main island group is in the Korean Archipelago in the Yellow Sea. The climate of Korea ranges from dry and extremely cold winters in the north to almost tropical conditions in parts of the south. The country once had large timber resources. Most of the remaining stands are in the north, where, despite excessive cutting during the Japanese occupation (1910–45), timber remains an important resource. Predominant trees are larch, oak,

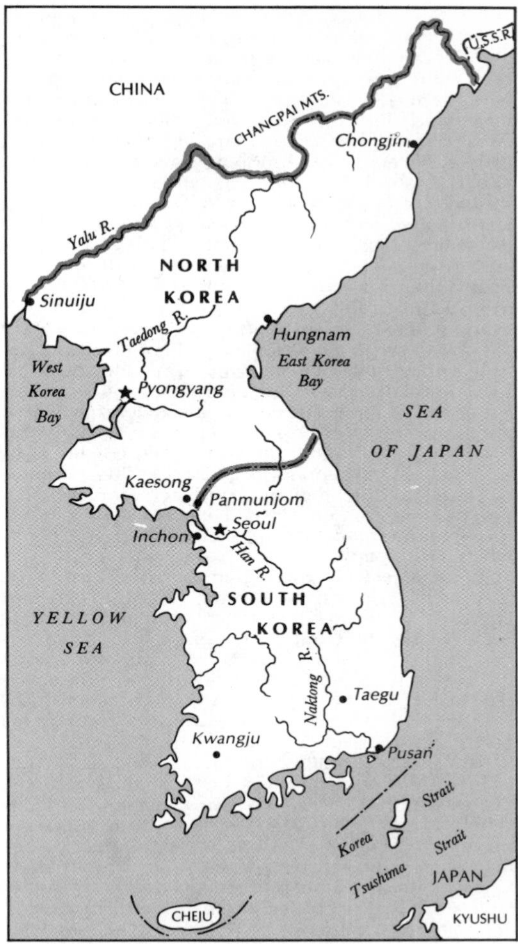

alder, pine, spruce, and fir. Intensive government conservation and reforestation programs have increased the supply, and timber occasionally appears on North Korean export lists. The south, on the other hand, is largely deforested—the result of illegal cutting after 1945 and damage during the Korean War (1950–53). Some forests remain, especially in the west central area of South Korea, and a government reforestation program has been initiated, but the dense population and extensive agriculture continue to encroach upon the small reserves and considerable timber has to be imported. Korea has great mineral wealth, most of it (80% to 90%) concentrated in the north. Of the peninsula's five major minerals—gold, iron ore, coal, tungsten, and graphite—only the tungsten and amorphous graphite are found principally in the south. South Korea has only 10% of the peninsula's rich coal and iron deposits. Its minerals are widely scattered, and mining operations are generally small-scaled, although tungsten is an important export item. In the north, modern mining methods have been instituted, and minerals and metals account for about 15% of the export revenue. North Korea is especially rich in iron and coal and has some 300 different kinds of minerals; in 1970 it ranked first among world producers of graphite and was among the world's top 10 in deposits and production of gold, tungsten, magnesite, zinc, barites, magnatite, molybdenum, limestone, mica, and fluorite. Other important minerals include copper, kaolin, lead, nickel, silver, and manganese. Because of the mountainous and rocky terrain, only about 20% of Korean land is arable. Rice is the chief crop, with wet paddy fields constituting about half of the farmland. Paddies are found along the coasts, in claimed tidal areas, and in river valleys. Barley, wheat, corn, soybeans, and grain sorghums are also extensively cultivated, especially in the uplands; other crops include cotton, tobacco, fruits, potatoes, beans, and sweet potatoes. Before the country was divided (1945), the colder and less fertile north depended heavily upon the south for food. Agricultural self-sufficiency has now become a major goal of the North Korean government, and the establishment of highly mechanized state farms has been a step in that direction. Both governments have recently expanded irrigation facilities; numerous dams are being constructed, and land reclamation projects are in progress. Livestock plays a minor role in Korean agriculture, especially in the north, where the steep and often barren hills are unsuitable for large-scale grazing. In the south, cattle are used largely as beasts of burden, and while chickens and rabbits are raised, relatively little meat is eaten. Fish remains the chief source of protein in the Korean diet. The fishing waters off Korea are among the best in the world; the long coastline and numerous islands, inlets, and reefs provide excellent fishing grounds, and the presence of both a warm and a cold current attracts a great variety of species—cuttlefish, anchovy, yellow corvina, hairtail, saury, pollack, flatfish, cod, sandfish, herring, and mackerel. Octopus and shrimp are also caught, and seaweed is valuable; agar (a seaweed product) is an important export item. Deep-sea fishing is expanding, and Korean ships now range into the Atlantic and Arctic Oceans. Almost all of the deep-sea catch (consisting largely of tuna) is canned and exported. The Korean economy was shattered by the war of 1950 to 1953. Postwar reconstruction was abetted by enormous amounts of foreign aid (in the north, from Communist countries and in the south, chiefly from the United States) and intensive government economic development programs. The greatest industrial advances were made during the 1960s; in that decade the south experienced an 85% increase in productivity and a 250% rise in per capita gross national product. The north has changed from a predominantly agricultural society (in 1946) to an industrial one; 70% of its national product is now derived from manufacturing and mining. Major North Korean products include iron, steel, and other metals, machinery, textiles (synthetics, wool, cotton, silk), and chemicals. In the south the traditional consumer goods industries (textiles, garments, food-processing) are still dominant, but heavy industry has been established and a great variety of products are now manufactured; these include electrical and electronic equipment, chemicals, ceramic goods, and plywood (made from imported lumber; in 1972 South Korea was the world's leading plywood exporter). The industrialization of both north and south has been accompanied by improved transportation. By the end of the Korean War the rail system had been destroyed, and paved highways were almost nonexistent. The railroads have been extensively rebuilt, and the South Korean government has completed a series of superhighways connecting Seoul with numerous major cities. There is domestic air service, and international airports are located at both Seoul and Pyongyang. Educational facilities have expanded enormously. South Korea has some 200 institutions of higher learning, about one half of which are in Seoul; these include colleges and universities, graduate schools, junior colleges, and other specialized institutions. The emphasis in North Korea has been on specialized and technical education. There are many technical colleges, and the major university, Kim Il Sung, is on the outskirts of Pyongyang. Most Koreans are Confucianists or Buddhists, although the people tend to be eclectic in their religious practices. Korean Confucianism, for example, has developed into more of an ethical system than a religion, and its influence is wide and pervasive. Of the various indigenous religions, Chon-do-gyo (a native mixture of Buddhism, Confucianism, and Taoism) is the most influential. South Korea has a large number of practicing Christians; the Christian religion was introduced by missionaries in the late 19th cent. and had a particular appeal during the years of Japanese occupation. The North Korean government has actively suppressed religion as contrary to Marxist belief.

History. Chinese and Japanese influences have been strong throughout Korean history, but the Koreans, descended from Tungusic tribal peoples, are a distinct racial and cultural group. The documented history of Korea begins in the 12th cent. B.C., when a Chinese scholar, Ki-tze (Kija), founded a colony at Pyongyang. After 100 B.C. the Chinese colony of Lolang, established near Pyongyang, exerted a strong cultural influence on the Korean tribes settled in the peninsula. The kingdom of Koguryo, the first native Korean state, arose in the north near the Yalu River in the 1st cent. A.D., and by the 4th cent. it had conquered Lolang. In the south, two kingdoms emerged, that of Paekche (A.D. c.250) and the powerful kingdom of Silla (A.D. c.350). With Chinese support, the kingdom of Silla conquered Koguryo and Paekche in the 7th cent. and unified the peninsula. Under Silla rule, Korea prospered and the arts flourished; Buddhism, which had entered Korea in the 4th cent., became dominant in this period. In 935 the Silla dynasty was peacefully overthrown by Wang Kon, who established the Koryo dynasty (the name was selected as an abbreviated form of Koguryo). During the Koryo period, literature was cultivated, and although Buddhism remained the state religion, Confucianism—introduced from China during the Silla years—controlled the pattern of government. In 1231, Mongol forces invaded from China, initiating a war that was waged intermittently for some 30 years. Peace came when the Koryo kings accepted Mongol rule, and a long period of Koryo-Mongol alliance followed. In 1392, Yi Songgye, with the aid of the Ming dynasty (which had replaced the Mongols in China) seized the throne. The Yi dynasty, which was to rule until 1910, built a new capital at Seoul and established Confucianism as the official religion. Early in the Yi period (mid-15th cent.) an efficient Korean phonetic alphabet as well as printing with movable metal type were developed. In 1592 an invasion of the Japanese conqueror Hideyoshi was driven back by the Yi dynasty with Chinese help, but only after six years of great devastation and suffering. Manchu invasions in the first half of the 17th cent. resulted in Korea being made

(1637) a vassal of the Manchu dynasty. Korea attempted to close its frontiers and became so isolated from other foreign contact as to be called the Hermit Kingdom. All non-Chinese influences were excluded until 1876, when Japan forced a commercial treaty with Korea. To offset the Japanese influence, trade agreements were also concluded (1880s) with the United States and the countries of Europe. Japan's control was tightened after the First SINO-JAPANESE WAR (1894–95) and the RUSSO-JAPANESE WAR (1904–5), when Japanese troops moved through Korea to attack Manchuria. These troops were never withdrawn, and in 1905 Japan declared a virtual protectorate over Korea and in 1910 formally annexed the country. The Japanese instituted vast social and economic changes, building modern industries and railroads, but their rule (1910–45) was harsh and exploitative. Sporadic Korean attempts to overthrow the Japanese were unsuccessful, and after 1919 a provisional Korean government, under Syngman Rhee, was established at Shanghai. In World War II, at the Cairo Conference (1943), the United States, Great Britain, and China promised Korea independence. At the end of the war Korea was arbitrarily divided into two zones as a temporary expedient; Soviet troops were north and Americans south of the line of lat. 38°N. The Soviet Union thwarted all UN efforts to hold elections and reunite the country under one government. When relations between the Soviet Union and the United States worsened, trade between the two zones ceased; great economic hardship resulted, since the regions were economically interdependent, industry and trade being concentrated in the north and agriculture in the south. In 1948 two separate regimes were formally established—the Republic of Korea in the south, and the Democratic People's Republic under Communist rule in the north. By mid-1949 all Soviet and American troops were withdrawn, and two rival Korean governments were in operation, each eager to unify the country under its own rule. In June, 1950, the North Korean army launched a surprise attack against South Korea, initiating the KOREAN WAR, and with it, severe hardship, loss of life, and enormous devastation. After the war the boundary was stabilized along a line running from the Han estuary northeast across the 38th parallel, with a "no-man's land," 1.24 mi (2 km) wide and occupy-

Pyongyang, the capital of North Korea (above).

Seoul, the capital of South Korea (below).

ing a total of 487 sq mi (1,261 sq km), on either side of the boundary. Throughout the 1950s and 60s an uneasy truce prevailed; thousands of soldiers were poised on each side of the demilitarized zone, and there were occasional shooting incidents. In 1971 negotiations between North and South Korea provided the first hope for peaceful reunification of the peninsula; in Nov., 1972, an agreement was reached for the establishment of joint machinery to work toward unification. The difficulty of real concessions being made by both sides persisted, however, and Korea remained divided. **North Korea,** or Democratic People's Republic of Korea (1973 est. pop. 14,900,000), 46,540 sq mi (120,538 sq km), founded on May 1, 1948, has its capital at PYONGYANG, the largest city. After the Korean War, the Communist government of North Korea, under the leadership of KIM IL SUNG, used the region's rich mineral and power resources as the basis for an ambitious program of industrialization and rehabilitation. With Chinese and Soviet aid, railroads, industrial plants, and power facilities were rebuilt. Farms were collectivized, and industries were nationalized. In a series of three-year, five-year, seven-year, and six-year economic development plans, the coal, iron, and steel industries were greatly expanded, new industries were introduced, and the mechanization of agriculture was pushed. A serious population loss, resulting from the exodus of several million people to the south, was somewhat offset by Chinese colonists and Koreans from Manchuria and Japan. North Korea has maintained close relations with the Soviet Union and Communist China (military aid treaties were signed with both countries in 1961), but has sought to retain a degree of independence; the Sino-Soviet rift has facilitated this. Relations with the United States have remained uncompromisingly hostile, as dramatized by the seizure (1968) of the U.S. intelligence ship *Pueblo* and the imprisonment of its crew for 11 months, and the shooting down of an American plane in 1969. North Korea, although nominally a republic governed by a representative assembly, is actually ruled by the Communist party (known in Korea as the Korea Workers' Party). All governmental institutions are controlled by Kim Il Sung, who has been leader since the country's inception in 1948. **South Korea,** or Republic of Korea (1973 est. pop. 33,400,000), 38,022 sq mi (98,477 sq km), formally proclaimed on Aug. 15, 1948, has its capital at SEOUL, the largest city. PUSAN, the second largest city, is the country's chief port, with an excellent natural harbor near the delta of the Naktong River. Other important cities are TAEGU and INCHON. Syngman RHEE was elected first president in 1948. Traditionally the agricultural region of the Korean peninsula, South Korea faced severe economic problems after partition. Attempts to establish an adequate industrial base were hampered by limited resources and an acute lack of power, most of which, prior to 1948, had been supplied by the north. War damage and the flood of refugees from North Korea further intensified the economic problem. The country depended upon foreign aid, chiefly from the United States, and the economy was characterized by runaway inflation, highly unfavorable trade balances, and mass unemployment. The increasingly authoritarian rule of President Syngman Rhee, with government corruption and injustice, added to the discontent of the people. The elections of March, 1960, in which Rhee won a fourth term, were marked by widespread violence, police brutality, and accusations by Rhee's opponents of government fraud. A student protest march on April 19, 1960, in which 125 students were shot down by the police, triggered a wave of uprisings across the country. The government capitulated, and Rhee resigned and went into exile. A Second Republic of Korea, under the leadership of Dr. John M. Chang (Chang Myun), was unable to correct the economic problems or maintain order, and in May, 1961, the South Korean armed forces seized power in a bloodless coup. A military junta under Gen. Park Chung Hee established firm control over civil freedoms, the press, and the economy, somewhat relaxing restrictions as its power solidified. General Park was elected president in 1963, reelected in 1967, and, following a constitutional amendment permitting a third term, again in 1971. His government was remarkably successful in fighting graft and corruption and in reviving the economy. Successive five-year economic development plans, first launched in 1962, brought dramatic changes. Between 1962 and 1972 manufacturing was established as a leading economic sector and exports increased at an average annual rate of 41%. In Oct., 1972, President Park proclaimed martial law and dissolved the national assembly, asserting that such measures were necessary to improve South Korea's position in the reunification talks with North Korea. Constitutional changes greatly increasing the presidential power were approved by a national referendum in 1972; by 1975, Park had assumed near-dictatorial powers. The Communist victories in Indochina (1975) created new tensions with North Korea and precipitated a government crackdown against dissidents. A scandal involving alleged Korean influence-peddling in the U.S. Congress, along with President Jimmy Carter's announced intention to withdraw 42,000 U.S. troops from South Korea, caused uncommon strains with the United States in 1977. See K. G. Clare et al., *Area Handbook for the Republic of Korea* (1969); Rinn-Sup Shinn et al., *Area Handbook for North Korea* (1969); Pow-Key Sohn et al., *The History of Korea* (1970); B. Y. Choy, *Korea: A History* (1971); D. C. Cole, *Korean Development* (1971); Yung-hwan Jo, comp., *Korea's Response to the West* (1971); Se-Jin Kim, *The Politics of Military Revolution in Korea* (1971); P. M. Bartz, *South Korea* (1972); U-gun Hang, *The History of Korea* (tr. 1972); W. E. Henthorn, *A History of Korea* (1972); R. A. Scalapino and Chong-Sik Lee, *Communism in Korea* (2 vol., 1973).

Korean, language of uncertain relationship. It is thought by some scholars to be akin to Japanese, by others to be a member of the Altaic subfamily of the Ural-Altaic family of languages (see URALIC AND ALTAIC LANGUAGES), and by still others to be unrelated to any known language. The Korean tongue is spoken by about 36 million people in Korea (27 million in South Korea and 9 million in North Korea) and by nearly 1 million others in Japan. Unlike Chinese, Korean does not use tones to make semantic distinctions. Its syntax, however, is similar to that of Chinese, while its morphology resembles that of Japanese. Korean is an agglutinative language in which different linguistic elements, each of which exists separately and has a fixed meaning, are often joined to form one word. A distinctive feature of Korean is the use of a number of different forms to indicate the respective social positions of the speaker, the individual spoken to, and the individual spoken about. The literature in the language dates from the 7th cent. A.D. Once written in Chinese characters, modern Korean has its own phonetic alphabet, called Hankul (or *onmun*), which was devised in the 15th cent. See Edward W. Wagner, *Elementary Written Korean* (3 vol., 1963–71); S. E. Martin et al, *Beginning Korean* (1969).

Korean War, conflict between Communist and non-Communist forces in Korea from June 25, 1950, to July 27, 1953. At the end of World War II, Korea was divided at the 38th parallel into Soviet (North Korean) and U.S. (South Korean) zones of occupation. In 1948 rival governments were established: The Republic of Korea was proclaimed in the South and the People's Democratic Republic of Korea in the North. Relations between them became increasingly strained, and on June 25, 1950, North Korean forces invaded South Korea. The United Nations quickly condemned the invasion as an act of aggression, demanded the withdrawal of North Korean troops from the South, and called upon its members to aid South Korea. On June 30, U.S. President Truman authorized the use of American land, sea, and air forces in Korea; a week later, the United Nations placed the forces of 15 other member nations under U.S. command, and Truman appointed Gen. Douglas MACARTHUR supreme commander. In the first weeks of the conflict the North Korean forces met little resistance and advanced rapidly. By Sept. 10 they had driven the South Korean army and a few American troops to the Pusan area at the southeast tip of Korea. A counteroffensive began on Sept. 15, when UN forces made a daring landing at Inchon on the west coast. North Korean forces fell back and MacArthur received orders to pursue them into North Korea. On Oct. 19, the North Korean capital of Pyongyang was captured; by Nov. 24, North Korean forces were driven almost to the Yalu River, which marked the border of Communist China. As MacArthur prepared for a final offensive, the Chinese Communists joined with the North Koreans to launch (Nov. 26) a successful counterattack. The troops were forced back, and in Jan., 1951, the Communists again advanced into the South, capturing Seoul, the South Korean capital. After months of heavy fighting, the center of the conflict was returned to the 38th parallel, where it remained for the rest of the war. MacArthur, however, wished to mount another invasion of North Korea. When a letter of his was read in Congress, urging a full-scale war against Communism, Truman removed (April 10, 1951) MacArthur from command and installed Gen. Matthew B. RIDGWAY as commander-in-chief. Ridgway began (July 10, 1951) truce negotiations with the North Koreans and Chinese, while small unit actions, bitter but indecisive, continued to take place. Negotiations broke down in Oct., 1952, over repatriation of prisoners of war, but were resumed the following April. After much difficulty, an armistice agreement was signed (July 27, 1953). Casualties in the war were heavy. U.S. losses were placed at over 54,000 dead and 103,000 wounded, while North and South Korean casualties were each at least 10 times as high. See John Miller, Jr., *Korea, 1951–53* (1956); Robert Leckie, *Conflict: The History of the Korean War, 1950–53* (1962); David Rees, *Korea: The Limited War* (1964, repr. 1970); H. J. Middleton, *The Compact History of the Korean War* (1965); M. B. Ridgway, *The Korean War* (1967); L. C. Gardener, ed., *The Korean War* (1972).

United Nations troops during a battle in the Korean War.

Koreish: see KURAISH.

Korhogo (kôrhō'gō), town (1967 est. pop. 30,000), N Ivory Coast. It is an administrative and processing center for a mountainous region where cotton, kapok, rice, millet, groundnuts, maize, and yams are grown and sheep and goats are raised. Diamonds are mined in the area. Korhogo was on an important precolonial trade route to the Atlantic coast.

Korin, Ogata (ōgä'tä kō'rēn), 1658–1716, Japanese decorator and painter. He is renowned for his lacquer work and paintings on screens, decorated with bold designs and striking color contrasts, and his masterful compositional use of empty space. These works show the influence of two earlier artists, Koetsu and Sotatsu, but he departed from conventions, creating his own nearly abstract style. Korin also excelled as a teacher. See study by Doanda Randall (1960).

Kórinthos, Greece: see CORINTH.

Koritsa: see KORÇË, Albania.

Koriyama (kōrē'yämä), city (1970 pop. 241,673), Fukushima prefecture, N Honshu, Japan, on the Abukuma River. It is a major commercial and communications center with industries producing textiles, electrical appliances, and food products.

Körmendi, Ferenc (fĕ'rĕnts kör'mĕndē), 1900–1972, Hungarian novelist. His *Escape to Life* (1932) won the international novel competition of 1932. Among his translated novels are *The Happy Generation* (1934, tr. 1945) and *That One Mistake* (1938, tr. 1947).

Kornberg, Arthur, 1918–, American biochemist, b. Brooklyn, grad. College of the City of New York (B.S., 1937) and Univ. of Rochester (M.D., 1941). In 1942 he joined the U.S. Public Health Service and became (1951) medical director. He was a staff member (1942–52) of the National Institutes of Health, Bethesda, Md. He taught at Washington Univ., St. Louis, and became chairman (1959) of the department of biochemistry at Stanford. Kornberg shared the 1959 Nobel Prize in Physiology and Medicine with Severo Ochoa for their work in the discovery of the mechanisms in the biological synthesis of deoxyribonucleic acid (DNA) and ribonucleic acid (RNA).

Kornilov, Lavr Georgyevich (lä'vər gēyôr'gyĭvĭch kərnyē'ləf), 1870–1918, Russian general, anti-Bolshevik commander during the civil war (1918–20). He fought in the Russo-Japanese War, and in World War I he was captured (1915) by the Austrians and escaped (1916). After the February Revolution of 1917, he was made commander in chief by Kerensky and proceeded to restore discipline among the troops. Conservative elements rallied to Kornilov, who hoped to reconstruct the provisional government on more conservative lines. In Sept., 1917 (Aug., 1917, O.S.) he sent troops to Petrograd (now Leningrad) to carry out these plans. Kerensky—who feared that Kornilov planned to establish a military dictatorship—dismissed Kornilov and, upon Kornilov's refusal to accept dismissal, arrested him and his assistants, including Denikin. Shortly after the October Revolution of 1917, Kornilov escaped from Petrograd and joined M. V. ALEKSEYEV in S Russia. Their volunteer army was greatly weakened by the virtual defection of the Don Cossacks early in 1918; under Kornilov's leadership the army fell back to the Kuban region. He was killed while attacking Ekaterinodar (now Krasnodar) and was succeeded by Denikin as anti-Bolshevik commander in the south.

Korolenko, Vladimir Galaktionovich (vlədyē'mĭr gələktyô'nəvĭch kərəlyĕn'kə), 1853–1921, Russian short-story writer and publicist. A member of a Populist circle, he was arrested in 1879 and exiled to Siberia until 1885. There he wrote many of his lyrical tales, notable for their descriptions of desolate nature. His most famous story, "Makar's Dream" (1885, tr. 1954 in *Korolenko's Siberia*), describes a dying peasant's dream of heaven. After 1895, Korolenko devoted himself to liberal journalism. Greatly honored in Russia by 1903, he welcomed the revolution but later opposed the Bolshevik regime. See his autobiography, ed. by Neil Parsons (1972).

Körös or **Harmás Körös** (här'mŏsh kö'rösh) [Hung.,=triple Körös], Rum. *Criş,* river, c.345 mi (560 km) long, formed in E Hungary by the junction of three headstreams that rise in Transylvania, NW Rumania. It meanders west through farmland to the Tisza River at Csongrád. The Körös is used for irrigation.

korrigum: see DAMALISK.

Korsør (kôrsör'), city (1970 com. pop. 19,864), Vestsjaelland co., S central Denmark, a seaport on the Store Baelt. In the city are fisheries and factories producing glass and processed food.

Kortrijk (kôrt'rīk), Fr. *Courtrai,* city (1970 pop. 44,961), West Flanders prov., SW Belgium, on the Leie River. It is an important linen and textile-manufacturing center. Kortrijk was one of the earliest (14th cent.) and most important cloth-manufacturing towns of medieval Flanders. In 1302, Flemish burghers defeated French knights there in the first BATTLE OF THE SPURS. The Church of Notre Dame (13th cent.) in the city contains Anthony Van Dyck's *Elevation of the Cross* (1631). The Gothic city hall dates from the 16th cent.

Koruk, Algerian corsair: see BARBAROSSA.

Koryak National Okrug: see KAMCHATKA, peninsula, USSR.

Korzybski, Alfred Habdank (kôrzĭb'skē), 1879–1950, Polish-American linguist, b. Warsaw. In his system, which he called General Semantics, Korzybski aimed at a distinction between the word and the object it describes and between the individual objects all described by the same word, insisting also that the effect of time be taken into consideration. In 1949, Korzybski lectured at Yale on his system; he wrote two books describing it (1921 and 1933). See Kelly Thurman, *Semantics* (1960).

Kós (kŏs, kôs), Lat. *Cos,* island (1971 pop. 16,650), 111 sq mi (287 sq km), SE Greece, in the Aegean Sea; 2d largest of the DODECANESE, near the Bodrum peninsula of Turkey. Although it rises to c.2,870 ft (875 m) in the southeast, the island is mostly low-lying. Fishing and sponge diving are important occupations. Grain, tobacco, olive oil, and wine are produced, and cattle, horses, and goats are raised. Kós has mineral deposits and several sulfur springs. The island's main town is Kós (1971 pop. 7,828), situated on the northeast shore. In ancient times the island was controlled in turn by Athens, Macedon, Syria, and Egypt. A cultural center, it was the site of a school of medicine founded in the 5th cent. B.C. by Hippocrates. Kós later enjoyed great prosperity as a result of its alliance with the Ptolemaic dynasty of Egypt, which valued the island as a naval base. The island became part of modern Greece in 1947. It is called Coos in Acts 21.1.

Kosala (kō'sələ), ancient Indian kingdom, corresponding roughly in area with the region of OUDH. Its capital was Ajodhya. It was a powerful state in the 6th cent. B.C. but was weakened by a series of wars with the neighboring kingdom of Magadha and finally (4th cent. B.C.) absorbed by it. Kosala was the setting of much Sanskrit epic literature including the RAMAYANA. Buddha and Mahavira, founder of Jainism, taught in the kingdom.

Kosciusko, Thaddeus (kŏs"ēŭs'kō), Pol. *Tadeusz Andrzej Bonawentura Košciuszko,* 1746–1817, Polish general. Trained in military academies in Warsaw and Paris, he offered his services to the colonists in the American Revolution because of his commitment to the ideal of liberty. Arriving in America in 1777, he took part in the Saratoga campaign and advised Horatio Gates to fortify Bemis Heights. Later he fortified (1778) West Point and fought (1780) with distinction under Gen. Nathanael Greene in the Carolina campaign. After his return to Poland he became a champion of Polish independence. He fought (1792–93) in the campaign that resulted in the second partition (1793) of Poland (see POLAND, PARTITIONS OF). In 1794 he issued a call at Kraków for a national uprising and led the Polish forces against both Russians and Prussians in a gallant but unsuccessful rebellion that ended with the final partition of Poland. He was imprisoned, and after being freed (1796) went to the United States and later (1798) to France, where after the fall of Napoleon he pleaded with Alexander I of Russia for Polish independence. He died in Solothurn, Switzerland, and is buried in Kraków. His devotion to liberty and Polish independence have made him one of the great Polish heroes. See Miecislaus Haiman, *Kosciuszko in the American Revolution* (1943, repr. 1972) and *Kosciuszko, Leader and Exile* (1946).

Kosciusko, Mount (kŏzēŭ'skō), 7,316 ft (2,230 m) high, SE New South Wales, Australia, in the Australian Alps; highest peak of Australia. Winter sports are held on its slopes.

Kose no Kanaoka: see KANAOKA.

kosher [Heb.,=proper, i.e., fit for use], term used in rabbinic literature to mean what is ritually correct, but most widely applied to food that is in accordance with the Jewish dietary laws based on Old Testament passages (primarily Lev. 11 and Deut. 14). Kosher meat is the flesh of animals that both chew the cud and have cloven hoofs (as the cow and sheep); the animal must have been slaughtered with a skillful stroke by a specially trained and highly learned and pious Jew; the meat must be carefully inspected, and, unless cooked by broiling, it must be salted and soaked to remove all traces of blood. Kosher fishes are those that have scales and fins. The rules that apply to the slaughter and preparation of fowl are the same as those for the slaughter of animals. The cooking and eating of milk products with, or immediately after, meats or meat products is unkosher; even the use of the same kitchen and table utensils and towels is forbidden. The cleansing of newly acquired utensils and the preparation of articles for Passover use are also called koshering. The antithesis of kosher is *tref* [from Heb.,=animal torn by wild beasts]. The origins and motivations for the dietary laws and customs have been variously given as hygienic, aesthetic, folkloric, ethical, and psychological. Reform Judaism does not require observance of the kosher laws.

Koshigaya (kōshē'gäyä), city (1970 pop. 139,168), Saitama prefecture, central Honshu, Japan, on the Motoara River. It is a suburb of Tokyo and is noted for its peach orchards.

Koshtan-Tau (kəshtän''-tou', kôsh''tän-), peak, c.16,880 ft (5,150 m) high, Kabardino-Balkar Autonomous SSR, S European USSR, in the central Greater Caucasus.

Košice (kô'shĭtsĕ), Ger. *Kaschau,* Hung. *Kassa,* city (1970 pop. 145,027), E Czechoslovakia, in Slovakia. It is a major industrial center and transportation hub and a market for the surrounding agricultural area. The city's industries include food processing, brewing and distilling, printing, and the manufacture of machinery, cement, and ceramics. A petroleum refinery and a modern iron and steel center are nearby. Originally a fortress town, Košice was chartered in 1241 and became an important trade center during the Middle Ages. It was frequently occupied by Austrian, Hungarian, and Turkish forces. By the Treaty of Trianon (1920) the city passed from Hungary to Czechoslovakia. Košice's most notable historic buildings are the Gothic Cathedral of St. Elizabeth (14th–15th cent.), the 14th-century Franciscan monastery and church, and an 18th-century town hall. The city also has a university and several cultural institutions.

Kosinski, Jerzy (jûr'zē kəzĭn'skē), 1933–, Polish-American writer, b. Łódź, Poland. He learned English after emigrating to the United States in 1957. His best-known work is *The Painted Bird* (1965), a novel depicting the nightmarish wanderings of a young boy among the brutal peasants of a nameless country during World War II. The horrors of war and the violation of a human being are rendered in language of remarkable beauty. Kosinski's other novels, *Steps* (1968), *Being There* (1971), and *The Devil Tree* (1973), echo the theme of character disintegration through cruelty and revenge. He also writes under the name Joseph Novak.

Köslin: see KOSZALIN, Poland.

Kosseir: see QUSAYR, AL, Egypt.

Kossel, Albrecht (äl'brĕkht kôs'əl), 1853–1927, German physiologist. He was professor at Heidelberg from 1901. He specialized in the physiological chemistry of the cell and its nucleus and of proteins, including nucleins. He discovered the purine adenine and the pyrimidine thymine. For this work he received the 1910 Nobel Prize in Physiology and Medicine. He wrote *Protamines and Histones* (tr. 1928).

Kossovo or **Kossovo-Metohija** (kô'sôvô-mĕtô'-khēä), Serbo-Croatian *Kosovo i Metohija* and *Kosmet,* autonomous region, 4,126 sq mi (10,686 sq km), SE Yugoslavia, in Serbia. PRIŠTINA is the chief city. The largely mountainous region includes the fertile valleys of Kossovo and Metohija and is drained by the Southern Morava River. Agriculture, stock raising, forestry, and lead and silver mining are the major occupations. Kossovo's population is mainly Albanian, Serbian, and Montenegrin. Settled by the Slavs in the 7th cent., the region passed to Bulgaria in the 9th cent. and to Serbia in the 12th cent. From the battle of Kossovo in 1389 until the Balkan War of 1913, it was under Turkish rule. Partitioned in 1913 between Serbia and Montenegro, it was incorporated into Yugoslavia after World War I. Following World War II, Kossovo became an autonomous region within Serbia. At **Kossovo Field,** Serbo-Croatian *Kosovo Polje,* in 1389, the Turks under Sultan Murad I defeated Serbia and its Bosnian, Montenegrin, Bulgarian, and other allies. Before the battle Milosh Obilich, a Serb, posing as a deserter, was taken into the tent of Murad, whom he stabbed to death; he was immediately slain, as was Prince Lazar of Serbia after being captured. The battle of Kossovo Field (the name means "field of the black birds") broke the power of Serbia and Bulgaria, which soon passed under Ottoman rule. The battle figures prominently in Serbian poetry. In another battle on the site in 1448, Sultan Murad II defeated an army led by John Hunyadi.

Kossuth, Louis (kŏsōōth'), Hung. *Kossuth Lajos,* 1802–94, Hungarian revolutionary hero. Born of a Protestant family and a lawyer by training, he entered politics as a member of the diet and soon won a large following. His liberal and nationalist program did not avoid the possibility of dissolving the union of the Hungarian and Austrian crowns. He was arrested in 1837, but popular pressure forced the Metternich regime to release him in 1840. Kossuth, a fiery orator, was one of the principal figures of the Hungarian revolution of March, 1848. When, in April, Hungary was granted a separate government, Kossuth became finance minister. He continued and intensified his anti-Austrian agitation. His principles were liberal, but his nationalism was opposed to the fulfillment of the national aspirations of the Slavic, Rumanian, and German minorities in Hungary and was particularly resented in Croatia. When the Austrian government, supported by the *ban* [governor] of Croatia, Count JELLACHICH DE BUZIM, prepared to move against Hungary, Kossuth became head of the Hungarian government of national defense. His government withdrew to Debrecen before the advance of the Austrians under Alfred WINDISCHGRÄTZ. In April, 1849, the Hungarian parliament declared Hungary an independent republic and Kossuth became president. The Hungarians won several victories, but in 1849, Russian troops intervened in favor of Austria, and Kossuth was obliged to resign the government to General GÖRGEY. The Hungarian surrender at Vilagos marked the end of the republic. Kossuth fled to Turkey. He visited England and the United States and received ovations as a champion of liberty. Kossuth lived in exile in England and (after 1865) in Italy. He was dissatisfied with the *Ausgleich* [compromise] of 1867, by which the AUSTRO-HUNGARIAN MONARCHY was created, and he refused an offer of amnesty in 1890. After his death at Turin, Italy, his body was returned to Budapest and buried in state. See biographies by Otto Zarek (tr. 1937, repr. 1970), Endre Sebestyen (1950), and P. C. Headley (1971); F. A. Pulszky, *White, Red, Black* (2 vol., 1853, repr. 1970).

Kostelanetz, André (än'drā kŏs''təlä'nĭts), 1901–, American pianist and conductor, b. St. Petersburg (now Leningrad), Russia. After studying at the St. Petersburg Conservatory of Music, he emigrated to the United States in 1922 and became a citizen in 1928. As a conductor Kostelanetz concentrates on popular and semiclassical works and on simplified versions of famous symphonies. He became popular while appearing regularly on radio and has made many records. He is conductor of the annual Promenade Concerts at Avery Fisher Hall at Lincoln Center in New York City.

Koster or **Coster, Laurens Janszoon** (lou'rəns yän'sōn kôs'tər), c.1370–c.1440, Dutch sexton of a church in Haarlem, one of the men to whom has been ascribed the invention of printing with movable types. His name was Laurens Janszoon, but he is known by his office, as Koster or Coster [sexton]. The evidence that his printing with movable type preceded Gutenberg's is inconclusive.

Kostroma (kəstrəmä'), city (1970 pop. 223,000), capital of Kostroma oblast, E European USSR, on the Volga at the mouth of the Kostroma River. It is a major linen-milling center. Metallurgy, ship repair, and the production of machinery, plywood, and footwear are also important. Founded in 1152, it was the capital of a principality in the 13th and 14th cent. It became an important commercial center after it was annexed by Moscow in 1364. At Kostroma in 1613, Michael Romanov was elected czar. Among the ancient buildings of Kostroma are the Ipatyev monastery (16th cent.) and the Uspensky Cathedral (c.1250).

Kosygin, Alexei Nikolayevich (əlyĭksyā' nyĭkəlī'əvĭch kəsē'gĭn), 1904–, Soviet political leader. A member of the Communist party from 1927, he joined its central committee in 1939. In the 1940s, as an aide to Joseph Stalin, he became recognized as an expert in economics and industry. He held various other government and party posts before becoming (1960) first deputy chairman of the USSR council of ministers. In 1964 he succeeded Nikita Khrushchev as premier, sharing overall power with Leonid BREZHNEV, general secretary of the Communist party. By the late 1960s, however, his importance in the party and government hierarchy had diminished in relation to that of Brezhnev, although Kosygin continued as premier. In this post he introduced various economic measures designed to reform and modernize Soviet agriculture, industry, and trade.

Alexei Kosygin (seated), with Leonid Brezhnev (left), and Andrei Gromyko (right).

Koszalin (kôshä'lēn), Ger. *Köslin,* city (1970 pop. 64,400), NW Poland, near the Baltic Sea. Its industries produce canned fish, metal products, and chemicals. It was founded in 1188, prospered from the 14th to the 16th cent., but suffered greatly in the Thirty Years War. There is a 14th-century Gothic cathedral in Koszalin. The city was transferred from Germany to Poland by the Potsdam Conference (1945).

Kota (kō'tə), city (1971 pop. 213,005), Rajasthan state, NW India, on the Chambal River. Kota, enclosed by a massive wall, is a district administrative center and a market for sugarcane, oilseed, and building stone. The city has an airport. The Mathureshi temple is the most famous of Kota's many temples.

Kota Baharu (kōt'ə bəhär'o͞o) or **Kota Bahru** (bär'o͞o), city (1971 pop. 55,052), capital of Kelantan state, Malaysia, central Malay Peninsula, on the South China Sea at the mouth of the Kelantan River. It is a modern city with an important power station. It was seized by Japan (Dec. 10, 1941) early in the campaign against Singapore during World War II.

Kota Kinabalu (kĭn"əbəlo͞o'), formerly **Jesselton,** town (1971 pop. 41,830), capital of Sabah, Malaysia, in N Borneo and on a small inlet of the South China Sea. It is the chief port of the state and is connected by road and rail with the interior. Rubber is exported. It was founded in 1899 and in 1947 replaced SANDAKAN as the capital of what was then British North Borneo.

Kotelny Island (kōtĕl'nē), largest island of the Anjou group of the NEW SIBERIAN ISLANDS, c.100 mi (160 km) long and c.60 mi (100 km) wide, off N Siberian USSR. The island was discovered in 1773 by Ivan Lyakhov, a Russian merchant. Polar foxes and deer inhabit the island.

Köthen (kö'tən), city (1970 pop. 36,587), Halle district, central East Germany. There are lignite mines, sugar refineries, textile mills, and chemical factories in the city. Known in 1115, Köthen was from 1603 to 1847 the residence of the dukes of Anhalt-Köthen, at whose court Johann Sebastian Bach was musical director from 1717 to 1723. A former spelling was Cöthen.

Kotka (kōt'kä), city (1970 pop. 34,349), Kymi prov., SE Finland, on the Gulf of Finland. It is a major export center for paper, pulp, and timber, and it has chemical industries. It was chartered in 1878.

koto (kō'tō), a Japanese string instrument related in structure to the ZITHER. It consists of an elongated rectangular wooden body, strung lengthwise with 7 to 13 silk strings. The uniformly long strings are tuned to one of several standard tunings by wooden bridges. The koto is placed horizontally on the floor with the player seated behind it, and it is plucked with the fingernails or with a plectum. The instrument flourished in Japanese art music from the 17th cent. until the middle of the 19th cent., when European music began to overshadow indigenous music in popularity.

Kotor (kô'tôr), Ital. *Cattaro,* town (1971 pop. 32,439), SW Yugoslavia, in Montenegro, on the Bay of Kotor, an inlet of the Adriatic. It is a seaport and a tourist center. The town was colonized by Greeks (3d cent.

Japanese woman playing koto (left).

B.C.) and later belonged to the Roman and Byzantine empires. In 1797 it passed to Austria and became an important naval base; in 1918 it was transferred to Yugoslavia. It has a medieval fort and town walls and a 16th-century cathedral.

Kottbus: see COTTBUS, East Germany.

Kotzebue, August von (ou'go͞ost fən kôt'səbo͞o), 1761–1819, German dramatist and politician. He wrote some 200 plays, including *Menschenhass und Reue* (1789, tr. *The Stranger,* 1798), *Die Spanier in Peru; oder, Rollas Tod* (1795, tr. *Rolla,* 1797), and *Die beiden Klingsberg* (1801, tr. *Father and Son,* 1914). Kotzebue was a gifted, though superficial, playwright; his comedies and operatic librettos remained popular throughout the 19th cent. Among those who set his librettos to music were Beethoven, Schubert, and C. M. von Weber. After a stay in Russia, Kotzebue returned to Germany as an agent of Czar Alexander I. He was detested for his reactionary propaganda; his assassination at Mannheim by a student led to the suppression of German student organizations (see BURSCHENSCHAFT) through the Carlsbad Decrees.

Kotzebue, Otto von (ô'tō), 1787–1846, Russian naval officer and explorer; son of A. F. F. von Kotzebue. He accompanied A. J. von Krusenstern on his circumnavigation (1803–6) and himself commanded two voyages around the world (1815–18, 1823–26). He discovered some 400 islands in the South Seas, checked the location of others, and gathered new information on the Pacific coast of Siberia. He sailed N through Bering Strait, explored the northwest coast of Alaska hoping to find a Northwest Passage, and in 1816 discovered and explored Kotzebue Sound. Scientists accompanying his expeditions made valuable reports on ethnography and natural history. Kotzebue's own narratives were translated into English as *A Voyage of Discovery* (3 vol., 1821) and *A New Voyage round the World* (2 vol., 1830, repr. 1967).

Kotzebue (kŏt'səbyo͞o), city (1970 pop. 1,696), NW Alaska, on Kotzebue Sound at the tip of Baldwin Peninsula; inc. 1958. It has one of the largest settlements of Eskimos in Alaska. A regional trade center, Kotzebue has a tourist industry. The city, set on a tundra, began in the 18th cent. as an Eskimo trading post for arctic Alaska and part of Siberia.

Koublai Khan: see KUBLAI KHAN.

Kouchibouguac National Park (ko͞o''shēbəkwăk'), 87 sq mi (225 sq km), on Kouchibouguac Bay, E N.B., Canada, near Richibuct; est. 1969. The park's scenic features include lagoons, bays, and offshore sandbars.

Koufax, Sanford (Sandy Koufax), 1935–, American baseball player, b. New York City. He played (1955–66) with the Dodgers, remaining on the team when the franchise was moved from Brooklyn, N.Y., to Los Angeles. He three times received the Cy Young Award for his outstanding pitching (1963, 1965, 1966). A left-hander with overwhelming speed and a brilliant curve, Koufax struck out 2,396 batters between 1955 and 1966 before being forced into premature retirement with an arm ailment. He was elected to the Baseball Hall of Fame in 1972.

koumiss (ko͞o'mĭs): see FERMENTED MILK.

Koundouritis, Paul: see KONDOURIOTIS, PAUL.

kouprey: see GAUR.

Koussevitzky, Serge (Sergei Aleksandrovich Koussevitzky) (sĕrzh ko͞osəvĭt'skē; syĭrgā' əlyĭksän'drəvĭch ko͞osyĭvēt'skē), 1874–1951, Russian-American conductor, studied in Moscow. He began his career as a double bass player, but in 1908 he made his debut as a conductor in Berlin. In 1910 he and his wife, Natalie, formed an orchestra that Koussevitzky conducted until 1918. In 1917 he was made conductor of the State Symphony Orchestra in Petrograd. Leaving Russia in 1920, he made Paris the center of his activity until he came to the United States in 1924, becoming a citizen in 1941. He was conductor (1924–49) of the Boston Symphony Orchestra and also directed (from 1936) the Berkshire Symphonic Festivals, today known as the Berkshire Festival. A champion of modern music, he repeatedly commissioned and performed new works by American composers, such as Aaron Copland, Samuel Barber, and William Schuman. See biographies by Moses Smith (1947) and Arthur Lourié (1931, repr. 1969); study by H. Leichtentritt (1946).

Kovalevsky, Sonya or **Sophie,** 1850–91, Russian mathematician. She studied at the universities of Heidelberg and Berlin (under K. T. Weierstrass) and in 1874 received a Ph.D in absentia from the Univ. of Göttingen for her remarkable thesis on partial differential equations. From 1884 she taught at the Univ. of Stockholm. In 1888 she won the Bordin Prize of the French Academy of Sciences for a memoir on the rotation of a solid body about a fixed point. Her childhood reminiscences, published in 1890, were translated as *Sonya Kovalevsky: Her Recollections of Childhood* (1895), with a biographical study by Anna Leffler Edgren. See biography by P. Ia. Polubarinova-Kochina (1957).

Kovel (kō'vəl, Rus. kô'vĭl), Pol. *Kowel,* city (1967 est. pop. 31,000), W European USSR, in the Ukraine, on the Tura River. A rail junction and agriculture center, it has food and peat processing plants, railroad shops, and sewing, flax, and woodworking industries. First mentioned in the 14th cent., Kovel belonged to Lithuania and passed to Poland when the two states were united in 1569. The city was taken by Russia during the third partition of Poland in 1795. It was again under Polish rule from 1921 to 1945, when it reverted to the USSR.

Kovno: see KAUNAS, USSR.

Kovrov (kərôf′), city (1970 pop. 123,000), central European USSR, on the Klyazma River. Kovrov is an industrial center that produces excavating machines, linen textiles, and machine tools.

Kowait: see KUWAIT.

Kowel: see KOVEL, USSR.

Kowloon: see HONG KONG.

Koxinga (kŏksĭng′gə), Mandarin *Kuo-hsing-yeh* [lord of the imperial surname], 1624–62, Chinese general, whose original name was Chêng Ch′êng-kung. From 1646 to 1660 he led many unsuccessful campaigns of Ming dynasty loyalists against the invading Ch′ing dynasty. Koxinga captured (1661) part of TAIWAN (Formosa) from the Dutch. The population of the southern coast of China was evacuated (1662) to facilitate the defense against his raids. After the death of his son Chêng Ching, Taiwan fell to the Ch′ing (1683).

Koya (kō′yä), peak, 2,858 ft (871 m) high, S Honshu, Japan. On its summit is a Buddhist monastery, founded in 816. The monastery has 120 temples and is visited by more than a million pilgrims annually. The peak is also known as Koyasan.

Koz, priestly family. Ezra 2.61; Neh. 3.4,21; 7.63. Hakkoz: 1 Chron. 24.10.

Kozhikode, India: see CALICUT.

Kozlov, Frol Romanovich (frōl rəmä′nəvĭch kŏz′-lŏf), 1908–65, Soviet Communist leader. Early in his career he joined the Communist party and rose in the party organization. Kozlov reached prominence as a close ally of Khrushchev and became (1957) a full member of the presidium. In 1960 he was made secretary of the party central committee. He suffered a stroke in 1963 and resigned his posts in Nov., 1964, after Khrushchev's removal.

Kozlov: see MICHURINSK, USSR.

Kr, chemical symbol of the element KRYPTON.

Kra, Isthmus of (krä), narrow neck of the Malay Peninsula, c.40 mi (60 km) wide, SW Thailand, between the Bay of Bengal and the Gulf of Siam. It has long been the proposed site of a ship canal that would bypass the congested Straits of Malacca.

Kraepelin, Emil (krĕpəlēn′), 1856–1926, German psychiatrist, educated at Würzburg (M.D., 1878). He also studied under Wilhelm Wundt in Leipzig. He was appointed professor of psychiatry at the Univ. of Dorpat, Heidelberg (1891) and at Munich (1903), where he also directed a clinic. He investigated (1883–92) the influence of fatigue and alcohol upon physical functions. He also classified mental diseases according to their cause, symptomatology, course, final stage, and pathological anatomical findings. He established the clinical pictures of dementia praecox (schizophrenia) in 1893 and of manic-depressive psychosis in 1899. He was concerned only with diagnostic classification and did not accept the theory of unconscious mental activity postulated by psychoanalysts. He contributed little toward understanding mental disorders, but he brought clarity into psychiatric thought and helped introduce scientific methods of investigation. His major work is his *Textbook of Psychiatry* (9th ed. 1927).

Krafft, Adam: see KRAFT, ADAM.

Krafft-Ebing, Richard von (rĭkh′ärt fən kräft-ā′-bĭng), 1840–1902, German physician and neurologist. Professor of psychiatry at Strasbourg (1872), Graz (1873), and Vienna (1889), he was recognized as an authority on deviant sexual behavior and its medicolegal aspects. His most noted work is *Psychopathia sexualis* (1886, tr. 1892).

Kraft or **Krafft, Adam** (both: ä′däm kräft), c.1455–1509, German sculptor of Nuremberg. He moved from an ornamental late Gothic style toward clarity, symmetry, and a powerful use of rounded, organically constructed figures. His decorations for the Schreyer family tomb (c.1490) in the Church of St. Sebald in Nuremberg and his openwork tabernacle (1493–96) for the Church of St. Lawrence typify his earlier style. His later manner may be seen in his *Stations of the Cross* (1505–8; Nuremberg). Kraft was notably adept at blending architectural and sculptural forms.

Krag, Jens Otto (yĕns ô′tō kräkh), 1914–, Danish political leader. A Social Democrat, he entered parliament in 1947 and played a leading role in shaping Denmark's postwar economic policies. He served as minister of commerce, industry, and shipping (1947–50), minister of economy and labor (1953–57), and minister of external economic affairs (1957–58). Minister of Foreign Affairs (1958–62,1966–67), he was twice prime minister (1962–68, 1971–72). In 1972 his goal of Common Market membership for Denmark was realized when his government won a resounding victory in a referendum on the issue; one day later Krag resigned the premiership for personal reasons.

Krak: see AL KARAK, Jordan.

Krakatoa (krākətō′ə, krä–) or **Krakatau** (kräkätou′), volcanic island, c.5 sq mi (13 sq km), W Indonesia, in Sunda Strait between Java and Sumatra; rising to 2,667 ft (813 m). A terrific volcanic explosion in 1883 blew up most of the island and altered the configuration of the strait; the accompanying tsunami caused great destruction and loss of life along the nearby coasts of Java and Sumatra. The explosion is classed as one of the largest volcanic eruptions in modern times; so great was the outpouring of ashes and lava that new islands were formed and debris was scattered across the Indian Ocean as far as Madagascar. Since then there have been lesser eruptions.

Kraków (kră′kou, Pol. krä′ko͞of), Ger. *Krakau,* city (1970 pop. 583,444), S Poland, on the Vistula. A river port and industrial center, it has varied manufactures including metals, machinery, electrical equipment, and chemicals. One of E Europe's largest iron and steel plants is in the city. Founded c.700 and made a bishopric c.1000, Kraków became (1320) the residence of the kings of Poland. The Kraków fire (1595) caused the transfer (1596) of the royal residence to Warsaw, but the kings were still crowned and buried in Kraków until the 18th cent. The city passed to Austria in the third partition of Poland (1795) and was included (1809) in the grand duchy of Warsaw. In 1815 the Congress of Vienna made the city and its vicinity into the republic of Kraków, a protectorate of Russia, Prussia, and Austria, and in 1846 it was included in Austria. The city reverted to Poland in 1919. Kraków has many historic landmarks and national relics. Its university (known sometimes as the Jagiellonian Univ.), founded in 1364 by Casimir the Great, has long been a leading European center of learning; Copernicus was one of its students. The city has some 50 old churches, many of which contain works of art. Standing on a hill, the Wawel, are the royal castle (rebuilt 16th cent. in Italian Renaissance style) and the Gothic cathedral (rebuilt in the 14th cent.), which contains the tombs of great Poles. The Rynek [market] square is noted for the Church of Our Lady (13th cent.), which has carvings by Veit Stoss; the 14th-century cloth hall; and the remaining tower of the 14th-century town hall.

Kramař, Charles or **Karel** (kä'rĕl krä'märsh), 1860–1937, Czechoslovakian political leader. Elected (1891) to the Austrian parliament, Kramař soon became leader of the liberal nationalist Young Czech party. An ardent Slavophile, he called (1898) for an alliance of Austria-Hungary and Russia against the Germans, whom he regarded as the implacable enemy of all Slavs. He publicly advocated Czech autonomy within the Austrian Empire but privately favored an independent Czech state within a Russian-led Slavic federation. In World War I he led the resistance movement of the Czech nationalists at home, while Thomas G. MASARYK and Eduard BENEŠ led it abroad. He received a death sentence (1916) for treason, but the sentence was commuted to life imprisonment. An amnesty (1917) brought about his release. On October 28, 1918, Kramař led a bloodless coup in Prague, making Czech independence from Austria a reality. He was (1918–19) the first premier of the new state under President Masaryk, but was forced to resign as a result of his opposition to land reform and other progressive measures. After 1919 he led a rightist minority against Masaryk and Beneš.

Kramatorsk (krəmətôrsk'), city (1970 pop. 150,000), S central European USSR, in the Donets Basin of the Ukraine. It is an iron and steel center with factories that produce equipment for coal-mining and chemical industries.

Kramer, Jack (John Albert Kramer), 1921–, American tennis player, b. Las Vegas, Nev. He excelled at tennis while still in high school. Kramer and Frederick (Ted) Schroeder won the U.S. national doubles championship in 1940 and again in 1941. While serving (1942–46) in the U.S. coast guard in World War II, Kramer continued to play tournament tennis, and in 1943 (with Frank Parker) he again won the national doubles title. In 1946–47 he led the U.S. teams that won the Davis Cup, and he also won the national singles title, the national doubles (with Ted Schroeder), the British singles, and the British doubles (with Bob Falkenburg). After turning professional (1947), he took the U.S. professional singles (1948), the world professional singles (1949), and (with Robert Riggs) the world professional doubles (1949) championships. He began promoting professional tennis tournaments in 1952, retiring in 1954 to continue these activities.

Kranach, Lucas: see CRANACH, LUCAS.

Krapp, George Philip, 1872–1934, American scholar, b. Cincinnati. Krapp joined the faculty of Columbia Univ. in 1897, was professor of English at the Univ. of Cincinnati (1908–10) and at Columbia (1910–34). An authority on Anglo-Saxon, he was the first editor of the "Anglo-Saxon Poetic Records," an edition of the existing body of Anglo-Saxon poetry. Besides his authoritative works *Modern English: Its Growth and Present Use* (1909) and *The English Language in America* (1925), Krapp wrote books on English language and literature, speech improvement, and grammar.

Krasicki, Ignacy (ēgnä'tsē kräsēts'kē), 1735–1801, Polish satirist. He is noted for the poems *Myszeis,* an allegory on political disorder, and *Monachomachia,* a witty inspection of monastic life, as well as for his novels, prose satires (e.g., *Satyry,* 1779), and fables. Krasicki enjoyed the favor of both Stanislaus II and Frederick the Great. Six years before his death he was made archbishop of Gniezo.

Krasiński, Zygmunt, Count (zĭg'mo͞ont kräsēn'yəskē), 1812–59, Polish romantic poet. An ardent patriot and Slavophile, he lived much of his life abroad. His majestic works, often set in classical antiquity, include *The Undivine Comedy* (1833, tr. 1875), an allegory of the tragic history of Poland entitled *Iridion* (1835, tr. 1927), *Dawn* (1843), and *The Psalms of the Future* (1845–48). His works transcend nationalist themes in their philosophical concern with the plight of modern man.

Krasnodar (krəs"nədär'), city (1970 pop. 465,000), capital of Krasnodar Kray, SE European USSR, on the Kuban River. A river port and railroad junction, it has petroleum refineries and machinery, metalworking, textile, chemical, and food-processing plants. Founded in 1794 by Zaporozhe (Black Sea) Cossacks upon orders from Catherine II, it was organized as their administrative center and called Ekaterinodar (Yekaterinodar). It served as a military center protecting Russia's Caucasian frontier. After 1918 it was the capital of the Kuban-Black Sea Soviet Republic and was renamed in 1920.

Krasnodar Kray or **Krasnodar Territory,** administrative division (1970 pop. 4,511,000), 32,317 sq mi (83,701 sq km), SE European USSR, extending E from the Sea of Azov and the Black Sea into the KUBAN steppe and straddling the northwestern end of the Greater Caucasus. Krasnodar is the capital. The territory includes the ADYGE AUTONOMOUS OBLAST. The main agricultural section is in the Kuban steppe and along the lower Kuban River. Most of the area has high quality black soil. The territory is one of the USSR's principal tobacco-growing regions. The subtropical Black Sea littoral produces fruit, tea, and wine and is dotted with health resorts, of which Sochi is the best known. There are petroleum, gas, machinery, cement, and lumber industries. Krasnodar, Maikop, and Armavir are the chief industrial centers; Tuapse is the main port. More than 90% of the population is Russian and Ukrainian; their dialect is a mixture of the two languages. The rest of the population is Adyge or Circassian. The area N of the Kuban belonged to the Crimean Khanate and was annexed by Russia in 1783. The Kuban Cossacks, who settled there, gradually displaced the native nomadic Nogay Tatars. The Black Sea littoral was ceded to Russia by Turkey in the Treaty of Adrianople (1829). The remainder, known as CIRCASSIA, was annexed in 1864. Krasnodar Kray was formed in 1937.

Krasnovodsk (krəsnəvôtsk'), city (1970 pop. 64,800), S Central Asian USSR, in the Turkmen Republic, on the Krasnovodsk Gulf of the Caspian Sea. It is the western terminus of oil and natural gas pipelines and of the Trans-Caspian RR, which links the Caspian region with central Asia. It is also a transshipment point for agricultural produce. The city was founded in 1869.

Krasnoyarsk (krəsnəyärsk'), city (1972 est. pop. 688,000), capital of Krasnoyarsk Kray, W Siberian USSR, on the Yenisei River. A major river port and rail center, it has industries producing heavy equipment for the Trans-Siberian RR, building and mining equipment, and farm and shipbuilding machinery. There are also plants producing cement, aluminum, and textiles. One of the world's largest hydroelectric plants is on the Yenisei at Krasnoyarsk. Founded in

1628 as the Cossack outpost of Krasny Yar, it grew rapidly after the discovery of gold and the construction of the Trans-Siberian RR (late 19th cent.). Krasnoyarsk is the seat of the Siberian Institute of Forestry.

Krasnoyarsk Kray or **Krasnoyarsk Territory,** administrative division (1970 pop. 2,962,000), c.928,000 sq mi (2,403,520 sq km), central Siberian USSR, extending from the Sayan Mts. and the Minusinsk basin in the south across the Siberian wooded steppe, taiga, and tundra to the Arctic Ocean. The territory stretches along the entire course of the Yenisei, comprising parts of the West Siberian lowland on the left bank and the central Siberian Plateau on the right bank. The Yenisei and its tributaries are important transportation routes and electric power sources. The Trans-Siberian RR crosses the southern section of the territory. There are deposits of brown coal, graphite, iron ore, manganese, gold, copper, nickel, aluminum, uranium, and mica. In the north is an extensive lumber industry. Grain is grown, cattle and reindeer are raised, and fur trapping is carried on. Krasnoyarsk, the capital, and Kansk, Achinsk, Norilsk, Minusinsk, and Igarka are the chief cities. The territory includes Krasnoyarsk proper (S and E of the Yenisei), the Khakass Autonomous Oblast (in the southwest), the Evenki National Okrug (in the east central section), and the Taymyr National Okrug and Peninsula (N of the Arctic Circle). The southern part of the territory contains 90% of the population, which includes Russians, Ukrainians, Belorussians, Khakass, Tatars, Evenki, Yakuts, and Nenets. The territory was organized in 1934. During Stalin's rule and after, the area was the site of labor camps.

Krasnoye Selo (kräs'nəyə syĭlô'), city (1969 est. pop. 22,000), NW European USSR. It is a rail terminus and has industries producing paper and plastics. Krasnoye Selo was a favorite summer resort of St. Petersburg before the Russian Revolution. Nearby are two of the former summer palaces.

Kraszewski, Józef Ignacy (yo͞o'zĕf ēgnä'tsē kräshĕf'skē), 1812–87, Polish writer. He was imprisoned for political activities in Lithuania and in Germany. Wandering in exile through Europe, he died in Geneva. A large part of Kraszewski's nearly 600-volume output (much of it in English translation) consists of historical novels in the manner of Gogol. His most important work is the epic *Anafielas* (1839–43), a trilogy concerning Lithuanian history.

Kraus, Karl (kärl krous), 1874–1936, Austrian essayist and poet, b. Bohemia. His satirical review the *Fackel* lashed out at hypocrisy, intellectual corruption, and the machine age. His voluminous works include *Worte in Versen* (9 vol., 1916–30, partial tr. *Poems,* 1930); *Die letzten Tage der Menschheit* (1919, tr. *The Last Days of Mankind,* 1974), a monumental drama of World War I; and volumes of essays, aphorisms, and epigrams.

Krauskopf, Joseph (krous'kŏpf), 1858–1923, American rabbi and humanitarian, b. Prussia. He went to the United States in 1872, enrolling (1875) in the first class of the Hebrew Union College, Cincinnati, and receiving ordination in 1883. From 1887 until his death he was rabbi of the Congregation Keneseth Israel, Philadelphia, which flourished under his leadership. He was founder and president of the National Farm School at Doylestown, Pa., which opened in 1897, and he studied agricultural conditions in Russia. Krauskopf was a leader of charitable activities and reform movements in Philadelphia and Pennsylvania and a leading spokesman for his people. His writings include *Evolution and Judaism* (1887). See biography by W. W. Blood (1973).

Krautheimer, Richard (krout'hīmər), 1897–, American art historian, b. Germany. In 1935, Krautheimer began teaching in American universities, becoming professor of fine arts at New York Univ. in 1952. He is an authority on Christian and Byzantine architecture, compiler of *The Early Christian Basilicas of Rome* (1937–) and author of *Early Christian and Byzantine Architecture* (1965). His biography of Lorenzo Ghiberti (1956) and his *Studies in Early Christian, Medieval, and Renaissance Art* (1969) are widely acclaimed.

Kravchinski, Sergei Mikhailovich: see STEPNIAK, S.

kray (krī) [Rus., = edge], administrative and territorial unit of the USSR. There are six krays, or territories, within the Russian Soviet Federated Socialist Republic (RSFSR), the largest of the country's 15 constituent republics. They are: ALTAI KRAY, KRASNODAR KRAY, KRASNOYARSK KRAY, PRIMORSKY KRAY, STAVROPOL KRAY, and KHABAROVSK KRAY. Historically, these areas were frontier zones at the edges of the Russian Empire and were gradually annexed by Moscow. The only kray outside the RSFSR is TSELINNY KRAY (Virgin Lands Territory), which was formed in 1960 in the Kazakh Republic.

Krebs, Sir Hans Adolf, 1900–, English biochemist, b. Germany, M.D. Univ. of Hamburg, 1925. He taught at Cambridge and at the Univ. of Sheffield and after 1954 was professor of biochemistry at Oxford. In 1939 he became an English citizen. He received the 1953 Nobel Prize in Physiology and Medicine, awarded jointly to him and to F. A. Lipmann, for his studies of intermediary metabolism. These studies included the elucidation of the cycle of chemical reactions called the citric acid, or Krebs, cycle, which has proved to be the major source of energy in living organisms.

Krebs cycle: see CITRIC ACID CYCLE.

Krefeld (krā'fĕlt), city (1970 pop. 222,250), North Rhine–Westphalia, W West Germany, a port on the Rhine River. It is the center of the West German silk and velvet industry. Other manufactures include quality steels, machinery, and dyes. Krefeld was chartered in 1373 and was an important linen-weaving center until it passed (1702) to Prussia. The silk industry, encouraged by a monopoly given to the city by Frederick II of Prussia, soon replaced linen weaving; and in the 20th cent. the manufacture of artificial silk became important. The city was heavily damaged in World War II. In 1929 the neighboring town of Uerdingen was incorporated into Krefeld. A former spelling is Crefeld.

Krehbiel, Henry Edward (krā'bēl), 1854–1923, American music critic, b. Ann Arbor, Mich. In 1880 he became music critic of the New York *Tribune.* He championed the music of Wagner, Brahms, and Tchaikovsky when it was little known in the United States. Krehbiel wrote many books on music and edited the English version of A. W. Thayer's biography of Beethoven, which appeared in 1921.

Kreisky, Bruno (bro͞o'nō krī'skē), 1911–, Austrian Socialist politician. He served as a diplomat and foreign affairs minister (1959–66). His goal of Austrian independence and neutrality was realized in a treaty in 1955 that he helped negotiate. Elected chairman of the Socialist party in 1967, he led the Socialists to victory in 1970 but failed to gain a majority of the

The Kremlin, the historic core of Moscow, USSR.

seats in parliament. After the People's party under Josef KLAUS refused to continue the long-standing coalition, Kreisky became chancellor and formed a minority government, the first single-party government in Austria since World War II.

Kreisler, Fritz (krīs'lər), 1875–1962, Austrian-American violinist, studied at the conservatories of Vienna and Paris. He first appeared in the United States in 1888. After studying medicine, then art, Kreisler returned to the violin, making a sensationally successful appearance in Berlin in 1899. In 1901 he played again in the United States and afterward was perhaps the most popular violinist in the country. He served briefly in the Austrian army in World War I; in 1939 he became a French citizen and in 1943 a U.S. citizen. He composed the operettas *Apple Blossoms* (1919) and *Sissy* (1933) and numerous famous violin pieces, including *Caprice Viennois, Tambourin chinois,* and *Polichinelle Sérénade.* In 1935 he revealed that a number of the pieces he had published as compositions of old masters were actually his own. See biography by L. P. Lochner (1950).

Kremenchug (krĕmĭnchōōk'), city (1970 pop. 148,000), S central European USSR, in the Ukraine, on the Dnepr River. It is the center of an industrial complex based on a hydroelectric plant; construction of the plant created the large Kremenchug Reservoir nearby. Kremenchug was founded in 1571 as a fortress.

Kremenets (krĕmĭnyĕts'), Pol. *Krzemieniec,* city (1967 est. pop. 20,000), W European USSR, in the Ukraine. It is a rail terminus, highway hub, and agriculture trade center. Food and tobacco processing and the manufacture of milling machinery, tiles, cement, and hats are important industries. Founded in the 11th cent., Kremenets was part of the Kievan duchy and in the 13th cent. became a fortified city of Galich-Volhynia. After the Polish-Lithuanian union in 1569, it served as a royal residence. The city passed to Russia during the third partition of Poland in 1795. It was again under Polish rule from 1919 to 1945, when it reverted to the USSR.

Kremer, Gerhard: see MERCATOR, GERARDUS.

kremlin (krĕm'lĭn), Rus. *kreml,* citadel or walled center of several Russian cities. During the Middle Ages, the kremlin served as an administrative and religious center and offered protection against military attacks. Thus a kremlin constituted a city in itself, containing palaces, government buildings, churches, marketplaces, and munitions stockpiles. Famous kremlins still preserved include those of Moscow, Astrakhan, Gorky, Kazan, Novgorod, and Pskov. That of Moscow is known simply as the **Kremlin.** Triangular and surrounded by crenellated walls, it occupies 90 acres (36.4 hectares) in the historic core of Moscow. It is bounded on the south by the Moscow River and Kremlin quay, on the east by Red Square with Lenin's tomb, the Moscow Historical Museum, and St. Basil's Cathedral, and on the west and south by the old Alexander Gardens. The Kremlin's walls, built in the 15th cent., are topped on each side by seven towers (20 towers altogether); among these is the Spasskaya [of the Savior], with famous chimes, above the main gate. In the center of the Kremlin is Cathedral Square, with the Uspenski [Assumption] Cathedral (late 15th cent. but containing rare icons of the 12th and 14th cent.), which was used for czarist state occasions, for the crowning of czars, and for the burial of church patriarchs; the Blagoveschenski [Annunciation] Cathedral (15th–16th cent.), which served as the private chapel for the czars' families; the Arkhangelski Cathedral (14th–17th cent.), which contains tombs of the czars; and the separate bell tower of Ivan the Great, c.266 ft (81 m) high, the golden cupola of which dominates the crosses, cupolas, and roofs of the other buildings. On a pedestal adjoining the bell tower is the Czar Bell (cast in 1735), the world's largest bell, with a height of 20 ft (6.1 m) and a weight of 200 tons. The Czar Cannon, located nearby, was cast in 1586 and weighs 40 tons. Along the Kremlin walls are large palaces, including the 15th-century Granovitaya Palata (the throne and banquet hall of the czars); the 19th-century Oruzheinaya Palata (Armory), built as a museum for crowns, scepters, thrones, costumes, and armor; and the 19th-century Grand Palace (Rus. *Bolshoi Dvorets*), rebuilt under the Communist regime and now housing the Supreme Soviet (parliament) of the USSR. The Kremlin's architectural history may be divided into the three periods of the wooden Kremlin (founded in the 13th cent.), the Italian Renaissance Kremlin, and the modern Kremlin started by Catherine the Great in the 18th cent. The Kremlin is almost the only part of Moscow that has escaped all of the city's numerous fires, including that of 1812, when Napoleon's headquarters were in Moscow. It suffered minor damage during the 1917 Bolshevik Revolution. The Kremlin was the residence of the czars until Peter the Great transferred the capital to St. Petersburg (see LENINGRAD) in 1712. Since 1918, when the capital was moved back to Moscow, the Kremlin has been the USSR's political and administrative center.

Křenek, Ernst (krĕ'nĕk, Czech kerzhĕ'nĕk), 1900–, Austrian-American composer, b. Vienna. Křenek was born to Czech parents. He studied in Vienna and Berlin, and in the early 1920s he composed chamber music, a violin concerto (1924), and two operas, in a neoclassical style. In 1925 he became conductor at the opera house in Kassel. His jazz opera *Johnny Strikes Up* (1926), about a Negro band leader, was extremely successful and has been translated into many languages. He returned to Vienna in 1928, and after a brief period of neo-Romanticism, during which he wrote the opera *Leben des Orest* (1930) and a Schubertian song cycle, he gradually adopted the 12-tone technique (see SERIAL MUSIC) originated by Arnold Schoenberg. His opera *Karl V* (1933) is entirely in the 12-tone system. In 1937, Křenek moved to the United States, where he taught and composed chamber, orchestral, and choral music and wrote the opera *Tarquin* (1940) and the chamber opera *Dark Waters* (1950). He wrote *Eleven Transparencies* (1956) for orchestra and electronic music. Křenek is also known as lecturer, pianist, and the author of *Studies in Counterpoint* (1940), *Self-Analysis* (1950), excerpts from an unpublished autobiography, and *Exploring* Music (tr. 1966).

Kresge Foundation, fund established (1924) by retail chain store owner Sebastian S. Kresge (1867–1966) as a broad-purpose philanthropic institution. The foundation describes its policy as "to favor grants providing for the maintenance, expansion, or perpetuation of existing organizations over grants which look to the establishment or initiating of new organizations or experimental projects." Prior to the middle 1960s the foundation gave most of its support to colleges and universities, hospitals, religious institutions, and child welfare agencies in Michigan and the Northeast. Since then, however, there has been a wider geographic distribution of grants and a decrease in support to religious programs. Most assistance goes to the construction and maintenance of buildings or other major capital equipment. Given an initial endowment of $1.3 million, in 1972 the foundation had assets totaling $887 million.

Kresilas: see CRESILAS.

Kretschmer, Ernest, 1888–1964, German psychiatrist, educated at Tübingen, Hamburg, and Munich (M.D., 1913). He served as director of the neurological clinic of the Univ. of Marburg (1926–46) and in 1946 became the director of the neurological clinic of the Univ. of Tübingen. He emphasized the morphological-physiological-psychological unity of the individual, correlating body types and personality characteristics. He maintained that a person's temperamental reaction tendencies are a reflection of his physical make-up. His theories have not found general acceptance.

Kreuger, Ivar (ē'vär kroo͞'gər), 1880–1932, Swedish financier. After studying engineering in Stockholm and engaging in construction enterprises in the United States, he returned to Sweden and organized the firm of Kreuger and Toll. In 1913 he began to form a TRUST to control all aspects of the production of matches in Sweden, and later throughout the world; it eventually became a huge international finance agency. Speculation and fraudulent practices during the 1920s wrecked the trust and led to Kreuger's suicide. Much of his money was obtained from U.S. backers. See studies by Allen Churchill (1957) and Robert Shaplen (1960).

Kreutzer, Rodolphe (kroit'sər, Fr. rôdôlf' krötzĕr'), 1766–1831, French composer and violinist. He was professor of violin at the Paris Conservatory from its founding in 1795 until 1826 and was one of the authors of the violin method taught there. Although he composed some 40 operas and numerous concertos and sonatas, he is remembered for his 40 études for the violin, which remain unsurpassed. Beethoven's *Kreutzer Sonata* is dedicated to him.

Kreuzlingen (kroits'lĭng"ən), town (1970 pop. 15,760), Thurgau canton, NE Switzerland, on the Lake of Constance. The town is contiguous with the German city of Constance. It is an industrial center with the oldest aluminum rolling mill in Switzerland. Foodstuffs, chemicals, and motor vehicles are also manufactured. The Augustinian monastery, founded in the 13th cent. and now a school, has a noted baroque church.

Kreymborg, Alfred (krām'bôrg), 1883–1966, American poet and anthologist, b. New York City. Originally one of the IMAGISTS, he wrote poems collected in *Mushrooms* (1916), *Manhattan Men* (1929), *Selected Poems* (1945), and *Man and Shadow* (1946). He chronicled American poetry in such works as the critical history *Our Singing Strength* (1929, 1934) and the anthology *Lyric America* (1930). His puppet plays were also popular. See his autobiography, *Troubadour* (1925).

Krieghoff, Cornelius (krēg'hŏf), 1812–72, Canadian painter, b. Düsseldorf, Germany. He traveled widely and took part in the Seminole Indian wars in Florida as a member of the U.S. army. Commissioned by the War Dept. to make paintings from many sketches done in these wars, he worked at Rochester, N.Y., and then moved to Canada, working first at Toronto, then at Montreal, and in 1853 at Quebec. He had a keen sense of the picturesque in French-Canadian life, and his numerous pictures are much sought after. See biography by C. M. Barbeau (1934).

Kriemhild: see NIBELUNGEN.

Kriens (krēēns'), town (1970 pop. 20,409), Lucerne canton, central Switzerland, at the foot of Mt. Pilatus. It is a suburb of Lucerne.

Krilenko, Nikolai Vasilyevich: see KRYLENKO.

krill: see CRUSTACEAN.

Krio, Cape (krēō'), Turk. *Deveboynu Burnu*, promontory, SW Turkey, on the Aegean Sea, on Reşadiye Peninsula north of the island of Rhodes. Ancient CNIDUS was situated there.

Krishna (krĭsh'nə) [Sanskrit, = black], one of the most popular deities in Hinduism, the eighth avatar, or incarnation of VISHNU. Krishna appears in the MAHABHARATA epic as a prince of the Yadava tribe and the friend and counselor of the Pandava princes. His divinity is proclaimed in several places in the epic, particularly in the BHAGAVAD-GITA. Krishna's childhood and youth are described in the *Harivamsa* (a supplement to the *Mahabharata*), the *Vishnu Purana,* and the *Bhagavata Purana,* the last being one of the most important texts of the Bhakti, or devotional, movement. As a young boy Krishna is the foster child of cowherds and shows his divine nature by conquering demons. As a youth he is the

Hindu deity Krishna (right) with the gopi Radha, depicted in an 18th-cent. Indian miniature.

lover of the *gopis* (milkmaids), playing his flute and dancing with them by moonlight. The play of Krishna and the *gopis* is regarded in Hinduism as an image of the soul's relationship with God. The love of Krishna and Radha, his favorite *gopi,* is celebrated in a great genre of Sanskrit and Bengali love poetry. See W. G. Archer, *The Loves of Krishna* in *Indian Painting and Poetry* (1953, repr. 1960); Milton Singer, ed., *Krishna: Myths, Rites and Attitudes* (1965).

Krishna, river: see KISTNA.

Krishnagar (krĭsh'nəgər), town (1971 pop. 86,354), West Bengal state, E central India, on the Jalangi River. It is a district administrative center. The main products of the area are rice, jute, sugar, ceramics, and plywood. Krishnagar was the residence of the rajas of the former princely state of Nadia.

Krishna Menon, Vengalil Krishnan (vĕngä'lēl krĭsh'nən krĭsh'nə mĕn'ĭn), 1897–1974, Indian diplomat. He was educated at the Presidency College and the Law College of Madras and at the London School of Economics and University College, London. During his long stay (1924–47) in England he joined the Labour party, was admitted (1934) to the English bar, and served (1934–47) as borough councilor of St. Pancras, London. As secretary (1929–47) of the India League and also as a journalist, he worked hard for Indian self-government and became closely associated with Jawaharlal Nehru. After Indian independence (1947), Krishna Menon served as high commissioner for India in Great Britain (1947–52) and as Indian delegate to the United Nations (1952–62), where he was an outspoken critic of the United States and a staunch supporter of mainland China. In 1957 he was appointed minister of defense, but in 1962, following the Chinese invasion of India's northern frontiers, he was severely criticized for India's lack of military preparedness and was relieved of office. In 1967 he lost his seat in the national legislature, where he had served since 1953, but he was reelected in 1969. See biography by T. J. S. George (1964); study by Michael Brecher (1968).

Krishnamurti, Jiddu (jĭd'o͞o krĭsh″nəmo͞or'tē), 1895–, Indian religious figure. Annie BESANT met him in 1909 and proclaimed that he was an incarnation of Maitreya, the messianic Buddha. In 1929, following a two-year tour of England and America with Annie Besant, Krishnamurti repudiated these claims and dissolved the World Order of the Star, a religious organization that he had founded in 1911. He retained some connection with the theosophical movement, however, and continued an active career of lecturing and writing. He finally settled in Ojai, Calif., where from 1969 he headed the Krishnamurti Foundation. His writings include *The Songs of Life* (1931), *Commentaries on Living* (1956–60), *Freedom from the Known* (1969), *The Urgency of Change* (1970), and *The Awakening of Intelligence* (1974). See Emily Lutyens, *Candles in the Sun* (1957); L. S. R. Vas, *The Mind of J. Krishnamurti* (1971).

Kristiania: see OSLO, Norway.

Kristiansand (krĭstyänsän'), city (1970 pop. 56,914), capital of Vest-Agder co., S Norway, a commercial and passenger port on the Skagerrak. Manufactures include ships, textiles, canned fish, and beer. The city was founded (1641) by Christian IV and became an episcopal see in 1682. Its Christiansholm Fortress (1662–72) now houses a restaurant. The Varodden Bridge (1956), one of the largest suspension bridges in N Europe, spans the nearby Randesund.

Kristianstad (krĭstyän'städ), city (1970 pop. 43,799), capital of Kristianstad co., SE Sweden, on the Helgaän River. Its nearby seaport, Åhus, is on the Baltic Sea. Kristianstad is a commercial and industrial center, located in a fertile agricultural region. Manufactures include textiles, machinery, and processed food. Founded (1614) by Christian IV of Denmark, Kristianstad changed hands frequently, but passed definitively to Sweden in 1678. A church built (12th cent.) by Archbishop Absalon is nearby.

Kristiansund (krĭstyänso͞on'), city (1970 pop. 18,508), Møre og Romsdal co., W Norway, a port on the Atlantic Ocean. It is the site of a large trawler fleet and has industries that produce ships and fish and forest products. Chartered in 1742, Kristiansund was destroyed (1940) by bombardment in World War II and has since been rebuilt on three islands enclosing the harbor.

Kristinehamn (krĭ″stĭnəhä'mən), city (1970 pop. 21,403), Värmland co., S central Sweden, a port on Lake Vänern. The city was first chartered in 1582 as Bro. It was rechartered in 1642 by Queen Christina and renamed Kristinehamn.

Kritios: see CRITIUS.

Krivoy Rog (krēvoi' rôk'), city (1972 est. pop. 600,000), SW European USSR, in the Ukraine, at the confluence of the Ingulets and Saksagan rivers. It is a rail junction, an industrial center, and a metallurgical and coking center of one of the world's richest iron-mining regions. Burial mounds in the area indicate that Scythians inhabited it and used the iron deposits. Founded in the 17th cent. by Zaporozhe Cossacks, the city received its name (Crooked Horn) because of the shape of the iron-mining area. Krivoy Rog's industrial growth dates from 1881, when French, Belgian, and other foreign interests founded a mining syndicate. The city has mining and pedagogical institutes.

Krk (kûrk), Ital. *Veglia,* island (1971 pop. 13,078), 157 sq mi (407 sq km), in the Adriatic, off the Dalmatian coast, NW Yugoslavia. The largest of Yugoslav islands in the Adriatic, it has several small seaside resorts. The chief town, Krk, has retained its medieval walls and castle and has a 13th-century Roman Catholic cathedral.

Krkonoše (kŭr'kônôshĕ), Ger. *Riesengebirge,* Pol. *Karkonosze,* highest range of the Sudetes, extending c.25 mi (40 km) along the border of N Czechoslovakia and SW Poland. Its highest peak, Sněžka (Ger. *Schneekoppe,* Pol. *Śnieżka*), rises to 5,258 ft (1,603 m). Paper and textile mills, which use the range's waterpower, are found on both sides of the border. Coal is mined near Zacléř, Czechoslovakia. There are numerous resorts and spas in the mountains; the most notable is Janské Lázně, Czechoslovakia. A national park (est. 1963) straddles the international border. The Labe (Elbe) River rises in the Krkonoše.

Krnov (kûr'nôf), Ger. *Jägerndorf,* city (1970 pop. 22,496), N Czechoslovakia, in Moravia, on the Opava River, near the Polish border. An industrial center, it manufactures machinery, textiles (especially woolens), and musical instruments (notably organs). The city was founded in 1221 and served as the capital of an independent duchy from 1377 to 1523. Krnov has an 18th-century castle and several fine churches and abbeys.

Krochmal, Nachman Kohen (näkh'män kō'hĕn krôkh'mäl), 1785–1840, Jewish secular historian and writer, b. Galicia. He was a leader in the movement of the Jewish enlightenment, a founder of the Conservative movement in Judaism, and a pioneer of modern Jewish scholarship. He applied his synthesis of religion and philosophy to the writing and teaching of Jewish history. His most important work, *Guide to the Perplexed of Our Age,* in Hebrew, was published posthumously in 1851.

Krock, Arthur, 1886–1974, American journalist, b. Glasgow, Ky. He left Princeton to take up reporting and worked in Louisville and Washington. In 1927 he joined the New York *Times,* becoming Washington correspondent in 1932. Krock's pungent and controversial columns generally espoused a conservative viewpoint. He was the only man to win four Pulitzer awards, two prizes (1935, 1938), a special commendation, and a special citation. His books include *Sixty Years On The Firing Line* (1968), *In the Nation: 1932–1966* (1969), *The Consent of the Governed and Other Deceits* (1971), and *Myself When Young: Growing Up in the 1890's* (1973).

Kroeber, Alfred Louis (krō'bər), 1876–1960, American anthropologist, b. Hoboken, N.J., Ph.D. Columbia, 1901. He taught (1901–46) at the Univ. of California and was director (1925–46) of the anthropological museum there. An authority on the Indians of North and South America, he participated in many expeditions in the Southwest and in Mexico and Peru. Like his teacher Franz BOAS, Kroeber upheld the tradition of broad scholarship, and he was a major figure in the founding of the modern science of anthropology. He set forth clearly the relationship of culture patterns to the individual and presented a new concept of society as the interaction of groups and persons. Kroeber wrote many influential articles, and his books include *Anthropology* (1923, rev. ed. 1948), *Configurations of Culture Growth* (1944), *The Nature of Culture* (1952), and *Style and Civilization* (1957). See biographies by his wife Theodora Kroeber (1970) and J. H. Steward (1973).

Krogh, Schack August Steenberg (shäk ou'go͝ost stān'bĕrg krôkh), 1874–1949, Danish physiologist. He taught at the Univ. of Copenhagen (1916–45) and studied respiration, circulation, and the effect of an exclusive meat diet on the Eskimo and of deep-sea conditions on living organisms. For his discovery of the regulation of the vasomotor mechanism of the capillaries he received the 1920 Nobel Prize in Physiology and Medicine. His writings include *The Anatomy and Physiology of Capillaries* (1922, rev. ed. 1959), *Osmotic Regulation in Aquatic Animals* (1939), and *Comparative Physiology of Respiratory Mechanisms* (1941).

Krohg, Christian (krĭs'tyän krōg), 1852–1925, Norwegian genre and portrait painter and author. After studying on the continent, Krohg returned to Norway in 1878 and became a well-known advocate of impressionism. He later taught in Paris and in 1909 became director of the Oslo Academy. In *The Struggle for Existence* (4 vol., 1920–21) he advocated the social mission of the arts.

Krolewska Huta: see CHORZÓW, Poland.

Kroll, Leon (krōl), 1884–1974, American painter and lithographer, b. New York City. Kroll studied in New York with J. H. Twachtman and later in Paris. He returned to New York, where he became a well-known teacher. His oils are characterized by clarity, strong color, and attention to modeling of forms. Kroll's work is represented in major galleries throughout the United States. His many murals include one for the Worcester War Memorial and one for the Justice Dept., Washington, D.C.

Kroměříž (krô'myĕrzhēsh), Ger. *Kremsier,* city (1970 pop. 22,308), central Czechoslovakia, in Moravia, on the Morava River. An agricultural center, it manufactures farm machinery and machine tools and has sugar refineries. Kroměříž was chartered in 1290 and served as the residence of the bishops of Olmütz. It was also the site of a meeting (Nov., 1848–March, 1849) of the first Austrian constituent parliament (see AUSTRIA). Among the city's present-day landmarks is an 18th-century palace with a large library and a ceremonial hall.

Kronborg castle: see HELSINGØR, Denmark.

Kronecker, Leopold (lā'ōpôlt krō'nĕk"ər), 1823–91, German mathematician. After making a fortune in business he devoted his attention to mathematics and became professor at the Univ. of Berlin in 1883. Noted as an algebraist, he was a pioneer in the field of algebraic numbers and in formulating the relationship between the theory of numbers, the theory of equations, and elliptic functions.

Kronos: see CRONUS.

Kronshtadt (krənshtät'), city, NW European USSR, on the small island of Kotlin in the Gulf of Finland, c.15 mi (20 km) from Leningrad. It is the chief naval base for the Soviet Baltic fleet. The harbor is icebound for several months each year. It was founded (1703) by Peter I as a port and a fortress to protect the site of St. Petersburg, and it was the commercial harbor of St. Petersburg until the 1880s. The port lost its commercial value after the development of St. Petersburg. The visit (1891) of a French naval squadron to Kronshtadt was followed by a Franco-Russian military agreement heralding the formation of the Triple Entente of France, England, and Russia. Mutinies of the naval garrison took place in 1825 and 1882 and played a part in the revolutions of 1905 and 1917 (see RUSSIAN REVOLUTION). A revolt of the sailors in March, 1921, was instrumental in establishing Lenin's NEW ECONOMIC POLICY. The general unrest among peasants and workers touched off this mutiny of the naval garrison that had been loyal to the Bolsheviks during the revolution. This was the climax of the anti-Bolshevik unrest in the country. In

World War II, Kronshtadt played a major role in the defense of Leningrad against the Germans. It is also spelled Cronstadt.

Kroonstad (kro͞on'stät), town (1970 pop. 50,898), Orange Free State, E central South Africa, on the Vals River. It is an agricultural and industrial center. There is a grain elevator, and grain is shipped from the town. Kroonstad is also an important rail junction and has large marshaling yards. The town's chief industries are clothing manufacture and mineral processing, and the production of machine parts. Kroonstad was founded in 1855. Its growth was stimulated by the discovery of gold in the region in the late 19th cent. After the fall of BLOEMFONTEIN during the SOUTH AFRICAN WAR, it was (March 13–May 11, 1900) the capital of the ORANGE FREE STATE. Kroonstad Technical College is in the town.

Kropotkin, Piotr Alekseyevich, Prince (pyô'tər əlyĭksyā'ĭvĭch krəpôt'kĭn), 1842–1921, Russian anarchist. He came from a wealthy princely family and as a boy was a page to the czar. Repelled by court life, he obtained permission to serve as an army officer in Siberia, where his explorations and scientific observations established his reputation as a geographer. After returning to European Russia, he became an adherent of the Bakuninist faction of the NARODNIKI and engaged in clandestine propaganda activities until arrested in 1874. Two years later he escaped to Western Europe, where he worked with various anarchist groups until his imprisonment in France (1883). Pardoned in 1886, partly as the result of the popular clamor for his release, he moved to England and spent the next 30 years mainly as a scholar and writer developing a coherent anarchist theory. In his most famous book, *Mutual Aid* (1902), he attacked T. H. Huxley and other Social Darwinists for their picture of nature and human society as essentially competitive. He insisted that cooperation and mutual aid were the norms in both the natural and social worlds. From this perspective he developed a theory of social organization—in *Fields, Factories and Workshops* (1898) and elsewhere—that was based upon communes of producers linked with each other through common custom and free contract. Returning to Russia following the February Revolution of 1917, he attempted to engender support for a continued Russian effort in World War I and to combat the rising influence of Bolshevism. Following the Bolshevik triumph in the October Revolution (1917), he retired from active politics. Consistently nonviolent in his anarchist beliefs, Kropotkin, as both thinker and man, was admired and acclaimed by many far removed from anarchist circles. See his *Memoirs of a Revolutionist* (1899, repr. 1968); biography by George Woodcock and Ivan Avakumović (1950, repr. 1971); J. W. Hulse, *Revolutionists in London* (1970); Paul Avrich, ed., *The Anarchists in the Russian Revolution* (1973).

Krüdener, Juliana, Baroness von (fən krüd'ənər), 1764–1824, Russian novelist and mystic. Born a Livonian aristocrat, she married a Russian diplomat. She left her husband (1801) for the pleasures of literary and social life in Paris and Switzerland. There Krüdener wrote a sentimental, largely autobiographical novel, *Valérie* (1804), which became a literary sensation. Converted to Moravian pietism, she devoted herself to preaching her faith and for a time held enormous influence over Alexander I of Russia. She claimed to have inspired the formation of the Holy Alliance of Russia, Austria, and Prussia. See E. J. Knapton, *The Lady of the Holy Alliance* (1939).

Kruger, Paul (Stephanas Johannes Paulus) (kro͞o'gər, Afrikaans stāfä'nəs yōhä'nəs pou'ləs krügər), 1825–1904, South African Transvaal statesman, known as Oom Paul. As a child he accompanied (1836) his family northward from the Cape Colony in the Great Trek that was eventually to cross the Vaal River and establish the Dutch-speaking republic of Transvaal (1852). Kruger's life was closely tied to the development of the country; he was a pioneer, soldier, farmer, and politician. The Transvaal was annexed by Great Britain in 1877. Kruger at first cooperated with the British but shortly thereafter was dismissed because of his demands for retrocession. He was one of the triumvirate (with Piet Joubert and Martinius Pretorius) who negotiated the Pretoria agreement with the British (1881) granting the Boers independence. Kruger was elected president in 1883 and reelected in 1888, 1893, and 1898. His policy was one of continual resistance to the British, who came to be personified in South Africa by Cecil RHODES. Colonization of Rhodesia N of the Transvaal and the increasing importance of gold mining merely brought much greater resistance on Kruger's part to Rhodes's dream of a unified South Africa. In the 1890s, Kruger adopted a stringent policy against the enfranchisement of the Uitlanders who were settling in the Transvaal. The Jameson Raid (see JAMESON, SIR LEANDER STARR) into the Transvaal (Dec., 1895), undertaken with Rhodes's knowledge, created an international crisis. The Kaiser congratulated Kruger (in the "Kruger telegram") for the successful repulsion of the British, with the implication that Germany had a right to interfere in the Transvaal. The message caused great indignation in England. Kruger fought in the early stages of the SOUTH AFRICAN WAR, but in 1900 he went to Europe on a Dutch cruiser in a vain effort to enlist aid for his country. He died an exile in Switzerland. See his memoirs (tr. 1902, repr. 1969); biography by Manfred Nathan (1941); studies by J. S. Marais (1962), D. M. Schreuder (1969), and C. T. Gordan (1970).

Kruger National Park, game reserve, c.8,000 sq mi (20,720 sq km), Transvaal, NE Republic of South Africa. One of the world's largest wildlife sanctuaries, it has almost every species of game in southern Africa. In its rivers are found hippopotamuses and crocodiles; everywhere countless varieties of birds can be seen. Tourists driving along the park's extensive (c.1,200-mi/1,930-km) road system can observe the animals at close quarters. The park was originally founded as the Sabi Game Reserve (1898) by S. J. P. Kruger; it was enlarged and made a national park in 1926.

Krugersdorp (kro͞o'gərzdôp), city (1970 pop. 91,202) Transvaal, NE South Africa. The chief industrial city of the W Witwatersrand, Krugersdorp is the center for a region where gold, manganese, asbestos, lime, and uranium are mined. The city has uranium extraction plants. It also serves as the trade center for the surrounding farming area. Founded in 1887, it was named for Paul Kruger, president of the Transvaal republic. The Paardekraal monument marks the spot where in 1880 BOERS pledged themselves to end British rule in the Transvaal. Nearby are the Sterkfontein Caves (an important archaeological site), Kromdei Paleontological Reserve, and Krugersdorp Game Reserve. The city has a technical college.

Krupp (kro͝op), family of German armament manufacturers. The family settled in Essen in the 16th cent. The core of the great Krupp industrial empire was started by **Friedrich Krupp**, 1787–1826, who built a small steel plant c.1810. His son, **Alfred Krupp**, 1812–87, known as the "Cannon King," introduced new methods for producing large quantities of cast steel. After the Franco-Prussian War he specialized more and more in armaments and acquired mines all over Germany. Under his son, **Friedrich Alfred Krupp** (Fritz Krupp), 1854–1902, who was interested in the financial rather than the technical aspects of the enterprise, the Krupp family vastly extended its operations. His daughter, Bertha Krupp (after whom the Big Berthas were named), married Gustav von Bohlen und Halbach, who assumed the name **Gustav Krupp von Bohlen und Halbach**, 1870–1950. He took over the management of the firm, which had become a public company in 1903. After 1933 the Krupp works became the center of German rearmament. In 1943, by a special order from Hitler, the company was again converted into a family holding and **Alfried Krupp von Bohlen und Halbach,** 1907–1967, son of Gustav and Bertha, took over the management. After Germany's defeat, he was tried as a war criminal and sentenced (1948) to imprisonment for 12 years. In 1951 he was released, and in 1953 he resumed control of the firm with the stipulation that he sell his major interests in iron, steel, and coal. The condition was not fulfilled, however. Shortly before his death in July, 1967, the firm's indebtedness caused Alfried to announce that the Krupp concern would become a public corporation. His son **Arndt von Bohlen and Halbach,** 1938–, relinquished his inheritance rights, and in 1968 the Krupp family ceased to control the firm. See Gert von Klass, *Krupps: The Story of an Industrial Empire* (1953, tr. 1954); Norbert Mühlen, *The Incredible Krupps* (1959); William Manchester, *The Arms of Krupp, 1587–1968* (1968).

Krusenstern, Adam Johann von (ä'däm yō'hän fən kro͞o'zənshtĕrn), 1770—1846, Russian navigator. From 1803 to 1806 he circumnavigated the globe. Although the voyage was undertaken to stimulate the fur trade of the Pacific coast and to revive trade with China and Japan, its real contribution was to the knowledge of the hydrography of the N Pacific coast of America. Krusenstern was director (1827–42) of the royal naval academy and was promoted to the rank of admiral. He wrote an account of his voyage (3 vol. and atlas, 1809–13; tr. 1813).

Krusenstjerna, Agnes von (äng'nās vôn kro͞osĕnshĕr'nä), 1894–1940, Swedish novelist. Krusenstjerna's works reflect the aristocratic and emotionally disturbed background from which she came. She frequently portrayed the degeneracy of the society from which she separated herself. Her works include the controversial novel cycles *Tony-böckerna* [the Tony books] (1922–26) and *Fröknarna von Pahlen* [the Misses von Pahlen] (1930–35). In these novels she presented for the first time in Swedish literature a candid picture of sexual problems. Her works are outstanding for the skill and psychological acuity of her writing.

Kruševac (kro͞o'shĕväts), town (1971 pop. 117,926), E Yugoslavia, in Serbia. A commercial center, it has chemical and munitions industries. The seat of the kings of Serbia until 1389, it has retained the ruins of a medieval castle.

Krušné Hory: see ERZGEBIRGE.

Krutch, Joseph Wood (kro͞och), 1893–1970, American author, editor, and teacher, b. Knoxville, Tenn., grad. Univ. of Tennessee, 1915, Ph.D. Columbia, 1923. He was on the editorial staff of the *Nation,* primarily as drama critic, from 1924 to 1952. From 1937 to 1953 he held a professorship at Columbia. Highly regarded as both a social and literary critic, Krutch is the author of such works as *Comedy and Conscience after the Restoration* (1924), *Edgar Allan Poe: A Study in Genius* (1926), *The Modern Temper* (1929), *The American Drama since 1918* (1939), *Samuel Johnson* (1944), *Henry David Thoreau* (1948), *The Measure of Man* (1954), and *Human Nature and the Human Condition* (1959). After he moved to Arizona, he turned also to the study of nature; his books in this field include *The Twelve Seasons* (1949), *The Desert Year* (1952), and *The Voice of the Desert: A Naturalist's Interpretation* (1955). See his autobiography, *More Lives than One* (1962); *A Krutch Omnibus: Forty Years of Social and Literary Criticism* (1970); *The Best Nature Writings of Joseph Wood Krutch* (1970).

Krylenko or **Krilenko, Nikolai Vasilyevich** (both: nyĭkəlī' vəsē'lyəvĭch krĭlyĕn'kō), 1885–1938, Russian revolutionary and jurist. In Nov., 1917, Trotsky promoted him from ensign to commander in chief of the Russian forces for the purpose of opening peace negotiations with the Central Powers. Krylenko resigned in 1918 and later became public prosecutor and commissar of justice. He was tried (1938) in the party purge trials instituted by Stalin and was executed.

Krylov, Ivan Andreyevich (ēvän' əndrā'əvĭch krĭlôf'), 1768–1844, Russian fabulist. Some of his more than 200 fables were adapted from Aesop and La Fontaine, but most were original. A moralist, Krylov used popular language to satirize human weaknesses, social customs, and political events. His works won him international renown. See translations by Bernard Pares (1926); *Russian Fables of Ivan Krylov* (tr. by Walter Morison, 1942); study by N. L. Stepanov (1973).

Krym: see CRIMEA, USSR.

kryolite: see CRYOLITE.

krypton (krĭp'tŏn) [Gr.,=hidden], gaseous chemical element; symbol Kr; at. no. 36; at. wt. 83.80; m. p. −156.6°C; b. p. −152.3°C; density 3.73 grams per liter at STP (see separate article); valence usually 0. Krypton is a colorless, odorless, tasteless gas. It is one of the so-called INERT GASES found in group 0 of the PERIODIC TABLE. It is a rare gas present in air at a concentration of about one part per million. Naturally occuring krypton is a mixture of six stable isotopes. It is produced commercially by fractional distillation of liquid air. Krypton is used to fill electric lamp bulbs and various electronic devices. Fluorescent lamps are filled with a mixture of krypton and argon. Krypton is also used in tungsten-filament photographic projection lamps and in very high-powered electric arc lights used at airports. A mixture of stable and unstable isotopes of krypton is produced by slow neutron fission of uranium in nuclear reactors. Krypton-85 (half-life about 10 years) is the most stable of the 17 radioactive isotopes known; it makes up about 5% by volume of the krypton produced in the nuclear reactor. It is used to detect leaks in sealed containers, to excite phosphors in light sources with no external source of energy, and in medicine to detect abnormal heart openings. Although krypton does not generally form chemical compounds in the normal sense, gram quantities of krypton difluoride have been prepared and several other compounds have been reported. Krypton has characteristic green and orange lines in its spectrum. In 1960 the meter was defined by inter-

National Mosque in Kuala Lumpur, capital of the Federation of Malaysia.

national agreement as exactly 1,650,763.73 times the wavelength (in a vacuum) of the orange-red line in the emission spectrum of krypton-86 (see WEIGHTS AND MEASURES). Krypton was discovered in 1898 by William RAMSAY and W. M. Travers in residue from the evaporation of a sample of liquid air from which oxygen and nitrogen had been removed.

Kuala Lumpur (kwä'lə lo͝om'po͝or), city (1971 pop. 451,278), capital of the Federation of Malaysia, S Malay Peninsula, at the confluence of the Klang and Gombak rivers. The chief inland city of Malaysia, Kuala Lumpur is the commercial center of a tin-mining and rubber-growing district and is a transportation hub. It was founded in 1857 by Chinese tin miners and superseded Klang in 1880 as the capital of Selangor. In 1896 it became the capital of the Federated Malay States (see MALAYSIA). Among the notable structures is the modern parliament building in Moorish style. The population is about two-thirds Chinese.

Kuala Terengganu (tərĕng-gä'no͞o) or **Kuala Trengganu** (trĕng-), city (1971 pop. 53,353), capital of Terengganu state, Malaysia, central Malay Peninsula, on the South China Sea at the mouth of the Terengganu River. It is a port and has a weaving industry. The residence of the sultan of Terengganu is in the city.

Kuang Hsü (gwäng shü), 1871–1908, emperor of China (1875–1908). Although he was not in the direct line of succession, he was appointed to the throne by his aunt, the dowager empress and regent, TZ'U HSI. He began his rule in 1889. In 1898, during the "hundred days of reform," he rebelled against her domination and issued many decrees modernizing the political and social structure of China. His aunt thereupon resumed the regency and kept him imprisoned for the remainder of his life while she ruled China in a conservative manner.

Kuang Wu Ti: see LIU HSIU.

Kuban (ko͞obăn', -bän', Rus. ko͞obä'nyə), river, c.570 mi (920 km) long, rising in the Greater Caucasus on the western slopes of Mt. Elbrus, S European USSR, and flowing north in a wide arc past Karachayevsk, Cherkessk, and Armavir, then W past Krasnodar, entering the Sea of Azov through two arms. Its upper course is precipitous and leads through several gorges; it then meanders slowly through the Kuban Steppe, a rich black-earth area and one of the major grain and sugar-beet districts of the USSR. The last 150 mi (240 km) are navigable. Russia annexed the khanate of Crimea, of which the Kuban area was a part, in 1783. Now mainly within the KRASNODAR KRAY, the Kuban region was from about the mid-18th cent. to 1920 the territory of the **Kuban Cossacks.** After Catherine II defeated (1775) the ZAPOROZHYE Cossacks in the Ukraine, some of them emigrated to Turkey, but in 1787 they were allowed to return and settle along the Black Sea between the Dnepr and the Bug rivers. Then known as the Black Sea Cossacks, they were in 1792 resettled in the Kuban region. Though they lost much of their freedom and their rights were restricted, they were granted local self-government in return for military service. In 1860 they were renamed the Kuban Cossacks, while defending the Kuban region from hostile Circassian mountaineers to the south. After the Bolshevik Revolution of 1917, the Kuban Cossacks proclaimed an independent republic and fought against the Bolsheviks. After the civil war of 1918–20 the Soviet regime abolished their government, and their traditional privileges were abrogated.

Kubelík, Jan (yän ko͞o'bəlĭk), 1880–1940, Czech violinist. Kubelík studied with Otakar Ševčik at the Prague Conservatory. He made his debut in Vienna in 1898 and was thereafter acclaimed for his great virtuosity and dramatic power by critics in England, on the Continent, and in the United States, where he first appeared in 1901. Kubelík composed six violin concertos, a symphony, and some chamber music. He performed very little after World War I. His son, **Rafael Kubelík,** 1914–, b. Býchory, Czechoslovakia, was conductor of the Chicago Symphony (1950–53) and later director of the Covent Garden Opera in London. He also composed the opera *Veronika*

(1947), as well as symphonic and instrumental works.

Kubitschek, Juscelino (zhōōsəlē'nōō kōō'bəchĕk), 1902–76, president of Brazil (1956–61). A surgeon who served as mayor of Belohorizonte and governor of Minas Gerais, he was elected president in 1955. He launched an immense public works program, borrowing heavily to construct buildings, highways, hydroelectric projects, and the new capital city, Brasília. He offered enormous incentives to industry, and the country's productive capacity soared. The huge deficit spending, however, sparked an inflationary spiral, and the national debt reached almost $4 billion. Kubitschek was succeeded in office by Janio Quadros. In 1964, after a military takeover in Brazil, Kubitschek was deprived of his political rights and went into exile temporarily.

Kublai Khan (kōō'blī kän), 1215?–1294, Mongol emperor, founder of the Yüan dynasty of China. From 1251 to 1259 he led military campaigns in S China. He succeeded (1260) his brother Mangu as khan of the empire that their grandfather JENGHIZ KHAN had founded. The empire reached its greatest territorial extent with Kublai's final defeat (1279) of the Sung dynasty of China; however, his campaigns against Japan (see KAMIKAZE), SE Asia, and Indonesia failed. Kublai's rule was nominal except in Mongolia and China. He recruited men of all nations for his civil service, but only Mongolians were permitted to hold the highest government posts. He promoted economic prosperity by rebuilding the Grand Canal, repairing public granaries, and extending highways. He fostered Chinese scholarship and arts. Although he favored Buddhism, other religions (except Taoism) were tolerated. Kublai encouraged foreign commerce, and his magnificent capital at Cambuluc (now Peking) was visited by several Europeans, notably Marco Polo, who described it. It is perhaps this city which figures in Coleridge's poem *Kubla Khan*. Kublai's name is also spelled Kubilai, Koublai, and Kubla.

Kuching (kōō'chĭng), city (1971 pop. 63,491), capital of Sarawak, Malaysia, in W Borneo and on the Sarawak River. It is the largest city in the state and a river port. Sago flour and pepper are exported. It was founded in 1839 by James BROOKE. In the city are Anglican and Roman Catholic cathedrals and a museum of Borneo folklore. The population is about two-thirds Chinese.

Kuchuk Kainarji, Treaty of (kōōchōōk' kīnär'jē, Turk. küchük' kī''närjä'), 1774, peace treaty signed at the end of the first of the Russo-Turkish Wars undertaken by Catherine II of Russia against Sultan Mustafa III of the Ottoman Empire (Turkey). It was signed at the village of Kuchuk Kainarji, now Kaynardzha, NE Bulgaria, in the Dobruja, near the Danube and SE of Silistra. The treaty ceded Kerch and several other Black Sea ports in the Crimea to Russia and declared the rest of the khanate of Crimea independent. Russian trading ships were allowed to navigate in Turkish waters. Moldavia and Walachia were restored to the suzerainty of the sultan, but Russia obtained the right of intervening with the Sublime Porte (the sultan's court) on behalf of those two principalities. Russia furthermore acquired certain rights of representation on behalf of the Greek Orthodox subjects of the sultan. By a separate treaty (1775) Turkey ceded Bukovina to Austria. The Treaty of Kuchuk Kainarji facilitated the eventual Russian annexation (1783) of the Crimea and was the basis of the later claims of Russia as protector of the Christians in the Ottoman Empire. The Russian ascendancy over Turkey, of which the treaty was a symptom, made the EASTERN QUESTION acute. Varied spellings include the forms Kutchuk and Kainardji.

Küçük Menderes, river, Turkey: see SCAMANDER.

Kudalur, India: see CUDDALORE.

Kudrun: see GUDRUN.

kudu (kōō'dōō), short-haired African ANTELOPE, genus *Strepsiceros*. The greater kudu, *Strepsiceros strepsiceros,* has a reddish brown coat with thin vertical white stripes on its sides. It is among the largest of the antelopes; males may reach a shoulder height of 5 ft (150 cm) and a weight of 500 lb (230 kg). The male has widely spread spiral horns with up to three full twists, sometimes exceeding 5 ft in length; it has a long throat fringe and a white chevron on the muzzle. Females are smaller and hornless, without a beard or nose markings. The greater kudu inhabits hilly brush country of E and S Africa, ranging to altitudes above the treeline. Members of this species are always found near water and are excellent swimmers. Kudus are primarily browsers, feeding on leaves and young shoots, but they may graze as well. Females and their young travel in small bands; males are solitary and join the band only during the mating season. The lesser kudu, *S. imberbia,* reaches a shoulder height of about 3 ft (90 cm) and has more numerous stripes and no throat fringe; it inhabits desert and semidesert areas of eastern Africa. Kudus are classified in the phylum CHORDATA, subphylum Vertebrata, class Mammalia, order Artiodactyla, family Bovidae.

kudzu (kŏŏd'zōō), plant of the family Leguminosae (PULSE family), native to Japan, and introduced in the United States c.1876 as a decorative vine now widely grown in the South. It is for use as a cover crop, for pasturage and hay, and for controlling soil erosion. Kudzu *(Pueraria thunbergiana)* has a woody stem, broad leaves, and clusters of large purple flowers. In the Orient it is cultivated for its edible tubers and hemplike fiber. Kudzu is classified in the division MAGNOLIOPHYTA, class Magnoliopsida, order Rosales, family Leguminosae.

Kuei-lin or **Kweilin** (both: gwā-lĭn'), city (1970 est. pop. 235,000), N Kwangsi Chuang Autonomous Region, S China, on the Kuei River. It is a transportation center, with connections by rail, river, and road. Paper products are manufactured in the city. The country's second largest tin mine is nearby, and tungsten, manganese, and antimony are also found in the area. Kuei-lin is known for its beautiful karst scenery, often pictured by Chinese landscape painters. A U.S. air force base was there during World War II. Kuei-lin was once capital of Kwangsi prov.

Kuei-yang or **Kweiyang** (both:gwā-yäng), city (1970 est. pop. 1,500,000), capital of Kweichow prov., SW China. On the main road from K'un-ming to Chungking, it is also a rail (since 1959) and industrial center. Textiles, chemical fertilizers, machine tools, petroleum products, cement, and paper are among its manufactures. Important coal fields are nearby. Kuei-yang's institutions of higher learning include Kweichow Univ.

Kufa (kōō'fə), former Mesopotamian city, near the Euphrates River, c.110 mi (177 km) S of Baghdad. Founded in 638, it soon rivaled Basra (Al Basrah) in size. The Arab governor of Iraq resided there until 702. For a time Kufa was the seat of the Abbasid caliphate, and Ali, the fourth caliph, was murdered there. Celebrated as a major seat of Arab learning, it was also a continual source of political and religious unrest. The city was repeatedly plundered by the Karmathians in the 10th cent. and lost its importance. It is now an uninhabited ruin surrounded by desert.

Kufstein (ko͝of'shtīn), city (1971 pop. 12,800), in Tyrol prov., W Austria, on the Inn River, near the West German border. It is a summer and winter resort. Manufactures include skis and chemicals. The fortress of Geroldseck, rebuilt by Emperor Maximilian I in the 16th cent. on 12th-century foundations, contains a modern organ famous for its great size and power.

Kuhlau, Friedrich (frē'drĭkh ko͞o'lou), 1786–1832, Danish composer, b. Germany. Kuhlau went to Denmark in 1810 to avoid Napoleon's conscription. Despite the loss in childhood of one eye, he became a flutist and pianist and a favorite of the Danish court. He composed a great deal of incidental music, many works for the flute, and a number of piano pieces that are often studied by beginners.

Kühlmann, Richard von (rĭkh'ärt fən kül'män), 1873–1948, German diplomat. Appointed foreign secretary in Aug., 1917, he led the delegation that negotiated (March, 1918) the Treaty of Brest-Litovsk, which removed Russia from World War I. In July, 1918, army leaders forced his removal from office for publicly declaring that the war could not be ended by military action alone and without recourse to diplomacy.

Kuhn, Bowie (bo͞o'ē kyo͞on), 1926–, American commissioner of baseball, b. Takoma Park, Md. A lawyer, he was (1950–69) legal counsel for baseball club owners before his election as baseball commissioner in 1969. He soon became known as the most vigorous and imaginative commissioner since Kenesaw Mountain Landis.

Kuhn, Richard (rĭkh'ärt ko͞on), 1900–1967, Austrian chemist, director of the Kaiser Wilhelm Institute, Heidelberg. For his research on the carotinoids (he prepared eight of them in pure form) and on vitamins (he isolated riboflavin, or B_2) he was awarded the 1938 Nobel Prize in Chemistry. A Nazi decree prevented his acceptance of the award until after World War II. Kuhn also isolated vitamin B_6.

Kuhn, Walt, 1880–1949, American painter, b. New York City. At the age of 19 he worked as a cartoonist in San Francisco, contributing later to *Life* magazine. After travel and study in Europe he devoted himself largely to oil painting. In 1913, in cooperation with his friend Arthur B. Davies, he was instrumental in assembling the famous Armory Show. He is best known for his bold and brilliant interpretive portraits and figure studies of circus and backstage types, of which *Blue Clown* (Whitney Mus., New York City) is a characteristic example. He is represented in the galleries of Andover, Mass.; Brooklyn, N.Y.; Denver; Los Angeles; San Francisco; Washington, D.C.; and Dublin, Ireland.

Kuhnau, Johann (yō'hän ko͞o'nou), 1660–1722, German musician. Kuhnau was J. S. Bach's predecessor as organist and cantor at St. Thomas Church in Leipzig. He wrote various treatises on music and composed the first harpsichord sonatas.

Kukai or **Kobo-Daishi** (ko͞o'kī, kō'bō-dī'shē), 774–835, Japanese priest, scholar, and artist, founder of the Shingon or "True Word" sect of Buddhism. Of aristocratic birth, he studied the Chinese classics as a young man, but left the university and became a wandering ascetic, eventually making a commitment to Buddhism. He was (804–806) a member of a Japanese embassy to T'ang China, where he studied the Buddhist TANTRA. He returned to Japan with many scriptures and art objects and was honored by the emperor. In 816 he founded the Kongobuji monastery on Mt. Koya, S of Kyoto. Kukai is famous as a calligrapher and is said to have invented (on the model of Sanskrit) hiragana, the syllabary in which, in combination with Chinese characters, Japanese is written. Mt. Koya is still a center of pilgrimage, and there is a folk belief that Kukai, who is buried there, is not dead but in deep meditation and will one day rise again. See collection of his major works ed. by Yoshito Hakeda (1972).

Ku K'ai-chih (go͞o kī-jûr), c.344–c.406, Chinese painter, one of the most eminent painters before the T'ang dynasty. He was especially noted for his portraits but also painted landscapes. None of his works survive today, but his genius can be surmised from ancient writings and from presumed copies of his works. *The Admonitions of the Instructress to Court Ladies* (British Mus.)—the oldest-known Chinese scroll—is thought to be a 7th-century copy of his painting. Another such scroll (early 12th cent.?), *The Nymph of the Lo River,* is at the Freer Gallery, Washington, D.C. These scrolls supply valuable information on paintings of the archaic period in China.

Kukawa (ko͞o'käwä") or **Kuka** (ko͞o'kä), town, NE Nigeria. It is in a farming and salt-mining region. Kukawa was founded in 1814 by Muhammad al-Kanemi of the state of BORNU. The capital and chief commercial center of Bornu, Kukawa was also the southern terminus of a trans-Saharan caravan route to TRIPOLI, Libya. In 1893, Kukawa was conquered and destroyed by forces under Rabih, a Sudanese slave trader. It was rebuilt by the British in 1902 as a garrison town.

Ku Klux Klan (kyo͞o klŭks klăn, ko͞o"), designation mainly given to two distinct secret societies that played a part in American history, although other less important groups have also used the name. The first Ku Klux Klan was an organization that thrived in the South during the RECONSTRUCTION period following the Civil War. The second was a nationwide organization that flourished after World War I. Subsequent groups calling themselves the Ku Klux Klan sprang up in much of the South after World War II and in response to civil rights activity during the 1960s. The original Ku Klux Klan was organized by ex-Confederate elements to oppose the Reconstruction policies of the radical Republican Congress and to maintain "white supremacy." After the Civil War, when local government in the South was weak or nonexistent and there were fears of black outrages and even of an insurrection, informal vigilante organizations or armed patrols were formed in almost all communities. These were linked together in societies, such as the Men of Justice, the Pale Faces, the Constitutional Union Guards, the White Brotherhood, and the Order of the White Rose. The Ku Klux Klan was the best known of these, and in time it absorbed many of the smaller organizations. It was organized at Pulaski, Tenn., in May, 1866. Its strange disguises, its silent parades, its midnight rides, its mysterious language and commands, were found to be most effective in playing upon fears and superstitions. The riders muffled their horses' feet and covered the horses with white robes. They themselves, dressed in flowing white sheets, their faces covered with white masks, and with skulls at their saddle horns, posed as spirits of the Confederate dead returned from the battlefields. Although the Klan was often able to achieve its aims by terror alone, whippings and lynchings were also used; not only against the blacks but also against the carpetbaggers and scalawags. A general organization of the local Klans was effected in April, 1867, at Nashville, Tenn. Gen. N. B. FORREST, the famous Confederate cavalry leader, was made Grand Wizard of the Empire and was assisted by ten Genii. Each state constituted a Realm under a Grand Dragon with eight Hydras as a staff; several counties formed a Dominion controlled by a Grand Titan and six Furies; a county was a Province ruled by a Grand Giant and four Night Hawks; the local Den was governed by a Grand Cyclops with two Night Hawks as aides. The individual members were called Ghouls. Control over local Dens was not as complete as this organization would seem to indicate, and reckless and even lawless local leaders sometimes committed acts that the leaders could not countenance. General Forrest, in Jan., 1869, seemingly under some apprehension as to the use of its power, ordered the disbandment of the Klan and resigned as Grand Wizard. Local organizations continued, some of them for many years. The Klan was particularly effective in systematically keeping black people away from the polls, so that the ex-Confederates gained political control in many states. Congress in 1870 and 1871 passed legislation to combat the Klan (see FORCE BILL). The Klan was especially strong in the mountain and Piedmont areas. In the Lower South the Knights of the White Camellia were dominant. That order, founded (1867) in Louisiana, is reputed to have had even more members than the Ku Klux Klan, but its membership was more conservative and its actions less spectacular. It had a similar divisional organization, with headquarters in New Orleans. The second Ku Klux Klan was founded in 1915 by William J. Simmons, an ex-minister and promoter of fraternal orders; its first meeting was held on Stone Mt., Ga. The new Klan had a wider program than its forerunner, for it added to "white supremacy" an intense nativism and anti-Catholicism (it was also anti-Semitic) closely related to that of the Know-Nothing movement of the middle 19th cent. Consequently its appeal was not sectional, and, aided after 1920 by the activities of professional promoters Elizabeth Tyler and Edward Y. Clarke, it spread rapidly throughout the North as well as the South. It furnished an outlet for the militant patriotism aroused by World War I, and it stressed fundamentalism in religion. Professing itself nonpolitical, the Klan nevertheless controlled politics in many communities and in 1922, 1924, and 1926 elected many state officials and a number of Congressmen. Texas, Oklahoma, Indiana, Oregon, and Maine were particularly under its influence. Its power in the Midwest was broken during the late 1920s when David C. Stephenson, a major Klan leader there, was convicted of second degree murder, and evidence of corruption came out that led to the indictment of the governor of Indiana and the mayor of Indianapolis, both supporters of the Klan. The Klan frequently took extralegal measures, especially against those whom it considered its enemies. As was the case with the earlier Klan, some of these measures, whether authorized by the central organization or not, were extreme. At its peak in the mid-1920s its membership was estimated at 4 million to 5 million. Although the actual figures were probably much smaller, the Klan nevertheless declined with amazing rapidity to an estimated 30,000 by 1930. The Klan spirit, however, was a factor in breaking the Democratic hold on the South in 1928, when Alfred E. Smith, a Roman Catholic, was that party's presidential candidate. Its collapse thereafter was largely due to state laws that forbade masks and eliminated the secret element, to the bad publicity the organization received through its thugs and swindlers, and apparently from the declining interest of the members. With the depression of the 1930s, dues-paying membership of the Klan shrank to almost nothing. Meanwhile, many of its leaders had done extremely well financially from the dues and the sale of Klan paraphernalia. After World War II, Dr. Samuel Green of Georgia led a concerted attempt to revive the Klan, but it failed dismally as the organization splintered and as state after state specifically barred the order. Southern civil rights activities during the 1960s gave the Klan a new impetus and led to revivals of scattered Klan organizations. The most notable of these were Mississippi's White Knights of the Ku Klux Klan, led by Robert Shelton. The newly revived Klan groups were responsible for violent attacks against blacks and civil rights workers in cities throughout the South, including Jacksonville and St. Augustine, Fla., Birmingham and Montgomery, Ala., and Meridian, Miss. In spite of its efforts, the new Klan was not strong, and by the end of the decade its power and membership had declined to practically nothing. A. W. Tourgée's *Fool's Errand* (1880) and Thomas Dixon's *Clansman* (1905), on which D. W. Griffith based his famous film *The Birth of a Nation*, were two popular novels about the original Klan. For other works on the Reconstruction era Ku Klux Klan see W. L. Fleming's edition (1905) of J. C. Lester and D. L. Wilson, *Ku Klux Klan*; S. F. Horn, *Invisible Empire: The Story of the Ku Klux Klan, 1866–1871* (1939, repr. 1973). The structure of the Klan after World War I is discussed in J. M. Mecklin, *The Ku Klux Klan* (1924); A. S. Rice, *The Ku Klux Klan in American Politics* (1962). David Lowe's *Ku Klux Klan: The Invisible Empire* (1967) deals with the final period of Klan activity, as does David M. Chalmer's *Hooded Americanism* (1968), which also discusses the first and second Klans.

Kükong: see SHAO-KUAN, China.

Kukulcán: see QUETZALCOATL.

Members of the Ku Klux Klan.

Kulakov, Feodor (fyô'dər ko͞o'läkôf), 1918–, Soviet political leader. A member of the Communist party after 1940, Kulakov held various agricultural management positions before becoming deputy minister of agriculture (1955–59) and then minister of grain products (1959–60) for the Russian Soviet Federated Socialist Republic. He headed the agriculture department of the Communist party central committee from 1964 to 1965. He was made a member of the party's central committee in 1961, one of its secretaries in 1965, and a politburo member in 1971.

kulan: see ASS.

Kuldiga (ko͝ol'dĭgä), Ger. *Goldingen,* town, W European USSR, in Latvia. Founded in 1244, Kuldiga was a residence of the dukes of Courland and still retains a medieval character. The city has two 17th-century churches.

Kuldja: see I-NING, China.

Kulikovo, battle of (ko͞olyĭkô'və), 1380, victory of Grand Duke DMITRI DONSKOI of Moscow over Khan Mamai of the Golden Horde. The battle was fought on a plain by the Don near the present village of Kurkino, RSFSR, SE of Tula. Although the victory was the first Russian defeat of the Tatars, it did not eliminate Mongol rule, which endured for another century.

Kulm: see CHEŁMNO, Poland.

Kulmbach, Hans von (häns fən ko͝olm'bäkh), c.1480–1522, German painter and graphic artist. His real name was Hans Süss. In general his work reveals the influence of Dürer, but he had little of the master's power. Von Kulmbach worked chiefly in Nuremberg, although he probably spent several years in Cracow as court painter. His masterpiece is the Tucher altarpiece for the Church of St. Sebald in Nuremberg. He also executed portraits and designs for painted glass.

Kulmbach, town (1970 pop. 23,647), Bavaria, E central West Germany, on the White Main River. It has breweries, textile and paper mills, and canneries. Known in 1035, Kulmbach became (1340) the residence of the margraves of Kulmbach (later known as the margraves of Bayreuth) of the house of Hohenzollern. In 1791 the town passed to Prussia, in 1807 it was taken by France, and in 1810 it was annexed by Bavaria and made part of Upper Franconia. On a nearby hill is the fortress (now a museum) of Plassenburg (12th cent.; rebuilt in Renaissance style 1560–70), which served as a prison from 1808 to the early 20th cent.

Kulturkampf (ko͝olto͝or'kämpf") [Ger.,=conflict of cultures], the conflict between the German government under BISMARCK and the Roman Catholic Church. The promulgation (1870) of the dogma of the INFALLIBILITY of the pope in matters of faith and morals within the church sparked the conflict; it implied that the pope was the defender of the church against incursions by states. The German bishops and most lay Catholics supported this dogma. Bismarck, who was anxious to strengthen the central power of the new German Empire, feared the strongly organized church, which found its political voice in the Catholic Center party (organized 1870). The Center party received additional support from particularists in Bavaria and from other disaffected minorities such as the suppressed Poles in Prussia and the Guelph party of HANOVER, which refused to recognize Hanover's annexation (1866) by Prussia. In his opposition to the church, Bismarck found himself in alliance with the liberals, the traditional opponents of the church. The struggle was initiated by the abolition (July, 1871) of the Catholic department in the Prussian ministry of culture. Feelings grew stronger when Bismarck gave support to the small group of churchmen led by DÖLLINGER who refused to accept the dogma of papal infallibility. In 1872, Bismarck gave the state direct control of the schools in Prussia and obtained the expulsion of the Jesuits, first from Prussia and then from Germany as a whole. The May Laws (of May, 1873) restricted the disciplinary powers of the church, placed the education of the clergy under state supervision, and provided for the punishment of those who refused to cooperate. Next, civil ceremonies became obligatory for marriages in Germany. The church resisted these laws, and many clerics were imprisoned or removed from office for their refusal to comply. Meanwhile, the Center party increased its strength significantly. After its large gains in the Reichstag elections of 1878, Bismarck began to moderate his policy, influenced also by the alienation of the liberals through his protective tariff policies. The death of Pope PIUS IX (1878) aided the gradual resolution of the conflict. Many of the antichurch laws were repealed or fell into disuse. In 1887 a modus vivendi was reached with Pope LEO XIII. In evaluating the Kulturkampf in Germany it is important to remember that the church was at odds with a number of European states during this period. See L. P. Walace, *The Papacy and European Diplomacy, 1869–1878* (1948); see also bibliography under BISMARCK, OTTO VON.

Kulun, Chinese name of ULAN BATOR.

Kum, Iran: see QOM.

Kumamoto (ko͞omä'mōtō), city (1970 pop. 439,886), capital of Kumamoto prefecture, W Kyushu, Japan. An agricultural market town, it has manufactures of bamboo ware and pottery. It was an important castle town in the 17th cent.; one of its castles (built 1651) still stands. There are also two universities and several shrines in the city. Kumamoto prefecture (1970 pop. 1,700,079), 2,872 sq mi (7,438 sq km), is noted for the Aso-san volcanic peaks and for its many islands.

Kumanovo (ko͞o'mänôvô), town (1971 pop. 113,382), S Yugoslavia, in Macedonia. It is the center of a tobacco-growing region. The Serbs won a decisive victory over the Turks at Kumanovo in 1912.

Kumans: see CUMANS.

Kumarajiva (ko͞omär'əjĭvə), 344–413, Buddhist scholar and missionary, b. Kucha, in what is now Sinkiang prov., China. When his mother, a Kuchean princess, became a nun, he followed her into monastic life at the age of seven. He grew up in centers of Hinayana BUDDHISM, but he was converted to Mahayana Buddhism in his teens and became a specialist in MADHYAMIKA philosophy. In 383, Chinese forces seized Kucha and carried Kumarajiva off to China. From 401 he was at the Ch'in court in the capital Chang-an (the modern Sian), where he taught and translated Buddhist scriptures into Chinese. More than 100 translations are attributed to him. Of these only about 24 can be authenticated, but they include some of the most important titles in the Chinese Buddhist canon. Kumarajiva's career had an epoch-making influence on Chinese Buddhist thought, not only because he made available important texts that were previously unknown, but also because he did much to clarify Buddhist terminology and philosophical concepts. He and his disciples established the Chinese branch of the

Madhyamika, known as the San-lun, or "Three Treatises" school.

Kumasi (ko͞omä'sē, -mä'-), city (1970 pop. 234,274), capital of the Ashanti Region, central Ghana. The second largest city in Ghana, it is a commercial and transportation center in a cocoa-producing region, and it has a large central market. Kumasi was founded c.1700 as the capital of the Ashanti confederacy. A fort built by the British in 1897 is of interest. A university of science and technology and other schools are in the city.

Kumbakonam (ko͞ombəkō'nəm), town (1971 pop. 112,971), Tamil Nadu state, SE India, on the Cauvery River. Its district, in the richest part of the river delta, has one of the highest population densities in India. The area is known for its betel vines. Manufactures include brassware, textiles, and jewelry. The town is a Brahmanic cultural center. The many Hindu temples along the river are visited by pilgrims every 12 years.

Kumbum (ko͞om'bo͞om'), large lamasery at Huang-ch'ang, NE Tsinghai prov., China, c.12 mi (20 km) SW of Hsi-ning. Long a renowned pilgrimage center, it stands on the spot where Tsong-kha-pa (b.1417), the great Tibetan reformer of Lamaism (see TIBETAN BUDDHISM), is said to have been born. Its Living Buddha became (1952) the 10th Panchen Lama of Tibet. The lamasery is sometimes spelled Gumbum.

Kumgang San (ko͞om'gäng' sän), mountain range, SE North Korea, rising to 5,374 ft (1,638 m). There are scenic ravines and caverns and many ancient Buddhist temples. The range is also known as the Diamond Mts.

kumiss (ko͞o'mĭs): see FERMENTED MILK.

kümmel (kĭm'əl, Ger. küm'əl), sweet LIQUEUR, popular in the Baltic states and produced chiefly in Latvia. Cumin and caraway seeds give the predominating flavor. A fine variety is Allasch kümmel, made in Allasch near Riga, now part of the Soviet Union.

kumquat (kŭm'kwŏt), ornamental shrub of the genus *Fortunella* of the family Rutaceae (RUE family), closely related to the orange and other CITRUS FRUITS. It has evergreen leaves, sweet-scented white flowers, and small, orange-yellow edible fruits which are eaten fresh or in preserves. Three or four types of the kumquat, which is probably native to China, are cultivated as house and hedge plants in the Gulf states and in California. They are much hardier than most oranges. The kumquat is also called kinkan. Kumquats are classified in the division MAGNOLIOPHYTA, class Magnoliopsida, order Sapindales, family Rutaceae.

Kun, Béla (bā'lŏ ko͞on), 1886–1939?, Hungarian Communist. A prisoner of war in Russia after 1915, he embraced Bolshevism. After the outbreak of the Russian Revolution in 1917 he was sent to Hungary as a propagandist. In 1919, Count Michael Károlyi and his government resigned and the Communists and Social Democrats formed a coalition government under Kun. Kun set up a dictatorship of the proletariat; nationalized banks, large businesses and estates, and all private property above a certain minimum; and ruthlessly put down all opposition. He raised a Red Army and overran Slovakia. The allies forced Kun to evacuate Slovakia, and a counterrevolution broke out. Kun was at first victorious over the counterrevolutionists, but he was defeated by a Rumanian army of intervention and was forced to flee to Vienna. Kun's Red Terror was followed by a White Terror. Nicholas HORTHY DE NAGYBANYA became regent of Hungary. Kun, after being held at an insane asylum in Vienna, went (1920) to Soviet Russia. He reappeared (1928) in Vienna and was briefly imprisoned but was allowed to return to the USSR. There he took an active part in the Comintern until he was accused of anti-Stalinism in the Communist party purges of the 1930s. It is usually thought that he died in prison or in exile in Siberia. In the late 1950s and 1960s his reputation was restored in the USSR. See Oszkár Jászi, *Revolution and Counter-Revolution in Hungary* (1924); R. L. Tökés, *Béla Kun and the Hungarian Soviet Republic* (1967).

kundalini: see YOGA.

Küng, Hans (häns küng), 1928–, Swiss Roman Catholic theologian and author. Ordained in 1954, he became (1960) professor of fundamental theology at Tübingen Univ. and later served (1962–65) as adviser to the Second Vatican Council. Having consistently criticized papal authority, he became the first major Roman Catholic theologian to reject the doctrine of papal infallibility in his book *Infallible? An Inquiry* (tr. 1971). His other works include *The Council in Action* (tr. 1963), *Structures of the Church* (tr. 1966), *Truthfulness: the Future of the Church* (tr. 1968), and *Why Priests?* (tr. 1972).

Kungälv (kŭng'ĕlv''), town (1970 pop. 11,500), Göteborg och Bohus co., SW Sweden, on the Götaälv River. Founded in the 10th cent., Kungälv was one of the chief cities of medieval Norway, known as Konghelle and mentioned in the sagas. The town was plundered (1135) by Wends, seized (1368) by Hansa merchants, and ceded (1658) to Sweden.

Kungei Ala-Tau, mountains, Asia: see ALA-TAU.

K'ung Hsiang-hsi (ko͞ong shyäng-shē), 1881–1967, Chinese banker and political leader, educated at Oberlin and at Yale. He deemed himself a direct descendant of Confucius in the 75th generation. Throughout his career he supported Sun Yat-sen and Chiang Kai-shek. His first important position was minister of industry and commerce (1928–31). After 1931 he belonged to the central executive committee of the Kuomintang. He was minister of finance (1933–44), and governor of the Bank of China (1933–45). One of China's wealthiest and most powerful men, he was married to Soong Ai-ling (see SOONG, family). K'ung Hsiang-hsi, also known as H. H. Kung, retired in 1945. After the fall of the Nationalist government (1949) he went to live in the United States.

Kunié, New Caledonia: see PINES, ISLE OF.

Kunigunde, Saint: see HENRY II, Holy Roman emperor.

Kunitz, Stanley (kyo͞o'nĭts), 1905–, American writer and editor, b. Worcester, Mass. He has taught poetry at many colleges and universities. His volumes of poetry, complex and metaphysical, include *Intellectual Things* (1930), *Selected Poems, 1928–1958* (1958; Pulitzer Prize), and *The Testing Tree* (1971). Kunitz is also known as the editor (with Howard Haycraft) of such reference books as *American Authors 1600–1900* (1938), *Twentieth Century Authors* (1942), and *British Authors Before 1800* (1952).

Kuniyoshi, Yasuo (yäso͞o-ō' ko͞on''ēyō'shē), 1892?–1953, American painter, b. Okayama, Japan. He came to the United States in 1906 and studied art in Los Angeles and at the Art Students League in New York City. He visited Europe in 1925 and in 1928. Kuniyoshi's work has been described as Oriental in spirit but Western in technique, with an inclination toward somber color. His paintings, drawings, and prints are rich in symbolism and fantasy. They are best seen in the galleries of New York City. Kuniyoshi was long a popular teacher at the Art Students League. See monograph by Atsuo Imaizumi and Lloyd Goodrich (1954).

Kunlun (ko͞on'lo͞on'), great mountain system of central Asia, between the Himalayas and the Tien Shan, extending c.1,000 mi (1,610 km) E from the Pamir mts., along the Tibet-Sinkiang prov. border of W China and into Tsinghai prov., where it branches into the mountain ranges of central China; it rises to 25,340 ft (7,724 m) in Ulugh Mus Tagh (Wu-lu-k'o Mu-shih), NE Tibet. The Kunlun's main branches are the A-erh-chin Shan-Mo (Altyn Tagh) and Nan Shan in the north; the Min Shan in the south; and the Tsinling Shan in the east. The Kunlun system acts as a natural barrier between N Tibet and the Tarim basin of Sinkiang; streams rising on the northern slope of the Kunlun disappear into the basin's desert sands. Great sections of the system are inaccessible and uninhabited; there is a very small nomad population, and yaks are the beasts of burden in the high mountain passes.

K'un-ming or **Kunming** (both: ko͞o-mĭng), city (1970 est. pop. 1,700,000), capital of Yünnan prov., S China, on the northern shore of Tien Ch'ih. It is a major administrative, commercial, and cultural center of S China and leading transportation hub (air, road, rail), with rail connections to North Vietnam. Coal is mined, and the city has an iron and steel complex. Other manufactures include phosphorus, chemicals, machinery, textiles, paper, and cement. K'un-ming has long been noted for its scenic beauty and equable climate. It consists of an old walled city, a modern commercial suburb, and a residential and university section. Although it was often the seat of kings in ancient times, K'un-ming's modern prosperity dates only from 1910, when the railroad from Hanoi was built. In World War II, K'un-ming was important as the Chinese terminus of the Burma Road. The city has an astronomical observatory, and its institutions of higher learning include Yünnan Univ. and a medical college. On the outskirts is a famed bronze temple, dating from the Ming dynasty. K'un-ming was formerly called Yünnanfu.

Kunsan (ko͞on'sän'), Jap. *Gunzan,* city (1970 est. pop. 112,500), SW South Korea, on the Yellow Sea at the Kum River estuary. It is a major port, especially for rice shipments, and is a commercial center for the rice grown in the Kum basin. Rice processing, fishing and fish processing, shipbuilding, and the production of salt, rubber, and alcohol are the chief industries. The city is also an important railroad hub. Originally a poor fishing village, Kunsan gained importance with the development of its port, which was opened to foreign trade in 1899. The Japanese, who ruled Korea from 1910 to 1945, further developed the city and port.

Kunya-Urgench: see URGENCH, ancient city, USSR.

Kuomintang (kwō'mĭntăng', ko͞o'ō-), [Chin.,=national people's party]. SUNG CHIAO-JEN organized this party in 1912 under the nominal leadership of SUN YAT-SEN to succeed the Revolutionary Alliance. The original Kuomintang program called for parliamentary democracy and moderate socialism. In 1913, Yüan Shih-kai, the president of China, suppressed the Kuomintang although it held a majority in the first national assembly. Under Sun Yat-sen, the party established unrecognized revolutionary governments at Canton in 1918 and 1921 and even sent a delegation to the Versailles Peace Conference. Sun accepted aid from the USSR, and after 1922 many Comintern agents, notably Michael Borodin and V. K. Blücher, helped reorganize the Kuomintang. At the party congress in 1924 at Canton, a coalition including Communists adopted Sun's political theory, which included the Three People's Principles (San Min Chu I), namely, nationalism, democracy, and a guaranteed livelihood. Sun thought that Chinese national reconstruction must follow a progression of stages: military government, tutelage under the Kuomintang, and popular sovereignty. In 1926, Kuomintang general CHIANG KAI-SHEK launched the NORTHERN EXPEDITION advancing N from Canton against the Peking government. After halting temporarily in 1927, when the Communists were purged and the civil war between the two factions began, Kuomintang forces finally captured Peking in 1928. The Kuomintang government at Nanking received diplomatic recognition in 1928 and began the period of tutelage. After several Kuomintang military campaigns, the Communists were forced (1934–35) to withdraw from their bases in S and central China and establish new strongholds in the northwest. The Kuomintang, except for the period between 1937 and 1940, continued to war against the Communists, greatly weakening its military capacity against the Japanese. Although plagued by bureaucratic inefficiency and corruption, it controlled the Chinese government absolutely until 1947, when it permitted some participation by minor liberal parties. Full-scale civil war, further complicated by inflation, characterized the years from 1945 to 1949. The power of the Kuomintang steadily declined, and by the end of 1949 the Communists controlled the mainland. Since then the Kuomintang, forced from the mainland, has governed TAIWAN. See G. T. Yu, *Party Politics in Republican China: The Kuomintang, 1912–1924* (1966); Hsieh Jan-chih, ed., *The Kuomintang* (1970).

Kuopio (ko͞o'ôpēō), city (1970 pop. 64,744), capital of Kuopio prov., central Finland, on Lake Kallavesi. Situated in a large forest region, its industries are based on timber. It is at the head of the Saimaa lake system and is a tourist and inland-navigation center. Kuopio was chartered in 1782. There are several colleges in the city.

Kupala, Janka (yäng'kä ko͞opä'lä), 1888–1942, Belorussian poet and writer, whose original name was Ivan Lutsevich. Kupala was a major figure of the Belorussian national and cultural revival. His prerevolutionary works, which stress national liberation, include the novel *Along the Path of Life* (1913), a collection of verse entitled *Heritage* (1922), and the drama *Ravaged Nest* (1919). Hostility toward Communism is evident in his poetry written between 1918 and 1928 and in the allegorical comedy *The Natives* (1922). Kupala's works after 1930 are of slight literary value.

Kupka, Frank or **František** (frän'tyĭshĕk ko͞op'kä), 1871–1957, Czech painter, etcher, and illustrator. Kupka illustrated works by Reclus and Leconte de Lisle and an edition of Aristophanes' *Lysistrata.* In 1911 he joined the ORPHISM movement led by DELAUNAY. He was one of the first painters to explore pure geometric abstraction. His decorative style was affected by the "machine esthetic" of the 1920s. Kupka is well represented in the Musée national d'Art moderne, Paris, and in the National Gallery, Prague.

Kuprili: see KÖPRÜLÜ.

Kuprin, Aleksandr Ivanovich (əlyĭksän'dər ēvä'nəvĭch ko͞o'prĭn), 1870–1938, Russian novelist and short-story writer. Kuprin was an army officer for several years before he resigned to pursue a writing career. He won fame with *The Duel* (1905, tr. 1916), a novel of protest against the Russian military system. In 1909, *The Pit* (tr. 1922), his novel dealing with prostitution in Odessa, created a sensation. Kuprin left Russia after the revolution but returned in 1937. Some of his best short stories of action and adventure appear in English in the collections *The River of Life* (1916) and *The Bracelet of Garnets* (1917).

Kura (ko͞orä'), ancient *Cyrus,* river, c.950 mi (1,530 km) long, the chief river of Georgian SSR and Azerbaijan SSR, S European USSR. It rises in NE Turkey, NW of Kars, and flows NE into the USSR, then SE, parallel to the Caucasus Mts., to the Caspian Sea. There are hydroelectric plants on the river near Tbilisi and Mingechaur; the extensive reservoir at Mingechaur is also used for irrigation. The lower Kura River, joined by the Araks River, its chief tributary, flows through an irrigated plain that extends into NW Iran. Cotton is the chief crop of the region, which lies partly below sea level. The Kura is navigable c.300 mi (480 km) upstream.

Kuraish (ko͞orĭsh'), ancient Bedouin tribe near Mecca to which Muhammad belonged. At one time camel drivers and caravan guides, they became, after acquiring custody of the KAABA (5th cent.), one of the most powerful tribes in central Arabia and the chief family of Mecca. They were at first bitter opponents of Muhammad but became his devoted followers when Muhammad retained the Kaaba, a source of pilgrim revenue, as a sanctuary of Islam. The great founders of the Umayyad, Abbasid, and Fatimid dynasties were of Kuraish origin. The modern Hashemite rulers of Jordan, the former Imam of Yemen, and the king of Morocco claim to be the descendants of Muhammad's tribe. The name also appears as Quraysh or Koreish.

Kurayoshi (ko͞orä'yōshē), city (1970 pop. 49,629), Tottori prefecture, W Honshu, Japan, on the Tenjin River. It is an agricultural and communications center with a textile industry.

Kurdistan (kûr'dĭstăn", ko͞ordĭstän'), an extensive plateau and mountain region in SW Asia (c.74,000 sq mi/191,660 sq km), inhabited mainly by Kurds and including parts of E Turkey, NE Iraq, NW Iran and smaller sections of NE Syria and Soviet Armenia. The region lies astride the Zagros mts. (Iran) and the eastern extension of the Taurus mts. (Turkey) and extends in the south across the Mesopotamian plain. Kurdistan includes the upper reaches of the Tigris and Euphrates rivers. There are an estimated 4 million Kurds in Turkey, 2 million in Iran, and 2 million in Iraq. In Turkey they dwell near the Iranian frontier around Lake Van, as well as in the vicinity of Diyarbakır and Erzurum. The Kurds in Iran live principally in Azerbaijan and Khurasan, with some in Fars. In Iraq the Kurds live mostly in the vicinity of Mosul, Kirkuk, and Sulaimaniyah. Ethnically close to the Iranians, the Kurds were traditionally nomadic herdsmen who are now mostly seminomadic or sedentary. Railroads have not penetrated far into Kurdistan; much transportation between Kurdish villages is by mule, donkey, ox, or pony. The majority of Kurds are devout Sunnite Muslims. Kurdish dialects belong to the northwestern branch of the Iranian languages. The Kurds have traditionally resisted subjugation by other nations. Commonly identified with the ancient Corduene, which was inhabited by the Carduchi (mentioned in Xenophon), Kurdistan was conquered by the Arabs and converted to Islam in the 7th cent. The region was held by the Seljuk Turks in the 11th cent., by the Mongols from the 13th to 15th cent., and then by the Ottoman Empire. Having struggled for centuries to free themselves from Ottoman rule, the Kurds were encouraged by the Turkish defeat in World War I and by U.S. President Woodrow Wilson's plea for self-determination for non-Turkish nationalities in the empire. The Kurds brought their claims for independence to the Paris Peace Conference in 1919. The Treaty of Sèvres (1920), which liquidated the Ottoman Empire, provided for the creation of an autonomous Kurdish state. Because of Turkey's military revival under Kemal Atatürk, however, the Treaty of Lausanne (1923), which superseded Sèvres, failed to mention Kurdistan. Revolts by the Kurds of Turkey in 1925 and 1930 were forcibly quelled, and manifestations of Kurdish nationalism there are still suppressed. The Kurds in Iran also rebelled during the 1920s, and at the end of World War II a Soviet-backed Kurdish "republic" existed briefly. Agitation among Iraq's Kurds for a unified and autonomous Kurdistan led in the 1960s to prolonged warfare between Iraqi troops and the Kurds under Gen. Mustafa al-Barzani. In 1970, Iraq finally promised local self-rule to the Kurds, with the city of Irbil as the capital of the Kurdish area. The Kurds refused to accept the terms of the agreement, however contending that the president of Iraq would retain real authority and demanding that Kirkuk, an important oil center, be included in the autonomous Kurdish region. In 1974 the Iraqi government sought to impose its plan for limited autonomy in Kurdistan. It was rejected by the Kurds, and heavy fighting erupted and continued throughout the year. Despite their lack of political unity throughout history, the Kurds, as individuals and in small groups, have had a lasting impact on developments in SW Asia. Saladin, who gained fame during the Crusades, is perhaps the most famous of all Kurds. See studies by Arfa Hassan (1966), Thomas Bois (tr. 1966), and Edgar O'Balliance (1973).

Kurds: see KURDISTAN.

Kure (ko͞o'rā), city (1970 pop. 234,184), Hiroshima prefecture, SW Honshu, Japan, on Hiroshima Bay. It is a major naval base and port, with shipbuilding yards. Steel, pulp, files, machinery, and tools are manufactured in Kure.

Kure Island or **Curé Island** (both: ko͞o'rā), formerly **Ocean Island,** circular atoll, c.15 mi (24 km) in circumference, in the NW part of the Hawaiian group, c.50 mi (80 km) NW of Midway Island. Kure is uninhabited but has a large variety of sea birds. The island was annexed in 1886 by the Kingdom of Hawaii and was worked for guano.

Kurgan (ko͞orgän'), city (1970 pop. 244,000), capital of Kurgan oblast, W Siberian USSR, on the Tobol River. Kurgan is the important junction of the western branches of the Trans-Siberian RR. Its factories produce agricultural and road-building equipment, machine tools, and food products. Kurgan was founded in the 17th cent. There are many ancient burial mounds (Turkic *Kurgan*) in the area.

Kuril Islands (ko͞o'rēl, ko͞or'ĭl) or **Kuriles,** Jap. *Chishima-Retto,* Rus. *Kurilskiye Ostrova,* island chain, c.6,020 sq mi (15,590 sq km), Sakhalin oblast, E USSR. They stretch c.775 mi (1,250 km) between S Kamchatka Peninsula and NE Hokkaido, Japan, and separate the Sea of Okhotsk from the Pacific Ocean. There are 30 large and numerous small islands; Iturup is the largest. Atlasova volcano (7,674 ft/2,339 m) on Atlasova Island is the highest point of the chain. The islands are mainly of volcanic origin. Active volcanoes are present and earthquakes are frequent. The low temperature, high humidity, and persistent fog make the islands unpleasant for human habitation. There are, however, communities engaged in sulfur mining, hunting, and fishing. In the 18th cent. both Russia and Japan penetrated the islands. In 1875, Japan gave up Sakhalin in return for Russian withdrawal from the Kuriles, and the Japanese held the islands until the end of World War II. The Yalta Conference ceded the islands to the USSR, and Soviet forces occupied the chain in Sept., 1945. Japan has challenged the Soviet right to the Kuriles, and failure to resolve the impasse has been a major obstacle to the signing of a peace treaty between Japan and the USSR.

Kurland: see COURLAND, USSR.

Kurnool (kərno͞ol′), town (1971 pop. 136,682), Andhra Pradesh state, S central India, at the confluence of the Tungabhadra and Hindri rivers. Formerly the state capital, Kurnool is now a district administrative center and a market for grain, hides, and cotton. There are ruins of a fort built by the Hindu Vijayanagar kings in the 16th cent. The town was overrun by Muslims in 1565 and was ceded to the British by the Nizam of Hyderabad in 1800. Kurnool is a center of pilgrimage and is surrounded by hill resorts.

Kurokawa, Noriaki (nôrēä′kē ko͝orō′käwä), 1934–, Japanese architect. Youngest of the group of architects known as the metabolists, who perceive architectural works as living organisms, Kurokawa plans for the growth or change of his buildings by addition or subtraction of modular units. The Takara Beautilion (1970, Osaka), the Toshiba IHI Pavilion, Hawaiian Dreamland (1966–67), and the Nitto Foods Co. plant in Sagae, Japan, are among his best-known designs.

Kuropatkin, Aleksey Nikolayevich (əlyĭksyā′ nyĭkəlī′əvĭch ko͝orŭpät′kĭn), 1848–1925, Russian general. He distinguished himself in the Russo-Turkish War of 1877–78. Made minister of war in 1898, he opposed the course that precipitated the Russo-Japanese War of 1904–5, but after its outbreak he took command of the troops in Manchuria. Kuropatkin resigned after the Russian defeat at Mukden. During World War I he was (1916–17) governor of Turkistan. See his book, *The Russian Army and the Japanese War* (tr. 1909).

Kurosawa, Akira (äkē′rä ko͝orō′säwä), 1910–, Japanese film director, scriptwriter, and producer, b. Tokyo. He is regarded as one of the world's great directors. His *Ikiru* (1952), a moving study of an elderly bureaucrat facing death by cancer, is an acknowledged classic. Among his other films are *Rashomon* (1950), about truth and illusion; *Seven Samurai* (1954), an epic adventure story; *Throne of Blood* (1957), an adaptation of *Macbeth;* and *Yojimbo* (1961), a rousing Japanese-style Western. See study by Donald Richie (1970).

Kuroshio, ocean current: see JAPAN CURRENT.

Kursk (ko͝orsk), city (1970 pop. 284,000), capital of Kursk oblast, central European USSR, at the confluence of the Tuskor and Seim rivers. An important rail junction, it has machine, chemical, and synthetic fiber plants. A large iron deposit is south of the city. Known since 1095, Kursk was destroyed by the Mongols in 1240 and was rebuilt as a Muscovite fortress in 1586. During World War II the Soviets won a major battle near Kursk in 1943.

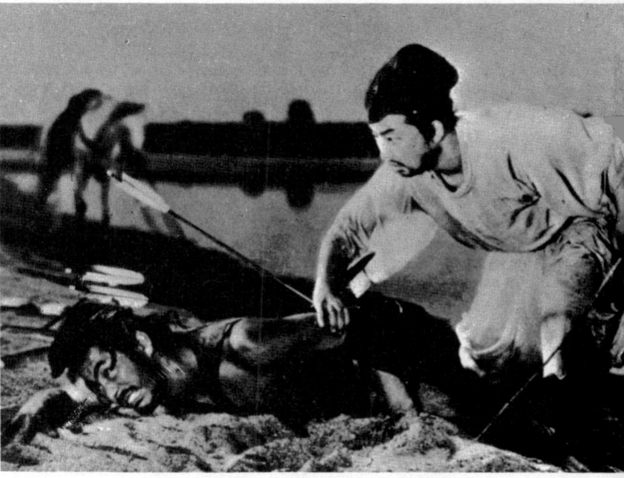

Scene from Akira Kurosawa's film Rashomon, *with Toshiro Mifune (left).*

Kursky Zaliv (ko͝or′skē zä′lēv) or **Courland Lagoon** (ko͝or′lănd), lagoon, 56 mi (90 km) long and 28 mi (45 km) wide, W USSR, in the Lithuanian and Russian republics. It is separated from the Baltic Sea by Courland Spit, a sandspit c.60 mi (100 km) long and 1 to 2 mi (1.6–3.2 km) wide, which leaves only a narrow opening at the Klaypeda Channel in the north. The Neman River empties into the lagoon.

Kurume (ko͞oro͞o′mā), city (1970 pop. 194,178), Fukuoka prefecture, W Kyushu, Japan, on the Chikugo Plain. It is a commercial and agricultural center and manufactures rubber and cotton goods. Kurume, a former castle town, is now the seat of a medical college.

Kurunegala (ko͝or″o͞onā′gələ), town (1968 est. pop. 23,000), W central Sri Lanka (Ceylon). It is an important road junction and the administrative and commercial center of a coconut, rice, and rubber plantation district. Overlooking the town is Elephant Hill, a stronghold in the 14th cent., when Kurunegala was the capital of a Sinhalese kingdom.

Kurusu, Saburo (sä″bo͞orō′ ko͞oro͞o′so͞o), 1886–1954, Japanese career diplomat. As ambassador to Germany from 1939 to 1941, he signed the Berlin Pact (Sept., 1940). A special envoy to Washington, he and Admiral Nomura were negotiating when Pearl Harbor was bombed on Dec. 7, 1941. Interned in the United States from Dec., 1941 to June, 1942, he returned to Japan and became (1945) a professor at Tokyo Univ.

Kurzeme: see COURLAND, USSR.

Kusatsu (ko͞osä′tso͞o), town (1970 pop. 46,610), Gumma prefecture, central Honshu, Japan. As early as the 12th cent. its hot sulfur springs were known for their medicinal properties.

Kush: see CUSH.

Kushaiah (ko͞oshā′yə), Levite. 1 Chron. 15.17. Kishi: 1 Chron. 6.44.

Kushiro (ko͞oshē′rō), city (1970 pop. 191,946), SE Hokkaido, Japan, on the Pacific Ocean. The main port of E Hokkaido and the island's only ice-free trading port, it exports timber, fish, and coal. Kushiro is also a major base for fishermen. The city is the center of the huge Kushiro coal field, which extends far out to sea; mining is carried on in the sea. Industrialization has made Kushiro important in the production of marine products, dairy products, lumber, paper, pulp, and fertilizer. The city is traversed by the Kushiro River.

Kuskokwim (kŭs'kōkwĭm), river, c.800 mi (1,290 km) long, rising on the northwest slopes of the Alaska Range, central Alaska, and flowing SW to the Bering Sea. The river is a potential source for hydroelectric power production.

Küssnacht am Rigi (küs'näkht äm rē'gē), town (1970 pop. 7,956), Schwyz canton, central Switzerland, on the Lake of Lucerne. A small resort, it is known chiefly as the scene of the killing of Gessler by William TELL. A nearby 17th-century chapel commemorates the legendary exploit.

Kustanay (ko͞ostənī'), city (1970 pop. 124,000), capital of Kustanay oblast, NW Central Asian USSR, in Kazakhstan, on the Tobol River. It is an agricultural center and producer of chemical fibers. Rich iron deposits are nearby.

Kütahya (kütä'yä), city (1970 pop. 62,060), capital of Kütahya prov., W central Turkey. An agricultural market center, the city has been famous since the 16th cent. for the manufacture of ceramics. It has a hydroelectric plant. Known in ancient history as Cotyaeum, it was occupied by the Seljuk Turks soon after the battle of Manzikert (1071). In the 15th cent. it passed to the Ottomans. A former spelling is Kutaiah.

Kutaisi (ko͞otəē'sē), city (1970 pop. 161,000), SE European USSR, in Georgia, on the Rioni River. An industrial center, it has industries producing trucks, mining and transport equipment, textiles, chemicals, and food products. Industry is aided by a large hydroelectric station on the Rioni. Kutaisi was the capital of ancient Colchis (8th cent. B.C.), and the capital of Imeritia in the 13th, 15th, and 16th cent. A.D. It was taken by the Russians in 1810. There is some notable medieval architecture, including the ruins of the 11th-century St. George Cathedral.

Kutb Minar: see QUTB MINAR.

Kutch or **Cutch** (both: kŭch, ko͝och), district, 17,000 sq mi (44,030 sq km), Gujarat state, W India, bounded on the N by Pakistan. It is largely barren except for a fertile band along the Arabian Sea. There is some horse and camel breeding. Bhuj and Mandvi, a port, are the chief towns. Formerly a princely state, Kutch was established in the 14th cent. by RAJPUTS, was often invaded from Sind, and passed under British rule in 1815. Kutch was incorporated into Gujarat in 1960. The Rann of Kutch, a salt waste (9,000 sq mi/23,310 sq km) mainly in the N of the district, was the scene of Indo-Pakistani fighting in 1965.

Kutchin Indians (kŭch''ĭn'), group of North American Indians of the ATHABASCAN branch of the Nadene linguistic stock (see AMERICAN INDIAN LANGUAGES). They inhabit the Yukon valley in NW Canada and E Alaska and also the valley of the Peel River, a tributary of the Mackenzie. In prehistoric times the Kutchin subsisted as caribou hunters. They practiced polygamy, and they sometimes practiced infanticide on female children to prevent overpopulation. Sir Alexander Mackenzie was the first European to visit (1789) this area, and by c.1810 a trading post was established. The Kutchin are extremely hospitable, sometimes entertaining guests for weeks at a time. In the mid-19th cent. they numbered some 1,200; presently they number about 1,500. The Kutchin are also called the Loucheux. See Cornelius Osgood, *Contributions to the Ethnography of the Kutchin* (1936).

Kutchuk Kainardji or **Kutchuk Kainarji, Treaty of:** see KUCHUK KAINARJI, TREATY OF.

Kut-el-Amara: see AL KUT, Iraq.

Kutenai Indians: see KOOTENAI INDIANS.

Kutná Hora (ko͞ot'nä hô'rä), Ger. *Kuttenberg,* city (1970 pop. 18,097), NW Czechoslovakia, in Bohemia. Now an agricultural center, it was an important silver-mining center in the Middle Ages. Its famous mint largely created the power and greatness of the medieval kings of Bohemia. In 1409, Emperor Wenceslaus IV issued a decree at Kutná Hora that changed the status of the Univ. of Prague. In 1421–24, Kutná Hora was captured by the Hussites, recaptured by Emperor Sigismund, and captured again and burned by John Žižka. Till then a stronghold of Catholicism, it became for two centuries the center of Bohemian Protestantism. The city suffered again in the Thirty Years War (1618–48) and lost its importance after the silver mines closed in the 17th cent. Kutná Hora is rich in medieval architecture; the Church of St. Barbara (14th cent.) is a splendid example of Bohemian Gothic, and the Gothic Cathedral of St. James (14th cent.) has a tower 266 ft (81 m) high. The "Italian Court," begun in the 13th cent., is a palace once used both as a mint and as a residence of the kings of Bohemia.

Kuttenberg: see KUTNÁ HORA, Czechoslovakia.

Kutuzov, Mikhail Ilarionovich (mēkhəyēl' ēləryôn'əvĭch ko͞oto͞o'zəf), 1745–1813, Russian field marshal. He fought against the Polish Confederation of Bar (see BAR, CONFEDERATION OF) and served in the RUSSO-TURKISH WARS of 1768–74 and 1787–92, in which he lost an eye. He took part (1805) in the battle of Austerlitz, which was fought against his advice. In 1811–12 he again took command against the Turks and defeated them in a brilliant campaign that brought Bessarabia to Russia. In Aug., 1812, Kutuzov replaced BARCLAY DE TOLLY as commander in chief against the invading armies of NAPOLEON I. Kutuzov was expected to engage the French in battle and to abandon his predecessor's delaying tactics. The battle of BORODINO was the result; after that butchery, Kutuzov resumed Barclay's wise policy of retreat, which eventually led to Napoleon's ruin. He pursued Napoleon relentlessly after the retreat of the *Grande Armée* from Moscow (1812–13). He was created prince of Smolensk for a victory there late in 1812.

kuvasz (pl. kuvaszok), (ko͞ov'äs, ko͞o'väs), breed of powerful WORKING DOG perfected in Hungary over many centuries. The kuvasz may stand as high as 30 in. (76 cm) at the shoulder and weigh up to 120 lb (54 kg). Its double coat of fine underhairs and thick, medium-length, straight or slightly wavy outercoat is pure white in color. Although both Tibet and Turkey have been cited as the original home of the kuvasz, recently assimilated evidence seems to support the contention that it was one of the sheepherding dogs used in Mesopotamia more than 7,000 years ago. Whatever its origins, its history in Hungary is well attested to, as is its service there, for a period of hundreds of years, as a guard, shepherd, and hunting dog. Today it is also raised for show competition and as a pet. See DOG.